FATHER of the
FATHERLESS

FATHER of the FATHERLESS

The Authorized Biography of Father Nelson Baker

Richard Gribble, CSC

PAULIST PRESS
New York / Mahwah, NJ

Except as otherwise noted, the Scripture quotations contained herein are from the New Revised Standard Version: Catholic Edition Copyright © 1989 and 1993, by the Division of Christian Education of the National Council of the Churches of Christ in the United States of America. Used by permission. All rights reserved.

IMPRIMI POTEST:
Rev. Thomas P. Looney, CSC
Provincial Superior of the Eastern Province of the Congregation of Holy Cross
Bridgeport, Connecticut
Feast of the Visitation, May 31, 2010

While the text portrays the virtuous life of Father Baker; his outstanding accomplishments on behalf of poor and abandoned children; his devotion to Mary, the Mother of God; and the testimony of many to his holiness—the text does not speak of Father Baker as a saint, nor does it contain any public prayers promoting his cause.

Jacket design by Sharyn Banks
Book design by Lynn Else

Library of Congress Cataloging-in-Publication Data

Gribble, Richard.
    Father of the fatherless : the authorized biography of Father Nelson Baker / Richard Gribble.
        p. cm.
    Includes bibliographical references and index.
    ISBN 978-0-8091-0596-0 (alk. paper)
    1. Baker, Nelson H. (Nelson Henry), 1841–1936. 2. Catholic Church—Clergy—New York (State)—Biography. 3. Orphanages—New York (State)—Lackawanna. I. Title.
    BX4705.B132G75 2011
    282.092—dc22
    [B]
2010054119

Published by Paulist Press
997 Macarthur Boulevard
Mahwah, New Jersey 07430

www.paulistpress.com

Printed and bound in the
United States of America

During his sixty years of priesthood, Venerable Nelson Baker, Apostle of Charity, touched the lives of tens of thousands of people through his work in the collective Institutions of St. Joseph's Orphan Asylum, St. John's Protectory, and the Infant Home, and through his role as pastor of St. Patrick Parish, which later became Our Lady of Victory in Buffalo, New York. His place in history can be found on many fronts, but it was his complete dedication to "Baker's Boys," the orphans and truants for whom he became a father, that he will always be best remembered. It is appropriate that this book be dedicated to the thousands of children who were saved from death and/or were provided the framework for life by Father Baker and his dedicated assistants, the Sisters of St. Joseph and the Brothers of the Holy Infancy and Youth of Jesus.

"We teach boys to be true and genuine....We teach boys to be pure in thought....We teach boys to be self-reliant and self-helpful....We teach boys to be unselfish, to care for the feelings and comforts of others."

—Father Nelson H. Baker, April 1929

Contents

Photographs on pages 64–70 and 156–160

Foreword

As the spiritual leader of the Diocese of Buffalo, it gives me great pleasure to introduce the first authoritative biography of Msgr. Nelson H. Baker, V.G., or "Father Baker" as he is most commonly known. While many who live in Western New York are aware of our hometown "Apostle of Charity," Father Gribble's work provides a wonderful opportunity to finally share this remarkable story with a global audience.

Father Baker was truly a modern-day saint, one whose life shows us that, with faith, one can accomplish tremendous things. It is my sincere hope, as word spreads about Father Baker, that he will inspire others to do great things for God's kingdom and for the poor and needy around them.

On my very first visit to Buffalo, after my appointment as bishop of the diocese, I had the opportunity to visit Father Baker's famed Our Lady of Victory National Shrine and Basilica. I will never forget the feeling I had as I stepped into the church: I felt that I was instantly transported to one of the breathtaking shrines in Europe and that I was on holy ground. At that moment, I knew I was in a very special place. As I learned more about Father Baker's life and legacy, I knew we needed to do everything possible to continue to promote his cause for canonization. This authoritative biography is an important part of that process.

As you enjoy this story of Father Baker's life, I am confident you will be moved by all this man was able to accomplish for others during his lifetime, as well as for the countless individuals who continue to be helped today through his legacy. I am grateful to Rev. Richard Gribble, CSC, for laying out Father Baker's life so well, and I ask for your prayers in our continued work to promote Father Baker's cause for canonization.

Father of the Fatherless

May God bless all who read this biography and may Father Baker's inspiration, Our Lady of Victory, protect you.

+ Most Rev. Edward U. Kmiec, DD
Bishop of Buffalo
The Feast of the Visitation, 2010

P. Sullivan
7. IX. 04

Preface

Venerable Nelson Baker (universally known simply and always as "Father Baker") first came to my attention in the summer of 2007. Although being a student of American Catholic history and with academic knowledge of the major players in the episcopal, priestly, diaconal, and lay ranks of the Church in the United States, I had never heard of him before this time. That summer I received an invitation from Our Lady of Victory Homes of Charity in Lackawanna, New York, to consider writing a biography of their founder, Father Baker. I had been recommended by a Niagara native, Kevin Carrizo di Camillo, who knew of my scholarship through his work at Paulist Press as my book editor. I traveled to Buffalo to "check out the sources" to ascertain if sufficient extant primary and secondary sources were available to complete such a project. Satisfied after my review of material that the project was possible, and with the proper permissions from the people in Buffalo, I began my work.

My research on the life of Father Baker gave me pause for at least two major reasons. First, I was amazed at the scope of Baker's work, his longevity, and the number of people he served. Priests and religious consider it a privilege to celebrate anniversaries of ordination or vows, with the silver and golden jubilees (twenty-five and fifty years, respectively) being of special significance. Baker, not ordained until he was thirty-four, some eight to ten years older than his contemporaries, completed sixty years as a priest and was active until almost the very end of his life, finishing his great project of the Basilica of Our Lady of Victory at age eighty-four (and lived another decade after that). My second surprise was my wonder and confusion as to why Baker was not better known. As a student of the field, I found it remarkable to think that Baker and his work are, regrettably, basically unknown outside the greater Western New York region. This book seeks to bring interest in him and his work with male youth and with unwed mothers and their children to a greater readership.

This project could not have been completed without the assistance of many people. First, I am grateful to all of the Our Lady of Victory Institutions, headed by Monsignor Paul J. E. Burkard, for their invitation and confidence in allowing me to research and write this biography. I was given full cooperation on all levels, including total access to extant sources, hospitality during my research visits, and financial support to complete the work in a timely manner. My name would not have been brought to the attention of the Our Lady of Victory family had it not been for the aforementioned Kevin Carrizo di Camillo of Paulist Press, who recommended me for this project, and whose family in Niagara Falls lavished me with Western New York hospitality. A special note of thanks must be extended to Mrs. Beth Donovan, head of public relations at Our Lady of Victory Homes of Charity. She took the time in that initial summer of 2007 visit to ferry me about Buffalo to do my research and provided me with my first visit to Niagara Falls. Additionally, she has been my contact person throughout the project. While in Lackawanna, I shared an office with Mrs. Jenny Brown, who always showed me the utmost in kindness and greeted me each morning with a bright smile to start the day. Gratitude also must be given to Sister Ann Louise Hentges, SSMN, archivist for the Diocese of Buffalo, for her assistance and support, and to the late Monsignor Walter Kern, who compiled significant amounts of information pertinent to Nelson Baker, which made my task much easier. Sister Elizabeth Savage, SSJ, was of great assistance in the Sisters of St. Joseph Archives. I also wish to thank Professors Christopher Kauffman, Timothy Allan, and Dennis Castillo, who read the manuscript and provided excellent suggestions for improvement. Mr. Ron Paszek, superintendent of Holy Cross Cemetery in Lackawanna, provided significant research assistance. To the men and women of the Our Lady of Victory family—who have assisted me in many ways through lunches, wonderful conversations, and encouragement—I extend my thanks. Special thanks go to the priests who live at Casa

Victoria, my residence in Lackawanna during research trips. They provided welcome, hospitality, and sincere friendship during my extended visits. Last, I wish to thank my dear friend Sister Tania Santander Atauchi, CDP, whose constant care, interest, support, and indomitable faith in all my projects has always helped me to succeed.

Richard Gribble, CSC

Acknowledgments

Most grateful, if posthumous, acknowledgment is to
Monsignor Robert C. Wurtz, PA (1932–2006),
who was the pastor of Our Lady of Victory Basilica
and allowed the Father Baker Archives to be opened for
this project.
Requiescat in Pace. Amen.

Introduction

Driving along Ridge Road in Lackawanna, New York, east from the Buffalo Skyway (Route 5) or west from the New York Thruway (Interstate 90), one observes at the midpoint a towering edifice of faith. Located at the corner of Ridge Road and South Park is the Basilica of Our Lady of Victory. This church, with its twin towers in front and its magnificent cupola dome, stands alone in the area, dominating the skyline. The sign across the street reads: "Welcome to Father Baker's. Our Lady of Victory, Pray for Us."

The Basilica of Our Lady of Victory, which was consecrated in May 1926, stands as a symbol of the life and career of Nelson Baker, whom Father Patrick Cormican, SJ, called the "Father of the Fatherless."[1] Nelson Henry Baker (1842–1936) even today is extremely well known in Western New York. During his sixty years of priesthood, he literally became a household name because of, as Cormican indicates, his work assisting orphans and troubled boys. For fifty-four years (1882–1936), he was superintendent of the Our Lady of Victory Institutions, beginning initially with St. Joseph's Orphan Asylum and St. John's Protectory, but adding over time Our Lady of Victory Infant Home for single mothers and their children, Our Lady of Victory General Hospital, and homes for working boys and girls to aid young adults in their transition to independent life. Sr. Mary Timothy Dempsey accurately captured the significance of Baker's work in his day: "Father Baker's Our Lady of Victory Institutions…[are] landmark[s] in the Western New York area."[2]

Baker's fame has manifested itself in varied ways. Casual conversations with local people will inevitably raise the name of this venerable priest. Although few people alive today can speak from any personal history or experience of Father Baker, that does not prevent many from waxing eloquently and with great pride about the accomplishments of this man. For at least three generations, parents have had in their arsenal of discipline for their recalcitrant children the threat: "If you don't behave, I'll send you to Father Baker's!" Many a young lad has heard these words. The warning was idle in content, but demonstrable of the respect—and "holy fear," from the perspective of young boys and girls—that this venerable priest generated. For a man who actively shunned the spotlight, he might be appalled at his contemporary celebrity status. Nevertheless, he would certainly be pleased that the work to which he dedicated his life has evolved in important ways in the early years of the twenty-first century.

A Brief Review of Former Biographical Works

Possibly due in large measure to the limited knowledge of Father Baker outside of the Buffalo area, published (and most especially) scholarly efforts to chronicle and analyze his life and apostolic works are few. The three major biographical extant sources are two popular and rather hagiographical biographies (one of which was written ten years *before* Father Baker actually died) and one scholarly doctoral dissertation, which addresses how the aura and heroic status of Baker were produced over time by what people said and wrote about him. Additionally, there are numerous summaries of his life, mostly drawn from the first two aforementioned sources and from many, many articles, published for the most part in Catholic magazines.

In 1925, Father Thomas Galvin, CSsR, who first met Baker as a resident at St. Joseph's Orphan Asylum, and who later as a priest worked closely with him in a specialized apostolate of evangelization to African Americans, produced the first book-length chronicle of Baker's life and his ministry to troubled youth. The monograph *Father Baker and His Lady of Victory Charities*—which was not authorized and, therefore, positively mortified Baker when published—provides the reader with some useful information from an insider's perspective. Divided into two parts, the book chronicles many of the events and accomplishments of Baker's life, using a topical rather than a chronological approach. This work is neither footnoted nor contextualized, save a bit of basic information about the locale in which the events occurred. Written by a former "Baker Boy" and a priest-colleague in ministry, the book is not intended as a critical analysis, but rather presents the reflections of one who owed his whole life, including his vocation as a priest, to Baker. One scholarly review of Galvin's work accurately described its strengths and weaknesses. Noting that the book provides important firsthand information and insight into the character of Baker, Dr. Heather Hartel also describes the monograph's shortcomings:

> However, the revivalist rhetorical devices that character-ize Galvin's recurring outpourings of praise for Baker ultimately end up revealing more about Galvin's own personal feelings about Baker, [his] defense of Catholic patriotism and enthusiasm for Catholic missionary efforts than Baker's personality. The portrait of Baker that emerges from Galvin's tribute is a highly inflated, but fairly accurate version of the positive attitude toward Baker's civil and religious contributions that was devel-oping during the 1920s in the Buffalo region.[3]

Thirty-five years later, Floyd Anderson, a writer from New Jersey, was commissioned to produce a popular biography of Baker. The monograph, *Apostle of Charity: The Father Nelson Henry Baker Story*, is a very succinct, readable, and generally accu-rate presentation of the life and work of Baker. Written almost twenty-five years after Baker's death, Anderson's book had several advantages not available to Galvin, including (most important) the perspective of looking back on Baker's whole life and understand-ing how Father Baker had been perceived by the people of his gen-eration. Like Galvin's effort, this book does not have footnotes and fails to place Baker within the historical context of his day. It is clear, however, that Anderson had more sources and used them effectively to generate his chronological account. Like Galvin's effort as well, the book is somewhat hagiographical in its tone, but it does address Baker's penchant for control and his at-times dom-ineering personality. Monsignor Walter Kern, former archivist of the Diocese of Buffalo, commented that Anderson's work was "historically accurate" and his judgments appropriately based on the evidence available to him. Hartel also generally perceives Anderson's work in a positive light:

> Although he relies heavily on anecdotal information and uses his creative license to reveal Baker's personality with literary embellishments, Anderson provides many verifiable historical details from Baker's diaries, newspaper reports, military records, diaries of Baker's companions at [the] seminary and the *Annals* and *Victorian*, citing his sources in a general manner within the flow of the text.[4]

The only critical (yet unpublished) scholarly work produced on the life of Nelson Baker is the aforementioned doctoral dissertation by Heather Hartel. This work, which is exhaustively researched and fully footnoted, does not purport to be a biography of the priest. Rather, Hartel seeks to combine historical material with a study of lived religion to show how the cause of Nelson Baker's sainthood could be a boon to economic recovery for the City of Lackawanna. In a very interesting study, she differentiates between the historical person and the figure generated by what people said about him. Thus, she shows how the passage of time and the inevitable growth in wonder at his accomplishments have made Baker the reverential figure he is today.

Contributions of This Current Monograph

This book is intended as a critical biography of the life and work of Father Baker. As with any similar project, the historian's efforts are framed by sufficient extant materials of the subject's life and effect upon society. More than one dozen archival repositories were consulted in the research phase of this project. Most of the relevant data is held by Our Lady of Victory, the Diocese of Buffalo, and the Buffalo and Erie County Public Library. Many additional smaller repositories provided invaluable information on certain specific elements of Baker's apostolic endeavors. Unfortunately, the one area of disappointment with respect to sources was the Archives of the Sisters of St. Joseph of Buffalo. This religious community played an integral role in the three major Institutions supervised by Baker: St. Joseph's Orphan Asylum, St. John's Protectory, and Our Lady of Victory Infant Home. Yet records of these Institutions, correspondence between various religious and Baker, and other related documents are not extant. One additional major lacuna is the almost total absence of any financial records for Baker's Institutions. The extant record available shows that annually Father Baker was asked to raise monies in the range of $100,000 or more. The basic explanation that Father Baker raised sufficient capital through mail solicitation and donations alone simply does not satisfy this writer's historical sensibility. Still, with the sources available, a complete narrative and analysis of Father Baker's life and work, within the context of American Catholic history of the period, is presented. This biography seeks to remove the hagiographic halo from the head of Father Baker and replace it with a detailed examination, allowing readers to draw their own conclusions concerning his sanctity. While spirituality is addressed briefly in the epilogue, it is *not* the intention of this writer to make suggestions concerning Father Baker's cause for canonization.

The accomplishments of Nelson Baker were numerous and noteworthy. His long life spanned the period of American history from the establishment of frontier outposts in the Wild West to the dark days of the Great Depression. Father Baker actually served in the Civil War as a member of New York's 74th Militia. Then, for a brief stint of approximately four years, he was a very successful businessman at the outset of the Gilded Age, when rising industrialism and organized labor were engaged in their epic confrontation. He finally found his true vocation and was ordained to the priesthood at age thirty-four, when most of his peers had already been settled in their life routine for some ten years. He came to prominence in the Buffalo area during the Progressive Era. His work with orphans and troubled boys resonated with those who were promoting social causes, characterized by the Protestant Social Gospel that was prominent during the era. During his later days, when the nation was forced to detour due to economic disaster, Father Baker also shifted to meet the need placed before him.

Nelson Baker's longevity provided the opportunity for him to achieve significant goals in his chosen vocation of priesthood. A priest for sixty years and a pastor for fifty-four years—at Saint

Patrick's Parish, which later became Our Lady of Victory—Baker served God's people by celebrating the sacraments, visiting the sick, burying the dead, and educating children. At age seventy-nine, when most priests had been retired for several years, Nelson Baker initiated the construction project of a lifetime, the National Shrine Basilica of Our Lady of Victory, which today stands as a physical reminder of his life, work, and enduring love and devotion to the Blessed Virgin Mary.

As superintendent of three major Institutions that cared for youth, Baker, from the perspective of many, set his mark on history. His supervisory role at the Orphanage and Protectory was certainly significant, but other men and women have done similar work. More significant were new Institutions that addressed contemporary problems. When, to his disgust and horror, Baker heard of infant skeletons being found in the sewers and storm drains of a local city, he responded immediately by starting what would be called the Our Lady of Victory Infant Home, where the needs of single mothers and their children were met in a safe Christian environment.[5] Ever mindful of the trust and confidence these women placed in him, Baker unswervingly held fast against New York State officials who demanded that he change his policies with respect to disclosure of information to prospective adoptive parents. Disagreements with other socially concerned Catholics who worked with children did not faze Baker. Backed by his local ordinary, Bishop William Turner, Baker carried the day in his fight against the State, until his death led to changes in the operation of the Institutions. Baker also supervised residences for young adults, his Working Boys and Working Girls Homes. Thus, Baker's Institutions provided service to youth from birth to maturity. All these projects, including construction of buildings and the day-to-day operations, were financed, according to remaining sources, as alluded to earlier, through a creative direct-mail campaign, the Association of Our Blessed Lady of Victory. Unique for its day, this financing plan, promoted through its two publications, the *Annals* and *The Victorian*, together with generous benefactors over the years, allowed Baker to serve thousands of children and by extension their families. Indeed, the historian Timothy Allan aptly summarized Baker's contribution:

> He compiled a record of personal spirituality, social
> uplift, material generosity, unstinting pastoral charity,
> Christian evangelism and outreach, development and
> construction which has rarely been matched and even
> more rarely exceeded.[6]

Nelson Baker was held in sufficient respect and wielded the necessary
clout to do what he wanted to do in meeting the needs of others.

Baker actually (and literally) wore three ministerial hats (a black
biretta, a miter, and a scarlet-trimmed biretta): superintendent of the
Our Lady of Victory Institutions, pastor of St. Patrick's parish (later
Our Lady of Victory), and vicar general (and twice administrator) of
the Diocese of Buffalo. While Father Baker's work in each area was
significant, the bulk of his time and energy went to the Institutions.
In a typical fashion for the day, Baker delegated much of his parish
ministry to curates. His diocesan duties were irregular and were
manifested most notably in his work with communities of women
religious. Thus, while some balancing was necessary, Baker, while
working in three different domains, could still concentrate his efforts
toward his Institutions in Lackawanna.

The engine that drove the machine of Nelson Baker was his
unwavering and popular devotion to the Blessed Virgin Mary, under
her title of Our Lady of Victory, and his great zeal toward frequent
reception of the Eucharist in Holy Communion, the latter idea preceding by twenty years a similar call by Pope (later Saint) Pius X. In
the late spring of 1874, while a seminarian, Baker participated in a
pilgrimage to Europe that allowed him to discover his patroness
when by chance he visited Notre Dame des Victoires Church in
Paris. For the rest of his life, Baker placed all of his endeavors and
projects under the patronage of Our Lady of Victory. He seems to
never have been disappointed. As a seminarian, he began a lifelong
commitment to frequent reception of the Eucharist, an idea which
he strongly promoted among his young charges in the Institutions.
Toward the end of his life, Baker reflected on his work and the heav-
enly dynamos that supported him:

> Everything has been going along nicely, and our num-
> ber of persons to care for has been growing, and we have

had a great deal of responsibility and many things to take care of, but Our Lord has been very good to us and He has blessed us in many ways and we never can thank Him sufficiently and His Holy Mother for the[ir] continual watchfulness over us and our cares.[7]

This biography seeks to bring to full light a remarkable figure in Catholic philanthropy, not one who gave up only monetary or material possession, but more important, one who gave his life for the cause of those who lived on the margins of society. One of Baker's close colleagues, Brother Stanislaus, a member of the Brothers of the Holy Infancy and Youth of Jesus, stated what many experienced in Nelson Baker:

I came here [Our Lady of Victory] to follow a trade and I stayed to follow a man. What really made me want to stay here more than anything else was that I wanted to live in the sunlight of Father Baker's spirit. The kindliness, the gentleness of the man, his understanding of boys, his love for all people, [and] his faith in the goodness in everybody—these things seemed far more precious to me than the half-hearted promise of the competitive work day world.[8]

Baker did not have the advantage of Hollywood or the services of an actor like Spencer Tracy, who in the 1938 film portrayed the famous Father Edward Flanagan of Boys Town to be his public promoter. Yet, for those who live in the Buffalo / Western New York area, Nelson Baker can match Father Flanagan stride for stride. One local Buffalo radio broadcaster, Jack McLean, commented: "Father Baker was a remarkable man. He was a builder, humanitarian, faithful disciple of the Master. No panegyric is needed now. His own life speaks for itself. No monument of marble is required to preserve his memory."[9] In November 1999, the *Buffalo News* named Baker the City's "most influential citizen of the 20th century."[10] One Buffalo priest, writing thirty years ago, offered an appropriate summary of the priest's life and contribution:

Nelson Baker was able to re-define his priesthood by incorporating much of the traditional virtues of the American priesthood with the dynamic styles of a charismatic churchman, a dedicated social worker, an astute businessman, and a "back-room" clerical politician, and play all the roles well.[11]

Nelson Baker's life and ministry continues today in the work of Baker Victory Services and its development affiliate, Our Lady of Victory Homes of Charity. With facilities that serve some of the most marginalized individuals, including those with severe physical and mental disabilities, as well as troubled youth, Father Baker's legacy continues to serve the people of Western New York. Under the experienced eyes of those who guide this charity today, it is clear that the dream inaugurated more than a century ago continues to be lived. With a paid staff of over 1,000 and annual budget of $55 million, over 5,000 people a year continue to be served as a result of the vision and inspiration of one man. Father Nelson H. Baker was a disciple of Jesus Christ and Our Lady of Victory; he was, as labeled by some, the "Padre of the Poor." In his heart, however, he was the "Father of the Fatherless," and proclaimed by his life Christ's message of love. His was a life to emulate and celebrate.

CHAPTER 1

Early Days in Buffalo (1842–1869)

America's victory over Great Britain in the War of 1812 paved the way for the new United States, now free from all European ties, to expand westward and fulfill what became known as its "Manifest Destiny"—and yet what today is seen by historians as a national myth. Americans began to pour over the Alleghenies in significant numbers, leading to the opening of the Midwest and eventually to expansion across the continent to the West Coast. The first wave of immigrants—dominated in the pre–Civil War, also known as antebellum, period by Germans and Irish—began to flock to America's shores seeking new lands, freedom, religious liberty, and, for many, a new lease on life. This westward expansion in the State of New York was greatly enhanced by the completion of the Erie Canal, which opened on October 26, 1825. Then referred to by many as the "Eighth Wonder of the World," the canal connected the Mohawk River (which connected to the Hudson) at Rome, New York, to Lake Erie, with its terminus in Buffalo. This engineering marvel allowed for the safe and rapid transportation of goods by water from the Atlantic Ocean to the Midwest. Additionally, it became the catalyst to the expansion and development of the City of Buffalo.

Nelson Baker, Buffalo, and Catholicism, 1821–1869

Like many great American cities, Buffalo had a simple foundation that was linked to the native peoples of the region. In 1792 and 1793, Robert Morris, one of the most celebrated financiers of the Revolutionary War era, sold a large tract of land in what is today western Pennsylvania and New York, but at the time was under the jurisdiction of the Commonwealth of Massachusetts. The buyers were a group of Dutch capitalists. Known in history as the "Holland Land Purchase," this region had never been legally procured from the Seneca Indian tribe that occupied the region. Thus, on September 15, 1797, after three weeks of constant negotiations, Morris, with the permission of the United States government, finalized a treaty with the Senecas for rights to the land. The Treaty of Big Tree (as it was called) gave Morris's investors more than 5,000 square miles of territory; it reserved a mere 130 square miles of land for the native population. Eventually, however, by 1842 the Senecas had sold all of this land as well.[1]

The newly acquired land was then surveyed to prepare it for new settlers, who soon began to arrive as part of the nation's westward expansion. Between 1798 and 1800, Joseph Elliott, who had earlier worked with his brother Andrew and the French city planner and architect Pierre L'Enfant in the layout of Washington, DC, surveyed the region, including a plan for the town of "New Amsterdam." In 1804, Timothy Dwight, the fabled Congregational minister and grandson of Jonathan Edwards, described this small village as "a casual collection of adventurers, living like most frontier folks in a state of relaxed religious discipline."[2]

The small village initially developed slowly, but with the completion of the Erie Canal, expansion was more rapid. In 1808, New Amsterdam was officially named Buffalo and was made the seat for Niagara County. In 1813, the town, then with a population of slightly over 2,000, was burned by the British, but the hearty frontiersmen quickly rebuilt what was lost and then expanded. In 1821, Niagara County was divided into northern and southern regions, with Buffalo part of the new southern Erie County. In 1832, the year of the town's incorporation, the population was 9,200, but with the Canal's boon to commercial enterprise, population in 1850 swelled to 42,261.[3] Still, Buffalo was not what one would call an attractive place. The historian Frances Trollope wrote of Buffalo in the 1830s: "Of the thousand and one towns I saw in America I think Buffalo is the queerest looking....All the buildings have the appearance of having been run up in a hurry, though everything has an air of great pretension."[4]

The commercial sector of the burgeoning city met the expanding population's needs with products shipped via the Canal, yet the development of the rest of the metropolitan area lagged. Streets remained unpaved and public spaces were underdeveloped or abused. Writing about Buffalo in the 1850s, the historian David Gerber concludes, "For those seeking beauty or culture, this [Buffalo] was hardly an inspired or inspiring landscape."[5]

While the physical development of Buffalo may have lagged, the religious growth of the region was rapid and significant. In the first half of the nineteenth century, the Western New York region from the Finger Lakes west to Rochester (referred to as the "Burned-Over District") was a haven for the establishment of several native-grown Christian groups and sects. Charles Finney, one of the most prominent preachers of the Second Great Awakening,[6] organized and preached numerous revivals in this region between September 1830 and June 1831[7] and conducted a two-month revival in Buffalo between April and June 1831.[8] This region, specifically Palmyra, New York, saw the birth of the Church of Jesus Christ of Latter Day Saints (the Mormons), which today continues to grow and flourish throughout the world. Millennial groups such as the Millerites, and utopian communities such as the Shakers, were popular in Western New York as well. Communitarian groups, such as the short-lived Oneida Community of John Humphrey Noyes and its radical and highly provocative concept of "complex marriage," were also present in the district.[9]

Catholicism's roots in the Greater Buffalo area find their origin in the early seventeenth century. In the fall of 1626, Franciscan friars from the Huron mission northwest of Lake Ontario visited this region. In 1821—almost two hundred years later—Bishop Henry Connolly of Philadelphia passed through the area while traveling to Quebec. That same year Patrick Kelly, an Irishman from Kilkenny College, became the first Catholic priest assigned to Western New York. After two years of difficult labor, he left the region, continuing west to Michigan. Father Michael McNamara followed Kelly, serving as a resident priest outside Rochester from 1825 to 1832.[10] During those periods when Buffalo had absolutely no priests, Catholics practiced their faith through family prayers and devotional literature. Periodically Catholics made the three hundred mile trek to Albany, where the closest priest resided, to validate marriages, confess their sins, and receive the Eucharist.

The initial lack of permanent clergy and Church organization was quickly rectified when Buffalo's enhanced status as the terminus of the Erie Canal prompted action. In 1804, Louis LeCouteulx took up residence as one of five Catholic families in a local population of one thousand. In January 1829, Father Stephen Badin, the first priest ordained in the United States, while returning to his station in the Diocese of Bardstown, Kentucky, met and stayed with LeCouteulx. When LeCouteulx agreed to cede a plot of land to start a parish and cemetery, Badin agreed to ask John DuBois, bishop of New York City, that he send a resident priest to Buffalo. Grateful for the benefaction, DuBois visited Buffalo that year and discovered to his pleasant surprise that, besides the small Catholic community headed by LeCouteulx, there were also eight hundred recently arrived Swiss and Alsatian Catholics in the area. In 1831, using money he had obtained in Europe, he erected a small wooden church, "The Lamb of God," which became St. Louis Parish. Eventually, DuBois assigned Father Nicholas Mertz as the founding pastor.[11]

When DuBois returned to Buffalo in 1831, he found a community that was divided with "considerable discord in the Church between its German and Irish members."[12] While the parish served principally the German and Alsatian communities, Irish immigrants and other new arrivals attended services at the church. In the early 1830s, with the number of Catholics rising, the capacity of St. Louis Church was exceeded. In 1833, the Irish decided to withdraw from the parish and start their own community. In 1837, Father Charles Smith was sent from Albany to Buffalo to serve the Irish community. Services were held in various places until 1841, when St. Patrick's Church was constructed. By 1843, St. Louis and St. Patrick were joined by St. Mary (a second German parish) as the three parishes serving Buffalo's Catholic community.[13]

The growing Catholic community of antebellum Buffalo was generally accepted by the Protestant majority. Buffalo's rough edges, manifested through its pioneer spirit and the aforementioned lack of physical development, necessitated some counter to keep stability. This antidote was supplied, as described by historian David Gerber, by the Catholic Church. Emphasizing the moral structure of Catholicism, he writes:

> A religion which could exact such disciplined behavior in behalf of order and benevolence from its clergy, could do so too from its lay adherents; and while such secular influence may have been criticized when it came to partisan politics, when the matter ultimately influenced the development of the type of moral character that kept people orderly and out of the poorhouse, it was deemed laudable...[He continues,] Protestantism...in comparison to Catholicism, seemed lacking in the structures which formed moral character.[14]

It was this growing, yet at times ethnically divided, Catholic community that welcomed Nelson Henry Baker, born on February 16, 1842,[15] the second son of Louis (Lewis) Baker and Caroline Donnellan. Baker and his three brothers,—Lewis (born 1839), Andrew (born 1845), and Ransom (born 1846)—practiced their father's Lutheran faith, but their mother was a faithful Catholic. Nelson's paternal grandfather was Christian Becker (*Baker* is the anglicized version of the German). Becker and his wife, Charlotte, emigrated with their son, Louis, aged seventeen, from the Grand Duchy of Hesse (Darmstadt, Germany) to a French port. They took passage on the *Henri IV* to the port of New York, arriving on October 25, 1834. They continued their journey west, settling in Buffalo.[16] Nelson's mother was Caroline Donnellan, who was born to an Irish father in London in 1816. As a child she emigrated to the United States, spending the last forty-six years of her life in Buffalo.[17] Through his father's influence, Nelson was baptized at St. John's Evangelical Lutheran Church, located near his home, on March 18, 1842.[18]

Baker was raised in a middle-class family that was typical in many ways. Louis Baker was a successful businessman who operated a grocery and general store on Batavia Street; the family residence was above the storefront.[19] Baker's family was also typical in that it was a inter-ethnic marriage—but quite atypical in its cross-ing of religious lines. His mixed ancestry typified the two major immigrant groups in antebellum America, and, as alluded to ear-lier, in Buffalo specifically.

Germans were clearly the strongest numerically of all immi-grant groups in Buffalo prior to the Civil War, yet divisions were present on many fronts. Nationally, between 1841 and 1860, almost 1.5 million Germans immigrated to America's shores. In 1855, 39 percent of Buffalo households were German-speaking, including Germans, Austrians, Alsatians, and Swiss. The commu-nity was not cohesive geographically in the city. Indeed, as histo-rian David Gerber points out, there was no one area of the city that German peoples occupied, although they were significantly present in wards 4, 5, 6, and 7. They were divided economically, but were generally financially prosperous. Social class, Gerber points out, "was a potential source of differentiation,"[20] as was religion. In 1839, in order to service German Lutherans, the German Evangelical Church of the Holy Trinity and the First German Evangelical Lutheran Trinity Church were established. Prior to the Civil War, six German Catholic churches, serviced by Redemptorists and Jesuits, were in operation.[21] These parishes served 10,000 people, representing about 60 percent of Buffalo's German-speaking Christians.[22] Indeed, because the Germans were largely serviced by religious orders (like the Jesuits and Redemptorists), the rule of the local bishop, John Timon, CM, "was at best indirect"[23] (because the bishop himself was of the Vincentian Religious Order, also known as the Congregation of the Mission, or the Lazarites). Lastly, intra-German rivalries existed based on whether people departed from Europe before or after 1848, when many wars of European revolution ended.

Significantly, however, despite the many divisions in the German-speaking community, "by the 1850s a strong sense of German identity and group commitment was becoming evident."[24] The community was held together by language, culture, and ide-ology; by an extensive pattern of secular, religious, and political associations; and even by occasional mobilizations in defense of what was common to all of them in their way of life. Indeed, Gerber succinctly captured the essence of division that creates unity: "There is a paradox in intra-ethnic conflict: the more members of the emergent group quarreled with one another, the more they became involved in being ethnic and in attempting to determine the destiny of the group."[25]

During these formative years for the Church in Buffalo, the Germans held control. Not only did they dominate St. Louis parish, but Timon recruited German Jesuits to establish St. Michael's parish (only a few blocks from St. Louis) to serve the needs of German Catholics (ironically, Germany as a unified country did not come into being until 1871).

The other significant players in the ethnic mix of Buffalo, as well as in the life of Nelson Baker, were the Irish. Nationally, between 1841 and 1860, nearly 1.7 million Irish immigrants established themselves in the United States. As with Irish immigration in general, the great catalyst that brought these people to Buffalo was the potato blight, which caused the Great Famine of the 1840s. Characteristically, the Irish were less educated, and possessed fewer technical skills than their German contemporaries. This was a formula for fewer opportunities, especially in the job market. Gerber accurately describes the situation most Irish workers faced: "Their lack of urban job experience and skills combined with the city's tremendous need for unskilled labor to guarantee them a secure foothold only in the secondary labor market."[26] Moreover, the poverty—as well as the lack of business acumen, technical skills, and education for the majority of the Irish population—curtailed this community's general economic development. Negative stereotypes abounded: The Irish male, "Pat," was seen as ignorant, cunning, lazy, self-indulgent, drunk, superstitious, and prone to violence. His female counterpart, "Bridget," was labeled with many of these same defects, but had her own unique ones as well—she was undependable and a horrible cook. When she wasn't stealing valuable household things (as a maid), she was breaking them.[27] Gerber suggests that while some of these stereotypes might be ascribed to "American poverty or the alienation resulting from the immigration and resettlement process...the roots lay deep within the fabric of Irish peasant culture."[28]

The Irish may have suffered on the low end of the labor and economic ladders for the laity, but with respect to the Church, the

Irish on the national level dominated and exercised significant control from their positions in the hierarchy, causing significant friction with the Germans. David Gerber points out that Irish interference in the Church "frequently irritated German Catholics, just as the prominence of the Irish in politics and government irritated German Democrats and most Americans."[29] Both nationally and locally in Buffalo, Irish churchmen flexed their muscles in ways that brought negative reactions from others, especially their ethnic rivals, the Germans. Their outright dominance in the ranks of the episcopacy alienated Germans, leading to conflicts in certain celebrated cases. Nationally this situation reached its apex (or, depending on your politics, its nadir) late in the century with the Abbelen Memorial of 1886 and its counterpart, the Lucerne Memorial of 1891, championed by Peter Paul Cahensly.[30] More locally, Germans reacted against the forceful style of many Irish clerics, who served in secular as well as Church leadership, due to the weakness of the Irish laity. Irish priests generated many enemies as a result of their tactics when operating in the secular sphere of society. Historian John Higham, best known for his studies on immigration, commented that the Irish priest maintained a particularly "combative and brutally repressive style of public leadership which infuriated Americans because of its self-confidence and terrified them because of its resourcefulness and single-mindedness."[31]

In defense of the Irish it must be noted that local mobilizations by the clergy generally defended the Church in the public sphere. The Church was responsible for giving birth to, guiding, and strengthening the formal organizations that emerged from the burgeoning ethnic diversity of American Catholicism.

The religious environment of Buffalo that surrounded Nelson Baker in his youth made no obvious impression on the boy, who exercised the responsibilities and freedoms of someone his age. Baker attended local public elementary school #12, which was at the corner of Batavia and Spring streets.[32] He then matriculated to Buffalo's first secondary school, Central High, from which he graduated at age seventeen.

Baker was described at the time as "a thin wiry boy who possessed a gentle, but strong disposition, a ready smile and a pleasant sense of humor."[33] He was talented in many ways, but most especially athletically and musically. He was an avid baseball player and liked to sing and play the piano and guitar. Joseph Edwards, who knew Baker as a boy, once commented, "There were some good musicians among the younger set in the neighborhood, but Nelson Baker was acknowledged the best player and singer."[34]

Baker was popular with his peers and would certainly have been classified as "the life of the party." Mary Winter Dole, one of his peers, stated many years later, "Nelson was a very popular young man at…parties because he could sing, dance, and play various instruments: piano, guitar, and snare drum. He even composed some pieces." He was considered a "real catch" by the girls.[35] And he was not above practical jokes. His biographer Floyd Anderson relates how Baker and his younger brother Ransom managed to switch the flags flying at the headquarter offices of the Republican and Democratic parties in Buffalo, to the shock of the politicians, but to the brothers' great delight.[36]

Upon graduation from Central High, Nelson joined his brother Lewis in their father's dry goods and grocery shop. He demonstrated a quick mind, was good with mathematics, and was enjoyed by all for his genial personality. It was clear that he possessed the requisite skills to be successful in business. Baker's physical and intellectual development was matched by an equally rich spiritual maturity.

There is no extant record that clearly explains the reason, but Baker was re-baptized a Catholic by Father Joseph Lennon on November 29, 1851, at St. Patrick's Parish. Lennon and family friend Anna Brooks served as his sponsors.[37] Assuredly, Baker's decision to enter the Roman Catholic Church came from the influence of his faithful mother. Years after his ordination, he wrote: "I thank God for having raised me to the dignity of the Catholic priesthood through the influence of an Irish Catholic mother."[38] From this start Baker began to develop a Catholic spirituality. When he was twelve years old, his parents gave him a dollar to spend any way he chose. He decided to purchase a porcelain statue of the Blessed Virgin Mary, a sacramental that he always kept close to him. His true devotion to Our Lady was present even at such a tender age. His actions at such a young age were a clear foreshadowing of his later devotion to Our Lady of Victory. A couple years later Baker completed his Christian initiation by receiving the sacraments of Holy Communion and Confirmation at St. Joseph's Cathedral.[39]

Nelson Baker's maturation in the faith came at a time when the Church in Buffalo was being formally established. The rapid expansion of commerce and the consequent influx of people, development of towns, and local governments led in 1847 to the division of the New York Diocese. Albany and Buffalo became their own dioceses. On October 17, 1847, at St. Patrick's Cathedral in New York, John Timon was consecrated the first bishop of Buffalo by Archbishop John Hughes. Timon, a Vincentian priest ordained in 1825, had worked in St. Louis and also as a missionary in Texas. In 1835, he was asked to head the American mission for his congregation. Between 1839 and 1847, he was asked on several occasions to take a diocese, but he rejected the offers. Finally, in 1847, feeling he could no longer refuse the repeated requests, Timon accepted his new assignment in Buffalo, delivered by the bishop of St. Louis.[40]

Timon spent the first two years of his time in Buffalo visiting the enormous, sprawling diocese and making an evaluation of its needs. His extensive visitation revealed the true poverty of the diocese. There were only eighteen priests, many of whom were elderly and infirm. Clerics were hard to recruit and could not be counted on to remain in the diocese if they came at all. In 1854, he started a seminary, but it produced very few vocations before inevitably closing. Many parishes did not possess the requisite sacred vessels (the chalice and paten) and other necessities to properly celebrate the sacraments.[41]

The situation in the diocese necessitated that Timon take action, especially to raise funds and seek religious and clergy for the many ministerial needs. Thus, on November 14, 1849, the bishop traveled to Europe seeking assistance. Fortunately, he was highly successful in his quest, raising significant monies for many projects, and bringing back to the diocese priests and religious sisters, who would be critical for the promotion and expansion of Catholic education. He returned on June 6, 1850, with $8,000 cash, many vestments and additional liturgical items, and, possibly most important, students for the seminary.[42]

Upon his return Timon set his sights for an expansion of the diocese on several fronts. His initial and primary goal was the construction of a cathedral. In 1851, he broke ground on the site, but without sufficient financing, the project slowed. However, he was able to secure the necessary money from Mexico and Spain so that St. Joseph's Cathedral was dedicated in 1855. The growing number of Catholics required yet more parish churches. Between 1850 and 1880, with the Catholic population moving from 70,000 to 100,000, the number of parishes in the diocese increased from 58 to 135 (national parishes rising from 5 to 24), and parish schools increased tenfold from 4 to 40. Clergy more than tripled from 53 to 166, and the number of women religious sky-rocketed from 19 to 407.[43]

Timon's contribution to the Church in Buffalo was certainly significant. While he might be faulted for his penchant to micromanage affairs, believing that anything important in any parish needed his sanction, he was responsible for organizing the diocese and placing it on a solid footing for the future. He was known as one who loved his priests, but his autocratic style of leadership demanded their obedience. He demonstrated great zeal (as will be described in detail later) for charitable and educational institutions. The historian David Gerber aptly captured Timon's commitment in the context of mid-nineteenth-century America: "Tailoring his own actions and the character of the diocese itself to suit the American environment, Timon was successful in demonstrating the usefulness of the church to a society that was hardly predisposed to be hospitable to it."[44] Maturing in the faith during this period, Nelson Baker was certainly aware of Timon's efforts on behalf of the diocese.

Catholicism during the early years of Nelson Baker's life in Buffalo was dominated by a major conflict between the lay trustees of St. Louis Church and Bishop Timon, a disagreement that became a cause célèbre on a national level. Almost immediately after his arrival, Timon took up residence in St. Louis Church, the first and primary parish in the city. The new bishop was perceptive enough to realize that, as described earlier, at least an awareness of conflict would exist between himself as an Irishman and the German-dominated community at St. Louis. Thus, he quickly appointed Father Francis Guth, pastor of St. Louis, as vicar general. Additionally, he managed to secure German-speaking Jesuits to serve in three of four new parishes, and established the *Aurora* as the diocesan German-language newspaper. Still, as David Gerber suggests, even Timon's more "indirect rule" over German Catholics did not achieve its desired end.[45]

The conflict between a bishop of Irish ancestry and the German-speaking lay majority at St. Louis was only half the problem. The more fundamental disagreement—and what would generate sufficient stir to cause papal intervention—was their differences of opinion on the concept of "lay trusteeism." In his authoritative study on this subject, the American Church historian Patrick Carey demonstrated how trusteeism became the basis for the formation of many parishes, and was generally accepted as a satisfactory way to expand the faith in regions where the Church had not been officially organized through the formation of a diocese. Basically, trusteeism was a system whereby a group of laymen served as overseers of a parish. Initially these trustees secured land, constructed a church, and, possibly most important, often *hired* the parish priest. This system worked well in most places, but celebrated cases in Virginia and New York City, where conflicts arose between the trustees and Bishop John Carroll—then the sole bishop in America—concerning control and decision making in the parish, doomed the system as any permanent method to establish parishes and expand the Church.[46]

The trustee model was attractive and in vogue in American Catholicism for at least two significant reasons. First, the system met the needs of a rapidly expanding Catholic population in areas before a diocese was formed. Second, the model was consistent with Protestant models that assisted a parish to function in the absence of episcopal control. The trustee situation at St. Louis was exacerbated when the European Franco-German tradition of lay administration was rejected by an Irish bishop, who perceived any conflict as lay disobedience. Gerber synthesizes the nature of the disagreement:

> The chaotic situation of ethnic Catholicism in the mid-
> nineteenth century, which is suggested by the miscon-
> strued ethnicities complicating the parish's relations
> with its bishops, led an accepted Old World religious tra-

dition to become the circumstance for New World disobedience.[47]

When the trustees at St. Louis parish refused to abide by Bishop Timon's order with respect to control of the parish, he resorted to extreme measures. He issued orders of excommunication for several trustees and placed the parish under interdict. Timon also informed the Vatican that "a few disgruntled laymen…wanted absolute control over ecclesiastical temporalities in his diocese." This case and similar problems in Philadelphia promoted Propaganda Fide (the Society for the Propagation of the Faith) to send Archbishop Gaetano Bedini to the United States in 1853 "to investigate the trustee troubles and to try and reconcile trustees to their bishops according to canon law and American legislation."[48] Bedini's mission was an abject failure, due in large measure to rabid anti-Catholicism that perceived the heavy hand of Pope Pius IX "crushing" the spirit of American democracy that trusteeism exhibited. Not until 1854, through the work of the Jesuit priest Francis Weninger, was a workable compromise concluded. Gerber accurately concluded: "The St. Louis struggle was one of the most bitter and prolonged in the history of the American Church."[49]

The trustee battle at St. Louis Church added fuel to a growing conflagration of anti-Catholicism that was popular and often virulent in antebellum America. This sometimes-pervasive prejudice was not a negative reaction to Catholic theological teaching, but rather to the general perception that Catholics, because of their loyalty to the pope, could not also be loyal to the Republic. Antebellum America was aflame with anti-Catholic rhetoric that was manifest in three principal areas: literature, politics, and education.[50] The famous inventor of the telegraph, Samuel F. B. Morse, in his book *Imminent Dangers to the Free Institutions of the United States Through Foreign Intervention* (1834), claimed that "Popery is opposed in its very nature to Democratic Republicanism; and it is, therefore, as a political system, as well as religious, opposed to civil and religious liberty and consequently to our form of government." In more lurid fashion, two supposedly "escaped nuns," Rebecca Reed and Maria Monk, in their respective works, *Six Months in a Convent* (1835)

13

and *Awful Disclosures of the Hotel Dieu Nunnery in Montreal* (1836), wrote fantastic tales of sexual liaisons between priests and nuns, murdered infants buried in convent basements, and similarly sordid incidents.[51]

Politically, anti-Catholicism was centered in the American, or "Know-Nothing," Party of the period 1850 to 1856. As described by the historian Tyler Anbinder, the Know-Nothings, whose nativist agenda claimed that Catholicism sought to dominate American religious and temporal life, gained a significant following locally and nationally.[52] Many state legislators and governors were Know-Nothings, as were many members of Congress. In 1856, Millard Fillmore, Buffalo native and the thirteenth president of the United States, ran a second time for the White House, this time on the Know-Nothing ticket, claiming his party was the only one that could bring harmony between North and South in their widening gap over the issue of slavery.

Education, more specifically, the existence of Catholic schools, was a third log on the fire of anti-Catholicism. Nativists and promoters of anti-Catholicism saw parochial schools as a means of separation from American society and a rejection of the common (public) school system. David Gerber commented on this point: "Many Protestants saw Catholic 'interference' in the public schools as an effort to subvert the one public agency which pre-pared the young for civic responsibility and participation in a self-governing republic."[53]

Catholics started their own schools to promote their faith, but also to remove their children from perceived damaging influ-ence of public schools, where the King James Version of the Bible, which was not approved by Roman Catholicism, was a standard text. Celebrated acts of violence against Catholic institutions in Charlestown, Massachusetts (1834), and in Philadelphia (1844) were perpetrated because of the education issue.[54]

Anti-Catholicism in Buffalo held some of these ideas, but was also rather unique for Northern urban centers. The historian Timothy Allan describes Buffalo as "a center of nineteenth century exclusivist attitudes."[55] This exclusion was fueled principally by the situation at St. Louis Church. Protestants welcomed the rebellion at the parish and supported the trustees whose fight against the

Church was perceived as right and appropriate. The institutional Church's (the Vatican's) response was perceived as a threat to republican liberty. Champions of anti-Catholicism were disappointed when the trustees eventually compromised in the aforementioned 1854 agreement, which had been brought about by the Jesuit Francis Weninger.

The Buffalo situation was also somewhat unique in that opposition to Catholicism was tempered by attitudes that spoke highly of the Church. David Gerber commented:

> The intense, organized, political anti-Catholicism of the 1850s may well have had a brief public life not because it served transitory political functions, but instead because large and important segments of Protestant opinion remained divided against themselves on the utility of the Church and the worthiness of Roman Catholicism.[56]

For example, Catholic clergy were not targeted as in other regions. Indeed, Gerber pointed out, "The Catholic clergy were models of compassionate charity, self-sacrifice, discipline, and under the ascetic Timon, not simply thrifty, but [given to] penury."[57] Additionally, while Buffalo's Protestants may have rejected Catholics on a more personal level, they applauded their social institutions, such as orphanages and hospitals, and their movements, such as the temperance campaign of Father Theobald Mathew, that passed through the city.

Anti-Catholicism, like the waves of immigration, went into hibernation during the period of the Civil War (1861–65) and Reconstruction (1865–77), but it emerged in the 1880s and beyond in new manifestations. This reemergence of anti-Catholic rhetoric was fueled by events that were largely outside the United States. While new immigrants from Southern and Eastern Europe, many of whom were Catholic, began to arrive once again on America's shores, raising the persistent nativist call for caution, most of the fuel actually came from events in Rome. Publication in 1864 of the "Syllabus of Errors," an appendix to Pope Pius IX's encyclical *Quanta Cura*, raised eyebrows by its perceived rejection

15

of the modern world and exaltation of the position of the pope. This latter idea became even more prominent in 1870 at the First Vatican Council with the declaration of papal infallibility proclaimed in *Pastor Aeternus*. Later still the publication of *Testem Benevolentiae* (January 1899), which ended the Americanist crisis, and *Lamentabili Sane Exitu* and *Pascendi Dominici Gregis* (both in 1907), condemning theological modernism, raised concerns in the minds of non-Catholics that the Church was anti-intellectual and a barrier to progress.[58]

But how did this rather pervasive anti-Catholic environment affect Nelson Baker, whose faith matured at this very same time? It would have been impossible for Baker, a bright young man who was gaining experience as a Catholic, to have missed newspaper criticism of Bishop Timon and the general anti-Catholic rhetoric of the day. Yet the experience does not seem to have had a major negative impact on him. If anything, anti-Catholicism may have inspired him to want to know more and work harder to understand his faith. The historian Timothy Allan has suggested:

> Somehow the youthful Baker must have escaped the harmful and corrosive influences of the ugly nativist, anti-Catholic, anti-immigrant, and exclusivist mentality which troubled the city of Buffalo during Baker's formative years. This escape apparently allowed Baker to grow to a maturity that evidenced no trace of reactive bitterness toward those who were anti-Catholic or anti-Irish (or anti-German) nor did he show any indication of acquired prejudices toward other immigrants or racial or ethnic groups.[59]

Civil War Duty

The election in November 1860 of Abraham Lincoln as sixteenth president of the United States placed in motion a series of events leading to the American Civil War. Certainly the underlying issues of slavery and states' rights, which divided North and South, had been brewing for many years, but Lincoln's election tipped the scales toward outright division, which began with the secession of

16

South Carolina on December 24, 1860. By the date of Lincoln's inauguration, March 4, 1861, seven states had seceded and formed the Confederate States of America. After the first salvo of the war was fired at Fort Sumter in Charleston Harbor on April 12, 1861, four more states joined the Confederate Union.[60]

American Catholics, from the hierarchy on down, supported the Union or the Confederacy generally based on geography: those in the North supported the Union, and those in the South the Confederacy.[61] Nationwide, however, Catholics generally had no significant problem with the actual concept of slavery. The practice was never condemned in the Bible, though both slavery and the slave trade had been by several popes, dating back to John VIII in AD 882 and through Gregory XVI in 1839. On a more practical level, poor and lesser-skilled Irish Catholics viewed emancipated blacks as competition for jobs. Therefore, non-Catholics in Buffalo feared that Bishop Timon and his "subjects" would be pro-Confederacy and antiwar.[62]

The fact that this attitude did not materialize lies principally in the personality and actions of Timon. He was not an abolitionist, but he hoped that slavery could be abolished without the disruption of the Union, an evil that (he felt) would be worse than slavery itself. However, when the Union dissolved and hostilities started, Timon asked his people to respond generously to the call of the nation for assistance. He stated, "The issue has been forced upon us. Our country calls; with patriotic zeal, with devoted hearts, we should obey her call."[63] He often preached to troops preparing to ship out for service. His attitude promoted duty to the Union, not vengeance toward the Confederacy:

> Our country it is our duty not to question, but to obey. So much the more holy will be the war, as it is not one of passion, but of duty. Those gallant soldiers do not rush to battle through enmity, hatred, or revenge. Ah no! They love their brothers of the South; they mourn over the necessity of arraying themselves in arms against their late beloved fellow citizens. A very few, the guilty authors of disunion are blamed, others are pitied as deceived, and all are still loved as brothers. But the

17

South began the war; the North cannot back out without forfeiting its manhood, its honor, and its glorious future. So says our lawful government, so say the wise and the good, throughout the length and breadth of our untainted land. This war, then, is not one of hatred or personal enmity; it is a war of duty, of lofty patriotism, of obedience to our country's call. It is a war to preserve the high standing of our beloved country among the nations of the earth. It is a war which if successful (as who can doubt) will be of benefit to patriotic citizens, in the South as well as the North.[64]

For the first two years of hostilities, New York in general, and Buffalo more specifically, did not really feel any significant effect from the situation. However, in June 1863, General Robert E. Lee led his Confederate army into Maryland and Pennsylvania. On June 15, in order to stem the tide of the invasion, the secretary of war, Edwin Stanton, requested twenty thousand New York State militia troops be prepared for service. Three days later, in response to the call, Nelson Baker, who was still working at his father's grocery business, enlisted as a private in the 74th Regiment of the New York Militia. The next day the 74th and twenty-five other regiments were mustered for service and left immediately for Pennsylvania. Baker's unit arrived at Harrisburg and then moved onto Mount Union to protect railroad lines and a canal in the area. The 74th was present on the outskirts of the Battle of Gettysburg before moving on July 5 to Chambersburg and eventually into Maryland, shadowing General Lee's army in its retreat from its disastrous defeat. By July 9, Baker's unit, which had seen no combat, was in Clear Spring, Maryland. There the 74th engaged in brief skirmishes with Confederate troops.[65]

Although Maryland returned to calm, an emergency situation arose in New York City, prompting the 74th to be ordered there on July 13. For five days, July 13 to 17, New York was rocked by some of the most destructive and deadly riots in the nation's history. Referred to as the "New York Draft Riots," white citizens, generally Irish, went on a rampage, burning buildings and murdering innocent people in response to the Federal Conscription Act of

March 1863. This law stated that all men twenty to thirty-five and all single men thirty-five to forty-five were eligible for military service. However, a provision in the act allowed one to "buy" a replacement—for $300. The Irish in New York, too poor to "buy" a substitute-soldier for themselves, believed the law doomed them to a fight in a war that was being waged to free the very people, slaves, who would be competition for their lower-paying jobs.[66]

Baker's unit was sent "with all possible dispatch" to help quell the riot. The 74th stayed in the city two days, doing what was possible to save homes and businesses, protect the innocent, and bring general calm to the situation. Unfortunately, by the time of their arrival the damage had largely been done. In the melee police were killed, street cars were blown up, a black orphanage was burned, businesses that employed blacks were looted, the mayor's house was attacked, and many free blacks were hunted down and killed. Ironically, however, most of the dead were the rioters themselves.[67] In a sad commentary, Civil War historian Bruce Catton wrote: "The draft riots were based on ignorance, misery, fear, and the inability of one class of men to understand another class; upon the fact that these really were 'classes of men' in a classless American society."[68]

When calm was restored in New York, Baker and his fellow soldiers returned to Buffalo. The unit was mustered out of service on August 3, 1863.

The situation in New York created fear that similar riots might erupt in other areas. Bishop Timon took the opportunity to issue a pastoral letter on July 16 urging calm:

> In New York many misguided men, yet very few, we believe, practical Catholics, have shed blood in the late riot...Dearly beloved, listen to the advice of a father who dearly loves you; submit to law and God will protect you. Should there be a draft, fewer would be drafted than would probably be killed in an unholy struggle against [the] law. And if any of you be drafted, we will try to protect and aid; God will protect, aid and bless, in more ways than we know or dare name...We exhort you to trust in God, and not to lend yourselves to excite mob violence, which leads so often to murder.[69]

Nelson Baker's military service was short, but it foreshadowed his future life. The 74th militia saw only limited combat in the war, but it did help restore order in a chaotic situation. The historian Timothy Allan has captured the significance of Baker's six weeks as a soldier: "As if a sign of things to come, Nelson Baker's military enlistment was marked more by a humanitarian peacekeeping cause than by the interests of death and destruction."[70]

Businessman in Buffalo

As is often the case, business throughout the nation, including Buffalo, profited during the period of the Civil War. By mid-1860, the number of factory workers had increased 50 percent from 1850 levels. In the same period, the number of firms in the city with fifty or more employees jumped from sixteen to twenty-three.[71]

Capitalizing on the business-rich environment and on his already-proven acumen for the discipline, Baker entered into a business partnership with Joseph Meyer. Located at 272 Washington Street, "Meyer and Baker" became a very successful feed and flour business.[72] The business was highly profitable due in large measure to the discipline of the owners and Baker's great business sense. Indeed, Baker's first biographer, Father Thomas Galvin, CSsR, wrote: "The businessmen of the city soon discovered in him [Baker] not only their equal but their superior in finance."[73] Years later a comment on Baker's business expertise rings true: "To the business man he is a hard headed, financial wizard, good natured in his business affairs, but severely honest, and insists that all with whom he deals be likewise."[74]

Despite his success in business and with a bright future almost assured, Nelson Baker felt a call in a new direction. His maturing Catholic faith prompted him to find ways to exercise his skills to assist God's people. During his days with Joseph Meyer, Baker was known for his piety. He became a member of the St. Vincent de Paul Society. He met and assisted Father Thomas Hines, who was superintendent of an orphanage and protectory for boys at Limestone Hill, five miles south of central Buffalo, by providing supplies and teaching Sunday School classes.[75] Additionally, in

1868, Baker contacted Father Joseph Durthaller, SJ, pastor of St. Michael's Church on Washington Street, asking for instructions in Latin. Durthaller agreed to assist Baker and two others, Daniel Walsh and John Fitzgerald, in learning the language.[76] Slowly but surely, Nelson Baker was discovering his true vocation.

Conclusion

Nelson Baker's youth and early adult years set a tone for his future ministry as priest and superintendent of large institutions for boys. He received broad experience through a good public school education and most especially his service as a Union soldier in the Civil War. Quick-witted, insightful, and intelligent, Baker parlayed these virtues into a brief but significant career as a successful local businessman. He learned much about commerce and acquired important tools that he would need later in life. Most especially, his somewhat-unexpected conversion to Catholicism, most probably coming as a result of his Irish Catholic mother's influence, set him in a direction to exercise his experience and gifts in service of God's people. For Nelson Baker this was a time of human formation that led exceptionally well into his formal religious formation upon which he would immediately enter.

CHAPTER 2

Seminary of Our Lady of Angels (1869–1876)

After the Civil War, the American scene was filled with uncertainty, yet driven by hope for a better future. The great wound that the Civil War inflicted on the nation had indeed begun to heal. Although the war had ended, the Union victory turned sour almost immediately when the great champion Abraham Lincoln was felled by an assassin's bullet at Washington's Ford's Theatre on Good Friday, April 14, 1865. The president's death left the country without leadership to successfully incorporate the North's military victory into a way forward for the nation as a whole. Unpopular with Congress and succeeding an icon in the person of the martyred Abraham Lincoln, the new president, Andrew Johnson, was ineffective in implementing a Reconstruction policy that could completely bind up the nation's wound. The bleeding had been stopped but more needed to be done. Social problems arose in many forms, including the great question of what to do with manumitted slaves. Laboring classes wanted a greater share of the economic pie and were ready to revolt to claim what they considered their just due. The nation was heading in a different direction, but it was not completely clear where it would lead.

Similarly, Nelson Baker was in a quandary. A mature man, a veteran of the war with a fine business sense, he had a bright future, but like the nation, he was not certain of his direction. He had proven his ability and was in good position to go forward in a successful career as a Buffalo businessman. But something did not feel quite right; he believed that there was more for him to do and accomplish. Worldly success had already been achieved, but some vague, nameless, and nagging emptiness remained. The next several years would allow Baker to answer the question of his vocation and find his true path. It would not be easy and his choice would be questioned by several people he loved and admired, but he placed his faith in himself, his Church, and most especially God, confident that he had made the proper choice, for him and the people he would serve.

The Decision to Enter the Priesthood

Nelson Baker's business acumen and ability to succeed in this arena had been demonstrated both by his time working with his father and, after his military service, by his partnership with Joseph Meyer. Yet, while Baker's future seemed bright and his direction clear, questions continued to nag the young man concerning his vocation. His volunteer service with the St. Vincent de Paul Society and his friendship with Father Hines gave him a forum from which to better clarify his future. While no personal record of his thoughts from this period is extant, the fact that he was spending considerable time in the service of others and on his Latin lessons clearly demonstrates that ideas beyond his present partnership with Meyer were percolating in his head.

An opportunity to solidify his decision presented itself in the summer of 1868. In July, Baker went with a friend, John Fitzgerald, with whom he was studying Latin at night, on a two-week vacation to New York City. While there, he spent five days at St. John's College in Fordham, a town just outside the city. (St. John's College was officially renamed Fordham University in 1907.) At St. John's, Baker participated in an Ignatian-style retreat under the direction of Jesuit Father Joseph Shea, rector of the college. Typical for the day, the retreat was highly structured, centered on thirteen meditations that included such topics as "Last End—Purpose of Life," "Sin of Adam," "On Avoiding Sin," "Death," "General Judgment," "Blessed Sacrament," and "Vocation."

Baker's retreat notes provide significant insight into his thinking at this critical stage of his life. A sense of urgency to make the right decision is evident in his thoughts. Interestingly, especially as will be seen in the development of his spirituality, Baker started his diary on January 1, 1868—later known as the Solemnity of Mary,

23

the Mother of God—with a long meditation on the Real Presence of Jesus in the Holy Eucharist. The journal then picks up months later during the Ignatian retreat. He centered his meditations, quite naturally, about his vocation decision. Reflecting on the ingratitude of the prodigal son (Luke 15:11–32), he wrote: "How much baser are we towards Almighty God, squandering the gifts which He gives us....How much more infinitely kind and merciful is our Father in opening his arms to us and receiving us back again in his arms."[1] And in a meditation on death, Baker spoke of the need to prepare oneself for God, a state he had not reached:

> We must all die, sooner or later, we know not the day or the hour, be ye always ready with our lamp lighted and our arrangements all made, like a traveler with his trunk packed at the depot waiting for the train [and] ready to jump aboard. Watch and pray for ye know not the day or the hour, like a thief in the night I will come.[2]

Baker's meditations demonstrate how he wrestled with his decision, yet ultimately trusted that God would show him a clear path. In a fashion typical for the day, he spoke of his unworthiness. Speaking of the Eucharist, he wrote, "Oh what graces ought we not ask for when receiving our dear Lord in the Holy Com[munion]. We can not [*sic*] ask to[o] much." He believed that if one was committed, the way would be shown to him. Rather than measuring oneself out, there was a need to give fully, trusting God every step of the way:

> Cast yourself entirely on your dear Lord and be willing to act in conformity to His divine will....Whatever be our vocation, let us show that we are Christians, that we have a soul to save, and let us try to induce others not to attach themselves to earthly things which soon vanish, but to remember that we are here only a little while and let us live in the world as though we were not in the world.[3]

When Baker returned to Buffalo, he sought advice to sort out the retreat and his general thoughts. Probably because of his past association and friendship, he sought counsel from Father Hines at Limestone Hill. The priest told Baker that one way to know if he had a vocation to the priesthood was to petition the bishop for entrance into the seminary. If the prelate said yes, that was a clear sign of God's will. Thus, he met with Bishop Stephen Ryan, Timon's successor, who welcomed him with open arms. Baker informed his business partner of his decision, stating that he would work one more year and then enter the seminary.[4]

Prior to entering the seminary, Baker took one more extended period to "clear his head" and give serious consideration to his future, most especially his relationship with God. Between June 24 and July 12, 1869, he took an eighteen-day trip on the Great Lakes, using the time to visit churches, pray, and mentally prepare himself for his major transition in life that was scheduled to begin in the fall. Baker left Buffalo on the steamer *Professor Winslow*. After twenty-six hours of travel he arrived in Detroit. Debarking from the ship, he attended two Masses at the cathedral, made a visit to St. Mary's Church, and finished the day at St. Anne's Parish with a celebration of vespers (the Church's "Evening Prayer"). Along the trip, taking different vessels, the *Professor Empire* and *Dean Richmond*, he stopped in Windsor, Port Huron, Presque Isle, Mackinac Island, Milwaukee, and Chicago. His diary describes the churches he visited and services attended, with emphasis on his frequent reception of the Eucharist—a form of piety that would become central to Baker's spirituality and that was far ahead of its time.[5]

Nelson Baker had made the decision to enter the seminary, informed his business partner of his choice, and made an effort to strengthen his decision through a retreat and extended trip. Yet possibly his greatest hurdle, that of informing his family, was still to come. Recall that Nelson was the only son of four to convert to his mother's Catholic faith; the others, like Nelson himself, were baptized into the Lutheran tradition of their father.[6] Additionally, the specter of anti-Catholicism was still present in Buffalo, even though it did not seem to have damaged Baker's perspective on religion or life in general. Speaking of the conflict in his family in his early days in the seminary, he wrote, "Father I think does not like to have me here nor my [business] partner, nor bro[ther]s, but

25

my mother and God and Mary do."[7] Concerning Baker's decision, the historian Timothy Allan commented, "In the end, Baker deliberately and consciously chose Church and Lord. In so doing he resisted the lure of success and a share in the wealth that powered the American dream and burnished the Gilded Age."[8]

Our Lady of Angels Seminary (1869–1874)

When Bishop John Timon came to Buffalo in 1847, his see, like most new dioceses, had limited clergy; the need to find more priests was imperative. From the time of the Council of Trent (1545–63)—which mandated the establishment of seminaries as a solution to the ignorance and poor training of clergy that was evident in the Reformation period—local ordinaries had the responsibility to establish a diocesan (or possibly regional) training ground for priests. Thus, in 1851, Timon engaged three priests from the Missionary Oblates of Mary Immaculate in Montreal to open a diocesan seminary in Buffalo. The initiative was not well planned or financed and the school closed in 1855. Not to be deterred, however, Timon immediately turned to his own religious community, the Vincentians, a congregation well known for seminary formation work, to launch an effort in Buffalo. He convinced Father (later Archbishop of Toronto) J. V. Lynch to head the effort. In late 1855, Lynch purchased a large tract of land (approximately two hundred acres) on the banks of the Niagara River two miles below the Suspension Bridge (the seminary later became Niagara University). It took a few more years, but on April 20, 1863, a charter for Our Lady of Angels Seminary was obtained. One year later, fire destroyed the seminary building, but Timon immediately came to the rescue with money and a new building was ready for seminarians in the fall of 1865.[9] The 1869–70 catalog described the seminary:

> The "Seminary of Our Lady of Angels" is an ecclesiastical institution for the education of young men who aspire to the holy state of the priesthood…Our course of studies embraces all that is required to prepare the youthful candidate for the sacred ministry.[10]

Having arranged his personal and business affairs in order to close one chapter in life, Nelson Baker opened this new chapter on September 2, 1869, with his entry into Our Lady of Angels Seminary. His diary relates little about the experience save the mechanics of his move: "On Monday [September 3 we] selected and arranged our little beds and decorated our little place with some holy pictures in the afternoon." Baker shared this experience with about twenty other new students.[11]

Baker entered this new life with much vigor and dedication, especially with respect to his very conservative, even abstemious, self-imposed rules on diet. He set high standards on sacramental participation, stating that he planned to receive Holy Communion every Sunday at 6 a.m. Mass and attend Mass each day at 8:30 a.m. Additionally, he promised to always assist at vespers, Eucharistic Benediction, and all other seminary prayer services. He began a lifelong practice of meager eating. He wrote:

> With thy help, O God, and the help of thy intercession, O Holy Mary, my queen, I hope to receive sufficient grace to avoid sin, and this most detestable vice of *Gluttony* [emphasis Baker]. Assist me to conform to these little rules and not to be controlled by my wicked passions.[12]

More specifically, he described his daily allotment of food. Breakfast: oatmeal, two and a half slices of graham bread, or four oatmeal cakes, and no drink. Dinner (lunch): cracked wheat, two and a half slices graham, or four oatmeal cakes, or a little meat and potato and vegetables, or a little soup and bread. Supper (dinner): two pieces of graham bread and oatmeal, or soak bread in tea and pour off tea and eat bread. He also promised to eat no peaches, pie, custard, bread pudding, bread pudding sauce, cakes, tomatoes, or molasses.[13] Father Baker, to absolutely no one's surprise, was a very thin man his entire life!

Baker entered the seminary's college program, which was normally five years long, but shortened for him because he had completed high school.[14] In his first year, he took Latin grammar and translations, English grammar and composition, German, history, math, ancient geography, declamation, and Christian doctrine. On January 29, 1870, he wrote in his diary: "I have [made] pretty good headway with God's help and the help of His Blessed Mother."[15]

Although he had entered the seminary, Baker did not forget his family members or his responsibilities to them. In his first semester he went home on three occasions, the last one over the New Year's holiday for the express purpose of giving his share of the business to his youngest brother, Ransom. Nelson gave his brother use of his capital and all the profits that would come to him. He hoped to take the interest from the profits to pay his expenses at the seminary and to give some to his parents.[16]

Baker's dedication to his new life was clearly evident in the way he became involved in all sorts of activities. In late September, almost immediately after his arrival, he became involved in organizing Our Lady of Angels Literary Association, serving as the group's first treasurer. As mentioned previously, Nelson Baker was not at all shy, but, rather, possessed an effusive personality that allowed him to be very popular with his peers. He brought these gifts and traits to his days at Our Lady of Angels. He was also active in the formation of the Philharmonic and Dramatic Association (PDA) on February 1, 1870, and served as the group's founding secretary.[17] The PDA's purpose was described in the seminary's history:

> This association was organized for the purpose of entertaining the social gatherings of the students and to cultivate a taste for vocal and instrumental music; also to develop the arts of declamation and of drama; or any such branch that tends to the mutual improvement of the members.[18]

During his first year, the PDA held several presentations, many of which featured Baker and his multiple talents. On February 22, he joined with two other seminarians in a variety skit, "Washington Crossing the Delaware." On the same program, this time playing the guitar, he teamed with the same two men in a medley of songs for guitar, violin, and flute. He rounded out his performance that evening playing the part of Rev. Joshua Drab in a "laughable farce" titled "Prince Arthur's Reception." Less than one month later on St. Patrick's Day, March 17, the PDA sponsored another show. The second play of the evening, titled "Phases of City Life," featured Baker as Abraham Clausen, a cloth dealer.[19]

Baker was equally if not more involved with various societies that fostered the spiritual development of the seminarians. In his first year, foreshadowing his lifelong dedication to the Blessed Virgin Mary, Baker helped initiate the Sodality of Our Lady of Angels (also referred to as the Sodality of the Immaculate Conception), so seminarians devoted to Mary could "reap all the graces and blessings attached to that devotion." In October 1869, he was elected treasurer of the sodality, initiating his association with a group that would claim much of his time for the next several years of his religious formation.[20] On January 6, 1870, about the midpoint of his first year, he helped in the formation of the Society for the Perpetual Adoration of the Blessed Sacrament. He organized the students into two groups, with members from each group alternating for fifteen-minute periods of prayer that did not interfere with studies. Among the needs raised in this time of prayer was the conversion of sinners, including those who would be influenced by their future priestly ministry.[21]

At the end of his first year, Nelson Baker could take great pride in his accomplishments. Besides his active involvement with many groups, for both entertainment and spiritual enrichment, he claimed several academic prizes as well. He received first honors in German, second prize in Latin grammar, and first honorable mention in algebra, history, and Christian doctrine. He could proudly write in his diary, "Have been very much pleased by the past year."[22]

Baker kept active during the summer, preparing for the next academic year and dealing with family matters. Scrupulous about his studies, Baker used the summer (and the following summer of 1871) to continue the study of Latin on his own. He hired a certain "Mr. Wilbert" to tutor him in Latin for 65 cents per session. Apparently the effort was worth the price, for he reported in November 1871, "Am doing pretty well, better than some, thank God and Mary....Commenced to speak Latin in class."[23] Besides Latin, Baker was forced to deal with the persistent call from his family and Joseph Meyer to return to his profitable business. Meyer assumed Baker would spend his summer vacation working in the store, but the latter had no intention to do so. He had made his decision and was not going to change his mind.[24]

Baker returned to Our Lady of Angels in September 1870, ready to continue his chosen path toward priesthood and service to God's people. He reported that he had to "work hard in Latin," continuing to believe himself academically behind other seminarians. Yet, he knew from his record the previous year that he could (and most probably would) excel. Thus, he reported at the outset of the year that he was "getting on nicely."[25]

During the next two years, the remainder of his college program (pre-philosophy and theology), Baker continued his impressive record of active participation and superior academic achievement. He was a popular man at the seminary and was noticed by others. John Reilly, one of Baker's classmates at the seminary and his roommate during their common year of philosophy (1872–73), spoke of the latter's daily constitutional, "trotting about the walk between rising time and morning prayer." He called Baker "wise as a serpent, simple as a dove; but the innocence of the dove is better than the virtue of many serpents."[26] The historian William Emerling noted Baker's ability to stand above others: "Nelson Baker revealed talents and abilities as a student and such powers of self-discipline and determination as a person, that he did stick out while some younger and stronger of his classmates fell by the way."[27]

Throughout his college and seminary days, Nelson Baker continued to be active in the Sodality of Our Lady of Angels. Members agreed to pray the Little Office of the Blessed Virgin Mary every Saturday. Each Wednesday, members attended a conference on various topics. Baker served two terms as prefect of the group, and was asked to continue in this capacity, but the rules of the sodality did not allow him to accept. Under his leadership the sodality welcomed many new members, to a total of seventy-five by the end of academic year 1870–71. Baker gave conferences to the sodality on temperance and strongly encouraged members to "take the pledge" for the summer. Historian and Buffalo diocesan archivist Walter Kern once commented, "By example and word he strongly promoted temperance all his life." Baker also organized outings for the sodality, including a trip to Hamilton, Ontario, in May 1871.[28]

Baker's devotion to the Blessed Virgin was strong, but it was not that unusual for the day. However, his strong commitment to the Eucharist, most notably frequent reception of the sacrament, was not only rare, but far ahead of the Universal Church, which only began to encourage such faithfulness in the early twentieth century under the direction of Pope St. Pius X. Baker promoted perpetual adoration of the Blessed Sacrament as before, but it was his strong belief in the efficacy of frequent Communion that set Nelson Baker apart from others. Indeed, as the historian of American Catholicism Jay P. Dolan has written, "Frequent communion was not customary for Catholics in the United States."[29] Noting that Irish parishes did not advocate first Communion until one was age fourteen, with Germans waiting until age eighteen, the historian Joseph Casino suggests that only monthly Communion or less was normative until the dawn of the twentieth century.[30] American Church historian Joseph Chinnici, OFM, however, has shown that in the 1890s, the Perpetual Adoration groups and Eucharistic leagues, which had sprung up in the United States, energetically promoted frequent Communion, attendance at Benediction, and other Eucharistic devotions.[31]

Baker's devotion to the Eucharist is clearly observed in various written comments as well as his frequent reception of Communion. In a meditation titled "The Sacred Heart: A Heart of Love," Baker expressed in romantic language, not uncommon for the day, his devotion to the Eucharist:

> His Loving Heart in the tabernacle is still sweetly drawing souls to itself and filling them with its own tender affection, and inspiring them to make heroic sacrifices for their own eternal interests, and the interests of the savior God.[32]

Presiding at a Good Friday service as a newly ordained priest, he wrote in his diary, "Was celebrant, carried Most Blessed Sacrament in procession back to altar, consumed it—oh! How I am favored."[33]

31

Additionally, his diary is sprinkled with many entries that contain passages associated with the Eucharist.

During his time at Our Lady of Angels, Baker's devotion to the Eucharist only grew greater, most profoundly through his almost daily reception of the sacrament. In the fall of 1872, at the outset of his philosophy year, he wrote, "Am at present receiving our Blessed Lord Wed[nesday], Sat[urday] and Sun[day]. And he is very kind to me, favoring me at times very much. All I want is his sweet love."[34] Speaking with his spiritual director, Father Robert Rice, he asked permission to increase his reception of the Eucharist from three to four times per week. When he began theological studies in September 1873, he again sought advice from Father Rice, who suggested, "Do as you did last year." Baker continues: "I am a little timid about going so often (5 times), but with God's help I will not fear the remarks of the boys. During vacation I went almost every week 5 times to Holy Communion."[35]

Baker's strong desire for frequent reception of the Eucharist marks him as a transitional figure in American Catholic practice.[36] While there is no certainty, the historian and archivist Walter Kern has conjectured that Baker's mother was the source of his devotion: "She [Baker's mother] was specially devoted to the Blessed Sacrament fervently receiving the Eucharist weekly, when few Catholics did so."[37] Timothy Allan asserts that Baker saw the Eucharist as a "vehicle through which love could be both obtained and exercised." It was a "Divine Gift, powerful in its effect on its recipient...and conveying perhaps a sense of acceptance into favored sonship."[38] It is clear, even at this early stage of his spiritual development, especially through his active participation in the Sodality of Our Lady of Angels, that Nelson Baker had strong devotion to the Blessed Virgin Mary. However, it was his dedication and fidelity to reception of the Eucharist that set him apart from contemporaries and provided him the spiritual engine that would drive his future herculean efforts on behalf of youth and the poor.

Nelson Baker's noteworthy advance in spirituality was equaled by his continued active participation in the seminary's nonacademic events. Plying his musical skill, Baker regularly sang first tenor and played in a quartet called the Niagara Harmonists. Additionally, he often performed with the seminary's Palestrina

Society. His classmates often asked for encores of two popular songs: "I am a Young Man from the Country, from Schenectady I Came," and "Oft in the Stilly Night." He was also a member of the Jobbers' Orchestra, a seven-member ensemble of which the seminary history states: "These gentlemen were ready to discourse sweet strains at a moment's notice, and the proficiency they possessed in the musical line was way beyond the plebian name which they affected for their association." In the fall of 1875, when funds were needed to pay for repairs to the seminary chapel, Baker participated in a "First Class Amateur Concert" that performed locally, as well as in Brooklyn and Albany.[39]

Beyond his musical talent, Baker demonstrated great ability in speech. He became well known throughout the seminary for his rendition of Edgar Allen Poe's famous, mysterious poem "The Raven." His classmate John Reilly said that Baker's presentation "charmed his classmates as well as his professors."[40] On a few occasions he gave eloquent talks to celebrate the birthday of George Washington. The *Niagara Index*, student newspaper for Our Lady of Angels, reported that on February 22, 1871, "Mr. Baker discoursed appropriately upon 'Our Country'—its progress since the days of Washington." The speech was described as "a lucid and precise history of the brilliant success which attended the country, the foundation of whose existence had been so well laid by Washington."[41] Five years later, the paper lauded Baker for another Washington's birthday speech, titled "Catholicity and the Republic":

> Rev. [Mr.] N. H. Baker's attempt was the best oratorical display of the evening. His matter showed much research, and the important part which Catholicity played in the colonization of our country, in the schemes of civilization and in the revolutionary drama was [*sic*] accurately sketched. Add to this that his delivery was almost flawless, and it may, with all justice, be said that his oration was the gem of the evening.[42]

Baker's remaining college days also saw him continue his association with the temperance movement and his garnering of academic prizes. He spoke when the situation presented itself to his peers on the evils of drinking and smoking, and presented his audience with the challenge to "take the pledge" for the summer months. He felt his message was successful as he wrote, unknowingly foreshadowing his future, "I have had good success with small boys." Academically, in June 1871, Baker claimed first prize in declamation and honorable mention premiums in Latin, English, composition, history, and Christian doctrine.[43]

Nelson Baker's transition to seminary life and his progress from the time of his entry were phenomenal, but a significant health challenge interrupted his peace. In December 1871, Baker contracted erysipelas, also known as St. Anthony's Fire, a very serious infectious disease of the skin. Initially he was treated unsuccessfully by two doctors from Niagara Falls. After spending seven weeks at the seminary and making little progress, he was sent to Buffalo Hospital under the care of the Sisters of Charity, where he stayed eleven weeks and received treatment from his family physician. Baker reported in his diary, "Received good care from Dr. Cronyn and the Sisters."[44] Baker returned to the seminary on April 8, but much more time for full recovery was needed. Father William Markoe, one of Baker's classmates, described both the situation and how Baker was respected by all:

> For several weeks we have had two boys at the point of death. One has been half devoured by erysipelas, but seems to be out of danger now. He is one of the two whom I mentioned in one of my first letters as being real saints, and he was [so] looked upon by the whole house. I had the pleasure of sitting with him night before last, and I can assure you I heard a saint talk. You can hardly imagine what it is to hear him talk and now that he is recovering, he speaks of being resigned to the will of God, and of being willing to live to please him as if it were hard for him to live as it is for most men to die![45]

By Easter he was walking with crutches, then with two canes; in July he still needed assistance. In October 1872, he wrote in his diary, "Am still upon one cane, but can walk some without it."[46]

Rather remarkably, Baker continued his studies without interruption, even with his severe illness. Finishing the college program, he spent the academic year 1872–73 in the seminary's philosophy program. Because of his illness, he was excused temporarily from Scripture and Church history courses, placing his main focus on moral theology. Reflecting on the year, which included winning second prize in moral philosophy, he wrote: "We have been examined. We all did well. I think I did remarkably well, better than expected."[47] In January 1873, Baker—using Scripture, the Church Fathers, saints, and other theologians—crafted a series of apologetic discourses on a wide range of topics that included the sacraments, the Spanish Inquisition, exclusive salvation, purgatory, the Blessed Virgin Mary, indulgences, infallibility, and celibacy.[48]

In September 1873, he started his study of theology, the last phase of his seminary education. He reported, "We commenced theology. I had almost the first call and did pretty well thank God." He added a description of the student body: "We [the seminary] are pretty full, about 64 [college students], 48 theologians, and 9 philosophers, about 140—that is very well." His courses that fall were dogma, moral theology, hermeneutics, canon law, and ceremonial and Scripture history.[49]

With the hurdles of college and philosophy education, as well as the severe challenge of ill health having been negotiated, Nelson Baker began to look toward the future in his ministry as priest. At the outset of the year Baker had a conversation with his local ordinary, Stephen Ryan. The bishop surprised Baker by suggesting that he study theology in Genoa, Italy, of all places. Baker asked to decline the invitation, citing his fear that theological study would be too difficult in Europe, especially considering the language difference. Baker had a surprise request of his own. As he wrote in his diary:

> I then told him [Ryan] that I desire to go west, when I finish, if I receive the grace and strength to persevere. He did not like it much, and thought he would not put obstacles in [my] way, but had better take advice about it. My excuses were too many friends in Buffalo, and the great need of priests in the West. But, if God does not

change me, I will go there, as we can get enough men for the East.[50]

At Christmas time, ministry in the West was still a plausible option in Baker's mind. He wrote, "Bishop Ryan...always notices me when the other boys are around, and has some remark to make. I think he wants to hold me, but 'God willing,' I expect and hope to go away from all my friends—West."[51]

Baker also started theology as he had his college program—with a commitment to a life of simplicity and self-denial. Commenting on a retreat taken at the outset of the year, he wrote, "God blessed me much on the 1st day. I enjoyed it [the retreat] very much; I received the Holy Grace to deny myself of *dessert* [emphasis Baker] or other delicate foods for the rest of the retreat. *Thank God* [emphasis Baker] that is ever one of my great weaknesses."[52]

Baker's years as a theologian, while still occupied with many of his activities of the past, provided him the opportunity for new and more challenging experiences and responsibilities.[53] His maturity and well-demonstrated talent for leadership brought him to the eye of the seminary staff. Thus, in September 1872, Baker was asked by the prefect, Father P. V. Kavanaugh, and his spiritual director and prefect of studies, Father Robert Rice, to serve as assistant prefect, initially for one week, but eventually a full semester. Baker reported, "I could not refuse."[54] Speaking of Baker's service as assistant prefect, the seminary history states:

> Possessing tact, gentleness of the proper consistency, and even a thorough knowledge of boys' ways, he proved himself a most efficient aid[e] to the overburdened first prefect, while winning without extra effort on his part from the entire household esteem and affection which the years succeeding have only increased and mellowed.[55]

In January, Baker's position was extended for the rest of the academic year. He described some of his duties: "I must take the boys to breakfast, say morning prayer and at night 'beads,' examine, visit and assist in all duties of Second Prefect."[56]

In the spring of 1873, he became conflicted with his position of assistant prefect. That semester two Vincentians left the seminary for other positions. Baker thought he might be elevated to prefect, but instead Father J. J. Lamey was selected for the position. Baker described the situation: "My self pride prompted to make me think that I would be acting officer, but it was a just humiliation for me to know that others had not as good an opinion of me as I did myself. I thank God for this humiliation and have prayed for that grace."[57] Baker's "humiliation" was surely not a real disappointment, however, for it seems the job was wearing him down. He wrote, "Am still 2nd Prefect—but am getting tired of it—I hope that I will not be forced into it next year—*Deo Assistente*."[58] Still, Baker considered the experience to be quite valuable. He wrote, "I have had very good success with the small boys, and I think most anything can be done with them, if one knows how to manage them."[59]

As he entered theology in September 1873, Baker was free of his duties as assistant prefect, but his responsibilities were shifted in a different direction. Father Rice, now president of Our Lady of Angels, appointed Baker to head the St. Vincent de Paul Society at the seminary. Although Baker was familiar with the society's work from his earlier volunteer efforts with Father Hines at Limestone Hill, nevertheless, he did not want the appointment. Baker explained:

> I tried to get out but he [Rice] walked off and when I told him that I did not think that I could do it, he laughed and said it was *humility* [emphasis Baker]. (I wish it was; there is too much presumption about me.) I will see him again and if he is in earnest, I suppose I must do my best, but I will need God's help very much and *Mary's* [emphasis Baker].[60]

Under Baker's leadership the society grew and prospered. Membership grew from twenty-one to thirty-seven between September and December 1873. Baker reported, "Society progressing well."[61] The society's membership produced a few short plays, including "Colonel Congressman," "Joseph in Egypt," and

"Hawkeye the Detective." The *Niagara Index* lauded the plays and their catalyst: "Of the entertainment as a whole we have nothing to say but that is [*sic* – it] was praiseworthy and highly creditable to its progenitor—Mr. Nelson H. Baker."[62]

Nelson Baker's seminary days allowed him to demonstrate his ability to take responsibility on various levels, but, as should be the case for one considering priestly ministry, it was the human dimension that was most critical. For Baker this critical aspect of his life was best seen in his friendship with Daniel Walsh, which blossomed during their common years at Our Lady of Angels. In August 1873, prior to their formal entry into theological study, the two friends took a vacation cruise on the steamer *Professor St. Louis* that toured the Great Lakes, with stops in Cleveland, Detroit, Mackinac Island, Milwaukee, and Chicago. The trip, which in some ways retraced the same route of Baker's cruise of the summer of 1869, was most notable for an encounter with two fellow passengers, Evans F. J. Wayne and an unnamed Yale College student, both of whom challenged his faith. Based on the thoroughness expressed in his list of "controversial subjects" compiled in January, Baker's defense of the faith must have been clear, consistent, and accurate. In response to the attack and his need to defend the Church, Baker wrote:

> Had the most severe attack of any in my life from a student at Yale, attacked "Infallibility," Immaculate Conception,…indulgences, praying to saints, etc. , forgiveness of sins, tradition, etc., etc., but thank God I think I was able to show him but for our inability, and hope with God's help, to be able to do better in [the] future. [63]

The trip must have been a bonding experience for the two seminarians for upon their return they actively engaged two separate apostolic endeavors. First, the two began teaching Christian doctrine to children at the Chapel of Our Lady of Mercy, the first organized mission of St. Joseph's Cathedral, located on Michigan Street in Buffalo. Their main effort, however, was to raise funds for the Sisters of Our Lady of Charity of the Refuge, commonly known as the

Good Shepherd Sisters. The Sisters' "Convent Book" reports their activity: "Burning with zeal for God's honor and glory and the salvation of souls, [Baker and Walsh] put their heads and hands together in endeavors to brighten the gloomy days for the Sisters and assist them in their heroic work of charity."[64] The two friends "gave entertainments for the benefit of the Sisters and performed many other kindly offerings for them." One fundraiser netted $500 to further the work of the Sisters' community.[65]

Baker's participation in the life of Our Lady of Angels continued to flourish during his days in theology. His expertise in rhetoric was demonstrated in two original essays, "The Young Man of the Period" and "Ambition," both of which were published in the *Niagara Index.*[66] He staged two plays, "Harvest Storm" and "A Reprise of Joseph in Egypt," for the students. Additionally, Baker's membership and participation with seminary organizations, such as the St. Vincent de Paul Society, and his leadership roles, granted him by peers and the seminary staff, continued to be strong.

Nelson Baker seemed settled in his chosen vocation and was well on his way toward the goal of ordination to the priesthood, but he could not ignore nor avoid his family and the business he left behind. Recall that it was Baker's initial hope that his younger brother Ransom would simply take his share of the business and work as partner with Joseph Meyer. However, by November 1871, it seemed Meyer's heart was no longer in the work; Ransom, too, wanted to take another route in life. Nonetheless, in the spring of 1873, Baker reported, "I handed over my business to Ransom, letting him use my capital and giving him all the profits." Still, the business did not run smoothly and financial problems ensued. Baker was forced to lament: "How my relationship with Ransom will end, *I do not know* [emphasis Baker]." In March 1874, Nelson prevailed upon Ransom to continue the business by partnering with their brother Andrew.[67]

As some sense of calm came to the business situation, Baker was able to achieve greater acceptance from his family for his decision to study for the priesthood. His mother continued to be the principal source of family support. In March 1873, he reported, "Mother was down to see me just a week ago, because I did not go home since Christmas, and brought me some apples, oranges, cookies, etc. *What a good mother* [emphasis Baker]." Later that fall he again praised her: "Oh, what a good mother. May God bless her, and preserve her until I can make her happy."[68] Midway through his last year at Our Lady of Angels, there appeared a small opening of acceptance on behalf of his brother Ransom. Speaking of his service as sub deacon at some Masses attended by his brother, Baker wrote, "Ransom wrote me a congratulatory letter, in answer to mine, very nice, says he will be pleased when he sees me in *possession* [emphasis Baker]."[69]

Pilgrimage to Rome—1874

Nelson Baker's latter years at Our Lady of Angels were a time when major events in the Universal Church created a significant impact on American Catholicism. The nineteenth century saw the rise of several ideologies that the Church viewed as hostile to Christian thought. Rationalism, socialism, liberalism, communism, and religious indifferentism were countered by Church documents and policies that sought to correct errors and reemphasize the central position of Catholicism in the life of people. The institutional Church was also under attack from within its own ranks. Gallicanism, known in some lands as Febronianism or Josephinism, which drew its name from the Gallican Articles of 1682, promoted the power of the local national church in decision making. Ultramontanism, on the other hand, was the belief that all answers to questions of faith must be found by literally looking ("over the mountains") to Rome. Beginning in August 1832, with the promulgation of Pope Gregory XVI's encyclical *Mirari Vos*, which attacked liberalism and religious indifferentism, the Vatican staunchly and consistently raised its voice against the ideologies of the age and its opponents within its own ranks. This stance reached its apex in the pontificate of Blessed Pius IX. In 1864, Pius IX issued "The Syllabus of Errors," a list of eighty contemporary propositions that the pope viewed as erroneous. However, the crowning event of the ultramontanist response to the nineteenth century was the proclamation of papal infallibility in *Pastor*

Aeternus, the principal document of the First Vatican Council (1869–70).[70]

The result of these events in Europe was in some measure a reignition of the fires of anti-Catholicism in the United States.[71] Greater centralization of power by the pope was viewed as undemocratic and was vehemently rejected. Pius IX thus became the lightning rod to which much of America's anti-Catholic sentiment was directed. In an effort to demonstrate support for the pontiff, Father Edward Sorin, CSC, who was the superior general of the Congregation of Holy Cross, and founder and former president of the University of Notre Dame, a man with a true spirit of *romanità,* advanced the idea of an American pilgrimage to Rome. Such a trip would bolster support for the pope and provide the pilgrims with a greater appreciation of the *romanità* spirit. He wrote, "They [the pilgrims] will return content, enchanted, and will fashion public opinion in the United States over the next decade, a very important thing."[72]

Realizing a member of the hierarchy could best serve as leader of the pilgrimage, Sorin asked his local ordinary, Bishop Joseph Dwenger of Fort Wayne, Indiana, to be the titular head of the group.[73] Dwenger agreed to Sorin's request. In a circular letter to the clergy of the diocese, he explained his rationale for the trip:

> Conscious of the awful responsibilities of my office, and of my own weakness and imperfections, I leave Fort Wayne the 10th of May next to make a pilgrimage to Lourdes, and to the shrines of the Apostles, hoping thereby to obtain special graces from God for the salvation of my poor soul, to obtain for myself and my Diocese the blessing of our venerable and saintly pontiff, Pius IXth, and to obtain other benefits for my Diocese.[74]

In the spring of 1874, Baker read in the newspaper about the pilgrimage and was immediately interested. Desiring to thank God for his physical recovery from erysipelas and seeing the possibility to visit some of the famous shrines of Europe were, according to his biographer Floyd Anderson, the principal motivations for Baker's participation in the pilgrimage. Baker describes his next

41

actions: "I have written to New York to try to go on the pilgrimage to Rome and go today to see what the bishop says." He continues, "Have seen the bishop and he makes no objections, says the intention is a good one, and the passage is cheap."[75] After also receiving the permission of the seminary rector, Father Rice, to serve as the school's representative on the trip, Baker sent in his deposit of $150.00. The *Index* reported:

> [Mr. Baker] has discontinued his studies for the remainder of the year...to be the bearer of a handsome donation from the faculty and the students to the Holy Father....We are confident that the tribute to be presented on behalf of the Sem[inary] of O[ur] L[ady of] A[ngels] will give His Holiness an assurance of the feelings of affection which animate his children and which the most distant separation cannot estrange. We wish Mr. Baker a bon voyage.[76]

Baker left Buffalo via train for New York on May 13, carrying with him gifts of money ($175) and a scroll for the pope. Arriving the next day at noon, he joined the group, which consisted of Bishop Dwenger, thirty-three priests, fifty lay men, and eighteen lay women. On May 16, Archbishop (later Cardinal) John McCloskey offered Mass at St. Patrick's Cathedral for the pilgrims who then, after a brief return to the Metropolitan Hotel, boarded the *S.S. Periere*, which set course for France.[77]

During the journey to Europe, a retreat-like regimen was maintained for the pilgrims as much as was possible. Initially, and not at all surprisingly, Baker and his fellow pilgrims had trouble adjusting to shipboard life and were frequently sick, but with calmer seas they fell into a general routine. Mass was celebrated by Dwenger each morning, with a novena and the Angelus at 11:30 a.m. At 2:30 p.m., all prayed the Rosary, which was followed by a short instruction by the bishop. In the evening, meditation and night prayer were observed. Maintaining his strong devotion to the Eucharist, Baker wrote in his diary, "About half of the pilgrims went to communion. I enjoyed the happy privilege, as it is Pentecost Sunday."[78]

On May 27, the *Periere* reached LeHavre, but the group pushed on to Paris, arriving the next day. Cardinal Joseph Guibert, archbishop of Paris, greeted the group at his private chapel where Mass was celebrated. Originally the plan called for a brief stay in Paris before moving south, but because the Shrine at Lourdes was overcrowded with pilgrims, the decision was made to stay in Paris a couple of extra days. This allowed the group to see many of Paris's churches, including the fabled Notre Dame Cathedral, Church of the Madelene, La Sainte-Chapelle, St. Clotilde, St. Genevieve, Holy Trinity, and St. Sulpice.[79]

The group also visited Notre Dame des Victoires, a rather small but renowned church in the city. After celebrating Mass, Dwenger told the pilgrims of his own devotion to Our Lady of Victory, whom he believed had interceded on his brother's behalf to bring about a miraculous healing.[80] Baker wrote in his diary about the experience:

> The church is ever in one continuous religious enthusiasm where eighteen secular priests minister to the people and where the greatest miracles of grace, in bringing back lost and hardened sinners, are daily being performed through the powerful intercession of *Our Immaculate Lady* [emphasis Baker].[81]

Considering Baker's future ministry that centered itself in devotion to Mary, under the title of Our Lady of Victory, his initial recorded reaction, while demonstrating his inspiration, was not quite as exultant as one might expect. Years later, Robert Doran, longtime editor of *The Victorian*, reflected on Baker's experience:

> He [Baker] was amazed as he entered the shrine. His eyes focused on the intensely appealing statue of a lady holding a little boy in her arms atop the main altar....He knelt at the communion rail, still gazing at the statue. And then his words came in a torrent of whispers: "From now on I shall devote my entire life to your service. I shall devote all my thoughts and actions to your

43

name. I will spread the devotion of Our Lady of Victory throughout America."[82]

After the delay in Paris, the pilgrims journeyed via Bordeaux to Lourdes on June 2 and stayed two days. The group then moved south onto Marseilles where they boarded the steamer *Et Jerome* for an overnight trip to Citta Vecchia in Italy. On June 8, the group arrived via train in Rome, the ultimate destination of their pilgrimage, where they stayed until June 20. On June 10, the pilgrims had an audience with Pope Pius IX. Bishop Dwenger introduced each person to the pontiff. Nelson Baker presented a personal gift to the pope, along with the $175 donation and scroll from the faculty and students at Our Lady of Angels.[83] Baker commented on his brief encounter with the Holy Father: "In health, he seemed strong and active, his voice sonorous, and his gestures most vigorous. He seemed as if he were inspired with new life, at the sight of so many of his faithful flock."[84]

The highlight of the pilgrimage having passed, and with more than a week before needing to set off again, Baker and the other pilgrims had several free days to explore Rome itself—"The Eternal City." Baker visited several of the more important churches in the city, including St. Paul Outside the Walls, St. Sebastian, St. John Lateran, Holy Cross of Jerusalem Basilica, St. Lawrence, St. Mary Major, Our Lady of Perpetual Help, Our Lady of Mt. Carmel, St. Clement, and St. Peter in Chains. Walter Kern, former Buffalo diocesan archivist, has commented about Baker's time in Rome: "Nelson examined all the art work honoring the Blessed Mother with some interest." Additionally, he visited the catacombs, Tre Fontane, Mamertine Prison, and the Roman Colosseum.[85]

On June 21, Baker and his fellow travelers began their trip home. He stopped first in Loretto, then moved on, passing through several Italian and French towns and cities before arriving once again in Paris on June 24. He went to the church of Notre Dame des Victoires once again, inspired from his initial visit. Thomas Galvin, CSsR, who had much association with Nelson Baker over the years, suggests this was the visit that convinced him that henceforth he would devote his life to the promotion of Our Lady of

Victory.[86] Eventually, Baker arrived in LeHavre on July 4 and New York eleven days later. He stayed in the city one extra week before arriving in Buffalo in late July. He spent a quiet summer, "perhaps trying to catch up a little on the weeks of classes he missed in May and June when he was on the pilgrimage."[87]

Journey to Ordination

During his last two years of theology, Baker continued to be an excellent student and was active in seminary activities, but the period was highlighted by reception of minor orders. He was originally scheduled for tonsure and the minor orders in May 1875, but due to some problems associated with his baptismal record, he was forced to wait. He received tonsure and the minor orders of acolyte and subdeacon on December 21.[88] (The dates of his reception of the other minor orders—porter, exorcist, and lector—are not known).

Having finished his training, Baker was ready to engage ministry. Commenting on Baker's overall formation at Our Lady of Angels, one Buffalo priest commented, "Baker's seminary education fostered a clericalism, a strict sense of obedience to authority, and a traditional discipline which also typified much of the Catholic Church of his time."[89]

In early March 1876, Baker and classmates James Lasher, John Long, and Maurice Lee were summoned to speak with Bishop Ryan. Traditionally, ordinations in Buffalo had been celebrated on Trinity Sunday, but Ryan told the men that an urgent need for priests in the diocese necessitated that their ordinations be advanced. Thus, these men were ordained deacons on March 11. Eight days later, on March 19, the Feast of St. Joseph, Nelson Baker and his three classmates were ordained to the priesthood by Bishop Ryan at St. Joseph's Cathedral. A brief description of the day was given by the *Catholic Echo*: "Many friends of the reverend gentlemen were present in the cathedral during the impressive ceremonies with whom we heartily join in offering congratulations, praying that a bright and fruitful future be the lot of our newly-ordained friends."[90] Years later, reflecting back on the event, Baker thanked God and his mother: "I thank God for having raised me

45

to the sublime dignity of the Catholic priesthood. For this favor, I thank Him alone; but after that I owe it to the influence of a good Irish Catholic mother."[91] Baker celebrated his first Mass in the presence of his whole family on March 22, 1876, in the chapel of Our Lady of Angels Seminary, an institution with which he would keep close association the rest of his life.[92]

Conclusion

The years of Nelson Baker's religious formation, leading to his ordination, placed him on a path of life from which he would never waver. During his years at Our Lady of Angels Seminary, Baker received not only the required theological training for his chosen vocation, but more important his spiritual rationale for ministry and a long list of contacts that would prove useful in future dealings with clergy in the Diocese of Buffalo. Baker's two visits to Notre Dame des Victoires in Paris during his 1874 pilgrimage to Rome provided him with the inspiration he needed to initially engage in and then continue his work with orphans and troubled boys. As will be seen, his devotion to the Blessed Mother, under her title of Our Lady of Victory, became the central focus of his priesthood. She was not only a patroness, but for Baker the source and continuing inspiration for his vitality and ability to accomplish goals far beyond the capability of most people. The seminary years were also instrumental in making Baker well known in the Diocese of Buffalo. His popularity at Our Lady of Angels Seminary at Niagara University and the respect he gained from peers and superiors alike would prove extremely helpful, especially in his future role as vicar general. First, however, Baker's training equipped him for ministry in a parish, the bread and butter of the secular clergy. His story of ministry must, therefore, start here.

CHAPTER 3

First Assignments (1876–1882)

In 1876, the United States ended its period of "Reconstruction," prompting the nation to find a new direction after the close of its darkest hour of the Civil War. Characterized by substantial growth in population, extravagant displays of wealth, and the beginnings of strife in organized labor, the age produced superrich industrialists and financiers such as Cornelius Vanderbilt, John D. Rockefeller, Andrew Carnegie, and J. P. Morgan. Often referred to as "robber barons" because of their overpowering and often unethical work practices, they were challenged by the rise of the union movement, as manifest in the establishment of the American Federation of Labor in 1886, with cigar maker Samuel Gompers as the founding president. Also called the Gilded Age, this period saw the creation of a modern industrial economy; the completion of the transcontinental railroad and of national communication systems allowed the corporation to become dominant and to advance business operations in the country. Contrarily, the period also saw the genesis of American philanthropy, sometimes referred to as the "Gospel of Wealth," which allowed the establishment of thousands of colleges, hospitals, museums, academies, public libraries, symphony orchestras, and other charities.

As the nation as a whole began to expand and grow in new ways, so Nelson Baker and the Church he was now ordained to serve sought fresh beginnings. Baker began his priestly ministry in an expanding Church that continued to gain new members through immigration from the new demographic of Southern and Eastern Europe, which consisted principally of Italians and Poles. Pope Leo XIII's *Rerum Novarum*, published in 1891, was the first social-justice encyclical. It became the Magna Carta for organized labor as it advocated and legitimated workers' associations and brought the social teachings of the Church to mainstream America. While the Church would continue to be saddled with new manifestations of anti-Catholicism, such as the American Protective Association in the 1890s and still later, in the 1920s, the reappearance of the Ku Klux Klan, nevertheless, Catholicism's increased strength and visibility gave its institutions and leaders more credence and acceptance within American society as a whole. Thus, Nelson Baker's entrance onto the scene of the Buffalo Church came at a time when opportunities for change and new directions were possible for those willing to be courageous and take the initiative.

The Gilded Age and the City of Buffalo

The Gilded Age, often defined by historians as the period from the end of Reconstruction (1876) to the onset of the Progressive Era (1900), was a time of national expansion and numerous internal tensions. Between 1876 and 1912, the remaining western portion of the continental United States was added to the Union. Between 1860 and 1900, the nation's population more than doubled, from 31 to 76 million. With the end of the Civil War, immigration once again became significant, with the demographics shifting to Southern and Eastern Europe, represented best by Italians and Poles. Between 1870 and 1900, there arrived 12 million new immigrants on America's shores. The nation's Gross National Product (GNP) rose from $7.4 to $35 billion between 1870 and 1910.

This huge expansion created several major tensions. The failure of Reconstruction left significant questions unanswered. What was the nation to do with freed slaves who had little education and few technical skills? How could the Union incorporate its victory in the war into a refreshed social vision? Rising incomes, robber baron employers, and dissatisfied workers led to a rise in labor unrest and the initiation of a serious campaign for organized workers. The drive for greater industrial output created huge problems in urban life when overcrowded slums became the locus for disease and misery.[1] Indeed the historian Francis Walter has concluded,

"The progress of industrialization had created a complex of social problems largely alien to the antebellum generation."[2]

The nation as a whole sought to respond to the social dilemma that had developed in many sectors of American life. While many individuals and groups can be credited with some form of relief, the best-known movement was the Settlement House system, created and operated by Jane Addams. Rapid changes in society, social dislocation, and the emergence of various radical elements created an unsettled state where the unfit, the sick, the orphans, the homeless, and in general the poor of society fell through the cracks. Addams's Hull House provided the basic services for those who had fallen off the societal train as it sped forward to greater financial, social, and political fortune.[3] The historian Phillip Paludan wrote of Addams, "She virtually invented social work."[4]

One of the most pressing social problems of the era was the burgeoning level of homeless and orphan children. Children found themselves on the streets through the death of their parents or through simple abandonment by their families. As described later (chapter 8) this situation drew national attention in the response of Charles Loring Brace and his Orphan Trains, a system that Nelson Baker totally rejected.[5]

The City of Buffalo responded in many significant ways to the social problems, beginning even before the "flood" of people generated during the Gilded Age. The County Poor House, established in 1829, was Buffalo's first institution dedicated to social service. This facility was expanded into a hospital and insane asylum by 1850. That same year the Buffalo Association for the Relief of the Poor was formed; it was incorporated two years later in 1852. This group was formed "to detect and relieve the needy and especially to remedy and remove public and professional begging." Unfortunately, neither of these institutions left a record of effective service.[6]

Buffalo's first institution that provided efficacious social service was the Charity Organization Society, established in 1877, when the city population stood at approximately 140,000. Under the direction of its president, Pascal Pratt, the society serviced almost 4,000 families, expending $112,000 in its first year. In

1881, the society was assisting 7,327 families, leading it to boast, "These figures prove that the Society is winning its fight against poverty in Buffalo....Poverty is a curable disease, and it is being cured in this city." The society continued its service into the new century, joining the efforts of local churches after 1895 in a common drive to bring relief to those who suffered.[7]

The Salvation Army was also prominent in Buffalo's fight to combat the social dislocation of the Gilded Age. William and Catherine Booth had founded the Army, originally called the "Christian Mission," in 1865 in London as a Christian evangelist group, but it quickly evolved into a social service agency when the majority of their converts were thieves, prostitutes, and the poor. In 1878, the group took the name "Salvation Army"[8] and quickly began to branch out beyond England. The first meeting of the Army in the United States was in Philadelphia in 1879. Five years later, a corps of the Army was established in Buffalo. In 1894, the Army opened the Industrial Home for Men, and in 1899, the Rescue Home for Fallen Women was established. The Army's most prominent institution in the city was the Industrial Home for Men. The historian J. N. Larned, when observing the Home's operation, commented, "The importance of this Industrial Home is widely appreciated by citizens and officials."[9]

Buffalo proudly was home to numerous other religious and secular agencies, groups, and societies, many of which established specific institutions to assist the poor in the city, a ministry in which Nelson Baker engaged par excellence. The Buffalo Orphan Asylum for the care of orphaned and destitute children was established in 1836 (incorporated in 1837) by an association of charitable women from various Protestant congregations. In 1838, Louis LeCouteulx, who had given the land for St. Louis Parish, gave another piece of property for a more substantial facility, but financial backing was not found immediately. Finally, in 1851, a larger facility, able to hold 150 children, was opened. The Young Men's Christian Association (YMCA), founded in London in 1844 by Sir George Williams,[10] came to Buffalo in April 1852, under the guidance of George W. Perkins and five associates. By 1907, the Association had 10,000 members in the city. In September 1858, the Charity Foundation of the Protestant Episcopal Church was established, with George W. Clinton as its first president. The Evangelical Lutheran Church opened St. John's Orphan Home in 1864.[11] The London Charity Organization, originally founded in England in 1869 to deal with pauperism, came to Buffalo in 1877, mostly through the efforts of the Reverend S. Humphreys Gurteen of St. Paul's Episcopal Church. Larned writes of Gurteen's efforts:

> By a course of Sunday evening lectures on the subject [pauperism] at St. Paul's, by discussion of it in newspapers and a vigorous pamphlet, and by an untiring propagandism privately pursued, he [a]woke interest in the proposition and won supporters so quickly that the organization he desired was accomplished before the close of the year. It was the first of its kind in the United States.[12]

Also, the Buffalo Deaconess Home of the Methodist Episcopal Church, an outgrowth of the Women's Home Missionary Society, was established in 1888. This was an organization of women who served as nurses and teachers and provided home visitations to shut-ins.[13]

State and other secular entities followed the lead of the churches through their establishment of various institutions for the poor. In 1867, the Home for the Friendless opened "for aged women who were homeless." One year later, the Guard of Honor, which "sought to aid homeless young men who needed work," was established at the Buffalo Female Academy. On April 23, 1870, the New York legislature authorized construction of the Buffalo State Hospital for the care and treatment of the insane. The facility opened in November 1880. The Women's Educational and Industrial Union of Buffalo was formed on February 5, 1884. This union provided a gymnasium; free reference library; Girls' Union Circle (a club); lectures on hygiene, health, and law; as well as classes for attendants on home nursing, cooking, and dressmaking. Westminster and Neighborhood Houses, social settlement homes in the style of Jane Addams's Hull House, were opened in September and November 1894, respectively.[14]

51

The Catholic Church's response to the social dilemma in postbellum America, which became Nelson Baker's raison d'être, was initiated by Buffalo's first bishop, John Timon, CM. J. N. Larned has commented, "Buffalo owes many and large debts to Bishop Timon for organizations of beneficent work that have wrought a constant increase of good to the community since his day."[15] When Timon arrived in 1847, he found only one institution, an orphan asylum in Rochester, which had been established in 1841 but incorporated in 1845.[16] He realized the need for additional institutions to aid orphans and thus, in 1848, he was able to obtain six Sisters of Charity from Baltimore to become the nuclear staff for St. Vincent's Orphan Asylum. Located adjacent to St. Patrick's Church in Buffalo, the asylum had separate homes for boys and girls. The facility's limits were tested almost immediately when an outbreak of cholera in 1849 left many children as orphans. Before his death in 1867, Timon inaugurated smaller facilities for the wayward, the sick, and the deaf.[17] One writer concluded, "[Timon] struggled valiantly in building institutions for orphans and destitute children."[18]

During the time of both Timon and his successor, Stephen Ryan, several additional institutions to serve the poor and disenfranchised were established by various religious congregations. The German Roman Catholic Orphan Asylum, founded in 1851, was serviced by the Sisters of the Third Order of St. Francis. In 1862, this same community opened St. Francis Asylum for the Aged and Infirmed. In 1855, the Sisters of Our Lady of Refuge, a French religious order, founded the Asylum of Our Lady of Refuge, also known as the Home of the Good Shepherd.[19] The Sisters' work was geared to "preserve and restore to society poor lost women, and to protect and educate destitute and wayward Roman Catholic female children."[20] In July 1861, the Sisters of Charity opened Providence Retreat for the care and treatment of the insane and of victims of alcoholism and drugs. The Guardian Mission, established in 1898 by the Sisters of St. Francis, was the pioneer Catholic effort in social settlement work in Buffalo.[21] The Catholic Total Abstinence Union of America (CTAUA) met in Buffalo in 1877, in league with the better known Women's Christian Temperance Union (WCTU), which was under the capable leadership of Frances Willard. Bishop Ryan commended the membership for its "holy cause" and the "most sacred trust" in which they were engaged. He suggested that such temperance societies should be established in every parish throughout the diocese.[22]

National parishes—that is, parishes that served specific ethnic groups—represented 18 percent of Buffalo's Catholic congregations by 1880;[23] these parishes established groups or reached out personally in service to their own people. First and foremost these parishes provided the Church's services in the vernacular languages of the various immigrant populations. Bishop Ryan and his successor, James Quigley, made every effort to provide each ethnic group with clergy who were native to their land and language. Noting that most parishes had a number of sodalities and societies to assist the poor and disperse charity, the historian David Gerber commented, "The Catholic parish cast a wide associational net far beyond attendance at Mass and the obligatory twice-a-year confession."[24]

Limestone Hill

On April 16, 1867, Bishop John Timon, the first local ordinary for the Diocese of Buffalo, died. He was succeeded by a fellow Vincentian religious, Stephen Ryan, who was consecrated bishop on November 8, 1868. Commenting on Ryan's time as bishop, one writer stated, "Bishop Ryan labored to extend the facilities of religion to his rapidly growing flock[,] to defend the working man against the excesses of capitalism and to combat the nativism which again appeared on the local scene."[25]

Ryan made his mark initially in his expansion of parishes and promotion of Catholic education. Within fifteen years of taking the see, Ryan had established ten new parishes, including the first Polish national parish, St. Stanislaus, in 1873.[26] The advancement of Christian education, considered by many in the hierarchy to be the central pillar to the maintenance of the faith, was Ryan's principal forte. Three years before the Third Plenary Council of Baltimore would mandate that all parishes establish schools,[27] Ryan was already promoting Catholic schools as integral to the development of the

Church, not only in Buffalo but nationally. He emphasized the cross-fertilization among school, family, and home: "The Christian Church is fed from the Christian school and this in turn filled from the Christian family, the Christian home. These constantly and necessarily act and re-act on each other and on society."[28]

In a pastoral letter issued on February 27, 1881, he wrote, "I believe to be of the first importance, viz: that of establishing, sustaining and improving our parish schools." He continued: "The Christian school must then be ready to take the child from the threshold of the Christian home and fit the young boy and the young girl to be consistent, instructed and faithful members of the Christian Church."[29]

Part of the territory under Bishop Ryan's jurisdiction was the region of Limestone Hill in the town of West Seneca, approximately five miles south of central Buffalo. Nelson Baker was familiar with this region from his preseminary days. Back in 1869, his conversations with Father Thomas Hines, pastor of the local parish, St. Patrick's, and superintendent of the Institutions for orphaned and wayward boys, had helped him make the decision to enter the seminary. Hines came to Limestone Hill in May 1857 after his ordination two months previous, replacing James Early, who had been the first superintendent. There was just Holy Cross Mission, a small wooden chapel (100 feet by 35 feet, built for $12,000).[30]

After several years it was clear to Hines that an expanding parish base required a more permanent church structure. Thus, beginning on July 15, 1873, with the laying of the cornerstone by Father William Gleason, the vicar general under Bishop Ryan, a new church in honor of St. Patrick was erected at Limestone Hill. Two years later on August 22, 1875, Ryan dedicated the new church with a sermon preached by another Vincentian priest, John Lynch, CM, the archbishop of Toronto, and later the founding president of Our Lady of Angels Seminary at Niagara University.[31]

From Baker's past experience in the area, it was probably not a major surprise that his first assignment after his ordination was to assist Father Hines at the parish and the Institutions of Limestone Hill. Additionally, his maturity and business acumen would be important assets in this multifaceted and complex ministry. *The*

Catholic Union reported the assignment: "Of the young clergy-men just ordained, Rev. Nelson Baker goes to the Reformatory [at] Limestone Hill to assist Father Hines—a most suitable appointment." Baker celebrated his first Mass at St. Patrick's on March 25, 1876, the Feast of the Annunciation, a date that might have been coincidental, but was certainly a reflection of his devotion to the Blessed Virgin Mary.[32]

Hines kept his new curate very busy in his first year as a priest. In his diary, Baker records celebrating Mass, hearing Confessions, and giving a few conferences to boys in the Institutions. In one talk he gave the boys, "3/4 hour on lying, giving scandal, prayer and obedience." He preached frequently and baptized many orphans, as well as other children from the parish. Hines gave him major roles in the Holy Week services as well as in administration of First Communion. Despite his busy schedule, Baker was able to go home periodically for family visits. He made every effort to assist his family financially, including buying furniture made by boys in the Protectory and bringing it to his parents' home.[33]

When Baker arrived at Limestone Hill, the Institutions to assist orphaned and wayward boys had been in place for some time. The historian Timothy Allan has accurately described the connection between the time period and the evolution of the Institutions:

> Indeed, it was largely in response to these unsettled conditions [of the Gilded Age] and the great social needs that arose from them that in 1872 the predecessor institutions of Father Baker's later Victory Homes, St. Joseph's Male Orphan Asylum and St. John's Protectory, were finally moved to and established in Limestone Hill after several previous relocations.[34]

The foundation of St. Joseph's Orphan Asylum can be traced prior to Bishop Timon's arrival in Buffalo in 1847. Although the Buffalo Orphan Asylum had been founded in 1836, the Church itself first reached out to orphans in 1841, when a home for this purpose was opened in Rochester. In 1848, Timon established St. Vincent's Female Ayslum. It was the cholera epidemic of 1849, however, that provided the catalyst for significant action to assist orphans. To meet the immediate need, male orphans were placed in a home on Niagara Street in Buffalo; girls were housed in another home on Ellicot Street, adjacent to St. Patrick's parish in the heart of the city. Only one year later, in 1850, Bishop Timon purchased land in Lancaster, New York, and built a facility to combine the efforts of the orphanages in Rochester and Buffalo. Incorporated on August 2, 1851, St. Joseph's Boys Orphan Asylum was not successful. Thus, on April 9, 1854, the home was closed and a similar institution opened on Best Street in Buffalo. The orphanage stayed there until August 27, 1856, when Timon purchased sixty acres of land contiguous with Holy Cross Cemetery at Limestone Hill. St. Joseph's Boys Orphan Asylum was moved to this new location. Father J. M. Early was initially placed in charge of the institution.[35]

In an effort to staff St. Joseph's, Timon wrote to Father Edward Sorin, CSC, at Notre Dame, asking for Holy Cross religious to serve the orphanage. As mentioned, Sorin was the person who would later initiate the idea of an American pilgrimage to Rome to bolster American support for Pius IX, who felt under siege from those who professed emerging ideologies contrary to Christianity. The "Book of Accounts" for the Sisters of Holy Cross reported: "In November 1856, Bishop Timon secured the services of four brothers and three sisters to found an orphan asylum."[36] The Holy Cross religious arrived on November 21. The *Buffalo Sentinel* reported that the Brothers "took charge of St. Joseph's Boys Asylum." The paper continued, "The good Sisters of the Holy Cross have also come to watch over, with a mother's care, the health and cleanliness of the poor orphans. God will bless their efforts."[37]

The ministry of the Holy Cross contingent in Buffalo was, however, short-lived. Sorin, seeking to assist financially his nascent congregation, sought a permanent agreement with Timon with respect to the services of his religious at St. Joseph's. However, Timon, who was concerned about financing his new cathedral project, was unwilling to make a permanent contract. Correspondence between Sorin and Timon indicates a certain sense of mistrust on both sides. Sorin felt Timon's refusal to cement the arrangements was inconsistent with his initial request. Timon responded by telling Sorin, "The Sisters are not at peace; some of them are not very efficient; the novice wants to leave; she complains of her superior." Addressing the Brothers, Timon complained, "It seems that they [the Brothers] cannot realize the object I had at heart, teaching trades to the boys." Timon concluded, "On the whole it is better to withdraw them, which I humbly invite you to do as soon as convenient."[38] Thus, in May 1857 after a very brief stay, Holy Cross religious returned to Notre Dame in Northern Indiana. To show he had no hard feelings toward Holy Cross, Timon wrote to Sorin congratulating him on reports recently received about the efficacious ministry conducted by members of the congregation. He concluded, "It made me wish that one day you might find some establishment in my diocese under better auspices than our first attempt."[39]

The withdrawal of Holy Cross religious from St. Joseph was quickly remedied. Bishop Timon asked the Sisters of St. Joseph, a local Buffalo congregation of religious women, to take charge of St. Joseph's Orphan Asylum. The Sisters had first arrived in Canadaigua, New York, from St. Louis on December 8, 1854. Four Sisters—Mother Veronica Chiers and Sisters Anselm McCourt, Anastasia Donovan, and Petronilla Roscoe—were assigned to the orphanage.[40] The environment at St. Joseph's was described at the time of the transition, this way: "Living conditions were primitive enough in the orphanage although the building was new, for it had none of the accessories of the modern institution. The furniture was meager, the bedding scanty, light and heat only what was barely necessary."[41]

Although the Sisters of Saint Joseph readily took to their new apostolate, it was clear almost from the outset that their work would not be easy. The most obvious problem was the facility, which was inadequate almost from the date of their arrival. The original structure was a wood frame building on the northwest corner of Ridge Road and South Park Avenue (coincidentally the present location of Our Lady of Victory Basilica and National Shrine). During the transition between Early and Thomas Hines, who took over St. Joseph and St. John's Protectory in 1857, a new larger orphanage was contemplated, but construction was not completed on the four-story brick building, located on the opposite side of Ridge Road, until January 1859. In 1860, three years after Hines took the reins as superintendent, the population at St. Joseph averaged 120 boys. However, by 1867 that number had risen to 190.[42] Another significant problem the Sisters faced was lack of financial resources. This situation forced the Sisters to routinely beg for their needs and those of the orphans. They took turns at this less-than-glorious but absolutely necessary task. One account, specifying the actions of one Sister, read: "Sister Michael was a familiar figure as she went door-to-door at the docks, in boiler shops, everywhere soliciting food and financial assistance for her 'dear boys,' for whom she cared with the tenderness of a mother."[43]

The financial panic of 1873, another major hurdle that the Sisters were forced to endure, almost ended the community's work at St. Joseph. One history of the period lauded the Sisters' efforts to keep St. Joseph in operation: "During these 'hard times' and the years of scarcity, it was the inner spirit and the individual personal energy and self-denial of the Sisters of St. Joseph which were the safeguards of the Home and guardians of the children's welfare."[44]

Bishop Timon's rescue plan for orphans, which evolved into St. Joseph's Orphan Asylum, was complemented by a similar initiative to assist wayward youths. Observing that some boys at St. Joseph needed more discipline, and realizing that destitute children, both those identified by the courts and others, were a burgeoning social problem, Timon instituted a plan for a correctional institution to complement St. Joseph. In 1863, a building, St. John's Protectory, was erected, and one year later on April 25, 1864, the institution was incorporated as the Society for the Protection of Destitute Roman Catholic Children at the City of Buffalo. A report to the New York State Board of Charities said, "The object of the Society is to change and provide support, education and training for such idle, truant, vicious, and homeless children."[45]

The establishment of St. John's was consistent with the call of the American bishops at the 1866 Second Plenary Council of Baltimore to provide such facilities. The bishops confessed, "It is a melancholy fact, and a very humiliating avowal for us to make, that a very large portion of the idle and vicious youth of our principal cities are children of Catholic parents." In response to this growing problem of crime among youth, the council's pastoral letter reads:

The only remedy for this great and daily augmenting evil is to provide Catholic protectories or industrial schools, to which such children may be sent; and where, under the only influence that is known to have reached the roots of vice, the youthful culprit may cease to do evil and learn to do good.

The bishops could say that some progress toward addressing this problem had been made, yet vigilance was necessary and more had to be accomplished. The pastoral letter continued:

We rejoiced that in some of our dioceses—would that we could say all—a beginning has been made in this good work, and we cannot too earnestly exhort our venerable brethren of the clergy to bring this matter before their respective flocks, to endeavor to impress on Christian parents the duty of guarding their children from the evils above referred to, and to invite them to make persevering and effectual efforts for the establishment of institutions, wherein, under the influence of religious teachers, the waywardness of youth may be corrected, and the good seed planted in the soil in which, while men slept, the enemy had sowed tares.[46]

Under the supervision of Thomas Hines, St. John's served the diocese and local youth, but not without its share of challenges. As was the case with St. Joseph, the Protectory was staffed by Sisters of St. Joseph—initially Sister Francis de Sales Dehahanty, Sister Philomena Fitzgerald, and Sister Vincent Callahan—who joined a fledgling group of religious, the Brothers of the Holy Infancy and Youth of Jesus. The Sisters supervised the residence while the Brothers oversaw the facility's educational trades programs. One of the greatest challenges was the attitude of the boys. Sister Mary Timothy Dempsey, the historian of educational facilities at Limestone Hill, stated: "Some boys were rude and coarse, desperate and rebellious and had no regard for persons—priests, Brothers, and Sisters included." This attitude and the need to keep order necessitated strong measures. Dempsey continues, "The result was the boys lived in a prison-like atmosphere with prison-like cells and iron barred windows."[47]

Trades education, supervised by the Brothers, was central to daily life at St. John's and one of the institution's most noteworthy contributions. Initially, shoes and chairs were the only two products produced on any significant level. In 1875, the New York State Board of Charities reported that the boys at the Protectory received on average four hours of trades' schooling daily; some with more ability received five hours of daily training, and those less skilled received three hours daily.[48]

Nelson Baker's introduction to St. John's was rather mixed. The almost prison-like environment at the Protectory grated severely against his understanding of the institution's mission. Speaking of St. Joseph's and St. John's, he reported in his diary, "We have about 140 boys. Some try almost daily to get away, but they are generally caught."[49] The financial situation, which forced the Sisters of St. Joseph to beg on the streets, was also distasteful to Baker. At least one partial solution to the problem was to sell chairs made by the boys at the Protectory to various parishes. However, the idea never moved from the drawing board. He reported on April 3, 1876: "Saw Bishop, asked to go selling—Not like it—Said he wanted me to look over the spiritual interests of the boys, and not *selling* [emphasis Baker]."[50] On the brighter side, it was obvious from the outset that Baker made a very positive impression on the youth in both Institutions. One youth at St. John's described the boys' experience of Baker: "It was a happy day for us when Father Baker came along. Every boy had a new friend and as the months went by that feeling was intensified." Brother Stanislaus, who would become Father Baker's most trusted assistant, wrote about the boys' collective experience of Baker: "Here they found friendliness, comfort, happiness and the friendship of a good man, a man of God, a father and a brother to them all."[51]

Ministry in Corning, New York

Nelson Baker continued to serve as Father Hines's assistant into the new decade of the 1880s, but in his mind the situation was becoming more untenable with the passing of time. He realized that Hines was not physically well, yet his past business experience told him the mounting debt that the Institutions were incurring required aggressive action. He came to the conclusion that unless something was done to resolve the debt he needed a transfer. Thus, he went to Ryan requesting a new assignment. The bishop agreed and assigned him, effective January 9, 1881, as a curate to Father Peter Colgan at St. Mary's Parish in Corning, New York, which was east of Buffalo.[52] The boys in the Institutions were greatly saddened by Baker's departure. One boy commented, "We were indeed very sorry when we were told that Bishop Ryan was sending Father [Baker] from us and appointing him to a parish in Corning, N.Y."[53]

The Church was first planted in Corning in 1842 through the efforts of Father P. Bradley. He said Masses in private homes, but also established a station that he visited four times per year to provide the sacraments for the local people. In 1852, Father Thomas Cunningham came to Corning as the first resident pastor. He was succeeded in 1860 by Colgan who remained there for over thirty years, during which time he built the stone edifice of St. Mary's Church.[54] Baptismal records show that Baker was present in the parish from at least February 6, 1881, to February 18, 1882. Even though Baker's time there was quite short, the historian Robert McNamara commented, "But even during those twelve months, he had endeared himself to the parishioners for his earnestness and piety, and even for his alleged ability to work miracles."[55]

Father Baker's time in Corning was centered around ministry to the sick, some of whom, it was reported, experienced miraculous cures. When Kate Dwyer recovered from typhoid fever after Baker prayed over her and applied water from Lourdes, it was firmly believed by many that his intervention was the catalyst to the cure. Similarly, Frank Walker's recovery from diphtheria was attributed to Baker's intercessory prayer. A third incident, Dennis McCarty's unexplained relief from a painful kidney ailment after a visit from Baker, provides more evidence to Baker's perceived miraculous power.[56]

Nelson Baker's ministry in Corning was highly efficacious, but mounting problems at Limestone Hill required Bishop Ryan to take action. In early January 1880, even before Baker's departure, Hines had been falsely accused of mismanagement of affairs at St. John's Protectory. Additionally, lingering anti-Catholic groups, looking for any opportunity to bash the Church, trumped up charges that he had "imprisoned" one of the boys. These events, Hines's deteriorating health, and the severe debt of the Institutions, which only continued to mount, led to his resignation on February 23, 1882. He was reassigned to St. Raphael (later Sacred Heart) Parish in Niagara Falls, New York. Buffalo diocesan historian Walter Kern claims that Ryan was looking for a replacement for Hines as early as May 1881, and when he could find no appropriate person, he decided to reassign Baker, but now as superintendent and pastor.[57]

Thus, after only one year in Corning, Nelson Baker returned to Limestone Hill. Although he possibly could not have imagined it, Baker would spend the rest of his priesthood—well over half a century—ensconced in this small borough south of Buffalo. Baker's significant contribution to the people at St. Mary's was noted in the *Corning Democrat*:

> Fr. Baker will be kindly remembered by St. Mary's people as a most devoted priest whose endearing qualities drew forth the encomiums of the masses. He well understands the dignity of his calling, for in him was well recognized the beautiful humility which in this age seems to counteract silently, but surely, the vile and rapid passions of man.[58]

Conclusion

The initial assignment and first years of a priest's ministry are often a time to ground him in the clerical vocation and gain valuable experience. Such was the case for Nelson Baker in his first assignment at Limestone Hill. There, he learned the ropes of sacramental ministry at St. Patrick's Parish, but his work in West Seneca also entailed significant association with two major Institutions, St. Joseph's Orphan Asylum and St. John's Protectory, which both served male youths. Most assuredly, Bishop Stephen Ryan must have assigned Baker to Limestone Hill in part because of the young priest's proven business savvy and experience. Thus, while not at this stage the superintendent, it is certain that Baker became engaged with the day-to-day activity at the Institutions, gaining valuable experience. Baker's frustration concerning the fiscal problems at the Institutions, which led to a brief sojourn at Corning, New York, did not alter Ryan's plan to place his new, but experienced priest in charge of the operation in West Seneca. The proverbial "writing was on the wall": Nelson Baker's first assignments served as warm-ups to the main event of his life, superintendent at Limestone Hill.

The Limestone Hill Institutions at the time of Father Baker's first assignment after ordination. Pictured are St. Patrick's Church (right foreground), St. John's Protectory (right background), and St. Joseph's Orphan Asylum (left), c. 1876.

Aerial illustration of Father Baker's "City of Charity"—the Our Lady of Victory Institutions, c. 1920. The illustration is prior to the construction of the Basilica, which started in 1921. Detail at the left shows an outdoor shrine dedicated to Our Lady of Victory.

Father Baker fulfilled his dream of a gift of thanksgiving to his patroness—the Our Lady of Victory National Shrine and Basilica, c. 1930.

In 1999, Father Baker's earthly remains were transferred from a nearby cemetery to a new tomb within Our Lady of Victory Basilica.

Father Baker with just a
few of his invaluable
helpmates, the
Sisters of St. Joseph,
c. 1890.

Newly ordained Father Nelson Baker,
age thirty-four, 1876.

Introducing his young
charges to music and the
arts was as important to
Father Baker as their
schooling and skills
training, c. 1890.

Father Baker with some of the youngest in his care, who would reside at the Our Lady of Victory Infant Home until they were five, c. 1930.

"Daddy Baker" made frequent visits to the courtyard to spend time with the boys, c. 1922.

Father Baker takes a moment to pose with young children from St. Joseph's Orphanage and some of his supporters, c. 1928.

Father Baker greets the faithful outside Our Lady of Victory Basilica, c. 1926.

One of Father Baker's proudest accomplishments was assisting hundreds of black Americans in converting to the Catholic faith. Here he poses with the Our Lady of Victory Colored Mission Society, c. 1933.

Extensive media coverage was devoted to Father Baker's passing on July 29, 1936, at age ninety-four. The column head at the right mistakenly says he is ninety-six.

In the week following Father Baker's passing, it is estimated that more than a half-million people visited Lackawanna to pay their last respects. On August 3, 1936, the day of his Mass of Christian Burial, a reported 50,000 onlookers lined the sidewalks, waiting for a glimpse of the funeral procession.

One of the services held in Our Lady of Victory Basilica to mark
Father Baker's passing, 1936.

CHAPTER 4

Ministry in the Gilded Age (1882–1900)

Nelson Baker returned to the site of his first assignment with some trepidation and surely with a sense that many challenges lay before him. Yet, he was a mature man of forty, with six years of priestly experience under his belt, and thus Bishop Ryan believed he had the necessary tools to take on a difficult ministry. It would be his task to move the Institutions and the parish forward. As superintendent, he would be challenged to bring his fresh ideas to a ministry that had limped along, especially due to financial problems, for several years. Not only did Baker need new ideas, he needed renewed energy and a sense of confidence supported by a strong faith that all is possible for one who believes. Few could have dreamed the heights to which Baker would bring his ministry, but what he accomplished was certainly not achieved overnight, of course. Rather, through a systematic approach, finding solutions to problems and situations as they arose, Baker built a reputation as a "Father to the Fatherless"—thousands of boys who saw him as the strong parent they never knew or appreciated. The challenges that Baker faced when he returned to Limestone Hill were multiple and significant. These required him to combine his business background and his knowledge of people, with a rarely seen faith in God, manifested most profoundly in his devotion to the Blessed Virgin Mary, to find answers that allowed him to serve God's people more fully and faithfully.

St. Patrick's Parish

When Nelson Baker returned to Limestone Hill in February 1882, the situation was anything but optimum. Although Baker had previous experience with the parish and the Institutions, he felt woefully unqualified to take the helm of such a major operation. Additionally, while he understood that Father Hines was sick and, therefore, had possibly not been aware of the situation, the debt when he left in February 1881 had mushroomed. Thus, Baker balked when initially asked to return. However, Bishop Ryan had few options, and, with Baker's added credential of significant business experience, he was the logical choice. Therefore, Baker accepted his new assignment. He immediately initiated efforts to stanch the economic bleeding of the Institutions and then find a way to place them on sturdy financial footing. He met with the many, many creditors, all of whom were demanding immediate and full payment. Baker assured each person that all debts would be met, but it would take time. If payment was demanded immediately, the liability would be met—but Baker would do no further business with any such creditors. However, if anyone was willing to take partial payment and work with him, Baker promised future business. Using what personal funds he still had from his business partnership, he was able to stabilize the situation.[1]

Despite the precarious financial situation that greeted Baker, he was able nonetheless to demonstrate great vigor and confidence in his new assignment. While there was much more to be done, the fact that Baker had at least pacified his creditors earned him plaudits. One local paper wrote of the situation, "Father Baker [brought] a chaotic, haphazard condition to a business-like order."[2] His ability to bring his businesslike determination and consequently strong hand to a tense situation "established confidence in his power to succeed."[3] He brought together his deep faith, sense of fairness, and business savvy in an effort to win souls for Christ. Many were amazed at his ability to combine so seemingly easily the two hats of pastor and business executive. A contemporary account described the positive and powerful effect Baker was able to produce from the outset:

The labors of Father Baker in providing homes for destitute Catholic children are well worthy of commendation. To many an abandoned child he supplies not only the necessities of this life, but the...[possibility] of eternal salvation. No more noble work could be contemplated than taking these little ones from the jaws of eternal ruin and placing them in good Catholic homes.[4]

Father Baker's pastoral sense was demonstrated from his first days as superintendent at Limestone Hill. While some admitted that Baker could be a bit "long-winded" in the pulpit, "he always preached about love and kindness....He talked on the love of God, love of the poor—he was very strong on it." Clara Balduf, who answered correspondence for Baker at the Protectory between 1916 and 1918, described Baker's preaching: "He had a 'reaching voice.' He was always praising and talking about Our Lady of Victory. His sermons always left you wanting to be better."[5] Baker's love and compassion for the unfortunate outweighed all his other interests. In the confessional he was described as "gentle and kind."[6] Baker's pastoral sense of compassion comes through clearly in a letter written to a woman after the death of her husband:

I appreciate very much your lonely condition after parting with our dear friend, Peter, and I know that no earthly person can take his place. Hence, it naturally leaves a void in your heart which nothing can fill. We are always living in the hope that when the cares of this life are over, and we are called upon to meet again, our old friendships will be renewed, but in a much higher and more intense and loving form, which will last always, because Our Lord promised us that we would enjoy with Him an eternity of celestial happiness without ending.[7]

It was a blessing that Baker's pastoral gifts found a home and were appreciated by those he served, but he could not avoid the realization that the economic situation was beyond him, and thus he sought assistance. Harking back to his pilgrimage to Rome in 1874 and to his transformative experience when visiting the Church

73

of Notre Dame des Victoires in Paris, Baker decided to dedicate his work to Our Lady of Victory and place the Institutions under her patronage.[8] His idea manifested itself in the initiation of the Association of Our Blessed Lady of Victory and the creation of one of the first direct-mail solicitation campaigns. The Association, established in 1883 to satisfy Baker's acute need for funds, but fueled through his combined business expertise and indomitable faith, was a bold and rather unique development program. Indeed, the historian Timothy Allan wrote: "Baker was…a pioneer in the art of direct promotional mailing."[9] Initially he wrote to postmasters throughout the country, asking to be supplied the names and addresses of Catholic women in their locales who might be willing to financially assist with his ministry with orphans and wayward boys. With the responses he received, Baker conducted a "full-court press" letter campaign, writing to thousands of women, explaining the Association and seeking their assistance. Membership in the Association was only 25 cents annually. Members agreed to the daily recitation of the Litany of Our Blessed Lady of Victory; other devotions, such as daily recitation of the Rosary, Benediction of the Blessed Sacrament, Perpetual Adoration, and daily Communion, were also highly encouraged. In turn, Association members received *The Appeal for Homeless and Destitute Children*, a newsletter that kept all abreast of Baker's work and his remembrance of them in several annual novenas, as well as in Masses celebrated at St. Patrick's and specific Marian shrines worldwide.[10]

In order for the Association to be sufficiently profitable to eliminate the crushing debt that Baker inherited, which was the group's principal raison d'être, the new superintendent pushed hard and used every avenue available to secure members. Association publications almost always carried an invitation, generally in the section "Notes for Solicitors," for new members and asked present members to seek others who could join. The campaign also offered membership to the *deceased*. One "Notes to Solicitors" column read:

We are often asked if the dead can be enrolled as members of the Association and participate in its many spiritual advantages, and in reply [we] will state that certificates of membership may be taken out in the names of the deceased, and they will participate in the many prayers and Masses offered for them.[11]

Besides his two principal reasons for establishing the Association of Our Lady of Victory—namely, to raise funds and to increase the spiritual enrichment of its members by promotion of devotion to Our Lady of Victory—Baker always had the physical and spiritual welfare of the boys in the Institutions as a first priority. The Association's purpose was described:

> The object of the Association is the temporary protection of destitute, homeless, orphan children who are in imminent danger of losing their Faith, in affording them a protecting care until they can be placed in good Catholic homes, and thus save them from the many dangers that beset their path.[12]

Baker also addressed the issue of groups that proselytized orphans, such as the Orphan Trains organized by Charles Loring Brace. (Briefly mentioned in chapter 3, Brace will be discussed more fully in chapter 8.):

> Our Association has been formed to prevent this wholesale proselytizing of our unfortunate little ones and we are making all necessary efforts to obtain control of this class of children, and to protect them from these dangers and place them into homes among our good people who will...educate them in the Faith in which they were born.[13]

From the outset, the Association published a magazine to inform members of Baker's work, to solicit more assistance, and to provide spiritual nourishment. The first publication, issued in August 1884 in English and German, was the *Appeal for Homeless and Destitute Children.* The one extant copy of this eight-page periodical, which sought to "promot[e] membership to O[ur]

L[ady of] V[ictory,]" described the Association's purpose as "the temporal protection of destitute, homeless, and orphan children, *wherever found* [emphasis Baker]," both physically and spiritually.[14]

The short-lived newsletter was replaced in July 1888 by the *Annals of the Association of Our Blessed Lady of Victory*. Baker welcomed readers in the inaugural issue:

> With this number the "Annals" makes its bow to the many friends of the Association of Our Blessed Lady of Victory, and comes with fondest greeting, buoyed with the brightest hope, that its object may be realized in encouraging and fostering devotion and love to the Blessed Mother of God.
>
> We have long had it in view to publish a little journal, in connection with our "Association," to act as a medium between it and its many friends, which would become a mutual means of communication, and tend to further advance the spiritual and temporal interests of the Association, and in so doing, increase devotion and honor to our Blessed Lady.[15]

At the outset, the *Annals* was a sixteen-page quarterly newsletter and magazine that described itself as "A Catholic Magazine Devoted to the Honor of the Blessed Mother of God." In the second issue, this description changed slightly, from "A Catholic Magazine" to a "Quarterly Magazine," with most articles dedicated to devotion to the Blessed Virgin Mary. The inaugural issue was dominated by such short articles as: "Confidence in Mary," "The Picture of the Blessed Virgin," "Mary Always Conquers," "A Great Generation's Devotion to the Rosary," and "The Sepulcher of the Blessed Virgin Mary." Additionally, each issue had sections dedicated to "Petitions," "Favors Granted to Members of the Association Through the Intercession of Our Blessed Lady of Victory," and "Sparkling Gems in Mary's Crown," the latter being a series of quotes from the saints on Mary.[16] Each issue also contained essays devoted to St. Joseph and the Sacred Heart of Jesus. Subscribers to the *Annals* grew, reaching an apex of 280,000 households nationwide.[17]

The successful launch of the *Annals* immediately generated increased membership. Equally important was the positive response received from readers. The second issue, October 1888, reported, "We are more than delighted with the generous greeting that welcomed the first number of our *Annals* into existence, and we have heard none but most cheering words of congratulation from friends on all sides, with the fondest wishes for its success and prosperity."[18]

Baker was integrally involved with the *Annals* as the magazine's chief writer. Under the byline NHB, Baker wrote many articles for the *Annals*, mostly on Mary, but analysis of other essays shows that he also penned many of them, on various religious and devotional topics. In her dissertation describing the "marketing" of Father Baker as a saint, religion scholar Heather Hartel commented about Baker's contribution to the *Annals*:

> His articles sought to ignite the same enthusiasm and devotion in others through descriptions of her [Mary's] intercession in various circumstance[s], explanations of church teachings regarding her status and power, and stories of her more famous "sentinels," like St. Vincent de Paul and St. John of the Cross.[19]

The *Annals* also published essays by prominent local and national figures. The local ordinaries, especially Bishop Charles Colton, often contributed essays that generally followed the basic themes of popular devotion, centered on Mary. For example, in the October 1906, issue Colton contributed two essays: "Our Lady, Queen of Angels" and "Queen of the Rosary." In 1907, he wrote two other essays: "June—The Month of the Sacred Heart" and "The Joy of Christmas."[20]

Baker was generally satisfied with the progress of the *Annals* and the ministry it was supporting. While it took some time, eventually the debt that he inherited when he became superintendent in 1882 was liquidated, allowing him to press forward and expand his facilities.[21] He reported in January 1889, "Through the aid furnished by the Association, we have enlarged our Institution, so as to afford better facilities for accommodating and caring for the many little children that are seeking protection beneath the shelter-ing mantle of Our Blessed Lady."[22] The growth of the Association was largely responsible for this expansion. In January 1890 and again in January 1894, Baker reported banner years for recruiting:

> The year of 1893 has been the most successful year of any since the inception of our Association: during it, more members have been enrolled, more favors and blessings bestowed, graces more [abundant] than ever before. Our Blessed Lady has been to us all remarkably generous during the year.[23]

The importance of this ministry was certainly not lost on Baker, and he felt obligated to do more: "The longer we are engaged in our work, the more we are impressed with its importance, so much so that we feel that with all our efforts, we are not doing all we should do or could do."[24]

Baker's plans for expansion focused on his ministry with youth and his desire to spread devotion to Our Lady of Victory, under whose patronage he had placed his whole apostolate. He realized that St. Joseph's Orphan Asylum and St. John's Protectory existed to shelter and protect children before they could be placed in good homes, but the reality was that the older a child was, the more difficult he was to place. Thus, Baker fore-saw the need to build and expand his facilities.[25] Speaking of the Association's connection with Mary, he wrote:

> As it is evidently God's holy will that His own Mother should be better known and more tenderly beloved, why not strive to carry out God's will in this regard, by doing all that we can to propagate this devotion by extending the influence of the Association which has as its object the cultivating and spreading of this beautiful devotion, resting assured that our efforts will not be unnoticed or unrewarded.[26]

Expansion of facilities necessitated more funds, but Baker was not averse to asking his benefactors to dig deeper, for he believed the cause was right and he knew (and felt) his patroness was assisting him at all times. In a typical appeal, Baker, in a manner not unlike contemporary televangelists, unabashedly professed his total confidence that people would respond to his request:

> The new building and all its improvements and accommodations will cost nearly $50,000 when completed; we started out to build this without the means, but with the implicit confidence that our Blessed Lady would inspire our friends to help us to meet this large sum, and we are not being disappointed, but we have yet much to pay. We hope our good friends will not lag in their zeal but continue to assist us as generously in the future as in the past, and I am sure that our Lord will not fail in generously rewarding them for so doing.[27]

Baker was pleased that his fellow clergy also assisted him monetarily. In a generic letter to his fellow priests, he expressed his gratitude for their contributions "in behalf of our many homeless and destitute Catholic children." He asked for their continued support, stating expansion would continue, "if we can obtain the financial aid necessary to carry on the work."[28] Brother Stanislaus, Baker's loyal and trusted associate at St. John's Protectory, recognized his mastery as a fundraiser: "His power to raise money was miraculous. The institutions had no endowment or direct source of income, but the money came somehow in a steady stream of contributions."[29]

The *Annals*, following on the heels of the *Appeal for Homeless and Destitute Children*, served as the Association's principal mouthpiece for eight years, but Baker's expansion of facilities generated an additional publication. *The Victorian*, first published in 1895, took its name from the Association's patroness.[30] Published as a monthly, rather than quarterly like the *Annals*, it was sold initially for 50 cents annually. By the time of Baker's death in 1936, it was $2.00.

The magazine was initially oriented toward a boy audience. An essay titled "A Boys' Paper" says that many publications purport to be boys' magazines, but "the papers are published for revenue and the boys' interest is of secondary consideration....Our aim in the future will be as in the past to make a paper that any boy can read, believe and enjoy." The essay suggests that many magazines orient their content

> for a race of boys that exist only in the imagination of "school marms." Our boys want something with life and snap in it; they want a paper that comes down to their plane, that uses their own language, that treats the questions of the day from their point of view....Such a paper we believe *The Victorian* to be, at least we aim to make it such.[31]

The magazine was edited by students, who rotated regularly, and printed at St. John's Protectory. This publication of forty-seven pages had several features in each issue: "Question Box," "Editorials," "All Praise to Our Blessed Lady," "Among Our Boys," "Household Recipes," "Junior League of Our Blessed Lady of Victory, and "Young Folks." Additionally, each issue had several freelance articles with such titles as "A Delightful Trip—Fictional Account of Marquette and Joliet," "Boy's Superstitions," "Facts in Natural History," "Marco Polo's Homecoming," plus regular installment series stories, such as "The Fortunes of a Family of Catholics." The magazine was very patriotic, even verging on jingoistic. Such vignettes as "Salute the Flag," and comments like "Every true American boy is a patriot," were common.[32]

While Father Baker's pen was not the central focus of *The Victorian*, as with the *Annals*, his close association with the magazine is evident in several dimensions. First, the magazine's affection for him comes through strongly. Heather Hartel suggested that from the outset, "*The Victorian* magazine frequently reflected the fondness and admiration for Baker present within the Institutes."[33] Second, Baker's persona and ideas were also readily apparent in the magazine. He suggested that the *Victorian* should serve four specific functions: spread devotion to Our Lady of Victory, defend the Church, interest people in social charity, and serve the Church family.[34] On a personal level he explained to Bishop Matthew Harkins of Providence, Rhode Island:

> The great object of our publication is to stimulate and
> encourage an interest in the work of Our Lady of
> Victory Home at Victoria, Lackawanna, N.Y. and its
> institutions, where we are caring for homeless and desti-
> tute children of every class.[35]

Last, through Baker's influence, the circulation of both magazines
(*The Victorian* and the *Annals*) flourished, allowing his message
and work to spread broadly throughout the country and internationally to Canada.[36]

The success of Baker's two principal publications led to their
merger in August 1929. Baker explained the move in the *Victorian*:

> Almost from the beginning of our work, we have also
> published a quarterly magazine of thirty-two pages,
> dedicated solely to the honor of Our Blessed Lady. In
> order to please our friends, we have combined these two
> publications into a book of sixty-four pages, beginning
> with the August 15 issue.[37]

Baker explained further to the Board of Managers of the
Society for the Protection of Destitute Roman Catholic Children
that, with circulation between the two magazines at approximately
300,000, he hoped that the combined new format might help to
raise circulation to 500,000.[38] The merger was more an absorption
of the *Annals* than a physical joining of the two magazines. First,
the merged publication dropped the name *Annals*, but kept *The
Victorian*. Second, while *The Victorian* had always published essays
on Catholic popular devotion, the level of demonstrable Marian
piety ever present in the *Annals* was not so clearly evident in the
merged magazine.[39]

Lifetime of Devotion to Our Lady of Victory

On an intellectual level, there was nothing truly remarkable
about late nineteenth-century American Catholicism. While it is
true many bishops and a few other clerics and Church thinkers battled each other during what was known as the Americanist crisis,

and fewer still took sides in the debate over theological modernism, most American Catholics had little stake in theological discussion.[40] Indeed, American Church historian James O'Toole has accurately captured the experience of the vast majority of Catholics in late nineteenth-century America:

> American Catholics, like their fellow Americans who went to other churches, lived their faith through countless unremarkable routines. Deep questions of theology usually meant little to them, but parishioners clung to deeply ingrained habits of devotion, both public and private. Particular devotions changed over time, waxing or waning in popularity, but the habits endured.[41]

Religious historian Colleen McDannell suggests that devotionalism was the unique contribution made by Catholics to American religion: "One way that Catholics successfully claimed a part of the American religious landscape was by creating a devotional life that spoke to their concepts of the supernatural."[42] Ann Taves, in her seminal work on Catholic devotionalism, specifies how popular piety eclipsed theological teaching in common practice:

> Forms of devotion...were promoted and widely adopted during the mid-nineteenth century....Evidence suggests that by the middle decades of the nineteenth century, the reception of the sacraments was overshadowed for most lay Catholics by devotional practices associated with Mary, Jesus, the Sacred Heart, and the Blessed Sacrament.[43]

Unlike twenty-first-century America, where religion is often a low priority or even ancillary to one's life, Americans in the late nineteenth century experienced religion as part of their daily routine. Robert Orsi, one of the foremost historians of Catholic popular religiosity, has proffered four essential ideas to understand religious practice:

1. A sense of the range of idiomatic possibility and limitation in a culture

2. An understanding of the knowledge of the body in the culture
3. An understanding of the structure of social experience
4. A sense of what sorts of characteristic tensions erupt within these particular structures

In a practical sense he believes religion cannot be compartmentalized in one's life: "Religion cannot be neatly separated from the other practices of everyday life....Nor can 'religion' be separated from the material circumstances in which specific instances of religious imagination and behavior arise and to which they respond."[44] He continues, "Religion comes into being in an ongoing, dynamic relationship with the realities of everyday life." Orsi suggests that religion is not a fixed dimension of one's person, but rather, "people appropriate religious idioms as they need them, in response to particular circumstances. All religious ideas and impulses are of the moment, invented, taken, borrowed, and improvised at the intersections of life."[45]

During much of the nineteenth century, the roots of Marian piety were found in France. After the French Revolution, when the "Cult of the Supreme Being" had challenged Catholic hegemony, the Church sought to reassert its authority. McDannell commented,

> After the Revolution the Church tried to re-establish itself in a changing social and political environment. The miracles, prophecies and supernaturalism of nineteenth century France reassured Catholics that their world was indeed blessed by God and would continue in spite of war and social change.[46]

Devotion to the Blessed Mother was strongly fostered through a series of Marian apparitions in Europe: Paris (1830), La Salette (1846), Lourdes (1858), and Pontmain (1871) in France; and Knock in Ireland (1879). Additionally, the proclamation of the dogma of the Immaculate Conception by Pope Pius IX in 1854 bolstered this devotion.[47]

In many ways, devotion to Mary defined Roman Catholic spirituality in the late nineteenth and early twentieth centuries.

While it is clear that Mary has played an integral role in Roman Catholicism from the apostolic era, the concentration of devotion in this time period is noteworthy. Again McDannel has commented on this phenomenon: "Although Catholics understood their Marian piety to be truly 'Catholic,' the expressions of that piety drew from the culture of the time."[48] Popular religious practices—such as recitation of the Rosary; devotion to the Immaculate Conception, the Sacred Heart of Jesus, and the Immaculate Heart of Mary; plus the use of various scapulars, such as the Brown Scapular of Our Lady of Mount Carmel, or the Green Scapular of the Immaculate Heart of Mary—were so common they largely defined the spirituality of the epoch.[49]

Quite obviously Nelson Baker possessed a great devotion to the Blessed Virgin, but the devotion developed over time. In the opinion of Buffalo Catholic historian Walter Kern, Baker's devotion to Mary at the seminary had rather ordinary roots:

> Nelson had a great devotion to the Blessed Mother, but it had only the form of general Marian prayers, the scapular of Our Lady of Mount Carmel, the Little Office, and Our Lady of Peace. There is no proof that he had devotion to Our Lady of Victory this early in life.[50]

When Baker made the pilgrimage to Europe in late spring of 1874, and by chance visited the Church of Notre Dame des Victoires, his devotion was strengthened, but his enthusiasm and zeal continued to deepen and mature with time.

The greatest manifestation of Baker's devotion to Mary was his unceasing and indomitable trust and confidence in her intercession. This was noted by many of his contemporaries. Thomas Galvin, CSsR, describes how Baker approached various projects:

> Solicitous? Yes, he was!...But discouraged and worried? Never! Trials, hunger, cold, troubles of every variety arose to test his courage, but never did he swerve from that self-abandonment to God's care and to confidence in his Blessed Lady of Victory, and never did she disappoint him.[51]

Clara Balduf, who worked at St. John's Protectory from 1916 to 1918, stated, "He put all his trust in Our Lord and Our Lady....When he prayed I really believe that he was sure it would be granted." Similarly, Sister Theophane Bwie, SSJ, commented, "His [Baker's] love for Our Lady of Victory was, not just love, it was confidence, it was trust."[52] Baker described the evolution of his confidence in Mary:

> If we have succeeded in our work, it is because we have had unbounded confidence in God's Holy Mother, as she has been pleased always to extend to us her gener-ous aid; in our poverty and want, surrounded by every need, when one hardly knew which way to turn, Mary always came to our rescue and opened to us the pathway of success.[53]

Nelson Baker saw Mary as a friend with whom he could talk on a personal level. His devotion to her, as expressed by Balduf, was never manifested from a distance: "From the way he preached about the power of Our Lady, you would think he had a close connection with her."[54] He often seemed to lose himself and even forget about others when looking at a statue of Mary and then speaking to her as if she was standing before him. One contempo-rary recalled her impression of Baker's relationship with Mary:

> There never was anyone with *greater* [emphasis in the original] faith in the Blessed Mother—and very few with as great faith in her—as Father Baker. He was always close to her. He'd talk to her as if she were a living per-son right there with him. He praised her for her favors and even scolded her when she kept him waiting for something he needed badly.[55]

Since Mary was his friend, it was quite logical for Baker to entrust all his projects to her protection and intercession. He once stated, "Our Blessed Lady is my friend. She understands me. She comforts me. I pray to her and she tells me the course I should pur-sue. I do nothing without her advice, and with her support I cannot

85

fail."[56] When people praised him for his great accomplishments, such as his ability to successfully obtain financing for a construction project, Baker set the record straight by giving her the credit:

> I had very little to do with it....The Blessed Mother is the manager. She is the banker. She financed the whole affair. I placed the institution under Her care. I am only the administrator. I never worry. If She wishes this undertaking to succeed it will, despite my infirmities.[57]

As his ministry expanded, so his confidence in Mary increased proportionally. In October 1924, with additional expansion of the Institutions in progress, Baker confidently wrote:

> We are still building and have many plans for the future, all to advance God's glory, and we continue to depend upon our dear Blessed Lady, that she will inspire our many good friends to continue to aid us in the future as in the past, and then we can promise to our kind friends, every blessing that heaven contains, and these will be obtained and bestowed through the generous hands of Our Dear Blessed Lady of Victory.[58]

Throughout his half century as superintendent of the Our Lady of Victory Institutions, Nelson Baker always met his financial responsibilities, save one request in 1934 for assistance from the diocese (see chapter 10). Near his death, the estimated value of the Institutions assets was $25 million. In response to this fact, he only said, "I haven't the slightest idea how it was paid for. It was the Mother of God who did it one way or another." For a man with Baker's business-trained mind, his explanation that he had no idea how his debts were paid does not seem to tell the whole story. However, without extant data, this will remain a mystery.[59]

Baker's love for Mary, and his total confidence that any project engaged in her name would be successful and secure from debt, prompted him to hope that others could share his belief and experience. He was sure this was possible since his own work had been generated by a proverbial mustard seed of faith and had blossomed into the great tree that covered thousands of homeless and destitute children. As his dependence on Mary became greater, so too his trust grew stronger. Considering it imperative for others to catch the same fire that glowed through him, he realized the responsibility, common to all, to promote devotion to the Blessed Mother.

> We must realize then the importance of making use of every opportunity to advance the interest of Our Blessed Lady, in speaking of her glories, extolling her virtues, and making known her great love for us, and thus we will inspire all hearts with an ardent desire of loving our Blessed Lady more and more, and of enkindling her love more ardently in our hearts, which will be to us a foretaste of the happiness which we will afterwards enjoy at her hands in heaven.[60]

This mandate, as he understood it, to foster devotion to Mary was evident throughout Baker's ministerial life.[61]

Closely allied with the more public vistas of Baker's devotion to Mary was his profound personal fidelity to her. Ruth Monk, who was baptized by Baker during his active evangelization of African Americans (see chapter 10), called Baker's personal Marian devotion "deep and sincere."[62] Baker was thankful to God for giving Mary as a great advocate and the one who showed perfect example. He wrote, "Mary's life we may not only study and admire, picture and paint,—we are to imitate it as much as we can." Baker saw Mary as the one who brought calm out of chaos.[63]

Baker was also a great champion and practitioner of devotional prayers and rituals honoring Mary. Very devoted to the Rosary, he wrote,

> This devotion, so charming, needs but little encouragement, as it is filled with happiest thought and sweetest consolation; it must be most dear to Our Blessed Lord, as we are thinking of Him from its beginning to the end; Jesus and Mary go with us hand in hand, as our fingers glide over the Rosary.[64]

Baker also regularly prayed the Stations of the Cross, but he was most devoted to, and took great time meditating on, the Fourth Station, when Jesus meets Mary on the *Via Dolorosa*. In 1894, desiring a place of reflection and prayer dedicated to Mary, Baker built a shrine to Our Lady of Victory adjacent to St. John's Protectory.[65]

The prayers and devotion offered by Father Baker and others, whether public or private, were often answered in remarkable ways. The *Annals* and *The Victorian* reported many favors granted by Our Lady of Victory. A typical report from a grateful mother read: "Our Lady of Victory has indeed proved herself a friend to me. Recently my son was in a terrible railroad accident, but thank God he escaped uninjured—He wore the miraculous medal of Our Blessed Lady of Victory."[66] One young woman described another favor granted:

> About four months ago I asked of our Blessed Mother a favor for my father which has been most beautifully granted. I asked to have my father's sight restored and also his hearing which was almost gone and I rejoice to state that both requests have been granted.[67]

While Nelson Baker's devotion to Mary was unswerving, powerful, and consistent, his zeal at times ascribed excessive powers to the Mother of God. In a meditation titled "Mary's Wonderful Power," Baker wrote:

> Mary is most powerful and omnipotent in heaven; she commands not only the angels but God himself, whose omnipotence is the omnipotence of Mary. Think now what Mary can do on earth, since she is so powerful in heaven. All power is given her in heaven and on earth.[68]

The Institutions of Our Lady of Victory

Nelson Baker's philosophy as superintendent of the Institutions of Our Lady of Victory viewed boys, even though at times wayward, as good and as redeemable from their flaws. Using every means available to him, he sought for each boy to reach his "maximum potential"; this was a guiding principle. How this could be accomplished was, of course, the great question. The challenge was articulated by one writer:

> It was the special task of Father Baker and his assistants to mold this heterogeneous collection of boys into educated, manly, and well-balanced individuals....He insisted that his charges be well-filled, by manual and mental training, to cope with the rigors of an exacting world [69]

Baker firmly believed that whatever could be done for his boys, in the name of God, would reap abundant rewards, sometimes in this life, but most assuredly in the next.[70]

Nelson Baker was motivated to assist orphaned and troubled youths for important reasons. First, he did not want these children to lose their Catholic faith, which often happened when families disintegrated. Thomas Galvin tells the story that, early in his priesthood, Baker encountered a group of homeless Catholic waifs in New York. Commenting on Baker's reaction, Galvin writes, "Father Baker's sense of justice and his indignation over the cruel injustice soon to be perpetrated on these unsuspecting little ones could not be hushed into silence."[71]

Second, Baker believed that the basic procedure of the day that placed youths who had committed petty crimes in the same category with adults was wrong. Such a situation only led to a life of crime. He believed youths were too young to be labeled "bad."[72] For Baker, the basic problem was a difficult home life. Since he could not reform their home life, he took as many boys as possible into his Institutions and gave them the training necessary to make them good American Catholics.[73] Baker explained:

> Our friends are continually asking us if we will take homeless and destitute children that are wandering about our cities and towns, and we always state that we are only too glad to give a home to these little homeless children, and we will strive to give them every advantage in an educational, religious and industrial manner, so

89

that they will afterwards be able to earn their own living, and we trust, be a credit to us, and to our holy faith.[74]

Baker's basic philosophy led him to extend a general invitation for boys to be sent to his Institutions. His longtime friend Brother Stanislaus articulated Baker's policy: "Father Baker had one simple rule, to accept any boy who needed care without question and without price, to keep him and teach him until he was able to go out into the world and make a living for himself."[75] Baker himself presented his ideas: "Our good friends must not be delicate about asking us to receive any little homeless infant, as we are now in a condition to receive all that may be sent, regardless of circumstances, parentage, or money."[76]

Baker's open-door policy brought boys from all across the country and Canada. In her history of the Sisters of St. Joseph, Sister Immaculata Maxwell commented: "From distant parts boys came to Father Baker's to seek shelter—the name of the orphanage was synonymous with refuge to those who are needy."[77] Each issue of the *Annals* contained letters Baker had received requesting that he take some child. Many of these children were not true orphans, but Baker's assistance was still sought for various reasons. While each case was somewhat unique, there was a common denominator: a mother (generally) or a father did not have the resources to provide for the boy(s), and the petitioner had total confidence in Baker and his program. In a typical request, a man from Iowa wrote to Baker:

> I address you on behalf of a poor mother who has a boy twelve years of age that she cannot take care of, and she has appealed to me to try and get him in some Catholic Institution; I thought of your good work having read in your *Annals* that you take boys from different parts of the country, and I ask your consideration of this poor child's care.[78]

A very different set of circumstances accompanied a second request from a woman in Cleveland: "There is a little boy here of about ten years of age that we would like to place in some institution like yours; the mother has just died and the father's whereabouts are unknown. Would you be kind enough to make a place for him in your Institution?" [79] The spiritual dimension of Baker's Institutions was noted by many and made a principal reason for the request. One woman wrote to Baker:

> My sister has two boys whose father has deserted them, and the authorities have placed them in a Protestant home, and as she is unable to support them, she is very anxious about their welfare, and desires me to write and see if you could take them into your home, and thus save them from the danger of losing their Faith.[80]

At times Baker's help was sought when children were in great misery. In January 1929, he received a request to take in three brothers. Their case was described to him:

> We have in our care three boys who have a rather unique history. When reported, the children were found in a two-room shack. The mother was dead and the father was reported to be in the neighborhood cutting wood. He did not buy food or clothing for the children, but was buying an automobile. The boys lived on groundhogs and what they could get from their neighbors.[81]

Using great sensitivity and manifesting his abundant generosity, Father Baker answered the pleas sent to him. In his succinct but effective style, Baker would typically write, "We shall be pleased to take the boy you write us about, and do the best we can for him, and the other two boys, if they are in danger of going wrong." When responding to priests who sought to send children, he also generally requested if possible that $4.00 per week be submitted for the child's care.[82]

The flood of requests, combined with Baker's general open acceptance, created a situation where facilities and resources were stretched to their limits. As early as 1893, Baker was forced to admit, "We have not been able to supply sufficient accommodations for the large numbers that are being continually brought to our doors."[83] This situation forced Baker to make a decision—restrict numbers or expand his facilities. For this man of faith, however, there was no option; the facilities needed to be expanded. Baker did not see the situation as problematic, but rather was pleased that his request had generated such a massive response. In 1932, in the period of the Great Depression (during the twilight of his life), he wrote:

> Since making this invitation general, we have been almost flooded with applications and with children, so much so that we have been unable to take care of them all; we hoped for this result, as we are trying to take such children regardless of expense, and without obligation on the parties sending them to us [without] bearing any expense in the matter and hence they come even more freely than we had anticipated.[84]

Despite the situation of growing numbers, Baker was convinced that the children were better off with him and equally certain that God, pleased with his work, would provide the resources to see a way forward: "We feel that God must surely bless the work and will raise up more friends to aid us in defraying the necessarily heavy expenses, as well as to find good Catholic homes for His own little children."[85]

Nelson Baker's rapport with the boys in his Institutions is best described as a father-son relationship. Indeed, many of the boys said, "When he [Baker] talked to you, you almost thought he was your real Father."[86] This perception was verified by Herbert Sisson, Buffalo superintendent for the poor, after an official visit to St. John's Protectory:

> During my visit to the Institution, I was struck by the friendliness between the little charges and Father Baker. The latter is like a real father to those youngsters. Whenever he appears where they are, they rush up to him, clinging to his clothes or are tossed up in the air by him. The children love and respect him.[87]

Like a loving father, Baker demonstrated gentleness and forgiveness, but in a powerful way. One observer commented:

> He forgave without punishment, but always in a manner so compelling it seemed punishment itself. A few words of reproof in his kindly tones were enough. That is the force that gave him such command over unruly boys; it was the method he used to make men of them, and there were few indeed who left his institutions without loving him as a father— as a guardian.[88]

Baker was even-handed in his relationships with the boys; he played no favorites, but rather treated all the same. He was much attuned to boys who in some way needed added attention. While in the recreation yard of the Protectory, he had the ability to scan the scene and then speak with a boy who seemed lonely. Brother Stanislaus once commented:

> I remember how he used to come walking through the yard in the evening. He would stop to speak with some despondent lad, some little fellow with gloom and despair in his face. And I have seen the boy's face lighted like a little candle that has been touched by a big one.[89]

Baker also took the time to interact with the boys in various activities, again as any loving father would do. He often played ball with them; on Sunday afternoons he sometimes took walks with a few boys to buy apples, potatoes, or some other item needed for dinner. He always had candy with him for any casual meeting; his care and concern was evident in the minutest detail. Thomas Galvin, who experienced Baker's fatherly care firsthand, wrote, "He [Baker] looks upon them [the boys] as treasures conferred by Divine Providence, and no father of a family goes to greater expense nor bestows more tender affection on his children."[90] He was their advocate in every situation.

His love for his boys was reciprocated in many significant ways. The boys, many of whom referred to him as "Daddy Baker" as a sign of their affection, almost seemed to be in competition to gain his attention. Remembering his experience as a "Baker Boy," Galvin wrote:

> His [Baker's] appearance in the play yard was the signal for a whoop and a hurrah and a scamper, the boys rivaling each other in their efforts to be the first to reach him....A mass of boys swarming around him, jostling, pushing, scrambling for points of vantage to talk to him....And how he enjoyed himself. He grew young again. He shouted and whooped with the most effusive of them.[91]

Baker was often feted by the boys on special occasions, especially on his birthday and anniversary of ordination. For example, on March 19, 1897, the boys gave him a surprise party, including a dramatic play, to celebrate his anniversary of ordination. One report stated, "Everything was done in secret, and done well, as all who attended the party testified."[92]

Baker's philosophy, which made his ministry with orphans and unruly boys so efficacious, was solidified by a dedicated work ethic. He used his gifts and talents to their maximum extent; he did not allow any ability to lie fallow. Brother Stanislaus once commented, "Father Baker succeeded because he used, [to] the fullest extent, a remarkable business ability and because of his deep piety and abiding faith."[93] Unlike the contemporary social theorist Father John Ryan, Baker was a man of action. He was, when it was necessary, a hard-nosed businessman who got the job done. Yet, he never lost sight of the fact that the spiritual dimension was the engine that drove the "train" of his life.[94]

Nelson Baker's philosophy of working with boys was put to use initially at St. Joseph's Orphan Asylum, the original institution at Limestone Hill. During his first years as superintendent, the population at St. Joseph averaged between 100 and 120, but with time, especially after Baker's general invitation in the *Annals* and *The Victorian* was more widely disseminated, this number grew substantially.[95] Baker's ministry at the orphanage paved a path that would be used to direct the rest of his life at Our Lady of Victory Institutions.[96]

Life at St. Joseph, like most all institutions, was governed by a daily routine. From rising at 6 a.m. to retirement at 8 to 8:30 p.m., the boys were scheduled to be at meals, in school or recreation, at religious exercises, or at study. Besides their responsibilities in school, the boys served in the kitchen, with such duties as setting tables prior to meals, clearing and cleaning after meals, or setting up for the next day. These tasks rotated based on conduct.[97] Baker tried to be flexible, but there were a few nonnegotiable rules. First, running away was punishable by being sent to St. John's Protectory, which the boys called the "hill" or the "ref," to designate it as a home for more incorrigible youth. Second, smoking, leaving the grounds, or using profane language led to additional daily duties.[98] On the other hand, rewards were also in evidence for exceptional school achievement and good conduct. An inspection report of 1904 commented: "Rewards are given for good conduct and for proficiency in school work. Corporal punishment is used occasionally, but the giving of tasks is the more common method of punishing. No record of punishments is kept."[99]

Education was the most significant activity at St. Joseph's. In the first years of the asylum, because the boys were so scattered in their knowledge, classes were conducted without specific grade levels. Rather, the Sisters of St. Joseph did their best to educate each boy "at his own speed and at his own level."[100] High school records show that many "Baker's Boys" graduated from high school with averages greater than 90 percent and fulfilled the requirements for the New York State Board of Regents Examinations. Sister M. Timothy Dempsey, chronicler of educational efforts at Limestone Hill, confidently asserted, "It can be safely assumed the education the boys were receiving at the turn of the century was of excellent caliber."[101]

Religious education and training were of course part and parcel of the daily regimen at St. Joseph's. Boys were kept in the Institutions if at all possible until they had completed their Christian initiation, "thus giving them a firm foundation in the faith in addition to sheltering them for a time longer."[102] The daily routine included a visit to the chapel for prayers and singing. During Lent it was customary for the boys to attend Mass each day as well.

When feast days came, the Sisters organized processions and parades around the theme of the day.[103]

In addition to religious activities, the boys at St. Joseph enjoyed many recreational moments as well. Sunday was special at the orphanage in many ways. It was visiting day, allowing the boys to receive family visitors. As a reward on Sundays, the Sisters took certain boys to a movie in town. In the afternoon, all the residents of St. Joseph crossed the street to the Protectory for a weekly movie, held in the auditorium.[104]

Knowledge and appreciation for Father Baker's work at St. Joseph's extended far beyond the borders of the City or Diocese of Buffalo. Cardinal James Gibbons of Baltimore, writing to Baker, expressed what many felt:

> If my words of encouragement and blessings can contribute to the success of a work so meritorious, which of itself should claim the attention of all who are interested in succoring the innocent, needy, and helpless, and which should receive the generous support of those who are in a position to give, it is with the greatest pleasure, that I approve of your good and great work.[105]

The first apostolic delegate to the United States, Archbishop (later Cardinal) Francesco Satolli, also energetically endorsed Baker's work: "I heartily approve of your great and holy work, of caring for the Homeless and Destitute Child; as our Blessed Lord was once a homeless child, he cannot fail to bless those who make it a work of their life, to offer a home to those in need."[106] In August 1908, Pope Pius X imparted his apostolic blessing, "with the wish that the Lord may prosper this work of religion and beneficence."[107]

The laudatory comments given to Father Baker must be shared with the Sisters of St. Joseph, whose presence and ministry were integral to the success of the Institutions. The community was first invested on October 15, 1650, at the orphanage at Le Puy, France, as a result of the vision of Bishop Henri de Maupas of Le Puy and Father Jean Paul Médaille, SJ, who sought to create a congregation that blended contemplative life with practical

charity. Thus, on March 10, 1651, the bishop formally authorized the congregation. The community, led by Mother St. John
Fontbonne, was suppressed during the French Revolution. Twelve
years later, she again took the habit on July 14, 1808. In 1836, the
Sisters came to St. Louis; in 1854, Bishop Timon asked for the
Sisters' services in Buffalo. Besides St. Joseph's Orphan Asylum
and St. John's Protectory at Limestone Hill, the Sisters of St.
Joseph were actively engaged in many other educational apostolates throughout Buffalo, including a school for the deaf that
opened on December 8, 1888.[108] When Baker became superintendent at Limestone Hill, Bishop Ryan placed the Sisters under
his direction.[109]

The Sisters' efforts at St. Joseph were led by Mother Mary
Anne Burke, who was superior of the community from 1869 to
1913. She was responsible for encouraging members of the
community to gain accreditation from the State of New York as
teachers. Additionally, along with Father Baker, she introduced
technical trades as part of the general curriculum for the boys at St.
John's Protectory. One writer commented on the efficacy of their
partnership: "The Reverend Mother was considered the perfect
foil for Father Nelson Baker who made the institutions famous.
Both are considered geniuses in their own right with phenomenal
business sense and devotion equal to the saints."[110]

The Sisters' efforts were well appreciated by all who observed
or experienced their dedicated ministry. Father Thomas Galvin
experienced the work of the Sisters of St. Joseph as an orphan himself and observed them as a fellow assistant to Baker. He wrote of
"the kind, wise, holy, and material training of these good daughters of St. Joseph," which allowed him to receive "a thoroughly
Catholic, pious, and religious education." He continued:

> I unhesitatingly declare that for good sense, deep wis-
> dom and practical piety, I have not yet found any sister-
> hood that surpassed those Sisters of St. Joseph in the
> training they gave us. The history of St. Joseph at
> Limestone Hill should be written in gold....No human
> pen or mortal tongue can ever adequately describe the

sublime heroism, the spirit of self-immolation, and the sublime virtues practiced by these noble women.[111]

Speaking at the diamond jubilee celebration of the arrival of the Sisters to Buffalo, Father Henry Laudenbach accurately captured the integral part played by these religious women: "At Father Baker's great social center, you have been his right and left hands."[112] Father Baker himself was very appreciative of the Sisters' significant contribution to his work at the Institutions. In an appreciative tone he later wrote:

> I had not the opportunity of expressing to you my gratitude for the many kindnesses you have bestowed upon us, in connection with our work here, and I know that Our Blessed Lord will more than abundantly reward you for your thoughtfulness in helping us to take care of the great work in our hands.[113]

Nelson Baker's philosophy and indefatigable work ethic, combined with the assistance of the Sisters of St. Joseph and the Brothers of the Holy Infancy and Youth of Jesus, were also exercised at St. John's Protectory, the sister institution to St. Joseph. When Baker returned to Limestone Hill in 1882, he found St. John's in a chaotic state. The Protectory was insolvent, having lost credit with all businesses in Buffalo. The boys at St. John's were described by one observer as possessing "a refractory, lawless, insubordinate disposition and [they] naturally chafed under their forced confinement behind bars, and locks and keys."[114] The almost prison-like atmosphere at the Protectory, an environment totally inconsistent with Baker's philosophy, was changed almost immediately after his return. Bars were removed from windows; such an environment was not conducive to learning. As Sister Mary Timothy Dempsey suggests, "He wanted his Institutions to be home and school, not a prison and labor camp."[115] Reaction to Baker's "new direction" was swift and positive. After a meeting of the managers of the Society for the Protection of Destitute Roman Catholic Children at the City of Buffalo, one local paper reported: "The good Priests and Sisters have reason to be proud of their success....The managers who frequently visit the establishment could not help remarking [about] the improvements in the Protectory and its surroundings."[116]

Baker's commitment to work with the residents at St. John's was clearly efficacious. His ability to disarm boys, often angry with their situation and the world in general, was remarkable. On one occasion a youth lashed out at Baker, telling him that he would not attend church; he had rejected religion in total. Baker responded, "Son, don't wait for a hearse to take you to church."[117] On another occasion, one of the boys could not control his temper. Baker told him, "Hold onto your temper, son, because nobody wants it but yourself."[118] Commenting on Baker's amazing rapport with youth, Otto Rosalsky, a famous New York City judge who worked with troubled youth, wrote: "The great humanitarian could put over more with one sentence than all the rest could do with a whole chapter."[119] Baker's policy to spare no expense in creating a proper home environment paid off as evidenced by the dearth of problems and the many success stories that emerged from the Protectory. In 1896, the district attorney of Buffalo, John Kenefick, remarked to a group of local citizens: "In tracing the antecedents of criminals for ten years past, [I] never discovered 'A Victory Boy' in the whole lot."[120]

Beyond the task of creating a new environment, Baker also found a need for new facilities. While a state report of 1885 said the boys "are given a good common school education, besides being instructed in trades," and complemented Baker and his associates for a number of improvements, still there were problems. While stating that the Protectory was scrupulously clean, the report also declared, "The building is old and in poor repair."[121]

Baker did not need the state report to know that his expanding population of boys and the physical condition of the Protectory required action. In a general appeal letter, he wrote: "The longer we are engaged in the work, the more we are convinced of its urgent necessity of the want of greater facilities for carrying it on, and the means necessary for success."[122] In 1884, even before the report was published, an expansion of St. John's was started, the first since the building was constructed in 1863. With his usual supreme confidence, Baker went forward without

99

the financial means, believing fully that Our Lady of Victory would help him to meet the challenge. The addition, which included more living space and a new chapel, was dedicated on June 26, 1889, with Baker the principal celebrant at the Mass and Bishop Ryan preaching the sermon.[123]

The initial addition was only the first of several expansions and renovations of St. John's before the close of the century. In 1893, a completely new section of the Protectory, dedicated solely to teaching technical trades, was added to the facility. One year later, another very large expansion was completed, adding 217 beds and 26 bathrooms, plus expanding the chapel to accommodate 500. As always, funding was a concern, but seemingly not for Baker. As the latter project, costing $50,000, neared completion, he wrote in the *Annals*: "Our Blessed Lady [will] inspire our friends to help us to meet this large sum and we are not disappointed."[124] In 1896, Victoria Hall, with a seating capacity for 1,500, was completed. This project allowed Baker to start a marching band, drill team, and cadet corps at St. John's. Finally, in 1897, a massive five-story addition was built. This gave the home a total of 700 beds, six large school rooms, six dining rooms, extensive bathing and lavatory facilities, plus the trade school.[125] One final cosmetic, yet important change was the name associated with the institution. While the official title remained, in 1897 St. John's became known as "Our Lady of Victory Home." Sister Immaculata Maxwell, the historian of the Sisters of St. Joseph in Buffalo, wrote: "With this gesture some of the blight that seemed attached to the idea of the establishment banished too."[126]

The routine and staffing at St. John's were very similar to that at St. Joseph's. The boys' days were highly structured, rising at 5:30 a.m. and retiring at 9:00 p.m., with school, recreation, meals, study, and religious services, including Mass and Eucharistic Benediction. Saturdays were dedicated to trades education and recreation. Sundays featured Mass, more recreation, and the aforementioned afternoon films, which were enjoyed by the boys from St. Joseph as well. The residents in the home were often wards of the city or state, but others were simply homeless children.[127]

St. John's educational program was staffed by the Sisters of St. Joseph, who served primarily as teachers of older boys, and the

Brothers of the Holy Infancy and Youth of Jesus, who taught the younger boys, assisted in the dormitories, and supervised the technical trades training. The Sisters had the necessary training, qualifications, and accreditation to teach and administer exams, including the Regents exams, to older boys. Baker sent some Brothers to Buffalo's Jesuit-staffed Canisius College for teacher training, but their principal contribution was in the maintenance of order and technical training. The *Buffalo Courier* in 1894 described the liberal arts education at St. John's:

> The boys devote five hours daily, except Sunday, to school work. Four good Sisters of St. Joseph teach them English composition, grammar, arithmetic, geography, history, and drawing. The school is thoroughly equipped with all appliances useful in a school room. There are four departments in as many rooms, each well lighted, well ventilated, and heated by steam....When the boys reach the age of sixteen, they had to leave the Protectory, but with a fair education and moral training, it was not difficult for them to get employment and a good home.[128]

People were impressed with the program at St. John's. One local paper commented on the quality of education: "The children astonished everyone by their proficiency and thoroughness in spelling, geography and arithmetic: their original essays were much admired as well for the composition as the penmanship."[129]

Baker's program sought to educate boys in mind and heart. Therefore, religion and patriotism were an important part of the curriculum. These ideas built character and provided them with all the requisite tools to deal with the vicissitudes of life. Father Baker's program was not designed simply to save children from the streets, but, equally important, to train and prepare them to be educated, morally sound, and productive members of society. People observed that Baker's Boys were prepared to face the world and earn a respectable livelihood for themselves and their families.[130] Specialized training in technical trades was the added

101

dimension so critical to the education program at St. John's. In 1894, the *Buffalo Courier* reported,

> Aside from the mental training, the boys receive five hours daily instructions in the industrial department of the institution under competent teachers. The opportunity is afforded each boy to follow any trade he may like and he then developes [*sic*] whatever natural ability he may possess.[131]

Over time the number of trades available for the boys to engage in grew significantly. When Baker arrived in 1876, the principal area was the manufacture of furniture, but by 1895 plumbing, gas and steam fitting, shoe making and tailoring, carpentry, and printing were also part of the program. Later still, baking, machining, painting and varnishing, barbering, and telegraphy were added.[132] The trade school's success and value were recognized in 1897 when inspectors from Albany accredited the program as the best in the State of New York, making special mention of the work of the Brothers in their report.[133] More important, however, was the positive effect this training had on the boys. Sister Mary Timothy Dempsey commented, "These trades became for them [the boys] their life and the signs by which they would be recognized as respectable citizens."[134] The training received at St. John's was also noted for the base it constructed for a successful life, both in business and in their Catholic faith. Dempsey continued: "The foundation was laid for later life to enable them to be professional men, businessmen, tradesmen, or artisans, but the greatest concern was that they be good husbands and fathers and possibly prominent Catholics and citizens of their community."[135]

Concerning St. John's, the *Buffalo Courier* offered the opinion that "there is no place in America where similar work is being done." The paper verified its comment by citing W. H. Grant, an agent for the Society of the Prevention of Cruelty to Children, who after visiting St. John's, declared that no institution in New York State could compare with it.[136] Indeed, Baker's work was also noted by the historian Thomas Donahue: "Under the care of Father Baker this institution has grown to one of the model protectories of the United States....Thousands of boys have left this institution and have grown up to be honorable members of society and faithful members of the Church."[137]

While the Sisters of St. Joseph made a significant contribution to the general education of boys at St. John's, it was the work of the Brothers of the Holy Infancy and Youth of Jesus that gave the institution its reputation for excellence in training. The origin of the Brothers is not clear from extant data. Some sources say that in 1854 Bishop Timon petitioned Pope Pius IX for a Brotherhood to assist at St. Joseph's Orphan Asylum. Other sources say he consulted with the Christian Brothers in the foundation. It is clear, however, that on January 25, 1856, John Harris, an Irish immigrant who had settled in Buffalo in 1849, Thomas Curran, and Francis Holmes were received as novices at St. Joseph's Cathedral by Timon's vicar general, Father Bernard O'Reilly. The three men were sent to Limestone Hill to assist Father Thomas Hines.[138]

Formal organization and growth of the Brothers took many years. Between 1882, when Baker returned to Limestone Hill, and 1905, when the community was formally organized, membership grew to a dozen men. That year, with Baker's assistance, a rule and constitution were written and approved. On July 16, under the direction of Father Baker, Brother Aloysius was elected brother superior; Brother Holy Infancy, assistant superior; Brother Mary Francis, master of novices, and Brothers Stanislaus, Francis, and Victory as the local council.[139]

The Brothers' ministries were exclusively associated with the apostolates of Father Baker. They worked principally at St. John's, but also at Our Lady of Victory Farm and as teachers at the school of Our Lady of Victory Mission (later Our Lady of the Sacred Heart—see chapter 7). They were a great help to the Sisters of St. Joseph, lessening their burden as teachers and supervisors for the younger children at St. John's. Clearly, their most significant contribution was as teachers in the trade school. It must be noted, however, that the formation program for the Brothers was minimal at best. There was no formal novitiate; rather, Brothers basically did the same work whether they were in the stage of initial formation or in perpetual vows. The community existed to serve at

Baker's Institutions; possibly for this reason the formalities of religious life were seemingly of little significance.

The relationship between the Brothers and Baker was generally harmonious. Baker was well respected as a person, but also for his position and the fact that he had fostered the community and encouraged vocations to it. Baker was even-handed in dealing with the Brothers; as with the boys in the Institutions, he played no favorites. Yet, as one might expect in an environment like St. John's, where tension and high levels of energy are constant, friction did naturally arise. One problem arose over methods of discipline. Baker did not tolerate any corporal punishment against the boys. When, at times, such was administered by one or more of the Brothers, Baker reacted strongly. The most significant conflict was waged over authority. Baker did not like to be contradicted or to lose control of any situation. One former Brother related a story that illustrates this point. Some of the Brothers wanted to move beyond the confinement of Baker's work. When Bishop John Mark Gannon of Erie, Pennsylvania, sought a group of religious brothers to supervise an institution for boys in his diocese, six Brothers of the Holy Infancy and Youth of Jesus volunteered to go. Not wanting to lose the Brothers, Baker told them they could go, but if the venture did not work out, they would not be welcome again at any of Baker's Institutions. The Brothers decided not to go to Erie.[140]

The Brothers' ministry was highly appreciated and viewed as integral to Baker's success at St. John's. Their central role as teachers in the trades' shops is most clear, but their presence as a positive male role model for boys with troubled pasts and a dim future is incalculable. One writer has synthesized their contribution: "For all the years of their dedicated service, the Brotherhood was an indispensable factor in the day-to-day management of the Institution and in the later success of Father Baker's Boys."[141]

St. Joseph's Orphan Asylum and St. John's Protectory were Father Baker's two Institutions at Limestone Hill prior to the twentieth century, but an additional ministry to assist working boys was added to his responsibilities. Institutions to assist orphans and troubled youths, like Baker's Institutions, were meeting many needs in the diocese, but nothing was being done for older youths and young adults who found themselves powerless, penniless, and homeless. There was a need for a residence to assist young people in their physical needs, but, equally important, to preserve their faith and morals. Thus, in November 1888, a group of one hundred women, meeting in the former Hammond Mansion near Niagara Square in downtown Buffalo, organized themselves as the Ladies Aid Society of the Working Boys Home. Mrs. Daniel O'Day was elected the Society's president. Working with Bishop Ryan, the Society prepared the Hammond Mansion to serve as a Working Boys Home. The facility opened in 1889 with Father Daniel Walsh, Baker's seminary friend, as the first director, and four Sisters of St. Joseph as assistants.[142]

In October 1897, Bishop James Quigley, who succeeded Ryan after the latter's death, transferred charge of the Working Boys Home to Baker. Although this added to Baker's workload, the new institution placed a cap on his already existent work to assist boys. As with his ministry at St. Joseph and St. John's, Baker was open to receiving boys. He wrote, "These [working boys] are invited to come and we offer them the advantages of our home and trade school, without demanding any compensation."[143] Baker could now see more plainly the fruits of his work with boys who had "graduated" from the Limestone Hill Institutions and the Working Boys Home, taking their place as productive citizens in society. He wrote,

> We are pleased to note how many of our poor boys who have graduated from the Working Boys Home have become prominent in the workings of society, as we have several amongst our clergy; also lawyers, doctors, and professional men, and we are pleased to note that the first Vice-President of one of our banks is also one of our graduates.[144]

In 1889, the Sisters of St. Joseph, citing the ministry as too arduous, left the Working Boys Home and were replaced by the Brothers of the Holy Infancy and Youth of Jesus.[145]

The Gas Well

The expansion of the Institutions at Limestone Hill only increased Father Baker's need for additional resources to cover costs and pay bills. He thought he had an answer to one rising cost; namely, heating the buildings during the long and often brutally bitter Buffalo winters. He had heard of natural gas deposits in Canada and placed his faith in the hope that gas could be found on the grounds of the Institutions. Thus, with his begging hand outstretched yet again, Baker went to Bishop Ryan asking for money to drill a well. Having heard of the bishop's recent receipt of a gift of $5,000, Baker hoped this might be used for his project. Initially, Ryan thought Baker's request to be folly, but Baker eventually left that day with $2,000, sufficient funds to hire a company and begin to drill.[146]

After securing the permission of his Board (the Society for the Protection of Destitute Roman Catholic Children at the City of Buffalo) and hiring Woodrich and Company of Pennsylvania to oversee the project, drilling commenced in January 1891. The operation went on for weeks and then months with no positive results. Baker was forced to return to Ryan and eventually convinced the bishop to give the remainder of the $5,000 gift toward the project. As time passed, however, even those in Baker's "house" became very skeptical. One Sister of St. Joseph reportedly told him, "We know you have literally performed miracles here, Father, and I am sure no project you have in mind could surprise us, but this is not a project. This is folly, sheer folly."[147]

Baker pressed on with full confidence, heedless of what others thought about his project. Finally on August 21 at a depth of 1,137 feet, a pocket of gas was breached. Not certain if the find was a small pocket or a significant deposit, drilling continued. The escaping gas was ignited by a nearby flame, causing an explosion and massive fire at the well site. Eight people were injured and drilling equipment was destroyed. The fire required experts from Pennsylvania to extinguish, but eventually the well was capped and made serviceable.[148] One local paper reported the event:

Father Baker of the West Seneca Catholic Protectory got more than enough gas to heat his institutions and light his trade school and school and other buildings. Excitement is great in the town and its people dream of untold fortunes. Everyone is talking of the miracle well which Father Baker calls the Victorian gas well. It appears to be the greatest gas well ever struck in America.[149]

The precise role of Nelson Baker in the discovery of the gas is a combination of fact and speculation. Extant data verifies that Baker's project, which was considered speculative at best, was financed by Bishop Ryan. Many stories abound about Baker's use of various religious processions to know where to drill, and of his faithful prayers, including novenas, when the process produced nothing for several months. Whether these devotions are part of the true history does not mask the clear faith he possessed in moving forward when all others believed nothing would come of the effort and expense. The well, which many sought to buy after its discovery, continues to supply gas in limited quantities today.[150]

Conclusion

Father Baker's return to Limestone Hill as superintendent at St. Joseph's Orphan Asylum and St. John's Protectory, as well as pastor of St. Patrick's Parish, was the environment in which the script of the remainder of his life would be played out. His first years at the helm of such a massive operation were critical in setting the course for the future. Baker's use of money solicitation by mail in an effort to seek fiscal stability and alleviate a crushing debt was rare and possibly unique for Catholic institutions of his day. Since the remainder of his time at Limestone Hill would continually be filled with fiscal challenges, the base established in his early days as superintendent was critical. Additionally, these first years saw the establishment of his relationship with the Brothers of the Holy Infancy and Youth of Jesus and with the Sisters of St. Joseph, the two religious communities with whom he would partner in ministry until his death in 1936. These communities supplied the personnel and the religious witness that Baker needed to teach and supervise his boys. Additionally, he obtained the services at the lowest possible cost. By the turn of the century, Baker had not only stabilized the Institutions, which were on their heels financially at the time he assumed control, but also made significant additions to the facilities and educational program that would allow his ministry to continue to serve thousands of boys over the next thirty-five years. Thus, Baker was ready to tackle a new ministry that somewhat fell into his lap. He met the need as it would unfold before him.

CHAPTER 5

The Infant Home (1908–1936)

The United States entered the twentieth century as a nation that was ascending in many ways. Victory in the short-lived but nonetheless significant Spanish-American War of 1898 suddenly elevated the United States onto the world scene. The defeat of a former world power in six months, while simultaneously gaining significant territories across the globe, made the United States an important player in international politics and economics. Having, at least for some significant moments, moved away from its staid policy of isolationism, the United States was poised and ready for a broader role in the world.

Similarly, the new century held excellent possibilities for Nelson Baker and his expanding ministry to youth in Western New York. By the turn of the century, Baker had been a priest for twenty-five years and for almost twenty years had served as superintendent of the Our Lady of Victory Institutions at Limestone Hill. An open-door policy for orphans and troubled youth and an expanding base (although never sufficient) of fiscal resources were a formula for more activity at St. Joseph's and St. John's, but Baker soon discovered a pressing need to assist the most vulnerable of society: infants and the unborn. The Institutions he inherited from Father Hines and Bishop Timon needed a complement to protect those who had previously been left out of the equation. Thus, consistent with the new direction the nation needed to traverse in its more worldwide role, Nelson Baker and his Our Lady of Victory ministry expanded and completed his dream of servicing God's children from birth to maturity.

The City of Lackawanna

The dawn of the twentieth century brought significant changes to the area of Limestone Hill, the community that played host to Father Baker's Institutions. Since 1852, the district had been formally named West Seneca, after the local Native American tribe. The town was actually incorporated on October 16, 1851, when portions of two other communities, Cheektowaga and Hamburg, were annexed under the town name of Seneca. Because the Erie County Board of Supervisors met infrequently, the incorporation was not made official until December. The name was changed the next year, however, to avoid confusion with another settlement of the same name in Eastern New York State.[1]

As Baker's Institutions became more established and his name and reputation began to spread widely, he proffered the idea of changing the name of the town to one more consistent with his work. He suggested Victory Hill, Our Lady of Victory, or Victoria. It was true that Baker's Institutions were the most identifiable portion of the town, but because his suggestions were too similar to names of other New York State post offices, the request was denied. Moreover, local opposition to the proposal was strong. The *Buffalo Evening News* chided Baker for his perceived arrogance: "Can nothing be done to extinguish the lawless name-fiend who delights in changing the name of some post office?" Baker, however, had more control over his own domain. The July 1904 issue of the *Annals* reported that the United States government had changed the town name from West Seneca to Victorhill. In a rather arrogant move, between 1905 and 1909 the masthead of the quarterly magazine proudly displayed "Victorhill" as the location of Baker's Institutions.[2]

While squabbles between Baker and local officials on the town's name are interesting, it was the arrival of Lackawanna Steel to the area that transformed the landscape and future of the region. In the latter months of 1899, Walter Scranton and Moses Taylor of the Lackawanna Iron and Steel Company, along with Buffalo capitalists John J. Albright, John G. Milburn, and Edmund Hayes, advanced $15 million to construct a steel plant in the Buffalo area. The company approved the transfer of operations from Scranton, Pennsylvania, in December. A two-square-mile, 1,600-acre plot of land was acquired along Lake Erie, just south of downtown Buffalo, for the plant. Construction began in May 1900; the first blast furnace was operational on February 13, 1903. Production began immediately, but the physical plant continued to expand, reaching its full extent of fifteen mills by 1918.[3]

The arrival of Lackawanna Steel was transformative to the region formerly dominated by Father Baker's Institutions. The plant led to significant growth in population and revenues, creating a sharp division between residents of West Seneca who lived near the plant and those on the east side of the town. People in the western section paid more taxes due to increased salaries, but the perception was that residents in the eastern half of the town benefited most from these revenues. Additionally, the steel plant required special infrastructure for proper operations. These factors eventually led to a division of the town. In 1909, the western half was incorporated as Lackawanna, taking the corporate name.[4] In May 1922, through the efforts of Charles Schwab, Lackawanna and Bethlehem Steel Corporations merged, taking the latter's name. Steel remained king in Lackawanna for the remainder of Baker's life. Indeed, religion scholar Heather Hartel accurately commented, "Lackawanna's history became intertwined with the story of the steel industry in the Buffalo region."[5]

Roman Catholicism in the city also expanded significantly in the early twentieth century, in response to the explosion of people and industry. The arrival of varied immigrant groups generated the construction of numerous national parishes. As stated previously, Buffalo was home to more than double the national average of national parishes. St. Barbara (1904) and St. Hyacinth (1910) served the Polish community; St. Anthony (1917) was home for the Italians; Assumption (1918) hosted the Hungarians; and Our Lady of the Sacred Heart of Jesus (1919, later renamed Our Lady of Bistrica) assisted the Croatian population. Additionally, St. Charles Borromeo (1903), Our Mother of Good Counsel (1904), and St. Michael's (1910) were established to serve the general population. In 1925, Lackawanna was home to nine Catholic churches and six parochial schools.[6]

The Infant Home

For over twenty years, Nelson Baker's work had taken home-less and wayward boys off the streets and provided them with edu-cation and a future, but as the new century began to unfold, a new and possibly even more pressing and disturbing situation came to his attention. While the source is not clear, Father Baker became aware that "in a certain city...the remains of over two hundred lit-tle ones were found in different stages of decay, sufficient to clot the sewer." Mortified at such a wanton destruction of human life, Baker, always a man of action, knew something needed to be done to save such infants.[7]

In the spring of 1906, Baker found an immediate albeit tem-porary solution to this problem through the assistance of Amelia Mathieson. Mrs. Mathieson owned a boarding house at 471 Pearl Street that she was willing to donate to Baker to be used as a home for unwanted infants. After securing a release to vacate from her residents, many of whom were willing to assist the new project with bedding and other essentials, she prepared the home for its new arrivals. When local police units heard about Baker's new project, babies began to arrive at Mrs. Mathieson's home. The facility was initially staffed by Mathieson, two other women volun-teers, and Sister Marcelline Brophy, SSJ, as superintendent.[8]

The addition of the Infant Home to his ministry brought some semblance of completion to Father's Baker's overall dream to assist youths in trouble. One local paper described the Home as "the missing link in the chain of institutions" that Baker con-trolled.[9] Baker himself commented on what the addition would mean for his work:

> Our work will then be complete. The Infant Home will be for children from infancy to five years of age; our Orphan Home for five to ten, and our Protectory from ten to fifteen years of age; then our Working Boys' Home will care for those over fifteen years of age, so that every class will be protected, from infancy to maturity.[10]

The home on Pearl Street met the current need, but as always, Nelson Baker almost immediately initiated plans for a permanent and larger facility to be located adjacent to the Orphan Asylum and the Protectory. Costs for a new building were estimated at $150,000. Utilizing his vast and growing network of friends, Baker made his initial plea for funds to his Association of Our Lady of Victory[11] in October 1906. Further, he made this direct appeal in the January 1907 issue of the *Annals*:

> As we are about to celebrate the joyful feast of the birth of the Divine Infant, we might be pardoned in making the suggestion that it would be a most beautiful and appropriate Christmas gift to the Divine Infant child an offering of A SINGLE DOLLAR to aid in erecting a home for His homeless little ones who are now as He once was, without a home, and forced to live in a rude stable.[12]

Baker's supreme confidence in his benefactors and Mary was evident when the cornerstone of the new building, adjacent to St. Joseph's Asylum and across the street from St. John's Protectory, was laid on March 25, 1907, the Feast of the Annunciation. He again wrote to Association members:

> We are depending on our good friends to assist us in this work, as we have always depended upon them, in all our works, and our confidence in them has not been in vain, as God has always inspired them to come to our assistance in all His works of charity, and we have always succeeded and he has always received the honor, to Whom it may be done.[13]

Some who responded to Baker's petitions expressed the desire to furnish a crib for an infant. Baker craftily transformed this suggestion into the establishment of the Crib Donors' Guild. Members agreed to donate $25 to furnish a crib, with mattress, pillow, and bedding. In return, Guild members would be remembered in Masses offered at the Home, "the pious prayers of the Sisters and children," and have their names inscribed on a brass tablet at the Home's entrance.[14]

113

Construction of the Infant Home went forward without problem, and the new facility was dedicated on Sunday, August 16, 1908, with Bishop Charles Colton present for the occasion. The home was built in the form of a straight-sided U, with the base 150 feet and each wing 144 feet in length.[15] The *Buffalo Courier* expressed what many in attendance that day were surely thinking: "The necessity of protecting and caring for abandoned newly-born infants has been apparent at all times, and Msgr. Baker recognizing the fact worked unceasingly to provide a home for the[se] unfortunate little ones."[16]

Baker continued to press hard as an advocate for the new Infant Home. On October 28, 1908, he established the Our Lady of Victory Aid Society to provide articles of clothing for the infants and young children at the Home. Additionally, Society members volunteered their time and expertise when help was needed in some way. Baker also promoted the Home in the *Annals* and *The Victorian*. Every issue published not-so-subtle prompts of the need to support the Home with articles titled "How to Befriend a Little Homeless Child," "An Infant Appeal," or "An Appeal from the Little Ones." The names of new members of the Crib Donors' Guild were always listed; photos of infants in each issue were another constant reminder.[17] As was always the case, Baker attributed his success to Mary:

> Since starting our Infant Home, She [Mary] has been to us particularly generous, in aiding us in defraying the immense expense, incident in building so large and expensive a Home, and then in sending us so many homeless little ones, which might otherwise be lost, both soul and body, and the saving of which, must be very dear to the Heart of Our Blessed Lord.[18]

Father Baker's open-door policy, similar to what he espoused with respect to his other Institutions, was central to the operation of the Infant Home. Children would be received and no questions asked. The *Annals* promoted this policy in a few ways. Besides publishing essays with titles such as "Send Us the Babies" each issue of the magazine spoke of the great kindness of people who supplied clothing and other necessities for the infants. Moreover, continuing his open-door policy, each installment had a plea from Baker for children to be sent without reservation:

> Our friends must not be delicate about asking us to receive any little homeless infants...as we intend to take any and all that are presented, regardless of circumstances of parentage or money, and we hope that others of our charitable friends will be glad to adopt a beautiful little infant into their own home if nature has not already provided them with children.[19]

With the new home operational, Baker told readers of *The Victorian* that children should be sent "as we are established for this purpose."[20] Baker's policy of accepting all children was manifest in a unique way as well. Local Buffalo writer Boniface Hanley described the procedure:

> One of the features of the home was a small bassinet, complete with pillow and blankets, that stood in the hallway just inside the unlocked outside door. Anyone could quietly open the door to the home in the middle of the night and leave a baby in the bassinet. There were no questions asked, no forms to be filled out, [and] no one to probe into the infant's background. For a number of years the bassinet remained, quietly receiving abandoned infants.[21]

Possibly because of the information provided in the *Annals* and *The Victorian*, women from across the country came to the Home to receive its services. The rationale for Baker's open-door policy is found in his desire to save children and his utter disgust at the horror stories that circulated about women who seemed to have few options when an unplanned pregnancy arose. For many women, the only plausible option was abortion, and generally this illegal and immoral infanticide was done using the most primitive of methods. In a 1924 report, he wrote,

Many of our so-called homes of charity refuse their protection to this class of needy ones and hence force them to resort to some desperate means of self-preservation which may mean the destruction of the child and the recklessness of the murderer mother, with a dark future before her and with blood-stained hands.[22]

He believed that an open-door policy was the only proper response to such possible wanton destruction of life. He offered the Infant Home as the proper alternative:

This spirit of charity will surely save innumerable souls and Our Lady of Victory Maternity Home and Infant Home has been erected for this purpose and we are only too glad to have the privilege of assisting as far as possible in mitigating and lessening this unfortunate condition.[23]

He wanted women to be guided to the Infant Home so they could be offered protective services regardless of financial consideration. He claimed, "We know of no other institution in the country that is willing to receive this class of unfortunate girls and their offspring."[24]

Baker understood that women were stigmatized by unwanted pregnancies, even though men were morally culpable for the situation. He wrote, "In most cases experience has taught that men are mostly to blame and quickly absolve [themselves] when harm is done."[25] Baker's policy to protect women and their children was premised on this attitude. He stated:

Our motive has been, regardless of experience, to protect the unfortunate young mother and her family, and save the life of her child, which we feel, under our system, has been most successful and that we have received upon it, God's special blessing.[26]

Baker felt a sacred trust that could not be violated with the women who came to him for assistance. He wrote to his bishop, William Turner: "In coming to us, they engage our sympathy and assistance in concealing the matter of their trouble and while we are glad to offer our services, we promise that we will protect them as it lies in our power."[27] The procedures followed at the Infant Home were based on his trust and confidence in the expectant mothers. Only information voluntarily given was obtained from them. They could be received under an assumed name; their true identity was kept in a special record available only to supervisors. An instruction and procedures booklet, "Care of Infants and Small Children," was very clear and specific:

> A full record of the child should be made particularly regarding baptism, doctor's examination and [a] statement of condition should also be given. In most cases *false names* and *false histories* [emphasis original] will be given for illegitimate infants; no other [information] should be exacted. Great prudence and secrecy should be observed in regard to illegitimate infants; they should not be the subject of conversation among the Sisters and *never* [emphasis original] with externs. No information concerning the children should be given to any parties presenting themselves except the mother of those who placed the children in the institution.

Privacy was strictly enforced; visitors were never allowed to roam through the house for fear they might accidently meet other women.[28]

Baker employed a rather ingenious method to keep the location of women secret, should this be their desire, but still maintain communication with family and friends. Staff personnel from the various Institutions who had family in other parts of the country were asked to serve as intermediary decoys. For example, a woman at the Infant Home could tell her family that she was in Washington, DC. A family relative of one of Baker's staff living in Washington would forward correspondence to the woman or family via the Washington address, making it appear the woman was indeed writing from that city. The system apparently worked quite well.[29]

Sisters, nurses, and other personnel were also given very specific instructions. However, as his trusted partners, the Sisters were

117

given more responsibility to supervise the lay staff. They were told to "attend personally to infants and small children." They were to be especially vigilant to assure that all procedures were followed. Baker possessed no tolerance for any violence toward a child. One worker related an incident when a nurse struck a little boy. Baker saw the altercation and within ten minutes the offending party had been dismissed, taking her clothes and pay.[30]

Father Baker realized that his ideas and policies might not be popular with some or accepted by others, but he was not to be swayed from what he firmly believed was just and proper. As has been noted previously, money was a constant concern for Baker. The Infant Home ran a substantial debt each year, causing some to question whether the work should be continued. Baker, noting that the Infant Home might be the only facility in the country that would take women with no questions asked, forcefully defended his work without apology:

> This is not a popular charity, but Our Lord and His Blessed Mother are behind us in this work, and we are not delicate about continuing it as we feel we are saving the young ladies to their friends and society and the little ones to our Holy Faith.[31]

Baker's confidence that his method was correct continued to grow with time. In one annual report for the Infant Home he wrote,

> The longer we are engaged in this work, the more we realize the benefits which accrue to this unfortunate class of young women who come to us for protection and care. We look upon this as one of the most serious problems of the present day, and one upon which depends the future of many an unfortunate creature and the destiny of her little one.[32]

After Baker's death, the *Brooklyn Tablet* synthesized the efficacy of his ministry and the method he used:

Father Baker was no theorist; he had no use for the modern jargon, its ideology, its methods or reports. Undoubtedly he would never have qualified for even an investigator's job in the modern relief system. But God's ways are different. He seeks the sincere, the genuine, the true lover of the poor where accomplishments in the treasury of Heaven may not occupy as much space as a single case work record, but that is sufficient and it speaks volumes.[33]

In the day-to-day operations of the Infant Home, Baker sought, as much as possible, to model a family environment. The pregnant women and young mothers were expected to assist in the kitchen with the preparation of meals. During the day the women attended spiritual and educational classes and presentations designed to steer them back onto the proper road. Typical presentations included "The Necessity of Being Good," "The Danger of Bad Companions," "The Unhappiness of a Sinful Life," and "The Possibility of Falling Again." Older children, who were also a significant concern, attended kindergarten classes to prepare them to start formal schooling the next year at St. Joseph's.[34] Speaking of the Home's daily operations, Baker wrote, "Our system is one mingling humanity and Christianity in an ennobling manner, in not only aiding the fallen to rise, but also assuring the future from its [the pregnancy's] repetition and preserving the respectability and dignity of the family home."[35]

As at St. Joseph's Orphan Asylum, the backbone to operations at the Infant Home was supplied by the Sisters of St. Joseph. Baker was very pleased and expressed his gratitude for their ministry in this new apostolate:

> I had not the opportunity of expressing to you my gratitude for the many kindnesses you have bestowed upon us in connection with our work here [Infant Home], and I know that Our Blessed Lord will more than abundantly reward you for your thoughtfulness in helping us take care of the great work in our hands.[36]

119

Father Baker's personal love for the children was clear from all observers. He regularly visited the Home, especially before age slowed his physical activity. He always attended functions, especially the annual Christmas party. When he visited he could not resist playing with the children and holding them in his lap. The children were special to him; in the end, it was for their preservation that this ministry was initiated.[37]

Daily operations at the Home were carried out in increasingly crowded conditions. The number of women and children served grew dramatically over time. In 1907, when the Home was on Pearl Street, 10 women and 51 children were served. In 1917, these numbers had jumped to 40 and 328; ten years later, in 1927, they increased further to 214 and 439. In 1926, Baker reported, "A great deal of difficulty has been experienced in keeping the number down to 200 and extraordinary efforts have been made to adopt the little ones into families."[38] Every available space was utilized, in the Home and, when necessary, other Institutions. Annual state reports on the conditions in the Home described the lack of physical space and inadequate staffing. As much as he hated to do so, as early as 1914 and as late as 1927, Baker was forced to restrict admissions. In a somber tone he reported,

> On account of the great increase in the number of our unmarried mothers our room capacity has been severely taxed and we have been obliged to turn away many infants for want of room, and we feel that some extraordinary effort must be made by us very soon in order to save the souls of these little ones.[39]

The overcrowded conditions at the Home became a crisis in the late spring of 1925 when a severe measles outbreak hit the area. In order to reduce contagion, only one child per crib was mandated, but the two hundred child quota was being exceeded. One nurse at the Infant Home warned Baker that there was "no *room* [emphasis original] or help to care for more than the quota."[40]

From the outset of its operation, Baker envisioned the Infant Home as a facility where women could come, with trust and anonymity, to have their children, but it was also the priest's hope that many of these children would soon be adopted into homes where their faith would be protected. He often solicited assistance in obtaining names of prospective parents. A typical appeal read: "Our little babies are still coming and coming pretty fast, and we are trying to get homes for them, and we wish our good friends could see their way to adopt a little child, which will surely bring sunshine and happiness into their home."[41] To this end, Baker held "days of exhibition" when the public was invited to come to the Home and "look over" the children for possible adoption.[42] Baker's desire to move children to homes did not, however, compromise his overall policy that children must be protected. Indeed, he often wrote to those in charge of adoptions expressing his concern for children. A typical letter read in part:

> Anything you can write us regarding these matters will be cared for very secretly, but we would like to know if the families with which they are placed are the proper ones to care for children and also to know if any families are boarding more children than they can properly care for.[43]

He was satisfied that many children were placed in homes of active Catholics.[44]

The situation of overcrowding, and the challenges he received pertinent to his adoption policy, prompted Father Baker to consider new directions, including expansion of his facilities. In a reflective statement he commented:

> When we began our Infant Home work, we did not expect to do more than care for infants and small children, but we feel that the maternity work has been forcing itself upon us, as we frequently have applications from unfortunate young women in poor circumstances, and often without friends or means, who present themselves and ask our assistance, to relieve them in their difficulty....We feel we have frequently done much good, like preventing acts of distruction [*sic*] on the part of the young lady, who is usually abandoned by her friends,

and she has threatened self-distruction [*sic*], as no hand is held out to help her.[45]

In 1911, only three years after the opening of the new home, a separate house for children with contagious diseases was constructed. Called "the Cottage," the eight-room addition cost $25,000. Baker was pleased with the facility. He called upon the readers of the *Annals* to assist with contributions, "so that we will soon have it free from debt."[46]

After the Infant Home had been open for only a few years, Baker revealed his plans to expand this ministry. In 1914, when New York State officials complained of overcrowding in their annual inspection report, Baker immediately began to consider expansion. In January 1916, he wrote in the *Annals*:

> We have already received over 2000 of these little waifs, and hence to be able to accommodate more we have planned to build a twin building to our present one, which will give us almost double our present accommodations, and we hope also, to assist in saving not only the infanticide, but perhaps the suicide of the unfortunate mother.[47]

In July 1927, due certainly to the constantly overcrowded conditions, Baker informed New York State officials that he planned to build a second infant home across the street and behind the new Basilica (see chapter 9). When it was suggested in reply that any monies for a new facility be placed into the operational home, Baker answered, "We are daily more and more convinced of the importance and grave necessity" of the new project. In a rare incident of backtracking, Baker reported in April 1929: "We have enlarged our capacity by spending $77,432.64 for improvements [in the current building]." This addition enabled the Infant Home to accommodate 100 more (a total of 300) infants and young children.[48]

Father Baker's ministry to infants and young children, while of great significance and joy to him personally, has been seen historically as possibly his greatest contribution. Herbert Sisson, superintendent for the poor in Buffalo, was quite impressed with all Baker's work after a tour of the facilities. Speaking of the Infant Home, he commented:

> I scarcely know how to frame words of praise in support of it....I doubt if there is a finer infants' home anywhere in this country. There certainly cannot be a better one....The infants' home is a real home with the added advantage that isn't to be found in every home, namely skilled and scientific help which is available at all times for the benefit of the tiny charges.[49]

Thomas Galvin called the Infant Home Baker's "most commendable achievement." He concluded, "If Father Baker did nothing else to entitle him to an eternal reward in the Kingdom of God, this Institution alone would be for him an unfailing passport to Heaven."[50]

Maternity Care Expands

Father Baker's dream to expand his outreach to infants and children, an idea necessitated by the overwhelming response to his open-door policy, was eventually fulfilled in an unexpected and slightly different way. Both Baker and the State realized the need and advocated action to resolve the congestion issue. He continued to explain to his Association via the *Annals* the need for an addition to the Home: "Our infants' home is filled to its utmost capacity, and unless we add more room, we must stop taking babies and small children, and this we do not wish to do." He informed his readers in July 1914 that a planned addition would soon proceed.[51]

On August 15, 1915, the Feast of the Assumption, the cornerstone was laid on a new maternity hospital, located on the adjacent east side of the Infant Home. Baker's decision to expand beyond the basic care of infants and children was premised on the numerous requests that had been received since the Infant Home's opening in 1908. Construction was placed on hold, however, due to a fire at St. Joseph's Orphan Asylum in January 1916, which forced Baker to divert funds toward the immediate need for repairs to provide shelter for the boys. Additionally, he showed some trepidation about moving forward, due to World War I. Uncharacteristically, he told his friends through the *Annals*, "We are afraid; we are all praying for it to cease, and then we will have courage to erect our new work."[52]

Baker's doubt did not last long and when funds were received the project continued forward. Exhibiting the strong faith that had guided him for over forty years as a priest, he wrote:

> We are soon to consecrate to her [Mary] a new work of love: a Home for the unfortunate of her sex, a haven of protection to the fallen, a maternity home for those in need. As we have clung to Mary in the past, we will still cling to her now, and as she has always guided and aided us, we will still place in her our confidence and our hopes, and we surely will listen to the sweet words of the Son as He cheerfully granted the requests of His Blessed Mother.[53]

The new Maternity Hospital, built for slightly over $240,000, opened on October 2, 1919. Three Sisters of St. Joseph—Geraldine Jordan (administrator), Josephine Hourihan (director of nursing), and Concordia Friel—were assigned to the new ministry. Dr. Michael Sullivan, a former Baker Boy and now a well-respected physician, was chief of staff.[54]

From the outset the Infant Home hired and trained nurses to work with the children, but the addition of the Maternity Hospital accelerated this training program. Beginning in 1912, most issues of the *Annals* and *The Victorian* ran an advertisement seeking nurses to be trained for work in the Infant Home. The program, which was fifteen months in length and did not require "so high an education," included child care, basic obstetrics, and various maternity issues.[55]

The basic program envisioned originally by Baker for the Maternity Hospital was forced to expand almost from the outset. Two factors, coming almost simultaneously, were the primary catalysts that led to the transformation of the new facility into a full-service hospital and not one that catered specifically to women and children. First, in 1920, the New York legislature passed a law that required registered nurses to receive their training in a hospital that served men and women of all ages and that handled surgery and disease cases. In its annual report, the New York State Board of Charities commented about the nurse-training situation at the Maternity Hospital: "In general the facilities are suitable and adequate, but the work has developed to such an extent that additional facilities will soon be needed in order to accommodate applicants."[56]

The international flu pandemic of 1918 was the second major factor leading to an expansion of the Maternity Hospital. Mercy Hospital on Tifft Street was the only hospital in the area, and it had only twenty-five beds. Dr. Sullivan and the Sisters of St. Joseph urged Baker to expand the Maternity Hospital's services. While Baker believed he was moving beyond his basic mission of aiding troubled youth, he acceded to the wishes of Sullivan and the Sisters.[57] Still, Baker continued to insist that the hospital's primary mission was "the protection of the young unmarried mother, to assist in saving the life of the unborn child and to throw about the young mother the necessary protection and care."[58] On October 14, 1932, Our Lady of Victory Hospital received full accreditation. The hospital record reported, "We received full approval by the American College of Surgeons. They commended highly the staff and the hospital for the high standards of service in the care of the patient." Additionally, in 1934 the American Medical Association approved the hospital for teaching resident physicians.[59]

The new state law and the expanded hospital required an advanced nurses' training program. The training, lasting twenty-eight to thirty months, and conferring the title of RN on its graduates, provided classes and field training for all types of medical, obstetrical, and surgical work, with accreditation coming from the State Board of Health. The first graduates of the new program, fourteen women, received their "RN hats" on January 21, 1921. While the expanded program recruited new candidates, women were also accepted in the older program, lasting fifteen months, for work solely with pregnant women, children, and young mothers.[60]

The expansion of the Infant Home and the new Our Lady of Victory Hospital were the catalysts that led Baker to construct two new homes for nurses. The first, authorized in 1922 and located behind the Infant Home, was ready for occupancy in 1923. It was a three-story home that could accommodate sixty nurses. *The Victorian* described the home: "We have completely equipped it with every modern convenience so as to make it a very pleasant and attractive home for the nurses, which will be an additional inducement to adopt the profession."[61]

As facilities and those they served continued to expand and increase, so too grew the need for proper housing for nurses in Father Baker's Institutions. As early as 1927, a second nurses' home, accommodating ninety, was being considered. In February 1929, Baker reported that the new building was under construction. This new home, which was located on the adjacent east side of the hospital and connected to the latter by an enclosed foot bridge, housed nurses working in the hospital. This allowed the original building to accommodate nurses and trainees for the Infant Home.[62] The new home, accommodating fifty-two and built for $240,000, opened in 1930.[63]

Conclusion

Nelson Baker's work with orphans and troubled boys was significant but not particularly unique. However, when he discovered a need to reach out to single mothers and their children, he entered a new phase of ministry that was rare indeed. Not only did Baker venture into untested territory, but he did so in his usual bold style, building on faith alone two new institutions, the Infant Home and the Maternity Hospital, which later became Our Lady of Victory General Hospital. These foundations allowed Father Baker to complete his grand scheme to provide support for children from birth through their secondary education, and even to early adulthood through his Working Boys Home. The Infant Home was also significant, for it demonstrated Baker's basic belief of never taking no for an answer. He always believed that his endeavors would be successful, through his own efforts and his total confidence in the assistance of his patroness, Our Lady of Victory.

Baker's role as superintendent of the Institutions was always his principal hat, but beginning in the early days of the twentieth century he was also called upon to serve in leadership for the diocese. His earlier contacts at Our Lady of Angels Seminary would be helpful as he tackled the challenges of serving as vicar general of the Roman Catholic Diocese of Buffalo, New York.

CHAPTER 6

Vicar General of Buffalo (1903–1936)

Nelson Baker's pioneering efforts to assist pregnant women and their children were far-reaching in their scope and progressive in their perspective. He challenged the prevailing wisdom and set his course in a new direction in order to meet the need that was presented to him. His efforts to aid many whom society had rejected or forgotten were consistent with the Progressive Era of American history, during which politicians, governments, social advocates, and religious figures, working from different perspectives, sought to remedy many of the ills of society that industrial progress, municipal growth, and technological advances had generated.

While his Institutions in Lackawanna occupied the bulk of his time and energy, Nelson Baker never divorced himself from his diocese and from the priests and religious who served God's people in parishes, schools, hospitals, and other important apostolic ventures. He adeptly met the needs of the diocese while maintaining direction of the Institutions he loved. Well respected by all his local ordinaries and his fellow clerics, Baker, over his long sixty-year priesthood, served the Diocese of Buffalo as vicar general and twice as diocesan administrator when (between bishops) the see was vacant. In the process he endeared himself to numerous religious communities of women, was instrumental in the progress and promotion of two Catholic colleges, and gained the admiration of Buffalo Catholics, whether or not they had been personally touched by his more well-known Institutions for youth.

Progressive-Era America

The political and social structures present in the United States during the first twenty years of the twentieth century have been labeled by historians as the "Progressive Era." Generally defined as the period between 1898 (the conclusion of the Spanish-American War) and 1917 (the commencement of American involvement in World War I), the Progressive Era was an urban and nationwide movement that stressed political and social reform. Moving beyond Populism and its agrarian and generally localized concerns, the Progressive Era stressed a more intimate and sympathetic look at urban problems, labor, social welfare, and municipal reform. Many of the ideas that had their genesis in Populist thought were adapted and enacted through legislation in the first two decades of the twentieth century.

Why was there a drive for national reform during a time of general prosperity, after America's triumph against Spain in the closing days of the nineteenth century? The noted historian Richard Hofstadter, in his seminal work *The Age of Reform: From Bryan to F.D.R.*, suggests that patterns of power had moved from the individual to the corporation during the Gilded Age. In response, individuals, often in an unorganized way, rebelled against industrial discipline and the consequences of organization. Thus, due to this more individualized approach, Progressive thinkers were not a unified group. Again, as Hofstadter stated, "Indeed the characteristic Progressive was often of two minds on many issues."[1] Some Progressives wanted to increase political influence and control of ordinary people, while others wanted to concentrate authority in experts. Many reformers sought to curtail the growth of large corporations and eliminate monopolies; others accepted "bigness in industry" because of the economic benefits it brought. In general, however, Progressive-Era thinkers sought to make life better for the individual. The historians Arthur S. Link and Richard L. McCormick aptly stated, "In general Progressives sought to improve the conditions of life and labor and to create as much social stability as possible."[2]

The Progressive Era and its desire for reform cannot be associated with any one group of people; it is the only reform movement that was experienced by the whole nation. Indeed, intellectuals, professionals, and opinion-making peoples of all stripes rallied behind the reform banner in a way rarely seen in American history. These people abandoned the status quo and joined the mainstream of liberal proponents. In a broad sense, Progressivism was the way a whole generation of Americans defined themselves politically and socially.

Political reform was started and found its greatest support in cities where structural and social reforms were initiated; state and national political reform lagged behind. Graft in cities was rooted out. This was most dramatically demonstrated on opposite ends of the country, in San Francisco and New York. During the first decade of the twentieth century, San Francisco's municipal government was controlled by a political machine headed by Abraham Ruef; nothing was accomplished in the City by the Bay without Boss Ruef's approval. Similarly, one generation earlier, Boss Tweed brought political corruption in New York's notorious Tammany Hall to an apogee. Progressive-Era reformers, intolerant of such abuses of power, led the drive that led to the downfall and eventual incarceration of both men.

Political reform took on a national tone during the presidency of Theodore Roosevelt. Roosevelt was able to inspire public opinion to guide people toward reform. People responded favorably to his drive for a change in thinking, leading to a more moral approach to government. Public opinion as an independent voice grew during the Roosevelt years. Roosevelt was also famous for busting large trusts (accomplished through the Sherman Antitrust Act) and for initiating measures to regulate business in an effort to root out unethical practices. Roosevelt's platform expressed the idea of the "corporate liberal state": big government working in harmony with large economic interests to regulate corporations (antitrust laws), to guarantee the rights of organized labor, and to protect the poor and weak in society.[3]

While little of significance concerning reform occurred during the administration of William Howard Taft (1908–12), his successor Woodrow Wilson and his "New Freedom" policy brought political Progressivism to new heights. Wilson, a Jeffersonian at heart, sought to regulate big business by attacking what he called the triple wall of privilege: tariffs, banks, and trusts. Additionally, Wilson was a great supporter of a federal child labor law, workmen's compensation measures, agricultural credits, and women's suffrage, the latter being one of Progressivism's greatest triumphs.

Progressive-Era reform in government was characterized by a fundamental shift from legislative to executive power. Lawmakers were forced to learn how to deal with less power, while simultaneously catering to the needs of persons, agencies, or boards that wielded an increased level of power. Most Progressive reformers believed that government regulation and authority had to be expanded to deal with the economic and social problems present in the United States. This led to further restrictions on legislative branches of government. For example, during this period, the Seventh Amendment to the Constitution took the election of senators away from state legislatures and gave it directly to the people.

Political and government Progressive policies were matched by renewed regulation in business. Indeed, this was one of Progressivism's distinctive and important achievements: antibusiness was a prime mover during the era. Various theories explained the causes and consequences of business regulation. One school, the Public Interest Interpretation, said that the regulation of business was undertaken to protect the general welfare of the public from the greed and wrongdoing of corporations. Thus, this reform was initiated by the people. Another theory, the Capture Thesis, inverted the public interest, saying that regulated businesses themselves—not the people—were the main beneficiaries of government regulation. A third school, the Pluralist Interpretation, suggested that a combination of diverse competing interests—consumers, corporations seeking restraints on rivals, and the supervised businesses themselves—had a hand in the details of regulation.[4]

Numerous acts of reform illustrate the advances made by Progressivism during this period of history. The Hepburn Act (1906) revitalized the Sherman Antitrust Act of 1890 and strengthened the Interstate Commerce Commission (1887). The Pure Food and Drug Act (1906), attributable in large measure to the muckraking novel *The Jungle* by Upton Sinclair, transformed American practices with respect to the proper handling of meats,

131

produce, and other food items. The Federal Reserve Act (1913) regulated banking procedures, while the creation of the Federal Trade Commission (1914) helped to eliminate corruption and fraud in the free trade of products. The Federal Farm Loan Act (1916) extended much-needed credit to farmers. Possibly the best illustration of the era was the Keating-Owen Child Labor Law (1916), which prohibited interstate shipment of goods produced by child labor.[5]

The Progressive Era was a period of significant gain for organized labor. The drive to smash monopolies and curtail corporate power was beneficial to workers. As one example, membership in Samuel Gompers' American Federation of Labor (AFL) grew fourfold from 500,000 to 2 million between 1900 and 1920.[6] Unions made great strides in several specific campaigns, most important the promotion of closed shop companies, advocacy of an eight-hour workday, and the achievement of just and adequate compensation for individuals and families through minimum-wage legislation. Overall, unions sought to have at least some voice in the day-to-day operations of business, a privilege they had not previously entertained, let alone enjoyed.[7]

The pulse of the country allowed the drive of organized labor to be successful. Labor's earlier crushing defeats in the Homestead strike (steel) and Pullman strike (railroad) of 1892 and 1894, respectively, were now being reversed; the heightened consciousness of the general public to the plight of the worker and the need for labor to organize gave unions sufficient notoriety and strength to begin the process of overcoming the behemoth of management. Not until the Wagner Act of 1935, however, would labor have the right, by law, to organize.

The Progressive Era and American Religion

The Progressive sentiment that caught fire and raged across the country in political, social, and government reform also found a welcome home in American religion. In general, the drive for reform in American religion during the Progressive Era has been labeled the "Social Gospel." Christians, in response to the Industrial Revolution and the consequent impact on individuals and families, were concerned about the human problem of industrial-caused strife, the wildly unequal distribution of wealth, and the worsening conditions for the urban poor. Thus, men and women of faith, under the banner of social reform and the teachings of Jesus, sought solutions to problems of the era.

The Social Gospel was a movement historically contiguous with Progressivism. Generally associated with Protestantism, the Social Gospel was defined by its disciples as the application of the teaching of Jesus and the total message of Christian salvation to society—economic life, social institutions, and individuals. In 1917, Walter Rauschenbush, generally considered the driving force behind the movement, wrote, "The social movement is the most important ethical and spiritual movement in the modern world, and the Social Gospel is the response of the Christian consciousness to it."[8] The Social Gospel was a crusade for justice and righteousness in all areas of common life. Although the movement used basic Christian principles, it did not preach the message of Christ: its aims were social, not theological. It was not an organized movement, but rather a network of different movements that operated in different contexts. It was generally a middle-class movement that drew ideas from Progressive thinkers who combined social action with individual rights and responsibilities.

In line with general Progressive-Era thought, individualism was replaced with a view toward greater solidarity. Thus, proponents of the Social Gospel emphasized social salvation, whereas the dominant evangelical tradition had long emphasized personal salvation. Consequently, the social sins of society, such as slavery, poverty, racism, and economic injustice, were the targets of reform for disciples of the Social Gospel—not personal sin.

Social Gospel proponents did not view their ideas as new or revolutionary, but simply the application of Christ's teaching to the reality of their day. There was no one way to achieve this reform; "Social Gospelers" worked in different ways and on varied levels to achieve similar ends. Where social workers, professionals, and coercion were used to effect change in political, government, and business abuses, the Social Gospel applied Christian principles in seeking answers to society's ills.

Three significant principles guided the Social Gospel move-

133

ment. First was the belief that the social principles of Jesus, as articulated in the Gospels, were reliable guides for both individuals and
groups in any historical period. In other words, the Gospel message was timeless. Second, proponents of the Social Gospel
believed in progress; they maintained that people could be educated to choose the good. For them, personal conversion and that
of society was possible. Finally, the Social Gospel preached the
belief that sin could be transmitted corporately; social sin was a
stain on society that needed to be removed.[9] These principles and
the movement in general aided both individuals and institutions to
make the difficult transition from the rural, small-town America of
the nineteenth century to the highly industrialized, urban society
of the twentieth century with all its consequent and ineluctable
social problems.

American Catholicism during the Progressive Era was not at
the forefront of reform and did not carry the banner of the Social
Gospel, but the period allowed the construction of a foundation
from which social reform later blossomed in the 1930s. As previously mentioned, the Church hierarchy and intellectuals found
themselves on the canvas after suffering almost a knockout from the
one-two punch delivered by the condemnation of Americanism in
1899 and then theological modernism in 1907. Additionally, the
Church continued to be dogged by anti-Catholic rhetoric, manifested in the last years of the nineteenth century by the American
Protective Association (APA), and the general level of distrust that
almost forced Catholics to wear the badge of second-class citizenship.[10] That said, the worldwide impact of Pope Leo's social encyclical, *Rerum Novarum*, was—and still is—a high-water mark from
the Universal Church on the rights of workers.

A significant seed for the future growth of the Church in the
United States was planted in the waning days of the Progressive Era.
In August 1917, the American bishops had formed a temporary and
voluntary association, the National Catholic War Council, to guide
the response of the American Church to World War I. In July 1919,
the Administrative Committee of the War Council met at the
University of Notre Dame with a group of other bishops. The assembled prelates agreed to form a permanent organization, the National
Catholic Welfare Council (NCWC), to provide a national Catholic

voice to address issues of relevance to the Church. The first official meeting of the NCWC took place at the Catholic University of America in September. The bishops elected an administrative committee, headed by Archbishop Edward Hanna of San Francisco, and formed themselves into five subcommittees of press, social service, mission, Catholic societies, and education. Paulist Father John J. Burke, CSP, was appointed as general secretary.[11]

In addition to the formation of the NCWC, the Progressive Era was also fertile ground for the formation of ideas that manifested themselves under the rubric of "Catholic Action" in the 1930s and 1940s. The most prominent Catholic social theorist of this period was John A. Ryan (1869–1945), a priest of the Archdiocese of St. Paul, Minnesota. Ryan's Catholic University doctoral dissertation, "A Living Wage," catapulted him to a place of leadership in the area of social reform for the American Church. He was the author of "The Bishops' Program for Social Reconstruction" (February 1919), the first major document issued by the American bishops in the twentieth century. Written as an American Catholic response to the social dislocation created by the war, the document advocated many Progressive reforms, several of which were later enacted in the New Deal policy of Franklin Delano Roosevelt. Ryan advocated for a minimum wage, social insurance, child labor laws, rights of organized labor, and equal pay for men and women engaged in the same amount and quality of work.[12]

Another leading light of the American Catholic social agenda rooted in Progressivism was Father Peter Dietz (1878–1947). His biographer, Mary Harrita Fox, suggests that Dietz's priesthood was inseparably linked with a desire to do something about "[the] working man's difficulties and possibilities."[13] While Ryan was more a theorist and academician in Catholic Progressivism, Dietz, like Nelson Baker, was the man "in the trenches" seeking to bring about social reform through the founding of societies, bringing Catholic influence into trade, providing a uniform policy for the Catholic press, and designing educational courses to enlighten workers. His most significant contribution was the Militia of Christ for Social Service, organized in 1909 during the American Federation of Labor's (AF of L) annual meeting. Dietz was convinced that some Catholic umbrella group, like his militia, was necessary for the protection of unions.[14]

The work of John Ryan, as a theorist, and Peter Dietz, as a leader on the ground, is a good example of Catholics who plowed the ground and sowed the seed that blossomed as Catholic Action during the interwar years. Drawing their inspiration from Pope Pius XI's encyclical *Ubi Arcano*, proponents of Catholic Action sought to join the efforts of the laity with those of the hierarchy to effect social reform in the United States.

As with their predecessors, the noteworthy efforts of those who worked under the banner of Catholic Action can be divided into theorists and practitioners. Possibly the leading theorist of the day was Father Paul Hanly Furfey, a sociologist and longtime professor at the Catholic University of America. Furfey used the philosophy of personalism, outlined best by the French scholar Emmanuel Mounier, to present his understanding of social reform. Furfey understood the Gospel as a radical call for action; it was the motivating and integrating force of his whole life. Furfey held a threefold strategy for the application of personalism to social reform. First, he believed that true Christians must separate themselves from society. Second, this separation leads directly to an attitude of nonparticipation: Christians must practice voluntary poverty and simplicity, and refuse to participate in systems that are injurious to others, especially the poor. Last, Furfey believed Christians must always bear witness to what they believed, emphasizing the positive aspects of Christian personalism in their words and actions.[15]

Practitioners of Catholic Action took the ideas of Furfey and others and manifested them in specific organizations to assist the poor and other disenfranchised peoples who stood on the margins of American society. The Catholic Worker Movement, started by Dorothy Day and Peter Maurin in 1933, is the best-known group that carried out the specifics of social reform to the most fragile in American society. The Catholic Worker program was threefold: (1) roundtable discussions of leading intellectuals who sought answers to social questions, (2) houses of hospitality for direct service to the poor, and (3) farm communes, where workers and intellectuals could labor and converse together in one community. It was the second part of the program— namely, the houses of hospitality—

which were most famous and gained for the group a very positive reputation among social reformers.[16] Catholic Worker houses flourish to this very day.

Nelson Baker and the Diocese of Buffalo

Progressive-Era America, most especially the Church's response to the "Social Question"—that is, the adverse fall-out in society as a result of the Industrial Revolution—provides the background for Father Baker's work in the twentieth century. His establishment of the Infant Home and Maternity Hospital, which later became Our Lady of Victory (General) Hospital, is a clear example of efforts consistent with the social agenda of the day. While not a task that is measured by social protocols, Baker's ministry to the Diocese of Buffalo, through his positions as vicar general and administrator, was conducted in a spirit of justice and fairness, hallmarks of the general drive for social reform so characteristic of the age.

Nelson Baker served his first twenty years as a priest under the guidance and leadership of Stephen Ryan, the second bishop of Buffalo. While he probably did not see it in 1882, Baker certainly had to be very happy that Ryan had demonstrated great wisdom in reassigning him to St. Patrick's and the Limestone Hill Institutions. Through this appointment he had found his life's work. Ryan showed ultimate confidence in Baker in 1891 when the latter asked for money to drill a gas well when everyone, including those closest to him, considered the venture utter folly. Thus, when Ryan died on April 10, 1896, it must have been a very sad day for Nelson Baker.

Ryan was succeeded by James Quigley, a Buffalo native, who was consecrated as bishop on February 24, 1897, at St. Joseph's Cathedral. Being a local man, Quigley was obviously well aware of Baker's work and his growing reputation. Thus, it was not a difficult decision for him, as mentioned previously, to appoint Baker as director of the Working Boys Home since the ministry was completely consistent with his work with youth at Limestone Hill.[17] While Quigley's tenure in Buffalo was quite short, he made his mark in preaching against socialism that threatened blue-collar workers, many of whom were Catholics. The historian Thomas Donahue commented:

> Bishop Quigley's condemnation of socialistic theories in the interests of working men was published throughout the United States, and it brought the Bishop of Buffalo prominently before the public; and the Catholic working man, as well as Church authorities, looked upon him as a champion of their rights.[18]

In January 1903, Quigley was appointed archbishop of Chicago, and was installed on March 8, leaving a vacancy in Buffalo. On August 24, 1903, Charles Colton was consecrated and installed as the fourth bishop of Buffalo by Archbishop John Farley at St. Patrick's Cathedral in New York. Colton was described as "a man of great faith and full of zeal for the glory of God."[19] His contribution to the diocese was significant. One account reads:

> In his short life of twelve years as head of the diocese, he spent what appeared to be unwavering energy in building up parishes, institutions and good works of every description; he lent himself without stint to all manner of functions and to anyone who desired his protection, or encouragement.[20]

Like Bishop Ryan, Colton recognized in Baker a man who possessed great talent and seemingly unlimited energy that needed to be tapped. Thus, on December 26, 1903, Colton appointed Baker as vicar general to "assist me in the administration of the Diocese."[21] Baker's appointment was received with marked demonstrations of "approval from all classes of citizens, Catholics and non-Catholics alike, the latter holding him in as high esteem as do the former."[22] A contemporary description of Baker in his new role demonstrates the respect afforded him:

> As to the personality of our new Vicar General, it is but a simple truth to aver that he is indeed an ideal priest—one after Christ's own heart—kind, generous, just, charitable,

merciful, true. He is surely a noble character adorned with the higher supernatural graces of the true priestly life, without a tinge of belittling vanity or selfishness to detract there from. We know of none among his fellow priests who will not offer hearty felicitations to Father Baker upon the unsought honor that has come to him.[23]

Baker accorded himself well in his new position. While there is hardly any surviving data that describes their personal relationship, it is clear that Baker's assistance was well appreciated by Colton. A local paper commented on Baker's service during a prolonged absence by Colton from the diocese:

> During Bishop Colton's absence in Europe, Msgr. Baker, his Vicar-General, administered the affairs of the diocese in a masterly manner and showed himself to be, if that were necessary, the skilled executive, and on the Right [sic] Reverend Bishop's return, he found as was to be expected, everything in the best possible condition.[24]

In his role as vicar general, serving under Colton and his two immediate successors, Denis Dougherty and William Turner, Baker was given many and varied responsibilities. As the bishop's right-hand man and second in command, he held the power of attorney "to sign and endorse notes and generally to transact any and all business of the corporation known as 'The Diocese of Buffalo.'"[25] He was often called upon to handle various canonical matters concerning Church properties, both purchased and sold, and the examination of novices and their admittance to vows in various religious communities. His most significant contribution was his handling of various personnel issues. Baker organized the annual clergy retreat, provided faculties to visiting clergy, and granted delegation to local clergy when individual pastors were not present to grant same. Baker also assisted the bishop in finding clergy to staff the growing number of national parishes in the diocese. Not being able to please all, Baker was viewed by some as heavy-handed in his dealings with the clergy. One of his contemporaries said that Baker at times acted "like the Lord Almighty

God."[26] However, overall Baker was commended for his work as vicar general. The historian Thomas Donahue commented, when observing Baker's work: "He [Baker] fulfills efficiently the onerous duties of the office, notwithstanding the multiplicity of other interests that claim his time and attention."[27] Baker successfully balanced his duties with the diocese and his Lackawanna Institutions.

Upon the death of Bishop Colton on May 9, 1915, Baker was appointed as administrator of the diocese and served in this capacity until June 16, 1916, when Denis Dougherty assumed responsibility as the fifth bishop of Buffalo. Baker continued his basic duties with respect to canonical matters, yet possibly with more personal investment than before. One religious sister claimed that, after assuming the position of administrator, "His [Baker's] solicitude for our community became even more tender."[28] As administrator, however, Baker was required to make more weighty decisions, such as personnel appointments. He rewarded hard work and fervor in ministry. For example, he wrote to one priest: "In consideration of your past pastoral work, I hereby appoint you as rector of the Church of St. Mary Magdalene. I hope you will manifest in your new and greater field the same zeal and administrative ability which you have shown in your former pastorates."[29]

Father Baker's most significant challenge during his year as administrator was to mount opposition against a proposed New York State tax on "all institutions of a religious nature." Upon hearing of this initiative, Baker immediately called a meeting of the clergy at the chancery to forge a strategy to stop the legislation before it got rolling with any speed. The proposed law would tax charitable, benevolent, hospice, and educational institutions, 0.25 percent of their assessed value. In his letter of invitation to a February 21, 1916, meeting he wrote, "If this law is enacted and enforced, it will place a very heavy tax upon all our institutions…and it behooves us to do what we can to prevent its being passed."[30] The meeting was well attended, with representatives from nearly all religious communities and institutions in the diocese. The participants, stating they were willing to make any sacrifice necessary to kill this proposal, formed a committee, with Judge John Kenefick as chairman. It was agreed that the committee would lobby all local legislative representatives to reject the proposal. Baker's response was efficacious as the State Senate dropped plans to entertain the bill. Baker warily wrote to the clergy, "We had better keep praying that this good news will continue."[31]

With the crisis averted, Baker turned his attention to assisting with the transition of Denis Dougherty from his present position in the Philippines to his new post in Buffalo. He informed Dougherty of a recent rash of clergy deaths and its negative impact on the operations of the diocese. Yet, in his generally confident and inspirational tone he wrote, "We have quite a number of students preparing for ordination, and we trust that when the time comes, you will be able to assist the Diocese very much with young clergy." Additionally, he informed the new bishop that the diocese's 1,700 religious priests, brothers, and sisters are "very successful in adding continually new members to their respective families."[32] Baker was also pastorally sensitive, realizing that Dougherty's physical transition would be significant, including the need to acclimate to a vastly different climate. He wrote,

> Kindly consider your good health in coming to be our Bishop, and while we are anxiously looking forward to this great pleasure, we would guard you specifically as our winter weather here drags through the month of April and sometimes part of May.[33]

Dougherty obviously heeded Baker's advice, only arriving and taking his position in mid-June 1916.

Baker's work as administrator was well appreciated by observers in his day. The *Catholic Union & Times* reported, "In spite of the years upon him, he has never wavered; indeed, if anything, he seems to have grown younger, eloquent testimony in favor of the old established fact that work never killed anyone." In a very laudatory article, the paper continued,

> It has been a strenuous year for Msgr. Baker, but he has done nobly. He has had different problems to solve, problems quite unknown to those outside and which required deepest thought and earnest prayer. He has, however, overcome every difficulty that has arisen and

141

hands over the diocese to the new ordinary in the very best condition possible.[34]

Bishop Dougherty's time, like that of James Quigley earlier, was cut short by his appointment as archbishop (and later cardinal) of Philadelphia on July 9, 1918. Baker, who had been reappointed by Dougherty as vicar general, was once again called upon by his metropolitan, Cardinal John Farley of New York, to serve as administrator of the diocese until March 30, 1919. Baker's nine-month tenure as interim head of the diocese came as the United States was engaged in World War I. Thus, one of his major concerns was the success of the United War Work Campaign. He wrote to the pastors in the diocese: "I have been requested to have you announce to your good people that the Fourth Liberty Loan has been launched, and we are called upon to meet it with the spirit of self-sacrifice and noble generosity which has characterized us in the previous loans."[35]

Coordinated by the National Catholic War Council, the campaign, held November 11 to 18, 1918, asked individuals to seek subscriptions to government war bonds from their family, friends, and work colleagues. In the spirit of patriotism, Baker again wrote to his fellow priests, asking their support:

> We must surely realize the grave necessity of this action taken by the government, as a means of utmost importance to us all, in [caring] generously for our boys who are exposing their lives and making heroic sacrifices and subjecting themselves to every manner of self-denial and deprivation, and the least we can do is to aid the government in affording them the very best possible care, in making their lot as agreeable as we are able. The Liberty Loan is essentially necessary to this end, and as we have so generously aided in the former loans, this one is even more vital and important, as the increasing demands of the war have grown so enormously, that for us now to fail in the support of the government would be to us all most disgraceful and humiliating.[36]

Baker was also asked to represent the diocese at special functions. In a rather uncharacteristic personal comment, yet one consistent with many Catholics of the day, Baker sought to avoid attending an "Ecclesial Reception" for Bishop Charles Brent of the Episcopal Diocese of Western New York, who had distinguished himself in the war. Responding to the request of Cardinal James Gibbons of Baltimore, Baker wrote,

> Personally I am averse to taking part in anything of this kind, but we might be criticized on account of the prominent part he has taken in the great war, which seems to have obliterated to a great extent what has here-to-fore kept us apart, and still I do not think that we ought to yield too much, even in celebrations of this nature.[37]

The successor to Denis Doughterty, William Turner, was consecrated bishop at Mount St. Sepulchre, Washington, DC, on March 30, 1919, and was installed as the sixth ordinary of Buffalo on April 9 at St. Joseph's Cathedral. Turner was an academic, having held the chair of the philosophy department at the Catholic University of America. He was an accomplished writer and exceptionally well known for his charity work.[38] Baker wrote to welcome his new bishop:

> We are looking forward with extreme pleasure to the time when we will enjoy the great honor of having you amongst us, as one of Our Lord's specially appointed servants, and we know you will find, especially your clergy, a most devoted, united, faithful and loyal class, and the people under them, have been trained to be true and loving children of the Church.[39]

From the outset Baker and Turner enjoyed a close professional and personal relationship. The latter asked Baker to serve as assistant priest at his consecration in Washington, DC. On the day of his installation, Turner reappointed Baker as vicar general, demonstrating the new bishop's confidence in, and respect for, the venerable priest. The bishop often called upon Baker, seeking his ideas and advice. He sought his counsel concerning names of priests from Buffalo who might be submitted as possible candidates for bishop. When the bishop wrote a pastoral letter, he sent it to Baker for his review. He asked: "Tell me candidly if you are satisfied with the reference to Our Lady of Victory Institutions. I am disposed to omit anything that you may object to or to include some additional matter if you so support."[40]

Turner also sought Baker's advice in certain delicate matters, such as the merging of two parishes, asking which priest should be appointed pastor in the new combined parish.[41] The bishop also gave Baker extended powers when he was away from the diocese. For example, in February 1930, Turner said that, during his forthcoming absence from the diocese, Baker would be given twelve additional faculties, including excardination and incardination, appointing and removing assistant pastors, and inflicting ecclesiastical penalties. Baker took these new responsibilities in stride, even though it took him away from his primary apostolate as pastor and superintendent.[42] He admitted, however, that at times the grind was severe: "We have gone all through the long series of congratulations, prize giving, and graduating exercises, and it seems this year as though there was no end to them."[43]

On a personal level, Baker's relationship with Turner was even closer. The bishop was pleased and proud of Baker's work with youth. He wrote, "God bless you and your noble work. In this, as in all else, you have my entire confidence and my appreciation of the blessings that this great charity brings to all who participate in it."[44] Baker regularly supported the ministerial works of the diocese with excess funds he received from the Association and from the operations of Holy Cross Cemetery, the latter associated with St. Patrick's Parish.[45] In a touching letter written while on vacation in Alabama, Turner spoke from the heart:

> All the time I am happy in thought that you are taking such good care of everything at home. Please ask your boys to say a[n] official prayer for me. And please give me a memento in your Mass. I will not forget you at the altar tomorrow on the beautiful Feast of the Purification.[46]

144

Turner was also concerned about Baker's health, especially as their friendship grew with time. After Baker had recovered from a bout of illness, Turner wrote, "I was delighted yesterday to find you in such good health."[47]

Nelson Baker's work as vicar general was appreciated by all the bishops with whom he served. Thomas Galvin wrote, "With unbounded confidence in his extraordinary leadership and wise management of affairs, they [the bishops] unhesitatingly gave him their blessing and cordial approbation."[48] Some accounts referred to "the almost superhuman work of Father Baker," as related by the bishops under whom he served. In 1929, the bishop-elect of Rochester, John Francis O'Hern, spoke of how many viewed Nelson Baker. In answering a note of congratulations sent by Baker to the new bishop, O'Hern commented: "No word of congratulations from our beloved 'Father Baker' will ever come too late to be appreciated by anyone who knows your wonderful self and all that you mean to the church in the United States in the cause of charity."[49]

During the years that Nelson Baker worked with his local ordinaries as vicar general and twice as administrator of the diocese, he received two significant honorific awards. In November 1904, Pope Pius X elevated Baker to the rank of domestic prelate with title of "monsignor" and "right reverend."[50] News of this honor was received in late December. *The Victorian* reported, "All here in Victorhill are most pleased, the little boys under his care making a most vociferous demonstration in his honor when they heard of his elevation."[51] Baker was vested at St. Joseph's Cathedral on March 23, 1905. He celebrated the Mass with 175 of his fellow priests present.[52] His elevation, while welcomed by all, did not change him, his mission, and most especially his approach to life and ministry. He always preferred to be called Father Baker, choosing the more familiar salutation over the honorific "monsignor." One news story reporting his vesture stated:

> The chief charm of Msgr. Baker lies in his simplicity, earnestness and disinterestedness, and there is not a priest or layman in the diocese who does not rejoice in

the honor conferred on him by the Holy Father at the instance of his appreciative Bishop.[53]

Baker's elevation to the rank of monsignor was capped on March 9, 1923, when Pope Pius XI named him protonotary apostolic, *ad instar participantium*, an honor that made him "eligible to participate in all special privileges of the Holy See."[54]

Father Baker's work in the Diocese of Buffalo, both as vicar general and twice as administrator, found its most significant manifestations in his work with many religious communities of women and his association with fellow clergy. Through his role as vicar general, he had close and regular contact with many religious priests, brothers, and sisters. Branching beyond his official duties, Baker, out of a desire to serve and his ever-magnanimous spirit, assisted many women's religious communities on a personal level.

He often served as an advocate for the Sisters when disagreements arose over contracts and other civil disputes. When property owned by the Dominican Sisters and damaged by D & L Railroad was not restored swiftly, Baker became the Sisters' advocate. He wrote to the mother superior: "I will push him [the attorney] a little harder than he has been pushed. These people have a good deal of business to attend to, and if you are easy with them, they will make no progress, but I will see if I can get some haste in this matter."[55] Still, he was realistic and when necessary advised religious to accept certain terms in order to avoid a nasty court fight. In a dispute between Dominican nuns and the architect and builder of their new convent, Baker was forced to concede:

> I am sorry to be obliged to advise you thus in this matter, but I am thinking of your own temporal and spiritual happiness, and I wish you to avoid, as far as possible, the serious annoyance which might come from not accepting the present conditions.[56]

Baker's business experience, from both the past and his present associations with those involved with the Institutions, helped him to assist religious with various financial matters and questions. In February 1905, Baker was instrumental in the formation of the

Mercy Hospital Aid Society. He emphasized the important role that religious women play in establishing and maintaining charitable institutions.[57] Baker was eager to assist with various fundraising drives. He wrote to one sister superior:

> I was pleased to learn that you have permission of your Right Reverend Bishop to enter into a campaign to raise funds to assist you in financing the new building. Now that the Catholic Charities Drive is over, your friends are all anxious to enter into the "battlefield" with you.[58]

Baker's responsibilities concerning canonical matters for the women's communities were performed on a regular basis. These included official visitations to convents for the canonical examination of Sisters preparing for first vows or final profession. He conducted these duties with a great pastoral sensitivity, consistent with his general approach to youth, finding this approach most conducive to both his personality and to fulfillment of his responsibilities. After one official visit, he wrote to Bishop Turner, "I found a splendid religious spirit among the members; all seem to be perfectly happy and contented, which was for me, perfectly satisfactory."[59]

While Father Baker diligently and properly fulfilled his official responsibilities toward women religious, it was his regular and heartfelt acts of kindness toward them that made their relationship close. On several occasions, Baker organized a trip on the Niagara River to which he invited communities of religious women. For example, in July 1922, he engaged the *Island Belle* for a day trip. Writing an invitation to religious superiors, he stated, "Will be delighted to welcome as many Sisters as you can spare, and I am sure they will enjoy it."[60] Baker's generosity was manifest through small but frequent monetary gifts to religious houses. A typical letter, with donation enclosed, read, "I thought you might be in need of something that would require a few dollars, so I take great pleasure in mailing you a check for that purpose, to make it pleasant for you and your good Sisters."[61] Baker was well known for bringing Christmas cheer through a letter and enclosing a check, along with his promise of prayers. It was not unusual at all for Baker to surprise various communities with seemingly random acts

147

of kindness. In 1905, he visited a Dominican convent and noticed there were insufficient chairs for all the Sisters to sit. Playfully he told the Sisters that he was sure the Blessed Mother would see to it that they had sufficient chairs. A few days later a truck arrived at the convent with two dozen new chairs for the community. On other occasions Baker would unexpectedly arrive at the convent and celebrate Benediction.[62]

Father Baker was gracious to *all* women religious sisters, but he held a special relationship with the Sisters of Our Lady of Charity. As related earlier, he and his seminary friend Daniel Walsh raised money for this community through their musical presentations. Years later, both in his role as vicar general and also from personal association, Baker continued this close association with the community. One contemporary account accurately described this relationship:

> Baker has been more or less identified with the work of the Sisters of the Refuge, and nobly has he acquitted himself of the duties of friend and benefactor, aiding them by his fatherly advice in unlooked for difficulties, assisting them in the advancement of their work, the salvation of erring souls, and befriending them generally. His gift of touching hearts has rendered him of immense usefulness in the Institution, as many of these souls committed to the care of the Sisters owe their perseverance to his timely intervention and his wholesome advice.[63]

Baker enjoyed the company of the community and was a regular guest throughout the year. The "Convent Book," a chronicle of the community, speaks of Baker's regularly coming to celebrate Mass and to visit. He never came empty-handed, but always had something to share with the Sisters. Various accounts say that annually Baker celebrated the feasts of Epiphany and St. Mary Magdalen with the community. Each year he treated the "consecrates" at the convent to a daylong picnic.[64] The Sisters acknowledged their special relationship with Nelson Baker. One letter from the religious superior is illustrative: "There are so many things which we would like to tell you, and about which we would like to ask your advice, as you have always been so generous and kind to us through many years."[65]

Father Baker's relationship with the priests of Buffalo, while cordial and certainly consistent with his basic pastoral approach to ministry, was experienced in ways quite different from his association with women religious. Possibly because he was "one of them," it seems that Baker was more direct and challenging to his fellow priests than to women religious. As administrator of the diocese, Baker was often requested to arbitrate disputes among his fellow priests, including the perceived infringement of one pastor into the geographic region of another, as well as disputes among the clergy within a particular parish rectory. When he felt a priest performed well, then that priest was rewarded. He wrote to one cleric, "It gives me great pleasure to appoint you to the Rectorship of the Church of St. Agnes in the City of Buffalo. Your splendid priestly work warrants me in bestowing this desirable parish upon you."[66]

Baker had high standards. Speaking of his relationship with his associates at St. Patrick's (later Our Lady of Victory Basilica), one Sister of St. Joseph commented, "They 'towed the mark,' I suppose while Father Baker was there. Oh, I think he'd be real good to them in his own way, but he expected them to be like him."[67] His high standards also applied to personal generosity. Responding to a letter that indicated that the clergy of the diocese had contributed little to the annual charity appeal, Baker wrote,

> It occurred to me, and I thought of it in other years, where our priests make very little of an effort towards making a success of the drive, and I have never suggested that it was needed for them to assist in any way, but it occurred to me this year, more particularly,...the plan of quietly suggesting to our clergy to contribute a small part of their salary and income, to make this successful...It don't [*sic*] seem right that our clergy, who, as a rule do very nicely financially, shall be exempt from adding a little to a cause of this kind.[68]

The historical record that survives to this day is not weighty, but there are clear indications that Nelson Baker at times crossed swords with some of his fellow clergy, most especially those in closest contact with him. Sister René Ruberto wrote: "Accounts of priests who worked with him tell that it was not easy. In his later years, he had many assistants who were transferred quite frequently because of this difficulty."[69] As indicated previously, Baker's own high personal standards and work ethic were often the mark he used to judge the competence and accomplishments of his peers. Additionally, because of his positions as pastor, superintendent of the Institutions, and vicar general of the diocese, he wielded significant clout that was used when necessary. One observer suggested that Baker had the ear of Bishop Turner with respect to clergy placements: "If he called the Bishop and said he wanted somebody transferred, they would be transferred tomorrow."[70] One of Baker's former assistants stated:

> I may add that those who are most intimately associated with Monsignor Baker and all those who lived with him would be among the first to oppose any effort to canonize him. Personally, I knew him very well and I never saw in him any evidence of heroic virtue.[71]

The most prominent and documented difficulty Baker faced with the clergy was with another assistant, Herman Gerlach, who served as a curate under Baker at St. Patrick's and Our Lady of Victory Basilica from 1913 to 1932. Initially Gerlach respected Baker. He was quoted in a local paper, "All of us who knew him [Baker] cannot help but love him. He is a memorable man and one of the saintliest I have ever known."[72] However, in late December 1932, Gerlach was reassigned quite suddenly as pastor of Our Lady of the Angels, a rural parish in Cuba, New York.[73] The following Sunday many parishioners walked out of the Basilica when Baker began to preach, perceiving that as pastor he was responsible for the transfer. A few years later Gerlach, speaking of his dismissal, wrote of "the dirty deal I got from Fr. Baker."[74]

The historical record, however, does not support the conclusions drawn by those who observed this incident from the outside. It seems that Baker's conflict with Gerlach was based on the latter's rough and discourteous treatment of the Brothers of the Holy

Infancy and Youth of Jesus and the Sisters of St. Joseph in the Institutions. Apparently not able to control his assistant, Baker was forced to go to the bishop. Turner told Gerlach:

> You do not know, I am sure, how many complaints I have received regarding your conduct both inside the Institutions and outside. Ordinarily, I should have confronted you with these accusations, but Monsignor Baker, in his kindness and long-suffering charity, made me to forbear....I can truly say that...you have corrupted every young man whom I have appointed to help Monsignor Baker. It is your loss that you, so near to him, could not improve your own spiritual condition.[75]

While some rough roads were traversed in his relationship with the clergy, in the end, Baker's decisions were supported by superiors and peers alike. In November 1915, during his first stint as administrator of the diocese, Baker allowed a parish bazaar to be held in the geographical jurisdiction of another parish. The pastor of the second church complained to the apostolic delegate, Archbishop Giovanni Bonzano, in Washington, DC. However, Bonzano's response not only upheld Baker's decision, but praised him for his wisdom:

> Consequently the decision of Monsignor Baker is neither contrary to good order, discipline or government, nor is there any reason why it should breed dissension or discord. To the contrary, it should be a means of bringing together the faithful of the two parishes and of improving relations between respective pastors, who unfortunately, as you inform me, are unfriendly to each other.[76]

Appreciation was also apparent from his curates as well. After serving with Baker for several years at St. Patrick's, one priest, who sought a transfer in order to be closer to his dying parents, wrote in gratitude:

> I want you to know that I have left your work with real regret. I have learned something by being associated

with you, something I never can forget and that is the beauty of holiness. I pray to Our Lady that she may obtain a portion of that beauty in my life.[77]

Additional Administrative Functions

Nelson Baker's work for the Diocese of Buffalo centered in activities associated with his roles as vicar general and administrator, but other aspects of Church life in the region also gained his attention. In 1849, Bishop John Timon purchased a small farm at Limestone Hill for $1,000. Soon thereafter he consecrated forty acres of the farm to be used as a cemetery. The mission church of Holy Cross, established in 1851, obtained its name from the cemetery.[78] During his more than half-century tenure as pastor, Baker wisely managed the cemetery, allowing it to serve its primary function, while at the same time be economically profitable. He had a good working relationship with the cemetery's local administrator, Margaret Kirby. He placed implicit trust in her judgment. Writing to her about a certain employee who was problematic, he concluded, "Whatever you think, we will carry out."[79]

The economic profitability of the cemetery was an added boon to Baker, especially to pay some of the huge debts he annually ran in the operations of his Institutions. For example, records show that between January 1, 1904, and December 1922, the cemetery had a net profit of $133,173.50. This surplus was shared with the Institutions, but additionally with the diocese for assistance in the construction of a new St. Joseph's Cathedral, and similar projects.[80] In a typical note, Baker wrote to Bishop Turner, "You will find enclosed a check for $3000, which I find we can spare from our cemetery accounts."[81] Additionally, during his stints as administrator, records showed that Baker lent monies from the cemetery surplus to various pastors in order to pay their bills.[82] Father Baker's ever-present kindness was manifested in his operation of the cemetery as well. He often wrote Kirby suggesting that pastoral sensitivity was more important than monetary gain or the opinions of society. When Virginia Reeves, an African American woman, was murdered near the Basilica, Baker wrote

Kirby telling her to accept the dead woman's husband's small contribution:

> The bearer is the husband of the Colored lady that was killed the other day, and he accompanies the undertaker, and you might be pleased to treat them as you would anybody else, and you need not put her in any position where you think the neighbors would find fault with them, and oblige.[83]

Operation of the cemetery also drew periodic complaints, mostly concerning maintenance of the facility. One irate attorney wrote to Bishop Turner, venting his frustration. He suggested that a board of directors be appointed to oversee and manage the affairs of the cemetery:

> It should be the aim of the clergy who have the cemeteries in their charge to do all they can to make things correspond with conditions of today and not what was a generation ago as your Superintendent seems to feel exists at present. For if any constructive criticism is offered for any remarks made for the betterment of the place, you are told that things suit Father Baker and that is sufficient. It is such conduct that is making the people leave the place and from the looks of things, it will not be long before the City of Lackawanna will be closing up the place on the ground[s] that the same is a public nuisance and should be abated.[84]

In addition to his administration of Holy Cross Cemetery, Baker was a significant player in the formation and fostering of Catholic colleges in the Buffalo area. In 1861, the Grey Nuns of Ottawa, Canada, started Holy Angels Academy. In 1907, due to long waiting lists for entry, a wing was added to one of the buildings initially erected in 1872. While touring the new building, Bishop Colton and his vicar Nelson Baker suggested that the Sisters augment the building for a new Catholic college for women, since there was no such institution in Western New York and only one in the entire state, the College of New Rochelle, just north of New York City. With the consent of the Sisters, Baker and Colton, working with lawyer Charles O'Connor, drafted and submitted directly to the New York legislature a charter for the new school, which was passed on April 4, 1908. Governor Charles Evans Hughes signed the legislation and on September 27, 1908, D'Youville College opened with nine students.[85]

Baker was closely allied with the college until his death. He accepted nomination to the Board of Governors and became vice chancellor of the college, beginning on June 8, 1912. He served continuously until 1935, missing only two of the Board's annual meetings. Baker's administrative assistance with the college poured over into his work with the Institutions. During the latter years of his life, students from D'Youville came each Christmas week to St. Joseph's Orphan Asylum and hosted a party for the boys. The coeds were assigned a boy for whom they supplied a gift. The day always ended with a visit to a local soda fountain in Lackawanna, where the boys had a full choice from the menu.[86]

Baker also had an excellent relationship with Canisius College, established by the Jesuits in 1870. As stated previously, Baker as a young man received instructions in Latin from Father Joseph Durthaller, SJ. He and others were the vanguard responsible for the foundation of Canisius. Baker was present at the college on numerous occasions, often in an official capacity representing the bishop. In 1920, he was awarded an honorary Doctor of Laws, an honor that he greatly appreciated.[87] Baker's contribution to the college was noted in the *Canisius Monthly*:

> Looking over the Roll Call of Honor I see none more likely to outlast this early pioneer of Canisius, as no man of them all gave his mind more singly to a purpose or more largely loved mankind as Buffalo's internationally known prelate, the Right Reverend Monsignor Nelson H. Baker....He is, perhaps, the best-loved man living today, for he asks nothing, receives much, and gives everything....His name will be loved, honored, and cherished while humanity remains human.[88]

Conclusion

For over thirty years, Nelson Baker enjoyed close association with priests and religious in the Diocese of Buffalo. This secondary hat as vicar general and twice administrator of the diocese was worn successfully. It was a new role that required additional skills not previously tapped and that forced him to deal closely with his peers, not with troubled youth. Baker admirably carried out all of his many canonical duties with religious and served his fellow priests as the need dictated. His association with several women's religious communities demonstrated his pastoral sense, while serving in an administrative capacity. As might be expected, at times Baker drew fire and ruffled the feathers of some fellow clerics, but his decisions were always made in a fair and equitable manner. Baker's role in the diocese was significant, especially the trust and respect he gained from his last local ordinary, Bishop William Turner. Yet, this role cannot be adequately compared to his work with the Institutions. When asked to serve by the bishop, Baker ably responded, but he always returned to his raison d'être in Lackawanna, a ministry that continued to expand throughout the first third of the twentieth century.

Right Reverend Monsignor Nelson
H. Baker, protonotary apostolic,
vicar general, c. 1930.

On the occasion of his ninety-fourth birthday, a couple of
Father Baker's young charges join in the celebration, 1936.

Father Baker enjoys a casual moment with friends, c. 1928.

As vicar general of the Diocese of Buffalo, Father Baker had the opportunity to participate in many diocesan events, including the laying of cornerstones, 1925.

Father Baker spent countless hours at his desk handling the extensive
responsibilities of the Our Lady of Victory Institutions, c. 1933.

Over a four-day period, an estimated 400,000 mourners waited in lines
for hours to enter the Basilica and pay their last respects
to Lackawanna's "Apostle of Charity."

Woodworking was just one of the skills mastered by the
young men at the massive trade school, c. 1920.

Father Baker updated his loyal donors across the country and
asked for their continued support, through *The Victorian*,
his monthly magazine, 1925.

St. Joseph's
Orphanage,
c. 1925.

St. John's
Protectory,
c. 1925.

Our Lady of Victory
Infant Home,
c. 1925.

CHAPTER 7

Father Baker's Boys (1900–1936)

Nelson Baker's contribution to the Diocese of Buffalo in his leadership roles as vicar general and administrator was significant; it added greatly to the harmony within religious communities and provided a sense of continuity for the whole diocese during times of transition. Yet, Father Baker's heart and soul were devoted to the Institutions in Lackawanna, beginning with the Orphanage and the Protectory, but now with an ever-increasing ministry to women and children at the Infant Home and General Hospital. During the first third of the twentieth century, these Institutions continued to expand their facilities and clientele, and improve their services. Baker's energy and dedication never waned but only seemed to grow greater and stronger with time. Somewhat lost in the notoriety, popularity, and daily hard work of the Institutions was the fact that Baker was also responsible for the pastoral needs of the people of St. Patrick's Parish, a need that led to the generation of two new mission churches and schools, plus expansion of educational facilities. Buoyed by the nation's general prosperity in the wake of World War I and the lavishness of the Roaring Twenties, Baker was inspired to extend his work as widely as possible, confident that, with the assistance and protection of Our Lady of Victory, success and prosperity would be brought to all his endeavors.

St. Joseph's Orphan Asylum

From the construction of the Infant Home in 1908, Father Baker's Our Lady of Victory Institutions, often referred to by local people as the "Second Holy City," was complete.[1] Baker's dream of assisting youth from birth to adulthood—providing them with education, a foundational faith, and a sense of purpose—continued to blossom throughout the Progressive Era, through the prosperity of the Roaring Twenties, and even through the gloom of the Great Depression. Always a man of the Church, when the Infant Home opened, he sought the blessing of the Vicar of Christ on earth, Pope Pius X:

> Monsignor Nelson H. Baker, Vicar-General of the Diocese of Buffalo, humbly implores of Your Holiness a special blessing upon himself, the priests, religious, and sisters under his care, and all the members of the Association of Our Blessed Lady of Victory, who have the care of the nine hundred and fifty homeless and destitute children.[2]

State inspection reports for St. Joseph and the other Institutions, almost all of which are extant, break down the population in the various homes in various categories. Geographic origins of residents are listed as "Erie County," "Other Counties," and "Borders." A second category was whether the boys were public charges supported by the State, or private charges, with the latter generally double or more the public count. Lastly, the reports always compare the total census population of the institution versus the capacity of that home as dictated by the State. *The Victorian* reported that between 1906 and 1926 the average census population was 1,084: with a breakdown of 510 at St. John's, 287 at St. Joseph's, 240 at the Infant Home, and 47 at the Working Boys Home. A review of the still-available state reports, however, shows these numbers to be somewhat inflated. The average population at St. Joseph's during this period was approximately 190.[3] Interestingly, despite the onset of the Great Depression, the population at St. Joseph between 1927 and 1933 was less, averaging 180 boys. In 1937, one year after Father Baker's death, the census had dropped to 135, a 25 percent reduction.[4]

The state reports for St. Joseph's from the start of the twentieth century to Father Baker's death in 1936 reveal some important details. While the population at the Asylum was always close to its maximum-allowed capacity, it was only occasionally over the limit; still, overcrowding became a major concern, particularly in the mind of the State.[5] As mentioned above, private admissions were significantly higher than public charges, ranging from a high ratio of 11.2 to 1 in 1924, to a low of 1.5 to 1 in 1912.[6] Of the private charges, at least 50 percent (generally the percentage was much higher) were listed as "free," meaning that they were fully supported by Baker's significant fundraising efforts. Stipends requested by Baker from the State and those private parties with the ability to pay, at least partially, varied with time. At the end of World War I, public admissions from Erie County were charged $5.00 per week; others, including boys admitted by private citizens, were asked to pay $4.00 per week. However, payment was never a criterion for any boy at any of the institutions.[7]

Annual New York State reports on St. Joseph's (sometimes more frequent) were generally complimentary toward the efforts of the Sisters of St. Joseph, but were quite critical of the overall lack of qualified personnel at the facility. The September 1931 report lauded the Sisters' efforts: "St. Joseph's Male Orphan Asylum is being ably administered by a group of intelligent, trained, and conscientious women who are keenly interested in the child-caring program being executed at the institution." However, critique of the administration of the Asylum was also noted. One state official, while appreciative of improvements made since the last annual inspection, concluded, "The administrative situation at this institution…cannot yet be regarded as satisfactory." The 1931 report that praised the Sisters also stated, "It is unfortunate that a more active board cannot meet with greater frequency to assist the Sisters in their making changes which they feel would benefit their charges."[8]

Overcrowding at the institution was by far the State's most prominent and consistent critique of St. Joseph's.[9] In part this situation arose due to Father Baker's consistent open-door policy, which became known throughout the country and Canada. Thomas Galvin claimed that in 1925 the residents of St. Joseph's came from thirty-seven different states and three Canadian provinces.[10] Baker's policies ran afoul of state regulations and common practice on two fronts. First, by the mid-1920s, prevailing policy in the State no longer supported the concept of orphanages. Baker himself commented on a report that New York has "condemned orphanages in the State, and will not allow them to be supported any longer, as all orphan children in the future are to be placed in boarding homes."[11] Second, the State sought to enforce laws that did not allow non–New York children to be assisted by Baker's Institutions. However, the priest's long-standing work and high reputation gave him clout during his life to fend off all efforts to both suspend his operations and remove non–New Yorkers from his Institutions. One contemporary observer commented: "He [Baker] was tough dealing with [the] State about the orphans being sent back to their state. He wouldn't let them go. He had a lot of power with the State. After his death, the kids were sent back."[12]

Possibly as an outgrowth from earlier progressive reforms, New York after World War I became much more proactive in identifying problems and making strong comments, leading to their rapid correction. In 1919 and 1921, the secretary of the New York State Board of Charities, James Foster, was especially harsh in his criticism of the Asylum. In November 1919, he wrote to Bishop Turner:

It appears that many of these [deficiencies] are easily remediable and that none are beyond a very moderate standard of care and training. We feel that the general character of many of the details noticed, for example, the condition of walls, toilets, and playgrounds and the lack of proper personal care for the children, indicate that the ideals of work in the institution are not in keeping with modern standards of childcare and it is our belief that those in charge of the work should carefully study, not only their own methods and practices, but those employed in other institutions of the better class as a basis for critical judgment of their own work. In the light of such comparison, we feel convinced that the present standards would be no longer tolerated and material improvement in the work done would be brought about.[13]

Two years later Foster addressed additional concerns to the bishop:

> It appears that the personal care of the children is not good....The reasons for this undesirable condition seem to lie in part, at least, in the want of sufficient adult help, either Sisters or lay employees to carry on the work of the place in a satisfactory and modern manner.

In conclusion, he hoped that Turner would understand that the State's call for improvement at St. Joseph's was based solely on promoting the good of the children in residence. He wrote:

> We believe that you will agree with us that very considerable improvements in the work of this institution are needed and can easily be made....I am sure that you quite understand that our purpose is solely to further the interests of the children cared for by the institution and to assist those who are directing and carrying out its work.[14]

State concern for deficiencies at St. Joseph's, while still voiced throughout the 1920s, became somewhat less aggressive. In 1926, the concern was that the physical building did not provide sufficient space for children to recreate in small groups. The next year, the report was more positive, but still reserved in its comments:

> May I express to you our appreciation of the numerous and important improvements that have been made since the...previous inspection and upon the general improvement in administrative conditions. We believe that better care and training are now being given to the voice of your institution than has heretofore been the case. There still remain, however, a number of matters which should have your attention.[15]

In 1928 and 1929, appreciation for administrative improvements was again given, and in the latter year, the state inspectors were pleased to report, "Changes made in the plant and administration in order to provide supervision in small groups are commendable."[16] Added vocational training was, in the opinion of the inspection team, "the most important need at St. Joseph's home at the present time."[17]

In the 1930s, St. Joseph's seems to have negotiated an important turn in direction that again pleased state inspectors. In 1931, the annual report was complimentary to the obvious improvements made in recent years. In part the report read, "General administrative conditions as to the cleanliness and care of [the] plant and as to personal care and training of children are excellent."[18] Two years later the report even praised the institution, especially considering its limited economic resources:

> The Asylum is unusual in the apparent effort being made by those in charge to understand the child's point of view and to provide surroundings which shall make him happy. While the ability to do this is limited here by lack of funds and perhaps also by institutional tradition, much has been done....Some of the playrooms are made delightful with a variety of gay pictures—mostly cut from magazines and calendars—toys, games, books, small objects made by the children, curios, plants, etc., which create an atmosphere not often found in this type of institution.[19]

State inspections of St. Joseph's were obviously important to Father Baker and his dedicated staff, but the ongoing day-to-day life at the Asylum was more significant to the boys in residence. As described earlier, daily life in this period, as in previous years, followed a regular regimen, from rising at 5:30 a.m. and retiring between 7 and 9 p.m. depending on age groups.[20] The schedule included daily Mass and prayer, meals, classes, recreation, and study. Beyond the ordinary daily routine, some boys worked in the Home for a modest stipend. One report stated, "Every child performing household duties has been placed on a 'boys' payroll list' receiving compensation for their weekly tasks."[21] Although it is not clear why, it seems this procedure was changed before Baker's death. The 1933 state inspection report commented that all boys over twelve were expected to assist with various chores. However, "no money allowance is given as a reward for this, the reason being entirely financial rather than disapproval of the practice."[22]

Sports were another important part of daily life at St. Joseph's. While physical education was not a mandated program at the Asylum until 1923, various sports activities were integral to the life of the boys. Basketball and baseball teams were formed for intramural competition, as well as a traveling team to compete against other Catholic schools in the local area. It was quite common as well for the boys at St. Joseph's to cross the street to the large enclosed yard at St. John's Protectory. One of the annual sports traditions was Decoration Day, which marked the opening of the baseball season. The Protectory band played, and the boys marched around the yard and ended at the baseball diamond. Each year Father Baker threw out the ceremonial first pitch of the season. Sister Mary Timothy Dempsey commented on the value of sports at the Asylum: "Sports programs endeavored to teach them the value of good sportsmanship, teamwork, and other qualities necessary for social adjustment."[23]

Sports were only part of a vast array of various activities that complemented life at St. Joseph's. The weekly Sunday afternoon movie at St. John's was a regular event greatly anticipated by all—indeed, many considered it the highlight of the week. While the regular daily regimen was important in a home with so many boys with varied backgrounds and interests, Baker, nonetheless, made every possible effort to remove from the minds of these children any idea that their home was an institution, let alone a prison. Thus, in an effort to break up the routine, Baker fostered various events that changed the pace. For example, July 4 was a carnival day, with games, as well as running, swimming, and wheelbarrow races.[24] When transportation could be arranged, he took the boys out from the Asylum. Some local citizens believed it was a bad idea to take these boys, many who had been wards of the State, into public places, even for a short time. Father Baker, however, believed in the value of such outings. Boys were treated to baseball games in Buffalo, a day at the circus, and most especially the annual "autoride." Each summer, the Automobile Club of Buffalo

167

arranged transportation so that all the boys could attend a day of
fun, food, and general recreation, usually held in Buffalo's Delaware
Park. A cadre of volunteers was assembled to transport and supervise Baker's Boys for the day. Children from other orphan homes
joined in the festivities.[25]

Education at St. Joseph's Orphan Asylum

Catholic education, central to Baker's program in the
Institutions, had been offered by the Diocese of Buffalo since the
time of Bishop Timon. Yet the early record of general secular education in the region was less than stellar. One historian of the
period remarked:

> In the appointment to positions within the educational
> system, the highest standards of public morality were
> not always observed. Instruction itself left much to be
> desired. Discipline in the classroom was excessive and all
> too often exercised by disinterested teachers whose
> methodology was largely memorization, an antiquated
> collection of textbooks, paid for by the students, con-
> tributed with crowded and obsolete physical properties
> to what one reforming Superintendent of Schools mod-
> estly referred to as "the generally low tone of the
> schools."[26]

Reform of Buffalo's public education system began with J. F.
Crocker, who served as superintendent of public schools from
1882 to 1892. Crocker instituted manual and physical education
as part of the curriculum and established a kindergarten program.
Henry P. Emerson, who succeeded Crocker as superintendent for
the next twenty-six years (1892–1918), continued the latter's
work in a common effort to modernize the school system. In addition to furthering the ideas of his predecessor, he inaugurated the
idea of free textbooks for students that would be owned by the
city. His most important service was his insistence on excellent
teachers, whose qualifications would be determined by examina-

tion. He established a teachers' retirement fund and a training school for educators.[27]

Catholic education, initiated by Bishop John Timon, was at least initially promoted largely out of fear that common schools would be injurious to the faith of children. This reality was noted by a historian of the period:

> The greatest increment in the number of private schools during this period was the result of the religious convictions of Roman Catholics and Lutherans who insisted that only in a parochial school could the child be adequately grounded in the faith of his fathers.[28]

It took some time, but Timon was able to establish parish schools and to furnish them with women religious and priests as teachers. By 1859, there were approximately 2,400 girls and 1,200 boys enrolled in Buffalo's diocesan schools.[29] Anticipating the action of the United States hierarchy in 1884, Bishop Stephen Ryan, in a November 1873 pastoral letter, wrote:

> Catholic parents cannot in conscience send their children to schools in which the faith and morals are imperiled. Such are schools where religious instruction is not executed. Such in general are public schools....Continue to send your children where faith and morals will be guarded from the risks and perils to which they must inevitably be exposed in schools where the first essential element of true education, that is religion, is executed or ignored....Let there be good parochial schools in every parish where all the children and especially the children of the poor may receive Christian education.[30]

Baker wanted his Institutions to be much more than correctional facilities; education was, therefore, critical to his overall program. Baker was convinced that, without a proper education, the mind and in some sense one's whole life was imperiled. He knew the contributions an educated person could make, and thus he spared no effort to make his youthful charges assets to society.

169

Sister Mary Timothy Dempsey described the educational philosophy practiced by Baker:

> Father Baker believed in the education of soul and body and high ideals were constantly kept before the boys' minds. He instilled civic and moral virtues and love of God and country. Both religion and patriotism, therefore, formed an essential part of the curriculum. Thus, the formation of character and the acquisition of knowledge kept pace with the religious and intellectual growth of "Father Baker's Boys."[31]

The molding of modern citizens through the combination of education with religion and patriotism was a prominent theme in Catholic education at this time. At a time when the Ku Klux Klan was once again raising the ever-present specter of anti-Catholicism, Church educators responded by demonstrating that a Catholic education called one to the duty of patriotism. The "muscular Catholicism" of the era was illustrated by a comment on what educational product Baker's Institutions produced: "They will become good citizens because they are being educated in the love of God, and the love of their country, and all that goes to make up the ideal Christian man."[32]

Father Baker's educational philosophy was defined at length in an April 1929 essay in *The Victorian*. His entire statement is both illustrative and instructive in understanding both him and what he sought in the education he provided, including Catholic masculinity:

> First, we hold up the Catholic ideal of manhood. It is to grow in the vigor of manliness, copying Him who came to show us the way of life. We put before our boys the picture of the Perfect Man....Nothing short of the perfect life of Christ is offered as the true good of a Catholic's endeavor. This is impressed with all its beauty and appealing force on the young minds that live under our roof.
>
> We teach the boys to be true and genuine. No education is worthy [of its] name that does not inculcate this

170

fundamental necessity. An ignorant man, true and genuine in his actions, is worth more than all the learning in the world.

We teach the boys to be pure in thought. Thoughts are the driving power of our actions....The body invigorated by a pure mind will not take pleasure in actions that are unchaste and unholy.

We teach the boys to be self-reliant and self-helpful. The boy who lacks confidence will never overcome in the battle of life. Self-confidence, not cock-sureness, will enoble [*sic*] all the faculties. To be industrious always and self-supporting is the right spirit to instill in youthful minds.

What else is there to teach you in this world of bustle, hurry and scurry, and so little accomplished in this age when pleasure and greed give no time to self-sacrifice and mortification; in a country where material gain has more devotees and worshipers than spiritual worth and God-like virtues.

We teach the boys to be unselfish, to care for the feelings and comforts of others. We try to have them think of doing something rather than getting; to give rather than receive; be generous, noble and manly; to respect the aged and holy things. To suffer one's self-respect rather than cause others pain.[33]

Father Baker's philosophy of education was integrated into the specifics of the program at St. Joseph's, including adequate physical space.[34] The Asylum had to meet the requirements of the State. The State Board of Charities rules regarding education read:

Children of school age, retained in any such institution in whole or in part at public expense, shall receive regular and suitable instruction as required by the Education Law, and provision shall be made for the manual and industrial training of children of 12 years of age and over in a manner approved by the State Board of Charities.[35]

The state mandate was aptly satisfied in the mind of the eminent historian Frederick Zwerlein. He wrote:

> The Managers [of St. Joseph's] seek to combine instruction in the common branches of an English education with useful labors and with some trade that will enable the poor orphans in...[later] life to gain more surely an honest living, and thus prevent them from becoming a burden to themselves or to their fellow citizens.[36]

The academic curriculum at St. Joseph's was not extensive, but was consistent with the needs of students in various grade levels. Reading, spelling, basic arithmetic, language, and geography were studied by all; these were integrated with more advanced subjects of drawing, history, and philosophy for older students. Long before public schools in the area realized the importance of technical training and made provision for the teaching of trades, Father Baker's Boys received such skills. Dempsey claimed that a short-lived (1903–4) industrial trades program operated at St. Joseph's. Normal procedure, however, was for the boys at St. Joseph's to receive technical training at St. John's, which had appropriate facilities. St. Joseph also offered limited musical, elocution, and drama education. Plays and musical presentations were presented in Victoria Hall at St. John's.[37]

Sister Mary Clotilda Wagner, SSJ, who served as superior of the Sisters of St. Joseph at the Orphanage from 1909 to 1915, introduced several important educational advancements to the Home's program. She improved the small library, especially through the addition of monthly and weekly publications. Additionally, she convinced Baker that one of the Brothers of the Holy Infancy and Youth of Jesus should teach the upper-grade boys in order that they have more of a male presence in the Orphanage. Routine night study became normative under her direction. Last, she opened a kindergarten class for young children who had not come from the Infant Home. To improve conditions for teachers, she insisted the class size be reduced by the addition of a new classroom.[38]

Father Baker himself was also responsible for some significant improvements in the educational system. In 1930, due to overcrowding in the school, he was forced to send some of his boys to the public schools of Lackawanna. In order to maintain the controlled environment he sought, Baker realized that an addition to the Orphanage, in order to accommodate sufficient students, would be necessary. Therefore, with the approval of Bishop Turner, a small addition, costing $40,000, was built and ready for use by September 1931.[39] A second improvement was a small program for those students who needed extra assistance in learning. The state inspection report of 1929 revealed that some boys had been diagnosed as borderline with respect to normal intelligence. In response, Baker placed Sr. Mary Virginia Rugg in charge of an instruction program for students performing at subpar levels. The class was successful. One observer commented, "Visitors to the special class were not only enlightened, but edified at the patience and care given these children."[40]

The education program at St. Joseph's, the centerpiece of the Institution, was a success story that produced dividends for the boys and American society. The local Buffalo press lauded Baker's efforts: "The educational facilities are exceptionally good, the best teachers being employed, and thus the highest standard of excellence is obtained."[41] Over the years, boys at St. Joseph's (and St. John's) did exceptionally well on the New York State Board of Regents Exams. In April 1928, the *Annals* reported that twenty-one of twenty-one boys passed the exam, averaging over 90 percent. Proudly *The Victorian* proclaimed, "The school that can turn out boys with a Regents certificate in their pockets and practical knowledge of a useful [trade] in their hands is accomplishing much for the next generation."[42] Indeed, most who came to St. Joseph's arrived friendless and in a helpless situation, but they left with a sense of courage and confidence, knowing they had sufficient knowledge and skill to be successful in the world. Dempsey aptly concluded:

> Father Baker gained a greater victory than those who were victorious in the Civil War—or any war—for he constructed rather than tore down a "City of God," producing God-fearing men. He was also able to award a majority of them the "V for Victory" over themselves

and their problems of social living. This was implanted in their hearts after their first triumphal victory either in the scholastic field or in manual skills. Life and living now had meaning and was [*sic*] worth continuing, where possibly a few months or years previously, it did not. What greater lesson could they learn![43]

The educational program at St. Joseph's was well respected and grew over time to meet specific needs, but there were still some gaps. John Sullivan, who lived in Baker's Institutions for eighteen years, was critical of the proportion of schooling to other activities as well as of his teachers. He commented, "We should have got[ten] a better education; everything was congested and there was no push for education." He continued, "There was a lot of support, but not much schooling, I wish we had more prepared people to train us."[44] The one significant omission in the program was a social dimension. Baker did not see any great value in participation in social functions where girls were present. Sister Mary Timothy Dempsey in her educational study of the Limestone Hill Institutions concluded: "In many cases this resulted in a warped personality regarding heterosexual relationships, later affecting their [the boys'] life and happiness."[45]

Education was certainly central to Father Baker's overall daily mission at St. Joseph's, but in a master plan for the Institution, he hoped his boys would one day ultimately be adopted and raised in good Catholic families. The *Annals* in its regular column "Notes for Solicitors" sought families for boys in the Asylum:

> We have nice little boys from 8 to 12 years whom we would like to adopt into good Catholic families. They are bright and intelligent and with some education, and it is to the interest of any good family to adopt one of these little boys, and bring them up as their own, and perhaps a future great credit will reflect upon their benefactors.[46]

In an effort to advance the adoption process, the Orphanage participated in what might be termed a "trial run program" where

174

local families agreed to host a boy in their home with the hope and desire to make the placement more permanent. Extant data shows that some of these placements worked quite well while, unfortunately, others were unsuccessful. One typical success story read: "Boys are real well. Give satisfaction. [Parent] wishes to take adoption papers for both. Wishes them to take his name." A similar story was related about two brothers:

> Had a pleasant surprise today. One of our boys...called and looked well and prosperous. Was placed out June 29/09 to...in Avon, N.Y. His brother Clarence was with him. Clarence was sent to W[orking] B[oys] Home, Sept 21/07. He also looked well and prosperous. Both are working. Both came on Oct 1, 1903. Poor boys from PA.

Unfortunately, success was not always possible. One entry in the "Record of Adoption" reads: "Ran away a few days after going to the above address—a wild boy. Do not know where he is." Another case was similar: "Said William is consistently changing; on the move he calls it, isn't satisfied with them. Does not know where he is most of the time."[47]

Religious Training at St. Joseph's Orphan Asylum

St. Joseph's Asylum was applauded for its work in the education and social adjustment of its residents; however, one of its lesser-known, but in Father Baker's mind, more important offerings, was its religious program. Baker's strong devotion to the Blessed Virgin Mary under her title of Our Lady of Victory was indeed powerful and central to his life and work. But, as his strong devotion to the Eucharist continued to develop from his days in the seminary, this was in some ways more significant because, it broke new ground in the religious terrain of the day.

The nineteenth century was a period of great Eucharistic devotion, but not, as outlined earlier (see chapter 2), an era that fostered frequent Communion. The American Catholic historian Margaret McGuinness commented, "By the beginning of the twentieth century it was a rare American Catholic parish that did not offer some form of Eucharistic devotion during the course of the liturgical year."[48] Prior to the twentieth century, even faithful Catholics were generally convinced that they should not receive the Eucharist with any great frequency. Indeed, to receive Communion was reserved for special occasions; it was not a privilege to be afforded each time one attended Mass.

The movement toward more frequent reception of the Eucharist, a practice Baker had adopted in the early 1870s, did not blossom until a generation later during the pontificate of Pius X (which lasted from 1903 until 1914). In a series of decrees issued between May 30, 1905, and July 14, 1907, the pope promoted frequent reception of the Eucharist. In *Sacra Tridentina Synodus,* issued on December 20, 1905, he wrote:

> Frequent and daily Communion, as a practice most earnestly desired by Christ our Lord and by the Catholic Church should be open to all the faithful, of whatever rank and condition of life; so that no one who is in the state of grace, and who approaches the Holy Table with a right and devout intention (*recta pinque mente*), can be prohibited therefrom.[49]

Thus, the instruction promoted frequent Communion, asking only that one have the intention to do God's will and not be in a state of mortal sin.[50] In addition to frequent reception of the Eucharist, the pope also advocated lowering the age for First Holy Communion by children. In a decree published on February 14, 1906, he wrote, "It is necessary that children be nourished by Christ before they are dominated by their passions so they can with greater courage resist the assaults of the devil, of the flesh, and of their other enemies, whether internal or external."[51] From this decree arose the more common contemporary practice of first receiving Communion at the age of reason, normally set at seven years.

Despite encouragement from the Holy Father, changing old habits and convincing people of the fruits of frequent Communion was difficult. The transition for most American Catholics required some "innovative" thinking. Virgil Michel, a Benedictine monk from Collegeville, Minnesota, became a leader in demonstrating how the Eucharist could promote social regeneration in the United States. Deriving the foundation of his teaching from the liturgical movement started in late nineteenth-century Europe, and from the initiation of Catholic Action in the United States in the early 1930s, Michel wrote extensively on the importance of the Eucharist as a source of renewal for the American Church. He used deductive reasoning to deliver his message: (1) Pope Pius X said the liturgy was the primary and indispensable source of true Christian spirit; (2) Pope Pius XI said a true Christian spirit is indispensable for social regeneration; therefore, (3) the liturgy is indispensable for social regeneration.[52]

Several other things were done to promote frequent Communion; one was to emphasize how the Eucharist could unite families. A contemporary writer stated, "What a display of active life and faith would soon be witnessed if parents and children would approach the Communion rail regularly, attend Mass frequently, and make the Eucharist the center of their devotion."[53] Mass times at parishes were adjusted so people could satisfy the Eucharistic fast and still receive Communion.[54] Additionally, Eucharistic confraternities, such as the Apostleship of Prayer (Sacred Heart League), were established along with the common practice of Communion breakfasts. The Catholic press also promoted frequent Communion through the publication of numerous books and pamphlets encouraging the practice.[55]

Eucharistic devotion and frequent Communion were also promoted through Eucharistic congresses. Five national Eucharistic congresses were held in the United States between 1895 and 1911. These meetings set the stage for the International Eucharistic Congress held in Chicago in 1926. The majesty and grandeur of the Chicago Congress was captured by Margaret McGuinness:

> Marching in public processions, filling Soldier Field and chartering special trains, Catholics demonstrated to the rest of America that they were a force to be reckoned with. No longer an insignificant minority on the American

scene, Catholics were ready to profess their faith publicly without fear of repercussions.[56]

The church historian Joseph Chinnici, OSF, concluded that the Eucharistic movement in the first half of the twentieth century "was the most vital spiritual movement of American Catholicism in these decades."[57]

Nelson Baker's personal devotion to the Eucharist remained an integral part of his life throughout his priesthood, but the direction set by the pope certainly served as a catalyst to instill in his boys a spirituality similar to his own. Indeed, Thomas Galvin remarked,

> With his usual reverence for Ecclesiastical Superiors and his characteristic docility to their instructions, he [Baker] unhesitatingly complied with the desire of Christ's Vicar on earth. *Roma locuta est, causa finita est* [Rome has spoken, the case is closed]—that settled the affair for him.[58]

Although the end of each day often found Baker quite tired from his many duties, "he was never too tired or too weary to devote at least a half hour before the Blessed Sacrament."[59] He shared his devotion to the Eucharist with religious and priests in the diocese. He encouraged devotion to the Eucharist in a letter to a group of Carmelite Sisters:

> I am enclosing a copy of several very beautiful devotions to Our Lord in the Blessed Sacrament, as your good daughters may be pleased to read from time to time, to encourage them very much in their love for our Dear Blessed Lord.[60]

Father Baker also instilled a love for the Blessed Sacrament into the hearts and heads of his boys, at both St. Joseph's and St. John's. He proudly wrote: "Daily Holy Communion for our little ones is now an established fact. Our orphaned and homeless children approach the Holy Altar daily to receive our Lord in the Most Blessed Sacrament of His love."[61]

The *Annals* and *The Victorian* promoted the practice as well and attributed much of the success of the boys to their frequent reception of Communion: "There can be no doubt that the innumerable blessings both spiritual and temporal that have been ours during the past year have come to us as a reward of our boys' loyalty, love, and remarkable devotion to Our Lord in the Blessed Sacrament."[62]

Father Baker also promoted frequent reception of the Eucharist by providing rewards for greater participation. Boys were granted additional periods of recreation if they demonstrated great love for the Eucharist. Most prominently, Baker held a monthly competition among the classes at St. Joseph's and St. John's centered on Eucharistic devotion. Classes competed to gain the highest percentage of daily Communion among their members. Each month Baker held a ceremony in the Protectory chapel at which a special banner was awarded to the class whose members received the Eucharist most frequently. Baker presented each boy in the winning class with a medal of Our Lady of Victory.[63]

Father Baker was very proud when his boys responded so devotedly to his call to receive Communion more frequently. The "Among the Boys" column in *The Victorian* read, "It has been a consolation to Father Baker to find his boys devoted to the Most Blessed Sacrament. Most of them receive Holy Communion every day and this is one of the things that seems to keep Father Baker young."[64] One local newspaper commented:

> It was always the subject for ecclesiastical comment in praise of Father Baker that in the cluster of buildings at the corners in Lackawanna upwards of 600 communions were received each day, making a total of more than 220,000 a year, a rather splendid record for institutions in a small parish.[65]

Ten years later *The Victorian* commented again: "His [Baker's] greatest consolation is to see his boys receive Holy Communion."[66]

Nelson Baker's love for the Eucharist and his desire to instill this same love into his boys was clear, but it is not equally evident that the venerable priest stressed frequent reception of the

Sacrament of Penance. It is at least worth noting that in all his many comments about the importance of the Eucharist, there is no accompanying emphasis on the need for proper preparation via Confession to receive Holy Communion. Most probably, in an age when people regularly—many as often as weekly—confessed their sins, the need to emphasize sacramental Penance was not considered important. Rather, it was assumed that people would only receive if they believed they were spiritually prepared.

St. Joseph's daily routine, educational opportunities, and religious regimen received a severe blow on January 9, 1916. That day a fire destroyed the upper floors of the Asylum and caused significant water damage to other parts of the home. The immediate crisis required that the boys be lodged temporarily in Baker's other Institutions. Initially, 97 younger children were placed at the Infant Home; 131 older children were sent to St. John's Protectory.[67] Seemingly unflappable by the setback, Baker diverted funds earmarked for the ongoing expansion of the Infant Home (which later became the Maternity Hospital) to initiate repairs at St. Joseph's. By 1918, the building was restored to full-service operations.[68]

Our Lady of Victory Farm and Camp Baker

Nelson Baker's Institutions provided boys from infancy through high school (and even beyond, through the Working Boys Home) with the home environment, education, and religious foundation that would allow them to take their place as upstanding Christian men in American society. Baker's program was, objectively speaking, sufficiently inclusive to meet its mission, but the wise priest saw significant advantage in adding one more dimension. Capital necessary to feed some six hundred boys, plus possibly eighty to one hundred nurses and religious sisters and brothers, was significant. As a way to lower costs, provide food, and help the boys gain valuable experience, Baker operated Our Lady of Victory Farm, just south of the Institutions on Martin Road.

The farm, approximately 270 acres, was part of a land purchase made in 1856. A small-scale farm was in operation on the land until Baker realized the possibilities, both financially and educationally, that the property could bring. He transformed the terrain for his specific use: a significant portion of the land was for crops, but pasture was also necessary. In 1914, Baker reported the farm had 80 head of cattle, 150 hogs, 350 chickens, and 8 horses. The next year he reported the farm's productivity as 31,027 gallons of milk; 50,317 pounds of beef; 22,262 pounds of pork; 600 bushels of potatoes; 960 bushels of oats; and 80 tons of fodder corn. This was sufficient for his needs and provided some surplus for sale to local residents. Baker was able to report that the farm "achiev[ed] a substantial profit for the year."[69] A few years later the farm's productivity seemed greater with 45 Holstein cows producing 130 gallons of milk daily, and 1,500 laying hens producing 900 eggs per day.[70]

The addition of Our Lady of Victory Farm was complemented by an additional source of summer recreation for the boys. In July 1925, Camp Turner, a diocesan summer facility, was opened in the Allegheny Mountains near Bradford, Pennsylvania, approximately eighty-five miles south of Buffalo. The camp was initially under the direction of Monsignor Edmund Britt, chancellor of the diocese.[71] Although the data that remains is not very specific, it appears that a similar recreation facility, Camp Baker, was established in East Eden, New York, in the spring of 1936.[72] The camp, located about twelve miles south of Baker's Institutions in Lackawanna, was forty-four acres of land, through which ran a beautiful creek. The facility boasted a swimming pool (similar to that at St. John's), a large common area, and several cabins. During the summers, the boys in groups of approximately sixty spent two weeks at the camp, participating in baseball, swimming, and other sports, as well as simply enjoying the beauty of nature. Speaking of Camp Baker, Brother Stanislaus stated, "It's the best investment we have ever made. It makes the boys happy and that's what we want."[73]

St. John's Protectory

St. John's Protectory, the brother institution to St. Joseph's Orphan Asylum, was administered through the Society for the Protection of Destitute Roman Catholic Children. The annual reports of this society present a dramatic picture of the magnitude of the ministry that Nelson Baker provided directly to children and, by extension, to the whole of Western New York. In review of the numbers of children, of the expense to run the operations in the various Institutions, and, possibly most significant, of the debt incurred each year, one wonders how the whole operation continued to function so well throughout Baker's extremely long life. Extant records show that while population at the Institutions fluctuated, operational expenses and debts continued to climb with time. While the populations in St. Joseph and St. John's remained relatively stable, the number of babies and young children present in the Infant Home varied greatly, thus creating inconsistencies in numbers of children served.

An appraisal of the society's annual reports that survive, a portion of which was generally published in the *Annals*, provides significant insight into the operations of the Institutions. The 1915 report states that the Our Lady of Victory Institutions assisted 1,704 children: 856 partly assisted by public funds, 284 partly assisted by private funds, and 568 supported completely by the society. Expenses for the year were $125,576.34, with a deficit of $62,396.53.[74] In 1919, the report states that 1,439 children—477 partially supported by public funds, and 962 totally supported by the society—were serviced at an annual expense of $206,520.60. By 1926, the population was 1,355, with 298 supported by public funds, 296 partially supported by private funds, and 761 fully supported by the society. That year's expenses ran $271,738.87; the debt was $119,886.64. In 1928 and 1929, the population in the Institutions remained relatively the same, but expenses rose significantly and, consequently, the debt—$168,929.90 in 1928 and $203,947.66 in 1929.[75]

In the 1930s, the annual reports actually show population in retreat, partially due to lower numbers at St. Joseph's and St. John's, but expenses and debts continued to be significant. In 1931, 867 children were assisted: 169 through public funds, 237 partially funded privately, and 461 fully supported by the society. Expenses that year were $476,500.74; the debt incurred was $292,415.29. In 1933, the population was down to 759, but a debt of $161,836.61 remained. In 1935, the last full year of Father Baker's life, 541 children were served—40 with public funds, 35 partially privately funded, and 464 supported by the society; they incurred a debt of $185,575.[76] After Baker's death, the numbers in the Institutions dropped dramatically. For example, St. John's went from a population of approximately 350 in 1936 to 170 in 1937.[77]

The numbers reported by the *Annals* and *The Victorian* force one to wonder how Baker was able to annually raise sufficient funds to keep the Institutions alive and functioning properly. No records exist to allow one to determine the sources of Baker's benefactions. Subscribers to the *Annals* and *Victorian*, as members of the Association of Our Lady of Victory, had always been the backbone. With the passing of time, the expansion of the Institutions, and Baker's greater influence and more widespread knowledge of his work, it is certainly plausible that more benefactors to his Institutions were gained. However, it seems highly unlikely that the huge debts just described could have been erased simply by annual subscriptions or even significant donations. Some additional and consistent source of revenue, such as real estate holdings or similar, would have been necessary to sustain such a massive operation. Indeed, in 1934, Baker reported, "The population of our neighborhood is growing so much that we have erected 15 houses, all of which are occupied and which bring us a fair-sized income each year." It is probable that a similar scenario was present earlier.[78] While this comment gives some insight, a clear picture that paints all the details on Baker's development efforts is simply not available. While this mystery exists, the bottom line remains that the number of children serviced and Baker's ability to overcome significant annual debts demonstrates an accomplishment far beyond the capabilities of most people. Between his commitment to ministry and his exceptional faith, Nelson Baker always managed to meet his goals and the needs of those around him.

Consideration of the financial situation at St. John's helps to place in context the exceptional achievements at the Protectory during the first third of the twentieth century. Throughout this period the institution was staffed by the Brothers of the Holy Infancy and Youth of Jesus and by the Sisters of St. Joseph, with the former serving as the anchor. The numbers of Brothers at the Institution varied, but averaged approximately fifty, serving principally as teachers in the trade school and supervisors in the dormitories. Their ministry at times led them to use corporal punishment on the boys, a response that was completely antithetical to Baker's philosophy of how to deal with unruly boys.[79] Sisters of St. Joseph, while serving in a more limited capacity, were nonetheless truly important in teaching boys in the upper grades and preparing them for the New York State Regents Examinations.[80]

Education at St. John's, as was the case at St. Joseph's, was a central daily activity and provided the basic skills boys needed for their future lives. The boys received a basic education at the hands of the Brothers of Holy Infancy, but from the outset the strength of the educational system was training in technical trades. Education in trades took a significant leap forward in 1903 when a massive four-story L-shaped addition was made to the Protectory. The addition allowed training in the fields of plumbing, gas fitting, steam fitting, carpentering, tailoring, shoe making, brick laying, lathing, plastering, blacksmithing, and painting.[81]

Trades education was primary at St. John's, but a small secondary school was available to its residents. Originally, only those boys who demonstrated potential were allowed to attend Our Lady of Victory Academy. Thus, since many boys "fell through the cracks" of the education system, Baker saw a need to expand the standard education beyond the elementary level, leading to the inauguration of a high school program in 1932. One year later, *The Victorian* described the secondary school curriculum: "The course conducted at the School is the classical course in accordance with the New York State Board of Regents. The boys are taught Latin, literature, biology, algebra, civics, religion, and elocution. The teachers are Brothers of the Holy Infancy."[82]

St. John's was not spared from its share of problems. On January 20, 1908, eight years prior to the devastating fire at St. Joseph's, a similar conflagration gutted a large portion of the newly built trades' school at the Protectory. The original fire was quite small, which led residents to believe the Protectory's internal fire squad could extinguish it, but the inability to pump water to the third-floor location of the fire led to a roaring conflagration. Normally one hundred boys were in this area of the building, but fortunately they were attending classes at the time. Estimated damage to the facility was $100,000.[83]

The Protectory's other area of concern was its relationship to the State of New York, but concerns raised were minimal compared to that of St. Joseph's. Extant records showed that annual state inspections of the former institution were, in fact, quite favorable. The one problematic year was 1920. Charles Johnson of the State Board of Charities outlined his concerns to Bishop Turner:

> The needs existing in the personal care and training of the children are those in which we are particularly interested and we shall be more than glad to discuss with you the possibilities for improvement in the work of manual and industrial training and recreational and social activities of the institution.[84]

The satisfactory negotiation of various difficulties and challenges at St. John's was noticed by observers inside and outside Baker's fold. Cardinal James Gibbons of Baltimore, who died in 1921, offered Baker words of congratulations for his "good and great work." The Buffalo diocesan newspaper spoke of the "herculean effort being made at Father Baker's to fulfill the sacred trust of protecting the homeless child and training [him] to become a fit and worthy citizen of this great republic."[85] Speaking of St. John's, the historian Thomas Donahue wrote, "Under the care of Father Baker this institution has grown to be one of the model protectories of the United States." Possibly the greatest compliment was made by Thomas Galvin, CSsR. Speaking of the transformative effect that Baker's Institutions had on the youth they served, he wrote: "They came as convicts and left as converts. They came with hatred for authority and left with a reverence for law and order. They came as reckless and daredevils, and left as self-respecting young men."[86]

Education and Mission Parishes

Nelson Baker's work with youth, manifested through his major Institutions of the Infant Home, St. Joseph's Orphan Asylum,

185

and St. John's Protectory, was the ministry that captured the attention of all in Western New York and carried his name and reputation far and wide. One must not forget, however, that Father Baker was a pastor responsible for the day-to-day needs of his faithful flock, who had no need for the services that made him famous. Since education was obviously important to him, based on the time and energy he placed into its establishment and growth in the Institutions, it should be no surprise that he placed equal emphasis on educating the youth of his own parish.

St. Patrick's School, serving children in his parish, was established in 1895. Housed in a relatively small two-story building, the school served 56 students in 1896; by 1901, the student population was 128. Enrollment at the school continued to climb, reaching 296 in 1904, but dropped to 150 in 1906, due to the establishment in West Seneca (about three miles from St. Patrick's) of St. Charles School, staffed by the Sisters of Mercy. In 1906, St. Patrick's School was renamed Our Lady of Victory School.[87]

Throughout the remaining years of the Progressive Era, enrollment at Our Lady of Victory School, staffed by the Sisters of St. Joseph, remained relatively stable, along with the number of religious serving as teachers.[88] In 1908, student population was 234, with four Sisters as teachers. By 1921, however, a new school building welcomed 371 students, who were taught by eight Sisters of St. Joseph. Throughout the 1920s and into the first six years of the 1930s, student enrollment and numbers of religious as teachers rose slowly, reaching 623 students and eleven Sisters of St. Joseph in 1936.[89]

In 1921, Our Lady of Victory School was complemented by the addition of a much-needed high school, Our Lady of Victory Academy. This high school, again staffed by the Sisters of St. Joseph, served graduates from the elementary school plus the most talented from St. Joseph's and the brightest and best behaved from St. John's.[90] The new school building, half of which served the elementary grades and the other half the Academy, was located on South Park Avenue, just south of St. Patrick's Church. Baker was quite pleased with this addition to his educational apostolate: "Our new high school has been very successful and we have graduated nearly all of our fourth year class." The next year he boasted that twenty-six out of twenty-seven students passed the State Board of Regents Examinations. However, he had to admit that the school was over-crowded. Thus, in 1930, with the approval of Bishop Turner, an addition was made to the building,[91] adding 67 percent to the original structure and costing $40,000. In January 1933, a second addition to the Academy section of the school was opened.[92]

Clearly, Father Baker was most concerned with the education of the youth in his parish and Institutions, but this did not mean his endeavors in this field were sufficient for all. The need for a parish and school to service the many and varied peoples who flocked to West Seneca to work in the burgeoning steel industry was apparent from the first years of the new century. Thus, in 1903, St. Charles Borromeo Parish opened, with Father John F. Ryan serving as the first pastor. Church and school occupied the same building; the church located upstairs and the school downstairs. For some years the parish was active, serving several different ethnic groups. However, with the establishment of several national parishes in the area, especially after 1917, large sections of the parishioner base at St. Charles were lost. For this reason primarily, and the onset of the Great Depression along with the consequent loss of income, the church and school were closed in 1929.[93]

The closure of St. Charles Borromeo School, coupled with Lackawanna's increasingly polyglot population, created a need for a new Catholic school. Observing the situation, Baker pressed his bishop to start a school for the many children in the area, suggesting the Felician Sisters as the responsible community because of their experience in working with diverse peoples. Thus, in December 1930, William Turner wrote to Mother Mary Angelina, superior of the local Felician community in Buffalo, asking her Sisters to staff a new school using the old facilities at St. Charles. He told her: "Monsignor Baker is very much in favor of this arrangement, and as he knows the neighborhood much better than I do, I suggest that you consult with him before you submit your answer."[94] After consultation with Mother Mary Bonaventure, the superior general, the Sisters agreed to the proposal to open a school "for the poorest of the poor in ethnic parishes which could not afford an educational institution."[95]

The Our Lady of Victory Annex School, also referred to as the American Catholic School, opened on January 5, 1931. Sister Mary Sylvina Perska (superior and principal), Sister Mary Felicita Lewandowska, and Sister Mary Amalia Trybus were teachers, and Sister Maryann Tokarczyk, a postulant, was assigned to domestic duties. During the first week, 47 students were present, but by June, 175 were in enrolled in six different grade levels and represented seventeen separate nationalities. Initially the school used the abandoned St. Charles Borromeo classrooms.[96] But almost from day one, Baker realized that the facilities would not be adequate for the future needs of the Annex School. Thus, on March 30, 1931, construction began on a new school. Built rapidly, the new two-story brick building—with twelve lighted classrooms, a library, an office, and a basement trade school, and costing $53,150—was ready for use on August 30, 1931. While the new school was under construction, Baker also realized the makeshift convent for the Sisters, which was the rather dilapidated former rectory at St. Charles, needed renovation. The remodeled convent sported six private bedrooms, a recreation room, and a dining room.[97]

The partnership in ministry between Nelson Baker and the Felician Sisters was appreciated on both sides. Mother Angelina was happy to be a part of Baker's team: "Thanking you again, Rt. Rev. Monsignor for all you did and are doing for the Sisters and the children. I consider it a great privilege to have my Sisters belong to Father Baker's Big Family."[98] In gratitude for the Sisters' willingness to unselfishly engage this new apostolate, Baker responded:

> Anything which I have furnished the Sisters and children during the month of January have all been as a small donation towards their comfort and I would like to retain the privilege of giving them, from time to time, something a little extra to add to their pleasure and comfort, as we are so happy to have the Sisters there [Our Lady of Victory Annex School] and we cannot show sufficiently our gratitude.[99]

The Annex School grew rapidly over the next few years. In September 1931, 390 students were welcomed to the new school;

by June 1932, 470 students from nineteen nationalities were enrolled.[100] Baker was highly satisfied with this new apostolate, writing to Mother Angelina, "I have been very much pleased so far with our school under the care of your good and devoted Sisters. We had a splendid session, the first one, and I'm quite sure the second will be even better." Baker's prediction proved true as, during the first half of the 1930s, enrollment leveled off at approximately 550 students.[101] As late as December 1935, he continued to express his gratitude: "We are so happy to know that your Sisters are so successful in our school in Lackawanna…and we cannot thank you enough for their constant and lovely acts of kindness."[102]

The main function of Our Lady of Victory Annex School was to provide Catholic education for the myriad ethnic groups that populated Western Lackawanna. However, as part of Father Baker's outreach to the African American community (see chapter 10), the school also doubled as a parish. Beginning shortly after the new school was completed and continuing for the remainder of Baker's life, each Sunday morning Masses were celebrated at 9 a.m., principally for black Catholics, and 11 a.m. for whites of various nationalities. Baker explained that his intent was not segregation but rather "to offer Black Americans an identity and full participation in services geared to their cultural needs."[103]

Besides the founding of educational institutions, Father Baker was also responsible for the establishment of two mission churches. In 1906, he founded Our Mother of Good Counsel parish and school in Blasdell. The school welcomed forty-four students and two Sisters of St. Joseph as teachers. Mission status for the parish was short-lived; in 1908, it gained autonomy with Father Lawrence Fell as pastor.[104] Then, in September 1920, Our Lady of Victory Mission Church was started on Abbott Road, to serve Italian and Polish immigrants. Baker celebrated the first Mass at the Mission on the Feast of All Saints, November 1, 1920. Two years later, a school opened at the Mission with the Brothers of the Holy Infancy and Youth of Jesus as teachers. The school was "prompted by the urgent need for an agency of this kind to meet the spiritual requirements of the many children in that vicinity."[105] During the week the church building doubled as a school.

The school and parish grew, but five years later, on April 1, 1929, a freak tornado destroyed the mission church and school. Baker wasted no time in making plans to rebuild. He rapidly received authorization from the bishop to make an appeal for funds to rebuild. On October 12, 1929, the cornerstone for the new church was laid. According to the parish history, the new chapel was ready for use in late November 1929.[106] In 1932, a new school was completed at a cost of slightly over $40,000. By the time of Baker's death, the school educated 102 students with five Brothers as teachers. Unfortunately, after Baker's death the Brothers could no longer sustain their commitment to the school, which was forced to close.[107]

Conclusion

During the first three decades of the twentieth century, Nelson Baker's Our Lady of Victory Institutions continued to provide a safe and wholesome life for thousands of boys. Never one to rest on his laurels, Baker continued to expand and improve his services, especially in the realm of education and trades training. He sought to build up American Catholics who were proud of their faith and their nation, an idea consistent with the general Catholic trend of the era that stressed "muscular Catholicism." The well-rounded Catholic boy was educated in the three R's, but also in the faith and in American culture. Baker sought to make life for his boys as normal as was possible in an institutional setting. Sports, summer camp, farm work, and various outings into Buffalo for picnics and special events helped to soften strong-willed youth and round off the edges of sharp personalities. Baker's work seemingly always caught the eye of the public, but the view was not always positive. Thus, Nelson Baker entered into the "battle of his life," with the State of New York, one based on principles and faith. He would not lose this fight.

CHAPTER 8

Struggles with the State Office of New York (1921–1936)

In 1882, when Father Baker arrived at Limestone Hill as superintendent of St. Joseph's Orphan Asylum and St. John's Protectory, these Institutions, while having been in existence for more than twenty years, were still in many way, in their infancy. During the remainder of the nineteenth and the first quarter of the twentieth centuries, Baker liquidated the debt; built significant additions; enhanced educational, religious, and recreational programs; and constructed a new Infant Home and General Hospital. Through these efforts, Baker and his Our Lady of Victory ministries became household names in Buffalo and gained respect from many individuals and groups, locally and across the nation. Baker's pioneering efforts, while respected by the faithful in Buffalo, generated significant concern from state officials in New York and led to the most significant crisis of his long and faithful ministry. The crisis was created when two vastly different philosophies with respect to care for children, most especially adoption policies, clashed. Even within American Catholicism, Father Baker was a maverick in many of his methods. While Baker received significant and constant support from his local ordinary, Bishop William Turner, this fight with the State of New York also demonstrated the favored status he had fought for, and secured, within the diocese and the local population as a result of his dedication to youth.

Orphans in Buffalo

Orphans and abandoned children were rather common in late nineteenth-century America, especially in large port cities like New York and Boston. Some of these children were offspring of parents who had died at sea during the process of immigration, or from disease or accident. Others came from hardworking families who simply could not afford to raise them. Still others were simply abandoned by one or both parents.

This situation generated a response from Protestant, Jewish, and Catholic communities. By far the best known response was that of Reverend Charles Loring Brace of New York, a young minister from a Calvinist background. Upon observing this tidal wave of abandoned children, he said, "Children were ruining the city and the city was ruining children." In 1853, after his return from Europe where he was appalled to see hordes of homeless children roaming the streets, Brace and a small group of social reformers founded the Children's Aid Society, a group that promoted the philosophy of "placing out" orphan children. He believed that a program that could deliver these abandoned youth to proper families, especially childless couples, would be helpful to both groups. He once stated, "The family is God's Reformatory; and every child of bad habits who can secure a place in a Christian home is in the best possible place for improvement."[1]

In 1854, Brace's Children's Aid Society sponsored the first "Orphan Train," which arrived in Dowagiac, Michigan, with forty-six children aboard. Between 1857 and 1929, some 150,000 children were sent from the East to the Midwest and Far West regions of the United States to begin new lives. In towns and cities where the Children's Aid Society planned to send the children, advertisements were generally placed in local papers a few weeks prior to the train's arrival. A typical advertisement read: "WANTED: HOMES FOR CHILDREN, OF VARIOUS AGES AND OF BOTH SEXES AND WELL-DISCIPLINED." The notice listed the Children's Aid Society's terms: "Education, religious training, and treatment IN EVERY WAY AS MEMBERS OF THE FAMILY."[2]

Father Baker strongly rejected the Orphan Train project and the basic philosophy upon which it was based. His main concern was that children would lose their faith; the Orphan Train project was the perfect machine for Brace to proselytize youth. Baker had addressed this issue with respect to his own Institutions. Conscious of the fact that protecting the faith of his boys was of paramount importance, Father Baker wrote:

> We must see to it, that these [St. Joseph's and St. John's] are institutions for the protection and proper training of our youth. *This matter must be grappled with* [emphasis Baker] or else thousands upon thousands more of our little ones will be lost to the Church.[3]

As early as 1893, he began to work with Catholics in large cities who are "our own agents in the courts and competing for the possession of these children, and then striv[ing] to place them in Catholic homes."[4] In an essay addressing both the clergy and the laity, Baker summarized his argument:

> Our friends in our large cities, who are engaged in the same cause, have organized to compete with the enemies' gigantic machinery who have made a business of obtaining our homeless little children by every means in their power, shipping them in car-load lots, to the far West, and distributing them into families who will certainly not rear them in the true Faith in which they were born.[5]

Father Baker's Institutions to assist orphans were complemented by other initiatives in Buffalo, both secular and religious in their origins. In 1838, Louis LeCouteulx bequeathed land for the express purpose to aid orphans. By 1850, a group of trustees, for what became the Buffalo Orphan Asylum, began to realize this goal. The New York State legislature granted $20,000 to initiate the project. The sale of some private property and additional gifts from benefactors added to this basic fund. In 1852, the asylum was opened on Virginia Street; in 1878, an infants' ward was added through a generous benefaction of $10,000.[6]

The Catholic Church also assisted orphans in the City of Buffalo. The same cholera epidemic of 1849 that had led to the foundation of St. Joseph's Orphan Asylum was the catalyst that prompted the Sisters of Notre Dame in their efforts to aid homeless youth. On September 8, 1852, the Sisters took charge of a small structure on Pine Street to house orphans. Six years later, the pastor of St. Mary's Parish on Broadway invited the Sisters to establish a more permanent home for these children. Twenty years later, in 1873, nine German national parishes in Buffalo, championed by the efforts of Father Elias Schauer, CSsR, pastor of St. Mary's Church, pooled their resources to finance and supervise an orphanage principally for German orphans. The institution was incorporated under the laws of the State of New York in 1874. The facility was formally opened on October 1, 1875, with the Sisters of St. Francis given supervision of the home.[7]

Nelson Baker vs. the State of New York

The New York State Board of Charities was established in 1867 by an act of the legislature. The rationale given for this establishment was twofold: (1) the protection of individuals who, because of some misfortune, could not be properly maintained by their family and, therefore, had become dependent on some form of organized charity; and (2) the protection of the integrity of funds, either raised by taxes or contributed by organized private charitable societies for the relief of individuals. In order to carry out this mandate the board was given two basic powers: (1) to visit charitable institutions, and (2) to report to the legislature.[8]

The board realized that abuse of orphans had occurred in the past due to general indifference and specific failures on the part of some public officials. In a state report published in February 1900, the lackadaisical attitude taken toward the orphan problem was addressed this way:

> Too much of this work, however, as it has been my experience to find, has been carried on in so indifferent and careless manner as to be to a considerable extent a source of reproach to many who have been engaged in it, and it accordingly seems to me that those who really desire the children's good should constantly be upon

the alert to secure correction of the evils and abuses too frequently incident in this form of work, in order that they who believe in the principle may also repose confidence in the practice.

The same document addressed the failures of individuals, most especially public officials, toward orphans:

On the one hand there are a number of private incorporations of high standing, and not a few public officials also, who from the best and most disinterested of motives are ready to carry on this work in that intelligent manner which is productive of beneficent results.... On the other hand, however, there are indifferent public officials, serving in some instances, perhaps a too niggardly constituency, who have apparently been interested solely to save money for their localities or to rid themselves of embarrassing charges.[9]

From the State's perspective, one key ingredient in the proper care of orphans was appropriate disclosure of information and accurate record-keeping. Rules adopted by the board in June 1927 called for the preservation in permanent form of information regarding each orphan, including name, sex, color, place and date of birth, and last residence, as well as extensive information about the father and mother of the child. The records were to be properly indexed and ready for inspection at any time.[10]

The proper placing out of children was also addressed by the board. William P. Letchworth, former president and longtime commissioner with the State Board of Charities, addressed this issue:

In the placing out of children two objects are to be considered—one is to save the county the expense of maintaining them, and the other is to save the children and make society better. The last consideration is by far the most important. If abandoned infants and street waifs, through the medium of good homes, can be converted into good citizens, the whole framework of society will be strengthened. If, on the other hand, dependent children are allowed to mature in an immoral atmosphere, pauperism and crime are increased. It is, therefore, of the utmost importance that the work of the county agents should not be perfunctorily or hurriedly performed, because of the large amount of it there is to do, or to save the county expense. It should be performed in the most painstaking and conscientious manner. For any child placed in an immoral home the public may later on be burdened with a multitudinous pauper and criminal progeny springing forth.[11]

Prevailing American Catholic views on the general issue of orphans and the specific question of placing out or adoption evolved during the Progressive Era, becoming more in line with the position held by the State. Although there were some who, like Nelson Baker, maintained that big institutions remained the best way to handle the large population of orphans, most Catholics involved with this type of apostolic work shifted their philosophy away from using orphanages to finding individual homes.[12] Many Catholic social activists at the dawn of the twentieth century seriously questioned the value of institutional homes for orphans.[13] Many of these facilities were so severely crowded that no possibility for individual love, care, and concern existed. This basic philosophy of placing out was adopted in 1898 through the foundation of the Catholic Home Bureau of New York. The bureau received the wholehearted support of Archbishop Michael Corrigan:

> The project of establishing a Catholic Home Bureau impresses me favorably and seems likely to accomplish good results. In the first place it will prevent overcrowding of our institutions, and relieve us of the care of many children who are now dependent on charity and not allow them to be self-reliant.[14]

The Catholic Home Bureau's philosophy with respect to the care of orphans became the preferred practice for ministry to homeless youth in the American Church. Beginning in New York, similar societies were established in Washington, DC, and in Detroit.[15] One contemporary observer wrote of this transformation: "As a permanent home for the early years of dependent children, the orphan asylum should go out of business. Its day is past. It is not a real childhood home and cannot by any courtesy of speech claim to be such."[16] John O'Grady, the historian of American Catholic charities, similarly commented: "There was no use in arguing that the institutional home could satisfy all the requirements of a child caring program. The old methods of placing children out from institutions were now discredited."[17]

The prevailing evolution of thought concerning orphans, even coming from Catholic sources, did not sway Father Baker from his staunch belief in the efficacy of orphanages. In a report he filed in February 1927, he noted that the "new method" had been a dismal failure in some places in Western New York. He referenced a situation in Boston, New York (a town southeast of Buffalo), where children placed with individual families were not provided proper sleeping or hygienic facilities. He asked Bishop Turner if he could write to the State in order to contradict statements made in recent documents issued from Albany. Baker feared that state policy would lead to the placement of some children in environments that were not conducive to proper growth and maturation, which were opportunities for the children to abandon their faith. Additionally, he rejected the State's claim that orphanages were obsolete. He wrote Turner:

> I would like to prove that the advantages of the orphanage to the orphan child are vastly superior to any that could be furnished by private families where a child might be boarded....I feel it is an injustice to our institutions and their faithful teachers, who have labored so long and so faithfully to permit these misrepresentations to go abroad without being in some manner corrected, as they are so evidently false.[18]

Nelson Baker's most significant battle to maintain his philosophy in the proper treatment of children was played out from the early 1920s until his death, in a long and sometimes rather heated

197

battle with the State of New York. While general procedures were at stake, it was the specifics of how Baker operated the Infant Home that became a great source of conflict and most assuredly consternation on his part. While, as described earlier, discrepancies had been noted at St. Joseph's, the problems at the Infant Home were much deeper; they drew criticism from the State and caused internal dissension within the Diocese of Buffalo.

Significant concerns from state officials about the Infant Home first surfaced in the mid-1920s. A report in April 1923 outlined inadequacies in staffing and an improper diet for children. The report also noted that the Home did not follow Board of Health regulations with respect to monthly examination of children. At the time of the inspection the census was 193 children, but the capacity was only 182. The report read:

> It is evident...that the number of persons engaged in the work is too small to give the children proper care. Those engaged in the work are not in most instances, properly trained and they are inadequately supervised. A larger staff is also an important need....Although the children are in good condition as to cleanliness, the need of more individual attention and study is apparent. The inadequacies of the staff are apparent. In addition, the general physical condition of the children could probably be improved by more careful study of individual diets.[19]

The 1924 report complimented the Infant Home for complying with state laws and regulations, and it noted improvements in administration of the Home, but one year later previous problems recurred and new problems arose.[20] In a harsh tone, the report stated:

> The defects of administration...may presumably be the cause of much of the illness and poor physical appearance of the babies and of lack of proper care and neglect of them through the incompetence of the caretakers and failure to establish proper methods of child care and even ordinary sanitary standards.[21]

The many problems noted in the April 1925 report led to a reinspection in November of the same year. While inspectors were pleased with administrative enhancements and noted that "the improvement in the health and general appearance of the children is remarkable," this second report raised new problems with record-keeping, specifically the Home's failure to disclose information. The report read, "The records are still meager concerning the history for the children." In a not-so-subtle hint, Charles Johnson, executive director of the State Board of Charities, sent Baker published materials on progressive methods for child care in institutions. The issue of disclosure would keep Baker and the State in a constant battle until the former's death.[22]

The State of New York's significant concerns over operations and policies at the Infant Home continued to increase during the latter half of the 1920s. The 1927 annual report noted, "The institution is overcrowded in departments occupied by the youngest groups of children." Possibly more problematic, however, was the fear that the children's development was being stifled: "In general the mental development of the children is apparently greatly retarded and they are in need of more individual attention." As in the past, the report was also highly critical of the home's shoddy record-keeping, noting that such failures violated regulations published by the State Board of Charities.[23] In March 1928, James Foster, secretary of the New York Department of Charities, wrote to William Turner. Stating that he was "especially interested in the work of this institution [Infant Home]," Foster wished to deliver a copy of a report by Dr. Clara H. Town, director of the Psychological Clinic of the Children's Aid Society in Buffalo. Dr. Town had just completed a study of the Infant Home and identified "children with questionable physical condition or mental status." These, she felt, should be placed in foster homes.[24]

In 1929, the State escalated its attack against Baker and his Infant Home by appealing directly to Bishop Turner for action. Foster petitioned Turner on behalf of children in the Home:

It is, I think, unnecessary to repeat what I have previously written to you as to the dissatisfaction of the State Board of Charities concerning the work of this institution [Infant Home] and of our concern for the welfare of the unfortunate children who are committed to it.[25]

Foster also described a rash of "infections, contusions, lacerations, sprains, infections, and fractures" (112 cases in a population of 350) that occurred at the home. The bishop, in turn, wrote to Baker asking, "Will you kindly write, after inquiry, so I can answer his [Foster's] letter in a way to satisfy him."[26]

Charles Johnson also increased his rhetoric, addressing the bishop with a sense of urgency:

> The policies and standards of this institution [Infant Home] as to the admission of children and treatment of the problems which their mothers present, as to the care of children while in the institution and as to the placement of children in foster homes are all widely at variance from the commonly accepted principles of present-day social work. The very fundamentals of the work [that] is carried on are in contradiction of the ideals of child welfare work as expressed by our best charitable and social work agencies, public and private, including those of all religious denominations.

Johnson asked for a personal meeting with Turner, indicating the importance to rectify problems at the Infant Home as soon as possible: "I feel that the conditions reported by our Inspectors are so serious as regards the welfare of the children for whom these institutions care, that we must discuss them frankly and fully."[27]

While no response from Turner is extant, it *is* clear that the bishop was worried because he consulted legal counsel about the whole issue. Turner's lawyer, Charles O'Connor, told the ordinary that the basic problem of having insufficient personnel to supervise a large number of children was a legitimate concern.[28]

In the 1930s, the tenor of the State's concerns was dampened considerably but was still present. Fear that had been raised in 1927—that the mental development of the children could be compromised because of conditions in the Home—was again voiced in late 1930: "The institution is failing completely to provide for the normal activities of the children and as a result their mental development is seriously retarded....There is little care or training aside from attention to physical needs."[29] By 1936, possibly due to a significantly lower census of children, the State report noted significant improvement in the institution: "A definite effort appears to have been made to better meet the requirements of the rules applicable to child-caring institutions."[30]

Nelson Baker's conflict with the State of New York went beyond the institutions and personalities in Buffalo and Albany. In November 1925, John O'Grady, secretary of the National Conference of Catholic Charities, wrote to Bishop Turner with concerns he had heard raised about "institutions at Lackawanna made by the State Board of Charities." While he stated that Baker's work "will stand out as one of the greatest contributions that has ever been made to Catholic Charities in the United States," he realized that anxiety over the criticism of Baker's institutions had to be removed. In order to achieve this goal, O'Grady volunteered to conduct (with two others) an independent and impartial review of the Institutions. He wrote:

> With your approval I would be glad to make a sympathetic and confidential study of the Lackawanna institutions. I know that such a study would be most helpful to you and Monsignor Baker. In order that it be successful I believe it is necessary that I be given a free hand. I am sure that Monsignor Baker can rely on my prudence and admiration for him to prevent me from doing anything rash.[31]

Turner wrote to Baker about O'Grady's fears and the offer he had made for an independent inspection. In a vote of confidence and support, Turner wrote,

> In regard to Dr. O'Grady's letter I have no wish except to do as you wish. If you are in any way disinclined to have such a "survey," the matter is ended so far as I am concerned, and I will, in such case, send Dr. O'Grady a negative answer.[32]

Baker responded to Turner, telling him such an inspection was "uncalled for and unnecessary."[33] While the immediate concern thus ended, the greater and longer-lasting question of what officials, both inside and outside Church circles, thought of Nelson Baker's philosophy and policies at the Infant Home remained outstanding.

Father Baker's conflict with the State of New York over his operation of the Infant Home began with concerns about overcrowding, lack of staff, and the mental development of the children, but it was the priest's philosophy concerning disclosure that brought the dispute to its boiling point. As described in chapter 5, Baker's whole philosophy was wrapped around the idea of saving children. In order to achieve this basic goal, it was imperative in his mind to provide complete anonymity to women who sought his assistance. William H. Meegan, a fellow priest and head of Buffalo's Catholic Charities' Placing Out Division, articulated Baker's philosophy in a letter to William Turner:

> He seems to feel that the first consideration is the reputation of the mother, especially her family; that every effort should be made to safeguard them especially as they are likely to commit an abortion or suicide if they could not be given this care in secrecy.[34]

This policy of anonymity, however, was repeatedly challenged by state officials for three basic reasons: First, it was contrary to established norms being practiced in secular and religious houses that offered services similar to those of Baker. Second, the policy could prove highly problematic for prospective adoptive parents. And finally, complete disclosure and proper documentation was part of the New York statutes on adoptions. Baker's policy also ran afoul of his fellow priests in the diocese, especially those working in Catholic Charities.

While it was clear almost from the outset that Baker's approach to the question of disclosure was in conflict with both state and fellow Catholic officials, the confrontation began to flare in 1925 over Buffalo diocesan policy with respect to adoptions. Father Baker was hopeful that Catholic Charities could assist his efforts in placing out children from the Infant Home. William Meegan was willing to assist, but suggested to Baker that prospective adoptive parents were more likely to take children if given full information about the mother. In June, Meegan wrote to Baker and presented a hypothetical situation of an adopted child who "has become insane." He asked Baker:

> In general what would you advise with reference to prospective foster parents who are becoming increasingly insistent on adequate information of the child's history before accepting it. It is our thought that many desirable foster homes are going to be procured if they know fully about the child in accordance with the standards of the State Board of Inspection and unless this policy is followed in practice, it may be inadvisable to try to place children....It seems almost essential in honesty to the foster homes that child placing agencies know fully about the children they place.[35]

Baker responded that, while he was pleased that Catholic Charities was willing to assist in the process of placing out of children, his basic policy of nondisclosure must be maintained. He wrote: "In consideration of the confidence placed in us by the mothers of the children, and our promise made to them in the protection of their characters, etc., we cannot be unfaithful to them and hence not divulge that which they hold so sacred." He also told Meegan that should any problem develop with children, "we will carefully permit them to be returned to the Institution and to our care, so that they [adoptive parents] will take no risk in the matter whatsoever."[36]

Baker's refusal to bend and his status in the diocese led Meegan to seek advice from Bishop Turner. Meegan was appreciative of Baker's efforts to safeguard the mothers and in general was sympathetic with Baker's position, but he told the bishop that he believed it was possible to follow state law without disclosing vital information. All records were secured and available only to essential personnel. Additionally, Meegan told the bishop that failure to follow state laws could lead to the revocation of Catholic Charities' license to place children, as well as make the agency guilty of a misdemeanor. Meegan summarized his position:

> It is most important in view of the requirements of Section #1301 of the State Charities Law, and in accordance with the recognized standards of placing-out work, that the department obtain as complete history as possible of each child referred for placement; institutions referring children should be required to institute means and to make a complete preliminary investigation of cases referred by individuals and further investigation if thought necessary in institutional cases.[37]

He concluded, "We are in a dilemma over these conflicting instructions and…respectfully submit the whole matter to you for [a] decision."[38]

The State entered this confrontation by its clear rejection of Baker's philosophy, and James Foster pressed his case with Meegan:

> To permit an unmarried mother to enter the institution where a child is born and to leave the child there and go her way without careful inquiry being made into the case is unfair to the mother and her child and is more than likely to deprive them of the kind of help that they most need. The idea that secrecy is the most important thing in cases of this kind is entirely out of date.[39]

He further told Meegan that a general agreement on the need for complete information was standard practice throughout the country. He concluded, "This principle is so well-established that it seems almost unnecessary to cite authorities for it."[40]

Father Baker wrote to Bishop Turner, responding to the critique by reasserting his unflinching belief that secrecy as a sacred trust could never be violated. He also addressed Foster's insistence that full disclosure was normative:

> This unnatural custom is neither legal nor practical in caring for these matters where the records of unfortu-

nate young women [are concerned], who, coming here, and reposing to us, [have] perfect confidence that their characters will be protected, and the good names of their families.

Under such circumstances, no Agent or Visitor of any Benevolent or Charitable Association should have the right to examine and copy the names of families for records that should be sacred and afterwards use them to the detriment of the unfortunate mother, her family and her friends.[41]

Baker expressed his hope to the bishop that his operation and that of the Child Placing Department of Catholic Charities might develop further. However, he concluded, "If we are formally obliged to disclose the information we have always held sacred and so inform our patients, it will surely be the beginning of the end."[42]

Turner saw merit in both points of view. He verified the veracity of the State's basic claim, but also acknowledged Baker's significant experience in the field and his wisdom. Therefore, he proposed a compromise whereby Buffalo Catholic Charities would follow state guidelines regarding disclosure, while Baker would be allowed to continue his work at the Infant Home as he had previously done. In August, Bishop Turner informed Baker concerning the first half of his proposed compromise:

> I am deeply concerned over the instructions of the State Board of Charities to the Placing Department concerning the records of children placed out from the institutions. I find, however, these instructions are in accord with the standard requirements of both Catholic and public placing out work. The program for Catholic Child Caring Homes, published by the National Conference of Catholic Charities, maintains [that] these records are essential....This principle seems grounded in justice to the foster parents whom the child placing agency must safeguard....Many other reasons occur to me which show the advantage of having a true history of the child in order to place it intelligently, but we are

205

confronted with the fact that this is necessary to place the children legally. Therefore, I am according to the representatives of the Placing Department the right to interview and communicate with the parents, and consult the records of the children who come to all the child caring homes of the diocese. I have so instructed the Child Placing Department.[43]

Turner believed that the best solution from Baker's perspective was to take the child placement aspect out of the domain of the Infant Home. However, one week later Turner again wrote to Baker proposing the second half of his compromise: "It seems to me that the cause of religion will best be served if you continue to carry on your work for the salvation of unfortunate unmarried mothers in the way you have been conducting it for so many years."[44] Stating that the all-important Catholic principle of safeguarding secrets must be maintained, Turner concluded, "Let our Catholic Charities placing out agency obey the state laws as it must, but with my consent and hearty approval, let *your* work be of increased efficiency and increased benefit to the unfortunate women [emphasis added]." Rather naively, Turner suggested that adoptive parents could forgo detailed information and take the risk of adopting based on data that Baker would make available to them.[45]

Turner's compromise solution may have satisfied his need for a response and mollified the concerns of both Baker and Meegan, but the State's criticism of Baker's policies continued. The 1927 state inspection report of the Infant Home retraced old ground with respect to the need for full disclosure, but James Foster went further in a personal letter to Baker. Taking a different tack, the State Department of Charities secretary raised the issue of moral accountability: "To relieve the mother of responsibility for the care of her child by simply allowing her to leave it and go her way is a thoroughly discredited method and abandoned by all progressive social agencies dealing with such cases."[46]

Two years later, the 1929 report continued to emphasize how Baker's policies were at wide variance with commonly accepted contemporary principles, but it also held out an olive branch, suggesting a possible way out of the impasse:

> I do not see how anything worthwhile can be accomplished to relieve this situation except through a careful study of the work of this institution as it is, of local needs in child welfare work, and of the principles by which the future of the institution should be determined.[47]

The split between Baker and the State of New York continued as an unbridgeable gap for the remainder of his life. Although the 1933 state inspection report spoke of "some improvement," it concluded, "A general policy of the institution has not changed."[48] In January 1936, another compromise of sorts was proposed. The report suggested that, prior to admission, each child's case should be thoroughly investigated to "determine what plan of care is best suited to the needs of the unmarried mother." If an emergency existed, the report continued, the woman should be admitted, but relevant information should be obtained prior to her discharge or the adoption of the child. A preliminary investigation by the State showed that many of the women in the Infant Home had at least one parent if not both who were aware of the situation. Thus, the report concluded, "This being the case, there is little reason for those in charge to feel that in these and similar cases investigation is a violation of confidence."[49] When Father Baker died just a few months later, the impasse remained.

The contentious issue of disclosure was an integral part of the larger concern of child adoptions. It is clear that Bishop Turner was concerned with Baker's adoption policies, for he sought guidance from his legal counsel, Charles O'Connor, on how to proceed. Turner wanted to know if Baker's Institutions were subject to state laws. After his review of the statutes, O'Connor told the bishop that Baker's Institutions were "subject to the Public Health Law and Domestic Relations Law in some matters."[50] Baker, however, defended his operational policy at the Infant Home. Noting that Sisters and nurses always took great care to investigate homes where children were to be placed, including a match of religion, he wrote to Turner, "We have always been very careful and exacting, as to furnishing the very best homes available for our little ones and we feel that we have been most successful."[51]

Charles Johnson continued to remind Turner that the Infant Home's adoption policy had been unsatisfactory for many years. State inspection reports continued to note discrepancies in two major areas: (1) prospective homes were insufficiently investigated, and (2) there was inadequate record-keeping.[52] Thus, the State Board of Charities recommended that the Infant Home cease its adoption program. The January 1929 report stated:

> As the institutional authorities have neither training, experience nor comprehension of placing out work, it is recommended that the placing out activities of this institution be discontinued and that full responsibility for this branch of the work be undertaken by the Buffalo Cath[olic] Char[ities].[53]

While there is no surviving response to the State, Baker did report in the *Annals* that additional inspection people had been hired to investigate prospective adoption parents "to see that they conform to all the requisites demanded by the State Board of Charities."[54] Despite Baker's initiative, the 1930–31 report continued to recommend that adoptions cease at the Infant Home.[55] However, by 1933, some improvement had been noted:

> The work of the placing out department apparently has improved since the last inspection, but more care in the investigation of homes, fuller records, a larger number of favorable references, a more careful fitting of the child to the home and more frequent visits is [*sic*] recommended.[56]

Throughout the confrontation between Father Baker and the State of New York, regarding both issues of disclosure and adoptions, Bishop William Turner gave consistent and unfailing support to his vicar general. In a letter to Charles Johnson, the bishop praised Baker as a person and extolled his work at the Institutions:

You are dealing, not with me, the nominal head of the institutions, but with a saintly man, in his eighty-seventh year, a national figure in the world of charity. We shall soon see, I hope, an end of petty persecution of him in the name of efficiency that is purely material, in that it overlooks the spiritual in view of material interests of the children. So far as concerns the efficiency and real charity, the work of all the institutions of which he is superintendent has been and is marvelously beneficent in accomplishment.[57]

Turner also defended Baker by attacking the inconsistencies of state policy and statutes:

The annual changing of the State Charities Law and kindred legislation makes it difficult for a force trained more particularly in the work of actual charity to comply fully with the frequently changing statistical requirements of theoretical charity and real charity might suffer by the dispensing with their services.[58]

Johnson fired back at Turner, rejecting the accusations and, moreover, speaking of his appreciation for Baker's work and devotion. He placed his critique within this context:

There is no such thing as persecution on our part, petty or otherwise, nor do we and our inspectors fail to appreciate Father Baker's high character, self devotion to the work which he has built up, and the motives which activate him and material success which he has achieved.

It is precisely because of the success of such work as his, which cannot be measured in terms of dollars and cents, brick and mortar, food and clothing, that our inspectors' reports and our letters addressed to you are critical of existing conditions in these institutions.[59]

The confrontation between Father Baker and the State of New York, the one significant trial of opposition he faced during his work with youth, requires some analysis. This author believes that Nelson Baker's heart was unquestionably in the right place. He wanted to save children; that was his bottom line. His discovery of a growing circle of unwanted children, many of whom had been aborted, convinced him that a safe house where women could have their children and maintain anonymity was essential. The bond of trust that developed between a woman and Baker could not be violated; to do so would compromise his whole rationale for the Home. Clearly, as seen by the thousands of women and children assisted by the Infant Home, Baker's policy saved many, many children. As stated, this facility was at least rare, and possibly even unique, in Catholic social outreach. The criticism Baker received from the State Board of Charities accusing him of absolving women of their responsibility for their actions is unjustified. Rather, it seems that he chose compassion over authority, believing that women would learn responsibility through the birth and rearing of their children. The mistake of an unexpected pregnancy had already been made; there was a need to move on and deal with the reality of the situation. Additionally, one could hardly expect a man of his advanced age, who had been operating in one way—with great success and public adulation—to change his procedures so drastically.

It is clear as well, however, that Father Baker was not open to any review of his policies; he kept full control of all avenues of his work. That said, it is not an uncommon attitude for a domestic prelate to possess. Prevailing methods for adoption, including full disclosure of family information for prospective adoptive parents, as understood by both state and religious organizations, did not seem important to him. Edmund J. Butler, executive secretary of the Catholic Home Bureau of New York City, and a contemporary of Baker's, described what had become standard practice in adoption procedures:

> It is necessary before undertaking to place out a child to secure definite information as to his family, religious affiliation, and physical and mental condition. Lack of such information may later create serious problems

detrimental to the interests of the child and his foster parents.

As the details of the history of the child and his parents and the results of the investigation are constantly necessary to meet legitimate inquiries concerning the child and his care or to solve problems or shape methods during the period of supervision, a complete system of records is necessary.[60]

In an article published shortly after his death, Baker was described as two-faced in his ideas. He supported the methods of Catholic Charities of Buffalo, but separated *his* work from the collective. He could not reconcile himself to new ideas. The anonymous author stated:

> He [Baker] did not criticize or find fault with the methods of the new generation. In fact he was willing to lend them his support. He gave his whole-hearted support to the forward-looking program of the Catholic Charities of Buffalo. In his own work, however, he was determined to follow his own ways.[61]

Baker's ideas were based on a policy of trust as absolutely inviolate, choosing compassion over law, and believing that his experience, which he believed demonstrated the soundness of his approach, was of more value than any statute.

This confrontation raises some additional questions that most assuredly arose during the years Father Baker supervised the Infant Home. What was his policy regarding his "contract" with a pregnant woman if she was a minor or was married? Would it be proper to inform parents or husband in such cases? The various annual reports show that many babies died; undoubtedly some mothers must also have died from childbirth or complications. How were such cases handled? This author believes such events were most likely handled on a case-by-case basis. Yet, especially in the case of a minor, parents have a right to know the location and physical condition of their children, especially when service is being rendered by the Church.

211

Nelson Baker's status in the community allowed him to continue his operation as he believed and deemed proper. He had served not only as priest, pastor, and superintendent of the Institutions, but repeatedly as vicar general and twice administrator of the diocese, Baker wielded significant clout within the presbyterate. When one couples this reality with his close friendship with Bishop William Turner, it becomes clear that no one could challenge Nelson Baker. Even though Turner forged a compromise between Baker and Buffalo Catholic Charities on the adoption and disclosure issues, his support for the venerable priest never wavered. Additionally, Baker held the respect and support of thousands of people who had been touched by his work in Lackawanna, not only the youth themselves, but parents and families of these boys, and the many observers who marveled at what he was doing. Baker's methods had been successful, and nobody wanted him to accept a program in which he did not believe. And no one, then or now, could argue with his seemingly miraculous level of success.

Father Baker's ability to maintain his philosophy and keep contradictory forces at bay was dramatically demonstrated after his death. He produced such success with his programs during his life that the State could "overlook" his failures to comply as long as he was alive. Upon his death in July 1936, however, things changed drastically and quickly. Abandoned babies could no longer be left at the Infant Home. The New York State law that forbade the importation of orphaned children external to the state was enforced. However, the ministry that Father Baker provided for single mothers continues today through the work of Baker Victory Services. Pregnant young women are welcomed in a group home setting or at the Dorothy Miller Residence.[62]

Conclusion

Father Baker's ministry to the marginalized of the world was, generally speaking, well appreciated by all peoples and without any serious opposition. Some complaints arose from the State of New York concerning conditions in the Institutions, especially the periodic problem with overcrowding, but there never was an ideological disagreement. Who could argue against a man who was sheltering, educating, and making decent citizens of hundreds of boys —boys who, as a result of various circumstances, found themselves as orphans or wards of the State? However, Baker's non-disclosure policy with respect to his work at the Infant Home created a significant ideological break with the State and even prevailing Catholic practice of the day. Nelson Baker, however, never flinched in continuing to do as he believed best, heedless of the State's mandates. Because of his long-standing commitment to youth, his almost iconic status with many in the local community, and the unswerving support he received from his own bishop, Baker won a prolonged battle with the New York State Office of Charities. The events demonstrate Baker's standing in the community and the power he wielded. While his view was somewhat understandable, his total refusal to bend or negotiate made clear his unwillingness to accept anything but his own way. This same determination would be seen as he engaged the most significant building project of his life: the construction of the Basilica of Our Lady of Victory.

CHAPTER 9

The Basilica of Our Lady of Victory (1921–1926)

Nelson Baker's Lackawanna Institutions for youth literally made the priest's name a household word in Western New York and in many other places across the country. However, there was one more critical part of his master plan, actually the crown jewel, that still needed to be built. While Baker never wrote anything formally about it, his experience at Notre Dame des Victoires in Paris during his 1874 pilgrimage to Rome transformed his life and gave him the inspiration that generated the faith and persistence he manifested in sixty years of priesthood. As mentioned in chapter 8, somewhat overshadowed by the scope and prominence of his work with youth was the fact that Baker was a pastor in Lackawanna for fifty-four years. He inherited St. Patrick's Parish, later adding an elementary school and later still Our Lady of Victory Academy. Additionally, he started mission churches and schools, such as Our Mother of Good Counsel and Our Lady of the Sacred Heart. But Baker wanted to create a truly monumental sanctuary to honor the Mother of God, his patroness and the one whose inspiration had guided his priestly ministry in all respects from the very outset. Exercising his great faith and unshakable belief that God desired it, Baker undertook the design and construction of a massive church of almost surreal proportions, the National Shrine of Our Lady of Victory—a church so immense that its central dome was second only to the Capitol building in Washington, DC. Even today it is the pride of people of faith throughout Western New York.

Initiation of the Project

When Nelson Baker arrived in 1882 as superintendent of the Institutions at Limestone Hill, he brought with him a strong devotion to the Mother of God under her title of Our Lady of Victory. From the time of his first encounter with his devotion during his participation in the 1874 pilgrimage to Rome, Our Lady of Victory was central to his spirituality and foundational to his work, as he placed all endeavors under her patronage. In 1883, under the burden of an oppressive debt incurred through the operations of St. Joseph's and St. John's, he started the Association of Our Blessed Lady of Victory, a unique solicitation by mail that rather remarkably brought the Institutions economic recovery and, therefore, the ability to expand operations in short order. Baker's two major publications, the *Annals* and the *The Victorian*, also found a patron in Mary. Images of Our Lady of Victory were positively ubiquitous. In 1889, when a new chapel was built in St. John's Protectory, a six-foot-high statue of Our Lady of Victory was placed in a prominent position. In 1894, Baker constructed a shrine specific to Our Lady of Victory adjacent to St. John's. Additional statues and other "reminders" of the patronage of Mary, Our Lady of Victory, were found throughout the Institutions.

Father Baker had demonstrated his true love for Mary, yet the one manifestation he truly sought, a church in her honor, eluded him. He had thought of such a project as early as 1906. While the Institutions that identified Baker's work in the Buffalo area were physically immense and generated lots of attention, the church at St. Patrick's was rather small and becoming more and more crowded with increased population, especially as the result of the steel industry at the turn of the century. However, at this time Baker's attention was fixed on the construction of the Infant Home as a way to address a significant moral issue in the community. Nonetheless, Baker's dream of a grand church was germinating. The *Annals* reported, "It is known by Father Baker's best friends that he is ambitious of giving his parish here one of the greatest churches in the world before his earthly career is ended and he is called to his reward for his saintly works."[1]

During the first two decades of the twentieth century, many challenges that required additions to existing Institutions and other concerns occupied Baker's time. In January 1916, as outlined in chapter 7, a devastating fire at St. Joseph's Orphan Asylum forced Baker to delay construction of his Maternity Hospital and concentrate on repairs to the Orphanage. Three months later, on April 8, a fire in the belfry of St. Patrick's Church eventually caused the steeple to collapse. Fortunately no one was injured, and the blaze was contained, but the event was an additional catalyst to drive Baker's master plan. Quite obviously, repairs were necessary to the church, but Father Baker ordered restoration only of those areas needed for worship. At a parish meeting held shortly after the fire, Baker announced his plans to build a magnificent church, one that would rival similar sanctuaries in Europe, as a way to give thanks to Our Lady of Victory for her constant patronage.[2]

By 1921, Baker's three major Institutions for homeless youth were operating relatively smoothly, despite the constant search for fiscal stability. This comparative calm allowed Baker to finally turn his full attention to building the monument to Our Lady of Victory. Remarkably, Baker initiated this massive project when he was seventy-nine years old. Yet he still possessed the requisite energy, stamina, and determination to see the project through to completion. In July he presented his motivation to his loyal benefactors:

> The time had come when our Blessed Lord thought the humble and lowly Shrine dedicated to His Blessed Mother should give way to a temple more worthy, as far as human beings could make it worthy, of His own dear Mother; a Shrine that would give expression of the sincere and devout love of the devoted lovers of Mary, to whom they had become so devoted, and to whose generous heart they were so much indebted.[3]

Three months later Father Baker gave some substance to his basic plan:

> While Mary's praises resound over the entire land, and all are to her intensely grateful, there seems to be one

universal demand, that this gratitude should manifest itself in the erection and dedication of a National Shrine in her honor; a Shrine that will in beauty, loveliness and grandeur, be worthy...to be consecrated to the august Mother of God under the title of titles, Our Blessed Lady of Victory. [4]

Baker hoped that the shrine would act as a stimulus for the conversion of hearts and souls. Additionally, he thought his magnificent church should manifest the unity of God's people. He wrote:

The Shrine will embody the truth of the essential oneness of God's children by its invitation for all to come and worship under its illumined dome. A Shrine for all people, where Holy Church will show her tenderness, her Motherly care and solicitude, where God's Mother will befriend all who watch at her doors.[5]

Construction of the Shrine

Father Baker's monumental edifice to the Mother of God, as with any of his other projects, began on the drawing board. Baker chose Emile Uhlrich to design the shrine. A Frenchman born in 1873, Uhlrich was a graduate of the École des Beaux-Arts in Paris and came to the United States in 1891, settling in Cleveland. Uhlrich's resumé, highlighting church design in the Cleveland area, was extensive. Working with a colleague, he completed work on the German-Wallace College (1897), St. John's Evangelical Lutheran Church (1901), St. Stanislaus Church (1904–6), St. Michael's Roman Catholic Church (1906), and the Nativity of the Blessed Virgin Mary School (1915).[6]

Nelson Baker most assuredly had in his mind some idea of the shrine's size and appearance, but he needed Uhlrich's architectural expertise to put his ideas on paper. Uhlrich too had ideas for the church. His design philosophy for the shrine was to both honor the Mother of God and create an edifice of grandeur and beauty. He wrote to Baker explaining his ideas:

217

I feel that this monument should be in an exuberant, exultant mood befitting a national expression of gratitude to Our Lady of Victory as a testimony to Her triumph over the modern spirit of irreligion like a trumpet blast on this prominent knoll, on this national Highway, fairly shouting Victory to all who may be inspired by the appeal of this striking monument to place themselves under the Blessed Mother's banner.[7]

Baker was somewhat concerned that Uhlrich would create in his mind a church that the priest could not, in reality, afford. He wrote to his architect, who was in Italy to gain ideas:

I am afraid that your visits to these beautiful places and seeing all these magnificent works will get your ideas so high, that we cannot meet them and I know that you would like to see the...work of our new shrine as beautiful as wealth could make it.[8]

Uhlrich, expressing the idea, "There is nothing I am not ready to do...to please you," was responsive to Baker, producing a design within the fiscal confines of the project.[9]

With some sense of urgency Baker pushed Uhlrich to deliver his completed design to avoid any construction delays. He wrote, "Wishing you would hurry up as rapidly as possible."[10] Again, Uhlrich responded, delivering complete blueprints for the project only one month after his formal proposal had been accepted by Baker. As a loyal servant of his bishop, Baker submitted Uhlrich's designs to Turner who upon review gave his blessing, but suggested that the massive twin towers that were to adorn the entrance of the church made it, in his opinion, "too Polish."[11] In a twist of fate, one of the original towers was hit by lightning, destroying it. Afterward, both towers were lowered to a less grandiose height.

In addition to a professional and experienced architect, Baker's prized project needed a similarly well-experienced and reliable contractor. He was fortunate to find the right candidate among his very own parish flock. Edward S. Jordan, a parishioner at St.

Patrick's, was hired in January 1921 as the general contractor for the shrine. Jordan had been the principal contractor for many buildings in Baker's "Second Holy City," including Our Mother of Good Counsel Church (for two years a mission of St. Patrick), the Maternity Hospital, and Our Lady of Victory Parochial School.[12] Jordan received a strong vote of confidence from Uhlrich, who described him as "so capable and trustworthy a man." Uhlrich wrote to Baker,

> At this stage of the work I intended to be a great deal more on the job than the once per month agreed. In fact, under ordinary circumstances, I would have remained at the site as much as Mr. Jordan. But we have really started work ahead of completely worked out details and [we] are still deeply in them. I find that I can be more useful here just now. Besides, you can, no doubt, trust Mr. Jordan. I have asked him to ask for information or any visit whenever it seems useful for the good of the work. Having not heard from him I suppose that he gets along all right.[13]

With his two major players for this massive undertaking in place, Father Baker could now turn his attention to the important task of financing this project. As in the past, Baker first went to his loyal Association of Our Blessed Lady of Victory, who had supported his efforts so significantly in the past. His first appeal appeared in the *Annals* in July 1921:

> We have then only to request our dear Lord to inspire our many devoted friends who are sincere friends to His dear Mother, to erect this Shrine as a loving testimony of their fondest affection and deepest gratitude for the countless blessings and graces that have been so generously bestowed upon them through her sacred hands.[14]

In July 1922, a new minicolumn, "A Block of Marble," appeared in the *Annals* asking for a $10 contribution "to furnish a block of marble for the National Shrine of Our Blessed Lady of

Victory."[15] In the column, Baker encouraged his benefactors by referencing the small contribution of the poor widow in the Gospel (Luke 21:1–4): "The faithful clients of Our Lady of Victory who wish a share in the graces which must come to those who help by their 'mites' in this glorious building, should endeavor at least to furnish a block of marble."[16] Baker was also able to convince religious orders, his fellow priests, and a few bishops to contribute more substantial funds to sponsor an altar or a statue of a particular saint.[17]

Nelson Baker's supreme confidence that his financial needs would be met through the intercession of his patroness, and the generosity of Association members and other friends, allowed him to boldly go forward even though adequate financing had not been achieved. His goal was to build the shrine and incur no debt. In the spirit of great faith and assurance, he wrote to a benefactor:

> We have great confidence in Almighty God in taking care of our work, as He has always been remarkably good to us, and has always made it easy and pleasant for us to care for this large group of dependents, and we feel if we did the external temporal work, He would see necessary means would be provided.[18]

Baker's supreme confidence was manifest in signing a contract for the exterior marble of the shrine. In a move that some might call foolhardy, he explained his actions and reasons:

> We have boldly made the contract with the Georgia Marble people for the exterior marble of $400,000.00. We had no hesitancy in believing our Blessed Lady would inspire our many friends to help us and this, while it seems an enormous amount, would not half pay the expense of the exterior, but we feel our Blessed Lady wishes something expensive on the exterior,...and we have launched into it, with the firm faith that when it is finished we will be able to consecrate it, free from debt, which will be in about two years.[19]

Baker's efforts to finance his great shrine to Our Lady of Victory were ongoing as construction began. Baker oversaw every aspect of the construction, sometimes acting as a mother hen and at other times more like a bothersome intruder. Always insistent that the project move forward, he pushed his workers, most especially Emile Uhlrich and Edward Jordan, to keep on schedule. At the outset, construction was ahead of design. Sarcastically, Baker wrote to Uhlrich exhorting him to forward plans to the contractor in order to keep the project moving:

> We were glad to hear from you and to know you are tiring yourself out, but we think it is very important that somebody should get tired, as our esteemed friend Mr. Jordan is getting thin in his anxiety and worry to get it [the foundation of the shrine] started.[20]

The first significant milestone in the construction of the shrine was the blessing of the cornerstone. In August 1921, after the completion of the annual novena for the Assumption, Bishop William Turner laid and blessed the cornerstone.[21] During the next four years of construction, with the razing of St. Patrick's Church, to make way for the new shrine, Mass for parishioners was celebrated in Our Lady of Victory School; later, when prepared, the new shrine crypt was the site for Mass.[22]

Construction of the shrine took five years and required the services of at least twenty-two significant contractors. Father Baker was always aware of his local source of support and, therefore, chose local contractors and personnel as much as possible. This began with the selection of Edward Jordan as chief contractor. The granite foundation upon which the church would be built was supplied by the Memorial Art Company of Buffalo. Other Buffalo-based contractors were the Daprato Statuary Company, responsible for supplying statues in the shrine, and the Machwirth Brothers, contracted to supply four copper angels to be placed facing north, south, east, and west on the dome of the shrine. Originally these eighteen-foot statues were slated to be gilded in gold, but Baker rejected the idea as unfeasible. In 1923, the J. W. Danforth Company was awarded the contract for heating and ven-

221

tilation in the shrine.[23] One of the more important contractors for aesthetic purposes was the Otto F. Andrle Stained Glass and Art Institute. Father Baker worked with his contractors, but was clearly very demanding in his desire for excellence. Apparently disappointed in the performance of Andrle's company, Baker received a letter from the former assuring him that he would receive the best possible service available:

> I am much grieved about your disposition toward me, but I am doing everything in my power to please you. Believe me I am working to deliver good work and I daresay I am indifferent about the compensation. I assure you I am giving you every value you can possibly get anywhere.[24]

Six months later, Andrle again wrote, "It is not a question of money with us, it is only to please you."[25]

As mentioned earlier, in February 1922, a contract was let to Georgia Marble Company of Tate, Georgia, for all exterior marble, costing more than $400,000.[26] Baker's shrewd business sense, which he had exercised throughout his priesthood, was a great benefit during this construction. When disagreements and difficulties arose with the Georgia Marble contract over what was and was not included in the contract price, Baker went on the offensive to support his side and to assure the project moved forward without delay. However, when he felt a contractor's concern or critique against another company was valid, he again came to the forefront. When Georgia Marble complained to Baker about design changes that were leading to delays, the venerable priest wrote to his architect, Emile Uhlrich: "We cannot urge upon you too strongly the importance of getting these details and models to us at the earliest possible moment. We have already been seriously delayed on account of not having them. Kindly rush all you can."[27]

Baker's business sense was important and very helpful to him in the construction of the shrine, but his pastoral sense was also evident and brought out the best in others. The priest's status and the respect that others gave to him made contractors desirous of being part of "the team." Such a relationship existed between

Baker and C. J. Poiesz, president of Cleveland Plastering Company. The contractor wrote to Baker:

> We wish to assure you that although we have suffered a financial loss in connection with our work for you, we feel that we have gained an enviable reputation and a sense of satisfaction in work well done. For those of us who are Catholics there is added to the above, knowledge that we have contributed with our own skill to the honor and glory of Him from whom all good things come.[28]

Throughout the construction process, Baker maintained close oversight on the project by observing daily activity and maintaining a lively and detailed correspondence with his architect. Baker was not averse to venting his frustration and disappointment when he believed construction had been slowed, especially due to design. In February 1922, Baker heard from one of his contractors that Uhlrich was considering design changes. In response he wrote to his architect:

> Mr. Uhlrich, we feel you ought to have made the plans specific as you knew what we need in this line and it ought to have been put in without coming now or in the future as we do not know where this will end, if you continue to make changes and we feel you have time enough to make the plans perfect when you could have foreseen this necessity.[29]

Later in May, Baker wrote a second time urging Uhlrich's cooperation: "You are holding up the work for proper information."[30] Uhlrich responded, "You need not fear, Right Reverend Monsignor, that I will be the cause of a moment's delay in this work on which I stand all my best efforts without stint."[31]

Although their relationship was at times a bit frazzled, Baker counted on Uhlrich to coordinate the efforts of the other contractors. In a report in October 1923, this relationship was clearly delineated:

The architect will furnish sufficient details to clearly illustrate all work required. Contractors for plastering, marble work, electric wiring, plumbing, bronze work, and decorating are particularly required to work in harmony together and with the general contractor, under the direction of the architect, to accomplish a perfect interior, free of corrections. No errors will be passed without redress at the expense of the responsible contractor, but all are cautioned to avoid mistakes by checking not only their work, but by consulting with others in regard to the proper placing of their work, when it is likely to affect their own trade.[32]

Uhlrich was also asked to be a second watchdog for Baker. For example, he wrote to the Lackawanna Bridge Works Corporation with significant concerns about their effort on the project:

I have to state to you our dissatisfaction with your manner of the erecting the steel work for the shrine at Lackawanna for which you have the contract, and I have to demand that you adopt forthwith acceptable methods and provide for proper equipment and labor to correct the serious defects already caused by your negligence and [that you] resume work in a safe and workmanlike way to ensure a correct setting in place of your work and avoid the further ruining of your work and ours and serious danger to life.[33]

In addition, Uhlrich provided Baker with periodic updates of progress and information pertinent to the project.

In 1923, other significant contractors were added to those already in place. In January, the Benzinger Marble Company of Pietrasanta, Italy, was contracted to prepare fifteen near life-size statues for the Stations of the Cross. (The biblical "Agony in the Garden" Station was added to the traditional fourteen stations, which begin with "Jesus Is Condemned to Death.") Benzinger also made two statues of the Blessed Virgin Mary (under her title of Our Lady of Victory), one at the main altar and a second at the front of the church. Later that same year, Gonippo Raggi, professor at St. Michael's Royal Art Academy in Rome, was entrusted with the interior decoration of the shrine. By 1923, Raggi, a native Italian who lived in Spring Lake, New Jersey, had become well established in the United States, and had offices in Boston, New York, and Philadelphia. He worked with a Buffalo resident, Marion Rzeznik, a Polish native who had studied painting and sculpture in Krakow, Vienna, and New York City before settling in Buffalo. Raggi was given several commissions to decorate the dome, Sacred Heart and St. Joseph's chapels, five smaller chapels in the sanctuary, plus some exterior work on the cupola of the dome. Later, he was also commissioned to decorate the altars to St. Patrick and St. Vincent de Paul, plus the Lourdes Chapel and the baptistry.[34]

The interior design of the colossal dome was Raggi's greatest challenge. His primary proposal to Baker was to create a scene with one subject, "which would give the impression of heaven." A second possibility was to divide the dome into panels, creating various figures and ornamentals in high relief. Baker chose the first option and reported to Uhlrich about his choice: "He [Raggi] has made a very beautiful sketch of the Assumption of Our Blessed Lady in which he brings countless angelic beings into the sketch....He has promised to give us something superior to anything he has done."[35] In preparing his sketches, Raggi visited the Infant Home and was touched by the faces of the children he saw. He wrote to Baker, "I would ask, feeling to please you, to use some of them as lovely models for the large crowd of angels around the Blessed Virgin in the dome."[36]

Most of the critical details concerning specific altars, statues, stained glass, and decoration of the magnificent dome had been covered by various contracts, yet the general interior work was still not contracted. While in Italy to speak with various peoples and suppliers of materials, Emile Uhlrich had received a bid of $500,000 from Lautz Corporation to furnish the shrine interior, not including the pulpit, vestibule, and other smaller yet detailed parts. However, in January 1924, the Tonetti Brothers Marble Company of Pietrasanta agreed to supply "all interior marble" work for $130,000. Uhlrich told Baker, "You have nothing to compare to the total price." He continued, "Tonetti Brothers say that they will spare no money or efforts to make your shrine the most beautiful in America." Baker was obviously pleased with the report and responded, "[I]t gave us great consolation to know you were...so successful and doing so nicely."[37]

While the price "sold" Baker in awarding the contract to Tonetti, their relationship was stormy throughout the latter period of the shrine's construction. The main point of disagreement concerned procedures for payment and fulfillment of the contract obligations. Tonetti kept pressing Baker for payment, but the priest responded that monies would be sent when the product arrived. In a rather angry tone, Baker expressed his concern: "I am very much ashamed and more or less indignant that you are treating us like so many children, in acting 'perfectly' regardless of our signing contracts which were to guide us up to the end of our work."[38]

Four months later, again irked by demands for payment from Tonetti, Baker responded, "I am very much surprised to find you sending us a draft for $27,000 through our bank here, and I was obliged to simply tell the bank that we did not owe that much." Claiming the required marble had not arrived, he continued,

> Notwithstanding this, you are foolishly sending drafts which you told me before would answer everything, but you pay no attention to any deficiencies. You know very well...you cannot expect the entire amount until these [missing] pieces [of marble] arrive and we have made a proper adjustment according to your contract.[39]

As the shrine rose majestically from the earth, the skyline of Lackawanna changed significantly. During the latter years of construction, Father Baker continued his vigilant and strict oversight of every aspect of the project. He was happy to report to Uhlrich, "Everything has gone along smoothly, as we have had no accidents and Almighty God has been very good to us, because everything has worked so pleasantly and safely."[40] The fact that construction had proceeded relatively smoothly was due largely to Father Baker's ability to wear several hats simultaneously in order to get the job done. He often served as a cheerleader, keeping all contractors and various other parties as happy as possible. His main function seems to have been an arbitrator when disputes arose between various contractors. When Gonippo Raggi complained that some stained glass would conflict with his design of the dome, Baker was quick to respond. A grateful Raggi wrote, "Therefore your interest in having me instruct the glass man in harmonizing his work with mine pleased me very much. [It] is the only way to have the best result."[41] In a similar way Baker eased tension with Tonetti concerning payments.[42] Beyond his roles as cheerleader and arbitrator, Baker was also the coordinator and point man who kept all parties informed.

Baker's main concern was to support his architect, Emile Uhlrich. Extant data shows that the two men had a close working relationship. In regular correspondence, Baker supported his architect in disputes. He once wrote, "I know you are working very hard and the climate is against you."[43] In response, Uhlrich sought to please Baker, knowing that the project was close to his heart. He told him, "Above all I desire to be useful to you and not abandon the work if anything could be helped by my presence."[44]

Construction of the shrine received two fortunate boosts that were not expected. Baker's biographer Floyd Anderson relates the story of two American soldiers in Europe after World War I. While traveling, they encountered a farmer in Spain whose home was adorned with pictures of Our Lady of Victory and Nelson Baker. The soldiers told the farmer of Baker's project to construct the shrine. The Spaniard in return told the Americans that he had some rare red marble on his property that he was willing to donate for the construction of the shrine. This stone now adorns the four corners of the main altar in the Basilica.[45] The other stroke of good fortune was that arrangements were made for Baker to receive all marble shipments for his shrine free of customs duty. The request was made to President Calvin Coolidge and the United States Congress, asking that "the marble [for the shrine] be admitted free of duty as we feel that the country owes this to the good Father for the interest he has taken in this great work of universal national charity."[46]

Dedication of the Basilica of Our Lady of Victory

In the summer of 1925, Father Baker began to make plans for the dedication of his new shrine to Our Lady of Victory.[47] Baker was very proud of his monument to the Mother of God, who had been his patroness in all endeavors from the beginning of his ministry. In July 1925, he happily wrote:

> Nothing has been spared to make the shrine one of the most beautiful in the world; its brilliantly white marble exterior glistening in the sunlight, while the tall stately cross-crowned spires pierce high into the clouds, and its magnificent dome surrounded with electric fire and surmounted with its brilliantly illuminated cross, all of which form a scene unequaled in splendor, seldom if ever witnessed.[48]

Emile Uhlrich expressed his gratitude for the opportunity given him to participate in this project.

> I wish to take this occasion to again tell you how happy and privileged I have been in serving you as the interpreter of your great vision. Now that it has been realized I pray that nothing will ever becloud it and that every remaining question will be settled to your satisfaction as all the worries that have been born so far have gradually vanished.

He continued to offer his services to Baker: "I wish to be useful to you as long as possible here. But no matter where I might go, you can always depend on me."[49]

Bishop Turner, while in Rome for his *ad limina*, requested and received the following three rescripts for the new shrine:

1. A plenary indulgence was granted to those who visit the church (gained once per year).

2. *Altare Privilegiatum* (a place for Eucharistic Adoration) was granted for the main altar, St. Patrick's altar, and St. Vincent de Paul's altar.
3. Permission was granted for perpetual Eucharistic Adoration on a side altar. The last rescript most assuredly must have been welcomed by Baker considering his consistent, fervent, and long-standing devotion to the Eucharist.[50]

The dedication of the shrine was originally scheduled for October 7, 1925, the Feast of Our Lady of Victory. Baker planned the dedication "with all the pomp and solemnity befitting the Mother of God, the Blessed Mother of Jesus." Bishop Turner was scheduled to bless the main altar, with visiting bishops and monsignors blessing the eight smaller altars for the Sacred Heart of Jesus, the Immaculate Conception, St. Joseph, St. Patrick, St. Vincent de Paul, St. Anne, St. Aloysius, and Our Lady of Lourdes.[51]

Unfortunately, the planned dedication had to be postponed. Baker reported, "Owing to a delay in receiving certain shipments of marble, which must come from abroad, we have been obliged to postpone." While disappointed, Baker always demonstrated a positive countenance, explaining that the shrine should not be dedicated until it was ready. He wrote:

> As we are very anxious that this, the Temple of Our Blessed Lady will be as beautiful as human beings can make it, we have been obliged to proceed very slowly....When the shrine is finally completed it will be something that cannot be equaled in this country, and our friends tell us that we have seen nothing more beautiful in any other country.[52]

Finally, in December 1925, the shrine was completed. Baker reported, "Our new and very beautiful shrine to Our Blessed Lord in honor of His Holy Mother has just been completed and is soon to be solemnly consecrated to their honor and glory."[53] Prior to the church's first services, Baker initiated a novena on December

17 to conclude on Christmas Eve. The first Mass celebrated in the shrine was on Christmas Day 1925.[54]

Completion of the shrine allowed Baker to reschedule the formal dedication. Appropriately, it was decided to hold this special event on March 19, 1926, Father Baker's fiftieth anniversary of his ordination. However, due to his own personal illness, the actual dedication was delayed until May 25.[55] The consecration ceremony began at 6 a.m., with Bishop Turner officiating. Baker was the celebrant at the dedication Mass held at 10:30 a.m., along with four hundred bishops and priests. Cardinal Patrick Hayes of New York in his sermon that day stated:

> I know of no church like this, so beautiful, so uplifting, so glorious—I know of no other church like this, consecrated to the Charities of Christ, Our Lord. It is a monument to the Buffalo Diocese, the city of Lackawanna, to our great Lady of Victory and to a modern Apostle of Charity—Father Baker.[56]

After a grand reception, Bishop Thomas Shahan, rector of the Catholic University of America, presided at Vespers at 4 p.m. Later, at 7:30 p.m., Bishop Joseph Conroy of Ogdensburg, New York, presided at Eucharistic Benediction.[57]

Monsignor Nelson Baker rightly took great pride at the dedication of the shrine. He was certain that Mary herself was pleased; her pleasure was evident in the array of peoples present. Reflecting on the day, Baker wrote:

> Our Blessed Lady, with a brilliant light shining upon her, stood up alone on the altar and viewed the immense concourse of people, as they tell us that over 30,000 were trying to squeeze into our shrine which could not hold more than four or five thousand. With the Cardinal present, also several bishops and our own four hundred clergymen, it was a most brilliant sight. I felt that Our Blessed Lady was pleased with so much honor as it was herself that attracted a vast concourse.[58]

230

The construction of the shrine was by far the most expensive project Father Baker ever engaged. Extant sources differ on the cost of the project, from $2.8 to $3.8 million. Included in these costs was the $50,500 fee to the architect, Emile Uhlrich, and $42,800 to the interior artist, Gonippo Raggi. All seemed satisfied with their compensation. Uhlrich, in general, spoke for the others: "I am quite satisfied with the settlement we have arrived at of my fee."[59]

Father Baker's monument to Our Blessed Lady of Victory is a testimony to his faith and desire to show gratitude for the success of his work. The church is built in the Renaissance neoclassical style, using forty-six different types of marble in its construction. The original twin towers at the front of the edifice rose 165 feet to the sky.[60] The dome, with a circumference of 251 feet, at the time second largest in United States only to the United States Capitol, is guarded on the outside by four mammoth copper angels; the inside is a beautiful mural of the Assumption of Mary, guarded by 11-foot statues of the four Evangelists. Life-sized Stations of the Cross are mounted throughout the aisles. Nine altars—especially the main altar, plus the three secondary altars to the Sacred Heart, St. Joseph, and St. Patrick—highlight the interior. Well over two thousand angels in painted and sculpted forms are present in the shrine. Prominent statues of Our Lady of Victory are found above the main altar and at the entrance to the church. A series of panels depicting Mary under her varied titles are also featured in the shrine.[61]

When completed, the shrine received significant adulation from many varied sources. The cardinal Secretary of State in the Vatican commented, "Among the churches of America, the Sanctuary of Our Lady of Victory is for many reasons to be counted as one of the greatest." *L'Osservatore Romano*, the semi-official Vatican newspaper, similarly described it as "one of the most superb shrines the Catholic Church possesses in the United States." One local Buffalo paper understandably was even more complementary: "No expense has been spared to fit the shrine with the necessaries to enkindle devotion and to awaken in the human heart the sentiments which make religion paramount in the life of man."[62] Father Baker also wanted to trumpet the shrine, but emphasized more its symbolic value than its aesthetic:

> The shrine of Our Lady of Victory will be emblematic of this unity among Catholics. As it will show forth the work of many nations, and call those of every tongue to worship within its walls, the devotee will appreciate more fully how universal is the church and how Catholic her appeal.[63]

One of the rescripts obtained by Bishop Turner during his *ad limina* visit to Rome was that of perpetual Eucharistic Adoration in the new shrine. In order to assure that someone was always present in the church, Baker started the Society of Adoration, a group consisting of Sisters, Brothers, nurses, and other interested people from the Infant Home and General Hospital as a base of people.[64]

The crowning accolade received for Father Baker's monument to Mary was its designation as a basilica by the Holy See. Even before the shrine was dedicated, Baker's close friend Bishop Thomas Walsh of Trenton, New Jersey, suggested that, with the approval of Bishop Turner, he apply to the pope to have the new church designated as a basilica. Walsh wrote Baker, "I am sure that His Excellency [Turner] will be pleased to obtain this signal honor for you from the Holy See." He promised, "I will do all in my power to have it granted."[65] Two months after the dedication, on July 28, *L'Osservatore Romano* reported that the shrine had been designated a basilica. The paper noted, "It is not its beauty, size, and magnificence that give the Sanctuary of Our Lady of Victory of Lackawanna its greatest importance. Its greatest value is that it is the center of a very large work of piety and charity."[66] The ceremony conferring this distinction on the shrine was held on October 3, 1926. Bishop Turner celebrated a Pontifical Mass at which Bishop Walsh, whom Baker considered the catalyst behind the honor, preached the sermon.[67]

The Basilica of Our Lady of Victory, only the second "minor" basilica in the United States at the time, was a major boon to the City of Lackawanna. *The Victorian* reported:

The Shrine of Our Blessed Lady of Victory is daily becoming more dear to our friends. During the past year many thousands passed through its portals. They went their way with hearts burning with greater love for God's Holy Mother, and with a renewed determination to serve with greater fidelity Her Divine Son.[68]

Similarly, religion scholar Heather Hartel commented, "It [the Basilica] brought national prestige to Lackawanna, greatly increased the visual impact of the institutes in the cityscape, and drew pilgrims from across the United States."[69]

Conclusion

In 1874, when Nelson Baker "accidently" encountered devotion to Our Lady of Victory, he could hardly imagine construction of a basilica in her honor, but that unexpected event was the original catalyst to his most significant life project. At an age when most men, whether priests or laity, have long retired, Baker took on the construction of a massive shrine to honor his patroness who, he firmly believed, was behind all his success at the Institutions. Undoubtedly, she was the inspiration that kept his fertile mind active and his slight but energetic body sufficiently healthy to tackle such a major endeavor. The Basilica of Our Lady of Victory, which even today dominates the skyline of the City of Lackawanna, is significant in Baker's life for a few important reasons. First, the project allowed him to complete his dream to honor the Mother of God in this special way. This was a task critical in satisfying Baker's spiritual journey. Second, the project was completed in a relatively short amount of time—five years—without any serious complications and, incredibly, the church was totally paid for by the time of its consecration in May 1926. When one considers the scope of the project in his day and how pastors today pay loans for years and even decades after construction of a new building— church, school, or parish hall—Baker's ability to complete the project safely and without incurring any debt is remarkable—if not miraculous.

The completion of the Basilica allowed Nelson Baker to concentrate his efforts in new directions. With his Institutions and new Basilica completed and operating without major problems, he sought new horizons. The onset of the Great Depression provided the environment and the motivation for him to serve God's people in new and different ways.

CHAPTER 10

Ministry during the Depression (1930–1936)

The interwar years of U.S. history record two very different periods, one of relative ease and prosperity and a second of misery and pain. The close of the Progressive Era and the onset of the 1920s brought America to new heights both internationally and domestically. The expanding horizons and influence that the nation had experienced after the Spanish-American War of 1898 only grew faster after the conclusion of World War I. While the United States chose not to be a member of the League of Nations, nonetheless, it was the significant work of President Woodrow Wilson that led to the organization's foundation. In 1921 to 1922, the United States hosted the Washington Arms Conference, seeking international disarmament. On the international front, the United States was emerging as the nation that would later lead the free world after World War II. Domestically the nation also enjoyed a period of euphoria as characterized by the flappers and freedom of the 1920s. Yet, with the sudden onset of the Great Depression, beginning with the crash of October 1929, the United States entered a period of severe economic decline and social dislocation. Business executives sold apples and frequented soup lines. "Hoovervilles"—named pejoratively after Herbert Hoover, the president during the Depression—sprang up on the outskirts of many towns and cities. Unemployment reached nearly 25 percent. Almost overnight, feast had turned to famine; hope had become despair.

During the 1930s, Nelson Baker, his Institutions, and the newly built Basilica of Our Lady of Victory were forced to walk a different road. Baker was able to maintain his invaluable ministry to youth, although the task of financing his work proved even more difficult than before. The Great Depression gave Baker an opportunity to assist two other populations that had traditionally been abandoned by society, but even more so under the curtain of economic disaster: the poor and African Americans. Father Baker seized the opportunity given him to reach out, meeting both material and spiritual needs of people in distress. It was a new ministry for an old priest, but Nelson Baker was ready for the task.

The Great Depression and American Catholics

The 1920s in the United States was a period when several issues dominated the national interest. Immigration restriction, seen most prominently through the passage of the 1917 literacy test, the 1921 Johnson Act, and the 1924 Johnson-Reed Act, drew the attention of the nation. Prohibition, enforced nationally through the ratification of the Eighteenth Amendment to the Constitution in January 1919 and the passage of the Volstead Act in October, divided the nation into "wets" and "drys." Implementation of the law was impossible as government enforcement agencies were ineffective and small production of alcohol was virtually impossible to stop. By the mid-1920s, it was obvious to all, save possibly the Women's Christian Temperance Union (WCTU), which had worked long and hard for its passage, that prohibition was a failure. In February 1933, Congress passed the Twenty-First Amendment, repealing America's "experiment." On December 5, the measure was ratified by Utah, the thirty-sixth and decisive state.

The decade was also a period of heightened religious tension. The clash between fundamentalism and modernism was played out most prominently in the summer of 1925 at the infamous "Scopes Monkey Trial." William Jennings Bryan, champion of the fundamentalists, and Clarence Darrow, defender of the modernists, locked horns over the teaching of Darwin's theory of evolution in Tennessee's public schools. While John Scopes, a high school biology teacher, was convicted of violating the Tennessee statute, the trial virtually destroyed the fundamentalist position in the minds of most Americans.[1]

In addition, the ever-present face of anti-Catholicism once again rose in this period through the reemergence of the Ku Klux

Klan, which under the direction of Hiram Wesley Evans continued to preach the nineteenth-century creed of Protestant, white, rural, and American. Short-lived in its ferocity, the Klan was shamed into obscurity when one of its "generals," D. C. Stephenson, was convicted of manslaughter in the death of a young woman with whom he was involved in a scandalous affair.[2]

Prohibition, immigration, and religious fundamentalism—and the euphoric environment of the 1920s in which these issues arose—were forced to the side almost overnight in October 1929. That month a series of severe market drops on the New York Stock Exchange transformed American economic prosperity into misery. On October 21, the market dipped sharply but recovered. Over the next week the market continued to fall with October 29, "Black Tuesday," seeing the greatest fall. By mid-November stock prices were down 40 percent. The economic fallout from the market crash was significant and palpable. Between 1929 and 1932, unemployment rose from 3.1 to 24 percent; in the same period, more than five thousand banks closed, with a cumulative loss to investors of over $2.3 billion. Production of goods and services declined 51 percent by 1932 from their 1929 high.[3]

President Herbert Hoover, who was personally wealthy but with a reputation as a compassionate man and a good organizer, sought answers to America's greatest financial disaster. As a champion of rugged individualism, Hoover, like many Americans, saw the crash initially as a temporary downturn; he never understood the basic weakness of the nation's financial base. He asked for a spirit of voluntarism to right America's economic ship, but when his methods did not work, he could not change his philosophy. He remained antistatist and was not convinced of the need for federal aid in the situation. Rather than the image of a tireless Progressive, Hoover was branded as an insensitive reactionary. Paulist priest and commentator on America James Gillis summarized well what many thought:

> Alas, poor President Hoover. Never since Washington have people expected more of a man elected to lead them, and never has any chief executive proved so disappointing. But one thing all good Americans desire—

a leader worthy of the name, to direct us in these distressing circumstances. May heaven send us one.[4]

President Franklin Delano Roosevelt, inaugurated on March 4, 1933, was the man the American people chose to lead them from the darkness of the Depression to a new day; the "New Deal" was his plan of action. After World War I, trends toward management, bureaucracy, and "bigness" were found in all aspects of American society. The New Deal, "a descendant of Progressive reform," was the tool used by Roosevelt to manage the "bigness" of society, which had come about through mergers and the establishment of vastly extended companies and businesses in the boon period of the 1920s. The historian David Shannon called the New Deal "a complex set of compromises" generated by outside pressures, which Roosevelt molded into a workable program.[5] The president believed in the full employment of the federal government in an effort to combat the Depression and to relieve those most sorely injured by it. He was thus willing to compromise and modify the traditional relationship of independence existent between government and private enterprise in the interest of the general welfare of the country. He was no opponent of capitalism, but felt that the reality of the situation necessitated bold and innovative steps that might be questionable in more normal economic conditions. From the perspective of American Catholics, Roosevelt referenced the papal social-justice encyclical entitled *Quadragesimo Anno* (1931) and the concept of social justice in his speeches.

Roosevelt wasted no time in implementing his plan, viewing his election as a mandate from the American people for immediate action. Within the first one hundred days following his assumption of office, the initial phase of the New Deal, based on recovery, had been enacted as the law of the land. The Depression was attacked from three different fronts: agriculture, unemployment, and business and labor.[6]

The National Industrial Recovery Act (NIRA) of June 16, 1933, became the heart of Roosevelt's New Deal with its formation of the National Recovery Administration (NRA). Written to stimulate both business and labor, the NIRA satisfied employers' demands for government backing of trade-association agreements

238

so as to stabilize production and prevent price slashing, while giving workers wage-and-hours protection and the right to bargain collectively. In the hope that consumers' buying power could be raised as rapidly as prices and wages, there was attached to the act a $3.3 billion public works appropriation to "prime the pump" of the economy.[7]

The nation, enthralled that finally some significant effort had been made to stem the tide of the Depression and effect recovery, began a honeymoon with Roosevelt and his New Deal. Businesses throughout the land placed the Blue Eagle (which stated "We Do Our Part") in shop windows to show their support for the NRA; the general tone of the nation was upbeat, positive, and forward looking. Catholics as a body were equally enthusiastic about the new president and his New Deal legislation, which brought hope that the horrible downward trend of the nation for the past four years could be reversed. Catholics also rejoiced that Roosevelt had chosen two of their own for cabinet positions,[8] which helped to raise the Church to its highest level to date of public recognition. Additionally, leading Catholic intellectuals of the day advocated social positions akin to that of the president, enhancing his popularity with the rank and file of the Church. The New Deal was also well received by Catholics because it was seen to be based on Catholic social teaching.[9] Catholics believed the government to be duty bound to provide for the needs of the unemployed and other marginalized people of society. Thus, when Roosevelt launched into his campaign to curtail the power of Wall Street and to place greater regulation on the economy, his efforts were initially fully supported. The hierarchy backed the president on both personal and organizational levels. Cardinals Patrick Hayes (New York), William O'Connell (Boston), and George Mundelein (Chicago), as well as Archbishop Edward Hanna (San Francisco) and Bishop Karl Alter (Toledo), were all in the Roosevelt camp. The best-known organizations, including the National Conference of Catholic Men (NCCM), the National Conference of Catholic Women (NCCW), and the National Catholic Welfare Conference (NCWC), strongly supported the NRA.[10] Nelson Baker, as well, was a strong Roosevelt supporter. In a letter to a local congressman he wrote of "the wonderful success that our new President is obtaining, so that we are

239

going to live in a Democratic atmosphere for the next four years and I hope it will be forty years before it is changed."[11]

Catholic support for the policies of Roosevelt, especially the NRA and the agencies it generated, is illustrated best in the activities of John A. Ryan and Francis Haas. Ryan, pejoratively labeled the "Right Reverend New Dealer" by his nemesis, Father Charles Coughlin, equated Roosevelt's economic policy with social justice. He served as a member of the Industrial Appeals Board of the NRA and promoted the president's New Deal through his work with the Social Action Department of the NCWC, his teaching, and his writings. His biographer Francis Broderick says, however, that Ryan's influence with the president should not be overstated; the two men met on four different occasions and corresponded a half-dozen times during their mutual tenures of service to the government.[12] Francis Haas was most closely associated with Roosevelt's labor policies. The Milwaukee cleric believed in and promoted a just wage and the need for industry, labor, and the government to work in harmony and mutual cooperation. During the life of the NRA, Haas served on the Labor Advisory Board and its successor, the National Labor Board.[13]

Aiding the Depression Poor

During his forty years of ministry at Limestone Hill, Nelson Baker became well known as a man who assisted the poor and their needs. His work with orphans and troubled youth and most especially his open door policy toward unwed mothers demonstrated that he believed in and practiced the basic Christian virtue of charity and did so without reservation. Anyone in need could find a welcome and giving hand in the person of Father Baker. His biographer Floyd Anderson wrote, "Father Baker's hand extended out to everyone who came to him in need. He was never parochial in his charity. To him everyone was God's creation."[14] Indeed, even at the end of his life, one local Buffalo paper accurately commented: "He ha[s] adhered to his policy of never turning a needy person away from his door, despite the added hundreds and thousands that have come, asking aid."[15]

Baker's charity to youth was well known; when, in a similar

way, a situation arose that required action for the poor, he responded fully and completely. Such an opportunity occurred in 1919 when workers at Bethlehem Steel, many of whom were Baker's parishioners, went on strike due to poor working conditions. Bethlehem Steel officials immediately ordered all strikers living in company-owned housing to vacate. Thus, a significant number of people found themselves homeless and out of work almost overnight. Father Baker wasted no time in securing relief, providing food, and sheltering workers and their families in a few homes he quickly rented. In other cases, he assisted strikers with their rent. The historian Timothy Allan captured both the inspiration and action of Baker in his service to the poor:

> Even when local municipal authorities and company officials tried to dissuade Baker from what was clearly a direct effort to sustain the workers in their strike he could not be deterred from what his conscience told him was right....During his declining years, with the nation sorely beset by the economic catastrophe of the Great Depression—Baker was still steadfast to the basic "vocation" of his life.[16]

Ten years later, when the Great Depression threw the United States into its worst economic disaster, Baker started a vast ministry providing food, clothing, shelter, and money to those in need. In a personal letter he explained his work, "We have for the past six months been caring for a large number of people who are without homes and friends, and we have been caring for them as best we could."[17] In September 1930, Baker started a new ministry called "City of Charity," which distributed clothes and made every effort to meet specific needs of those most ill and affected by the economic fallout. Between September 20, 1930, and January 7, 1933, without public funds for assistance from the diocese, Baker's new ministry provided 454,000 meals; 4,625 pairs of adult shoes; 2,125 coats; 800 men's suits; 1,100 women's dresses; 1,237 sets of underwear; 500 dresses for girls; and 300 pairs of children's shoes. Many boys in St. John's Protectory actually crafted these clothes, especially the shoes. During the period, more than 1,500 people received free medical attention. Additionally, Baker provided more than 20,000 nights of lodging for the homeless.[18]

Nelson Baker's most noteworthy direct assistance to the poor during the Great Depression was his initiation of daily meals served at St. John's Protectory. On Christmas Eve 1930, Baker sent out a general invitation to all the unemployed in the area to come the next day for a Christmas dinner.[19] Over the next three years Baker provided daily meals three times a day to the poor and unemployed of Lackawanna. One contemporary observer described the scene:

> The sober, orderly men form an undisturbed quiet procession at meal hours designated, just outside the basilica, and await their turns at the beautifully prepared tables [in the basement of the Protectory]. It seems like the miracle of the loaves and fishes to witness the members who are fed and occasionally Monsignor Baker gives them tobacco and a few coins. He and his guests seem to have a signal understanding, as he sends them daily away contented.[20]

Baker himself described his work in writing to a religious priest:

> We supply here daily from seven hundred to one thousand meals to the hungry and poor who are coming here daily to carry off with them bread for their hungry children and we feel that the whole work is one inspired by our Divine Master, and we are glad to have the opportunity of doing it.[21]

Daily meals continued to be served throughout 1931 and 1932. Baker reported to Bishop Turner about his work: "We are still feeding the poor unemployed and the number still increases: since January 1, 1931 our daily feeding has been from 140 to 429 men, making a total of 24,400 meals during that time." During the same time period he reported that 77,700 loaves of bread had been distributed to those in need.[22]

On January 7, 1933, Baker suspended operation of his soup kitchen, citing the expense and limited resources. He reported:

This cannot keep up forever. We have a budget the same as any other institution. Our work is done in the name of charity. When the number of free meals grew to such alarming proportions, we knew we could not keep up the distribution indefinitely. It may surprise you to know that for the year 1932 we [Our Lady of Victory] assumed a financial deficiency of approximately $159,000.[23]

The closure of the soup kitchen almost immediately prompted a delegation of the unemployed who met with Baker. He said his decision was partially based on news from Ernest Cole, director of the State Temporary Relief Administration, that there was a duplication of effort in the area. However, after the meeting, Baker walked away convinced that the State was not doing enough. Thus, he reported, "Our food kitchens will be reopened at the earliest opportunity....I will maintain a kitchen for the hungry men of Lackawanna until I'm compelled by financial necessity to close them."[24] Baker's efforts to assist the poor in the community were noted: "He is actively engaged in the development and building of the town—doing excellent work in solving home and employment problems."[25]

Father Baker's generosity to the hundreds of people that he served each day went beyond food, clothing, and shelter. He regularly went with the Sisters of St. Joseph to beg money from employed dockworkers. Later that day, as he walked down the soup line and visited with those awaiting their turn to eat, he would give men what he had, usually a quarter. He was once quoted, as saying, "The men have to have a little jingle in their pocket for self-respect."[26]

Father Baker's outreach to the poor and unemployed benefited many people, but not all approved of his work. In a conversation with a friend, Baker explained his general philosophy for assisting the poor:

I've often been criticized for taking care of these poor people. But let's put ourselves in their position. Some of them may have been careless. Some may have been lazy and didn't want to work and some maybe couldn't find

243

work. They are hungry and cold. What would we do if we were hungry and cold and had no means to take care of ourselves? We would probably go to the corner store and steal a loaf of bread or a bottle of milk and get into trouble. We do this for these men to keep them from getting into trouble....And God is blessing our work. Times are hard, but we manage.[27]

Baker was also criticized for his actions of giving money to the poor. He always replied, "I find the more we give away, the more we get." At times observers noticed that men in line would receive their quarter from Baker and then proceed to the back of the line and often receive money again. They cautioned him against this practice, but his response probably caught them off guard: "When I die, the good Lord will not ask me if they were worthy. But he might ask me if I gave."[28]

Nelson Baker's outreach to the unemployed of Buffalo was unquestionably a significant effort, but it is important to place his work within the broader context of the endeavors of Buffalo Catholic Charities to assist the poor. From 1880 forward, the Diocese of Buffalo was host to several institutions founded to assist the marginalized of society. Besides St. Joseph's and St. John's, the Sisters of St. Joseph were also responsible for St. Mary's Orphan Asylum and for Le Couteulx St. Mary's Institution for the Instruction of Deaf Mutes. St. Vincent's Female Orphan Asylum, Providence Lunatic Asylum, and the St. Mary's Asylum for Widows, Foundlings, and Infants were administered by the Sisters of Charity. The German Roman Catholic Orphan Asylum and St. Francis Asylum were sponsored by the Sisters of St. Francis. The Magdalene Asylum was operated by the Sisters of Our Lady of Refuge, and the Catholic Home for Young Girls out of Employment was sponsored by the Ladies of the Sacred Heart of Mary.[29]

The number of institutions to serve various groups was indeed impressive, but there was no coordination to their efforts. Thus, in 1917, the Catholic Charities Aid Association was incorporated as a preliminary step to the formation of a formal diocesan structure for charity work. Beginning in 1922 and continuing into 1923, a committee of six local Buffalo Catholics, chaired by Judge

Daniel J. Kenefick, met to organize formally. In October 1923, Catholic Charities of Buffalo was officially incorporated. One year later the Board of Catholic Charities was organized with Bishop Turner as chairman and Nelson Baker as vice chairman. Father J. C. Carr was appointed as director. The group comprised seventeen separate organizations, including many mentioned above, but none associated with Father Baker.[30] The Board of Charities was divided into four divisions: foundling asylums, child-care institutes, institutions for the aged, and family welfare.[31]

The board had been formed but, other than a small budget from the bishop, the body had no capital to do its work of coordination of and assistance to the various existent agencies in the diocese. Thus, in April 1924, with a "kickoff" letter from the bishop, a weeklong drive to raise funds for the board was initiated. Baker as vice chairman was the responsible party in this effort. His duties included setting up teams, with their captains, to lead a door-to-door fund drive.[32] The 1924 appeal was very successful, gaining $316,574.24.[33]

Baker stayed active with Catholic Charities until the time of his death. As vice chairman he was responsible for the annual fund drive and any capital projects the board entertained. He was also the spokesman for Catholic Charities, especially responding to invitations to speak on the radio.[34]

When the diocesan Board of Catholic Charities was formed, Father Baker's Institutions were not among the seventeen sponsored. As mentioned previously, Baker seemingly had almost a Midas touch in his ability to raise money for his Institutions, not only for their day-to-day maintenance, but to expand their ability to serve significantly. However, with the onset of the Great Depression, even Baker was eventually forced to extend his begging hand. In April 1934, for the first time, Baker petitioned the board to receive assistance for his Institutions. He explained in *The Victorian*:

> This is the first year I had the courage to ask the Bishop
> to include our institutions in the Appeal; but we are run-
> ning so far behind, contributions have dropped off
> $100,000 in the year, that I had to ask the Bishop to

help me; and he very graciously told me he would be glad to include our needs in the Appeal.[35]

He went on to say that he could not pay his bills and, therefore, realized he needed assistance. An appeal was made in *The Victorian* to be generous in the annual drive:

> Circumstances over which he has no control have forced the great benefactor of Our Lady of Victory institutions to ask for sixty thousand dollars in this year's Appeal. Divided among the families of this Diocese capable of giving it is a mere bagatelle. Sixty thousand dollars will scarcely support his institutions for two months. But he is willing with his great faith in Our Lady of Victory to secure the amount necessary for his institutions for the other 10 months.
>
> In making your donations, then, be mindful of the service rendered to this grand old priest whose life has been the practice of the virtue of Charity. Bring joy to his heart [in his] declining years by demonstrating your affection in [y]our esteem for the abundant labors of Father Baker at Lackawanna.[36]

Baker asked for and received a $60,000 supplement in 1934, but his appeal must have caught the ear and attention of his faithful benefactors, for there was no request in the remaining two years of his life. In fact, the next year Bishop Turner applauded Baker for his ability to keep the Institutions afloat financially: "I am most pleased to learn that, in spite of the almost insurmountable difficulties, you have been enabled to maintain the financial standing of the institutions of Our Lady of Victory."[37] William Meegan, director of Catholic Charities and someone who opposed Baker on issues associated with the Infant Home (chapter 8), reminded people of the great work Baker had done for Catholic Charities throughout his priestly ministry:

> Msgr. Baker, more than anyone else, has been a source of inspiration to the thousands who have labored in

annual appeals for the support of Catholic agencies of the diocese. He was not content, however, to set an example of courage and zeal in the divine work of charity, but each year took an active part in the annual appeal and followed its progress with remarkable attention for a man of his advanced age. The help that Msgr. Baker gave to us in the past has been of incalculable value.[38]

Black Catholics in the United States

The history of African Americans and Roman Catholicism in the United States is a story of much injustice, lack of acceptance, and inability on the part of the Church to adequately serve this marginalized group. Its early history is rooted in religious congregations: those formed for an exclusively black membership and those formed specifically to serve the African American Catholic community. The first black congregation of women religious, the Oblate Sisters of Providence—founded by Jacques Joubert, SS, and cofounded and led by Elizabeth Lange—took vows in 1829. The Sisters of the Holy Family were established in New Orleans in November 1842. The Missionary Franciscan Sisters of the Immaculate Heart, under the guidance of Mother Mathilda Beasley, were founded in Savannah, Georgia, in 1891. These communities sought to educate black children, as public education was largely unavailable to them.[39]

In the latter quarter of the century, three new congregations arose in the United States specifically to serve the African American community. The Mill Hill Fathers, founded in 1871 by Herbert Vaughn in England, came to the United States in 1893 as the Josephites. In September 1923, the Divine Word Missionaries opened St. Augustine Seminary in Bay St. Louis, Louisiana, as a training ground for black priests. A young Philadelphia heiress, Katharine Drexel, founded the Sisters of the Blessed Sacrament for Indians and Colored People in 1891. The histories of these congregations produced many stories of successful foundations and compassionate ministry, but their failures in moving the African American Catholic community toward equal status with other Catholics were often glaring.[40]

247

Possibly the most significant champion of the black Catholic cause in the late nineteenth century was Daniel Rudd. A former slave and the founder of the *American Catholic Tribune*, the first black Catholic newspaper, Rudd was the driving force behind a series of five lay black Catholic congresses, held between 1889 and 1897. These national meetings, which drew some of the most talented and best educated black Catholics, became venues to discuss many topics pertinent to African Americans of the day, including education, vocational training, labor issues, establishment of better housing, and the problem of racism in the Church.[41]

The twentieth century provided new leaders and some positive advances for the African American Catholic community. Thomas Wyatt Turner, longtime professor at Howard University, held no punches in his strong criticism of the segregationist policies in the Church. In his writings, he addressed five major areas where black Catholics had been subjugated: education, Catholic organizations, the Catholic University of America, black priests, and racism in the Church.

In 1924, Turner founded the Federated Colored Catholics, an organization to unite black Catholics, enhance their possibility for Catholic education, and raise the overall status of blacks within the Church through greater participation in the cause of racial justice. Jesuit priests John LaFarge and William Markoe were two other major proponents for black Catholics. LaFarge founded the Catholic Interracial Council (with its journal *Interracial Review*) and, as a result of this, the Northeast Clergy Conference for Negro Welfare. From his base in St. Louis, Markoe published the *St. Elizabeth's Chronicle* as a newspaper to support the rights of African Americans.[42]

In the City of Buffalo, African Americans in general and black Catholics in particular struggled for recognition and their rights. Prior to the Civil War, African Americans in Buffalo were very rare indeed. The first record of an African American in the region was in the 1770s when Joseph Hodges, a fur trapper, traversed the thirty-six-mile Niagara River, which connects Lake Erie and Lake Ontario. In the 1830s, the three hundred blacks in Buffalo began to make notable strides, especially in the establishment of churches. The first black church, Bethel African Methodist

Episcopal Church, was founded in 1831; in 1848, the first black public school was started. One black educator, Peyton Harris, commented about this foundation: "The education of colored youth, up to this point, has been shamefully limited. In very deed it has not reached the dignity and elevation of education."[43] One significant event for blacks in pre–Civil War Buffalo was in August 1843, when the city played host to the National Negro Convention Movement. This six-day event, held at the Bethel African Methodist Episcopal Church, promoted black solidarity through addressing questions of political and social change, including free residence (the freedom to live where one chose to live) and exclusion from education. The conference also featured antislavery speakers.[44]

The period just prior to, and ten years after, the Civil War was especially difficult for African Americans in Buffalo. The Fugitive Slave Act of 1850 forced many blacks to flee the city for Canada. Two years earlier, many Europeans escaping revolution arrived in the city and became competition to Buffalo's black population for jobs. Industrial development after the war was a time of regression for the black community as few had sufficient technical skills to participate in the new job market. Indeed, the historian T. J. Davis commented: "By 1870 the shape of Black Buffalo looked worse than it had in the 1850s." This decline continued throughout the Gilded Age, which saw fewer blacks working in trades, and neighborhoods becoming more segregated. While the African American population between 1855 and 1875 declined, the entire city population tripled. Davis thus concluded: "At mid-century Buffalo was indeed a Queen City in Black population along the Great Lakes; at the turn of the century it was a relatively poor handmaiden."[45]

At the dawn of the twentieth century, Buffalo, as a burgeoning industrial city, experienced the "Great Migration" north of many African Americans. Between 1905 and 1925, the black population rose from 1,059 to 7,413. The importance of this demographic shift was noted by Davis: "This rapid, sizeable increase in Blacks in the city was perhaps the most influential factor in shifting the direction and pace of community change."[46] Unfortunately the burgeoning black population did not mean that blacks in Buffalo found any greater toleration. African Americans were able to get jobs with Bethlehem Steel and other large companies, but they were only and always low-end positions. Davis commented, "The prevalent notion was that Blacks should stay in their place."[47]

The African American community's "second-class" status in Buffalo was a direct catalyst to the promotion of various organizations of blacks in the city. The Niagara Movement, founded by W. E. B. Du Bois in 1905, and the National Urban League, founded in 1911, established chapters in Buffalo. The principal organization in the city, however, was the National Association for the Advancement of Colored People (NAACP), founded in 1909–10. Indeed, it was this latter group in January 1915 that became the first black organization to formally inaugurate a chapter in the city.[48]

The presence of the NAACP and similar organizations could not, unfortunately, arrest the growing feeling of discrimination and subservience experienced by the African American community. The historian Lillian Williams suggests that, as the African American population grew, so too did the opposition of white citizens who devised new tactics of discrimination and segregation. The growing population also accented the distance between blacks and whites in the city. In order to counter this growing opposition, black leaders employed a philosophy predicated upon self-help and racial solidarity in devising and implementing pragmatic social programs. Williams writes, "Through self-help—i.e., self-reliance—Blacks were best able to ward off the debilitating psychological effects of racism and to launch a campaign of human dignity and equality, as well as for social, economic, and political improvement."[49] Despite these efforts, socioeconomic problems continued to plague the African American community. These were manifested most significantly in the lack of opportunity, prejudice, high rents and low wages, and insufficient protection of civil rights.[50]

The history of neglect, prejudice, discrimination, and frustration that accompanied the general African American community in Buffalo was also present, as had been seen nationally, in the Catholic community. Serge de Schoulipnikoff, vicar general for German- and French-speaking citizens during the time of Bishop Timon, was the first to minister to black Catholics in the area. When Schoulipnikoff left the region shortly after the Civil War, his ministry was not continued until 1911, when Father John D. Biden formed the St. Augustine's Club. In June Biden purchased the Dambach House on Michigan Avenue and renovated the three-story structure to accommodate a chapel, social and reading rooms, and a meeting hall. The chapel was serviced by priests from St. Joseph's Cathedral, with Father Henry A. Mooney assigned as the club's chaplain. In 1919, Bishop Turner invited the Josephites to oversee the club, but misunderstandings and factions developed that led the ordinary to once again place the club under the jurisdiction of the Cathedral. Finally in May 1933, Redemptorist priests (CSsR) from St. Mary's Church on Broadway formally took charge of St. Augustine's as a mission church, with Father Francis Litz as pastor and Father John Conway assigned to the mission.[51]

Father Baker's Black Apostolate

Nelson Baker's basic philosophy of assisting the poor and marginalized, manifested throughout his priesthood and his work with youth, was also demonstrated, late in his life, through his outreach to black Catholics. The roots of his desire to assist the African American community go back at least to his pilgrimage to Europe in 1874 and possibly to his Civil War service. Assuredly Baker's observations of the horrible carnage that resulted from the infamous Draft Riots in New York City must have given him some sympathy for the general cause and promotion of blacks in the country. Even more, however, during the voyage to Europe, Baker met a priest, Father T. R. Muelder, who had worked with blacks in Kentucky. He told Baker, "If you get a chance to help Negroes, Mr. Baker, I hope you will seize it."[52]

In a way similar to his assistance to single mothers and their children through the establishment of the Infant Home, Baker saw an opportunity with the black community and responded fully. He stated, "Once I thought that the only thing that would please me was when I built the Basilica. But this has pleased me more—to convert the Negroes to Jesus Christ and I know it is a blessing."[53] Baker demonstrated a genuine affection for this population. One woman who experienced Baker's outreached hand, commented,

Father Baker didn't seem to mind our ragged clothes or worn out shoes and sometimes runny noses. He tried to fix all of the above and more times succeeded quite well. Fr. Baker seemed to love us anyway. His hugs and kisses on the forehead or cheek were real and firm. You couldn't fool children, especially poor ones. We *knew* [emphasis original] he loved us.[54]

Baker explained his motivation in *The Victorian*:

Indeed, it is high time that we took some notice of these gentle, humble, unobtrusive people, who up to now have been mostly proselytized by the sects. The Negro has a soul just as his white brother, but why is it that he has so long been neglected? The Negro convert to the Catholic Faith is usually very true, devout, and faithful. The race is deeply religious, genial and kindly. They are deeply grateful for any favor the white man bestows upon them, are humble, and never intrude themselves where they are not wanted.[55]

Baker's desire to advance the temporal and spiritual needs of the African American community in Lackawanna took a major leap forward at Christmas 1931. Confined to bed due to a broken arm, Baker asked Brother Joachim, who was supervising the soup line, to ask some of the African Americans seeking assistance if they were interested in becoming Catholics. The reaction of the people was very positive, especially because Baker had been so good to them. One African American explained to Baker: "Father Baker, ...we were afraid to ask you [for catechesis] because nobody likes us poor Colored people. But because you are so good and kind we are glad that you will let us become Catholics."[56] In turn, Baker wrote to a fellow priest, "I was only too glad to welcome them."[57]

Inspired by the positive reaction to his invitation, Baker wasted no time in responding. In January 1932, he began to instruct thirty African Americans on the precepts of the faith. Quickly the numbers rose greatly and it was clear that Baker would need assistance. On February 2, based on the recommendation of

Bishop Turner, Father Thomas Galvin, CSsR, a former Baker Boy, joined his mentor in the instruction of African Americans. Galvin was born on March 10, 1864, in Buffalo, but when his parents died at age five he was sent to St. Joseph's. Father Baker took a special interest in the boy, speaking to him often about priesthood. Eventually he entered the Redemptorist Congregation, and was ordained a priest on December 7, 1892.[58] The two men held great mutual respect. Baker spoke of Galvin: "He was wonderfully brilliant and took naturally to religious subjects and this aptitude it seemed could best be developed by the good Fathers in their [Redemptorist] community."[59] Galvin referred to Baker as a "kind and saintly priest."[60] After serving five years in a parish in Boston, Galvin was sent to Brooklyn where he began his work with deaf mutes, becoming proficient in sign language and starting a ministry of retreats for this community.[61]

The small group of thirty students soon mushroomed, with five hundred under instruction, regularly or irregularly, during 1932. Initially classes were held in a small makeshift classroom in the basement of the Protectory. Baker and Galvin met the class each day (six days per week) between 4 and 5 p.m. Galvin was the principal instructor, but when he could not be present, Baker took the class. However, Baker almost daily gave a ten- to fifteen-minute exhortation to the students. Eventually in early March, due to the growing size of the class, Baker moved instruction upstairs to the refectory. However, "owing to a whispering campaign of persecution...Father Baker for fear of the state inspectors...was advised to partition or board off one end of the refectory for a classroom, thus making it a complete and separate apartment from the refectory."[62]

Students received three months of daily intensive instruction. All candidates for baptism were required to pass a test of thirty-five questions. Some of these simply were informational, others inquired about one's commitment, but others were catechetical. For example, typical questions in the latter section would be: What is the Holy Eucharist? What is Easter duty? Who is the Blessed Virgin Mary? The latter part of the examination required candidates to recite basic prayers, including the Our Father, Hail Mary, Apostles' Creed, and the Acts of Faith, Hope, and Charity.[63]

The fruits of the black apostolate were manifested in a profound way on Easter Sunday, March 27, 1932, when Father Baker baptized 10 black converts. By May 12, 98 more had been baptized. By the end of the year the statistics were very impressive: 333 baptisms, 343 reclaimed Catholics, 291 First Communions, and 204 Confirmations. By June 9, 1935, the number of baptisms was 698. Additionally, at least 7 weddings between couples in the classes were celebrated between November 1932 and June 1935.[64]

Baker's dedication to the black apostolate was so complete that he felt it necessary to apologize to some religious for his perceived failure to be attentive to their needs. He wrote to the superior of the local Carmelite community:

> The reason for my apparent indifference is that we have given so much—and really all of our time, to our Negro people, and have instructed and baptized 333 men, women and children, and they have taken so much of our time, but we have had to take it away from everything else, but it won't be long before I have the pleasure of calling on you.[65]

The success of the black apostolate was manifested not only in sacramental numbers, but in the joy that this ministry brought to Baker. He was thrilled that the people in his class were "anxious to be educated and received as members of the Catholic Church." In a letter to a fellow priest he confided, "The work is giving us [Baker and Galvin] very great pleasure and we feel the Lord is not displeased with us, and everything seems to be going along smoothly and pleasantly."[66] In another letter to a friend, he continued his same theme of joy:

> This venture has been to us a most pleasant one, and has afforded us a great deal of happiness in having an opportunity of educating those [who] perhaps never have known anything of the Catholic Faith before, and we made it so attractive, since we did not invite a single one of this number, to continue to present themselves for instruction.[67]

Baker also voiced his joy to his local ordinary: "The work has been a very pleasant one, principally on account of the high appreciation these good people have had of our work among them."[68]

Father Baker's sacramental outreach to the African American community was significant but short-lived. The program was active in 1932, as many received sacraments, but various roadblocks began to appear before the end of the year. One day after Christmas, Galvin was informed of his transfer from Buffalo. Galvin spent mid-June to mid-July in Maryland due to ill health. When his partner in ministry returned in late July, Baker wrote to the Redemptorist provincial expressing how skillful Galvin had become in working with blacks and to Baker had become a "beloved friend for the work we have in hand."[69] Like Baker, Galvin was appreciative of the opportunity he had received to work with the African American community. In December 1932, he wrote, "I am thankful to God that He allows me the opportunity and just sufficient health to promote His honor and glory and to save the souls of this most abandoned class of people."[70]

Galvin never fully recovered, however, from his illness and died on September 20, 1933. At his funeral Baker led the final prayers at the cemetery. Speaking of his former Baker Boy and colleague in ministry, he commented,

> For the past two years, he has been called upon to give instructions to large numbers of colored people, who are living and rearing their children without a knowledge of the True Faith, and his devotion to them became very tender, and he had the pleasure of seeing many of them embracing, through his efforts, a knowledge of that Faith which has been established by Our Blessed Lord Himself.
>
> These good, poor people, became so much attached and devoted to their new teacher, that they have grieved very intensely at the thought that they have lost such a dear, good friend, and they feel that Almighty God must bless him most generously for the kindness he has shown them, and he left positive orders to have this

kindness continued. The general loss of the good Father is considered irreparable.[71]

The loss of Thomas Galvin as a partner in the black apostolate was a significant blow, but other obstacles also raised their heads against Baker's ministry to African Americans. The general antagonism against blacks, as described earlier, plus the "pain" of the Great Depression, set many people against Baker's work from the outset. Soon after Baker initiated his apostolate, police in Lackawanna began to arrest blacks in the area, labeling them as vagrants. Some of these people were homeless, but they had not been arrested by the police prior to this. At times members of the convert class were required to leave the Protectory under the cloud of darkness and secrecy. Galvin reflected upon his experience: "Immediately the powers of darkness raised up an incessant and bitter persecution which made life so miserable for Father Baker, myself and the converts, that if the undertaking were not the work of the right-hand of the Most High it would have collapsed into a disgraceful failure."[72]

In order to neutralize the police purge against the black community, Father Baker rented two apartment houses for those in catechesis. No longer on the street, the people could not be labeled vagrants and, therefore, were not subject to the city's ordinance against vagrants. Appealing to a judge on behalf of forty-eight blacks who had been arrested, Baker stated, "These men were being provided a home and meals by me. The police had no right to arrest the[m] just because conditions have thrown them on the mercies of their fellow men."[73] Nonetheless, Lackawanna authorities continued to press their case. In turn, Baker organized a meeting with the mayor of Lackawanna, a Polish Catholic, and with a municipal judge to discuss the issue, but both officials failed to appear, without the courtesy of informing Baker of their plans. This persecution forced Baker to shelter those scheduled to celebrate the Sacrament of Confirmation at the Working Boys Home. Eventually these candidates were confirmed in Buffalo. Galvin commented on the persecution brought against Baker and his work: "These municipal officials would not wait [un]til these people [Blacks] were baptized, but mercilessly drove them away, or imprisoned them; and this to a great extent thwarted Father Baker's benevolent and holy project, and also prevented many souls from being saved for God in heaven."[74]

Opposition to Father Baker's ministry to African Americans came not only from civic officials but, ironically, from some in his own house as well. Thomas Galvin described the situation in graphic terms:

> There existed in Father Baker's household a spirit of hostility and vindictiveness against any project that Father Baker might inaugurate in favor of the "Dirty Nigger Bums" as they were styled. The animosity and inimical sentiments were so intense that life would become nigh intolerable for any visiting priest who would be induced to take charge of the work.[75]

Criticism came in the form of general prejudice and discrimination, but specifics with respect to Baker's catechetical method were most prominent. Baker's critics suggested catechesis should be done once per week for two-years, not every day for a shorter period of time. Baker rejected the criticism and baptized candidates when he believed they were ready.[76]

Father Baker's critics were present, but his supporters were equally vocal and much more numerous. Chief among his cadre of disciples was Bishop Turner, who wrote to his vicar general in a generic sense applauding his ministry:

> You are entirely right in your attitude, and between our-selves, it is significant to know that when it is a question of *institutional* [emphasis original] care of colored chil-dren, they must turn to us. Nice white boys may find houses; the poor little darkies who also have souls, go begging for Catholic institutional homes as the only means of caring for them.[77]

Baker was appreciative of Turner's support. He wrote, "Your very kind letter came to hand, including a generous offering to assist us in caring for our colored converts, for which we are exceedingly grateful."[78] Several years after his death, Baker was still being applauded for his work with African Americans. Pope Pius XII, in writing to Bishop John Duffy of Buffalo, praised Baker for his efforts:

> We are particularly grateful to learn that there has been added to the long list of beneficent enterprises a flourishing mission for the Negro peoples whose welfare in the United States of America is one of Our most fatherly concerns. It had therefore seemed good to Us to confer on those who are responsible for this praiseworthy undertaking, namely the Association of Our Lady of Victory of Lackawanna, N. Y., some sign of Our particular benevolence that they may be encouraged to continue with unabated zeal their noble labors for the honor of God and the salvation of souls.[79]

The Working Girls Homes

The Great Depression generated in Father Baker two major new ministries of outreach: direct service to the poor through food and clothing, and his work of evangelization among African Americans. During the same period, however, Baker engaged in a familiar ministry to a new group of people, working to establish a home for young adult women in need of some assistance. He wrote in *The Victorian* concerning the rationale for his new work: "We learned that many of our poor girls who came here for the purpose of obtaining a livelihood fell in with bad companions and were numbered, after a while with the wicked women of the city."[80] In 1932, in a move similar to the establishment of the Working Boys Home before the turn of the century, Baker teamed with Inspector John S. Marmon, former superintendent of police, and the Junior Board of the Ladies Aid Society of the Working Boys Home to establish a Working Girls Home on Auburn Street in Buffalo.[81] The home was established "for working girls who were out of employment as a means of protecting that class, as they were easily led astray and brought into houses of ill-repute, and there was nothing left for them but a life of misery and wickedness."[82]

The success of the Working Girls Home on Auburn Street led to the establishment in 1935 of a second similar home on Jersey Street. Baker commented, about both homes: "We are saving many girls from entering the houses conducted by bad women, and thus saving the poor girls from a bad life."[83]

Conclusion

The Great Depression brought economic collapse to the United States on a scale never previously seen. Like many, Nelson Baker, seeing a need before him, answered the call by adding to his already-heavy plate of responsibilities and began to serve the hungry and homeless with food and shelter. This additional work, while helpful to many, was only one of many measures employed by peoples in both private and civic realms to assist the poor in their need. However, this new work led Father Baker into an active apostolate of evangelization to African Americans, something that was indeed very rare for Catholics in the 1930s. Breaking through a barrier that had seldom seen blacks as worthy of evangelization, Baker's pioneering efforts to catechize hundreds in this community was a local example of a more regional effort championed by the Northeast Clergy Conference for Negro Welfare and the efforts of John LaFarge, SJ. Baker rejected periodic criticism of his work, but rather pressed forward, assisted by Thomas Galvin, CSsR, to meet the spiritual needs of a neglected population.

Father Baker's work with African Americans occurred well into the twilight of his life. He had accomplished much, but his many duties, combined with growing infirmities of advanced age and ill health, began to take their toll on this dutiful servant of God. However, he continued to serve as best he could under the patronage of Our Lady of Victory.

CHAPTER 11

Final Years and Death (1926–1936)

The hundred-year period of 1840 to 1940 encompassed some of the most significant events in U.S. history, and demonstrated the ability of its citizens to adapt while holding fast to the nation's fundamental principles, articulated in the Declaration of Independence and the Constitution. America sustained itself through the horrors of four significant wars and national economic depression; it met the challenge of industrialization and the demand for social reform; it emerged as a significant player on the world's political and economic scene. While Americans were forced to adapt to changing times and situations, their ability to maintain focus on their basic national beliefs, while never forgetting their foundational roots, allowed the country to move in new directions and meet the challenges of the future.

In a similar way, Nelson Baker, who lived during this same historical period, adapted to the times and situations to meet the needs of the people to whom he ministered. As a young man, he answered the call of his nation by taking up arms in the Civil War. Using his business expertise, he started a successful feed and flour business. But it was the call of the priesthood and ministry to God's people that would be his life's vocation. While Father Baker's apostolic work focused principally on youth, he adapted, added, and moved in different directions as the situation dictated. He was not afraid to take on challenges, whether that meant raising money for the needs of his Institutions, building the truly magnificent and massive Basilica of Our Lady of Victory, or fighting the State of New York to maintain what he believed to be a sacred trust. He met these challenges as a man of faith with absolute trust that his patroness, Our Lady of Victory, would never fail him. As Baker entered the twilight of his life he continued to faithfully serve others as he had been ordained to do. Nelson Baker never lost sight of his dreams, inspiring others to do likewise.

A Priest Forever

Nelson Baker chose his eventual path in life much later than most of his contemporaries, but he always was one who rejoiced in his reality: "You are a priest forever, according to the order of Melchizedek" (Heb 7:17, NRSV). As described earlier (chapter 1), Baker's childhood and early adult years provided him with an education superior to most of his day and with business experience that demonstrated his ability to be economically successful. Yet, he followed the call of the Lord and entered Our Lady of Angels Seminary at Niagara University and was eventually ordained a priest on March 19, 1876. These events demonstrate that Nelson Baker willingly chose his path, even in the face of family opposition. He was proud to be a priest, which was always central in his long life. Therefore, whenever the opportunity arose to commemorate the vocation God had given him, he and his friends celebrated that reality.

The course of his ministerial life brought him into contact with thousands of boys and placed him in a close association with his bishops. Thus, when important anniversaries of Baker's priesthood arose, it was these people who took the initiative to show their love and appreciation for his ministry to them. On March 19, 1896, Father Baker was feted on his twentieth anniversary of priesthood by a celebration held at St. John's Protectory. The party, organized by the boys at the two Institutions, featured the singing of the Victoria Boys and the formal opening of the Victoria Gymnasium and Drill Hall. Additionally, a program of song and recitation performed by the students was capped by a short play.[1]

The dawn of the new century provided the opportunity to once again celebrate Father Baker's priesthood. His silver jubilee was marked by a grand celebration that was supervised by a priest friend, J. F. Kelly. A solemn high Mass, celebrated by Father Baker at Our Lady of Victory Chapel at St. John's, was the centerpiece of the celebration. Daniel Walsh, with whom he had assisted the Sisters of Our Lady of Charity of the Refuge, served as deacon and John Biden as a subdeacon. Bishop James Quigley preached the homily. A banquet served after the Mass in Victoria Hall hosted many priests, as well as Quigley, and Bishop Bernard McQuaid from the neighboring Diocese of Rochester. Father Baker received numerous gifts for his anniversary, including a solid silver monstrance, a gold chalice, a ciborium, as well as vestments and personal items of furniture. Possibly even more special to him, the boys at St. Joseph pooled their money and bought Father Baker a music box, cassock, and cloak. Boys at the Protectory presented him with a china closet; those at the Working Boys home gave him a humeral veil for the celebration of Eucharistic Benediction.[2] Five years later, Bishop Charles Colton led the celebration on the occasion of his thirtieth anniversary. He commented, "Father Baker's life work began on St. Joseph's Day, and his was the same work as St. Joseph's work. He has always been guarding and watching over the little ones."[3]

The time between Father Baker's silver and golden jubilees was the most significant for his work with troubled youth and included his establishment of the Infant Home and its extension the Maternity (later General) Hospital. Thus, when the occasion for his golden jubilee arrived, there was certainly much to celebrate. As previously mentioned, Father Baker's fiftieth anniversary of priesthood coincided with the planned opening of his new shrine, but illness required that both celebrations be delayed. He celebrated his jubilee on Easter Sunday, April 4, 1926. The boys at St. Joseph and St. John's led the entertainment that day. This included flag drills, a performance by the Our Lady of Victory Band, and a short play titled "Ketchum and Killem Medical Dispensary." Many guest speakers were present for the occasion, including Walter J. Lohr, mayor of Lackawanna, who presented Father Baker with a check for $4,000 from various local parishes. Additionally, he received many spiritual bouquets from his boys.[4]

This grand event was certainly an opportunity for both accolades and personal reflection. Father Matthew Walsh, CSC, president of the University of Notre Dame, wrote Baker with regrets that he could not attend the dedication of the new shrine.

However, he congratulated Baker for his efforts, concluding, "I need not say that to you personally go the prayers and greetings of all on the occasion of your glorious anniversary."[5] Baker himself offered a reflection on his life and priesthood: "Today I celebrated my golden jubilee. Indeed it is golden. Every day in my 50 years as a priest has been golden because of the joy and happiness I experienced. My life has been nothing but happiness and God has blessed me with happy surroundings."[6]

Few priests are privileged to celebrate their golden jubilees, but those able to celebrate sixty years as presbyters are quite rare—especially when not ordained until age thirty-four. Father Baker was one of those few selected by God for such a celebration. Due to his age and rather feeble condition, the occasion was not marked with significant pomp as his earlier anniversaries, but such an accomplishment was noted by many, including the president of the United States, Franklin Delano Roosevelt, who wrote to Baker on this incredible occasion:

> There are indeed notable anniversaries and I desire to join with your other friends in extending hearty congratulations with all good wishes that you may long enjoy peaceful days and the supreme happiness which must come to one who has earned from a grateful people the title Priest of the Poor.[7]

Father Baker himself, demonstrating both thankfulness and humility, reflected upon this significant event:

> The cheer and privilege of attaining such an anniversary is such a rare occurrence but I must be particularly thankful for having been one of those selected. I only desire that He may record me still a brief span in which to attempt to accomplish some of the work I would like to do in His name.[8]

Unfortunately, the extended time asked by both the president and Father Baker to enjoy peaceful days and continue his ministry would be very short.

Nelson Baker's active life of ministry occupied his daily life and was the reason for many celebrations of his priesthood, but he never forgot his roots—and the family that gave him life and formed his core value system. Baker, as we recall, was the only member of his family who followed his mother's Catholic faith. Yet, as years passed, possibly as a result of his influence and notoriety in the area, other members of his family did seek entrance into the Church. In 1894, responding at the point of death to his priest son's question if anything could be done for him, Louis Baker is reported to have said, "If there is anything that will separate me from your dead mother, I want to remove it." Grateful to God for the opportunity, Father Baker, in the presence of two Sisters of St. Joseph, baptized his father in the Roman Catholic Church.[9] A few hours later his father died. In 1930, Baker's brother Ransom was also received into the Church, expressing his great pleasure in the privilege of receiving the Lord in the Blessed Sacrament.[10]

Neither Father Baker's advanced age nor his commitment to his family could keep his fertile mind from always considering new and important ways to serve God's people. He never missed an opportunity to assist others, but time and physical limitations take their toll on all. Baker had several projects in his mind, even in his later years. As education was always an important driving force in his work with youth, Baker wanted to close a gap in his educational offerings by establishing a junior college. Such a facility would allow boys in the Institutions, with sufficient skill, to progress from kindergarten through college.[11]

Although no plans were definitively made for this proposal, a clearer picture was presented for two other projects. The first was consistent with his lifetime commitment to troubled youth, as Father Baker sought to reach out to another marginalized group; namely, children with mental challenges. When state inspectors informed Baker that some of his charges stood on the margins of average intellect, he acted to provide proper teachers and facilities to meet their needs. In order to provide greater service, Baker made plans to construct a facility dedicated to the education of the mentally challenged. He shared his thoughts with one religious sister: "We are now planning to build a large home for weak-minded children in a building practically as large as our hospital....The building is very much needed, as there are so many weak-minded children in need of care, and no effort is made to improve them."[12] He planned to canvas local businesses for donations to construct the facility.[13] Father Baker's second future institution must have been close to his heart, but for different reasons. Possibly due to his own advancing years, Baker's mind turned to ministry to the aged. His friend Brother Stanislaus explained his dream: "He cherished a hope that someday he would build a home for the aged, and those friends who helped him in his early struggles would be welcome to come here and spend their last days under the protection of Our Lady of Victory."[14]

Certainly these projects would have been beneficial to many. However, pressing concerns during the Great Depression, his ongoing battle with the State of New York, and his own at-times precarious health did not allow these last projects to find fruition.

Health Problems and Diminished Capacity

Nelson Baker lived a long, fruitful, and exceptional life that was generally free from serious illness, although there were two significant trials in his younger adult years. During his days at Our Lady of Angels Seminary, he suffered through a long and painful ordeal with erysipelas, but fortunately had no complications later in life from this serious attack. A quarter century later, in February 1898, Baker battled a bad case of pneumonia. He was ordered by doctors to a warmer climate for full recovery. Thus, he went with his friend Daniel Walsh to Southern Pines, North Carolina. After two months he returned rested and fully recovered.[15]

God's blessing of general good health continued, allowing Baker the strength and stamina to guide to completion the construction of the Basilica of Our Lady of Victory, but he did suffer a few significant health problems during the last ten years of his life. In April 1926, a severe cold forced him to escape the harsh winter of Buffalo for the more temperate climate in Washington, DC. In September, his friend Thomas Walsh, bishop of Trenton, wrote with great concern about Baker's health: "I was horribly shocked by your recent breakdown. I hope and pray that you are fully and lastingly restored to perfect health and vigor."[16] In

November Baker's physician declared him to be in "good condition," yet recommended, if he wished to continue his wonderful work, he should conserve and restore his energy by passing the winter in the warmer climate of the South, leaving after the holidays if not before.[17] Apparently Baker did not heed the advice, because a friend wrote to him the ensuing February:

> We wish you would arrange your affairs so that you can come down and spend a month here with us in the sunshine of Florida while we are here. The sunshine and air would do you an immense amount of good, and it would be nice for you to get away from the harsh February and March winds....It will help build you up so that you can return to your work strengthened and fortified to carry on your great work for God.[18]

Baker's most serious bout with ill health began unexpectedly in December 1927. On his way to celebrate a requiem Mass for his friend Sr. Mary Anne Burke, SSJ, he told his driver he could not see out of his right eye and was in great pain. An examination by a specialist revealed that his eye was badly infected. Eventually it was surgically removed. In early January he wrote to some friends indicating that he was confined to his room "on account of some trouble in my eyes." He continued, "I sincerely hope, with God's help, to be around soon."[19] Bishop Thomas Walsh of Trenton wrote to Baker with a sense of heartache over the news: "I was shocked and saddened beyond words by the gloomy intelligence of your serious illness. I am consoled in the happy, glorious information that you are now out of danger and that you are well on the road to complete and lasting recovery and health."[20]

Initially, it seems, his recovery went well, but a full recovery took several months. In mid-January he wrote to a religious sister: "I am pleased to state that I am improving nicely in every way"; at the same time, one of Baker's attending physicians wrote to the bishop: "Our good old friend Father Baker seems to be doing very well. I saw him last week and he was quite chipper."[21] Unfortunately, Baker's personal prognosis for a rapid recovery did not materialize. In early March, at the request of Bishop Turner,

Baker left Our Lady of Victory Hospital and took up residence at Providence Hospital in Washington, DC. His stay in Washington was buoyed by letters of support he received from many and varied peoples. One friend wrote, "We hope that you will be greatly benefited by your stay there [Washington] and will return to Lackawanna in far better health than before your recent illness."[22]

By mid-May Baker was back at the Protectory. He received a heartfelt and most sincere welcome home from the boys. In an unsigned letter, their love for Baker comes through clearly and powerfully:

> We, the voice of St. John's Protectory, are sorry you were ill. We missed you and each day prayed earnestly for your recovery. Hence, it is with joyful hearts we welcome you back. In Father Baker we have a friend whose kind fatherly care for us knows no limits. Well we know that another Father Baker could not be found on this planet called Earth. Perhaps you realize now our joy in having you with us.[23]

Although Baker had returned to his active pace, now sporting a glass right eye, he continued to suffer from small accidents. In November 1928, an "injury to one of [his] limbs" kept him close to home and thus unable to participate in certain activities or to associate with his many friends. In February 1932, Baker was once again on "restricted duty," recovering from a broken shoulder suffered in a fall while walking near his room in the Protectory.[24]

Father Baker's physical age with its consequent limits to human capabilities, coupled with his recent illnesses, diminished his capacity to exercise his leadership role, with both the Institutions and the diocese. Yet, he continued to generate respect and even awe simply through his presence. In 1934, one commentator observed: "[He] receives callers almost daily in the old-fashioned reception room of St. John's Protectory where he autographs holy pictures, blesses penitents [and] gives away hundreds of Our Lady of Victory souvenir medals and scapulars."[25] In January 1935, he reported an illness had kept him from the Christmas celebration that had just passed. He wrote:

I felt awfully ashamed, but I have not been in the church during the nine days of the Novena until Christmas night, and I stole away to get there, as my doctor holds me down tight, and I can't leave my room without telling him and getting permission to do so.[26]

In mid-March a local paper reported: "The Rt. Rev. Msgr. Nelson Baker, 93 on Feb. 16, is weary. The Depression has heaped burden after burden on his shoulders, frail from age. His stout spirit has driven him beyond his physical strength for years." Later that same month, another report read: "Still a frail man, he [Baker] is desperately in need of rest and his physicians have ordered him to stay in bed. He may not go across the hall to his chapel to say Mass."[27] Baker rallied sufficiently to attend his eighteenth consecutive spring luncheon hosted by the Ladies Aid Society of the Working Boys Home. However, he was not able to participate in Holy Week services that same spring.[28]

Father Baker's evident decline continued apace and was readily noticed by all who encountered him. One friend noted, "I have just been advised that there is little hope for his complete mental recovery. My lifelong friend and advisor lies helpless, in a pitiful state that brings tears to my eyes."[29] Baker himself wrote to the chancellor of the diocese, Edmund Britt, admitting his limitations: "Our medical doctor is keeping me under his control and has asked me not to climb stairs anymore than is really necessary."[30] *The Victorian*'s description of Baker indicated that death was on the horizon:

He tried to smile as he waves a greeting to the youngsters, but it is only a feeble effort. The tears stream down his cheeks as he reflects upon his helplessness....His wan face is almost motionless. His eyes are closed. The small mouth moves in silent prayer. Occasionally the nurse reaches over a shrunken form to wipe away a tear that has trickled down his wrinkled cheeks....This saintly priest is now in the twilight of his well-spent life. The Angel of Death is slowly winding her black mantle round his wasted frame.[31]

A few months later, in the spring of 1936, Baker began to fail noticeably. Again, *The Victorian* described the venerable priest's decline:

> The footsteps of Father Baker have lost their sprightliness; the once strong voice has grown feeble and thin; his eyes no longer sparkle with their former luster; but the courage which years ago prompted him to carry on in the face of disaster is as strong today as it was the day he assumed responsibility of St. John's Protectory.[32]

Father Baker's infirmed condition led some to seek profit based on his name. Ten years earlier, Lackawanna police were informed of a man claiming to be Dr. Sullivan, Father Baker's personal physician, soliciting buyers for a book, "The Life of Father Baker," at a cost of two dollars per copy. Additionally, this scurrilous imposter was selling various "medical tonics" for fourteen dollars per bottle.[33] In June 1935, a different but nonetheless fake scheme to raise money for Baker's Institutions was reported to the chancellor, Edmund Britt. An organization called "Victory Club" was asking for a two dollar donation that would gain the contributor rosaries and Masses at the Basilica. Baker had no knowledge of this program, let alone approved of same.[34]

Nelson Baker's inability to continue his past, almost herculean, efforts in service to youth and the diocese required that his responsibilities be reduced. Brother Stanislaus realized that the one-man industry that Baker had ably controlled for almost fifty years simply could not continue. Thus, over the last two years of his life, Baker was slowly relieved of all his major responsibilities. In May 1932, Bishop Turner assigned Monsignor John Nash to assist Baker with his duties in the diocese, telling Baker it was so as "not to put you to any unnecessary strain."[35] In the summer of 1933, Turner informed Baker that doctors had told the former to take a month's rest. Mindful of Baker's condition, he placed diocesan matters in the hands of a committee. He explained to his vicar general with a note of affection:

One of the happiest results of this arrangement has been the removal from your shoulders of this kind of responsibility during my enforced absence. You, also, are under doctor's orders and it is my wish that you follow my example and obey. You remain, of course, Vicar General, in the full enjoyment of your powers, so discreetly and wisely exercised during my previous absences. But I beg you, and the whole Diocese that loves you and venerates you begs you to avoid all care and worry about our Diocesan affairs....We beg you, then, to spare yourself the fatigue of routine attendance at the chancery.[36]

In March 1934, Bishop Turner told Baker that, due to the latter's burden with the Institutions and his new work with African Americans, he was asking the chancellor, Edmund Britt, to take responsibility for Catholic cemeteries in the diocese.[37] In February 1936, Turner again placed Monsignor Nash in charge, "as I do not wish to trouble you with any added burdens at this time."[38]

The need to reduce Father Baker's responsibilities in the diocese was also evident with his many burdens associated with his Institutions for youth. In late fall 1935, Turner gave Edmund Britt the power of attorney with respect to all Our Lady of Victory operations, including the transfer of control of bank funds. In September 1935, Britt was elected vice president of the Society for the Protection of Destitute Roman Catholic Children at the City of Buffalo, replacing Baker. On December 18, 1935, Britt, in turn, hired Irving E. Geary to run the day-to-day operations of the Institutions. Father Baker remained a titular head, especially for fundraising and public relations.[39] In September 1935, Bishop Turner appointed Father James Lucid to head operations for Father Baker. He wrote, "In view of the condition of Monsignor Baker's health, you are hereby appointed Administrator of the Basilica and parish of Our Lady of Victory and all the institutions under Father Baker's care."[40] In late February 1936, Father Austin Crotty was appointed administrator in place of Lucid.[41]

Death and Tribute

The death spiral that would finally claim the life of Father Baker began in earnest on April 30, 1936, when he was admitted to Our Lady of Victory Hospital, suffering from pneumonia. He recovered from this bout of ill health but was very much weakened. News of Father Baker's condition spread as far as Rome. Cardinal Secretary of State Eugenio Pacelli (later Pope Pius XII) sent the message: "The Holy Father sends your Reverence his affectionate apostolic benediction, invoking fortitude and divine comfort in your illness."[42] Baker's condition was well known to his friend and bishop, William Turner. The bishop prepared a funeral oration for his friend. Claiming that he was not "fit for the task" and "I have not even the words to convey my inadequate thoughts in a manner worthy of the occasion," Turner nonetheless provided a beautiful and powerful summary of Baker's life. Taking a slightly different direction than might be expected, he addressed what made his friend's life so useful to the world:

> His humanity was more than human....It took its inspiration from above, and like the rose it got its splendor of color and its softness of hue, its gorgeous growth and its glorious perfume not from the roots that, as you all know, struck deep in the human earth from which we spring, but from the radiant sunshine of religion and revelation that is above us and around us and that wrapped him more than any other in our dull dismal days in its warmth, in the life-giving vitalizing force, that made his life so useful to those who lived in his day and age, and so beautiful in the sight of those who knew him as well.[43]

Ironically, Turner died on July 10, 1936, and never gave his homily.[44]

In mid-July, Baker was once again admitted to Our Lady of Victory Hospital. Friends who visited said that he was generally unconscious or delirious and did not recognize them, even though they had been friends for many years. In lucid moments he expressed the desire to die on August 15, Feast of the Assumption.[45] On July 17, Baker received Extreme Unction, the last rites of the Church, from one of his curates, Austin Crotty, who was then serving as

271

administrator of the parish and Institutions. When it was clear to all that death was imminent, some twenty Sisters of St. Joseph and Brothers of the Holy Infancy and Youth of Jesus gathered outside his room to recite the Litany for the Dying and the Rosary. Surrounded by Monsignor John Nash, administrator of the diocese, Father Joseph Burke, and Dr. Michael Sullivan, Nelson Baker died on July 29, 1936, at 9:20 a.m. The cause of death was listed as cardiac exhaustion and dilation.[46]

Nelson Baker left the world the way he entered it: a poor man who sought only God's glory. His will, written on July 7, 1922, with three other accompanying codicils demonstrated his poverty. He wrote:

> I have no money in the bank, no bonds nor securities of any kind or form. I am indebted to no one financially, and no one is indebted to me....There is no salary due me [from any source]....I have no property of any kind, except certain chattels donated to me by kind friends during my life, such as books, altar furniture, certain articles of furniture, clothing, etc. and I wish the Institutions which have been under my charge in Lackawanna to have these.[47]

In the codicils he spoke of the joy of his priesthood, his absolute faith in the intercession of Our Lady of Victory, and his desire for the Institutions to continue through the good work of the Sisters of St. Joseph.[48]

Baker's death immediately generated published tributes from officials in Lackawanna and Buffalo. The proclamation of Mayor George J. Zimmermann of Buffalo praised Baker for molding "the bodies, souls, and characters of more than 60,000 boys to the principles of Christianity and citizenship." Zimmermann described Baker as the "leading figure in the spiritual, social, and economic advancement of the City of Buffalo and its environs, where his kindly advice and sage counsel, his unstinting gift of time and energy and faith have aided every important function for the enduring benefit of his birthplace."[49] Both Zimmermann and John

Askler, mayor of Lackawanna, declared official periods of mourning until Baker's funeral.[50]

The next few days saw an outpouring of love and gratitude never previously witnessed in the area. At 4 p.m., on July 30, Father Baker's body was transferred to the Basilica of Our Lady of Victory while many priests of the diocese chanted the Office of the Dead. From then until the morning of the funeral, August 3, people near and far, from all walks of life, in orderly fashion though often waiting many hours in the hot sun, filed by the casket to pay their final respects to the Father of the Fatherless, whose body lay in state. Estimates vary, saying that from 300,000 to 500,000 people filed by during this period.[51]

On August 3, the day of the funeral, some 25,000 to 50,000 people gathered in and around the Basilica, hoping in some way to participate. For the first time since the Basilica opened, there was no morning Mass celebrated so as to prepare for the funeral. As a sign of tribute to the priest who did so much for so many, nearly all stores in Lackawanna posted a sign on their front business windows that read: "As a token of respect to our beloved Father Baker, we will be closed from 10 a.m. to noon." The mayor of Lackawanna ordered the day to be a public holiday in honor of our "first citizen for many years."[52]

The funeral Mass procession began at St. John's Protectory with some two thousand participants. In the line of order were representatives of the Knights of St. John, Knights of Columbus (Fourth Degree), American Legion, Holy Name Society, St. Vincent de Paul Society, St. Ann's Colored Society, and the Catholic Daughters of the Americas. These were followed by fifty Sisters of St. Joseph and Brothers of the Holy Infancy and Youth of Jesus, fifty nurses, the clergy, and those celebrating the Mass.[53] One local paper described the scene:

> At least 50,000 persons—men, women, and children that Father Baker loved—stood in solid phalanx all along Ridge Rd. from South Park Ave. to far beyond the cemetery gates. Ten to 15 deep they stood, straining at the ropes stretched along the curb for a glimpse of the final act of the funeral drama that had marked its climax

273

in the white marble basilica that Father Baker had built for the great[er] honor of God.[54]

The Mass was broadcast over WEBR and WKBW, with Francis A. Gowney, professor of English at the Little Seminary of St. Joseph and the Little Flower, as the commentator.[55]

Once the procession had entered the Basilica, the Mass began. The principal celebrant was Thomas Walsh, now bishop of Newark, while Thomas Hickey, retired bishop of Rochester, preached the homily. Bishop George L. Leech of Harrisburg, Pennsylvania, was also present in the sanctuary. Monsignor Edmund Britt, chancellor of the diocese, was the master of ceremonies at the funeral Mass.[56] In his funeral oration Hickey described how his own interest in assisting troubled youth had drawn him to Baker's ministry. He praised Baker, identifying the spiritual flowers of faith, hope, and charity as the roots of his humility. Referencing Jesus' words to seek the things of heaven and not of earth, Hickey offered Baker's life as the perfect manifestation of the Lord's challenge. Most important, Baker was lauded for his belief that whatever he did was actually God's work. Hickey proclaimed:

> He [Baker] knew no limit in placing what he had to offer in the hands of God....His faith was such that he never wavered; he knew no limit in his fidelity. His hope never wavered for the outcome of his work. Of his charity, it must be said that he remembered that while loving God is the first commandment, loving one's fellow men is the second. His whole life was a life spent in the love of God, and in the love and care of God's children. Of his humility, we may say that he never forgot the words of Christ, "I am meek and humble of heart."[57]

Commenting on the funeral, one local Buffalo newspaper stated, "No greater tribute has been paid to any man in Western New York history."[58]

Nelson Baker was buried in Holy Cross Cemetery with his parents, Louis and Caroline, on each side of him. In a semicircle around him were the graves of many Sisters of St. Joseph and Brothers of the Holy Infancy and Youth of Jesus who worked with him at St. Joseph's and St. John's for more than fifty years. In October 1936, Father Joseph Maguire, pastor of St. Agatha's Church in Buffalo, was chosen by Monsignor John Nash, administrator of the diocese, as the next superintendent of Our Lady of Victory Homes of Charity and administrator of the Basilica and Parish of Our Lady of Victory.[59]

Father Baker's death was front-page news for several days in the Buffalo area and generated an outpouring of tributes to a man who had lived his life in the image of his Master. Religion scholar Heather Hartel accurately stated: "The loss of Baker's respected and loved persona and community leadership was a highly charged emotional event for many residents of Lackawanna and Buffalo."[60] *The Victorian* reported: "He extended the charity of the Nazarene…regardless of creed, race, or position in life" in ways that would never be forgotten. Father Baker was gone but his spirit would continue to guide his followers to work on behalf of God's little ones.[61]

Tributes to the life and ministry of Nelson Baker poured forth from every realm of society and many parts of the world. Cardinal Pacelli, writing on behalf of Pope Pius XI, extended the sympathy of the Holy Father with the assurance of prayers for "the eternal repose [of this] faithful servant of God and His poor."[62] Monsignor Joseph Maguire, Baker's successor as superintendent of the Institutions, stated: "Truly has he been called the "Father of the Poor"—for in his many ministrations of true honest to goodness charity, he never neglected anyone, regardless of creed or race."[63] The *Buffalo Times* spoke clearly of the legacy of Baker's great compassion: "And so passes a man whose greatness was not in stone, or eloquence, or statecraft, but in a compassionate heart. He will feel at home among the saints. And then we will give thanks that he had lived and bless his memory."[64] The *Buffalo Courier-Express* emphasized the example that Baker's life was for others: "Father Baker was a remarkable man. He was builder, humanitarian, faithful disciple of the Master. No panegyric is needed now. His own life speaks for itself."[65] The *Niagara Gazette* captured Baker's motivation and contribution:

A great and good man—he devoted his entire life to the unselfish service of others. Meek and gentle, kind and loving father to each soul in his care, all loved him; gracious and affable and sincerely sympathetic, none feared to approach him. Charitable to a fault, saintly in life, a model to his people and to his clergy, and sanctified in his labors, he leaves to posterity a monument to his zeal for God's glory that is symbolic of his life and labors.[66]

The breadth of Father Baker's influence in the community was expressed by an outpouring of sympathy from many Protestant church leaders. Samuel A. Keen, superintendent of the Buffalo District Methodist Episcopal Church, illustrated this sentiment:

Father Baker has made a unique and magnificent contribution to the better life of Buffalo and of America. While we wonder at his splendid abilities to bring things to pass in a large and substantial way, we are more deeply impressed by the reality and tenderness of his love for the poor, the unfortunate, and the suffering.

There is no higher position for any person than to be a lover of God's little ones. In this regard Father Baker takes second place to no archbishop or cardinal. His memory will be nobly perpetuated in the institutions he has established; it will be even more substantially enshrined in the undying admiration and affection of those who [have] been served by him and those who shall be blessed in learning about his Christ-like life.[67]

In addition, the universal desire for goodness that Baker manifested in so many ways was highlighted by Bishop Cameron J. Davis of the Protestant Episcopal Diocese of Western New York: "He [Baker] has for many years expressed the highest principles of Christian service. His gentle, loving characteristics have made their impression for the good of scores of citizens. They will always live with us."[68]

Similarly many leaders of business and government extolled Baker's life. One government official, Martin Bement, said of

Baker: "A man's success in life should be measured by the friends he makes and the good he does. Measured by this rule Father Baker was the most successful man in this country, and probably in the world."[69] In her study of the factors and influences that have generated much of the contemporary knowledge of Baker's work, Heather Hartel suggested that Baker's death and the outpouring of sentiment that followed it help to "secur[e] his status as a celebrated local personality and further establish his reputation as a saintly figure."[70]

Conclusion

Nelson Henry Baker, a Catholic priest of the Diocese of Buffalo, New York, Father to the Fatherless, lived a long and fruitful life of ministry with its central focus on assisting orphans and troubled youth. Baker served the poor of Buffalo for sixty years; he provided homes, food, education, and hope to thousands of children who had been abandoned by their parents or the State. Throughout his time as pastor of St. Patrick's Parish (later Our Lady of Victory Basilica), and as superintendent of his three principal Institutions for youth—St. Joseph's Orphan Asylum, St. John's Protectory, and Our Lady of Victory Infant Home—Baker adapted, advanced, and promoted his work as the situation and personnel dictated. As the nation traversed a path from relative obscurity on the world scene to a position of international prominence, so Nelson Baker's work evolved from a rather small operation serving the local community to a ministry that welcomed all with no questions asked or payment required. Seemingly in possession of endless energy and never cowed by the challenges placed before him, Baker ended his life as he began it: penniless yet, like his patroness Our Lady of Victory, "full of grace."

Father Nelson Baker:
Portrait and Legacy

Nelson Baker lived an extraordinary life in many ways. His ninty-four years of life, sixty years of priesthood, and fifty-four years as pastor speak of great longevity. The experiences of being a soldier in the Civil War, a successful businessman, and a well-respected clergyman demonstrate his ability to adapt and use his multiple talents in vastly different ways. His dedication as an administrator of institutions for youth, his near-miraculous ability as a fund-raiser, and his determination as one who battled the State of New York to maintain his method of operation shows his perseverance, courage, and great faith. His ministry to the poor and to African Americans during the Great Depression made crystal clear his compassion and unbiased outreach to any and all in need.

Yet, despite his long life, numerous activities, and grand record of accomplishments, Father Baker's legacy cannot be confined solely to measurable criteria. The richness of his life provided a mark of excellence and care for many agencies and institutions dedicated to the poor, issued a challenge to the advancement of social-justice Catholicism nationwide, and made an indelible imprint on the minds and hearts of the people of Western New York. These rather intangible but very real aspects of Father Baker's life require some analysis. His legacy is a product of his accomplishments, plus his personality, his spirituality, and the kindness and humility that characterized his life. It is fitting in closing this story to examine the less visible but nonetheless critical aspects that made Nelson Baker the man, priest, and minister who was thought by some in his day to be a miracle worker and considered by many today to be a saint.

Baker's Driving Forces

Nelson Baker was a man of great talent and genius who also possessed seemingly endless energy, and who persevered through many trials, producing significant results—in many cases life-changing, if not life-saving results—for thousands of people in the process. He used his business acumen to do the work and his faith to lead him in the proper direction. The driving force of his life was undoubtedly his love for the Blessed Virgin Mary under her title of Our Lady of Victory. Indeed one writer in 1915 stated: "Of all Father Baker's works, the one dearest to his heart, the one upon which all is builded [sic] is his zeal in spreading devotion to Our Blessed Lady of Victory."[1] Another contemporary offered a similar comment: "I think he was so consumed with his work for the Blessed Mother that it was foremost in his mind all the time."[2]

Father Baker's devotion to Mary was manifested in many ways. Like most Catholics of his time period, Baker practiced popular devotions, including the Rosary, which received a huge boost in popularity through the apparitions of Mary at Fatima, Portugal, in 1917. One of the Baker's Boys commented: "He'd [Baker] always have a rosary in his hand, always even at work. Many times we used to go to his office and he would have a rosary in his hand."[3] Images of Our Lady of Victory could be found throughout the Institutions that he supervised for more than half a century. The majestic statues of Mary that adorn the Basilica's main altar and greet those who enter the church are prominent examples, but they only represent a more general mind-set in Baker's thinking. Small statues of Our Lady of Victory along with medals of her image were often the prizes awarded to boys in the Institutions for various good works, including, as mentioned earlier, the class that won the monthly contest for the highest percentage of reception of the Holy Eucharist. Baker's devotion to Mary was demonstrated repeatedly in his two publications, the *Annals* and *The Victorian*. Each issue contained various articles that addressed in some way devotion to Mary.[4] Father Baker himself spoke of Mary as his motivating force: "I placed myself and my work in the hands of Our Blessed Lady of Victory. I besought her aid and intercession in carrying on our sorely needed work.

280

Through her powerful aid have our buildings grown to their present proportions."[5]

Unquestionably the Blessed Virgin Mary is central to understanding Nelson Baker's spirituality and the principal driving force behind his apostolic work, but as we have seen, his devotion to the Eucharist was also at the root of his life. While Baker's 1874 chance encounter with devotion to Our Lady of Victory was the chief catalyst to his later devotion, his piety associated with the Eucharist was more self-motivated. The Buffalo diocesan historian Walter Kern claims that Baker's devotion to the Eucharist, especially his desire for more frequent Communion, was initiated through conversations he had with confessors during those critical years of his business partnership with Joseph Meyer. Kern further asserts that Baker's devotion grew stronger through ordination. He wrote: "With the right to celebrate Mass once a day, and when necessary to do it twice, his [Baker's] Eucharistic piety continued to grow."[6] The encouragement Baker gave to his boys to receive the Eucharist, especially the monthly contest, and his promotion of exposition of the Blessed Sacrament and Benediction became almost legendary in his Institutions. In his role as vicar general, he gave permission in some communities for weekly exposition and often came, many times unannounced, to celebrate Eucharistic Benediction with various communities of Sisters.[7]

While Father Baker's devotion to the Eucharist was manifested primarily through his own piety and his promotion of the devotion in his institutions, he also provided insight through his writings. In 1918, he wrote attributing his success to Our Lady of Victory, but also recognized the essential role of Jesus in his work:

> Our expenses have been enormous considering the high cost of living, but our Lord being the friend of the homeless and destitute would not permit us to suffer....He is now aiding us in the erection of a Home for Maternity purposes, and we feel that an immense good will [has] come from the same, but we never could do it without His holy help, and we feel that His Blessed Mother will also be honored in this work, as we have always tried to have her in all our works.[8]

Father Baker's motivating forces of devotion to Our Lady of Victory and the Blessed Sacrament were exercised daily through prayer. Baker raised up his requests for his Institutions, whether seeking monetary funds or the faith and strength to persevere through difficult times, by means of prayer. The many novenas prayed annually for and by members of the Association of Our Blessed Lady of Victory, the celebration of the Eucharist, plus important popular devotions such as the Rosary and Eucharistic Benediction were public demonstrations of prayer. These outward manifestations were joined by other devotions of particular importance to Father Baker, but possibly less visible to the outside world. He always held a strong devotion to the Sacred Heart of Jesus. In one meditation he wrote: "We owe much to the Sacred Heart of Jesus, and should show that we are not unmindful of His great love for us, not unfeeling for His intense sufferings, prompted by love for us, and the least we can do is to love Him in return."[9]

In the Communion of Saints, Father Baker held special devotions to St. Joseph, St. Vincent de Paul, and St. Alphonsus Liguori. As husband of Mary and foster father to Jesus, St. Joseph certainly holds an important place in salvation history, yet his role is often overshadowed by Mary and Jesus and obscured due to his silence in the Scriptures and the prevalence of information and writings on other saintly figures. However, Father Baker still held a special devotion to St. Joseph, publishing in the *Annals* and *The Victorian* personal reflections and various articles dedicated to him. He once wrote of St. Joseph:

> My dear readers, every one of you now holding this book in your hand must die. There will come an hour when your heart will cease to beat, when you will close your eyes and fold your hands in death. Happy you if your death has the assistance of St. Joseph. Then, no matter if flames devour you, or waters overwhelm you, or disease slays you, the prayers of St. Joseph will throw around you, an all protecting mantle of defense.
>
> St. Joseph is the patron of a happy death because he died in the arms of Jesus and Mary, and was the first of the patriarchs who entered heaven with our Lord.[10]

Baker's devotion to St. Vincent de Paul began during his days as a businessman when he assisted Father Thomas Hines at Limestone Hill with obtaining food and other items for St. Joseph's and St. John's. This was done through the St. Vincent de Paul Society. Baker's devotion was strengthened during his days at Our Lady of Angels Seminary and Niagara University when he supervised the Society's outreach to others. Baker's devotion to St. Alphonsus Liguori was closely associated with his devotion to Mary, as this pioneer of moral theology and founder of the Redemptorist order was also a great proponent of Marian piety.[11]

Father Baker's dedication to prayer was seldom directed inward to his own requests, but rather outward to the needs of others. Besides his obvious prayer for the Institutions he supervised and the thousands of boys they served, Baker never forgot parishioners and other individuals who came to him seeking his prayers. Brother de Sales of the Brothers of the Holy Infancy and Youth of Jesus claimed that, from about 1909 forward, Baker always carried with him two small, red-covered books. One contained the names of people who had asked for his prayers; the other contained names of those who had made contributions to the Institutions. He placed these books on the altar each day he said Mass and left them before the altar each evening before retiring. A third notebook was inscribed with the names of those he daily met and who sought his prayers. Each evening a secretary would transfer names from this daily entry into the red-covered book, assuring people that Father Baker would not forget their requests. One writer commented, "The 'Little Red Book' was precious to Father Baker."[12]

The goal of Father Baker's personal devotion to Mary, the Eucharist, and popular saints was the salvation of souls. After his death, one news story commented: "He [Baker] loves Christ and his soul burns with the desire to give souls to Christ, his own first and then countless others."[13] The historian Timothy Allan captured the essence of Baker's apostolic work:

> As a priest, Nelson Baker was, clearly, activist rather than theorist…combining in his life and work an extraordinary example of the synthesis of the spiritual and practical.…Father Baker was inspired by one unchangeable

thought, and that was the overriding mission of the ordained priest to save souls for God.[14]

Obviously, Baker's desire to save souls was oriented in a preferential way toward orphans, troubled boys, and infants. His love and compassion for those living on the margins outweighed all other interests. Shortly after the Infant Home opened he wrote, "It is needless to notify our friends that we shall take homeless and destitute children wherever they may be found, as this is the object of our work."[15]

Nelson Baker's magnetic personality, personal motivation, and strong devotion were held together by the glue of his great faith. This faith had many aspects and was manifested in numerous ways. His faith was centered in the Christian life and anchored in God. He once wrote:

The religious man is the only successful man. Nothing fails with him. Every shaft reaches the mark, if the mark be God. He has wasted no energies. Every hope has been fulfilled beyond his expectations. Every means has turned out marvelously to be an end because it had God in it, Who is our single end.[16]

Baker's faith was exercised most prominently in the service of others. Possessing the proverbial mustard seed of faith that would allow a mulberry tree to be uprooted and planted in the ocean (Luke 17:6), Baker outwardly did not worry about monies needed for various projects; he was convinced that needed revenues would be found. He believed that God would always respond in munificent ways if men and women were willing to do their part. He once wrote, "God can turn every blade of grass into greenbacks. He can put into the hearts of people [the idea] to help you...He will not be outdone in generosity."[17] His faith was ever confirmed through what he accomplished in life. One observer commented:

His [Baker's] success has given his faith the most beautiful confirmation. Never once have failed the needs of the large works of Our Lady of Victory; never once one of its shops had to suspend operations because there was no money to pay the workmen on Saturday. Nevertheless almost every week started without one knowing on whom to count to settle accounts.[18]

Father Baker experienced numerous challenges and troubles in his life, both personally and with respect to his apostolic work, but these hurdles never swayed his faith. He believed that "God assigns to each [person] a share of suffering that will chasten the soul to more noble ideals and finally to heights of sanctity."[19] Baker always seemed to ride on the crest of the waves; he never seemed cowed or subdued. His friend Brother Stanislaus commented after Baker's death: "I never knew him to be discouraged. I never knew him to be worried by any difficulties. He had an unfailing faith in his work, which to him was a work of religion."[20] Baker went forward with projects where others would hold back. He was "reckless…in his full trust in God," a trait that allowed him to serve more fully and achieve significant results.[21] One member of his family aptly described his work ethic and faith: "The family thought Father Baker was a dreamer, but he was different from most people. Through his prayers and great faith, his dreams became reality. He worked all the time and consequently got things done."[22]

Characteristics of a Lifetime

Nelson Baker was a man of small stature but enormous personality. He was actually quite short, only 5'4", with a very slender build and maturing gray hair. He was once described as "a stately man, alert and smiling." He usually wore a Prince Albert coat, with celluloid collar and cuffs in his ever-present clerical black. His genteel nature, his always positive countenance, and his optimistic outlook on life—things that had made him the "life of the party" as a youth growing up in Buffalo—were equally evident and appreciated by others during his sixty years of priesthood.[23] Baker possessed a good sense of humor and a very affirming attitude toward people. He especially liked to "joke around" with the boys and at times his fellow priests and religious. He often offered off-the-cuff quips and jokes. When a photographer used an explosive flash taking an indoor shot, Baker was often heard saying, "Well, nobody was killed!" In the last years of his life, one of the nurses at the Infant Home remembered Baker saying, "I am half blind but I can still see the pretty girls."[24] At times his humor extended to his professional relationships. During the depths of the Great Depression, he wrote to Margaret Kirby, his administrator of Holy Cross Cemetery, mixing contemporary reality with comic relief:

> I am so glad to know that you are continuing to do business although undertakers are telling us, with tears in their eyes, that their business is dropping off, and I guess the reason is that it costs so much to die that nobody wants to do it....We had Brother Thomas' brother-in-law here for a few days, and his good wife, and he mourned very much that there was so little business doing in his town in Vermont, and he was watching the telephone all the time, hoping to get word that somebody important had died so that he could hurry back and get the job.[25]

Inside Father Baker's small physical size, genteel personality, and grand sense of humor lay a very private, optimistic, and patient man with whom all felt comfortable. He was a man who always shunned the limelight; his apostolic work was to aid children and to promote the greater glory of God. Therefore, in March 1925, he was aghast when he learned that Thomas Galvin—former Baker Boy and now fellow priest—had published a book about his life.[26] Father Baker also demonstrated supreme patience, as evidenced by his work with youth and his longtime battle with the State Office of New York. Indeed, one writer commented: "Outside of his love for Our Lady of Victory and his child-like confidence in her, his one outstanding characteristic was his patience."[27] Father Baker was always approachable, due in large part to his open-mindedness and his ability to look at both sides of all issues. His soft speech and the twinkle he always had in his eye drew people to him like a magnet.

While Father Baker's personality and the way he approached people were attractive to all, he was not a man who liked to delegate responsibility; he had a penchant for control, a trait not uncommon in clerical ranks. Still, toward the end of his life he was forced to delegate some responsibility. Herman Gerlach, who served as one of Baker's curates from 1913 to 1932, aided the venerable priest at the Institutions. One news report, published after Gerlach's death in 1937, stated:

> While at Father Baker's he [Gerlach] aided the noted Padre of the Poor in his charitable endeavors, being the beloved prelate's principal assistant in planning and carrying out his work. He played a prominent role in the building of the world famous basilica and several homes and institutions of Our Lady of Victory.[28]

While records are sparse, it appears that Baker ceded more responsibility to his curates in the day-to-day activities at the parish. The baptismal and interment records of St. Patrick's Parish show that, during his first twenty-five years as pastor, Baker was very active in sacramental ministry. However, after 1907, his name is infrequently seen listed in the sacramental registers.[29] Nonetheless, Baker was the one from whom all ideas pertinent to his apostolic works flowed; he was the one who stood at the center of all fundraising initiatives. His biographer Floyd Anderson claimed that Baker "never learned to delegate authority in major matters."[30] Baker's philosophy of control could, however, be viewed as dedication. A comment from one former student at Our Lady of Victory Mission School, who was later an employee at Holy Cross Cemetery, speaks to both of these possibilities: "No matter how insignificant a matter it was, it was not too small for him [Baker] to [take] care of personally. He never passed anything important on to anyone else. There would [never] be anything he thought too insignificant for him to do."[31]

Baker's predilection for control was partially based on his demanding nature, for both himself and others. His almost superhuman volume of energy and extraordinary work ethic produced very high standards. This allowed him to do more than the average person, but possibly placed unreal expectations on others. One Sister of St. Joseph recalled an incident when one of Baker's curates praised the Sisters and Brothers of the Holy Infancy and

Youth of Jesus for their exceptional work. To this comment, Baker replied, "That's nice, but I wish it were true."[32] People who worked at the Institutions were fully aware that Baker was "the boss." When he wanted it done, he wanted it done. "One did not challenge a decision made by Father Baker."[33]

Any tendency present in the personality of Father Baker to hold control could not in any way, however, obscure his virtues of kindness and humility. His contemporaries spoke of his "heart of gold" and of how he "always had time for those who came to him, and he never turned anyone away."[34] As mentioned previously, Baker was unassuming, preferring the spotlight to be placed on others. One person wrote, "He is determinedly uncommunicative about his own life and achievements....His main concern is with [the] men."[35] He was not concerned with their religion or their political ideology; his only concern was their need—or needs. It seemed no matter how busy he was with all of the business associated with the institutions, he always had time for everybody.[36]

One significant element of his kindness was how he manifested charity through generosity. Baker was generous almost to a fault, to family, friends, and often people he did not even know. As a young businessman, he used his assets to assist his family on many occasions. When he arrived at Limestone Hill as superintendent of the Institutions, he calmed the stormy waters created by his many creditors by offering to pay them partially from his own assets. Later, especially during the period of the Great Depression, he gave clothes, shelter, and even pocket change to those in need. One of Baker's contemporaries commented: "Men would stop him and ask him for a hand-out, and he always gave it to them. He was very, very good to all people regardless of who they were."[37] At Holy Cross Cemetery, he often gave free service to the poor, believing that everyone deserved a proper Christian burial. He also demonstrated great charity toward various religious sisters and brothers in the diocese, both through cash allotments and his expert advice on various business matters. One description of Baker captures this important feature of his personality: "To the widow, the poor, and the unfortunate, he is a kind hearted angel of mercy, never turning a deaf ear to a worthy cause, always willing to help the oppressed."[38]

Father Baker was a humble man, as demonstrated by his simplicity of life, deference toward superiors, and rejection of titles of authority, especially "monsignor" in favor of simply "father." Baker's abstemious eating practices during his seminary days continued throughout his life. His dress was equally simple; he often wore clothes until they were faded and threadbare. One observer commented, "He always wore the same old suit or cassock—nothing new." The material side of life held no attraction to Nelson Baker. One Sister of St. Joseph stated, "He lived as though he was poor....His meals and everything were very plain and he wasn't hard to please at all."[39] A contemporary writer of the day offered his opinion: "Father Baker's whole life is curiously medieval in its simplicity and asceticism."[40] Baker always demonstrated filial piety toward his ecclesiastical superiors; his docility to their least desire and his respect for their authority and person were noted by his contemporaries. While Baker had been named a monsignor in 1905 and a protonotary apostolic in 1923, he never used these titles, always preferring to be addressed simply as "Father Baker." His humility was also present in that he never held himself apart from others. He never saw patchy clothes or a life in disarray; he saw the person. While his fame spread, he remained a quiet unassuming gentleman who centered his thoughts on those who had been placed in his care.[41] A prayer that Baker wrote speaks clearly of his priorities, including his humility: "To be silent, to suffer, to judge no one without necessity, and to listen to the voice of God within us—this will be a continual prayer and sacrifice of self." [42]

The Figure of a Saint

The task of a biographer is to report the facts and narrate the events of the subject's life, interpreting them in the context of the time period to determine their significance to the individual and to the world in which the person lived. Thus, the determination of sanctity, especially with respect to the Roman Catholic Church and its highly specialized and detailed processes of beatification and canonization, has not been entertained in this work on the life of Nelson Henry Baker. However, both during Baker's life and now, over seventy years after his death, numerous stories, with varying degrees of historical merit, have arisen that many claim to be miracles effected by the celebrated priest's intercession. Interestingly, the only critically researched work on Baker, that of Dr. Heather Hartel, addresses this issue by analyzing the "cult" of Father Baker and its impact on the people of Western New York. She writes: "The diversity of representations of Baker and the Institutes created by both ecclesiastic and popular agents demonstrate that Baker's story is deeply ingrained within the imaginative life of the greater Buffalo region."[43] She concludes, "I assume that Baker's sanctity exists in the fluid world of discourse. Simply put, Baker as a saint exists in what is said about him, and what is said about him can change."[44] This theoretical analysis, while helpful for scholarship, seems to ignore the saintly virtues Father Baker clearly demonstrated in his life, as described in this biography.

How did the contemporaries of Father Baker view his life? This biography clearly demonstrates the positive impact he had on others and the general respect and love that others held for him. This grew with time but, so too, must the love and respect for any person, for it is based on what one experiences from the person in question. Some saw Nelson Baker as Christ-like. One religious sister wrote to him:

> I could see in you, dear Monsignor Baker, another Christ on earth, a soul that existed only to please Jesus and His Blessed Mother. Yes, you are the real priest of God, and if the Lord would accept it I would give the years of my existence to give to you [a] longer and prosperous life to make you continue such great work.[45]

In the eulogy for Baker he never delivered, Bishop Turner stated: "He had Christ's love for the poor; he had Christ's compassion for those who suffer; he had Christ's tender care for children; he had Christ's courtesy if I may so call it, towards the downfall of, the unfortunate, but rejected by smug society, the victims of our too pharisaical social order."[46] Turner further said that non-Catholics viewed Baker "not as a Catholic, but as a citizen, as a doer of good deeds, as a worker of wonders in social betterment, as a true representative…of the Spirit of Christ."[47] He was one who served and did so faithfully.

As might be expected, most people centered their comments on Baker's work with youth. Thomas Galvin described him as a "public-spirited citizen…who endures all manner of personal sacrifices, persecution, misunderstanding, financial outlays, and even loss of health and fortune if necessary, in order to provide the happiness, eternal and temporal, of others."[48] One contemporary writer offered a similar comment:"His [Baker's] labor on behalf of homeless children is known far and wide and is commended by all right-thinking men because it is a work of religion, of charity, of patriotism."[49]

Baker's Christ-like work, his simplicity of life, and his virtues of great charity and kindness made him the central figure in several reported miracles, both during his life and after his death. Local Buffalo writer John Koerner has addressed the phenomenon of reported miracles in Baker's life in two recently published books. Koerner's works are not intended to report verifiable facts, but rather, using a more hagiographic technique, to chronicle stories that have circulated for years about unexplained physical healings and other phenomena that people believe happened through the intercession of Father Baker. These books enhance a "cult understanding" of Father Baker, thus verifying the basic thesis of Heather Hartel.

Numerous accounts of miraculous healings have been reported by various writers. Thomas Galvin, in his 1925 biography of Baker, was the first to recount specific incidents that were inexplicable and thus "miraculous." He reported four cures, all as a result of people's participation in the various novenas to Our Lady of Victory. Sister René Ruberto reported three other miracles during Baker's life, including the case of a nurse at the Infant Home who was pronounced dead but, when Baker knelt by her bed and prayed the Rosary, she returned to life. Between 1927 and 1935, even while Baker was still alive, *The Victorian* reported numerous cures, most of which came as a result of participation in the novenas, but others, it was believed, came as a direct result of Baker's personal prayer for the individual. Robert McNamara reported three incidents in Corning, New York, during Baker's brief one-year stay there, that people believed to be miraculous (see chapter 3).[50]

Following Baker's death, miracles resulting from his intercession continued to be reported. One story related by Koerner speaks of two women in the Basilica who, when praying, saw Father Baker pass by them. One of the women, deaf in one ear, told Baker about her condition. He responded by putting his hands over her head and prayed over her. When the woman left the church she was able to hear.[51]

The many miracles reported as by the hands of Father Baker beg the inevitable question: "Was Nelson Baker a saint?" There is no question that people both during his life and after his death believed that he was. Father Patrick Cormican, SJ, who knew Baker in his last years, commented immediately after the latter's death: "To my certain knowledge Father Baker has performed miraculous cures and I have reason to hope that he will someday be formally declared a saint by the Catholic Church."[52] In August 1935, a Baker devotee, Francis van Eich, stated: "He [Baker] surely is a living saint." In late July 1947, Monsignor Joseph Maguire, who succeeded Baker as pastor of the Basilica of Our Lady of Victory, expressed in a sermon preached at Mass that Baker would one day be named a saint.[53]

Nelson Baker's exemplary life, reports of miracles by his hand, and the belief in the minds of many that he was a saint, led diocesan officials shortly after his death to speak of his canonization. Hartel suggests that people believed the cause to be important but it was overshadowed by more immediate financial and pragmatic concerns. Joseph Maguire showed interest in the cause but had to put his efforts into reorganizing the Institutions. Bishop John O'Hara (1945–51) expressed his intent to pursue the cause, but felt it would be appropriate to wait longer to initiate matters. Monsignor Joseph McPherson, who headed Our Lady of Victory operations from 1949 to 1979, commissioned Floyd Anderson's non-footnoted biography, but, like O'Hara, he did not want to initiate the cause as the diocese and the institutions did not have sufficient personnel or funds to support such an effort.[54]

Finally, in May 1986, the fiftieth anniversary of the priest's death, the cause for Father Baker's canonization was resurrected.

Through the combined efforts of Monsignors Walter Kern (diocesan archivist), Robert Wurtz (president of Our Lady of Victory Institutes), and Robert Murphy (pastor of Our Lady of Victory Parish), a proposal was made to Bishop Edward D. Head, but the local ordinary decided to move cautiously until all proper documentation could be obtained. In January 1987, with these requirements met, Bishop Head publicly announced that diocese had begun to study Baker's life with the intention of beginning the canonization process. Ten months later on October 7, the Feast of Our Lady of Victory, the Vatican declared Nelson Baker a "Servant of God." In November 1994, censors reported there was "nothing unacceptable" in Baker's published writings.[55] In January 2011, the Vatican named him "Venerable Nelson Baker."

Nelson Baker's Legacy

Unquestionably Nelson Baker left a legacy that for the foreseeable future will continue to mark Lackawanna, Buffalo, and the whole of Western New York. During his day and even to the present hour, Baker's name remains a household word. Buffalo residents can mark their youth by the first time they were introduced to two local icons: the Buffalo Bills professional football team and the name of Father Baker. This phenomenon was impressed upon the author the first time I arrived in Buffalo. Taking a cab from the airport, I told the driver, whose accent immediately told me he was an immigrant, that I wanted to go to the Basilica of Our Lady of Victory in Lackawanna. The driver immediately went into a panegyric on Father Baker as if he personally knew this priest who had died more than seventy years earlier. Indeed, a comment made after Baker's death has proven true: "Legends adorn the fame of saints long dead, but here was a man who became a legend in his own time. To have known Father Baker was to marvel at his energy and that the works that flowed from it."[56] Yes, Nelson Baker truly was a legend in his own time.

Baker's legacy is found in his uncompromising devotion to his apostolic endeavors and his undying faith. He certainly accomplished much. Again, Hartel aptly noted: "Documentary and anecdotal evidence leaves little doubt that Nelson H. Baker was an extraordinarily appealing Catholic personality. His humility, shrewd fund raising instincts, and persistence in caring for others remained dominant characteristics until the end of his life."[57] Baker's legacy is also found in his Institutions and care for youth. One writer has captured the essence of this gift: "Thus Father Baker left behind not only a record written in stone, brick and marble, but an enduring monument in the hearts of men."[58] One must not forget, as well, his legacy of the stunningly magnificent Basilica, which stands as a tangible symbol of one man's faith in God and devotion to Mary.

The heritage Father Baker left might well be explained by his devotion to St. Vincent de Paul, from whom he most assuredly received inspiration in his early life. Like the founder of the Vincentian order of priests, Baker gave away his life to those less fortunate, most especially to the young. His success rested on his ability to offer a Christian response to the serious problem of homeless and delinquent children in the United States. In praising Baker, one comment in a local Buffalo newspaper captured this aspect of his contribution to society: "Only what a man gives away is he allowed to take with him to the grave. Father Baker has given all they had to give."[59] For well-over half a century he supervised the Institutions that gave away everything so that children would prosper as productive and faith-filled members of American society.

Who was Nelson Henry Baker? This question was ably addressed by the canon lawyer Father Joseph Klos:

> To some he was a shrewd businessman, driven to succeed by a remarkable vision. To others, he was a protector, an advocate for the rights and well-being of all people, regardless of ability, race or creed. And to still others, he was a spiritual leader of incredible faith, giving all to God in the name of Our Lady of Victory.[60]

Nelson Baker's ninety-four years of life covered a broad spectrum of triumph and defeat in American society. Active as an adult from the time of the Civil War through the interwar period of the 1930s, he has left a significant footprint in history. The historian Timothy Allan summarized Baker's legacy and history: "An impor-

tant aspect of Father Baker's adult life is that it embraced and illu-
minated the noblest historical impulses of his times while it also
soared above and disdained the mean and the ignoble."[61]

Conclusion

Father Theodore Hesburgh, CSC, was president of the
University of Notre Dame for thirty-five years (1952–87), advisor
to United States presidents, friend of popes, president of the
Board of Trustees of Harvard University, and inspiration to thousands by his exemplary life. His significant work for Catholic
higher education, and his service to the nation—as well as having
more honorary degrees awarded him than any other person now
living—mark his importance. He wrote a trenchant comment in
the introduction to his autobiography, *God, Country, and Notre
Dame*. He said the one and *only* word he wants on his tombstone
is *Priest*. As a member of Father Hesburgh's religious family, the
Congregation of Holy Cross, I know that this wish will not be fulfilled, but the thinking behind his request is, to say the least,
indicative of his humility. With a uniquely broad resumé that
demonstrates significant achievement in many areas of society,
sacred and secular, an equally wide-ranging group of friends and
associates, and exploits that were reported in newspapers and
whose names are and will be found in history books, Father
Hesburgh's request might seem a bit odd. But for him, his life
centered on the priesthood; the other accomplishments were secondary.

Nelson Baker, builder of institutions, advocate for the poor,
and "Father to the Fatherless" was, above all things, a priest, a servant of Jesus Christ. His legacy of assistance to orphans and troubled youth, the construction of the Basilica of Our Lady of
Victory, and the many ways he touched the hearts and minds of
thousands of people were, for Father Baker, sources of spiritual
enrichment that nurtured his vocation to serve God's people as a
priest. This is what he leaves to history and to all of those who
admire his life and work.

Afterword

As a young boy growing up in Western New York and now, as a priest of the Diocese of Buffalo, I had more than a passing knowledge of Father Baker and his work. Like almost every youngster in the Buffalo area, I had the threat of being sent to "Father Baker's" held over my head whenever I misbehaved. My pastorate prior to coming to Our Lady of Victory was the neighboring parish of Our Lady of the Sacred Heart, which was founded by Father Baker in the 1920s as a mission of the Basilica. I was surrounded by the image of Father Baker and the goals he set for his ministry. It was with true humility (and a certain amount of trepidation) that I entered into my current assignment as pastor of the Basilica, president of Baker Victory Services, executive vice president of Our Lady of Victory Homes of Charity, and vice postulator for Father Baker's Cause for Canonization. It is in the role as vice postulator that I am able to share with you the history and status of efforts to have Father Baker canonized.

In his lifetime, Father Baker was considered a saintly man by many who knew him. After his death, his reputation as a holy man, if not an actual saint, continued to grow. In the minds of many in the Buffalo area and beyond, it would be only a matter of time until he was considered for formal canonization.

In 1987, when the Vatican Congregation for the Causes of Saints accepted the proposal of then-bishop Edward D. Head to open the case for Father Baker's canonization, they set into motion a thousand-year-old process for naming a saint. Once a local bishop proposes someone for potential canonization, he appoints a person in the diocese whose responsibility it will be to make the life and works of the person better known, and, on a diocesan scale, make others aware of the possibility of canonization.

In the early stage of the diocesan effort to promote Father Baker's cause, Monsignor Robert Wurtz was named the postulator. At the time he was the administrator of the Our Lady of Victory Homes of Charity and Baker Victory Services. Monsignor Robert Murphy, then pastor of Our Lady of Victory Basilica, was named vice postulator, and Monsignor Walter Kern, diocesan archivist, who had already done much work on the life and times of Father Baker, was named notary, or canonical secretary, for the process.

Once the Vatican officially accepts the cause for a proposed saint, the administrative structure surrounding the cause changes. At this point, the role of postulator moves to a canon lawyer who resides in Rome, representing the cause "on the scene" as it proceeds. The former diocesan postulator becomes the vice postulator, continuing to promote awareness of the potential saint. In light of the Holy See's formal acceptance of Father Baker's case, Buffalo's Bishop Henry J. Mansell (presently archbishop of Hartford, Connecticut) selected the Roman canon lawyer Dr. Andrea Ambrosi as postulator. At the same time, he named Monsignor Robert Wurtz as vice postulator. Since Monsignor Kern's health was no longer strong, his role as notary was given to Ms. Dianne Bellagamba, Monsignor Wurtz's secretary.

Monsignor Wurtz had given over thirty years of service to the Father Baker Institutions. At the heart of his ministry was his strong desire to see Father Baker canonized. He worked tirelessly to bring this about and his efforts laid the groundwork for all that was to come. Chief among his accomplishments was the 1999 transfer of Father Baker's coffin from its original burial site in Holy Cross Cemetery near the Basilica to the chapel of Our Lady of Lourdes *inside* the Basilica. During one of Monsignor Wurtz's meetings with the Congregation for the Causes of Saints in Rome, the Congregation recommended this move to allow more people access to Father Baker's remains so that they could pray near his body. Presently more than 20,000 pilgrims visit the church and pray at Father Baker's tomb each year. The unexpected death of Monsignor Wurtz in December 2006 led to my appointment, by Bishop Edward U. Kmiec, as head of the OLV Institutions and vice postulator for Father Baker's cause.

As we stand now, Father Baker is on the first of three steps to canonization. On January 14, 2011, Pope Benedict XVI approved the decree on the life and holiness of Father Baker, naming him "Venerable." This approval opens the door to the second step: *beatification*. With the approval of one miracle, Father Baker will be named "Blessed." At this time, more public devotion to Father Baker is possible, including an annual feast day in the church calendar. After that, with the acceptance by Rome of one more miracle, the third step, *canonization*, will take place, and he will be named St. Nelson Baker. I am honored to be able to shepherd this process for such a holy man and a great example of Christian service—a truly great man and priest.

❧

This authoritative biography on Father Baker is long overdue. There have been many published works through the years, and much "urban legend" has grown over the decades. I am grateful to Rev. Richard Gribble, CSC, for his efforts to bring an accurate accounting of Father Baker's life and work to print. Father Gribble embraced this task as if he were one of us—a born and raised Buffalonian giving his hometown hero his due. I can't thank Father Gribble enough for this gift to Father Baker's legacy.

To Buffalo Bishop Edward U. Kmiec, who has been unsurpassable in his support for Father Baker's cause and for the publication of this biography, my heartfelt gratitude.

I also appreciate the commitment of former Paulist Press editor Kevin di Camillo. While for years representatives from the OLV Institutions recognized the need to commission Father Baker's official biography, it was Kevin's vision, his polite persistence, and his personal dedication that made this project finally come to fruition. We are also grateful for the work of managing editor Donna Crilly and the Paulist Press staff.

Finally, I ask for the prayers of all of you—to and for Father Baker—that the Father of the Fatherless may one day be canonized and be officially named as having taken his place among God's holy ones.

+ Rev. Msgr. Paul J. E. Burkard
The Feast of the Presentation, 2011

Notes

Introduction

1. *Victorian* 41 (3) (March 1935): 6; Archives of Our Lady of Victory Homes of Charity (hereafter AOLV), Lackawanna, NY.

2. Sr. Mary Timothy Dempsey, SSJ, "History of Education at Limestone Hill: Father Baker's Institutions, Lackawanna, NY, 1856–1964" (master's thesis, Mount St. Joseph College of Education, 1965), 2.

3. Heather A. Hartel, "Producing Father Nelson H. Baker: The Practices of Making a Saint for Buffalo, N.Y." (PhD diss., University of Iowa, 2006), 96.

4. Ibid., 122.

5. Baker's previous biographers tell the story of his discovery of the skeletal remains of babies in the sewers of Buffalo and the Erie Canal. However, extant news stories to verify this claim could not be located. The one source found from the pen of Nelson Baker himself that speaks of the remains of babies being found "in a certain city" is *Annals* 32 (3) (January 1920): 1. The former Buffalo diocesan archivist Walter Kern believed this city to be Toronto.

6. Timothy Allan, "Nelson Henry Baker, Priest and Servant of God: An Overview of His Life within Its Historical Context," 14, unpublished essay, AOLV.

7. Nelson Baker to Sr. Margaret Mary, September 27, 1934, Personal File, AOLV.

8. *Buffalo Times*, n.d., clipping, Brother Stanislaus File, AOLV.

9. Quoted in Sr. René Ruberto, "Father Baker—Folk Hero: Legendary Study of the Life of Nelson H. Baker, 1841–1936" (master's thesis, SUNY Buffalo State College, 1976), 37.

10. Quoted in Joseph Klos, "Children in Father Baker's Institutions and Their Reception of Selected Sacraments" (JCL thesis, Catholic University of America, 2002), 2.

11. Gregory Dobson, "Daddy Baker: A Man for His Times," unpublished essay, December 1979, Personal Papers of Timothy Allan (hereafter PPTA), Hamburg, NY.

Chapter 1

1. William Wyckoff, *The Developer's Frontier: The Making of the Western New York Landscape* (New Haven, CT: Yale University Press, 1988), 2. Wyckoff says the total land obtained in the Holland Land Purchase was over 3 million acres. See also Heather A. Hartel, "Producing Father Nelson H. Baker: The Practices of Making a Saint for Buffalo, N.Y." (PhD diss., University of Iowa, 2006), 26–27. Also see Mark Stein, *How the States Got Their Shapes* (Washington, DC: Smithsonian, 2008).

2. See John Theodore Horton, Edward Williams, and Harry S. Douglas, *History of Northwestern New York: Erie, Niagara, Wyoming, Genesee, and Orleans Counties*, vol. 1 (Lewiston, NY: Lewiston Historical Publishing Company, Inc., 1942), 36.

3. Hartel, "Producing Father Baker," 28.

4. Frances M. Trollope, *Domestic Manners of the Americans* (New York: Howard Wilford Bell, 1904), 353.

5. David Gerber, "Ambivalent Anti-Catholicism: Buffalo's American Protestant Elite Faces the Challenge of the Catholic Church, 1850–1860," *Civil War History* 30 (Summer 1984): 138.

6. The Second Great Awakening, approximately 1790 to 1840, was a time of significant religious fervor, evidenced by widespread Christian evangelism and conversions at revivals and camp meetings. It was named after the Great Awakening, a similar period in the 1730s to 1740s, led by Jonathan Edwards. The Second Great Awakening generated great religious fervor throughout New England, the mid-Atlantic region, and the South. Some of the more notable preachers of the period were Charles Finney, Lyman Beecher, Barton Stone, and Peter Cartwright. This period also saw the creation of several new American-born sects and denominations in the Burned-Over District of Western New York.

7. A brief summary of the work of Charles Finney is provided in Sydney Ahlstrom, *A Religious History of the American People* (New Haven, CT: Yale University Press, 1972), 458–61.

8. Francis Walter, "Some Considerations on the Times and Environment in Which Monsignor Nelson H. Baker Lived and Labored," unpublished essay, n.d., 9, AOLV.

9. Noyes believed that too many people in society were weak and not useful. Thus, he initiated the concept of "complex marriage" in which sexual unions were planned between men and women to generate children who were stronger and more fit, mentally and physically. The Oneida Community did not survive after Humphrey's death. For an in-depth description of the religious fervor of the Burned-Over District, see Ahlstrom, *Religious History of the American People*, 491–509.

10. J. N. Larned, *A History of Buffalo: Delineating the Evolution of the City*, vol. 1 (New York: The Progress of the Empire State Company, 1911), 68–69; Thomas Donahue, *History of the Catholic Church in the Western New York Diocese of Buffalo* (Buffalo, NY: Catholic Historical Publishing Company, 1904), 41–42, 69.

11. Thomas Donahue, *History of the Diocese of Buffalo* (Buffalo, NY: The Buffalo Catholic Publishing Company, 1929), 43, 69; Larned, *History of Buffalo*, 69; David A. Gerber, *The Making of an American Pluralism: Buffalo, New York, 1825–1860* (Urbana: University of Illinois Press, 1989), 284–85. In 1843, when a permanent St. Louis Church was built, there were 1,600 Catholics in Buffalo.

12. Larned, *History of Buffalo*, 70.

13. Ibid., 71.

14. Gerber, "Ambivalent Anti-Catholicism," 135–36.

15. Nelson Baker's birth date has been debated in the historical record. In his book *Father Baker and His Lady of Victory Charities* (Buffalo, NY: Buffalo Publishing Company, Inc., 1925), Thomas Galvin, CSsR, who knew Baker well—both as an orphan in St. Joseph Orphan Asylum and later as a fellow priest, working with him closely in a specialized apostolate to African Americans—indirectly supports the date of 1841 by suggesting that Baker was eighty-five when he celebrated his fiftieth anniversary of ordination

in 1926. Baker's tomb in Our Lady of Victory Basilica lists 1841 as the year of his birth. The main supporting evidence for the 1841 date is his Catholic baptismal record (1851), which says he was in his tenth year at the time of baptism; however, all relevant historical accounts (save Galvin), including his military record and the records in the Archives of the Diocese of Buffalo concerning his ordination, confirm the 1842 date.

16. "Arrival of Bakers and Donnellans," biographical information, Baker Papers, Box 4a, Diocese of Buffalo Chancery Archives (hereafter DBCA), Buffalo, NY; Patrick J. Cormican, SJ, "Monumental Achievements of Msgr. Nelson Baker, Padre of the Poor," *The Echo* (August 6, 1936), A71, found in Walter Kern, Baker Papers, vol. 1, AOLV.

17. Walter Kern, "Life and Times of Father Baker," #60, Kern, Baker Papers, vol. 1, AOLV; Floyd Anderson, *Apostle of Charity: The Father Nelson Henry Baker Story* (Buffalo, NY: Our Lady of Victory Homes of Charity, 1960), 8. The extant record has conflicting information on Caroline Donnellan's birth date. Kern says 1816; Anderson says March 17, 1817. She died on September 20, 1884. Lewis Baker's birth date is not extant; he died in 1896.

18. Nelson Baker, "Protestant Baptism," biographical information, Baker Papers, Box 4a, DBCA.

19. Anderson, *Apostle of Charity*, 8–9; Directories, City of Buffalo, 1858 and 1868, found in Kern, Baker Papers, vol. 1, AOLV.

20. For statistics on German immigrants, see W. S. and E. S. Woytinsky, *World Population and Production* (New York: Twentieth Century Fund, 1953), 75–77; Gerber, *Making of a Pluralism*, 164.

21. The parishes that served the German-speaking peoples of Buffalo were St. Louis (1829), St. Mary's (1843), St. Francis Xavier (1848), St. Boniface (1849), St. Michael's (1851), and St. Ann's (1858).

22. Gerber, *Making of a Pluralism*, 163, 174, 191–93; Walter, "Some Considerations," AOLV.

23. Gerber, *Making of a Pluralism*, 193.
24. Ibid., 166.

25. Ibid., 168.

26. Ibid., 124; for Irish immigration statistics, see W. S. and E. S. Woytinsky, *World Population*, 75–77.

27. Gerber, *Making of a Pluralism*, 138–40.

28. Ibid., 133.

29. Ibid., 142.

30. In 1886, Father Peter Abbelen of Milwaukee submitted to the Holy See a document (which became known as the Abbelen Memorial) virtually *demanding* that more German national parishes be established and that a higher percentage of bishops be of German ancestry. The document warned that unless this was done there would be great losses to the faith. The plea was rejected by most of the American bishops, but it caused quite a stir in the American Church at the outset of what became known as the Americanist crisis, which pitted more traditionalist bishops against those more transformationalist in their thinking. In Lucerne, Switzerland, in 1891, delegates to an international conference of the St. Raphaelsverein, an organization formed in 1871 to assist German Catholic emigrants worldwide, published a document claiming that American bishops had neglected the spiritual welfare of immigrant German Catholics. As with the Abbelen Memorial, the American hierarchy vigorously objected to the insinuations in the Lucerne Memorial, causing more tension between Germans and Irish. For more information on these two famous documents and a more complete description and analysis of the situation, see Colman Barry, OSB, *The Catholic Church and German Americans* (Milwaukee, WI: The Bruce Publishing Company, 1953), especially 62–75 and 131–82.

31. Quoted in Gerber, *Making of a Pluralism*, 146–47.

32. It is interesting and somewhat confusing that Baker's mother did *not* send him to Catholic schools. Bishop Timon lauded St. Patrick's school, and St. Mary's was located very close to Baker's home.

33. Walter Kern, "Life and Times of Father Baker," #3, Kern, Baker Papers, vol. 1, AOLV.

34. See *Catholic Union and Times*, August 2, 1934, found in Kern, Baker Papers, vol. 1, AOLV.

35. Kern, "Life and Times of Father Baker," #9, Kern, Baker Papers, vol. 1, AOLV.

36. Anderson, *Apostle of Charity*, 9–10.

37. Baptismal record, Cathedral of St. Joseph, found in Kern, Baker Papers, vol. 1, AOLV.

38. Quoted in Anderson, *Apostle of Charity*, 8.

39. Kern, "Life and Times of Father Baker," #4, Kern, Baker Papers, vol. 1, AOLV. It is not clear precisely *when* Baker received these sacraments, but based on the general practice of the day, he was probably aged fourteen, which would be 1856.

40. Donahue, *History of the Diocese of Buffalo*, 70, 136; Hartel, "Producing Father Baker," 29; Gerber, *Making of a Pluralism*, 288.

41. Donahue, *History of the Diocese of Buffalo*, 139.

42. Ibid., 77–80; Gerber, *Making of a Pluralism*, 296–303. Timon was able to obtain monetary pledges from the three major European mission societies: $110,000 from the Society for the Propagation of the Faith, $10,920 from the Ludwigsmissionverein (Munich), and $6,800 from the Leopoldine Society (Vienna). While Timon was successful raising funds outside Buffalo, his efforts at home were not generally well received.

43. Jay P. Dolan, *The American Catholic Parish* (New York / Mahwah, NJ: Paulist Press, 1987), 109. During this same period, the percentage of Catholics in the city rose significantly as overall population actually dropped from 840,326 to 530,856.

44. Gerber, *Making of a Pluralism*, 316.

45. Ibid., 290; Donahue, *History of the Diocese of Buffalo*, 71.

46. Patrick Carey, *People, Priests and Prelates: Ecclesiastical Democracy and the Tensions of Trusteeism* (Notre Dame, IN: University of Notre Dame Press, 1987). In 1786, a dispute arose between Father John Carroll—then de facto, and later ordained, bishop of America—and the trustees at St. Peter's Church in New York over his decision to replace one priest with another, perceiving the latter to be a better preacher. Later Carroll and trustees in Norfolk, Charleston, Philadelphia, and other cities butted heads over authority and jurisdictional rights. In each case, after a nasty fight, Carroll was able to gain control.

47. David A. Gerber, "Modernity in the Service of Tradition:

Catholic Lay Trustees at Buffalo's St. Louis Church and the Transformation of European Communal Traditions, 1829–1855," *Journal of Social History* 15 (June 1982): 671; Gerber, *Making of a Pluralism*, 286.

48. Carey, *People, Priests and Prelates*, 272.

49. Gerber, *Making of a Pluralism*, 286.

50. Articles and monographs that illustrate and analyze anti-Catholicism in mid-nineteenth-century America, both nationally and locally, abound. Some of the more prominent sources are Ray Allen Billington, *The Protestant Crusade: A Study of the Origins of American Nativism* (New York: Rinehart & Company, 1952); Sr. Marie Leonore Fell, *The Foundations of Nativism in American Textbooks, 1783–1860* (Washington, DC: Catholic University of America Press, 1941); Gustavus Myers, *History of Bigotry in the United States* (New York: Random House, 1943); Charles Deusner, "The Know-Nothing Riots in Louisville," *Records of the Kentucky Historical Society* 61 (April 1963): 122–47; Thomas M. Keefe, "Chicago's Flirtation with Political Nativism, 1854–1856," *Records of the American Catholic Historical Society of Philadelphia* 82 (September 1971): 131–58.

51. Quoted in Edwin S. Gaustad, ed., *A Documentary History of Religion in America to the Civil War* (Grand Rapids, MI: William B. Eerdmans Publishing Company, 1993), 460. The tracts by Monk and Reed were actually penned by promoters of anti-Catholic rhetoric.

52. Tyler Anbinder, *Nativism & Slavery: The Northern Know-Nothings & the Politics of the 1850s* (New York: Oxford University Press, 1992). Along these lines, the historian David Gerber has written: "It was not religious dogma nor the daily, public activities of the Catholic clergy that the Protestant public had to fear and guard against, but rather the political engineering of the Romish Church—the most subtle and widespreading ever devised by the wit of man." See Gerber, "Ambivalent Anti-Catholicism," 126.

53. Gerber, "Ambivalent Anti-Catholicism," 128.

54. Sources that describe these two incidents are James J. Kenneally, "The Burning of the Ursuline Convent: A Different View," *Records of the American Catholic Historical Society of Philadelphia* 90 (1979): 15–22; Michael Feldberg, *The Philadelphia*

Riots of 1844: A Study of Ethnic Conflict (Westport, CT: Greenwood Press, 1975); Vincent P. Lannie and Bernard C. Diethorn, "For the Honor and Glory of God," *History of Education Quarterly* 8 (Spring 1968): 44–106; Elizabeth B. Geffen, "Violence in Philadelphia in the 1840s and 1850s," *Pennsylvania History* 36 (October 1969): 381–410.

55. Allan, "Nelson Henry Baker," 3, AOLV.

56. Gerber, "Ambivalent Anti-Catholicism," 121.

57. Ibid., 135.

58. Anti-Catholicism in the United States in the late nineteenth century was centered about the actions of the American Protective Association (APA), founded in 1887 in Clinton, Iowa, by Henry Bowers. The APA lingered into the twentieth century, but by that time was less effective. For information on the APA, see Michael Williams, *The Shadow of the Pope* (New York: McGraw-Hill Company, 1932), 103–4. The best volume on the APA is Donald Kinzer, *An Episode in Anti-Catholicism: The American Protective Association* (Seattle: University of Washington Press, 1964). Recent publications that demonstrate that anti-Catholicism has never died in the United States are Philip Jenkins, *The New Anti-Catholicism: The Last Acceptable Prejudice* (Oxford, England: Oxford University Press, 2003) and Mark Massa, SJ, *Anti-Catholicism in America: The Last Acceptable Prejudice* (New York: Crossroad, 2003).

59. Allan, "Nelson Henry Baker," 3, AOLV.

60. A basic summary of these important events is provided in James West Davidson et al., *Nation of Nations: A Concise Narrative of the American Republic* (Boston: McGraw-Hill, 2006), 418–22.

61. For example, in the North, Francis Kenrick (Philadelphia and Baltimore) and John Hughes (New York) were strong supporters of the Union position, whereas Patrick Lynch (Charleston) and Augustine Verot (St. Augustine) backed the South. Those in border states, such as Martin Spalding (Louisville, later Baltimore), rode the fence on the issues that generated the war (some historians see him as more favorable to the South). A good summary of this period and the principals involved is found in James Hennesey, SJ, *American Catholics: A History of the Roman Catholic Community in the United States* (New York: Oxford University Press, 1981), 143–57.

62. Leonard R. Riforgiato, "Bishop Timon, Buffalo and the Civil War," *The Catholic Historical Review* 73 (1) (January 1987): 65.

63. Quoted in ibid., 73.

64. Quoted in ibid.

65. Anderson, *Apostle of Charity*, 14; Walter Kern, "Life and Times of Father Baker," #10, Kern, Baker Papers, vol. 1, AOLV; report, "The 74th Regiment National Guard State of New York, 1899," Military File, AOLV.

66. Iver Bernstein, *The New York City Draft Riots: Their Significance for American Society and Politics in the Age of the Civil War* (New York: Oxford University Press, 1990), 708; Bruce Catton, *Never Call Retreat* (New York: Doubleday & Company, 1965), 215. Surviving records show that of 79,975 conscripts examined under the 1863 law, 6,998 procured a substitute.

67. Anderson, *Apostle of Charity*, 9; Catton, *Never Call Retreat*, 214–17.

68. Catton, *Never Call Retreat*, 214.

69. Quoted in Riforgiato, "Bishop Timon," 79.

70. Allan, "Nelson Henry Baker," 5.

71. Gerber, *Making of a Pluralism*, 238.

72. Anderson, *Apostle of Charity*, 21–22; Buffalo City and Erie County Register and Business Directory, 1870, found in Kern, Baker Papers, vol. 1, AOLV.

73. Thomas A. Galvin, CSsR, *Father Baker and His Lady of Victory Charities* (Buffalo, NY: Buffalo Catholic Publishing Company, Inc., 1925), 12.

74. *Victorian* 33 (3) (March 1927): 3–4, AOLV.

75. Brother Stanislaus, "Father Baker Dedicated All His Efforts to Our Lady of Victory," clipping, n.d., found in Kern, Baker Papers, vol. 1, AOLV.

76. Patrick J. Cormican, SJ, "Father Baker—Modern Apostle of Charity," in *Catholic Union and Times*, Centenary Edition: Commemorating One Hundred Years of Catholic History in Buffalo and Western New York and the Founding of the City of Buffalo and Diocese of Buffalo, 1931, AOLV.

Chapter 2

1. Nelson Baker Diary, Retreat Notes, July 9–13, 1868, AOLV.

2. Ibid.

3. Ibid.

4. Floyd Anderson, *Apostle of Charity: The Father Nelson Henry Baker Story* (Buffalo, NY: Our Lady of Victory Homes of Charity, 1960), 24–26; Boniface Hanley, "Servant of God Msgr. Nelson Baker, 1841–1936: One Lifetime," *The Anthonian* 53 (2) (1971): 8. Bishop Timon died in 1867 and was succeeded by Stephen Ryan.

5. Baker Diary, June 24–27, June 30, and July 7–8, all 1869, AOLV; Anderson, *Apostle of Charity*, 27–29; Walter Kern, "Life and Times of Father Baker," #19, in Kern, Baker Papers, vol. 1, AOLV. St. Anne's parish in Detroit had been the home of Father Gabriel Richard, a tireless priest as Baker would become; Richard died in 1832 while ministering to victims of a cholera epidemic.

6. Record of Baptisms, St. John's Evangelical Lutheran Parish, PPTA.

7. Baker Diary, January 29, 1870, AOLV.

8. Allan, "Nelson Henry Baker," 8, AOLV.

9. J. N. Larned, *A History of Buffalo: Delineating the Evolution of the City*, vol. 1 (New York: The Progress of the Empire State Company, 1911), 75; Thomas Donahue, *History of the Diocese of Buffalo* (Buffalo, NY: The Buffalo Catholic Publishing Company, 1929), 86; Thomas Donahue, *History of the Catholic Church in the Western New York Diocese of Buffalo* (Buffalo, NY: Catholic Historical Publishing Company, 1904), 200, 319. It should be noted that in 1883 the seminary was formed into Niagara University by the regents of the State of New York. Additionally, in the mid-1850s, Bishop Timon invited Italian Franciscans to come to the diocese to start a school, now St. Bonaventure University. A portion of this school was also a seminary, now Christ the King Seminary in East Aurora, NY. This Institution today serves the Diocese of Buffalo.

10. Catalog, "Officers and Students Seminary of Our Lady of Angels, 1869–1870," Archives of Niagara University (hereafter ANU), Niagara Falls, NY.

11. Baker Diary, September 2–4, 1869, AOLV; Anderson, *Apostle of Charity*, 25; Hanley, "One Lifetime," 8. Baker reported his per annum costs at the seminary. Tuition, room and board, washing and mending: $250; bedding: $12; use of musical instrument, from $40 (violin, flute, or clarinet) to $60 (piano or guitar). See Walter Kern, "Life and Times of Father Baker," #19 in Kern, Baker Papers, vol. 1, AOLV.

12. Baker Diary, September 16, 1869, and February 26, 1870, AOLV.

13. Ibid., February 26, 1869, AOLV; Anderson, *Apostle of Charity*, 32.

14. Our Lady of Angels Catalog, 1869–70, found in Kern, Baker Papers, vol. 1, AOLV. The seminary's full five-year collegiate department program, as listed in the catalog, is as follows:

> **Year I**: Latin, Greek, Modern History, Chemistry, Astronomy, Christian Doctrine
> **Year II**: Latin, Greek, Ancient History, Differential and Integral Calculus, Natural Philosophy, Christian Doctrine
> **Year III**: Latin, Greek, Ancient History, Surveying, Navigation, Analytical Geometry, Christian Doctrine
> **Year IV**: Latin Grammar, Greek Grammar, English Grammar, Composition and Declamation, History, French or German, Ancient Geography, Trigonometry, Christian Doctrine
> **Year V**: Latin Grammar, Orthography, English Grammar, Compendium of History, English Composition and Declamation, Bookkeeping, Arithmetic, Christian Doctrine

15. Quoted in Kern, "The Life and Times of Father Baker," #22, in Kern, Baker Papers, vol. 2, AOLV.

16. Baker Diary, January 29, 1870, AOLV.

17. Anderson, *Apostle of Charity*, 33–35; *History of the Seminary of Our Lady of Angels Niagara University, Niagara County, N.Y., 1856–1906* (Buffalo, NY: The Matthews-Northrup Works, 1906), 305, 310. These two sources disagree on what Baker's position was in the PDA: Anderson claims Baker was vice president; the seminary history claims Baker was secretary. I assume the history of the Institution is probably more accurate. Either way,

however, it is clear that Baker was highly involved with the organization from the very outset.

18. *History of Our Lady of Angels*, 310.

19. Ibid., 310–13.

20. Heather A. Hartel, "Producing Father Nelson H. Baker: The Practices of Making a Saint for Buffalo, N.Y." (PhD diss., University of Iowa, 2006), 25; Baker Diary, January 29, 1870, AOLV.

21. Kern, "Life and Times of Father Baker," #23, in Kern, Baker Papers, vol. 2, AOLV.

22. Ibid., catalog, "Officers and Students Seminary of Our Lady of Angels, 1869–1870," ANU; Baker Diary, January 29, 1870, AOLV.

23. Baker Diary, August 1, 1870, AOLV; Kern, "Life and Times of Father Baker," #27, in Kern, Baker Papers, vol. 2, AOLV.

24. Baker Diary, April 1 and June 29, 1870, AOLV.

25. Ibid., September 1, 1870, AOLV.

26. *Victorian* 42 (9) (September 1936): 33; John L. Reilly to *Catholic Union & Times*, March 9, 1936, in Kern, Baker Papers, vol. 2, AOLV.

27. William M. Emerling, *The History of Lackawanna* (Lackawanna, NY: The Lackawanna Bicentennial Commission, 1976), 71.

28. Kern, "Life and Times of Father Baker," #26 and #29, Kern, Baker Papers, vol. 2, AOLV. Interestingly, as will be mentioned in chapter 10, during the Great Depression, Baker looked forward to the repeal of prohibition during the Roosevelt administration. See Nelson Baker to James Mead, March 16, 1933, PPTA.

29. Jay P. Dolan, *The Immigrant Church: New York's Irish and German Catholics, 1815–1865* (Notre Dame, IN: University of Notre Dame Press, 1983), 55.

30. Cited in Allan, "Nelson Henry Baker," 22, AOLV.

31. Joseph Chinnici, OFM, *Living Stones: The History and Structure of Catholic Spiritual Life in the United States* (New York: Macmillan Company, 1989), 146–56.

32. *Annals* 19 (3) (January 1907): 10, AOLV.

33. Baker Diary, April 12, 1876, AOLV.

34. Kern, "Life and Times of Father Baker," #28, Kern, Baker Papers, vol. 2, AOLV.

35. Baker Diary, September 7, 1873, AOLV.

36. Allan, "Nelson Henry Baker," 26, AOLV.

37. Walter Kern, "Father Baker Running Out of Space," unpublished essay in Kern, Baker Papers, vol. 4, AOLV.

38. Allan, "Nelson Henry Baker," 23–24, AOLV.

39. Catalog, "Our Lady of Angels Seminary," 1873–74, 18–19, ANU; Baker Diary, March 19, 1873, AOLV; Kern, "Life and Times of Father Baker," #42, #29, #27B, Kern, Baker Papers, vols. 2 and 3, AOLV; *History of Our Lady of the Angels*, 267.

40. *Victorian* 42 (9) (September 1936): 49; Kern, "Life and Times of Father Baker," #27B, AOLV.

41. Quoted in Kern, "Life and Times of Father Baker," #25, Kern, Baker Papers, vol. 2, AOLV; Anderson, *Apostle of Charity*, 35.

42. *Niagara Index* 8 (12) (March 1, 1876): 9, ANU.

43. Baker Diary, June 17, 1873, and June 20, 1871, AOLV; Kern, "Life and Times of Father Baker," #26 and #31, Kern, Baker Papers, vol. 2, AOLV.

44. Kern, "Life and Times of Father Baker," #27, Kern, Baker Papers, vol. 2, AOLV; Baker Diary, July 7, 1872, AOLV.

45. "An Interesting Letter," *Victorian* 30 (3) (March 1924): 44. See also Anderson, *Apostle of Charity*, 36–37.

46. Baker Diary, October 9, 1872, AOLV.

47. Kern, "Life and Times of Father Baker," #28, #30, and #34, Kern, Baker Papers, vol. 2, AOLV; Baker Diary, September 21, 1873, AOLV.

48. Nelson Baker, "Notebook on Controversial Subjects," January 1, 1873, AOLV. The complete list of topics was sacraments, indifference in religion, rule of faith, Spanish Inquisition, grace, angel guardians, Immaculate Conception, exclusive salvation, Blessed Virgin Mary, purgatory, indulgences, infallibility, veneration of images, errors in the Protestant Bible, celibacy, and penance.

49. Baker Diary, September 7, 1873, and September 21, 1873, AOLV.

50. Ibid., September 7, 1873, AOLV.

51. Ibid., December 23, 1873, AOLV.

52. Ibid., October 1, 1873, AOLV.

53. Actually Baker began to be entrusted with greater responsibilities during his philosophy year, 1872–73.

54. Baker Diary, January 2, 1873, AOLV.

55. *History of Our Lady of Angels*, 203.

56. Quoted in Kern, "Life and Times of Father Baker," #29, Kern, Baker Papers, vol. 2, AOLV.

57. Baker Diary, May 9, 1873, AOLV.

58. Quoted in Kern, "Life and Times of Father Baker," #29, Kern, Baker Papers, vol. 2, AOLV.

59. Baker Diary, June 17, 1873, AOLV. Almost two years later, in April 1875, Baker was again asked to serve as second prefect, continuing to the end of the semester.

60. Ibid., September 22, 1873, AOLV.

61. Ibid., September 28, 1873; December 9, 1873; and October 29, 1873, AOLV.

62. Quoted in Kern, "Life and Times of Father Baker," #42, Kern, Baker Papers, vol. 3, AOLV.

63. Baker Diary, August 26, 1873, AOLV.

64. "Convent Book," Archives of the Sisters of Our Lady of Charity Buffalo (hereafter ASLCB), Hamburg, NY.

65. Donahue, *History of the Diocese of Buffalo*, 152; Kern, "Life and Times of Father Baker," #27B, Kern, Baker Papers, vol. 2, AOLV.

66. Kern, "Life and Times of Father Baker," #36, Kern, Baker Papers, vol. 2, AOLV.

67. Baker Diary, November 1, 1871; November 5, 1873; and March 5, 1874, AOLV. Also Kern, "Life and Times of Father Baker," #22, Kern, Baker Papers, vol. 3, AOLV. Baker indicates that the significant financial downturn of 1873 (the Panic of 1873) was a severe blow to the business. Extant information leads one to conclude that there was not a warm relationship between the Baker siblings. It seems the Baker brothers treated each other rather harshly. Andrew, the third son in age, actually cut himself off from the family and died alone in California.

68. Baker Diary, March 19, 1873 and October 22, 1873, AOLV.

69. Ibid., December 30, 1875, AOLV. Baker's use of the word *possession* seems to be a reference to a future assignment as a priest, a reality that would happen in only a few months.

70. Many fine books and articles provide amplifying information on this critical period in Church history. Some of these include Roger Aubert et al., *The Church in a Secularized Society* (New York: Paulist Press, 1978); Aubert et al., *The Church in the Age of Liberalism* (New York: Crossroad, 1981); Austin Gough, *Paris and Rome: The Gallican Church and the Ultramontane Campaign, 1848–1853* (Oxford, England: Clarendon Press, 1986); Derek J. Holmes, *The Triumph of the Holy See* (London: Burns & Oates, 1978); Don Cuthbert Butler, *The Vatican Council 1869–1870* (Westminster, MD: The Macmillan Company, 1962). Papal infallibility, as defined in *Pastor Aeternus*, says that the pope can speak infallibly only when speaking from the chair (as pope) to the universal Church on a teaching in the deposit of revelation on faith and morals, with the *sensus fidelium.*

71. United States bishops were divided in three camps over the definition of papal infallibility. One relatively small group wholeheartedly endorsed the definition; a very few opposed the teaching. The majority, however, while believing the definition to be theologically sound, thought that its definition at the time was highly problematic for American Catholics. Since the papacy had always been one of the great roadblocks that fueled Protestant animosity toward Catholics, the United States bishops perceived that the definition of papal infallibility would be seen as a move for greater Vatican power and would lead directly to increased hostility toward American Catholics. For more information on this idea, see James Hennesey, SJ, *First Council of the Vatican: The American Experience* (New York: Herder and Herder, 1963).

72. Quoted in Marvin O'Connell, *Edward Sorin* (Notre Dame, IN: University of Notre Dame Press, 2001), 641.

73. In reality, Sorin believed himself to be the true leader of the group. In a rather arrogant tone he wrote, "In fact, it is I who will be the pilot of the pilgrimage. Nobody has crossed the ocean twenty-seven times as I have done, and nobody knows Rome and Lourdes better than I....Perhaps I suffer from illusion, but it seems clear that Divine Providence has disposed these matters so as...to

allow me to render to the Holy Father a signal service." See ibid., 641–42.

74. Joseph Dwenger, "Circular Letter to Rev. Clergy of the Diocese of Fort Wayne," April 28, 1874, 1/06 Dwenger Papers, Archives of the University of Notre Dame (hereafter AUND), Notre Dame, IN.

75. Anderson, *Apostle of Charity*, 38–40; Baker Diary, March 5, 1874, AOLV; Kern, "Life and Times of Father Baker," #36, Kern, Baker Papers, vol. 3, AOLV.

76. *Niagara Index* V (17) (May 15, 1874): 125, ANU; Baker Diary, April 6, 1874, AOLV. The full passage for the pilgrimage was $350.00.

77. Kern, "Life and Times of Father Baker," #37, Kern, Baker Papers, vol. 3, AOLV; Baker Diary, May 16, 1874, AOLV; clipping, *Freeman's Journal*, August 22, 1874, Bishop Dwenger Papers, AUND; Anderson, *Apostle of Charity*, 39–40.

78. Baker Diary, May 24, 1874, AOLV; Anderson, *Apostle of Charity*, 41.

79. Hanley, "One Lifetime," 10; Kern, "Life and Times of Father Baker," #39, Kern, Baker Papers, vol. 3, AOLV.

80. Hanley, "One Lifetime," 10; *New York Times*, June 21, 1874, Bishop Dwenger Papers, AUND. Apparently Dwenger's brother was a victim of alcoholism whose condition had been "cured" by prayers to Our Lady of Victory.

81. Kern, "Life and Times of Father Baker," #38, Kern, Baker Papers, vol. 3, AOLV.

82. Sr. René Ruberto, "Father Baker—Folk Hero: Legendary Study of the Life of Nelson H. Baker, 1841–1936" (master's thesis, SUNY Buffalo State College, 1976), 11.

83. Kern, "Life and Times of Father Baker," #40, Kern, Baker Papers, vol. 3, AOLV.

84. Quoted in ibid., AOLV.

85. Ibid., #41, Kern, Baker Papers, vol. 3, AOLV.

86. Galvin, *Father Baker*, 20–21.

87. Kern, "Life and Times of Father Baker," #41 and #42, Kern, Baker Papers, vol. 3, AOLV.

88. Baker Diary, May 22, 1875, and December 30, 1875, AOLV; Kern, "Life and Times of Father Baker," #43, Kern, Baker

Papers, vol. 3, AOLV; Anderson, *Apostle of Charity*, 48; Priest
Ordination Book, DBCA. It is possible, although not certain, that
Baker's two baptisms, initially as a Lutheran and later as a Catholic,
were the cause of the confusion.

89. Gregory Dobson, "Daddy Baker," 6, PPTA.

90. Kern, "Life and Times of Father Baker," #44, Kern, Baker
Papers, vol. 3, AOLV.

91. Ibid., #18, vol. 1, AOLV.

92. Ibid., #45, vol. 3, AOLV. Shortly after his ordination,
Baker supplied the seminarians' recreation hall with chairs as a
form of thanks. The *Index* stated, "We have only then to publicly
thank Father Baker for his substantial consideration, even if, in
thus publicly expressing our gratitude, we obtrude upon the reverend gentleman praise which he fain would have remained unspo-
ken." See *Niagara Index* 9 (6) (December 1, 1876): 1, ANU. In
later years Baker served as the president of the Niagara Alumni
Association (which he helped start in 1881), regularly attended
alumni events, and contributed monetarily to the seminary. See
Niagara Alumni Bulletin 1 (1) (January 1915), ANU.

Chapter 3

1. See George Tindall and David Shi, *The Essential America:
A Narrative History*, vol. 2 (New York: W. W. Norton, 1996),
877–925 for more details; Allan, "Nelson Henry Baker," 6, 9–10,
AOLV. A good overview of this whole historical period is presented in Sean Dennis Cashman, *America in the Gilded Age: From
the Death of Lincoln to the Rise of Theodore Roosevelt* (New York:
New York University Press, 1984).

2. Francis Walter, "Some Considerations on the Times and
Environment in Which Monsignor Nelson H. Baker Lived and
Labored," 41, unpublished essay, n.d., AOLV.

3. An excellent synopsis of the Settlement House Movement
and the work of Jane Addams is found in Walter I. Trattner, *From
Poor Law and Welfare State: A History of Social Welfare in America*
(New York: Free Press, 1989), 147–72. The best title on Addams's
work specifically is her own—Jane Addams, *Twenty Years at Hull
House* (Boston: Bedford / St. Martin's Press, 1999).

4. Quoted in Allan, "Nelson Henry Baker," 10, AOLV.

5. Walter Kern, "Father Baker and the Orphan Trains," unpublished essay, Kern, Baker Papers, AOLV.

6. J. N. Larned, *A History of Buffalo: Delineating the Evolution of the City*, vol. 1 (New York: The Progress of the Empire State Company, 1911), 82.

7. Ibid., 84–87, 96.

8. Booth was reading a printer's proof of the 1878 annual report when he noticed the statement "The Christian Mission is a volunteer army." Crossing out the words *volunteer army*, he penned in *Salvation Army*. From those words came the basis of the foundation deed of the Salvation Army.

9. Larned, *A History of Buffalo*, 98–100.

10. The Young Men's Christian Association (YMCA) was originally called the Young Men's Christian Union, to avoid confusion with a similarly named group. In 1870, the more familiar title that has endured was appropriated.

11. Larned, *A History of Buffalo*, 87–93, 108, 115–17.

12. Ibid., 82–84.

13. Ibid., 100–101.

14. Ibid., 96–97, 101–5, 120.

15. Ibid., 111.

16. Thomas Donahue, *History of the Diocese of Buffalo* (Buffalo, NY: The Buffalo Catholic Publishing Company, 1929), 81, 190.

17. Ibid., 81–83, 190; Larned, *A History of Buffalo*, 110.

18. "Father Baker: Apostle of Three Generations," *Catholic Charities Review* (September 1936): 212.

19. Larned, *A History of Buffalo*, 111, 114–16.

20. Ibid., 114–15. The German Roman Catholic Orphan Asylum was incorporated in 1874. See the short history of German Roman Catholic Orphan Asylum, German Roman Catholic Orphan Asylum File, DBCA.

21. Ibid., 107, 116.

22. "Dr. Walter's Secular History of Fr. Baker's Time," 37–38, unpublished essay, AOLV.

23. Dolan, *American Catholic Parish*, 16. Buffalo's national, or ethnic, parishes represented 18 percent of the City's total Catholic

congregations—more than double the country's average of 7 percent.

24. "Dr. Walter's Secular History of Fr. Baker's Time," 21, 23, unpublished essay, AOLV; David A. Gerber, *The Making of an American Pluralism: Buffalo, New York, 1825–1860* (Urbana: University of Illinois Press, 1989), 152.

25. "Dr. Walter's Secular History of Fr. Baker's Time," 21, unpublished essay, AOLV.

26. Larned, *A History of Buffalo,* 76–78. The list of parishes is St. John the Baptist (1868), St. Mary of Sorrows (1872), St. Stanislaus (1873), St. Nicholas (1874), St. Stephen's (1875), Sacred Heart (1875), Church of the Assumption (1882), St. Agnes (1883), Church of the Holy Name (1874), and St. Adalbert's (1886).

27. The Third Plenary Council of Baltimore mandated that all parishes have a Catholic school. If one was not present, parishes were given two years to meet this requirement. The bishops' charge emphasized how significant the hierarchy considered Catholic schools and the priority they held. It should be noted, however, that many parishes already had schools at the time of this mandate. Thus, the bishops' message was oriented toward those parishes that still needed schools.

28. Donahue, *History of the Diocese of Buffalo*, 115.

29. Ibid., 114.

30. Thomas Galvin, CSsR, *Father Baker and His Lady of Victory Charities* (Buffalo, NY: Buffalo Publishing Company, Inc., 1925), 206; Donahue, *History of the Diocese of Buffalo*, 291; Alice M. Pytak, *A Christian Commitment: The Story of Father Nelson Henry Baker, 1841–1936* (Lackawanna, NY: Our Lady of Victory Homes of Charity, 1986), 6. The first recorded sacrament at Holy Cross Mission was a marriage witnessed by Father Hines on February, 5, 1858. See marriage register, Church of Holy Cross, Our Lady of Victory Basilica.

31. Galvin, *Father Baker*, 206.

32. Floyd Anderson, *Apostle of Charity: The Father Nelson Henry Baker Story* (Buffalo, NY: Our Lady of Victory Homes of Charity, 1960); Boniface Hanley, "Servant of God Msgr. Nelson Baker, 1841–1936: One Lifetime," *The Anthonian* 53 (2) (1971): 12; Heather A. Hartel, "Producing Father Nelson H. Baker: The

Practices of Making a Saint for Buffalo, N.Y." (PhD diss., University of Iowa, 2006), 26; *The Catholic Union*, March 30, 1876, 5.

33. Baker Diary, March 24–June 3, 1876, AOLV; Walter Kern, "Life and Times of Father Baker," #49 and #55 in Kern, Baker Papers, vol. 4, AOLV.

34. Allan, "Nelson Henry Baker," 10–11, AOLV.

35. Donahue, *History of the Diocese of Buffalo*, 190; Galvin, *Father Baker*, 209–10; Hartel, "Producing Father Baker," 30; Sr. Mary Timothy Dempsey, SSJ, "History of Education at Limestone Hill: Father Baker's Institutions, Lackawanna, NY, 1856–1964" (master's thesis, Mount St. Joseph College of Education, 1965), 3–4; Mary O'Leary, "A History of Our Lady of Victory Homes of Charity," unpublished essay, 1967, 3–4, AOLV.

36. "Large Book of Accounts," 119; "New York: Buffalo Orphanage, 1856–1857," S03.6, Archives of the Sisters of Holy Cross (hereafter ASHC), St. Mary's College, Notre Dame, IN. The record lists the original personnel that the Sisters sent, but nothing about whom the Brothers sent. The Sisters in the original group were Sr. M. Circumcision (Chanson), CSC, directress; Sr. M. Eudoxie (Davies); and Sr. M. Alberta (Albertine) (Mechan). No extant data for the Brothers of Holy Cross relevant to this apostolate could be located.

37. *Buffalo Sentinel*, November 29, 1856, 2, clipping found in Kern, Baker Papers, vol. 4, AOLV.

38. John Timon to Edward Sorin, CSC, December 20, 1856; April 16, 1857; and April 5, 1857, Sorin Papers, Archives of the Holy Cross Fathers, Indiana Province (hereafter AHCFI), Notre Dame, IN; also Sr. Mary Immaculata Maxwell, SSJ, *Like a Swarm of Bees: Sisters of St. Joseph of Buffalo* (Derby, NY: Society of St. Paul, 1956), 117. In a letter to the Sisters of St. Joseph, Timon explained further his rationale for dismissing Holy Cross: "You are aware that we had the Brothers and Sisters of the Holy Cross, a few months, in charge of our Boys Orphan Asylum, [but] finding the Brothers unable to teach trades, as they promised, and not satisfied with the arrangements, I requested M. Sorin to withdraw them." See Timon to "Dear and Respected Sister" (copy), May 6, 1857,

Timon to Sisters of St. Joseph Correspondence, Archives of the Sisters of St. Joseph of Buffalo (hereafter ASSJB), Clarence, NY.

39. John Timon to Edward Sorin, September 30, 1858, Sorin Papers, AHCFI.

40. Sr. Mary of the Sacred Heart, *The Congregation of St. Joseph of the Diocese of Buffalo, 1854–1933* (Buffalo, NY: The Holling Press, 1934), 89; "Extracts from the Congregation of Saint Joseph of Buffalo," n.d., unpublished essay, AOLV; "A Century of Love," *Victorian* 60 (12) (December 1954): 51, 53.

41. Sr. Mary of the Sacred Heart, *The Congregation of St. Joseph*, 90.

42. Dempsey, "History of Education at Limestone Hill," 5–6; *The Metropolitan Catholic Almanac and Laity Directory for the United States, Canada, and the British Provinces*, 1860, in Kern, Baker Papers, vol. 3, AOLV; John Timon to "D. Sister," January 21, 1859, Timon to the Sisters of St. Joseph Correspondence, ASSJB.

43. *Victorian*, n.d. [1936], clipping found in Baker Papers; "The Orphanage & Protectory at Lackawanna," St. John's Protectory History, ASSJB; Sr. Mary of the Sacred Heart, *The Congregation of St. Joseph*, 90. Sr. Mary Michael Dooley, SSJ, "left an enduring movement in the community for her care of the orphans and the boys at the Protectory." She was not only a fixture in town begging for the orphans, but, as she reported in a reflection written later in life, she also baked bread at St. Joseph's for twenty-eight years. See Maxwell, *Like a Swarm of Bees*, 125; and Sr. Michael Dooley, Personal Reflection, Sr. Michael Dooley Personnel File, ASSJB.

44. "The History of Lackawanna," Homes of Charity History, Baker Papers, ASSJB.

45. Maxwell, *Like a Swarm of Bees*, 114; Galvin, *Father Baker*, 15–16, 233; Joseph Klos, "Children in Father Baker's Institutions and Their Reception of Selected Sacraments" (JCL thesis, Catholic University of America, 2002), 6; O'Leary, "A History of Our Lady of Victory Homes of Charity," unpublished essay, 1967, 3–4, AOLV. The State of New York Charter for St. John's Protectory stated that the Institution could admit three groups of children: "[1] Children under the age of fourteen years, who by consent in

writing of their parents or guardians may be entrusted to it for their protection or reformation;…[2] Children of Roman Catholic parentage between seven and fourteen years of age may be committed from the City of Buffalo to the care of such corporation as idle, truant, vicious, homeless or vagrant children, by the order of the judgment of any magistrate or police justice of the County of Erie, empowered by law to make committal of children for any such causes;…[3] Children of the like parentage and age who have been placed in the County Poor House of Erie County from the City of Buffalo may be transferred at the option of the Superintendents of the Poor of the County of Erie, but no such transfer shall be made except upon the order in writing, signed by all the Superintendents." It should be noted that Father Hines was one of the original trustees of the Protectory.

46. Pastoral letter, Second Plenary Council of Baltimore, October 21, 1866, in Hugh J. Nolan, *Pastoral Letters of the United States Catholic Bishops*, vol. 1 (Washington, DC: National Conference of Catholic Bishops, 1984), 200.

47. Dempsey, "History of Education at Limestone Hill," 15–16.

48. Ibid., 7–8, 11.

49. Baker Diary, July 17, 1876, AOLV.

50. Ibid., April 3, 1876, AOLV.

51. Brother Stanislaus, "Every Boy Had a Friend in Father Baker," *Victorian* 47 (2) (February 1941): 58; "Father Baker's Life Related by Associates," clipping, July 30, 1936, in Kern, Baker Papers, vol. 4, AOLV. Brother Stanislaus, born John J. Gilhina, did yeoman service as Baker's "right-hand man" for years. At various times he was prefect of discipline, head of the printing plan for the *Annals* and *Victorian*, and editor of the publications. He was the constant companion of Father Baker for forty-four years. After the priest's death, Stanislaus wrote a series of historical reflections on their relationship that was published in the *Victorian*.

52. Kern, "Life and Times of Father Baker," #54, in Kern, Baker Papers, vol. 4, AOLV; Allan, "Nelson Henry Baker," 13, AOLV.

53. Stanislaus, "Every Boy Had a Friend in Father Baker," 59.

54. Donahue, *History of the Diocese of Buffalo*, 317.

55. Robert F. McNamara, *A Century of Grace: The History of St. Mary's Roman Catholic Parish, Corning, N.Y., 1848–1948* (Corning, NY: St. Mary's Church, 1979), 106.

56. Ibid., 227; John Koerner, *The Mysteries of Father Baker* (Buffalo, NY: Western New York Wares, Inc., 2005), 52.

57. Kern, "Life and Times of Father Baker," no number (January 1996), in Kern, Baker Papers, vol. 4, AOLV.

58. Quoted in McNamara, *A Century of Grace*, 106.

Chapter 4

1. Floyd Anderson, *Apostle of Charity: The Father Nelson Henry Baker Story* (Buffalo, NY: Our Lady of Victory Homes of Charity, 1960), 51–52; Heather A. Hartel, "Producing Father Nelson H. Baker: The Practices of Making a Saint for Buffalo, N.Y." (PhD diss., University of Iowa, 2006), 35; Boniface Hanley, "Servant of God Msgr. Nelson Baker, 1841–1936: One Lifetime," *The Anthonian* 53 (2) (1971): 12–14. Hartel cites Galvin, who claims that the Institutions were bankrupt when Baker arrived in 1882. Anderson claims in 1881 the debt at St. John's was $56,000. There is no precise extant data that shows the actual financial condition of the Institutions in 1882.

2. *Buffalo Times*, n.d., [1936], clipping, Personal Papers of Ron Paszck, hereafter PPRP, Lackawanna, NY.

3. Sr. Mary of the Sacred Heart, *The Congregation of St. Joseph of the Diocese of Buffalo, 1854–1933* (Buffalo, NY: The Holling Press, 1934), 92; James Burke, interview with the author, August 7, 2008, AOLV.

4. *Catholic Union & Times*, March 30, 1884, clipping in Kern, Baker Papers, vol. 4, AOLV.

5. Bruce Dickinson, interview with Walter Kern, July 31, 1990; Mr. Reno (first name unknown), interview with Walter Kern, November 29, 1987; Clara Balduf, interview with Walter Kern, May 22, 1990, Baker Canonization Files, AOLV.

6. Balduf, interview with Walter Kern, May 22, 1990, AOLV; Alice M. Pytak, "Because of Father Baker," *Catholic Digest* 45 (October 1981): 62.

7. Nelson Baker to Catherine McNeal, January 3, 1927, PPRP.

8. Walter Kern, "Life and Times of Father Baker," #58, Kern, Baker Papers, vol. 4, AOLV. Baker's idea to seek Our Lady of Victory as his patroness came from his heart and past experience, but it was a devotion with roots in the French Church. In December 1836, a dejected French priest, Abbé Desgenettes, was saying Mass at the Church of Our Lady of Victory in Paris. He was dejected due to the fact that people were not attending Mass or the sacraments. As he celebrated Mass, a voice came to him: "Consecrate your parish to the Holy and Immaculate Heart of Mary." Buoyed with confidence, he called a meeting of parishioners for one week later. To his great and pleasant surprise, five hundred people showed up for the meeting. This was the initiation of the Archconfraternity of Our Lady of Victory.

9. Allan, "Nelson Henry Baker," 15. It must be noted that no primary source extant data could be found to verify the initiation of the mail solicitation campaign. It *is* clear, however, with the passing of time more and more people were receiving Baker's two publications, the *Annals* and later the *Victorian*. The increase of his subscription base certainly had some connection to mail solicitation, as well as word of mouth.

10. Anderson, *Father Baker*, 53; Hanley, "One Lifetime," 14–16; Thomas Galvin, CSsR, *Father Baker and His Lady of Victory Charities* (Buffalo, NY: Buffalo Publishing Company, Inc., 1925), 129–34; *The Appeal for the Homeless and Destitute Child*, n.d., [1932], Miscellaneous File, AOLV; *Victorian* 34 (4) (April 1928): 3, AOLV. The seven annual novenas (still prayed today, but on different dates) for members of the Association were: (1) March 17–25, Annunciation; (2) June 12–20, Sacred Heart; (3) August 7–15, Assumption; (4) October 18–25, Our Lady of Victory; (5) November 2–10, Suffering Souls; (6) November 30–December 8, Immaculate Conception; and (7) December 17–25, Nativity of the Lord. Baker promised Association members remembrance in twenty-five Masses per week with those on Wednesday, Friday, and Saturday especially for the deceased. Additionally, he arranged for one hundred Masses to be celebrated at *each* of seven Marian shrines in Europe: (1) Our Lady of Victory

in Paris (for solicitors); (2) Lourdes (for those who no longer lived the faith); (3) Loretto (for the concerns of the faith); (4) Our Lady of Perpetual Help in Rome; (5) Our Lady of Mount Carmel in Rome (for needs at the hour of death); (6) Our Lady of Knock in Ireland (for perseverance of members); and (7) Shrine of the Sacred Heart in Paray-le-Monial, France (to encourage devotion to the Blessed Mother). See Kern, "Life and Times of Father Baker," #59, Kern, Baker Papers, vol. 4, AOLV. The story of Baker's direct mail campaign has been retold by all who have written about his new start at Limestone Hill in 1882. The story itself has no verifiable evidence and seems a stretch of the historical record. It is highly unlikely that postmasters in various cities would have had lists of Catholics in their region. Moreover, it is even less likely that such information would have been divulged. It is also questionable how many would have responded to an appeal letter from an unknown priest who lived, in many cases, in another state or even a distant area of the country.

11. *Annals* 26 (3) (January 1914): 13; 36 (3) (July 1923): 14, AOLV.

12. Galvin, *Father Baker*, 21–22.

13. *Annals* 6 (1) (July 1893): 1, AOLV. Chapter 8 has more amplifying information on Brace, the Children's Aid Society, and Orphan Trains.

14. Hartel, "Producing Father Baker," 69; Kern, "Life and Times of Father Baker," #59, Kern, Baker Papers, vol. 4, AOLV.

15. *Annals*, 1 (1) (July 1888): 1, AOLV.

16. Ibid., 1–16, AOLV.

17. Hartel, "Producing Father Baker," 69–70.

18. *Annals* 1 (2) (October 1888): 1, AOLV.

19. Hartel, "Producing Father Baker," 73. Hartel says that experts at Canisius College who compared "signed" essays by Baker and other essays in the *Annals* suggest that there is a high degree of certainty that Baker penned many more essays in the magazine than those with his NHB byline.

20. *Annals* 19 (2) (October 1906): 4; 19 (4) (April 1907): 10, AOLV.

21. Alice M. Pytak, *A Christian Commitment: The story of Father Nelson Henry Baker, 1841–1936* (Lackawanna, NY: Our

Lady of Victory Homes of Charity, 1986), 14. Pytak claims that by 1885 the debt on the Institutions had been liquidated. This would mean that the debt was paid in three years, which seems a bit optimistic. There is no extant data of precise debts and receipts from the Association to verify this claim.

22. *Annals* 1 (3) (January 1889): 1, AOLV.

23. Ibid., 2 (3) (January 1890): 1; 7 (3) (January 1894), clipping, Baker Published Writings File, AOLV.

24. Ibid., 1 (4) (April 1889): 1, AOLV.

25. Ibid., 6 (1) (July 1893): 1, AOLV.

26. Ibid., 4 (1) (January 1891), clipping, Baker Published Writings File, AOLV.

27. Ibid., 7 (4) (April 1894), clipping, Baker Published Writings File, AOLV. Baker's strong appeal to his support base was accompanied by his belief that Our Lady of Victory would always assist him.

28. Nelson Baker to "Rev. Dear Friend," February 10, 1886, Stephan Ryan Files, DBCA.

29. *Buffalo Times*, n.d. [August 1936], clipping, PPRP. This source claims that Baker needed to annually raise approximately $600,000. As will be discussed later with respect to the deficits run by St. Joseph's, St. John's, and other Institutions, the number might be reasonable, but seems greatly inflated.

30. Extant data is confusing on the date for the start of the *Victorian*. The *Victorian* itself in vol. 38 (1) (January 1932) says that the organ had been published for the past thirty-one years, with a circulation of 300,000. Vol. 39 (1) (January 1933) says the magazine "has been in existence for the past 32 years." Yet, the volume numbers show these statements to be inaccurate. Additionally, the Archives of Our Lady of Victory has an extant copy of vol. 2 (1) (May 1896). This extant data, plus the secondary sources of John Koerner and Heather Hartel, suggest 1895 is the best date for the inauguration of the *Victorian*.

31. *Victorian* 5 (2) (February 1899): 26, AOLV.

32. Ibid., 4 (3) (March 1898): 36, AOLV.

33. Hartel, "Producing Father Baker," 79.

34. *Western New York Catholic*, clipping, November 1987, Baker Papers, ASLCB.

35. Nelson Baker to Matthew Harkins, September 11, 1920, Miscellaneous File, AOLV.

36. *Victorian* 34 (1) (January 1928): 6, AOLV. Baker reported the *Victorian*'s circulation at 100,000 and the *Annals*'s at 260,000.

37. Ibid., 35 (8) (August 1929): 3, AOLV.

38. "Report of Nelson Baker to the Board of Managers of the Society for the Protection of Destitute Roman Catholic Children," November 12, 1929, Annual and Additional Reports File, AOLV.

39. Hartel, "Producing Father Baker," 79–80.

40. Americanism, which played out between approximately 1884 and 1899, pitted the more transformationalist bishops against those who were more traditionalist. The basic question of Americanism: Could Catholicism be in any way adapted to meet the unique situation the faith encountered in the United States? In the end Pope Leo XIII, writing in *Testem Benevolentiae* (January 1899), answered "No." The pope wrote, "It [Americanism] raises the suspicion that there are some among you who conceive and desire a church in America different from that which is in the rest of the world." See John Tracy Ellis, ed., *Testem Benevolentiae* in *Documents of American Catholic History* (Milwaukee, WI: The Bruce Publishing Company, 1962), 542. While numerous sources on Americanism are in the literature, the only one-volume account of this time period is Thomas G. McAvoy, CSC, *The Great Crisis in American Catholic History, 1895–1900* (Chicago: Henry Regnery Company, 1957). Theological modernism, which originated in Europe but which had some American proponents, was based on two premises: (1) promotion of the historical-critical method of Scripture study, and (2) the concept of the development of doctrine. Modernism was declared the "synthesis of all heresies" by Pope Pius X in his encyclical *Pascendi Dominici Gregis* (1907). Like Americanism, modernism has many scholarly sources. The one volume that links modernism with Americanism in the United States is R. Scott Appleby, *"Church and Age Unite!": The Modernist Impulse in American Catholicism* (Notre Dame, IN: University of Notre Dame Press, 1992). In his seminal 1955 article, the eminent Church historian John Tracy Ellis decried the inability of American Catholic intellectualism to move forward due

to its failure to concentrate the efforts of scholars in the intellectual life. See John Tracy Ellis, "American Catholics and the Intellectual Life," *Thought* 30 (Fall 1955): 351–88.

41. James O'Toole, ed., *Habits of Devotion: Catholic Religious Practice in Twentieth-Century America* (Ithaca, NY: Cornell University Press, 2004), 1.

42. Colleen McDannell, *Material Christianity: Religions and Popular Culture in America* (New Haven, CT: Yale University Press, 1995), 133.

43. Ann Taves, *Household of Faith: Roman Catholic Devotions in Mid-Nineteenth-Century America* (Notre Dame, IN: University of Notre Dame Press, 1986), vii–viii.

44. Robert Orsi, "Everyday Miracles: The Study of Lived Religion," in David Hall, ed., *Lived Religion in America: Toward a History of Practice* (Princeton, NJ: Princeton University Press, 1997), 6–7.

45. Ibid., 7–8.

46. McDannell, *Material Christianity*, 137.

47. Ibid., 137–39.

48. Ibid., 133.

49. Taves, *Household of Faith*, 36–38.

50. Kern, "Life and Times of Father Baker," #33, Kern, Baker Papers, vol. 2, AOLV.

51. Galvin, *Father Baker*, 100–101. Galvin continued, "This trust in his Blessed Lady of Victory is the secret of his success. It is the most precious flower in the garden of the soul."

52. Balduf, interview with Walter Kern, May 22, 1990; Sr. Theophane Bwie, SSJ, interview with Kern, November 29, 1987, AOLV.

53. *Annals* 25 (4) (April 1913): 5, AOLV.

54. Balduf, interview with Walter Kern, May 22, 1990, AOLV.

55. Josephine Quirk, "A Man to Remember," *Victorian* 56 (1) (1950): 19.

56. Quoted in *Buffalo Times*, July 29, 1936, in Sr. René Ruberto, "Father Baker—Folk Hero: Legendary Study of the Life of Nelson H. Baker, 1841–1936" (master's thesis, SUNY Buffalo State College, 1976), 39–40.

57. "Read This About Father Baker," *Victorian* clipping, n.d., in Kern, Baker Papers, vol. 2, AOLV.

58. *Annals* 37 (3) (October 1924): 3, AOLV.

59. Pytak, *Christian Commitment*, 20. One further example of Baker's total faith in Mary to liquidate all financial responsibilities is given in an essay, "The Glorious Festival of Our Lady of Victory." He writes: "The financial means required to erect buildings for our enormous family has ever been a serious problem, but our generous Lady has ever looked upon us with compassion and inspired the hearts of our good friends, and their kind offerings seem to grow and be multiplied, and thus our difficulties seem to meet and melt, through the help of our dear Lady of Victory." See *Annals* 40 (4) (October 1927): 3, AOLV. Nelson Baker's faith in Mary and her ability to assist never wavered. Yet, his comment that he did not have the slightest idea of the origins of the money simply cannot be true. This is another example of the mystery of how Baker financed his operation, a mystery that remains unsolved due to lack of extant information.

60. *Annals* 19 (3) (January 1907): 6, AOLV.

61. One further example of Baker's strong belief that all had a responsibility to bring others to greater devotion to Mary is provided: "We trust that all lovers of Our Blessed Lady will prove their fidelity to her, by striving to attract others to her love, by infusing into their hearts some of that love for her, which they find by God's grace, burning in their own, and then they will be fulfilling God's will, and draw down upon themselves special grace from heaven." See *Annals* 4 (1) (January 1891), clipping in Baker Published Writings File, AOLV.

62. Ruth Monk, interview with the author, August 9, 2008, AOLV.

63. *Annals* 24 (2) (October 1911): 5; 17 (1) (July 1904): 5, AOLV.

64. Ibid., 24 (2) (October 1911): 1, AOLV.

65. "Father Baker's—A History of Charity," publication of Our Lady of Victory Homes of Charity, 1979, 2, AOLV.

66. *Annals* 17 (1) (July 1904): 3, AOLV.

67. Ibid. Baker wrote his own prayer asking Mary for favors: "O Victorious Lady, thou who hast ever such powerful influence

with thy Divine Son in conquering the hardest of hearts, intercede for those for whom we pray, that, their hearts being softened by Divine Grace, they may return to the unity of the true faith, through Christ our Lord. Amen." See Kern, "Life and Times of Father Baker," #59, in Kern, Baker Papers, vol. 4, AOLV.

68. *Annals* 12 (1) (July 1899): 11, AOLV.

69. Mary O'Leary, "A History of Our Lady of Victory Homes of Charity," unpublished essay, 13–14, AOLV.

70. Ruberto, "Father Baker—Folk Hero," 38.

71. Galvin, *Father Baker*, 231–32.

72. Stanislaus, "Father Baker and Juvenile Delinquency," *Victorian* 49 (4) (April 1943): 32, AOLV.

73. Ibid.

74. *Annals* 20 (1) (July 1907): 13, AOLV.

75. Stanislaus, "A Father to Orphans," *Victorian* 46 (7) (July 1940): 15, AOLV.

76. *Annals* 21 (4) (April 1909): 12, AOLV.

77. Sr. Mary Immaculata Maxwell, SSJ, *Like a Swarm of Bees: Sisters of St. Joseph of Buffalo* (Derby, NY: Society of St. Paul, 1956), 129.

78. *Annals* 17 (1) (July 1904): 15, AOLV.

79. Ibid.

80. Ibid., 12 (1) (July 1899), 8, AOLV.

81. Mary Yager to "Father Baker's School," January 23, 1929, Everett Arlin Arbogast File, St. Joseph's Orphan Asylum, AOLV.

82. Nelson Baker to Sr. Mary Evangelist, August 24, 1926, Miscellaneous Correspondence File, AOLV; Baker to Karl Alter, March 30, 1919, Religious General File, Box 4a, Baker Papers, DBCA. There is no extant data to verify whether or not Baker's request for financial aid in the care of the boys was received.

83. *Annals* 4 (1) (July 1893): 1, AOLV.

84. "The Appeal for the Homeless and Destitute Child," n.d. [1932], Miscellaneous File, AOLV.

85. *Annals* 23 (3) (January 1911): 1; Nelson Baker to "Our Friends of the Rev. Clergy and Laity," short essay, n.d., Orphan Train File, AOLV.

86. Earnest Denn, "Testimony," n.d., Questionnaire for Former Wards of Father Baker, AOLV.

87. *Catholic Union & Times*, September 24, 1908, clipping in Newsclips 1896–1936, Box 4a, Baker Papers, DBCA.

88. *Catholic Union & Times*, August 6, 1936, Non-Catholic/Ecumenical File, AOLV.

89. *Buffalo News*, n.d. [July 1936], clipping in Kern, Baker Papers, vol. 1, AOLV. Many testimonies express the love and affection Baker demonstrated to the boys. One youth named Harry Haynes commented, "I came here when I was 9 years old. My father had died and my mother couldn't support us. I was crying that first day in a corner of the Asylum yard when an old man came up and talked to me. He talked gently to me for a long time and I wasn't homesick any longer. I didn't know it was Father Baker until afterwards." Clipping, n.d. [1936], PPRP.

90. Galvin, *Father Baker*, 55. Many reports state that Baker always had candy with him and gave it to any boys he encountered.

91. Quoted in Hartel, "Producing Father Baker," 82–83.

92. *Victorian* 3 (3) (March 1897): 40, AOLV.

93. Brother Stanislaus, "Father Baker Dedicated His Entire Life to OLV," *Victorian* 48 (7) (July 1942): 29, AOLV.

94. George Edward Smith, interview with Walter Kern, May 25, 1993, AOLV.

95. *Sadlier Catholic Directory Almanac and Ordo for Various Dioceses in the United States, British America, England, Ireland, and Scotland*, in Kern, Baker Papers, vol. 3, AOLV. Between 1901 and 1905, the population at St. Joseph's averaged 216. See St. Joseph Orphan Asylum Inspection Reports, 1901 to 1905, Inspection Reports, AOLV.

96. Nelson Baker used St. Joseph's Orphan Asylum (and St. John's Protectory) to "cut his teeth" in ministry, initially to boys, but later extended to unwed mothers and their children. The lessons learned at St. Joseph were instructive for the rest of his life.

97. St. Joseph Male Orphan Asylum Inspection, July 8, 1902, Inspection Reports, AOLV. The routine at St. Joseph's was this:

6:00 a.m.	Rise	1:15–3:30 p.m.	School
6:15 a.m.	Chapel	3:30–5:00 p.m.	Recreation
7:00 a.m.	Breakfast	5:00 p.m.	Rosary

7:30 a.m.	Lavatory	5:30 p.m.	Supper
8:00 a.m.	House duties	6:00 p.m.	Lavatory
9–11:30 a.m.	School	7:00 p.m.	Study
11:30 a.m.	Dinner	8–8:30 p.m.	Retire

98. A. P. Nemeth, *Father Baker's Children* (New York: Vantage Press, 1976), 3, 10–11.

99. St. Joseph Male Orphan Asylum Inspection, March 23, 1904, Inspection Reports, AOLV. A June 21, 1926, General Inspection Report stated, "Corporal punishment inflicted only by the Superintendent, consists of 'spanking' the child or striking the hand with a rubber tube. Corporal punishment is said to be seldom used."

100. Maxwell, *Swarm of Bees*, 129–30.

101. Dempsey, "Education at Limestone Hill," 34, AOLV.

102. Ibid., 20, AOLV.

103. Nemeth, *Father Baker's Children*, 13.

104. Ibid., 12, 27–29; John Phillips, interview with the author, August 10, 2008, AOLV. Sometimes the Sisters took the boys on field trips to Buffalo, traveling on street cars. It might be a trip to see a movie, attend the circus, or simply enjoy a public park. See Robert and Anthony Massaro Testimony, July 20, 2000, Massaro File, Lackawanna Institutes, ASSJB.

105. Quoted in "The Appeal for Destitute Children," State Charities File, AOLV.

106. Apostolic Delegate [Satolli] to Nelson Baker, May 12, 1895, Letters 1895–1936, Baker Papers, DBCA.

107. Quoted in *Annals* 21 (4) (April 1909): 4, AOLV.

108. Galvin, *Father Baker*, 217–23; Thomas Donahue, *History of the Catholic Church in the Western New York Diocese of Buffalo* (Buffalo, NY: Catholic Historical Publishing Company, 1904), 321–22; Kern, "Life and Times of Father Baker," #50, Kern, Baker Papers, vol. 4, AOLV. The Sisters of St. Joseph of Buffalo came originally from St. Louis and arrived at Canandaigua, NY, on December 8, 1854.

109. Maxwell, *Swarm of Bees*, 119–20.

110. *Western New York Catholic Supplement*, March 8, 1981, Baker Papers, ASLCB.

111. Galvin, *Father Baker*, 47; quoted in Ruberto, "Father

Baker—Folk Hero," 16; Thomas Galvin to "Father Master," April 1887, Galvin Papers, Archives of the Redemptorist Fathers in Baltimore (hereafter ARFB), Brooklyn, NY.

112. *Catholic Union & Times*, December 12, 1929, clipping found in Diamond Jubilee of Sisters of St. Joseph of Buffalo Scrapbook, December 8, 1929, Scrapbook #2, ASSJB.

113. Nelson Baker to Mother M. Constantia, March 27, 1935, Baker Papers, ASSJB.

114. Anderson, *Apostle of Charity*, 67; Galvin, *Father Baker*, 7, 9.

115. "Father Baker: Apostle of Three Generations," 213; Galvin, *Father Baker*, 16, 231–32; Dempsey, "Education at Limestone Hill," 24.

116. *Catholic Union & Times*, July 14, 1884, 4, clipping in Kern, Baker Papers, vol. 4, AOLV.

117. Josephine Quirk, "A Man to Remember," Part I, *Victorian* 56 (1) (1950): 18, AOLV.

118. Josephine Quirk, "A Man to Remember," Part II, *Victorian* 56 (2) (1950): 22, AOLV.

119. Quoted in Quirk, "A Man to Remember," Part I, *Victorian* 56 (1) (1950): 18, AOLV.

120. Quoted in Galvin, *Father Baker*, 238–39. The official prospectus of St. John's read: "Saint John's Protectory, Lackawanna, NY, by consent of its Managers, now offers to parents and guardians an opportunity of giving their boys, inclined to truancy, disobedience of willfulness, a good common school education, and a thorough knowledge of some useful trade which may be of service in obtaining for them a livelihood in the future." See Galvin, *Father Baker*, 16.

121. "Report of the Standing Committee on Reformatories," January 27, 1885, A0010–78, printed report, State Board of Charities Papers, New York State Archives (hereafter NYSA), Albany, NY.

122. Nelson Baker to "Our Many Friends of the Rev. Clergy and Laity," n.d., Orphan Train File, AOLV.

123. "Extraordinary Building Activities," Working Boys Home File, Baker Papers, Box 4a, DBCA; *Annals* 2 (1) (July 1889): 1, AOLV.

124. *Annals* 7 (4) (April 1894), clipping found in Baker's Writings File, AOLV.

125. Emerling, *The History of Lackawanna*, 73; Dempsey, "Education at Limestone Hill," 26.

126. Donald J. Monin, "A History and Reflection on the Brothers of the Holy Infancy and Youth of Jesus" (master's thesis, Christ the King Seminary, 1993), 9; Joseph Klos, "Children in Father Baker's Institutions and Their Reception of Selected Sacraments" (JCL thesis, Catholic University of America, 2002), 7; Maxwell, *Swarm of Bees*, 126.

127. John Phillips, interview with Walter Kern, December 1, 1987; Phillips, interview with author, August 10, 2008, AOLV; J. N. Larned, *A History of Buffalo: Delineating the Evolution of the City*, vol. 1 (New York: The Progress of the Empire State Company, 1911), 112.

128. Quoted in Dempsey, "Education at Limestone Hill," 24.

129. *Catholic Union & Times*, July 14, 1884, 4, clipping in Kern, Baker Papers, vol. 4, AOLV.

130. Galvin, *Father Baker*, 27; Dempsey, "Education at Limestone Hill," 13.

131. Quoted in Dempsey, "Education at Limestone Hill," 20.

132. Ibid., 25; also *Catholic Union & Times*, n.d. [1930–31], clipping in OLV Institutions File, AOLV.

133. Dempsey, "Education at Limestone Hill," 27.

134. Ibid., 28.

135. Ibid.

136. Quoted in ibid., 24.

137. Donahue, *History of Church in Western New York*, 322–23.

138. Galvin, *Father Baker*, 226–27; Monin, "Brothers of the Holy Infancy," 10, 14; Alfred Barrett, "The Charity of Father Baker, *America* 54 (26) (April 4, 1936): 612. Some sources suggest the investiture of Harris was actually in January 1855, but Monin says the diary of Timon, which gives January 1856 as the proper date for the reception of the three men as religious brothers, is the most accurate.

139. Monin, "Brothers of the Holy Infancy," 25; Brothers of the Holy Infancy Record Book, AOLV. Galvin states that the Brothers' Rule was not given episcopal approbation until June 1920. See Galvin, *Father Baker*, 229–30.

140. Monin, "Brothers of the Holy Infancy," 31; Raymond Thomas, interview with Robert Wurtz, December 3, 1987; John Phillips, interview with Walter Kern, December 1, 1987; George Edward Smith, interview with Walter Kern, April 11, 1989, AOLV. After Baker's death, the Brothers of the Holy Infancy and Youth of Jesus found themselves abandoned. Some joined other religious communities, others left religious life, and a few continued in their original vocations, but without any support from the Institutions. The loss of the basic apostolate for which the Brothers existed (St. John's population was drastically cut after Baker's death) meant the men had little to do and no apparent reason to continue in their work. Additionally, Baker's successor, Monsignor Joseph McGuire, had no association with them. See George Smith, interview with Walter Kern, n.d., PPTA.

141. Emerling, *History of Lackawanna*, 79. Ruberto wrote, "No one could deny the insurmountable amount of good work these men [the Brothers] did in the education of the boys." See Ruberto, "Father Baker—Folk Hero," 52.

142. Galvin, *Father Baker*, 247–48; Maxwell, *Swarm of Bees*, 131; the booklet "Opening and Dedication of Working Boys Home," October 27–28, 1897, Miscellaneous Papers, AOLV.

143. Galvin, *Father Baker*, 249; *Victorian* 37 (1) (January 1931): 9, AOLV.

144. "Report of Infant Home," n.d., Letters 1895–1936, Box 4a, Baker Papers, DBCA.

145. "A Century of Love," *Victorian* 60 (12) (December 1954): 53.

146. Anderson, *Apostle of Charity*, 55–61.

147. Galvin, *Father Baker*, 252–54; James R. Cleary, "Father Baker's Gas Wells," *Catholic Digest* 13 (November 1948): 6.

148. Anderson, *Apostle of Charity*, 55–61; Galvin, *Father Baker*, 254–58; *Buffalo Evening News*, August 22, 1891, 1.

149. Quoted in Cleary, "Gas Wells," 7–8.

150. The accounts by Anderson and Galvin have Baker using

a procession and a statue of Our Lady of Victory to know precisely where to drill. During the long months of the drilling operation, these same accounts say Baker prayed various novenas asking for Mary's intercession. Since his devotion to Our Lady of Victory, as indicated in this biography, was so complete, there is every reason to believe that such actions of popular devotion were utilized by him. Various sources quote offers proffered for the well, but the greatest was $60,000. A second gas well was discovered in 1911. See Cleary, "Gas Wells," 6–8.

Chapter 5

1. Ethelyn Weller, *A History of the Town of West Seneca* (Buffalo, NY: Buffalo and Erie County Historical Society, 1972), 1, 4; Thomas Galvin, CSsR, *Father Baker and His Lady of Victory Charities* (Buffalo, NY: Buffalo Publishing Company, Inc., 1925), 200–202; Heather A. Hartel, "Producing Father Nelson H. Baker: The Practices of Making a Saint for Buffalo, N.Y." (PhD diss., University of Iowa, 2006), 31.

2. Dobson, "Daddy Baker," 14, PPTA; Floyd Anderson, *Apostle of Charity: The Father Nelson Henry Baker Story* (Buffalo, NY: Our Lady of Victory Homes of Charity, 1960), 65; Galvin, *Father Baker*, 93; *Annals* 17 (1) (July 1904): 1, AOLV.

3. Emerling, *History of Lackawanna*, 55–57; Hartel, "Producing Father Baker," 39–40; Memorandum [no specific addressees], September 15, 1933, PPRP.

4. Hartel, "Producing Father Baker," 40–44; Weller, *A History of West Seneca*, 6; Emerling, *History of Lackawanna*, 58; Mary O'Leary, "A History of Our Lady of Victory Homes of Charity," unpublished essay (1967), 18–19, AOLV.

5. Hartel, "Producing Father Baker," 40.

6. Ibid., 42; "A History of Our Lady of the Sacred Heart Parish," Our Lady of the Sacred Heart Papers, DBCA; Galvin, *Father Baker*, 197–99.

7. Anderson, *Apostle of Charity*, 75; Sr. Mary Venard, SSM, Testimony, n.d., "Signed Recollections of NHB by Others," AOLV. Anderson and other secondary sources state that the human remains were discovered in Buffalo, but there is no extant

data to verify this claim. See *Annals* 32 (3) (January 1920): 1. Walter Kern was convinced that the unnamed city was Toronto.

8. Galvin, *Father Baker*, 269, 274; Sr. Mary Immaculata Maxwell, SSJ, *Like a Swarm of Bees: Sisters of St. Joseph of Buffalo* (Derby, NY: Society of St. Paul, 1956), 132–33.

9. *Buffalo News*, April 21, 1907, Baker Scrapbook, Buffalo Erie County Public Library (hereafter BEPL), Buffalo, NY.

10. Quoted in *Annals* 19 (1) (July 1906): 3, AOLV.

11. Ibid., 19 (2) (October 1906): 1; 19 (3) (January 1907): 1–2, AOLV.

12. Quoted in ibid., 19 (3) (January 1907): 4.

13. "The Appeal for the Homeless and Destitute Child," n.d., Miscellaneous File, AOLV.

14. Hartel, "Producing Father Baker," 44; Boniface Hanley, "Servant of God Msgr. Nelson Baker, 1841–1936: One Lifetime," *The Anthonian* 53 (2) (1971): 26; Anderson, *Apostle of Charity*, 77.

15. *Annals* 19 (1) (July 1906): 8; 21 (1) (January 1908): 3, AOLV.

16. *Buffalo Courier*, August 16, 1908, Baker Scrapbook, BEPL.

17. Yearbook 1908–1926, OLV Aid Society, AOLV; Hartel, "Producing Father Baker," 72.

18. *Annals* 22 (1) (July 1909): 1, AOLV.

19. Ibid., 20 (1) (July 1907): 14; 21 (4) (April 1909): 13, AOLV.

20. *Victorian* 23 (10) (October 1920): 4, AOLV.

21. Hanley, "One Lifetime," 26.

22. "Report of Nelson Baker to Board of Managers of Society for the Protection of Destitute Roman Catholic Children," November 20, 1924, Annual Reports File, AOLV.

23. Ibid.

24. Quoted in *Annals* 41 (2) (April 1928): 5, AOLV.

25. "Report of Nelson Baker to Board of Managers of Society for the Protection of Destitute Roman Catholic Children," November 20, 1924, Annual Reports File, AOLV.

26. Nelson Baker to James Foster, September 23, 1927, Reports, Box 5, Baker Papers, DBCA.

27. Nelson Baker to William Turner, June 4, 1928, State Charities File, AOLV. One nurse who worked at the Infant Home commented about Baker: "He was very protective of the unwed mothers. He didn't want us to know much about them. He wanted that protected." See Ellen Hayes, interview with Walter Kern, December 27, 1989, Interviews, Box 5, Baker Papers, DBCA.

28. "Care of Infants and Small Children," 1920, Board of Charities File, AOLV.

29. Peg Kessler, interview with the author, August 11, 2008, AOLV.

30. "Care of Infants and Small Children," 1920, Board of Charities File; Mr. Reno (first name unknown), interview with Walter Kern, November 29, 1987, AOLV.

31. "Report of Infant Home," n.d., Letters 1895–1936, Box 4a, Baker Papers, DBCA. As one example, in 1933 the Infant Home ran a debt of $76,000. See *Victorian* 39 (1) (January 1933): 5–6, AOLV.

32. Quoted in *Annals* 41 (2) (April 1928): 5, AOLV.

33. Quoted in *Victorian* 42 (9) (September 1936): 41, AOLV.

34. Lucie Beckett, interview with the author, August 9, 2008; Peg Kessler, interview with the author, August 11, 2008, AOLV; Dempsey, "Education at Limestone Hill," 48.

35. Nelson Baker to James Foster, September 23, 1927, State Reports, Box 5, Baker Papers, DBCA.

36. Nelson Baker to Mother Constantia, March 27, 1935, Mother Constantia File, ASSJB.

37. Ellen Hayes, interview with Walter Kern, December 27, 1989, Interviews, Box 5, Baker Papers, DBCA; Bruce Dickenson, interview with Walter Kern, July 31, 1990; Lucie Beckett, interview with the author, August 9, 2008, AOLV.

38. Chart enclosure to booklet, "Our Lady of Victory Infant Home, 1907–1967," Sisters of St. Joseph File, AOLV; *Annals* 39 (2) (July 1926): 5, AOLV.

39. *Annals* 40 (2) (April 1927): 5, AOLV. In 1914, he had reported similarly: "We have been obliged also to refuse receiving the poor mothers for the time being, as we have not the accom-

modations." See "Report of Nelson Baker to Board of Managers of Society for the Protection of Destitute Roman Catholic Children in the City of Buffalo," March 13, 1914, Annual and Other Reports, AOLV.

40. Elizabeth Finigan to Nelson Baker, May 19, 1925, Board of Charities File, AOLV.

41. *Annals* 24 (1) (July 1911): 13; *Victorian* 36 (1) (January 1930): 4, AOLV.

42. One account given by a Sr. Stanislaus, SSMN, from Lowell, MA, says Baker took small groups of children to various parishes and lined them up at the communion rail for adoption. See Lydia Fish, "Father Baker: Legends of a Saint in Buffalo," *New York Folklore* 10 (3–4) (Summer/Fall 1984): 25.

43. Nelson Baker to "Reverend Dear Father," January 24, 1927, Miscellaneous File, AOLV. It should also be noted that Baker was disappointed in an apparent attempt by the State to keep children away from his Home. He wrote to his board of managers, "There seems to have been a determined opposition to sending any infants or small children to our institutions by the Poor Department." See "Report of Nelson Baker to Board of Managers of Society for the Protection of Destitute Roman Catholic Children," December 4, 1923, Annual and Other Reports, AOLV.

44. *Annals* 39 (2) (October 1916): 3, AOLV.

45. "Report of Nelson Baker to Board of Managers of Society for the Protection of Destitute Roman Catholic Children," April 28, 1910, Annual and Other Reports, AOLV.

46. *Annals* 24 (1) (July 1911): 1; 23 (4) (April 1911): 1; Lucie Beckett, interview with the author, August 9, 2008, AOLV.

47. *Annals*, 27 (1) (July 1914): 8; 28 (3) (January 1916): 3, AOLV.

48. Nelson Baker to Charles Johnson, July 11, 1927; Baker to James Foster, September 23, 1927, State Reports, Box 5, Baker Papers, DBCA; *Annals* 42 (2) (April 1929): 3, AOLV.

49. Quoted in *Catholic Union & Times*, September 24, 1908, Newsclips 1896–1936, Box 4a, Baker Papers, DBCA.

50. Galvin, *Father Baker*, 268–69, 275.

51. Quoted in Anderson, *Apostle of Charity*, 82; *Annals* 27 (1) (July 1914): 3, AOLV.

52. *Annals* 28 (4) (April 1916): 2; 27 (3) (January 1915): 3, AOLV; Galvin, *Father Baker*, 276.

53. *Annals* 30 (4) (April 1918): 1, AOLV.

54. "Extraordinary Building Activities," Working Boys Home File, Box 4a, Baker Papers, DBCA; *Annals* 32 (3) (January 1920): 5, AOLV; "Fifty Years of Community Service, 1919–1969," Father Baker File, Lackawanna Institutions, ASSJB.

55. *Annals* 24 (4) (April 1912): 5; 28 (3) (July 1916): 5, AOLV.

56. State of New York, State Board of Charities, Annual Report, October 22, 1926, State Board of Charities File, AOLV.

57. Galvin, *Father Baker*, 277; "History of Our Lady of Victory Hospital" and "Logging for OLV," OLV Institutions Historical Items, DBCA; brochure, "Fifty Years of Community Service, 1919–1969," OLV Hospital, PPRP.

58. Quoted in *Annals* 36 (4) (October 1923): 14, AOLV.

59. "History of Our Lady of Victory Hospital," OLV Institutions Historical Items, DBCA; "Fifty Years of Community Service, 1919–1969," OLV Hospital, PPRP.

60. Dempsey, "Education at Limestone Hill," 48–50; "Fifty Years of Community Service, 1919–1969," OLV Hospital, PPRP; *Annals* 32 (2) (October 1919): 6; 37 (2) (April 1924): 14; 41 (3) (July 1928): 4–5. Extant sources differ on the graduation date. One says it was January 3, not January 21. The School of Nursing closed in 1952.

61. Brochure, "Fifty Years of Community Service, 1919–1969," OLV Hospital, PPRP; *Victorian* 30 (2) (February 1924): 24; "Supplementary Report for the Society for the Protection of Destitute Roman Catholic Children," December 4, 1923, Annual and Other Reports, AOLV.

62. *Buffalo Times*, March 18, 1927, Baker Scrapbook, BEPL; *Annals* 42 (2) (April 1929): 3.

63. "Report of Infant Home," n.d., Letters 1895–1936, Box 4a, Baker Papers, DBCA; *Victorian* 39 (1) (January 1933): 6, AOLV.

Chapter 6

1. Richard Hofstadter, *The Age of Reform: From Bryan to F.D.R.* (New York: Alfred A. Knopf, 1960), 3–22, 134.

2. Arthur S. Link and Richard L. McCormick, *Progressivism* (Arlington Heights, IL: Harlan Davidson, Inc., 1983), 2.

3. A good short summary of Theodore Roosevelt's Progressive politics is provided in George Tindall and David Shi, *The Essential America: A Narrative History*, vol. 2 (New York: W. W. Norton, 1996), 1014–22.

4. Link and McCormick, *Progressivism*, 63–66.

5. Tindall and Shi, *The Essential America*, vol. 2, 1030–43.

6. Ibid., 867. Also, there is an excellent summary of the progress of organized labor during Progressive-Era America on 857–74.

7. Foster Rhea Dulles and Melvyn Dubofsky, *Labor in America: A History* (Wheeling, IL: Harlan Davidson, 1993). See 175–99 on organized labor in the Progressive Era.

8. Robert T. Handy, *The Social Gospel in America, 1870–1920* (New York: Oxford University Press, 1966), 3–16; Walter Rauschenbush, *A Theology for the Social Gospel* (Nashville: Abingdon Press, 1987), 4–5.

9. Handy, *The Social Gospel*, 3–16.

10. The American Protective Association was formed in March 1887 by Henry F. Bowers and six associates. Its basic agenda was to remove *all* Catholic influence from American life. As one example, the secret oath of the American Protective Association (October 31, 1893) stated: "I do most solemnly promise and swear that I will always, to the utmost of my ability, labor, plead and wage a continuous warfare against ignorance and fanaticism; that I will use my utmost power to strike the shackles and chains of blind obedience to the Roman Catholic church from the hampered and bound consciences of a priest-ridden and church-oppressed people." See John Tracy Ellis, ed., *Documents of American Catholic History* (Milwaukee, WI: The Bruce Publishing Company, 1962), 480.

11. Douglas Slawson, *The Foundation and First Decade of the National Catholic Welfare Council* (Washington, DC: Catholic University of America Press, 1992), 45–95.

12. The genesis of Ryan's famous document on social reconstruction is fully discussed in Joseph M. McShane, SJ, *"Sufficiently Radical": Catholicism, Progressivism, and the Bishops' Program of 1919* (Washington, DC: Catholic University of America Press, 1986); "Program of Social Reconstruction," Administrative Committee National Catholic War Council, February 12, 1919. The reconstitution of national meetings of the American hierarchy was highly significant. In the nineteenth century, the American bishops had met in seven provincial and three plenary councils. The last time the bishops had met collectively prior to their reorganization in 1917 was in 1884 in Baltimore. However, the *arch*bishops did meet periodically during this same period.

13. Mary Harrita Fox, *Peter E. Dietz: Labor Priest* (Notre Dame, IN: University of Notre Dame Press, 1953), 21.

14. Ibid., 43–68.

15. The writing corpus of Paul Hanly Furfey is extensive. One good synthesis of his thought is provided in Mary Elizabeth Walsh and Paul Hanly Furfey, *Social Problems and Social Action* (Englewood Cliffs, NJ: Prentice-Hall, 1958). A more recent article that analyzes Furfey's work is Nicholas Rademacher, "Paul Hanly Furfey and the Social Services: Liberal, Radical, and Revolutionary," *U.S. Catholic Historian* 25 (4) (Fall 2007): 23–43. For a book of the period that best presents his ideas, see Paul Hanly Furfey, *Fire on the Earth* (New York: Macmillan, 1936).

16. Many fine sources are available to provide details about Dorothy Day, Peter Maurin, and the Catholic Worker Movement. Some of the best are Mel Piehl, *Breaking Bread: The Catholic Worker and the Origins of Catholic Radicalism in America* (Philadelphia: Temple University Press, 1982); Patrick G. Coy, ed., *Revolution of the Heart: Essays on the Catholic Worker* (Philadelphia: New Society Publishers, 1988); Dorothy Day, *The Long Loneliness: An Autobiography* (San Francisco: Harper, 1952); William Miller, *Dorothy Day: A Biography* (San Francisco: Harper & Row, 1982); Mark and Louise Zwick, *The Catholic Worker Movement: Intellectual and Spiritual Origins* (New York: Paulist Press, 2005); Nancy Roberts, *Dorothy Day & the Catholic Worker* (Albany: State University of New York Press, 1984); Dorothy Day, *Peter Maurin: Apostle to the World* (Maryknoll, NY: Orbis Books, 2004).

17. Thomas Donahue, *History of the Diocese of Buffalo* (Buffalo, NY: The Buffalo Catholic Publishing Company, 1929), 134; J. N. Larned, *A History of Buffalo: Delineating the Evolution of the City*, vol. 1 (New York: The Progress of the Empire State Company, 1911), 78–80.

18. Thomas Donahue, *History of the Catholic Church in the Western New York Diocese of Buffalo* (Buffalo, NY: Catholic Historical Publishing Company, 1904), 234–35.

19. Donahue, *History of the Diocese of Buffalo*, 140.

20. Sr. Mary of the Sacred Heart, *Congregation of St. Joseph*, 148–49.

21. *Catholic Union & Times*, December 31, 1903, Newsclips 1896–1936, Box 4a, Baker Papers, DBCA.

22. *Buffalo Courier*, January 3, 1904, clipping, Baker Scrapbook, BEPL.

23. *Catholic Union & Times*, December 31, 1903, Newsclips 1896–1936, Box 4a, Baker Papers, DBCA.

24. Clipping, March 23, 1905, Newsclips 1896–1936, Box 4a, Baker Papers, DBCA.

25. William Turner to Nelson Baker, April 27, 1922, Letters 1895–1936, Box 4a, Baker Papers, DBCA.

26. Nelson Baker to Denis Dougherty, February 23, 1917, and William Turner to Nelson Baker, April 27, 1922, Letters 1895–1936, Box 4a, Baker Papers, DBCA; retreat schedule for secular clergy of Buffalo, 1917, Vicar General File; Nelson Baker to Sr. St. John of the Cross, July 10, 1925, Religion File, AOLV; Nelson Baker to Charles Bocham, September 21, 1916, Unmarked File, Box 4a, Baker Papers, DBCA; Francis J. Hall, interview with Walter Kern, July 7, 1987, AOLV.

27. Donahue, *History of the Diocese of Buffalo*, 143.

28. Sr. Mary of Jesus, OP, "Msgr. Baker," unpublished reflection, Dominican Sisters File, AOLV.

29. Nelson Baker to John Pfluger, March 7, 1916, Vicar General File, AOLV.

30. Nelson Baker to "Dear Friend," February 18, 1916, Religious Communities Letter Collection, AOLV.

31. Nelson Baker to Sr. Mary Dolores, February 29, 1916, Sisters of Mercy File, Box 4a, Baker Papers, DBCA; Nelson Baker

to "Dear Friend," n.d. [1916], Religious Communities Letter Collection, AOLV.

32. Nelson Baker to Denis Dougherty, February 29, 1916, Vicar General File, AOLV.

33. Ibid.

34. *Catholic Union & Times*, June 8, 1916, Newsclips 1896–1936, Box 4a, Baker Papers, DBCA.

35. Nelson Baker to "Reverend Dear Father," September 21, 1918, Vicar General File, AOLV.

36. Ibid.

37. Nelson Baker to James Gibbons, January 24, 1919, Vicar General File, AOLV.

38. Sr. Mary of the Sacred Heart, *Congregation of St. Joseph*, 149.

39. Nelson Baker to William Turner, February 15, 1919, Miscellaneous Papers, AOLV; Donahue, *History of the Diocese of Buffalo*, 141.

40. William Turner to Nelson Baker, March 13 [?] (unprocessed); Turner to Baker, March 4, 1927, Miscellaneous Papers, AOLV.

41. William Turner to Nelson Baker, July 9, 1928, Miscellaneous File, AOLV.

42. William Turner to Nelson Baker, February 24, 1930, Letters 1895–1936, Box 4a, Baker Papers, DBCA; Baker to Mother Mary of St. John of the Cross, October 30, 1931, Religious File, AOLV.

43. Nelson Baker to Sr. Margaret Mary, July 10, 1930, Personal File, AOLV.

44. William Turner to Nelson Baker, June 12, 1928, Miscellaneous Papers, AOLV.

45. William Turner to Nelson Baker, July 7, 1926, Miscellaneous Papers, AOLV.

46. William Turner to Nelson Baker, February 1, 1924 (unprocessed), AOLV.

47. William Turner to Nelson Baker, March 29, 1926, Miscellaneous Papers, AOLV.

48. Thomas Galvin, CSsR, *Father Baker and His Lady of Victory Charities* (Buffalo, NY: Buffalo Publishing Company, Inc., 1925), 103.

49. John Francis O'Hern to Nelson Baker, January 21, 1929, Letters 1895–1936, Box 4a, Baker Papers, DBCA.

50. Transcription of papal proclamation, November 19, 1904, Letters 1895–1936, Box 4a, Baker Papers, DBCA.

51. *Victorian* 11 (1) (January 1905): 26, AOLV.

52. Ibid., 11 (4) (April 1905): 143, AOLV.

53. Clipping, March 23, 1905, Newsclips 1896–1936, Box 4a, Baker Papers, DBCA.

54. *Annals* 36 (3) (July 1923): 3, AOLV; *Buffalo Times*, March 30, 1930, clipping, Baker Scrapbook, BEPL. Heather Hartel claims that when Baker received the title protonotary apostolic, he was one of only five clerics in the United States to hold the designation. See Heather A. Hartel, "Producing Father Nelson H. Baker: The Practices of Making a Saint for Buffalo, N.Y." (PhD diss., University of Iowa, 2006), 50–51.

55. Nelson Baker to Mother St. Agnes, June 30, 1921, Religious File, AOLV.

56. Nelson Baker to Rev. Mother of the Blessed Sacrament, February 4, 1922, Religious File, AOLV.

57. Sr. Mary Innocentia Fitzgerald, *A Historical Sketch of the Sisters of Mercy in the Diocese of Buffalo, 1857–1942* (Buffalo, NY: Mount Mercy Academy, 1942), 81–82.

58. Nelson Baker to Sr. Agnes, August 4, 1926, Dominican Sisters Letter Collection, AOLV.

59. Nelson Baker to William Turner, November 26, 1927, Religious File, AOLV. Under Turner, Baker was given complete responsibility for canonical examination of the various communities of religious women in the diocese. See Nelson Baker to Rev. Mother Helena, June 16, 1922, Religious File, AOLV.

60. Nelson Baker to "Dear Mother," July 17, 1922, Religious File, AOLV.

61. Nelson Baker to Mother of St. John of the Cross, March 4, 1931, Religious File, AOLV.

62. Nelson Baker to Sisters of St. Dominic, December 20, 1916, Religious File, AOLV; Sr. Mary of Jesus, OP, "Msgr. Baker," unpublished reflection, Dominican Sisters File, AOLV; "Convent Book," ASLCB.

63. "Historical Sketches of the Institutions of Our Lady of

Charity of the Refuge, Buffalo, NY," 34, AOLV. The Sisters of Our Lady of Charity of Buffalo were also called the Sisters at the Refuge and the Good Shepherd Sisters.

64. Consecrates were women who lived the religious life of the Sisters of Charity without the profession of formal vows of poverty, chastity, and obedience.

65. "Convent Book"; Sr. Mary of St. Anne to Nelson Baker, n.d. [1928], Baker Papers, ASLCB.

66. Nelson Baker to John Kiefer, March 7, 1916, Vicar General Papers, AOLV.

67. Sr. Heronime Murphy, SSJ, interview with Walter Kern, December 27, 1987, AOLV.

68. Nelson Baker to Leo Geary, March 21, 1934, Vicar General Papers, AOLV.

69. Sr. René Ruberto, "Father Baker—Folk Hero: Legendary Study of the Life of Nelson H. Baker, 1841–1936" (master's thesis, SUNY Buffalo State College, 1976), 51.

70. John Phillips, interview with Walter Kern, December 1, 1987, AOLV.

71. Luke Sharkey to Bishop Smith, July 11, 1952, Priest Assistants to NHB File, AOLV. Sr. Heronime Murphy, SSJ, relates another incident. Baker and one of his assistants, Michael Regan, had a falling out. Murphy remembers Regan intentionally turning a hanging photo of Father Baker against the wall. See Sr. Heronime Murphy, SSJ, interview with Walter Kern, December 27, 1987, AOLV. It was at times reported that Baker could be vindictive when his fellow clergy complained about his policies. For example, after completion of the Basilica of Our Lady of Victory, Baker often gave permission for couples outside his parish boundaries to celebrate marriages in the new church. When priests complained about this rather indiscriminate policy of granting this privilege without securing the required permissions of the pastor(s) of the couple, the "offending" priest was often transferred. See Dobson, "Daddy Baker," 16, PPTA.

72. *Buffalo Times*, n.d., clipping, Priest Assistants to NHB, AOLV.

73. William Turner to Herman Gerlach, December 27, 1932,

Gerlach File, AOLV; Turner to Nelson Baker, December 27, 1932, Information and Interviews File, AOLV.

74. John Joseph Rooney, interview with Walter Kern, July 1, 1987, AOLV. Herman Gerlach to John Nash, August 12, 1936, PPTA. Rooney claims that conflict arose between Baker and Gerlach over the payment of bills. While Gerlach was not specific in his letter to Nash, it is clear that he felt he was treated unfairly by Baker.

75. William Turner to Herman Gerlach, December 27, 1932, Gerlach File, AOLV.

76. Apostolic delegate [Giovanni Bonzano] to Felix Scullin, November 24, 1950, Miscellaneous Correspondence, AOLV.

77. Henry Shaw to Nelson Baker, June 15, 1925, Miscellaneous Correspondence, AOLV.

78. *The Sentinel,* 1861 Holy Cross Cemetery, September 7, 1891, Holy Cross Cemetery File, DBCA. One account says that Holy Cross Cemetery was officially established as a parish cemetery in 1853, although records show burials as early as 1830. Since the cemetery antedated the small mission church, it is logical that the mission, Holy Cross, received its name from the cemetery.

79. Nelson Baker to Margaret Kirby, October 4, 1921, PPRP.

80. General Statement of Holy Cross Cemetery, 1904 to December 1, 1922, Holy Cross Cemetery File, DBCA. A similar General Statement of December 31, 1915, to December 1, 1922, gives a new surplus of $77,579.79. However, according to the statement, this surplus was used to purchase extra land and prepare it for cemetery use.

81. General Statement of Holy Cross Cemetery, from 1904 to December 1, 1922, Holy Cross Cemetery; Nelson Baker to William Turner, April 17, 1931, OLV Institutions Correspondence (1930s), Box 4a, Baker Papers, DBCA.

82. Nelson Baker to Margaret Kirby, September 17, 1930, Cemetery Files, AOLV.

83. Nelson Baker to Margaret Kirby, December 31, 1933, PPRP. Baker's veiled language was a code to Kirby to bury the woman like all others; the woman was not placed in a pauper's grave simply because her husband could not adequately pay. However, Baker was prudent enough to realize that some might

be upset if their loved ones were buried next to a murdered black woman. Thus, Baker was also telling Kirby to bury the woman in a plot that would not raise the ire of others. See Holy Cross Cemetery Burial Records, November 2, 1933.

84. W. E. McCorran to William Turner, August 28, 1923, PPRP.

85. Sr. Mary Kathleen Duggan, GNSH, "Father Baker and D'Youville College," e-mail to the author, August 6, 2009. See also Nelson Baker to Sr. Margaret Mary, January 3, 1933, Miscellaneous Papers, AOLV.

86. Duggan e-mail to the author, August 6, 2009.

87. Honorary Doctorate, Canisius College, 1920, Biographical Information, Box 4a, Baker Papers, DBCA.

88. *Canisius Monthly* 12 (?) (March 1928): 329, Newsclips 1896–1936, Box 4a, Baker Papers, DBCA.

Chapter 7

1. *Buffalo News*, July 29, 1936, Baker Scrapbook, BEPL.

2. Special blessing, Rome, August 12, 1908, Letters 1895–1936, Box 4a, Baker Papers, DBCA.

3. *Victorian* 32 (12) (December 1926): 6, AOLV.

4. St. Joseph's Male Orphan Asylum Inspection Reports, February 18, 1927; February 27, 1928; March 29, 1929; April 9, 1930; September 14, 1931; April 3, 1933; February 26, 1937: in Inspection Reports, AOLV. One possible reason for the population decline during the Depression was lack of money to take care of more boys. The drop after Baker's death is certainly attributable to that fact that, without Baker's control and influence, state laws with respect to not housing non–New York State children were enforced.

5. Census population and capacity at St. Joseph's were generally very close. In 1904, census and capacity were equal at 223. In 1910, 1912, and 1915, capacity was breached, with 1912 being the worst with the number of residents 19 over its capacity. It is interesting that the state reports for these years, however, do not emphasize overcrowding as a significant problem at the Asylum. See St. Joseph Male Orphan Asylum Inspection Reports, March

23, 1904; November 10, 1910; September 11, 1912; March 22, 1915: in Inspection Reports, AOLV.

6. St. Joseph Male Orphan Asylum Inspection Reports, September 11, 1912, and December 2, 1924, Inspection Reports, AOLV.

7. St. Joseph Male Orphan Asylum Inspection Reports, August 3, 1921, Inspection Reports, AOLV. Extant records that provide details on government payment for the boys in the Institutions could not be located. Thus, it is difficult to know whether or not the government (state or local) actually ever met its fiscal responsibility to Baker.

8. James Foster to Nelson Baker, October 22, 1925; Report of General Inspection of St. Joseph's Male Orphan Asylum, September 14, 1931, Inspection Reports, AOLV.

9. Some of the more common discrepancies found in annual state reports: (1) State Charities Board's rule violations on overcrowding, (2) unsanitary outside latrines, (3) inadequate bathrooms, (4) insufficient dental care, (5) limited recreation facilities, and (6) recommendations for more trades training.

10. Thomas Galvin, CSsR, *Father Baker and His Lady of Victory Charities* (Buffalo, NY: Buffalo Publishing Company, Inc., 1925), 300–305.

11. "Report of Chancery Work Performed During the Absence of the Right Reverend Bishop Turner," February 1–March 3, 1927, Miscellaneous Correspondence File, AOLV.

12. Bruce Dickenson, interview with Walter Kern, July 31, 1990, AOLV.

13. James Foster to William Turner, November 19, 1919, Inspection Reports, AOLV.

14. James Foster to William Turner, October 19, 1921, Inspection Reports, AOLV.

15. Charles Johnson to Nelson Baker, April 21, 1927, Board of Charities File, AOLV.

16. Charles Johnson to Nelson Baker, March 26, 1928; "Report of General Inspection of St. Joseph's Male Orphan Asylum," March 29, 1929, Inspection Reports, AOLV.

17. Charles Johnson to Nelson Baker, April 29, 1929, Inspection Reports, AOLV.

18. "New York State Department of Charities Annual Report, September 14, 1931, for St. Joseph Asylum," Relationship of Father Baker with New York State Department of Charities File, AOLV.

19. "Report of General Inspection of St. Joseph Male Orphan Asylum," April 3, 1933, Inspection Reports, AOLV.

20. A typical daily schedule at St. Joseph's:

5:30 a.m.	Older boys rise	3:30 to 5 p.m.	Recreation
6 a.m.	Mass	5:30 p.m.	Supper with recreation/ study
6:30 a.m.	Younger boys rise	7 p.m.	Retire for younger boys
7 a.m.	Breakfast	7 to 8:30 p.m.	Study
8:30 to 11:30 a.m.	Classes	8 p.m.	Bedtime for older boys
11:30 a.m.	Dinner	8:30 p.m.	Prayer for oldest boys
1:00 to 3:30 p.m.	Classes	8:45 p.m.	Retire for oldest boys

21. "Report of General Inspection of St. Joseph's Male Orphan Asylum," April 9, 1930, Inspection Reports, AOLV.

22. "Report of General Inspection of St. Joseph's Male Orphan Asylum," April 3, 1933, Inspection Reports, AOLV.

23. Sr. Mary Timothy Dempsey, SSJ, "History of Education at Limestone Hill: Father Baker's Institutions, Lackawanna, NY, 1856–1964" (master's thesis, Mount St. Joseph College of Education, 1965), 45–47; Joseph Kelly, interview with author, August 1, 2008, AOLV.

24. Galvin, *Father Baker*, 141–43; *Victorian* 31 (7) (July 1925): 33; "Report of General Inspection of St. Joseph's Male Orphan Asylum," June 21, 1926, Inspection Reports, AOLV.

25. *Victorian* 31 (7) (July 1925): 33; 38 (6) (June 1932): 33; Joseph Kelly, interview with author, August 1, 2008; John Phillips, interview with author, August 10, 2008, AOLV.

26. "Dr. Walter's Secular History of Fr. Baker's Time," 13–14, AOLV.

27. Ibid., 14–15.

28. Ibid., 15.

29. David A. Gerber, *The Making of an American Pluralism: Buffalo, New York, 1825–1860* (Urbana: University of Illinois Press, 1989), 308. Some Catholic school foundations of the period were St. Joseph College and Cathedral Parish School (1848); Canisius College (1870); Holy Angels Academy (1861); Buffalo Female Academy (1852); Buffalo Academy of the Sacred Heart (1874); St. Vincent's Technical School (1887). See J. N. Larned, *A History of Buffalo: Delineating the Evolution of the City*, vol. 1 (New York: The Progress of the Empire State Company, 1911), 146–70. It should be noted that the number enrolled in Catholic schools was probably higher as Catholic academies were not listed in the Catholic Directory under "Catholic diocesan schools."

30. "Dr. Walter's Secular History of Fr. Baker's Time," 15–16, AOLV.

31. Dempsey, "Education at Limestone Hill," 23.

32. *Annals* 37 (2) (April 1924): 3, AOLV. The need for Catholicism to demonstrate its undivided loyalty and patriotic fervor for the United States was manifested clearly in a dramatic way in 1924. Thousands of members of the Holy Name Society marched in Washington, DC, to counter a similar demonstration by the Ku Klux Klan. Baker's desire to instill patriotism in his boys was completely consistent with the general patriotic fervor of American Catholics in the 1920s.

33. *Victorian* 35 (4) (April 1929): 35–37, AOLV.

34. Baker's educational philosophy was also applied to the physical space where lessons were taught. Taking pride in his school and system, he insisted the classrooms be painted either a dull yellow or a standard gray to enhance their economical permanence. However, while Baker saw this as a boon, such was not the case for all his charges who sat in the classroom. One "Baker Boy" commented, "The dark and dreary classrooms left us restless, troublesome, and uninterested in our studies." See A. P. Nemeth, *Father Baker's Children* (New York: Vantage Press, 1976), 67.

35. State Board of Charities Rules—Amended, June 30, 1927, State Reports, Box 5, Baker Papers, DBCA.

36. Quoted in Sr. Marie Patrice Gallagher, OSF, *The History of Catholic Elementary Education in the Diocese of Buffalo,*

1847–1944 (Washington, DC: Catholic University of America Press, 1944), 39.

37. Dempsey, "Education at Limestone Hill," 29, 36–37, 69.

38. Ibid., 37–39.

39. Ibid., 70; *Victorian* 37 (1) (January 1931): 8, AOLV.

40. Report of General Inspection of St. Joseph's Male Orphan Asylum, March 29, 1929, Inspection Reports, AOLV; Dempsey, "Education at Limestone Hill," 60–61.

41. *Buffalo Courier*, April 10, 1904, clipping, Baker Scrapbook, BEPL.

42. *Annals* 41 (2) (April 1928): 6; *Victorian* 38 (9) (September 1932): 34.

43. Dempsey, "Education at Limestone Hill," 33.

44. Personal Reflection, John Sullivan, n.d. (unprocessed), AOLV.

45. Dempsey, "Education at Limestone Hill," 57. Dempsey does not elaborate on her comment about the lack of social development in the boys.

46. *Annals* 24 (1) (July 1911): 13, AOLV.

47. Our Lady of Victory Adoption Book, various entries, July 1, 1910; July 4, 1913; February 3, 1914.

48. Margaret McGuinness, "Let Us Go to the Altar: American Catholics and the Eucharist, 1926–1976," in James O'Toole, ed., *Habits of Devotion: Catholic Religious Practice in Twentieth-Century America* (Ithaca, NY: Cornell University Press, 2004), 190.

49. Quoted in Francis Thornton, *The Burning Flame: The Life of Pope Pius X* (Boston: Benziger Brothers, 1952), 156.

50. Owen Chadwick, *A History of the Popes, 1830–1914* (Oxford, England: Clarendon Press, 1998), 362.

51. Quoted in Igino Giordani, *Pius X: A Country Priest* (Milwaukee, WI: The Bruce Publishing Company, 1954), 94–95.

52. Virgil Michel, OSB, "Frequent Communion and Social Regeneration," *Orate Fratres* 10 (March 1936): 198–203. Michel wrote, "Frequent Communion which includes frequent Mass is Christ's essential way of effecting the death of disruptive selfishness in men and effecting the union of supernatural charity, both of which are essential to the good life here on Earth. Without

Christ there is increasing individualism and its consequent social disruption."

53. Joseph Forst, "Eucharist and Family Life," *Catholic Mind* 29 (July 8, 1931): 332.

54. Prior to the Second Vatican Council (1962–65), in order to prepare properly for reception of the Eucharist, Catholics were required to fast from food and drink from midnight before receiving Communion. After the Council this procedure was modified. Today Catholics are asked to fast for only one hour prior to receiving the Eucharist.

55. McGuinness, "Let Us Go to the Altar," 193–95.

56. Ibid., 189.

57. Joseph Chinnici, OFM, *Living Stones: The History and Structure of Catholic Spiritual Life in the United States* (New York: Macmillan Company, 1989), 146.

58. Galvin, *Father Baker*, 74.

59. Josephine Pilkington, "Father Baker's Little Red Book," *Victorian* 51 (7) (July 1945): 47.

60. Nelson Baker to Mother Mary of St. John of the Cross, July 16, 1931, Religious Communities File, AOLV.

61. *Annals* 35 (3) (July 1922): 3, AOLV.

62. *Victorian* 37 (10) (October 1931): 33; 31 (2) (February 1925): 31, AOLV.

63. *Buffalo Courier-Express*, July 30, 1936, clipping in Kern, Baker Papers, vol. 4, AOLV; clipping, n.d., PPRP.

64. *Victorian* 31 (2) (February 1925): 33, AOLV.

65. Clipping, n.d., PPRP.

66. *Victorian* 41 (2) (February 1935): 34, AOLV.

67. Nelson Baker Memorandum to State Board of Charities, May 6, 1960, Relationship of Father Baker with the New York State Department of Charities, AOLV.

68. *Annals* 28 (4) (April 1916): 3; AOLV; Boniface Hanley, "Servant of God Msgr. Nelson Baker, 1841–1936: One Lifetime," *The Anthonian* 53 (2) (1971): 29; Dempsey, "Education at Limestone Hill," 42.

69. Report of Father Baker to Board of Managers of the Society for the Protection of Destitute Roman Catholic Children, March 13, 1914, Annual Reports, AOLV; Dempsey, "Education

at Limestone Hill," 38–40. It is difficult to equate numbers of animals with the production of milk, beef, and pork. The productivity figures of 1915 seem high based on the previous year's number of animals. However, extant data does not allow for greater clarity.

70. *Buffalo Courier-Express*, n.d., Baker Scrapbook, BEPL.

71. *The Echo*, July 3, 1930, DBCA.

72. Meeting of Board of Managers of the Society for the Protection of Destitute Roman Catholic Children of the City of Buffalo, August 21, 1936, Reports, AOLV. The report, in outlining expenses between January 1 and July 31, 1936, speaks of "the establishment of Camp Baker for the boys at East Eden, N.Y." No earlier verification of the existence of this camp is extant.

73. *Buffalo News*, January 26, 1993, BEPL; Josephine Pilkington, "Father Baker's Best Investment," *Victorian* 51 (8) (August 1945): 49–50.

74. *Annals* 28 (2) (October 1915): 3, AOLV. The author is aware that, according to the breakdown of children serviced in the report, the total number should be 1,708, but the numbers as reported in the extant document are provided.

75. Ibid., 31 (3) (January 1919): 3; 39 (3) (July 1926): 4–5; 40 (2) (April 1927): 6; 41 (2) (April 1928): 6; 42 (2) (April 1929): 5, AOLV. *Victorian* 34 (1) (January 1928): 3–4, AOLV.

76. *Victorian* 37 (1) (January 1931): 4–8; 39 (1) (January 1933): 4–7; 41 (4) (April 1935): 4–6, AOLV.

77. Bruce Dickenson, interview with Walter Kern, July 31, 1990, AOLV.

78. "Chancery," Report of Nelson Baker to Board of Catholic Charities, 1934, 18, PPTA.

79. Mr. Reno (first name unknown), interview with Walter Kern, November 29, 1987; Clara Balduf, interview with Kern, May 22, 1990; Bruce Dickenson, interview with Kern, July 31, 1990, AOLV. One former Baker Boy said of his experience, "Well, if you had it coming, you got it. If they [the Brothers] didn't do it, there would be no control." Another resident of the Protectory asserts "that boys always got 'the whip,'" a piece of wood with nine straps when they were punished. He continued, "[Baker] never knew of it. If he had, he wouldn't have allowed it."

80. Dempsey, "Education at Limestone Hill," 73; Sr. René

Ruberto, "Father Baker—Folk Hero: Legendary Study of the Life of Nelson H. Baker, 1841–1936" (master's thesis, SUNY Buffalo State College, 1976), 18.

81. *Buffalo Courier-Express*, December 8, 1903, Baker Scrapbook; "Father Baker's Home," n.d., clipping, Baker Scrapbook, BEPL.

82. Dempsey, "Education at Limestone Hill," 72.

83. *Commercial*, January 21, 1908, Charities in Buffalo Scrapbook; *Express* (Buffalo), January 26, 1908, Baker Scrapbook, BEPL. Extant data does not show when repairs were completed.

84. Charles Johnson to William Turner, July 16, 1920, State Reports, Box 5, Baker Papers, DBCA.

85. Quoted in Galvin, *Father Baker*, 104; *Catholic Union & Times*, August 12, 1920, Newsclips 1896–1936, Box 4a, Baker Papers, DBCA.

86. Thomas Donahue, *History of the Diocese of Buffalo* (Buffalo, NY: The Buffalo Catholic Publishing Company, 1929), 390; quoted in Dempsey, "Education at Limestone Hill," 16.

87. "Extraordinary Building Activities," Working Boys Home File, Box 4a, Baker Papers, DBCA; *Sadlier Directory*, 1896; *Catholic Directory Almanac*, 1901, 1903, 1904, 1905, 1906, 1907.

88. *Catholic Directory Almanac*, 1904 through 1918. The *Catholic Directory* is the only consistent extant source that reports the numbers of students and religious serving as teachers. However, the numbers provided are clearly only estimates, based on the numbers reported. For example, between 1912 and 1918, inclusive, the *Directory* reports the number of students at Our Lady of Victory School as 209 with 4 Sisters of St. Joseph as teachers. Similarly between 1923 and 1932, the *Directory* reports enrollment at 481 students with 11 Sisters as teachers. It is not realistic to think that the numbers of students and religious during these two periods of time did not change at all.

89. *Catholic Directory Almanac*, 1921 through 1936. Enrollment records and the numbers of religious who were teachers remain estimates. Unfortunately, no extant data is held by the Sisters of St. Joseph to indicate how many Sisters were assisting at the school at any one time.

90. Sr. Mary Timothy Dempsey claims that the most gifted students from Baker's Institutions were sent either to Our Lady of Victory Academy or to Canisius High School in Buffalo. Those who attended the latter school, operated by the Jesuits, lived at the Working Boys Home.

91. *Victorian* 34 (1) (January 1928): 5; 37 (1) (January 1931): 8; Report of Nelson Baker to Board of Managers of the Society for the Protection of Destitute Roman Catholic Children, November 12, 1929, Annual and Other Reports; Nelson Baker to Sr. Margaret Mary, July 10, 1930, Personal File, AOLV.

92. *Victorian* 39 (1) (January 1933): 9. The magazine reported enrollments of 150 and 706 in the high school and elementary schools respectively. These numbers cannot be verified through the *Catholic Directory*, but as noted earlier the latter source is clearly not accurate. Therefore, what the *Victorian* reports is probably more accurate.

93. "Queen of All Saints Church," unpublished essay, December 1978, Queen of All Saints Papers, DBCA; Donahue, *History of Buffalo*, 302; St. Charles Borromeo Baptismal Record, July 1903 to November 1914, St. Anthony Church Rectory, Lackawanna, NY.

94. William Turner to Mother Mary Angelina, December 6, 1930, Archives of the Felician Sisters of Buffalo (hereafter AFSB), Buffalo, NY.

95. Sr. Mary Bonaventure Grabowski, *Felician Sisters: History of the Congregation of the Sisters of St. Felix of Cantalice* (Newark, NJ: Johnston Letter Co., Inc., 1993), 373, 854; Roderick Brown, OP, "A Gathering at the River: 150 Years of Black Catholic History in the Diocese of Buffalo," essay, 1997, 6, AOLV.

96. Grabowski, *Felician Sisters*, 373; Brown, "Gathering at the River," 6; Sr. Ellen Marie Kuznicki, "Journey in Faith," n.d., essay, AFSB; *Victorian* 39 (1) (January 1933): 9–11. The nationalities served were Hungarian, Croatian, Negro, Italian, Polish, Ukrainian, Slavic, Spanish, American, Russian, Syrian, German, Bulgarian, Serbian, Mexican, Canadian, and Macedonian. The Annex School received its second name, "American Catholic School," because it served the immigrant population that had built American Catholicism in the nineteenth century.

97. *Victorian* 39 (1) (January 1933): 11; Brown, "Gathering at the River," 7, AOLV.

98. Mother Angelina to Nelson Baker, January 31, 1931, AFSB.

99. Nelson Baker to Mother Angelina, February 9, 1931, AFSB.

100. Brown, "Gathering at the River," 6–7, AOLV.

101. Nelson Baker to Mother Mary Angelina, January 5, 1932, AFSB.

102. Nelson Baker to Mother Mary Simplicata, December 27, 1935, AFSB.

103. Brown, "Gathering at the River," 6; Sr. Ellen Marie Kuznicki, "Journey in Faith," n.d., essay, AFSB. Father Baker's mission school eventually became a canonical parish. In June 1949, Bishop John F. O'Hara, CSC, established Queen of All Saints parish and school. The parish served the local community for fifty-four years until it was closed on June 20, 1984.

104. *Catholic Directory Almanac*, 1907 and 1908; "Out of the Past," *The Sun* (Hamburg, NY), n.d., clipping in Vertical File, BEPL.

105. "A History of Our Lady of the Sacred Heart Parish," 7, Box 4a, Baker Papers, DBCA; clipping, n.d., OLV Basilica File, Box 4a, Baker Papers, DBCA; Heather A. Hartel, "Producing Father Nelson H. Baker: The Practices of Making a Saint for Buffalo, N.Y." (PhD diss., University of Iowa, 2006), 47.

106. "A History of Our Lady of the Sacred Heart Parish," 10, 12, Box 4a, Baker Papers, DBCA. This date is at best suspicious. Possibly the parish history is referring to a useable chapel, but not the completed new church. It is inconceivable that the new church was completed in only six *weeks*.

107. "A History of Our Lady of Sacred Heart," 11, Box 4a, Baker Papers, DBCA; *Victorian* 39 (1) (January 1933): 9, AOLV. Baker reported the mission church "taking all our ready cash." See Nelson Baker to George Zimmerman, September 13, 1929, Miscellaneous Papers, AOLV.

Chapter 8

1. Patricia J. Young and Frances E. Marks, *Tears of Paper: Orphan Train History* (Springdale, AK: Orphan Train Heritage Society of America, 1992), 17–35, 44.

2. Ibid., 21–22; Walter Kern, "Father Baker and the Orphan Trains," unpublished essay, Kern, Baker Papers, vol. 4, AOLV.

3. Nelson Baker, "To Our Many Friends of the Rev. Clergy and Laity," unpublished essay, Orphan Train File, AOLV.

4. *Annals* 6 (1) (July 1893): 1, AOLV.

5. "Appeal for the Homeless and Destitute Child," August 1890, 2, Orphan Train File, AOLV.

6. *Buffalo Courier-Express*, May 23, 1909, HV 99 B86/B72, BEPL.

7. "Short History," German Roman Catholic Orphan Asylum Papers, DBCA. Efforts to protect Catholic children from the Orphan Trains of New York are chronicled in Elizabeth McKeown and Dorothy Brown, "Saving New York's Children," *U.S. Catholic Historian* 13 (3) (Summer 1995): 77–95.

8. William Stewart, "The Necessary and Reasonable Powers of a State Board of Charities," A0010–78, Printed Reports, New York State Board of Charities Papers, NYSA.

9. "Dangers Attendant Upon Careless Method of Placing Out Children," February 19, 1900, A0010–78, Box 1, New York State Board of Charities Papers, NYSA.

10. State Board of Charities, Amended Rules, June 30, 1927, State Reports, Box 5, Baker Papers, DBCA.

11. "Dangers Attendant Upon Careless Method of Placing Out Children," February 19, 1900, A0010–78, Box 1, New York State Board of Charities Papers, NYSA.

12. One person who followed the basic perspective of Baker was Father W. L. Blake of New York City. Blake rejected the Orphan Train mentality. In response to the need in the City, he started St. Vincent's Home for Boys in Brooklyn. He reported that requests for entry exceeded the Institution's capacity. See *Catholic Union & Times*, February 4, 1903, 21.

13. Mary J. Oates, *The Catholic Philanthropic Tradition in America* (Bloomington: Indiana University Press, 1995), 56–57.

14. Quoted in John O'Grady, *Catholic Charities in the United States* (New York: Arno Press, 1971), 251–52.

15. Ibid., 253.

16. R. R. Reeder, "Our Orphan Asylums," *Survey Graphic* (June 1925): 3.

17. O'Grady, *Catholic Charities*, 252.

18. Nelson Baker, "Report of Chancery Work Performed during the Absence of Right [*sic*] Reverend Bishop Turner," February 1927, Relationship of Father Baker with New York State Department of Charities File, AOLV. (N.B.: Normally bishops are addressed as "Most Reverend.")

19. New York State Report, Department of Charities Annual Report on OLV Infant Home, April 3–4, 1923, Relationship of Father Baker with New York State Department of Charities File, AOLV.

20. New York State Report, Department of Charities Annual Report on OLV Infant Home, May 1924, Relationship of Father Baker with New York State Department of Charities File, AOLV.

21. New York State Report, Department of Charities Annual Report on OLV Infant Home, April 15, 1925, Relationship of Father Baker with New York State Department of Charities File, AOLV.

22. New York State Report, Department of Charities Annual Report on OLV Infant Home, April 11–14, 1927, Relationship of Father Baker with New York State Department of Charities File, AOLV; Charles Johnson to Nelson Baker, December 26, 1926, State Board of Charities File, AOLV.

23. New York State Report, Department of Charities Annual Report on OLV Infant Home, November 4–5, 1925, Relationship of Father Baker with New York State Department of Charities File, AOLV.

24. New York State Report, Department of Charities Annual Report on OLV Infant Home, March 7, 1928, Relationship of Father Baker with New York State Department of Charities File, AOLV; James Foster to William Turner, March 7, 1928; Report of

State Board of Charities Concerning Infant Home, November–
December 1928, State Reports, AOLV.

25. James Foster to William Turner, March 1, 1929, State
Board of Charities, File I, AOLV.

26. William Turner to Nelson Baker, March 4, 1929, State
Board of Charities, File I, AOLV.

27. Charles Johnson to William Turner, April 10, 1929, State
Board of Charities, File I, AOLV.

28. Charles O'Connor to William Turner, May 13, 1929,
State Board of Charities, File I, AOLV.

29. New York State Report, Department of Charities Annual
Report on OLV Infant Home, December 1930–January 1931,
Relationship of Father Baker with New York State Department of
Charities File, AOLV.

30. New York State Report, Department of Charities Annual
Report on OLV Infant Home, January–February 1936, Relationship of Father Baker with New York State Department of Charities
File, AOLV. The report listed 114 children in the Home, with a
capacity of 213.

31. John O'Grady to William Turner, November 10, 1925,
State Charities File, AOLV.

32. William Turner to Nelson Baker, November 20, 1925,
Miscellaneous File, AOLV.

33. Nelson Baker to William Turner, December 1, 1925,
State Board of Charities, File I, AOLV.

34. William H. Meegan to William Turner, July 24, 1925,
State Charities File, AOLV.

35. William H. Meegan to Nelson Baker, June 24, 1925,
State Board of Charities, File I, AOLV.

36. Nelson Baker to William H. Meegan, July 17, 1925, State
Reports, Box 5, Baker Papers, DBCA. Brother Stanislaus illustrated Baker's adamant objection to reviewing information about
women in the Infant Home: "If those who came seeking a child
from the Infant's Home chose to proceed by stern science and
cold eugenics—I mean, if they demanded to know the parentage
of the child so they could be assured of its qualities, they came to
the wrong place. Never did he give them any clues to the identity
of the mother. A Christ-like work he believed this work to be. He

was following in the footsteps of the Master." See *Buffalo Times*, n.d. [1936], *Victorian* Papers, AOLV.

37. William H. Meegan to William Turner, July 24, 1925, State Reports, Box 5, Baker Papers, DBCA.

38. Ibid.

39. James Foster to William H. Meegan, August 7, 1925, State Reports, Box 5, Baker Papers, DBCA.

40. Ibid.

41. Nelson Baker to William Turner, August 20, 1925, State Board of Charities, File I, AOLV.

42. Ibid.

43. William Turner to Nelson Baker, August 24, 1925, State Board of Charities, File I, AOLV.

44. William Turner to Nelson Baker, September 3, 1925, Miscellaneous Papers, AOLV.

45. Ibid.

46. New York State Report, Department of Charities Annual Report on OLV Infant Home, April 11–14, 1927, Board of Charities File, AOLV; James Foster to Nelson Baker, August 5, 1927, State Reports, Box 5, Baker Papers, DBCA.

47. Charles Johnson to William Turner, April 10, 1929, Relationship of Father Baker with New York State Department of Charities File, AOLV.

48. New York State Report, Department of Charities Annual Report on OLV Infant Home, April–May 1933, Relationship of Father Baker with New York State Department of Charities File, AOLV.

49. New York State Report, Department of Charities Annual Report on OLV Infant Home, January–February 1936, Relationship of Father Baker with New York State Department of Charities File, AOLV.

50. Charles L. O'Connor to William Turner, May 10, 1928, State Charities File, AOLV.

51. Nelson Baker to William Turner, June 4, 1928, State Charities File, AOLV.

52. One report read, "OL of V Infant Home resumed their placing out activities on September 22, 1927....Investigations of foster homes are not in all respects regarded as adequate....

Records regarding the history of the 45 children placed by the department are decidedly inadequate." See New York State Report, Department of Charities Annual Report on OLV Infant Home, November–December 1928 to January 1929, AOLV.

53. Ibid.

54. *Annals* 42 (2) (April 1929): 3, AOLV.

55. New York State Report, Department of Charities Annual Report on OLV Infant Home, December 1930–January 1931, Relationship of Father Baker with New York State Department of Charities File, AOLV.

56. New York State Report, Department of Charities Annual Report on OLV Infant Home, April–May 1933, Relationship of Father Baker with New York State Department of Charities File, AOLV.

57. William Turner to Charles Johnson, April 23, 1929, State Charities File, AOLV.

58. Ibid.

59. Charles Johnson to William Turner, April 29, 1929, Relationship of Father Baker with New York State Department of Charities File, AOLV.

60. Quoted in James Foster to William H. Meegan, August 7, 1925, State Charities File, AOLV.

61. "Father Baker: Apostle of Three Generations," *Catholic Charities Review* (September 1936): 213.

62. Sr. René Ruberto, "Father Baker—Folk Hero: Legendary Study of the Life of Nelson H. Baker, 1841–1936" (master's thesis, SUNY Buffalo State College, 1976), 52; George Edward Smith, interview with Walter Kern, April 11, 1989; Beth Donovan, interview with author, December 14, 2009, AOLV.

Chapter 9

1. *Annals* 19 (1) (July 1906): 8, AOLV.

2. *Buffalo Evening News*, April 8, 1916, 2. The damage estimate to the church from the fire, believed to be caused by defective wiring, was $5,000.

3. *Annals* 34 (3) (July 1921): 1–2.

4. Ibid., 34 (4) (October 1921): 3.

5. Ibid., 38 (2) (April 1925): 3.

6. Fiske Report, Our Lady of Victory Basilica, n.d. [1991]; Index of List of Uhlrich Buildings, November 13, 1989, Miscellaneous File, AOLV.

7. Emile Uhlrich to Nelson Baker, March 24, 1921, Miscellaneous Papers; Fiske Report [1991], AOLV.

8. Fiske Report [1991], AOLV.

9. Ibid.

10. Nelson Baker to Emile Uhlrich, December 21 [1920], Miscellaneous Papers; Fiske Report [1991], AOLV.

11. Nelson Baker to Emile Uhlrich, March 22, 1921, Miscellaneous Papers, AOLV.

12. Thomas Galvin, CSsR, *Father Baker and His Lady of Victory Charities* (Buffalo, NY: Buffalo Publishing Company, Inc., 1925), 174–76.

13. Quoted in Fiske Report [1991], AOLV.

14. *Annals* 34 (3) (July 1921): 3, AOLV.

15. Ibid., 35 (3) (July 1922): 6, AOLV. Lucie Beckett, who worked as a nurse at the Infant Home in the latter years of Baker's life, recalls contributions of $5.00 for a block of marble were also graciously accepted.

16. Ibid., 36 (3) (July 1923): 5–6, AOLV.

17. Heather A. Hartel, "Producing Father Nelson H. Baker: The Practices of Making a Saint for Buffalo, N.Y." (PhD diss., University of Iowa, 2006), 136.

18. Nelson Baker to John Sullivan, January 29, 1922, Basilica File, AOLV.

19. Ibid. Another example of Baker's faith being fulfilled was his request for contributions to have an ornate luna and monstrance constructed for the new shrine. He was so overwhelmed with contributions of gold and various jewels, that he contracted with Tiffany & Co. of New York for this project. See Tiffany & Co. to Nelson Baker, November 16, 1926, Basilica File, AOLV.

20. Nelson Baker to Emile Uhlrich, June 27, 1921, Miscellaneous Papers, AOLV.

21. *Annals* 34 (4) (October 1921): 3, AOLV.

22. "A History of Our Lady of the Sacred Heart Parish," 8, Our Lady of the Sacred Heart Papers, DBCA.

23. Fiske Report [1991], AOLV.

24. Otto Andrle to Nelson Baker, November 4, 1925, Miscellaneous File, AOLV.

25. Otto Andrle to Nelson Baker, April 13, 1926, Miscellaneous File, AOLV.

26. Fiske Report [1991], AOLV.

27. Nelson Baker to Emile Uhlrich, July 7, 1922, Miscellaneous File, AOLV.

28. C. J. Poiesz to Nelson Baker, February 8, 1926, Basilica Construction Papers, AOLV.

29. Nelson Baker to Emile Uhlrich, February 27, 1922, Miscellaneous File, AOLV.

30. Nelson Baker to Emile Uhlrich, May 1, 1922, Miscellaneous File, AOLV.

31. Emile Uhlrich to Nelson Baker, May 21, 1922, Miscellaneous File, AOLV.

32. Specifications for Lathing, Plastering, and Acoustic Treatment for the National Shrine of OLV, October 15, 1923, Miscellaneous File, AOLV.

33. Emile Uhlrich to Lackawanna Bridge Works Corporation, July 13, 1922, Miscellaneous File, AOLV.

34. Fiske Report [1991], AOLV; Alice M. Pytak, *A Christian Commitment: The Story of Father Nelson Henry Baker, 1841–1936* (Lackawanna, NY: Our Lady of Victory Homes of Charity, 1986), 31.

35. Quoted in Fiske Report [1991], AOLV.

36. Ibid.

37. Ibid.; Emile Uhlrich to Nelson Baker, February 6, 1924, Miscellaneous File, AOLV.

38. Nelson Baker to Renzo Mevoglione, February 19, 1926, Miscellaneous File, AOLV. Baker's comment "acting 'perfectly'" is a reference to his perception that Tonetti employees were acting as if they were innocent of any responsibility in upholding their end of the contract.

39. Nelson Baker to Renzo Mevoglione, June 30, 1926, Miscellaneous File, AOLV.

40. Nelson Baker to Emile Uhlrich, February 19, 1924, Miscellaneous File, AOLV.

41. Gonippo Raggi to Nelson Baker, March 17, 1924, Miscellaneous File, AOLV.

42. Nelson Baker to Fratelli Tonetti, May 16, 1924, Miscellaneous File, AOLV. Baker wrote, "I know you have been bothered very much, and I was sorry for it, although, I... [informed] you by cablegram, that we had placed the amount of money specified on your contract with our bank here on the first day of April, and that it was to have been deposited here, and they were to notify you by letter the same day."

43. Nelson Baker to Emile Uhlrich, February 19, 1924, Miscellaneous File, AOLV.

44. Emile Ulrich to Nelson Baker, October 19, 1925, Miscellaneous File, AOLV.

45. Floyd Anderson, *Apostle of Charity: The Father Nelson Henry Baker Story* (Buffalo, NY: Our Lady of Victory Homes of Charity, 1960), 89–90. Anderson says this story was related by Francis Van Eich, a devotee to Baker. The author could find no extant sources to verify the story.

46. "Father Baker's Home for Charity," pamphlet, New York State Library, n.d. [1926], 974.79609, L141–96.9564, NYSA, Charles L. O'Connor to Nelson Baker, July 6, 1926, Basilica File, AOLV.

47. In 1924, Baker had received permission to change the name of the parish to Our Lady of Victory.

48. *Annals* 38 (3) (July 1925): 3, AOLV.

49. Emile Uhlrich to Nelson Baker, May 29, 1926, Miscellaneous File, AOLV.

50. William Turner to Nelson Baker, May 20, 1925, Miscellaneous File, AOLV.

51. *Annals* 38 (3) (July 1925): 1–2, AOLV.

52. Ibid., 38 (4) (October 1925): 5, AOLV.

53. *Victorian* 31 (12) (December 1925): 2, AOLV.

54. Anderson, *Apostle of Charity*, 89.

55. *Buffalo Morning Express*, April 5, 1926, Baker Scrapbook, BEPL.

56. "Masterpiece in Marble," clipping, n.d., Vertical File, Nelson Baker, BEPL.

57. *Buffalo Morning Express*, May 24, 1926, Baker Scrapbook, BEPL.

58. Nelson Baker to Dominican Sisters, June 5, 1926, Dominican Sisters Letter Collection, AOLV.

59. Miscellaneous Notes, Baker Papers, DBCA; Francis Van Eich, "National Shrine of OLV," n.d., 21; Emile Uhlrich to Nelson Baker, September 29, 1926; List of Services, Emile Uhlrich, n.d., Account List of Payments, n.d. [1927], Miscellaneous File, AOLV. Extant data does not provide the total compensation for the contractor, Edward Jordan.

60. In 1941, lightning from a severe storm struck one of the towers, creating severe damage. Additionally, the harsh Buffalo winter weather was too much for the original marble, causing excessive expansion and contraction, creating cracks. Because of these factors, the tower was not restored, but rather its twin tower was lowered so both now rise to the present heights of seventy-eight feet. This reconstruction took two years and cost $150,000.

61. The panels depict Mary under various titles: (1) *Regina Patriacharum*, or "Queen of Patriarchs"; *Regina Apostolorum*, or "Queen of Apostles"; (3) *Regina Angelorum*, or "Queen of Angels"; (4) *Regina Prophetarum*, or "Queen of Prophets"; and (5) *Regina Martyrum*, or "Queen of Martyrs." See Francis Van Eich, "National Shrine of OLV," n.d., 5–11, AOLV.

62. Peter Cardinal Gasparri, proclamation, July 20, 1926, Collection of Diocesan Records, AOLV; Boniface Hanley, "Servant of God Msgr. Nelson Baker, 1841–1936: One Lifetime," *The Anthonian* 53 (2) (1971): 29; Buffalo, *Live Wire* 17 (3) (March 1926): 20, Baker Scrapbook, BEPL.

63. *Annals* 38 (2) (April 1925): 3, AOLV.

64. Josephine Pilkington, "Father Baker Loved the Blessed Sacrament," *Victorian* 50 (10) (October 1944): 53.

65. Thomas Walsh to Nelson Baker, April 21, 1926: Walsh to William Turner, May 15, 1926, Miscellaneous File, AOLV.

66. "Father Baker's—A History of Charity," Publication of Our Lady of Victory Homes of Charity, 1979, 10, AOLV.

67. Nelson Baker to "Dear Friend," September 23, 1926, Information and Interviews File, AOLV; Nelson Baker to Sr. Mary Agnes of Jesus, October 4, 1926, Religious File, AOLV. In his let-

ter it is clear that Baker believed his longtime friend was encouraging Turner to have the shrine designated as a basilica.

68. *Victorian* 35 (1) (January 1929): 4, AOLV.

69. Hartel, "Producing Father Baker," 138.

Chapter 10

1. Many fine books look at religious fundamentalism in the United States. Two excellent examples are George M. Marsden, *Fundamentalism and American Culture: The Shaping of Twentieth-Century Evangelicalism, 1870–1925* (Oxford, England: Oxford University Press, 1980); see 184–88 about the Scopes trial. Also see George Marsden, *Fundamentalism and Evangelicalism* (Grand Rapids, MI: William B. Eerdmans Publishing Company, 1991).

2. The full story of the affair between Stephenson and Madge Oberholtzer is related in Wyn Craig Wade, *The Fiery Cross: The Ku Klux Klan in America* (New York: Simon and Schuster, 1987), 239–48. See also Kenneth T. Jackson, *The Ku Klux Klan in the City, 1915–1930* (New York: Oxford University Press, 1967), 157–59.

3. Arthur S. Link, William A. Link, and William B. Catton, *American Epoch: A History of the United States Since 1900*, vol. 1., 1900–1945 (New York: Alfred A. Knopf, 1987), 228.

4. James Gillis, "Editorial Comment," *Catholic World* 134 (December 1931): 363.

5. David A. Shannon, *Between the Wars: America 1919–1941* (Boston: Houghton Mifflin, 1965), 149.

6. The Agricultural Adjustment Act (AAA) of May 13, 1933, the first branch of the three-pronged attack, aimed to establish a better balance between the prices of agricultural products (which had dropped so significantly and in the process bankrupted many farmers) and the prices of industrial products, so as to bring them into the same ratio as existed in the period 1909 to 1914. The legislation did raise farm prices, but the renewed prosperity of farmers eventually forced sharecroppers off the land with a consequent loss of livelihood. Unemployment was attacked by the establishment of the Federal Emergency Relief Administration (FERA) and the Public Works Administration (PWA), both of which produced

numerous government jobs. Initially, however, in order to free capital for use in the economy, the Emergency Banking Act was passed by Congress on March 9, which was followed by the more "reform minded" legislation of the Glass-Steagall Banking Act in June 1933, which established the Federal Deposit Insurance Corporation (FDIC) to insure funds and restore consumer confidence.

7. General Hugh S. Johnson, administrator of the NRA, worked with committees representing each industry. Fair codes of practice within the industry, which were desired by capital, were worked out, and at the same time set labor standards, which in many cases eliminated sweat shops and child labor. Before the codes were negotiated, Johnson asked the nation to accept an interim blanket code that set work standards of thirty-five to forty hours per week, a minimum pay of 30 to 40 cents per hour, and the elimination of child labor. In 1935, the U.S. Supreme Court unanimously declared the National Recovery Act unconstitutional. However, the provisions that assisted workers' rights, including organized labor, were restored in the Wagner Act passed later that same year.

8. Roosevelt appointed James Farley (New York) as postmaster general and Thomas Walsh (Montana) as attorney general.

9. In his campaign speeches, Roosevelt had effectively quoted from the two foundational social encyclicals *Rerum Novarum* (1891) and *Quadragesimo Anno* (1931). This misled many into thinking that the New Deal was based on the Church's social teaching. Roosevelt was a shrewd politician and courted the Catholic vote throughout his administration. David O'Brien has correctly stated, "The New Deal was essentially a political procedure seeking simultaneously to satisfy the frantic demands of savagely conflicting interests and to re-establish a workable economic order." See David O'Brien, *American Catholics and Social Reform—The New Deal Years* (New York: Oxford University Press, 1968), 234.

10. Several authors have fully discussed the support given by the Church to the initial efforts of Roosevelt. See O'Brien, *American Catholics and Social Reform*, 47–69; George Q. Flynn, *American Catholics and the Roosevelt Presidency, 1932–1936* (Lexington: University of Kentucky Press, 1968), 36–60, 78–102;

Aaron Abell, *American Catholicism and Social Action: A Search for Social Justice, 1865–1950* (Garden City, NY: Hanover House, 1960), 230–40. It should be noted that not all Catholics supported the New Deal, even in this early stage. Al Smith and Frederick Kenkel, editor of the Central Verein's *Central-Blatt and Social Justice*, for example, saw Roosevelt's policy as socialism. Later Charles Coughlin, the "Radio Priest," and James Gillis, CSP, editor of *The Catholic World*, became severe critics of Roosevelt.

11. Nelson Baker to James Mead, March 16, 1933, PPTA.

12. Francis L. Broderick, *Right Reverend New Dealer—John A. Ryan* (New York: The Macmillan Company, 1963), 211–43.

13. Thomas Blantz, CSC, *A Priest in Public Service: Francis J. Haas* (Notre Dame, IN: University of Notre Dame Press, 1982), 66–88.

14. Floyd Anderson, *Apostle of Charity: The Father Nelson Henry Baker Story* (Buffalo, NY: Our Lady of Victory Homes of Charity, 1960), 93.

15. *Buffalo Times*, March 12, 1935, clipping, Baker Scrapbook, BEPL.

16. Anderson, *Apostle of Charity*, 84; Allan, "Nelson Henry Baker," 19–20.

17. Nelson Baker to Sr. Margaret Mary, June 28, 1932, Personal File, AOLV.

18. Anderson, *Apostle of Charity*, 99–100; Walter Kern, "Baker and Black Catholics," unpublished essay, 1988, 1–2, AOLV. See also "Colored Congregation of Our Lady of Victory, Lackawanna, New York," Sacramental Records 1932–1949, copy in AOLV; and Nelson Baker to James Mead, Match 16, 1933, PPTA.

19. Elizabeth M. Finigan, "A Refuge of the Jobless," *The Commonweal* 15 (74) (April 13, 1932): 663. Extant data has conflicting information when the soup line began. One source suggests the ministry was initiated in September 1930, not at Christmas. See *Buffalo Courier-Express*, January 12, 1933, clipping, Baker News Clippings File, Buffalo Historical Society Library (hereafter BHSL), Buffalo, NY.

20. Finigan, "A Refuge of the Jobless," 664.

21. Nelson Baker to Andrew Kuhn, CSsR, July 27, 1932, Evangelization of Blacks File, AOLV. Residents of St. John's

Protectory and St. Joseph's Orphan Asylum remember the soup line. Many were asked to guide those in line to the Protectory basement where the meals were served. See Joseph Feeney, interview with Walter Kern, n.d., Interviews, Box 5, Baker Papers, DBCA.

22. Nelson Baker to William Turner, April 17, 1931, Colored Congregation of Our Lady of Victory File, AOLV.

23. *Buffalo Courier-Express*, January 12, 1933, clipping, Baker News Clippings File, BHSL.

24. Ibid. Extant records show that Baker served over 450,000 meals from the outset of his soup kitchen ministry to its temporary cessation on January 7, 1933. These same records show that between September 12, 1930, and August 31, 1933, the Our Lady of Victory collective expended $51,536.26 for medicine, food, shelter, and some utility payments for the poor unemployed. See Account Listing, n.d. [September 1933], State Board of Charities, File II, AOLV; Information Sheet, Collection of Diocesan Records, AOLV. It should also be noted that Baker was at this time petitioning his local congressman, James Mead, to lobby Harry Hopkins, head of the NRA, for additional monies to fund his feeding program. See Nelson Baker to James Mead, March 16, 1933, PPTA.

25. *Canisius Monthly* 12 (6) (March 1928): 330, in Newsclips 1896–1936, Box 4a, Baker Papers, DBCA.

26. Lydia Fish, "Father Baker: Legends of a Saint in Buffalo," *New York Folklore* 10 (3–4) (Summer/Fall 1984): 25; "Father Baker: A Fund-Raising Pioneer," clipping, Nelson Baker Vertical File, BEPL. Baker kept meticulous records of his charity. Between 1903 and 1932 inclusive, he gave away over $9,000. See "Report of Cash Given to the Unemployed," OLV Institutional Correspondence 1930s, Box 4a, Baker Papers, DBCA.

27. Quoted in Anderson, *Apostle of Charity*, 93.

28. "Father Baker Would Not Judge," *Catholic Digest* 60 (November 1996): 126; John Phillips, interview with Walter Kern, December 1, 1987, AOLV. Phillips claims it was such a disagreement over money that was partially the reason Herman Gerlach and Baker crossed swords, leading to the former's dismissal from the Basilica. Concerning Baker's belief that giving away money actually generated more money, Phillips offered the following

example: One day he was on a street and a poor woman told him that she was being evicted from her home because she could not pay the rent. Baker asked the woman how much she needed and she responded $12. It so happened that was precisely how much money Baker had in his vest pocket. He gave the money to her and told her to pay the rent and enjoy her home for another month. The woman went away joyful. Shortly thereafter, Baker entered a building and a man stepped up and pressed something into his hand and said, "Here, Father, is something to do some good with." Baker looked down and there in his palm was a $20 bill. He concluded, "I gave away $12 and receive $20. That's the way God works." See Anderson, *Apostle of Charity*, 93–94.

29. Diocese of Buffalo Directory, 1880, 167, DBCA.

30. Catholic Charities of Buffalo Fact Sheet, September 18, 1997, Catholic Charities File, DBCA.

31. *Catholic Union & Times*, March 6, 1924, Catholic Charities File, AOLV.

32. Parish Organization Plans Catholic Charities Campaign, April 6–13, 1924, Catholic Charities, 1921–1929 File, DBCA.

33. Catholic Charities Campaign Listing, "History of Catholic Charities," DBCA.

34. Charles Getman to Nelson Baker, August 25, 1926, Miscellaneous File, AOLV; Heather A. Hartel, "Producing Father Nelson H. Baker: The Practices of Making a Saint for Buffalo, N.Y." (PhD diss., University of Iowa, 2006), 51.

35. *Victorian* 40 (4) (April 1934): 9, AOLV.

36. Ibid.

37. William Turner to Nelson Baker, November 9, 1935, State Board of Charities, File II, AOLV.

38. *Buffalo Courier*, March 10, 1935, clipping, Baker Scrapbook, BEPL.

39. Religious communities were basically segregated until the 1950s.

40. The best book on the history of African American Catholics in the United States is Cyprian Davis, OSB, *The History of Black Catholics in the United States* (New York: Crossroad, 1990). For an analysis of the struggle for black Catholic priests, see Stephen Ochs, *Desegregating the Altar: The Josephites and the*

Struggle for Black Priests, 1871–1960 (Baton Rouge: Louisiana State University Press, 1990).

41. See Davis, *Black Catholics*, 164–72, for a synthesis on Daniel Rudd and the lay black Catholic congresses. Two additional sources are Sr. M. Adele Francis [Gorman], OSF, "Lay Activity and the Catholic Congresses of 1889 and 1893," *Records of the American Catholic Historical Society of Philadelphia* 74 (March 1963): 3–23; and David [Thomas] Spalding, CFX, "The Negro Catholic Congresses, 1889–1894," *Catholic Historical Review* 55 (October 1969): 337–57.

42. Davis, *Black Catholics*, 225–29. Lafarge's work is best presented in his own book *Interracial Justice* (New York: America Press, 1937).

43. T. J. Davis, "A Historical Overview of Black Buffalo's Work, Community and Protest," in Henry Lewis Taylor, Jr., *African Americans and the Rise of Buffalo's Post-Industrial City, 1940 to Present*, vol. 2 (Buffalo, NY: Buffalo Urban League, 1990), 9, 11, 14. For more information on this topic, see Stephen Gredal, *People of Our City and County*, vol. 13 (Buffalo, NY: Buffalo and Erie County Historical Society, 1965).

44. Davis, "Historical Overview," 12.

45. Ibid., 17–18.

46. Ibid., 19. Another source says the 1915 population was 9,000. See Lillian Serece Williams, *Strangers in the Land of Paradise: The Creation of an African American Community, Buffalo, New York, 1900–1940* (Bloomington: Indiana University Press, 1999), 1–3.

47. Davis, "Historical Overview," 19.

48. Ibid., 18; Williams, *Strangers in the Land of Paradise*, 155–56.

49. Williams, *Strangers in the Land of Paradise*, 189–91.

50. Davis, "Historical Overview," 20.

51. Roderick Brown, OP, "A Gathering at the River: 150 Years of Black Catholic History in the Diocese of Buffalo," essay, Diocese of Buffalo, 1997, 304, 8, AOLV. Litz claimed that there were 15,000 African Americans living in the parish boundaries of St. Mary's. See Francis Litz, "Black Apostolate," unpublished essay, Black Apostolate File, AOLV.

52. Brown, "A Gathering at the River," 24; quoted in Anderson, *Apostle of Charity*, 42; "Father Baker's—A History of Charity," 5, AOLV.

53. Quoted in Anderson, *Apostle of Charity*, 120.

54. Sylvia Hall Griffin, statement to Walter Kern, July 2, 1990, Interviews, Box 5, Baker Papers, DBCA.

55. Quoted in Clare Hampton, "Our Colored Brethren," *Victorian* 37 (1) (January 1931): 47, AOLV.

56. Quoted in Galvin, "Report of the Negro Apostolate in Lackawanna, N.Y.," 1932, Galvin Papers, ARFB.

57. Nelson Baker to Andrew Kuhn, CSsR, July 27, 1932, Evangelization of Blacks File, AOLV.

58. Rev. Thomas A. Galvin, CSsR, Notes, Galvin Papers, ARFB.

59. *Buffalo Catholic Union*, September 28, 1933, clipping, Galvin Papers, ARFB.

60. Thomas Galvin to "Father Master," April 1887, Galvin File, ARFB.

61. Galvin, "Report of the Negro Apostolate in Lackawanna, N.Y.," ARFB. Baker commented concerning Galvin, "His mind became very much attached to the needs of deaf mute people, who were unable to be instructed by the ordinary means, and he studied their language and improved much upon it, until he had developed a language of his own, and gave missions amongst a large number of this class." See Buffalo *Catholic Union*, September 28, 1933, Clipping, Galvin Papers, ARFB.

62. Nelson Baker to John Sullivan, April 11, 1932, Colored Congregation of Our Lady of Victory, AOLV; Galvin, "Report of the Negro Apostolate in Lackawanna, N.Y.," ARFB. Galvin reported that, due to marriage irregularities, some who desired to convert could not do so. He writes, "Those who were refused Baptism...left with tears and sorrow and protestations of love and admiration for the Catholic Church."

63. Galvin, "Report of the Negro Apostolate in Lackawanna, N.Y.," ARFB.

64. Brown, "A Gathering at the River," 25–26; Sacramental Register, Colored Congregation of Our Lady of Victory Mission Church, 1932–1935, AOLV. Sources differ on the precise num-

bers of baptisms and confirmations. The numbers reported here come from the baptismal registry, which seems the most reliable.

65. Nelson Baker to Mother St. John of the Cross, January 9, 1933, Religious Communities File, AOLV.

66. Nelson Baker to Andrew Kuhn, CSsR, July 27, 1932, Evangelization of Blacks File, AOLV.

67. Nelson Baker to John Sullivan, April 11, 1932, Colored Congregation of Our Lady of Victory File, AOLV.

68. Nelson Baker to William Turner, November 11, 1932, Evangelization of Blacks File, AOLV.

69. *Annals*, St. Mary's Parish, Buffalo, June 17, 1932, ARFB; Nelson Baker to Andrew Kuhn, CSsR, July 27, 1932, Evangelization of Blacks File, AOLV.

70. Thomas Galvin to Frater Connolly, December 26, 1932, Galvin Papers, ARFB.

71. Buffalo *Catholic Union*, September 28, 1933, Clipping, Galvin Papers, ARFB.

72. Galvin, "Report of the Negro Apostolate in Lackawanna, N.Y.," ARFB.

73. *The Echo*, January 28, 1932, clipping, Evangelization of Blacks File, AOLV; Ruth Monk, interview with the author, August 9, 2008, AOLV. Anderson, *Apostle of Charity*, 100–101; Buffalo *Courier*, May 8, 1932, clipping, Baker Scrapbook, BEPL.

74. Galvin, "Report of the Negro Apostolate in Lackawanna, N.Y.," ARFB.

75. Ibid.

76. Anderson, *Apostle of Charity*, 105–6. It seems that some Buffalo clergy believed the catechesis received by the black converts was inadequate. Some said Baker made exceptions in their training because they had been so poorly treated in the past. See Dobson, "Daddy Baker," 18.

77. William Turner to Nelson Baker, June 12, 1928, Miscellaneous File, AOLV.

78. Nelson Baker to William Turner, November 11, 1932, OLV Institution Correspondence (1930s), Box 4a, Baker Papers, DBCA.

79. Quoted from "Our Lady of Victory Colored Mission,"

WBER Radio Broadcast, March 18, 1941, Queen of All Saints File, DBCA.

80. *Victorian* 39 (1) (January 1933): 61, AOLV.

81. Ibid., 41 (4) (April 1935): 8, AOLV.

82. Ibid., 39 (1) (January 1933): 61, AOLV.

83. Report of the Infant Home, n.d., Letters 1895–1936, Box 4a, Baker Papers, DBCA.

Chapter 11

1. *Victorian* 1 (10) (March 1896), Newsclips 1896–1936, Box 4a, Baker Papers, DBCA.

2. Thomas Galvin, CSsR, *Father Baker and His Lady of Victory Charities* (Buffalo, NY: Buffalo Publishing Company, Inc., 1925), 261–65.

3. Quoted in Buffalo *Express*, March 20, 1906, Clipping, Baker Scrapbook, BEPL.

4. Buffalo *Express*, April 5, 1926, Clipping, Baker Scrapbook, BEPL.

5. Matthew Walsh, CSC, to Nelson Baker, April 12, 1926, UPWL 3/3, Walsh Papers, AUND.

6. *Buffalo Courier*, April 5, 1926, Clipping, Baker Scrapbook, BEPL.

7. Ibid., July 30, 1936, Clipping, Baker Scrapbook, BEPL.

8. Ibid., March 20, 1936, Clipping, Baker Scrapbook, BEPL.

9. *Victorian* 49 (7) (July 1943): 66, AOLV. See also Sacramental Records for St. Patrick's Parish, held at Our Lady of Victory Basilica, Lackawanna, NY.

10. Herman Gerlach to Nelson Baker, March 16, 1928, Miscellaneous File, AOLV.

11. Dempsey, "Education at Limestone Hill," 73.

12. Nelson Baker to Sr. Margaret Mary, July 10, 1930, Personal File, AOLV.

13. Heather A. Hartel, "Producing Father Nelson H. Baker: The Practices of Making a Saint for Buffalo, N.Y." (PhD diss., University of Iowa, 2006), 50.

14. Josephine Pilkington, "Father Baker's Dream Not Realized," *Victorian* 50 (3) (1944): 57.

15. Press Clippings, February 10, 1898, February 17, 1898, and April 1, 1898, Health File, AOLV.

16. Nelson Baker to Catherine McNeil, April 26, 1926, PPRP; Thomas Walsh to Nelson Baker, September 13, 1926 (in process), AOLV.

17. Henry Buswell to Nelson Baker, November 18, 1926, Miscellaneous File, AOLV.

18. Mark H. Lally to Nelson Baker, February 16, 1927, Miscellaneous File, AOLV.

19. Nelson Baker to Catherine McNeil, January 3, 1928; Baker to Thomas Walsh, April 19, 1928, Personal File, AOLV.

20. Thomas Walsh to Nelson Baker, January 4, 1928, Personal File, AOLV.

21. Nelson Baker to Mother Mary St. John of the Cross, January 18, 1928, Religious File, AOLV; Arthur Bennett to William Turner, January 25, 1928, Personal File, AOLV.

22. M. F. Lally to Nelson Baker, April 3, 1928, Baker Papers, ASLCB.

23. Anonymous [Boys at St. John's Protectory] to Father Baker, n.d. [May 1928], Personal File, AOLV.

24. Nelson Baker to Mother Mary St. John of the Cross, November 30, 1928, Religious File, AOLV; *Buffalo News*, February 16, 1932, Clipping, Baker Scrapbook, BEPL.

25. Quoted in John Koerner, *The Mysteries of Father Baker* (Buffalo, NY: Western New York Wares, Inc., 2005), 124–25.

26. Nelson Baker to Frank Twist, January 3, 1935, Personnel File, AOLV.

27. *Buffalo Times*, March 12, 1935, clipping; *Buffalo News*, March 21, 1930, Baker Scrapbook, BEPL.

28. *Buffalo Times*, May 19, 1935, clipping, Baker Scrapbook, BEPL; Nelson Baker to Edmund Britt, April 16, 1935, Personal File, AOLV.

29. Francis van Eich to William Turner, August 27, 1935, Religious General, Box 4a, Baker Papers, DBCA.

30. Nelson Baker to Edmund Britt, November 23, 1935, Miscellaneous File, AOLV.

31. *Victorian* 41 (10) (1935): 16–17, AOLV.

32. Ibid., 42 (3) (1936): 4, AOLV.

33. Angelo Cardemone to Nelson Baker, December 27, 1926; R. Gilson to Nelson Baker, January 24, 1927 (in process), AOLV.

34. Brother Liguori to Msgr. Edmund Britt, June 11, 1935, OLV Institutions and Correspondence (1930s), Box 4a, Baker Papers, DBCA.

35. William Turner to Nelson Baker, May 28, 1932, William Turner Papers, DBCA. Turner told Baker that Nash would take care of Chancery business on Thursday and Saturday afternoons and would be given full faculties in all matters. Baker remained as vicar general.

36. William Turner to Nelson Baker, July 31, 1933, Miscellaneous File, AOLV.

37. William Turner to Nelson Baker, March 22, 1934, Letters 1895–1936, Box 4a, Baker Papers, DBCA.

38. William Turner to Nelson Baker, March 27, 1936, State Charities File, AOLV.

39. Monin, "Brothers of the Holy Infancy," 35; Meeting Board of Managers of the Society for the Protection of Destitute Roman Catholic Children of the City of Buffalo, August 21, 1936, and September 3, 1935, Inspection Reports, AOLV.

40. William Turner to James Lucid, September 30, 1935, Diminishing Authority File, AOLV.

41. Edmund Britt (chancellor of Diocese of Buffalo) to Rev. Austin Crotty, February 27, 1936, Priest Assistants to NHB File, AOLV.

42. *Buffalo Courier-Express*, May 1, 1936: 26, clipping, Baker Scrapbook, BEPL; quoted in Floyd Anderson, *Apostle of Charity: The Father Nelson Henry Baker Story* (Buffalo, NY: Our Lady of Victory Homes of Charity, 1960), 110.

43. Quoted in Hartel, "Producing Father Baker," 103.

44. John Koerner claims that Catholic officials in Buffalo had prepared for Baker's death. Besides Turner's eulogy, some significant discussions had been made with respect to traffic control, fearing that thousands might rush to Baker's grave. A similar situation had occurred in 1929 in Malden, Massachusetts. On

November 14, 1929, the *Catholic Union & Times* reported that some 100,000 people were drawn to the grave of one Father Patrick Power when it was reported that some who passed by his grave had been cured of various physical ailments. Power had died more than fifty years earlier. It seems Buffalo Catholic administrators wished to head off any possible similar behavior over Baker's death. See Koerner, *Mysteries of Father Baker*, 62–64.

45. Clippings, *Buffalo Courier-Express*, July 30, 1936; *Buffalo News*, August 3, 1936, Baker Scrapbook, BEPL.

46. Anderson, *Apostle of Charity*, 110; *Buffalo Times*, July 29, 1936, clipping, Baker Scrapbook, BEPL; *Victorian* 42 (8) (August 1936): 1; Death Certificate of Nelson Baker, Miscellaneous File, AOLV.

47. *Buffalo News*, August 14, 1936, clipping, Baker Scrapbook, BEPL. Baker's codicils were added on January 11, 1928, and June 10 and 24, 1935.

48. Anderson, *Apostle of Charity*, 119–20.

49. Clipping, n.d. [July 1936], PPRP.

50. *Buffalo News*, July 30, 1936, clipping, Baker Scrapbook, BEPL.

51. Anderson, *Apostle of Charity*, 112–13; *Victorian* 42 (9) (September 1936): 7; *Buffalo News*, July 29, 1936, clipping, Baker Scrapbook, BEPL.

52. *Buffalo Times*, August 3, 1936, *Buffalo Courier-Express* July 30, 1936, clippings, Baker Scrapbook, BEPL.

53. *Buffalo Times*, August 3, 1936, clipping, Baker Scrapbook, BEPL; *Victorian* 42 (9) (September 1936): 11, AOLV.

54. *Buffalo Times*, August 3, 1936, clipping, Baker Scrapbook, BEPL.

55. *Victorian* 42 (9) (September 1936): 11, AOLV.

56. Ibid. The pallbearers for Baker's body were Frs. Austin Crotty, Walter Hutch, Joseph McPherson, Hugh O'Boyle, Raymond Tally, and James Reddington.

57. *Victorian* 42 (9) (September 1936): 17–19, AOLV; *Buffalo Times*, August 3, 1936, clipping, Baker Scrapbook, BEPL.

58. *Buffalo News*, August 3, 1936, clipping, Baker Scrapbook, BEPL.

59. Administrator [John Nash] to Joseph Maguire, October 12, 1936, Diminishing Authority File, AOLV.

60. Hartel, "Producing Father Baker," 51.

61. *Victorian* 42 (9) (September 1936): 3, AOLV.

62. Telegram, July 31, 1936, Funeral Telegrams and News-clips 1936, Box 4a, Baker Papers, DBCA.

63. *Victorian* 42 (9) (September 1936): 5, AOLV.

64. Quoted in ibid., 35.

65. Ibid., 37.

66. Ibid., 43.

67. Quoted in *Buffalo News*, July 29, 1936, clipping, Baker Scrapbook, BEPL.

68. Quoted in *Victorian* 42 (9) (September 1936): 23, AOLV.

69. Ibid., 27.

70. Hartel, "Producing Father Baker," 103.

Epilogue

1. Dennis J. Markham, "Another Milestone," *Annals* 27 (4) (April 1915): 3.

2. Kathryn Leary, interview with Walter Kern, November 6, 1988, AOLV.

3. John Phillips, interview with Walter Kern, December 1, 1987, AOLV.

4. Some examples of the articles that were regularly published in the *Annals* and the *Victorian*: "Devotion to Mary Rewarded," "Origin of the Paschal Anthem to Our Lady," "Our Blessed Lady of Miracles," "Reasons Why Protestants Do Not Appreciate Devotion to the Blessed Virgin," "Mary, Our Life, Our Sweetness, and Our Hope," "Mary, the Hope of Sinners," and "The Holy Name of Mary: A Power against Hell."

5. Quoted in Buffalo *Sunday Times*, n.d., clipping, Priest Assistants to NHB, AOLV.

6. Walter Kern, "Life and Times of Father Baker," #8, vol. 1, #54, vol. 4, Kern, Baker Papers, AOLV.

7. Sr. Mary Thomas Wolfe, OP, testimony, October 2, 1987, Signed Recollections of NHB by Others, AOLV.

8. Quoted in *Annals* 30 (3) (January 1918): 3, AOLV.

9. Quoted in ibid., 1 (1) (July 1888): 10, AOLV.

10. Ibid., 1 (3) (January 1889): 4, clipping, Published Writings File, AOLV.

11. Thomas Galvin, CSsR, *Father Baker and His Lady of Victory Charities* (Buffalo, NY: Buffalo Publishing Company, Inc., 1925), 11.

12. John Koerner, *The Mysteries of Father Baker* (Buffalo, NY: Western New York Wares, Inc., 2005), 88–89; Josephine Pilkington, "Father Baker's Little Red Book," *Victorian* 51 (7) (July 1945): 49.

13. *Buffalo Evening News*, n.d. [August 1936], clipping, PPRP. In a similar way, Thomas Galvin wrote, "The keynote in Father Baker's charities is zeal for the salvation of souls." See Galvin, *Father Baker*, 38.

14. Allan, "Nelson Henry Baker," 29, 31.

15. Pytak, "Because of Father Baker," 62; *Annals* 21 (1) (July 1908): 14, AOLV.

16. Quoted in *Annals* 12 (1) (July 1899): 5, AOLV.

17. Quoted in Fitzgerald, *Sisters of Mercy*, 86. Fitzgerald gives another example of Baker's belief that God responds to those who do their part. In a letter to the Mother Superior of the Sisters of Mercy, Baker wrote, "God does not need us, but when through obedience we undertake His work, we put Him under an obligation to help us."

18. *Annals* 40 (4) (October 1927): 7, AOLV. It must be stated, as mentioned earlier, that Baker's ability to keep the Institutions fiscally sound must have more substance than mail solicitation and donations. However, without extant data, this mystery will remain.

19. Nelson Baker, "The Feast of Our Blessed Lady of Victory," *Victorian* 34 (10) (October 1928): 4.

20. *Buffalo Times*, n.d. [August 1936], clipping, PPRP.

21. *Buffalo Evening News*, n.d. [August 1936], PPRP.

22. Press release, Our Lady of Victory, August 7, 1981, Nelson Baker Clipping File, BHSL.

23. Elizabeth Hefner, interview with Walter Kern, March 2, 1989; Rev. Francis J. Hall, interview with Walter Kern, July 7,

1987; Sr. Theophane Bwie, SSJ, interview with Walter Kern, November 29, 1987, AOLV.

24. John Phillips, interview with Walter Kern, December 1, 1987; Lucie Beckett, interview with author, August 9, 2008, AOLV; clipping, n.d. [August 1936], PPRP.

25. Nelson Baker to Margaret Kirby, July 15, 1932, Cemetery File, AOLV.

26. Nelson Baker to Brother Stanislaus, March 13, 1925, in Kern, "Life and Times of Father Baker," vol. 2, Kern, Baker Papers, AOLV. Father Baker wrote, "I trust he [Galvin] has obeyed me and sincerely hope he has, as I would not for all the world permit a book to go out to the public with any history of my work while I live." Baker had a standing order among his friends that nothing would be written about him during his lifetime. His disappointment in Thomas Galvin was based solely on his humble and unassuming manner.

27. Pilkington, "Little Red Book," 47.

28. News clipping, July 16, 1937, PPTA.

29. Baptismal and Interment Registers, St. Patrick's Parish, Our Lady of Victory Basilica. It should be noted that it was very common in Baker's day for curates to take care of sacramental ministry in parishes. Thus, Baker's "absence" from the registers was not unusual. Ellen Hayes, interview with Walter Kern, December 27, 1989; Ruth Monk, interview with author, August 9, 2008; John Phillips, interview with Walter Kern, December 1, 1987; Kathryn Leary, interview with Walter Kern, November 6, 1988, AOLV.

30. Floyd Anderson, *Apostle of Charity: The Father Nelson Henry Baker Story* (Buffalo, NY: Our Lady of Victory Homes of Charity, 1960), 81.

31. Recollections of George Smith, n.d. [1987], Signed Statements, AOLV.

32. Ibid. Sr. Heronime Murphy, SSJ, interview with Walter Kern, December 27, 1987, AOLV.

33. While it was probably an aberration, Smith, who at the time was a Brother of the Holy Infancy and Youth of Jesus, recalled an incident in 1924 where one of the boys at St. John's had died from a fall. At the funeral, Baker "bawled out" the boy's

parents, saying that their neglect led the boy to the Protectory. See George Smith, interview with Walter Kern, May 25, 1993, AOLV.

34. Kathryn Leary, interview with Walter Kern, November 6, 1988, AOLV.

35. Quoted in Heather A. Hartel, "Producing Father Nelson H. Baker: The Practices of Making a Saint for Buffalo, N.Y." (PhD diss., University of Iowa, 2006), 98.

36. John Joseph Rooney, interview with Walter Kern, July 1, 1987; Kathryn Leary, interview with Walter Kern, November 6, 1988, AOLV.

37. John Rooney, interview with Walter Kern, July 1, 1987, AOLV.

38. Cemetery Records, Account Logs, Holy Cross Cemetery, Lackawanna, NY; *Victorian* 33 (3) (March 1927): 4, AOLV.

39. Mr. Reno (first name unknown), interview with Walter Kern, November 29, 1987; Sr. Heronime Murphy, SSJ, interview with Walter Kern, December 27, 1987, AOLV.

40. Fred T. Alther, "Humanitarian Padre," *Town Tidings* (December 1930): 23.

41. Galvin, *Father Baker*, 102; St. Veronica Anne, SSJ, interview with Walter Kern, October 11, 1987; Sylvia Hall Griffin, interview with Walter Kern, July 2, 1990, Interviews, Box 5, Baker Papers, DBCA; Sr. René Ruberto, "Father Baker—Folk Hero: Legendary Study of the Life of Nelson H. Baker, 1841–1936" (master's thesis, SUNY Buffalo State College, 1976), 33.

42. *Annals*, n.d., clipping, Published Writings File, AOLV.

43. Hartel, "Producing Father Baker," 224.

44. Ibid., 10.

45. St. Moretta Ionata to Nelson Baker, October 13, 1926 (in process), AOLV.

46. *Victorian* 42 (9) (September 1936): 37.

47. Ibid.

48. Galvin, *Father Baker*, 135–36.

49. Markham, "Another Milestone," 3.

50. Galvin, *Father Baker*, 47–49; Ruberto, "Father Baker—Folk Hero," 46–91; Koerner, *Mysteries of Father Baker*, 91, 97, 122–23; Robert F. McNamara, *A Century of Grace: The History of*

St. Mary's Roman Catholic Parish, Corning, N.Y., 1848–1948 (Corning, NY: St. Mary's Church, 1979), 106–7.

51. Koerner, *Mysteries of Father Baker*, 119–20.

52. *Buffalo Courier* July 30, 1936, clipping, Baker Scrapbook, BEPL.

53. Francis van Eich to William Turner, August 27, 1935, Religious General File, Box 4a, Baker Papers, DBCA; *Buffalo Courier-Express*, July 30, 1947, clipping, Baker Scrapbook, BEPL.

54. Hartel, "Producing Father Baker," 192–93.

55. Ibid., 207, 229–32; *Buffalo Evening News*, October 7, 1987, clipping, Baker Scrapbook, BEPL.

56. *Buffalo News*, July 29, 1936, clipping, Baker's Death File, AOLV.

57. Hartel, "Producing Father Baker," 6, 276.

58. Mary O'Leary, "A History of Our Lady of Victory Homes of Charity," unpublished essay, 1967, AOLV.

59. Quoted in Ruberto, "Father Baker—Folk Hero," 31.

60. Joseph Klos, "Children in Father Baker's Institutions and Their Reception of Selected Sacraments" (JCL thesis, Catholic University of America, 2002), 1–2.

61. Allan, "Nelson Henry Baker," 1, AOLV.

Bibliography

Archives and Primary Source Repositories

Archives of the Felician Sisters of Buffalo (AFSB). Buffalo, NY.

Archives of the Holy Cross Fathers, Indiana Province (AHCFI). Notre Dame, IN.

Archives of Niagara University (ANU). Niagara Falls, NY.

Archives of Our Lady of Victory Homes of Charity (AOLV). Lackawanna, NY.

Archives of the Redemptorist Fathers of Baltimore (ARFB). Brooklyn, NY.

Archives of the Sisters of the Holy Cross (ASHC). Notre Dame, IN.

Archives of the Sisters of Our Lady of Charity of Buffalo (ASLCB). Hamburg, NY.

Archives of the Sisters of St. Joseph of Buffalo (ASSJB). Clarence, NY.

Archives of the University of Notre Dame (AUND). Notre Dame, IN.

Buffalo and Erie County Public Library (BEPL). Buffalo, NY.

Buffalo Historical Society Library (BHSL). Buffalo, NY.

Diocese of Buffalo Chancery Archives (DBCA). Buffalo, NY.

New York State Archives and Library (NYSA). Albany, NY.

Personal Papers of Timothy Allan (PPTA).

Personal Papers of Ronald Paszek (PPRP).

Primary Sources

Baker, Nelson. "The Assumption of the Blessed Virgin Mary." *Annals* 41 (3) (July 1928): 1–3.

————. "The Assumption of the Blessed Virgin Mary." *Victorian* 34 (8) (August 1928): 2–4.

————. "The Assumption of Our Blessed Lady." *Annals* 40 (3) (July 1927): 1–3.

————. "The Dignity of St. Joseph." *Annals* 24 (92) (October 1911): 11.

————. "The Feast of Our Blessed Lady of Victory." *Victorian* 41 (4) (October 1928): 1–3.

————. "Our Lady's Sorrows and Easter Joys." *Victorian* 36 (4) (April 1930): 2–3.

————. "Jesus and Mary: The Harmony of Their Lives." *Annals* 19 (3) (January 1907): 8.

————. "Lovers of Mary Should Always Speak Her Praises." *Annals* 19 (3) (January 1907): 6.

————. "Our Lady's Assumption." *Victorian* 41 (8) (August 1935): 2–4.

————. "The Sacred Heart, A Heart of Love." *Annals* 19 (3) (January 1907): 10.

Secondary Sources

Allan, Timothy R. "Nelson Henry Baker, Priest and Servant of God: An Overview of His Life within Its Historical Context." Unpublished paper, Our Lady of Victory Homes of Charity, n.d.

Alther, Fred T. "Humanitarian Padre." *Town Tidings* (December 1930): 22–23.

Anbinder, Tyler. *Nativism & Slavery: The Northern Know-Nothings & the Politics of the 1850s.* New York: Oxford University Press, 1992.

Anderson, Floyd. *Apostle of Charity: The Father Nelson Henry Baker Story.* Buffalo, NY: OLV Homes of Charity, 1960.

Appleby, R. Scott. *"Church and Age Unite!": The Modernist Impulse in American Catholicism.* Notre Dame, IN: University of Notre Dame Press, 1992.

Barrett, Alfred. "The Charity of Father Baker." *America* 54 (26) (April 4, 1936): 611–13.

Barry, Richard V. "A History of St. Joseph's Male Orphan Asylum, 1851–1951." Master's thesis, Canisius College, 1952.

The Basilica of Our Lady of Victory, 1851–1976: The Parish, 125 Years of Faith. White Plains, NY: Monarch Publishing, Inc., 1976.

Bernstein, Iver. *The New York City Draft Riots: Their Significance for American Society and Politics in the Age of the Civil War.* New York: Oxford University Press, 1990.

Blantz, Thomas, CSC. *A Priest in Public Service: Francis J. Haas.* Notre Dame, IN: University of Notre Dame Press, 1982.

Broderick, Francis L. *Right Reverend New Dealer—John A. Ryan.* New York: The Macmillan Company, 1963.

Brown, Roderick, OP. "A Gathering at the River: 150 Years of Black Catholic History in the Diocese of Buffalo." Essay, Diocese of Buffalo, 1997.

Carey, Patrick. *People, Priests and Prelates: Ecclesiastical Democracy and the Tensions of Trusteeism.* Notre Dame, IN: University of Notre Dame Press, 1987.

Catton, Bruce. *Never Call Retreat.* New York: Doubleday and Company, 1965.

"A Century of Love." *Victorian* 60 (12) (December 1954): 51–53, 61.

Chadwick, Owen. *A History of the Popes, 1830–1914.* Oxford, England: Clarendon Press, 1998.

Chinnici, Joseph, OFM. *Living Stones: The History and Structure of Catholic Spiritual Life in the United States.* New York: Macmillan, 1989.

Cleary, James R. "Father Baker's Gas Wells." *Catholic Digest* 13 (November 1948): 6–8.

Collins, Joseph B., ed. *Catechetical Documents of Pope Pius X.* Paterson, NJ: St. Anthony Guild Press, 1946.

Cormican, Patrick J., SJ. "Father Baker—Modern Apostle of Charity." In *Catholic Union and Times*, Centenary Edition: Commemorating One Hundred Years of Catholic History in Buffalo and Western New York and the Founding of the City of Buffalo and Diocese of Buffalo. Diocese of Buffalo, NY, 1931.

Cronin, Patrick. *Memorial of the Life and Labors of Rt. Rev. Stephen Vincent Ryan, D.D., Second Bishop of Buffalo, N.Y.* Buffalo, NY: Buffalo Catholic Publication Company, 1896.

Cross, Whitney R. *The Burned-Over District: The Social and Intellectual History of Enthusiastic Religion in Western New York, 1800–1850.* New York: Harper & Row, 1965.

Daughters of St. Paul. *Heroes From Every Walk of Life.* Boston: Daughters of St. Paul, 1981.

Davidson, James West, et al. *Nation of Nations: A Concise Narrative of the American Republic.* Boston: McGraw-Hill, 2006.

Davis, Cyprian, OSB. *The History of Black Catholics in the United States.* New York: Crossroad, 1990.

DeGweck, Joseph. "A Father's Devotion." *After 50* (June 2009): 2, 3, 6, 16–17.

Dempsey, Sr. Mary Timothy, SSJ. "History of Education at Limestone Hill: Father Baker's Institutions, Lackawanna, NY, 1856–1964." Master's thesis, Mount St. Joseph College of Education, 1965.

Deuther, Charles G. *The Life and Times of the Rt. Rev. John Timon, D.D., First Roman Catholic Bishop of the Diocese of Buffalo.* Buffalo, NY: The Sage, Sons and Company, 1870.

Dobson, Gregory. "Daddy Baker: A Man for His Times." Unpublished essay, December 1979.

Dolan, Jay P. *The American Catholic Experience.* Notre Dame, IN: University of Notre Dame Press, 1992.

———. *The American Catholic Parish.* New York: Paulist Press, 1987.

———. *The Immigrant Church: New York's Irish and German Catholics, 1815–1865.* Notre Dame, IN: University of Notre Dame Press, 1983.

Donahue, Thomas. *History of the Catholic Church in the Western New York Diocese of Buffalo.* Buffalo, NY: Catholic Historical Publishing Co., 1904.

———. *History of the Diocese of Buffalo.* Buffalo, NY: The Buffalo Catholic Publishing Company, 1929.

Doran, Robert K. "The Unconquerable." Unpublished manuscript, Our Lady of Victory Homes of Charity, n.d.

Dulles, Foster Rhea, and Melvyn Dubofsky. *Labor in America: A History.* Wheeling, IL: Harlan Davidson, 1993.

Emerling, William M. *The History of Lackawanna.* Lackawanna, NY: The Lackawanna Bicentennial Commission, 1976.

"Father Baker: Apostle of Three Generations." *Catholic Charities Review* (September 1936): 212–13.

"Father Baker's—A History of Charity." Publication of Our Lady of Victory Homes of Charity, 1979.

Feldberg, Michael. *The Philadelphia Riots of 1844: A Study of Ethnic Conflict.* Westport, CT: Greenwood Press, 1975.

Finigan, Elizabeth M. "A Refuge of the Jobless." *The Commonweal* 15 (74) (April 13, 1932): 663–64.

Fish, Lydia. "Father Baker: Legends of a Saint in Buffalo." *New York Folklore* 10 (3–4) (Summer/Fall 1984): 23–34.

Fitzgerald, Sr. Mary Innocentia. *A Historical Sketch of the Sisters of Mercy in the Diocese of Buffalo, 1857–1952.* Buffalo, NY: Mount Mercy Academy, 1942.

Forst, Joseph. "Eucharist and Family Life." *Catholic Mind* 29 (July 8, 1931): 329–40.

Fox, Mary Harrita. *Peter E. Dietz: Labor Priest.* Notre Dame, IN: University of Notre Dame Press, 1953.

Gallagher, Sr. Marie Patrice, OSF. *The History of Catholic Elementary Education in the Diocese of Buffalo, 1847–1944.* Washington, DC: Catholic University of America Press, 1944.

Galvin, Thomas A., CSsR. *Father Baker and His Lady of Victory Charities.* Buffalo, NY: Buffalo Catholic Publication Company, Inc., 1925.

Geffen, Elizabeth B. "Violence in Philadelphia in the 1840s and 1850s." *Pennsylvania History* 36 (October 1969): 381–410.

Gerber, David. "Ambivalent Anti-Catholicism: Buffalo's American Protestant Elite Faces the Challenge of the Catholic Church, 1850–1860." *Civil War History* 30 (Summer 1984): 120–43.

———. *The Making of an American Pluralism: Buffalo, New York, 1825–1860.* Urbana: University of Illinois Press, 1989.

———. "Modernity in the Service of Tradition: Catholic Lay Trustees at Buffalo's St. Louis Church and the Transformation of European Communal Traditions, 1829–1855." *Journal of Social History* 15 (June 1982): 655–84.

Gillis, James. "Editorial Comment." *Catholic World* 134 (December 1931): 363.

Giordani, Igino. *Pius X: A Country Priest.* Milwaukee, WI: The Bruce Publishing Company, 1954.

Grabowski, Sr. Mary Bonaventure. *Felician Sisters: History of the Congregation of the Sisters of St. Felix of Cantalice.* Newark, NJ: Johnston Letter Co., Inc., 1993.

Gredel, Stephen. "Buffalo's Polish Pioneers." *Polish-American Studies* 21 (2) (July–December 1964): 107–17.

———. *People of Our City and County.* Vol. 13. Buffalo, NY: Buffalo and Erie County Historical Society, 1965.

Hall, David., ed. *Lived Religion in America: Toward a History of Practice.* Princeton, NJ: Princeton University Press, 1997.

Hampton, Clare. "Our Colored Brethren." *Victorian* 37 (1) (January 1931): 46–49.

Handy, Robert T. *The Social Gospel in America, 1870–1920.* New York: Oxford University Press, 1966.

Hanley, Boniface. "Servant of God Msgr. Nelson H. Baker, 1841–1936: One Lifetime." *The Anthonian* 53 (2) (1971): 3–31.

Hartel, Heather A. "Producing Father Nelson H. Baker: The Practices of Making a Saint for Buffalo, N.Y." PhD diss., University of Iowa, 2006.

Hennesey, James, SJ. *American Catholics: A History of the Roman Catholic Community in the United States.* New York: Oxford University Press, 1981.

Hickey, Thomas. "Eulogy Given by Archbishop Hickey." *Victorian* 42 (9) (September 1936): 15–21.

Hofstadter, Richard. *The Age of Reform: From Bryan to F.D.R.* New York: Alfred A. Knopf, 1960.

Horton, John Theodore, Edward T. Williams, and Harry S. Douglas. *History of Northwestern New York, Erie, Niagara, Wyoming, Genesee, and Orleans Counties.* Lewiston, NY: Lewiston Historical Publishing Company, Inc., 1942.

Jordan, John W. *History of the Juniata Valley and Its Peoples.* Lewiston, NY: Lewiston Historical Publishing Company, 1913.

Kenneally, James J. "The Burning of the Ursuline Convent: A Different View." *Records of the American Catholic Historical Society of Philadelphia* 90 (1979): 15–22.

Ketchum, William. *An Authentic and Comprehensive History of Buffalo with Some Account of Its Early Inhabitants Both Savage and Civilized.* Buffalo, NY: Rockwell, Baker & Hall Printers, 1865. Republished by Michigan Scholarly Press, 1970.

Kinzer, Donald. *An Episode in Anti-Catholicism: The American Protective Association.* Seattle: University of Washington Press, 1964.

Klos, Joseph. "Children in Father Baker's Institutions and Their Reception of Selected Sacraments." JCL thesis, Catholic University of America, 2002.

Koerner, John. *The Father Baker Code.* Buffalo, NY: Western New York Wares, Inc., 2009.

———. *The Mysteries of Father Baker.* Buffalo, NY: Western New York Wares, Inc., 2005.

Kolash, Bernard. "The Padre of the Poor." *Ave Maria* 72 (November 4, 1950): 583–86.

Lackawanna Diamond Jubilee: Commemorating Seventy-Five Years of Progress. Lackawanna, NY: The City of Lackawanna 75th Anniversary Committee, 1984.

Lannie, Vincent P., and Bernard C. Diethorn. "For the Honor and Glory of God." *History of Education Quarterly* 8 (Spring 1968): 44–106.

Lapresta, Anthony. "It's Up to You to Make Good Today: An Unusual Tribute to Father Baker." *Victorian* 46 (6) (June 1940): 25–26.

Larned, J. N. *A History of Buffalo: Delineating the Evolution of the City.* Vol. 1. New York: The Progress of the Empire State Company, 1911.

Leary, Thomas E., and Elizabeth C. Sholes. *From Fire to Rust: Business Technology and Work at the Lackawanna Steel Plant,*

1899–1983. Buffalo, NY: Buffalo and Erie County Historical Society, 1987.

Link, Arthur S., William A. Link, and William B. Catton. *American Epoch: A History of the United States Since 1900*. Vol. 1, 1900–1945. New York: Alfred A. Knopf, 1987.

Link, Arthur S., and Richard L. McCormick. *Progressivism*. Arlington Heights, IL: Harlan Davidson, Inc., 1983.

Lynch, William C. "Development of Devotion to the Holy Eucharist in Seminarians." *National Catholic Education Association Proceedings*, 1931: 774–83.

Markham, Dennis J. "Another Milestone." *Annals* 27 (4) (April 1915): 3–5.

———. "Forty Years." *Annals* 28 (4) (April 1916): 4–7.

Mary of the Sacred Heart, Sr. *The Congregation of St. Joseph of the Diocese of Buffalo, 1854–1933*. Buffalo, NY: The Holling Press, 1934.

Maxwell, Sr. Mary Immaculata, SSJ. *Like a Swarm of Bees: Sisters of St. Joseph of Buffalo*. Derby, NY: Society of St. Paul, 1956.

McAvoy, Thomas G., CSC. *The Great Crisis in American Catholic History, 1895–1900*. Chicago: Henry Regnery Company, 1957.

McConnell, Oviatt. "Father Baker, Saint Likened by Archbishop." Buffalo *Times*, August 3, 1936, 1.

McDannell, Colleen. *Material Christianity: Religions and Popular Culture in America*. New Haven, CT: Yale University Press, 1995.

McDonnell, James R. "Treating Men Like Dirty Dogs." *New York Folklore* 10 (3–4) (1984): 65–75.

McKeown, Elizabeth, and Dorothy Brown. "Saving New York's Children." *U.S. Catholic Historian* 13 (3) (Summer 1995): 77–95.

McNamara, Robert F. *A Century of Grace: The History of St. Mary's Roman Catholic Parish, Corning, N.Y., 1848–1948*. Corning, NY: St. Mary's Church, 1979.

McShane, Joseph M., SJ. *"Sufficiently Radical": Catholicism, Progressivism, and the Bishops' Program of 1919*. Washington, DC: Catholic University of America Press, 1986.

Michel, Virgil, OSB. "Frequent Communion and Social Regeneration." *Orate Fratres* 10 (March 1936): 198–203.

Monin, Donald J. "A History and Reflection on the Brothers of the Holy Infancy and Youth of Jesus." Master's thesis, Christ the King Seminary, 1993.

Morgan, David. *Visual Piety.* Berkeley: University of California Press, 1998.

Morgan, David, and Sally Promey. *The Visual Culture of American Religions.* Berkeley: University of California Press, 2001.

Murphy, J. "Development of Devotion to the Blessed Sacrament." *Clergy Review* 11 (May–June 1936): 353–62, 449–59.

Nemeth, A. P. *Father Baker's Children.* New York: Vantage Press, 1976.

Niagara University. *History of the Seminary of Our Lady of Angels: Niagara University, Niagara County, N.Y., 1856–1906.* Buffalo, NY: The Matthews-Northrup Works, 1906.

Nolan, Hugh J. *Pastoral Letters of the United States Catholic Bishops.* Washington, DC: National Conference of Catholic Bishops, 1984.

Oates, Mary J. *The Catholic Philanthropic Tradition in America.* Bloomington: Indiana University Press, 1995.

O'Connell, Marvin. *Edward Sorin.* Notre Dame, IN: University of Notre Dame Press, 2001.

O'Grady, John. *Catholic Charities in the United States.* New York: Arno Press, 1971.

———. *The Catholic Church and the Destitute.* New York: The Macmillan Company, 1929.

O'Toole, James M. *Habits of Devotion: Catholic Religious Practice in Twentieth-Century America.* Ithaca, NY: Cornell University Press, 2004.

"Our Jubilarian." *Victorian* 1 (10) (March 1896): 1.

Pientka, A. M. "The Real Father Baker." Buffalo *Courier-Express,* May 3, 1981, 17, 21, 23.

Pilkington, Josephine. "Almost 90, Father Baker Receives a Staggering Cross." *Victorian* 50 (12) (December 1944): 53–54.

———. "Father Baker Gave Freely." *Victorian* 50 (1) (January 1944): 53–54.

————. "Father Baker and His Novena." *Victorian* 50 (6) (June 1944): 53, 55.

————. "Father Baker Loved the Blessed Sacrament." *Victorian* 50 (10) (October 1944): 53, 55.

————. "Father Baker's Best Investment." *Victorian* 51 (8) (August 1945): 49–50.

————. "Father Baker's Dream Not Realized." *Victorian* 50 (3) (March 1944): 57–58.

————. "Father Baker's Little Red Book." *Victorian* 51 (7) (July 1945): 47.

————. "Father Baker's Special Devotion." *Victorian* 50 (8) (August 1944): 53, 55.

————. "The More He Gave the More He Received." *Victorian* 51 (5) (May 1945): 53.

————. "The Prediction of Father Baker." *Victorian* 50 (2) (February 1944): 53–54.

————. "Saintly Personality of Father Baker." *Victorian* 52 (3) (February 1946): 53.

————. Sister Sings for Father Baker." *Victorian* 51 (2) (February 1945): 49–50.

Proceedings of the Conference on the Care of the Dependent Children. January 25–26, 1909. Washington, DC: Government Printing Office, 1909.

Pytak, Alice M. *The Basilica of Our Lady of Victory, 1851–1976.* White Plains, NY: Monarch Publishing, Inc., 1976.

————. "Because of Father Baker." *Catholic Digest* 45 (October 1981): 56–63.

————. *A Christian Commitment: The Story of Father Nelson Henry Baker, 1841–1936.* Lackawanna, NY: Our Lady of Victory Homes of Charity, 1986.

————. "Father Baker's Boys." *New York Alive* 8 (3) (May/June 1988): 59–62.

————. "Father Baker Would Not Judge." *Catholic Digest* 61 (November 1996): 126–30.

Quirk, Josephine. "A Man to Remember," pts. 1 and 2. *Victorian* 56 (1) (1950): 14–20; 56 (2) (1950): 20–22.

Rauschenbush, Walter. *A Theology for the Social Gospel.* Nashville: Abingdon Press, 1987.

Reeder, R. R. "Our Orphan Asylums." *Survey Graphics* (June 1925): 3–8.

Rich, Victoria. "Our Lady of Victory." Master's thesis, Hunter College, 2000.

Riforgiato, Leonard R. "Bishop Timon, Buffalo and the Civil War." *The Catholic Historical Review* 73 (1) (January 1987): 62–80.

Ruberto, Sr. René. "Father Baker—Folk Hero: Legendary Study of the Life of Nelson H. Baker, 1841–1936." Master's thesis, SUNY Buffalo State College, 1976.

Slawson, Douglas. *The Foundation and First Decade of the National Catholic Welfare Council.* Washington, DC: Catholic University of America Press, 1992.

Slominska, Sr. M. Donata, CSSF. "Rev. John Pitass, Pioneer Priest of Buffalo." *Polish-American Studies* 17 (1–2) (January–June, 1960): 28–41.

Stanislaus, Brother. "Anyone Could Talk to Father Baker." *Victorian* 49 (6) (June 1943): 30.

———. "Baker Never Knew an Unhappy Day." *Victorian* 46 (3) (March 1940): 9.

———. "The Faith of Father Baker." *Victorian* 46 (5) (May 1940): 7.

———. "Father Baker Dedicated His Entire Life to OLV." *Victorian* 48 (7) (July 1942): 29.

———. "Father Baker a Grandfather?" *Victorian* 48 (5) (May 1942): 24–25.

———. "A Father to Orphans." *Victorian* 46 (7) (July 1940): 14–15.

———. "Every Boy Had a Friend in Father Baker." *Victorian* 47 (2) (February 1941): 58–59.

———. "Father Baker and His Babies." *Victorian* 46 (4) (April 1940): 34–35.

———. "Father Baker and Juvenile Delinquency." *Victorian* 49 (4) (April 1943): 31–32.

———. "Fifty Years at Father Baker's." *Victorian* 47 (9) (September 1941): 41–42.

———. "Little Glimpses of Father Baker." *Victorian* 44 (4) (April 1938): 27.

————. "The Loyalty of Father Baker's Boys." *Victorian* 46 (9) (September 1940): 13–14.

Taves, Ann. *The Household of Faith: Roman Catholic Devotions in Mid-Nineteenth Century America.* Notre Dame, IN: University of Notre Dame Press, 1986.

Taylor, Henry Louis, Jr., ed. *African Americans and the Rise of Buffalo's Post-Industrial City, 1940 to Present.* Buffalo, NY: Buffalo Urban League, 1990.

Thomas, William B., and Kevin J. Moran. "Centralization and Ethnic Coalition in Buffalo, NY, 1918–1922." *Journal of Social History* 23 (1) (Autumn 1989): 137–53.

Thornton, Francis. *The Burning Flame: The Life of Pope Pius X.* Boston: Benziger Brothers, 1952.

Tindall, George, and David Shi. *The Essential America: A Narrative History.* New York: W. W. Norton, 1996.

Trattner, Walter I. *From Poor Law and Welfare State: A History of Social Welfare in America.* New York: Free Press, 1989.

Trollop, Frances M. *Domestic Manners of the Americans.* New York: Howard Wilford Bell, 1904.

Valaik, J. David, Edward Patton, Michael N. Vogel, and John H. Carlin. *Celebrating God's Life in Us: Catholic Diocese of Buffalo, 1847–1997.* Buffalo, NY: The Heritage Press, 1997.

Van Eich, Francis. "A Twentieth-Century Apostle of Charity." *The Canisius Monthly* 12 (6) (March 1928): 329–32.

"Victory: The Story of the OLV Institutions." Lackawanna, NY: Our Lady of Victory Homes of Charity, 2004.

Wade, Wyn Craig. *The Fiery Cross: The Ku Klux Klan in America.* New York: Simon and Schuster, 1987.

Walsh, Mary Ann. "Father Baker's: An Easter Story." *Our Sunday Visitor Magazine* 70 (April 11, 1982): 10–12.

————. "Father Baker's Folly." *Liguorian* 69 (June 1981): 26–31.

Walsh, Mary Elizabeth, and Paul Hanly Furfey. *Social Problems and Social Action.* Englewood Cliffs, NJ: Prentice-Hall, 1958.

Walter, Francis. "Some Considerations on the Times and Environment in Which Monsignor Nelson H. Baker Lived and Labored." Unpublished essay, Our Lady of Victory Homes of Charity, n.d.

Wellar, Ethelyn. *A History of the Town of West Seneca*. Buffalo, NY: Buffalo and Erie County Historical Society, 1992.

Williams, Lillian Serece. *Strangers in the Land of Paradise: The Creation of an African American Community, Buffalo, New York, 1900–1940*. Bloomington: University of Indiana Press, 1999.

Wyckoff, William. *The Developer's Frontier: The Making of the Western New York Landscape*. New Haven, CT: Yale University Press, 1988.

Young, Patricia J., and Frances E. Marks. *Tears of Paper: Orphan Train History*. Springdale, AK: Orphan Train Heritage Society of America, 1992.

Yzermans, Vincent A., ed. *All Things in Christ: Encyclicals and Selected Documents of Saint Pius X*. Westminster, MD: The Newman Press, 1954.

Index

(10-7)

$$t = \frac{M_1 - M_2}{S_{\text{Difference}}}$$

The t score is the difference between the two population means divided by the standard deviation of the distribution of differences between means.

(11-1)

$$S^2_{\text{Within}} \text{ or } MS_{\text{Within}} = \frac{S_1^2 + S_2^2 + \cdots + S_{\text{Last}}^2}{N_{\text{Groups}}}$$

The within-groups population variance estimate (or mean squares within) is the sum of the population variance estimates based on each sample, divided by the number of groups.

(11-2)

$$S_M^2 = \frac{\Sigma(M - GM)^2}{df_{\text{Between}}}$$

The estimated variance of the distribution of means is the sum of each sample mean's squared deviation from the overall mean, divided by the degrees of freedom for the between-groups population variance estimate.

(11-4)

$$S^2_{\text{Between}} \text{ or } MS_{\text{Between}} = (S_M^2)(n)$$

The between-groups population variance estimate (or mean squares between) is the estimated variance of the distribution of means times the number of scores in each group.

(11-5)

$$F = \frac{S^2_{\text{Between}}}{S^2_{\text{Within}}} \text{ or } \frac{MS_{\text{Between}}}{MS_{\text{Within}}}$$

The F ratio is the between-groups population variance estimate (or mean squares between) divided by the within-groups population variance estimate (or mean squares within).

(12-2)

$$S^2_{\text{Between}} = \frac{\Sigma(M - GM)^2}{df_{\text{Between}}} \text{ or } MS_{\text{Between}} = \frac{SS_{\text{Between}}}{df_{\text{Between}}}$$

The between-groups population variance estimate is the sum of squared deviations of each scores's group's mean from the grand mean divided by the degrees of freedom for the between-groups population variance estimate.

(12-3)

$$S^2_{\text{Within}} = \frac{\Sigma(X - M)^2}{df_{\text{Within}}} \text{ or } MS_{\text{Within}} = \frac{SS_{\text{Within}}}{df_{\text{Within}}}$$

The within-groups population variance estimate is the sum of squared deviations of each score from its group's mean divided by the degrees of freedom for the within-groups population variance estimate.

(13-1)

$$SS_{\text{Rows}} = \Sigma(M_{\text{Row}} - GM)^2$$

The sum of squared deviations for rows is the sum of each score's row's mean's squared deviation from the grand mean.

(13-3)

$$SS_{\text{Interaction}} = \Sigma[(X - GM) - (X - M) - (M_{\text{Row}} - GM) - (M_{\text{Column}} - GM)]^2$$

The sum of squared deviations for the interaction is the sum of the squares of each score's deviation from the grand mean minus its deviation from its cell's mean, minus its row's mean's deviation from the grand mean, minus its column's mean's deviation from the grand mean.

(13-4)

$$SS_{\text{Within}} = \Sigma(X - M)^2$$

The sum of squared deviations within cells is the sum of each score's squared deviation from its cell's mean.

(14-1)

$$\chi^2 = \Sigma \frac{(O - E)^2}{E}$$

Chi-square is the sum, over all the categories or cells, of the squared difference between observed and expected frequencies divided by the expected frequency.

(14-2)

$$E = \left(\frac{R}{N}\right)(C)$$

A cell's expected frequency is the number in its row divided by the total, multiplied by the number in its column.

STATISTICS FOR PSYCHOLOGY

Third Edition

Arthur Aron

State University of New York at Stony Brook

Elaine N. Aron

State University of New York at Stony Brook

Prentice
Hall

Upper Saddle River, New Jersey 07458

Library of Congress Cataloging-in-Publication Data

Aron, Arthur.
    Statistics for psychology / Arthur Aron and Elaine N. Aron.—3rd ed.
        p. cm.
Includes bibliographical references and index.
    ISBN 0-13-035810-X
    1. Psychology—Statistical methods. I. Aron, Elaine. II. Title.
    BF39 .A69 2003
        150'.7'27—dc21

                                                    2002003905

Editor-in-Chief: *Leah Jewell*
Senior Acquisition Editor: *Jayme Heffler*
Editorial Assistant: *Kevin Doughten*
Production Liaison: *Fran Russello*
Project Manager: *Patty Donovan/Pine Tree Composition, Inc.*
Prepress and Manufacturing Buyer: *Tricia Kenny*
Art Director: *Jayne Conte*
Cover Designer: *Kiwi Design*
Cover Art: *Wolfe/Getty Images Stone*
Permission Specialist: *Ann Sieger*
Director, Image Resource Center: *Melinda Reo*
Manager, Rights and Permissions: *Zina Arabia*
Interior Image Specialist: *Beth Boyd-Brenzel*
Cover Image Specialist: *Karen Sanatar*
Executive Marketing Manager: *Sheryl Adams*

Printed in the United States of America
10 9 8 7 6 5 4

ISBN 0-13-035810-X

Pearson Education Ltd., *London*
Pearson Education Australia, Pty, Limitd, *Sydney*
Pearson Education Singapore, Pte. Ltd.
Pearson Education North Asia Ltd. *Hong Kong*
Pearson Education Canada, Ltd., *Toronto*
Pearson Educacion de Mexico, S.A. de C.V.
Pearson Education—Japan, *Tokyo*
Peasron Education Malaysia, Pte. Ltd.
Pearson Education, *Upper Saddle River, New Jersey*

CONTENTS

PREFACE TO THE INSTRUCTOR

The heart of this book was written over a summer in a small apartment near the Place Saint Ferdinand, having been outlined in nearby cafés and on walks in the Bois de Boulogne. It is based on our 35 years of experience teaching, researching, and writing. We believe that the book we wrote is as different from the conventional lot of statistics texts as Paris is from Calcutta, yet still comfortable and stimulating to the long-suffering community of statistics instructors.

Our approach was developed over three decades of successful teaching—successful not only in the sense that students have consistently rated the course (a statistics course, remember) as a highlight of their major, but also in the sense that students come back to us later saying, "I was light-years ahead of my fellow graduate students because of your course," or "Even though I don't do research, your course has really helped me read the journals in my field."

The response to the first and second edition has been overwhelming. We have received hundreds of thank-you e-mails and letters from instructors (and from students themselves!) from all over the English-speaking world. Of course, we were also delighted by the enthusiastic review in *Contemporary Psychology* (Bourgeois, 1997).

In this third edition we have tried to maintain those things that have been especially appreciated, while reworking the book to take into account the feedback we have received, our own experiences, and advances and changes in the field. We have also added new pedagogical features to make the book even more accessible for students. However, before turning to the third edition, we want to reiterate what we said in the first edition about how this book from the beginning has been quite different from other statistics texts.

A BRIEF HISTORY OF THE STATISTICS TEXT GENRE

In the 1950s and 1960s statistics texts were dry, daunting, mathematical tomes that quickly left most students behind. In the 1970s, there was a revolution—in swept the intuitive approach, with much less emphasis on derivations, proofs, and mathematical foundations. The approach worked. Students became less afraid of statistics courses and found the material more accessible, even if not quite clear.

The intuitive trend continued in the 1980s, adding in the 1990s some nicely straightforward writing. A few texts have now also begun to encourage students to use the computer to do statistical analyses. However, discussions of intuitive understandings are becoming briefer and briefer. The standard is a cursory overview of the key idea and sometimes the associated definitional formula for each technique. Then come the procedures and examples for actually doing the computation, using another "computational" formula.

Even with all this streamlining, or perhaps because of it, at the end of the course most students cannot give a clear explanation of the logic behind the techniques they have learned. A few months later they can rarely carry out the procedures either. Most important, the three main purposes of the introductory statistics course are not accomplished: Students are not able to make sense of the results of psychology research articles, they are poorly prepared for further courses in statistics (where instructors must inevitably spend half the semester reteaching the introductory course), and the exposure to deep thinking that is supposed to justify the course's meeting general education requirements in the quantitative area has not occurred.

WHAT WE HAVE DONE DIFFERENTLY

We continue to do what the best of the newer books are already doing well: emphasizing the intuitive, de-emphasizing the mathematical, and explaining everything in direct, simple language. But what we have done differs from these other books in 11 key respects.

1. *The definitional formulas are brought to center stage* because they provide a concise symbolic summary of the logic of each particular procedure. All our explanations, examples, practice problems, and test bank items are based on these definitional formulas. (The amount of data to be processed in practice problems and test bank items are reduced appropriately to keep computations manageable.)

Why this approach? To date, statistics texts have failed to adjust to technological reality. What is important is not that the students learn to calculate a *t* test with a large data set—computers can do that for them. What is important is that students work problems in a way that they remain constantly aware of the underlying logic of what they are doing. Consider the population variance—the average of the squared deviations from the mean. This concept is directly displayed in the definitional formula (once the student is used to the symbols): Variance $= \Sigma(X - M)^2/N$. Repeatedly working problems using this formula engrains the meaning in the student's mind. In contrast, the usual computational version of this formula only obscures this meaning: Variance $= [\Sigma X^2 - (\Sigma X)^2/N]/N$. Repeatedly working problems using this formula does nothing but teach the student the difference between ΣX^2 and $(\Sigma X)^2$!

Teaching the old computational formulas today is an anachronism. Researchers do their statistics on computers now. At the same time, the use of statistical software makes the understanding of the basic principles, as they are symbolically expressed in the definitional formulas, more important than ever. Students still need to work lots of problems by hand to learn the material. But they need to work them using the definitional formulas that reinforce the concepts, not using the computational formulas that obscure them. Those formulas once made some sense as time-savers for researchers who had to work with large data sets by hand, but they were always poor teaching tools. (Because some instructors may feel naked without them, we still provide the computational formulas, usually in a brief footnote, at the point in the chapter where they would traditionally have been introduced.)

2. *Each procedure is taught both verbally and numerically—and usually visually as well.* In fact, when we introduce *every* formula, it has attached to it a concise statement of the formula in words. Typically, each example lays out the procedures in worked-out formulas, in words (often with a list of steps), and illustrated with an easy-to-grasp figure. Practice problems and test bank items, in turn, require the student to calculate results, write a short explanation in layperson's language of what they have done, and make a sketch (for example of the distributions involved in a *t* test). The chapter material completely prepares the student for these kinds of practice problems and test questions.

It is our repeated experience that these different ways of expressing an idea are crucial for permanently establishing a concept in a student's mind. Many psychology students are more at ease with words than with numbers. In fact, some have a positive fear of all mathematics. Writing the formula in words and providing the lay-language explanation gives them an opportunity to do what they do best.

3. A main goal of any introductory statistics course in psychology is to ***prepare students to read research articles.*** The way a procedure such as a *t* test or an analysis of variance is described in a research article is often quite different from what the student expects from the standard textbook discussions. Therefore, as this book teaches a statistical method, it also gives examples of how that method is reported in the journals (excerpts from current articles). And we don't just leave it there. The practice problems and test bank items also include excerpts from articles for the student to explain.

4. The book is ***unusually up to date.*** For some reason, most introductory statistics textbooks read as if they were written in the 1950s. The basics are still the basics, but statisticians and researchers think far more subtly about those basics now. Today, the basics are undergirded by a new appreciation of effect size, power, the accumulation of results through meta-analysis, the critical role of models, the underlying unity of difference and association statistics, the growing prominence of regression and associated methods, and a whole host of new orientations arising from the central role of the computer. We are much engaged in the latest developments in statistical theory and application, and this book reflects that engagement. For example, we devote an entire early chapter to effect size and power and then return to these topics as we teach each technique.

5. We ***capitalize on the students' motivations.*** We do this in two ways. First, our examples emphasize topics or populations that students seem to find most interesting. The very first example is from a real study in which 151 students in their first week of an introductory statistics class rate how much stress they feel they are under. Other examples emphasize clinical, organizational, social, and educational psychology while being sure to include sufficient interesting examples from cognitive, developmental, behavioral and cognitive neuroscience, and other areas to inspire students with the value of those specialties. (Also, our examples continually emphasize the usefulness of statistical methods and ideas as tools in the research process, never allowing students to feel that what they are learning is theory for the sake of theory.)

Second, we have worked to make the book extremely straightforward and systematic in its explanation of basic concepts so that students can have frequent "aha" experiences. Such experiences bolster self-confidence and motivate further learning. It is quite inspiring to *us* to see even fairly modest students glow from having mastered some concept like negative correlation or the distinction between failing to reject the null hypothesis and supporting the null hypothesis. At the same time, we do not constantly remind them how greatly oversimplified we have made things, as some books do. Instead, we show students, in the controversy sections in particular, how much there is for them to consider deeply, even in an introductory course.

6. *We emphasize statistical methods as a living, growing field of research.* We take the time to describe the issues, such as the recent upheaval about the value of significance testing. In addition, each chapter includes one or more "boxes" about famous statisticians or interesting side-lights. The goal is for students to see statistical methods as human efforts to make sense out of the jumble of numbers generated by a research study; to see that statistics are not "given" by nature, not infallible, not perfect descriptions of the events they try to describe but rather constitute a language that is constantly improving through the careful thought of those who use it. We hope that this orientation will help them maintain a questioning, alert attitude as students and later as professionals.

7. *Chapter 16 integrates the major techniques that have been taught,* explaining that the *t* test is a special case of the analysis of variance and that both the *t* test and the analysis of variance are special cases of correlation and regression. (In short, we introduce the general linear model.) In the past, when this point has been made at all, it has usually been only in advanced texts. But many students find it valuable for digesting and retaining what they have learned, as well as for sensing that they have penetrated deeply into the foundations of statistical methods.

8. *The final chapter looks at advanced procedures* without actually teaching them in detail. It explains in simple terms how to make sense out of these statistics when they are encountered in research articles. Most psychology research articles today use methods such as analysis of covariance, multivariate analysis of variance, hierarchical multiple regression, factor analysis, or structural equation modeling. Students completing the ordinary introductory statistics course are ill-equipped to comprehend most of the articles they must read to prepare a paper or study a course topic in further depth. This chapter makes use of the basics that students have just learned (along with extensive excerpts from current research articles) to give a rudimentary understanding of these advanced procedures. This chapter also serves as a reference guide that students can keep and use in the future when reading such articles.

9. The accompanying *Student's Study Guide and Computer Workbook* focuses on mastering concepts and also includes instructions and examples for working problems on the computer. Most study guides concentrate on plugging numbers into formulas and memorizing rules (which is consistent with the emphasis of the textbooks they accompany). For each chapter, our *Student's Study Guide and Computer Workbook* provides learning objectives, a detailed chapter outline, the chapter's formulas (with all symbols defined), and summaries of steps of conducting each procedure covered in the chapter, plus a set of self tests, including multiple-choice, fill-in, and problem/essay questions. In addition, for each procedure covered in the chapter, the study guide furnishes a thorough outline for writing an essay explaining the procedure to a person who has never had a course in statistics (a task they are frequently given in the practice problems and test bank items.).

Also, our *Student's Study Guide and Computer Workbook* provides the needed support for teaching students to carry out analyses on the computer. First, there is a special appendix on getting started with SPSS. Then, in each chapter corresponding to the text chapters, there is a section showing in detail how to carry out the chapter's procedures with SPSS. (These sections include step-by-step instructions, examples, and illustrations of how each menu and each output appears on the screen.) There are also special activities for using the computer to strengthen understanding. As far as we know, no other statistics textbook package provides this much depth of explanation.

10. We have written an ***Instructor's Resource Manual that really helps teach the course.*** The manual begins with a chapter summarizing what we have gleaned from our own teaching experience and the research literature on effectiveness in college teaching. The next chapter discusses alternative organizations of the course, including tables of possible schedules and a sample syllabus. Then each chapter, corresponding to the text chapters, provides full lecture outlines and additional *worked-out examples not found in the text* (in a form suitable for copying onto transparencies or for student handouts). These worked-out examples are especially useful to new instructors or those using our book for the first time, since creating good examples is one of the most difficult parts of preparing statistics lectures.

11. Our ***Test Bank makes preparing exams easy.*** We supply approximately 40 multiple-choice, 25 fill-in, and 10 to 12 problem/essay questions for each chapter. Considering that the emphasis of the course is so conceptual, the multiple-choice questions will be particularly useful for those of you who do not have the resources to grade essays.

INFLUENCES ON THE THIRD EDITION

We did the revision for the third edition over a summer in Tiburon, a small town overlooking the San Francisco Bay. We hope that this has not resulted in a loss of whatever romance the first edition gained from being written in Paris. On the other hand, this edition has been leavened by some beautiful Bay views.

More important, this revision is enriched by what we learned teaching with the first and second editions and by what we learned from the many instructors and students who have written to us about their experiences using the book. This revision is also informed by our own use of statistical methods. The last several years have been quite productive for the two of us in our own research programs in personality and social psychology. (For overviews of our main research programs, see A. Aron et al., 2001; E. Aron, 2000.) Our most recent adventure has been in social neuroscience, learning brain-imaging techniques, which it turns out are almost as fascinating for the statistical analysis challenges they pose as for the opportunities they provide for deepening knowledge of the issues we were previously studying with more conventional methods. Perhaps particularly useful has been that one of us (A. A.) has been serving as an associate editor for the *Journal of Personality and Social Psychology*. This has kept us in touch with how the best researchers are using statistics (as well as how reviewers assess their colleagues' use of statistics). In addition to reworking the book to keep it up to date in obvious and subtle ways, we have made a special effort in this edition to bring in to the text significant new pedagogical features.

SPECIFIC CHANGES IN THE THIRD EDITION

1. New pedagogic features. The most obvious changes to those familiar with the book will be the following additions we made to ease the learning process:

- ■ **"How Are You Doing?" sections.** These are brief self-tests focusing on concepts, inserted at three or four appropriate points in each chapter. These give students a chance to check that they have learned what they have just read, help them identify the central material in what they have just read, reinforce this material before going on to the next section, and divide the chapter into more accessible "chunks."

- ■ **Doubling the number of practice problems**. Each chapter now has at least 20. This provides the instructor with greater flexibility in the kinds and numbers of problems to assign.

- ■ **Examples of Worked-Out Computational Problems.** These are included just before the practice problems at the end of each chapter. These give the student the chance to check their knowledge before starting their assigned problems and provide a model to follow when working them out, thus easing anxiety and helping the student do the problems correctly.

- ■ **With each new formula there is a boxed concise statement of the formula in words**. This is important for helping students who fear symbols and math to see the underlying principle embedded in the formula, and keeps this verbal understanding directly available to them as they become accustomed to working with the symbols.

2. *Writing.* We have once again in this revision thoroughly reviewed every sentence, simplifying constructions and terminology wherever possible and sometimes rewriting from scratch entire paragraphs or sections. It is hard enough to learn statistics without having to read complicated sentences.

3. *Updating examples.* We have replaced over 60 examples from the second edition with new ones published in the last year or two. This is particularly important for the sections on how to understand and evaluate statistics in research articles.

4. *Updating content and controversies.* Most obvious to those familiar with earlier editions will be the discussion of the APA Task Force report and the new *APA Publication Manual*'s statements on data analysis. But the updates are everywhere in subtle ways—even with newly identified anecdotes about historical figures in the boxes!

5. *Reworking of some specific topics students had found difficult.* We have substantially reworked our treatment of a few topics that some students were struggling with, including grouped frequency tables, raw-score regression, confidence intervals, and effect size in analysis of variance. We have also made some changes in emphasis and coverage in response to instructors' suggestions, including more on the issue of causality and correlation and a fuller treatment of multiple comparisons in analysis of variance.

6. *There is now a unique Web page* available to instructors who adopt the book and to their students. We are particularly excited about the potential of the Web for aiding learning of statistics. Elliot Coups, has created an outstanding, dramatically innovative site. Some unique features (in addition to the usual chapter outline and objectives) include

- ■ For instructors: Powerpoint presentation materials for teaching the course, including examples from the text and examples from the *Instructor's Resource Manual* that are not in the text.

- Downloadable mini-chapter for students on applying statistics in their own research projects.
- Downloadable mini-chapter for students on repeated measures analysis of variance.
- Chapter objectives
- Downloadable mini-chapter on the logic and language of research (this was Appendix A in the earlier editions)
- Tips for Success: What to practice, and what to study.
- Learn More! sections: Practice problems that include tables from the text on the Web, giving the students the opportunity to use the tables to work through problems.
- On-line student study guide, including practice problems, true/false questions, and fill in the blanks.
- Flash card exercises for each chapter's key terms.
- All formulas
- Links to statistic sites

Some changes we have not made. The 11 points listed earlier in this Preface remain as the central, unique features of this book. Also, except in a few cases where we felt we could make a significant improvement in pedagogy, we have not changed each chapter's major teaching examples. Instructors using the second edition told us they have built their lectures around these examples and don't want to have to start from scratch with new ones.

KEEP IN TOUCH

Our goal is to do whatever we can to help you make your course a success. If you have any questions or suggestions, please write or e-mail (Arthur.Aron@ sunysb.edu will do for either of us). Also, if you should find an error somewhere, for everyone's benefit, please let us know right away. When errors have come up in the past, we have usually been able to fix them in the very next printing.

ACKNOWLEDGMENTS

First and foremost, we are grateful to our students through the years, who have shaped our approach to teaching by rewarding us with their appreciation for what we have done well, as well as their various means of extinguishing what we have done not so well. We also much appreciate all those instructors who have sent us their ideas and encouragement.

We remain grateful to all those who helped us with the first two editions of this book, as well as to those who helped with the first and second edition of the *Brief Course* version. For this third edition of *Statistics for Psychology*, we want to thank Jayme Heffler of Prentice Hall who led us through the long revision process with a combination of carrot and stick; Amy Lawrence who helped us locate wonderful research article examples; and Greg Strong and Anne-Lise Smith who helped us with the tedious work of cross-checking the accuracy of changes across different editions. We deeply appreciate the outstanding work that Elliot Coups did in creating our new Web site, as well as his wonderful contributions and many good ideas for improving the book itself. We also deeply appreciate Rachel Foster-Lifson's thoughtful and painstaking work on revising the *Students*

Study Guide and Computer Workbook. Finally, for their very helpful input on the development of this edition, we are very grateful to Linda Palm, Coastal Carolina University; Maria Czyzewska, Southwest Texas State University; Dennis Jowaisas, Oklahoma City University; Bryan Auday, Gordon College; and Elliot Coups, Rutgers University.

CREDITS

Data on pages 111, 324, 325, 360, 361, 482, 527, 528, and 576 based on tables in Cohen, J. (1988), *Statistical power analysis for the behavioral sciences.*

INTRODUCTION TO THE STUDENT

The goal of this book is to help you *understand* statistics. We emphasize meaning and concepts, not just symbols and numbers.

This emphasis plays to your strength. Most psychology majors are not lovers of mathematics but are keenly attuned to ideas. And we want to underscore the following, based on our 35 years of teaching experience: *we have never had a student who could do well in other college courses who could not also do well in this course.* (However, we will admit that doing well in this course may require more work than doing well in others.)

In this introduction, we discuss why you are taking this course and how you can gain the most from it.

WHY LEARN STATISTICS? (BESIDES FULFILLING A REQUIREMENT)

1. *Understanding statistics is crucial to being able to read psychology research articles.* Nearly every course you will take as a psychology major will emphasize the results of research studies, and these almost always are expressed using statistics. If you do not understand the basic logic of statistics—if you cannot make sense of the jargon, the tables, and the graphs that are at the heart of any research report—your reading of research will be very superficial.

2. *Understanding statistics is crucial to doing research yourself.* Many psychology majors eventually decide to go on to graduate school. Graduate study in psychology—even in clinical and counseling psychology and other applied areas—almost always involves *doing* research. In fact, learning to do research on your own is often the main focus of graduate school, and doing research almost always involves statistics. This course gives you a solid foundation in the statistics you need for doing research. Further, by mastering the basic logic and ways of thinking about statistics, you will be unusually well prepared for the advanced courses, which focus on the nitty-gritty of analyzing research results.

Many psychology programs also offer opportunities for undergraduates to do research. The main focus of this book is understanding statistics, not using statistics. Still, you will learn the basics you need to analyze the results of the kinds of research you are likely to do. (Also, the Web page that accompanies this book has a special mini-chapter to help you with practical issues in using what you learn in this book for analyzing results of your own research.)

3. *Understanding statistics develops your analytic and critical thinking.* Psychology majors are often most interested in people and in improving things in the practical world. This does not mean that you avoid abstractions. In fact, the students we know are exhilarated most by the almost philosophical levels of abstraction where the secrets of human experience so often seem to hide. Yet even this kind of abstraction often is grasped only superficially at first, as slogans instead of useful knowledge. Of all the courses you are likely to take in psychology, this course will probably do the most to help you learn to think precisely, to evaluate information, and to apply logical analysis at a very high level.

HOW TO GAIN THE MOST FROM THIS COURSE

There are five things we can advise:

1. *Keep your attention on the concepts.* Treat this course less like a math course and more like a course in logic. When you read a section of a chapter, your attention should be on grasping the principles. When working the exercises, think about why you are doing each step. If you simply try to memorize how to come up with the right numbers, you will have learned very little of use in your future studies—nor will you do very well on the tests in this course.

2. *Be sure you know each concept before you go on to the next.* Statistics is cumulative. Each new concept is built on the last one. There are short "How Are You Doing?" self-tests at the end of each main chapter section. Be sure you do them. And if you are having trouble answering a question—or even if you can answer it but aren't sure you really understand it—*stop.* Reread the section, rethink it, ask for help. Do whatever you need to do to grasp it. Don't go on to the next section until you are completely confident you have gotten this one. (If you are not sure, and you've already done the "How Are You Doing?" questions, try working a practice problem on this material from the end of the chapter.)

Having to read the material in this book over and over does not mean that you are stupid. Most students have to read each chapter several times. And each reading in statistics is usually much slower than that in other textbooks. Statistics reading has to be pored over with clear, calm attention for it to sink in. Allow plenty of time for this kind of reading and rereading.

3. *Keep up.* Again, statistics is cumulative. If you fall behind in your reading or miss lectures, the lectures you then attend will be almost meaningless. It will get harder and harder to catch up.

4. *Study especially intensely in the first half of the course.* It is particularly important to master the material thoroughly at the start of the course. Everything else you learn in statistics is built on what you learn at the start. Yet the beginning of the semester is often when students study least seriously.

If you have mastered the first half of the course—not just learned the general idea, but really know it—the second half will be easier. If you have not mastered the first half, the second half will be close to impossible.

5. *Help each other.* There is no better way to solidify and deepen your understanding of statistics than to try to explain it to someone who is having a harder time. (Of course, this explaining has to be done with patience and respect.) For those of you who are having a harder time, there is no better way to work through the difficult parts than by learning from another student who has just mastered the material.

Thus, we strongly urge you to form study groups with one to three other students. It is best if your group includes some who expect this material to come easily and some who don't. Those who learn statistics easily will get the most from helping others who have to struggle with it—the latter will tax the former's supposed understanding enormously. Those who fear trouble ahead need to work with those who do not—the blind leading the blind is no way to learn. Pick group members who live near you so that it is easy for you to get together. Also, meet often—between each class, if possible.

A FINAL NOTE

Believe it or not, we love teaching statistics. Time and again, we have had the wonderful experience of having beaming students come to us to say, "Professor Aron, I got a 90% on this exam. I can't believe it! Me, a 90 on a statistics exam!" Or the student who tells us, "This is actually fun. Don't tell anyone, but I'm actually enjoying . . . statistics, of all things!" We hope you will have these kinds of experiences in this course.

Arthur Aron
Elaine N. Aron

CHAPTER 1

DISPLAYING THE ORDER
IN A GROUP OF NUMBERS

Welcome to this book on statistics. We imagine you to be like other psychology students we have known who have taken this course. You have chosen this major because you are fascinated by people—by the visible behaviors of the people around you, perhaps too by their inner lives as well as by your own. Some of you are highly scientific sorts; others are more intuitive. Some of you are fond of math; others are less so, or even afraid of it. Whatever your style, we welcome you. We want to assure you that if you give this book some special attention (perhaps a little more than most textbooks require), you *will* learn statistics. The approach used in this book has successfully taught all sorts of students before you, including people who had taken statistics previously and done poorly. With this book and your instructor's help, you will learn statistics and learn it well.

More importantly, we want to assure you that whatever your reason for studying psychology, this course is not a waste of time. You need statistics—to read the work of other psychologists, to do your own research if you so choose, and to hone both your reasoning and your intuition. What is statistics, really? It is a tool that has evolved from a basic thinking process that every psychologist—every human—employs: You observe a thing; you wonder what it means or what caused it; you have an insight or make an intuitive guess; you observe again, but now in detail, or you try making some little changes in the process to test your intuition. Then you face the eternal problem: Was your hunch confirmed, or not? What are the chances that what you observed this second time will happen again and again, so that you can announce your insight to the world as something probably true?

Statistics is a method of pursuing truth. At least, statistics can tell you the likelihood that your hunch is true in this time and place, with these sorts of people. This pursuit of truth, or at least future likelihood, is the essence of psychology, of science, and of human evolution. Think of the first research questions: What will the mammoths do next spring? What will happen if I eat this root? It is easy to see how the accurate have survived. You are among them. Because your ancestors exercised brains as well as brawn, you are here. Do those who come after you the same favor: Think carefully about outcomes. Statistics is one good way to do that.

Psychologists use statistical methods to help them make sense of the numbers they collect when conducting research. The issue of how to design good research is a topic in itself, summarized in Appendix A. But in this book we confine ourselves to the statistical methods for making sense of the data collected through research.

THE TWO BRANCHES OF STATISTICAL METHODS

There are two main branches of statistical methods:

Descriptive statistics

1. **Descriptive statistics.** Psychologists use descriptive statistics to summarize and make understandable—to describe—a group of numbers from a research study

Inferential statistics

2. **Inferential statistics.** Psychologists use inferential statistics to draw conclusions and make inferences that are based on the numbers from a research study, but go beyond these numbers

In this chapter and the next three, we focus on descriptive statistics. This topic is important in its own right, but it also prepares you to understand inferential statistics. Inferential statistics are the focus of the remainder of the book.

In this chapter we introduce you to some basic concepts, and then you learn to use tables and graphs to describe a group of numbers. The purpose of descriptive statistics is to make a group of numbers easy to understand. Tables and graphs help a great deal.

SOME BASIC CONCEPTS

VARIABLES, VALUES, AND SCORES

As part of a larger study (Aron, Paris, & Aron, 1995), researchers gave a questionnaire to 151 students in an introductory statistics class during the first week of the course. One question asked was, How stressed have you been in the last 2 ½ weeks, on a scale of 0 to 10, with 0 being *not at all stressed* and 10 being *as stressed as possible*? (How would *you* answer?)

variable
values
score

In this example, level of stress is a **variable,** which can have **values** from 0 to 10, and the value of any particular person's answer is the person's **score.** If you had answered 6, your score would be 6; it would have a value of 6 on the variable called level of stress.

TABLE 1–1	Some Basic Terminolgy	
Term	Definition	Examples
Variable	Condition or characteristic that can have different values	Stress level, age gender, religion
Value	Number or category	0, 1, 2, 3, 4, 25, 85, female, Catholic
Score	A particular person's value on a variable	0, 1, 2, 3, 4, 25, 85, female, Catholic

More formally, a variable is a condition or characteristic that can have different values. In short, it can *vary*. In our example, the variable was level of stress, which can have the different values of 0 through 10. Height is a variable, social class is a variable, score on a creativity test is a variable, type of psychotherapy received by patients is a variable, speed on a reaction time test is a variable, number of people absent from work on a given day is a variable, and so forth.

A value is just a number, such as 4, –81, or 367.12. A value can also be a category, such as male or female, or a psychiatric diagnosis—major depression, post-traumatic stress disorder—and so forth.

Finally, on any variable, each person studied has a particular number or score that is his or her value on the variable. As we've said, your score on the stress variable might have a value of 6. Another student's score might have a value of 8. We use the word *score* for a particular person's value on a variable because much psychology research involves scores on some type of test.

Psychology research is about variables, values, and scores (see Table 1–1.) The formal definitions are a bit abstract, but in practice, the meaning usually is obvious.

LEVELS OF MEASUREMENT (KINDS OF VARIABLES)

Most of the variables psychologists use are like those in the stress ratings example: The scores are numbers that tell you how much there is of what is being measured. In the stress rating example, the higher the number, the more stress. It is a **numeric variable.** Numeric variables are also called *quantitative variables*.

numeric variable

There are several kinds of numeric variables. In psychology research the most important distinction is between two types. One type, **equal-interval variables,** are variables in which the numbers stand for about equal amounts of what is being measured.[1] For example, grade point average (GPA) is a roughly equal-interval variable, since the difference between a GPA of 2.5 and 2.8 means about as much as the difference between a GPA of 3.0 and 3.3 (both are a difference of .3 of a GPA). Most psychologists also consider scales like the 0 to 10 stress ratings as roughly

equal-interval variables

[1]Some researchers emphasize two distinctions about equal-interval variables. First, some equal-interval variables are also on a *ratio* scale of measurement. For example, twice as large is twice as much of the variable. Most counts or accumulations of things are ratio variables. For example, age is a ratio variable—a person who is 40 years old is exactly twice as old as someone who is 20. Similarly, number of siblings or number of times a person has experienced a strong depression are ratio variables. On the other hand, most variables in psychology are not on a ratio scale. It doesn't make sense to think of a GPA of 4 as exactly twice as high as a GPA of 2 or of an SAT score of 600 as exactly twice as good as an SAT of 300.

The other distinction is between *discrete* and *continuous* variables. A discrete variable has specific values, with none in between. Number of siblings is a discrete variable—you can't have 2.4 siblings! But age is a continuous variable—you can be 20.74 years old.

rank-order variables

equal interval—that, for example, a difference between stress ratings of 4 and 6 means about as much difference in degree of stress as a difference between 7 and 9.

The other main type of numeric variable, **rank-order variables,** are variables in which the numbers stand only for relative ranking. (Rank-order variables are also called *ordinal variables.*) A student's standing in his or her graduating class is an example. The difference between being second and third in class standing could be a very unlike amount of difference in underlying GPA than the difference between being eighth and ninth.

There is less information in a rank-order variable than in an equal-interval variable. That is, the difference from one rank to the next doesn't tell you the exact difference in amount of what is being measured. However, psychologists often use rank-order variables because they are the only information available. Also, when people are being asked to rate something, it is sometimes easier and less arbitrary for them to make rank-order ratings. For example, when rating how much you like each of your friends, it may be easier to rank them by how much liked than to rate your liking for each on a scale. Yet another reason researchers often use rank-order variables is that asking people to do ratings forces them to make distinctions. For example, if asked to rate how much you like each of your friends on a scale, you might rate several of them as exactly the same level—but ranking would avoid ties.

nominal variables

Another major type of variable used in psychology research, which is not a numeric variable at all, are **nominal variables** in which the values are names or categories. The term *nominal* comes from the idea that its values are names. (Nominal variables are also called *categorical variables* because their values are categories.) One example is gender, which has the values of female and male. A person's "score" on the variable gender is one of these two values. Another example is psychiatric diagnosis, which has values such as major depression, post-traumatic stress disorder, schizophrenia, and obsessive-compulsive disorder.

levels of measurement

These different kinds of variables are based on different **levels of measurement** (see Table 1–2). Suppose a researcher is studying the effects of a particular type of brain injury on being able to recognize objects. One approach the researcher might take would be to measure the number of different objects an injured person could observe at once. This would be an example of an equal-interval level of measurement. Alternately, the researcher might rate people as able to observe no objects (rated 0), only one object at a time (rated 1), one object with a vague sense of other objects (rated 2), or ordinary vision (rated 3). This would be a rank-order approach. Finally, the researcher might divide people into those who are completely blind (rated B), those who can identify the location of an object but not what the object is (rated L), those who can identify what the object is but not locate it in space (rated I), those who can both locate and identify an object but

TABLE 1–2	**Levels of Measurement**	
Level	Definition	Example
Equal-interval	Numeric variable in which differences between values correspond to differences in the underlying thing being measured	Stress level, age
Rank-order	Numeric variable in which values correspond to the relative position of things measured	Class standing, position finished in a race
Nominal	Variable in which the values are categories	Gender, religion

have other abnormalities of object perception (rated O), and those with normal visual perception (rated N). This would be a nominal level of measurement.

Throughout this book, as in the vast majority of psychology research, we work with numeric, equal-interval variables (or variables that roughly approximate equal-interval variables). We discuss statistical methods for working with rank-order variables in Chapter 15 and methods for working with nominal variables in Chapter 14.

BOX 1-1 Important Trivia for Poetic Statistics Students

The word *statistics* comes from the Italian word *statista,* a person dealing with affairs of state (from *stato,* "state"). It was originally called "state arithmetic," involving the tabulation of information about nations, especially for the purpose of taxation and planning the feasibility of wars.

Statistics derives from a wide variety of sources. The whole idea of collecting statistics came from governmental requirements but also from the need in ancient times to figure the odds of shipwrecks and piracy for marine insurance to encourage voyages of commerce and exploration to far flung places. The modern study of mortality rates and life insurance descended from the 17th-century plague pits—counting bodies cut down in the bloom of youth. The theory of errors (covered in Chapter 4 in this book) began in astronomy, from stargazing; the theory of correlation (Chapter 3) in biology, from the observation of parent and child differences. Probability theory (Chapter 5) came to us from the tense environs of the gambling table. The theory of analysis of experiments (Chapters 9 to 13) began in breweries and out among waving fields of wheat, where correct guesses might determine not only the survival of a tasty beer but also of thousands of marginal farmers. Theories of measurement and factor analysis (Chapter 17) derived from personality psychology, where the depths of human character were first explored with numbers. And chi-square (Chapter 14) came to us from sociology, where it was often a question of class.

In the early days of statistics, in the 17th and 18th centuries, it was popular to use the new methods to prove the existence of God. For example, John Arbuthnot discovered that more male than female babies were born in London between 1629 and 1710. In what is considered the first use of a statistical test, he proved that the male birthrate was higher than could be expected by chance (assuming that 50:50 was chance in this case), concluding that there was a plan operating, since males face more danger to obtain food for their families, and such planning, he said, could only be done by God.

In 1767, John Michell also used probability theory to prove the existence of God when he argued that the odds were 500,000 to 1 against six stars being placed as close together as those in the constellation Pleiades—their placement had to have been a deliberate act of the Creator.

Statistics helped win the Revolutionary War for what became the United States. John Adams obtained critical aid from Holland by pointing out certain vital statistics, carefully gathered by the clergy in local parishes, demonstrating that the colonies had doubled their population every 18 years, adding 20,000 fighting men per annum. "Is this the case of our enemy, Great Britain?" Adams wrote. "Which then can maintain the war the longest?"

Similar statistics were observed by U.S. President Thomas Jefferson in 1786. He wrote that his people "become uneasy" when there are more of them than 10 per square mile and that given the population growth of the new country, within 40 years these restless souls would fill up all of their country's "vacant land." Some 17 years later, Jefferson doubled the size of that "vacant land" through the Louisiana Purchase.

Statistics in the "state arithmetic" sense are legally endorsed by most governments today. For example, the first article of the U.S. Constitution requires a census.

Who said that statistics have no soul, no human side?

HOW ARE YOU DOING?

1. A father rates his daughter as a 2 on a 7-point scale (from 1 to 7) of crankiness. In this example, (a) what is the variable, (b) what is the particular score, and (c) what is the range of values?
2. What is the difference between a numeric and a nominal variable?
3. Give the level of measurement of each of the following variables: (a) a person's nationality (Mexican, American, Canadian, Australian, etc.); (b) a person's score on a standard IQ test, (c) a person's place on a waiting list (first in line, second in line, etc.).

ANSWERS:

1. (a) crankiness, (b) 2, (c) 1 to 7.
2. A numeric variable has values that are numbers that tell you the degree or extent of what the variable measures; a nominal variable has values that are different categories and have no particular numeric order.
3. (a) nominal, (b) equal-interval, (c) rank-order.

TABLE 1–3 | **Number of Students Rating Each Value of the Stress Scale**

Stress Rating	Frequency	Percent
10	14	9.3
9	15	9.9
8	26	17.2
7	31	20.5
6	13	8.6
5	18	11.9
4	16	10.6
3	12	7.9
2	3	2.0
1	1	0.7
0	2	1.3

Note: Data from Aron, et al. (1995).

frequency table

FREQUENCY TABLES

AN EXAMPLE

Let's return to the stress-rating example. Recall that in this study, students in an introductory statistics class during the first week of the course answered the question "How stressed have you been in the last 2 ½ weeks, on a scale of 0 to 10, with 0 being *not at all stressed* and 10 being *as stressed as possible*?" The 151 students' scores (their ratings on the scale) were as follows:

4, 7, 7, 7, 8, 8, 7, 8, 9, 4, 7, 3, 6, 9, 10, 5, 7, 10, 6, 8, 7, 8, 7, 8, 7, 4, 5, 10, 10, 0, 9, 8, 3, 7, 9, 7, 9, 5, 8, 5, 0, 4, 6, 6, 7, 5, 3, 2, 8, 5, 10, 9, 10, 6, 4, 8, 8, 8, 4, 8, 7, 3, 8, 8, 8, 8, 7, 9, 7, 5, 6, 3, 4, 8, 7, 5, 7, 3, 3, 6, 5, 7, 5, 7, 8, 8, 7, 10, 5, 4, 3, 7, 6, 3, 9, 7, 8, 5, 7, 9, 9, 3, 1, 8, 6, 6, 4, 8, 5, 10, 4, 8, 10, 5, 5, 4, 9, 4, 7, 7, 7, 6, 6, 4, 4, 4, 9, 7, 10, 4, 7, 5, 10, 7, 9, 2, 7, 5, 9, 10, 3, 7, 2, 5, 9, 8, 10, 10, 6, 8, 3

Looking through all these scores gives some sense of the overall tendencies. But this is hardly an accurate method. One solution is to make a table showing how many students used each of the 11 values the ratings can have (0, 1, 2, and so on, through 10). We have done this in Table 1–3. We also figured the percentage each value's frequency is of the total number of scores. Tables like this sometimes give only the raw-number frequencies and not the percentages, or only the percentages and not the raw-number frequencies.[2]

Table 1–3 is called a **frequency table** because it shows how frequently (how many times) each score was used. A frequency table makes the pattern of numbers easy to see. In this example, you can see that most of the students rated their stress level around 7 or 8, with few rating it very low.

HOW TO MAKE A FREQUENCY TABLE

Here are the four steps for making a frequency table.

---

[2]In addition, some frequency tables include, for each value, the total number of scores with that value and all values preceding it. These are called *cumulative frequencies* because they tell how many scores are accumulated up to this point on the table. If percentages are used, cumulative percentages also may be included. Cumulative percentages would give, for each value, the percentage of scores up to and including that value. The cumulative percentage for any given value (or for a score that has that value) is also called a *percentile*.

❶ **Make a list down the page of each possible value, from highest to lowest.** In the stress rating results, the list goes from 10, the highest possible rating, down through 0, the lowest possible rating.[3] Note that even if one of the ratings between 10 and 0 had not been used, you would still include that value in the listing, showing it as having a frequency of 0. For example, if no one had given a stress rating of 2, you would still include 2 as one of the values on the frequency table.

❷ **Go one by one through the scores, making a mark for each next to its value on your list.** This is shown in Figure 1–1.

❸ **Make a table showing how many times each value on your list is used.** That is, add up the number of marks beside each value.

❹ **Figure the percentage of scores for each value.** Do this by taking the frequency for that value and dividing it by the total number of scores. You may need to round off the percentage. As a rough guideline, with less than 10 values in your frequency table, round percentages to the nearest whole percentage; with 10 to 20 values, round to one decimal place; with more than 20 values, round to two decimal places. Note that because of the rounding, your percentages will not usually add up to exactly 100% (but it should be close).

An aside, the above steps assume you are using numeric variables, the most common situation. However, researchers also make frequency tables for nominal variables. With a nominal variable, the table shows the frequency for each value of the nominal variable. For example, a developmental psychologist might make a frequency table showing the number of fathers who use each of seven different discipline styles.

ANOTHER EXAMPLE

Tracy McLaughlin-Volpe and her colleagues (2001) had 94 introductory psychology students keep a diary of their social interactions for a week during the regular semester. Each time a participant had a social interaction lasting 10 minutes or longer, he or she would fill out a card. The card had questions about various aspects of the conversation and the conversation partner. Excluding family and work situa-

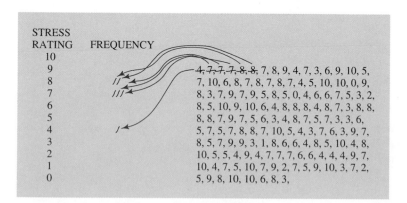

FIGURE 1–1   *Making a frequency table for the stress rating scores. (Data from Aron et al., 1995.)*

[3]Most statistics authorities follow the procedure we recommend here—going from highest at the top to lowest at the bottom. However, frequency tables in research articles are actually more likely to have the lowest number at the top and the highest at the bottom.

48 - /	31 -	15 - /
47 - //	30 - //	14 - ///
46 -	29 - ////	13 - //
45 -	28 - /	12 - /
44 - /	27 - /	11 - ////
43 -	26 - //	10 - 7𝓗𝓛 /
42 -	25 - ///	9 - ///
41 - /	24 - /	8 - 7𝓗𝓛 /
40 - /	23 - /	7 - //
39 -	22 - ///	6 - //
38 - /	21 - ////	5 - ///
37 -	20 -	4 - ////
36 -	19 - ////	3 - 7𝓗𝓛
35 - //	18 - 7𝓗𝓛	2 - /
34 -	17 - ////	1 - //
33 - /	16 - //	0 -
32 - /		

FIGURE 1–2 *Making a frequency table of students' social interactions over a week. (Data from McLaughlin-Volpe et al., 2001.)*

Tip for Success

You can cross-check your work by adding up the frequencies for all the values. This sum should equal the total number of scores you started with.

tions, the number of social interactions 10 minutes or longer over a week for these students were as follows:

48, 15, 33, 3, 21, 19, 17, 16, 44, 25, 30, 3, 5, 9, 35, 32, 26, 13, 14, 14, 47, 47, 29, 18, 11, 5, 19, 24, 17, 6, 25, 8, 18, 29, 1, 18, 22, 3, 22, 29, 2, 6, 10, 29, 10, 21, 38, 41, 16, 17, 8, 40, 8, 10, 18, 7, 4, 4, 8, 11, 3, 23, 10, 19, 21, 13, 12, 10, 4, 17, 11, 21, 9, 8, 7, 5, 3, 22, 14, 25, 4, 11, 10, 18, 1, 28, 27, 19, 24, 35, 9, 30, 8, 26

Now, let's follow our four steps for making a frequency table.

❶ **Make a list down the page of each possible value, from highest to lowest.** In this study, the highest number of interactions could be any number. However, the highest actual number in this group is 48, so we can use 48 as the highest value. The lowest possible number of interactions is 0. Thus, the first step is to list these values down a page. (It might be good to use several columns so that you can have all the scores on a single page.)

❷ **Go one by one through the scores, making a mark for each next to its value on your list.** Figure 1–2 shows this.

❸ **Make a table showing how many times each value on your list is used.** Table 1–4 is the result.

❹ **Figure the percentage of scores for each value.** We have *not* done so in this example because it would not help much for seeing the pattern of scores. However, if you want to check your understanding of this step, the first six percentages would be 1.06%, 2.13%, 0%, 0%, 1.06%, and 0%. (These are the percentages for frequencies of 1, 2, 0, 0, 2, and 0, rounded to two decimal places.)

TABLE 1–4 | **Frequency Table for Number of Social Interactions During a Week for 94 College Students**

Score	Frequency	Score	Frequency	Score	Frequency
48	1	31	0	15	1
47	2	30	2	14	3
46	0	29	4	13	2
45	0	28	1	12	1
44	1	27	1	11	4
43	0	26	2	10	6
42	0	25	3	9	3
41	1	24	2	8	6
40	1	23	1	7	2
39	0	22	3	6	2
38	1	21	4	5	3
37	0	20	0	4	4
36	0	19	4	3	5
35	2	18	5	2	1
34	0	17	4	1	2
33	1	16	2	0	0
32	1				

Note: Data from McLaughlin-Volpe et al. (2001).

GROUPED FREQUENCY TABLES

Sometimes there are so many possible values that an ordinary frequency table is too awkward to give a simple picture of the scores. The last example was a bit like that, wasn't it? The solution is to make groupings of values that include all values within a certain range. Consider the stress-ratings example. Instead of having a separate frequency figure for the students who rated their stress as 8 and another for those who rated it as 9, you could have a combined category of 8 and 9. This combined category is a range of values that includes these two values. A combined category like this is called an **interval.** This particular interval of 8 and 9 has a frequency of 41 (the 26 scores with a value of 8 plus the 15 scores with a value of 9).

interval

A frequency table that uses intervals is called a **grouped frequency table.** Table 1–5 is a grouped frequency table for the stress ratings example. (Note that in this example the full frequency table has only 11 different values. Thus, a grouped frequency table was not really necessary.) Table 1–6 is a grouped frequency table for the 94 students' number of social interactions over a week.

grouped frequency table

A grouped frequency table can make information even more directly understandable than an ordinary frequency table can. Of course, the greater understandability of a grouped frequency table is at a cost. You lose some information—details of the breakdown of frequencies within each interval.

When setting up a grouped frequency table, it makes a big difference how many intervals you use. There are guidelines to help researchers with this, but in practice it is done automatically by the researcher's computer. Thus, we will not focus on it in this book. However, should you have to make a grouped frequency table on your own, the key is to experiment with the interval size until you come up with an interval size that is a round number (such as 2, 3, 5, or 10) and that creates about 5 to 15 intervals. Then, when actually setting up the table, be sure you set the

TABLE 1–6	Grouped Frequency Table for Number of Social Interactions During a Week for 94 College Students

Interval	Frequency	Percent
45–49	3	3.2
40–44	3	3.2
35–39	3	3.2
30–34	4	4.3
25–29	11	11.7
20–24	10	10.6
15–19	16	17.0
10–14	16	17.0
5–9	16	17.0
0–4	12	12.8

Note: Data from McLaughlin-Volpe et al. (2001).

TABLE 1–5	Grouped Frequency Table for Stress Ratings

Stress Rating Interval	Frequency	Percent
10–11	14	9
8–9	41	27
6–7	44	29
4–5	34	23
2–3	15	10
0–1	3	2

Note: Data from Aron, et al. (1995).

BOX 1-2   Math Anxiety, Statistics Anxiety, and You: A Message for Those of You Who Are Truly Worried About This Course

Let's face it: Many of you dread this course, even to the point of having a full-blown case of "statistics anxiety" (Zeidner, 1991). If you become tense the minute you see numbers, we need to talk about that right now.

First, this course is a chance for a fresh start with the digits. Your past performance in (or avoidance of) geometry, trigonometry, calculus, or similar horrors need not influence in any way how well you comprehend statistics. This is largely a different subject.

Second, if your worry persists, you need to decide where it is coming from. Math or statistics anxiety, test anxiety, general anxiety, and general low self-confidence each seem to play their own role in students' difficulties with math courses (Cooper & Robinson, 1989; Dwinell & Higbee, 1991).

Is your problem mainly math/statistics anxiety? There are wonderful books and Web sites to help you. Do a search ("math anxiety" or "statistics anxiety"), or try *http://www.mathanxiety.net, http://www.math-power.com,* or *http://www.mathmatters.net.* We highly recommend Sheila Tobias's (1995) *Succeed with Math: Every Student's Guide to Conquering Math Anxiety* (but there are others books described at these Web sites). Tobias, a former math avoider herself, suggests that your goal be "math mental health," which she defines as "the willingness to learn the math you need when you need it" (p. 12). (Could it be that this course in statistics is one of those times?)

Tobias explains that math mental health is usually lost in elementary school, when you are called to the blackboard, your mind goes blank, and you are unable to produce the one right answer to an arithmetic problem. What confidence remained probably faded during timed tests, which you did not realize were difficult for everyone except the most proficient few.

Tobias says that students who are good at math are not necessarily smarter than the rest of us, but they really know their strengths and weaknesses, their styles of thinking and feeling around a problem. They do not judge themselves harshly for mistakes. In particular, they do not expect to understand things instantly. Allowing yourself to be a "slow learner" does not mean that you are less intelligent. It shows that you are growing in math mental health.

One recommendation Tobias makes is to divide your sheet of paper in half and work your statistics problems on the right half. When your statistics anxiety is blocking your work, use the left side to note your thoughts. These will usually be negative thoughts, like "I'll never get this." You then replace these with more reasonable, positive thoughts, like "It just takes time, and I can always get help if I stay stuck for too long" or "Look at all the statistics I have learned already." That way, you never stop working—on the problem or the psychological obstacles to solving it.

Is your problem test anxiety? Then you need to learn to handle anxiety better. Test-taking requires the use of the thinking part of our brain, the prefrontal cortex. When we are anxious, we naturally "downshift" to more basic, instinctual brain systems. And that ruins our thinking ability. Anxiety produces arousal, and one of the best understood relationships in psychology is between arousal and performance. Whereas moderate arousal helps performance, too much or too little dramatically reduces performance. Things you have learned become harder to recall. Your mind starts to race, and this creates more anxiety, more arousal, and so on. The phenomenon has been demonstrated in many areas, including test-taking—anxious, aroused test-takers perform worse than those who are calm (Piasecki et al., 2001). In particular, during a test, students are likely to move from a fear that they are performing poorly to a much larger fear that they are "no good and never will be." You want to avoid that jump. Rethink beforehand your true abilities and consider the actual reasons for any past failures—you had not prepared or were hampered by overarousal and anxiety, which you will now be better able to handle.

There are many ways to reduce anxiety and arousal in general, such as learning to breathe properly and to take a quick break to relax deeply. Your counseling center should be able to help you or direct you to some good books on the subject. Again, there are also many Web sites about reducing anxiety.

When arousal is the root of the problem, it helps just to know that there is nothing wrong with the "hardware"—nothing wrong with your brain, your intelligence, or your studying of the material. You really do know it. Mueller et al. (1993) demonstrated this by directly and indirectly testing how well a list of words had been learned, and found that anxious participants did worse than nonanxious participants when tested directly but just as well when tested indirectly.

Test anxiety specifically can be reduced by over-preparing for a few tests, so that you go in with the certainty that you cannot possibly fail, no matter how aroused you become. The best time to begin applying this tactic is when preparing for the first test of this course: There will be no old material to review, success will not depend on having understood previous material, and it will help you do better throughout the course. (You also might enlist the sympathy of your instructor or teaching assistant. Bring in a list of what you have studied, state why you are being so exacting, and ask if you have missed anything.) Your preparation must be ridiculously thorough, but only for a few exams. After these successes, your test anxiety should decline.

Also, create a practice test situation as similar to a real test as possible, so that more aspects of the exam situation are familiar (less arousing). Make a special effort to duplicate the aspects that bother you most. If feeling rushed is the troubling part, once you think you are well prepared, set yourself a time limit for solving some homework problems. Make yourself write out answers fully and legibly. This may be part of what makes you feel slow during a test. If the presence of others bothers you—the sound of their scurrying pencils while yours is frozen in midair—do your practice test with others in your course. Even make it an explicit contest to see who can finish first.

Finally, if it is practical for your instructor to arrange it, you may find you do better with untimed tests. On untimed tests, anxious students score the same as others and finish just as quickly; but on timed tests they do worse (Onwuegbuzie, 1994).

Is your problem a general lack of confidence? Is there something else in your life causing you to worry or feel badly about yourself? Then we suggest that it is time you tried your friendly college counseling center.

Could you be highly sensitive? A final word about anxiety and arousal: About 15% to 20% of humans (and all higher animals) seem to be born with a temperament trait that has been seen traditionally as shyness, hesitancy, or introversion (Eysenck, 1981; Kagan, 1994). But this shyness or hesitancy seems actually due to a preference to observe and an ability to notice subtle stimulation and process information deeply (Aron, 1996; Aron & Aron, 1997). This often causes highly sensitive persons (HSPs) to be very intuitive or even gifted. But it also means they are more easily overaroused by high levels of stimulation, like tests.

You might want to find out if you are an HSP (at *http://www.hsperson.com*). If you are, appreciate the trait's assets and make some allowances for its one disadvantage: this tendency to become easily overaroused. It has to affect your performance on tests. What matters is what you actually know, which is probably quite a bit. This simple act of self-acceptance—that you are *not* less smart but *are* more sensitive—may in itself help ease your arousal when trying to express your statistical knowledge.

By the way, if you can work through your statistics anxiety as an undergraduate, it will be a great advantage in graduate school, where 80% are handicapped by statistics anxiety, which is strongly associated with overall academic procrastination (Onwuegbuzie, 2001).

So good luck to all of you. We wish you the best while taking this course and in your lives.

low end of each interval to a multiple of the interval size and the top end of each interval to the number that is just below the low end of the next interval. For example, Table 1–5 uses six intervals with an interval size of 2, and each interval starts with a multiple of 2. Table 1–6 uses 10 intervals with an interval size of 5, and each interval starts with a multiple of 5.

HOW ARE YOU DOING?

1. What is a frequency table?
2. Why would a researcher want to make a frequency table?
3. Make a frequency table for the following scores: 5, 7, 4, 5, 6, 5, 4
4. What does a grouped frequency table group?

ANSWERS:

1. A systematic listing of the number of scores (the frequency) of each value in the group studied.
2. It makes it easy to see the pattern in a large group of scores.
3.

Value	Frequency	Percent
7	1	14
6	1	14
5	3	43
4	2	29

4. It groups together the frequencies of adjacent values into intervals.

FREQUENCY GRAPHS

A graph is another good way to make a large group of scores easy to understand. "A picture is worth a thousand words"—and sometimes a thousand numbers. A straightforward approach is to make a graph of the frequency table. There are two main kinds of such graphs: histograms and frequency polygons.

HISTOGRAMS

histogram

One way to graph the information in a frequency table is to use a kind of bar chart called a **histogram.** In a histogram, the height of each bar is the frequency of each value in the frequency table. Ordinarily, in a histogram all the bars are put next to each other with no space in between. The result is that a histogram looks a bit like a city skyline. Figure 1–3 shows two histograms based on the stress ratings example (one based on the ordinary frequency table and one based on the grouped frequency table). Figure 1–4 shows a histogram based on the grouped frequency table for the example of the numbers of students' social interactions in a week.

Researchers also make histograms based on a frequency table for a nominal variable. For example, the developmental psychologist we mentioned earlier might make a histogram for the number of fathers who use each of seven different discipline styles. Histograms for nominal variables are different in one main way: The bars are usually slightly separated, making a more ordinary-looking bar graph.

HOW TO MAKE A HISTOGRAM

Here are the four steps for making a histogram.

❶ **Make a frequency table.**
❷ **Put the values along the bottom of the page, from left to right, from lowest to highest.** For a grouped frequency table, the histogram is of the intervals, and you mark the center of each interval—the point half way between the start of the interval *and the start of the next.*
❸ **Make a scale of frequencies along the left edge of the page that goes from 0 at the bottom to the highest frequency for any value.**
❹ **Make a bar above each value with a height for the frequency of that value.**

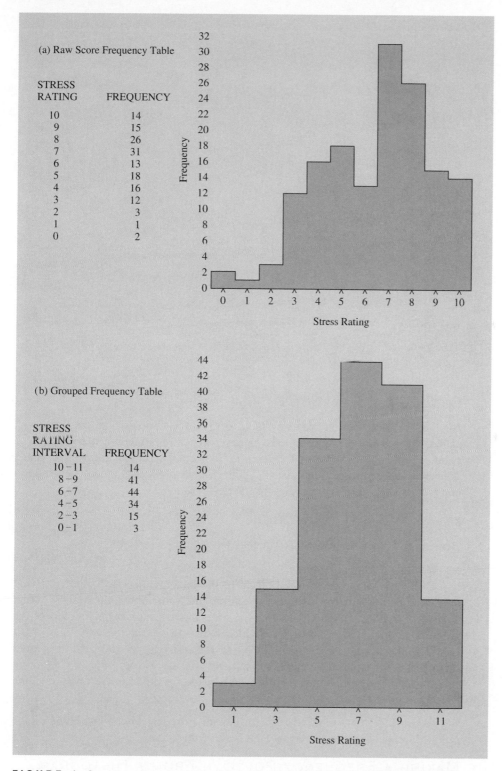

(a) Raw Score Frequency Table

STRESS RATING	FREQUENCY
10	14
9	15
8	26
7	31
6	13
5	18
4	16
3	12
2	3
1	1
0	2

(b) Grouped Frequency Table

STRESS RATING INTERVAL	FREQUENCY
10–11	14
8–9	41
6–7	44
4–5	34
2–3	15
0–1	3

FIGURE 1–3 *Histograms based on (a) frequency table and (b) a grouped frequency table for the stress ratings example. (Data from Aron et al.,1995.)*

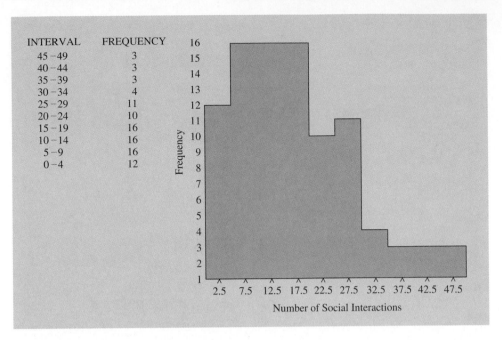

INTERVAL	FREQUENCY
45−49	3
40−44	3
35−39	3
30−34	4
25−29	11
20−24	10
15−19	16
10−14	16
5−9	16
0−4	12

FIGURE 1–4 *Histogram for number of social interactions during a week for 94 college students, based on grouped frequencies. (Data from McLaughlin-Volpe et al., 2001.)*

FREQUENCY POLYGONS

frequency polygon

Another way to graph a frequency table is to make a special kind of line graph called a **frequency polygon.** In a frequency polygon, the line moves from point to point. The height of each point shows the number of scores that have that value. This creates a kind of mountain-peak skyline. Figure 1–5 shows the frequency polygons for the frequency table in the stress ratings example.

HOW TO MAKE A FREQUENCY POLYGON

Tip for Success

Making a histogram or frequency polygon is easiest if you use graph paper.

Here are five steps for making a frequency polygon.

❶ **Make a frequency table.**
❷ **Put the values along the bottom of the page, from left to right, starting one value below the lowest value and ending one value above the highest value.** You need the extra values so that the line starts and ends along the baseline of the graph, at zero frequency. This creates a closed, or *polygon* figure.
❸ **Make a scale of frequencies along the left edge of the page that goes from 0 at the bottom to the highest frequency for any value.**
❹ **Mark a point above each value with a height for the frequency of that value.**
❺ **Connect the points with a line.**

Figure 1–6 shows the five steps for making a frequency polygon based on the grouped frequency table for the students' social interactions.

MAKING A FREQUENCY POLYGON FROM A HISTOGRAM

Suppose you have already made a histogram. To make it into a frequency polygon, just mark a dot at the center of the top of each bar and connect them. However, you do have to be sure to add dots for the empty value at the start and end, so the poly-

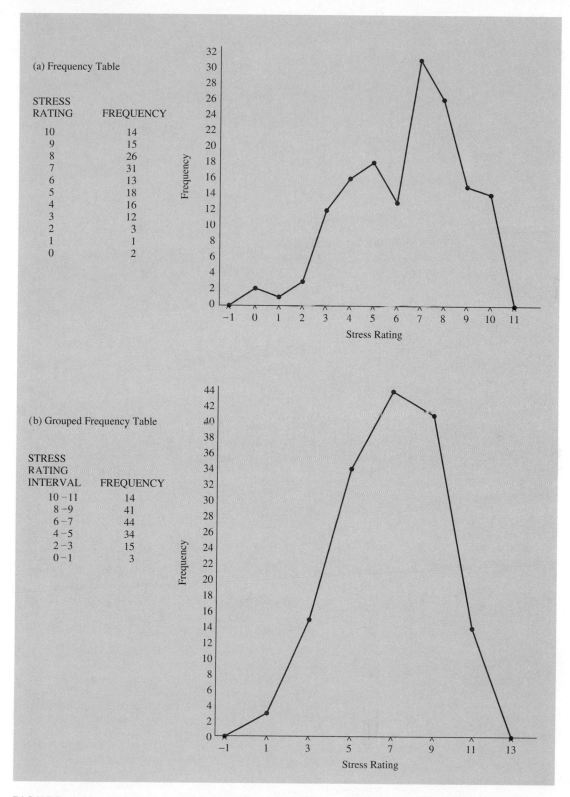

(a) Frequency Table

STRESS RATING	FREQUENCY
10	14
9	15
8	26
7	31
6	13
5	18
4	16
3	12
2	3
1	1
0	2

(b) Grouped Frequency Table

STRESS RATING INTERVAL	FREQUENCY
10 – 11	14
8 – 9	41
6 – 7	44
4 – 5	34
2 – 3	15
0 – 1	3

FIGURE 1–5 *Frequency polygons based on (a) a frequency table and (b) a grouped frequency table for the stress ratings example. (Data from Aron et al., 1995.)*

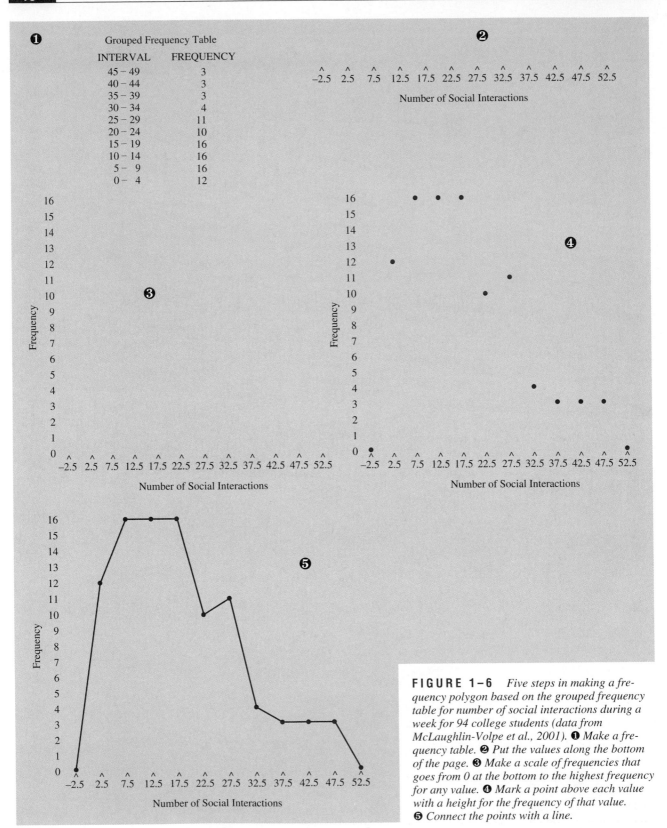

FIGURE 1–6 *Five steps in making a frequency polygon based on the grouped frequency table for number of social interactions during a week for 94 college students (data from McLaughlin-Volpe et al., 2001).* ❶ *Make a frequency table.* ❷ *Put the values along the bottom of the page.* ❸ *Make a scale of frequencies that goes from 0 at the bottom to the highest frequency for any value.* ❹ *Mark a point above each value with a height for the frequency of that value.* ❺ *Connect the points with a line.*

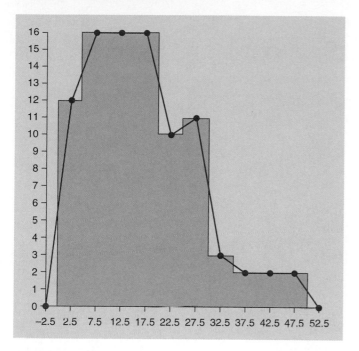

FIGURE 1–7   *Making a frequency polygon from a histogram, using the histogram for the students' social interactions example. (Data from Mclaughlin-Volpe et al., 2001).*

gon begins and ends at 0 frequency. Figure 1–7 shows all this, using the students' social interactions example.

1. Why do researchers make frequency graphs?
2. When making a histogram from a frequency table, (a) what goes along the bottom, (b) what goes along the left edge, and (c) what goes above each value?
3. Based on this frequency table, make (a) a histogram and (b) a frequency polygon:

Value	Frequency
5	2
4	5
3	8
2	4
1	3

4. How are histograms and frequency polygons (a) similar and (b) different?
5. Why does a frequency polygon include an extra value at the start and end along the bottom?

Answers:

1. To visually show the pattern in a frequency table.
2. (a) The values, from lowest to highest; (b) the frequencies from 0 at the bottom to the highest frequency of any value at the top; (c) a bar with a height of the frequency for that value.
3. See Figure 1–8.
4. (a) Both show the frequency table visually, with heights for each value for the frequency of that value. (b) A histogram uses bars; a frequency polygon is a line graph.
5. The extra values make the line start and end at zero frequency so that the line and the bottom of the graph together make a closed figure (a polygon).

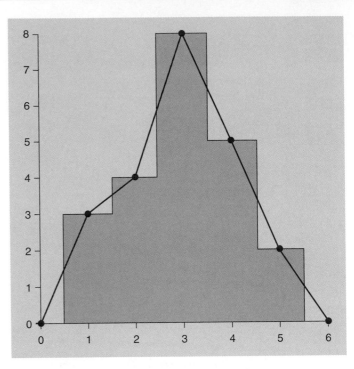

FIGURE 1–8   *Histogram and frequency polygon for "How Are You Doing?" question 3.*

SHAPES OF FREQUENCY DISTRIBUTIONS

frequency distribution

A frequency table, histogram, or frequency polygon describes a **frequency distribution.** That is, these show the pattern or shape of how the frequencies are spread out, or "distributed."

Psychologists also describe this shape in words. Describing the shape of a distribution is important both for the descriptive statistics of this chapter and for the inferential statistics of later chapters.

UNIMODAL AND BIMODAL FREQUENCY DISTRIBUTIONS

One question is whether a distribution's shape has only one main high point: one high "tower" in the histogram or one main "peak" in the frequency polygon. For example, in the stress ratings study, the most frequent value is 7, giving a graph with only one very high area. This is a **unimodal distribution.** If a distribution has two fairly equal high points, it is a **bimodal distribution.** Any distribution with two or more high points is also a **multimodal distribution.** (Strictly speaking, a distribution is bimodal or multimodal only if the peaks are exactly equal. However, psychologists use these terms more informally to describe the general shape.) Finally, a distribution with values of all about the same frequency is a **rectangular distribution.** Figure 1–9 shows examples of these frequency distribution shapes.

The scores from most psychology studies are usually an approximately unimodal distribution. Bimodal and other multimodal distributions occasionally turn up. A bimodal example would be the distribution of the number of employees

unimodal distribution
bimodal distribution
multimodal distribution

rectangular distribution

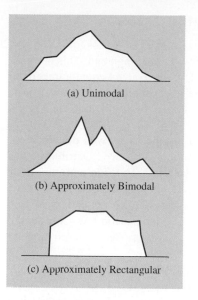

FIGURE 1–9 *Examples of (a) unimodal, (b) approximately bimodal, and (c) approximately rectangular frequency polygons.*

whose names have come to the attention of higher level managers. If you made a frequency distribution for the quality of work of such employees, the large frequencies would be at the values for a quality of work that is either very low or very high. An example of a rectangular distribution is the number of children at each grade level at an elementary school. There would be about the same number in first grade, second grade, and so on. Figure 1–10 shows these examples.

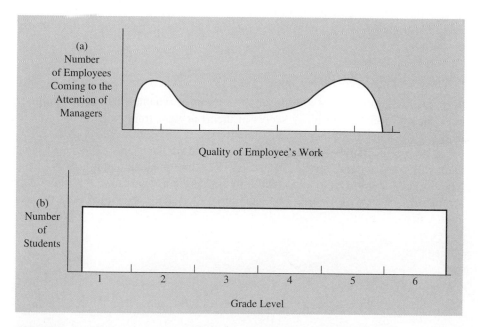

FIGURE 1–10 *Fictional examples of distributions that are not unimodal. (a) A distribution of the number of employees with different levels of quality of work who come to the attention of managers (bimodal distribution). (b) A distribution of the number of students at different grade levels in an elementary school (rectangular distribution).*

SYMMETRICAL AND SKEWED DISTRIBUTIONS

symmetrical distribution

skewed distribution

Look again at the frequency graphs of the stress ratings example (Figures 1–3 and 1–5). The distribution is lopsided, with more scores near the high end. This is somewhat unusual. Most things we measure in psychology have about equal numbers on both sides of the middle. That is, most of the time in psychology, the scores follow an approximately **symmetrical distribution** (if you fold the graph of a symmetrical distribution in half, the two halves look the same).

A distribution that clearly is not symmetrical is called a **skewed distribution.** The stress ratings distribution is a skewed distribution. A skewed distribution has one side that is long and spread out, somewhat like a tail. The side with the *fewer* scores (the side that looks more like a tail) is considered the direction of the skew. Thus, the stress study example, which has too few scores at the low end, is skewed to the left. However, the social interaction example, which has too few scores at the high end, is skewed to the right. Figure 1–11 shows examples of approximately symmetrical and skewed distributions.

A distribution that is skewed to the right is also called *positively skewed.* A distribution skewed to the left is also called *negatively skewed.*

floor effect

Strongly skewed distributions come up in psychology research mainly when what is being measured has some upper or lower limit. A situation in which many scores pile up at the low end because you can't have a lower score is called a **floor effect.** The number of social interactions example has a floor effect because no one can have less than 0 interactions.

ceiling effect

A skewed distribution caused by an upper limit is shown in Figure 1–12. This is a distribution of adults' scores on a multiplication table test. This distribution is strongly skewed to the left. Most of the scores pile up at the right, the high end (a perfect score). This shows a **ceiling effect.** The stress ratings example also shows a mild ceiling effect. This is because many students had high levels of stress, the maximum rating was 10, and people often do not like to use ratings right at the maximum.

NORMAL AND KURTOTIC DISTRIBUTIONS

normal curve

Psychologists also describe a distribution in terms of whether its tails are particularly "heavy" (thick, with many scores in them) or light (thin, with few scores in them). The standard of comparison is a bell-shaped curve. In psychology research and in nature generally, distributions often are quite similar to this bell-shaped standard, called the **normal curve.** We discuss this curve in some detail in later chapters. For now, however, the important thing is that the normal curve is a unimodal, symmetrical curve with average tails—the sort of bell shape shown in Figure 1–13a.

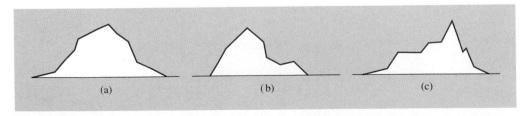

FIGURE 1–11 *Examples of frequency polygons of distributions that are (a) approximately symmetrical, (b) skewed to the right (positively skewed), and (c) skewed to the left (negatively skewed).*

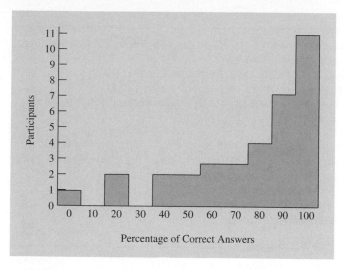

FIGURE 1–12 *A distribution skewed to the left due to a ceiling effect: fictional distribution of adults' scores on a multiplication table test.*

Both the stress ratings and the social interactions examples approximate a normal curve in a very general way—although, as we noted, both are somewhat skewed. In our experience, most distributions that result from psychology research are closer to the normal curve than are these two examples.

Kurtosis is how much the shape of a distribution differs from a normal curve in terms of whether its tails are heavier (thicker) or lighter (thinner) than the normal curve (DeCarlo, 1997). Kurtosis comes from the Greek word *kyrtos*, "curve." Figure 1–13b shows a kurtotic distribution with tails thicker than the normal curve. Figure 1–13c shows an extreme example of a kurtotic distribution, one with no tails at all. (A rectangular distribution would be even more extreme.)

Kurtosis

Distributions that have tails that are heavier or lighter than a normal curve also tend to have a different shape in the middle. Those with heavy tails are usually more peaked than the normal curve (see Figure 1–13b). It is as if the normal curve got pinched in the middle and some of it went up into a sharp peak and the rest spread out into thick tails. Those with light tails are usually flatter than the normal curve (see Figure 1–13c). It is as if the tails and the top of the curve both got sucked in to right near the middle on both sides. However, even though peakedness or flatness usually go along with kurtosis, the heaviness or lightness of the tails is what matters most.

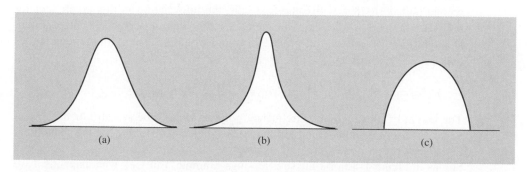

FIGURE 1–13 *Examples of (a) normal, (b) heavy-tailed, and (c) light-tailed distributions. (Adapted from DeCarlo, 1997.)*

HOW ARE YOU DOING?

1. Describe the difference between a unimodal and multimodal distribution in terms of (a) a frequency graph and (b) a frequency table.
2. What does it mean to say that a distribution is skewed to the left?
3. What kind of skew is created by (a) a floor effect and (b) a ceiling effect?
4. When a distribution is described as heavy tailed or light tailed, what is it being compared to?

ANSWERS:

1. (a) A unimodal distribution has one main high point; a multimodal distribution has more than one main high point; (b) a unimodal distribution has one value with a higher frequency than all the other frequencies; a multimodal distribution has more than one value with large frequencies compared to the values around it.
2. Fewer scores have low values than have high values.
3. (a) Skewed to the right; (b) skewed to the left.
4. The normal curve.

CONTROVERSY: MISLEADING GRAPHS

The most serious controversy about frequency tables, histograms, and frequency polygons is not among psychologists, but among the general public. The misuse of these procedures by some public figures, advertisers, and the media seem to have created skepticism about the trustworthiness of statistics in general and statistical tables and charts in particular. Everyone has heard that "statistics lie."

Of course, people can and do lie with statistics. It is just as easy to lie with words, but you may be less sure of your ability to recognize lies with numbers. In this section, we note two ways in which frequency tables and graphs can be misused and tell how to recognize such misuses. (Much of this material is based on the excellent and entertaining discussion of these issues in Tufte, 1983.)

FAILURE TO USE EQUAL INTERVAL SIZES

A key requirement of a grouped frequency table or graph is that the size of the intervals be equal. If they are not equal, the table or graph can be very misleading. Tufte (1983) gives an example, shown in Figure 1–14, from the respectable (and usually accurate) *New York Times*. This chart gives the impression that commissions paid to travel agents dropped dramatically in 1978. However, a close reading of the graph shows that the third bar for each airline is for only the first half of 1978. Thus, only half a year is being compared to each of the preceding full years. Assuming that the second half of 1978 was like the first half, the information in this graph actually tells us that 1978 would show an increase rather than a decrease. (For example, Delta Airlines' estimated full-year 1978 figure would be $72 million, much higher than 1977's $57 million.)

EXAGGERATION OF PROPORTIONS

The height of a histogram or frequency polygon usually begins at 0 or the lowest value of the scale and continues to the highest value of the scale. At the same time, the overall proportion of the graph should be about 1 to 1.5 times as wide as it is tall, as in Figure 1–15a for the stress ratings example. But look what happens if we make the graph much taller or shorter, as shown in Figures 1–15b and 1–15c. The effect is like that of a fun house mirror—the true picture is distorted.

FIGURE 1–14 *Misleading illustration of a frequency distribution due to unequal interval sizes. (From* New York Times, *August 8, 1978, p. D-1. © 1978 by the New York Times Company. Reprinted by permission.)*

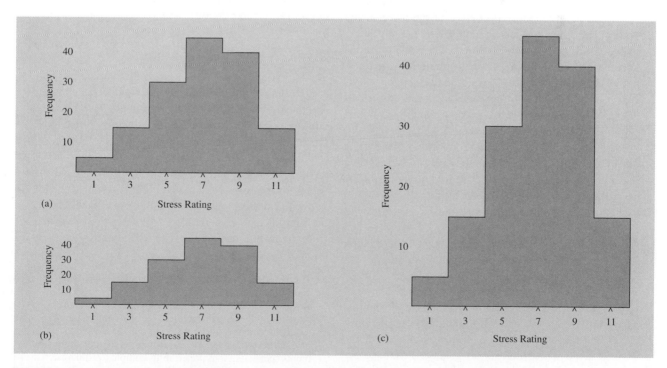

FIGURE 1–15 *Histograms of students' stress ratings distorted from the standard of width 1.5 times height. (Data from Aron, et al. 1995.)*

BOX 1-3   Gender, Ethnicity, and Math Performance

From time to time, someone tries to argue that because some groups of people score better on math tests and make careers out of mathematics, this means that these groups have some genetic advantage in math (or statistics). Other groups are said or implied to be innately inferior at math. The issue comes up about gender and also racial and ethnic groups, and of course in arguments about overall intelligence as well as math. There's *no* evidence for such genetic differences that can not be refuted (a must-see article: Block, 1995). But the stereotypes persist.

The impact of these stereotypes has been well established in research by Steele (1997) and his colleagues, who have done numerous studies on what they call "stereotype threat," which occurs when a negative stereotype about a group you belong to becomes relevant to you because of the situation you are in, such as taking a math test, and provides an explanation for how you will behave. A typical experiment creating stereotype threat (Spencer et al., 1999) involved women taking a difficult math test. Half were told that men generally do better on the test and the other half that women generally do equally well. When told that women do worse, the women did indeed score substantially lower. In the other condition there was no difference. (In fact, in two separate studies men performed a little worse when they were told there was no gender difference, as if they had lost some of their confidence.)

The same results occur when African Americans are given parts of the Graduate Record Exam—they do fine on the test when they are told no racial differences in the scores have been found, and do worse when they are told such differences have been found (Steele, 1997).

These results certainly argue against there being any inherent differences in ability in these groups. But that is nothing new. Many lines of research indicate that prejudices, not genetics, are the probable cause of differences in test scores between groups. For example, the same difference of 15 IQ points between a dominant and minority group has been found all over the world, even when there is no genetic difference between the groups', and in cases where opportunities for a group have changed, as when they emigrate, differences have rapidly disappeared (Block, 1995).

If groups such as women and African Americans are not inherently inferior in any area of intellectual endeavor, but perform worse on tests, what might be the reasons? The usual explanation is that they have internalized the "dominant" group's prejudices; however, Steele thinks the problem might not be so internal, but have to do with the situation. The stigmatized groups perform worse when they know that is what is expected—when they experience the threat of being stereotyped.

Of course in Steele's studies everyone tested had roughly the same initial educational background so that they knew the answers under the nonthreatening condition. Under the threatening condition, there is evidence that they try even harder. Too hard. And become anxious. Just as often, however, members of groups expected to do poorly simply stop caring about how they do. They disidentify with the whole goal of doing well in math, for example. They avoid the subject or take easy classes and just shrug off any low grades.

WHAT CAN YOU DO FOR YOURSELF?

So, do you feel you belong to a group that is expected to do worse at math? (This includes white males who feel they are among the "math dumbbells.") What can you do to get out from under the shadow of "stereotype threat" as you take this course?

First, care about learning statistics. Don't discount it to save your self-esteem and separate yourself from the rest of the class. Fight for your right to know this subject. What a triumph for those who hold the prejudice if you give up. Consider these words, from the former president of the Mathematics Association of America:

> The paradox of our times is that as mathematics becomes increasingly powerful, only the powerful seem to benefit from it. The ability to think mathematically—broadly interpreted—is absolutely crucial to advancement in virtually every career. Confidence in dealing with data, skepticism in analyzing arguments, persistence in penetrating complex problems, and literacy in communicating about technical mat-

ters are the enabling arts offered by the new mathematical sciences. (Steen, 1987, p. xviii)

Second, once you care about succeeding at statistics, realize you are going to be affected by stereotype threat. Think of it as a stereotype-induced form of test anxiety and work on it that way—see Box 1–2.

Third, in yourself, root the effects of that stereotype out as much as you can. It takes some effort. That's why we are spending time on it here. Research on stereotypes shows that they can be activated without our awareness (Fiske, 1998) even when we are otherwise low in prejudice or a member of the stereotyped group. To keep from being prejudiced about ourselves or others, we have to consciously resist stereotypes. So, to avoid unconsciously handicapping yourself in this course, as those in Steele's experiments probably did, you must make an active effort. You must consciously dismantle the stereotype and think about its falsehood.

SOME POINTS TO THINK ABOUT

- Women: Every bit of evidence for thinking that men are genetically better at math can and has been well disputed. For example, yes, the very top performers tend to be male, but the differences are slight, and the lowest performers are not more likely to be female, as would probably be the case if there were a genetic difference. But Tobias (1982) cites numerous studies providing nongenetic explanations for why women might not make it to the very top in math. For example, in a study of students identified by a math talent search, it was found that few parents arranged for their daughters to be coached before the talent exams. Sons were almost invariably coached. In another study, parents of mathematically gifted girls were not even aware of their daughters' abilities, whereas parents of boys invariably were. In general, girls tend to avoid higher math classes, according to Tobias, because parents, peers, and even teachers often advise them against pursuing too much math. So, even though women are earning more PhDs in math than ever before, it is not surprising that math is the field with the highest dropout rate for women.
- We checked the grades in our own introductory statistics classes and simply found no reliable difference for gender. More generally, Schram (1996) analyzed results of 13 independent studies of performance in college statistics classes and found an overall average difference of almost exactly zero (the slight direction of difference favored females). It has never even occurred to us to look for racial or ethnic differences, as they are so obviously not present.
- Persons of color: Keep in mind that only 7% of the genetic variation in humans is between races (Block, 1995). Mostly, we are all the same.
- Associate with people who have a positive attitude about you and your group. Watch for subtle signs of prejudice and reject it. For example, Steele found that the grades of African Americans in a large midwestern university rose substantially when they were enrolled in a transition-to-college program emphasizing that they were the cream of the crop and much was expected of them, while African Americans students at the same school who were enrolled in a "remedial program for minorities" received considerable attention, but their grades improved very little and many more of them dropped out of school. Steele argues that the very idea of a remedial program exposed those students to a subtle stereotype threat.
- Work hard during this course. If you are stuck, get help. If you work at it, you can do it. This is not about genetics. Think about a study cited by Tobias (1995) comparing students in Asia and the United States on an international mathematics test. The U.S. students were thoroughly outperformed, but more important was why: Interviews revealed that Asian students saw math as an ability fairly equally distributed among people and thought that differences in performance were due to hard work. U.S. students thought some people are just born better at math, so hard work matters little.

In short, our culture's belief that "math just comes naturally to some people" is false and harmful. It especially harms students who hear it early in their career with numbers and believe it explains their difficulties, when their real problem is due to gender or racial stereotypes or difficulty with English. But once you vow to undo the harm done to you, you can overcome effects of prejudice. Doing well in this course may even be more satisfying for you than for others. And it will certainly be a fine thing that you have modeled that achievement for others in your group.

Any particular shape is in a sense accurate. But the 1 to 1.5 proportion has been adopted to give people a standard for comparison. Changing this proportion misleads the eye.

FREQUENCY TABLES, HISTOGRAMS, AND FREQUENCY POLYGONS IN RESEARCH ARTICLES

Psychology researchers mainly use frequency tables, histograms, and frequency polygons as a step in more elaborate statistical analyses. They are usually not included in research articles—and when they are, just because they are so rare, they are often not standard in some way. When they do appear, they are most likely to be in survey studies.

An example of a frequency table in a research article is a study by Meyers and his colleagues (2001) of the careers of 433 sports psychologists who returned questionnaires sent to all the members of the two major professional organizations for sports psychologists. Table 1–7 (reproduced from Table 2 of Meyers et al.) is a frequency table for different categories of employment setting. Look at the results for all respondents' primary employment setting: 203 of them (46.9%) work in academic settings (that is, they are university professors or researchers), 158 (36.5%) are in private practice, and the rest work in various other settings, such mental health clinics and mental hospitals.

Histograms and frequency polygons are even more rare in research articles (except in articles *about* statistics), but they do appear occasionally. For example, Fritzon (2001) analyzed cases of arson from police files, focusing on the distance traveled to commit the crime in relation to different motivations for arson. Figure 1–16 (reproduced from Figure 1 in her article) is based on a grouped frequency table. It shows the frequency of crimes ("Number of offenses") committed at various distances for what

TABLE 1–7 Frequency of Primary and Secondary Employment Settings for All Survey Respondents and for Those Respondents Engaged in Paid Sport Psychology Work

| | All respondents | | | | Paid sport psychology respondents | | | |
| | Primary | | Secondary | | Primary | | Secondary | |
Employment setting	n	%	n	%	n	%	n	%
Academia	203	46.9	74	17.1	132	51.4	43	38.7
Private practice	158	36.5	76	17.6	101	39.2	43	38.7
Mental health clinic	24	5.5	12	2.8	12	4.7	3	2.7
Medical hospital	23	5.3	12	2.8	9	3.5	9	8.1
Public school system	8	1.8	4	1.7				
Managed care corp.	4	0.9			1	0.4		
Research firm	3	0.7			1	0.4		
Correctional facility	3	0.7	1	0.4				
Federal government	2	0.5						
Professional sport org.	1	0.2	26	6.0	1	0.4	13	11.7
Health club	1	0.2						
Other	3	0.6						

Note: corp. = corporation; org. = organization.
Source: Meyers et al., 2001.

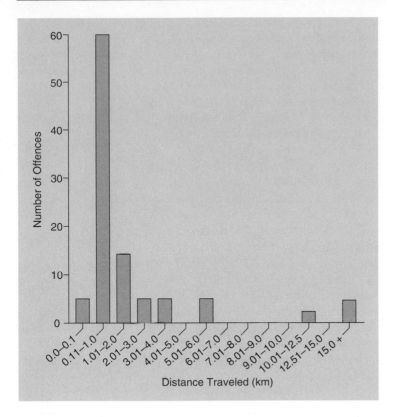

FIGURE 1–16   *Distances traveled to Damage* (n = 42). *(Source: Fritzon 2001.)*

she calls the "Damage" (opportunistic) type of arson. For example, the table shows that there were about four such cases within .1 kilometers from the arsonist's home, about 60 cases between .11 and 1 km, about 13 between 1.01 and 2 km, 4 between 2.1 and 3 km, and so forth. Notice that the intervals are not entirely equal. The researcher divides up the first km into two parts to emphasize that although most cases occur near home, very few occur at home or for an immediate neighbor. Similarly, the last categories (10.01–12.50, 12.51–15, and 15+) are larger because there are so few arsons at that distance. The decision to use unequal intervals is appropriate in this example—and is well labeled so that it is not misleading. Nevertheless, the use of different interval sizes does somewhat distort the shape of the distribution. Still, it is clear that the distribution is highly skewed to the right (that is, the long tail is to the right). In this study, the skew is due in part to a natural floor effect—you can't be less than 0 km from home.

Histograms and frequency polygons are only rarely used in research articles, and you are more likely to see a brief comment on the shape of the distribution of the scores collected in a study. This is particularly likely if the distribution seems to deviate from normal. We consider some examples of this in Chapter 15.

SUMMARY

1. Psychologists use descriptive statistics to describe—to summarize and make understandable—a group of numbers from a research study.
2. A value is a number or category; a variable is a characteristic that can have different values; a score is a particular person's value on the variable.

3. Most variables in psychology research are numeric with approximately equal intervals. However, some numeric variables are rank order (where the values are ranks), and some variables are not numeric at all (where the values are categories).
4. A frequency table organizes the scores into a table of each of the possible values with the frequency and percentage of scores that have that value.
5. When there are many different values, a grouped frequency table is more useful. It is like an ordinary frequency table except that the frequencies are given for intervals that include a range of values.
6. The pattern of frequencies in a distribution can be shown visually with a histogram, a kind of bar graph in which the height of each bar is the frequency for a particular value. An alternative is a frequency polygon, in which a line connects dots, the height of each of which is the frequency for a particular value.
7. The general shape of a histogram or frequency polygon can be unimodal (having a single peak), bimodal, multimodal (including bimodal), or rectangular (having no peak); it can be symmetrical or skewed (having a long tail) to the right or the left; and compared to the bell-shaped normal curve, it can be kurtotic (having tails that are too heavy or light).
8. Statistical graphs for the general public are sometimes distorted in ways that mislead the eye, such as failing to use equal intervals or exaggerating proportions.
9. Frequency tables, histograms, and frequency polygons are rarely shown in research articles. When they are, they often follow nonstandard formats or involve frequencies (or percentages) for a nominal variable. Shapes of distributions are more often described.

KEY TERMS

bimodal distribution (p. 18)
ceiling effect (p. 20)
descriptive statistics (p. 2)
equal-interval variables (p. 3)
floor effect (p. 20)
frequency distribution (p. 18)
frequency polygon (p. 14)
frequency table (p. 6)
grouped frequency table (p. 9)

histogram (p. 12)
inferential statistics (p. 2)
interval (p. 9)
kurtosis (p. 21)
levels of measurement (p. 4)
multimodal distribution (p. 18)
nominal variables (p. 4)
normal curve (p. 20)
numeric variable (p. 3)

rank-order variables (p. 4)
rectangular distribution (p. 18)
score (p. 2)
skewed distribution (p. 20)
symmetrical distribution (p. 20)
unimodal distribution (p. 18)
values (p. 2)
variable (p. 2)

EXAMPLE WORKED-OUT COMPUTATIONAL PROBLEMS

Ten first year students rated their interest in graduate school on a scale from 1 = no interest at all to 6 = high interest. Their scores were as follows: 2, 4, 5, 5, 1, 3, 6, 3, 6, 6.

MAKING A FREQUENCY TABLE

See Figure 1–17.

MAKING A HISTOGRAM

See Figure 1–18.

Interest in Graduate School	Frequency	Percent	
6	3	30	///
5	2	20	//
4	1	10	/
3	2	20	//
2	1	10	/
1	1	10	/

2,4,5,5,1,3,6,3,6,6

FIGURE 1–17 *Answer to example worked-out problem for making a frequency table.* ❶ *Make a list down the page of each possible value, from highest to lowest.* ❷ *Go one by one through the scores, making a mark for each next to its value on your list.* ❸ *Make a table showing how many times each value on your list is used.* ❹ *Figure the percentage of scores for each value.*

MAKING A FREQUENCY POLYGON

See Figure 1–19.

PRACTICE PROBLEMS

These problems involve tabulation and making graphs. Most real-life statistics problems are done on a computer. However, even if you have a computer and statistics software, do these by hand to ingrain the method in your mind.

For practice in using a computer to solve statistics problems, refer to the computer section of each chapter of the *Student's Study Guide and Computer Workbook* that accompanies this text.

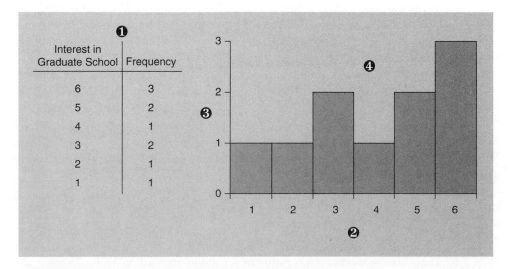

FIGURE 1–18 *Answer to example worked-out problem for making a histogram.* ❶ *Make a frequency table.* ❷ *Put the values along the bottom of the page, from left to right, from lowest to highest.* ❸ *Make a scale of frequencies along the left edge of the page that goes from 0 at the bottom to the highest frequency for any value.* ❹ *Make a bar above each value with a height for the frequency of that value.*

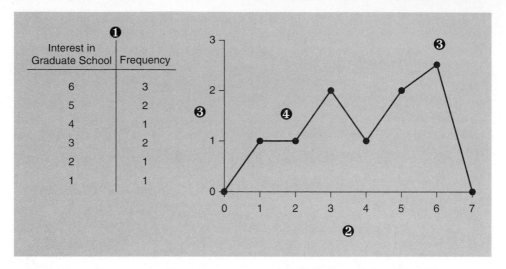

FIGURE 1–19 *Answer to example worked-out problem for making a frequency polygon.* ❶ *Make a frequency table.* ❷ *Put the values along the bottom of the page, from left to right, starting one value below the lowest value and ending one value above the highest value.* ❸ *Make a scale of frequencies along the left edge of the page that goes from 0 at the bottom to the highest frequency for any value.* ❹ *Mark a point above each value with a height for the frequency of that value.* ❺ *Connect the points with a line.*

All data are fictional unless an actual citation is given.

Answers to most Set I problems are given at the back of the book.

SET I

1. A client rates her satisfaction with her vocational counselor on a 4-point scale from 1 = not at all satisfied to 4 = very satisfied. What is the (a) variable, (b) possible values, and (c) score?

2. Give the level of measurement for each of the following variables: (a) ethnic group to which a person belongs, (b) number of times an animal makes a wrong turn in a maze, and (c) position one finishes in a race.

3. A particular block in a suburban neighborhood has 20 households. The number of children in these households is as follows: 2, 4, 2, 1, 0, 3, 6, 0, 1, 1, 2, 3, 2, 0, 1, 2, 1, 0, 2, 2.

    Make (a) a frequency table, (b) a histogram, and (c) a frequency polygon. Then, (d) describe the general shape of the distribution.

4. Fifty students were asked how many hours they had studied this weekend. Here are their answers:

    11, 2, 0, 13, 5, 7, 1, 8, 12, 11, 7, 8, 9, 10, 7, 4, 6, 10, 4, 7, 8, 6, 7, 10, 7, 3, 11, 18, 2, 9, 7, 3, 8, 7, 3, 13, 9, 8, 7, 7, 10, 4, 15, 3, 5, 6, 9, 7, 10, 6.

    Make (a) a frequency table, (b) a histogram, and (c) a frequency polygon. Then, (d) describe the general shape of the distribution.

5. These are the scores on a measure of sensitivity to smell taken by 25 chefs attending a national conference:

    96, 83, 59, 64, 73, 74, 80, 68, 87, 67, 64, 92, 76, 71, 68, 50, 85, 75, 81, 70, 76, 91, 69, 83, 75.

Make (a) a frequency table and (b) histogram. (c) Make a grouped frequency table using intervals of 50–59, 60–69, 70–79, 80–89, and 90–99. Based on the grouped frequency table, (d) make a histogram and (e) describe the general shape of the distribution.

6. Below are the number of minutes it took each of a group of 10-year-olds to do a series of abstract puzzles:

   24, 83, 36, 22, 81, 39, 60, 62, 38, 66, 38, 36, 45, 20, 20, 67, 41, 87, 41, 82, 35, 82, 28, 80, 80, 68, 40, 27, 43, 80, 31, 89, 83, 24.

   Make (a) a frequency table and (b) a frequency polygon. (c) Make a grouped frequency table using intervals of 20–29, 30–39, 40–49, 50–59, 60–69, 70–79, and 80–89. Based on the grouped frequency table, (d) make a histogram and (e) describe the general shape of the distribution.

7. Describe the shapes of the three distributions illustrated.

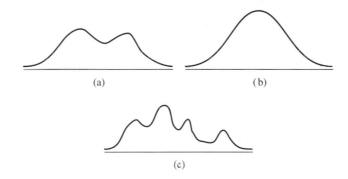

(a)   (b)

(c)

8. Draw an example of each of the following distributions: (a) symmetrical, (b) rectangular, and (c) skewed to the right.

9. Explain to a person who has never had a course in statistics what is meant by (a) a symmetrical unimodal distribution and (b) a negatively skewed unimodal distribution. (Be sure to include in your first answer an explanation of what is meant by a distribution.)

10. McKee and Ptacek (2001) asked 90 college students about a time they had "delivered bad news" to someone. Table 1–8 (their Table 1) shows the results for the type of bad news given. (a) Using this table as an example, explain the idea

TABLE 1–8	Descriptive Statistics for the Type of News Given		
Category		Frequency	Percentage
1. Relationship with family		19	21.1
2. School		1	1.1
3. Job/work		6	6.7
4. Relationship with actual/potential girlfriend/boyfriend		17	18.9
5. Personal health		1	1.1
6. Finance		1	1.1
7. Relationship with friends		21	23.3
8. Health of family member/friend		23	25.6
9. Other		1	1.1

Source: Eberhardt, McKee & Ptacek, 2001.

of a frequency table to a person who has never had a course in statistics. (b) Explain the general meaning of the pattern of results.

SET II

11. A participant in a cognitive psychology study is given 50 words to remember and later asked to recall as many as he can of those 50 words. This participant recalls 17. What is the (a) variable, (b) possible values, and (c) score?

12. Explain and give an example for each of the following types of variables: (a) equal-interval, (b) rank-order, and (c) nominal.

13. An organizational psychologist asks 20 employees in a particular company to rate their job satisfaction on a 5-point scale from 1 = very unsatisfied to 5 = very satisfied. The ratings were as follows:

    3, 2, 3, 4, 1, 3, 3, 4, 5, 2, 3, 5, 2, 3, 3, 4, 1, 3, 2, 4.

    Make (a) a frequency table, (b) a histogram, and (c) a frequency polygon. Then, (d) describe the general shape of the distribution.

14. A social psychologist asked 15 college students how many times they "fell in love" (or had a strong infatuation) before they were 11 years old. The numbers of times were as follows:

    2, 0, 6, 0, 3, 1, 0, 4, 9, 0, 5, 6, 1, 0, 2.

    Make (a) a frequency table, (b) a histogram, and (c) a frequency polygon. Then, (d) describe the general shape of the distribution.

15. Following are the speeds of cars clocked by radar on a particular road in a 35-mph zone on a particular afternoon:

    30, 36, 42, 36, 30, 52, 36, 34, 36, 33, 30, 32, 35, 32, 37, 34, 36, 31, 35, 20, 24, 46, 23, 31, 32, 45, 34, 37, 28, 40, 34, 38, 40, 52, 31, 33, 15, 27, 36, 40.

    Make (a) a frequency table, (b) a histogram, and (c) a frequency polygon. Then, (d) describe the general shape of the distribution.

16. Here are the number of holiday gifts purchased by 25 families randomly interviewed at a local mall at the end of the holiday season:

    22, 18, 22, 26, 19, 14, 23, 27, 2, 18, 28, 28, 11, 16, 34, 28, 13, 21, 32, 17, 6, 29, 23, 22, 19.

    Make (a) a frequency table and (b) a frequency polygon. (c) Make a grouped frequency table using intervals of 0–4, 5–9, 10–14, 15–19, 20–24, 25–29, and 30–34. Based on the grouped frequency table, (d) make a histogram and (e) describe the general shape of the distribution.

17. Pick a book and page number of your choice (select a page with at least 30 lines; *do not pick a textbook or any book with tables or illustrations.*) Make a list of the number of words on each line; use that list as your data set. Make (a) a frequency table, (b) a histogram, and (c) a frequency polygon. Then, (d) describe the general shape of the distribution. (Be sure to give the name, author, publisher, and year of the book you used, along with the page number, with your answer.)

18. Explain to a person who has never taken a course in statistics the meaning of (a) grouped frequency table and (b) frequency polygon.

19. Give an example of something having these distribution shapes: (a) bimodal, (b) approximately rectangular, and (c) positively skewed. Do not use an example given in this book or in class.

20. Find an example in a newspaper or magazine of a graph that misleads by failing to use equal interval sizes or by exaggerating proportions.

TABLE 1–9 Competition for Members and Other Resources

	Question: How much competition does this group face from other groups with similar goals for members and other resources?	
Answer	*Percentage*	*Number*
No competition	20	118
Some competition	58	342
A lot of competition	22	131
Total	100	591

Note: There were no statistically significant differences between states. For full results of significance tests, contact the author.

From "Policy Conflict and the Structure of Interest Communities" by Anthony J. Nownes, *American Politics Quarterly,* Vol. 28, No. 3, July 2000, p. 316, copyright © 2000. Reprinted by permission of Sage Publications Inc.

21. Nownes (2000) surveyed representatives of interest groups who were registered as lobbyists of three U.S. state legislatures. One of the issues he studied was whether interest groups are in competition with each other. Table 1–9 (Nownes' Table 1) shows the results for one such question. (a) Using this table as an example, explain the idea of a frequency table to a person who has never had a course in statistics. (b) Explain the general meaning of the pattern of results.

TABLE 1–10 Dominant Category of Explanation for Intimate Aggression by Gender and Perpetrator Status

	Group							
	Female				Male			
	Comparisons (*n* = 36)		Perpetrators (*n* = 33)		Comparisons (*n* = 32)		Perpetrators (*n* = 25)	
Category	*f*	%	*f*	%	*f*	%	*f*	%
Self-defense	2	6	3	9	3	9	1	4
Control motives	8	22	9	27	9	28	3	12
Expressive aggression	4	11	3	9	3	9	8	32
Face/self-esteem preservation	1	3	2	6	2	6	3	12
Exculpatory explanations	5	14	3	9	3	9	3	12
Rejection of perpetrator or act	12	33	6	18	10	31	7	28
Prosocial/acceptable explanations	0	0	0	0	0	0	0	0
Tied categories	4	11	7	21	2	6	0	0

Note: f = frequency. % = percentage of respondents in a given group who provided a particular category of explanation.

Source: Mouradian, 2001

22. Mouradian (2001) surveyed college students selected from a screening session to include two groups: (a) "Perpetrators"—students who reported at least one violent act (hitting, shoving, etc.) against their partner in their current or most recent relationship—and (b) "Comparisons"—students who did not report any such uses of violence in any of their last three relationships. At the actual testing session, the students first read a description of an aggressive behavior such as "Throw something at his or her partner" or "Say something to upset his or her partner." They then were asked to write "as many examples of circumstances of situations as [they could] in which a person might engage in behaviors or acts of this sort with or towards their significant other." Table 1–10 (Mouradian's Table 3) shows the "Dominant Category of Explanation" (the category a participant used most) for females and males, broken down by comparisons and perpetrators. (a) Using this table as an example, explain the idea of a frequency table to a person who has never had a course in statistics. (b) Explain the general meaning of the pattern of results.

CHAPTER 2

THE MEAN, VARIANCE, STANDARD DEVIATION, AND Z SCORES

Are You Ready?
What You Need to have Mastered Before Starting This Chapter:

- Chapter 1

As we noted in Chapter 1, the purpose of descriptive statistics is to make a group of scores understandable, and you learned some ways to do that with tables and graphs. In this chapter you learn the main ways to use numbers to describe a group of scores. These numbers are the mean, variance, standard deviation, and Z scores. The mean is the average score. The variance and standard deviation are about the amount of variation among the scores. A Z score makes use of the mean and variance to describe a particular score.

THE MEAN

mean
central tendency

Usually the best single number for describing a group of scores is the ordinary average, the sum of all the scores divided by the number of scores. In statistics this is called the **mean.** The average, or mean, of a group of scores shows the **central tendency,** or the typical or most representative value of the group of scores. You also will learn some other ways besides the mean for describing the central tendency of a group of scores.

Suppose a psychotherapist noted how many sessions her last 10 patients had taken to complete brief therapy with her. The numbers of sessions were as follows: 7, 8, 8, 7, 3, 1, 6, 9, 3, 8.

The mean of these 10 scores is 6 (the sum of 60 sessions divided by 10 patients). That is, on the average, her last 10 patients had each come for 6 sessions. The information for the 10 patients is thus summarized by the single number 6.

You can visualize the mean as a kind of balancing point for the distribution of scores. Try it by visualizing a board balanced over a log, like a rudimentary teeter-totter. Imagine piles of blocks set along the board according to their values, one for each score in the distribution (like a histogram made of blocks). The mean is the point on the board where the weight of the blocks on each side balances exactly. Figure 2–1 shows this for the sessions attended by the 10 patients.

Some other examples are shown in Figure 2–2. Notice that there need not even be a block right at the balance point. That is, the mean doesn't have to be a score actually in the distribution. The mean is the average of the scores, the balance point. The mean could even be a number that cannot possibly occur in the distribution, as when a mean is a decimal number, but all the scores in the distribution have to be whole numbers (2.3 children, for example). (By the way, this analogy to blocks on a board, in reality, would work out precisely only if the board had no weight of its own.)

FORMULA FOR THE MEAN AND STATISTICAL SYMBOLS

The rule for figuring the mean is to add up all the scores and divide by the number of scores. This can be stated as the following formula:

The mean is the sum of the scores divided by the number of scores.

$$M = \frac{\Sigma X}{N} \tag{2-1}$$

M

M is a symbol for the mean. An alternative, $\overline{X}$ ("X-bar"), is sometimes used. However *M* is most common in research articles. In fact, there is not a general agreement for most of the symbols used in statistics. (In this book we generally use the symbols most widely found in psychology research articles.)

Σ, the capital Greek letter sigma, is the symbol for "sum of." It means "add up all the numbers for what follows." It is the most common special arithmetic symbol used in statistics.

X stands for the scores in the distribution of the variable *X*. We could have picked any letter. However, if there is only one variable, it is usually called *X*. In

FIGURE 2–1 *Mean of the distribution of the number of therapy sessions attended by 10 patients, illustrated using blocks on a board balanced on a log.*

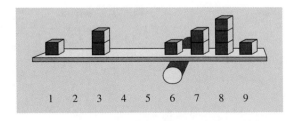

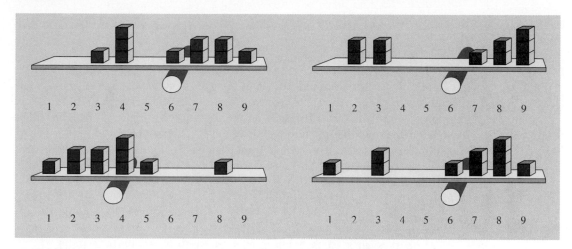

FIGURE 2–2 *Means of various distributions illustrated with blocks on a board balanced on a log.*

later chapters we use formulas with more than one variable. In those formulas, we use a second letter along with X (usually Y) or subscripts (such as X_1 and X_2).

ΣX is "the sum of X." This tells you to add up all the scores for the variable X. Suppose X is the number of therapy sessions of our 10 patients: ΣX then is 60, the sum of $7 + 8 + 8 + 7 + 3 + 1 + 6 + 9 + 3 + 8$.

N is for number—the number of scores in a distribution. In our example, there are 10 scores. Thus, N equals 10 [1] N

Overall, the formula says to divide the sum of all the scores in the distribution of the variable X by the total number of scores, N. In the therapy sessions example, this means you divide 60 by 10. Put in terms of the formula,

$$M - \frac{\Sigma X}{N} = \frac{60}{10} = 6$$

ADDITIONAL EXAMPLES OF FIGURING THE MEAN

Consider the examples from Chapter 1. The stress ratings of the 151 students in the first week of their statistics class (Aron et al., 1995) were as follows:

4, 7, 7, 7, 8, 8, 7, 8, 9, 4, 7, 3, 6, 9, 10, 5, 7, 10, 6, 8, 7, 8, 7, 8, 7, 4, 5, 10, 10, 0, 9,
8, 3, 7, 9, 7, 9, 5, 8, 5, 0, 4, 6, 6, 7, 5, 3, 2, 8, 5, 10, 9, 10, 6, 4, 8, 8, 8, 4, 8, 7, 3, 8,
8, 8, 8, 7, 9, 7, 5, 6, 3, 4, 8, 7, 5, 7, 3, 3, 6, 5, 7, 5, 7, 8, 8, 7, 10, 5, 4, 3, 7, 6, 3, 9, 7,
8, 5, 7, 9, 9, 3, 1, 8, 6, 6, 4, 8, 5, 10, 4, 8, 10, 5, 5, 4, 9, 4, 7, 7, 7, 6, 6, 4, 4, 4, 9, 7,
10, 4, 7, 5, 10, 7, 9, 2, 7, 5, 9, 10, 3, 7, 2, 5, 9, 8, 10, 10, 6, 8, 3.

In Chapter 1 we summarized all these numbers into a frequency table (Table 1–3). You can now summarize all this information as a single number by figuring the mean. You figure the mean by adding up all the stress ratings and dividing by the number of stress ratings. That is, you add up the stress ratings: $4 + 7 + 7 + 7 + 8 + 8$ and so on, for a total of 975. Then you divide this total by the number of scores, 151. In terms of the formula,

---

[1] In more formal, mathematical statistics writing, the symbols can be more complex. This complexity allows formulas to handle intricate situations without confusion. However, in books on statistics for psychologists, even fairly advanced texts, the symbols are kept simple. The simpler form rarely creates ambiguities in the kinds of statistical formulas psychologists use.

$$M = \frac{\Sigma X}{N} = \frac{975}{151} = 6.46$$

This tells you that the average stress rating was 6.46 (after rounding off). This is clearly higher than the middle of the 0–10 scale. You can also see this on a graph. Think again of the histogram as a pile of blocks on a board and the mean of 6.46 as the point where the board balances on the fulcrum (see Figure 2–3). This single number much simplifies the information in the 151 stress scores.

Similarly, consider the example from Chapter 1 of students' social interactions (McLaughlin-Volpe et al., 2001). The number of interactions over a week for the 94 students were as follows:

48, 15, 33, 3, 21, 19, 17, 16, 44, 25, 30, 3, 5, 9, 35, 32, 26, 13, 14, 14, 47, 47, 29, 18, 11, 5, 19, 24, 17, 6, 25, 8, 18, 29, 1, 18, 22, 3, 22, 29, 2, 6, 10, 29, 10, 21, 38, 41, 16, 17, 8, 40, 8, 10, 18, 7, 4, 4, 8, 11, 3, 23, 10, 19, 21, 13, 12, 10, 4, 17, 11, 21, 9, 8, 7, 5, 3, 22, 14, 25, 4, 11, 10, 18, 1, 28, 27, 19, 24, 35, 9, 30, 8, 26.

Again, in Chapter 1 we organized the original scores into a frequency table (Table 1–4). We can now take these same 94 scores, add them up, and divide by 94 to figure the mean:

$$M = \frac{\Sigma X}{N} = \frac{1{,}635}{94} = 17.40$$

This is illustrated in Figure 2–4.

FIGURE 2–3
Analogy of blocks on a board balanced on a fulcrum showing the mean for 151 statistics students' ratings of their stress level. (Data from Aron et al., 1995.)

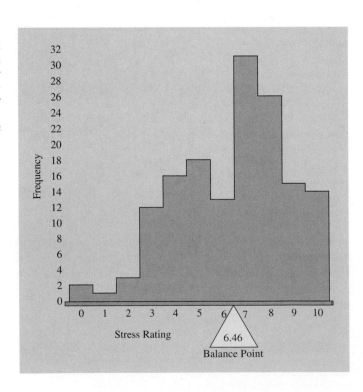

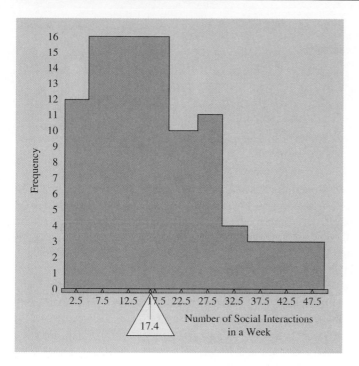

FIGURE 2–4 *Analogy of blocks on a board balanced on a fulcrum showing the mean for number of social interactions during a week for 94 college students. (Data from McLaughlin-Volpe et al., 2001.)*

STEPS FOR FIGURING THE MEAN

You figure the mean in two steps:

❶ **Add up all the scores.** That is, figure ΣX.
❷ **Divide this sum by the number of scores.** That is, divide ΣX by N.

OTHER MEASURES OF CENTRAL TENDENCY

The mean is only one of several ways to describe central tendency, the typical or representative value in a group of scores.

THE MODE

One alternative to the mean is the **mode.** The mode is the most common single number in a distribution. In our therapy sessions example, the mode is 8. This is because there are three patients with 8 sessions and no other number of sessions with as many patients. Another way to think of the mode is that it is the value with the largest frequency in a frequency table, the high point or peak of a distribution's frequency polygon or histogram (as shown in Figure 2–5).

    In a perfectly symmetrical unimodal distribution, the mode is the same as the mean. However, what happens when the mean and the mode are not the same? In that situation, the mode is usually not a very representative value for the scores in

mode

FIGURE 2-5 *The mode as the high point in a distribution's histogram, shown in the example of the number of therapy sessions attended by 10 patients.*

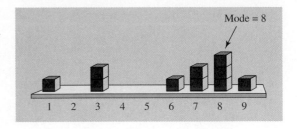

the distribution. In fact, sometimes researchers compare the mode to the mean in order to show that the distribution is *not* perfectly symmetrical and unimodal. Also, the mode can be a particularly unrepresentative value because it does not reflect many aspects of the distribution. For example, you can change some of the scores in a distribution without affecting the mode—but this is not true of the mean, which is affected by any single change in the distribution (see Figure 2–6).

On the other hand, the mode *is* the usual way of describing the central tendency for a nominal variable. For example, if you know the religions of a particular group of people, the mode tells you which religion is the most frequent. However, when it comes to the numerical variables that we use most often in psychology research, the mode is rarely used.

FIGURE 2-6 *The effect on the mean and on the mode of changing some scores, shown in the example of the number of therapy sessions attended by 10 patients.*

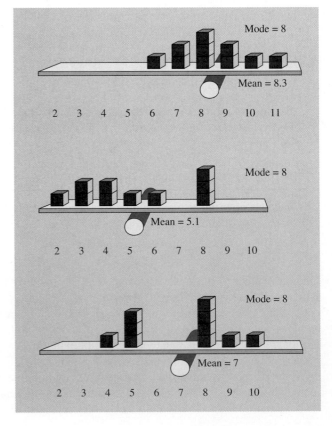

THE MEDIAN

Another alternative to the mean is the **median.** If you line up all the scores from lowest to highest, the middle score is the median. Figure 2–7 shows the scores for the number of therapy sessions attended lined up from lowest to highest. In this example, the fifth and sixth scores (the two middle ones), are both 7s. Either way, the median is 7.

When you have an even number of scores, the median can be between two different numbers. One solution is to use the average of the two middle scores. (There are more sophisticated solutions that take into account the pattern of scores on both sides of the middle. However, for most practical purposes, it is close enough just to use the average of the two middle scores.)

Sometimes, the median is better than the mean as a typical or representative value. This happens when there are a few extreme scores that would strongly affect the mean but would not affect the median. Reaction time results are a common example in psychology research of when the median might be better than the mean. Suppose you are asked to press a key as quickly as possible when a certain kind of pattern is shown on the computer screen. On five showings of the pattern, your times (in seconds) to respond are .74, .86, 2.32, .79, and .81. The mean of these five scores is 1.104 (that is, $\Sigma X/N = 5.52/5 = 1.104$). However, this mean is very much influenced by the one very long time (2.32 seconds). (The reason this time is so long might be because you were distracted just when the pattern was shown.) On the other hand, the median is much less affected by the extreme score. The median of these five scores is .81—a much more representative figure of most of the scores. That is, using the median to describe the central tendency might be better because it de-emphasizes the one extreme time, which is probably appropriate.

The importance of whether you use the mean, median, or mode can be seen in a recent controversy among psychologists studying the evolutionary basis of human mate choice. One set of theorists (e.g., Buss & Schmitt, 1993) argue that over their lives, men should prefer to have many more partners than women. According to this view, evolution should make women prefer to have just one reliable partner. This is because a woman can have only a small number of children in a lifetime and her genes are most likely to survive if those few children are well taken care of. Men, however, can have a great many children in a lifetime. Therefore, according to the theory, a shotgun approach is best for many men. Their genes are most likely to survive if they have a great many partners. Consistent with this assumption, evolutionary psychologists have found that men report wanting far more partners than do women.

Other theorists (e.g., Miller & Fishkin, 1997), however, have questioned this view. They argue that women and men should prefer about the same number of partners. This is because individuals with a basic predisposition to seek a strong intimate bond are most likely to survive infancy. This desire for strong bonds, they argue, remains (and has other benefits) in adulthood. These theorists also asked women and men how many partners they wanted. They found the same result as the

median

Tip for Success

One of the most common errors statistics students make when figuring the median is to forget to first line the scores up from lowest to highest.

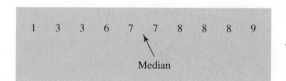

FIGURE 2–7 *The median is the middle score when scores are lined up from lowest to highest, shown in the example of the number of therapy sessions attended by 10 patients.*

TABLE 2–1	Responses of 106 Men and 160 Women to the Question: "How many partners would you ideally desire in the next 30 years?"		
	Mean	Median	Mode
Women	2.8	1	1
Men	64.3	1	1

Note: Data from Miller & Fishkin, 1997.

previous researchers when using the mean—men wanted an average of 64.32, women an average of 2.79. However, the picture looks drastically different if you look at the median or mode (see Table 2–1). Figure 2–8, taken directly from their article, shows why. Most women and most men want just one partner. A few want more, some many more. The big difference is that there are a lot more men in the small group that want many more than one partner.

So which theory is right? You could argue either way from these results. The point is that just focusing on the mean can clearly misrepresent the reality of the distribution.

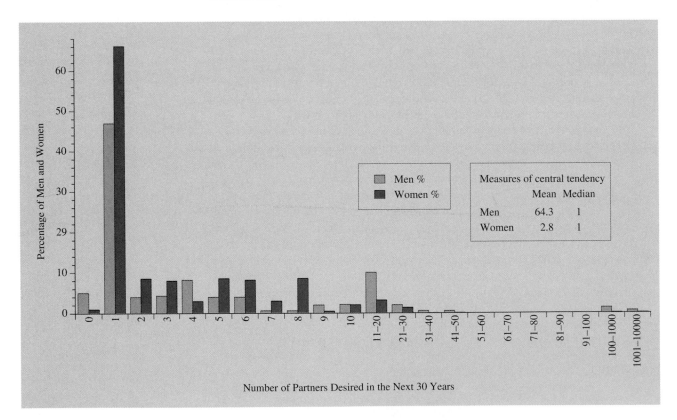

FIGURE 2–8   *Distributions for men and women for the ideal number of partners desired over 30 years. Note: To include all of the data, we collapsed across categories further out on the tail of these distributions. If every category represented a single number, it would be more apparent that the tail is very flat and that distributions are even more skewed than is apparent here. [From Miller & Fishkin, 1997, fig. 8–1. On the dynamics of human bonding and repro-ductive success: Seeking windows on the adapted-for-human-environmental interface. In J. A. Simpson & D. T. Kendrick (Eds.),* Evolutionary Social Psychology. *Mahwah, NJ: Erlbaum.]*

More generally, the median is most likely to be used when where there are a few extreme scores that would make the mean unrepresentative of the main body of scores. There are also times when psychologists use the median as part of more complex statistical methods. However, unless there are extreme scores, psychologists almost always use the mean as the measure of central tendency. In fact, the mean is a fundamental building block for most other statistical techniques.

STEPS FOR FINDING THE MEDIAN

The procedure for finding the median can be summarized as three steps:

❶ **Line up all the scores from lowest to highest.**

❷ **Figure how many scores there are to the middle score. If you have an odd number of scores, divide the number of scores in half and add ½. If an even number of scores, divide the number in half—this and the score above it are the middle scores.** For example, with 29 scores, an odd number, half is 14 ½; adding ½ gives you 15. The 15th score is the middle score. If there are 50 scores, an even number, half is 25. The 25th and 26th scores are the middle scores.

❸ **Count up to the middle score. If you have an odd number of scores, this is the median. If an even number of scores, the median is the average of the two middle scores.**

HOW ARE YOU DOING?

1. Name and define three measures of central tendency.
2. Write the formula for the mean and define each of the symbols.
3. Figure the mean of the following scores: 2, 8, 3, 6, and 6.
4. For the following scores find (a) the mode and (b) the median: 5, 4, 2, 8, 2.

ANSWERS:

1. The mean is the ordinary average—the sum of the scores divided by the number of scores. The mode is the most frequent score in a distribution. The median is the middle score—that is, if you line the scores up from lowest to highest, it is the score halfway along.
2. $M = \Sigma \, X/N$. M is the mean; Σ is the symbol for "sum of"—add up all the scores that follow; X is for the variable whose scores you are adding up; N is the number of scores.
3. $M = \Sigma \, X/N = (2 + 8 + 3 + 6 + 6) / 5 = 5$.
4. (a) 2. (b) 4.

THE VARIANCE AND THE STANDARD DEVIATION

Suppose you were asked, "How old are the students in your statistics class?" At a city-based university with many returning and part-time students, the mean age might be 38. You could answer, "The average age of the students in my class is 38." However, this would not tell the whole story. For example, you could have a mean of 38 because every student in the class was exactly 38 years old. Or you could have a mean of 38 because exactly half the class was 18 and the other half was 58. These are two quite different situations.

Distributions with the same mean can have very different amounts of spread around the mean; also, distributions with different means can have the same amount of spread around the mean. Figure 2–9a shows histograms for three different fre-

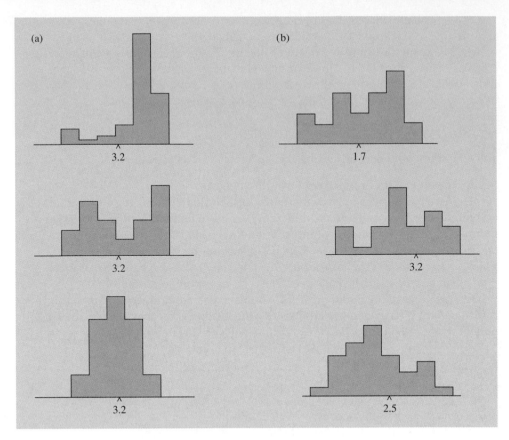

FIGURE 2−9 *Examples of distributions with (a) the same mean but different amounts of spread, and (b) different means but the same amount of spread.*

quency distributions with the same mean but different amounts of spread around the mean, and Figure 2–9b shows three different frequency distributions with different means but the same amount of spread.[2]

THE VARIANCE

variance

The **variance** of a group of scores tells you how spread out the scores are around the mean. To be precise, the variance is the average of each score's squared difference from the mean.

Here are the four steps to figure the variance:

deviation score

❶ **Subtract the mean from each score.** This gives each score's **deviation score.** The deviation score is how far away the actual score is from the mean.

squared deviation score

❷ **Square each of these deviation scores** (multiply each by itself). This gives each score's **squared deviation score.**

---

[2]This section focuses on the variance and standard deviation as indicators of spread, or dispersion. There is also another way to describe the spread of a group of scores, the *range*—the highest score minus the lowest score. Suppose that for a particular class the highest score on a midterm is 98 and the lowest score on the midterm is 60; the range is 38 (that is, 98 − 60 = 38). Psychology researchers rarely use the range because it is such an imprecise way to describe the spread. It is imprecise because it does not take into account how clumped together the scores are within the range.

❸ **Add up the squared deviation scores.** This total is called the **sum of squared deviations.**

❹ **Divide the sum of squared deviations by the number of squared deviations** (that is, divide the sum of squared deviations by the number of scores). This gives the average, or mean, of the squared deviations, which is the variance.

Suppose one distribution is more spread out than another. The more spread-out distribution has a larger variance because being spread makes the deviation scores bigger. If the deviation scores are bigger, the squared deviation scores are also bigger. Thus, the average of the squared deviation scores (the variance) is bigger.

In the example of the class in which everyone was exactly 38 years old, the variance would be exactly 0. That is, there would be no variance. (In terms of the numbers, each person's deviation score would be $38 - 38 = 0$; 0 squared is 0. The average of a bunch of zeros is 0.) By contrast, the class of half 18-year-olds and half 58-year-olds would have a rather large variance of 400. (The 18-year-olds would each have deviation scores of $18 - 38 = -20$. The 58-year-olds would have deviation scores of $58 - 38 = 20$. All the squared deviation scores, which are either -20 squared or 20 squared, come out to 400. The average of all 400s is 400.)

The variance is extremely important in many statistical procedures you will learn about later. However, the variance is rarely used as a descriptive statistic. This is because the variance is based on *squared* deviation scores, which do not give a very easy-to-understand sense of how spread out the actual, nonsquared scores are. For example, a class with a variance of 400 clearly has a more spread-out distribution than one whose variance is 10. However, the number 400 does not give an obvious insight into the actual variation among the ages, none of which are anywhere near 400.[3]

THE STANDARD DEVIATION

The most widely used way of *describing* the spread of a group of scores is the **standard deviation,** the positive square root of the variance. There are two steps to figure the standard deviation:

❶ **Figure the variance.**
❷ **Take the square root.**

If the variance of a distribution is 400, the standard deviation is 20. If the variance is 9, the standard deviation is 3.

The variance is about squared deviations from the mean. Therefore, its square root, the standard deviation, is about direct, ordinary, nonsquared deviations from the mean. *Roughly speaking, the standard deviation is the average amount that*

[3]Why don't statisticians just use the deviation scores themselves, make all deviations positive, and use the average of these? In fact, the average of the deviation scores (treating all deviations as positive) has a formal name—the *average deviation* or *mean deviation.* This procedure was actually used in the past, and some psychologists have recently raised the issue again, noting some subtle advantages of the average deviation (Catanzaro & Taylor, 1996). However, the average deviation does not work out very well as part of more complicated statistical procedures. In part, this is because it is hard to do algebraic manipulations with a formula that ignores the signs of some of its numbers.

A deeper reason for using the squared approach is that it gives more influence to large deviations (squaring a deviation of 4 gives a squared deviation of 16; squaring a deviation of 8 gives a squared deviation of 64). As you learn in later chapters, deviation scores often represent "errors": The mean is expected, and deviations from it are errors or discrepancies from what is expected. Thus, using squared deviations has the effect of "penalizing" large errors to a greater extent than small errors.

scores differ from the mean. For example, consider a class where the ages have a standard deviation of 20 years. This would tell you that the ages are spread out, on the average, about 20 years in each direction from the mean. Knowing the standard deviation gives you a general sense of the degree of spread.

The standard deviation does not, however, perfectly describe the distribution. For example, suppose the distribution of the number of children in families in a particular country has a mean of 4 and standard deviation of 1. Figure 2–10 shows several possibilities of the distribution of number of children, all with a mean of 4 and a standard deviation of 1.

It is also important to remember that the standard deviation is not *exactly* the average amount that scores differ from the mean. To be precise, the standard deviation is the square root of the average of scores' squared deviations from the mean. This squaring, averaging, and then taking the square root gives a slightly different result from simply averaging the scores' deviations from the mean. Still, the result of this approach has technical advantages that outweigh the slight disadvantage of giving only an approximate description of the average variation from the mean (see footnote 3).

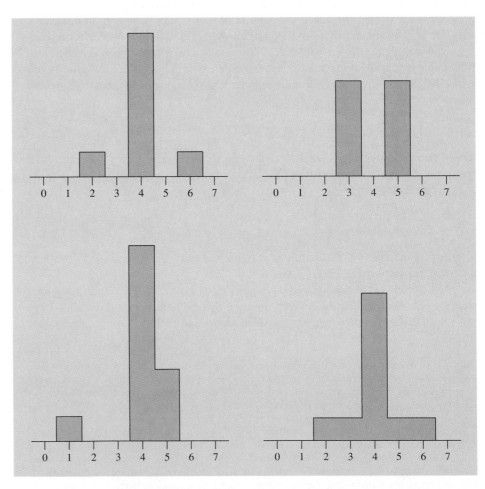

FIGURE 2–10 *Some possible distributions for family size in a country where the mean is 4 and the standard deviation is 1.*

FORMULAS FOR THE VARIANCE AND THE STANDARD DEVIATION

Here is the formula for the variance

(2-2)
$$SD^2 = \frac{\Sigma(X - M)^2}{N}$$

> The variance is the sum of the squared deviations of the scores from the mean, divided by the number of scores.

SD^2 is the symbol for the variance. (Later, you will learn its other symbols, S^2 **SD^2** and σ^2—the lowercase Greek letter sigma squared. The different symbols are for different situations in which the variance is used. In some cases, it is figured slightly differently.) SD is short for *standard deviation,* emphasizing that the variance is the standard deviation squared.

The top part of the formula is the sum of squared deviations. X is for each score and M is the mean. Thus, $X - M$ is the score minus the mean, the deviation score. The exponent 2 tells you to square each deviation score. Finally, the sum sign (Σ) tells you to add together all these squared deviation scores.

The sum of squared deviations, which is called the **sum of squares** for short, is   **sum of squares** an important part of many statistical procedures and has its own symbol, **SS.** Thus,   **SS** the variance formula can be written using SS instead of $\Sigma(X - M)^2$:

(2-3)
$$SD^2 = \frac{SS}{N}$$

> The variance is the sum of the squared deviations divided by the number of scores.

Whether you use the simplified symbol SS or the full description of the sum of squared deviations, the bottom part of the formula is just N, the number of scores. That is, the formula says to divide the sum of the squared deviation scores by the number of squared deviation scores (the number of scores in the distribution).

The standard deviation is the square root of the variance. So, if you already know the variance, the formula is

(2-4)
$$SD = \sqrt{SD^2}$$

> The standard deviation is the square root of the variance.

The formula for the standard deviation, starting from scratch, is the square root of what you figure for the variance:

(2-5)
$$SD = \sqrt{\frac{\Sigma(X - M)^2}{N}}$$

> The standard deviation is the square root of the result of taking the sum of the squared deviations of the scores from the mean divided by the number of scores.

or

(2-6)
$$SD = \sqrt{\frac{SS}{N}}$$

> The standard deviation is the square root of the result of taking the sum of the squared deviations divided by the number of scores.

EXAMPLES

Table 2–2 shows the figuring for the variance and standard deviation for the therapy sessions example. (The table assumes you have already figured the mean to be 6 sessions.) Usually, it is easiest to do your figuring using a calculator, especially one with a square root key. The standard deviation of 2.57 tells you that roughly speaking, on the average, the number of therapy sessions attended vary by about 2 ½ from the mean of 6.

Table 2–3 shows the figuring for the variance and standard deviation for the example of students' numbers of social interactions during a week (McLaughlin-Volpe et al., 2001). (To save space, the table shows only the first few and last few scores.) Roughly speaking, this result tells you that a student's number of social interactions in a week varies from the mean by an average of 11.49 interactions. This can also be shown on a histogram (Figure 2–11).

COMPUTATIONAL AND DEFINITIAL FORMULAS

In actual research situations, psychologists must often figure the variance and the standard deviation for distributions with a great many scores, often involving decimals or large numbers. This can make the whole process quite time consuming, even with a calculator. To deal with this problem, over the years researchers developed a number of shortcuts to simplify the figuring. A shortcut formula of this type is called a **computational formula.**

The computational formula for the variance is

computational formula

The variance is the sum of the squared scores minus the result of taking the sum of all the scores, squaring this sum and dividing by the number of scores, then taking this whole difference and dividing it by the number of scores.

$$SD^2 = \frac{\Sigma X^2 - (\Sigma X)^2 / N}{N}$$ (2-7)

TABLE 2–2 **Figuring the Variance and Standard Deviation in the Number of Therapy Sessions Example**

Score (Number of Sessions)	−	Mean Score (Mean Number of Sessions)	=	Deviation Score	Squared Deviation Score
7		6		1	1
8		6		2	4
8		6		2	4
7		6		1	1
3		6		−3	9
1		6		−5	25
6		6		0	0
9		6		3	9
3		6		−3	9
8		6		2	4
				Σ: 0	66

$$\text{Variance} = SD^2 = \frac{\Sigma(X - M)^2}{N} = \frac{SS}{N} = \frac{66}{10} = 6.6$$

$$\text{Standard deviation} = SD = \sqrt{SD^2} = \sqrt{6.6} = 2.57$$

TABLE 2–3	**Figuring the Variance and Standard Deviation for Number of Social Interactions During a Week for 94 College Students**			
Number of Interactions	−	Mean Number of Interactions	=	Deviation Score	Squared Deviation Score
48		17.40		30.60	936.36
15		17.40		−2.40	5.76
33		17.40		15.60	243.36
3		17.40		−14.40	207.36
21		17.40		3.60	12.96
.		.		.	.
.		.		.	.
.		.		.	.
35		17.40		17.60	309.76
9		17.40		−8.40	70.56
30		17.40		12.60	158.76
8		17.40		−9.40	88.36
26		17.40		8.60	73.96
			Σ:	0.00	12,406.44

$$\text{Variance} = SD^2 = \frac{\Sigma(X - M)^2}{N} = \frac{12{,}406.44}{94} = 131.98$$

$$\text{Standard deviation} = \sqrt{SD^2} = \sqrt{131.98} = 11.49$$

Note: Data from McLaughlin-Volpe et al. (2001).

ΣX^2 means that you square each score and then take the sum of these squared scores. However, $(\Sigma X)^2$ means that you first add up all the scores and then take the square of this sum. This formula is easier to use than the one you learned before if you are figuring the variance for a lot of numbers by hand, because you do not have to first find the deviation score for each raw score.

However, these days computational formulas are mainly of historical interest. They are used by researchers only when computers with statistics software are not readily available to do the figuring. In fact, even many hand calculators are set up so that you need only enter the scores and press a button or two to get the variance and the standard deviation.

In this book we give a few computational formulas (mainly in footnotes) just so you will have them if you someday do a research project with a lot of numbers and you don't have access to a computer with statistical software. However, we recommend *not* using the computational formulas when you are learning statistics. The computational formulas tend to make it harder to understand the *meaning* of what you are figuring.

It is much better to use the regular formulas we give when doing the practice problems. These are the formulas designed to help strengthen your understanding of what the figuring *means*. Thus, the usual formula we give is called a **definitional formula.**

definitional formula

The purpose of this book is to help you understand statistical procedures, not to turn you into a computer by having you memorize computational formulas you will rarely, if ever, use. (To simplify the actual figuring, however, our practice problems generally use small groups of whole numbers. For students who have access to a

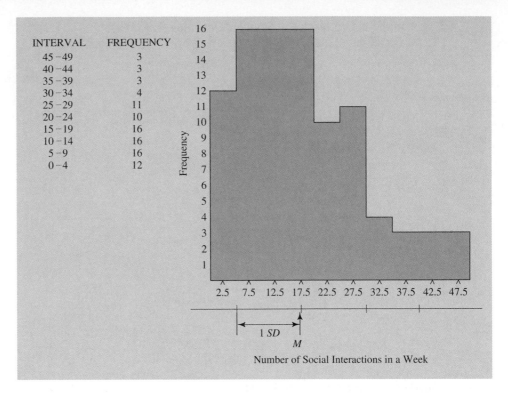

INTERVAL	FREQUENCY
45–49	3
40–44	3
35–39	3
30–34	4
25–29	11
20–24	10
15–19	16
10–14	16
5–9	16
0–4	12

FIGURE 2–11 *The standard deviation as the distance along the base of a histogram, using the example of number of social interactions in a week. (Data from McLaughlin-Volpe et al., 2002.)*

computer and statistics software, the *Student's Study Guide and Computer Workbook* accompanying this textbook includes material designed to give you experience doing statistics as psychologists normally would, working with standard statistics programs on a computer.)

THE VARIANCE AS THE SUM OF SQUARED DEVIATIONS DIVIDED BY *N* − 1

Researchers often use a slightly different kind of variance. We have defined the variance as the average of the squared deviation scores. Using that definition, you divide the sum of the squared deviation scores by the number of scores (that is, the variance is *SS* /*N*). But you will learn in Chapter 9 that for many purposes it is better to define the variance as the sum of squared deviation scores divided by *1 less than the number of scores*. In other words, for those purposes the variance is the sum of squared deviations dividing by *N* −1 (that is, variance is *SS*/[*N* − 1]). (You will learn in Chapter 9 that you use this dividing by *N* − 1 approach when you have scores from a particular group of people and you want to estimate what the variance would be for people in general who are like the ones you have scores for.)

The variances and standard deviations given in research articles are often figured using *SS*/(*N* − 1). Also, when calculators or computers give the variance or the standard deviation automatically, they are sometimes figured in this way. But don't worry. The approach you are learning in this chapter of dividing by *N* (that is, figuring variance as *SS*/*N*) is entirely correct for our purpose here, which is describing the variation in a group of scores. It is also entirely correct for the material covered in the rest of this chapter (Z scores of the kind we are using) and for the material you learn in Chapters 3 through 8. We mention this other approach (variance as $SS/[N-1]$) now only so that you will not be confused when you read about variance or standard deviation in other places or if your calculator or a computer program gives a surprising result. To keep things simple, we wait to discuss the dividing by $N-1$ approach until it is needed, starting in Chapter 9.

HOW ARE YOU DOING?

1. (a) Define the variance and (b) indicate what it tells you about a distribution and how this is different from what the mean tells you.
2. (a) Define the standard deviation, (b) describe its relation to the variance, and (c) explain what it tells you approximately about a group of scores.
3. Give the full formula for the variance and indicate what each of the symbols mean.
4. Figure the (a) variance and (b) standard deviation for the following scores: 2, 4, 3, and 7 ($M = 4$).
5. Explain the difference between a definitional and a computational formula.

ANSWERS:

1. (a) The variance is the average of the squared differences of each score from the mean. (b) The variance tells you about how spread out the scores are while the mean tells you the central tendency of the distribution.
2. (a) The standard deviation is the square root of the average of the squared deviations from the mean. (b) The standard deviation is the square root of the variance. (c) The standard deviation tells you approximately the average amount that scores differs from the mean.
3. $SD^2 = \Sigma(X - M)^2 / N$. SD^2 is the variance. Σ means the sum of what follows. X is for the scores for the variable being studied. M is the mean of the scores. N is the number of scores.
4. (a) $SD^2 = \Sigma(X - M)^2 / N = [(2 - 4)^2 + (4 - 4)^2 + (3 - 4)^2 + (7 - 4)^2] / 5 = 14/5 = 2.8$
   (b) $SD = \sqrt{SD^2} = \sqrt{3.5} = 1.87$.
5. A definitional formula is the standard formula that is in the straightforward form that shows the meaning of what the formula is figuring. A computational formula is a mathematically equivalent variation of the definitional formula that is easier to use if figuring by hand with a lot of scores, but it tends to obscure the underlying meaning.

Z SCORES

So far in this chapter you have learned how to describe a group of scores in terms of its mean and variation. In this section you learn how to describe a particular score in terms of where it fits into the overall group of scores. That is, you learn to describe a score in terms of whether it is above or below the average and how much it is above or below the average.

Suppose you are told that a patient, Alan, had seen the psychotherapist (the one we have been considering in this chapter) for 9 sessions. Now suppose also we do not know anything about how many sessions other patients have had with this therapist. In this situation, it is hard to tell whether Alan has attended a lot or a few sessions in relation to other patients. However, suppose we know that for the 10 patients of this therapist, the mean is 6 and the standard deviation is 2.57. With this knowledge, we can see that Alan attended an above-average number of sessions. We can also see that the amount Alan has attended more than the average (3 sessions more than average) was a bit more than this therapist's patients typically vary from the average. This is all shown in Figure 2–12.

FIGURE 2-12 *Number of sessions attended by patient Alan in relation to the overall distribution of number of sessions attended by all patients of the example psychotherapist.*

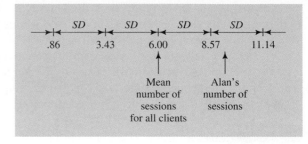

BOX 2–1   The Sheer Joy (Yes, Joy) of Statistical Analysis

You are learning statistics for the fun of it, right? No? Or maybe so, after all. Because if you become a psychologist, at some time or other you will form a hypothesis, gather some data, and analyze them. (Even if you plan a career as a psychotherapist, you will probably eventually wish to test an idea about the nature of your patients and their difficulties.) That hypothesis, your own original idea, and the data you gather to test it are going to be very important to you. Your heart may well be pounding with excitement as you analyze the statistics.

Consider some of the comments of social psychologists we interviewed for our book *The Heart of Social Psychology* (Aron & Aron, 1989). Deborah Richardson, who studies interpersonal relationships, confided that her favorite part of being a social psychologist is looking at the statistical output of the computer analyses:

> It's like putting together a puzzle. . . . It's a highly arousing, positive experience for me. I often go through periods of euphoria. Even when the data don't do what I want them to do . . . [there's a] physiological response. . . . It's exciting to see the numbers come off—Is it actually the way I thought it would be?—then thinking about the alternatives.

Harry Reis, former editor of the *Journal of Personality and Social Psychology,* sees his profession the same way:

By far the most rewarding part is when you get a new data set and start analyzing it and things pop out, partly a confirmation of what led you into the study in the first place, but then also other things. . . . "Why is that?" Trying to make sense of it. The kind of ideas that come from data. . . . I love analyzing data.

Bibb Latane, an eminent psychologist known for, among other things, his work on why people don't always intervene to help others who are in trouble, reports eagerly awaiting

> . . . the first glimmerings of what came out . . . [and] using them to shape what the next question should be. . . . You need to use everything you've got, . . . every bit of your experience and intuition. It's where you have the biggest effect, it's the least routine. You're in the room with the tiger, face to face with the core of what you are doing, at the moment of truth.

Bill Graziano, whose work integrates developmental and social psychology, calls the analysis of his data "great fun, just great fun." And in the same vein, Margaret Clark, who studies emotion and cognition, declares that "the most fun of all is getting the data and looking at them."

So you see? Statistics in the service of your own creative ideas can be a pleasure indeed.

WHAT IS A Z SCORE?

A **Z score** is the number of standard deviations the actual score is above the mean (if the score is positive) or below the mean (if the score is negative). The standard deviation now becomes a kind of yardstick, a unit of measure in its own right. In the psychotherapy example, Alan, who attended 9 sessions, has a Z score of +1.17. This is because Alan is 1.17 standard deviations above the mean (a little more than 1 standard deviation of 2.57 sessions above the mean). Another patient, Sarah, saw the therapist for 6 sessions. She has a Z score of 0 because her score is exactly the mean. That is, her score is 0 standard deviations above or below the mean. What about a patient who attended only 1 session? That patient attended 5 sessions less than average. This would be nearly 2 standard deviations below the mean (a Z score of −1.95). In terms of number of sessions, this patient would be about twice as far below average as patients of this therapist typically vary from average.

Z scores have many practical uses. They also are part of many of the statistical procedures you learn in this book. It is important that you become very familiar with them.

Z score

Z SCORES AS A SCALE

Figure 2–13 shows, for the therapy session example, a scale of Z scores lined up against a scale of raw scores. A **raw score** is an ordinary score as opposed to a Z score. The two scales are something like a ruler with inches lined up on one side and centimeters on the other.

raw score

Suppose that a developmental psychologist observed 3-year-old Peter in a laboratory situation playing with other children of the same age. During the observation, the psychologist counted the number of times Peter spoke to the other children. The result, over several observations, is that Peter spoke to other children about 8 times per hour of play. Without any standard of comparison, it would be hard to draw any conclusions from this. Let's assume, however, that it was known from previous research that under similar conditions, the mean number of times children speak is 12, with a standard deviation of 4. With that information, we can see that Peter spoke less often than other children in general, but not extremely less often. Peter would have a Z score of −1 ($M = 12$ and $SD = 4$, thus a score of 8 is 1 SD below M).

Suppose Ian was observed speaking to other children 20 times in an hour. Ian would clearly be unusually talkative, with a Z score of +2. Ian would speak not merely more than the average but more by twice as much as children tend to vary from the average! (See Figure 2–14.)

Z SCORES AS PROVIDING A GENERALIZED STANDARD OF COMPARISON

Another advantage of Z scores is that scores on completely different variables can be made into Z scores and compared. With Z scores, the mean is always 0 and the standard deviation is always 1.

Z score:	−2	−1	0	+1	+2
Raw score:	.86	3.43	6	8.57	11.14

FIGURE 2–13 *Scales of Z scores and raw scores in the psychotherapy session example.*

F I G U R E 2 – 1 4 *Number of times each hour that two children spoke, shown as raw scores and Z scores.*

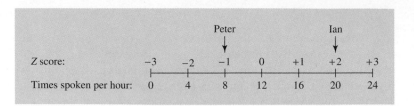

Suppose the same children in our example were also measured on a test of language skill. In this situation, we could directly compare the *Z* scores on language skill to the *Z* scores on speaking to other children. Let's say Peter had a score of 100 on the language skill test. If the mean on that test was 82 and the standard deviation was 6, then Peter is much better than average at language skill, with a *Z* score of +3. Thus, it seems that Peter's less than usual amount of speaking to other children is not due to poorer-than-usual language skill (see Figure 2–15).

Notice in this latest example that by using *Z* scores, you can directly compare the results of both the psychologist's observation of amount of talking and the language skill test. This is almost as wonderful as being able to compare apples and oranges! Converting a number to a *Z* score is a bit like converting words for measurement in various obscure languages into one language that everyone can understand—inches, cubits, and zingles (we made up that last one), for example, into centimeters. It is a very valuable tool.

FORMULA TO CHANGE A RAW SCORE TO A *Z* SCORE

As we have seen, a *Z* score is the number of standard deviations the raw score is above (or, if negative, below) the mean. To figure a *Z* score, subtract the mean from the raw score, giving the deviation score. Then divide the deviation score by the standard deviation. In symbols, the formula is

A *Z* score is the raw score minus the mean, divided by the standard deviation.

$$Z = \frac{X - M}{SD} \tag{2-8}$$

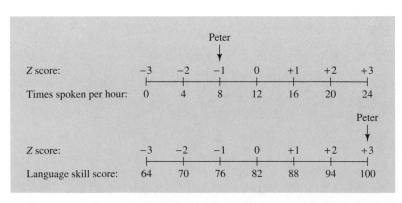

F I G U R E 2 – 1 5 *Scales of Z scores and raw scores for number of times spoken per hour and language skill, showing the first child's score on each.*

For example, using the formula for the child who scored 100 on the language test,

$$Z = \frac{X - M}{SD} = \frac{100 - 82}{6} = \frac{18}{6} = 3$$

STEPS TO CHANGE A RAW SCORE TO A Z SCORE

❶ **Figure the deviation score: Subtract the mean from the raw score.**
❷ **Figure the Z score: Divide the deviation score by the standard deviation.**

Using these steps for the child who scored 100 on the language test,

❶ **Figure the deviation score: Subtract the mean from the raw score.** $100 - 82 = 18$.
❷ **Figure the Z score: Divide the deviation score by the standard deviation.** $18/6 = 3$

FORMULA TO CHANGE A Z SCORE TO A RAW SCORE

To change a Z score to a raw score, the process is reversed: You multiply the Z score by the standard deviation and then add the mean. The formula is

(2-9) $$\boxed{X = (Z)(SD) + M}$$

> The raw score is the Z score times the standard deviation, plus the mean.

Suppose a child has a Z score of -1.5 on the language ability test. This child is 1.5 standard deviations below the mean. Because the standard deviation in this example is 6 raw score points, the child is 9 raw score points below the mean. The mean is 82. Thus, 9 points below this is 73. Using the formula,

$$X = (Z)(SD) + M = (-1.5)(6) + 82 = -9 + 82 = 73$$

STEPS TO CHANGE A Z SCORE TO A RAW SCORE

❶ **Figure the deviation score: Multiply the Z score by the standard deviation.**
❷ **Figure the raw score: Add the mean to the deviation score.**

Using these steps for the child with a Z score of -1.5 on the language test:

❶ **Figure the deviation score: Multiply the Z score by the standard deviation.** $-1.5 \times 6 = -9$
❷ **Figure the raw score: Add the mean to the deviation score.** $-9 + 82 = 73$.

ADDITIONAL EXAMPLES OF CHANGING Z SCORES TO RAW SCORES AND VICE VERSA

Consider again the stress ratings example. The mean of the 151 statistics students was 6.46, and the standard deviation was 2.30. Figure 2–16 shows the raw score and Z score scales. Suppose a student's stress raw score is 9. That student is well above the mean. Specifically, using the formula,

$$Z = \frac{X - M}{SD} = \frac{9 - 6.46}{2.30} = 1.10$$

That is, the student's stress level is 1.10 standard deviations above the mean.

Another student has a Z score of -2.37, a stress level well below the mean. You can find the exact raw stress score for this student using the formula

$$X = (Z)(SD) + M = (-2.37)(2.30) + 6.46 = -5.45 + 6.46 = 1.0$$

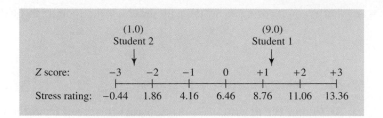

FIGURE 2–16   *Raw score and Z score scales for 151 statistics students' ratings of their stress level, showing scores of two sample students. (Data from Aron et al., 1995.)*

Let's also consider some examples from the study of students' number of social interactions in a week. The mean is 17.4 and the standard deviation is 11.49. A student who had 17 interactions in a week has a deviation score of $-.4$ (that is, $17 - 17.4 = -.4$). The Z score is then $-.03$ (that is, $-.4/11.49 = -.03$). This number of interactions is just below the mean. Similarly, a student who has 36 social interactions in a week has a deviation score of 18.6 (that is, $36 - 17.4 = 18.6$). The Z score is 1.62 (that is, $18.6/11.49 = 1.62$). This student is 1.62 standard deviations above the mean in terms of social interactions in a week.

To go the other way, suppose a student's Z score is .57. This student's raw score is the Z score times the standard deviation, plus the mean: $(.57)(11.49) + 17.4 = 23.95$ (rounded off, this person had 24 social interactions). This is all shown in Figure 2–17.

THE MEAN AND STANDARD DEVIATION OF Z SCORES

The mean of any distribution of Z scores is always 0. This is because when you change each raw score to a Z score, you take the raw score minus the mean. So the mean is subtracted out of all the raw scores, making the overall mean come out to zero. To put this another way, in any distribution, the sum of the positive Z scores must always equal the sum of the negative Z scores. Thus, when you add them all up, you get zero.

The standard deviation of any distribution of Z scores is always 1. This is because when you change each raw score to a Z score, you divide by the standard deviation. (Also, because the standard deviation is 1, the variance, the standard deviation squared, is always 1.)

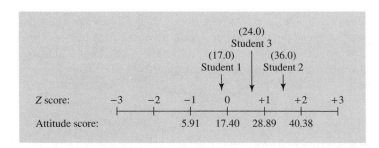

FIGURE 2–17   *Raw score and Z score scales for 94 students' number of social interactions in a week, showing scores of three sample students. (Data from McLaughlin-Volpe et al., 2002.)*

TABLE 2–4	**Figuring the Mean and the Standard Deviation of Z Scores in the Number of Therapy Sessions Example**

Number of Sessions (Raw Score)	Z Score for Number of Sessions	Z Score Mean	Z Score Deviation	Squared Z Score Deviation
7	.39	0	.39	.15
8	.78	0	.78	.61
8	.78	0	.78	.61
7	.39	0	.39	.15
3	−1.17	0	−1.17	1.37
1	−1.95	0	−1.95	3.80
6	0.00	0	0.00	0.00
9	1.17	0	1.17	1.37
3	−1.17	0	−1.17	1.37
8	.78	0	.78	.61
	Σ: 0.00			10.04[a]

$$M = \frac{\Sigma X}{N} = \frac{0}{10} = 0$$

$$SD^2 = \frac{\Sigma(X - M)^2}{N} = \frac{SS}{N} = \frac{10}{10} = 1$$

$$SD = \sqrt{1} = 1$$

[a]If there were no rounding error, this would equal exactly 10.

Table 2–4 shows the Z scores for the therapy session example, along with the figuring for the mean and standard deviation of the Z scores. As must be the case with Z scores, the mean comes out to 0 and the standard deviation (and variance), to 1.

A Z score is sometimes called a **standard score.** This is because Z scores have these standard values for the mean and the standard deviation. It is also because, as we saw earlier, Z scores provide a kind of standard scale of measurement for any variable. (However, sometimes the term *standard score* is used only when the Z scores are for a distribution that is a normal curve. You will learn in Chapter 5 that Z scores are even more useful when the distribution is a normal curve.)

standard score

Also, scores similar to Z scores are sometimes used in which the mean is a number other than 0 and the standard deviation is a number other than 1. For example, on some tests used by clinical psychologists, special scales are used in which the mean is 50 and the standard deviation is 10. Thus, a score on this scale of 65 would equal a Z score of 1.5.

HOW ARE YOU DOING?

1. What is a Z score (that is, how is it related to a raw score)?
2. Write the formula for changing a raw score to a Z score, and define each of the symbols.
3. For a particular group of scores, $M = 20$ and $SD = 5$. Give the Z score for (a) 30, (b) 15, (c) 20, and (d) 22.5.
4. Write the formula for changing a Z score to a raw score, and define each of the symbols.
5. For a particular group of scores, $M = 10$ and $SD = 2$. Give the raw score for a Z score of (a) +2, (b) +.5, (c) 0, and (d) −3.

6. Suppose a person has a *Z* score for overall health of $+2$ and a *Z* score for overall sense of humor of $+1$. What does it mean to say that this person is healthier than she is funny?

ANSWERS:

1. A *Z* score is the number of standard deviations a raw score is above or below the mean.
2. $Z = (X - M)/SD$. *Z* is the *Z* score; *X* is the raw score; *M* is the mean; *SD* is the standard deviation.
3. (a) $Z = (X - M)/SD = (30 - 20)/5 = 10/5 = 2$; (b) -1; (c) 0; (d) $+.5$
4. $X = (Z)(SD) + M$. *X* is the raw score; *Z* is the *Z* score; *SD* is the standard deviation; *M* is the mean.
5. (a) $X = (Z)(SD) + M = (2)(2) + 10 = 4 + 10 = 14$; (b) 11; (c) 10; (d) 4.
6. This person is more above the average in health (in terms of how much people typically vary from average in health) than this person is above the average in humor (in terms of how much people typically vary from the average in humor).

CONTROVERSY: THE TYRANNY OF THE MEAN

Looking in psychology research journals, you would think that statistics are the discipline's sole tool or language. But there has always been an undercurrent of dissatisfaction with a purely numerical approach. Throughout this book we want to keep you informed about controversies among psychologists about statistics; one place to begin seems to be the controversy about the overuse of statistics itself.

It's rarely discussed, but the "father of psychology," Wilhelm Wundt, thought experiments and statistics should be limited to topics such as perception and memory. The proper approach to all of the rest of psychology was the analysis and interpretation of meaning, without numbers (McLeod, 1996).

Behaviorism is often portrayed as the school of psychology historically most dedicated to keeping the field strictly scientific. Behaviorism began around 1913 with the rejection of the study of inner states because they are impossible to observe objectively. (Today most research psychologists attempt to measure inner events indirectly but objectively.) But behaviorism's most ardent spokesperson, B. F. Skinner, was utterly opposed to statistics. Skinner even said, "I would much rather see a graduate student in psychology taking a course in physical chemistry than in statistics. And I would include [before statistics] other sciences, even poetry, music, and art" (Evans, 1976, p. 93).

Why was Skinner so opposed to statistics? He held that observing behavior is the best way to understand it, and that means observing individual cases. He constantly pointed to the information lost by averaging the results of a number of cases. For instance, Skinner (1956) cited the example of three overeating mice—one naturally obese, one poisoned with gold, and one whose hypothalamus had been altered. Each had a different learning curve (pattern of rate of learning) to press a bar for food, revealing much about the eating habits created by each condition. If these learning curves had been summed or merged statistically, the result would have failed to represent actual eating habits of any real mouse. As Skinner said, "These three individual curves contain more information than could probably ever be generated with measures requiring statistical treatment, yet they will be viewed with suspicion by many psychologists because they are single cases" (p. 232).

A different voice of caution was raised by humanistic psychology, which began in the 1950s as a "third force" in reaction to both behaviorism and the main alternative at the time, Freudian psychoanalysis. The point of humanistic psychology was that human consciousness should be studied intact, as a whole, as it is experienced by individuals. Although statistics can be usefully applied to ascertain the mathematical relationships between phenomena, including events in consciousness, human experience can never be fully explained by reducing it to numbers (any more than it can be reduced to words). Each individual's experience is unique.

In clinical psychology and the study of personality, voices have often been raised to argue that much more of what really matters in psychology can be learned from the in-depth study of one person than from averages of persons—the *idiographic* versus the *nomothetic* approaches, to use the terms Gordon Allport borrowed from Wilhelm Windelband (see Hilgard, 1987). The philosophical underpinnings of the in-depth study of individuals can be found in phenomenology, which began in Europe after World War I (see Husserl, 1970).

Phenomenology is a philosophical position opposed to logical positivism. Logical positivism argues that there is an objective reality to be known. This is the philosophical position that traditionally underlies scientific efforts. Science is said to be able to uncover this objective or true reality because science uses experiments that anyone can observe or repeat to obtain the same results. Phenomenologists argue, however, that even these repeated observations are really private events in consciousness. You can never know whether what you mean by "green" or "the rat pressed the bar seven times" is what anyone else means by those words.

According to phenomenologists, science ought to be founded on the study of the filter through which all scientific data must come—human consciousness. Husserl sought to uncover through reflection the basic structures of consciousness, whatever is common to all human descriptions of a given experience. He hoped to "bracket" the psychologist's own personal assumptions about the experience so that only the other's experience was being considered. Later, the existential phenomenologists such as Heidegger focused on these essences as being inextricably bound up with our participation in experience. The essences are not in us alone, but a product of our being-in-the-world. No amount of reflection can bracket all of the effects of our habitual thinking about the world and the particular language we speak, which gives us the very words we have available for doing phenomenology.

More recently, we have seen an even broader spectrum of possible assumptions to be taken when analyzing data, from a continued faith in a discoverable reality to more postmodern thinking—"post" referring to after the loss of faith by some in a vision of inevitable human progress through a science based on logical positivism. These new views range from assuming there is a true reality but we will never know it completely to feeling all knowledge is socially constructed by those in power—lacking any basis in true reality—and should be challenged for the sake of the powerless (Highlen & Finley, 1996).

Today's main challenge to statistics comes from the strong revival of interest in "qualitative" research methods. There has been a growing concern among some psychologists that after 100 years of quantitative statistical research, psychology has yielded what they believe to be very little useful social knowledge (Jessor, 1996). Their hope is that carefully studying a few humans in context, as a whole, will do better.

Qualitative methods include case studies, ethnography, phenomenology, symbolic interactionism, systems studies, and "action inquiry" (Highlen & Finley, 1996). These methods were developed mainly in anthropology, where behaviorism and logical positivism never gained the hold that they did in psychology. Qualitative methods typically involve long interviews or observations of a few individuals, with the highly skilled researcher deciding as the event is taking place what is important to remember, record, and pursue through more questions or observations. According to this approach, the mind of the researcher is the main tool because only that mind can find the important relationships among the many categories of events arising in the respondent's speech.

Phenomenological psychology is a good example of an alternative to quantitative research, one that has been in use for 30 years. It leads to a detailed account of an experience, which we can presume is being shared by others like the individual studied. Evidence for its usefulness comes from research by Hein and Austin (2001) that compared two methods to study a single individual's experience, the experience of trying to balance work and family life. One method (used by Hein in this research) was empirical phenomenology, the most common form of phenomenological research. It tries to reflect on actual events described in the interview, sometimes tabulates data from the interview, states the steps that led to its findings so others can replicate them, and stresses rigor over creativity, although still recognizing that the researcher has to some degree interpreted or participated in shaping the results.

The other method (used by Austin in this research) was hermeneutical phenomenology, which makes no attempt to describe a systematic method or to bracket the researcher's experience. Rather, it seeks to use the researcher's personal exploration of the experience through interviews, reading, studying art work about the experience, and living it, all in order to arrive at one view of the phenomenon, a deep uncovering, which the reader can then continue.

When Hein and Austin compared what each had learned using their respective methods, they found it was highly similar, an encouraging sign that phenomenological psychologists can indeed "reveal meaning despite . . . the difficulties associated with interpreting meaning" (2001, p. 3).

Some psychologists (e.g., Kenny, 1995; McCracken, 1988) argue that quantitative and qualitative methods can and should complement each other. We should first discover the important categories through a qualitative approach, then determine their incidence in the larger population through quantitative methods. Too often, these psychologists argue, quantitative researchers jump to conclusions about the important categories without first exploring the human experience of them through free-response interviews or observations.

Finally, we want to mention the quite different thoughts of psychiatrist Carl Jung on what he called the "statistical mood." As the Jungian analyst Marie Louise von Franz (1979) expressed it, we are in the statistical mood when we walk down a street and observe the hundreds of blank faces and begin to feel diminished. We feel just one of the crowd, ordinary. Or when we are in love, we feel that the other person is unique and wonderful. Yet in a statistical mood, we realize that the other person is ordinary, like many others.

Von Franz points out, however, that if some catastrophe were to happen, each person would respond uniquely. There is at least as much irregularity to life as ordinariness.

> The fact that this table does not levitate, but remains where it is, is only because the billions and billions and billions of electrons which constitute the table tend statistically to behave like that. But each electron in itself could do something else. (p. IV-17)

Jung did not cherish individual uniqueness just to be romantic about it, however. He held that the important contributions to culture tend to come from people thinking at least a little independently or creatively, and their independence is damaged by this statistical mood.

The statistical mood is damaging to love and life, according to von Franz. To counteract it, "An act of loyalty is required towards one's own feelings" (p. IV-18). Feeling "makes your life and your relationships and deeds feel unique and gives them a definite value" (pp. IV-18–IV-19). In particular, feeling the importance of our single action makes immoral acts—war and killing, for example—less possible. We cannot count the dead as numbers but must treat them as persons with emotions and purposes, like ourselves.

In short, there have always been good reasons for limiting our statistical thinking to its appropriate domains and leaving our heart free to rule in others.

THE MEAN AND STANDARD DEVIATION IN RESEARCH ARTICLES

The mean and the standard deviation (and occasionally, the variance) are very commonly reported in research articles. Z scores, though extremely important as steps in advanced procedures you will learn later, are rarely reported directly in research articles.

Sometimes the mean and standard deviation are included in the text of an article. For example, our fictional psychotherapist might write, "The mean number of sessions for the last 10 patients was 6.0 ($SD = 2.57$)."

Means and standard deviations are also often listed in tables, especially if a study includes several groups or several different variables. For example, Payne (2001) gave participants a computerized task in which they first see a face and then a picture of either a gun or a tool. The task was to press one button if it was a tool and a different one if it was a gun. Unknown to the participants while they were doing the study, the faces served as a "prime" (something that starts you thinking a particular way) and half the time were of a black person and half the time of a white person.

Table 2–5 (reproduced from Payne's Table 1) shows the means and standard deviations for reaction times (time to decide if the picture is of a gun or a tool) after either a black or white prime under the different conditions. For example, in Experi-

---

TABLE 2–5 **Mean Reaction Times (in Milliseconds) in Identifying Guns and Tools in Experiments 1 and 2**

| | Prime | | | |
| | Black | | White | |
Target	M	SD	M	SD
Experiment 1				
Gun	423	64	441	73
Tool	454	57	446	60
Experiment 2				
Gun	299	28	295	31
Tool	307	29	304	29

Source: Payne, 2001.

ment 1, after a black prime, it took participants a mean of 423 milliseconds (thousandths of a second) to recognize the gun pictures; but after a white prime it took 441 milliseconds. (The results for Experiment 2 show a different pattern because in that study participants were told to decide as fast as possible. In another table Payne shows that when rushing, participants were more *accurate* at seeing something as a gun with the black prime.)

Table 2–6 (reproduced from Table 7 in Norcross et al., 1996) is a particularly interesting example. It does not give standard deviations, but it does give both means and medians. For example, in 1992 the mean number of applicants to doctoral counseling psychology programs was 120.2, but the median was only 110. This suggests that there were some programs with very high numbers of applicants that skewed the distribution. In fact, you can see from the table that for almost every kind of program, and for both applications and enrollments, the means are typically higher than the medians. (You may also be struck by just how competitive it is to get into doctoral programs in many areas of psychology. It is our experience that one of the factors that makes a lot of difference is doing well in statistics courses!)

SUMMARY

1. The mean is the ordinary average—the sum of the scores divided by the number of scores. In symbols, $M = \Sigma X/N$.

TABLE 2–6 Application and Enrollment Statistics by Area and Year: Doctoral Programs

| | Applications | | | | | | | | | Enrollments | |
| | N of programs | | | M | | | Mdn | | | M | Mdn |
Program	1973[a]	1979[a]	1992	1973[a]	1979[a]	1992	1973[a]	1979[a]	1992	1992	1992
Clinical	105	130	225	314.4	252.6	191.1	290	234	168	12.0	8
Cognitive			47			24.6			22	2.6	2
Community	4	2	5	90.5		24.4	60		23	3.2	2
Counseling	29	43	62	133.4	90.9	120.2	120	84	110	7.3	6
Developmental	56	72	97	54.1	38.9	27.6	41	30	24	2.8	2
Educational	23	28	30	67.8	39.7	20.0	34	26	12	6.0	4
Experimental and general	118	127	78	56.2	33.2	31.3	42	25	26	4.4	3
Health			7			40.7			30	4.4	5
Industrial/organizational	20	25	49	39.9	54.7	66.2	37	48	70	4.9	4
Personality	23	15	10	42.5	24.7	12.3	33	17	6	1.0	1
Perception/psychophysics			15			8.3			6	1.4	1
Physiological/biopsychology	40	43	76	33.2	29.3	20.0	29	24	20	3.9	2
School	30	39	56	78.5	54.0	31.3	53	34	32	5.4	5
Social	58	72	59	46.7	30.9	47.1	40	24	37	3.3	3
Other	47	37	273	61.6	74.1	26.6	27	25	15	3.3	2
Total	566	645	1,089	106.1	85.2	69.4			31	5.6	4

Note: The academic years correspond to the 1975–1976, 1981–1982, and 1994 editions of *Graduate Study in Psychology,* respectively.
[a]Data are from Stoup and Benjamin (1982).

From J. C. Norcross, J. M. Hanych, & R. D. Terranova, tab. 7. "Graduate study in psychology: 1992–1993" *American Psychologist,* 51, 631–643. Copyright © 1996 by The American Psychological Association. Reprinted with permission of the authors and the American Psychological Association.

2. Other, less commonly used ways of describing the central tendency of a distribution of scores are the mode (the most common single value) and the median (the value of the middle score when all the scores are lined up from lowest to highest).

3. The variation among a group of scores can be described by the variance—the average of the squared deviation of each score from the mean. In symbols, $SD^2 = \Sigma(X - M)^2/N$. The sum of squared deviations is also symbolized as SS. Thus $SD^2 = SS/N$.

4. The standard deviation is the square root of the variance. In symbols, $SD = \sqrt{SD^2}$. It can be best understood as approximately the average amount that scores differ from the mean.

5. A Z score is the number of standard deviations a raw score is above or below the mean. Among other uses, with Z scores you can compare scores on variables that have different scales.

6. There have always been a few psychologists who have warned against statistical methodology because in the process of creating averages, knowledge about the individual case is lost.

7. Means and standard deviations are often given in research articles in the text or in tables. Z scores are rarely reported in research articles.

KEY TERMS

central tendency (p. 35)
computational formula (p. 48)
definitional formula (p. 49)
deviation score (p. 44)
mean (M) (p. 35, 36)
median (p. 41)

mode (p. 39)
N (p. 37)
raw score (p. 53)
squared deviation score (p. 44)
standard deviation (SD) (p. 45)

standard score (p. 57)
sum of squared deviations (SS) (p. 45)
sum of squares (SS) (p. 47)
variance (SD^2) (p. 44)
Z score (p. 53)
Σ (p. 36)

EXAMPLE WORKED-OUT COMPUTATIONAL PROBLEMS

FIGURING THE MEAN

Find the mean for the following scores: 8, 6, 6, 9, 6, 5, 6, 2.
You can figure the mean using the formula or the steps.
Using the formula: $M = \Sigma X/N = 48/8 = 6$.
Using the steps:

❶ **Add up all the scores.** $8 + 6 + 6 + 9 + 6 + 5 + 6 + 2 = 48$.
❷ **Divide this sum by the number of scores.** $48/8 = 6$.

FINDING THE MEDIAN

Find the median for the following scores: 1, 7, 4, 2, 3, 6, 2, 9, 7.

❶ **Line up all the scores from lowest to highest.** 1, 2, 2, 3, 4, 6, 7, 7, 9.
❷ **Figure how many scores there are to the middle score. If you have an odd number of scores, divide the number of scores in half and add ½. If an even number of scores, divide the number in half—this and the score above it are the two middle scores.** There are an odd number of scores, so the middle score is half of 9 plus ½. This comes out to 4 ½ plus ½, which is 5. The middle score is the fifth score.

❸ **Count up to the middle score. If you have an odd number of scores, this is the median. If an even number of scores, the median is the average of the two middle scores.** The fifth score from the bottom is a 4. There are an odd number of scores, so the median is 4.

FIGURING THE SUM OF SQUARES AND THE VARIANCE

Find the sum of squares and the variance for the following scores: 8, 6, 6, 9, 6, 5, 6, 2. (These are the same scores used above for the mean. $M = 6$.)

You can figure the sum of squares and the variance using the formulas or the steps.

Using the formulas:

$$SS = (X - M)^2 = (8 - 6)^2 + (6 - 6)^2 + (6 - 6)^2 + (9 - 6)^2 + (6 - 6)^2$$
$$+ (5 - 6)^2 + (6 - 6)^2 + (2 - 6)^2$$
$$= 2^2 + 0^2 + 0^2 + 3^2 + 0^2 + -1^2 + 0^2 + -4^2 = 4 + 0 + 0 + 9 + 0 + 1$$
$$+ 16 = 30$$
$$SD^2 = SS/N = 30/8 = 3.75$$

Table 2–7 shows the figuring, using the following steps:

❶ **Subtract the mean from each score.**
❷ **Square each of these deviation scores.**
❸ **Add up the squared deviation scores.**
❹ **Divide the sum of squared deviations by the number of squared deviations.**

FIGURING THE STANDARD DEVIATION

Find the standard deviation for the following scores: 8, 6, 6, 9, 6, 5, 6, 2. (These are the same scores used above for the mean, sum of squares, and variance. $SD^2 = 3.75$.)

You can figure the standard deviation using the formula or the steps.

Using the formula: $SD = \sqrt{SD^2} = \sqrt{3.75} = 1.94$.

Using the steps:

❶ **Figure the variance.** The variance (from above) is 3.75.
❷ **Take the square root.** The square root of 3.75 is 1.94.

TABLE 2–7 **Figuring for Worked-Out (Computational Problem for the Variance Using Steps**

		❶	❷
Score	Mean	Deviation	Squared Deviation
8	6	2	4
6	6	0	0
6	6	0	0
9	6	3	9
6	6	0	0
5	6	−1	1
6	6	0	0
2	6	−4	16
			Σ = 30 ❸

❹ Variance = 30/8 = 3.75

CHANGING A RAW SCORE TO A Z SCORE

A distribution has a mean of 80 and a standard deviation of 20. Find the Z score for a raw score of 65.

You can change a raw score to a Z score using the formula or the steps.

Using the formula: $Z = (X - M)/SD = (65 - 80)/20 = -15/20 = -.75$

Using the steps:

❶ **Figure the deviation score: Subtract the mean from the raw score.** $65 - 80 = -15$.

❷ **Figure the Z score: Divide the deviation score by the standard deviation.** $-15/20 = .75$

CHANGING A Z SCORE TO A RAW SCORE

A distribution has a mean of 200 and a standard deviation of 50. A person has a Z score of 1.26. What is the person's raw score?

You can change a Z score to a raw score using the formula or the steps.

Using the formula: $X = (Z)(SD) + M = (1.26)(50) + 200 = 63 + 200 = 263$

Using the steps:

❶ **Figure the deviation score: Multiply the Z score by the standard deviation.** $1.26 \times 50 = 63$

❷ **Figure the raw score: Add the mean to the deviation score.** $63 + 200 = 263$

PRACTICE PROBLEMS

These problems involve figuring. Most real life statistics problems are done on a computer. However, even if you have a computer and statistics software, do these by hand (with the help of a calculator) to ingrain the method in your mind. Also, in all problems involving figuring, be sure to show your work.

For practice in using a computer to solve statistics problems, refer to the computer section of each chapter of the *Student's Study Guide and Computer Workbook* that accompanies this text.

All data are fictional unless an actual citation is given.

Answers to Set I problems are given at the back of the book.

SET I

1. Find the (a) mean, (b) median, (c) sum of squared deviations, (d) variance, and (e) standard deviation for the following scores:

   32, 28, 24, 28, 28, 31, 35, 29, 26

2. Find the (a) mean, (b) median, (c) sum of squared deviations, (d) variance, and (e) standard deviation for the following scores:

   6, 1, 4, 2, 3, 4, 6, 6

3. Here are the noon temperatures (in degrees Celsius) in a particular Canadian city at noon on December 26 for the 10 years from 1993 through 2002: -5, -4, -1, -1, 0, -8, -5, -9, -13, and -24. Describe the typical temperature and the amount of variation to a person who has never had a course in statistics. Give three ways of describing the typical temperature and two ways of describing its variation, explaining the differences and how you figured each. (You will learn more if you try to write your own answer first, before reading our answer at the back of the book.)

4. A researcher is studying the amygdala (a part of the brain involved in emotion). Six participants in a particular fMRI (brain scan) study are measured for the increase in activation of their amygdala while they are viewing pictures of violent scenes. The activation increases are .43, .32, .64, .21, .29, and .51. Figure the (a) mean and (b) standard deviation for these six activation increases. (c) Explain what you have done and what the results mean to a person who has never had a course in statistics.

5. On a measure of anxiety, the mean is 79 and the standard deviation is 12. What are the *Z* scores for each of the following actual scores? (a) 91, (b) 68, and (c) 103.

6. On a particular intelligence test, the mean number of items correct is 231, and the standard deviation is 41. What are the actual (raw) scores on this test for people with IQs of (a) 107, (b) 83, and (c) 100? (IQ is figured as 100, plus the *Z* score times 16. That is, an IQ score is set up to have a mean of 100 and a standard deviation of 16.) (*Note:* To do this problem, first figure the *Z* score for the particular IQ score; then use that *Z* score to find the raw score.)

7. Six months after a divorce, the former wife and husband each take a test that measures divorce adjustment. The wife's score is 63, and the husband's score is 59. Overall, the mean score for divorced women on this test is 60 (*SD* = 6); the mean score for divorced men is 55 (*SD* = 4). Which of the two has adjusted better to the divorce in relation to other divorced people of the same gender? Explain your answer to a person who has never had a course in statistics.

8. A researcher studied the number of dreams recounted over a 2-week period by 30 people in psychotherapy. In an article describing the results of the study, the researcher reports: "The mean number of dreams was 6.84 (*SD* = 3.18)." Explain these results to a person who has never had a course in statistics.

9. In a study by Gonzaga et al. (2001), romantic couples answered questions about how much they loved their partner and also were videotaped while revealing something about themselves to their partner. The videotapes were later rated by trained judges for various signs of affiliation. Table 2–8 (reproduced from their Table 2) shows some of the results. Explain to a person who has never had a course in statistics the results for self-reported love for the partner and for the number of seconds "leaning toward the partner."

TABLE 2–8   Mean Levels of Emotions and Cue Display in Study 1

Indicator	Women (*n* = 60)		Men (*n* = 60)	
	M	*SD*	*M*	*SD*
Emotion reports				
Self-reported love	5.02	2.16	5.11	2.08
Partner-estimated love	4.85	2.13	4.58	2.20
Affiliation-cue display				
Affirmative head nods	1.28	2.89	1.21	1.91
Duchenne smiles	4.45	5.24	5.78	5.59
Leaning toward partner	32.27	20.36	31.36	21.08
Gesticulation	0.13	0.40	0.25	0.77

Note: Emotions are rated on a scale of 0 (*none*) to 8 (*extreme*). Cue displays are shown as mean seconds displayed per 60 s.
Source: Gonzaga et al., 2001.

SET II

10. (a) Describe and explain the difference between the mean, median, and mode. (b) Make up an example (not in the book or in your lectures) in which the median would be the preferred measure of central tendency.

11. (a) Describe the variance and standard deviation. (b) Explain why the standard deviation is more often used as a descriptive statistic.

12. Find the (a) mean, (b) median, (c) sum of squared deviations, (d) variance, and (e) standard deviation.

   2, 2, 0, 5, 1, 4, 1, 3, 0, 0, 1, 4, 4, 0, 1, 4, 3, 4, 2, 1, 0

13. Find the (a) mean, (b) median, (c) sum of squared deviations, (d) variance, and (e) standard deviation.

   1,112; 1,245; 1,361; 1,372; 1,472

14. Find the (a) mean, (b) median, (c) sum of squared deviations, (d) variance, and (e) standard deviation.

   3.0, 3.4, 2.6, 3.3, 3.5, 3.2

15. Find the (a) mean, (b) median, (c) sum of squared deviations, (d) variance, and (e) standard deviation.

   8, −5, 7, −10, 5

16. Make up three sets of scores: (a) one with the mean greater than the median, (b) one with the median and the mean the same, and (c) one with the mode greater than the median. (Each made-up set of scores should include at least 5 scores.)

17. A psychologist interested in political behavior measured the square footage of the desks in the official office of four U.S. governors and of four chief executive officers (CEOs) of major U.S. corporations. The figures for the governors were 44, 36, 52, and 40 square feet. The figures for the CEOs were 32, 60, 48, and 36 square feet. (a) Figure the mean and standard deviation for the governors and for the CEOs. (b) Explain what you have done to a person who has never had a course in statistics. (c) Note the ways in which the means and standard deviations differ, and speculate on the possible meaning of these differences, presuming that they are representative of U.S. governors and large corporations' CEOs in general.

18. A developmental psychologist studies the number of words seven infants have learned at a particular age. The numbers are 10, 12, 8, 0, 3, 40, and 18. Figure the (a) mean, (b) median, and (c) standard deviation for the number of words learned by these seven infants. (d) Explain what you have done and what the results mean to a person who has never had a course in statistics.

19. On a measure of artistic ability, the mean for college students in New Zealand is 150 and the standard deviation is 25. Give the Z scores for New Zealand college students who score (a) 100, (b) 120, (c) 140, and (d) 160. Give the raw scores for persons whose Z scores on this test are (e) −1, (f) −.8, (g) −.2, and (h) +1.38.

20. On a standard measure of hearing ability, the mean is 300 and the standard deviation is 20. Give the Z scores for persons who score (a) 340, (b) 310, and (c) 260. Give the raw scores for persons whose Z scores on this test are (d) 2.4, (e) 1.5, (f) 0, and (g) −4.5.

21. A person scores 81 on a test of verbal ability and 6.4 on a test of quantitative ability. For the verbal ability test, the mean for people in general is 50 and the standard deviation is 20. For the quantitative ability test, the mean for people in general is 0 and the standard deviation is 5. Which is this person's stronger ability: verbal or quantitative? Explain your answer to a person who has never had a course in statistics.

TABLE 2–9 Descriptive Statistics for News Coverage Variables Aggregated by Month, *New York Times Index,* January 1981–November 1992.

	Mean	Standard Deviation	Range	Total
Total Front-Page Articles	5.84	4.10	0–22	835
Positive Front-Page Articles	1.64	1.33	0–6	261
Negative Front-Page Articles	1.83	1.92	0–11	234

Note: From "Media Coverage of the Economy and Aggregate Economic Evaluations" by Robert K. Goidel and Ronald E. Langley, *Political Research Quarterly,* Vol. 48, #2, June 1995. Reprinted by permission of the University of Utah, Copyright Holder.
Source: New York Times Index.

22. A study involves measuring the number of days absent from work for 216 employees of a large company during the preceding year. As part of the results, the researcher reports, "The number of days absent during the preceding year ($M = 9.21$; $SD = 7.34$) was. . . ." Explain what is written in parentheses to a person who has never had a course in statistics.

23. Goidel and Langley (1995) studied the positivity and negativity of newspaper accounts of economic events in the period just before the 1992 U.S. Presidential election. Table 2–9, reproduced from their report, describes the numbers of front-page articles on economic news in the *New York Times* for the 23 months preceding the election. Explain the results in the Mean and Standard Deviation columns to a person who has never had a course in statistics. (Be sure to explain some specific numbers as well as the general principle.)

CHAPTER 3

CORRELATION

Are You Ready?
What You Need to Have Mastered Before Starting this Chapter:

- Chapters 1 and 2

One hundred thirteen married people in the small college town of Santa Cruz, California, responded to a questionnaire in the local newspaper about their relationships. (This was part of a larger study reported by Aron et al., 2000). Consider one of the findings: The more they engaged in exciting activities with their partner, the more satisfied they reported being in their marriage.

Figure 3–1 is a graph of the results for these 113 people. The horizontal axis is for responses to the question "How exciting are the things you do together with your partner?" answered on a scale from 1 Not exciting at all to 5 Extremely exciting. The vertical axis is for scores on the standard measure of marital satisfaction used in this study. (This marital satisfaction questionnaire included items such as "In general, how often do you think that things between you and your partner are going well?") Each person's score is shown as a dot.

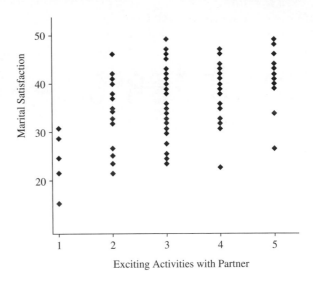

FIGURE 3–1 *Scatter diagram showing the correlation for 113 married individuals between doing exciting activities with their partner and their marital satisfaction. (Data from Aron et al., 2000.)*

correlation

The overall pattern is that the dots go from the lower left to the upper right. That is, lower scores on one variable more often go with lower scores on the other variable, and higher with higher. Even though the pattern is far from one to one, you can see a general trend. This general pattern of high scores on one variable going with high scores on the other variable, low scores going with low scores, and moderate with moderate, is an example of a **correlation.**

There are countless examples of correlation: Among students, there is a correlation between high school grades and college grades; in children, there is a correlation between age and coordination skills; in the marketplace, we often assume that a correlation exists between price and quality—that high prices go with high quality and low with low.

This chapter explores correlation, including how to describe it graphically, different types of correlations, how to figure the correlation coefficient (which describes the degree of correlation), correlation and causality, and issues about how to interpret a correlation coefficient. Chapter 4 discusses how you can use correlation to predict a person's score on one variable based on that person's score on another variable (for example, to predict a student's college grades based on his or her high school grades). In considering correlation and prediction, we move from the statistics for a single variable (Chapters 1 and 2) to statistics about the relationship between two or more variables.

GRAPHING CORRELATIONS: THE SCATTER DIAGRAM

scatter diagram

Figure 3–1, showing the correlation between exciting activities and marital satisfaction, is an example of a **scatter diagram** (also called a *scatterplot*). A scatter diagram shows you at a glance the degree and pattern of the relationship between the two variables.

HOW TO MAKE A SCATTER DIAGRAM

There are three steps to making a scatter diagram:

❶ **Draw the axes and decide which variable goes on which axis.** Often, it doesn't matter which variable goes on which axis. However, sometimes the logic of the study is that one variable is thought of as predicting or causing the other. In that situation, the one that is doing the predicting goes on the horizontal axis and the variable that is being predicted goes on the vertical axis. In Figure 3–1, we put exciting activities on the horizontal axis and marital satisfaction on the vertical axis because in the context of the study, we were working from a theory that exciting activities predict marital satisfaction. (We will have more to say about this later in the chapter when we discuss causality and also in Chapter 4 when we discuss prediction.)

❷ **Determine the range of values to use for each variable and mark them on the axes.** Your numbers should go from low to high on each axis, starting from where the axes meet. Usually, your low value on each axis is 0. However, you can use a higher value to start each axis if the lowest value your measure can possibly have is a lot higher than 0 in the group you are studying. For example, if a variable is age and you are studying college students, you might start that axis with 16 or 17, rather than 0.

The axis should continue to the highest value your measure can possibly have. When there is no obvious highest possible value, make the axis go to a value that is as high as people ordinarily score in the group of people of interest for your study.

In Figure 3–1, the horizontal axis is for the question about exciting activities, which participants answered on a scale of 1 to 5. We start the axis at 0 because this is standard, even though the lowest possible score on the scale is 1. We went up to 5, because that is the highest possible value on the scale. Similarly, the vertical axis goes from 0 to 60, since the highest possible scores on the marital satisfaction test is 60. (The test had 10 items, each answered on a 1 to 6 scale).

Note also that scatter diagrams are usually made roughly square, with the horizontal and vertical axes being about the same length (a 1:1 ratio). This is different from the histogram and frequency polygon graphs described in Chapter 1, which are usually wider than they are high (about a 1.5:1 width-to-height ratio).

❸ **Mark a dot for each person's pair of scores.** Find the place on the horizontal axis for that person's score on the horizontal-axis variable. Next, move up to the height for the person's score on the vertical-axis variable. Then mark a clear dot. Sometimes there are two persons with the same pair of scores so that their dots would go in the same place. When this happens, you can put a second dot as near as possible to the first—touching, if possible—but making it clear that there are in fact two dots in the one place. Alternatively, you can put the number 2 in that place.

AN EXAMPLE

Suppose a researcher is studying the relation of sleep to mood. As an initial test, the researcher asks 10 students in her morning seminar two questions:

1. How many hours did you sleep last night?
2. How happy do you feel right now on a scale from 0 Not at all happy to 8 Extremely happy?

The (fictional) results are shown in Table 3–1. (In practice, a much larger group would be used in this kind of research. We are using an example with just 10 to keep things simple for learning. In fact, we have done a real version of this study. Results of the real study are similar to what we show here, except not as strong as the ones we made up to make the pattern clear for learning.)

Tip for Success

When making a scatter diagram, it is easiest if you use graph paper.

TABLE 3–1 Hours Slept Last Night and Happy Mood Example (Fictional Data)

Hours Slept	Happy Mood
7	4
9	5
8	3
9	7
8	4
6	1
8	3
7	2
10	6
8	5

❶ **Draw the axes and decide which variable goes on which axis.** Because sleep comes before mood, it makes most sense to think of sleep as the predictor. Thus, we put hours slept on the horizontal axis and happy mood on the vertical axis. (See Figure 3–2a.)

❷ **Determine the range of values to use for each variable and mark them on the axes.** For the horizontal axis, we start at 0 as usual (and the minimum amount of sleep possible is 0 hours). We do not know the maximum possible, but let us assume that students rarely sleep more than 12 hours. The vertical axis goes from 0 to 8, the lowest and highest scores possible on the happiness question. (See Figure 3–2b.)

❸ **Mark a dot for each person's pair of scores.** For the first student, the number of hours slept last night was 7. Move across to 7 on the horizontal axis. Then, move up to the point across from the 4 (the happy mood rating for the first student)

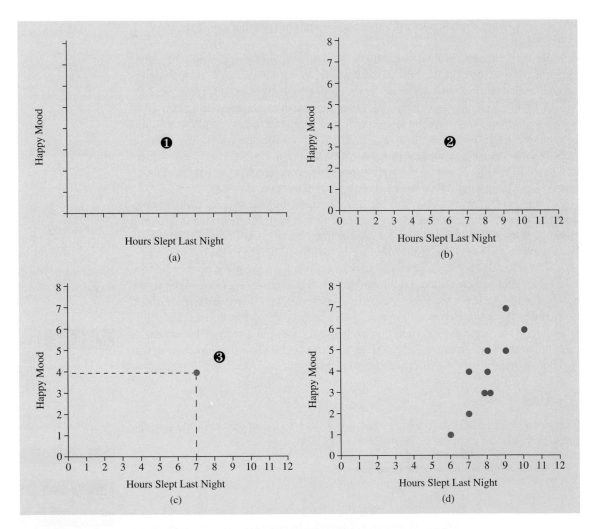

FIGURE 3–2 *Steps for making a scatter diagram. (a)* ❶ *Set up the axes—the predictor variable (hours slept last night) on the horizontal axis, the other (Happy Mood) on the other axis. (b)* ❷ *Determine the range of values and mark them on the axes. (c)* ❸ *Place a dot for the pair of scores for the first student. (d)* ❸ *continued: Place dots for the pairs of scores for all 10 students.*

on the vertical axis. Place a dot at this point. (See Figure 3–2c.) Do the same for each of the other nine students. The result should look like Figure 3–2d.

A SECOND EXAMPLE

Suppose that a memory researcher does an experiment to test a theory predicting that the number of exposures to a word increases the chance that the word will be remembered. Two research participants are randomly assigned to be exposed to the list of 10 words once, two participants to be exposed to the list twice, and so forth, up to a total of eight exposures to each word. This makes 16 participants in all, 2 for each of the eight levels of exposure.

Results are shown in Table 3–2. (An actual study of this kind would probably show a pattern in which the relative improvement in recall is less at higher numbers of exposures.)

❶ **Draw the axes and decide which variables go on which axis.** In this experiment, the number of exposures is intended to predict how many words will be recalled. Thus, the number of exposures goes on the horizontal axis, the number of words recalled, on the vertical axis (see Figure 3–3a).

❷ **Determine the range of values to use for each variable and mark them on the axes.** The number of exposures varies in the study from 1 to 8. Thus, we start with 0 for the sake of convention and go across to 8. The number of words remembered cannot be lower than 0 or more than 10, the total number on the list. (See Figure 3–3b.)

❸ **Mark a dot for each person's pair of scores.** The first dot goes above 1 on the horizontal axis and across from 4 on the vertical axis. Marking a dot for each person in the same way completes the scatter diagram (see Figure 3–3c).

TABLE 3–2	**Effect of Number of Exposures to Words on the Number of Words Recalled (Fictional Data)**	
Participant ID Number	Number of Exposures	Number of Words Recalled
1	1	4
2	1	3
3	2	3
4	2	5
5	3	6
6	3	4
7	4	4
8	4	6
9	5	5
10	5	7
11	6	2
12	6	9
13	7	6
14	7	8
15	8	9
16	8	8

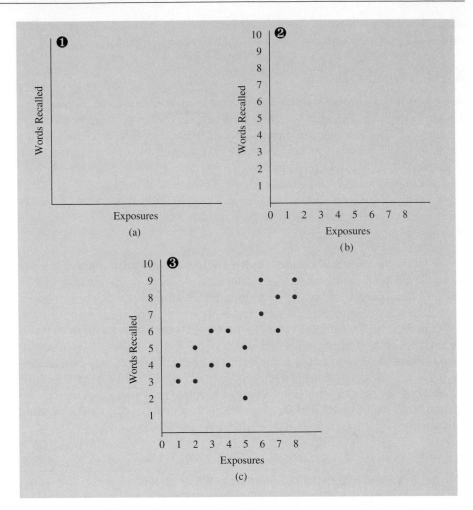

FIGURE 3–3 *Steps for making a scatter diagram for the scores in Table 3–2. (a)* ❶ *Set up the axes—the predictor variable (exposures) on the horizontal axis, the other (words recalled) on the other axis. (b)* ❷ *Determine the range of values and mark them on the axes. (c)* ❸ *Place a dot for each of the 16 participants' pair of scores. (Fictional data.)*

HOW ARE YOU DOING?

1. What does a scatter diagram show, and what does it consist of?
2. (a) Which variable goes on the horizontal axis? (b) Which on the vertical axis?
3. Make a scatter diagram for the scores shown below for four people who were each tested on two variables, X and Y. X is the variable we are predicting from; it can have scores ranging from 0 to 6. Y is the variable being predicted; it can have scores from 0 to 7.

Person	X	Y
A	3	4
B	6	7
C	1	2
D	4	6

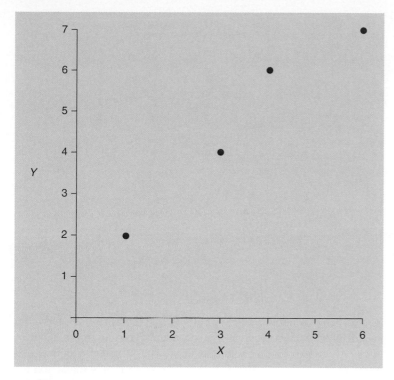

FIGURE 3–4 *Scatter diagram for scores in "How Are You Doing" question.*

ANSWERS:

1. A scatter diagram is a graph that shows the relation between two variables. One axis is for one variable; the other axis, for the other variable. The graph has a dot for each person's pair of scores. The dot for each person is placed above that person's score on the horizontal axis variable and directly across from that persons' score on the vertical axis variable.
2. (a) The variable that is doing the predicting. (b) The variable that is being predicted about.
3. See Figure 3–4.

PATTERNS OF CORRELATION

LINEAR AND CURVILINEAR CORRELATIONS

In each example so far, the pattern in the scatter diagram very roughly approximates a straight line. Thus, each is an example of a **linear correlation.** In the scatter diagram for the study of exciting activities and marital satisfaction (Figure 3–1), you could draw a line showing the general trend of the dots, as we have done in Figure 3–5. Similarly, you could draw such a line in the mood and sleep study example, as shown in Figure 3–6. Notice that the scores do not all fall right on the line, far from it in fact. But that the line does describe their general tendency. (In Chapter 4 you learn the precise rules for drawing such lines.)

      Sometimes, however, the general relationship between two variables does not follow a straight line at all, but instead follows the more complex pattern of a **curvilinear correlation.** For example, it is known that up to a point, more physiological

linear correlation

curvilinear correlation

FIGURE 3–5   *The scatter diagram of Figure 3–1 with a line drawn in to show the general trend. (Data from Aron et al., 2000.)*

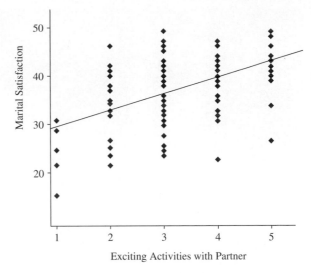

arousal makes you do better on almost any kind of task (such as on a math test). Beyond that point, still greater physiological arousal makes you do worse. That is, going from being nearly asleep to a moderate level of arousal makes you more effective. Beyond that moderate level, further increases in arousal may make you too "keyed up" to do well. This particular curvilinear pattern is illustrated in Figure 3–7. Notice that you could not draw a straight line to describe this pattern. Some other examples of curvilinear relationships are shown in Figure 3–8.

The usual way of figuring the degree of correlation (the one you learn shortly in this chapter) gives the degree of *linear* correlation. If the true pattern of association is curvilinear, figuring the correlation in the usual way could show little or no correlation. Thus, it is important to look at scatter diagrams to unearth these richer relationships rather than automatically figuring correlations in the usual way, assuming that the only relationship is a straight line.

FIGURE 3–6   *The scatter diagram of Figure 3–2d with a line drawn in to show the general trend.*

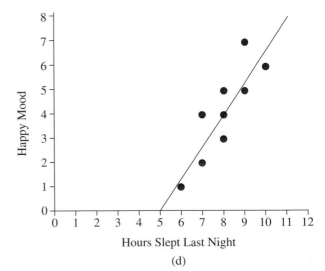

(d)

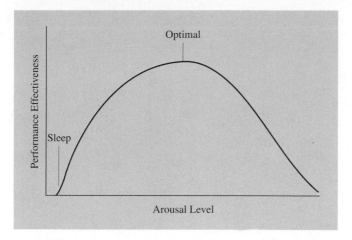

FIGURE 3–7   *Example of a curvilinear relationship—task performance and arousal.*

No Correlation

It is also possible for two variables to be essentially unrelated to each other. For example, if you were to do a study of income and shoe size, your results might appear as shown in Figure 3–9. The dots are spread everywhere, and there is no line, straight or otherwise, that is any reasonable representation of a trend. There is simply **no correlation.**

no correlation

Positive and Negative Linear Correlations

In the examples so far of linear correlations, such as exciting activities and martial satisfaction, high scores go with high scores, lows with lows, and mediums with mediums. This is called a **positive correlation.** (One reason for the term "positive" is that in geometry, the slope of a line is positive when it goes up and to the right on a graph like this. Notice that in figures 3–5 and 3–6 the lines go up and to the right.)

positive correlation

Sometimes, however, high scores go with low scores and lows with highs. This is called a **negative correlation.** For example, in the newspaper survey about marriage, the researchers also asked about boredom with the relationship and the partner. Not surprisingly, the more bored a person was, the *lower* was the person's marital satisfaction. That is, low scores on one variable went with high scores on the other. This is shown in Figure 3–10, where we also put in a line to emphasize the general trend. You can see that as it goes from left to right, it slopes slightly downward. (Compare this to the result for the relation of exciting activities and marital satisfaction shown in Figure 3–5, which slopes upward.)

negative correlation

Another example of a negative correlation is from organizational psychology. A well-established finding in that field is that absenteeism from work had a negative linear correlation with satisfaction with the job (e.g., Mirvis & Lawler, 1977). That is, the higher the level of job satisfaction, the lower the level of absenteeism. Put another way, the lower the level of job satisfaction, the higher the absenteeism.

Importance of Identifying the Pattern of Correlation

The procedure you learn in the next main section is for figuring the degree of linear correlation. As we suggested earlier, the best approach to such a problem is *first* to make a scatter diagram and use it to identify the pattern of correlation. If the pattern

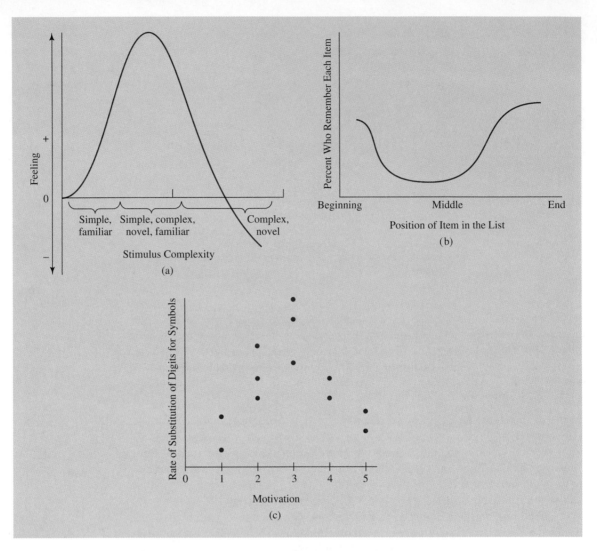

FIGURE 3-8 *Examples of curvilinear relationships: (a) the way we feel and the complexity of a stimulus; (b) the number of people who remember an item and its position on a list; and (c) children's rate of and motivation for substituting digits for symbols.*

is curvilinear, then you would not go on to figure the degree of linear correlation. This is important because figuring the degree of linear correlation when the true correlation is curvilinear would be misleading. (For example, you might conclude that there is little or no correlation when in fact it is large, just not linear.)

If the correlation appears to be roughly linear, it is also important to "eyeball" the scatter diagram a bit more. The idea is to note the direction (positive or negative) of a linear correlation and also to make a rough guess as to the degree of correlation—whether it is "small" (you can barely tell there is a correlation at all), "large" (it is near perfect—the dots fall almost exactly on a straight line), or "moderate" (somewhere in between). Noting the direction and making a rough guess as to the degree of correlation is important because it lets you check to see whether you have made a major mistake when you then do the figuring you learn in the next section.

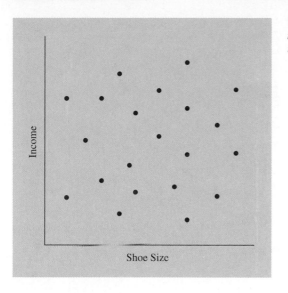

FIGURE 3–9 *Two variables with no association with each other—income and shoe size. (Fictional data.)*

HOW ARE YOU DOING?

1. What is the difference between a linear and curvilinear correlation in terms of how they appear in a scatter diagram?
2. What does it mean to say that two variables have no correlation?
3. What is the difference between a positive and negative linear correlation? Answer this question in terms of (a) the patterns in a scatter diagram and (b) what those patterns tell you about the relationship between the two variables.
4. For each of the scatter diagrams shown in Figure 3–11, say whether the pattern is roughly linear, curvilinear, or no correlation. If the pattern is roughly linear, also say if it is positive or negative.
5. Give two reasons why it is important to identify the pattern of correlation in a scatter diagram before proceeding to figure the degree of correlation.

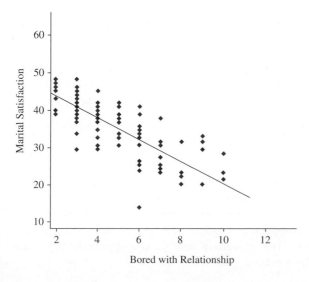

FIGURE 3–10 *Scatter diagram with the line drawn in to show the general trend for negative correlation between two variables: Greater boredom with the relationship goes with lower marital satisfaction. (Data from Aron et al., 2000.)*

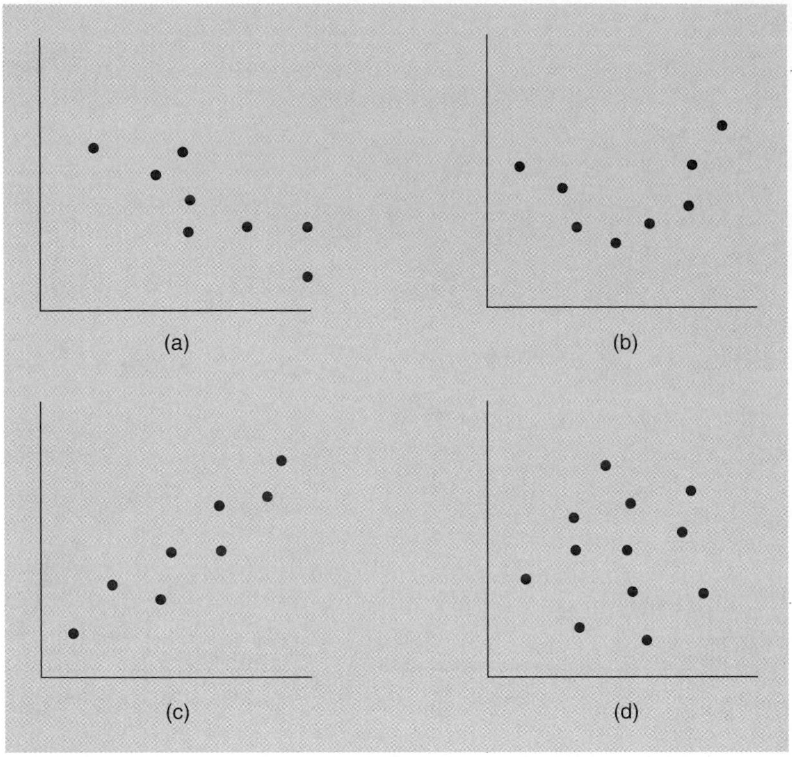

FIGURE 3–11 *Scatter diagrams for "How Are You Doing?" question 4.*

ANSWERS:

1. In a linear correlation, the pattern of dots roughly follow a straight line; in a curvilinear correlation, there is a clear pattern to the dots, but it is not a straight line.
2. There is no pattern of relationship between the two variables.
3. (a) In a scatter diagram for a positive linear correlation, the line that roughly describes the pattern of dots goes up and to the right; in a negative linear correlation, the line goes down and to the right. (b) In a positive linear correlation, the basic pattern is that high scores on one variable go with high scores on the other, mediums go with mediums, and lows go with lows; in a negative linear correlation, high scores on one variable go with low scores on the other, mediums go with mediums, and lows go with highs.
4. (a) linear, negative. (b) curvilinear. (c) linear, positive. (d) no correlation.
5. Identifying whether it is linear or not tells you whether it is appropriate to use the standard procedures for figuring a linear correlation. If it is linear, identifying the direction and approximate degree of correlation before doing the figuring lets you check the results of your figuring when you are done.

THE DEGREE OF LINEAR CORRELATION: THE CORRELATION COEFFICIENT

Looking at a scatter diagram gives you a rough idea of the type and degree of relationship between two variables. But it is not a very precise approach. What you need is a number that gives the precise degree of correlation.

DEGREE OF CORRELATION

What we mean by the *degree of correlation* is how much there is a clear pattern of some particular relationship between two variables. For example, we saw that a positive linear correlation is when high scores go with highs, mediums with mediums, lows with lows. The degree of such a correlation, then, is how much highs go with highs, and so on. Similarly, the degree of negative linear correlation is how much highs on one variable go with lows on the other, and so forth. In terms of a scatter diagram, a high degree of linear correlation means that the dots all fall very close to a straight line (the line sloping up or down depending on whether the linear correlation is positive or negative). A perfect linear correlation means all the dots fall exactly on the straight line.

LOGIC OF FIGURING THE DEGREE OF LINEAR CORRELATION

The first thing you need to figure the degree of correlation is some way to gauge what is a high and what is a low—and how high a high is and how low a low is. This means comparing scores on different variables in a consistent way. As we saw in Chapter 2, you can solve this problem of comparing apples and oranges by using Z scores.

To review, a Z score is the number of standard deviations a score is from the mean. Whatever the range of values of the variable, if you convert your raw scores to Z scores, a raw score that is high (that is, above the mean of all the scores on that variable) will always have a positive Z score, and a raw score that is low (below the mean) will always have a negative Z score. Further, regardless of the particular measure used, Z scores tell you in a very standard way just how high or low each score is. A Z score of 1 is always exactly 1 standard deviation above the mean and a Z score of 2 is twice as many standard deviations above the mean. Z scores on one variable are directly comparable to Z scores on another variable.

There is an additional reason why Z scores are so useful when figuring the degree of correlation. It has to do with what happens if you multiply a score on one variable by a score on the other variable, which is called a *cross-product*. When using Z scores, this is called a **cross-product of Z scores.** If you multiply a high Z score by a high Z score, you will always get a positive cross-product. This is because no matter what the variable, scores above the mean are positive Z scores, and a positive times a positive is a positive. Further—and here is where it gets interesting—if you multiply a low Z score by a low Z score, you also get a positive cross-product. This is because no matter what the variable, scores below the mean are negative Z scores, and a negative times a negative gives a positive.

cross-product of Z scores

If highs on one variable go with highs on the other, and lows on one go with lows on the other, the cross-products of Z scores always will be positive. Considering a whole distribution of scores, suppose you take each person's Z score on one variable and multiply it by that person's Z score on the other variable. The result of doing this when highs go with highs and lows with lows is that the multiplications all come out positive. If you sum up these cross-products of Z scores for all the people in the study, which are all positive, you will end up with a big positive number.

On the other hand, with a negative correlation, highs go with lows and lows with highs. In terms of Z scores, this would mean positives with negatives and negatives with positives. Multiplied out, that gives all negative cross-products. If you add all these negative cross-products together, you get a large negative number.

Finally, suppose there is no linear correlation. In this situation, for some people highs on one variable would go with highs on the other variable (and some lows

BOX 3-1   Galton: Gentleman Genius

Francis Galton is credited with inventing the correlation statistic. (Karl Pearson, the hero of our Chapter 14, worked out the formulas, but Pearson was a student of Galton and gave Galton all the credit.) Statistics at this time was a tight little British club. In fact, most of science was an only slightly larger club. Galton also was influenced greatly by his own cousin, Charles Darwin.

Galton was a typical, eccentric, independently wealthy gentleman scientist. Aside from his work in statistics, he possessed a medical degree, had explored "darkest Africa," invented glasses for reading underwater, experimented with stereoscopic maps, dabbled in meteorology and anthropology, and wrote a paper about receiving intelligible signals from the stars.

Above all, Galton was a compulsive counter. Some of his counts are rather infamous. Once while attending a lecture, he counted the fidgets of an audience per minute, looking for variations with the boringness of the subject matter. While twice having his picture painted, he counted the artist's brush strokes per hour, concluding that each portrait required an average of 20,000 strokes. While walking the streets of various towns in the British Isles, he classified the beauty of the female inhabitants by fingering a recording device in his pocket to register good, medium, or bad.

Galton's consuming interest, however, was the counting of geniuses, criminals, and other types in families. He wanted to understand how each type was produced so that science could improve the human race by encouraging governments to enforce eugenics—selective breeding for intelligence, proper moral behavior, and other qualities—to be determined, of course, by the eugenicists. (Eugenics has since been generally discredited.) The concept of correlation came directly from his first simple efforts in this area, the study of the relation of the height of children to their parents.

At first, Galton's method of exactly measuring the tendency for "one thing to go with another" seemed almost the same as proving the cause of something. For example, if it could be shown mathematically that most of the brightest people came from a few highborn British families and most of the least intelligent people came from poor families, that seemed at first to "prove" that intelligence was caused by the inheritance of certain genes (provided that you were prejudiced enough to overlook the differences in educational opportunities). Now the study only proves that if you were a member of one of those highborn British families, history would make you a prime example of how easy it is to misinterpret the meaning of a correlation.

References: Peters (1987); Salsburg (2001); Tankard (1984).

would go with lows), making positive cross-products. For other people, highs on one variable would go with lows on the other variable (and some lows would go with highs), making negative cross-products. Adding up these cross-products for all the people in the study would result in the positive cross-products and the negative cross-products canceling each other out, giving a result of 0.

In each situation, we changed all the scores to Z scores, multiplied each person's two Z scores by each other, and added up these cross-products. The result was a large positive number if there was a positive linear correlation, a large negative number if there was a negative linear correlation, and a number near 0 if there was no linear correlation.

However, you are still left with the problem of figuring the *degree* of a positive or negative correlation. The larger the number, the bigger the correlation. But how large is large, and how large is not very large? You can't judge from the sum of the cross-products alone, which gets bigger just by adding the cross-products of more persons together. (That is, a study with 100 people would have a larger sum of cross-products than the same study with only 25 people.)

The solution is to divide this sum of the cross-products by the number of people in the study. That is, you figure the *average of the cross-products of Z scores.* It turns out that because of the nature of Z scores this average can never be more than $+1$, which would be a positive linear perfect correlation. It can never be less than -1, which would be a negative linear perfect correlation. In the situation of no linear correlation, the average of the cross-products of Z scores is 0.

For a positive linear correlation that is not perfect, which is the usual situation, the average of the cross-products of Z scores is between 0 and $+1$. To put this another way, if the general trend of the dots is upward and to the right, but they do not fall exactly on a single straight line, the average of the cross-products of Z scores is between 0 and $+1$. The same rule holds for negative correlations: They fall between 0 and -1.

THE CORRELATION COEFFICIENT

The average of the cross-products of Z scores is called the **correlation coefficient.**   **correlation coefficient**
It is also called the *Pearson correlation coefficient* (or the *Pearson product-moment correlation coefficient,* to be very traditional). It is named after Karl Pearson (whom you will meet in Chapter 14, Box 14–1). Pearson, along with Francis Galton (see Box 3–1), played a major role in developing the correlation coefficient. The correlation coefficient is abbreviated by the letter **r,** which is short for *regression,* a concept closely related to correlation (see Chapter 4).

Figure 3–12 shows scatter diagrams and the correlation coefficients for several examples.

FORMULA FOR THE CORRELATION COEFFICIENT

The correlation coefficient, as we have seen, is the average of the cross-products of Z scores. Put as a formula,

(3-1)

$$r = \frac{\Sigma Z_X Z_Y}{N}$$

> The correlation coefficient is the sum, over all the people in the study, of the product of each person's two Z scores divided by the number of persons.

r is the correlation coefficient. Z_X is the Z score for each person on the X variable and Z_Y is the Z score for each person on the Y variable; $Z_X Z_Y$ is Z_X times Z_Y (the cross-product of the Z scores) for each person; and $\Sigma Z_X Z_Y$ is the sum of the cross-products of Z scores over all the people in the study. N is the number of people in the study.[1]

---

[1]There is also a "computational" version of this formula that is mathematically equivalent and thus gives the same result:

$$r = \frac{N\Sigma(XY) - \Sigma X \Sigma Y}{\sqrt{[N\Sigma X^2 - (\Sigma X)^2]} \ \sqrt{[N\Sigma Y^2 - (\Sigma Y)^2]}} \qquad (3\text{-}2)$$

This formula is easier to use when computing by hand when you have a large number of people in the study, because you don't have to first figure out all the Z scores. However, as we emphasized in Chapter 2, researchers rarely use computational formulas like this any more because most the actual figuring is done by a computer. As a student learning statistics, it is much better to use the definitional formula (3-1). This is because when solving problems using the definitional formula, you are strengthening your understanding of what the correlation coefficient means. In all examples in this chapter, we use the definitional formula and we urge you to use it in doing the chapter's practice problems.

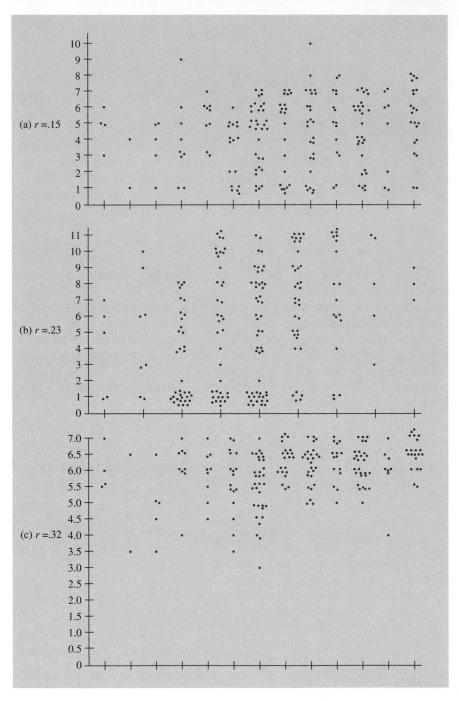

FIGURE 3–12   *Scatter diagrams and correlation coefficients for fictional studies with different correlations.*

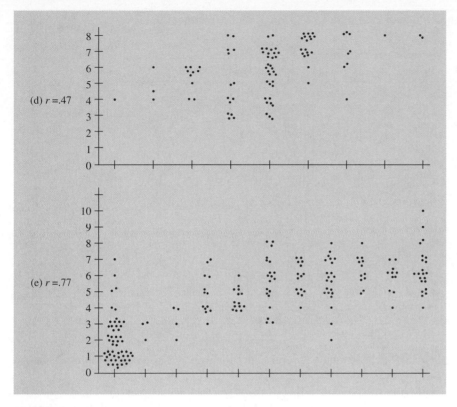

FIGURE 3–12   *Continued*

STEPS FOR FIGURING THE CORRELATION COEFFICIENT

Here are the four steps for figuring the correlation coefficient.

❶ **Change all scores to Z scores.** This requires figuring the mean and the standard deviation of each variable, then changing each raw score to a Z score (using the method from Chapter 2).

❷ **Figure the cross-product of the Z scores for each person.** That is, for each person, multiply the person's Z score on one variable by the person's Z score on the other variable.

❸ **Add up the cross-products of Z scores.**

❹ **Divide by the number of people in the study.**

Tip for Success

When changing the raw scores to Z scores, it is easiest (and you will make fewer errors) if you do all the Z scores for one variable and then all the Z scores for the other variable. Also, to make sure you have done it correctly, when you finish all the persons' Z scores for a variable, add them up—they should add up to 0 (within rounding error).

AN EXAMPLE

Let us try these steps with the sleep and mood example.

❶ **Change all scores to Z scores.** Starting with the number of hours slept last night, the mean is 8 (sum of 80 divided by 10 students), and the standard deviation is 1.10 (sum of squared deviations, 12, divided by 10 students, for a variance of 1.2, the square root of which is 1.10). For the first student, then, a number of hours slept of 9 is 1 hour above the mean of 8, and 1 divided by 1.10 is .91. Thus, the first score is .91 standard deviations above the mean, or a Z score of .91. We figured the rest of

TABLE 3–3 | **Figuring the Correlation Coefficient for the Sleep and Mood Study (Fictional Data)**

Number of Hours Slept (X)				Happy Mood (Y)				Cross-Products
	Deviation	Dev Squared			Deviation	Dev Squared		
X	X–M	$(X-M)^2$	Z_X ❶	Y	Y–M	$(Y-M)^2$	Z_Y ❶	$Z_X Z_Y$ ❷
7	−1	1	−.91	4	0	0	0	.00
9	1	1	.91	5	1	1	.58	.53
8	0	0	.00	3	−1	1	−.58	.00
9	1	1	.91	7	3	9	1.73	1.58
8	0	0	.00	4	0	0	.00	.00
6	−2	4	−1.82	1	−3	9	−1.73	3.15
8	0	0	.00	3	−1	1	−.58	.00
7	−1	1	−.91	2	−2	4	−1.16	1.05
10	2	4	1.82	6	2	4	1.16	2.10
8	0	0	.00	5	1	1	.58	.00 ❸
$\Sigma = 80$		$\Sigma(X-M)^2 = 12$	$\Sigma = 40$		$\Sigma(Y-M)^2 = 30$			$\Sigma Z_X Z_Y = 8.41$
$M = 8$		$SD^2 = 1.20$	$M = 4$		$SD^2 = 3.00$			$r = .841/10 = .84$ ❹
		$SD = 1.10$			$SD = 1.73$			

the Z scores in the same way and show them in the appropriate columns in Table 3–3.

❷ **Figure the cross-product of the Z scores for each person.** For the first student, multiply .91 by .58. This gives .53. The cross-products for all the students are shown in the last column of Table 3–3.

❸ **Add up the cross-products of Z scores.** Adding up all the cross-products of Z scores, as shown in Table 3–3, gives a sum of 8.41.

❹ **Divide by the number of people in the study.** Dividing 8.41 by 10 (the number of students in the study), gives a result of .841. This rounds off to .84. This is the correlation coefficient.

In terms of the correlation coefficient formula,

$$r = \Sigma Z_X Z_Y / N = 8.41/10 = .84.$$

Because this correlation coefficient is positive and near 1, the highest possible value, this is a very strong positive linear correlation.

A SECOND EXAMPLE

Now let's try these steps with the word memory experiment example we used earlier to make a scatter diagram. The steps are shown in Table 3–4.

❶ **Change all scores to Z scores.** The mean of the number of exposures is 4.50, with a standard deviation of 2.29. Thus, the first score of 1 is 3.5 exposures below the mean, which is 1.53 standard deviations below the mean, or $Z = -1.53$. Using the same procedure for all the other scores gives the Z scores shown in Table 3–4. (The table does not show the steps for figuring the deviation and squared deviation scores used to get the standard deviations.)

❷ **Figure the cross-product of the Z scores for each person.** The first cross-product is −1.53 times −.74, which equals +1.13. All the cross-products are shown in Table 3–4.

TABLE 3–4 Figuring the Correlation Coefficient for the Effect of Number of Exposures to Each Word on the Number of Words Recalled (Fictional Data)

Participant ID Number	Number of Exposures (Predictor Variable)		Number of Words Recalled (Criterion Variable)		Z-Score Cross-Product
	X	Z_X ❶	Y	Z_Y	$Z_X Z_Y$ ❷
1	1	−1.53	4	− .74	1.13
2	1	−1.53	3	−1.21	1.85
3	2	−1.09	3	−1.21	1.32
4	2	−1.09	5	− .26	.28
5	3	− .65	6	.21	− .14
6	3	− .65	4	− .74	.48
7	4	− .22	4	− .74	.16
8	4	− .22	6	.21	− .05
9	5	.22	5	− .26	− .06
10	5	.22	7	.68	.15
11	6	.65	2	−1.68	−1.09
12	6	.65	9	1.62	−1.05
13	7	1.09	6	.21	.23
14	7	1.09	8	1.15	1.25
15	8	1.53	9	1.62	2.48
16	8	1.53	8	1.15	1.76
					❸
Σ:	72		89		10.80
M:	4.50		5.56		$r = 10.80/16 = .68$ ❹
$SD = \sqrt{84/16} = 2.29$			$\sqrt{72/16} = 2.12$		

❸ **Add up the cross-products of the Z scores.** They add up to 10.80.

❹ **Divide by the number of people in the study.** The sum of the cross-products of Z scores (10.80) divided by the number of persons (16) comes out to .68. That is, $r = .68$.

In terms of the correlation coefficient formula,

$$r = \Sigma Z_X Z_Y / N = 10.80/16 = .68.$$

This correlation coefficient is positive and well above 0, but not very close to 1. This is a moderately strong positive linear correlation. (You will learn later that correlations above .5 are considered fairly strong.)

HOW ARE YOU DOING?

1. Give two reasons why we use Z scores for figuring the degree of linear correlation between two variables, thinking of correlation as how much highs go with highs and lows go with lows (or vice versa for negative correlations).
2. When figuring the correlation coefficient, why do you divide the sum of cross-products of Z scores by the number of people in the study?
3. Write the formula for the correlation coefficient and define each of the symbols.
4. Figure the correlation coefficient for the Z scores shown below for three people who were each tested on two variables, X and Y.

Person	Z_X	Z_Y
K	.5	−.7
L	−1.4	−.8
M	.9	1.5

ANSWERS:

1. First, Z scores put both variables on the same scale of measurement so that a high or low score (and how much it is high or low) means the same thing for both variables. Second, high Z scores are positive and low are negative. Thus, if highs go with highs and lows with lows, the cross-products will all be positive. Similarly, with a negative correlation where highs go with lows and lows with highs, the cross-products will all be negative.
2. Otherwise, the more people in the study, the bigger the sum of the cross-products, even if the degree of correlation is the same. Dividing by the number of people corrects for this.
3. $r = \Sigma Z_X Z_Y/N$. r is the correlation coefficient. Σ is the symbol for sum of—add up all the scores that follow (in this formula, you add up all the cross-products that follow). Z_X is the Z score for each person's raw score on one of the variables (the one labeled X) and Z_Y is the Z score for each person's raw score on the other variable (labeled Y). N is the number of people in the study.
4. $r = \Sigma Z_X Z_Y/N = [(.5)(−.7) + (−1.4)(−.8) + (.9)(1.5)]/3 = [−.35 + 1.12 + 1.35]/3 = 2.12/3 = .71$.

CORRELATION AND CAUSALITY

direction of causality

If two variables have a clear linear correlation, we normally assume that there is something causing them to go together. However, you can't know the **direction of causality** (what is causing what) just from the fact that the two variables are correlated.

THREE POSSIBLE DIRECTIONS OF CAUSALITY

Consider the example with which we started the chapter, the correlation between doing exciting activities with your partner and satisfaction with the relationship. It could be that doing exciting activities together causes the partners to be more satisfied with their relationship. But it could also be that people who are more satisfied with their relationship choose to do more exciting activities together. Yet another possibility is that something like having less pressure (versus more pressure) at work makes people happier in their marriage and also gives them more time and energy to do exciting activities with their partner. (See Figure 3–13a.)

The principle is that for any correlation between variables X and Y, there are at least three possible directions of causality: X could be causing Y, Y could be causing X, or some third factor could be causing both X and Y. It is also possible (and often likely) that there is more than one direction of causality making two variables correlated. This is illustrated in Figure 3–13b.

RULING OUT SOME POSSIBLE DIRECTIONS OF CAUSALITY

Sometimes you can rule out one or more of these three possible directions based on additional knowledge of the situation. For example, the correlation between sleep the night before and happy mood the next day cannot be due to happy mood the

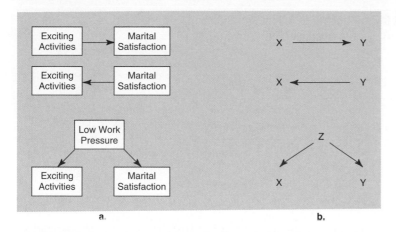

FIGURE 3–13 *Three possible directions of causality (shown with arrows) for a correlation for (a) the exciting activities and marital satisfaction example and (b) the general principle for any two variables* X *and* Y.

next day causing you to sleep more the night before (causality doesn't go backwards in time). But we still do not know if the sleep the night before caused the happy mood, or whether some third factor, such as a general tendency to be happy, caused people both to sleep well and to be happy on any particular day.

Another way we can rule out alternative directions of causality is by conducting a true experiment. In a true experiment, participants are randomly assigned to a particular level of a variable and then measured on another variable. An example of this is the study in which participants were randomly assigned to different numbers of exposures to a list of words, and then the number of words they could remember was measured. There was a .68 correlation between number of exposures and number of words recalled. In this situation, any causality has to be from the variable that was manipulated (number of exposures) to the variable that is measured (words recalled). Number of words recalled can't cause more exposures, because the exposures came first. And a third variable can't be causing both number of exposures and words recalled because number of exposures was determined randomly—nothing can be causing it other than the random method we used (such as flipping a coin).

CORRELATIONAL STATISTICAL PROCEDURES VERSUS CORRELATION RESEARCH METHODS

Discussions of correlation and causality in psychology research is often confused by there being two uses of the word *correlation*. Sometimes the word is used as the name of a statistical procedure, the correlation coefficient (as we have done in this chapter). At other times, the term correlation is used to describe a kind of research design. A **correlational research design** is any research design other than a true experiment. Ordinarily, a correlational research design is statistically analyzed using the correlation coefficient, and an experimental research design is analyzed using procedures you will learn in chapters 9 through 13. Hence the confusion.

However, there are exceptions. The word-exposure-memory experiment is an example. It is a true experiment (because participants were randomly assigned to conditions) that is properly analyzed using the correlation coefficient. There are

correlational research design

TABLE 3–5	Correlational Statistical Methods and Correlational Research Designs (Four Possibilities)	

	Statistical Method	
Type of Research Design	Correlation	Other
Correlational	Most common	Sometimes used
True Experiment	Sometimes used	Most common

also examples we consider later in the book in which researchers use a correlational research design that is most straightforwardly analyzed with a statistical procedure usually used for true experiments.

This distinction between correlational statistical methods and correlational research design is summarized in Table 3–5.

HOW ARE YOU DOING?

1. If anxiety and depression are correlated, what are three possible directions of causality that might explain this correlation?
2. If high school and college grades are correlated, what directions of causality can and cannot be ruled out by the situation?
3. A researcher randomly assigns participants to eat various numbers of cookies and then asks them how full they feel. The number of cookies eaten and feeling full are highly correlated. What directions of causality can and cannot be ruled out?
4. What is the difference between correlation as a statistical procedure and a correlational research design?

ANSWERS:

1. Being depressed can cause a person to be anxious; being anxious can cause a person to be depressed; some third variable (such as some aspect of heredity or childhood traumas) could be causing both anxiety and depression.
2. College grades cannot be causing high school grades (causality doesn't go backwards), but high school grades could be causing college grades (maybe knowing you did well in high school gives you more confidence), and some third variable (such as general academic ability) could be causing students to do well in both high school and college.
3. Eating more cookies can cause participants to feel full. Feeling full cannot have caused participants to have eaten more cookies, because the cookies were eaten first. Third variables can't cause both because how many cookies were eaten was determined randomly.
4. The statistical procedure of correlations is about using the formulas for the correlation coefficient, regardless of how the study was done. A correlational research design is a method of setting up a study in which you cannot definitely sort out the direction of causality, whatever the method of statistical analysis.

BOX 3-2   Illusory Correlation: When You Know Perfectly Well that if It's Big, It's Fat—and You Are Perfectly Wrong

The concept of correlation was not really invented by statisticians. It is one of the most basic of human mental processes. The first humans must have thought in terms of correlation all the time—at least those who survived. "Every time it snows, the animals we hunt go away. Snow belongs with no animals. When the snow comes again, if we follow the animals, we may not starve."

In fact, correlation is such a typically human and highly successful thought process that we seem to be psychologically organized to see more correlation than is there—like the Aztecs, who thought that good crops correlated with human sacrifices (let's hope they were wrong), and like the following examples from social psychology of what is called *illusory correlation* (Hamilton, 1981; Hamilton & Gifford, 1976; Johnson & Mullen, 1994).

Illusory correlation is the term for the overestimation of the strength of the relationship between two variables (the term has also had other special meanings in the past). Right away, you may think of some harmful illusory correlations related to ethnicity, race, gender, and age. One source of illusory correlation is the tendency to link two infrequent and therefore highly memorable events. Suppose Group B is smaller than Group A, and in both groups one third of the people are known to commit certain infrequent but undesirable acts. In this kind of situation, research shows that Group B, whose members are less frequently encountered, will in fact be blamed for far more of these undesirable acts than Group A. This is true even though the odds are greater that a particular act was committed by a member of Group A, since Group A has more members. The problem is that infrequent events stick together in memory. Membership in the less frequent group and the occurrence of less frequent behaviors form an illusory correlation. One obvious consequence is that we remember anything unusual done by the member of a minority group better than we remember anything unusual done by a member of a majority group.

Illusory correlation due to "paired distinctiveness" (two unusual events being linked in our minds) may occur because when we first encounter distinctive experiences, we think more about them, processing them more deeply so that they are more accessible in memory later (Johnson & Mullen, 1994). If we encounter, for example, members of a minority we don't see often, or negative acts that we rarely see or hear about, we really think about them. If they are paired, we study them both and they are quicker to return to memory. It also seems that we can continue to process information about groups, people, and their behaviors without any awareness of doing so. Sometime along the way, or when we go to make a judgment, we overassociate the unusual groups or people with the unusual (negative) behaviors (McConnell et al., 1994). This effect is stronger when information about the groups or people is sparse, as if we try even harder in ambiguous situations to make sense of what we have seen (Berndsen et al., 2001).

Most illusory correlations, however, occur simply because of prejudices. Prejudices are implicit, erroneous theories that we carry around with us. For example, we estimate that we have seen more support for an association between two social traits than we have actually seen: driving skills and a particular age group; level of academic achievement and a specific ethnic group; certain speech, dress, or social behaviors and residence in some region of the country. One especially interesting example is that most people in business believe that job satisfaction and job performance are closely linked, when in fact the correlation is quite low. People who do not like their job can still put in a good day's work; people who rave about their job can still be lazy about doing it.

By the way, some people form their implicit theories impulsively and hold them rigidly; others seem to base them according to what they remember about people and change their theories as they have new experiences (McConnell, 2001). Which are you?

The point is, next time you ask yourself why you are struggling to learn statistics, it might help to think of it as a quest to make ordinary thought processes more righteous. So again, we assert that statistics can be downright romantic: It can be about conquering dark, evil mistakes with the pure light of numbers, subduing the lie of prejudices with the honesty of data.

ISSUES IN INTERPRETING THE CORRELATION COEFFICIENT

There are a number of subtle cautions in interpreting a correlation coefficient.

THE STATISTICAL SIGNIFICANCE OF A CORRELATION COEFFICIENT

The correlation coefficient by itself is a descriptive statistic. It describes the degree and direction (positive or negative) of linear correlation in the particular group of people studied. However, when doing research in psychology, you often are more interested in a particular group of scores as representing some larger group that you have not studied directly. For example, the researcher studying sleep and mood tested only 10 individuals, but the researcher's intention in such a study would be that the scores from these 10 would tell us something about the sleep and mood for people more generally. (In practice, you would want a much larger group than 10 for this purpose. We used small numbers of people in our examples to make them easier to learn from.)

There is a problem, however, in studying only some of the people in the larger group you want to know about. It is possible that, by chance, the ones you pick to study happen to be just those people for whom highs happen to go with highs and lows with lows—even though, had you studied all the people in the larger population, there might really be no correlation.

statistically significant

We say that a correlation is **statistically significant** if it is unlikely that you could have gotten a correlation as big as you did if in fact the overall group had no correlation. Specifically, you figure out whether that likelihood is less than some small degree of probability (p), such as 5% or 1%. If the probability is that small, we say that the correlation is "statistically significant" with "$p < .05$" or "$p < .01$" (spoken as "p less than point oh five" or "p less than point oh one").

The method and logic of figuring *statistical significance* is the main focus of this book, starting with Chapter 5. We would be jumping ahead to try to explain it fully now. However, by the time you complete the later chapters, the details will be quite clear. (The needed details for applying the general principles of statistical significance you learn in those chapters to figuring statistical significance of a correlation coefficient is in the appendix to this chapter. But we suggest that you leave this appendix at least until you have completed Chapter 9.) We bring up this topic now only to give you a general idea of what is being talked about if you see mentions of statistical significance, $p < .05$, or some such phrase, when reading a research article that reports correlation coefficients.

THE CORRELATION COEFFICIENT AND THE PROPORTIONATE REDUCTION IN ERROR OR PROPORTION OF VARIANCE ACCOUNTED FOR

A correlation coefficient tells you the strength of a linear correlation. Bigger rs (values farther from 0) mean a higher degree of correlation. That is, an r of .6 is a stronger correlation than an r of .3. However, most researchers would hold that an r of .6 is *more than* twice as strong as an r of .3. To compare correlations with each other, most researchers square the correlations (that is, they use r^2 instead of r). This

proportionate reduction in error
proportion of variance accounted for

is called, for reasons you will learn in Chapter 4, the **proportionate reduction in error** (and also the **proportion of variance accounted for**).

For example, a correlation of .3 is an r^2 of .09 and a correlation of .6 is an r^2 of .36. Thus, a correlation of .6 is actually four times as strong as one of .3 (that is, .36 is four times as big as .09).

RESTRICTION IN RANGE

Suppose an educational psychologist studies the relation of grade level to knowledge of geography. If this researcher studied students from the entire range of school grade levels, the results might appear as shown in the scatter diagram in Figure 3–14a. That is, the researcher might find a strong positive correlation. But suppose the researcher had studied students only from the first three grades. The scatter diagram (see Figure 3–14b) would show little, if any, correlation (the correlation coefficient would be near 0). However, the researcher would be making a mistake by concluding that grade level is unrelated to geography over all grades.

The problem in this situation is that the correlation is based on people that include only a limited range of the possible values on one of the variables. (In this example, there is a limited range of grade levels.) It is misleading to think of the correlation as if it applied to the entire range of values the variable might have. This situation is called **restriction in range.**

restriction in range

It is easy to make such mistakes in interpreting correlations. (You will occasionally see them even in published research articles.) Consider another example. Businesses sometimes try to decide whether their hiring tests are correlated with how successful the persons hired turn out on the job. Often, they find very little relationship. What they fail to take into account is that they hired only people who did well on the tests. Their study of job success included only the subgroup of high scorers. This example is illustrated in Figure 3–15.

Yet another example is any study that tries to correlate intelligence with other variables that uses only college students. The problem here is that college students do not include many lower or below average intelligence students. Thus, a researcher could find a low correlation in such a study. But if the researcher did the same study with people who included the full range of intelligence levels, there could well be a high correlation.

UNRELIABILITY OF MEASUREMENT

Suppose number of hours slept and mood the next day have a very high degree of correlation. However, suppose also that in a particular study the researcher had asked people about their sleep on a particular night 3 weeks ago and about their

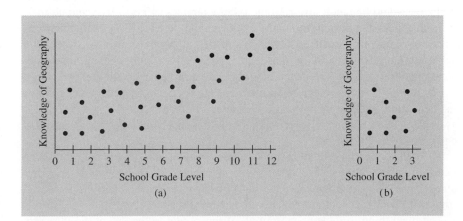

FIGURE 3–14 *Example of restriction in range comparing two scatter diagrams (a) when the entire range is shown (of school grade level and knowledge of geography) and (b) when the range is restricted (to the first three grades).*

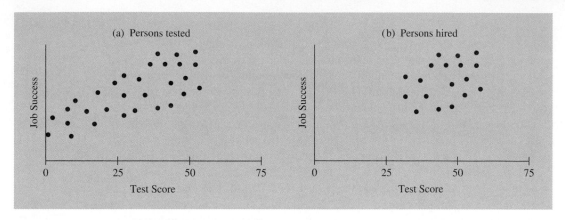

FIGURE 3–15   *Additional example of restriction in range comparing two scatter diagrams (a) when the entire range is shown (of all persons tested) and (b) when the range is restricted (to just those persons who were hired).*

mood on the day after that particular night. There are many problems with this kind of study. But one problem is that the measurement of hours slept and mood would not be very accurate. For example, what a person recalls about how many hours were slept on a particular night 3 weeks ago is probably not very close to how many hours the person actually slept. Thus, the true correlation between sleep and mood could be high, but the correlation in the particular study might be quite low, just because there is lots of "random noise" (random inaccuracy) in the scores.

Here is another way to understand this issue: Think of a correlation in terms of how close the dots in the scatter diagram fall to a straight line. One of the reasons why dots may not fall close to the line is inaccurate measurement.

Consider another example. Height and social power have been found in many studies to have a moderate degree of correlation. However, if someone were to do this study and measure each person's height using an elastic measuring tape, the correlation would be much lower. Some other examples of not fully accurate measurement are personality questionnaires that include items that are difficult to understand (or are understood differently by different people), ratings of behavior (such as children's play activity) that require some subjective judgment, or physiological measures that are influenced by things like ambient magnetic fields.

reliable   Often in psychology research our measures are not perfectly accurate or **reliable** (this idea is discussed in more detail in Chapter 17). The result is that a correlation between any two variables is lower than it would be if you had perfect measures of the two variables.

The reduction in a correlation due to unreliability of measures is called *attenuation.* More advanced statistics texts and psychological measurement texts describe formulas for *correction for attenuation* that can be used under some conditions. However, studies using such procedures are relatively rare in most areas of psychology research.

The main thing to remember from all of this is that to the extent the measures used in a study are less than perfectly accurate, the correlations reported in that study usually underestimate the true correlation between the variables (the correlation that would be found if there was perfect measurement).

1. What does it mean to say that a particular correlation coefficient is statistically significant?
2. (a) What numbers do psychologists use when they compare the size of two correlation coefficients? (b) What is this called?
3. (a) What is restriction in range? (b) What is its effect on the correlation coefficient?
4. (a) What is unreliability of measurement? (b) What is its effect on the correlation coefficient?

ANSWERS:

1. The probability is very low of getting a correlation this big between these two variables in the group of people studied if in fact there is no correlation between these two variables for people in general.
2. (a) The correlation coefficient squared. (b) The proportionate reduction in error or proportion of variance accounted for.
3. (a) Restriction in range is a situation in correlation in which the scores of the group of people studied on one of the variables do not include the full range of scores that are found among people more generally. (b) The effect is often to drastically reduce the correlation compared to what it would be if people more generally were included in the study (presuming there would be a correlation among people more generally).
4. (a) Unreliability of measurement is when the procedures used to measure a particular variable are not perfectly accurate. (b) The effect is to make the correlation smaller than it would be if perfectly accurate measures were used (presuming there would be a correlation if perfectly accurate measures were used).

CONTROVERSY: WHAT IS A LARGE CORRELATION?

An ongoing controversy about the correlation coefficient is, What is a "large" r? Traditionally, in psychology a large correlation is considered to be about .50 or above, a moderate correlation to be about .30, and a small correlation to be about .10 (Cohen, 1988). In fact, in psychology it is rare to find correlations that are greater than .40. Even when we are confident that X causes Y, X will not be the *only* cause of Y. For example, doing exciting activities together may cause people to be happier in their marriage. (In fact, we have done a number of true experiments supporting this direction of causality; Aron et al., 2000). However, exciting activities is still only one of a great many factors that affect marital satisfaction. All those other factors are not part of our correlation. No one correlation could possibly tell the whole story. Low correlations are also due to the unavoidably low reliability of many measures in psychology.

It is traditional to caution that a low correlation is not very important even if it is statistically significant. (As you will learn, a low correlation can be statistically significant if the study includes a very large number of participants.) After all, a correlation of .10 is equivalent to only a 1% proportionate reduction in error.

Furthermore, even experienced research psychologists tend to treat any particular size of correlation as meaning more of an association between two variables than it actually does. Michael Oakes (1982) at the University of Sussex gave 30 research psychologists the two columns of numbers shown in Table 3–6. He then asked them to estimate r (without doing any calculations). What is your guess? The intuitions of the British researchers (who are as a group at least as well trained in statistics as psychologists anywhere in the world) ranged from −.20 to +.60, with a mean of .24. You can figure the true correlation for yourself. It comes out to .50! That is,

TABLE 3–6	Table Presented to 30 Psychologists to Estimate r	
	X	Y
	1	1
	2	10
	3	2
	4	9
	5	5
	6	4
	7	6
	8	3
	9	11
	10	8
	11	7
	12	12

Note: Based on Oakes (1982).

what psychologists think a correlation of .50 means in the abstract is a much stronger degree of correlation than what they think when they see the actual numbers (which even at $r = .50$ only *look* like .24).

Oakes gave a different group of 30 researchers just the X column and asked them to fill in numbers in the Y column that would come out to a correlation of .50 (again, just using their intuition and without any figuring.) When Oakes figured the actual correlations from their answers, these correlations averaged .68. In other words, once again, even experienced researchers think of a correlation coefficient as meaning more linkage between the two variables than it actually does.

In contrast, other psychologists hold that small correlations can be very important theoretically. They also can have major practical implications in that small effects may accumulate over time (Prentice & Miller, 1992).

To demonstrate the practical importance of small correlations, Rosnow and Rosenthal (1989b) give an example of a now famous study (Steering Committee of the Physicians' Health Study Research Group, 1988) in which doctors either did or did not take aspirin each day. Whether or not they took aspirin each day was then correlated with heart attacks. The results were that taking aspirin was correlated $-.034$ with heart attacks.[2] That is, it produces about a .1% proportionate reduction in error. However, Rosnow and Rosenthal point out that this correlation of "only 3.4" meant that among the more than 20,000 doctors who were in the study, there were 72 more heart attacks in the group that did not take aspirin. (In fact, there were also 13 more heart attack deaths in the group that did not take aspirin.)

Certainly, this difference in getting heart attacks is a difference we care about. At the same time, however, the .1% proportionate reduction in error is still accurate. That is, taking aspirin is only a small part of what affects people getting heart attacks—99.9% of the variation in whether people get heart attacks is due to other factors (diet, exercise, genetic factors, etc.).

Another argument for the importance of small correlations emphasizes research methods. Prentice and Miller (1992) explain:

> Showing that an effect holds even under the most unlikely circumstances possible can be as impressive as (or in some cases, perhaps even more impressive) than showing that it accounts for a great deal of variance. (p. 163)

Some examples they give are studies showing correlations between attractiveness and judgments of guilt or innocence in court cases (e.g., Sigall & Ostrove, 1975). The point is that "legal judgments are supposed to be unaffected by such extraneous factors as attractiveness." Thus, if studies show that attractiveness is associated with legal judgments even slightly, we are persuaded of just how important attractiveness could be in influencing social judgments in general.

CORRELATION IN RESEARCH ARTICLES

Scatter diagrams are occasionally included in research articles. For example, Sheline and her colleagues (1999) were interested in a theory that depression creates

---

[2]To figure the correlation between getting a heart attack and taking aspirin, you would have to make the two variables into numbers. For example, you could make getting a heart attack equal 1 and not getting a heart attack equal 0; similarly, you could make being in the aspirin group equal 1 and being in the control group equal 0. It would not matter which two numbers you used for the two values for each variable. Whatever two numbers you use, the result will come out the same after converting to Z scores. The only difference which two numbers you use makes is that which value gets the higher number determines whether the correlation will be positive or negative.

chemical changes that injure the hippocampus, a region of the brain involved in memory. In their study, 24 depressed psychotherapy patients completed questionnaires, which the researchers used to figure the number of days each participant had been depressed during his or her life. Participants in this study then completed a brain-scan session to measure the size of their hippocampus. Sheline et al.'s results are shown in Figure 3–16. As predicted, there was a clear linear negative trend. (They also show a squared correlation of .36—the square root of this is a large r of .60.)

Thus, this scatter diagram suggests that the more days depressed, the smaller the hippocampus. Of course, this is a correlational result, so it is also possible that something about having a smaller hippocampus causes depression, or that some other factor, such as general life stress, causes both depression and a decrease in hippocampus size. (Also, you should know that although this result is very consistent, even those with the most days depressed still had plenty of hippocampus remaining.)

Correlation coefficients are very commonly reported in research articles, both in the text of articles and in tables. The result with which we started the chapter would be described as follows: There was a positive correlation ($r = .51$) between excitement of activities done with partner and marital satisfaction. (Often, the statistical significance of the correlation will also be reported—in this example, it would be $r = .51, p < .05$.)

Tables of correlations are common when several variables are involved. Usually, the table is set up so that each variable is listed down the left and also across the top. The correlation of each pair of variables is shown inside the table. This is called a **correlation matrix.**

correlation matrix

Table 3–7 is from a study of adolescents' strategies for coping with cultural diversity (Coleman et al., 2001). The researchers asked 398 students at a U.S. midwestern middle school (grades 6–8) to rate how likely they were to use each of nine different coping methods. Table 3–7 shows the correlations among the methods.

This example illustrates several features that are typical of the way correlation matrixes are laid out. First, notice that the correlation of a variable with itself is not

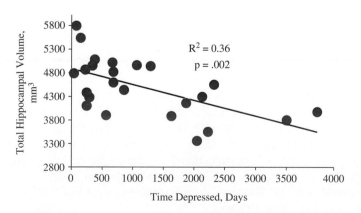

FIGURE 3-16 *Correlation between duration of depression and hippocampal volume. The Pearson correlation between cumulative lifetime total days of major depression was derived from the Diagnostic Interview for Genetic Studies using the Post Life Charting Method (Post et al., 1988) and the total hippocampal gray matter volumes. (From "Depression Duration But Not Age Predicts Hippocampal Volume Loss in Medically Healthy Women with Recurrent Major Depression" by Yvette I. Sheline, Milan Sanghav, et al.,* The Journal of Neuroscience, *June 15, 1999, 19(12), p. 5039. Copyright 1999 by the Society for Neuroscience. Reprinted by permission.*

TABLE 3–7	Correlations Among Strategies for Coping With Cultural Diversity					
Strategy	1	2	3	4	5	6
1. Acculturation	—					
2. Alternation	.62	—				
3. Assimilation	.56	.55	—			
4. Fusion	.46	.78	.48	—		
5. Integration	.45	.75	.39	.84	—	
6. Separation	.35	.21	.24	.14	.11	—

Note: All correlations were significant at $p < .05$.
Source: Coleman et al., 2001.

given. In this example, a short line is put in instead; sometimes they are just left blank. Also notice that only the lower triangle is filled in. This is because it would be repetitive to fill in the other half. For example, the correlation of acculturation with alternation (which is .62) has to be the same as the correlation of alternation and acculturation (so there is no point in putting .62 again in the upper part of the table). Another shortcut saves space across the page: The names of the variables are listed only on the side of the table, with the numbers for them put across the top.

Looking at this example, among other results, you can see that there are very strong correlations among some ways of coping, such as the .84 correlation between integration and fusion. (Integration in Coleman et al.'s terms means associating with both cultures at once but not trying to combine them; fusion involves trying to combine them.) On the other hand, as you might expect, the correlation is quite low between separation (trying to keep the cultures separate) and fusion (.14).

Also, notice the note at the bottom of the table that all correlations were statistically significant at $p < .05$. In a table in which some correlations are and some are not significant, it is common for the table to put stars by the significant ones.

SUMMARY

1. A scatter diagram shows the relation between two variables. The lowest to highest possible values of one variable (the one you are predicting from if the two variables are distinguishable) are marked on the horizontal axis. The lowest to highest possible values of the other variable are marked on the vertical axis. Each individual's pair of scores is shown as a dot.

2. When the dots in the scatter diagram generally follow a straight line, this is called a linear correlation. In a curvilinear correlation, the dots follow a line pattern other than a simple straight line. There is no correlation when the dots do not follow any kind of line. In a positive linear correlation, the line goes upward to the right (so that low scores go with lows and highs with highs). In a negative linear correlation, the line goes downward to the right (so that low scores go with highs and highs with lows).

3. The correlation coefficient (r) gives the degree of linear correlation. It is the average of the cross-products of Z scores. The correlation coefficient is highly positive when there is a strong positive linear correlation. This is because positive Z scores are multiplied by positive, and negative by negative. The correlation coefficient is highly negative when there is a strong negative linear correlation. This is because positive Z scores are multiplied by negative Z scores and negative by positive. The correlation coefficient is 0 when there is no linear correlation. This is because pos-

itives are sometimes multiplied by positives and sometimes by negatives (and vice versa), so that positive and negative cross-products cancel each other out.

4. The maximum positive value of r is $+1$. $r = +1$ when there is a perfect positive linear correlation. The maximum negative value of r is -1. $r = -1$ when there is a perfect negative linear correlation.

5. Correlation does not tell you the direction of causation. If two variables, X and Y, are correlated, this could be because X is causing Y, Y is causing X, or a third factor is causing both X and Y.

6. A correlation figured using scores from a particular group of people is often intended to apply to people in general. A correlation is statistically significant when statistical procedures (taught later in this book) make it highly unlikely that you would get a correlation as big as the one found with the group of people studied if in fact there were no correlation between these two variables among people in general.

7. Comparisons of the degree of linear correlation are considered most accurate in terms of the correlation coefficient squared (r^2), called the proportionate reduction in error or proportion of variance accounted for.

8. A correlation coefficient will be lower than the true correlation if it is based on scores from a group selected for study that is restricted in its range of scores (compared to people in general) or if the scores are based on unreliable measures.

9. Studies suggest that psychologists tend to think of any particular correlation coefficient as meaning more association than actually exists. However, small correlations may have practical importance and may also be impressive in demonstrating the importance of a relationship when a study shows the correlation holds even under what would seem to be unlikely conditions.

10. Correlational results are usually presented in research articles either in the text with the value of r (and sometimes the significance level) or in a special table (a correlation matrix) showing the correlations among several variables.

KEY TERMS

correlation (p. 70)
correlation coefficient (r)
  (p. 83)
correlation matrix
  (p. 97)
correlational research
  design (p. 89)
cross-product of Z scores
  (p. 81)

curvilinear correlation
  (p. 75)
direction of causality
  (p. 88)
linear correlation (p. 75)
negative correlation
  (p. 77)
no correlation (p. 77)
positive correlation (p. 77)

proportion of variance accounted for (r^2) (p. 92)
proportionate reduction
  in error (r^2) (p. 92)
reliable (p. 94)
restriction in range (p. 93)
scatter diagram (p. 70)
statistically significant
  (p. 92)

EXAMPLE WORKED-OUT
COMPUTATIONAL PROBLEMS

MAKING A SCATTER DIAGRAM AND DESCRIBING
THE GENERAL PATTERN OF ASSOCIATION

Make a scatter diagram and describe in words the general pattern of association, based on the class size and average achievement test scores shown below for five elementary schools.

Elementary School	Class Size	Achievement Test Score
Main Street	25	80
Casat	14	98
Harland	33	50
Shady Grove	28	82
Jefferson	20	90

The steps of solving the problem are described below; Figure 3–17 shows the scatter diagram with markers for each step.

❶ **Draw the axes and decide which variable goes on which axis.** It seems more reasonable to think of class size as predicting achievement test scores rather than the other way around. Thus, you can draw the axis with class size along the bottom. (However, the prediction was not explicitly stated in the problem, so the other direction of prediction is certainly possible. Thus, putting either variable on either axis would be acceptable.)

❷ **Determine the range of values to use for each variable and mark them on the axes.** We will assume that the achievement test scores go from 0 to 100. We don't know the maximum class size, so we guessed 50. (The range of the variables was not given in the problem; thus any reasonable range would be acceptable so long as it includes the values of the scores in the actual study.)

❸ **Mark a dot for the pair of scores for each person.** For example, to mark the dot for Main Street School, you go across to 25 and up to 80.

The general pattern is roughly linear. Its direction is negative (it goes down and to the right, with larger class sizes going with smaller achievement scores and vice versa). It is a quite strong correlation, since the dots all fall fairly close to a straight line—it should be fairly close to -1. In words, it is a strong, linear, negative correlation.

F I G U R E 3 – 1 7 *Scatter diagram for scores in "Worked-Out Examples of Computational Problems."* ❶ *Set up the axes.* ❷ *Determine the range of values and mark them on the axes.* ❸ *Place a dot for each school's pair of scores.*

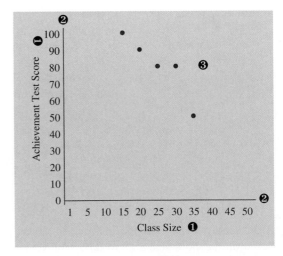

TABLE 3-8	Figuring Correlation Coefficient for Answer to "Worked-Out Examples of Computational Problems"

School	Class Size		Achievement Test Score		Cross-Product
	X	Z_X ❶	Y	Z_Y ❶	$Z_X Z_Y$ ❷
Main Street	25	.15	80	.00	0.00
Casat	14	−1.53	98	1.10	−1.68
Harland	33	1.38	50	−1.84	−2.53
Shady Grove	28	.61	82	.12	.08
Jefferson	20	− .61	90	.61	− .38
Σ:	120		400		−4.52 ❸
M:	24		80	$r = -4.52/5 = -.90$	❹
SD:	$\sqrt{214/5} = 6.54$		$\sqrt{1,328/5} = 16.30$		

FIGURING THE CORRELATION COEFFICIENT

Figure the correlation coefficient for the class size and achievement test example given above. You can figure the correlation using either the formula or the steps. The basic figuring is shown in Table 3–8 with markers for each of the steps.

Using the formula,

$$r = \Sigma Z_X Z_Y / N = -4.52/5 = -.90.$$

Using the steps,

❶ **Change all scores to Z scores.** For example, the mean for class size is 24, and the standard deviation is 6.54; thus, the Z score for the first class size, of 25, is $(25 - 24)/6.54 = .15$.

❷ **Figure the cross-product of the Z scores for each person** (in this case for each school). For example, for Main Street School, the cross-product is .15 times 0, which is 0; for Casat School, it is −1.53 times 1.10, which equals −1.68.

❸ **Add up the cross-products of the Z scores.** The total is −4.52.

❹ **Divide by the number of people in the study** (in this case, the number of schools). The sum (−4.52) divided by 5 is −.90; that is, $r = -.90$.

PRACTICE PROBLEMS

These problems involve figuring. Most real-life statistics problems are done on a computer. However, even if you have a computer and statistics software, do these by hand (with the help of a calculator) to ingrain the method in your mind. Also, in all problems involving figuring, be sure to show your work.

For practice in using a computer to solve statistics problems, refer to the computer section of each chapter of the *Student's Study Guide and Computer Workbook* that accompanies this text.

All data are fictional unless an actual citation is given.

Answers to most Set I problems are given at the back of the book.

SET I

1. For each of the following scatter diagrams, indicate whether the pattern is linear, curvilinear, or no correlation; if it is linear, indicate whether it is positive or negative and approximately how strong the correlation is.

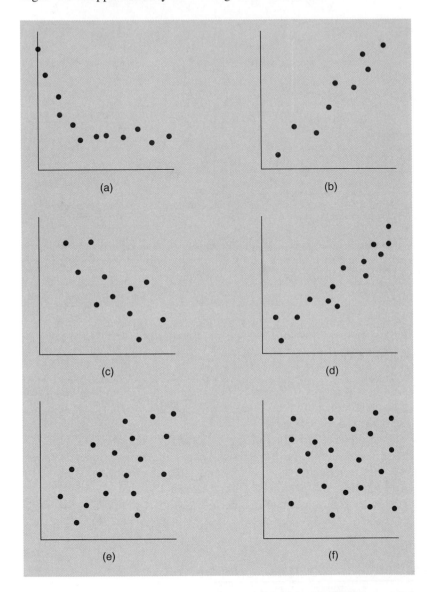

For problems 2 and 3, do the following: (a) Make a scatter diagram of the raw scores; (b) describe in words the general pattern of correlation, if any; (c) figure the correlation coefficient; (d) explain the logic of what you have done, writing as if you are speaking to someone who has never had a statistics course (but who does understand the mean, standard deviation, and Z scores); and (e) give three logically possible directions of causality, saying for each whether it is a reasonable direction in light of the variables involved (and why).

2. A researcher studied the relation between psychotherapists' degree of empathy and their patients' satisfaction with therapy. As a pilot study, four patient–therapist pairs were studied. Here are the results:

Pair Number	Therapist Empathy	Patient Satisfaction
1	70	4
2	94	5
3	36	2
4	48	1

3. An instructor asked five students how many hours they had studied for an exam. Here are the number of hours studied and the students' grades:

Hours Studied	Test Grade
0	52
10	95
6	83
8	71
6	64

4. In a study of people first getting acquainted with each other, researchers reasoned the amount of self-disclosure of one's partner and one's liking for one's partner. Here are the results:

Partner's Self-Disclosure		Liking for Partner	
Actual Score	Z Score	Actual Score	Z Score
18	.37	8	1.10
17	.17	9	1.47
20	.80	6	.37
8	−1.72	1	−1.47
13	− .67	7	.74
24	1.63	1	−1.47
11	−1.09	3	− .74
12	− .88	5	.0
18	.38	7	.74
21	1.00	3	−.74

In this problem, the Z scores are given to save you some figuring. (a) Make a scatter diagram of the raw scores; (b) describe in words the general pattern of correlation, if any; and (c) figure the correlation coefficient.

5. The following have been prepared so that data sets B through D are slightly modified versions of data set A. Make scatter diagrams and figure the correlation coefficients for each data set.

Data Set A		Data Set B		Data Set C		Data Set D	
X	Y	X	Y	X	Y	X	Y
1	1	1	1	1	5	1	1
2	2	2	2	2	2	2	4
3	3	3	3	3	3	3	3
4	4	4	5	4	4	4	2
5	5	5	4	5	1	5	5

6. A researcher is interested in whether a new drug affects the development of a cold. Eight people are tested: Four take the drug and four do not. (Those who take it are rated 1; those who don't, 0.) Whether they get a cold (rated 1) or not (0) is recorded. Four possible results are shown. Figure the correlation coefficient for each.

Possibility A		Possibility B		Possibility C		Possibility D	
Take Drug	Get Cold	Take Drug	Get Cold	Take Drug	Get Cold	Take Drug	Get Cold
0	1	0	1	0	1	0	1
0	1	0	1	0	1	0	1
0	1	0	1	0	0	0	1
0	1	0	0	0	0	0	0
1	0	1	1	1	1	1	0
1	0	1	0	1	1	1	0
1	0	1	0	1	0	1	0
1	0	1	0	1	0	1	0

7. For each of the following situations, indicate why the correlation coefficient might be a distorted estimate of the true correlation (and what kind of distortion you would expect):
(a) Scores on two questionnaire measures of personality are correlated.
(b) Comfort of living situation and happiness are correlated among a group of millionaires.

8. Chapman et al. (1997) interviewed 68 inner-city pregnant women and their husbands (or boyfriends) twice during their pregnancy, once between 3 and 6 months into the pregnancy and again between 6 and 9 months into the pregnancy. Table 3–9 shows the correlations among several of their measures. ("Zero-Order Correlations" means the same thing as ordinary correlations.) Most important in this table are the correlations among women's reports of their own stress, men's reports of their partners' stress, women's perception of their partners support at the first and at the second interviews, and women's depression at the first and at the second interviews.

Explain the results on these measures as if you were writing to a person who has never had a course in statistics. Specifically, (a) explain what is meant by a correlation coefficient using one of the correlations as an example; (b) study the

TABLE 3–9	Zero-Order Correlations for Study Variables									
Variable	1	2	3	4	5	6	7	8	9	10
1. Women's report of stress	—									
2. Men's report of women's stress	.17	—								
3. Partner Support 1	−.28*	−.18	—							
4. Partner Support 2	−.27*	−.18	.44***	—						
5. Depressed Mood 1	.23*	.10	−.34**	−.17	—					
6. Depressed Mood 2	−.50***	.14	−.42***	−.41***	.55***	—				
7. Women's age	.06	.16	.04	−.24*	−.35*	−.09	—			
8. Women's ethnicity	−.19	−.09	−.16	−.14	.11	.13	−.02	—		
9. Women's marital status	−.18	.01	.12	.24*	−.04	−.20	.05	−.34**	—	
10. Parity	.19	.13	−.11	−.17	.10	.16	.26*	.31*	−.12	

*$p < .05.$ **$p < .01.$ ***$p < .001.$

Note: Data from Chapman, H. A., Hobfoll, S. E., & Ritter, C. (1997), tab. 2. Partners' stress underestimations lead to women's distress: A study of pregnant inner-city women. *Journal of Personality and Social Psychology, 73,* 418–425. Copyright, 1997, by the American Psychological Association. Reprinted with permission.

table and then comment on the patterns of results in terms of which variables are relatively strongly correlated and which are not very strongly correlated; and (c) comment on the limitations of making conclusions about direction of causality based on these data, using a specific correlation as an example (noting at least one plausible alternative causal direction and why that alternative is plausible).

SET II

9. For each of the following scatter diagrams, indicate whether the pattern is linear, curvilinear, or no correlation; if it is linear, indicate whether it is positive or negative and approximately how strong the correlation is.

10. Make up a histogram with 10 dots for each of the following situations: (a) perfect positive linear correlation, (b) strong but not perfect positive linear correlation, (c) weak positive linear correlation, (d) strong but not perfect negative linear correlation, (e) no correlation, (f) clear curvilinear correlation.

For Problems 11 to 13, do the following: (a) Make a scatter diagram of the raw scores; (b) describe in words the general pattern of correlation, if any; (c) figure the correlation coefficient; (d) explain the logic of what you have done, writing as if you are speaking to someone who has never had a statistics course (but who does understand the mean, standard deviation, and Z scores); and (e) give three logically possible directions of causality, indicating for each direction whether it is a reasonable explanation for the correlation in light of the variables involved (and why).

11. Four research participants take a test of manual dexterity (high scores mean better dexterity) and an anxiety test (high scores mean more anxiety). The scores are as follows.

Person	Dexterity	Anxiety
1	1	10
2	1	8
3	2	4
4	4	−2

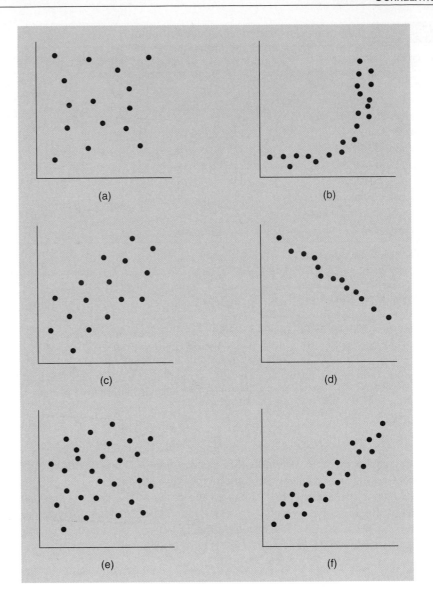

12. Four young children were monitored closely over a period of several weeks to measure how much they watched violent television programs and their amount of violent behavior toward their playmates. The results were as follows:

Child's Code Number	Weekly Viewing of Violent TV (hours)	Number of Violent or Aggressive Acts Toward Playmates
G3368	14	9
R8904	8	6
C9890	6	1
L8722	12	8

13. Five college students were asked about how important a goal it is to them to have a family and about how important a goal it is for them to be highly successful in their work. Each variable was measured on a scale from 0 Not at all important goal to 10 Very important goal.

Student	Family	Work
A	7	5
B	6	4
C	8	2
D	3	9
E	4	1

For problems 14 to 16, (a) make a scatter diagram of the raw scores; (b) describe in words the general pattern of correlation, if any; and (c) figure the correlation coefficient. In these three problems, the Z scores are given to save you some figuring.

14. The Louvre Museum is interested in the relation of the age of a painting to public interest in it. The number of people stopping to look at each of 10 randomly selected paintings is observed over a week. The results are as shown:

Painting Title	Approximate Age (Years)		Number of People Stopping to Look	
	X	Z_X	X	Z_Y
The Entombment	465	1.39	68	−.69
Mys Mar Ste Catherine	515	1.71	71	−.59
The Bathers	240	−.09	123	1.19
The Toilette	107	−.96	112	.82
Portrait of Castiglione	376	.80	48	−1.38
Charles I of England	355	.67	84	−.14
Crispin and Scapin	140	−.75	66	−.76
Nude in the Sun	115	−.91	148	2.05
The Balcony	122	−.86	71	−.59
The Circus	99	−1.01	91	.10

15. A schoolteacher thought that he had observed that students who dressed more neatly were generally better students. To test this idea, the teacher had a friend rate each of the students for neatness of dress. Following are the ratings for neatness, along with each student's score on a standardized school achievement test.

Child	Neatness Rating		Score on Achievement Test	
	X	Z_X	X	Z_Y
Janet	18	−.52	60	−.66
Gareth	24	1.43	58	−1.09
Grove	14	−1.82	70	1.47
Kevin	19	−.20	58	−1.09
Joshua	20	.13	66	.62
Nicole	23	1.11	68	1.04
Susan	20	.13	65	.40
Drew	22	.78	68	1.04
Marie	15	−1.50	56	−1.51
Chad	21	.46	62	−.23

16. A developmental psychologist studying people in their 80s was interested in the relation between number of very close friends and overall health. The scores for six research participants are shown below.

Research Participant	Number of Friends		Overall Health	
	X	Zx	Y	Zy
A	2	0	41	−.88
B	4	1.29	72	.96
C	0	−1.29	37	−1.12
D	3	.65	84	1.68
E	2	0	52	−.23
F	1	−.65	49	−.41

17. As part of a larger study, Speed and Gangestad (1997) collected ratings and nominations on a number of characteristics for 66 fraternity men from their fellow fraternity members. The following paragraph is taken from their "Results" section:

... men's romantic popularity significantly correlated with several characteristics: best dressed ($r = .48$), most physically attractive ($r = .47$), most outgoing ($r = .47$), most self-confident ($r = .44$), best trendsetters ($r = .38$), funniest ($r = .37$), most satisfied ($r = .32$), and most independent ($r = .28$). Unexpectedly, however, men's potential for financial success did not significantly correlate with romantic popularity ($r = .10$). (p. 931)

Explain these results as if you were writing to a person who has never had a course in statistics. Specifically, (a) explain what is meant by a correlation coefficient using one of the correlations as an example; (b) explain in a general way what is meant by "significantly" and "not significantly," referring to at least one specific example; and (c) speculate on the meaning of the pattern of results, taking into account the issue of direction of causality.

18. Gable and Lutz (2000) studied 65 children, 3 to 10 years old, and their parents. One of their results was "Parental control of child eating showed a negative association with children's participation in extracurricular activities ($r = .34$; $p < .01$)." Another result was "Parents who held less appropriate beliefs about children's nutrition reported that their children watched more hours of television

TABLE 3–10	Intercorrelations Between Measures of Victimization				
Measure	1	2	3	4	5
1. Peer (Schwartz et al., 1997)	—	.80**	.21*	.26**	.34**
2. Peer (Perry et al., 1988)		—	.32**	.21*	.22**
3. Self-report			—	.34**	.07
4. Diary				—	.08
5. Observe					—

*p < .05. ** p < .01.

Table 2 from "An Empirical Comparison of Methods of Sampling Aggression and Victimization in School Settings," by A. D. Pellegrini and Mara Bartini, *Journal of Educational Psychology*, June 2000. Vol. 92. No. 2. Copyright © 2000 by The American Psychological Association. Reprinted with permission.

per day ($r = .36$; $p < .01$)." (Both quotes from page 296.) Explain these results as if you were writing to a person who has never had a course in statistics. Be sure to comment on possible directions of causality for each result.

19. Table 3–10 is from a study by Pellegrini and Bartini (2000) of bullying and victimization among 367 middle-school students. Victimization was measured in several ways in the study, including two kinds of ratings by peers (fellow students), an overall self-report questionnaire, a monthly diary completed by the students about their experiences of bullying and aggression in the last 24 hours, and direct observations by the research team watching the students at breaks between classes, lunch, and so forth.

Explain the results as if you were writing to a person who has never had a course in statistics. Specifically, (a) explain what is meant by a correlation coefficient using one of the correlations as an example; (b) study the table and then comment on the patterns of results in terms of which variables are relatively strongly correlated and which are not very strongly correlated; and (c) comment on the limitations of making conclusions about direction of causality based on these data, using a specific correlation as an example (noting at least one plausible alternative causal direction and why that alternative is plausible).

20. Arbitrarily select eight full personal names, each from a different page of the telephone directory. Make a scatter diagram and figure the correlation coefficient for the relation between number of letters in first and last name. Describe the result in words, and suggest a possible interpretation for your results.

CHAPTER APPENDIX: HYPOTHESIS TESTS AND POWER FOR THE CORRELATION COEFFICIENT

This material is for students who have completed at least through Chapter 9 and are now returning to this chapter.

SIGNIFICANCE OF A CORRELATION COEFFICIENT

Hypothesis testing of a correlation coefficient follows the usual steps. However, there are three important points to note:

1. Usually, the null hypothesis is that the correlation in a population like that studied is no different from a population in which the true correlation is 0.
2. If the data meet assumptions (explained below), the comparison distribution is a *t* distribution with degrees of freedom equal to the number of people minus 2.

3. You figure the correlation coefficient's score on that t distribution using the formula

The t score is the correlation coefficient times the square root of 2 less than the number of people in the study, divided by the square root of 1 minus the correlation coefficient squared.

$$t = \frac{(r)(\sqrt{N-2})}{\sqrt{1-r^2}}$$

(3-2)

4. Note that the significance tests of a correlation, like a t test, can be either one-tailed or two-tailed. A one-tailed test means that the researcher has predicted the sign (positive or negative) of the correlation.[3]

Assumptions for the significance test of a correlation coefficient are that (a) the populations for both variables are normally distributed and (b) in the population, the distribution of each variable at each point of the other variable has about equal variance. However, as with the t test and analysis of variance, moderate violations of these assumptions are not fatal.

AN EXAMPLE

In the sleep and mood study example, let's suppose that the researchers predicted a positive correlation between number of hours slept and mood the next day, to be tested at the .05 level.

❶ **Restate the question as a research hypothesis and a null hypothesis about the populations.** There are two populations:

Population 1: People like those in this study.
Population 2: People for whom there is no correlation between number of hours slept the night before and mood the next day.

The null hypothesis is that the two populations have the same correlation. The research hypothesis is that Population 1 has a higher correlation than Population 2. (That is, the prediction is for a population correlation greater than 0.)

❷ **Determine the characteristics of the comparison distribution.** Assuming we meet the assumptions (in practice, it would be hard to tell with only 10 people in the study), the comparison distribution is a t distribution with $df = 8$. (That is, $df = N - 2 = 10 - 2 = 8$.)

❸ **Determine the cutoff sample score on the comparison distribution at which the null hypothesis should be rejected.** The t table (Table A–2 in Appendix A) shows that for a one-tailed test at the .05 level, with 8 degrees of freedom, you need a t of at least 1.860.

❹ **Determine your sample's score on the comparison distribution.** We figured a correlation of $r = .84$. Applying the formula to find the equivalent t, we get

$$t = \frac{(r)(\sqrt{[N-2]})}{\sqrt{[1-r^2]}} = \frac{(.84)(\sqrt{8})}{\sqrt{(1-.71)}} = \frac{(.84)(2.83)}{\sqrt{.29}} = \frac{2.38}{.54} = 4.41.$$

[3]Dunlap and Myers (1997) give a shortcut for finding the significance of a correlation coefficient. It turns out that the r needed for significance at the .05 level (two-tailed) is closely approximated by $2/\sqrt{N}$. For example, for $N = 5$, you would need a correlation of .89 ($2/\sqrt{5} = 2/2.24 = .89$). Dunlap and Myers also provide a shortcut for approximating the number of participants needed for power in the range of 80% to 90%, for a two-tailed test at the $p < .05$ significance level. The needed sample size is 8 divided by r^2. For example, using this formula, for $r = .10$, the needed number of participants is $8/.10^2$, which comes to 800.

TABLE 3–11 Approximate Power of Studies Using the Correlation Coefficient (*r*) for Testing Hypotheses at the .05 Level of Significance

		Effect Size		
		Small (r = .10)	Medium (r = .30)	Large (r = .50)
Two-tailed				
Total *N*:	10	.06	.13	.33
	20	.07	.25	.64
	30	.08	.37	.83
	40	.09	.48	.92
	50	.11	.57	.97
	100	.17	.86	[a]
One-tailed				
Total *N*:	10	.08	.22	.46
	20	.11	.37	.75
	30	.13	.50	.90
	40	.15	.60	.96
	50	.17	.69	.98
	100	.26	.92	[a]

[a]Nearly 1.00.

❺ **Decide whether to reject the null hypothesis.** The *t* score of 4.41 for our sample correlation is more extreme than the minimum needed *t* score of 1.860. Thus, you can reject the null hypothesis, and the research hypothesis is supported.

EFFECT SIZE AND POWER

The correlation coefficient itself is a measure of effect size. (Thus, in the example, effect size is $r = .84$.) Cohen's (1988) conventions for the correlation coefficient are .10 for a small effect size, .30 for a medium effect size, and .50 for a large effect size. Table 3–11 gives approximate power, and Table 3–12 gives minimum sample size for 80% power (also see footnote 3). More complete tables are provided in Cohen (1988, pp. 84–95, 101–102).

TABLE 3–12 Approximate Number of Participants Needed for 80% Power for a Study Using the Correlation Coefficient (*r*) for Testing a Hypothesis at the .05 Significance Level

	Effect Size		
	Small (r = .10)	Medium (r = .30)	Large (r = .50)
Two-tailed	783	85	28
One-tailed	617	68	22

CHAPTER 4

PREDICTION

Are You Ready?
What You Need to Have Mastered Before Starting this Chapter:

- Chapters 1, 2, and 3

In this chapter, building on what you learned in Chapter 3, we consider a major practical application of statistical methods—making predictions. Psychologists of various kinds are called on to make informed (and precise) guesses about such things as how well a particular job applicant is likely to perform if hired, how much a reading program is likely to help a particular third grader, or how likely a potential parolee is to commit a violent crime if released. Learning the intricacies of statistical prediction also deepens your insight into other statistical topics and prepares you for central themes in more advanced statistics courses.

We first consider procedures for making predictions about one variable, such as college grade point average (GPA), based on information about another variable, such as SAT scores. We then examine how to estimate the expected accuracy of the predictions we make using these procedures. Finally, we introduce situations in which predictions about one variable, such as college GPA, are made based on information about two or more other variables, such as using both SAT scores and high school GPA.

PREDICTOR AND CRITERION VARIABLES

predictor variable (X)
criterion variable (Y)

With correlation it does not matter much which variable is which. But with regression you have to decide which variable is being predicted from and which variable is being predicted to. The variable being predicted from is called the **predictor variable.** The variable being predicted to is called the **criterion variable.** In equations the predictor variable is usually labeled X, the criterion variable, Y. That is, X predicts Y. In the example we just considered, SAT scores would be the predictor variable or X, and college grades would be the criterion variable or Y. (See Table 4–1.)

PREDICTION USING Z SCORES

It is easier to learn about prediction if we first consider prediction using Z scores. (We get to prediction using ordinary scores shortly.)

THE PREDICTION MODEL

prediction model

standardized regression coefficient (β)

The **prediction model,** or *prediction rule* to make predictions with Z scores is that a person's predicted Z score on the criterion variable is found by multiplying a particular number, called a **standardized regression coefficient,** by that person's Z score on the predictor variable. The standardized regression coefficient is symbolized by the Greek letter beta (β).

   Beta is called a standardized regression *coefficient* because a coefficient is a number you multiply by another number. It is called a standardized *regression* coefficient because the statistical method for prediction is sometimes called regression (for reasons we discuss later in the chapter). Finally, it is called a *standardized* regression coefficient because you are working with Z scores, which are also called standard scores.

FORMULA FOR THE PREDICTION MODEL USING Z SCORES

Here is the formula for the prediction model using Z scores:

A person's predicted Z score on the criterion variable is the standardized regression coefficient times that person's Z score on the predictor variable.

$$\hat{Z}_Y = (\beta)(Z_X)$$ (4-1)

TABLE 4–1	Predictor and Criterion Variables	
	Variable Predicted From	Variable Predicted To
Name	Predictor variable	Criterion variable
Symbol	X	Y
Example	SAT scores	College GPA

In this formula, $\hat{Z}_Y$ is predicted value of the particular person's Z score on the criterion variable Y. The hat symbol means "predicted value of." β is the standardized regression coefficient. Z_X is the particular person's Z score on the predictor variable X. Thus, $(\beta)(Z_X)$ means multiplying the standardized regression coefficient by the person's Z score on the predictor variable.

For example, suppose that at your school the standardized regression coefficient (β) is .3 for predicting college GPA at graduation from SAT at admission. A person applying to your school has an SAT score that is 2 standard deviations above the mean (that is, a Z score of $+2$). The predicted Z score for this person's GPA would be .3 times 2, which is .6. That is, this person's predicted Z score for his or her college GPA is .6 standard deviations above the mean. In symbols,

$$\hat{Z}_Y = (\beta)(Z_X) = (.3)(2) = .6$$

STEPS FOR THE PREDICTION MODEL USING Z SCORES

Here are the steps for the prediction model using Z scores:

❶ **Determine the standardized regression coefficient.**
❷ **Multiply the standardized regression coefficient by the person's Z score on the predictor variable.**

We can illustrate the steps using the same example as above for predicting college GPA of a person at your school with an entering SAT 2 standard deviations above the mean.

❶ **Determine the standardized regression coefficient.** In the example, it was .3.
❷ **Multiply the standardized regression coefficient by the person's Z score on the predictor variable.** In the example, the person's Z score on the predictor variable is $+2$. Multiplying .3 and 2 gives .6. Thus, .6 is the person's predicted Z score on the criterion variable (college SAT).

THE STANDARDIZED REGRESSION COEFFICIENT (β)

It can be proved mathematicallly that the best number to use for the standardized regression coefficient in bivariate prediction is the correlation coefficient. That is, in bivariate prediction, $\beta = r$.

It may help you to understand this to consider two extreme situations. First, consider the situation when the correlation between two variables is perfect: In this situation $r = 1$. Thus, $\beta = 1$. If beta is 1, then the person's predicted Z score on the criterion variable is 1 times the person's Z score on the predictor variable. The result is that a person's predicted Z score on the criterion variable is the same as the person's Z score on the predictor variable. In terms of the formula, when $r = 1$,

$$\hat{Z}_Y = (\beta)(Z_X) = (1)(Z_X) = Z_X.$$

That is, $\hat{Z}_Y = Z_X$.

This makes sense, since if the correlation is perfect, the Z scores of the predictor and criterion variable should be the same.

Now consider the extreme situation when there is no correlation between the predictor and criterion variables, where $r = 0$. In this situation, the standardized regression coefficient is 0. Thus, whatever the person's score on the predictor variable, when you multiply it by the standardized regression coefficient of 0, the result is 0. In other words, when there is no correlation between a predictor and criterion variable, the predicted Z score on the criterion variable is always 0. A Z score of 0 is the same as the mean. Thus, when there is no correlation between the predictor and criterion variable, the prediction rule says you should predict that the person's score on the criterion variable will be the mean. In terms of the formula, when $r = 0$,

$$\hat{Z}_Y = (\beta)(Z_X) = (0)(Z_X) = 0.$$

This makes sense because when you have no information to go on (because the information you have, the predictor variable, tells you nothing about the criterion variable), your best bet is to predict the person will have an average score on the criterion variable. For example, if you had to predict a person's income and all you know about the person is the person's shoe size, your best bet is to predict the person has an average (mean) income.

In sum, when the correlation between predictor and criterion variables is 1, the best number for the standardized regression coefficient is 1, and when the correlation is 0, the best number for the standardized regression coefficient is 0. Thus, it is not surprising that in the intermediate cases, when r is between 0 and 1, the best number for the standardized regression coefficient is also between 0 and 1.

EXAMPLES

Consider again the example from Chapter 3 in which 10 students had a correlation of .84 between number of hours slept the night before and happy mood that day. Because the correlation is .84, the standardized regression coefficient is also .84. That is $r = .84$, thus $\beta = .84$. This means that the model for predicting a person's Z score for happy mood is to multiply .84 by the person's Z score for the number of hours slept the night before.

Suppose you were thinking about staying up so late one night you would get only 5 hours sleep. This would be a Z score of -2.73 on numbers of hours slept— that is, nearly 3 standard deviations less sleep than the mean. (We changed 5 hours to a Z score using the mean and standard deviation for the scores in this example and applying the procedure you learned in Chapter 2 for changing raw scores to Z scores: $Z = (X - M)/SD$.) We could then predict your Z score on happy mood the next day by multiplying .84 by -2.73. The result comes out to -2.29. This means that based on the results of our little study, if you sleep only 5 hours tonight, tomorrow we would expect you to have a happy mood that is more than 2 standard deviations below the mean (that is, you would be very unhappy). In terms of the formula,

$$\hat{Z}_Y = (\beta)(Z_X) = (.84)(-2.73) = -2.29.$$

In terms of the steps,

❶ **Determine the standardized regression coefficient.** Because the correlation coefficient is .84, the standardized regression coefficient is also .84.

❷ **Multiply the standardized regression coefficient by the person's Z score on the predictor variable.** Your Z score on the predictor variable is -2.73. Multiplying .84 by -2.73 gives a predicted Z score on happy mood of -2.29.

By contrast, if you planned to get 9 hours sleep, the prediction model would predict that tomorrow you would have a Z score for happy mood of .84 times .91 (the Z score when the number of hours slept is 9), which is $+.76$. You would be somewhat happier than the average. In terms of the formula,

$$\hat{Z}_Y = (\beta)(Z_X) = (.84)(.91) = .76.$$

WHY PREDICTION IS ALSO CALLED REGRESSION

Psychologists often call this kind of prediction *regression*. Regression means, literally, going back or returning. We use the term regression here because in the usual situation in which there is less than a perfect correlation between two variables, the criterion variable Z score is some fraction of the predictor variable Z score. This fraction is beta. In our sleep and mood example, beta is .84; thus the fraction is 84/100. This means that a person's predicted Z score on the criterion variable is 84/100 of the person's Z score on the predictor variable. As a result, the predicted Z score on the criterion variable is closer to the mean of 0 than is the Z score on the predictor variable. (In our sleep and mood example, when the Z score on the predictor variable was .91, the Z score predicted for the criterion variable was .76, a number closer to 0 than .91.) That is, the Z score on the criterion variable regresses, or goes back, toward a Z of 0.

Tip for Success

When making predictions using Z scores, you can check your work by being sure that a person's predicted Z score on the criterion variable is closer to 0 than the person's Z score on the predictor variable.

HOW ARE YOU DOING?

1. What is the prediction model using Z scores?
2. Why does the *standardized regression coefficient* have this name? (That is, explain the meaning of each of the three words that make up the term: standardized, regression, and coefficient.)
3. Write the formula for the prediction model using Z scores, and define each of the symbols.
4. Figure the predicted Z score on the criterion variable (Y) in each of the following situations:

Situation	r	Z_X
a	.2	1.2
b	.5	2.0
c	.8	1.2

ANSWERS:

1. A person's predicted Z score on the variable being predicted about (the criterion variable) is the standardized regression coefficient times the person's score on the variable being predicted from (the predictor variable).
2. It is called *standardized* because you are predicting with Z scores, which are also called standard scores. It is called a *regression* coefficient because it is used in prediction, which is also called regression. (Prediction is called regression because the result of the prediction process is a predicted score on the criterion variable that is closer to the mean—goes back towards the mean—than is the score on the predictor variable.) It is called a *coefficient* because it is a number you multiply by another number.
3. $\hat{Z}_Y = (\beta)(Z_X)$. $\hat{Z}_Y$ is the predicted Z score on the criterion variable. (The hat symbol means it is the predicted score.) β is the standardized regression coefficient. Z_X is the Z score on the predictor variable.
4. a. $(.2)(1.2) = .24$
   b. $(.5)(2.0) = 1.00$
   c. $(.8)(1.2) = .96$

RAW-SCORE PREDICTION USING THE *Z*-SCORE PREDICTION MODEL

Based on what you have learned, you can now also make predictions involving raw scores. One method of doing this is to change the raw score on the predictor variable to a Z score, make the prediction using the prediction model with Z scores, and then change the predicted Z score on the criterion variable to a raw score.

STEPS OF RAW-SCORE PREDICTION USING THE Z-SCORE PREDICTION MODEL

❶ **Change the person's raw score on the predictor variable to a Z score.** That is, change X to Z_X. Based on the formula from Chapter 2, $Z_X = (X - M_X)/SD_X$.

❷ **Multiply the standardized regression coefficient by the person's predictor variable Z score.** That is, multiply β (which is the same as r) by Z_X. This gives the predicted Z score on the criterion variable ($\hat{Z}_Y$). This is formula (4–1):

$$\hat{Z}_Y = (\beta)(Z_X).$$

Or in terms of the correlation coefficient, $\hat{Z}_Y = (r)(Z_X)$.

❸ **Change the person's predicted Z score on the criterion variable to a raw score.** That is, change $\hat{Z}_Y$ to $\hat{Y}$. Based on the formula from Chapter 2, $\hat{Y} = (SD_Y)(\hat{Z}_Y) + M_Y$.

EXAMPLES

Recall our example from the sleep and mood study in which we wanted to predict your mood the next day if you sleep 5 hours the night before. In the sleep and mood example, the mean for sleep was 8 and the standard deviation was 1.10; for happy mood, the mean was 4 and the standard deviation was 1.73. The correlation between sleep and mood was .84.

❶ **Change the person's raw score on the predictor variable to a Z score.** $Z_X = (X - M_X)/SD_X = (5 - 8)/1.10 = -3/1.10 = -2.73$. That is, as we saw earlier, the Z score for 5 hours sleep is -2.73.

❷ **Multiply the standardized regression coefficient by the person's predictor variable Z score.** $\hat{Z}_Y = (r)(Z_X) = (.84)(-2.73) = -2.29$. That is, as we also saw earlier, your predicted Z score for mood if you sleep only 5 hours is -2.29.

❸ **Change the person's predicted Z score on the criterion variable to a raw score.** $\hat{Y} = (SD_Y)(\hat{Z}_Y) + M_Y = (1.73)(-2.29) + 4 = -3.96 + 4 = .04$. In other words, using the regression procedure for the model based on the little study of 10 students, we would predict that if you sleep only 5 hours tonight, tomorrow you will rate your happy mood as about a zero!

Table 4–2 shows these steps worked out for sleeping 9 hours tonight.

Tip for Success

In using these steps, be careful when changing raw scores to Z scores and Z scores to raw scores to use the mean and standard deviation for the correct variable. In Step 1, you are working only with the score, mean, and standard deviation for the predictor variable (X). In Step 3, you are working only with the score, mean, and standard deviation for the criterion variable (Y).

TABLE 4–2 Raw-Score Prediction Using the Z-Score Prediction Model: Steps, Formulas, and Example

Step	Formula	Example
❶	$Z_X = (X - M_X)/SD_X$	$Z_X = (9-8)/1.10 = .91$
❷	$Z_Y = (\beta)(Z_X)$	$Z_Y = (.84)(.91) = .76$
❸	$\hat{Y} = (SD_Y)(\hat{Z}_Y) + M_Y$	$\hat{Y} = (1.73)(.76) + 4 = 5.31$

1. Explain the principle behind raw-score prediction using the Z-score prediction model.
2. List the steps of making raw-score predictions using the Z-score prediction model.
3. For a variable X, the mean is 10 and the standard deviation is 3. For a variable Y, the mean is 100 and the standard deviation is 10. The correlation of X and Y is .6. (a) Predict the score on Y for a person who has a score on X of 16. (b) Predict the score on Y for a person who has a score on X of 7.
4. For a variable X, the mean is 20 and the standard deviation is 5. For a variable Y, the mean is 6 and the standard deviation is 2. The correlation of X and Y is .8. (a) Predict the score on Y for a person who has a score on X of 20. (b) Predict the score on Y for a person who has a score on X of 25.

ANSWERS:

1. The principle is that you first change the raw score you are predicting from to a Z score, then make the prediction, then change the predicted Z score to a predicted raw score.
2. ❶ **Change the person's raw score on the predictor variable to a Z score.**
   ❷ **Multiply the standardized regression coefficient by the person's predictor variable Z score.**
   ❸ **Change the person's predicted Z score on the criterion variable to a raw score.**
3. (a) $Z_X = (X - M_X)/SD_X = (16 - 10)/3 = 6/3 = 2$.
   $\hat{Z}_Y = (r)(Z_X) = (.6)(2) = 1.2$.
   $\hat{Y} = (SD_Y)(\hat{Z}_Y) + M_Y = (10)(1.2) + 100 = 12 + 100 = 112$.
   (b) $Z_X = (X - M_X)/SD_X = (7 - 10)/3 = -3/3 = -1$.
   $\hat{Z}_Y = (r)(Z_X) = (.6)(-1) = -.6$.
   $\hat{Y} = (SD_Y)(\hat{Z}_Y) + M_Y = (10)(-.6) + 100 = -6 + 100 = 94$.
4. (a) $Z_X = (X - M_X)/SD_X = (20 - 20)/5 = 0/5 = 0$.
   $\hat{Z}_Y = (r)(Z_X) = (.8)(0) = 0$.
   $\hat{Y} = (SD_Y)(\hat{Z}_Y) + M_Y = (2)(0) + 6 = 0 + 6 = 6$.
   (b) $Z_X = (X - M_X)/SD_X = (25 - 20)/5 = 5/5 = 1$.
   $\hat{Z}_Y = (r)(Z_X) = (.8)(1) = .8$.
   $\hat{Y} = (SD_Y)(\hat{Z}_Y) + M_Y = (2)(.8) + 6 = 1.6 + 6 = 7.6$.

RAW-SCORE PREDICTION USING THE DIRECT RAW-SCORE PREDICTION MODEL

In practice, if you are going to make predictions for many different people, you would use a **raw-score prediction model** that allows you to just plug in a particular person's raw score on the predictor variable and then solve directly to get the person's predicted raw score on the criterion variable.

raw-score prediction model

DIRECT RAW-SCORE PREDICTION MODEL

The direct raw-score prediction model is that a person's predicted raw score on the criterion variable is found by starting with a number called the **regression constant** and adding to it the result of multiplying a **raw-score regression coefficient** by the person's raw score on the predictor variable.

regression constant (a)
raw-score regression coefficient (b)

FORMULA FOR DIRECT RAW-SCORE PREDICTION MODEL

Here is the formula for the direct raw-score prediction model:

A person's predicted score on the criterion variable equals the regression constant plus the raw-score regression coefficient times that person's score on the predictor variable.

$$\hat{Y} = a + (b)(X) \qquad\qquad (4\text{-}2)$$

In this formula, $\hat{Y}$ is the person's predicted raw score on the criterion variable; a is the regression constant, b is the raw-score regression coefficient, and X is the person's raw score on the predictor variable.

EXAMPLES

In the sleep and happy mood example the regression constant is -6.57 and the raw-score regression coefficient is 1.33. This means that to predict a person's score on mood, you start with a mood of -6.57 and add 1.33 times the number of hours sleep. In terms of the formula,

$$\hat{Y} = a + (b)(X) = -6.57 + (1.33)(X).$$

Or in terms of the variable names,

$$\text{Predicted mood} = -6.57 + (1.33)(\text{hours of sleep}).$$

Applying this formula to predicting mood after getting 5 hours sleep,

$$\text{Predicted mood} = -6.57 + (1.33)(5) = -6.57 + 6.65 = .08.$$

Predicting mood if you sleep 9 hours,

$$\text{Predicted mood} = -6.57 + (1.33)(9) = -6.57 + 11.97 = 5.40.$$

These results differ slightly from the results we got making raw-score predictions using the Z-score prediction model only because of rounding error. The underlying mathematics are identical.

Table 4–3 shows the worked-out raw-score prediction formula for the predicted mood scores for scores on sleep ranging from 0 hours to 16 hours. You can see from this table that, as we said earlier, it is much easier to do predictions with raw scores using the direct raw-score prediction formula.

An important thing to notice from Table 4–3 is that in actual prediction situations it is not a good idea to predict from scores on the predictor variable that are much higher or lower than those in the study you used to figure the original correlation. You can see in this example that when a person sleeps a very small number of hours, you predict negative scores on the mood scale, which is impossible (the scale goes from 0 to 8); and when the person sleeps a great many hours, you predict happiness scores on the mood scale that are higher than the limits of the scale. (In fact, it does not even make sense—sleeping 16 hours would not really make you incredibly happy.) This is why a prediction model should be used for making predictions only within the same range of scores that were used to come up with the original correlation on which the prediction model is based. (However, as we shall see in the next section, making predictions based on a predictor variable score of exactly 0 has a special purpose that is very important regardless of whether you would use this for making actual predictions.)

FIGURING THE REGRESSION CONSTANT

To do direct raw-score prediction, you need to figure the regression constant (a) and the raw-score regression coefficient (b). Fortunately, you can figure these numbers using what you already know from raw-score prediction using Z-scores.

TABLE 4–3	Direct Raw-Score Prediction in the Sleep and Mood Example for 0 to 16 Hours of Sleep

Predicted mood $= -6.57 + (1.33)$(hours of sleep)

0 hours sleep	$-6.57 + (1.33)(0) = -6.57 + 0 = -6.57$
1 hour sleep	$-6.57 + (1.33)(1) = -6.57 + 1.33 = -5.24$
2 hours sleep	$-6.57 + (1.33)(2) = -6.57 + 2.66 = -3.91$
3 hours sleep	$-6.57 + (1.33)(3) = -6.57 + 3.99 = -2.58$
4 hours sleep	$-6.57 + (1.33)(4) = -6.57 + 5.32 = -1.25$
5 hours sleep	$-6.57 + (1.33)(5) = -6.57 + 6.65 = .08$
6 hours sleep	$-6.57 + (1.33)(6) = -6.57 + 7.98 = 1.41$
7 hours sleep	$-6.57 + (1.33)(7) = -6.57 + 9.31 = 2.74$
8 hours sleep	$-6.57 + (1.33)(8) = -6.57 + 10.64 - 4.07$
9 hours sleep	$-6.57 + (1.33)(9) = -6.57 + 11.97 = 5.40$
10 hours sleep	$-6.57 + (1.33)(10) = -6.57 + 13.30 = 6.73$
11 hours sleep	$-6.57 + (1.33)(11) = -6.57 + 14.63 = 8.06$
12 hours sleep	$-6.57 + (1.33)(12) = -6.57 + 15.96 = 9.39$
13 hours sleep	$-6.57 + (1.33)(13) = -6.57 + 17.29 = 10.72$
14 hours sleep	$-6.57 + (1.33)(14) = -6.57 + 18.62 = 12.05$
15 hours sleep	$-6.57 + (1.33)(15) = -6.57 + 19.95 = 13.38$
16 hours sleep	$-6.57 + (1.33)(16) = -6.57 + 21.28 = 14.71$

Look again at Table 4–3. Notice that when a person sleeps exactly 0 hours, the predicted raw score for mood is -6.57. This is exactly the same as the regression constant.

This is a general principle: *The regression constant is the predicted raw score on the criterion variable when the raw score on the predictor variable is 0.* The reason this works is the regression constant is the number you always add in—a kind of baseline number, the number you start with. And it is reasonable that the best baseline number would be the number you predict from a predictor score of 0.

You can also see from the formula why the regression constant has to be the predicted score when the predictor variable is 0. If X is 0, then whatever b is, $(b)(X)$ is 0 (anything multiplied by 0 is 0). And if $(b)(X)$ equals 0, that only leaves a. In terms of formulas, If $X = 0$, then $\hat{Y} = a + (b)(0) = a + 0 = a$.

So how do you figure the regression constant? You do raw-score prediction with Z-scores and predict the criterion raw score when the prediction raw score is 0.

In the sleep and mood example, the Z score on hours slept (the predictor variable) for 0 hours is -7.27. That is,

$$Z_X = (X - M_X)/SD_X = (0 - 8)/1.10 = -8/1.10 = -7.27.$$

Using the Z score prediction model, this gives a predicted mood Z score of -6.11. That is,

$$\hat{Z}_Y = (r)(Z_X) = (.84)(-7.27) = -6.11.$$

Finally, changing the predicted Z score of -6.11 to a raw score gives -6.57. That is,

$$\hat{Y} = (SD_Y)(\hat{Z}_Y) + M_Y = (1.73)(-6.11) + 4 = -10.57 + 4 = -6.57.$$

Thus, the regression constant (a) is -6.57.

To repeat, you can figure the regression constant for the direct raw-score prediction formula by using raw-score prediction with Z scores to find the predicted criterion variable score when the predictor variable score is 0.

FIGURING THE RAW-SCORE REGRESSION COEFFICIENT

You can also figure the raw-score regression coefficient (b) with raw-score prediction using Z-scores. Look once again at Table 4–3. Notice that for each additional hour's sleep in the predictor variable, the predicted mood increases by exactly 1.33. For example, from 0 hours to 1 hour sleep, predicted mood goes from -6.57 to -5.24, an increase of exactly 1.33. Similarly, from 5 hours to 6 hours sleep, predicted mood goes up from .08 to 1.41—again, an increase of exactly 1.33. Recall that in the raw-score prediction formula, 1.33 is exactly b, the regression coefficient.

Here is the principle: The raw-score regression coefficient is how much the predicted criterion variable increases for every increase of 1 on the predictor variable. The reason this works is that the regression coefficient is what you multiply by the predictor variable. Thus, for each increase of 1 in the predictor variable, the result of the multiplication is increased by b, the raw-score regression coefficient.

The raw-score regression coefficient is a kind of "rate of exchange." That is, it tells you how many predicted units of the criterion variable you get for any particular number of units of the predictor variable. It is like knowing that on a given day, one Canadian dollar buys 80 Japanese Yen. (However, don't carry the analogy too far. When exchanging money, you are making a relatively exact transaction. With prediction models, the exchange is of an actual amount in the predictor variable in return for predicted amount in the criterion variable. Except in the case of a perfect correlation, that prediction will not be exact.)

You can also see from the raw-score prediction formula why b is the same as the increase in the predicted criterion variable when you increase the predictor's score by 1. For example, look at what happens when you go from a predictor score of 0 to a predictor score of 1:

$$\hat{Y} = a + (b)(X).$$
$$\text{If } X = 0, \hat{Y} = a + (b)(1) = a + 0 = a.$$
$$\text{If } X = 1, \hat{Y} = a + (b)(0) = a + (b)(1) = a + b.$$

The difference between a and $a + b$ is just b.

You can use this principle to figure b. That is, to find b, you figure the raw-score predicted value when the predictor is 1, do the same when the predictor is 0, and subtract. (Since when finding a you will have already figured the prediction value when the predictor is 0, the second part of this is done for you.) Most important, you can do all this with raw-score prediction using the Z-score prediction model.

STEPS FOR DIRECT RAW-SCORE PREDICTION

Here are the overall steps for direct raw-score prediction:[1]

❶ **Figure the regression constant.** To do this, figure the predicted raw-score on the criterion variable when the predictor variable is 0 with raw-score prediction using the Z-score prediction model.

---

[1]As usual, when extensive figuring is involved, there are also computational formulas. For the regression constant and the raw-score regression coefficient, $b = (\beta)(SD_Y/SD_X)$ and $a = M_Y - (b)(M_X)$. However, we strongly recommend that you use the procedures described in these steps involving changing to and from Z scores to figure a and b when doing the practice problems. This approach reinforces the underlying principles, which is the main thing you are trying to learn. (In actual research practice, you would figure a and b by computer. So what matters is understanding what these numbers mean.)

❷ **Figure the raw-score regression coefficient.** To do this, first figure the predicted raw score on the criterion variable when the predictor variable is 1 with raw-score prediction using the Z-score prediction model; then take this number minus the regression constant (from Step 1).

❸ **Find the person's predicted raw score on the criterion variable.** To do this, multiply the raw-score regression coefficient (from Step 2) by the person's score on the predictor variable, then add this result to the regression constant (from Step 1).

All of this may seem rather tedious. But as we pointed out earlier, this method is easier if you will be making many raw-score predictions. This is because once you have figured the regression constant and raw-score regression coefficient, you can make all of your predictions without having to change raw scores to and from Z scores.

EXAMPLE

Consider the example from Chapter 3 of the study of effect of number of exposures to a list of words and the number of words recalled (see Table 3–2 and Figure 3–3) . Specifically, suppose you want to predict how many words a person will recall if the person sees the list six times. In this example, for the number of times the list was presented (the predictor variable), the mean was 4.5 and the standard deviation was 2.29. For the number of words recalled (the criterion variable), the mean was 5.56 and the standard deviation was 2.12. The correlation between number of exposures and number of words recalled was .68.

❶ **Figure the regression constant.** To do this, figure the predicted raw score on the criterion variable when the predictor variable is 0 with raw-score prediction using the Z-score prediction model:

$$Z_X = (X - M_X)/SD_X = (0 - 4.5)/2.29 = -4.5/2.29 = -1.97.$$
$$\hat{Z}_Y = (r)(Z_X) = (.68)(-1.97) = -1.34.$$
$$\hat{Y} = (SD_Y)(\hat{Z}_Y) + M_Y = (2.12)(-1.34) + 5.56 = -2.84 + 5.56 = 2.72.$$

Thus, the regression constant (a) is 2.72.

❷ **Figure the raw-score regression coefficient.** To do this, first figure the predicted raw-score on the criterion variable when the predictor variable is 1 with raw-score prediction using the Z-score prediction model:

$$Z_X = (X - M_X)/SD_X = (1 - 4.5)/2.29 = -3.5/2.29 = -1.53.$$
$$\hat{Z}_Y = (r)(Z_X) = (.68)(-1.53) = -1.04.$$
$$\hat{Y} = (SD_Y)(\hat{Z}_Y) + M_Y = (2.12)(-1.04) + 5.56 = -2.20 + 5.56 = 3.36.$$

Then, take this number minus the regression constant (from Step 1). We already saw that the predicted raw score for a person with a number of exposures raw score of 0 comes out to 2.72. Thus, the final step is to subtract: $3.36 - 2.72 = .64$. The raw-score regression coefficient (b) is .64.

The direct raw-score prediction rule is that the predicted number of words recalled equals 2.72 plus .64 times a person's number of exposures to the list. That is, $\hat{Y} = 2.72 + (.64)(X)$.

❸ **Find the person's predicted raw score on the criterion variable.** To do this, multiply the raw score regression coefficient (from Step 2) by the person's score on the predictor variable, then add this result to the regression constant (from Step 1). We are predicting in this example for a person who had six exposures.

TABLE 4–4 Direct Raw-Score Prediction in the Number of Exposures and Number of Words Recalled Example for 1 to 8 Exposures

Predicted number recalled $= 2.72 + (.64)$(number of exposures)

1 exposure	$2.72 + (.64)(1) = 2.72 + .64 = 3.36$
2 exposures	$2.72 + (.64)(2) = 2.72 + 1.28 = 4.00$
3 exposures	$2.72 + (.64)(3) = 2.72 + 1.92 = 4.64$
4 exposures	$2.72 + (.64)(4) = 2.72 + 2.56 = 5.28$
5 exposures	$2.72 + (.64)(5) = 2.72 + 3.20 = 5.92$
6 exposures	$2.72 + (.64)(6) = 2.72 + 3.84 = 6.56$
7 exposures	$2.72 + (.64)(7) = 2.72 + 4.48 = 7.20$
8 exposures	$2.72 + (.64)(8) = 2.72 + 5.12 = 7.84$

Thus, we multiply .64 times 6 (which comes out to 3.84), then add this result to 2.72, which comes out to 6.56. Using the formula,

$$\hat{Y} = a + (b)(X) = 2.72 + (.64)(6) = 2.72 + 3.84 = 6.56.$$

In other words, if a person is exposed to the list six times, we predict he or she will recall between 6 and 7 words.

Table 4–4 applies this prediction rule to predictions for numbers of exposures from 1 to 8.

HOW ARE YOU DOING?

1. What is the advantage of direct raw-score prediction over raw-score prediction using the Z-score prediction model?
2. Write the formula and define each of the symbols for the direct raw-score prediction model.
3. Describe the meaning (the effect on prediction) of the regression constant and the raw-score regression coefficient.
4. For a variable X, the mean is 10 and the standard deviation is 3. For a variable Y, the mean is 100 and the standard deviation is 10. The correlation of X and Y is .6. (a) Figure the regression constant, (b) figure the raw-score regression coefficient, and (c) write the formula for the raw-score prediction model. Then, (d) predict the score on Y for a person who has a score on X of 16, and (e) predict Y for $X = 7$. (f) Compare your answers to the "How Are You Doing?" results for the same numbers, but using raw-score prediction with the Z score prediction rule.
5. For a variable X, $M = 20$, $SD = 5$; for Y, $M = 6$, $SD = 2$; $r = .8$. (a) Figure the regression constant, (b) figure the raw-score regression coefficient, and (c) write the formula for the raw-score prediction model. Then, predict $\hat{Y}$ for (d) $X = 20$ and (e) $X = 25$. Compare your answers to the "How Are You Doing?" results for the same numbers, but using raw-score prediction with the Z score prediction rule.

ANSWERS:

1. If you are making many predictions, it is less work. That is, once you have come up with the direct raw-score prediction model formula, you can make all the predictions you want without having to keep changing raw scores to and from Z scores.
2. $\hat{Y} = a + (b)(X)$. $\hat{Y}$ is the person's predicted raw score on the criterion variable; a is the regression constant, b is the raw-score regression coefficient, and X is the person's raw score on the predictor variable.
3. The regression constant tells you what a person's predicted score would be on the criterion variable if the person's score on the predictor variable was 0. The raw-score regression coefficient tells you how much a person's predicted score on the criterion variable increases for each 1-point increase in the person's score of the predictor variable.

4. (a) For $X = 0$, $Z_X = (X - M_X)/SD_X = (0 - 10)/3 = -10/3 = -3.33$.
    $\hat{Z}_Y = (r)(Z_X) = (.6)(-3.33) = -2$.
    $\hat{Y} = (SD_Y)(\hat{Z}_Y) + M_Y. = (10)(-2) + 100 = -20 + 100 = 80$.
    Thus, $a = 80$.
    (b) For $X = 1$, $Z_X = (X - M_X)/SD_X = (1 - 10)/3 = -9/3 = -3$.
    $\hat{Z}_Y = (r)(Z_X) = (.6)(-3) = -1.8$.
    $\hat{Y} = (SD_Y)(\hat{Z}_Y) + M_Y = (10)(-1.8) + 100 = -18 + 100 = 82$.
    For $X = 0, \hat{Y} = 80$.
    Thus, $b = 82 - 80 = 2$.
    (c) $\hat{Y} = a + (b)(X) = 80 + (2)(X)$.
    (d) $\hat{Y} = 80 + (2)(X) = 80 + (2)(16) = 80 + 32 = 112$.
    (e) $\hat{Y} = 80 + (2)(X) = 80 + (2)(7) = 80 + 14 = 94$.
    (f) Results are identical.
5. (a) for $X = 0$, $Z_X = (X - M_X)/SD_X - (0 - 20)/5 = \quad 20/5 = -4$.
    $\hat{Z}_Y = (r)(Z_X) - (.8)(-4) = \quad 3.2$.
    $\hat{Y} = (SD_Y)(\hat{Z}_Y) + M_Y = (2)(-3.2) + 6 = -6.4 + 6 = -.4$.
    Thus, $a = -.4$.
    (b) For $X = 1$, $Z_X = (X - M_X)/SD_X = (1 - 20)/5 = -19/5 = -3.8$.
    $\hat{Z}_Y = (r)(Z_X) = (.8)(-3.8) = -3.04$.
    $\hat{Y} = (SD_Y)(\hat{Z}_Y) + M_Y = (2)(-3.04) + 6 = -6.08 + 6 = -.08$.
    For $X = 0, \hat{Y} = -.4$
    Thus, $b = -.08 - -.4 = .32$.
    (c) $\hat{Y} = a + (b)(X) = -.4 + (.32)(X)$.
    (d) $\hat{Y} = -.4 + (.32)(X) = -.4 + (.32)(20) = -.4 + 6.4 = 6$.
    (e) $\hat{Y} = -.4 + (.32)(X) - .4 + (.32)(25) = .4 + 0 - 7.0$.
    (f) Results are identical.

THE REGRESSION LINE

You can visualize a prediction model as a line on a graph set up like a scatter diagram. The line is called a **regression line.** It shows the relation between the predictor variable and predicted values of the criterion variable.

     regression line

     Figure 4–1 shows the regression line for the hours slept and happy mood example. The regression line gives the predicted mood score from any particular number of hours slept. The dotted lines show the prediction we figured for having 9 hours sleep the night before.

SLOPE OF THE REGRESSION LINE

The steepness of the regression line, called its **slope,** is the amount the line moves up for every unit it moves across. In the example in Figure 4–1, the line moves up 1.33 on mood for every additional hour slept the night before. In fact, the slope of the line is exactly *b,* the raw-score regression coefficient.

     slope

THE INTERCEPT OF THE REGRESSION LINE

The point at which the regression line crosses (intercepts) the vertical axis is called the **intercept**—or sometimes the *Y intercept.* (This assumes you have drawn the vertical axis so it is at the 0 point on the horizontal axis.) The intercept is the predicted criterion variable score for someone with a score of 0 on the predictor vari-

     intercept

FIGURE 4–1 *The regression line for the hours slept and happy mood example, showing predicted mood for a person with 9 hours sleep.*

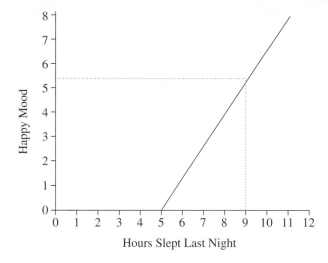

able. If Figure 4–1 included lower values of mood, the line would cross the vertical axis at −6.57. That is, when a person has slept 0 hours, he or she is predicted to have a mood score of −6.57. In fact, the intercept of the line is exactly *a,* the regression constant.

HOW TO DRAW THE REGRESSION LINE

The first steps are setting up the axes and labels of your graph—the same steps that you learned in Chapter 3 for setting up a scatter diagram. The regression line is a straight line. Thus, you only have to figure the location of any two points and draw the line that passes through them. There are four steps:

❶ **Draw and label the axes for a scatter diagram.** Remember to put the predictor variable on the horizontal axis.

❷ **Figure the predicted value on the criterion variable for a low value on the predictor variable, and mark the point on the graph.** The predictions are made using the procedures we have already covered. (If you were using raw-score prediction, you will already have figured this for when the predictor variable is 0.)

❸ **Do the same thing again, but for a high value on the predictor variable.** It is best to pick a value much higher than you used in Step 2. This makes the dots fairly far apart, so your drawing will be more accurate.

❹ **Draw a line that passes through the two marks.** This is the regression line.

EXAMPLES

Here is how you would draw the regression line for the sleep and mood example. (The steps are shown in Figure 4–2.)

❶ **Draw and label the axes for a scatter diagram.**

❷ **Figure the predicted value on the criterion variable for a low value on the predictor variable, and mark the point on the graph.** We saw earlier that when a person slept 5 hours the night before (that is, the score on the predictor variable is 5), the predicted mood score is .04. (When we used the direct raw-score method, we got a slightly different result due to rounding error. Either result would give almost the same line.) Thus, you mark this point ($X = 5, \hat{Y} = .04$) on the graph.

Tip for Success

To help you remember which variable goes on which axis, you can use the mnemonic "what's known forms a stable basis for what's predicted or envisioned up high."

Tip for Success

You can check the accuracy of your line by predicting any third point. It should also fall on the line.

Tip for Success

If you have figured the raw-score prediction formula, you can check the accuracy of your line by figuring the amount the line goes up for each point across. This should be the same as b. You can also note where the line crosses the vertical axis (presuming the vertical axis is set at 0 on the horizontal axis). This should be the same as a.

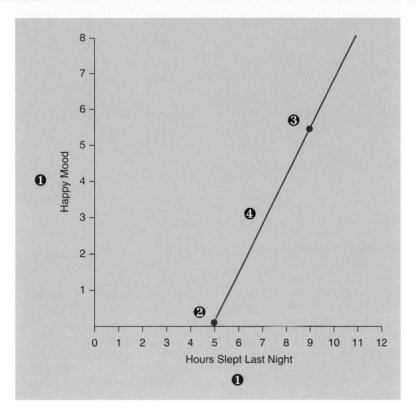

FIGURE 4-2 *Steps in drawing a regression line using the sleep and mood example.* ❶ *Draw and label the axes,* ❷ *mark a point for a low value of the predictor variable and its predicted value on the criterion variable,* ❸ *mark a point for a high value of the predictor variable and its predicted value on the criterion variable, and* ❹ *draw the regression line.*

❸ **Do the same thing again, but for a high value on the predictor variable.** We also saw earlier that if a person sleeps 9 hours the night before, we predict a mood score of 5.31. Thus, you make this point ($X = 9$, $\hat{Y} = 5.31$) on the graph.

❹ **Draw a line that passes through the two marks.**

Figure 4–3 shows the regression line for the word recall example. We made the regression line using predictor scores of 4 and 7 exposures.

HOW ARE YOU DOING?

1. What does the regression line show?
2. (a) What is the slope of the regression line? (b) What is it equivalent to in the direct raw-score prediction formula?
3. (a) What is the intercept of the regression line? (b) What is it equivalent to in the direct raw-score prediction formula?
4. Draw the regression line for X and Y as described in the "How Are You Doing?" for the previous section, where for X, $M = 10$, $SD = 3$; for Y, $M = 100$, $SD = 10$; and $r = .6$.
5. Draw the regression line for variables X and Y as described in the "How Are You Doing?" for the previous section, where $X = 20$, $SD = 25$; for Y, $X = 6$, $SD = 2$; and $r = .8$.

ANSWERS

1. The relation between the predictor variable and predicted values of the criterion variable.
2. (a) The amount the line goes up for every one it moves across. (b) b, the raw-score regression coefficient.

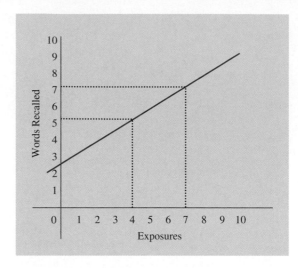

FIGURE 4–3 *The regression line for the word recall example, showing predicted number of words recalled for individuals with four and with seven exposures to each word.*

3. (a) The point at which the regression line crosses the vertical axis (assuming the vertical axis is at 0 on the horizontal axis). (b) *a*, the regression constant.
4. See Figure 4–4.
5. See Figure 4–5.

ERROR AND PROPORTIONATE REDUCTION IN ERROR

How accurate are the predictions you make using regression? Normally, you predict the future, so there is no way to know how accurate you are in advance. However, you can estimate your likely accuracy. What you do is figure how accurate your prediction model would have been if you had used it to make "predictions" for the scores you used to figure the correlation coefficient in the first place.

Here is how this works: First, you figure the prediction model in the usual way based on the correlation coefficient for the particular group of people you have studied. Next, you use this prediction model to make a "prediction" for each of the people in your study. (You make "predictions" for each person in the sense that you put the person's predictor variable score into the prediction formula and figure the person's "predicted" criterion variable score. We put the words "prediction" and "predicted" in quotes here because you already know each person's criterion variable score. You are using the prediction rule, but to predict something you already know.) You then compare each of these "predicted" scores to the person's actual score on the criterion variable. If the prediction rule is a good one, then these "predicted" criterion variable scores should be very close to the actual criterion variable scores.

Consider the sleep and mood example. There is no way to know for sure how accurate predictions will be for people who were not in the study. But you could ask, "Suppose I had used this model to predict the mood for the students I did study? How accurate would those 'predictions' have been?" Consider the 10 students we used in Chapter 3 to figure the correlation coefficient (which came out to

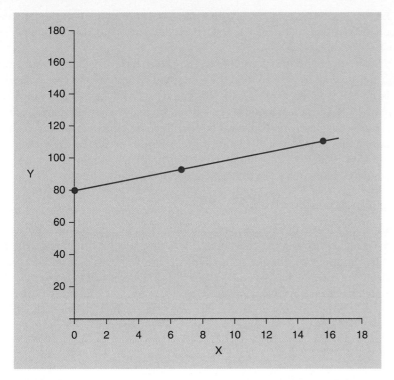

FIGURE 4–4   *Regression line for "How Are You Doing?" question 4.*

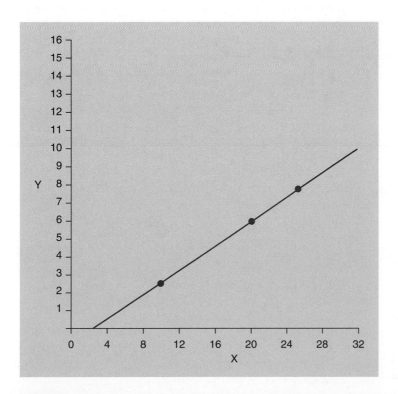

FIGURE 4–5   *Regression line for "How Are You Doing?" question 5.*

.84). Earlier in this chapter we saw that the raw-score prediction model based on this correlation (and the means and standard deviations for this example) worked out to $\hat{Y} = -6.57 + (1.33)(X)$.

We can now apply that formula back to these same 10 students. For example, one of the students slept 7 hours. Using the prediction rule, the "predicted" mood for this student is $-6.57 + (1.33)(7)$. This comes out to a "predicted" mood for this student of 2.74. The actual mood score for this student was 4—a figure close to, but not the same as, what we predicted. The first three columns of Table 4–5 show the number of hours slept, the actual mood score, and the "predicted" mood score using the prediction model. Notice that overall, the "predicted" mood scores are moderately close to, but not the same as, the actual mood scores.

ERROR AND SQUARED ERROR

The next step is to use these predictions about the original people we studied to estimate the accuracy of the prediction rule. To do this, you first figure how far off the predictions you make using the prediction rule are from the actual scores of these individuals you originally studied. How far off you are is called **error.** That is, for each individual, *error is the actual score minus the predicted score.*

error

The next thing you do is square each error to get *squared errors.* That is,

A person's squared error is the square of the difference between the person's actual criterion variable score and the person's predicted criterion variable score.

$$Error^2 = (Y - \hat{Y})^2 \qquad (4\text{-}3)$$

Using squared errors solves the problem that some errors will be positive numbers (we predicted too low) and some, negative numbers (we predicted too high). If you do not square the errors, when you eventually add them up, the positive and negative errors will offset each other. (Recall that you did the same thing in Chapter 2 when working with deviations from the mean.)

The errors and squared errors from our sleep and mood example are shown in Table 4–5.

TABLE 4-5 **Figuring Errors and Squared Errors for the Sleep and Mood Example**

| Hours Slept | Happy Mood | | Error | Squared Error |
	Actual	Predicted		
X	Y	$\hat{Y}$	$(Y - \hat{Y})$	$(Y - \hat{Y})^2$
7	4	2.74	1.26	1.59
9	5	5.40	$-.40$	.16
8	3	4.07	-1.07	1.15
9	7	5.40	1.60	2.56
8	4	4.07	$-.07$	.00
6	1	1.41	$-.41$	.17
8	3	4.07	-1.07	1.15
7	2	2.74	$-.74$	.55
10	6	6.73	$-.73$	.53
8	5	4.07	.93	.86
				Σ 8.72

GRAPHIC INTERPRETATION OF ERROR

Figure 4–6 shows the scatter diagram for the sleep and mood example with the regression line drawn in. In this graph, the 10 actual scores are shown as dots; predicted mood scores for all values of number of hours slept are on the regression line. Thus, the error for any particular student is the vertical distance between the dot for the student's actual mood score and the regression line. We have drawn dotted lines to show the error for each student.

PROPORTIONATE REDUCTION IN ERROR

Now, how are errors and squared errors useful? The most common way to think about the accuracy of a prediction model is to compare the amount of squared error using your prediction model to the amount of squared error you would have without the model.

First, you figure the amount of squared error using the prediction model. Next, you figure the squared error you would make predicting without the model. Finally, you compare the two amounts of squared error.

The squared error using the prediction model is the **sum of the squared errors.** **sum of the squared error** That is, you just add up the squared errors of the individuals in the study. In the sleep and mood example, this is the sum of the last column in Table 4–5, which is 8.72. The sum of squared errors is abbreviated as SS_{Error}. In our example, $SS_{Error} = 8.72$. SS_{Error}

How do you figure the amount of squared error predicting without the model? If you cannot use the prediction model, the most accurate prediction for anyone will be the criterion variable's mean. In our example, suppose you knew nothing about how much a person slept the night before. Your best strategy for any student would be to predict that the student will have an average score on happy mood. That is, your best strategy would be to predict a mood score of 4. Consider another example. Suppose you wanted to predict a person's college GPA, but you had no information about any predictor variables. Your best bet here is to predict that person will have the average college GPA for students at that college.

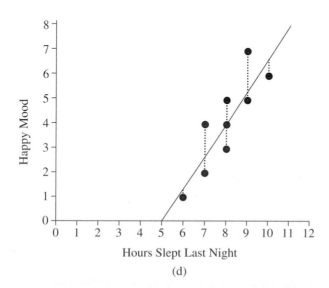

FIGURE 4–6 *Scatter diagram for the sleep and mood example with the regression line drawn in and dotted lines showing errors.*

Thus, predictions without a model means predicting the mean. This means that *the amount of squared error when predicting without a model is the amount of squared error when predicting each score to be the mean.* Error in general is the actual score minus the predicted score. When the predicted score is the mean, error is the actual score minus the mean. Squared error is the square of this number. The sum of these squared errors is the **total squared error when predicting from the mean**; we call this number SS_{Total}. (What we are now calling SS_{Total} is the same as what we called SS in Chapter 2 when figuring the variance. In Chapter 2, we defined SS as the sum of squared deviations from the mean. A deviation from the mean is the score minus the mean. This is exactly the same as the error that results when our prediction is the mean.)

total squared error when predicting from the mean (SS_{Total})

The worth of a prediction model is how much less error you make using the prediction model (SS_{Error}) compared to using the mean (SS_{Total}). With a good prediction model, SS_{Error} should be much smaller than SS_{Total}.

proportionate reduction in error

The key comparison is the **proportionate reduction in error:** The reduction in error ($SS_{Total} - SS_{Error}$), divided by the total amount that could be reduced (SS_{Total}). In terms of a formula,

> The proportionate reduction in error is the sum of squared error when predicting from the mean minus the sum of squared error when predicting from the bivariate prediction rule, all divided by the sum of squared error when predicting from the mean.

$$\text{Proportionate reduction in error} = \frac{SS_{Total} - SS_{Error}}{SS_{Total}} \qquad (4\text{-}4)$$

To put this another way, using the mean to predict is not a very precise method because it leaves a lot of error. So, now you are seeing how much better you can do—how much the proportion of the squared error you would make using the mean is reduced by using the prediction rule.

Suppose a prediction model is no improvement over predicting from the mean. In this situation, SS_{Error} equals SS_{Total} (SS_{Error} can never be worse than SS_{Total}). The prediction model has reduced zero error ($SS_{Total} - SS_{Error} = 0$), and it has reduced 0% of the total error ($0/SS_{Total} = 0$).

Now suppose a prediction model gives perfect predictions with no error whatsoever. The prediction model has reduced the error by 100%. (In terms of the equation, if $SS_{Error} = 0$, then the numerator will be $SS_{Total} - 0$, or SS_{Total}; dividing SS_{Total} by SS_{Total} gives 1, or 100%.)

In most actual situations, the proportionate reduction in error will be somewhere between 0% and 100%.

STEPS FOR FIGURING THE PROPORTIONATE REDUCTION IN ERROR

❶ **Figure the sum of squared errors using the mean to predict: Take each score minus the mean, square it, and add these up.** This gives SS_{Total}.

❷ **Figure the sum of squared errors using the prediction model: Take each score minus the predicted score for this person, square it, and add these up.** This gives SS_{Error}.

❸ **Figure the reduction in squared error: This is the sum of squared errors using the mean to predict (from Step 1) minus the sum of squared error using the prediction model (from Step 2).**

TABLE 4–6 Figuring Proportionate Reduction in Error for the Sleep and Mood Example

Actual	Predicting Using Mean ❶			Using Prediction Model ❷		
Y	Mean	Error	Error²	$\hat{Y}$	Error	Error²
4	4	0	0	2.74	1.26	1.59
5	4	1	1	5.40	−.40	.16
3	4	−1	1	4.07	−1.07	1.15
7	4	3	9	5.40	1.60	2.56
4	4	0	0	4.07	−.07	.00
1	4	−3	9	1.41	−.41	.17
3	4	−1	1	4.07	−1.07	1.15
2	4	−2	4	2.74	−.74	.55
6	4	2	4	6.73	−.73	.53
5	4	1	1	4.07	.93	.86
		$SS_{Total} = 30$			$SS_{Error} = 8.72$	

Proportionate reduction in error ❸ $\dfrac{SS_{Total} - SS_{Error}}{SS_{Total}} = \dfrac{30 - 8.72}{30} = \dfrac{21.28}{30} = .71$ ❹

❹ **Figure the proportionate reduction in squared error. This is the reduction in squared error (from Step 3) divided by the total squared error when using the mean to predict (from Step 1).**

EXAMPLES

Table 4–6 shows the scores, predicted scores, errors, squared errors, sums of squared errors, and proportionate reduction in error for the sleep and mood example. Using the steps,

❶ **Figure the sum of squared errors using the mean to predict: Take each score minus the mean, square it, and add these up.** From Table 4–6, $SS_{Total} = 30$.

❷ **Figure the sum of squared errors using prediction model: Take each score minus the predicted score for this person, square it, and add these up.** From Table 4–6, $SS_{Error} = 8.72$.

❸ **Figure the reduction in squared error: This is the sum of squared errors using the mean to predict (from Step 1) minus the sum of squared errors using the prediction model (from Step 2).** Reduction in squared error = 30 − 8.72 = 21.28.

❹ **Figure the proportionate reduction in squared error. This is the reduction in squared error (from Step 3) divided by the total squared error when using the mean to predict (from Step 1).** Proportionate reduction in squared error = 21.28/30 = .71.

Thus, when predicting happy mood from sleep the night before, the prediction model, based on the scores from our group of 10 students, provides a 71% reduction in error over using the mean to predict.

Table 4–7 shows the score, predicted scores, errors, and squared errors for the word recall study. As you can see, the sum of squared error is 40.13. From previous figuring (in Chapter 3 when figuring the variance) we know that SS_{Total} is 72. Thus, the reduction in squared error is $72 - 40.13$, which is 31.87. The proportionate reduction in squared error is this reduction in squared error, 31.87, divided by the total squared error, 72. Dividing 31.87 by 72 gives .44.

PROPORTIONATE REDUCTION IN ERROR AS r^2

The proportionate reduction in error turns out to equal the correlation coefficient squared. That is,

The proportionate reduction in error is equal to the correlation coefficient squared.

$$\text{Proportionate reduction in error} = r^2 \qquad (4\text{-}5)$$

Because of this equivalence, r^2 is typically used as the symbol for the proportionate reduction in error.

For example, in the sleep and mood study, the correlation coefficient was .84, and .84 squared is .71. That is, $r^2 = .71$. Notice that this number (.71) is exactly the same as we just figured by finding predicted scores, errors, squared errors, sums of squared errors, and proportionate reduction in squared error. Similarly, for the word recall study, the correlation was .68, which when squared, gives .46, the same number (within rounding error) that we just figured for proportionate reduction in error the long way.

We figured the proportionate reduction in error so laboriously in these examples only to help you understand this important concept. (It will be important for

TABLE 4–7 **Squared Error for the Experiment on the Effect of Number of Exposures on Number of Words Recalled**

Subject	Number of Exposures X	Number of Words Recalled Y	$\hat{Y}$	Error	Error^2
1	1	4	3.4	.6	.36
2	1	3	3.4	− .4	.16
3	2	3	4.0	−1.0	1.00
4	2	5	4.0	1.0	1.00
5	3	6	4.6	1.4	1.96
6	3	4	4.6	− .6	.36
7	4	4	5.3	−1.3	1.69
8	4	6	5.3	.7	.49
9	5	5	5.9	− .9	.81
10	5	7	5.9	1.1	1.21
11	6	2	6.6	−4.6	21.16
12	6	9	6.6	2.4	5.76
13	7	6	7.2	−1.2	1.44
14	7	8	7.2	.8	.64
15	8	9	7.8	−1.3	1.69
16	8	8	7.8	.2	.40
				$SS_{Error} =$	40.13

you to do so with some additional examples, such as those in the practice problems, to ingrain this logic in your mind.) However, in an actual research situation, you would use the simpler procedure of squaring the correlation coefficient. (Also note that this works in reverse also. If you know the proportionate reduction in error, you can find the correlation coefficient by taking the square root of the proportionate reduction in error.)

PROPORTIONATE REDUCTION IN ERROR AS THE PROPORTION OF VARIANCE ACCOUNTED FOR

The proportionate reduction in error is sometimes called the **proportion of variance accounted for.** This name is used because SS_{Total} is a kind of measure of variance from the criterion variable's mean and is closely related to the variance of the criterion variable. (SS_{Total} is the same as SS in the variance formula—the number that, when divided by N, gives the usual variance.) Proportionate reduction in error is how much of SS_{Total} is reduced, or accounted for, by the prediction model. Thus, proportionate reduction in error is also a kind of proportion of variance that is reduced.

proportion of variance accounted for

HOW ARE YOU DOING?

1. Explain in words how you figure (a) the sum of squared error predicting from the mean, and (b) the sum of squared error using the prediction model.
2. Write the formula for figuring the proportionate reduction in error and define each of its symbols in words.
3. Explain why the procedure for figuring the proportionate reduction in error tells you about the accuracy of the prediction model.
4. Explain how you would show error in a graph.
5. Below are scores and predicted scores for four people on a particular criterion variable using a prediction model based on the scores from these four people. Figure the proportionate reduction in error and correlation coefficient.

Score	Predicted Score
6	5.7
4	4.3
2	2.9
8	7.1

ANSWERS:

1. (a) You figure the sum of squared error predicting from the mean by taking each criterion variable score minus the mean of the criterion variable scores, squaring this difference, then summing up all these squared differences.
   (b) You figure the sum of squared error using the prediction model by taking each criterion variable score minus what you would predict for that person's criterion variable score using the prediction model, squaring this difference, then summing up all these squared differences.
2. Proportionate reduction in error = $(SS_{Total} - SS_{Error})/SS_{Total}$. SS_{Total} is the sum of squared differences between criterion variable scores and the criterion variable mean; SS_{Error} is the sum of squared differences between criterion variable scores and that person's predicted criterion variable score using the prediction model.
3. The procedure for figuring the proportionate reduction in error tells you about the accuracy of the prediction model because it tells you the proportion of total error (the error you would make if just predicting from the mean) you are reducing by using the prediction model (where your error is based on predicting from the prediction model). That is, the larger proportion of total error you reduce, the more accurate your prediction model. Perfect prediction would be 100% reduction.

4. A scatter diagram with the regression line drawn in shows error as the vertical distance between the dot for the actual score and the regression line.

5.

Score	Mean	Error	Error^2	Score	Predicted	Error	Error^2
6	5	1	1	6	5.7	.3	.09
4	5	−1	1	4	4.3	−.3	.09
2	5	−3	9	2	2.9	−.9	.81
8	5	3	9	8	7.1	.9	.81
		$SS_{\text{Total}} = 20$				$SS_{\text{Error}} = 1.80$	

Proportionate reduction in error $= (SS_{\text{Total}} - SS_{\text{Error}})/SS_{\text{Total}} = (20 - 1.8)/20 = 18.2/20 = .91$
$r = \sqrt{r^2} = \sqrt{.91} = .95.$

MULTIPLE REGRESSION

bivariate prediction

So far, we have predicted a person's score on a criterion variable using the person's score on a single predictor variable. That is, each example so far was for **bivariate prediction** (bivariate means two variables) and the prediction models we used were *bivariate prediction models.*

Suppose you could use more than one predictor variable. For example, in predicting happy mood, all you had to work with was the number of hours slept the night before. Suppose you also knew how well the person had slept or how many dreams the person had had. With this added information, you might be able to make a much more accurate prediction of mood.

multiple correlation
multiple regression

The association between a criterion variable and two or more predictor variables is called **multiple correlation.**[2] Making predictions in this situation is called **multiple regression.**

We explore these topics only briefly because the details are beyond the level of an introductory book. However, multiple regression and correlation are frequently used in research articles in psychology, so it is valuable for you to have a general understanding of them. (We also have more to say about multiple regression in chapters 16 and 17.)

MULTIPLE REGRESSION PREDICTION MODELS

In multiple regression, each predictor variable has its own regression coefficient. The predicted Z score of the criterion variable is found by multiplying the Z score for each predictor variable by its standardized regression coefficient and then adding up the results. For example, here is the Z-score multiple regression formula with three predictor variables:

The predicted Z score for the criterion variable is the standardized regression coefficient for the first predictor variable times the person's score on the first predictor variable, plus the standardized regression coefficient for the second predictor variable times the person's score on the second predictor variable, plus the standardized regression coefficient for the third predictor variable times the person's score on the third predictor variable.

$$\hat{Z}_Y = (\beta_1)(Z_{X_1}) + (\beta_2)(Z_{X_2}) + (\beta_3)(Z_{X_3})$$

(4-6)

---

[2]There are also procedures that allow you to use more than one criterion variable. For example, you might want to know how good a predictor hours slept is for both mood and peace of mind. Procedures involving more than one criterion variable are called "multivariate statistics" and are quite advanced. We introduce you to some examples in Chapter 17.

$\hat{Z}_Y$ is the person's predicted score on the criterion variable. β_1 is the standardized regression coefficient for the first predictor variable; β_2 and β_3 are the standardized regression coefficients for the second and third predictor variables. Z_{X1} is the person's Z score for the first predictor variable; Z_{X2} and Z_{X3} are the person's Z scores for the second and third predictor variables. $(\beta_1)(Z_{X1})$ means multiplying β_1 by Z_{X1}, and so forth.

For example, in the sleep and mood study, a multiple regression model for predicting mood (Y) using the predictor variables of number of hours slept, which we could now call X_1, and also a rating of how well you slept (X_2) and number of dreams during the night (X_3), might be as follows:

$$\hat{Z}_Y = (.53)(Z_{X1}) + (.28)(Z_{X2}) + (.03)(Z_{X3}).$$

Suppose you were asked to predict the mood of a student who had a Z score of -1.82 for number of hours slept, a Z score of 2.34 for how well she slept, and a Z score of .94 for number of dreams during the night. That is, the student did not sleep very long, slept very well, and had a few more dreams than average. You would figure the predicted Z score for happy mood by multiplying .53 times the number-of-hours-slept Z score, 2.34 times the how-well-slept Z score, and .94 times the number-of-dreams Z score, then adding up the results:

$$\hat{Z}_Y = (.53)(-1.82) + (.28)(2.34) + (.03)(.94).$$
$$= -.96 + .66 + .03 = -.27.$$

Thus, under these conditions, you would predict a happy mood Z score of $-.27$. This means a happy mood about one-quarter of a standard deviation below the mean. You can see that how well the student slept partially offset getting fewer hours sleep. Given the very low β for dreams in this model, number of dreams would in general make very little difference in mood the next day, no matter how many or how few.

AN IMPORTANT DIFFERENCE BETWEEN MULTIPLE REGRESSION AND BIVARIATE PREDICTION

There is one particularly important difference between multiple regression and bivariate prediction. In ordinary bivariate prediction, $\beta = r$. That is, the standardized regression coefficient is the same as the correlation coefficient. But in multiple regression, the standardized regression coefficient (β) for a predictor variable is *not* the same as the ordinary correlation coefficient (r) of that predictor with the criterion variable.

Usually, a β will be closer to 0 than r. The reason is that part of what makes any one predictor successful in predicting the criterion will usually overlap with what makes the other predictors successful in predicting the criterion variable. In multiple regression, the standardized regression coefficient is about the unique, distinctive contribution of the variable, excluding any overlap with other predictor variables.

Consider the sleep and mood example. When we were predicting mood using just the number of hours slept, β was the same as the correlation coefficient of .84. Now, with multiple regression, β for number of hours slept is only .53. It is less because part of what makes number of hours slept predict mood overlaps with what makes sleeping well predict mood (in this fictional example, people who sleep more hours usually sleep well).

multiple correlation coefficient (R)

In multiple regression, the correlation between the criterion variable and all the predictor variables taken together is called the **multiple correlation coefficient** and is symbolized as **R.** However, because of the usual overlap among predictor variables, the multiple correlation is usually smaller than the sum of the individual rs of each predictor with the criterion variable.

SOME IMPORTANT SIMILARITIES WITH BIVARIATE PREDICTION

One important similarity of multiple regression with bivariate prediction is that both can be done with either raw scores or Z scores. We emphasized Z scores to keep the discussion simple. But when doing multiple regression with raw scores, the prediction model has a single overall regression constant (a), but different raw-score regression coefficients (b_1, b_2, etc.) for each predictor.

Another important similarity is that for both, the squared correlation coefficient is the proportionate reduction in error. In bivariate prediction, the symbol is r^2. In multiple regression it is R^2.

LIMITATIONS OF REGRESSION

All of the limitations for correlation we discussed in Chapter 3 apply to prediction. The procedures we have considered in this chapter are inaccurate if the correlation is curvilinear, the group studied is restricted in range, or the measures are unreliable. That is, in each of these situations the regression coefficients (whether bivariate or multiple) are smaller than they should be to reflect the true association of the predictor variables with the criterion variable. Nor do these prediction procedures by themselves tell you anything about the direction of causality. Even in published articles, researchers sometimes overlook these limitations when considering complex regression results.

HOW ARE YOU DOING?

1. What is multiple regression?
2. Write the multiple regression prediction model with two predictors (using Z-score prediction), and define each of the symbols.
3. In a Z-score multiple regression model, the standardized regression coefficient for the first predictor variable is .4 and for the second predictor variable is .7. What is the predicted criterion variable Z score for (a) a person with a Z-score of $+1$ on the first predictor variable and a Z score of $+2$ on the second predictor variable, and (b) a person with a Z score of $+2$ on the first predictor variable and a Z score of $+1$ on the second predictor variable?
4. In multiple regression, why are the standardized regression coefficients for each predictor variable often smaller than the ordinary correlation coefficient of that predictor variable with the criterion variable?
5. How is a raw-score multiple regression model different from a Z-score multiple regression model?
6. List three conditions in which regression coefficients you figure will be closer to zero than they would be if they represented the true regression model.

ANSWERS:

1. The procedure for predicting a criterion variable from a prediction rule that includes more than one predictor variable.
2. $\hat{Z}_Y = (\beta_1)(Z_{X1}) + (\beta_2)(\beta_{X2})$.
   $\hat{Z}_Y$ is the person's predicted score on the criterion variable. β_1 is the standardized regression coefficient for the first predictor variable, β_2 is the standardized regression coefficient for

the second predictor variable. Z_{X1} is the person's Z score for the first predictor variable, and Z_{X2} is the person's Z score for the second predictor variable.

3. (a) $\hat{Z}_Y = (.4)(Z_{X1}) + (.7)(Z_{X2}) = (.4)(1) + (.7)(2) = .4 + 1.4 = 1.8$.
   (b) $\hat{Z}_Y = (.4)(Z_{X1}) + (.7)(Z_{X2}) = (.4)(2) + (.7)(1) = .8 + .7 = 1.5$.

4. In multiple regression, a predictor variable's association with the criterion variable usually overlaps with the other predictor variables' association with the criterion variable. Thus, the unique association of a predictor variable with the criterion variable (the standardized regression coefficient) is usually smaller than the ordinary correlation of the predictor variable with the criterion variable.

5. In a raw-score multiple regression model there is a regression constant and there is a raw-score regression coefficient (instead of a standardized regression coefficient) for each predictor variable.

6. Restriction in range, curvilinear relations, and unreliable measurement.

CONTROVERSY: COMPARING PREDICTORS

One ongoing controversy about multiple regression is how to judge the relative importance of each predictor variable in predicting the criterion variable. As we noted, a regression coefficient tells you the unique contribution of the predictor variable to the prediction, over and above all the other predictors. When predicting by itself, without considering the other predictors (that is, using its ordinary correlation with the criterion variable), a predictor variable may seem to have a quite different importance relative to the other predictor variables. For example, if there are three predictors, the βs could be .4, .6, and .8. But in that particular study, the rs for these three predictors might be .4, .2, and 3. Thus, if you looked at the βs, you would think the third predictor was most important; but if you looked at the rs, you would think the first predictor was most important.

Many approaches to this problem have been considered over the years, but all are controversial. What most experts recommend is to use all the information you have—consider *both* the rs *and* the βs, keeping in mind the difference in what they tell you. The r tells you the overall association of the predictor variable with the criterion variable. The β tells you the unique association of this predictor variable, over and above the other predictor variables, with the criterion variable.

In addition to these and other controversies relating to the statistical aspects, there has been an ongoing controversy for many years about the superiority of statistical prediction over more intuitive, humanistic, or clinical approaches. This issue is addressed in Box 4–1.

BOX 4–1   Clinical Versus Statistical Prediction

Fifty years ago, Paul Meehl (1954) wrote an unsettling little book called *Statistical Versus Clinical Prediction*. He argued that when experts such as clinical psychologists (or business managers, economic forecasters, engineers, or doctors, among others) use the kinds of unspecified internal cognitive processes that are usually called "trained intuitions," they are not very accurate. On the average their decisions are no better than those anybody at all could make by using very simple, straightforward prediction *formulas*. For example, in psychiatric diagnosing, a supposedly well-trained clinician's interview and diagnosis are less useful than a mere rule such as "if the person has been admitted to the hospital twice before, is over 50,

(continued)

and appears suicidal, then . . ."—the kind of rule generated by using a multiple regression model.

In the first decade after Meehl questioned the accuracy of experts, considerable efforts were made to disprove him. But on the whole, Meehl's discovery has held up (Dawes et al., 1993; Kleinmuntz, 1990): Unaided human cognition is, on the average, less accurate in making predictions than the statistical method of using regression models, and these predictions matter. We're talking about diagnoses, parole decisions, business decisions, engineering decisions.

Remember, this is an issue of prediction, and statistical methods cannot do all that well at prediction either. Their main advantage is consistency, like a gambler with a system. Humans may be better at explaining why something happened after it happened, because then we know where to look for the cause. But since these predictions often have serious consequences, it is still a shock to find that human logic or intuition following lengthy interviews or testing can be so poor compared to a simple formula.

Naturally, the focus has turned to how cognition operates, why it is flawed, and what, if anything, can be done to improve it. The flaws are mainly that people make illusory correlations (see Chapter 3, Box 3–2). Or they are overconfident; they do not keep a record of their successes and failures to see whether they are in fact accurate, but instead put too much weight on their remembered successes and forget their failures. Also, overconfidence comes in part from lack of feedback—clinicians may make hundreds of diagnoses without learning whether they were correct. Finally, human memory and cognition may not have the capacity to handle the information and operations required to make certain complex decisions. And that capacity varies. Some people have a high "need for cognition," the desire to think about things. Those with a low need are less consistent and accurate (Ruscio, 2000).

A great deal of research has addressed how to "debias" human decisions. People can be shown when they can rely on their intuition—for example, when there is not time to apply a formula or when simple averaging will suffice. At other times they need to understand that a formula is more accurate—for example, when rules are complicated.

There is also considerable work on decision aids, such as computer programs with built-in decision rules supplied by experts. Sometimes, more intuitive or subjective information can be added at the last minute by experts knowledgeable about the particular situation (Holzworth, 1996; Whitecotton, 1996). Although decision aids seem like they would be inflexible and therefore "inhuman," these aids and formulas can be modified as often as necessary. What cannot be allowed with any decision aid is that it be abandoned when someone has a hunch they can do better without the aid.

The use of decision support systems is on the rise. For example, expert chess players have developed aids that can sometimes outwit their own creators, merely by being thoroughly consistent. Thus, some chess players have become comfortable using decision support systems to keep themselves on track during a game.

When the stakes are high, however, as when involving life and death, most people still have more faith in human decisions, perhaps because of the hope that inspired intuition can beat the odds in a particular case. But as health care is forced to become more cost conscious, it may have to use impartial decision aids about who receives what treatment. And the public may benefit. For example, a decision aid for helping doctors who are not dermatologists decide if something might be skin cancer and require referral to a specialist was found to decrease errors by 64% (Gerbert et al., 1999). Another decision aid reduced serious medication errors by 55% (Bates et al., 1998).

It may take time, but we all will need to appreciate that it can be more humane to avoid subjective, caring judgments when objective decision aids exist.

PREDICTION IN RESEARCH ARTICLES

It is rare for bivariate prediction models to be reported in psychology research articles; usually, simple correlations are reported. Sometimes, however, you will see regression lines from bivariate predictions. This is usually done when there is more than one group and the researcher wants to illustrate the difference in the prediction rule between the two groups.

For example, consider an experiment Oettingen and her colleagues (2001) conducted with German university students. This experiment focused on the students' thoughts about the possibility of studying abroad. First, the students were asked about how much they expected to succeed (that is, how likely it was that they would study abroad). In the next part of the study, participants were divided into one of three groups. Participants in the positive fantasy group were instructed to spend some time thinking about specific positive aspects of studying abroad; those in the negative reality group, were instructed to spend some time thinking about specific obstacles in the current reality that stand in the way of studying abroad; and those in the contrast group were instructed to spend some time thinking about both positive possibilities and negative realities. Afterwards, participants answered questions about how disappointed they would be if they were never able to study abroad.

Figure 4–7 (Oettingen et al.'s Figure 2) shows a regression line for each of the three experimental groups. Each regression line shows how much expectation of success predicts anticipated disappointment. The major result is shown in the dark blue line: For students in the contrast group (those who thought about both the positive possibilities and realistic obstacles), the greater their initial expectations of success, the more disappointed they would be if they were not able to study abroad.

The researchers see the pattern for the contrast group as what would be expected—that people are most disappointed when they expect to succeed and least disappointed when they don't. But either having positive fantasies or dwelling on

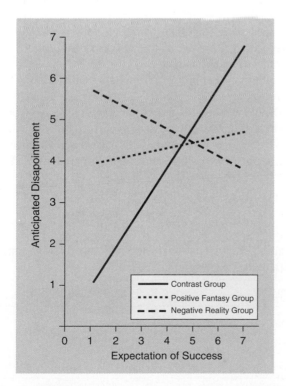

FIGURE 4–7 *Regression lines depicting the link of expectation of success to anticipated disappointment as a function of self-regulatory thought. (Source: Oettingen et al., 2001.)*

negative obstacles interferes with this normal process, so level of disappointment is much less related to expectations of success.

As we noted earlier, multiple regression results are common in research articles and are often reported in tables. Usually, the table lays out the regression coefficient for each predictor variable, which can be either standardized (β), unstandardized (b), or both, along with the overall R or R^2 in a note at the bottom of the table. The table may also give the correlation coefficient (r) for each predictor with the criterion variable. This lets you compare the unique association of each predictor to the criterion variable (what the regression coefficient tells you) with the overall association (what the correlation coefficient tells you). As we saw in Chapter 3 with correlation tables, regression tables also usually give the statistical significance for the various statistics reported. Finally, many tables will provide a variety of other statistics that go beyond what we have covered. But if you understand the basics, you should be able to make good sense of the key information in such tables.

Consider an example from a study (Hahlweg et al., 2001) of a treatment method for agoraphobia, a condition that affects about 4% of the population and involves unpredictable panic attacks in public places such as crowded restaurants, buses, or movie theaters. Table 4–8 (Hahlweg et al.'s Table 4) shows the correlation coefficients (rs) and standardized regression coefficients (βs) for four variables predicting the effectiveness of the treatment. (The actual criterion variable is labeled "Average Intragroup Effect Size at Postassessment." The article explains that this is each patient's change from before to after treatment, averaged across several measures of mental health.)

Looking at the β column, you can see that the standardized regression coefficients were very small for number of sessions attended and the duration of the disorder. At the same time, age and BDI (a measure of depression at the start of treatment) were much more important unique predictors of the outcome of treatment. Also notice (from the bottom of the table) that the overall correlation of the four predictors with treatment outcome had an R of .36 and an R^2 of .13. This is a moderate overall relationship, but not substantial—that is, only 13% of the overall variance in treatment outcome was predicted by these four variables. Notice also the r column. For BDI and age, the βs and rs are about the same. Note, however, that number of sessions and durations have larger rs than βs. This suggests that these two variables have considerable overlap with each other or other variables in the prediction model, so that their unique contribution to predicting treatment outcome is rather small.

TABLE 4–8 | **Multiple Regression Analysis Predicting Average Intragroup Effect Size at Postassessment**

Independent variable	r	β
BDI	.30***	.30***
Age	−.21***	.20**
No. of sessions	.12*	.08
Duration of disorder	−.13*	−.02

Note. $R = .36$; $R^2 = .13$. BDI = Beck Depression Inventory.
* $p < .05$.   ** $p < .01$.   *** $p < .000$.
Source: Hahlweg et al., 2001.

SUMMARY

1. Prediction (or regression) makes predictions about scores on a criterion variable based on scores on a predictor variable. The best model for predicting a person's Z score on the criterion variable is to multiply the standardized regression coefficient (ß) by the person's Z score on the predictor variable. The best number to use for the standardized regression coefficient is the correlation coefficient (r).

2. Predictions with raw scores can be made by changing a person's score on the predictor variable to a Z score, multiplying it by the standardized regression coefficient, and then changing the predicted criterion variable Z score to a raw score.

3. You can do direct raw-score-to-raw-score prediction using a prediction model which includes a regression constant (a) that you add to the result of multiplying a raw-score regression coefficient (b) by the predictor variable raw score. a is the predicted score on the criterion variable when the predictor variable is 0; b is the amount that the predicted criterion variable increases when you increase the predictor variable score by 1. (These can be figured using the method in point 2 above.)

4. A regression line, which is drawn in the same kind of graph as a scatter diagram, shows the predicted criterion variable value for each value of the predictor variable. The slope of this line equals b; a is where this line crosses the vertical axis.

5. The proportionate reduction in error, an indicator of the accuracy of a prediction model, is figured by applying the prediction model to the scores on which the original correlation was based. The sum of squared error when using the prediction model (SS_{Error}) is the sum of the squared differences between each actual score and the predicted score for that individual; the sum of squared error total (SS_{Total}) is the sum of the squared differences between each actual score and the mean; the proportionate reduction in error is the reduction in squared error gained by using the model ($SS_{Total} - SS_{Error}$) divided by the squared error when predicting from the mean (SS_{Total}). The proportionate reduction in error (or proportion of variance accounted for) equals the correlation coefficient squared (r^2).

6. In multiple regression, a criterion variable is predicted from two or more predictor variables. In a multiple regression model, each predictor variable is multiplied by its own regression coefficient, and the results are added up to make the prediction. (When raw scores are used, there is also a regression constant.) Each regression coefficient tells you the unique relation of the predictor to the criterion variable in the context of the other predictor variables. The multiple correlation coefficient (R) is the overall degree of association between the criterion variable and the predictor variables taken together. R^2 is the overall proportionate reduction in error.

7. Bivariate prediction and multiple regression have the same limitations as ordinary correlation. In addition, in multiple regression there is ambiguity in interpreting the relative importance of the predictor variables.

8. Bivariate prediction results are rarely described directly in research articles, but regression lines are sometimes shown when prediction models for more than one group are being compared. Multiple regressions are commonly reported in articles, often in a table that includes the regression coefficients and overall proportionate reduction in error.

KEY TERMS

bivariate prediction (p. 136)

criterion variable (Y) (p. 114)

error (p. 130)

intercept (p. 125)

multiple correlation (p. 136)

multiple correlation coefficient (R) (p. 138)

multiple regression (p. 136)

prediction model (p. 114)

predictor variable (X) (p. 114)

proportion of variance accounted for (r^2, R^2) (p. 135)

proportionate reduction in error (r^2, R^2) (p. 132)

raw-score prediction model (p. 119)

raw-score regression coefficient (b) (p. 119)

regression constant (a) (p. 119)

regression line (p. 125)

slope (p. 125)

standardized regression coefficient (β) (p. 114)

sum of the squared error (SS_{Error}) (p. 131)

total squared error when predicting from the mean (SS_{Total}) (p. 132)

EXAMPLE WORKED-OUT COMPUTATIONAL PROBLEMS

The bivariate problems below are based on the following data set. (This is the same data for the example worked-out computational problems in Chapter 3). In this study, the researchers want to predict achievement test score from class size.

Elementary School	Class Size	Achievement Test Score
Main Street	25	80
Casat	14	98
Harland	33	50
Shady Grove	28	82
Jefferson	20	90
M	24	80
SD	6.54	16.30
$r = -.9$		

BIVARIATE PREDICTION OF Z SCORES

Predict the Z scores for achievement for schools that have class sizes with Z scores of -2, 1, 0, $+1$, and $+2$.

This can be done using either the formula or the steps. Using the formulas,

$$\hat{Z}_Y = (\beta)(Z_X) = (-.9)(-2) = 1.8.$$
$$(-.9)(-1) = .9.$$
$$(-.9)(0) = 0.$$
$$(-.9)(+1) = -.9.$$
$$(-.9)(+2) = -1.8.$$

Using the steps,

❶ **Determine the standardized regression coefficient.** β in bivariate prediction is the same as r. Thus, $\beta = -.9$.

❷ **Multiply the standardized regression coefficient by the person's Z score on the predictor variable.** $-.9 \times -2 = 1.8$; $-.9 \times -1 = .9$; $-.9 \times 0 = 0$; $-.9 \times 1 = -.9$; $-.9 \times 2 = -1.8$.

DETERMINING THE RAW-SCORE PREDICTION FORMULA

Determine the raw-score prediction formula for predicting achievement test scores from class size.

❶ **Figure the regression constant.** To do this, figure the predicted raw score on the criterion variable when the predictor variable is 0 with raw-score prediction using the Z-score prediction model. Using the formulas,

$$Z_X = (X - M_X)/SD_X = (0 - 24)/6.54 = -24/6.54 = -3.67.$$
$$\hat{Z}_Y = (r)(Z_X) = (-.9)(-3.67) = 3.30.$$
$$\hat{Y} = (SD_Y)(\hat{Z}_Y) + M_Y = (16.30)(3.30) + 80 = 53.79 + 80 = 133.79.$$

Thus, a is 133.79.

❷ **Figure the raw-score regression coefficient.** To do this, first figure the predicted raw score on the criterion variable when the predictor variable is 1 with raw-score prediction using the Z-score prediction model; then take this number minus the regression constant (from Step 1). Using the formulas,

$$\text{For } X = 1: Z_X = (X - M_X)/SD_X = (1 - 24)/6.54 = -23/6.54 = -3.52.$$
$$\hat{Z}_Y = (r)(Z_X) = (-.9)(-3.52) = 3.17.$$
$$\hat{Y} = (SD_Y)(\hat{Z}_Y) + M_Y = (16.30)(3.17) + 80 = 51.67 + 80 = 131.67.$$

From Step 1, the predicted raw score for a school with class sizes of 0 is 26.21. Thus, $b = 131.67 - 133.79 = -2.12$. The raw-score prediction model formula is thus

$$\text{Predicted Achievement Test Score} = 133.79 + (-2.12)(\text{Class Size}).$$

USING THE RAW-SCORE PREDICTION FORMULA TO MAKE PREDICTIONS

Use the raw score prediction formula to find the predicted average achievement test score for each school.

$$\text{Predicted Achievement Test Score} = 133.79 + (-2.12)(\text{Class Size}).$$

School	
Main Street	$133.79 + (-2.12)(25) = 133.79 + -53.00 = 80.79$
Casat	$133.79 + (-2.12)(14) = 133.79 + -29.68 = 104.11$
Harland	$133.79 + (-2.12)(33) = 133.79 + -69.96 = 63.83$
Shady Grove	$133.79 + (-2.12)(28) = 133.79 + -59.36 = 74.43$
Jefferson	$133.79 + (-2.12)(20) = 133.79 + -42.40 = 91.39$

MAKING A REGRESSION LINE

Draw the scatter diagram and put the regression line into it for class size predicting achievement test score.

The result of each step is shown in Figure 4–8.

❶ **Draw and label the axes for a scatter diagram.** In this question, you are also asked to make the complete scatter diagram, which means putting in the dots for the actual scores.

❷ **Figure the predicted value on the criterion variable for a low value on the predictor variable, and mark the point on the graph.** From the answer to the

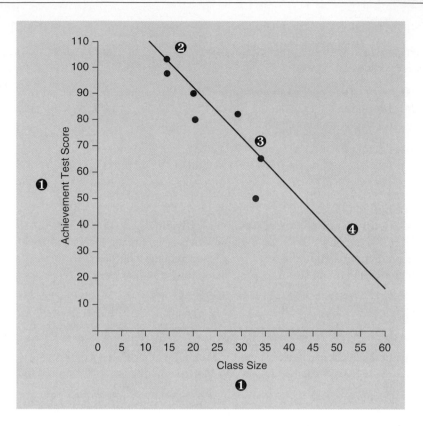

FIGURE 4–8 *Steps of making regression line for class size and achievement test example worked out problem:* ❶ *Draw and label the axes,* ❷ *mark a point for a low value of the predictor variable and its predicted value on the criterion variable,* ❸ *mark a point for a high value of the predictor variable and its predicted value on the criterion variable;* ❹ *draw the regression line.*

previous problem, the predicted achievement test score for a school with a class size of 14 is 104.11. Thus, you mark the point $(X = 14, \hat{Y} = 104.11)$.

    ❸ **Do the same thing again, but for a high value on the predictor variable.** From the answer to the previous problem, the predicted achievement test score for a school with a class size of 33 is 63.83. Thus, you mark the point $(X = 33, \hat{Y} = 63.83)$.

    ❹ **Draw a line that passes through the two marks.**

FIGURE THE PROPORTIONATE REDUCTION IN ERROR

Find the proportionate reduction in error for predicting achievement test score from class size.

    ❶ **Figure the sum of squared error using the mean to predict: Take each score minus the mean, square it, and add these up. From Table 4–9, $SS_{\text{Total}} = 1328$.**

    ❷ **Figure the sum of squared errors using the prediction model: Take each score minus the predicted score for this person, square it, and add these up.** From Table 4–9, $SS_{\text{Error}} = 288.45$.

    ❸ **Figure the reduction in squared errors: This is the sum of squared errors using the mean to predict (from Step 1) minus the sum of squared errors using the prediction model (from Step 2).**

| TABLE 4–9 | Steps 1 and 2 of Figuring Proportionate Reduction in Error for Class Size and Achievement Test Worked-Out Example Problem |

School	Actual	Prediction Using Mean			Using Prediction Model		
		Mean	Error	Error^2	Predicted	Error	Error^2
Main Street	80	80	0	0	80.79	.79	.62
Casat	98	80	18	324	104.11	6.11	37.33
Harland	50	80	−30	900	63.83	−13.83	191.27
Shady Grove	82	80	2	4	74.43	7.57	57.30
Jefferson	90	80	10	100	91.39	−1.39	1.93
				$SS_{Total} = 1328$			$SS_{Error} = 288.45$

Reduction in squared error $= 1328 - 288.45 = 1039.55$.

❹ **Figure the proportionate reduction in squared error. This is the reduction in squared error (from Step 3) divided by the total squared error when using the mean to predict (from Step 1).**

Proportionate reduction in squared error $= 1039.55/1328 = .78$.

Note: The square root of the proportionate reduction in error should approximately equal the correlation. In this problem, $\sqrt{.78} = \pm .88$. The correlation we began with was .9. This is well within the rounding error we would expect given the amount of figuring (and the rounding off at each point) to come up with the proportionate reduction in error.

MULTIPLE REGRESSION PREDICTIONS

A (fictional) psychologist studied the talkativeness of children in families with a mother, father, and one grandparent. The psychologist found that the child's happiness score depended on the quality of the child's relationship with each of these people. The multiple regression prediction model using Z scores is as follows:

Predicted talkativeness Z score of the child $= (.32)(Z$ mother$) +$
$(.21)(Z$ father$) + (.41)(Z$ grandparent$)$

Predict a child's talkativeness Z score who had Z scores for relationship quality of .48 with mother, $-.63$ with father, and 1.25 with grandparent).

Predicted talkativeness Z score of the child $= (.32)(Z$ mother$) +$
$(.21)(Z$ father$) + (.41)(Z$ grandparent$)$.

$= (.32)(.48) + (.21)(-.63) + (.41)(1.25) = .15 + -.13 + .51 = .53$

PRACTICE PROBLEMS

These problems involve figuring. Most real-life statistics problems are done on a computer. However, even if you have a computer and statistics software, do these by hand (with the help of a calculator) to ingrain the method in your mind. Also, in all problems involving figuring, be sure to show your work.

For practice in using a computer to solve statistics problems, refer to the computer section of each chapter of the *Student's Study Guide and Computer Workbook* that accompanies this text.

All data are fictional unless an actual citation is given.

Answers to Set I problems are given at the back of the book.

SET I

1. A sports psychologist working with hockey players found that knowledge of physiology correlates .4 with number of injuries received over the subsequent year. The psychologist now plans to test all new athletes and use this information to predict the number of injuries they are likely to receive. (a) Indicate the predictor variable, (b) criterion variable, and (c) standardized regression coefficient. (d) Write the Z-score prediction model. Indicate the predicted Z scores for number of injuries for athletes whose Z scores on the physiology test are (e) –2, (f) –1, (g) 0, (h) +1, and (i) +2.

2. A professor has found that in her classes scores on the midterm exam predict scores on the final exam. The raw-score prediction formula is

Predicted final exam score = 40 + (.5)(midterm exam score).

Figure the predicted final exam scores for each of eight students whose scores on the midterm were (a) 30, (b) 40, (c) 50, (d) 60, (e) 70, (f) 80, (g) 90, and (h) 100.

3. For each of the following, (a) through (d), determine the raw-score prediction model. Then (e) make a single graph showing all the regression lines, labeling each by its letter. (Be sure to make your graph large enough so that the lines are clearly separate.)

	Criterion Variable (Y)		Predictor Variable (X)		
	M	SD	M	SD	r
(a)	10	2.0	10	2.0	.4
(b)	20	2.0	10	2.0	.4
(c)	10	2.0	20	2.0	.4
(d)	10	2.0	10	4.0	.4

4. Problem 3 in Chapter 3 was about an instructor who asked five students how many hours they had studied for an exam. The number of hours studied and their grades, along with means and standard deviations, are shown here. The correlation was .84, and SS_{Total} for test grade was 1,110. (a) Determine the raw-score prediction formula for predicting test grade from hours studied; (b) use this formula to find the predicted test grades for each of the five students; (c) draw the scatter diagram and put the regression line into it; (d) figure the error and squared error for each of the five predictions; (e) find the proportionate reduction in error (using SS_{Error} and SS_{Total}); (f) take the square root of the proportionate reduction in error you figured to see if it matches the correlation coefficient within rounding error; and (g) explain what you have done to someone who understands mean, standard deviation, Z scores, and correlation coefficient, but does not know any more about statistics.

	Hours Studied (X)	Test Grade (Y)
	0	52
	10	95
	6	83
	8	71
	6	64
M	6	73
SD	3.35	14.90

5. Repeat problem 4, doing parts (a) through (f), but this time predicting hours studied from test grade. (SS_{Total} for predicting hours studied from the mean is 56.)

6. Problem 2 in Chapter 3 described a pilot study of the relation between psychotherapists' degree of empathy and their patients' satisfaction with therapy. Four patient–therapist pairs were studied. The results are presented here, including the means and standard deviations. The correlation coefficient is .90, and SS_{Total} for patient satisfaction is 10.

Pair Number	Therapist Empathy(X)	Patient Satisfaction (Y)
1	70	4
2	94	5
3	36	2
4	48	1
M	62	3
SD	22.14	1.58

(a) Determine the raw-score prediction formula for predicting satisfaction from empathy; (b) use this formula to find the predicted satisfaction scores for each of the four patient–therapist pairs; (c) draw the scatter diagram and put the regression line into it; (d) figure the error and squared error for each of the four predictions; (e) find the proportionate reduction in error (using SS_{Error} and SS_{Total}); (f) take the square root of the proportionate reduction in error you figured to see if it matches the correlation coefficient (within rounding error); and (g) explain what you have done to someone who understands mean, standard deviation, Z scores, and correlation coefficient, but does not know any more about statistics.

7. Repeat problem 6, doing parts (a) through (f), but this time predicting empathy from satisfaction. (SS_{Total} for predicting empathy from the mean is 2,068.) Then (g) indicate which results are different from and which one the same as in problem 6.

8. In the Oettingen et al. (2001) study described earlier (in the "Prediction in Research Articles" section), in addition to studying anticipated disappointment, the researchers conducted an experiment focusing on number of plans and on taking responsibility. Their results are shown in Figure 4–9. Explain the meaning of each graph to a person who has never had a course in statistics.

9. Mize and Petit (1997) were interested in the impact of a mother's style of helping her child understand social interactions on the child's social life. These researchers arranged for 43 volunteer mothers and their 3- to 5-year-old children to be video-

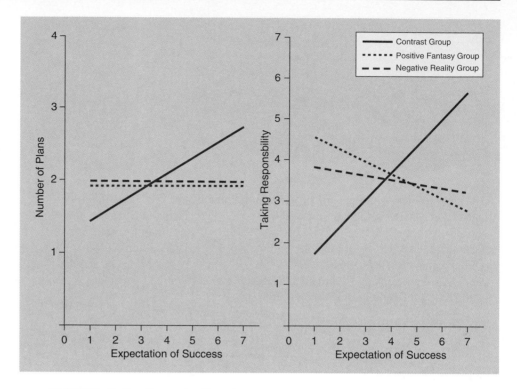

FIGURE 4–9 *Regression lines depicting the link of expectation of success to formulating plans (left) and to taking responsibility (right) as a function of self-regulatory thought. (Source: Oettingen et al., 2001.)*

taped in three separate sessions. In the key session, the mothers and children were shown videotapes of other children behaving in hostile or rejecting ways with each other; then the mothers discussed the tapes with their children. Later, the psychologists rated each mother for "social coaching"—such as how well the mothers helped the children understand what they had seen and suggested more positive ways to handle the situation. Tapes of the mothers and children playing together were rated for the mothers' "responsive style"—warmth and attunement to the children. Finally, in the last session, tapes of the children solving a puzzle were rated for the mothers' "nonsocial teaching"—how well they helped the children develop problem-solving skills. In another part of the study, the researchers had all the children answer questions about how much they liked the other children. Using this information, they were able to come up with an overall measure of how much each child was liked, which they called "peer acceptance."

The researchers hypothesized that the extent to which a mother was good at social coaching would predict her child's peer acceptance. They also hypothesized that the relation of a mother's social coaching to peer acceptance would hold up even in a multiple regression equation that included nonsocial coaching and would also hold up in a regression equation that included responsive style. (That is, including the other predictors in the model would still leave a substantial unique association of social coaching with peer acceptance.)

The Peer Acceptance section of Table 4–10 shows their results. Equation 1 is the multiple regression model in which nonsocial teaching and social coaching are included as predictors of peer acceptance. Equation 2 is the multiple regression model in which responsive style and social coaching are included as

TABLE 4–10 Simultaneous Regression Analyses Predicting Teacher-Rated Social Skills, Aggression, and Peer Acceptance in Study 1

	Criteria											
	Peer Acceptance				Social Skills				Aggression			
Predictor Variables	r	R^2	sr_1	Beta	r	R^2	sr_1	Beta	r	R^2	sr_1	Beta
Equation 1:												
Nonsocial teaching	.21*		.10	.10	.15		.05	.06	−.35*		−.23	−.24
Social coaching	.36*	.14*	.30	.32	.31*	.10	.28	.29	−.41***	.22**	−.32	−.33*
Equation 2:												
Responsive style	.34*		.26	.27	.25		.18	.18	−.26		−.16	−.17
Social coaching	.36*	.19*	.28	.29	.31*	.13	.25	.26	−.41***	.20*	−.36	−.37*

Note: sr_1 = semipartial correlation; n = 38.

*$p < .10$; **$p < .05$; ***$p < .01$.

Data from Mize, J., & Pettit, G. S. (1997), tab. 2. Mothers' social coaching, mother-child relationship style, and children's peer competence: Is the medium the message? *Child Development, 68,* 312–332. Copyright, 1997, by the Society for Research in Child Development, Inc. Reprinted with permission.

predictors of peer acceptance. Explain the meaning of the peer acceptance results as if you were writing to a person who understands correlation but has never had any exposure to regression or multiple regression analysis. (You can ignore the column for sr_1, the semipartial correlation. All the information you need to interpret this table is included in the r, R^2, and beta columns.)

10. (a) Based on Table 4–10 (discussed in problem 9), Peer Acceptance section, write out Mize and Petit's Equation 1 (a regression equation for Z scores). Then figure the predicted Z score for peer acceptance for children whose mothers have the following Z scores.

Mother	Nonsocial Teaching	Social Coaching
A	−2	0
B	0	0
C	2	0
D	0	−2
E	0	2
F	2	2
G	−1	−2

(b) Now write out Equation 2 and figure the predicted Z score for Peer Acceptance for children whose mothers have the following Z scores:

Mother	Responsive Style	Social Coaching
A	−2	0
B	0	0
C	2	0
D	0	−2
E	0	2
F	2	2
G	−1	−2

SET II

11. A personnel psychologist studying adjustment to the job of new employees found a correlation of .3 between amount of education and rating by job supervisors 2 months later. The psychologist now plans to use amount of education to predict supervisors' later ratings. Indicate the (a) predictor variable, (b) criterion variable, and (c) beta; (d) Write the Z-score prediction model; give the predicted Z scores for supervisor ratings for employees with amount of education Z scores of (e) -1.5, (f) -1, (g) $-.5$, (h) 0, (i) $+.5$, (j) $+1$, and (k) $+1.5$.

12. A clinical psychologist has found that score on a new depression scale predicts satisfaction with psychotherapy. The raw-score prediction formula is

$$\text{Predicted therapy satisfaction} = 1 + (.4)(\text{depression score}).$$

Figure the predicted satisfaction with therapy for each of six patients whose scores on the depression test were (a) 5, (b) 6, (c) 7, (d) 8, (e) 9, and (f) 10.

13. For each of the following, (a) through (d), determine the raw-score prediction model. Then make a single graph showing all the regression lines, labeling each by its letter. (Be sure to make your graph large enough so that the lines are clearly separate.)

	Criterion Variable (Y)		Predictor Variable (X)		
	M	SD	M	SD	r
(a)	1	2	5	2	.6
(b)	5	2	1	2	.6
(c)	5	2	1	3	.6
(d)	5	2	1	2	$-.6$

14. For each of the following, (a) through (e), determine the Z-score prediction model and the raw-score prediction model. Then make a single graph showing all the (raw score) regression lines, labeling each by its letter, (a) through (e), and making your graph large enough so that the lines are clearly separated.

	Criterion Variable (Y)		Predictor Variable (X)		
	M	SD	M	SD	r
(a)	0	1.0	0	1.0	.3
(b)	5	1.0	5	1.0	.3
(c)	0	5.0	0	5.0	.3
(d)	0	1.0	5	5.0	.3
(e)	0	1.0	0	1.0	.0

15. In problem 11 of Chapter 3, four individuals were given a test of manual dexterity (high scores mean better dexterity) and an anxiety test (high scores mean more anxiety). The scores, means, and standard deviations are given here. First, figure the correlation between dexterity and anxiety (or refer to your answer from Chapter 3). SS_{Total} for anxiety was 84.

(a) Determine the raw-score prediction formula for predicting anxiety from dexterity; (b) use this formula to find the predicted anxiety scores for each of the four individuals studied; (c) draw the scatter diagram and put the regression line into it; (d) figure the error and squared error for each of the four predictions; (e) find the proportionate reduction in error (using SS_{Error} and SS_{Total}); (f) take the square root of the proportionate reduction in error you calculated to see if it matches the correlation coefficient; and (g) explain what you have done to someone who understands mean, standard deviation, Z scores, and correlation coefficient, but does not know any more about statistics.

Person	Dexterity	Anxiety
1	1	10
2	1	8
3	2	4
4	4	−2
M	2	5
SD	1.22	4.58

16. Repeat problem 15, doing parts (a) though (f), but this time predicting dexterity from anxiety. Then (g) indicate which results are different from and which are the same as in problem 15. (SS_{Total} for dexterity is 6.)

17. Problem 12 from Chapter 3 was about the amount of violent television watched and the amount of violent behavior toward their playmates for four young children. The scores are given here. First, figure the correlation between amount of violent TV watched and violence towards playmates (or refer to your answer from Chapter 3).

(a) Determine the raw-score prediction formula for predicting violence from television watching; (b) use this formula to find the predicted violence towards playmates scores for each of the four individuals studied; (c) draw the scatter diagram and put the regression line into it; (d) figure the error and squared error for each of the four predictions; (e) find the proportionate reduction in error (using SS_{Error} and SS_{Total}); (f) take the square root of the proportionate reduction in error you figured to see if it matches the correlation coefficient; and (g) explain what you have done to someone who understands mean, standard deviation, Z scores, and correlation coefficient, but does not know any more about statistics. The results were as follows:

Child's Code Number	Weekly Viewing of Violent TV (hours)	Number of Violent or Aggressive Acts Toward Playmates
G3368	14	9
R8904	8	6
C9890	6	1
L8722	12	8

18. Repeat problem 17, doing parts (a) though (f), but this time predicting violent TV viewing from violent acts. Then (g) indicate which results are different from and which are the same as in problem 17.

19. In problem 13 from Chapter 3, five college students were asked about how important a goal it is for them to have a family and about how important a goal it is for them to be highly successful in their work. Each variable was measured on a scale from 0 not at all important goal to 10 very important goal. First figure the correlation between importance of family and work goals (or refer to your answer from Chapter 3).

(a) Determine the raw-score prediction formula for predicting importance of work goals from importance of family goals; (b) use this formula to find the predicted importance of work goals for each of the four students studied; (c) draw the scatter diagram and put the regression line into it; (d) figure the error and squared error for each of the four predictions; (e) find the proportionate reduction in error (using SS_{Error} and SS_{Total}); (f) take the square root of the proportionate reduction in error you figured to see if it matches the correlation coefficient; and (g) explain what you have done to someone who understands mean, standard deviation, Z scores, and correlation coefficient, but does not know any more about statistics. The results were as follows:

Student	Family	Work
A	7	5
B	6	4
C	8	2
D	3	9
E	4	1

20. Repeat problem 19, doing parts (a) though (f), but this time predicting importance of family goals from importance of work goals. Then (g) indicate which results are different from and which are the same as in Problem 19.

21. Nezlek et al. (1997) had participants first write self-descriptions and then exchange them with four other students also taking part in the study. Then, the students privately ranked the other students on how much they would like to work with them on the next task. One group of participants were then told that they had been selected to work on the next task with the rest of the group—this was the inclusion condition. The remaining participants were told that they had not been chosen to work with the others and would work alone—the exclusion condition. At this point, participants were asked about how accepted they felt. Earlier, at the start of the study, they had completed a self-esteem scale. Figure 4–10 shows regression lines for the two experimental groups. Explain what these two lines mean to a person who understands correlation but knows nothing about prediction.

22. Social psychologists studying criminal justice issues have long been interested in what influences people's attitudes about punishment of criminal offenders. Graham and her colleagues (1997) took advantage of the very public trial of U.S. football star O. J. Simpson to test some basic issues in this area. In the first few days after Simpson was accused of having murdered his ex-wife, the researchers asked people a series of questions about the case. The researchers were mainly interested in the responses of the 177 individuals who believed Simpson was probably guilty, particularly their belief about retribution—how much they agreed or disagreed with the statement "The punishment should make O. J. suffer as he made others suffer." The researchers were interested in a number of possible influences on this belief. These included "control" (how

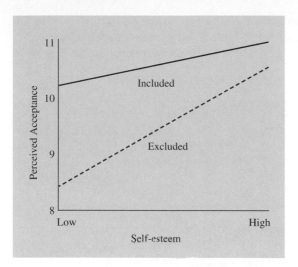

FIGURE 4–10   *Effects of inclusion/exclusion and trait self-esteem on perceived acceptance. [From Nezlek, J. B., Kowalski, R. M., Leary, M. R., Blevins, T., & Holgate, S. (1997), fig. 1. Personality moderators of reactions to interpersonal rejection: Depression and trait self-esteem.* Personality and Social Psychology Bulletin, 23, *1235–1244.]*

much control they believed Simpson had over his actions at the time of the crime), "responsibility" (how much they believed he was responsible for the crime), "anger" they felt towards him, "sympathy" they felt for him, "stability" (how much they believed his actions represented a stable versus temporary way of behaving), and "expectancy" (if they thought he would commit such a crime again). Graham and her colleagues reported

. . . Table [4–11] reveals partial support for our hypotheses. As expected, the strongest predictors of the retributive goal of making Simpson suffer were inferences about responsibility and the moral emotions of anger and sympathy. [S]tability and expectancy . . . were relatively weak [predictors]. (p. 337)

Explain these results as if you were writing to a person who understands correlation but has never had any exposure to regression or multiple regression analysis. (Refer only to the retribution part of the table. You may ignore the *t* column, which is about statistical significance of the results.)

TABLE 4–11   Multiple Regressions Predicting Punishment Goals From the Attributional Variables, Study 1

	Punishment Goal							
	Retribution		Rehabilitation		Protection		Deterrence	
Predictors	β	*t*	β	*t*	β	*t*	β	*t*
Control	−.05	<1	−.05	<1	−.03	<1	.15	1.90
Responsibility	.17	2.07*	−.00	<1	−.04	<1	.19	2.15*
Anger	.30	4.04***	.11	1.54	−.03	<1	−.04	<1
Sympathy	−.30	−3.68***	.39	5.18***	−.07	<1	−.13	−1.54
Stability	−.01	<1	−.34	−4.85***	−.19	2.33*	.04	<1
Expectancy	−.10	−1.33	−.06	<1	−.27	3.36***	.08	1.04
R^2		.27		.37		.17		.18

Note: β = standardized regression coefficient.
*p < .05; ***p < .001.
Data from Graham, S., Weiner, B., & Zucker, G. S. (1997), tab. 4. An attributional analysis of punishment goals and public reactions to O. J. Simpson. *Personality and Social Psychology Bulletin, 23,* 331–346. Copyright, 1997, by the Society for Personality and Social Psychology, Inc. Reprinted by permission of Sage Publications, Inc.

23. Based on Table 4–11 from problem 22, write out the regression equation for predicting retribution. Then figure the predicted Z score for retribution for persons A through J, whose Z scores on each predictor variable are shown below.

Person	A	B	C	D	E	F	G	H	I	J
Control	1	0	0	0	0	0	1	0	1	−1
Responsibility	0	1	0	0	0	0	1	0	1	−1
Anger	0	0	1	0	0	0	1	1	1	−1
Sympathy	0	0	0	1	0	0	0	1	1	−1
Stability	0	0	0	0	1	0	0	0	1	−1
Expectancy	0	0	0	0	0	1	0	0	1	−1

24. Think of something that you would like to be able to predict and what information would be useful in predicting it. (This should be different from any example given in class or in the textbook, and both variables should be measured on numeric scales.) (a) Write a Z-score prediction model, noting the name of the predictor variable and the name of the criterion variable. Also, (b) estimate a number for the standardized regression coefficient that you think makes some sense based on what you know about the things you are making predictions about. Finally, (c) explain why you picked the regression coefficient size you did.

25. Think of something that you would like to be able to predict and what information would be useful in predicting it. (This should be different from any example given in class, in the textbook, or that you used for a previous problem. Also, it should be something where both variables are measured on a numeric scale.) (a) Write a raw-score prediction model, noting the name of the predictor variable and the name of the criterion variable. Also, (b) estimate numbers for the regression constant and the raw-score regression coefficient that you think makes some sense based on what you know about the things you are making predictions about. Finally, explain why you picked (c) the regression constant and regression (d) coefficient size you did.

26. Think of something that you would like to be able to predict and what information would be useful in predicting it—with more than one variable as predictors. (This should be different from any example given in class, in the textbook, or used in a previous problem. All variables should be measured on numeric scales.) (a) Write a Z score prediction model, noting the name of the predictor variables and the name of the criterion variable. Also, (b) estimate numbers for the standardized regression coefficients for each predictor variable that you think makes some sense based on what you know about the things you are making predictions about. Finally, (c) explain why you picked the regression coefficient sizes you did.

27. Ask five other students of the same gender as yourself (each from different families) to give you their own height and also their mother's height. Figure the correlation coefficient, determine the raw-score prediction model for predicting a person's height from his or her mother's height, and make a graph showing the regression line. Finally, based on your prediction model, predict the height of a person of your gender whose mother's height is (a) 5 feet, (b) 5 feet 6 inches, and (c) 6 feet. (Note: Either convert inches to decimals of feet or do the whole problem using inches.)

CHAPTER 5

SOME KEY INGREDIENTS FOR INFERENTIAL STATISTICS:

THE NORMAL CURVE, PROBABILITY, AND POPULATION VERSUS SAMPLE

Are You Ready?
What You Need to have Mastered Before Starting This Chapter:

- Chapters 1 and 2

Ordinarily, psychologists conduct research to test some theoretical principle or the effectiveness of some practical procedure. For example, a psychophysiologist might measure changes in heart rate from before to after solving a difficult problem. These measurements would then be used to test a theory that predicts that heart rate should change following successful problem solving. An applied social psychologist might examine the effectiveness of a program of neighborhood meetings intended to promote water conservation. Such studies are carried out with a particular group of research participants. But researchers use inferential statistics to make more general conclusions about the theoretical principle or procedure being studied. These conclusions go beyond the particular group of research participants studied.

This chapter and Chapters 6, 7, and 8 introduce inferential statistics. In this chapter, we consider three topics: the normal curve, probability, and population none of the positive influences show up. Thus, in general, the person remembers a middle amount, an amount in which all the opposing influences cancel each other out. Very high or very low scores are much less common.

This creates a unimodal distribution—most of the scores near the middle and fewer at the extremes. It also creates a distribution that is symmetrical, because the number of letters recalled is as likely to be above as below the middle. Being a unimodal symmetrical curve does not guarantee that it will be a normal curve; it could be too flat or too pointed. However, it can be shown mathematically that in the long run, if the influences are truly random, and the number of different influences being combined is large, a precise normal curve will result. Mathematical statisticians call this principle the *central limit theorem*. We have more to say about this principle in Chapter 7.

THE NORMAL CURVE AND THE PERCENTAGE OF SCORES BETWEEN THE MEAN AND 1 AND 2 STANDARD DEVIATIONS FROM THE MEAN

The shape of the normal curve is standard. Thus, there is a known percentage of scores above or below any particular point. For example, exactly 50% of the scores in a normal curve are below the mean, because in any symmetrical distribution, half the scores are below the mean. More interestingly, as shown in Figure 5–2, approximately 34% of the scores are always between the mean and 1 standard deviation from the mean. (Notice, incidentally, from Figure 5–2, that the 1 standard deviation point on the normal curve is at the place where the curve starts going more out than down.)

Consider IQ scores. On many widely used intelligence tests, the mean IQ is 100, the standard deviation is 16, and the distribution of IQs is roughly a normal curve (see Figure 5–3). Knowing about the normal curve and the percentage of scores between the mean and 1 standard deviation above the mean tells you that about 34% of people have IQs between 100, the mean IQ, and 116, the IQ score 1 standard deviation above the mean. Similarly, because the normal curve is symmetrical, about 34% of people have IQs between 100 and 84 (the score 1 standard deviation below the mean), and 68% (34% + 34%) have IQs between 84 and 116.

As you can also see from looking at the normal curve, there are many fewer scores between 1 and 2 standard deviations from the mean than there are between the mean and 1 standard deviation from the mean. It turns out that about 14% of the scores are between 1 and 2 standard deviations above the mean (see Figure 5–2). (Similarly, because the normal curve is symmetrical, about 14% of the scores are between 1 and 2 standard deviations below the mean.) Thus, about 14% of people have IQs between 116 (1 standard deviation above the mean) and 132 (2 standard deviations above the mean).

You will find it very useful to remember the 34% and 14% figures. These figures tell you the percentage of people above and below any particular score whenever you know that score's number of standard deviations above or below the mean. You can also reverse this approach and figure out a person's number of standard deviations from the mean from a percentage. Suppose you are told that a person scored in the top 2% on a test. Assuming that scores on the test are approximately normally distributed, the person must have a score that is at least 2 standard deviations above the mean. This is because a total of 50% of the scores are above the mean, but 34% are between the mean and 1 standard deviation above the mean, and another 14% are between 1 and 2 standard deviations above the mean. That leaves 2% (that is, 50% – 34% – 14% = 2%).

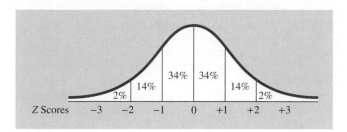

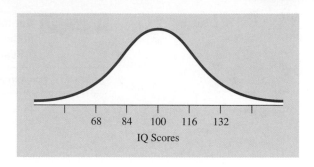

FIGURE 5–2   *Normal curve with approximate percentages of scores between the mean and 1 and 2 standard deviations above and below the mean.*

FIGURE 5–3   *Distribution of IQ scores on many standard intelligence tests (with a mean of 100 and a standard deviation of 16).*

Similarly, suppose you were selecting animals for a study and needed to consider their visual acuity. Suppose also that visual acuity was normally distributed and you wanted to use animals in the middle two thirds (a figure close to 68%) for visual acuity. In this situation, you would select animals that scored between 1 standard deviation above and 1 standard deviation below the mean. (That is, about 34% are between the mean and 1 standard deviation above the mean and another 34% are between the mean and 1 standard deviation below the mean.) Also, remember from Chapter 2 that a Z score is the number of standard deviations a score is above or below the mean—which is just what we are talking about here. Thus, if you knew the mean and the standard deviation of the visual acuity test, you could figure out the raw scores (the actual level of visual acuity) for being 1 standard deviation below and 1 standard deviation above the mean (that is, Z scores of +1 and −1). You would do this using the methods of changing raw scores to Z scores and vice versa that you learned in Chapter 2, which are

$$Z = (X - M)/SD \text{ and } X = (Z)(SD) + M$$

THE NORMAL CURVE TABLE AND Z SCORES

The 50%, 34%, and 14% figures are important practical rules for working with scores that have a normal distribution. However, in many research and applied situations, psychologists need more precise information. Because the normal curve is mathematically exact, you can figure the exact percentage of scores between any two points on the normal curve, not just those that happen to be right at 1 or 2 standard deviations from the mean. For example, exactly 68.59% of scores have a Z score between +.62 and −1.68; exactly 2.81% of scores have a Z score between +.79 and +.89; and so forth.

You can figure these percentages using calculus, based on the formula for the normal curve. However, you can also do this much more simply. Statisticians have worked out tables for the normal curve that give the percentage of scores between the mean (a Z score of 0) and any other Z score. Suppose you want to know the percentage of scores between the mean and a Z score of .64. You just look up .64 in the table and it tells you that 23.89% of the scores in a perfect normal distribution are between the mean and this Z score.

We have included such a **normal curve table** in Appendix A (Table A–1).   **normal curve table**
Table 5–1 shows the first part of the full table. The leftmost column in the table lists

TABLE 5–1 Normal Curve Areas: Percentage
of the Normal Curve Between the Mean and the
Z Scores Shown (First part of table only: full table in Appendix A)

Z	% Mean to Z	Z	% Mean to Z	Z	% Mean to Z
.00	.00	.45	17.36	.90	31.59
.01	.40	.46	17.72	.91	31.86
.02	.80	.47	18.08	.92	32.12
.03	1.20	.48	18.44	.93	32.38
.04	1.60	.49	18.79	.94	32.64
.05	1.99	.50	19.15	.95	32.89
.06	2.39	.51	19.50	.96	33.15
.07	2.79	.52	19.85	.97	33.40
.08	3.19	.53	20.19	.98	33.65
.09	3.59	.54	20.54	.99	33.89
.10	3.98	.55	20.88	1.00	34.13
.11	4.38	.56	21.23	1.01	34.38
.12	4.78	.57	21.57	1.02	34.61
.13	5.17	.58	21.90	1.03	34.85
.14	5.57	.59	22.24	1.04	35.08
.15	5.96	.60	22.57	1.05	35.31
.16	6.36	.61	22.91	1.06	35.54
.17	6.75	.62	23.24	1.07	35.77
.18	7.14	.63	23.57	1.08	35.99
.19	7.53	.64	23.89	1.09	36.21
.20	7.93	.65	24.22	1.10	36.43
.21	8.32	.66	24.54	1.11	36.65
.22	8.71	.67	24.86	1.12	36.86
.23	9.10	.68	25.17	1.13	37.08
.24	9.48	.69	25.49	1.14	37.29
.25	9.87	.70	25.80	1.15	37.49
.26	10.26	.71	26.11	1.16	37.70
.27	10.64	.72	26.42	1.17	37.90
.28	11.03	.73	26.73	1.18	38.10
.29	11.41	.74	27.04	1.19	38.30
.30	11.79	.75	27.34	1.20	38.49
.31	12.17	.76	27.64	1.21	38.69
.32	12.55	.77	27.94	1.22	38.88
.33	12.93	.78	28.23	1.23	39.07
.34	13.31	.79	28.52	1.24	39.25
.35	13.68	.80	28.81	1.25	39.44
.36	14.06	.81	29.10	1.26	39.62
.37	14.43	.82	29.39	1.27	39.80
.38	14.80	.83	29.67	1.28	39.97
.39	15.17	.84	29.95	1.29	40.15
.40	15.54	.85	30.23	1.30	40.32
.41	15.91	.86	30.51	1.31	40.49
.42	16.28	.87	30.78	1.32	40.66
.43	16.64	.88	31.06	1.33	40.82
.44	17.00	.89	31.33	1.34	40.99

the Z score and the column next to it gives the percentage of scores between the mean and that Z score. Notice that the table lists only positive Z scores. This is because the normal curve is perfectly symmetrical. Thus, the percentage of scores between the mean and, say, a Z of $+.64$ is exactly the same as the percentage of scores between the mean and a Z of $-.64$.

In our example, you would find .64 in the "Z" column and then, right next to it in the "% Mean to Z" column, you would find 23.89.

You can also reverse the process and use the table to find the Z score for a particular percentage of scores. For example, suppose you were told that Janice's creativity score was in the top 30% of ninth-grade students. Assuming that creativity scores follow a normal curve, you could figure out her Z score as follows: First, you would reason that if she is in the top 30%, then 20% of the students have scores between her score and the mean. That is, there are 50% above the mean, and she is in the top 30% of scores overall, which leaves 20% between her score and the mean. This is all shown in Figure 5–4. Then, you would look at the "% Mean to Z" column of the table until you found a percentage that was very close to 20%. In this example, the closest you could come would be 19.85%. Finally, you would look at the "Z" column to the left of this percentage. The Z score for 19.85% is .52. Thus, Janice's Z score for her level of creativity (as measured on this test) is .52. If you know the mean and standard deviation for ninth-grade students' creativity scores, you can figure out Janice's actual raw score on the test by changing her Z score of .52 to a raw score using the usual method of changing Z scores to raw scores.

Tip for Success

The normal curve table in Appendix B repeats the basic two columns several times on the page. Be sure to look across only one column.

STEPS FOR FIGURING THE PERCENTAGE ABOVE OR BELOW A PARTICULAR RAW SCORE OR Z SCORE USING THE NORMAL CURVE TABLE

Here are the six steps for figuring percentage of scores.

❶ **If you are beginning with a raw score, first change it to a Z score.**

❷ **Draw a picture of the normal curve, where the Z score falls on it, and shade in the area for which you are finding the percentage.** (When marking where the Z score falls on the normal curve, be sure to put it in the right place above or below the mean according to whether it is a positive or negative Z score.)

❸ **Make a rough estimate of the shaded area's percentage based on the 50%–34%–14%–percentages.** You don't need to be very exact—it is enough just

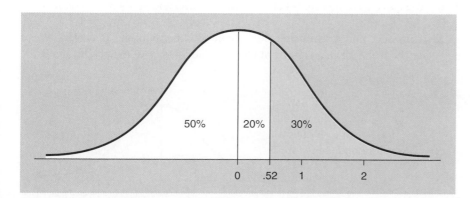

FIGURE 5–4 *Distribution of creativity test scores showing area for top 30% and Z score where this area begins.*

to estimate a range in which the shaded area has to fall, figuring it is between two particularly whole Z scores.

❹ **Find the exact percentage using the normal curve table.** Look up the Z score in the "Z" column of Table A–1 and find the percentage in the "% Mean to Z" column next to it. If you want the percent of scores between the mean and this Z score, this would be your final answer.

❺ **If needed, add or subtract 50% from this percentage.** Often, you need to add 50% to the percentage figured in Step 4. You need to do this if the Z score is positive and you want the total percent below this Z score, or if the Z score is negative and you want the total percent above this Z score. Other times, you have to subtract this percentage from 50%. You have to do this if the Z score is positive and you want the percent higher than it (as in the creativity test example above), or if the Z score is negative and you want the percent lower than it. However, don't try to memorize rules about adding or subtracting the 50%. It is much easier to make a picture for the problem and reason out whether the percentage you have from the table is correct as is or if you need to add or subtract 50%.

❻ **Check that your exact percentage is similar to your rough estimate from Step 3.**

EXAMPLES

Here are two examples using IQ scores where $M = 100$ and $SD = 16$.

Example 1: If a person has an IQ of 125, what percentage of people have higher IQs?

❶ **If you are beginning with a raw score, first change it to a Z score.** Using the usual formula from Chapter 2, $Z = (125 - 100)/16 = +1.56$.

❷ **Draw a picture of the normal curve, where the Z score falls on it, and shade in the area for which you are finding the percentage.** This is shown in Figure 5–5 (along with the exact percentages figured later).

❸ **Make a rough estimate of the shaded area's percentage based on the 50%–34%–14% percentages.** If the shaded area started at a Z score of 1, it would have 16% above it. If it started at a Z score of 2, it would have only 2% above it. So, with a Z score of 1.56, the number of scores above it has to be somewhere between 16% and 2%.

❹ **Find the exact percentage using the normal curve table.** In Table A–1, 1.56 in the "Z" column goes with 44.06 in the "% Mean to Z" column. Thus, 44.06% of people have IQ scores between the mean IQ and an IQ of 125 (Z score of +1.56).

❺ **If needed, add or subtract 50% from this percentage.** Because 50% of people are above the mean on any normal curve and 44.06% of the people above the

FIGURE 5–5 *Distribution of IQ scores showing percentage of scores above an IQ score of 125 (shaded area).*

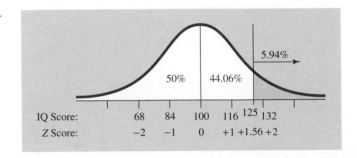

mean are below this person's IQ, that leaves 5.94% above this person's IQ (that is, 50% − 44.06% = 5.94%). This is the answer to our problem.

❻ **Check that your exact percentage is within the range of your rough estimate from Step 3.** Our result, 5.94%, is within the 16% to 2% range we estimated.

Example 2: Suppose a person has an IQ of 95. What is the percentage of people with IQs lower than this person?

❶ **If you are beginning with a raw score, first change it to a Z score.** $Z = (95 − 100)/16 = −.31$.

❷ **Draw a picture of the normal curve, where the Z score falls on it, and shade in the area for which you are finding the percentage.** This is shown in Figure 5–6 (along with the percentages figured later).

❸ **Make a rough estimate of the shaded area's percentage based on the 50%–34%–14% percentages.** You know that 50% of the curve is below the mean. So, the shaded area has to be less than 50%. You also can figure that 16% of the curve is below a Z score of −1. (This is because 34% is between 0 and −1, leaving 16% below −1.) Thus, this Z score of −.31 has to have between 50% and 16% of scores below it.

❹ **Find the exact percentage using the normal curve table.** The table shows that 12.17% of scores are between the mean and a Z score of .31.

❺ **If needed, add or subtract 50% from this percentage.** The percentage below a Z score of −.31 is the total of 50% below the mean, less the 12.17% between the mean and −.31, leaving 37.83% (that is, 50% − 12.17% = 37.83%).

❻ **Check that your exact percentage is similar to your rough estimate from Step 3.** Our result, 37.83%, is within the 50% to 36% range.

FIGURING Z SCORES AND RAW SCORES FROM PERCENTAGES USING THE NORMAL CURVE TABLE

Going from a percentage to a Z score or raw score is similar to going from a Z score or raw score to a percentage. However, you use just the reverse procedure for the part of figuring the exact percentage. Also, any necessary changes from a Z score to a raw score are done at the end. Here are the steps.

❶ **Draw a picture of the normal curve, and shade in the approximate area for your percentage using the 50%–34%–14% percentages.**

❷ **Make a rough estimate of the Z score where the shaded area starts.**

❸ **Find the exact Z score using the normal curve table (including adding or subtracting 50% if necessary before looking it up).** Looking at your picture, figure out the percentage between the mean and where the shading starts or ends. For

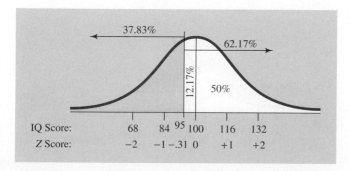

FIGURE 5–6 *Distribution of IQ scores showing percentage of scores below an IQ score of 95 (shaded area).*

example, if your percentage is the top 8%, then the percentage from the mean to where that shading starts is 42%. If your percentage is the bottom 35%, then the percentage from where the shading starts is 15%. If your percentage is the top 83%, then the percentage from the mean to where the shading stops is 33%.

Once you have the percentage from the mean to where the shading starts or stops, look up the closest number you can find to it in the "% Mean to Z" column of the normal curve table and find the Z score in the "Z" column next to it. That Z will be your answer—except it may be negative. The best way to tell if it is positive or negative is by looking at your picture.

❹ **Check that your exact Z score is similar to your rough estimate from Step 2.**
❺ **If you want to find a raw score, change it from the Z score.**

EXAMPLES

Here are three examples. Once again, we use IQ for our examples, with $M = 100$ and $SD = 16$.

Example 1: What IQ score would a person need to be in the top 5%?

❶ **Draw a picture of the normal curve, and shade in the approximate area for your percentage using the 50%–34%–14% percentages.** We wanted the top 5%. Thus, the shading has to begin above (to the right of) 1 SD (there are 16% of scores above 1 SD). However, it cannot start above 2 SD because there are only 2% of scores above 2 SD. But 5% is a lot closer to 2% than to 16%. Thus, you would draw in the shading starting a small way to the left of the 2 SD point. This is shown in Figure 5–7.

❷ **Make a rough estimate of the Z score where the shaded area starts.** The Z score is between +1 and +2.

❸ **Find the exact Z score using the normal curve table (including adding or subtracting 50% if necessary before looking it up).** Because 50% of people have IQs above the mean, at least 45% have IQs between this person's IQ and the mean (that is, 50% – 5% = 45%). Looking in the "% Mean to Z" column of the normal curve table, the closest figure to 45% is 44.95% (or you could use 45.05%). This goes with a Z score of 1.64 in the "Z" column.

❹ **Check that your exact percentage is similar to your rough estimate from Step 2.** As we estimated, +1.64 is between +1 and +2.

❺ **If you want to find a raw score, change it from the Z score.** Using the formula from Chapter 2, $X = M + (Z)(SD) = 100 + (1.64)(16) = 126.24$. In sum, to be in the top 5%, a person would need an IQ of at least 126.24.

FIGURE 5–7 *Finding the Z score and IQ raw score for where the top 5% start.*

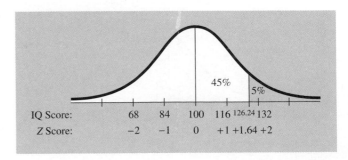

IQ Score:	68	84	100	116	126.24	132
Z Score:	−2	−1	0	+1	+1.64	+2

Example 2: What IQ score would a person need to be in the lowest 1%?

❶ Draw a picture of the normal curve and shade in the approximate area for your percentage using the 50%–34%–14% percentages. You want the bottom 1%. Thus, the shading has to begin below (to the left of) −2 *SD* (there are 2% of scores below −2 *SD*). You would draw in the shading starting to the left (below) the −2 *SD* point. This is shown in Figure 5–8.

❷ Make a rough estimate of the *Z* score where the shaded area starts. The *Z* score has to be below −2.

❸ Find the exact *Z* score using the normal curve table (including adding or subtracting 50% if necessary before looking it up). Being in the bottom 1% means that at least 49% of people have IQs between this IQ and the mean (that is, 50% − 1% = 49%). In the normal curve table, 49% in the "% Mean to *Z*" column (or as close as you can get, which is 49.01%) goes with a *Z* score of 2.33. Because you are below the mean, this becomes −2.33.

❹ Check that your exact percentage is similar to your rough estimate from Step 2. As we estimated, −2.33 is below −2.

❺ If you want to find a raw score, change it from the *Z* score. *X* = 100 + (−2.33)(16) = 62.72. In sum, a person in the bottom 1% on IQ has a score that is 62.72 or below.

Example 3: What range of IQ scores includes the 95% of people in the middle range of IQ scores?

This kind of problem, of finding the middle percentage, may seem odd. However, it is actually a very common situation used in procedures you will learn in later chapters.

The best way to think of this kind of problem is in terms of finding the particular scores that go with the upper and lower ends of this percentage. Thus, in this example, you are really trying to find the points where the bottom 2.5% ends and the top 2.5% begins (which, out of 100%, leaves the middle 95%).

❶ Draw a picture of the normal curve and shade in the approximate area for your percentage using the 50%–34%–14% percentages. Let's start with the point where the top 2.5% begins. This has to be higher than 1 *SD* (there are 16% of scores higher than 1 *SD*). However, it cannot start above 2 *SD* because there are only 2% of scores above 2 *SD*. But 2.5% is very close to 2%. Thus, you would figure that the top 2.5% starts just to the left of the 2 *SD* point. Similarly, the point where the bottom 2.5% comes in would be just to the right of −2 *SD*. The result of all this is that we will shade in the area starting just above −2 *SD* and continuing up to just below +2 *SD*. This is shown in Figure 5–9.

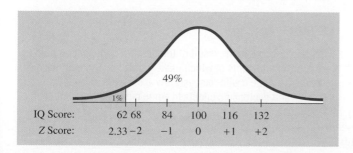

FIGURE 5–8 *Finding the Z score and IQ raw score for where the bottom 1% start (going down).*

FIGURE 5-9 *Finding the Z scores and IQ raw scores for where the middle 95% of IQ scores begin and end.*

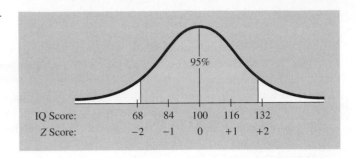

| IQ Score: | 68 | 84 | 100 | 116 | 132 |
| Z Score: | -2 | -1 | 0 | +1 | +2 |

❷ **Make a rough estimate of the Z score or raw score where the shaded area starts**. You can see from the picture that the Z score for the upper limit of the shaded area has to be between +1 and +2, but quite close to +2. Similarly, the lower limit of the shaded area has to be between -1 and -2, but quite close to -2.

❸ **Find the exact Z score using the normal curve table (including adding or subtracting 50% if necessary before looking it up).** Being in the top 2.5% means that at least 47.5% of people have IQs between this IQ and the mean (that is, 50% - 2.5% = 47.5%). In the normal curve table, 47.5% in the "% Mean to Z" column goes with a Z score of 1.96. The normal curve is entirely symmetrical. Thus, the Z score for the bottom 2.5% should be -1.96.

❹ **Check that your exact percentage is similar to your rough estimate from Step 2.** As we estimated, 1.96 is between 1 and 2 and is very close to 2, and -1.96 is between -1 and -2 and very close to -2.

❺ **If you want to find a raw score, change it from the Z score.** For the high end, $X = 100 + (1.96)(16) = 131.36$. For the low end, $X = 100 + (-1.96)(16) = 68.64$. In sum, the middle 95% of IQ scores run from 68.64 to 131.36.

HOW ARE YOU DOING?

1. Why is the normal curve (or at least a curve that is symmetrical and unimodal) so common in nature?
2. Without using a normal curve table, about what percentage of scores on a normal curve are (a) above the mean, (b) between the mean and 1 *SD* above the mean, (c) between 1 and 2 *SD*s above the mean, (d) below the mean, (e) between the mean and 1 *SD* below the mean, and (f) between 1 and 2 *SD*s below the mean?
3. Without using a normal curve table, about what percentage of scores on a normal curve are (a) between the mean and 2 *SD*s above the mean, (b) below 1 *SD*, (c) above 2 *SD*s below the mean?
4. Without using a normal curve table, about what *Z* score would a person have who is at the start of the top (a) 50%, (b) 16%, (c) 84%, (d) 2%?
5. Using the normal curve table, what percentage of scores are (a) between the mean and a *Z* score of 2.14, (b) above 2.14, (c) below 2.14?
6. Using the normal curve table, what *Z* score would you have if (a) 20% are above you, (b) 80% are below you.

ANSWERS:

1. It is common because any particular score is the result of the random combination of many effects, some of which make it larger and some of which make it smaller. Thus, on the average these effects balance out near the middle with relatively few at each extreme, because it is unlikely for most of the increasing and decreasing effects to come out in the same direction.
2. (a) 50%, (b) 34%, (c) 14%, (d) 50%, (e) 34%, (f) 14%.
3. (a) 48%, (b) 84%, (c) 98%.
4. (a) 0, (b) 1, (c) -1, (d) 2.

5. (a) 48.38%, (b) 1.62%, (c) 98.38%.
6. (a) .84, (b) .84.

PROBABILITY

The purpose of most psychological research is to examine the truth of a theory or the effectiveness of a procedure. But scientific research of any kind can only make that truth or effectiveness seem more or less likely; it cannot give us the luxury of knowing for certain. Probability is very important in science. In particular, probability is very important in inferential statistics, the methods psychologists use to go from results of research studies to conclusions about theories or applied procedures.

Probability has been studied for centuries by mathematicians and philosophers. Yet even today, the topic is full of controversy. Fortunately, however, you need to know only a few key ideas to understand and carry out the inferential statistical procedures you learn in this book. These few key points are not very difficult—indeed, some students find them obvious.

INTERPRETATIONS OF PROBABILITY

In statistics we usually define **probability** as the expected relative frequency of a particular outcome. An **outcome** is the result of an experiment (or just about any situation in which the result is not known in advance, such as a coin coming up heads or it raining tomorrow). *Frequency* is how many times something happens. The *relative frequency* is the number of times something happens relative to the number of times it could have happened. That is, relative frequency is the proportion of times it happens. (A coin might come up heads 8 times out of 12 flips, for a relative frequency of 8/12, or 2/3.) **Expected relative frequency** is what you expect to get in the long run if you repeated the experiment many times. (In the case of a coin, in the long run you would expect to get 1/2 heads). This is called the **long-run relative-frequency interpretation of probability.**

probability (p)
outcome

expected relative frequency

long-run relative-frequency interpretation of probability

We also use probability to mean how certain we are that a particular thing will happen. This is called the **subjective interpretation of probability.** Suppose that you say there is a 95% chance that your favorite restaurant will be open tonight. You could be using a kind of relative frequency interpretation. This would imply that if you were to check whether this restaurant was open many times on days like today, on 95% of those days you would find it open. However, what you mean is probably more subjective: On a scale of 0% to 100%, you would rate your confidence that the restaurant is open at 95%. To put it another way, you would feel that a bet was fair that had odds based on a 95% chance of the restaurant's being open.

subjective interpretation of probability

The interpretation, however, does not affect how probability is figured. We mention these interpretations for two reasons. First, we want to give you some deeper insight into the meaning of the term *probability*, which is such a prominent concept throughout statistics. Second, familiarity with both interpretations helps you understand some of the deepest controversies in statistics—one of which we introduce at the end of this chapter.

FIGURING PROBABILITIES

Probabilities are usually figured as the proportion of successful possible outcomes, the number of possible successful outcomes divided by the number of *all* possible outcomes. That is,

BOX 5-2   Pascal Begins Probability Theory at the Gambling Table, Then Learns to Bet on God

Whereas in England statistics were used to keep track of death rates and to prove the existence of God (see Chapter 1, Box 1–1), the French and the Italians developed statistics at the gaming table. In particular, there was the "problem of points"—the division of the stakes in a game after it has been interrupted. If a certain number of plays were planned, how much of the stakes should each player walk away with, given the percentage played so far?

The problem was discussed at least as early as 1494 by Luca Pacioli, a friend of Leonardo da Vinci. But it was unsolved until 1654, when it was presented to Blaise Pascal by the Chevalier de Méré. Pascal, a French child prodigy, attended meetings of the most famous adult French mathematicians and at 15 proved an important theorem in geometry. In correspondence with Pierre Fermat, another famous French mathematician, Pascal solved the problem of points and in so doing began the field of probability theory and the work that would lead to the normal curve.

By the way, not long after solving this problem, Pascal suddenly became as religiously devout as the English statisticians. He was in a runaway coach on a bridge and was saved from drowning only by the traces of the team breaking at the last possible moment. He took this as a warning to abandon his mathematical work in favor of religious writings and later formulated "Pascal's wager": that the value of a game is the value of the prize times the probability of winning it; therefore, even if the probability is low that God exists, we should gamble on the affirmative because the value of the prize is infinite, whereas the value of not believing is only finite worldly pleasure.

Reference: Tankard (1984).

$$\text{Probability} = \frac{\text{Possible successful outcomes}}{\text{All possible outcomes}}$$

Consider the probability of getting heads when flipping a coin. There is one possible successful outcome (getting heads) out of two possible outcomes (getting heads or getting tails). This makes a probability of 1/2, or .5. In a throw of a single die, the probability of a 2 (or any other particular side of the six-sided die) is 1/6, or .17. This is because there can be only one particular successful outcome out of six possible outcomes. The probability of throwing a die and getting a number 3 or lower is 3/6, or .5. There are three possible successful outcomes (a 1, a 2, or a 3) out of six possible outcomes.

Now consider a slightly more complicated example. Suppose a class has 200 people in it, and 30 are seniors. If you were to pick someone from the class at random, the probability of picking a senior would be 30/200, or .15. This is because there are 30 possible successful outcomes (getting a senior) out of 200 possible outcomes.

STEPS FOR FINDING PROBABILITIES

❶ Determine the number of possible successful outcomes.
❷ Determine the number of all possible outcomes.
❸ Divide the number of possible successful outcomes (Step 1) by the number of all possible outcomes (Step 2).

Applying these steps to the probability of getting a number 3 or lower on a throw of a die,

❶ **Determine the number of possible successful outcomes.** There are three outcomes of 3 or lower—a 1, 2, or 3.

❷ **Determine the number of possible outcomes.** There are six possible outcomes in the throw of a die—a 1, 2, 3, 4, 5, or 6.

❸ **Divide the number of possible successful outcomes (Step 1) by the number of all possible outcomes (Step 2).** 3/6 = .5.

RANGE OF PROBABILITIES

A probability is a proportion, the number of possible successful outcomes to the total number of possible outcomes. A proportion cannot be less than 0 or greater than 1. In terms of percentages, proportions range from 0% to 100%. Something that has no chance of happening has a probability of 0, and something that is certain to happen has a probability of 1. Notice that when the probability of an event is 0, the event is completely *impossible;* it cannot happen. But when the probability of an event is low, say 5% or even 1%, the event is *improbable* or *unlikely,* but not impossible.

PROBABILITIES EXPRESSED AS SYMBOLS

Probability is usually symbolized by the letter p. The actual probability number is usually given as a decimal, though sometimes fractions or percentages are used. A 50-50 chance is usually written as $p = .5$, but it could also be written as $p = ½$ or $p = 50\%$. It is also common to see probability written as being less than some number, using the "less than" sign. For example, $p < .05$ means "the probability is less than .05."

PROBABILITY RULES

As we noted above, our discussion only scratches the surface of probability. One of the topics we have not considered are the rules for figuring probabilities for multiple outcomes (for example, what is the chance of flipping a coin twice and both times getting heads?). These are called probability rules, and they are important in the mathematical foundation of many aspects of statistics. However, you don't need to know these probability rules to understand what we cover in this book. Also, these rules are rarely used directly in analyzing results of psychology research. Nevertheless, you will occasionally see such procedures referred to in research articles. Thus, the most widely mentioned probability rules are described in the Chapter Appendix.

PROBABILITY AND THE NORMAL DISTRIBUTION

So far, we have mainly discussed probabilities of specific events that might or might not happen. We also can talk about a range of events that might or might not happen. The throw of a die coming out 3 or lower is an example (it includes the range 1, 2, and 3). Another example is the probability of selecting someone on a city street who is between the ages of 30 and 40.

If you think of probability in terms of proportion of scores, probability fits in well with frequency distributions (see Chapter 1). In the frequency distribution shown in Figure 5–10, 10 of the total of 50 people scored 7 or higher. If you were selecting people from this group of 50 at random, there would be 10 chances (possible successful outcomes) out of 50 (all possible outcomes) of selecting one that was 7 or higher. Thus, $p = 10/50 = .2$.

You can also think of the normal distribution as a probability distribution. With a normal curve, the proportion of scores between any two Z scores is known. As we

FIGURE 5–10 *Frequency distribution (shown as a histogram) of 50 people in which p = .2 (10/50) of randomly selecting a person with a score of 7 or higher.*

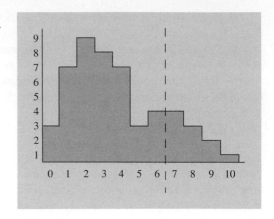

are seeing, the proportion of scores between any two Z scores is the same as the probability of selecting a score between those two Z scores. For example, the probability of a score being between the mean and a Z score of $+1$ is about 34%; that is, $p = .34$.

In a sense, it is merely a technical point that the normal curve can be seen as either a frequency distribution or a probability distribution. We mention this only so that you will not be confused when we talk later about the probability of a score coming from a particular portion of the normal curve.

HOW ARE YOU DOING?

1. The probability of an event is defined as the expected relative frequency of a particular outcome. Explain what is meant by (a) relative frequency and (b) outcome.
2. List and explain two interpretations of probability.
3. Suppose you have 400 pennies in a jar and 40 of them are more than 9 years old. You then mix up the pennies and pull one out. (a) What is the probability of getting one that is more than 9 years old? In this problem, (b) what is the number of possible successful outcomes? and (c) what is the number of all possible outcomes?
4. Suppose people's scores on a particular personality test are normally distributed with a mean of 50 and a standard deviation of 10. If you were to pick a person completely at random, what is the probability you would pick someone with a score on this test higher than 60?
5. What is meant by $p < .01$?

ANSWERS

1. (a) Relative frequency is the number of times something happens in relation to the number of times it could have happened.
   (b) An outcome is the result of an experiment—what happens in a situation where what will happen is not known in advance.
2. (a) The long-run relative frequency interpretation of probability is that probability is the proportion of times we expect something to happen (relative to how often it could happen) if the situation were repeated a very large number of times. (b) The subjective interpretation of probability is that probability is our sense of confidence that something will happen rated on a 0% to 100% scale.
3. (a) 40/400 = .10. (b) 40. (c) 400.
4. 16%.
5. The probability is less than .01.

SAMPLE AND POPULATION

We are going to introduce you to some important ideas by thinking of beans. Suppose you are cooking a pot of beans and taste a spoonful to see if they are done. In this example, the pot of beans is a **population,** the entire set of things of interest. The spoonful is a **sample,** the part of the population about which you actually have information. This is illustrated in Figure 5–11a. Figures 5–11b and 5–11c are other ways of showing the relation of a sample to a population.

population
sample

In psychology research, we typically study samples not of beans but of individuals to make inferences about some larger group. A sample might consist of 50 Canadian women who participate in a particular experiment, whereas the population might be intended to be all Canadian women. In an opinion survey, 1,000 people might be selected from the voting-age population and asked for whom they plan to vote. The opinions of these 1,000 people are the sample. The opinions of the larger voting public in that country, to which the pollsters hope to apply their results, is the population (see Figure 5–12).[2]

WHY SAMPLES INSTEAD OF POPULATIONS ARE STUDIED

If you want to know something about a population, your results would be most accurate if you could study the entire population rather than a subgroup from that population. However, in most research situations this is not practical. More important, the whole point of research usually is to be able to make generalizations or predictions about events beyond your reach. We would not call it scientific research if you tested three particular cars to see which gets better gas mileage—unless you hoped to say something about the gas mileage of those models of cars in general. In other words, a researcher might do an experiment on the way in which people store words in short-term memory using 20 students as the participants in the experiment. But the purpose of the experiment is not to find out how these particular 20 students respond to the experimental versus the control condition. Rather, the purpose is to learn something about human memory under these conditions in general.

The strategy in almost all psychology research is to study a sample of individuals who are believed to be representative of the general population (or of some particular population of interest). More realistically, researchers try to study people who do not differ from the general population in any systematic way that should matter for that topic of research.

The sample is what is studied, and the population is an unknown that researchers draw conclusions about based on the sample. Most of what you learn in the rest of this book is about the important work of drawing conclusions about populations based on information from samples.

METHODS OF SAMPLING

Usually, the ideal method of picking out a sample to study is called **random selection.** The researcher starts with a complete list of the population and randomly selects some of them to study. An example of random selection is to put each name on

random selection

---

[2]Strictly speaking, *population* and *sample* refer to scores (numbers or measurements), not to the research participants measured. Thus, in the first example, the sample is really the scores of the 50 Canadian women, not the 50 women themselves; the population is really what the *scores* would be if all Canadian women were measured.

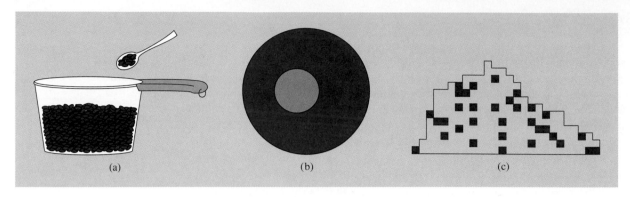

FIGURE 5–11 *Populations and samples: In (a), the entire pot of beans is the population and the spoonful is a sample. In (b), the entire larger circle is the population and the circle within it is the sample. In (c), the histogram is of the population and the particular shaded scores together make up the sample.*

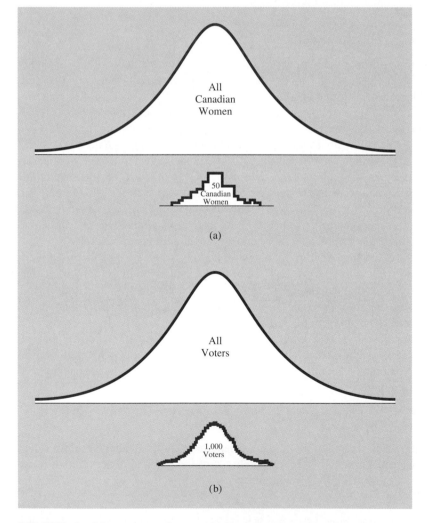

FIGURE 5–12 *Additional examples of populations and samples. In (a), the population is the scores of all Canadian women and the sample is the scores of the 50 particular Canadian women studied. In (b), the population is the voting preferences of the entire voting-age population and the sample is the voting preferences of the 1,000 voting-age people who were surveyed.*

a table tennis ball, put all the balls into a big hopper, shake it up, and have a blind-folded person select as many as are needed. (In practice, most researchers use a computer-generated list of random numbers. Just how computers or persons can create a list of truly random numbers is an interesting question in its own right that we examine in Chapter 15, Box 15–1.)

It is important not to confuse truly random selection with what might be called **haphazard selection**; for example, just taking whoever is available or happens to be first on a list. When using haphazard selection, it is surprisingly easy accidentally to pick a group of people to study that is really quite different from the population as a whole. Consider a survey of attitudes about your statistics instructor. Suppose you give your questionnaire only to other students sitting near you in class. Such a survey would be affected by all the things that influence where students choose to sit, some of which have to do with just what you are studying—how much they like the instruc-tor or the class. (Thus, for example, asking students who sit near you would result in opinions more like your own than a truly random sample would.)

Unfortunately, it is often impossible to study a truly random sample. Much of the time, in fact, studies are conducted with whoever is willing or available to be a research participant. At best, as noted, a researcher tries to study a sample that is not systematically unrepresentative of the population in any known way. For example, suppose a study is about a process that is likely to differ for people of different age groups. In this situation, the researcher may attempt to include people of all age groups in the study. Alternatively, the researcher would be careful to draw conclu-sions only about the age group that was studied.

Methods of sampling is a complex topic that is discussed in detail in research methods textbooks (also see Box 5–3) and the research methods mini chapter on the website for this book.

haphazard selection

STATISTICAL TERMINOLOGY FOR SAMPLES AND POPULATIONS

The mean, variance, and standard deviation of a population are called **population pa-rameters.** A population parameter usually is unknown and can only be estimated from what you know about a sample taken from that population. You do not taste all the beans, just the spoonful. "The beans are done" is an inference about the whole pot.

Population parameters are usually shown as Greek letters. The symbol for the mean of a population is μ, the Greek letter mu. The symbol for the variance of a population is σ^2, and the symbol for its standard deviation is σ, the lowercase Greek letter sigma. You won't see these symbols often, except while learning statis-tics. This is because, again, researchers seldom know the population parameters.

The mean, variance, and standard deviation you figure for the scores in a sam-ple are called **sample statistics.** A sample statistic is figured from known informa-tion. Sample statistics are what we have been figuring all along and are expressed with the symbols we have been using all along: M, SD^2, and SD. These various symbols are summarized in Table 5–2.

population parameters

μ
σ^2
σ

sample statistics

HOW ARE YOU DOING?

1. Explain the difference between the population and a sample in relation to a research study.
2. Why do psychologists usually study samples and not populations?
3. Explain the difference between random sampling and haphazard sampling.
4. Explain the difference between a population parameter and a sample statistic.
5. Give the symbols for the population parameters for (a) the mean and (b) the standard deviation.

BOX 5–3   Surveys, Polls, and 1948's Costly "Free Sample"

It is time to make you a more informed reader of polls in the media. Usually, the results of properly done public polls will be accompanied, somewhere in fine print, by a statement like "From a telephone poll of 1,000 American adults taken on June 4 and 5. Sampling error ±3%." What does all this mean?

The Gallup poll is as good an example as any (Gallup, 1972), and there is no better place to begin than 1948, when all three of the major polling organizations—Gallup, Crossley (for Hearst papers), and Roper (for *Fortune*)—wrongly predicted Thomas Dewey's victory over Harry Truman for the U.S. presidency. Yet Gallup's prediction was based on 50,000 interviews and Roper's on 15,000. By contrast, to predict George H. Bush's 1988 victory, Gallup used only 4,089. Since 1952, the pollsters have never used more than 8,144—but with very small error and no outright mistakes. What has changed?

The method used before 1948, and never repeated since, was called "quota sampling." Interviewers were assigned a fixed number of persons to interview, with strict quotas to fill in all the categories that seemed important, such as residence, sex, age, race, and economic status. Within these specifics, however, they were free to interview whomever they liked. Republicans generally tended to be easier to interview. They were more likely to have telephones and permanent addresses and to live in better houses and better neighborhoods. This slight bias had not mattered prior to 1948. Democrats had been winning for years anyway. In 1948, the election was very close and the Republican bias produced the embarrassing mistake that changed survey methods forever.

Since 1948, all survey organizations have used what is called a "probability method." Simple random sampling is the purest case of the probability method, but simple random sampling for a survey about a U.S. presidential election would require drawing names from a list of all the eligible voters in the nation—a lot of people. Each person selected would have to be found, in diversely scattered locales. So instead, "multistage cluster sampling" is used. The United States is divided into seven size-of-community strata, from large cities to rural open country; these groupings are divided into seven geographic regions (New England, Middle Atlantic, and so on), after which smaller equal-sized groups are zoned, and then city blocks are drawn from the zones, with the probability of selection being proportional to the size of the population or number of dwelling units. Finally, an interviewer is given a randomly selected starting point on the map and is required to follow a given direction, take households in sequence, and ask for the youngest man 18 or older or, if no man is at home, the oldest woman 18 or older. (This has been found to compensate best for the tendencies for young men, and then all men, and then older women, in that order, to be not at home and hence underrepresented.)

Actually, telephoning is often the favored method for polling today. Phone surveys cost about one third of door-to-door polls. Since most people now own phones, this method is less biased than in Truman's time. Phoning also allows computers to randomly dial numbers, and unlike telephone directories, this method calls unlisted numbers.

Whether the survey is by telephone or face to face, there will be about 35% nonrespondents after three attempts. This creates yet another bias, reckoned with through questions about how much time a person spends at home, so that a slight extra weight can be given to the responses of those who were reached but usually at home less, to make up for those missed entirely.

What happened in 2000? Obviously, polls lost some of their credibility. Actually, the polls before the election were quite accurate, predicting Gore winning the national popular vote by a very slight margin—which he did. The exit polls may not have been completed with as much care—the issue is still being debated.

Now you know quite a bit about opinion polls. But we have left two important questions unanswered: Why are only about 1,000 included in a poll meant to describe all U.S. adults, and what does the term sampling error mean? For these answers, you must wait for Chapter 7 (Box 7–1).

TABLE 5-2	Population Parameters and Sample Statistics	
	Population Parameter (Usually Unknown)	**Sample Statistic** (Figured from Known Data)
Basis:	Scores of entire population	Scores of sample only
Symbols:		
Mean	μ	M
Standard deviation	σ	SD
Variance	σ^2	SD^2

ANSWERS:

1. The population is the entire group to which results of a study are intended to apply. The sample is the particular, smaller group of individuals actually studied.
2. It is not practical in most cases to study the entire population.
3. In random sampling, the sample is chosen from among the population using a completely random method, so that any particular individual has an equal chance of being included in the sample. In haphazard sampling, the researcher selects to be studied whoever is available or convenient.
4. A population parameter is about the population (such as the mean of all the scores in the population); a sample statistic is about a particular sample (such as the mean of the scores of the people in the sample).
5. (a) μ. (b) σ.

CONTROVERSIES: IS THE NORMAL CURVE REALLY NORMAL?, WHAT DOES PROBABILITY REALLY MEAN?, AND USING NONRANDOM SAMPLES

Basic as they are, there is considerable controversy about all three topics we have introduced in this chapter: the normal curve, probability, and sample and population. In this section we consider a major controversy about each.

IS THE NORMAL CURVE REALLY SO NORMAL?

We said earlier that real distributions in the world often closely approximate the normal curve. Just how often real distributions closely follow a normal curve turns out to be very important, and not just because normal curves make Z scores more useful. As you learn in later chapters, the main statistical methods psychologists use assume that the samples studied come from populations that follow a normal curve. Researchers almost never know the true shape of the population distribution, so if they want to use the usual methods, they have to just *assume* it is normal, making this assumption because most populations are normal. Yet, there is a long-standing debate in psychology about just how often populations really are normally distributed. The predominant view has been that given the way psychology measures are developed, a bell-shaped distribution "is almost guaranteed" (Walberg et al., 1984, p. 107). Or, as Hopkins and Glass (1978) put it, measurements in all disciplines are such good approximations to it that one might think "God loves the normal curve!"

On the other hand, there has been a persistent line of criticism about whether nature really packages itself so neatly. Micceri (1989) showed that many measures commonly used in psychology are *not* normally distributed "in nature." His study included achievement and ability tests (such as the SAT and the GRE) and personality tests (such as the MMPI). Micceri examined the distributions of scores of 440 psychological and educational measures that had been used on very large samples. All of the measures he examined had been studied in samples of over 190 individuals, and the majority had samples of over 1,000 (14.3% even had samples of 5,000 to 10,293). Yet large samples were of no help. No measure he studied had a distribution that passed all checks for normality (mostly, Micceri looked for skewness, kurtosis, and "lumpiness"). Few measures had distributions that even came reasonably close to looking like the normal curve. Nor were these variations predictable: "The distributions studied here exhibited almost every conceivable type of contamination" (p. 162), although some were more common with certain types of tests. Micceri discusses many obvious reasons for this nonnormality, such as "ceiling" or "floor" effects (see Chapter 2).

How much has it mattered that the distributions for these measures were so far from normal? According to Micceri, it is just not known. And until more is known, the general opinion among psychologists will no doubt remain supportive of traditional statistical methods, with the underlying mathematics based on the assumption of normal population distributions.

What is the reason for this nonchalance in the face of findings such as Micceri's? It turns out that under most conditions in which the standard methods are used, they give results that are reasonably accurate even when the formal requirement of a normal population distribution is not met (e.g., Sawilowsky & Blair, 1992). In this book, we generally adopt this majority position favoring the use of the standard methods in all but the most extreme cases. But you should be aware that a vocal minority of psychologists disagrees. Some of the alternative statistical techniques they favor (ones that do not rely on assuming a normal distribution in the population) are presented in Chapter 15.

Galton, one of the major pioneers of statistical methods (recall Chapter 3, Box 3–1), said of the normal curve, "I know of scarcely anything so apt to impress the imagination. . . . [It] would have been personified by the Greeks and deified, if they had known of it. It reigns with serenity and in complete self-effacement amidst the wild confusion" (1889, p. 66). Ironically, it may be true that in psychology, at least, it truly reigns in pure and austere isolation, with no even close-to-perfect real-life imitators.

WHAT DOES PROBABILITY REALLY MEAN?

We have already introduced the major controversy in the area of probability theory as it is applied to statistics in psychology, the dispute between the long-term relative-frequency interpretation and the subjective degree-of-belief interpretation. In most cases, though, it really does not much matter which interpretation is used; the statistics are the same. But among the minority of theorists who favor the subjective interpretation, some hold a rather critical view of the mainstream of statistical thinking. In particular, they have advocated what has come to be called the Bayesian approach (for example, see Phillips, 1973). The approach is named after Thomas Bayes, an early-18th-century nonconformist English clergyman who developed a probability theorem now appropriately known as Bayes' theorem.

Bayes' theorem itself can be proved mathematically and is not controversial. However, its applications in statistics are hotly debated. The details of the approach are beyond the scope of an introductory text, but the main point of dispute can be made clear here: According to the Bayesians, science is about conducting research in order to adjust our preexisting beliefs in light of evidence we collect. Thus, conclusions drawn from an experiment are always in the context of what we believed about the world before doing the experiment. The mainstream view, by contrast, says that it is better not to make any assumptions about prior beliefs. We should just look at the evidence as it is, judging whether the experiment has shown any reliable effects at all. Some statisticians in the mainstream do acknowledge that the Bayesian description of science may be more accurate. However, they are still uncomfortable with using Bayesian statistical methods in research practice because the conclusion drawn from each study would then depend too heavily on the subjective belief of the particular scientist doing the study. The same experimental results from different scientists could lead to different conclusions.

USING NONRANDOM SAMPLES

Most of the procedures you learn in the rest of this book are based on mathematics that assume that the sample studied is a random sample of the population. As we pointed out, however, in most psychology research the samples are nonrandom, including whatever individuals are available to participate in the experiment. Most studies are done with college students, volunteers, convenient laboratory animals, and the like.

Some psychologists are concerned about this problem and have suggested that researchers need to use different statistical approaches that make generalizations only to the kinds of people that are actually being used in the study.[3] For example, these psychologists would argue that if your sample has a particular nonnormal distribution, you should assume that you can generalize only to a population with the same particular nonnormal distribution. We will have more to say about their suggested solutions in Chapter 15.

Sociologists, as compared to psychologists, are much more concerned about the representativeness of the groups they study. Studies reported in sociology journals (or in sociologically oriented social psychology journals) are much more likely to use formal methods of random selection and large samples, or at least to address the issue in their articles.

Why are psychologists more comfortable with using nonrandom samples? The main reason is that psychologists are mainly interested in the *relationships* among variables. If in one population the effect of experimentally changing X leads to a change in Y, this relationship should probably hold in other populations. This relationship should hold even if the actual levels of Y differ from population to population. Suppose that a researcher conducts the experiment we used as one of the examples in chapters 3 and 4, testing the relation of number of exposures to a list of words to number of words remembered. Suppose further that this study is done with college students and that the result is that the greater the number of exposures, the greater the number of words remembered. The actual number of words remembered from the list might well be different for people other than college students. For ex-

[3]Frick (1998) argues that in most cases psychology researchers should not think in terms of samples and populations at all. Rather, he argues, researchers should think of themselves as studying processes. An experiment examines some process in a group of individuals. Then the researcher evaluates the probability that the pattern of results could have been caused by chance factors. For example, the researcher examines whether a difference in means between an experimental and a control group could have been caused by factors other than by the experimental manipulation. Frick claims that this way of thinking is much closer to the way researchers actually work, and argues that it has various advantages in terms of the subtle logic of inferential statistical procedures. (Reichardt & Gollob, 1999, present a related argument.) It will be interesting to see the reaction to Frick's proposal over the next few years. In any case, following the more standard approach (as taught in this book) yields exactly the same results and is consistent with the way most psychologists understand statistical reasoning.

ample, chess masters (who probably have highly developed memories) may recall more words; people who have just been upset may recall fewer words. However, even in these groups, we would expect that the more times exposed to the list, the more words will be remembered. That is, the *relation* of number of exposures to number of words recalled will probably be about the same in each population.

In sociology, the representativeness of samples is much more important. This is because sociologists are more concerned with the actual mean and variance of a variable in a particular society. Thus, a sociologist might be interested in the average attitude towards older people in the population of a particular country. For this purpose, how sampling is done is extremely important.

NORMAL CURVES, PROBABILITIES, SAMPLES, AND POPULATIONS IN RESEARCH ARTICLES

You need to understand the topics we covered in this chapter to learn what comes next. However, the topics of this chapter are rarely mentioned directly in research articles (except articles *about* methods or statistics). Sometimes you see the normal curve mentioned, usually when a researcher is describing the pattern of scores on a particular variable. (We say more about this and give some examples from published articles in Chapter 15, where we consider situations in which the scores do not follow a normal curve.)

Probability is also rarely discussed directly, except in relation to statistical significance, a topic we mentioned briefly in Chapter 3. In almost any article you look at, the results section will be strewn with descriptions of various methods having to do with statistical significance, followed by something like "$p < .05$" or "$p < .01$." The p refers to probability, but the probability of what? This is the main topic of our discussion of statistical significance in Chapter 6.

Finally, you will sometimes see a brief mention of the method of selecting the sample from the population. For example, a major survey study of various influences on job satisfaction (such as the quality of social relations at work), used the following sampling method:

> The sampling procedure consisted of two steps: First, 20 municipalities in the Netherlands . . . were drawn. Next, 2,800 home addresses of persons in the aforementioned age groups [18, 22, and 26] were randomly selected from the registry offices in these municipalities. (Taris & Feij, 2001, p. 59)

Even with such careful procedures, researchers check whether their sample is similar to the population as a whole based on any information they may have about the overall population (for example, from census records). Thus, in this study, the researchers report that "The sample was almost representative of the Dutch population in the age groups mentioned above: the sample consisted of a wide range of occupations and job levels" (p. 59).

In contrast, even survey studies typically are not able to use such rigorous methods and have to rely on more haphazard methods of getting their samples. For example, in a recent study of relationship distress and partner abuse, the researchers describe their method of gathering research participants to interview as follows: "Seventy-four couples of varying levels of relationship adjustment were recruited through community newspaper advertisements" (p. 336). In a study of this kind, one cannot very easily recruit a random sample of abusers since there is no list of all abusers to recruit from! This could be done with a very large national random sample of couples, who would then include a random sample of abusers. Indeed, the authors of this study are very aware of the issues. At the end of the article, when discussing "cautions necessary when interpreting our results," they note that before their conclusions can be taken as definitive "our study must be replicated with a representative sample" (p. 341).

SUMMARY

1. The scores on many variables in psychology research approximately follow a bell-shaped, symmetrical, unimodal distribution called the normal curve. Because the shape of this curve follows an exact mathematical formula, there is a specific percentage of scores between any two points on a normal curve.

2. A useful working rule for normal curves is that 50% of the score are above the mean, 34% between the mean and 1 standard deviation above the mean, and 14% between 1 and 2 standard deviations above the mean.

3. A normal curve table gives the percentage of scores between the mean and any particular positive Z score. Using this table, and knowing that the curve is symmetrical and that 50% of the scores are above the mean, you can figure the percentage of scores above or below any particular Z score. You can also use the table to figure the Z score for the point where a particular percentage of scores begins or ends.

4. Most psychology researchers consider the probability of an event to be its expected relative frequency. However, some think of probability as the subjective degree of belief that the event will happen. Probability is usually figured as the proportion of successful outcomes to total possible outcomes. It is symbolized by p and has a range from 0 (event is impossible) to 1 (event is certain). The normal curve provides a way to know the probabilities of scores being within particular ranges of values.

5. A sample is an individual or group that is studied—usually as representative of some larger group or population that cannot be studied in its entirety. Ideally, the sample is selected from a population using a strictly random procedure. The mean, variance, and so forth of a sample are called sample statistics. When of a population, they are called population parameters and are symbolized by Greek letters—μ for mean, σ^2 for variance, and σ for standard deviation.

6. There are controversies about each topic in this chapter. One is about whether normal distributions are truly typical of the populations of scores for the variables we study in psychology. Another debate, raised by advocates of a Bayesian approach to statistics, is whether we should explicitly take the researcher's initial subjective expectations into account. Finally, some researchers have questioned the use of standard statistical methods in the typical psychology research situation that does not use strict random sampling.

7. Research articles rarely discuss normal curves (except briefly when a variable being studied seems not to follow a normal curve) or probability (except in relation to statistical significance). Procedures of sampling, particularly when the study is a survey, are sometimes described, and the representativeness of a sample when random sampling could not be used may be discussed.

KEY TERMS

expected relative
    frequency (p. 169)
haphazard selection
    (p. 175)
long-run relative-
    frequency interpretation
    of probability (p. 169)
normal curve (p. 158)

normal curve table (p. 161)
normal distribution
    (p. 158)
outcome (p. 169)
population (p. 173)
population parameters
    (p. 175)
probability (p) (p. 169)

random selection (p. 173)
sample (p. 173)
sample statistics (p. 175)
subjective interpretation
    of probability (p. 169)
μ (p. 175)
σ (p. 175)
σ^2 (p. 175)

EXAMPLE WORKED-OUT COMPUTATIONAL PROBLEMS

FIGURING THE PERCENTAGE ABOVE OR BELOW A PARTICULAR RAW SCORE OR Z SCORE

Suppose a test of sensitivity to violence is known to have a mean of 20, a standard deviation of 3, and to follow a normal curve. What percentage of people have scores above 24?

❶ **If you are beginning with a raw score, first change it to a Z score.** $Z = (24 - 20)/3 = 1.33$.

❷ **Draw a picture of the normal curve, where the Z score falls on it, and shade in the area for which you are finding the percentage.** This is shown in Figure 5–13.

❸ **Make a rough estimate of the shaded area's percentage based on the 50%–34%–14% percentages.** If the shaded area started at a Z score of 1, it would include 16%. If it started at a Z score of 2, it would include only 2%. So with a Z score of 1.56, it has to be somewhere between 16% and 2%.

❹ **Find the exact percentage using the normal curve table.** In Table A–1 (Appendix A), 1.33 in the "Z" column goes with 40.82 in the "% Mean to Z" column.

❺ **If needed, add or subtract 50% from this percentage.** Because 50% of people are above the mean on any normal curve, and 40.82% of the people above the mean are below this score, that leaves 9.18% above this person's score (that is,

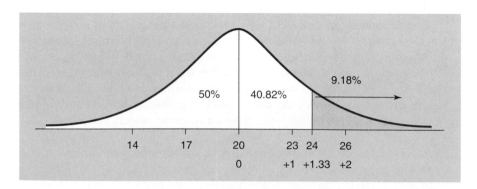

FIGURE 5–13   *Distribution of sensitivity to violence scores showing percentage of scores above a score of 24 (shaded area).*

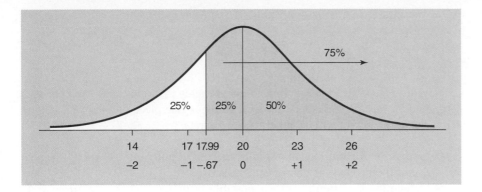

FIGURE 5-14   *Finding the Z score and sensitivity to violence raw score for where the top 75% start.*

50% − 40.82 = 9.18%). That is the answer to the problem: 9.18% of people have a higher score than 24 on the sensitivity to violence measure.

➏ **Check that your exact percentage is within the range of your rough estimate from Step 3.** Our result, 9.18%, is within the 16% to 2% range estimated.

Note: If the problem involves Z scores that are all 0, 1, or 2 (or −1 or −2), you can work the problem using the 50%–34%–14% figures and without using the normal curve table. The only steps are making the figure and adding or subtracting 50% as necessary.

FIGURING Z SCORES AND RAW SCORES FROM PERCENTAGES

Consider the same situation: A test of sensitivity to violence is known to have a mean of 20, a standard deviation of 3, and to follow a normal curve. What is the minimum score a person needs to be in the top 75%?

➊ **Draw a picture of the normal curve and shade in the approximate area for your percentage using the 50%–34%–14% percentages.** The shading has to begin between the mean and 1 *SD* below the mean. (There are 50% above the mean and 84% above 1 *SD* but below the mean). This is shown in Figure 5–14.

➋ **Make a rough estimate of the Z score where the shaded area starts.** The Z score has to be between −1 and 0.

➌ **Find the exact Z score using the normal curve table (including adding or subtracting 50% if necessary before looking it up).** Since 50% of people have IQs above the mean, for the top 75% you need to include the 25% below the mean. Looking in the "% Mean to Z" column of the normal curve table, the closest figure to 25% is 24.86, which goes with a Z of .67. Since we are interested in below the mean, we want −.67.

➍ **Check that your exact percentage is similar to your rough estimate from Step 2.** −.67 is between 0 and −1.

➎ **If you want to find a raw score, change it from the Z score.** $X = M + (Z)(SD) = 20 + (−.67)(3) = 20 − 2.01 = 17.99$. That is, to be in the top 75%, a person would need to have a score on this test of at least 18.

Note: If the problem instructs you not to use a normal curve table, you should be able to work the problem using the 50%–34%–14% figures. The only steps are making the figure, adding or subtracting 50% as necessary, and possibly changing the results to raw scores.

FINDING A PROBABILITY

A candy dish has four kinds of fruit-flavored candy: 20 apple, 20 strawberry, 5 cherry, and 5 grape. If you close your eyes and pick one piece of candy at random, what is the probability it will be either cherry or grape?

❶ **Determine the number of possible successful outcomes.** There are 10 possible successful outcomes—5 cherry and 5 grape.

❷ **Determine the number of all possible outcomes.** There are 50 possible outcomes overall: $20 + 20 + 5 + 5 = 50$.

❸ **Divide the number of possible successful outcomes (Step 1) by the number of all possible outcomes (Step 2).** $10/50 = .2$. Thus, the probability of picking either a cherry or grape candy is .2 or 20%.

PRACTICE PROBLEMS

These problems involve figuring. Most real-life statistics problems are done on a computer. However, even if you have a computer and statistics software, do these by hand (with the help of a calculator) to ingrain the method in your mind. Also, in all problems involving figuring, be sure to show your work. In this chapter, in addition, it is important to draw the diagrams for the normal curve problems.

For practice using a computer to solve statistics problems, refer to the computer section of each chapter of the *Student's Study Guide and Computer Workbook* that accompanies this text.

All data are fictional unless an actual citation is given.

Answers to Set I problems are given at the back of the book.

SET I

1. Suppose the people living in a particular city have a mean score of 40 and a standard deviation of 5 on a measure of concern about the environment. Assume that these concern scores are normally distributed. Approximately what percentage of people have a score (a) above 40, (b) above 45, (c) above 30, (d) above 35, (e) below 40, (f) below 45, (g) below 30, and (h) below 35? (Do not use a normal curve table; use the 50%–34%–14% figures for this problem.)

2. Using the information in problem 1, what is the minimum score a person has to have to be in the top (a) 2%, (b) 16%, (c) 50%, (d) 84%, and (e) 98%? (Do not use a normal curve table; use the 50%–34%–14% figures for this problem.)

3. A psychologist has been studying eye fatigue using a particular measure, which she administers to students after they have worked for 1 hour writing on a computer. On this measure, she has found that the distribution follows a normal curve. Using a normal curve table, what percentage of students have Z scores (a) below 1.5, (b) above 1.5, (c) below -1.5, (d) above -1.5, (e) above 2.10, (f) below 2.10, (g) above .45, (h) below -1.78, and (i) above 1.68?

4. In the previous problem, the test of eye fatigue has a mean of 15 and a standard deviation of 5. Using a normal curve table, what percentage of students have scores (a) above 16, (b) above 17, (c) above 18, (d) below 18, (e) below 14?

5. In the eye fatigue example of problems 3 and 4, using a normal curve table, what score on the eye fatigue measure would a person need to have to be in (a) the top 40%, (b) the top 30%, (c) the top 20%?

6. Using a normal curve table, give the percent of scores between the mean and a Z score of (a) .58, (b) .59, (c) 1.46, (d) 1.56, (e) –.58.

7. Assuming a normal curve, (a) if a person is in the top 10% of his or her country on mathematics ability, what is the lowest Z score this person could have? (b) If the person is in the top 1%, what would be the lowest Z score this person could have?

8. Consider a test of coordination that has a normal distribution, a mean of 50, and a standard deviation of 10. (a) How high a score would a person need to be in the top 5%? (b) Explain your answer to someone who has never had a course in statistics.

9. The following numbers of individuals in a company received special assistance from the personnel department last year:

Drug/alcohol	10
Family crisis counseling	20
Other	20
	—
Total	50

If you were to select someone at random from the records for last year, what is the probability that the person would be in each of the following categories (a) drug/alcohol, (b) family, (c) drug/alcohol or family, (d) any category except "Other," (e) any of the three categories? (f) Explain your answers to someone who has never had a course in statistics.

10. A research article is concerned with the level of self-esteem of Australian high-school students. The methods section emphasizes that it surveyed a "random sample" of Australian high school students. Explain to a person who has never had a course in statistics or research methods what this means and why it is important.

11. Altman et al. (1997) conducted a telephone survey of the attitudes of the U.S. adult public towards tobacco farmers. In the method section of their article, they explained that their respondents were "randomly selected from a nation-wide list of telephone numbers" (p. 117). Explain to a person who has never had a course in statistics or research methods what this means and why it is important.

Set II

12. The amount of time it takes to recover physiologically from a certain kind of sudden noise is found to be normally distributed with a mean of 80 seconds and a standard deviation of 10 seconds. Approximately what percentage of scores (on time to recover) will be (a) above 100, (b) below 100, (c) above 90, (d) below 90, (e) above 80, (f) below 80, (g) above 70, (h) below 70, (i) above 60, and (j) below 60? (Do not use a normal curve table; use the 50%–34%–14% figures for this problem.)

13. Using the information in problem 12, what is the longest time to recover a person can have and still be in the bottom (a) 2%, (b) 16%, (c) 50%, (d) 84%, and

(e) 98%? (Do not use a normal curve table; use the 50%–34%–14% figures for this problem.)

14. Suppose that the scores of architects on a particular creativity test are normally distributed. Using a normal curve table, what percentage of architects have Z scores (a) above .10, (b) below .10, (c) above .20, (d) below .20, (e) above 1.10, (f) below 1.10, (g) above −.10, and (h) below −.10?

15. In the example in problem 14, using a normal curve table, what is the minimum Z score an architect can have on the creativity test to be in the (a) top 50%, (b) top 40%, (c) top 60%, (d) top 30%, and (e) top 20%?

16. In the example in problem 14, assume that the mean is 300 and the standard deviation is 25. Using a normal curve table, what scores would be the top and bottom score to find (a) the middle 50% of architects, (b) the middle 90% of architects, and (c) the middle 99% of architects?

17. Suppose that you are designing an instrument panel for a large industrial machine. The machine requires the person using it to reach 2 feet from a particular position. The reach from this position for adult women is known to have a mean of 2.8 feet with a standard deviation of .5. The reach for adult men is known to have a mean of 3.1 feet with a standard deviation of .6. Both women's and men's reach from this position is normally distributed. If this design is implemented, (a) what percentage of women will not be able to work on this instrument panel? (b) What percentage of men will not be able to work on this instrument panel? (c) Explain your answers to a person who has never had a course in statistics.

18. You are conducting a survey at a college with 800 students, 50 faculty members, and 150 administrative staff members. Each of these 1,000 individuals has a single listing in the campus phone directory. Suppose you were to cut up the directory and pull out one listing at random to contact. What is the probability it would be (a) a student, (b) a faculty member, (c) an administrative staff member, (d) a faculty or administrative staff member, and (e) anyone except staff or administration? (f) Explain your answers to someone who has never had a course in statistics.

19. You apply to 20 graduate programs, 10 of which are in clinical psychology, 5 of which are in counseling psychology, and 5 of which are in social work. You get a message from home that you have a letter from one of the programs you applied to, but nothing is said about which one. Give the probabilities it is from (a) a clinical psychology program, (b) a counseling psychology program, (c) from any program other than social work. (d) Explain your answers to someone who has never had a course in statistics.

20. Suppose you want to conduct a survey of the attitude of psychology graduate students studying clinical psychology towards Freudian methods of psychotherapy. One approach would be to contact every psychology graduate student you know and ask them to fill out a questionnaire about it. (a) What kind of sampling method is this? (b) What is a major limitation of this kind of approach?

21. A recent large study of how people make future plans and its relation to their life satisfaction (Prenda & Clachman, 2001) obtained their participants "through random-digit dialing procedures." These are procedures in which phone numbers to call potential participants are selected at random from all phone numbers in a particular country. Explain to a person who has never had a course in statistics (a) why this method of sampling might be used and (b) why it may be a problem if not everyone called agreed to be interviewed.

22. Suppose that you were going to conduct a survey of visitors to your campus. You want the survey to be as representative as possible. How would you select the people to survey? Why would that be your best method?

CHAPTER APPENDIX: PROBABILITY RULES AND CONDITIONAL PROBABILITIES

Probability rules are procedures for figuring probabilities in more complex situations than we have considered so far. This appendix considers the two most widely used such rules and also explains the concept of conditional probabilities that is used in advanced discussions of probability.

ADDITION RULE

The *addition rule* (also called the *and rule*) is used in situations where there are two or more *mutually exclusive outcomes*. Mutually exclusive means that if one outcome happens, the others can't happen. For example, heads or tails on a single coin flip are mutually exclusive because the result has to be one or the other, but can't be both. With mutually exclusive outcomes, the total probability of getting either outcome is the sum of the individual probabilities. Thus, on a single coin flip, the total chance of getting either heads (which is .5) or tails (also .5) is 1.0 (.5 plus .5). Similarly, on a single throw of a die, the chance of getting either a 3 (1/6) or a 5 (1/6) is 1/3 (1/6 + 1/6). If you are picking a student at random from your university in which 30% are seniors and 25% are juniors, the chance of picking someone who is either a senior or a junior is 55%.

Even though we have not used the term "addition rule," we have already used this rule in many of the examples we considered in this chapter. For example, we used this rule when we figured that the chance of getting a 3 or lower on the throw of a die is .5.

MULTIPLICATION RULE

The *multiplication rule* (also called the *or rule*), however, is completely new. You use the multiplication rule to figure the probability of getting *both* of two (or more) *independent outcomes*. Independent outcomes are outcomes in which getting one has no effect on getting the other. For example, getting heads or tails on one flip of a coin is an independent outcome from getting heads or tails on a second flip of a coin. The probability of getting both of two independent outcomes is the product (the result of multiplying) the individual probabilities. For example, on a single coin flip, the chance of getting heads is .5. On a second coin flip, the chance of getting heads (regardless of what you got on the first flip) is also .5. Thus, the probability of getting heads on *both* coin flips is .25 (.5 times .5). On two throws of a die the chance of getting a 5 on *both* throws is 1/36—the probability of getting a 5 on the first throw (1/6) times the probability of getting a 5 on the second throw (1/6). Similarly, on a multiple choice exam with four possible answers to each item, the chance of getting both of two questions correct just by guessing is 1/16—that is, the chance of getting one question correct just by guessing (1/4) times the chance of getting the other correct just by guessing (1/4). To take one more example, suppose you have a 20% chance of getting accepted into one particular graduate school and a 30% chance of getting accepted into a different particular graduate school. Your chance of getting accepted at *both* graduate schools is just 6% (that is, 20% × 30% is 6%).

CONDITIONAL PROBABILITIES

There are several other probability rules, some of which are combinations of the addition and multiplication rules. Most of these other rules have to do with what are called *conditional probabilities*. A conditional probability is the probability of one outcome, assuming some other particular outcome will happen. That is, the probability of the one outcome depends on, is *conditional* on, the probability of the other outcome. Thus, suppose that college A has 50% women and college B has 60% women. If you select a person at random, what is the chance of getting a woman? If you know the person is from college A, the probability is 50%. That is, the probability of getting a woman, conditional upon her coming from college A, is 50%.

CHAPTER 6

INTRODUCTION TO HYPOTHESIS TESTING

hypothesis testing

Are You Ready?
What You Need to have Mastered Before Starting This Chapter:

- Chapters 1, 2, and 5

In this chapter, we introduce the crucial topic of **hypothesis testing.** Hypothesis testing is a systematic procedure for deciding whether the results of a research study, which examines a sample, support a particular theory or practical innovation, which applies to a population. Hypothesis testing is the central theme in all the remaining chapters of this book, as it is in most psychology research.

We should warn you that many students find the most difficult part of the course to be mastering the basic logic of this chapter and the next two. This chapter in particular requires some mental gymnastics. Even if you follow everything the first time through, you will be wise to review it thoroughly. Hypothesis testing involves a grasp of ideas that make little sense covered separately, so this chapter covers a fairly large number of new ideas all at once. However, a benefit of this is that once you understand the material in this chapter and the two that follow, your mind will be used to this sort of thing, and the rest of the course should seem easier.

At the same time, we have kept this introduction to hypothesis testing as simple as possible, putting off what we could for later chapters. For example, real-life psychology research almost always involves samples of many individuals. However, to simplify how much you have to learn at one time, all of this chapter's examples are about studies in which the sample is a single individual. To do this, we had to create some odd examples. Just remember that you are building a foundation that will, by Chapter 9, prepare you to understand hypothesis testing as it is actually carried out.

A HYPOTHESIS-TESTING EXAMPLE

Here is our first necessarily odd example that we made up to keep this introduction to hypothesis testing as straightforward as possible. A large research project has been going on for several years. In this project, new babies are given a particular vitamin and then the research team follows their development during the first 2 years of life. So far, the vitamin has not speeded up babies' development. The ages at which these and all other babies start to walk is shown in Figure 6–1. Notice that the mean is 14 months, the standard deviation is 3 months, and the ages follow a normal curve. Looking at the distribution, you can see that less than 2% start walking before 8 months of age; these are the babies who are 2 standard deviations below the mean. (This fictional distribution actually is close to the true distribution psychologists have found for European babies, although that true distribution is slightly skewed to the right [Hindley et al., 1966].)

One of the researchers working on the project has an idea. If the vitamin the babies are taking could be more highly refined, perhaps the effect of the vitamin would be dramatically greater: Babies taking the highly purified version should start walking much earlier than other babies. (We will assume that the purification process could not possibly make the vitamin harmful.) However, refining the vitamin in this way is extremely expensive for each dose, so the research team decides to try the procedure with just enough purified doses for one baby. A newborn in the project is then randomly selected to take the highly purified version of the vitamin, and the researchers then follow this baby's progress for 2 years. What kind of result should lead the researchers to conclude that the highly purified vitamin allows babies to walk earlier?

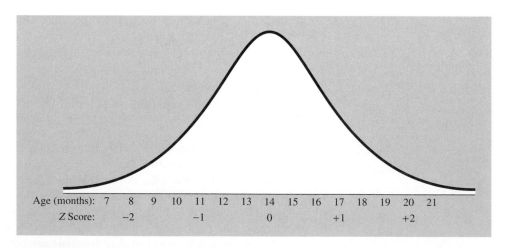

FIGURE 6–1   *Distribution of when babies begin to walk (fictional data).*

This is an example of a hypothesis-testing problem. The researchers want to draw a general conclusion about whether the purified vitamin allows babies in general to walk earlier. The conclusion about the babies in general, however, will be based on results of studying only a sample. (In this strange example, the sample is of a single baby.)

THE CORE LOGIC OF HYPOTHESIS TESTING

There is a standard way researchers approach a hypothesis-testing problem like this one. They use the following reasoning. Ordinarily, the chance of a baby's starting to walk at age 8 months or earlier would be less than 2%. Thus, walking at 8 months or earlier is highly unlikely. But what if the randomly selected baby in our study does start walking by 8 months? If that happens, we will *reject* the idea that the specially purified vitamin has *no* effect. If we reject the idea that the specially purified vitamin has no effect, then we must also *accept* the idea that the specially purified vitamin *does* have an effect. (The logic of this example is central to everything else we do in the book. You may want to read this paragraph again.)

The researchers first spelled out what would have to happen for them to conclude that the special purification procedure makes a difference. Having laid this out in advance, the researchers can then go on to carry out their study. In this example, carrying out the study means giving the specially purified vitamin to a randomly selected baby and watching to see how early that baby walks. Suppose the result of the study is that the baby starts walking before 8 months. The researchers would then conclude that it is unlikely the specially purified vitamin makes no difference and thus also conclude that it does make a difference.

This kind of opposite-of-what-you-predict, roundabout reasoning is at the heart of inferential statistics in psychology. It is something like a double negative. One reason for this approach is that we have the information to figure the probability of getting a particular experimental result if the situation of there being no difference is true. In the purified vitamin example, the researchers know what the probabilities are of babies walking at different ages if the specially purified vitamin does not have any effect. It is the probability of babies walking at various ages that is already known from studies of babies in general—that is, babies who have not received the specially purified vitamin. (Suppose the specially purified vitamin has no effect. In that situation, the age at which babies start walking is the same whether or not they receive the specially purified vitamin. Thus, the distribution is that shown in Figure 6–1, based on ages at which babies start walking in general.)

Without such a tortuous way of going at the problem, in most cases you could just not do hypothesis testing at all. In almost all psychology research, whether involving experiments, surveys, or whatever, we base our conclusions on this question: What is the probability of getting our research results if the opposite of what we are predicting were true. That is, we are usually predicting an effect of some kind. However, we decide on whether there *is* such an effect by seeing if it is unlikely that there is *not* such an effect.

THE HYPOTHESIS-TESTING PROCESS

Let's look at our example once again, going over each step in some detail. Along the way, we cover the special terminology of hypothesis-testing. Most important, we introduce five steps of hypothesis testing you use for the rest of this book.

STEP 1: RESTATE THE QUESTION AS A RESEARCH HYPOTHESIS AND A NULL HYPOTHESIS ABOUT THE POPULATIONS

First, note that the researchers in our example are interested in the effects on babies in general (not just this particular baby). That is, the purpose of studying any sample is to know about populations. Thus, it is useful to restate the research question in terms of populations. In the present example, we can think of two populations of babies:

Population 1: Babies who take the specially purified vitamin
Population 2: Babies who do not take the specially purified vitamin

Population 1 are those babies who receive the experimental treatment. In our example, there is only one real-life baby in Population 1. Yet this one baby represents an as-yet-unborn future group of many babies to whom the researchers want to apply their results. Population 2 is a kind of baseline of what is already known.

The prediction of the research team is that Population 1 babies (those who take the specially purified vitamin) will on the average walk earlier than Population 2 babies (those who do not take the specially purified vitamin). This prediction is based on the researchers' theory of how these vitamins work. A prediction like this about the difference between populations is called a **research hypothesis.** Put more formally, the prediction is that the mean of Population 1 is lower (babies receiving the special vitamin walk earlier) than the mean of Population 2. In symbols, the research hypothesis is $\mu_1 < \mu_2$.

research hypothesis

The opposite of the research hypothesis is that the populations are not different in the way predicted. Under this scenario, Population 1 babies (those who take the specially purified vitamin) will on the average *not* walk earlier than Population 2 babies (those who do not take the specially purified vitamin). That is, this prediction is that there is no difference in when Population 1 and Population 2 babies start walking. They start at the same time. A statement like this, about a lack of difference between populations, is the crucial *opposite* of the research hypothesis. It is called a **null hypothesis**. It has this name because it states the situation in which there is no difference (the difference is "null") between the populations. In symbols, the null hypothesis is $\mu_1 = \mu_2$.[1]

null hypothesis

The research hypothesis and the null hypothesis are complete opposites. In fact, the research hypothesis is sometimes called the *alternative hypothesis*—that is, it is the alternative to the null hypothesis. This is actually a bit ironic. As researchers, we care most about the research hypothesis. But when doing the steps of hypothesis testing, we use this roundabout method of seeing whether or not we can reject the null hypothesis so that we can decided about its alternative (the research hypothesis).

STEP 2: DETERMINE THE CHARACTERISTICS OF THE COMPARISON DISTRIBUTION

Recall that the overall logic of hypothesis testing involves figuring out the probability of getting a particular result if the null hypothesis is true. Thus, you need to

[1]We are oversimplifying a bit in here to make the initial learning easier. The research hypothesis is that one population will walk earlier than the other, $\mu_1 < \mu_2$. Thus, to be precise, its opposite is that the other group will either walk at the same time or later. That is, the opposite of the research hypothesis in this example includes both no difference and a difference in the direction opposite to what we predicted. In terms of symbols, if our research hypothesis is $\mu_1 < \mu_2$, then its opposite is $\mu_1 \geq m_2$ (the symbol $\geq$ means "greater than or equal to"). We discuss this issue in some detail later in the chapter.

know about what the situation would be if the null hypothesis were true. In our example, we start out knowing all about Population 2 (see Figure 6–1). If the null hypothesis is true, Population 1 and Population 2 are the same—in our example, this means Populations 1 and 2 both follow a normal curve, have a mean of 14 months, and a standard deviation of 3 months.

In the hypothesis-testing process, you want to find out the probability that you could have gotten a sample as extreme as what you got (say a baby walking very early) if your sample were from a distribution of the sort you would have if the null hypothesis were true. Thus, in this book we call this distribution a **comparison distribution**. (The comparison distribution is sometimes called a *statistical model* or a *sampling distribution*—an idea we discuss in Chapter 7.) That is, in the hypothesis-testing process, you compare the actual sample's score to this distribution.

comparison distribution

STEP 3: DETERMINE THE CUTOFF SAMPLE SCORE ON THE COMPARISON DISTRIBUTION AT WHICH THE NULL HYPOTHESIS SHOULD BE REJECTED

Ideally, well before conducting a study, researchers set a target against which they will compare their result—how extreme a sample score they would need to draw a confident conclusion. Specifically, they determine the score the sample would need to have to decide against the null hypothesis—how extreme it would have to be for it to be too unlikely that they could get such an extreme score if the null hypothesis were true. This is called the **cutoff sample score.** (The cutoff sample score is also known as the *critical value*.)

cutoff sample score

Consider our purified vitamin example in which the null hypothesis is that it doesn't matter whether a baby is fed the specially purified vitamin. The researchers might decide that if the null hypothesis were true, a randomly selected baby walking before 8 months would be very unlikely. With a normal distribution, being 2 or more standard deviations below the mean (walking by 8 months) could occur less than 2% of the time. Thus, based on the comparison distribution, the researchers set their cutoff sample score even before doing the study. They decide in advance that *if* the result of their study is a baby who walks by 8 months, they will reject the null hypothesis.

On the other hand, what if the baby does not start walking until after 8 months? If that happens, the researchers will not be able to reject the null hypothesis.

When setting in advance how extreme a score needs to be to reject the null hypothesis, researchers use Z scores and percentages. In our purified vitamin example, the researchers might decide that if a result were less likely than 2%, they would reject the null hypothesis. Being in the bottom 2% of a normal curve means having a Z score of about -2 or lower. Thus, the researchers would set -2 as their Z-score cutoff point on the comparison distribution for deciding that a result is extreme enough to reject the null hypothesis.

Suppose that the researchers are even more cautious about too easily rejecting the null hypothesis. They might decide that they will reject the null hypothesis only if they get a result that could occur by chance 1% of the time or less. They could then figure out the Z-score cutoff for 1%. Using the normal curve table, to have a score in the lower 1% of a normal curve, you need a Z score of -2.33 or less. (In our example, a Z score of -2.33 means 7 months.) In Figure 6–2, we have shaded the 1% of the comparison distribution in which a sample would be considered so extreme that the possibility that it came from a distribution like this would be rejected.

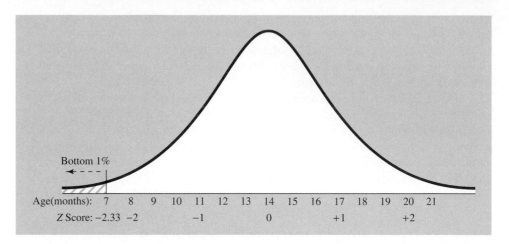

FIGURE 6–2 *Distribution of when babies begin to walk, with bottom 1% shaded (fictional data).*

**conventional levels
of significance**

statistically significant

In general, psychology researchers use a cutoff on the comparison distribution with a probability of 5% that a score will be at least that extreme. That is, researchers reject the null hypothesis if the probability of getting a result this extreme (if the null hypothesis were true) is less than 5%. This probability is usually written as $p < .05$. However, in some areas of research, or when researchers want to be especially cautious, they use a cutoff of 1% ($p < .01$).[2] These are called **conventional levels of significance.** They are described as the *.05 significance level* or the *.01 significance level.* When a sample score is so extreme that researchers reject the null hypothesis, the result is said to be **statistically significant.**

STEP 4: DETERMINE YOUR SAMPLE'S SCORE ON THE COMPARISON DISTRIBUTION

The next step is to carry out the study and get the actual result for your sample. Once the results are in for the sample, you figure the Z score for the sample's raw score based on the mean and standard deviation of the comparison distribution.

Assume that the researchers did the study and the baby who was given the specially purified vitamin started walking at 6 months. The mean of the comparison distribution to which we are comparing these results is 14 months and the standard deviation is 3 months. Thus, a baby who walks at 6 months is 8 months below the mean. This puts this baby 2 2/3 standard deviations below the mean. The Z score for this sample baby on the comparison distribution is thus -2.67. Figure 6–3 shows the score of our sample baby on the comparison distribution.

---

[2]These days, when hypothesis testing is usually done on the computer, you have to decide in advance only on the cutoff probability. The computer prints out the exact probability of getting your result if the null hypothesis were true. You then just compare the printed-out probability to see if it is less than the cutoff probability level you set in advance. However, to *understand* what these probability levels mean, you need to learn the entire process, including how to figure the Z score for a particular cutoff probability.

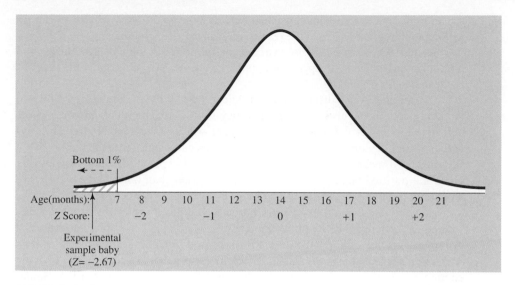

FIGURE 6–3 *Distribution of when babies begin to walk, showing both the bottom 1% and the single baby that is the sample studied (fictional data).*

STEP 5: DECIDE WHETHER TO REJECT THE NULL HYPOTHESIS

To decide whether to reject the null hypothesis, you compare your actual sample's Z score (from Step 4) to the cutoff Z score (from Step 3). In our example, the actual result was -2.67. Let's suppose the researchers had decided in advance that they would reject the null hypothesis if the sample's Z score was below -2. Since -2.67 is below -2, the researchers would reject the null hypothesis.

Or, suppose the researchers had used the more conservative 1% significance level. The needed Z score to reject the null hypothesis would then have been -2.33. But, again, the actual Z for the randomly selected baby was -2.67. Thus, even with this more conservative cutoff, they would still reject the null hypothesis. This situation is shown in Figure 6–3.

If the researchers reject the null hypothesis, what remains is the research hypothesis. In this example, the research team can conclude that the results of their study support the research hypothesis, that babies who take the specially purified vitamin walk earlier than other babies.

IMPLICATIONS OF REJECTING OR FAILING TO REJECT THE NULL HYPOTHESIS

It is important to emphasize two points about the conclusions you can make from the hypothesis-testing process. First, suppose you reject the null hypothesis so that your results support the research hypothesis (as in our example). You would still not say that the results *prove* the research hypothesis or that the results show that the research hypothesis is *true*. This would be too strong because the results of research studies are based on probabilities. Specifically, they are based on the probability being low of getting your result if the null hypothesis were true. Proven and true are okay in logic and mathematics, but to use these words in conclusions from scientific research is quite unprofessional. (It is okay to use *true* when speaking hypothetically—for example, "*if* this hypothesis *were* true, then . . ."—but not when speaking of conclusions about an actual result.) What you do say when you can reject the null hypothesis is that the results are *statistically significant*.

Second, when a result is not extreme enough to reject the null hypothesis, you do not say that the result supports the null hypothesis. You simply say the result is *not statistically significant*.

A result that is not strong enough to reject the null hypothesis means only that the study was inconclusive. The results may not be extreme enough to reject the null hypothesis, but the null hypothesis might still be false (and the research hypothesis true). Suppose that in our example the specially purified vitamin had only a slight but still real effect. In that case, we would not expect to find any single baby given the purified vitamin to be walking a lot earlier than other babies. Thus, we would not be able to reject the null hypothesis, even though it is false.

Showing that the null hypothesis is true would mean showing that there is absolutely no difference between the populations. It is always possible that there is a difference between the populations but that the difference is much smaller than what the particular study was able to detect. Therefore, when a result is not extreme enough to reject the null hypothesis, the results are simply inconclusive. Sometimes, however, if studies have been done using large numbers and accurate measuring procedures, evidence may build up in support of something close to the null hypothesis—that there is at most very little difference between the populations. (We have more to say on this important issue later in this chapter and in Chapter 8.)

SUMMARY OF STEPS OF HYPOTHESIS TESTING

Here is a summary of the steps of hypothesis testing:

❶ **Restate the question as a research hypothesis and a null hypothesis about the populations.**

❷ **Determine the characteristics of the comparison distribution.**

❸ **Determine the cutoff sample score on the comparison distribution at which the null hypothesis should be rejected.**

❹ **Determine your sample's score on the comparison distribution.**

❺ **Decide whether to reject the null hypothesis.**

A SECOND EXAMPLE

Here is another fictional example. Two happy-go-lucky personality psychologists are examining the theory that happiness comes from positive experiences. In particular, these researchers argue that if people have something very fortunate happen to them, they will become very happy and stay happy for a long time. So the researchers plan the following experiment: A person will be randomly selected from the North American adult public and given $1 million. Six months later, this person's happiness will be measured. It is already known (in this fictional example) what the distribution of happiness is like in the general population of North American adults, and this is shown in Figure 6–4. On the test being used, the mean happiness score is 70, the standard deviation is 10, and the distribution is approximately normal.

The psychologists now carry out the hypothesis-testing procedure. That is, the researchers consider how happy the person would have to be before they can confidently reject the null hypothesis that receiving that much money does not make people happier 6 months later. If the researchers' result shows a very high level of happiness, the psychologists will reject the null hypothesis and conclude that getting $1 million

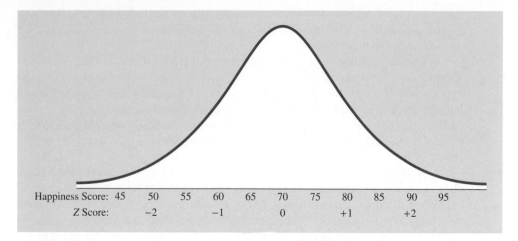

FIGURE 6-4 *Distribution of happiness scores (fictional data).*

probably does make people happier 6 months later. But if the result is not very extreme, these researchers would conclude that there is not sufficient evidence to reject the null hypothesis, and the results of the experiment are inconclusive.

Now let us consider the hypothesis-testing procedure in more detail in this example, following the five steps.

❶ **Restate the question as a research hypothesis and a null hypothesis about the populations.** There are two populations of interest:

Population 1: People who 6 months ago received $1 million
Population 2: People who 6 months ago did not receive $1 million

The prediction of the personality psychologists, based on their theory of happiness, is that Population 1 people will on the average be happier than Population 2 people: In symbols, $\mu_1 > \mu_2$. The null hypothesis is that Population 1 people (those who get $1 million) will not be happier than Population 2 people (those who do not get $1 million).

❷ **Determine the characteristics of the comparison distribution.** Eventually, we want to compare our score to the situation in which the null hypothesis is true. If the null hypothesis is true, the distributions of both Populations 1 and 2 are the same. We know Population 2's distribution, so it can serve as the comparison distribution.

❸ **Determine the cutoff sample score on the comparison distribution at which the null hypothesis should be rejected.** What kind of result would be extreme enough to convince us to reject the null hypothesis? In this example, assume that the researchers decided in advance to reject the null hypothesis as too unlikely if the results could occur less than 5% of the time if this null hypothesis were true. Because we know that the comparison distribution is a normal curve, we can find that the top 5% of scores from the normal curve table begin at a Z score of about 1.64. So the researchers might set as the cutoff point for rejecting the null hypothesis a result in which the sample's Z score on the comparison distribution is at or above 1.64. (Since the mean of the comparison distribution is 70 and the standard deviation is 10, the null hypothesis would be rejected if the sample result was at or above 86.4.)

❹ **Determine your sample's score on the comparison distribution.** Now for the results: Six months after giving this randomly selected person $1 million, the researchers give their now wealthy research participant the happiness test. The person's score is 80. As you can see from Figure 6–4, a score of 80 has a Z score of +1 on the comparison distribution.

❺ **Decide whether to reject the null hypothesis.** The Z score of the sample individual is +1. The researchers set the minimum Z score needed to reject the null hypothesis at +1.64. Thus, the sample score is not extreme enough to reject the null hypothesis. The experiment is inconclusive; researchers would say the results are "not statistically significant." Figure 6–5 shows the comparison distribution with the top 5% shaded and the location of the sample millionaire.

You may be interested to know that Brickman et al. (1978) carried out a more elaborate study based on the same question, in which they studied lottery winners as examples of people suddenly having a very positive event happen to them. Their results were similar to those in our fictional example, with the group winning the money being not much happier 6 months later than people who did not win the money. Also, another group they studied, people who had become paraplegics through a random accident, were found to be not much less happy than other people 6 months later. These researchers studied fairly large numbers of individuals and explored the issue in several different ways. Their conclusion was that if a major event does have a lasting effect on happiness, it is probably not a very big one. So it looks like the lottery isn't the answer. (This pattern has also been found in other studies; e.g., Suh et al., 1996.)

HOW ARE YOU DOING?

1. A sample is given an experimental treatment intended to make them score higher than the general public on a particular measure. State (a) the null hypothesis and (b) the research hypothesis.
2. (a) What is a comparison distribution. (b) What role does it play in hypothesis testing?
3. What is the cutoff sample score?
4. Why do we say that hypothesis testing involves a double negative logic?

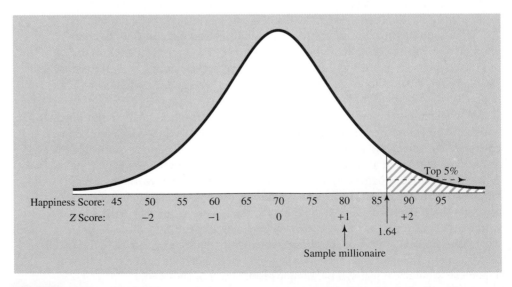

FIGURE 6–5 *Distribution of happiness scores with upper 5% shaded and showing the location of the sample millionaire (fictional data).*

5. What can you conclude when (a) a result is so extreme that you reject the null hypothesis, and (b) a result is not so extreme that you can reject the null hypothesis?

6. A training program to increase friendliness is tried on one individual randomly selected from the general public. Among the general public (who do not get this procedure) the mean on the friendliness measure is 30 with a standard deviation of 4. The researchers want to test their hypothesis at the 5% significance level. After going through the procedure, this individual's score on the friendliness measure is 40. What should the researchers conclude?

ANSWERS:

1. (a) The population of people like those who get the experimental treatment do not score higher than the population of individuals who do not get the experimental treatment. (b) The population of people like those who get the experimental treatment score higher than the population of people who do not get the experimental treatment.

2. (a) A distribution to which you compare the results of your study. (b) In hypothesis testing, the comparison distribution is the distribution for the situation when the null hypothesis is true. To decide whether to reject the null hypothesis, you check how extreme the score of your sample is on this comparison distribution—how likely it would be to get a sample with a score this extreme if your sample came from this distribution.

3. The Z score at which, if the sample's Z score is more extreme than it on the comparison distribution, you reject the null hypothesis.

4. Because we are interested in the research hypothesis, but we test whether it is true by seeing if we can reject its opposite, the null hypothesis.

5. (a) The research hypothesis is supported; the result is statistically significant. (b) The result is not statistically significant; the result is inconclusive.

6. Reject the null hypothesis; the research hypothesis is supported; the result is statistically significant. Thus, the training program increases friendliness. (The cutoff sample Z score is 1.64. The actual sample's Z score is 2.5.)

ONE-TAILED AND TWO-TAILED HYPOTHESIS TESTS

Our hypothesis-testing examples so far were about situations in which the researchers were interested in only one direction of result. In the purified vitamin example, the researchers tested whether the baby would walk *earlier* than other babies. In the happiness example, the personality psychologists predicted the person who received $1 million would be *happier* than other people. The researchers in these studies were not really interested in the possibility that giving the specially purified vitamins would cause babies to start walking later or that people getting $1 million might actually become less happy.

DIRECTIONAL HYPOTHESES AND ONE-TAILED TESTS

The purified vitamin and happiness studies are examples of **directional hypotheses.** Both studies focused on a specific direction of effect. When a researcher makes a directional hypothesis, the null hypothesis is also, in a sense, directional. Suppose the research hypothesis is that getting $1 million will make a person happier. The null hypothesis, then, is that the money will either have no effect or make the person less happy. (In symbols, if the research hypothesis is $\mu_1 > \mu_2$, and the null hypothesis is $\mu_1 \leq \mu_2$.). Thus, in Figure 6–5, for the null hypothesis to be rejected, the sample had to have a score in the top 5%—the upper extreme or tail of the comparison distribution. (When it comes to rejecting the null hypothesis with a directional hypothesis, a score at the other tail would be the same as a score in the middle.) For

directional hypotheses

one-tailed test

this reason, the test of a directional hypothesis is called a **one-tailed test.** A one-tailed test can be one-tailed in either direction. In the happiness study example, the tail for the predicted effect was at the high end. In the purified vitamin example, the tail for the predicted effect was at the low end (that is, the prediction tested was that babies would start walking unusually early).

NONDIRECTIONAL HYPOTHESES AND TWO-TAILED TESTS

Sometimes, a research hypothesis states that an experimental procedure will have an effect, without specifying whether it will produce a very high score or a very low score. For example, an organizational psychologist may be interested in the impact of a new social-skills program on productivity. The program could improve productivity by making the working environment more pleasant. Or, the program could hurt productivity by encouraging people to socialize instead of work. The research hypothesis is that the skills program *changes* the level of productivity; the null hypothesis is that the program does not change productivity one way or the other. In terms of symbols, the research hypothesis is $\mu_1 \neq \mu_2$ ($\neq$ is the symbol for not equal); the null hypothesis is $\mu_1 = \mu_2$.

nondirectional hypothesis

When a research hypothesis predicts an effect but does not predict a particular direction for the effect, it is called a **nondirectional hypothesis.** To test the significance of a nondirectional hypothesis, you have to take into account the possibility that the sample could be extreme at either tail of the comparison distribution. Thus, this is called a **two-tailed test.**

two-tailed test

DETERMINING CUTOFF POINTS WITH TWO-TAILED TESTS

There is a special complication in a two-tailed test. You have to divide up the significance percentage between the two tails. For example, with a 5% significance level, you would reject a null hypothesis only if the sample was so extreme that it was in either the top 2.5% or the bottom 2.5%. In this way, the overall chance of the null hypothesis being true is kept at a total of 5%.

Note that a two-tailed test makes the cutoff Z scores for the 5% level $+1.96$ and -1.96. For a one-tailed test at the 5% level, the cutoff was not so extreme—only $+1.64$ or -1.64, but only one side of the distribution was considered. These situations are illustrated in Figure 6–6a.

Using the 1% significance level, a two-tailed test (.5% at each tail) has cutoffs of $+2.58$ and -2.58, while a one-tailed test's cutoff is either $+2.33$ or -2.33. These situations are illustrated in Figure 6–6b.

WHEN TO USE ONE-TAILED OR TWO-TAILED TESTS

If the researcher decides in advance to use a one-tailed test, then the sample's score does not need to be so extreme to be significant, as it would need to be with a two-tailed test. Yet there is a price: With a one-tailed test, if the result is extreme in the direction opposite to what was predicted, no matter how extreme, the result cannot be considered significant.

In principle, you plan to use a one-tailed test when you have a clearly directional hypothesis and a two-tailed test when you have a clearly nondirectional hypothesis. In practice, it is not so simple. Even when a theory clearly predicts a particular result, the actual result may come out opposite to what you expected. Sometimes, this opposite may even be more interesting than what you had predicted. (What if, as in all the fairy tales about wish-granting genies and fish, receiving $1 million and being able to ful-

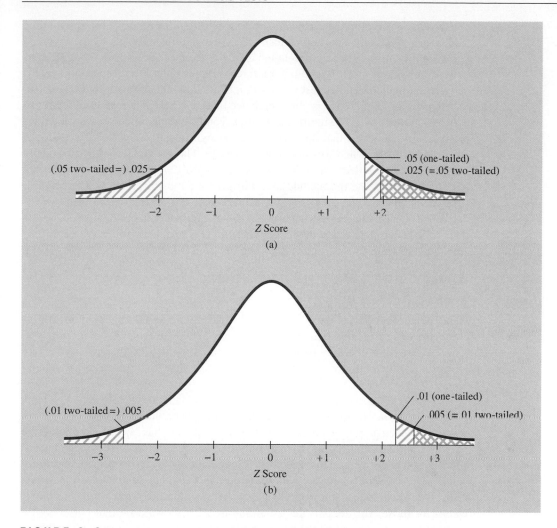

FIGURE 6–6 *Significance level cutoffs for one-tailed and two-tailed tests: (a) .05 significance level; (b) .01 significance level. (The one-tailed tests in these examples assume the prediction was for a high score. You could instead have a one-tailed test where the prediction is for the lower, left tail.)*

fill almost any wish had made that one individual miserable?) By using one-tailed tests, we risk having to ignore possibly important results.

For these reasons, researchers disagree about whether one-tailed tests should be used, even when there is a clearly directional hypothesis. To be safe, many researchers use two-tailed tests for both nondirectional and directional hypotheses. If the two-tailed test is significant, then the researcher looks at the result to see the direction and considers the study significant in that direction.[3] In practice, this is a

---

[3]Leventhal and Huynh (1996) argue that this procedure is technically incorrect. If you are testing a nondirectional hypothesis, you should only make nondirectional conclusions. A better procedure, they suggest, is to use a "directional two-tailed test"—what amounts to two simultaneous one-tailed tests (one in each direction). Thus, if you want an overall significance level of .05, you would use a directional two-tailed test in which the two one-tailed subparts each used the .025 level. (See also Jones & Tukey, 2000, for a related approach.) Leventhal and Huynh's way of thinking about two-tailed tests does seem to be more logical and to have some technical advantages. However, researchers have not yet adopted this approach, and for most purposes the outcome is the same. Thus, in this book we stick to the more traditional approach.

conservative procedure, because the cutoff scores are more extreme for a two-tailed test, so it is less likely a two-tailed test will give a significant result. Thus, if you do get a significant result with a two-tailed test, you are more confident about the conclusion. In fact, in most psychology research articles, unless the researcher specifically states that a one-tailed test was used, it is assumed that it was a two-tailed test.

In practice, however, it is our experience that most research results are either so extreme that they will be significant whether you use a one-tailed or two-tailed test or so far from extreme that they would not be significant no matter what you use. But what happens when a result is less certain? The researcher's decision about one-tailed or two-tailed tests now can make a big difference. In this situation the researcher tries to use the method that will give the most accurate and noncontroversial conclusion. The idea is to let nature—and not a researcher's decisions—determine the conclusion as much as possible. Further, whenever a result is less than completely clear one way or the other, most researchers will not be comfortable drawing strong conclusions until more research is done.

EXAMPLE OF HYPOTHESIS TESTING WITH A TWO-TAILED TEST

Here is one more fictional example, this time using a two-tailed test. Clinical psychologists at a residential treatment center have developed a new type of therapy to reduce depression that they believe is more effective than the therapy now given. However, as with any treatment, it is also possible that it could make patients do worse. Thus, the clinical psychologists make a nondirectional hypothesis.

The psychologists randomly select an incoming patient to receive the new form of therapy instead of the usual. (In a real study, of course, more than one patient would be selected; but let's assume that only one person has been trained to do the new therapy and she has time to treat only one patient.) After 4 weeks, the patient fills out a standard depression scale that is given automatically to all patients after 4 weeks. The standard scale has been given at this treatment center for a long time. Thus, the psychologists know in advance the distribution of depression scores at 4 weeks for those who receive the usual therapy: It follows a normal curve with a mean of 69.5 and a standard deviation of 14.1. (These figures correspond roughly to the depression scores found in a national survey of 75,000 psychiatric patients given the Minnesota Multiphasic Personality Inventory (MMPI), a widely used standard test; Dahlstrom et al., 1986). This distribution is shown in Figure 6–7.

The researchers then carry out the hypothesis-testing:

❶ **Restate the question as a research hypothesis and a null hypothesis about the populations.** There are two populations of interest:

Population 1: Patients diagnosed as depressed who receive the new therapy
Population 2: Patients diagnosed as depressed who receive the usual therapy

The research hypothesis is that when measured on depression 4 weeks after admission, patients who receive the new therapy (Population 1) will on the average score differently from patients who receive the current therapy (Population 2). In symbols, the research hypothesis is $\mu_1 \neq \mu_2$. The opposite of the research hypothesis, the null hypothesis, is that patients who receive the new therapy will have the same average depression level as the patients who receive the usual therapy. (That is, the depression level measured after 4 weeks will have the same mean for Populations 1 and 2.) In symbols, the null hypothesis is $\mu_1 = \mu_2$.

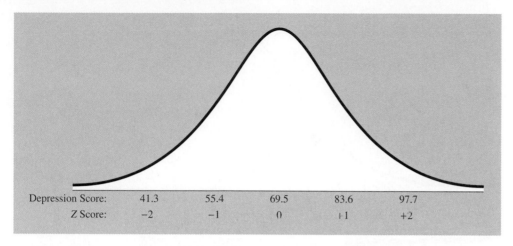

Depression Score:	41.3	55.4	69.5	83.6	97.7
Z Score:	−2	−1	0	+1	+2

FIGURE 6–7 *Distribution of MMPI depression scale scores at 4 weeks after admission for diagnosed depressed psychiatric patients receiving the standard therapy (fictional data).*

❷ **Determine the characteristics of the comparison distribution.** If the null hypothesis is true, the distributions of Populations 1 and 2 are the same. We know the distribution of Population 2, so we can use it as our comparison distribution. As noted, it follows a normal curve with $\mu = 69.5$ and $\sigma = 14.1$.

❸ **Determine the cutoff sample score on the comparison distribution at which the null hypothesis should be rejected.** The clinical psychologists select the 5% significance level. They have made a nondirectional hypothesis and will therefore use a two-tailed test. Thus, they will reject the null hypothesis only if the patient's depression score on the comparison distribution is in either the top or bottom 2.5% of the comparison distribution. In terms of Z scores, these cutoffs are $+1.96$ and -1.96 (see Figure 6–8).

❹ **Determine your sample's score on the comparison distribution.** The patient who received the new therapy was measured 4 weeks after admission. The patient's score on the depression scale was 41, which is a Z score on the comparison distribution of -2.02.

❺ **Decide whether to reject the null hypothesis.** A Z score of -2.02 is slightly more extreme than a Z score of -1.96, which is where the lower 2.5% of the comparison distribution begins. This is a result so extreme that it is unlikely to have occurred if this patient were from a population no different from Population 2. Therefore, the clinical psychologists reject the null hypothesis. They can thus say that the result is statistically significant and supports their research hypothesis that the new therapy does indeed change patients' depression level more than the usual therapy.

HOW ARE YOU DOING?

1. What is a nondirectional hypothesis test?
2. What is a two-tailed test?
3. Why do you use a two-tailed test when testing a nondirectional hypothesis?
4. What is the advantage of using a one-tailed test when your theory predicts a particular direction of result.
5. Why might you use a two-tailed test even when your theory predicts a particular direction of result?

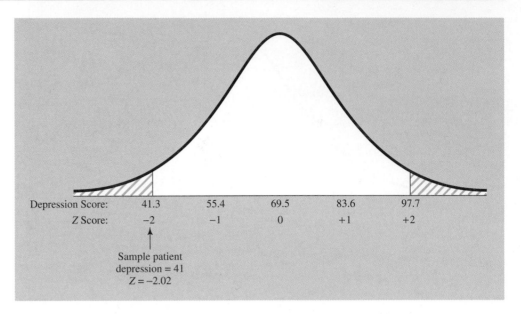

| Depression Score: | 41.3 | 55.4 | 69.5 | 83.6 | 97.7 |
| Z Score: | −2 | −1 | 0 | +1 | +2 |

Sample patient
depression = 41
Z = −2.02

FIGURE 6–8   *Distribution of MMPI depression scale scores with upper and lower 2.5% shaded and showing the sample patient who received the new therapy (fictional data).*

6. A researcher predicts that making a person hungry will affect how he or she does on a co-ordination test. A randomly selected person agrees not to eat for 24 hours before taking a standard coordination test and gets a score of 400. For people in general of this age group and gender tested under normal conditions, coordination scores are normally distributed with a mean of 500 and a standard deviation of 40. Using the .01 significance level, what should the researchers conclude?

ANSWERS:

1. A nondirectional hypothesis test is a hypothesis test in which you do not predict a particular direction of difference.
2. A two-tailed test is one in which the overall percentage for the cutoff is evenly divided between the two tails of the comparison distribution.
3. You use a two-tailed test when testing a nondirectional hypothesis because an extreme result in either direction would support the research hypothesis.
4. The cutoff for a one-tailed test is not so extreme; thus, if your result comes out in the predicted direction, it is more likely to be significant. The cutoff is not so extreme because the entire percentage (say 5%) is put on one tail instead of being divided between two.
5. It lets you count as significant an extreme result in either direction; if you used a one-tailed test and the result came out opposite to your prediction, it would have to be ignored.
6. The cutoffs are ±2.58. The sample person's Z score is $(400 − 500)/40 = −2.5$. The result is not significant; the study is inconclusive.

CONTROVERSY: SHOULD SIGNIFICANCE TESTS BE BANNED?

The last few years has seen a major controversy about significance testing itself, with a concerted movement on the part of a small but vocal group of psychologists to ban significance tests completely! This is a radical suggestion with far-reaching implications (for at least half a century, nearly every research study in psychology has used significance tests). There probably has been more written in the major psychology journals recently about this controversy than ever before in history about any issue having to do with statistics.

The discussion has gotten so heated that one article began as follows:

> It is not true that a group of radical activists held 10 statisticians and six editors hostage at the 1996 convention of the American Psychological Society and chanted, "Support the total test ban!" and "Nix the null!" (Abelson, 1997, p. 12)

Since this is by far the most lively and important controversy in years regarding statistics as used in psychology, we discuss the issues in at least three different places. In this chapter we focus on some basic challenges to hypothesis testing. In chapters 7 and 8, we cover other topics that relate to aspects of hypothesis testing that you will learn about in those chapters.

Before discussing this controversy, you should be reassured that you are not learning about hypothesis testing for nothing. Whatever happens in the future, you absolutely have to understand hypothesis testing to make sense of virtually every research article published in the past. Further, in spite of the controversy that has raged for the last few years, it is extremely rare to see new articles that do not use significance testing. Thus, it is doubtful that there will be any major shifts in the near future. Finally, even if hypothesis testing is completely abandoned, the alternatives (which involve procedures you will learn about in chapters 7 and 8) require understanding virtually all of the logic and procedures we are covering here.

So, what is the big controversy? Some of the debate concerns subtle points of logic. For example, one issue relates to whether it makes sense to worry about rejecting the null hypothesis when a hypothesis of no effect whatsoever is extremely unlikely to be true. We discuss this issue briefly in Box 6–1. Another issue is about the foundation of hypothesis testing in terms of populations and samples, since in most experiments the samples we use are not randomly selected from any definable population. We discussed some points relating to this issue in Chapter 5. Finally, some have questioned the appropriateness of concluding that if the data are inconsistent with the null hypothesis, this should be counted as evidence for the research hypothesis. This controversy becomes rather technical, but our own view is that given recent considerations of the issues, the way researchers in psychology use hypothesis testing is reasonable (Nickerson, 2000).

However, the biggest complaint against significance tests, and the one that has received almost universal agreement, is that they are misused. In fact, opponents of significance tests argue that even if there were no other problems with the tests, they should be banned simply because they are so often and so badly misused. There are two main ways in which they are misused; one we can consider now, the other must wait until we have covered a topic you learn in Chapter 8.

A major misuse of significance tests is the tendency for researchers to decide that if a result is not significant, the null hypothesis is shown to be true. We have emphasized that when the null hypothesis is not rejected, the results are inconclusive. The error of concluding the null hypothesis is true from failing to reject it is extremely serious, because important theories and methods may be considered false just because a particular study did not get strong enough results. (You learn in Chapter 8 that it is quite easy for a true research hypothesis not to come out significant just because there were too few people in the study or the measures were not very accurate. In fact, Hunter [1997] argues that in about 60% of psychology studies, we are likely to get nonsignificant results even when the research hypothesis is actually true.)

BOX 6-1   To Be or Not to Be—But Can Not Being Be? The Problem of Whether and When to Accept the Null Hypothesis

The null hypothesis states that there is no difference between populations represented by different groups or experimental conditions. As we have seen, the usual rule in statistics is that a study cannot find the null hypothesis to be true. A study can only tell you that you cannot reject the null hypothesis. That is, a study that fails to reject the null hypothesis is simply uninformative. Such studies tend not to be published, obviously. However, much work could be avoided if people knew what interventions, measures, or experiments had not worked. Indeed, Greenwald (1975) reports that sometimes ideas have been assumed too long to be true just because a few studies found results supporting them, while many more, unreported, had not.

Frick (1995), has pointed out yet another serious problem with being rigidly uninterested in the null hypothesis: Sometimes it may be true that one thing has no effect on another. This does not mean that there would be a zero relationship of no correlation or no difference at all—a result that is almost impossible in many situations. It would only mean that the effect was so small that it probably represented no real, or at least no important, relationship or difference.

The problem is knowing when to conclude that the null hypothesis (or something close to it) might be true. Frick (1995) gives three criteria. First, the null hypothesis should seem possible. Second, the results in the study should be consistent with the null hypoth-esis and not easily interpreted any other way. Third, and most important, the researcher has to have made a strong effort to find the effect that he or she wants to conclude is not there. Among other things, this means studying a large sample and having very thorough and sensitive measurement. If the study is an experi-ment, the experimenter should have tried to produce the difference by using a strong manipulation and rig-orous conditions of testing.

Frick points out that all of this leaves a subjective element to the acceptance of the null hypothesis. Who decides when a researcher's effort was strong enough? Subjective judgments are a part of science, like it or not. For example, reviewers of articles sub-mitted for publication in the top scientific journals have to decide if a topic is important enough to com-pete for limited space in those journals. Further, the null hypothesis is being accepted all the time anyway. (For example, many psychologists accept the null hy-pothesis about the effect of extrasensory perception.) It is better to discuss our basis for accepting the null hypothesis than just to accept it.

What are we to make of all this? It is clear that just failing to reject the null hypothesis is not the same as supporting it. Indeed, equating these is a serious mis-take. But Frick reminds us that there are situations in which the evidence ought to convince us that some-thing like the null hypothesis is likely to be the case.

What should be done? The general consensus seems to be that we should keep significance tests, but better train our students not to misuse them (hence, the em-phasis on these points in this book). We should not, as it were, throw the baby out with bathwater. To address this controversy, the American Psychological Associa-tion (APA) established a committee of eminent psychologists renowned for their statistical expertise. The committee met over a 2-year period, circulated a prelimi-nary report, and considered reactions to it from a large number of researchers. In the end, they strongly condemned various misuses of significance testing of the kind we have been discussing, but they left its use up to the decision of each researcher. In their report they concluded

Some had hoped that this task force would vote to recommend an outright ban on the use of significance tests in psychology journals. Although this might eliminate some abuses, the committee thought there were enough counterexamples (e.g.,

Abelson, 1997) to justify forbearance. (Wilkinson & Task Force on Statistical Inference)

Recently, Nickerson (2000) systematically reviewed more than 400 articles on this controversy. His conclusion, with which we agree (as do probably most psychology researchers), is that significance testing "is easily misunderstood and misused but that when applied with good judgment it can be an effective aid in the interpretation of experimental data" (p. 241).

HYPOTHESIS TESTS IN RESEARCH ARTICLES

In general, hypothesis testing is reported in research articles as part of one of the specific methods you learn in later chapters. For each result of interest, the researcher usually first says whether the result was statistically significant. Next, the researcher usually gives the symbol associated with the specific method used in figuring the probabilities, such as t, F, or χ^2 (covered in chapters 9 to 14). Finally, there will be an indication of the significance level, such as $p < .05$ or $p < .01$. (The researcher will usually also provide much other information, such as sample scores and relevant means and standard deviations.) For example, Barron and Harackiewics (2001), reported that "participants in the difficulty condition ($M = 12.42$, $SD = 4.33$) completed significantly fewer problems than did participants in the success condition ($M = 24.35$, $SD = 6.81$), $t(152) = 12.83$, $p < .001$." There is a lot here that you will learn about in later chapters, but the key thing to understand now about this result is the "$p < .001$." This means that the probability of their results if the null hypothesis (of no difference between the populations their groups represent) were true is less than .001 (.1%).

When a result is close, but does not reach the significance level chosen, it may be reported anyway as a "near significant trend," with $p < .10$, for example. When a result is not even close to being extreme enough to reject the null hypothesis, it may be reported as "not significant" or the abbreviation ns will be used. Finally, whether or not a result is significant, it is increasingly common for researchers to report the exact p level—such as $p = .03$ or $p = 27$. The p reported here is based on the proportion of the comparison distribution that is more extreme than the sample score information that you could figure from the Z score for your sample and a normal curve table.

Finally, the results of hypothesis testing may be shown only as asterisks in a table of results. In such tables, a result with an asterisk is significant, while a result without one is not. For example, Table 6–1 shows results of part of a study by Stipek and Ryan (1997) comparing economically disadvantaged and advantaged preschoolers. This table gives figures for variables measured by observing the children in the classroom, including means, standard deviations, and F statistics (an indication of the procedure used in this study to test significance, a procedure you will learn in chapters 11 to 13). The important thing to look at for purposes of the present discussion are the asterisks (and the notes at the bottom of the table that go with them) telling you the significance levels for the various measures. For example, for calling attention to their accomplishments, disadvantaged children ($M = .20$) scored significantly higher than advantaged children ($M = .04$). The reverse pattern was seen for "Smiles after completing the task."

On the other hand, making positive social comparisons did not differ significantly between the groups (the means were .71 and .61, but these were not different enough to be significant in this study). Thus, we cannot conclude that for preschool-

TABLE 6–1 | Mean Scores for Classroom-Observed Motivation Variables by Socioeconomic Status

Motivation Variable	Disadvantaged		Advantaged		
	M	SD	M	SD	F(1, 196)
Calls attention to accomplishment	0.20	0.51	0.04	0.20	9.94**
Smiles after completing task	0.14	0.42	0.05	0.22	4.49*
Positive social comparison	0.71	0.45	0.64	0.48	.01
Negative social comparison	0.12	0.34	0.36	0.48	21.24****
Competence comments	4.14	1.83	5.74	1.78	25.39****
Seeks help	0.01	0.10	0.09	0.33	5.14*
Noncompliance	0.12	0.35	0.13	0.53	.07
Disciplined	0.10	0.30	0.16	0.47	2.26
Sad	1.03	0.17	1.02	0.14	.15
Bored	1.05	0.21	1.29	0.46	25.29***
Frustrated	1.03	0.17	1.03	0.17	.02
Effort rating	1.34	0.93	1.36	0.95	.28

$*p < .05; **p < .01; ***p < .001; ****p < .0001.$

Note. Data from Stipek, D. J., & Ryan, R. H. (1997), tab. 4. Economically disadvantaged preschoolers: Ready to learn but further to go. *Developmental Psychology, 33,* 711–723. Copyright, 1997, by the American Psychological Association. Reprinted with permission.

ers, being disadvantaged has any relation to making positive social comparisons. It would also be wrong to conclude that being disadvantaged has no relation to making positive social comparisons. Once again, when a result is not strong enough to reject the null hypothesis, normally our best conclusion is that the results are inconclusive.

In reporting results of significance testing, researchers rarely make explicit the research hypothesis or the null hypothesis, or describe any of the other steps of the process in any detail. It is assumed that the reader understands all of this very well.

SUMMARY

1. Hypothesis testing considers the probability that the result of a study could have come about even if the experimental procedure had no effect. If this probability is low, the scenario of no effect is rejected and the theory behind the experimental procedure is supported.

2. The expectation of an effect is the research hypothesis, and the hypothetical situation of no effect is the null hypothesis.

3. When a result is so extreme that the result would be very unlikely if the null hypothesis were true, the null hypothesis is rejected and the research hypothesis supported. If the result is not that extreme, the study is inconclusive.

4. Psychologists usually consider a result too extreme if it is less likely than 5%, though psychologists sometimes use a more stringent 1%, or even .1%, cutoff.

5. The cutoff percentages is the probability of the result being extreme in a predicted direction in a directional or one-tailed test. The cutoff percentages are the probability of the result being extreme in either direction in a nondirectional or two-tailed test.

6. Five steps of hypothesis-testing follow:

❶ **Restate the question as a research hypothesis and a null hypothesis about the populations.**

❷ **Determine the characteristics of the comparison distribution.**

❸ **Determine the cutoff sample score on the comparison distribution at which the null hypothesis should be rejected.**

❹ **Determine your sample's score on the comparison distribution.**

❺ **Decide whether to reject the null hypothesis.**

7. Recently, there has been much controversy about significance tests, including critiques of the basic logic and, especially, that they are often misused. One major way significance tests are misused is when researchers interpret not rejecting the null hypothesis as demonstrating that the null hypothesis is true.

8. Research articles typically report the results of hypothesis testing by saying a result was or was not significant and giving the probability level cutoff (usually 5% or 1%) the decision was based on.

KEY TERMS

comparison distribution (p. 193)

conventional levels of significance ($p < .05, p < .01$) (p. 194)

cutoff sample score (p. 193)

directional hypotheses (p. 199)

hypothesis testing (p. 189)

nondirectional hypotheses (p. 200)

null hypothesis (p. 192)

one-tailed test (p. 200)

research hypothesis (p. 192)

statistically significant (p. 194)

two-tailed test (p. 200)

EXAMPLE WORKED-OUT COMPUTATIONAL PROBLEMS

A randomly selected individual, after going through an experimental treatment, has a score of 27 on a particular measure. The scores of people in general on this measure are normally distributed with a mean of 19 and a standard deviation of 4. The researcher predicts an effect, but does not predict a particular direction of effect. Using the 5% significance level, what should you conclude? Solve this problem explicitly using all five steps of hypothesis testing and illustrate your answer with a sketch showing the comparison distribution, the cutoff (or cutoffs), and the score of the sample on this distribution.

❶ **Restate the question as a research hypothesis and a null hypothesis about the populations.** There are two populations of interest:

Population 1: People who go through the experimental procedure.
Population 2: People in general (that is, people who do not go through the experimental procedure).

The research hypothesis is that Population 1 will score differently than Population 2 on the particular measure. The null hypothesis is that the two populations are not different on the measure.

❷ **Determine the characteristics of the comparison distribution:** $\mu = 19$, $\sigma = 4$, normally distributed.

❸ **Determine the cutoff sample score on the comparison distribution at which the null hypothesis should be rejected.** For a two-tailed test at the 5% level (2.5% at each tail), the cutoff is ±1.96.

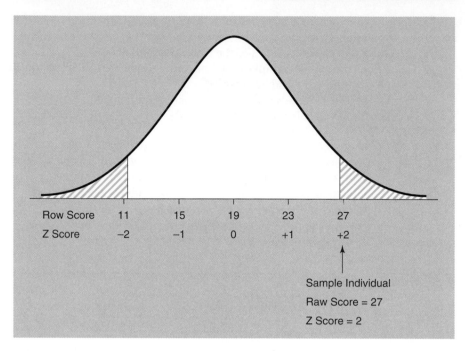

FIGURE 6–9   *Diagram for Example Worked-Out Computation Problem showing comparison distribution, cutoffs (2.5% shaded area on each tail), and sample score.*

❹ Determine your sample's score on the comparison distribution. $Z = (27 - 19)/4 = 2$.
   ❺ Decide whether to reject the null hypothesis. A Z score of 2 is more extreme than the cutoff Z of ± 1.96. Reject the null hypothesis; the result is significant. The experimental procedure affects scores on this measure. The diagram is shown in Figure 6–9.

PRACTICE PROBLEMS

These problems involve figuring. Most real-life statistics problems are done on a computer. However, even if you have a computer and statistics software, do these by hand (with the help of a calculator) to ingrain the method in your mind. Also, in all problems involving figuring, be sure to show your work.
   For practice in using a computer to solve statistics problems, refer to the computer section of each chapter of the *Student's Study Guide and Computer Workbook* that accompanies this text.
   All data are fictional unless an actual citation is given.
   Answers to Set I problems are given at the back of the book.

SET I

1. Define the following terms in your own words: (a) hypothesis-testing procedure, (b) .05 significance level, and (c) two-tailed test.
2. When a result is not extreme enough to reject the null hypothesis, explain why it is wrong to conclude that your result supports the null hypothesis.

3. For each of the following, (a) say what two populations are being compared, (b) state the research hypothesis, (c) state the null hypothesis, and (d) say whether you should use a one-tailed or two-tailed test and why.

   (i) Do Canadian children whose parents are librarians score higher than Canadian children in general on reading ability?

   (ii) Is the level of income for residents of a particular city different from the level of income for people in the region?

   (iii) Do people who have experienced an earthquake have more or less self-confidence than the general population?

4. Based on the information given for each of the following studies, decide whether to reject the null hypothesis. For each, give the Z-score cutoff (or cutoffs) on the comparison distribution at which the null hypothesis should be rejected, the Z score on the comparison distribution for the sample score, and your conclusion. Assume that all populations are normally distributed.

Study	Population		Sample Score	Cutoff p	Tails of Test
	μ	σ			
A	10	2	14	.05	1 (high predicted)
B	10	2	14	.05	2
C	10	2	14	.01	1 (high predicted)
D	10	2	14	.01	2
E	10	4	14	.05	1 (high predicted)

5. Based on the information given for each of the following studies, decide whether to reject the null hypothesis. For each, give the Z-score cutoff (or cutoffs) on the comparison distribution at which the null hypothesis should be rejected, the Z score on the comparison distribution for the sample score, and your conclusion. Assume that all populations are normally distributed.

Study	Population		Sample Score	p	Tails of Test
	μ	σ			
A	70	4	74	.05	1 (high predicted)
B	70	1	74	.01	2
C	70	2	76	.01	2
D	72	2	77	.01	2
E	72	2	68	.05	1 (low predicted)

6. A psychologist studying the senses of taste and smell has carried out many studies in which students are given each of 20 different foods (apricot, chocolate, cherry, coffee, garlic, and so on). She administers each food by dropping a liquid on the tongue. Based on her past research, she knows that for students overall at the university, the mean number of these 20 foods that students can identify correctly is 14, with a standard deviation of 4, and the distribution of scores follows a normal curve. The psychologist wants to know whether people's accuracy on this task has more to do with smell than with taste. Thus, she sets up special procedures that

keep a person from being able to use the sense of smell during the test. The psychologist then tries the procedure on one randomly selected student. This student is able to identify only 5 correctly. Using the .05 significance level, what should the researcher conclude? Solve this problem explicitly using all five steps of hypothesis testing and illustrate your answer with a sketch showing the comparison distribution, the cutoff (or cutoffs), and the score of the sample on this distribution. Then explain your answer to someone who has never had a course in statistics (but who is familiar with mean, standard deviation, and Z scores).

7. A psychologist is working with people who have had a particular type of major surgery. This psychologist proposes that people will recover from the operation more quickly if friends and family are in the room with them for the first 48 hours after the operation. It is known that time to recover from this kind of surgery is normally distributed with a mean of 12 days and a standard deviation of 5 days. The procedure of having friends and family in the room for the period after the surgery is tried with a randomly selected patient. This patient recovers in 18 days. Using the .01 significance level, what should the researcher conclude? Solve this problem explicitly using all five steps of hypothesis testing and illustrate your answer with a sketch showing the comparison distribution, the cutoff (or cutoffs), and the score of the sample on this distribution. Then explain your answer to someone who has never had a course in statistics (but who is familiar with mean, standard deviation, and Z scores).

8. What is the effect of going through a natural disaster on the attitude of police chiefs about the goodness of the people in their city? A researcher studying this expects a more positive attitude (because of many acts of heroism and helping of neighbors), but a more negative attitude is also possible (because of looting and scams). It is known that in general police chiefs' attitudes about the goodness of the people in their cities is normally distributed with a mean of 6.5 and a standard deviation of 2.1. A major earthquake has just occurred in an isolated city, and shortly afterwards, the researcher is able to give the attitude questionnaire to the police chief of that city. The chief's score is 8.2. Using the .05 significance level, what should the researcher conclude? Solve this problem explicitly using all five steps of hypothesis testing and illustrate your answer with a sketch showing the comparison distribution, the cutoff (or cutoffs), and the score of the sample on this distribution. Then explain your answer to someone who has never had a course in statistics (but who is familiar with mean, standard deviation, and Z scores).

9. Robins and John (1997) carried out a study on narcissism (self-love), comparing people who scored high versus low on a narcissism questionnaire. (An example item was "If I ruled the world it would be a better place.") They also had other questionnaires, including one that had an item about how many times the participant looked in the mirror on a typical day. In their results section, the researchers noted ". . . as predicted, high-narcissism individuals reported looking at themselves in the mirror more frequently than did low narcissism individuals (Ms = 5.7 vs. 4.8), . . . p <.05" (p. 39). Explain this result to a person who has never had a course in statistics. (Focus on the meaning of this result in terms of the general logic of hypothesis testing and statistical significance.)

10. Reber and Kotovsky (1997), in a study of problem solving, described one of their results comparing a specific group of participants within their overall control condition as follows: "This group took an average of 179 moves to solve the puzzle, whereas the rest of the control participants took an average of 74 moves, $t(19)$ = 3.31, p <.01" (p. 183). Explain this result to a person who has never had a course in statistics. (Focus on the meaning of this result in terms of the general logic of hypothesis testing and statistical significance.)

SET II

11. List five steps of hypothesis testing and explain the procedure and logic of each.
12. When a result is significant, explain why is it wrong to say the result "proves" the research hypothesis?
13. For each of the following, (a) say what two populations are being compared, (b) state the research hypothesis, (c) state the null hypothesis, and (d) say whether you should use a one-tailed or two-tailed test and why.

    (i) In an experiment, people are told to solve a problem by focusing on the details. Is the speed of solving the problem different for people who get such instructions compared to people who are given no special instructions?

    (ii) Based on anthropological reports in which the status of women is scored on a 10-point scale, the mean and standard deviation across many cultures are known. A new culture is found in which there is an unusual family arrangement. The status of women is also rated in this culture. Do cultures with the unusual family arrangement provide higher status to women than cultures in general?

    (iii) Do people who live in big cities develop more stress-related conditions than people in general?

14. Based on the information given for each of the following studies, decide whether to reject the null hypothesis. For each, give the Z-score cutoff (or cutoffs) on the comparison distribution at which the null hypothesis should be rejected, the Z score on the comparison distribution for the sample score, and your conclusion. Assume that all populations are normally distributed.

Study	Population		Sample Score	p	Tails of Test
	μ	σ			
A	5	1	7	.05	1 (high predicted)
B	5	1	7	.05	2
C	5	1	7	.01	1 (high predicted)
D	5	1	7	.01	2

15. Based on the information given for each of the following studies, decide whether to reject the null hypothesis. For each, give the Z-score cutoff (or cutoffs) on the comparison distribution at which the null hypothesis should be rejected, the Z score on the comparison distribution for the sample score, and your conclusion. Assume that all populations are normally distributed.

Study	Population		Sample Score	p	Tails of Test
	μ	σ			
A	100.0	10.0	80	.05	1 (low predicted)
B	100.0	20.0	80	.01	2
C	74.3	11.8	80	.01	2
D	16.9	1.2	80	.05	1 (low predicted)
E	88.1	12.7	80	.05	2

16. A researcher wants to test whether certain sounds will make rats do worse on learning tasks. It is known that an ordinary rat can learn to run a particular maze correctly in 18 trials, with a standard deviation of 6. (The number of trials to learn this maze is normally distributed.) The researcher now tries an ordinary rat on the maze, but with the sound. The rat takes 38 trials to learn the maze. Using the .05 level, what should the researcher conclude? Solve this problem explicitly using all five steps of hypothesis testing and illustrate your answer with a sketch showing the comparison distribution, the cutoff (or cutoffs), and the score of the sample on this distribution. Then explain your answer to someone who has never had a course in statistics (but who is familiar with mean, standard deviation, and Z scores).

17. A family psychologist developed an elaborate training program to reduce the stress of childless men who marry women with adolescent children. It is known from previous research that such men, 1 month after moving in with their new wife and her children, have a stress level of 85 with a standard deviation of 15, and the stress levels are normally distributed. The training program is tried on one man randomly selected from all those in a particular city who during the preceding month have married a woman with an adolescent child. After the training program, this man's stress level is 60. Using the .05 level, what should the researcher conclude? Solve this problem explicitly using all five steps of hypothesis testing and illustrate your answer with a sketch showing the comparison distribution, the cutoff (or cutoffs), and the score of the sample on this distribution. Then explain your answer to someone who has never had a course in statistics (but who is familiar with mean, standard deviation, and Z scores).

TABLE 6–2 Selected Indicators of Change in Tobacco Use, ETS Exposure, and Public Attitudes Toward Tobacco Control Policies—Massachusetts, 1993–1995

	1993	1995
Adult Smoking Behavior		
Percentage smoking >25 cigarettes daily	24	10*
Percentage smoking <15 cigarettes daily	31	49*
Percentage smoking within 30 minutes of waking	54	41
Environmental Tobacco Smoke Exposure		
Percentage of workers reporting a smokefree worksite	53	65*
Mean hours of ETS exposure at work during prior week	4.2	2.3*
Percentage of homes in which smoking is banned	41	51*
Attitudes Toward Tobacco Control Policies		
Percentage supporting further increase in tax on tobacco with funds earmarked for tobacco control	78	81
Percentage believing ETS is harmful	90	84
Percentage supporting ban on vending machines	54	64*
Percentage supporting ban on support of sports and cultural events by tobacco companies	59	53*

Source: Biener and Roman. 1996.
$*p < .05$
Note. Data from Siegel, M., & Biener, L. (1997), tab. 4. Evaluating the impact of statewide anti-tobacco campaigns: The Massachusetts and California tobacco control programs. *Journal of Social Issues, 53,* 147–168. Copyright © 1997 by the Society for the Psychological Study of Social Issues. Reprinted with permission.

18. A researcher predicts that listening to music while solving math problems will make a particular brain area more active. To test this, a research participant has her brain scanned while listening to music and solving math problems, and the brain area of interest has a percent signal change of 58. From many previous studies with this same math-problems procedure (but not listening to music), it is known that the signal change in this brain area is normally distributed with a mean of 35 and a standard deviation of 10. Using the .01 level, what should the researcher conclude? Solve this problem explicitly using all five steps of hypothesis testing and illustrate your answer with a sketch showing the comparison distribution, the cutoff (cutoff), and the score of the sample on this distribution. Then explain your answer to someone who has never had a course in statistics (but who is familiar with mean, standard deviation, and Z scores).

19. Pecukonis (1990), as part of a larger study, measured ego development (a measure of overall maturity) and ability to empathize with others among a group of 24 aggressive adolescent girls in a residential treatment center. The girls were divided into high and low ego development groups, and the empathy ("cognitive empathy") scores of these two groups were compared. In his results section, Pecukonis reported, "The average score on cognitive empathy for subjects scoring high on ego development was 22.1 as compared with 16.3 for low scorers, . . . p < .005" (p. 68). Explain this result to a person who has never had a course in statistics. (Focus on the meaning of this result in terms of the general logic of hypothesis testing and statistical significance.)

20. In an article about anti-tobacco campaigns, Siegel and Biener (1997) discuss the results of a survey of tobacco usage and attitudes, conducted in Massachusetts in 1993 and 1995; Table 6–2 shows the results of this survey. Focusing on just the first line (the percentage smoking >25 cigarettes daily), explain what this result means to a person who has never had a course in statistics. (Focus on the meaning of this result in terms of the general logic of hypothesis testing and statistical significance.)

CHAPTER 7

HYPOTHESIS TESTS WITH MEANS OF SAMPLES

Are You Ready?
What You Need to have Mastered Before Starting This Chapter:

- Chapters 1, 2, 5, and 6

In Chapter 6, we introduced the basic logic of hypothesis testing. We used as examples studies in which the sample was a single individual. As we noted, however, in actual practice, psychology research almost always involves a sample of many individuals. In this chapter, we build on what you have learned so far and consider hypothesis testing involving a sample of more than one. Mainly, this requires examining in some detail what we call a distribution of means.

THE DISTRIBUTION OF MEANS

Hypothesis testing in the usual research situation, where you are studying a sample of many individuals, is exactly the same as you learned in Chapter 6—with an important exception. When you have more than one person in your sample, there is a special problem with Step 2, determining the characteristics of the comparison distribution. The problem is that the score you care about in your sample is the *mean of the group of scores.* The comparison distributions we have considered so far were distributions of *individual scores* (such as the population of ages when individual babies start walking). Comparing the mean of a sample of, say, 50 individuals to a distribution of individual scores is a mismatch—like comparing apples and oranges. Instead, when you have a mean of a sample of 50, you need a comparison distribution that is a distribution of means of samples of 50. Such a comparison distribution we call a **distribution of means.**

distribution of means

A distribution of means is a distribution of the means of each of a very large number of samples of the same size, with each sample randomly taken from the same population of individuals. (Statisticians also call this distribution of means a *sampling distribution of the mean.* In this book, however, we use the term *distribution of means* to keep it clear we are talking about populations of *means*, not samples or some kind of distribution of samples.)

The distribution of means is the proper comparison distribution when there is more than one person in a sample. Thus, in most research situations, determining the characteristics of a distribution of means is necessary for Step 2 of the hypothesis-testing procedure, determining the characteristics of the comparison distribution.

BUILDING A DISTRIBUTION OF MEANS

To help you understand the idea of a distribution of means, we consider how you could build up such a distribution from an ordinary population distribution of individuals. Suppose our population of individuals was of the grade levels of the 90,000 elementary and junior-high schoolchildren in a particular region. Suppose further (to keep the example simple) that there are exactly 10,000 children at each grade level, from first through ninth grade. This population distribution would be rectangular, with a mean of 5, a variance of 6.67, and a standard deviation of 2.58 (see Figure 7–1).

Next, suppose that you wrote each child's grade level on a table tennis ball and put all 90,000 plastic balls into a giant tub. The tub would have 10,000 balls with a 1 on them, 10,000 with a 2 on them, and so forth. Stir up the balls in the tub, and then take two of them out. You have taken a random sample of two balls. Suppose one ball has a 2 on it and the other has a 9 on it. The mean grade level of this sample of two children's grade levels is 5.5, the average of 2 and 9. Now you put the balls back, mix up all the balls, and select two balls again. Maybe this time you get two 4s, making the mean of your second sample 4. Then you try again; this time you get a 2 and a 7, making your mean 4.5. So far you have three means: 5.5, 4, and 4.5.

These three numbers (each a mean of a sample of grade levels of two school children) can be thought of as a small distribution in its own right. The mean of this little distribution of three numbers is 4.67 (the sum of 5.5, 4, and 4.5, divided by 3). The variance of this distribution is .39 (the variance of 5.5, 4, and 4.5). The standard deviation is .62 (the square root of .39). A histogram of this distribution of three means is shown in Figure 7–2.

If you continued the process, the histogram of means would continue to grow. Figure 7–3a shows an example after 10 samples, each of two randomly drawn balls. Figure 7–3b shows the histogram of the distribution of means after 20 samples, each of two randomly drawn balls. After 100 such samples, the histogram of the distribution of the means might look like that in Figure 7–3c; after 1,000, like Figure 7–3d. (We actually made the histograms shown in Figure 7–3 using a computer to make the random selections instead of using 90,000 table tennis balls and a giant tub.)

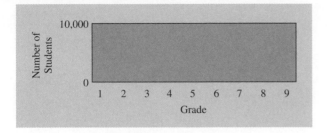

FIGURE 7–1 *Distribution of grade levels among 90,000 schoolchildren (fictional data).*

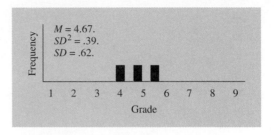

FIGURE 7–2 *Distribution of the means of three randomly taken samples of two schoolchildren's grade levels each from a population of grade levels of 90,000 schoolchildren (fictional data).*

In practice, researchers almost never take many different samples from a population. It is quite a lot of work to come up with a single sample and study the people in that sample. Fortunately, however, you can figure out the characteristics of a distribution of means directly, using some simple rules, without taking even one sample. The only information you need is (a) the characteristics of the population distribution of individuals and (b) the number of scores in each sample. (Don't worry for now about how you could know the characteristics of the population of individuals.) The laborious method of building up a distribution of means in the way we have just considered and the concise method you learn shortly give the same result. We have had you think of the process in terms of the painstaking method only because it helps you understand the idea of a distribution of means.

CHARACTERISTICS OF A DISTRIBUTION OF MEANS

Notice three things about the distribution of means we built in our example, as shown in Figure 7–3d:

1. The mean of the distribution of means is about the same as the mean of the original population of individuals (both are 5).
2. The spread of the distribution of means is less than the spread of the distribution of the population of individuals.
3. The shape of the distribution of means is approximately normal.

The first two characteristics, regarding the mean and the spread, are true for all distributions of means. The third, regarding the shape, is true for most distributions of means. These three observations, in fact, illustrate three basic rules you can use to find the mean, variance, and shape of any distribution of means without having to write on plastic balls and take endless samples. (The three rules, to which we turn shortly, are based on the *central limit theorem,* a fundamental principle in mathematical statistics we mentioned in Chapter 5.)

Now, let's examine the three rules. The first is for the **mean of the distribution of means**.

> Rule 1: The mean of a distribution of means is the same as the mean of the population of individuals.

Stated as a formula,

(7-1)
$$\mu_M = \mu$$

mean of the distribution of means

The mean of the distribution of means is the mean of the population of individuals.

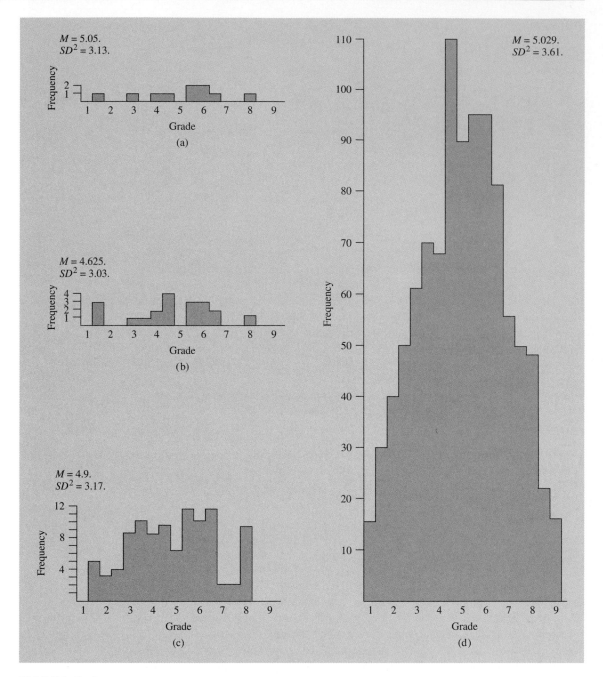

FIGURE 7–3 *Distributions of the means of samples, of two randomly drawn balls each, from a population of 90,000 balls, consisting of 10,000 with each of the numbers from 1 through 9. Numbers of sample means in each distribution shown are (a) 10 sample means, (b) 20 sample means, (c) 100 sample means, and (d) 1,000 sample means. (Actual sampling simulated by computer.)*

μ_M is the mean of the distribution of means (it uses a Greek letter because the distribution of means is also a kind of population). μ is the mean of the population of individuals.

Each sample is based on randomly selected individuals from the population of individuals. Thus, the mean of a sample will sometimes be higher and sometimes be lower than the mean of the whole population of individuals. However, because the selection process is random and we are taking a very large number of samples, eventually the high means and the low means perfectly balance each other out.

You can see in Figure 7–3 that with a large number of samples, the mean of the distribution of means becomes very similar to the mean of the population of individuals, which in this example was 5. If we had shown an example with 10,000 means of samples, the mean of the means of these 10,1000 samples would be even closer to 5. It can be proven mathematically that if you took an infinite number of samples, the mean of the distribution of means of these samples would come out to be exactly the same as the mean of the distribution of individuals.

The second rule is about spread. Rule 2A is for the **variance of the distribution of means**.

variance of the distribution of means

Rule 2a: The variance of a distribution of means is the variance of the population divided by the number of individuals in each of the samples.

Here is the reason that a distribution of means will be less spread out than the distribution of individuals from which the samples are taken: Any one score, even an extreme score, has some chance of being included in any particular random sample. The chance is less of two extreme scores both being included in the same random sample. Further, for a particular random sample to have an extreme mean, the two extreme scores would both have to be extreme in the same direction (both very high or both very low). Thus, having more than a single score in each sample has a moderating effect on the mean of such samples. In any one sample, the extremes tend to be balanced out by a middle score or by an extreme in the opposite direction. This makes each sample mean tend toward the middle and away from extreme values. With fewer extreme means, the variance of the means is less.

Consider again our example. There were plenty of 1s and 9s in the population, making a fair amount of spread. That is, about a ninth of the time, if you were taking samples of single scores, you would get a 1, and about a ninth of the time you would get a 9. If you are taking samples of two at a time, you would get a sample with a mean of 1 (that is, in which *both* balls were 1s) or a mean of 9 (both balls 9s) much less often. Getting two balls that average out to a middle value such as 5 is much more likely. (This is because several combinations could give this result—a 1 and a 9, a 2 and an 8, a 3 and a 7, a 4 and a 6, or two 5s).

The more individuals in each sample, the less spread out will be the means of those samples. This is because with several scores in each sample, it is even rarer for extremes in any particular sample not to be balanced out by middle scores or extremes in the other direction. In terms of the plastic balls in our example, we rarely got a mean of 1 when taking samples of two balls at a time. If we were taking three balls at a time, getting a sample with a mean of 1 (all three balls would have to be 1s) is even less likely. Getting middle values for the means becomes even more likely.

Using samples of two balls at a time, the variance of the distribution of means came out to about 3.33. This is half of the variance of the population of individuals, which was 6.67. If we had built up a distribution of means using samples of three balls each, the variance of the distribution of means would have been 2.22. This is one third of the variance of our population of individuals. Had we randomly selected five balls for each sample, the variance of the distribution of means would have been one fifth of the variance of the population of individuals.

These examples follow a general rule—our Rule 2a for the distribution of means: the variance of a distribution of means is the variance of the distribution of the population divided by the number of individuals in each of the samples. This rule holds in all situations and can be proven mathematically.

Here is Rule 2a stated as a formula:

The variance of a distribution of means is the variance of the population of individuals divided by the number of individuals in each sample.

$$\sigma_M^2 = \frac{\sigma^2}{N} \qquad (7\text{-}2)$$

σ_M^2 is the variance of the distribution of means, σ^2 is the variance of the population of individuals, and N is the number of individuals in each sample.

In our example, the variance of the population of individual children's grade levels was 6.67, and there were two schoolchildren's grade levels in each sample. Thus,

$$\sigma_M^2 = \frac{\sigma^2}{N} = \frac{6.67}{2} = 3.34$$

To use a different example, suppose a population had a variance of 400 and you wanted to know the variance of a distribution of means of 25 individuals each:

$$\sigma_M^2 = \frac{\sigma^2}{N} = \frac{400}{25} = 16$$

standard deviation of the distribution of means

The second rule also tells us about the **standard deviation of the distribution of means**.

Rule 2b: The standard deviation of a distribution of means is the square root of the variance of the distribution of means.

Stated as a formula,

The standard deviation of a distribution of means is the square root of the variance of the distribution of means and also is the square root of the result of dividing the variance of the population of individuals by the number of individuals in each sample.

$$\sigma_M = \sqrt{\sigma_M^2} = \sqrt{\frac{\sigma^2}{N}} \qquad (7\text{-}3)$$

σ_M is the standard deviation of the distribution of means.

Sometimes, this formula is algebraically manipulated to emphasize the relation between the standard deviation of the population of individuals and the standard deviation of the distribution of means:

The standard deviation of a distribution of means is the standard deviation of the population of individuals divided by the square root of the number of individuals in each sample.

$$\sigma_M = \frac{\sigma}{\sqrt{N}} \qquad (7\text{-}4)$$

standard error of the mean
standard error

The standard deviation of the distribution of means also has a special name of its own, the **standard error of the mean,** or the **standard error**, for short. (Thus, σ_M also stands for the standard error.) It has this name because it tells you how much the means of samples are typically "in error" as estimates of the mean of the population of individuals. That is, it tells you how much the particular means in the distribution of means deviate from the mean of the population. We have more to say about the standard error later in the chapter.

Finally, the third rule for finding the characteristics of a distribution of means focuses on its shape.

Rule 3: The shape of a distribution of means is approximately normal if either (a) each sample is of 30 or more individuals or (b) the distribution of the population of individuals is normal.

Whatever the shape of the distribution of the population of individuals, the distribution of means tends to be unimodal and symmetrical. In the grade-level example, the population distribution was rectangular. (It had an equal number at each value.) However, the shape of the distribution of 1,000 sample means (Figure 7–3d) was roughly that of a bell—unimodal and symmetrical. Had we taken many more than 1,000 samples, the shape would have been even more clearly unimodal and symmetrical.

A distribution of means tends to be unimodal because of the same basic process of extremes balancing each other out that we noted in the discussion of the variance: Middle scores for means are more likely, and extreme means are less likely. A distribution of means tends to be symmetrical because lack of symmetry (skew) is caused by extremes. With fewer extremes, there is less asymmetry. In our grade-level example, the distribution of means we built up also came out so clearly symmetrical because the population distribution of individual grade levels was symmetrical. Had the population distribution of individuals been skewed to one side, the distribution of means would have still been skewed, but not as much.

The more individuals in each sample, the closer the distribution of means will be to a normal curve. In fact, with samples of 30 or more individuals, even with a nonnormal population of individuals, the approximation of the distribution of means to a normal curve is very close and the percentages in the normal curve table will be extremely accurate.[1, 2] Finally, whenever the population distribution of individuals is normal, the distribution of means will be normal, regardless of the number of individuals in each sample.

SUMMARY OF RULES AND FORMULAS FOR DETERMINING THE CHARACTERISTICS OF A DISTRIBUTION OF MEANS

Rule 1: The mean of a distribution of means is the same as the mean of the population of individuals: $\mu_M = \mu$.

---

[1]We have ignored that a normal curve is a smooth theoretical distribution, while in most real-life distributions, scores are only at specific numbers, such as a child being in a particular grade and not in a fraction of a grade. So, one difference between our example distribution of means and a normal curve is that the normal curve is smooth. However, in psychology research, even when our measurements are at specific numbers, we usually assume that the underlying thing being measured is continuous.

[2]We have already considered this principle of a distribution of means tending toward a normal curve in Chapter 5. Though we had not yet discussed the distribution of means, we still used this principle to explain why the distribution of so many things in nature follows a normal curve. In that chapter, we explained it as the various influences balancing each other out, to make an averaged influence come out with most of the scores near the center and a few at each extreme. Now we have made the same point using the terminology of a distribution of means. Think of any distribution of individual scores in nature as about a situation in which each score is actually an average of a random set of influences on that individual. Consider the distribution of weights of pebbles. Each pebble's weight is a kind of average of all the different forces that went into making the pebble have a particular weight.

Rule 2a: The variance of a distribution of means is the variance of the distribution of the population divided by the number of individual in each of the samples: $\sigma_M^2 = \sigma^2/N$.

Rule 2b: The standard deviation of a distribution of means is the square root of the variance of the distribution of means: $\sigma_M = \sqrt{\sigma_M^2}$.

Rule 3: The shape of a distribution of means is approximately normal if either (a) each sample is of 30 or more individuals or (b) the distribution of the population of individuals is normal.

Figure 7–4 shows these three rules graphically.

EXAMPLE

Consider the population of scores of students who have taken the Graduate Record Examinations (GRE): Suppose the distribution is approximately normal with a mean of 500 and a standard deviation of 100. What will be the characteristics of the distribution of means for samples of 50 students?

Rule 1: The mean of a distribution of means is the same as the mean of the population of individuals. The mean of the population is 500. Thus, the mean of the distribution of means will also be 500. That is, $\mu_M = \mu = 500$.

Rule 2a: The variance of a distribution of means is the variance of the distribution of the population divided by the number of individual in each of the samples.

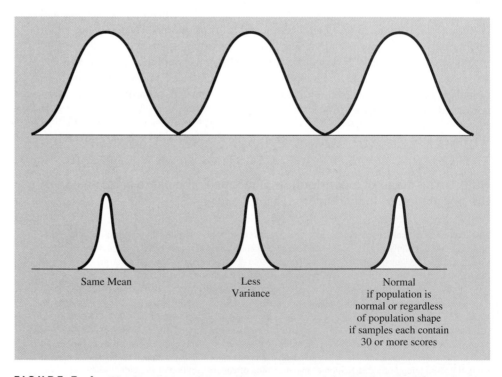

Same Mean Less Variance Normal if population is normal or regardless of population shape if samples each contain 30 or more scores

FIGURE 7–4 *The distribution of means (lower curves) and the distribution of the population of individuals (upper curves).*

Rule 2b: The standard deviation of a distribution of means is the square root of the variance of the distribution of means. The standard deviation of the population of individuals is 100; thus, the variance of the population of individuals is 10,000. The variance of the distribution of means is therefore 10,000 divided by 50 (the size of the sample). This comes out to 200. That is, $\sigma_M^2 = \sigma^2/N = 10,000/50 = 200$. The standard deviation of the distribution of means is the square root of 200, which is 14. That is, $\sigma_M = \sqrt{\sigma^2} = \sqrt{200} = 14$.

Rule 3: The shape of a distribution of means is approximately normal if either (a) each sample is of 30 or more individuals or (b) the distribution of the population of individuals is normal. Our situation meets both of these conditions—the sample of 50 students is more than 30, and the population of individuals follows a normal distribution. Thus, the distribution of means will follow a normal curve. (It would have been enough even if only one of the two conditions had been met.)

REVIEW OF THE DIFFERENT KINDS OF DISTRIBUTIONS

We have considered three different kinds of distributions: (a) the distribution of a population of individuals, (b) the distribution of a particular sample of individuals from that population, and (c) the distribution of means. Figure 7–5 shows these three kinds of distributions graphically and Table 7–1 describes them.

HOW ARE YOU DOING?

1. What is a distribution of means?
2. Explain how you could create a distribution of means by taking a large number of samples of four individuals each.
3. (a) Why is the mean of the distribution of means the same as the mean of the population of individuals? (b) Why is the variance of a distribution of means smaller than the variance of the distribution of the population of individuals?
4. Write the formula for the variance of the distribution of means and define each of the symbols.
5. (a) What is the standard error? (b) Why does it have this name?
6. A population of individuals has a mean of 60 and a standard deviation of 10. What are the characteristics of a distribution of means from this population for samples of four each?

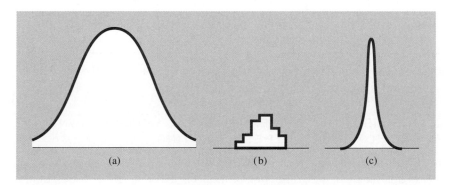

(a)   (b)   (c)

FIGURE 7–5   *Three kinds of distributions: (a) the distribution of a population of individuals, (b) the distribution of a particular sample from that population, and (c) the distribution of means.*

TABLE 7–1	Comparison of Three Types of Distributions		
	Population's Distribution	Particular Sample's Distribution	Distribution of Means
Content	Scores of all individuals in the population	Scores of the individuals in a single sample	Means of samples randomly taken from the population
Shape	Could be any shape, often normal	Could be any shape	Approximately normal if samples have ≥ 30 individuals in each or if population is normal
Mean	μ	$M = \Sigma X/N$	$\mu_M = \mu$
Variance	σ^2	$SD^2 = \Sigma(X - M)^2/N$,	$\sigma_M^2 = \sigma^2/N$
Standard deviation	σ	$SD = \sqrt{SD^2}$	$\sigma_M = \sqrt{\sigma_M^2} = \sigma/\sqrt{N}$

ANSWERS:

1. It is a distribution of the means of a very large number of samples of the same size randomly taken from the population of individuals.
2. Take a random sample of four from the population and figure its mean. Repeat this a very large number of times. Make a distribution of these means.
3. (a) With randomly taken samples, some will have higher means and some lower means than those of the population of individuals; these should balance out. (b) You are less likely to get a sample of several scores with an extreme mean than you are to get a single extreme score. This is because in any random sample it is highly unlikely to get several extremes in the same direction—extreme scores tend to be balanced out by middle scores or extremes in the opposite direction.
4. $\sigma_M^2 = \sigma^2/N$. σ_M^2 is the variance of the distribution of means; σ^2 is the variance of the population of individuals; N is the number of individuals in your sample.
5. (a) The standard deviation of the distribution of means. (b) It tells you about how much means of samples typically (standardly) differ from the population mean, and thus the typical amount that means of samples are in error as estimates of the population mean.
6. $\mu_M = 60$; $\sigma_M^2 = 25$ (that is, $10^2/4 = 25$); $\sigma_M = 5$; shape = normal.

HYPOTHESIS TESTING WITH A DISTRIBUTION OF MEANS

Now we are ready to turn to hypothesis testing when there is more than one individual in the study's sample.

THE DISTRIBUTION OF MEANS AS THE COMPARISON DISTRIBUTION IN HYPOTHESIS TESTING

In the usual research situation, a psychologist studies a sample of more than one person. In this situation, the distribution of means is the comparison distribution. It is the distribution whose characteristics need to be determined in Step 2 of the hypothesis-testing process. The distribution of means is the distribution to which you compare your sample's mean to see how likely it is that you could have selected a sample with a mean that extreme if the null hypothesis were true.

BOX 7-1   More About Polls: Sampling Errors and Errors in Thinking About Samples

If you think back to Box 5–3 on surveys and the Gallup poll, you will recall that we left two important questions unanswered about fine print included with the results of a poll, which read something like "From a telephone poll of 1,000 American adults taken on June 4 and 5. Sampling error ±3%." First, you might wonder how such small numbers, like 1,000 (but rarely much less), can be used to predict the opinion of the entire U.S. public. Second, after working through the material in this chapter on the standard deviation of the distribution of means, you may wonder what a "sampling error" means when a sample is not randomly sampled but rather selected by the complicated probability method used for polls.

Regarding sample size, you know from this chapter that large sample sizes, like 1,000, greatly reduce the standard deviation of the distribution of means. That is, the curve becomes very high and narrow, gathered all around the population mean. The mean of any sample of that size is very close to being the population mean.

Still, you might persist in an intuitive feeling that the number required to represent all of the huge U.S. public might need to be larger than just 1,000. However, if you think about it, when a sample is only a small part of a very large population, the sample's ab-

solute size is the only determiner of accuracy. This absolute size determines the impact of the random errors of measurement and selection. What remains important is reducing bias or systematic error, which can be done only by careful planning.

As for the term *sampling error,* when simple random sampling is not used, sampling error is not quite the same as the standard deviation of a distribution of means, or the confidence interval based on it, as described in this chapter. Instead, the sampling error for polls is worked out according to past experience with the sampling procedures used. It is expressed in tables for different sample sizes (usually below 1,000, because that is where error increases dramatically).

So, now you understand opinion polls even better. The number of people polled is not very important (provided that it is at least 1,000 or so). What matters very much, however, is the method of sampling and estimating error, which will not be reported even in the fine print in the necessary detail to judge if the results are reliable. The reputation of the organization doing the survey is probably the best criterion. If the sampling and error-estimating approach is not revealed, be cautious. (As for the 2000 election, the TV networks claim that the organizations doing the exit polls for the media did not do a good job.)

FIGURING THE *Z* SCORE OF A SAMPLE'S MEAN ON THE DISTRIBUTION OF MEANS

There can be some confusion in figuring the location of your sample on the comparison distribution in hypothesis testing with a sample of more than one. In this situation, you are finding a Z score of your sample's mean on a distribution of means. (Before, you were finding the Z score of a single individual on a distribution of a population of single individuals.) The method of changing the sample's mean to a Z score is the same as the usual way of changing a raw score to a Z score. However, you have to be careful not to get mixed up because more than one mean is involved. It is important to remember that you are treating the sample mean like a single score. In other words, the ordinary formula (from Chapter 2) for changing a raw score to a Z score is $Z = (X - M)/SD$. In the present situation, you are actually using the following formula:

| The Z score (for the sample's mean on the distribution of means) is the sample's mean minus the mean of the distribution of means, divided by the standard deviation of the distribution of means. |

$$Z = \frac{(M - \mu_M)}{\sigma_M}$$ (7-5)

For example, suppose your sample's mean is 18 and the distribution of means has a mean of 10 and a standard deviation of 4. The Z score of this sample mean is $+2$. Using the formula,

$$Z = \frac{(M - \mu_M)}{\sigma_M} = \frac{18 - 10}{4} = \frac{8}{4} = 2$$

This is shown in Figure 7–6.

EXAMPLE

Suppose a team of educational psychologists is interested in the effects of instructions on timed school achievement tests. These educational researchers have a theory that predicts that people will do better on a test if they are told to answer each question with the first response that comes to mind. To test this theory, the researchers give a standard school achievement test to 64 randomly selected fifth-grade schoolchildren. They give the test in the usual way, except that they add to the instructions a statement that children are to answer each question with the first response that comes to mind.

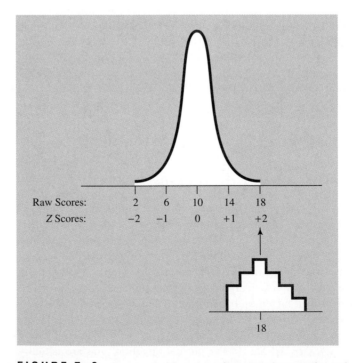

| Raw Scores: | 2 | 6 | 10 | 14 | 18 |
| Z Scores: | −2 | −1 | 0 | +1 | +2 |

18

FIGURE 7–6   *Z score for the mean of a particular sample on the distribution of means.*

When given in the usual way, the test is known to have a mean of 200, a standard deviation of 48, and an approximately normal distribution. This distribution is shown in Figure 7–7a.[3]

Now let's follow the five steps of hypothesis testing you learned in Chapter 6:

❶ **Restate the question as a research hypothesis and a null hypothesis about the populations.** The two populations are these:

Population 1: Fifth graders who get the special instructions
Population 2: Fifth graders who do not get the special instructions

The research hypothesis is that the population of fifth graders who take the test with the special instructions will on the average have higher scores than the population of fifth graders who take the test in the normal way: $\mu_1 > \mu_2$. The null hypothesis is that Population 1's scores will not on the average be higher than Population 2's: $\mu_1 \leq \mu_2$. Note that these are directional hypotheses. The researchers want to know if their special instructions will increase test scores; results in the opposite direction would be irrelevant.

❷ **Determine the characteristics of the comparison distribution.** The result of the study will be a mean of a sample of 64 individuals (of fifth graders in this case). Thus, the comparison distribution has to be the distribution of means of samples of 64 individuals each. This comparison distribution will have a mean of 200 (the same as the population mean). Its variance will be the population variance divided by the number of individuals in the sample. The population variance is 2,304 (the population standard deviation of 48 squared); the sample size is 64. Thus, the variance of the distribution of means will be 2,304/64, or 36. The standard deviation of the distribution of means is the square root of 36, or 6. Finally, because there are more than 30 individuals in the sample, the shape of the distribution of means will be approximately normal. Figure 7–7b shows this distribution of means.

❸ **Determine the cutoff sample score on the comparison distribution at which the null hypothesis should be rejected.** Let's assume the researchers decide to use the standard 5% significance level and as we noted in Step 1, they are making a directional prediction. Hence, the researchers will reject the null hypothesis if the result is in the top 5% of the comparison distribution. The comparison distribution (the distribution of means) is a normal curve. Thus, the top 5% can be found from the normal curve table. It starts at a Z of +1.64. This top 5% is shown as the shaded area in Figure 7–7b.

❹ **Determine your sample's score on the comparison distribution.** The result of the (fictional) study is that the 64 fifth graders given the special instructions had a mean of 220. (This sample's distribution is shown in Figure 7–7c.) A mean of 220 is 3.33 standard deviations above the mean of the distribution of means:

$$Z = \frac{(M - \mu_M)}{\sigma_M} = \frac{220 - 200}{6} = \frac{20}{6} = 3.33$$

[3]This study would be much better if the researchers also had another group of fifth graders who were randomly assigned to be tested by the same researchers under the same conditions, but without the special instruction added. Relying on the general scores for fifth graders taking this test is a bit hazardous because the circumstances in the experiment might be somewhat different from that of the usual testing situation. However, we have taken liberties with this example to help introduce the hypothesis-testing process to you one step at a time. In this example and the others in this chapter, we use situations in which a single sample is contrasted with a "known" population. Starting in Chapter 9, we extend the hypothesis-testing procedure to more realistic research situations, those involving more than one group of participants and those involving populations whose characteristics are not known.

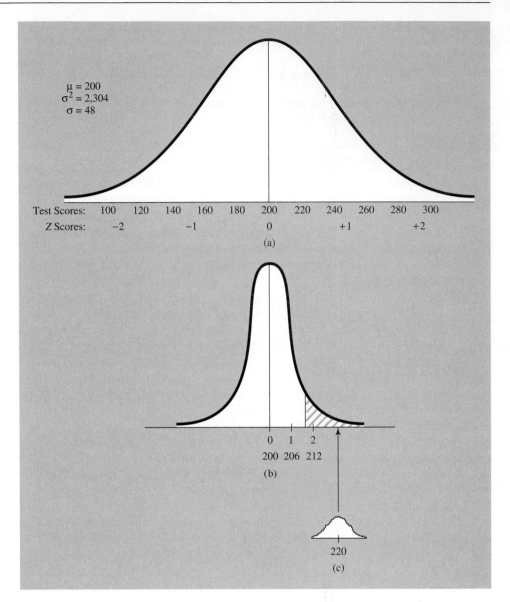

$\mu = 200$
$\sigma^2 = 2,304$
$\sigma = 48$

Test Scores: 100   120   140   160   180   200   220   240   260   280   300

Z Scores: -2 -1 0 $+1$ $+2$

(a)

      0   1   2

    200   206   212

(b)

220

(c)

FIGURE 7–7   *For the fictional study of performance on a standard school achievement test, (a) the distribution of the population of individuals, (b) the distribution of means (the comparison distribution), and (c) the sample's distribution.*

❺ **Decide whether to reject the null hypothesis.** We set the minimum Z score to reject the null hypothesis to $+1.64$. The Z score of the sample's mean is $+3.33$. Thus, the educational psychologists can reject the null hypothesis and conclude that the research hypothesis is supported. To put this another way, the result is statistically significant at the $p < .05$ level. You can see this in Figure 7–7b. Note how extreme the sample's mean is on the distribution of means (the distribution that would apply if the null hypothesis were true). The final conclusion is that among fifth graders like those studied, the special instructions do improve test scores.

A SECOND EXAMPLE

Suppose a researcher is interested in whether memory is affected by stress. The researcher conducts a study in which 25 participants are told that they have to give a talk to a large audience, which is quite stressful for most people. While the participants are preparing their talk, they are given a memory task. The memory task is that they are first shown a large number of pictures; a half hour later they are shown these pictures again, mixed up with pictures they have not seen before; for each picture, they have to say whether or not they have seen it before. In our fictional example, we will suppose that people generally get an average of 53 correct with a standard deviation of 7, and the scores in the general population are normally distributed (see Figure 7–8a). However, the 25 participants in this study had a mean

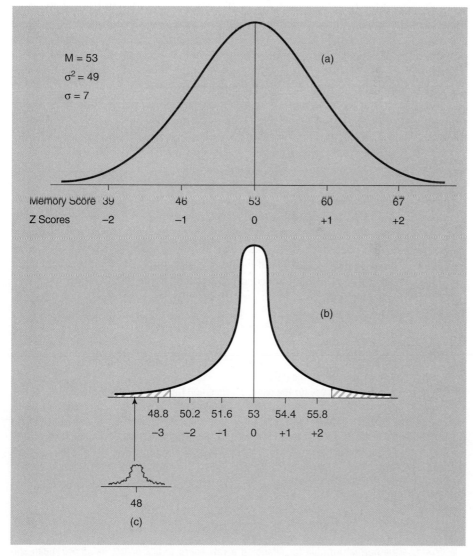

FIGURE 7–8   *For the fictional study of memory under stress, (a) the distribution of the population of individuals, (b) the distribution of means (the comparison distribution), and (c) the sample's distribution.*

correct of only 48. The researcher wants to use the 1% significance level and an effect would be important in either direction (that is, it is possible that stress could make memory worse or better).

❶ **Restate the question as a research hypothesis and a null hypothesis about the populations.** The two populations are these:

Population 1: People under stress
Population 2: The general population (people not under stress)

The research hypothesis is that the population of people who do the memory task under stress will on the average score differently than the general population when doing this task not under any particular stress: $\mu_1 \neq \mu_2$. The null hypothesis is that Population 1's scores are on the average the same as Population 2's: $\mu_1 = \mu_2$.

❷ **Determine the characteristics of the comparison distribution.** This comparison distribution will be a distribution of means. It will have a mean of 53 (the same as the population mean). Its variance will be the population variance divided by 25, the number of individuals in the sample: $\sigma_M^2 = \sigma^2/N = 7^2/25 = 49/25 = 1.96$; $\sigma_M = \sqrt{\sigma_M^2} = \sqrt{1.96} = 1.4$. The shape will be normal, since the population of individuals is normally distributed. (Figure 7–8b shows the comparison distribution.)

❸ **Determine the cutoff sample score on the comparison distribution at which the null hypothesis should be rejected.** Based on the normal curve table for the top and bottom .5% (.495), the cutoffs are ± 2.57. (See tiny shaded areas in Figure 7–8b.)

❹ **Determine your sample's score on the comparison distribution.** The sample's mean was 48 (see Figure 7–8c). This comes out to a Z of −3.57 on the comparison distribution: $Z = (48 - 53)/1.4 = -5/1.4 = -3.57$.

❺ **Decide whether to reject the null hypothesis.** The Z score of the sample's mean is −3.57. Thus, the researchers can reject the null hypothesis and conclude that the research hypothesis is supported. To put this another way, the result is statistically significant at the $p < .01$ level. You can see this in Figure 7–8b. Note how extreme the sample's mean is on the distribution of means (the distribution that would apply if the null hypothesis were true). The final conclusion is that among fifth graders like those studied, the special instructions do improve test scores.

HOW ARE YOU DOING?

1. How is hypothesis testing with a sample of more than one person different from hypothesis testing with a sample of a single person?
2. How do you find the Z score for the sample's mean on the distribution of means?
3. A researcher predicts that showing a certain film will change people's attitudes towards alcohol. The researchers then randomly select 36 people, show them the film, and give them an attitude questionnaire. The mean score on the attitude test for these 36 people is 70. The score for people in general on this test is 75, with a standard deviation of 12. Using the five steps of hypothesis testing and the 5% significance level, does showing the film change people's attitudes towards alcohol?

ANSWERS:

1. In hypothesis testing with a sample of more than one person, the comparison distribution is a distribution of means.
2. You use the normal formula for changing a raw score to a Z score, using the mean and standard deviation of the distribution of means.
3. ❶ **Restate the question as a research hypothesis and a null hypothesis about the populations.** The two populations are these:
   Population 1: People shown the film

Population 2: People in general
The research hypothesis is that the population shown the film have different average attitude scores than the population of people in general; the null hypothesis is that the populations have the same average attitude score.
❷ **Determine the characteristics of the comparison distribution.** $\mu_M = 70$; $\sigma_M^2 = \sigma^2/N =$
144/36 = 4; $\sigma_M = 2$; shape is normal.
❸ **Determine the cutoff sample score on the comparison distribution at which the null
hypothesis should be rejected.** Two-tailed cutoff, 5%, is ±1.96.
❹ **Determine your sample's score on the comparison distribution.** $Z = (70 - 75)/2 = -2.5$.
❺ **Decide whether to reject the null hypothesis.** The result, 2.5, is more extreme than
±1.96; reject the null hypothesis. Seeing the film does change attitudes.

ESTIMATION, STANDARD ERRORS, AND CONFIDENCE INTERVALS

Hypothesis testing is our main focus in this book. However, there is another kind of
statistical question related to the distribution of means that is also important in psychology: estimating an unknown population mean based on the scores in a sample.
Traditionally, this has been very important in survey research. In recent years it is
also becoming important in experimental research (e.g., Wilconson and Task Force
on Statistical Inference, 1999) and can even serve as an alternative approach to hypothesis testing.

ESTIMATING THE MEAN: POINT ESTIMATES

The best estimate of the population mean is the sample mean. In the study of fifth
graders who were given the special instructions, the mean score for the sample of
64 fifth graders was 220. Thus, 220 is the best estimate of the mean for the
unknown population of fifth graders who would ever receive the special instructions.

The mean of the sample is the best estimate because you are more likely to get
a sample mean from a population with a mean of 220 than from a population with
any other mean. Consider Figure 7–9. Suppose the true distribution of means has
the same mean as our sample, as would be the case in this figure if the true distribution of means was distribution c. In this situation, it is very likely that a mean from
this distribution of means would be close to our sample's mean. But suppose the
true distribution of means was like distribution d. In this case, many fewer means
are near to our sample's mean.

In this example, you are estimating the specific value of the population mean.
When you estimate a specific value of a population parameter, it is called a **point   point estimate
estimate.**

THE ACCURACY OF A POINT ESTIMATE

How accurate is this point estimate of the mean? A way to get at this question is to
ask, How much do means from a distribution of means vary? One indication of such
variation, we know, is the standard deviation of the distribution of means. Like any
standard deviation, it tells you how much scores in the distribution typically vary. In
this case, the "scores" are sample means. Because our interest is in making an estimate of the population mean, any variation is error. Thus, the amount of variation is
the amount you can expect means of scores from a population like the one we stud-

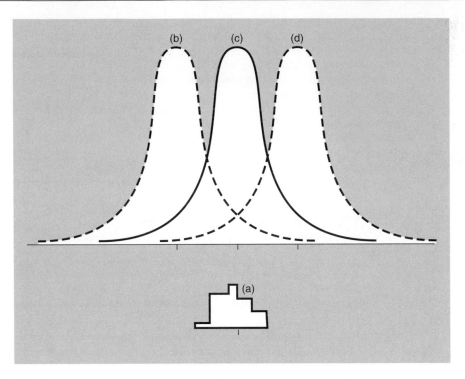

FIGURE 7-9   *A sample and three distributions of sample means. The mean of a particular sample (a) is more likely to have come from a distribution of means with the same mean (c) than from any other distribution of means (such as b and d).*

ied are likely to be in error as an estimate of the true, unknown population mean.[4] As we briefly noted earlier when introducing the standard deviation of the distribution of means, this is why it is also known as the standard error of the mean, or the standard error for short. The accuracy of our estimate of 220 for the mean of the population of fifth-graders who get the special instructions would be the standard error, which we figured earlier to be 6.

INTERVAL ESTIMATES

interval estimate

You can also estimate the *range* of possible means that are likely to include the population mean. This is called an **interval estimate**.

Consider our point estimate of 220 with a standard error of 6. It seems reasonable that a mean between 220 and 226 (one standard error above 220) is 34% likely. This is because the distribution of means is a normal curve, the standard error is 1 standard deviation on that curve, and 34% of a normal curve is between the mean and 1 standard deviation above the mean. From this reasoning, we could also figure that another 34% should be between 220 and 214 (1 standard error below 220). Putting this together, we have a region from 214 to 226 that we are 68% confident

[4]You don't know the true distribution of means for the population your sample comes from. But in the examples we have considered in this chapter, you do know the variance and shape of the distribution of means for a similar population (Population 2). It is reasonable to assume that even if the mean is different, the variance and shape of the distribution of the population your sample comes from is the same. Thus, you can use this distribution of means to estimate the amount that a sample mean from any population with the same variance and shape is likely to vary from its population mean.

should include the population mean. (See Figure 7–10a). This is an example of a confidence interval. We would call it the "68% confidence interval." The upper and lower ends of a confidence interval are called **confidence limits**. In this example, the confidence limits for the 68% confidence interval are 214 and 226.

    Normally, however, you would want to be more than 68% confident about your estimates. Thus, it is standard when figuring confidence intervals to use 95% or even 99% confidence intervals. These are figured based on the distribution of means for the area that includes the middle 95% or middle 99%. For the **95% confidence interval**, you want the area in a normal curve on each side between the mean and the Z score that includes 47.5% The normal curve table shows this to be 1.96. Thus, in terms of Z scores, the 95% confidence interval is from -1.96 to $+1.96$ on the distribution of means. Changing these Z scores to raw scores for the school achievement test example gives an interval of 208.24 to 231.76 (see Figure 7–10b). That is, for the lower confidence limit, $(-1.96)(6) + 120 = -11.76 + 120 = 208.24$; for the upper confidence limit, $(1.96)(6) + 120 = 11.76 + 120 = 231.76$. In sum, based on the sample of 64 fifth graders who get the special instructions, you can be 95% confident that the true population mean for such fifth graders is between 208.24 and 231.76.

    For a **99% confidence interval**, you use the Z scores for the middle 99% of the normal curve (the part that includes 49.5% above and below the mean). This comes out to ± 2.57. Changing this to raw scores, the 99% confidence interval is from 204.58 to 235.42.

confidence limits

95% confidence interval

99% confidence interval

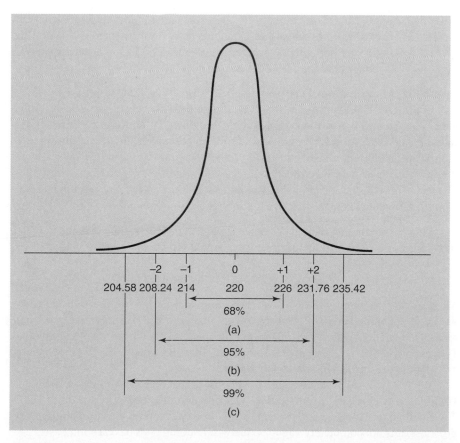

FIGURE 7–10 *A distribution of means and the (a) 68%, (b) 95%, and (c) 99% confidence intervals for fifth graders taking a test with special instructions (fictional data).*

Notice in Figure 7–10 that the greater the confidence, the broader the confidence interval. In our example, you could be 68% confident that the true population mean is between 214 and 226; but you could be 95% confident that it is between 208.24 and 231.76 and 99% confident it is between 204.58 and 235.42. This is a general principle. It makes sense that you need a wider range of possibility to be more sure you are right.

STEPS FOR FIGURING CONFIDENCE LIMITS

There are two steps for figuring confidence limits:

❶ **Figure the standard error.** That is, find the standard deviation of the distribution of means in the usual way:

$$\sigma_M = \sqrt{\sigma^2/N}$$

❷ **For the 95% confidence interval, figure the raw scores for 1.96 standard errors above and below the sample mean; for the 99% confidence interval, figure the raw scores for 2.57 standard errors above and below the sample mean.** To figure these raw scores, you multiply 1.96 or 2.57 times the standard error and subtract this from the mean (for the lower limit) or add this to the mean (for the upper limit).

EXAMPLE

Let's find the 99% confidence interval for the stress and memory example from earlier in the chapter. Recall that in that example, scores on the memory task in the general population are normally distributed with a mean of 53 and a standard deviation of 7. The score of the sample of 25 tested under stress was 48.

❶ **Figure the standard error.** $\sigma_M = \sqrt{\sigma^2/N} = \sqrt{7^2/25} = \sqrt{1.96} = 1.4$.

❷ **For the 95% confidence interval, figure the raw scores for 1.96 standard errors above and below the sample mean; for the 99% confidence interval, figure the raw scores for 2.57 standard errors above and below the sample mean.** You want the 99% confidence interval. Thus, you first multiply 2.57 by 1.4 to get 3.6, which is how far the confidence limit is from the mean. You then subtract this distance from 48, the mean of the sample: $48 - 3.6 = 44.4$. For the upper confidence limit, you add this distance to the sample mean: $48 + 3.6 = 51.6$.

Thus, based on this sample of 25 participants, you can be 99% confident that an interval from 44.4 to 51.6 includes the true population mean.

THE SUBTLE LOGIC OF CONFIDENCE INTERVALS

There is one problem with all this: Strictly speaking, what we are figuring to be, say, a 95% confidence interval is the range of means that are 95% likely to come from a population with a true mean that happens to be the mean of our sample. However, what we really want to know is the range that is 95% likely to include the true population mean. This we cannot know.

What we can say is that we are 95% *confident* that the true mean is in this range. Confidence is closer to the subjective interpretation of probability we discussed in Chapter 5. In fact, confidence is meant to be a little vaguer term than probability. Nevertheless, it is not completely vague. What we are doing does have a solid basis.

Here is how to understand this: Suppose in our fifth grader example, the true mean was indeed 220. As we have seen, this would give a 95% confidence interval

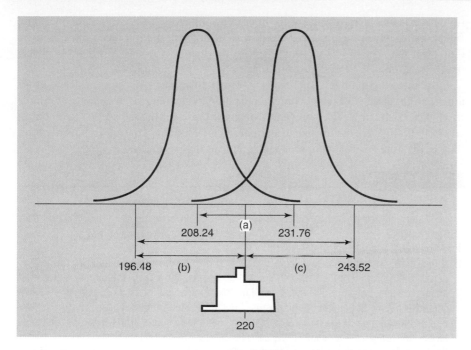

FIGURE 7–11 *(a) 95% confidence interval based on sample mean of 220 for fifth graders taking a test with special instruction (fictional data); (b) range including 95% of sample means, based on distribution of means shown above it with* μ_{Mb} = *lower limit of the of the 95% confidence interval for M* = *220; (c) range including 95% of sample means, based on distribution of means shown above it with* μ_{Mc} = *upper limit of the 95% confidence interval for M* = *220.*

of 208.24 to 231.76, as shown in Figure 7–11a. We don't know what the true population mean is. But suppose the true population mean was 208.24. The range that includes 95% of sample means from this population's distribution of means would be from 196.48 to 220, as shown in Figure 7–11b. (You can work this out yourself following the two steps for figuring confidence limits.) Similarly, for the population with a mean of 231.76, the range that includes 95% of sample means from this population's distribution of means is from 220 to 243.52, as shown in Figure 7–11c.

What this shows is a general principle: For a 95% confidence interval, the lower confidence limit is the lowest possible population mean that would have a 95% probability of including our sample mean; the upper confidence limit is the highest possible population mean that would have a 95% probability of including our sample mean.

This convoluted logic is a bit like the double-negative logic behind hypothesis testing. This is no accident, since both are making inferences from samples to populations using the same information.

CONFIDENCE INTERVALS AND HYPOTHESIS TESTING

A practical implication of the link of confidence intervals and hypothesis testing is that you can use confidence intervals to do hypothesis testing! If the confidence interval does not include the mean of the null hypothesis distribution, then the result is significant. For example, in the fifth-grader study, the 95% confidence interval for those who got the special instructions was from 208.24 to 231.76. However, the population that did not get the special instructions had a mean of 200. This population mean is outside the range of the confidence interval. Thus, if you are 95% confident that the true range is 208.24 to 231.76 and the population mean for those who didn't get the special instructions is not in this range, you are 95% confident that that population is not the same as the one your sample came from.

Another way to understand this is in terms of the idea that the confidence limits are the points at which a more extreme true population would not include your sample mean 95% of the time. The population mean for those getting the special instructions was 200. If this were the true mean also for the group that got the special instructions, 95% of the time it would not produce a sample as high as the one we got.

HOW ARE YOU DOING?

1. (a) What is the best estimate of a population mean, and (b) why?
2. (a) What number is used to indicate the accuracy of an estimate of the population mean, and (b) why?
3. What is a 95% confidence interval?
4. A researcher predicts that showing a certain film will change people's attitudes towards alcohol. The researchers then randomly select 36 people, show them the film, and give them an attitude questionnaire. The mean score on the attitude test for these 36 people is 70. The score for people in general on this test is 75, with a standard deviation of 12. (a) Find the best point estimate of the mean of people who see the film and (b) its 95% confidence interval. (c) Compare this result to the conclusion you drew when you used this example in the "How Are You Doing?" section for hypothesis testing.
5. (a) Why is it wrong to say that the 95% confidence interval is the region in which there is a 95% probability of finding the true population mean? (b) What is the basis for our 95% confidence?

ANSWERS:

1. (a) The sample mean. (b) It is more likely to have come from a population with the same mean than from any other population.
2. (a) The standard error. (b) The standard error is roughly the average amount that means vary from the mean of the distribution of means.
3. The range of values that you are 95% confident includes the population mean, estimated based on the scores in a sample.
4. (a) Best estimate is the sample mean: 70.
   (b) Standard error is 2 (that is, $\sqrt{144/36} = 2$). Lower confidence limit = $(-1.96)(2) + 70 = -3.92 + 70 = 66.08$; upper confidence limit = $(1.96)(2) + 70 = 3.92 + 70 = 73.92$.
   (c) The confidence interval does not include the mean of the general population (which was 75). Thus, you can reject the null hypothesis that the two populations are the same. This is the same conclusion as when using this example for hypothesis testing.
5. (a) It is wrong because you do not know the true population mean, so you have no way of knowing for sure what to start with when figuring 95% probability.
   (b) The lower confidence limit is the point at which a true population any lower would not have a 95% probability of including a sample with our mean; similarly, the upper confidence limit is the point at which a true population any higher would not have a 95% probability of including a sample with our mean.

CONTROVERSY: CONFIDENCE INTERVALS OR SIGNIFICANCE TESTS?

You may recall from Chapter 6 that currently there is a lively debate among psychologists about significance testing. Among the major issues in that debate is a proposal that psychologists should use confidence intervals instead of significance tests.

Those who favor replacing significance tests with confidence intervals (e.g., Cohen, 1994; Hunter, 1997; Schmidt, 1996) cite several major advantages. First, as we noted above, confidence intervals contain all the key information in a significance test,[5] but also give additional information—the estimation of the range of values that you can be quite confident include the true population mean. A second advantage is that they focus attention on estimation instead of hypothesis testing. Some researchers argue that the goal of science is to provide numeric estimates of effects, not just decisions as to whether an effect is different from zero. That is, with estimation (point and interval estimates), you have a clear idea of how big the effect is and how accurate you are about that estimate. With hypothesis testing, you draw conclusions about whether the effect is in the predicted direction, but not how big this effect is in that direction.

Confidence intervals are particularly valuable when the results are not significant (Frick, 1995), because knowing the confidence interval gives you an idea of just how far from no effect you can be confident that the true mean is to be found. If the entire confidence interval is near to no effect, you can feel confident that even if there is some true effect, it is probably small. For example, suppose a group of people is tested after receiving a procedure that claims to affect IQ. The mean for the group is 102, and the 99% confidence interval is 98 to 106. This would be a nonsignificant finding because it includes 100, the mean IQ of the population who do not receive the special procedure. At the same time, since the confidence interval includes numbers other than 100, it is certainly possible that there is a real effect. Nevertheless, the key point is that if there is a real effect, it is likely to be very small, since we are 99% confident it won't be more than a 1-point decrease or a 6-point increase. On the other hand, suppose the confidence interval for this same study was 89 to 115. This result would also be nonsignificant (because it includes 100). However, it would tell us that the study is really very inconclusive: It is possible that there is little or no effect (that the population mean of those who receive the procedure is around 100), but it is also possible that there is a substantial effect (that the true population mean for those who receive the procedure involves a decrease of as much as 11 IQ points or an increase of as much as 15 IQ points).

A third advantage claimed by proponents of confidence intervals over significance testing is that researchers are less likely to misuse them. As we noted in Chapter 6, a common error in the use of significance tests is to conclude that a nonsignificant result means there is no effect. With confidence intervals, it is harder to fall into this kind of error. The confidence interval with a nonsignificant result will include the mean expected for no effect. However, it will also include other possible values. Thus, you are reminded that the true population mean may very well be other than the no effect mean.

In light of these various advantages, confidence intervals are starting to be used more in psychology research. In fact, the recently revised *Publication Manual of the American Psychological Association* (2001) takes the position that "The use of confidence intervals is . . . strongly recommended" (p. 22).

In spite of these apparent advantages, it is still relatively uncommon to find confidence intervals in most types of psychology research articles. In part, this is

[5]Some proponents of confidence intervals over significance testing argue that we should ignore the link with hypothesis testing. This is the most radical anti-significance-test position. That is, these psychologists argue that our entire focus should be on estimation, and significance testing of any kind should be irrelevant. In Chapter 8, we will discuss the rationale for their position, along with the counter arguments.

probably due to tradition and to most psychologists having been trained with and more used to significance tests. Confidence intervals also require more description in a research article. For example, consider a larger table of results. It is easy to put in a star for each number to show its significance, and it is easy to read such a table. With confidence intervals, instead of a star, you would need two extra numbers (the upper and lower confidence limit) for each result.

Other psychologists (e.g., Abelson, 1997; Harris, 1997; Nickerson, 2000) emphasize two reasons for not abandoning significance testing in favor of confidence intervals. First, for some advanced statistical procedures, it is possible to do significance testing but not to figure confidence intervals. Second, just as it is possible to make mistakes with significance tests, it is also possible to make other kinds of mistakes with confidence intervals—especially since most research psychologists are less experienced in using them. Indeed, as we have seen, the seemingly simple logic of confidence intervals in fact relies on some fairly subtle reasoning. In considering these issues, Abelson wrote: "Under the Law of Diffusion of Idiocy, every foolish application of significance testing will beget a corresponding foolish practice for confidence limits" (p. 13).

Whatever the outcome of this controversy about confidence intervals, it is important to understand them, since you will run into them occasionally when reading research literature, and you are likely to see them more often in the future. On the other hand, they now appear only occasionally, and there is no sign that they are likely to replace significance testing any time soon. For this reason (and to keep the amount of material to be learned manageable), we decided not to emphasize confidence intervals in subsequent chapters of this book, which are mainly on significance testing in various types of research situations.

HYPOTHESIS TESTS ABOUT MEANS OF SAMPLES, STANDARD ERRORS, AND CONFIDENCE INTERVALS IN RESEARCH ARTICLES

As we have noted several times, research in which there is a known population mean and standard deviation is quite rare in psychology. We have asked you to learn about this situation mainly as a building block for understanding hypothesis testing in more common research situations. In the rare case in which research with a known population distribution is conducted, the hypothesis test is called a **Z test,** because it is the Z score that is checked against the normal curve.

Z test

Here is an example. As part of a larger study, Wiseman (1997) gave a loneliness test to a group of college students in Israel. As a first step in examining the results, Wiseman checked that the average score on the loneliness test was not significantly different from a known population distribution based on a large U.S. study of university students that had been conducted earlier by Russell et al. (1980). Wiseman reported:

> . . . [T]he mean loneliness scores of the current Israeli sample were similar to those of Russell et al.'s (1980) university sample for both males (Israeli: $M = 38.74$, $SD = 9.30$; Russell: $M = 37.06$, $SD = 10.91$; $z = 1.09$, NS) and females (Israeli: $M = 36.39$, $SD = 8.87$; Russell: $M = 36.06$, $SD = 10.11$; $z = .25$, NS). (p. 291)

In this example, the researcher gives the standard deviation for both the sample studied (the Israeli group) and the population (the data from Russell). However, in the steps of figuring each Z (the sample's score on the distribution of means), they would have used the standard deviation only of the population. Notice also that the researcher took the nonsignificance of the difference as support for the sample means being "similar" to the population means. However, the researcher was very careful not to claim that these results showed there was no difference.

Of the topics we have covered in this chapter, the one you are most likely to see in a research article is the standard deviation of the distribution of means, used to describe the amount of variation that might be expected among means of samples of a given size from this population. In this context, it is usually called the *standard error*, abbreviated *SE* or *SEM* (for standard error of the mean). For example, Foertsch and Gernsbacher (1997) conducted a study to examine the effect of using the pronoun *they* to avoid fixing the gender of the person referred to, though this use is traditionally considered grammatically improper. Foertsch and Gernsbacher hypothesized that using *they* in this way would not have much effect on reading time. Consider the sentence "A truck driver should never drive while sleepy, even if she may be struggling to make a delivery on time, because many accidents are caused by drivers who fall asleep at the wheel." In their study, the researchers measured the reading time for this version of the sentence, as well as for two other versions, one substituting *he* for *she* and one substituting *they* for *she*. In this sentence, the antecedent (the first clause) was about a truck driver, a stereotypically masculine profession. In other sentences they used, the antecedents were stereotypically feminine (a nurse) or neutral (a runner). Here are some of their results:

> For masculine antecedents, *she* clauses ($M = 59.5$, $SE = 2.05$) were read significantly more slowly than *he* clauses ($M = 54.8$, $SE = 1.77$) or *they* clauses ($M = 55.3$, $SE = 1.77$). . . . For feminine antecedents, *he* clauses ($M = 58.7$, $SE = 1.66$) were read significantly more slowly than either *she* clauses ($M = 52.9$, $SE = 1.64$) or *they* clauses ($M = 52.7$, $SE = 1.67$) . . ." (p. 108)

This report gives you the sample means and a clear idea of the accuracy of these sample means as estimates of the population means. Consider the implications of the first standard error (2.05). Knowing this tells you that the mean reading time of sentences with masculine antecedents for *she* clauses (59.5) is more than 2 standard errors higher than the reading time for either *he* or *they* clauses (54.8 and 55.3).

When researchers report the standard error of a result, they also give you information to figure the confidence interval. For example, let's assume a normal curve and figure the 95% confidence interval for masculine antecedents sentences with *she* clauses. Since the *SE* (which is another name for the standard deviation of the distribution of means) is 2.05, the upper 95% confidence limit is the mean plus the result of 1.96 times 2.05. This comes out to 59.5 plus 1.96 times 2.05, which is 63.52. The lower limit is 55.48. Thus, you can be 95% confident that the interval from 55.48 to 63.52 includes the true population mean.

Standard errors are also often shown in research articles as lines that go above the tops of the bars in a bar graph. These lines that go above the main bars are called *standard error bars*. For example, Figure 7–12, reproduced from Foertsch and Gernsbacher's article, shows the same results we listed above (plus some additional ones). Error bars on graphs are actually very common in psychology research articles, particularly in the more experimental areas such as perception and cognitive neuroscience. However, be careful to read the fine print. Sometimes the bars are not standard errors but are instead standard deviations or confidence intervals! In the Foertsch and Gernsbacher article, you would only know by reading the text (where

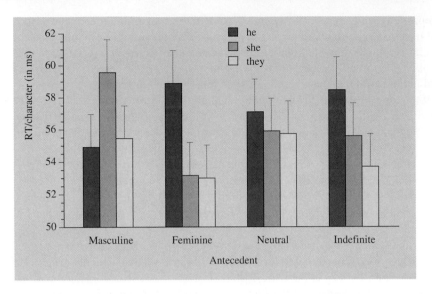

FIGURE 7–12 *Effects of antecedent type (masculine, feminine, neutral, or indefinite) and pronoun (he, she, or they) on per-character reading time (RT) when sentences were used nonreferentially (Experiment 1). [From Foertsch, J., & Gernsbacher, M. A. (1997), fig. 1. In search of gender neutrality: Is singular* they *a cognitively efficient substitute for generic* he? Psychological Science, 8, 108. Copyright, 1997, by the American Psychological Society. Reprinted with permission.]*

they describe the figures as standard errors). Sometimes what the bars represent is given in the figure caption.

As we noted, confidence intervals (usually abbreviated as CI), while far from standard, are becoming increasingly common in research articles. An organizational psychologist might explain that the average number of overtime hours worked in a particular industry is 3.7 with a 95% confidence interval of 2.5 to 4.9. This would tell you that the true average number of overtime hours is probably somewhere between 2.5 and 4.9. For example, Anderson et al. (2000) report that "Responses from the NHIS [National Health Interview Survey] indicate that by 1995, 39.7% of adults (95% CI = 38.8%, 40.5%) had been tested at least once. . . ." (p. 1090). This means that we can be 95% confident that the true percentage of people who have been tested is between 38.8% and 40.5%.

A shortcut that many researchers find helpful in reading research articles that give standard errors but not confidence intervals is that the 95% confidence interval is approximately 2 standard errors in both directions (it is exactly 1.96 *SEs*) and the 99% confidence interval is approximately 2.5 standard errors in both directions (it is exactly 2.57 *SEs*).

SUMMARY

1. When studying a sample of more than one individual, the comparison distribution in the hypothesis-testing process is a distribution of means. It can be thought of as what would result from (a) taking a very large number of samples, each of the same number of scores taken randomly from the population of individuals, and then (b) making a distribution of the means of these samples.

2. The distribution of means has the same mean as the population of individuals. However, it has a smaller variance because the means of samples are less likely to be extreme than individual scores. (In any one sample, extreme scores are likely to be balanced by middle scores or extremes in the other direction.) Specifically, its variance is the variance of the population divided by the number of individuals in each sample. Its standard deviation is the square root of its variance. The shape of the distribution of means approximates a normal curve if either (a) the samples are each of 30 or more scores or (b) the population of individuals follows a normal curve.

3. Hypothesis tests with a single sample of more than one individual and a known population are done the same way as the hypothesis tests of Chapter 6 (where the studies were of a single individual compared to a population of individuals). The main exception is that the comparison distribution is a distribution of means.

4. The best point estimate for the population mean is the sample mean. Its accuracy is the standard deviation of the distribution of means (the standard error), which tells you roughly the amount means vary. You can figure an interval estimate of the population mean based on the distribution of means. When the distribution of means follows a normal curve, the 95% confidence interval includes the range from 1.96 standard deviations below the sample mean (the lower confidence limit) to 1.96 standard deviations above the sample mean (the upper confidence limit). Strictly speaking, the 95% confidence interval around a sample mean is the range in which the lower limit is the mean of the lowest population whose population would have a 95% probability of including a sample with this sample mean and the upper limit is the corresponding mean of the highest population.

5. An aspect of the current debate about significance tests is whether researchers should replace them with confidence intervals. Proponents of confidence intervals argue that they provide additional information, put the focus on estimation, and reduce misuses common with significance tests. Confidence intervals are becoming more common but are still relatively unusual in psychology research articles, in part due to tradition and unfamiliarity with them, and to the awkwardness of describing them. In addition, opponents of relying exclusively on confidence intervals argue that they cannot be used in some advanced procedures, estimation is not always the goal, and they can have misuses of their own.

6. The kind of hypothesis testing described in this chapter (the Z test) is seldom used in research practice; you have learned it as a stepping-stone. The standard deviation of the distribution of means (the standard error) is commonly used to describe the expected variability of means, particularly in bar graphs. When confidence intervals are reported, it is usually with the abbreviation CI.

KEY TERMS

confidence limits (p. 235)
distribution of means (p. 218)
interval estimate (p. 234)
mean of the distribution of means (μ_M) (p. 219)
95% confidence interval (p. 235)

99% confidence interval (p. 235)
point estimate (p. 233)
standard deviation of a distribution of means (σ_M) (p. 222)
standard error (SE) (p. 222)

standard error of the mean (SE) (p. 222)
variance of the distribution of means (σ_M^2) (p. 221)
Z test (p. 240)

EXAMPLE WORKED-OUT COMPUTATIONAL PROBLEMS

FIGURE THE STANDARD DEVIATION OF THE DISTRIBUTION OF MEANS

Find the standard deviation of the distribution of means for a population with $\sigma = 13$ and a sample size of 20. Using Rule 2a and 2b for the characteristics of a distribution of means,

The variance of a distribution of means is the variance of the distribution of the population divided by the number of individuals in each of the samples. The standard deviation of a distribution of means is the square root of the variance of the distribution of means. The variance of the population is 169 (that is, 13 squared is 169); divided by 20 gives a variance of the distribution of means of 8.45. The square root of this, 2.91, is the standard deviation of the distribution of means.

Using the formula,

$$\sigma_M = \sqrt{\sigma^2/N} = \sqrt{13^2/20} = \sqrt{169/20} = \sqrt{8.45} = 2.91$$

HYPOTHESIS TESTING WITH A SAMPLE OF MORE THAN ONE

A sample of 75 given an experimental treatment had a mean of 16 on a particular measure. The general population of individuals has a mean of 15 on this measure and a standard deviation of 5. Carry out the full five steps of hypothesis testing with a two-tailed test at the .05 significance level and make a drawing of the distributions involved.

❶ **Restate the question as a research hypothesis and a null hypothesis about the populations. The two populations are these:**

Population 1: Those given the experimental treatment
Population 2: The general population (those not given the experimental treatment)

The research hypothesis is that the population given the experimental treatment will score differently on the particular measure used than the population in general (those not given the experimental treatment). The null hypothesis is that the populations have the same average score on this measure.

❷ **Determine the characteristics of the comparison distribution.** $\mu_M = \mu = 15$; $\sigma_M^2 = \sigma^2/N = 5^2/75 = 25/75 = .33$; $\sigma_M = \sqrt{\sigma_M^2} = \sqrt{.33} = .57$; shape is normal (sample size is greater than 30).

❸ **Determine the cutoff sample score on the comparison distribution at which the null hypothesis should be rejected.** Two-tailed cutoff, 5%, is ± 1.96.

❹ **Determine your sample's score on the comparison distribution.** $Z = (16 - 15)/.57 = 1/.57 = 1.75$.

❺ **Decide whether to reject the null hypothesis.** The result, 1.75, is *not* more extreme than ± 1.96; do not reject the null hypothesis. Results are inconclusive. The distributions involved are shown in Figure 7–13.

FINDING CONFIDENCE INTERVALS

Find the 99% confidence interval for the sample mean in the study described above.

❶ **Figure the standard error.** The standard error is the standard deviation of the distribution of means. In the problem above, it was .57.

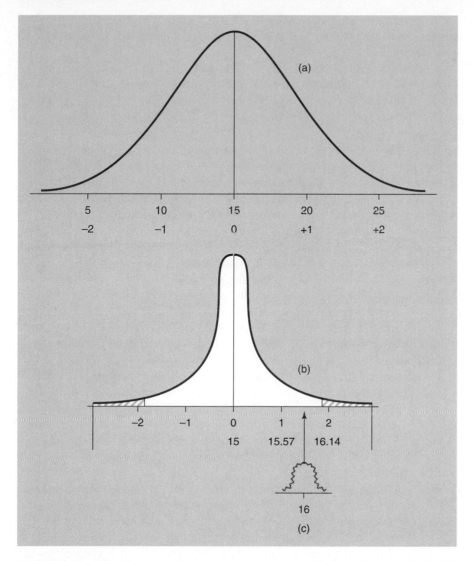

FIGURE 7–13 *For answer to hypothesis-testing problem in Example Worked-Out Computational Problems: (a) the distribution of the population of individuals, (b) the distribution of means (the comparison distribution), and (c) the sample's distribution.*

❷ **For the 95% confidence interval, figure the raw scores for 1.96 standard errors above and below the sample mean; for the 99% confidence interval, figure the raw scores for 2.57 standard errors above and below the sample mean.** For the 99% confidence interval, lower limit = 16 − (.57)(2.57) = 16 − 1.46 = 14.54; upper limit = 16 + (.57)(2.57) = 16 + 1.46 = 17.46.

PRACTICE PROBLEMS

These problems involve figuring. Most real-life statistics problems are done on a computer. However, even if you have a computer and statistics software, do these by hand (with the help of a calculator) to ingrain the method in your mind. Also, in all problems involving figuring, be sure to show your work.

For practice in using a computer to solve statistics problems, refer to the computer section of each chapter of the *Student's Study Guide and Computer Workbook* that accompanies this text.

All data are fictional unless an actual citation is given.

Answers to Set I problems are given at the back of the book.

SET I

1. Why is the standard deviation of the distribution of means generally smaller than the standard deviation of the distribution of the population of individuals?

2. For a population that has a standard deviation of 10, figure the standard deviation of the distribution of means for samples of size (a) 2, (b) 3, (c) 4, and (d) 9.

3. For a population that has a standard deviation of 20, figure the standard deviation of the distribution of means for samples of size (a) 2, (b) 3, (c) 4, and (d) 9.

4. Figure the 95% confidence interval (that is, the lower and upper confidence limits) for each part of problem 2. Assume that in each case the researcher's sample has a mean of 100 and that the population of individuals is known to follow a normal curve.

5. Figure the 99% confidence interval (that is, the lower and upper confidence limits) for each part of problem 3. Assume that in each case the researcher's sample has a mean of 10 and that the population of individuals is known to follow a normal curve.

6. For each of the following samples that were given an experimental treatment, test whether they are different from the general population: (a) a sample of 10 with a mean of 44, (b) a sample of 1 with a mean of 48. The general population of individuals has a mean of 40, a standard deviation of 6, and follows a normal curve. Carry out the full five steps of hypothesis testing with a two-tailed test at the .05 significance level, make a drawing of the distributions involved, and figure the 95% confidence interval.

7. For each of the following samples that were given an experimental treatment, test whether they scored significantly higher than the general population: (a) a sample of 100 with a mean of 82, (b) a sample of 10 with a mean of 84. The general population of individuals has a mean of 81, a standard deviation of 8, and follows a normal curve. Carry out the full five steps of hypothesis testing with a one-tailed test at the .01 significance level, make a drawing of the distributions involved, and figure the 99% confidence interval.

8. Twenty-five women between the ages of 70 and 80 were randomly selected from the general population of women their age to take part in a special program to decrease (speed) reaction time. After the course, the women had an average reaction time of 1.5 seconds. Assume that the mean reaction time for the general population of women of this age group is 1.8, with a standard deviation of .5 seconds. (Also assume that the population is approximately normal.) What should you conclude about the effectiveness of the course? (a) Carry out the steps of hypothesis testing (use the .01 level). (b) Make a drawing of the distributions involved. (c) Figure the 99% confidence interval. (d) Explain your answer to someone who is familiar with the general logic of hypothesis testing, the normal curve, Z scores, and probability, but is not familiar with the idea of a distribution of means or confidence intervals.

9. A large number of people were shown a particular film of an automobile collision between a moving car and a stopped car. Each person then filled out a questionnaire about how likely it was that the driver of the moving car was at

fault, on a scale from *not at fault* = 0 to *completely at fault* = 10. The distribution of ratings under ordinary conditions follows a normal curve with μ = 5.5 and σ = .8. Sixteen randomly selected individuals are tested in a condition in which the wording of the question is changed so the question asks, "How likely is it that the driver of the car who crashed into the other was at fault?" (The difference is that in this changed condition, instead of describing the event in a neutral way, the question uses the phrase "crashed into.") Using the changed instruction, these 16 research participants gave a mean at-fault rating of 5.9. Did the changed instructions significantly increase the rating of being at fault? (a) Carry out the steps of hypothesis testing (use the .05 level). (b) Make a drawing of the distributions involved. (c) Figure the 95% confidence interval. (d) Explain your answer to someone who has never taken statistics.

10. Lee et al. (2000) tested a theory of the role of distinctiveness in face perception. In their study, participants indicated whether or not they recognized each of 48 faces of male celebrities when they were shown rapidly on a computer screen. A third of the faces were shown in caricature form, in which facial features were electronically modified so that distinctive features were slightly exaggerated; a third were shown in veridical form, in which the faces were not modified at all; and a third were shown in anticaricature form, in which facial features were modified to be slightly more like the average of the celebrities' faces. The average percent correct across their participants is shown in Figure 7–14. Explain the meaning of the error bars in this figure to a person who understands mean, standard deviation, and variance, but nothing else about statistics.

11. Chiu et al. (1997) studied the tendency of some individuals to believe that people's traits are fixed; Chiu et al. labeled these individuals as "entity theorists" because they see other people as fixed entities. In particular, the researchers wanted to test whether entity theorists would be more likely to take

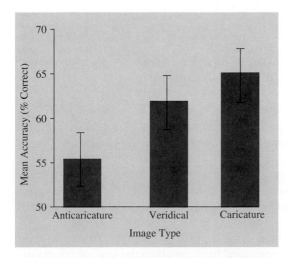

FIGURE 7–14   *Identification accuracy as a functionof image type. Standard error bars are shown. (From "Caricature Effects, Distinctiveness, and Identification: Testing the Face-Space Framework" by Kieran Lee, Graham Byatt, and Gillian Rhodes.* Psychological Science, *Vol. 11, September, 2000, p. 381. Reprinted by permission of Blackwell Publishers Journals.)*

a single event as evidence that a person has a fixed trait. As part of the study, they described to the research participants a situation in which one person behaved in a more friendly way than another, and then asked them which person would be more likely to be friendly in the future. Chiu et al. reported one of their findings about entity theorists as follows: "For them, if one person was found to be friendlier than another person in a particular situation, this relation would more likely than not generalize to a completely different situation" (p. 23). The statistical support for this was described as follows: "Entity theorists' overall prediction [of how likely the person was to be friendly] was significantly greater than .50 (95% CI = .5583 ± .0348)" (p. 23). Explain what "95% CI = .5583 ± .0348" means to a person who understands hypothesis testing with the mean of a sample of more than one but has never heard of confidence intervals.

SET II

12. Under what conditions is it reasonable to assume that a distribution of means will follow a normal curve?
13. Indicate the mean and the standard deviation of the distribution of means for each of the following situations.

	Population		Sample Size
	Mean	Variance	
(a)	100	40	10
(b)	100	30	10
(c)	100	20	10
(d)	100	10	10
(e)	50	10	10
(f)	100	40	20
(g)	100	10	20

14. Figure the standard deviation of the distribution of means for a population with a standard deviation of 20 and sample sizes of (a) 10, (b) 11, (c) 100, and (d) 101.
15. Figure the 95% confidence interval (that is, the lower and upper confidence limits) for each part of problem 13. Assume that in each case the researcher's sample has a mean of 80 and the population of individuals is known to follow a normal curve.
16. Figure the 99% confidence interval (that is, the lower and upper confidence limits) for each part of problem 14. Assume that in each case the researcher's sample has a mean of 50 and that the population of individuals is known to follow a normal curve.
17. For each of the following studies, the samples were given an experimental treatment and the researchers compared their results to the general population. For each, carry out the full five steps of hypothesis testing for a two-tailed test, make a drawing of the distributions involved, and figure the 95% confidence interval. (Assume all populations are normally distributed.)

	Population		Sample Size	Sample Mean	Significance Level
	μ	σ	(N)		
(a)	36	8	16	38	.05
(b)	36	6	16	38	.05
(c)	36	4	16	38	.05
(d)	36	4	16	38	.01
(e)	34	4	16	38	.01

18. For each of the following studies, the samples were given an experimental treatment and the researchers compared their results to the general population. For each, carry out the full five steps of hypothesis testing for a two-tailed test at the .01 level, make a drawing of the distributions involved, and figure the 99% confidence interval.

	Population		Sample Size	Sample Mean
	μ	σ	(N)	
(a)	10	2	50	12
(b)	10	2	100	12
(c)	12	4	50	12
(d)	14	4	100	12

19. A researcher is interested in whether North Americans are able to identify emotions correctly in people from other cultures. It is known that, using a particular method of measurement, the accuracy ratings of adult North Americans in general are normally distributed with a mean of 82 and a variance of 20. This distribution is based on ratings made of emotions expressed by other North Americans. In the present study, however, the researcher arranges to test 50 adult North Americans rating emotions of individuals from Indonesia. The mean accuracy for these 50 individuals was 78. Using the .05 level, what should the researcher conclude? (a) Carry out the steps of hypothesis testing. (b) Make a drawing of the distributions involved. (c) Figure the 95% confidence interval. (d) Explain your answer to someone who knows about hypothesis testing with a sample of a single individual but knows nothing about hypothesis testing with a sample of more than one individual or about confidence intervals.

20. A psychologist is interested in the conditions that affect the number of dreams per month that people report in which they are alone. We will assume that based on extensive previous research, it is known that in the general population the number of such dreams per month follows a normal curve, with $\mu = 5$ and $\sigma = 4$. The researcher wants to test the prediction that the number of such dreams will be greater among people who have recently experienced a traumatic event. Thus, the psychologist studies 36 individuals who have recently experienced a traumatic event, having them keep a record of their dreams for a month. Their mean number of alone dreams is 8. Should you conclude that people who have recently had a traumatic experience have a significantly different number of dreams in which they are alone? (a) Carry out the steps of hypothesis testing (use the .05 level). (b) Make a drawing of the distributions involved. (c) Figure the

95% confidence interval. (d) Explain your answer to a person who has never had a course in statistics.

21. A government-sponsored telephone counseling service for adolescents tested whether the length of calls would be affected by a special telephone system that had a better sound quality. Over the past several years, the lengths of telephone calls (in minutes) were normally distributed with $\mu = 18$ and $\sigma = 8$. They arranged to have the special phone system loaned to them for one day. On that day, the mean length of the 46 calls they received was 21 minutes. Test whether the length of calls has changed using the 5% significance level. (a) Carry out the steps of hypothesis testing. (b) Make a drawing of the distributions involved. (c) Figure the 95% confidence interval. (d) Explain your answer to someone who knows about hypothesis testing with a sample of a single individual but knows nothing about hypothesis testing with samples of more than one individual or about confidence intervals.

22. Li et al. (2001) compared older (aged 60 to 75) and younger (aged 20 to 30) adults on the impact on memory of making some aspect of what they were doing more difficult. Figure 7–15 shows some of their results. In the figure caption they note that "Error bars represent ± 1 *SEM*" (standard error of the mean). Explain the meaning of this statement, using one of the error bars as an example, to a person who understands mean and standard deviation, but knows nothing else about statistics.

23. Bushman and Anderson (2001) studied news reports of the effects of media violence on aggression over a 30-year period. Some of their results are shown in Figure 7–16. In the figure caption they note that "Capped vertical bars denote 95% confidence intervals." Explain what this means, using one of the vertical

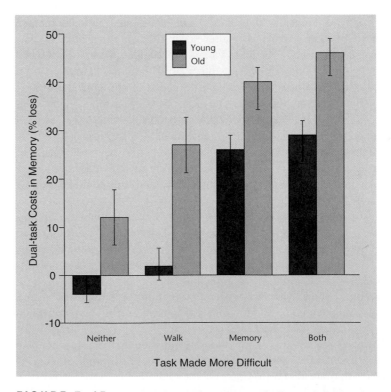

FIGURE 7–15 *Dual-task costs in memory recall as a function of age group and difficulty condition. Error bars represent ±1 SEM.*

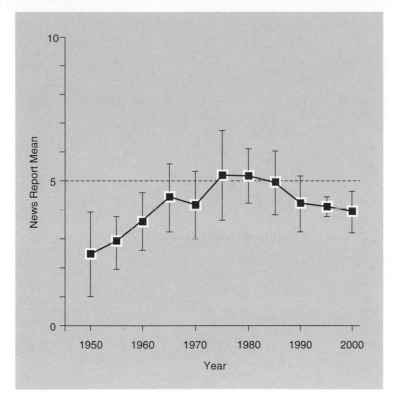

FIGURE 7–16 *News reports of the effect of media violence on aggression.* Note: *News report means are the average rated conclusions of newspaper and magazine articles. A rating of 0 indicates that the article said there was no relationship between violent media and aggression. A rating of 5 indicates that the article urged parents to discourage their children from consuming violent media. A rating of 10 indicates that the article said that viewing violence caused an increase in aggression. Capped vertical bars denote 95% confidence intervals. (Source: Li et al., 2001.)*

    bars as an example, to a person who understands standard error bars, but has never heard of confidence intervals.

24. Cut up 90 small slips of paper, and write each number from 1 to 9 on 10 slips each. Put the slips in a large bowl and mix them up. (a) Take out a slip, write down the number on it, and put it back. Do this 20 times. Make a histogram, and figure the mean and the variance of the result. You should get an approximately rectangular distribution. (b) Take two slips out, figure out their mean, write it down, and put the slips back.[6] Repeat this process 20 times. Make a histogram, then figure the mean and the variance of this distribution of means. The variance should be about half of the variance of this distribution of means. (c) Repeat the process again, this time taking three slips at a time. The distribution of means of three slips each should have a variance of about a third of the distribution of samples of one slip each. Also note that as the sample size increases, your distributions are getting closer to normal. (Had you begun with a normally distributed distribution of slips, your distributions of means would have been fairly close to normal regardless of the number of slips in each sample.)

[6]Technically, when taking the samples of two slips, this should be done by taking one, writing it down, putting it back, then taking the next, writing it down, and putting it back. You would consider these two scores as one sample for which you figure a mean. The same applies for samples of three slips. This is called sampling *with replacement*. However, with 90 slips in the bowl, taking two or three slips at a time and putting them back, will be a close enough approximation for this exercise and will save you some time.

CHAPTER 8

MAKING SENSE OF STATISTICAL SIGNIFICANCE:

EFFECT SIZE, DECISION ERRORS, AND STATISTICAL POWER

Are You Ready?
What You Need to have Mastered Before Starting This Chapter:

- Chapters 1, 2, 5, 6, and 7

Statistical significance is extremely important in psychology research, but sophisticated researchers and readers of research understand that there is more to the story of a study's result than $p < .05$ or *ns*. This chapter helps you become sophisticated about making sense of significance. Gaining this sophistication means learning about three closely interrelated issues: effect size, decision errors, and statistical power.

EFFECT SIZE

Consider again our example from Chapter 7 of giving special instructions to fifth graders taking a standard achievement test. In the hypothesis-testing process for this example, we compared two populations:

Population 1: Fifth graders receiving special instructions
Population 2: Fifth graders not receiving special instructions

The research hypothesis was that Population 1 would score higher than Population 2. Population 2 (that is, how fifth graders perform on this test when given in the usual way) is known to have a mean of 200. In the example, we said the researchers found that their sample of 64 fifth graders who were given the special instructions had a mean score on the test of 220. Following the hypothesis-testing procedure, we rejected the null hypothesis that the two populations are the same, because it was extremely unlikely that we would get a sample with a score as high as 220 from a population like Population 2. (See Figure 8–1, which is the same as Figure 7–7 from the last chapter.) Thus, we could conclude the result is "statistically significant." In this example, the best estimate of the mean of Population 2 is the sample's mean, which is 220. Thus, we can estimate that giving the special instructions has an average effect of increasing a fifth graders score by 20 points.

Now look again at Figure 8–1. Suppose the sample's score had been only 210. The result would still have been significant. (The standard deviation of the distribution of means was 6, so a sample mean of 210 would have a Z score of 1.67, which is more extreme than the cutoff in this example, which was 1.64). However, in this situation we would estimate that the average effect of the special instructions was only 10 points.

Notice that both results are significant, but in one example the effect is twice as big as in the other example. The point is that knowing statistical significance does not give you much information about the size of the effect. Significance tells us that the results of the experiment should convince us that there is an effect (that it is not "due to chance"). But significance does not tell us how big this nonchance effect is.

effect size (d)

Put another way, **effect size** is the amount that two populations do *not* overlap—that is, how much they are separated. In the fifth-grader example, Population 2 (the known population) had a mean of 200; based on our original sample's mean of 220, we estimated that Population 1 (those getting the special instructions) would have a mean of 220. The left curve in Figure 8–2 is the distribution (*of individual scores*) for Population 2, the right curve is the distribution for Population 1. Now look at Figure 8–3. Again, the left curve is for Population 2 and is the same as in Figure 8–2. However, this time the right curve for Population 1 is estimated based on a sample getting the special instructions with a mean of 210. Here you can see that the effect size is smaller, the two populations overlap even more. The amount that two populations do not overlap is called the effect size because it is the extent to which the experimental procedure has an *effect* of separating the two populations.

We often very much want to know not just whether a result is significant, but how big the effect is. As we will discuss later, an effect could well be statistically significant, but not of much practical significance. (That is, suppose an increase of only 10 points on the test is not considered very important.) Further, we may want to compare the results of this procedure to that of other procedures studied in the past. For these reasons, the latest edition of the *Publication Manual of the American Psychological Association* (APA, 2001), the accepted standard for how to present psychology research results, now states, "For the reader to fully understand the importance of your findings, it is almost always necessary to include some index of effect size. . . ."

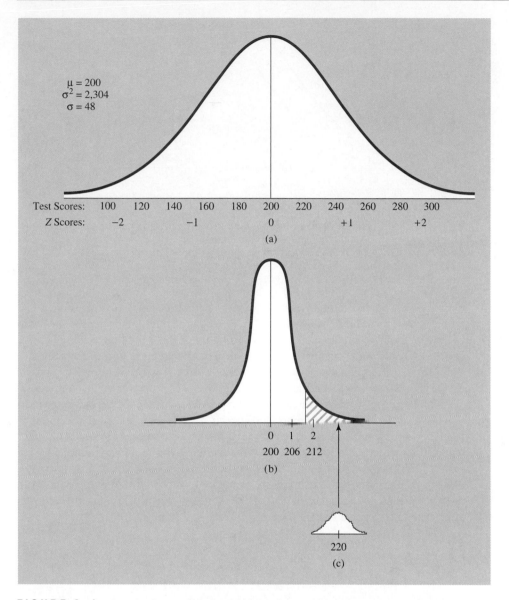

$\mu = 200$
$\sigma^2 = 2{,}304$
$\sigma = 48$

FIGURE 8-1 *For the fictional study of fifth graders' performance on a standard school achievement test, (a) the distribution of the population of individuals, (b) the distribution of means (the comparison distribution), and (c) the sample's distribution. (See discussion in Chapter 7.)*

(p. 25). Thus, whenever you use a hypothesis-testing procedure, you should also figure effect size. You should think of it as like a sixth step of our standard hypothesis-testing procedure: *figure the effect size.* As you will see later in the chapter, effect size plays an important role in two other important statistical topics—meta-analysis and power.

FIGURING EFFECT SIZE

With effect sizes, you can compare results from different studies, including studies that use different kinds of measures. For example, some other researchers may have tried special instructions on a completely different school achievement test in which the mean and standard deviation for those not getting the special instruction are

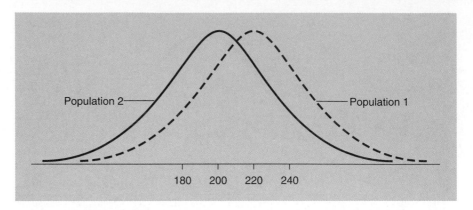

FIGURE 8–2   *For the fictional study of fifth graders' performance on a standard school achievement test, distribution of individuals for Population 1, those given the special instructions (right curve), and for Population 2, those not given special instructions (left curve). Population 1's mean is estimated based on the sample mean of 220, as originally described in Chapter 7; its standard deviation of 48 is assumed to be the same as Population 2's, which is known.*

quite different. Thus, knowing that the special instructions increased the score by 20 points is hard to compare to another study in which instructions increased the score by, say, 58 points—but on a completely different test that might have, for example, a mean of 1,000 and a standard deviation of 300. The solution to this problem is to use a *standardized effect size*—that is, to divide the raw score difference in points by the population standard deviation.

In the original fifth-grader example, the population standard deviation (of individuals) was 48. Thus, an increase of 20 points is 20/48 of a standard deviation, or .42. The increase of 58 on the test with a standard deviation of 300 would be a standardized increase of 58/300 or .19. (Notice that what you are doing is basically the same as figuring Z scores. And, like when figuring Z scores, you can compare apples to oranges in the sense that you can compare results on different measures with different means and standard deviations.) Usually, when psychologists refer to an effect size, they mean a standardized effect size.

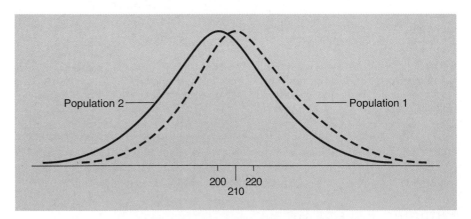

FIGURE 8–3   *For the fictional study of fifth graders' performance on a standard school achievement test, distribution of individuals for Population 1, those given the special instructions (right curve), and for Population 2, those not given special instructions (left curve). Population 1's mean is estimated based on a sample with a mean of 210; its standard deviation of 48 is assumed to be the same as Population 2's, which is known.*

Stated as a formula,

(8-1) $$d = \frac{\mu_1 - \mu_2}{\sigma}$$

In this formula, d is a symbol for effect size (also known as *Cohen's d*). (In later chapters, you will learn other measures of effect size, appropriate to different hypothesis-testing situations, that use other symbols.) μ_1 is the mean of Population 1 (the mean for the population that receives the experimental manipulation); μ_2 is the mean of Population 2 (the known population, the basis for the comparison distribution); and σ is the population standard deviation.

Notice that when figuring effect size, you don't use σ_M, the standard deviation of the distribution of means. Instead, you use σ, the standard deviation of the population of individuals. Also notice that you are only concerned with one population's standard deviation. This is because in hypothesis testing you usually assume that both populations have the same standard deviation. (We say more about this in later chapters.)

In our first example in this chapter (Figures 8–1 and 8–2), the mean of Population 1 was 220, the mean of Population 2 was 200, and the population standard deviation was 48. (In hypothesis-testing situations you don't know the mean of Population 1, so you actually use an estimated mean; thus, you are actually figuring an estimated effect size.). Using these numbers,

$$d = (\mu_1 - \mu_2)/\sigma = (220 - 200)/48 = 20/48 = .42.$$

For the example in which the sample mean was 210, we thus estimated Population 1's mean to be 210. Thus,

$$d = (\mu_1 - \mu_2)/\sigma = (210 - 200)/48 = 10/48 = .21.$$

However, suppose the procedure actually reduced the score—so that those who were given the special instructions had a mean of 170.

$$d = (\mu_1 - \mu_2)/\sigma = (170 - 200)/48 = -30/48 = -.63.$$

The minus sign means that the effect is a decrease.

EFFECT SIZE CONVENTIONS

What should you consider to be a "big" effect, and what is a "small" effect? Jacob Cohen (1988, 1992), a psychologist who developed the effect size measure among other major contributions to statistical methods, has helped solve this problem. Cohen came up with some **effect size conventions** based on the effects found in psychology research in general. Specifically, Cohen recommended that for the kind of situation we are considering in this chapter, we should think of a small effect size as about .2. With a d of .2, the populations of individuals have an overlap of about 85%. This small effect size of .2 is, for example, the average difference in height between 15- and 16-year-old girls (see Figure 8–4a), which is about a half-inch difference with a standard deviation of about 2.1 inches. Cohen considered a medium effect size to be .5, which means an overlap of about 67%. This is about the average difference in heights between 14- and 18-year-old girls (see Figure 8–4b). Finally, Cohen defined a large effect size as .8. This is only about a 53% overlap. It is about

effect size conventions

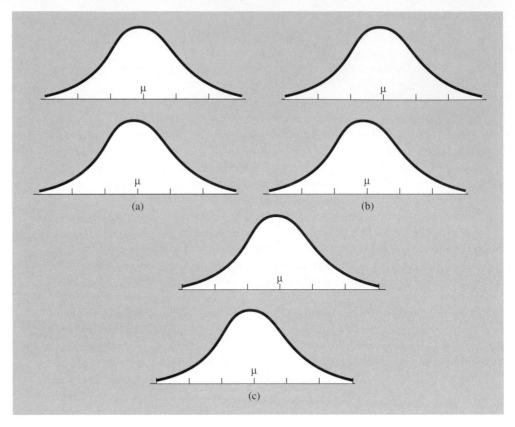

FIGURE 8–4   *Comparisons of pairs of population distributions of individuals showing Cohen's conventions for effect size: (a) small effect size (d = .2), (b) medium effect size (d = .5), and (c) large effect size (d = .8).*

TABLE 8–1	Summary of Cohen's Effect Size Conventions for Mean Differences

Verbal Description	Effect Size (d)
Small	.20
Medium	.50
Large	.80

the average difference in height between 13- and 18-year-old girls (see Figure 8–4c). These three effect size conventions are summarized in Table 8–1.

Consider another example. As we noted earlier in the book, many IQ tests have a standard deviation of 16 points. An experimental procedure with a small effect size would create an increase in IQ of 3.2 IQ points. (A difference of 3.2 IQ points between the mean of the population who goes through the experimental procedure and the mean of the population that does not, divided by the population standard deviation of 16, gives an effect size of .20. That is, $d = 3.2/16 = .20$.) An experimental procedure with a medium effect size would increase IQ by 8 points. An experimental procedure with a large effect size would increase IQ by 12.8 points.

Cohen's effect sizes provide a standard for deciding on the importance of the effect of a study in relation to what is typical in psychology.

META-ANALYSIS

meta-analysis

Meta-analysis is an important development in recent years in statistics that has had a profound effect on psychology. This procedure combines results from different studies, even results using different methods of measurement. When combining results, the crucial thing combined is the effect sizes. As an example, a social psychologist might be interested in the effects of cross-race friendships on prejudice, a topic on which there has been a large number of studies. Using meta-analysis, the social psychologist could combine the results of these studies. This would provide an overall effect size. It would also tell how effect sizes differ for studies done in different countries or about prejudice towards different ethnic groups. (For an example of such a meta-analysis, see Pettigrew & Meertens, 1997. For another example of meta-analysis, see Box 8–1.)

Reviews of the collection of studies on a particular topic that use meta-analysis are an alternative to the traditional "narrative" literature review article. Such traditional reviews describe and evaluate each study and then attempt to draw some overall conclusion. Table 8–2 is based on what was being done more than 15 years ago. Since then, the number of reviews using meta-analysis has increased dramatically in recent years but the emphasis on applied topics remains.

BOX 8–1   Effect Sizes for Relaxation and Meditation: A Restful Meta-Analysis

In the 1970s and 1980s, the results of research on meditation and relaxation were the subject of considerable controversy. Eppley et al. (1989) decided to look at the issue systematically by conducting a meta-analysis of the effects of various relaxation techniques on trait anxiety (that is, ongoing anxiety as opposed to a temporary state). Eppley and colleagues chose trait anxiety for their meta-analysis because it is a definite problem related to many other mental health issues, yet in itself is fairly consistent from test to test with the same measure and from one measure to another measure of it.

Following the usual procedure, the researchers culled the scientific literature for studies—not only research journals but also books and unpublished doctoral dissertations. Finding all the relevant research is one of the most difficult parts of meta-analysis.

To find the "bottom line," Eppley et al. compared effect sizes for each of the four main methods of meditation and relaxation that have been studied in systematic research. The result was that the average effect size for the 35 Transcendental Meditation (TM) studies was .70 (meaning an average difference of .70 standard deviation in anxiety scores between those who practiced this meditation procedure versus those in the control groups). This effect size was significantly larger than the average effect size of .28 for the 44 studies on all other types of meditation, the average effect size of .38 for the 30 studies on "progressive relaxation" (a widely used method by clinical psychologists), and the average effect size of .40 for the 37 studies on other forms of relaxation.

But the meta-analysis had really just begun. There were many subvariables of interest. For example, looking at different populations of research participants, they discovered that people who were screened to be highly anxious contributed more to the effect size, and prison populations and younger participants seemed to gain more from TM. There was little or no impact on effect size of the skill of the instructors, expectations of the subjects, whether subjects had volunteered or been randomly assigned to conditions, experimenter bias (the TM results were actually stronger when any apparently pro-TM researchers' studies were eliminated), the various measures of anxiety, and the research designs.

The researchers thought that one clue to TM's high performance might be that techniques involving concentration produced a significantly smaller effect, whereas TM makes a point of teaching an "effortless, spontaneous" method. Also, TM uses Sanskrit mantras (special sounds) said to come from a very old tradition and selected for each student by the instructor. Results were lower for methods employing randomly selected Sanskrit sounds or personally selected English words.

Whatever the reasons, the authors conclude that there are "grounds for optimism that at least some current treatment procedures can effectively reduce trait anxiety" (p. 973). So if you are prone to worry about little matters like statistics exams, consider these results.

| TABLE 8–2 | Number of Meta-Analytic Articles Published in Various Fields of Psychology (Through Mid-1987) |

Subdiscipline	Frequency
Education	115
Psychological therapy	100
Industrial/organizational psychology	44
Social psychology	43
Sex differences	28
Health psychology	27
Mental health	26
Personality	16
Experimental psychology	13
Developmental psychology	8

Note: From Cooper, H. M., & Lemke, K. M. (1991), tab. 1. On the role of meta-analysis in personality and social psychology. *Personality and Social Psychology Bulletin, 17,* 245–251. Copyright, 1991, by the Society for Personality and Social Psychology, Inc. Reprinted by permission of Sage Publications Inc.

HOW ARE YOU DOING?

1. What does effect size add to just knowing whether or not a result is significant?
2. Why do researchers usually use a standardized effect size?
3. Write the formula for effect size in the situation we have been considering and define each of the symbols.
4. On a standard test, the population is known to have a mean of 500 and a standard deviation of 100. Those receiving an experimental treatment have a mean of 540. What is the effect size?
5. (a) Why are effect size conventions useful? (b) What are the effect size conventions for d?
6. (a) What is meta-analysis? (b) What is the role of effect size in a meta-analysis?

ANSWERS:

1. A significant result can be just barely big enough to be significant or much bigger than necessary to be significant. Thus, knowing effect size tells you how big the effect is.
2. It makes results of studies using different measures comparable.
3. $d = (\mu_1 - \mu_2)/\sigma$. d is effect size; μ_1 is the mean of Population 1 (the mean for the population that receives the experimental manipulation); μ_2 is the mean of Population 2 (the known population, the basis for the comparison distribution); and σ is the population standard deviation.
4. $d = (\mu_1 - \mu_2)/\sigma = (540 - 500)/100 = .4$.
5. (a) Effect size conventions allow you to compare the effect size of a particular study to what is typically found in psychology research. (b) Small = .2, medium = .5, large = .8.
6. (a) A systematic procedure for combining results of different studies. (b) Meta-analyses usually come up with average effect sizes across studies and compare effect sizes for different subgroups of studies.

DECISION ERRORS

Another crucial topic for making sense of statistical significance is the kinds of errors that are possible in the hypothesis-testing process. The kind of error we consider here is about how, in spite of doing all your figuring correctly, your conclusions from hypothesis-testing can still be incorrect. It is *not* about making mistakes in calculations or even about using the wrong procedures. That is, **decision errors** are situations in which the right procedures lead to the wrong decisions.

decision errors

Decision errors are possible in hypothesis-testing because you are making decisions about populations based on information in samples. The whole hypothesis-testing process is based on probabilities. The hypothesis-testing process is set up to make the probability of decision errors as small as possible. For example, we only decide to reject the null hypothesis if a sample's mean is so extreme that there is a very small probability (say, less than 5%) that we could have gotten such an extreme sample if the null hypothesis is true. But a very small probability is not the same as a zero probability! Thus, in spite of your best intentions, decision errors are always possible.

There are two kinds of decision errors in hypothesis testing: Type I error and Type II error.[1]

TYPE I ERROR

You make a **Type I error** if you reject the null hypothesis when in fact the null hypothesis is true. Or, to put it in terms of the research hypothesis, you make a Type I error when you conclude that the study supports the research hypothesis when in reality the research hypothesis is false.

Type I error

Suppose you carried out a study in which you had set the significance level cutoff at a very lenient probability level, such as 20%. This would mean that it would not take a very extreme result to reject the null hypothesis. If you did many studies like this, you would often (about 20% of the time) be deciding to consider the research hypothesis supported when you should not. That is, you would have a 20% chance of making a Type I error.

Even when you set the probability at the conventional .05 or .01 levels, you can still make a Type I error sometimes (5% or 1% of the time). Consider again the example of giving special instructions to make fifth graders' perform better on a standard achievement test. Suppose the special instructions in reality make no difference whatsoever. However, in randomly picking a sample of fifth graders to study, the researchers might just happen to pick a group of fifth graders who would do unusually well on the test no matter what kind of instructions they received. Randomly selecting a sample like this is unlikely, because in general a random sample, especially one of 64 individuals, will have a mean that is close to the population mean. But such extreme samples are possible, and should this happen, the researchers would reject the null hypothesis and conclude that the special instructions do make a difference. Their decision to reject the null hypothesis would be wrong—a Type I error. Of course, the researchers could not know they had made a decision error of this kind. What reassures researchers is that they know from the logic of hypothesis testing that the probability of making such a decision error is kept low (less than 5% if you use the .05 significance level).

---

[1]You may also occasionally hear about a Type III error. This is concluding there is a significant result in a particular direction, when the true effect is in the opposite direction.

Still, the fact that Type I errors can happen at all is of serious concern to psychologists, who might construct entire theories and research programs, not to mention practical applications, based on a conclusion from hypothesis testing that is in fact mistaken. It is because these errors are of such serious concern that they are called Type I.

As we have noted, researchers cannot tell when they have made a Type I error. However, they can try to carry out studies so that the chance of making a Type I error is as small as possible.

What is the chance of making a Type I error? It is the same as the significance level you set. If you set the significance level at $p < .05$, you are saying you will reject the null hypothesis if there is less than a 5% (.05) chance that you could have gotten your result if the null hypothesis were true. When rejecting the null hypothesis in this way, you are allowing up to a 5% chance that you got your results even though the null hypothesis was actually true. That is, you are allowing a 5% chance of a Type I error.

alpha (α)

The significance level, which is the chance of making a Type I error, is called **alpha** (the Greek letter α). The lower the alpha, the smaller the chance of a Type I error. Researchers who do not want to take a lot of risk set alpha lower than .05, such as $p < .001$. In this way the result of a study has to be very extreme in order for the hypothesis testing process to reject the null hypothesis.

Using a .001 significance level is like buying insurance against making a Type I error. However, as when buying insurance, the better the protection, the higher the cost. There is a cost in setting the significance level at too extreme a level. We turn to that cost next.

TYPE II ERROR

If you set a very stringent significance level, such as .001, you run a different kind of risk. With a very stringent significance level, you may carry out a study in which in reality the research hypothesis is true, but the result does not come out extreme enough to reject the null hypothesis. Thus, the decision error you would make is in *not* rejecting the null hypothesis when in reality the null hypothesis is false. To put this in terms of the research hypothesis, you make this kind of decision error when the hypothesis-testing procedure leads you to decide that the results of the study are inconclusive when in reality the research hypothesis is true. This is called a **Type II**

Type II error
beta (β)

error. The probability of making a Type II error is called **beta** (the Greek letter β). (Do not confuse this beta with the standardized regression coefficient discussed in Chapter 4, which is also called beta.)

Consider again our fifth grader example. Suppose that, in truth, giving the special instructions *does* make fifth graders do better on the test. However, in conducting your particular study, the results are not strong enough to allow you to reject the null hypothesis. Perhaps the random sample that you selected to try out the new instructions happened to include mainly fifth graders who do very poorly on this kind of test regardless of the instructions given. As we have seen, even though the special instructions might help them do better than they would have otherwise, their scores may still not be much higher than the average of all fifth graders. The results would not be significant. Having decided not to reject the null hypothesis, and thus refusing to draw a conclusion, would be a Type II error.

Type II errors especially concern psychologists interested in practical applications, because a Type II error could mean that a valuable practical procedure is not used.

As with a Type I error, you cannot know when you have made a Type II error. But researchers can try to carry out studies so as to reduce the probability of making one. One way of buying insurance against a Type II error is to set a very lenient significance level, such as $p < .10$ or even $p < .20$. In this way, even if a study results in only a very small effect, the results have a good chance of being significant. There is a cost to this insurance policy too.

RELATION OF TYPE I AND TYPE II ERRORS

When it comes to setting significance levels, protecting against one kind of decision error increases the chance of making the other. The insurance policy against Type I error (setting a significance level of, say, .001) has the cost of increasing the chance of making a Type II error. (This is because with a stringent significance level like .001, even if the research hypothesis is true, the results have to be quite strong to be extreme enough to reject the null hypothesis.) The insurance policy against Type II error (setting a significance level of, say, .20) has the cost of increasing the chance of making a Type I error. (This is because with a level of significance like .20, even if the null hypothesis is true, it is fairly easy to get a significant result just by accidentally getting a sample that is higher or lower than the general population before doing the study.)

The trade-off between these two conflicting concerns usually is worked out by compromise—thus the standard 5% and 1% significance levels.

SUMMARY OF POSSIBLE OUTCOMES OF HYPOTHESIS TESTING

The entire issue of possibly correct or mistaken conclusions in hypothesis testing is diagramed in Table 8–3. Along the top of this table are the two possibilities about whether the null hypothesis or the research hypothesis is really true. (You never actually know this.) Along the side is whether, after hypothesis testing, you decide that the research hypothesis is supported (reject the null hypothesis) or decide that the results are inconclusive (do not reject the null hypothesis). Table 8–3 shows that there are two ways to be correct and two ways to be in error in any hypothesis-testing situation. We have more to say about these possibilities after we consider the topic of statistical power.

TABLE 8–3   **Possible Correct and Incorrect Decisions in Hypothesis Testing**

		Real Situation (in practice, unknown)	
		Null Hypothesis True	*Research Hypothesis True*
Conclusion Using Hypothesis-testing Procedure	*Research hypothesis supported (reject null hypothesis)*	Error (Type I) α	Correct decision
	Study is inconclusive (do not reject null hypothesis)	Correct decision	Error (Type II) β

HOW ARE YOU DOING?

1. What is a decision error?
2. (a) What is a Type I error? (b) Why is it possible? (c) What is its probability? (d) What is this probability called?
3. (a) What is a Type II error? (b) Why is it possible? (c) What is its probability called?
4. If you set a lenient alpha level (say .25), what is the effect on the probability of (a) Type I error and (b) Type II error?
5. If you set a stringent alpha level (say .001) , what is the effect on the probability of (a) Type I error and (b) Type II error?

ANSWERS:

1. A decision error is a conclusion from hypothesis testing that does not match reality.
2. (a) Rejecting the null hypothesis (and thus supporting the research hypothesis) when the null hypothesis is actually true (and the research hypothesis false) is a Type I error. (b) You reject the null hypothesis when a sample's result is so extreme it is unlikely you would have gotten that result if the null hypothesis is true. However, even though it is unlikely, it is still possible. (c) Its probability is the significance level (such as .05). (d) Alpha.
3. (a) Failing to reject the null hypothesis (and thus failing to support the research hypothesis) when the null hypothesis is actually false (and the research hypothesis true) is a Type II error. (b) You reject the null hypothesis when a sample's result is so extreme it is unlikely you would have gotten that result if the null hypothesis is true. However, the null hypothesis could be false, but the true population mean not different enough from the known population to produce samples extreme enough to reject the null hypothesis. (c) Beta.
4. (a) It is high; (b) it is low.
5. (a) It is low; (b) it is high.

STATISTICAL POWER

statistical power

Power is the ability to achieve your goals. A goal of a researcher conducting a study is to get a significant result—but only *if* the research hypothesis really is true. The **statistical power** of a research study is the probability that the study will produce a statistically significant result if the research hypothesis is true.

Notice that the power of an experiment is about the situation *if* the research hypothesis is true. If the research hypothesis is false, you do not want to get significant results. (That would be a Type I error.) Remember, however, even if the research hypothesis is true, an experiment will not automatically give a significant result—the particular sample that happens to be selected from the population may not turn out to be extreme enough to reject the null hypothesis.

Statistical power is important for several reasons. As you will learn later in the chapter, figuring power when planning a study helps you determine how many participants you need. As you will also learn later in the chapter, understanding power is extremely important when you read a research article, particularly for making sense of results that are not significant or results that are statistically but not practically significant.

Consider once again our example of giving special instructions to fifth graders taking a standard achievement test. Recall that we compared two populations:

Population 1: Fifth graders receiving special instructions
Population 2: Fifth graders not receiving special instructions

Also recall that the research hypothesis was that Population 1 would score higher than Population 2.

The top curve in Figure 8–5 shows the distributions of means for one possible situation the researchers might predict in which this research hypothesis would be true.

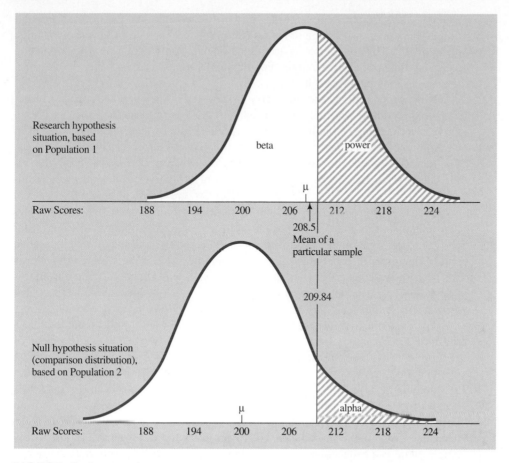

FIGURE 8-5 *Distributions of mean test scores of 64 fifth graders from a fictional study of fifth graders taking a standard achievement test. The lower distribution of means is based on a known distribution of individual test scores of fifth graders who do not receive any special instructions (Population 2). The upper distribution of means is based on a predicted distribution of individual test scores of fifth graders who receive the special instructions (Population 1). The researchers predict a mean of 208 for this population. Shaded sections of both distributions show the area in which the null hypothesis will be rejected.*

The bottom curve shows the distribution of means for Population 2. (Be careful: When discussing effect size, we showed figures, such as Figures 8–2 and 8–3, for populations of individuals; now we are back to focusing on distributions of means.)

The bottom distribution of means is a comparison distribution, the distribution of means that you would expect for both populations if the null hypothesis were true. The shaded part of this bottom distribution is the area where you would reject the null hypothesis if, as a result of your study, the mean of your sample was in this area. The shaded rejection area begins at 209.84 (a Z score of 1.64), taking up 5% of this comparison distribution.

The top curve is the distribution of means that the researchers *predict* for the population receiving special instructions (Population 1). We have never considered this predicted distribution before. This was partly because this population is quite imaginary—*unless* the research hypothesis is true. If the null hypothesis is true, the true distribution for Population 1 is the same as the distribution based on Population 2. The Population 1 distribution would not be set off to the right.

However, to learn about power, we now consider the situation in which a researcher predicts the research hypothesis to be true. In this situation, for this example, the mean of Population 1 is farther to the right than the mean of Population 2. The upper distribution of means (for predicted Population 1) is shown with a mean of 208. The comparison distribution's mean is only 200. Thus, the population receiving the special instructions (Population 1) is predicted to have, on the average, scores that are 8 points higher.

Now, suppose the researchers carry out the study. They give the special instructions to a randomly selected group of 64 fifth graders and find their mean score on the test. Remember, if the research hypothesis is true as they predict, the mean of their group of 64 students is from a distribution like the upper distribution of means.

In this example, however, this upper distribution of means (from the researchers' prediction about Population 1) is only slightly to the right of the comparison distribution. That is, the psychologists are predicting that the special instructions will produce only a small increase in scores (8 points). What this picture tells us is that most of the means from this upper distribution will not be far enough to the right on the lower distribution to reject the null hypothesis. Less than half of the upper distribution is shaded. Put another way, if the research hypothesis is true as the researchers predict, the sample we study is a random sample from this Population 1 distribution of means. However, there is less than a 50–50 chance that the random sample from this distribution will be in the shaded area.

For example, suppose the particular sample of 64 fifth graders studied had a mean of 208.5, as shown by the arrow in the figure. However, you need a mean of at least 209.84 to reject the null hypothesis. Thus, the result of this experiment would not be statistically significant. It would not be significant even though the research hypothesis really is true. (This is how you would make a Type II error.)

It is entirely possible that the researchers might happen to select a sample from Population 1 with a mean far enough to the right (that is, with a high enough mean test score) to be in the shaded area. However, given the way we have set up the example, there is a better-than-even chance that the study will *not* turn out significant, *even though we know the research hypothesis is true.* (Of course, once again, the researcher would not know this.) When a study like the one in this example has only a small chance of being significant even if the research hypothesis is true, we say the study has *low power.*

Suppose, on the other hand, the situation was one in which the upper curve was expected to be way to the right of the lower curve, so that almost any sample taken from the upper curve would be in the shaded rejection area in the lower curve. (Figure 8–7, later in the chapter, is an example of this kind.) In that situation, the study would have high power.

AN EXAMPLE

Consider again Figure 8–5, showing the distributions of means for the fifth-grader testing example. The population of individuals not receiving special instructions had a mean of 200 and a standard deviation of 48 (a variance of 2,304). The researchers studied a sample of 64 fifth graders. Thus, in Chapter 7 we figured the standard deviation of the distribution of means to be 6; that is, $\sqrt{2{,}304/64} = 6$. We have presumed that our researchers predicted the special instructions would raise the mean to 208. Figure 8–6 shows the Z scores for both distributions based on these numbers.

In Chapter 7, we found that using the 5% significance level, one-tailed, you need a Z score for the mean of your sample of at least 1.64 to reject the null hypothesis. Using the formula for converting Z scores to raw scores, this comes out to a raw score of 209.84; that is, 200 + (1.64)(6) = 209.84. This cutoff score is 1.84 test

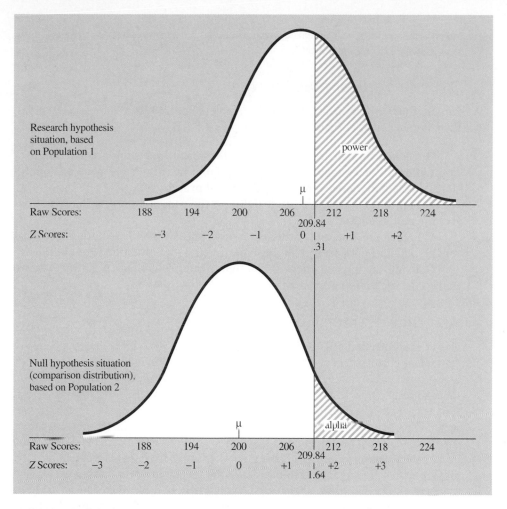

Research hypothesis
situation, based
on Population 1

power

μ

Raw Scores:	188	194	200	206	212	218	224

209.84

Z Scores:		−3	−2	−1	0	+1	+2	

.31

Null hypothesis situation
(comparison distribution),
based on Population 2

μ

alpha

Raw Scores:	188	194	200	206	212	218	224

209.84

Z Scores:	−3	−2	−1	0	+1	+2	+3

1.64

FIGURE 8–6 *Distributions of means of 64 test scores based on predicted (upper) and known (lower) populations of individuals. (From a fictional study of fifth graders taking a standard achievement test.) Scores are shown on both distributions for the significance cutoff for the lower distribution (the cutoff for p < .05, one-tailed). Power = 38%.*

points above the overall mean of 208 on that distribution, giving a Z score on that distribution of .31; that is, $(209.84 - 208)/6 = .31$. The normal curve table (Table A–1 in Appendix A) shows that 12% of a normal curve is between the mean and a Z of .31. Thus, 38% remains beyond a Z of .31. In other words, 38% of the predicted Population 1 distribution of means is above a Z score of .31 (and therefore 38% of the means are above a raw score of 209.84).

Here is the conclusion: Assuming the researchers' prediction is correct, the researchers have only a 38% chance that the sample of 64 students they study will have a mean high enough to make the result significant. That is, there is only a 38% chance of getting a mean higher than 209.84, even assuming the research hypothesis is true. Hence, we say that the power of this experiment is 38%.

Notice that power, the probability of getting a significant result if the research hypothesis is true, is just the opposite of beta, the probability of not getting a significant result if the research hypothesis is true. Thus, beta is 1 − power. In this example, power is 38%. Thus, beta for this example is 62% (that is, $1 - 38\% = 62\%$).

Finally, notice that the way we figured power had nothing to do with the actual results of the study. It was based on predictions. In fact, researchers usually figure power *before* doing the study.

STEPS FOR FIGURING POWER

In our situation (the mean of a single sample compared to a known population), there are four steps to figure power:

❶ Gather the needed information: the mean and standard deviation of Population 2 (the comparison distribution) and the predicted mean of Population 1 (the population given the experimental procedure).

❷ Figure the raw-score cutoff point on the comparison distribution to reject the null hypothesis.

❸ Figure the Z score for this same point, but on the distribution of means for the population that receives the experimental manipulation (Population 1).

❹ Using the normal curve table, figure the probability of getting a score more extreme than that Z score.[2]

ANOTHER EXAMPLE

Consider another fictional example. A large organization is trying to decide whether to start a new health promotion policy. Under this new policy, employees are examined and given needed training and advice on various health-related behaviors (exercise, diet, smoking, etc.). To test the effectiveness of the policy, the company's organizational psychologists plan the following study. Eighty employees will be randomly selected to participate. They will be measured at the end of a year on a standard test of their overall health. The researchers know (from past records) that in the organization as a whole, the mean score on the standard health test is 58, the standard deviation is 14, and the scores are normally distributed. For the program to be worth implementing, there must be an improvement of at least 5 points (that is, the predicted mean has to be at least 63). The organizational psychologists plan to use the .05 significance level. The distributions of means for the known populations (Population 2) and for the minimum-useful-improvement situation (Population 1) are shown in Figure 8–7.

What is the power of this experiment?

❶ Gather the needed information. In this example, the mean of the comparison distribution is 58. The predicted mean (that is, in this case, the minimal useful improvement situation) of the population that will receive the experimental procedure is 63. The variance of the population is 196 (that is, $14^2 = 196$). Thus, the variance of the distribution of means, the comparison distribution, is 2.45 (that is, 196/80 = 2.45). This gives a standard deviation of 1.57 (that is, $\sqrt{2.45} = 1.57$).

❷ Figure the raw-score cutoff point on the comparison distribution to reject the null hypothesis. For the 5% significance level, one-tailed, the Z score cutoff is +1.64. A Z of +1.64 equals a raw score of 60.57; that is, 58 + (1.64)(1.57) = 60.57. Thus, in the lower curve (the comparison distribution) in Figure 8–7, we have shaded the area to the right of 60.57. This is the alpha region.

Tip for Success

When figuring power, it is very helpful to make a diagram of the two distributions, similar to that in Figure 8–6.

WHAT D

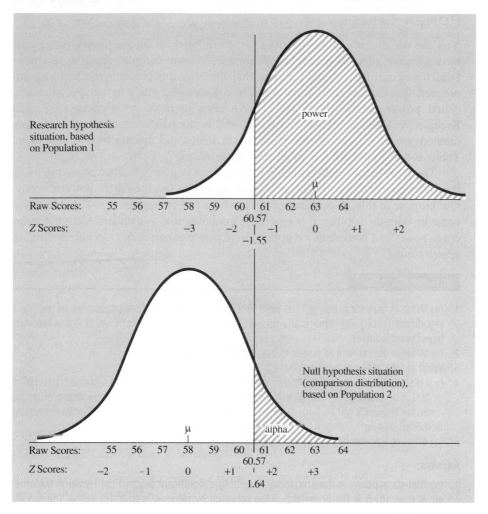

Row

Z Sc

FIGU
tions fo

FIGURE 8-7 *Distributions of means of 80 scores based on predicted (upper) and known (lower) distributions of populations in a fictional study of employees receiving a new health promotion program. Z scores and raw scores are shown on both distributions for the significance cutoff point on the lower distribution (significance cutoff based on p < .05, one-tailed).*

❹ U
than
plus
(b)
(c) E
5. (a)
sam
situ:

WH/

The st
fect si
(the sa
one-ta

EFF

Figure
which

❸ **Figure the Z score for this same point, but on the distribution of means for the population that receives the experimental manipulation (Population 1).** On this distribution (based on the predicted scores for Population 1), a raw score of 60.57 is the same as a Z score of −1.55; that is, (60.57 − 63)/1.57 = −1.55. Thus, in the upper curve in Figure 8–7, we have shaded the area to the right of −1.55. This shaded area shows the power of the study, the area in which a mean of an actual sample would turn out to be significant on the comparison distribution.

❹ **Using the normal curve table, figure the probability of getting a score more extreme than that Z score.** The normal curve table shows about 44% between the mean and a Z of 1.55. We are interested in all the area to the right of −1.55. Thus, there is a total of 44% between −1.55 and the mean, plus the 50% above the mean. This adds up to 94%. The power of this experiment is 94%. (Beta is thus 1 − 94% = 6%.)

1, the upper curve) would have a mean score 8 points higher than fifth graders in general (Population 2, the lower curve). Figure 8–9 shows the same study for a situation in which the researchers predicted that those given the special instructions would have a mean 16 points higher than fifth graders in general. Comparing Figure 8–9 to Figure 8–6, you are more likely to get a significant result in the situation shown in Figure 8–9. In fact, we figured earlier that the Figure 8–6 situation, in which the researchers predict a mean of 208, has a power of 35%. However, the Figure 8–9 situation, in which the researchers predict a mean of 216, comes out to a power of 85%. In any study, the bigger the difference you expect between the two populations, the more power in the study.

The difference in means between populations we saw earlier is part of what goes in to effect size. Thus, the bigger the effect size, the greater the power. The effect size for the situation in Figure 8–6, in which the researchers predicted Population 1 to have a mean of 208, is .17. That is, $d = (\mu_1 - \mu_2)/\sigma = (208 - 200)/48 =$

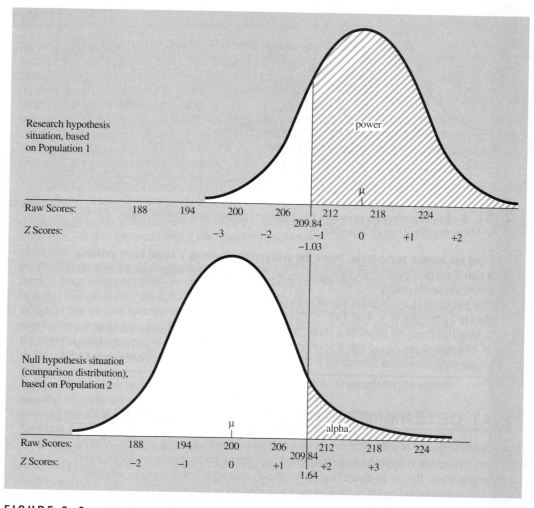

FIGURE 8–9 *Distributions of means of 64 test scores based on predicted (upper) and known (lower) distributions of populations of individuals. (From a fictional study of fifth graders receiving special instructions prior to taking a standard achievement test.) Scores are shown on both distributions for the significance cutoff on the lower distribution (the cutoff for p <.05, one-tailed). In this example, the predicted mean of the upper distribution is 216. Power = 85%.*

$8/48 = .17$. The effect size for the situation in Figure 8–9, in which the researchers predicted Population 1 to have a mean of 216, is .33. That is, $d = (\mu_1 - \mu_2)/\sigma = (216 - 200)/48 = .33$.

Effect size, however, is also affected by the population standard deviation. The smaller the standard deviation, the bigger the effect size. In terms of the formulas, this is because if you divide by a smaller number, the result is bigger. In terms of the actual distributions, this is because if two distributions which are separated are narrower, they overlap less. Figure 8–10 shows two distributions of means based on

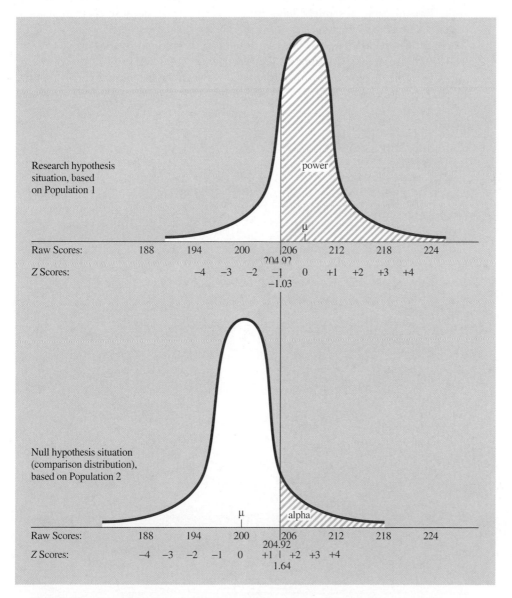

FIGURE 8–10 *Distributions of means of 64 test scores based on predicted (upper) and known (lower) distributions of populations of individuals. (From a fictional study of fifth graders taking a standard achievement test.) Scores are shown on both distributions for the significance cutoff on the lower distribution (the cutoff for p <.05, one-tailed). In this example, the predicted population mean is 208 but the population standard deviation is half as large as that shown for this example in previous figures. Power = 85%.*

the same example. However, this time we have changed the example so that the variance is much smaller (the standard deviation in the distribution of means is exactly half of what it was). In this version, the predicted mean is the original 208. However, both distributions of means are much narrower. Therefore, there is much less overlap between the upper curve and the lower curve (the comparison distribution). The result is that the power is 85%, much higher than in the original situation. The idea here is that the smaller the variance, the greater the power.

Overall, these examples illustrate the general principle that the less overlap between the two distributions, the more likely that a study will give a significant result. Two distributions might have little overlap either because there is a large difference between their means (as in Figure 8–9) or because they have so little variance that even with a small mean difference they do not overlap much (Figure 8–10). This principle is summarized more generally in Figure 8–11.

Notice that these two factors, difference between the means and variance of the population, are exactly what goes in to figuring effect size. That is, effect size is the

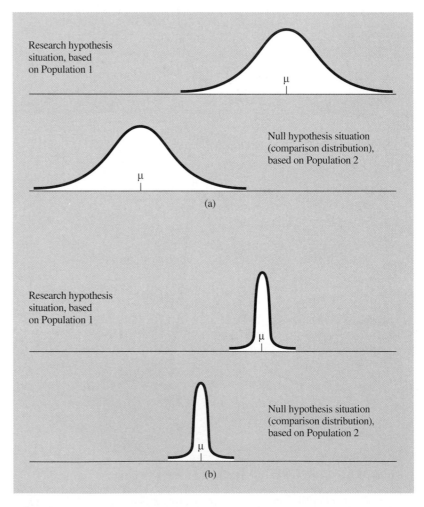

FIGURE 8–11 *The predicted and comparison distributions of means might have little overlap (and thus the study would have high power) because either (a) the two means are very different or (b) the variance is very small.*

difference between the means divided by the population standard deviation— $d = (\mu_1 - \mu_2)/\sigma$. Thus, the larger the difference expected between the two population means (that is, the larger $\mu_1 - \mu_2$ is), the greater the effect size; and the smaller the variance within the two populations (that is, the smaller σ^2 is and thus, the smaller σ is), the greater the effect size. And the greater the effect size, the greater the power. In fact, you may have noticed that we increased the power to exactly 85% both by doubling the predicted increase in means (as shown in Figure 8–9) and by cutting in half the standard deviation of the distribution of means (as in Figure 8–10). This is because in both examples we have the same effect size of .33. In the Figure 8–10 example, the standard deviation of the population distribution was 24. Thus, $d = (\mu_1 - \mu_2)/\sigma = (208 - 200)/24 = .33$.

When figuring power in advance of doing a study, the difference between the means of the two populations is a difference between the known population mean (Population 2) and the researcher's prediction for the population to be given the experimental manipulation (Population 1). This prediction is based on some precise theory, on previous experience with research of this kind, or on what would be the smallest difference that would be useful. In the situations we have considered so far, the population standard deviation, the other number you need to figure the effect size, is known in advance.

FIGURING POWER FROM PREDICTED EFFECT SIZES

Sometimes, instead of predicting a particular mean, researchers predict an effect size. Especially when studying something for the first time, researchers make this prediction using Cohen's conventions. That is, they may have only a fairly vague idea of how big an effect to expect, so if they expect a small effect, for example, they use a predicted effect size of .2.

Once the researchers have predicted an effect size, in whatever way, they can use their predicted effect size to figure the predicted mean (the mean for Population 1), and then figure power in the usual way. Consider our example in which the known population (Population 2) has a mean of 200 and a standard deviation of 48. Suppose the researchers predict an effect size of .2 (a small effect size, using Cohen's conventions). In this situation, the predicted mean has to be enough higher than 200 so that the overall effect size, after dividing by 48, comes out to .2. That is, the mean difference has to increase by .2 standard deviations. In the example .2 of 48 is 9.6. Thus, the predicted mean has to be 9.6 higher than the known mean. In this example, the known mean is 200, so the predicted mean for an effect size of .2 would be 209.6.

Stating this principle in terms of a formula,

(8-2)
$$\text{Predicted } \mu_1 = \mu_2 + (d)(\sigma).$$

| Predicted mean of the population to which the experimental procedure will be applied is the known population mean plus the result of multiplying the predicted effect size times the known population standard deviation. |

Suppose in our example the researchers predicted an effect size of .5 (a medium effect size). Using the formula,

$$\text{Predicted } \mu_1 = \mu_2 + (d)(\sigma) = 200 + (.5)(48) = 200 + 24 = 224.$$

Figure 8–12 shows for our fifth-grade example, the distributions of means for small (middle curve) and medium (upper curve) predicted effect sizes, along with the power for each situation.

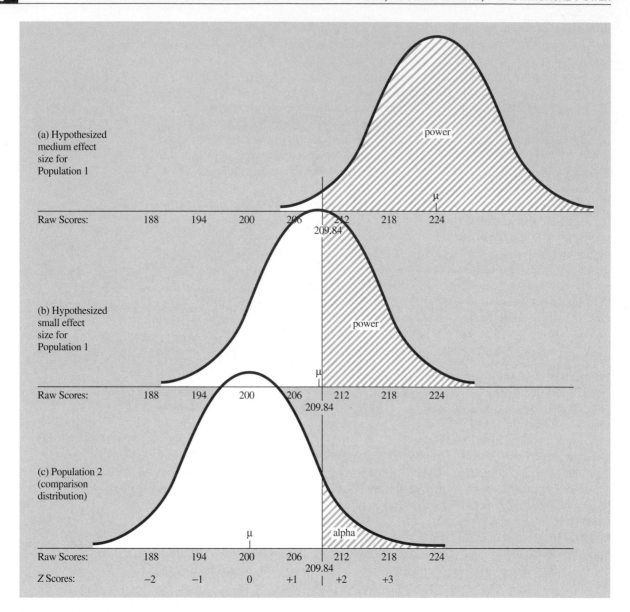

FIGURE 8-12 *Distributions of means of 64 test scores based on predicted (a, b) and known (c) distributions of populations of individuals. (From a fictional study of fifth graders taking a standard achievement test.) Scores are shown on distributions a and b for the significance cutoff for distribution c (the cutoff for p <.05, one-tailed.) In this example, (a) is the predicted distribution with a medium effect size (d = .5, power = 99%); and (b) is the predicted distribution with a small effect size (d = .2, power = 48%).*

SAMPLE SIZE

The other major influence on power, besides effect size, is the number of people in the sample that is studied, the sample size. Basically, the more people there are in the study, the more power.

Sample size affects power because the larger the sample size, the smaller the standard deviation of the distribution of means. If these distributions have a smaller standard deviation, they are narrower. And if they are narrower, there is less overlap between them. Figure 8–13 shows the situation for our fifth-grader example if the study included 100 fifth graders, instead of the 64 in the original example, with a predicted mean of 208 and a population standard deviation of 48. The power now is 51%. (It was 38% with 64 fifth graders). With 500 participants in the study, power is 98% (see Figure 8–14).

Don't get mixed up. The distributions of means can be narrow (and thus have less overlap and more power) for two very different reasons. One reason is that the population of individuals may have a small standard deviation; this has to do with effect size. The other reason is that the sample size is large. This reason is completely separate. Sample size has nothing to do with effect size. Both effect size and sample size affect power. However, as we will see shortly, these two different influences on power lead to completely different kinds of practical steps for increasing power when planning a study.

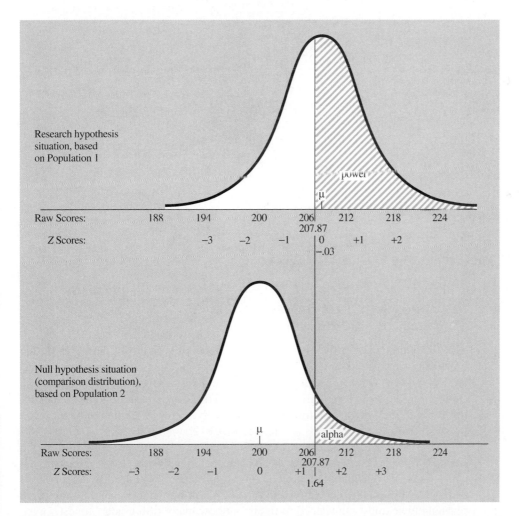

FIGURE 8–13 *Distributions of means of 100 test scores based on predicted (upper) and known (lower) populations of individuals. (From a fictional study of fifth graders taking a standard achievement test.) Scores are shown on both distributions for the significance cutoff for the lower distribution (the cutoff for p < .05, one-tailed). Power = 51%. Compare this example to the original example (Figure 8–6) in which the sample size was 64 (and power was 38%).*

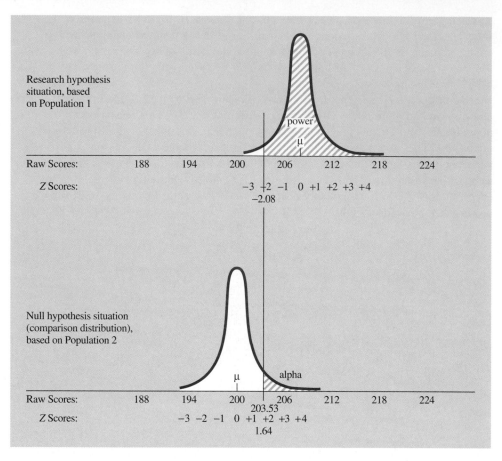

FIGURE 8–14 *Distributions of means of 500 test scores based on predicted (upper) and known (lower) populations of individuals. (From a fictional study of fifth graders taking a standard achievement test.) Scores are shown on both distributions for the significance cutoff for the lower distribution (the cutoff for p <.05, one-tailed). Power = 99%. Compare to figures 8–6 and 8–13.*

FIGURING NEEDED SAMPLE SIZE FOR A GIVEN LEVEL OF POWER

When planning a study, the main reason researchers figure power is to help decide how many participants to include in the study. Sample size has an important influence on power. Thus, a researcher wants to be sure to have enough people in the study for the study to have fairly high power. (Too often, researchers carry out studies in which the power is so low that it is unlikely they will get a significant result even if the research hypothesis is true. See Box 8–2.)

A researcher can figure out the needed number of participants by turning the steps of figuring power on their head. You begin with the level of power you want—say, 80%—and then figure how many participants you need to get that level of power. Suppose the educational psychologists in our fifth-grader example were planning their study and wanted to figure out how many fifth graders to test. Given their predicted mean difference of 8 and their known population standard deviation of 48, it turns out that they would need 222 fifth graders to have 80% power. We won't go into the computational details here. (However, you might want to try figuring this out on your own. See if you can get the same answer as we did, using

BOX 8-2   The Power of Typical Psychology Experiments

More than four decades ago, Jacob Cohen (1962), a psychologist specializing in statistical methods, published in the *Journal of Abnormal and Social Psychology* a now well-known analysis of the statistical power of studies. He had observed that great attention was given to significance, or the issue of whether a Type I error had been made (that the null hypothesis was mistakenly rejected and some effect was being assumed from the results that in fact did not exist). But essentially no attention was given to the possibility of a Type II error (that the null hypothesis had been mistakenly not rejected and a real effect was ignored because of inconclusive results—indeed, often treated as nonexistent). Power was not even discussed in these studies.

Cohen computed the power for the results in these articles. Not being familiar with the many content areas involved, he looked at power under three assumptions of effect size: small, medium, and large. If small, he found, the studies published had only one chance in six of detecting a significant effect. Not one had a better than 50–50 chance. If he assumed a medium effect in the population, the studies had a slightly better than 50–50 chance of detecting this effect. One quarter still had less than one chance in three. Only assuming large effects gave the studies as they were designed a good chance of rejecting the null hypothesis. As Cohen put it, "A generation of researchers could be suitably employed in repeating interesting studies which originally used inadequate sample sizes" (p. 153).

These experiments that "failed," when in fact their hypotheses were never adequately tested, represented tremendous knowledge that may have been lost, perhaps never to be explored again. And this loss was simply because of a failure to be concerned about power—most often a failure to calculate, through a consideration of effect size, significance level, and power, the sample size that would best test the hypothesis.

Several other similar analyses of the power of studies in a given journal have been conducted since Cohen's (e.g., Brewer's 1972 analysis of the *American Educational Research Journal* and Chase & Chase's 1976 study of the *Journal of Applied Psychology*). Meanwhile, Cohen published a handbook for analyzing power in the social sciences in 1969, and a revised version appeared in 1988. Still, in an article published in 1989, Sedlmeier and Gigerenzer observed that Cohen's admonitions apparently had no effect during the intervening years. In fact, the power of studies in the same journal that Cohen had studied (now the *Journal of Abnormal Psychology*) had actually decreased over those years. And low power still went unnoticed. Only 2 of 64 experiments even discussed power, and these two had not estimated it. Meanwhile, in 11% of the studies published in that issue, nonsignificance was considered a confirmation of the null hypothesis, perhaps in an attempt to adhere to the traditional admonitions we questioned in Chapter 6, Box 6–1. Yet Sedlmeier and Gigerenzer found that the median power in these particular studies was only .25. Certainly, if we are to consider it valuable information in itself when results favor the null hypothesis (again, see Box 6–1), it can only be taken that way when power is high enough so that if the research hypothesis was true, the study would at least have an even chance of showing it.

This stubborn failure by researchers to consider power is a bit shocking. More often than not, it means that researchers are going through all their work for nothing. The odds are against their finding what they seek, even if it is true. And it seems that methodology in psychology is so monolithic and fixed that it cannot be budged. But in an article in *American Psychologist* titled "Things I Have Learned (So Far)," Jacob Cohen (1990) looked back over the decades philosophically:

> I do not despair. I remember that W. S. Gosset, the fellow who worked in a brewery and appeared in print modestly as "Student," published the *t* test a decade before we entered World War I, and the test didn't get into the psychological statistics textbooks until after World War II.
>
> These things take time. So, if you publish something that you think is really good, and a year or a decade or two go by and hardly anyone seems to have taken notice, remember the *t* test, and take heart. (p. 1311)

the procedures you have learned, but starting with 80% power and following the steps backwards to get the number of participants needed.)

In practice, researchers use special tables that tell you how many participants you need in a study to have a high level of power, given a certain predicted effect size. We provide simplified versions of such tables for each of the main hypothesis-testing procedures you learn in upcoming chapters.

OTHER INFLUENCES ON POWER

Three other factors, besides effect size and sample size, affect power.

1. *Significance level (alpha).* Less extreme significance levels (such as .10 or .20) mean more power. More extreme significance levels (.01 or .001) mean less power. Less extreme significance levels result in more power because the shaded rejection area on the lower curve is bigger. Thus, more of the area in the upper curve is shaded. More extreme significance levels result in less power because the shaded rejection region on the lower curve is smaller. Suppose in our fifth-grader testing example we had used the .01 significance level instead. The power would have dropped from 38% to only 16%. (See Figure 8–15).

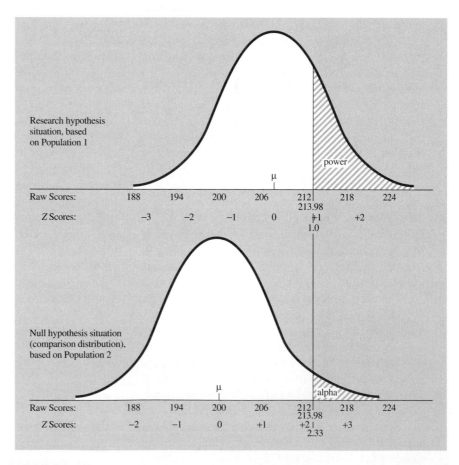

FIGURE 8–15 *Distributions of means of 64 test scores based on predicted (upper) and known (lower) populations of individuals. (From a fictional study of fifth graders taking a standard achievement test.) Scores are shown on both distributions for the significance cutoff for the lower distribution—the cutoff now for p <.01, one-tailed. Power = 16%. Compare this to the original example (Figure 8–6) in which the cutoff was p <.05 and power was 38%.*

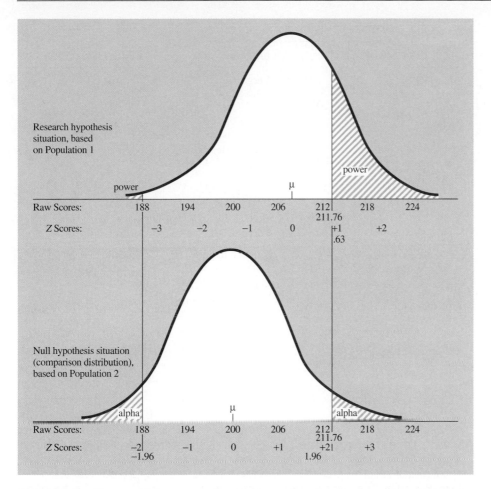

FIGURE 8–16 *Distributions of means of 64 test scores based on predicted (upper) and known (lower) populations of individuals. (From a fictional study of fifth graders taking a standard achievement test.) Scores are shown on both distributions for the significance cutoffs on the lower distribution—the cutoffs now for p <.05, two-tailed. Power = 26%. Compare this to the original example (Figure 8–6) in which the cutoff was p .05, one-tailed, and power was 38%.*

2. *One- versus two-tailed tests.* Using a two-tailed test makes it harder to get significance on any one tail. Thus, keeping everything else the same, power is less with a two-tailed test than with a one-tailed test. Suppose in our fifth-grader testing example we had used a two-tailed test instead of a one-tailed test (but still using 5% overall). As shown in Figure 8–16, power would be only 26% (compared to 38% in the original one-tailed version).

3. *Type of hypothesis-testing procedure.* Sometimes the researcher has a choice of more than one hypothesis-testing procedure to use for a particular study. We have not considered any such situations so far in this book, but we will do so in Chapter 15.

SUMMARY OF INFLUENCES ON POWER

Table 8–4 summarizes the effects of various factors on the power of a study.

TABLE 8–4   Influences on Power

Feature of the Study	Increases Power	Decreases Power
Effect size (d) ($d = [\mu_1 - \mu_2]/\sigma$)	Large d	Small d
Effect size combines the following two features:		
Hypothesized difference between population means ($\mu_1 - \mu_2$)	Large differences	Small differences
Population standard deviation (σ)	Small σ	Large σ
Sample size (N)	Large N	Small N
Significance level (α)	Lenient, high α (such as .05 or .10)	Stringent, low α (such as .01 or .001)
One-tailed versus two-tailed test	One-tailed	Two-tailed
Type of hypothesis-testing procedure used	Varies	Varies

HOW ARE YOU DOING?

1. (a) What are the two ways that effect size affects power? For each (b and c), explain how and why it affects power.
2. In a planned study involving a standard test, the population is known to have a mean of 500 and a standard deviation of 100. The researchers predict that their planned experimental procedure will produce a large effect (that is, they predict an effect size of .8). What is the predicted mean of the population that will be given the experimental procedure?
3. (a) How and (b) why does sample size affect power?
4. (a) How and (b) why does the significance level used affect power?
5. (a) How and (b) why does using a one-tailed versus a two-tailed test affect power?

ANSWERS:

1. (a) The two ways are the difference between the known and predicted population means and the population standard deviation.
   (b) The more difference between the means, the more power. This is because it makes the distribution of means further apart and thus have less overlap, so the area in the predicted distribution more extreme than the cutoff in the known distribution is greater.
   (c) The smaller the population standard deviation, the more power. This is because it makes the distribution of means narrower and thus have less overlap, so the area in the predicted distribution more extreme than the cutoff in the known distribution is greater.
2. Predicted $\mu_1 = \mu_2 + (d)(\sigma) = 500 + (.8)(100) = 580$.
3. (a) The larger the sample size, the more power. (b) This is because it makes the distribution of means narrower (because the standard deviation of the distribution of means is the population variance divided by the sample size) and thus have less overlap, so the area in the predicted distribution more extreme than the cutoff in the known distribution is greater.
4. (a) The more liberal the significance level (for example, .10 versus .05), the more power. (b) This is because it makes the cutoff in the known distribution less extreme, so the corresponding area more extreme than this cutoff in the predicted distribution of means is larger.
5. (a) A study with a one-tailed test has more power (for a result in the predicted direction) than a two-tailed test. (b) This is because with a one-tailed test, the cutoff in the predicted direction in the known distribution is less extreme, so the corresponding area more extreme

than this cutoff in the predicted distribution of means is larger. There is an added cutoff in the opposite side, but this is so far out on the distribution that it has little effect on power.

THE ROLE OF POWER WHEN PLANNING A STUDY

Figuring out power is very important when planning a study. If you do a study in which the power is low, even if the research hypothesis is true, this study will probably not give statistically significant results. Thus, the time and expense of carrying out the study would probably not be worthwhile. So when the power of a planned study is found to be low, researchers look for practical ways to increase the power to an acceptable level.

What is an acceptable level of power? A widely used rule is that a study should have 80% power to be worth doing (see Cohen, 1988). Obviously, the more power the better. However, the costs of greater power, such as studying more people, often make even 80% power beyond your reach.

How can you increase the power of a planned study? In principle, you can increase the power of a planned study by changing any of the factors summarized in Table 8–4. Let's consider each.

1. *Increase effect size by increasing the predicted difference between population means.* You can't just arbitrarily predict a bigger effect. There has to be a basis for your prediction. Thus, to increase the predicted difference, your method in carrying out the study must make it reasonable to expect a bigger effect. Consider again our example of the experiment about the impact of special instructions on fifth graders' test scores. One way to increase the expected mean difference might be to make the instructions more elaborate, spending more time explaining them, perhaps allowing time for practice, and so forth. A disadvantage of this approach is that it can be difficult or costly. Another disadvantage is that you may have to use an experimental procedure that is not like the one to which you want the results of your study to apply.

2. *Increase effect size by decreasing the population standard deviation.* You can decrease the population standard deviation in a planned study in at least two ways. One way is to study a population that has less variance within it than the one originally planned. With the fifth-grader testing example, you might only use fifth graders in a particular suburban school system. The disadvantage is that your results will then apply only to the more limited population.

   Another way to decrease the population standard deviation is to use conditions of testing that are more standardized and measures that are more precise. For example, testing in a controlled laboratory setting usually makes for less variation among scores in results (meaning a smaller standard deviation). Similarly, using tests with very clear wording and clear procedures for marking answers also reduces variation. When practical, this is an excellent way to increase power, but often the study is already as rigorous as it can be.

3. *Increase the sample size.* The most straightforward way to increase power is to study more people. Of course, if you are studying astronauts who have walked on the moon, there is a limit to how many are available. In most research situations, though, sample size is the main way to change a planned study to raise its power.

| TABLE 8–5 | Summary of Practical Ways of Increasing the Power of a Planned Experiment | |

Feature of the Study	Practical Way of Raising Power	Disadvantages
Predicted difference between population means $(\mu_1 - \mu_2)$	Increase the intensity of experimental procedure.	May not be practical or may distort study's meaning.
Standard deviation (σ)	Use a less diverse population.	May not be available; decreases generalizability.
	Use standardized, controlled circumstances of testing or more precise measurement.	Not always practical.
Sample size (N)	Use a larger sample size.	Not always practical; can be costly.
Significance level (α)	Use a more lenient level of significance (such as .1).	Raises alpha, the probability of Type I error.
One-tailed versus two-tailed test	Use a one-tailed test.	May not be appropriate to the logic of the study.
Type of hypothesis-testing procedure	Use a more sensitive procedure.	None may be available or appropriate.

4. *Use a less stringent level of significance.* Ordinarily, the level of significance you use should be the least stringent that reasonably protects against Type I error. Normally, in psychology research, this will be .05. It is rare that much can be done to improve power in this way.

5. *Use a one-tailed test.* Whether you use a one-tailed or a two-tailed test depends on the logic of the hypothesis being studied. As with significance level, it is rare that you have much of a choice about this factor.

6. *Use a more sensitive hypothesis-testing procedure.* This is fine if alternatives are available. We consider some options of this kind in Chapter 15. Usually, however, the researcher begins with the most sensitive method available, so little more can be done.

Table 8–5 summarizes some practical ways to increase the power of a planned experiment.

THE IMPORTANCE OF POWER WHEN EVALUATING THE RESULTS OF A STUDY

Understanding statistical power and what affects it is very important in drawing conclusions from the results of research.

WHEN A RESULT IS SIGNIFICANT: STATISTICAL SIGNIFICANCE VERSUS PRACTICAL SIGNIFICANCE

You have learned that a study with a larger effect size is more likely to come out significant. It also is possible for a study with a very small effect size to come out significant. This happens when a study has high power due to other factors, especially a large sample size. Consider a study in which among all students who take the SAT in a particular year, a sample of 10,000 whose first name begins with a particular letter are randomly selected. Suppose that their mean Verbal SAT is 504, compared to the overall population's mean SAT of 500 ($\sigma = 100$). This result would be significant at the .001 level. Its effect size is a tiny .04. That is, the significance test tells you that you can be confident there is a real difference—that the population of students whose first name begins with this letter have higher Verbal SAT scores than the general population of students. At the same time, the difference is not very important. The effect size makes it clear that this difference is very slight. The distributions of the two populations overlap so much that it would be of little use to know what letter a person's first name begins with.

The message here is that in judging a study's results, there are two questions. First, is the result statistically significant? If it is, you can consider there to be a real effect. The next question then is whether the effect size is large enough for the result to be useful or interesting. This second question is especially important if the study has any practical implications. (Sometimes, in a study testing purely theoretical issues, it may be enough just to be confident there is an effect at all in a particular direction. We have more to say about this later when discussing controversies.)

If the sample was small, you can assume that a statistically significant result is probably also practically important. On the other hand, if the sample size is very large, you must consider the effect size directly, as it is quite possible that the effect size is too small to be useful.

The implications of what we just said may seem a bit of a paradox. Most people assume that the more participants in the study, the more important its results. In a sense, just the reverse is true. All other things being equal, if a study with only a few participants manages to be significant, that significance must be due to a large effect size. A study with a large number of people in it that is statistically significant may or may not have a large effect size. This is why the American Psychological Association now urges researchers to include effect size when they describe results of studies in research articles.

Also notice that it is usually not a good idea to compare the significance level of two studies to see which has the more important result. For example, a study with a small number of participants that is significant at the .05 level might well have a large effect size. At the same time, a study with a large number of participants that is significant at the .001 level might well have a small effect size.

The level of significance does tell you something. It tells you how confident you can be that you can reject the null hypothesis, that there is a nonzero effect. The lower the p level, the stronger the evidence for a nonzero effect (Frick, 1996). However, it is definitely *not* the case that the smaller the p level, the larger the effect. If two studies were identical in every other way, a smaller p level would mean a bigger effect. But if the studies differ, especially if they differ in sample size, p level is ambiguous in its relation to effect size. A small p level could be due to a large effect size, but it could just as well be due to a large sample size. Thus, the p level tells you the strength of the evidence that there is a nonzero effect. The p level does not tell you how big that nonzero effect is.

The most important lesson from all this is that the word *significant* in statistically significant has a very special meaning. It means that you can be pretty confident that there is some real effect. But it does *not* mean that the effect is significant in a practical sense, that it is important or noteworthy.

ROLE OF POWER WHEN A RESULT IS NOT STATISTICALLY SIGNIFICANT

We saw in Chapter 6 that a result that is not significant is inconclusive. Often, however, we really would like to conclude that there is little or no difference between the populations. Can we ever do that?

Consider the relation of power to a nonsignificant result. Suppose you carried out a study that had low power and did not get a significant result. In this situation, the result is entirely inconclusive. Not getting a significant result may have come about because the research hypothesis was false or because the study had too little power (for example, it had too few participants).

On the other hand, suppose you carried out a study that had high power and you did not get a significant result. In this situation, it seems unlikely that the research hypothesis is true. In this situation (where there is high power), a nonsignificant result is a fairly strong argument against the research hypothesis. This does not mean that all versions of the research hypothesis are false. For example, it is possible that the populations are only very slightly different (and you figured power based on predicting a large difference).

In sum, a nonsignificant result from a study with low power is truly inconclusive. However, a nonsignificant result from a study with high power does suggest that either the research hypothesis is false or that there is less of an effect than was predicted when figuring power.

SUMMARY OF THE ROLE OF POWER WHEN EVALUATING RESULTS OF A STUDY

Table 8–6 summarizes the role of significance and sample size in interpreting experimental results.

HOW ARE YOU DOING?

1. (a) What are the two basic ways of increasing the effect size of a planned study? For each (b and c), how can it be done, and what are the disadvantages?
2. What is usually the easiest way to increase the power of a planned study?
3. What are the disadvantages of increasing the power of a planned study by (a) using a more lenient significance level, or (b) using a one-tailed test rather than a two-tailed test?
4. Why is statistical significance not the same as practical importance?
5. You are comparing two studies in which one is significant at $p < .01$ and the other is significant at $p < .05$. (a) What can you conclude about the two studies? (b) What can you *not* conclude about the two results?
6. When a result is significant, what can you conclude about effect size if the study had (a) a very large sample size or (b) a very small sample size?
7. When a result is not significant, what can you conclude about the truth of the research hypothesis if the study had (a) a very large sample size or (b) a very small sample size?

ANSWERS:

1. (a) Increase the predicted difference between population means and reduce the population standard deviation.

TABLE 8–6 Role of Significance and Sample Size in Interpreting Experimental Results

Outcome Statistically Significant	Sample Size	Conclusion
Yes	Small	Important result
Yes	Large	Might or might not have practical importance
No	Small	Inconclusive
No	Large	Research hypothesis probably false

(b) You can increase the predicted difference by making the experimental procedure more impactful. The disadvantages are that it might not be practical and it may change the meaning of the procedure you really want to study.

(c) You can decrease the population standard deviation by using a less diverse population (which has the disadvantage of not permitting you to apply your results to a more general population) and by using more standardized procedures or more accurate measurement (which may not be practical).

2. Increase the sample size.

3. (a) It increases the probability of a Type I error. (b) This may not be appropriate to the logic of the study; and if the result comes out opposite to predictions, in principle, it would have to be considered nonsignificant.

4. A statistically significant result means that you can be confident the effect did not occur by chance; It does not, however, mean it is a large or substantial effect.

5. (a) We can be more confident that the first study's result is not due to chance. (b) We cannot conclude which one has the bigger effect size.

6. (a) It could be small or large. (b) It is probably large.

7. (a) It is probably not true (or has a much smaller effect size than predicted). (b) You can conclude very little.

CONTROVERSY: STATISTICAL SIGNIFICANCE CONTROVERSY CONTINUED—EFFECT SIZE VERSUS STATISTICAL SIGNIFICANCE

In chapters 6 and 7 we discussed an ongoing, heated controversy about the value of significance tests, including the argument that they are so often misused. We said that there were two main ways that significance tests are misused that seriously concerns psychologists, one of which is that nonsignificant results are unthinkingly interpreted as showing there is in fact no effect. In light of this chapter, you should be able to see even more clearly why this mistake is a problem: Nonsignificant results could be due to either little or no true effect or simply to low power of the experiment.

In Chapter 6, we said we would postpone discussing the other way significance tests are often misused until we had covered material in a later chapter. That material was effect size, and we are now in a position to examine this issue. This misuse occurs when a significant result is unthinkingly interpreted as being an "important" result; that is, significance is confused with a large effect size.

Loosely speaking, statistical significance is about the probability that we could have gotten our pattern of results by chance. As Frick (1996) put it, significance is about the strength of the evidence that we have a nonzero effect. If our result is significant at the .05 level, that is pretty good evidence. If it is significant at the .01 level, that is even better evidence.

However, as we have seen in this chapter, a significant result may not be important in the sense of meaning a large effect size. For example, if the sample size was large, a result with a tiny effect size could be statistically significant at $p < .001$. In this situation we would be very confident that the true effect was other than zero. But the size of this true nonzero effect would still be very small. We would be concluding that we have a real, but slight effect. Similarly, if the sample size was small enough, a result with a huge effect size could be not statistically significant at all. In this situation, our best estimate of the size of the effect is that it is large. But we would have no confidence that this effect is really there at all—it could be that the true effect is very small or even in the opposite direction.

One prominent psychologist writing about this problem (Scarr, 1997) noted that the word *significant* is unfortunate, because in ordinary language it means "important." Indeed, she recommended that we change the name to something like "reliable." (This new name would have its own problems, since reliability is not quite the same as what significance tells us; Nickerson, 2000.) In any case, it is unlikely that the name will change soon. Thus, it is important that when reading or conducting psychology research, you keep in mind the distinction between the special way the word *significance* is used in psychology versus the way it is used in ordinary language. As we noted in Chapter 6, most psychologists do not see the misuses as reason to abandon significance testing. Instead, they argue, we should make more of an effort to prevent such misuse.

However, this is not the end of the matter. Many of those who oppose significance testing argue that even if properly used, significance testing misses the point. What psychology is fundamentally about, they argue, is effect size. It is not about whether a result is nonzero. We already saw a version of this argument in Chapter 7, with the suggestion that researchers use confidence intervals instead of significance testing. The full version of that proposal is that researchers should really be reporting effect sizes (ideally, with confidence intervals around the effect sizes).

Proponents of emphasizing effect size argue that effect sizes provide information that can be compared to other studies and used in accumulating information over independent studies as research in a field progresses. Effect sizes are crucial ingredients in meta-analysis, and many of the proponents of effect size see meta-analysis as *the* wave of the future of psychology.

There are, however, counterarguments in favor of significance testing (and against using effect sizes alone). One such counterargument is that when sample size is small, it is still possible for a study to come out with a large effect size just by chance. Thus, if we are interested in the result of a particular study that used a small sample, significance tests protect against taking the results of such a study too seriously. Similarly, there are times when a very small effect size is nevertheless important (see the discussion of this issue in Chapter 3). In such a situation, it is crucial to know whether the result should be trusted as not due to chance. Still, many of those making these counterarguments agree that significance has been overemphasized. Most hold that significance should always be reported but that effect size should also be given more emphasis in the discussion of results.

There is yet another view: In some circumstances effect sizes are actually misleading, and we should rely only on significance testing. Chow (1988, 1996), for example, makes a distinction between applied and theoretically oriented research. In applied research, psychologists want to know the actual amount of effect a particular program has or how big is the actual difference between two particular groups. In these circumstances, Chow agrees, effect size is a good idea. However, when doing theoretical research, Chow argues, the situation is quite different. It is in this situation, he says, that effect sizes are irrelevant and even misleading.

Consider an experiment on the effect of familiarity on recognizing information. The point of such a study is to examine the basic way that familiarity affects information processing. A particular study might show people familiar and unfamiliar words to see how many milliseconds it takes to recognize them. The effect size of such a study would tell us very little to help interpret the results of the study. It depends on all sorts of details of how the study was done, such as just how familiar and unfamiliar the different words used were, the specific way the words were presented, and so forth. What matters in a study like this, Chow says, is that (a) the prediction of a difference in recognizing familiar versus unfamiliar words was based on theory, (b) the results were consistent with what was predicted (as shown by the statistical significance), and (c) the theory is thus supported.

It is not only in cognitive psychology that research is primarily theoretical in this way. Some other examples of research that are primarily theoretical include experimental studies of motivations for interpersonal attraction, of how neural processes are influenced by chemical changes, of how infants develop language, or of how memory differs for emotional and nonemotional events.

In fact, the current balance of the use of significance tests and effect sizes is probably just what one might expect from the points that Chow makes. In applied areas of psychology, there is an increasing emphasis on effect size. But in more theoretical areas of psychology, explicit mentions of effect size are less common. The prevailing view among statistics experts in psychology seems to be that even in theoretically oriented research, the potential loss (due to misplaced emphasis) by including effect size is probably offset by, among other benefits, the usefulness to future researchers of having such information to help them in figuring power when planning their own studies and, most important, for future meta-analysts who will combine the results of this study with other related studies.

EFFECT SIZE, DECISION ERRORS, AND POWER IN RESEARCH ARTICLES

It is increasingly common for articles to mention effect size. For example, Moorehouse and Tobler (2000) studied the effectiveness of an intervention program for "high-risk, multiproblem, inner-city, primally African-American and Latino youth." The authors reported, "Youth who received 5–30 hours of intervention ([the high dosage group], $n = 101$) were comparted with those who received 1–4 hours (the low-dosage group, $n = 31$). . . . The difference between the groups in terms of reduction in [alcohol and drug] use was highly significant. A between-groups effect size of .68 was achieved for the high-dosage group when compared with the low-dosage group." (Their wording about the study is a bit confusing—they are using "dosage" here to mean the amount of intervention, not the amount of drugs anyone was taking!) The meaning of the .68 effect size is that the group getting 5 to 30 hours of intervention was .68 standard deviations higher in terms of reduction on their drug and alcohol use than the group getting only 1 to 4 hours of the intervention. This is a medium to large effect size.

TABLE 8-7	Target Classes and Effect Size			
			Mean Effect	
Target Class	N	%	Size	SD
Anxiety and depression	30	7	.67	.62
Phobias	76	18	1.28	.88
Physical and habit problems	106	26	1.10	.85
Social and sexual problems	76	18	.95	.75
Performance anxieties	126	30	.80	.71

Note: From Shapiro, D. A., & Shapiro, D. (1983), tab. 5. Comparative therapy outcome research: Methodological implications of meta-analysis. *Journal of Consulting and Clinical Psychology, 51,* 42–53. Copyright, 1983, by the American Psychological Association. Reprinted by permission of the author.

Effect size is most commonly reported in meta-analyses, in which results from different articles are being combined and compared. We have given several examples of such meta-analytic studies, including one in Box 8–1. As an example of how these studies actually describe results in terms of effect size, consider a famous meta-analysis conducted by Shapiro and Shapiro (1983). They reviewed 143 studies of the effects of psychotherapy that used reasonably sound methods. Among their results was a comparison of the effectiveness of therapies in general on different types of patients (which they called the "target class"). Table 8–7 shows the number of studies (N), the percentage that this number represents of all the studies reviewed, the average effect size, and the standard deviation of the effect sizes. From this table you can see that the largest benefit from psychotherapy was found in studies focusing on people with phobias and the smallest benefit in studies focusing on people with anxiety and depression. Based on Cohen's conventions, however, even the smallest effect size was still large.

You mainly think about decision error and power when planning research. (Power, for example, is often a major topic in research-funding proposals and in thesis proposals.) As for research articles, power is sometimes mentioned in the final section of an article where the author discusses the meaning of the results or in discussions of results of other studies. In either situation, the emphasis tends to be on the meaning of nonsignificant results. Also, when power is discussed, it may be explained in some detail. This is because it has been only recently that most psychologists have begun to be knowledgeable about power.

For example, Denenberg (1999), in discussing the basis for his own study, makes the following comments about a relevant previous study by Mody et al. (1997) that had not found significant results.

[T]hey were confronted with the serious problem of having to accept the null hypothesis. . . . we can view this issue in terms of statistical power. . . . A minimal statistical power of .80 is required before one can consider the argument that the lack of significance may be interpreted as evidence that Ho [the null hypothesis] is true. To conduct a power analysis, it is necessary to specify an expected mean difference, the alpha level, and whether a one-tailed or two-tailed test will be used. Given a power requirement of .8, one can then determine the N necessary. Once these conditions are satisfied, if the experiment fails to find a significant difference, then one can make the following kind of a statement: "We have designed an experiment with a .8 probability of finding a significant difference, if such exists in the population. Because we failed to find a significant effect, we think it quite unlikely that one exists. Even if it does exist, its contribution would appear to be minimal. . . ."

Mody et al. never discussed power, even though they interpreted negative findings as proof of the validity of the null hypothesis in all of their experiments. . . . Because the participants were split in this experiment, the *n*s were reduced to 10 per group. Under such conditions one would not expect to find a significant difference, unless the experimental variable was very powerful. In other words, it is more difficult to reject the null hypothesis when working with small *n*s. The only meaningful conclusion that can be drawn from this study is that no meaningful interpretation can be made of the lack of findings.

SUMMARY

1. Effect size is the degree of separation of the known population and the population that is given the experimental treatment. A widely used standardized measure of effect size, Cohen's *d*, is the difference between population means divided by the population standard deviation. Cohen's effect size conventions consider a small effect to be .2, a medium effect to be .5, and a large effect to be .8.

2. Meta-analysis is a procedure for systematically combining and comparing effect sizes of separate studies.

3. There are two kinds of decision errors one can make in hypothesis testing. A Type I error is when a researcher rejects the null hypothesis, but the null hypothesis is actually true. A Type II error is when a researcher does not reject the null hypothesis, but the null hypothesis is actually false.

4. The statistical power of a study is the probability that it will give a statistically significant result if the research hypothesis is true.

5. To figure power (in the situation of a known population and a single sample), you first find the cutoff point for significance, in raw-score terms, on the comparison distribution. Based on a specific predicted mean, you can find the *Z* score for this cutoff on the distribution of means for the population, given the experimental procedure. Power is the probability of exceeding this *Z* score, the area greater than this *Z* score, which you can find from the normal curve table.

6. The larger the effect size, the greater the power. This is because the greater the difference between means or the smaller the population standard deviation (the two ingredients in effect size), the less overlap between the known and predicted populations' distributions of means, so that the area in the predicted distribution more extreme than the cutoff in the known distribution is greater. Also, if you know or predict the effect size, you can figure the predicted mean; it will be the known mean plus the effect size times the population standard deviation. You can then use this to figure power.

7. The larger the sample size, the greater the power. This is because the larger the sample, the smaller the variance of the distribution of means, so that for a given effect size there is less overlap between distributions of means.

8. Power is also affected by significance level (the more extreme, such as .01, the lower the power), by whether a one-tailed or two-tailed test is used (with less power for a two-tailed test), and by the type of hypothesis-testing procedure used (in the occasional situation where there is a choice of procedure).

9. Statistically significant results from a study with high power (such as one with a large sample size) may not have practical importance. Results that are not sta-

tistically significant from a study with low power (such as one with a small sample size) leave open the possibility that significant results might show up if power were increased.

10. Psychologists disagree about whether significance or effect size is more important in interpreting experimental results; theoretically oriented psychologists seem to emphasize significance, and applied researchers emphasize effect size.

11. Research articles increasingly report effect size, and effect sizes are almost always reported in meta-analyses. Research articles rarely mention decision errors, but sometimes include discussions of power, especially when evaluating nonsignificant results.

KEY TERMS

alpha (α) (p. 262)
beta (β) (p. 262)
decision errors (p. 261)
effect size (d) (p. 254)

effect size conventions
  (p. 257)
meta-analysis (p. 258)
power tables (p. 270)

statistical power (p. 264)
Type I error (p. 261)
Type II error (p. 261)

EXAMPLE WORKED-OUT COMPUTATIONAL PROBLEMS

Each problem below is based on a known population with a normal distribution, $\mu = 40$, and $\sigma = 10$.

FIGURING THE EFFECT SIZE

A sample given an experimental treatment has a mean of 37. What is the effect size? Is this approximately small, medium, or large?

$d = (\mu_1 - \mu_2)/\sigma = (37 - 40)/10 = -.3/10 = -.3$ Approximately small.

FIGURING POWER

The researcher plans to conduct a new study with a sample of 25 and predicts that when given a new experimental treatment, this group will have a mean of 49. The researcher plans to use the 1% significance level (one-tailed). What is the power of the planned study? What is beta? Make a diagram of the overlapping distributions on which you show the area for alpha, beta, and power.

❶ **Gather the needed information the mean and standard deviation of Population 2 (the comparison distribution) and the predicted mean of Population 1 (the population given the experimental procedure).** Mean of the comparison distribution is 40. The predicted mean of the population that receives the experimental procedure is 49. The standard deviation of the distribution of means is $\sqrt{10^2/25} = \sqrt{100/25} = \sqrt{4} = 2$.

❷ **Figure the raw-score cutoff point on the comparison distribution to reject the null hypothesis.** A Z of $+2.33$ (for the 1% significance level) gives a raw score of $40 + (2.33)(2) = 44.66$.

❸ **Figure the Z score for this same point, but on the distribution of means for the population that receives the experimental treatment (Population 1).** A

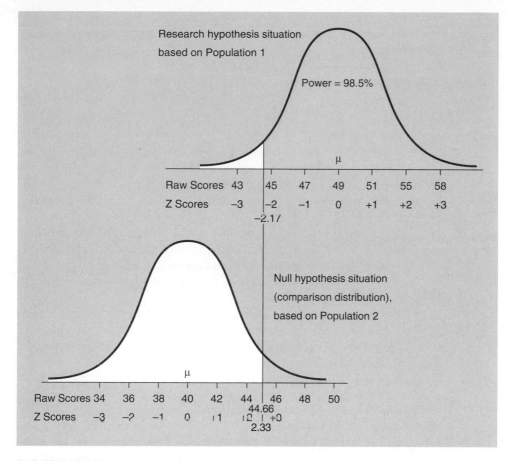

FIGURE 8–17 *Distributions of means for predicted (upper) and known (lower) distributions for "Examples of Worked-Out Computational Problems" for figuring power.*

raw score of 44.66 on the distribution that will be given the experimental treatment is a Z score of $(44.66 - 49)/2 = -4.34/2 = -.2.17$.

❹ **Using the normal curve table, figure the probability of getting a score more extreme than that Z score.** From the normal curve table, the area between the mean and a Z of 2.17 is 48.5%. Since −2.17 is below the mean, and there is another 50% above the mean, power = 98.5%.

The distributions involved are shown in Figure 8–17.

Beta is 1 − power. Thus, beta = 1 − 98.5% = 1.5%.

FIND THE PREDICTED MEAN FROM AN EFFECT SIZE

The researcher predicts a small negative effect size. What is the predicted mean?

A small negative effect size is −.2. Predicted $\mu_1 = \mu_2 + (d)(\sigma) = 40 + (-.2)(10) = 40 + (-2) = 38$.

PRACTICE PROBLEMS

These problems involve figuring. Most real-life statistics problems are done on a computer. However, even if you have a computer and statistics software, do these by hand (with the help of a calculator) to ingrain the method in your mind. Also, in all problems involving figuring, be sure to show your work.

For practice in using a computer to solve statistics problems, refer to the computer section of each chapter of the *Student's Study Guide and Computer Workbook* that accompanies this text.

All data are fictional unless an actual citation is given.

Answers to Set I problems are given at the back of the book.

SET I

1. Define *alpha* and *beta*.
2. In a completed study, there is a known population with a normal distribution, $\mu = 25$, and $\sigma = 12$. What is the estimated effect size if a sample given an experimental procedure has a mean of (a) 19, (b) 22, (c) 25, (d) 30, and (e) 35? For each part, also indicate whether the effect is approximately small, medium or large.
3. In a planned study, there is a known population with a normal distribution, $\mu = 50$, and $\sigma = 5$. What is the predicted effect size (d) if the researchers predict that those given an experimental treatment have a mean of (a) 50, (b) 52, (c) 54, (d) 56, and (e) 47? For each part, also indicate whether the effect is approximately small, medium, or large.
4. For each of the following studies, make a chart of the four possible correct and incorrect decisions, and explain what each would mean. (Each chart should be laid out like Table 8–3, but put into the boxes the possible results, using the names of the variables involved in the study.)
   (a) A study of whether increasing the amount of recess time improves schoolchildren's in-class behavior.
   (b) A study of whether color-blind individuals can distinguish gray shades better than the population at large.
   (c) A study comparing individuals who have ever been in psychotherapy to the general public to see if they are more tolerant of other people's upsets than is the general population.
5. In a planned study, there is a known population with a normal distribution, $\mu = 15$, and $\sigma = 2$. What is the predicted mean if the researcher predicts (a) a small positive effect size, (b) a medium negative effect size, (c) a large positive effect size, (d) an effect size of $d = .35$, and (e) and effect size of $d = -1.5$?
6. Here is information about several possible versions of a planned experiment. Figure effect size and power for each; sketch the distributions involved, showing the area for alpha, beta, and power. (Assume all populations have a normal distribution.)

	Population		Predicted Mean	N	Significance Level	One- or Two-Tailed
	μ	σ				
(a)	90	4	91	100	.05	1
(b)	90	4	92	100	.05	1
(c)	90	2	91	100	.05	1
(d)	90	4	91	16	.05	1
(e)	90	4	91	100	.01	1
(f)	90	4	91	100	.05	2

7. Based on a particular theory of creativity, a psychologist predicts that artists will be greater risk takers than the general population. The general population

is normally distributed with a mean of 50 and a standard deviation of 12 on the risk-taking questionnaire this psychologist plans to use. The psychologist expects that artists will score, on the average, 55 on this questionnaire. The psychologist plans to study 36 artists and test the hypothesis at the .05 level. (a) What is the power of this study? (b) Sketch the distributions involved, showing the area for alpha, beta, and power. (c) Explain your answer to someone who understands hypothesis testing with means of samples but has never learned about power.

8. On a particular memory task in which words are learned in a random order, it is known that people can recall a mean of 11 words with a standard deviation of 4, and the distribution follows a normal curve. A cognitive psychologist, to test a particular theory, modifies that task so that the words are presented in a way in which words that have a related meaning are presented together. The cognitive psychologist predicts that under these conditions, people will recall so many more words that there will be a large effect size. She plans to test this with a sample of 20 people, using the .01 significance level, two-tailed. (a) What is the power of this study? (b) Sketch the distributions involved, showing the area for alpha, beta, and power. (c) Explain your answer to someone who understands hypothesis testing involving means of samples but has never learned about effect size or power.

9. You read a study in which the result is significant ($p < .05$). You then look at the size of the sample. If the sample is very large (rather than very small), how should this affect your interpretation of (a) the probability that the null hypothesis is actually true, and (b) the practical importance of the result? (c) Explain your answers to a person who understands hypothesis testing but has never learned about effect size or power.

10. Aron et al. (1997) placed strangers in pairs and asked them to talk together following a series of instructions designed to help them become close. At the end of 45 minutes, individuals privately answered some questions about how close they now felt to their partners. (The researchers combined the answers into a "closeness composite.") One key question was whether closeness would be affected by either (a) matching strangers based on their attitude agreement or (b) leading participants to believe that they had been put together with someone who would like them. The result for both agreement and expecting to be liked was that "there was no significant differences on the closeness composite" (p. 567). The researchers went on to argue that the results suggested that there was little true effect of these variables on closeness:

> There was about 90% power in this study of achieving significant effects . . . for the two manipulated variables if in fact there were a large effect of this kind ($d = .8$). Indeed, the power is about 90% for finding at least a near-significant ($p < .10$) medium-sized effect ($d = .5$). Thus, it seems unlikely that we would have obtained the present results if in fact there is more than a small effect. . . . (p. 567).

Explain this result to a person who understands hypothesis testing but has never learned about power or effect size.

11. How does each of the following affect the power of a planned study?
   (a) A larger predicted difference between the means of the populations
   (b) A larger population standard deviation
   (c) A larger sample size
   (d) Using a more stringent significance level (e.g., .01 instead of .05)
   (e) Using a two-tailed test instead of a one-tailed test

12. List two situations in which it is useful to consider power, indicating what the use is for each.

SET II

13. In a completed study, there is a known population with a normal distribution, $\mu = 122$, and $\sigma = 8$. What is the estimated effect size if a sample given an experimental procedure has a mean of (a) 100, (b) 110, (c) 120, (d) 130, and (e) 140? For each part, also indicate whether the effect is approximately small, medium, or large.

14. In a planned study, there is a known population with a normal distribution, $\mu = 0$, and $\sigma = 10$. What is the predicted effect size (d) if the researchers predict that those given an experimental treatment have a mean of (a) -8, (b) -5, (c) -2, (d) 0, and (e) 10? For each part, also indicate whether the effect is approximately small, medium, or large.

15. For each of the following studies, make a chart of the four possible correct and incorrect decisions, and explain what each would mean. (Each chart should be laid out like Table 8–3, but put into the boxes the possible results, using the names of the variables involved in the study.)
    (a) A study of whether infants born prematurely begin to recognize faces later than do infants in general.
    (b) A study of whether high school students who receive an AIDS prevention program in their school are more likely to practice safe sex than are other high school students.
    (c) A study of whether memory for abstract ideas is reduced if the information is presented in distracting colors.

16. In a planned study, there is a known population with a normal distribution, $\mu = 17.5$, and $\sigma = 3.2$. What is the predicted mean if the researcher predicts (a) a small positive effect size, (b) a medium negative effect size, (c) an effect size of $d = .4$, (d) an effect size of $d = -.4$, (e) an effect size of $d = 3$?

17. Here is information about several possible versions of a planned experiment, each with a single sample. Figure effect size and power for each; then sketch the distributions involved, showing the area for alpha, beta, and power. (Assume all populations have a normal distribution.)

	Population		Predicted Mean	N	Significance Level	One- or Two-Tailed
	μ	σ				
(a)	0	.5	.1	50	.05	1
(b)	0	.5	.5	50	.05	1
(c)	0	.5	1.0	50	.05	1
(d)	0	.5	.5	100	.05	1
(e)	0	.5	.5	200	.05	1
(f)	0	.5	.5	400	.05	1

18. A psychologist is planning a study on the effect of motivation on performance on an attention task. In this task, participants try to identify target letters in a stream of letters passing by at a rapid rate. The researcher knows from long experience that under ordinary experimental conditions, the population of students who participate in this task identify a mean of 71 of the key letters; the

standard deviation is 10; and the distribution is approximately normal. The psychologist predicts that if the participant is paid a dollar for each letter identified correctly, the number correctly identified will increase to 74. The psychologist plans to test 20 participants under these conditions, using the .05 level. (a) What is the power of this study? (b) Sketch the distributions involved, showing the area for alpha, beta, and power. (c) Explain your answer to someone who understands hypothesis testing involving means of samples but has never learned about power.

19. An organizational psychologist predicts that assembly workers will have a somewhat higher level of job satisfaction if they are given a new kind of incentive program (that is, he predicts a medium effect size). On a standard job satisfaction scale, for assembly workers in this company overall, the distribution is normal, with $\mu = 82$ and $\sigma = 7$. The psychologist plans to provide the new incentive program to 25 randomly selected assembly workers. (a) What is the power of this study (using $p < .01$)? (b) Sketch the distributions involved, showing the area for alpha, beta, and power. (c) Explain your answer to someone who understands hypothesis testing involving means of samples but has never learned about effect size or power.

20. A team of personality psychologists predict that people who experienced a disaster during their childhood will score slightly higher on a measure of fear of disasters (that is, the researchers predict a small positive effect size). It is known from extensive previous testing, using this measure with the population in general, that scores are normally distributed, with a mean of 58 and a standard deviation of 6. The researchers then test their prediction by giving the measure to 120 people who grew up in an area that experienced a devastating forest fire when they were children. (a) What is the power of this study (using the .05 level? (b) Sketch the distributions involved, showing the area for alpha, beta, and power. (c) Explain your answer to someone who understands hypothesis testing involving means of samples but has never learned about effect size or power.

21. You read a study that just barely fails to be significant at the .05 level. That is, the result is not significant. You then look at the size of the sample. If the sample is very large (rather than very small), how should this affect your interpretation of (a) the probability that the null hypothesis is actually true and (b) the probability that the null hypothesis is actually false? (c) Explain your answers to a person who understands hypothesis testing but has never learned about power.

22. Caspi et al. (1997) analyzed results from a large-scale longitudinal study of a sample of children born around 1972 in Dunedin, New Zealand. As one part of their study, Caspi et al. compared the 94 in their sample who were, at age 21, alcohol dependent (clearly alcoholic) versus the 863 who were not alcohol dependent. The researchers compared these two groups in terms of personality test scores from when they were 18 years old. After noting that all results were significant, they reported the following results:

> Young adults who were alcohol dependent at age 21 scored lower at age 18 on Traditionalism ($d = .49$), harm avoidance ($d = .44$), Control ($d = .64$), and Social Closeness ($d = .40$), and higher on Aggression ($d = .86$), Alienation ($d = .66$), and Stress Reaction ($d = .50$).

Explain these results, including why it was especially important for the researchers in this study to give effect sizes, to a person who understands hypothesis testing but has never learned about effect size or power.

23. You are planning a study that you compute as having quite low power. Name six things that you might do to increase power.

CHAPTER 9

INTRODUCTION TO THE t TEST

Are You Ready?
What You Need to have Mastered Before Starting This Chapter:

- Chapters 1, 2, and 5 through 8

At this point, you may think you know all about hypothesis testing. Here's a surprise: What you know will not help you much as a researcher. Why? The procedures for testing hypotheses described up to this point were, of course, absolutely necessary for what you will now learn. However, these procedures involved comparing a group of scores to a known population. In real research practice, you often compare two or more groups of scores to each other, without any direct information about populations. For example, you may have two scores for each of several people, such as scores on an anxiety test before and after psychotherapy, or number of familiar versus unfamiliar words recalled in a memory experiment. Or you might have one score per person for two groups of people, such as an experimental group and a control group in a study of the effect of sleep loss on problem solving.

These kinds of research situations are among the most common in psychology, where usually the only information available is from the samples. Nothing is known about the populations that the samples are supposed to come from. In particular, the researcher does not know the variance of the populations involved, which is a crucial ingredient in step 2 of the hypothesis-testing process (determining the characteristics of the comparison distribution).

In this chapter, we first examine the solution to the problem of not knowing the population variance by focusing on a special situation, the comparison of the mean of a single sample to a population with a known mean but an unknown variance. Then, having seen how to handle this problem of not knowing the population variance, we go on to consider the situation in which there is no known population at all—the situation in which all we have are two scores for each of a number of people.

The hypothesis-testing procedures you learn in this chapter, those in which the population variance is unknown, are examples of **t tests.** The *t* test is sometimes called "Student's *t*" because its main principles were originally developed by William S. Gosset, who published his articles anonymously using the name "Student" (see Box 9–1).

t tests

THE *t* TEST FOR A SINGLE SAMPLE

Let's begin with an example. Suppose your college newspaper reports an informal survey showing that students at your college study an average of 2.5 hours each day. However, you think that the students in your particular dormitory study much more than that. You randomly pick 16 students from your dormitory and ask them how much they study each day. (We will assume that they are all honest and accurate.) Your result is that these 16 students study an average of 3.2 hours per day. Should you conclude that students in general in your dormitory study more than the college average? Or should you conclude that your results are so close to the college average that the small difference of .7 hours might well be due to your having accidentally picked 16 of the more studious residents in your dormitory?

t test for a single sample

The situation in this example is that you have scores for a sample of individuals and you want to compare the mean of this sample to a population for which you know the mean but not the variance. Hypothesis testing in this situation is called a **t test for a single sample.** (It is also called a *one-sample* t *test.*) The *t* test for a single sample works basically the same way as the procedure you learned in Chapter 7. In the studies we considered in Chapter 7, you had scores for a sample of individuals (such as a group of 64 fifth graders who had taken a standard test with special instructions) and you wanted to compare the mean of this sample to a population (such as fifth graders in general). However, in the studies we considered in Chapter 7, you knew both the mean and variance of the general population to which you were going to compare your sample. In the situations we are now going to consider, everything is the same, but you don't know the population variance. This presents two important new wrinkles having to do with the details of how you carry out two of the steps of the hypothesis-testing process.

The first important new wrinkle is in step 2. Because the population variance is not known, you have to estimate it. So the first new wrinkle we consider is how to estimate an unknown population variance. The other important new wrinkle affects both steps 2 and 3. When the population variance has to be estimated, the shape of the comparison distribution is not quite a normal curve, so the second new wrinkle we consider is the shape of the comparison distribution (for step 2) and how to use a special table to find the cutoff (step 3) on what is a slightly differently shaped distribution.

Let's return to the amount of studying example. Step 1 of the hypothesis-testing process is to restate the problem as hypotheses about populations. There are two populations:

BOX 9-1   William S. Gosset, Alias "Student": Not a Mathematician, but a Practical Man

William S. Gosset graduated from Oxford in 1899 with a degree in mathematics and chemistry. It happened that in the same year the Guinness brewers in Dublin, Ireland, were seeking a few young scientists to take a first-ever scientific look at beer making. Gosset took one of these jobs and soon had immersed himself in barley, hops, and vats of brew.

The problem was how to make beer less variable, and especially to find the cause of bad batches. A proper scientist would say, "Conduct experiments!" But a business such as a brewery could not afford to waste money on experiments involving large numbers of vats, some of which any brewer worth his hops knew would fail. So Gosset was forced to contemplate the probability of, say, a certain strain of barley producing terrible beer when the experiment could consist of only a few batches of each strain. Adding to the problem was that he had no idea of the variability of a given strain of barley—perhaps some fields planted with the same strain grew better barley. (Does this sound familiar? Poor Gosset, like today's psychologists, had no idea of his population's variance.)

Gosset was up to the task, although at the time only he knew that. To his colleagues at the brewery, he was a professor of mathematics and not a proper brewer at all. To his statistical colleagues, mainly at the Biometric Laboratory at University College in London, he was a mere brewer and not a proper mathematician. In short, Gosset was the sort of scientist who was not above applying his talents to real life.

In fact, he seemed to revel in real life: raising pears, fishing, golfing, building boats, skiing, cycling (and lawn bowling, after he broke his leg by driving his car, a two-seater Model T Ford that he called "The Flying Bedstead," into a lamppost). And especially he reveled in simple tools that could be applied to anything, simple formulas that he could compute in his head. (A friend described him as an expert carpenter but claimed that Gosset did almost all of his finer woodwork with nothing but a penknife!)

So Gosset discovered the *t* distribution and invented the *t* test—simplicity itself (compared to most of statistics)—for situations when samples are small and the variability of the larger population is unknown. Most of his work was done on the backs of envelopes, with plenty of minor errors in arithmetic that he had to weed out later. Characteristically, he published his paper on his "brewery methods" only when editors of scientific journals demanded it. However, the Guiness brewery did not allow its scientists to publish papers, because one Guiness scientist had revealed brewery secrets. To this day, most statisticians call the *t* distribution "Student's *t*" because Gosset wrote under the anonymous name "Student" so that the brewery would not know about his writings or be identified through his being known to be its employee. A few of his fellow statisticians knew who "student" was, but apparently meetings with others involved secrecy worthy of a spy-novel. Supposedly, the brewery learned of his scientific fame only at his death, when colleagues wanted to honor him.

In spite of his great achievements, Gosset often wrote in letters that his own work provided "only a rough idea of the thing" or so-and-so "really worked out the complete mathematics." He was remembered as a thoughtful, kind, humble man, sensitive to others' feelings. Gosset's friendliness and generosity with his time and ideas also resulted in many students and younger colleagues making major breakthroughs based on his help. And it led to his becoming the mediator in a famous feud between two less humble giants in the field, Karl Pearson and Ronald Fisher, whom you will meet later.

References: Peters (1987); Slasburg (2001); Stigler (1986); Tankard (1984).

Population 1: The kind of students who live in your dormitory
Population 2: The kind of students at your college generally

The research hypothesis is that Population 1 students study more than Population 2 students; the null hypothesis is that Population 1 students do not study more than Population 2 students. So far, the problem is no different from those in Chapter 7.

The degrees of freedom is the number of scores in the sample minus 1.

$$df = N - 1 \tag{9-3}$$

df

df is the degrees of freedom.

In our example, $df = 16 - 1 = 15$. (In some situations you learn about in later chapters, the degrees of freedom are figured a bit differently. This is because in those situations, the number of scores free to vary is different. For all the situations you learn about in this chapter, $df = N - 1$.)

The formula for the estimated population variance is often written using *df* instead of $N - 1$:

The estimated population variance is the sum of squared deviations divided by the degrees of freedom.

$$S^2 = \frac{\Sigma(X - M)^2}{df} = \frac{SS}{df} \tag{9-4}$$

THE STANDARD DEVIATION OF THE DISTRIBUTION OF MEANS

Once you have figured the estimated population variance, you can figure the standard deviation of the comparison distribution using the same procedures you learned in Chapter 7. As always, when you have a sample of more than one, the comparison distribution is a distribution of means, and the variance of a distribution of means is the variance of the population of individuals divided by the sample size. You have just estimated the variance of the population. Thus, you can estimate the variance of the distribution of means by dividing the estimated population variance by the sample size. The standard deviation of the distribution of means is the square root of its variance. Stated as formula,

The variance of the distribution of means based on an estimated population variance is the estimated population variance divided by number of scores in the sample.

$$S_M^2 = \frac{S^2}{N} \tag{9-5}$$

The standard deviation of the distribution of means based on an estimated population variance is the square root of the variance of the distribution of means based on an estimated population variance.

$$S_M = \sqrt{S_M^2} \tag{9-6}$$

Tip for Success

Be careful. To find the variance of a distribution of means, you always divide the population variance by the sample size. This is true whether the population's variance is known or only estimated. It is only when making the estimate of the population variance that you divide by the sample size minus 1. That is, the degrees of freedom are used only when estimating the variance of the population of individuals.

Note that with an estimated population variance, the symbols for the variance and standard deviation of the distribution of means use *S* instead of σ.

In the example, the sample size was 16 and the estimated population variance we just worked out was .64. The variance of the distribution of means, based on that estimate, will be .04. That is, .64 divided by 16 equals .04. The standard deviation is .2, the square root of .04. In terms of the formulas,

$$S_M^2 = \frac{S^2}{N} = \frac{.64}{16} = .04$$

$$S_M = \sqrt{S_M^2} = \sqrt{.04} = .2$$

THE SHAPE OF THE COMPARISON DISTRIBUTION WHEN USING AN ESTIMATED POPULATION VARIANCE: THE *t* DISTRIBUTION

In Chapter 7 you learned that when the population distribution follows a normal curve, the shape of the distribution of means will also be a normal curve. However, this changes when you do hypothesis testing with an estimated population variance. When you are using an estimated population variance, you have less true information and more room for error. The mathematical effect is that there are likely to be slightly more extreme means than in an exact normal curve. Further, the smaller your sample size, the bigger this tendency. This is because, with a smaller sample size, your estimate of the population variance is based on less information.

The result of all this is that when doing hypothesis testing using an estimated variance, your comparison distribution will not be a normal curve. Instead, the comparison distribution will be a slightly different curve called a ***t* distribution.**

t distribution

Actually, there is a whole family of *t* distributions. They vary in shape according to the degrees of freedom in the sample used to estimate the population variance. However, for any particular degrees of freedom, there is only one *t* distribution.

Generally, *t* distributions look to the eye like a normal curve—bell-shaped, symmetrical, and unimodal. A *t* distribution differs subtly in having heavier tails (that is, slightly more scores at the extremes). Figure 9–2 shows the shape of a *t* distribution compared to a normal curve.

This slight difference in shape affects how extreme a score you need to reject the null hypothesis. As always, to reject the null hypothesis, your sample mean has to be in an extreme section of the comparison distribution of means, such as the top 5%. However, if the comparison distribution has more of its means in the tails than a normal curve would have, then the point where the top 5% begins has to be further out on this comparison distribution. Thus, it takes a slightly more extreme sample mean to get a significant result when using a *t* distribution than when using a normal curve.

Just how much the *t* distribution differs from the normal curve depends on the degrees of freedom, the amount of information used in estimating the population variance. The *t* distribution differs most from the normal curve when the degrees of freedom are low (because your estimate of the population variance is based on a very small sample). For example, using the normal curve, you may recall that 1.64 is the cutoff for a one-tailed test at the .05 level. On a *t* distribution with 7 degrees of freedom (that is, with a sample size of 8), the cutoff is 1.895 for a one-tailed test at the .05 level. If your estimate is based on a larger sample, say a sample of 25 (so that *df* = 24), the cutoff is 1.711, a cutoff much closer to that for the normal curve. If your sample size is infinite, the *t* distribution is the same as the normal curve. (Of course, if your sample size were infinite, it would include the entire population!)

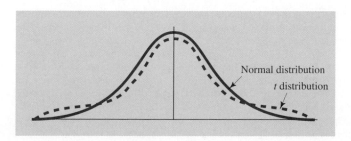

FIGURE 9–2 *The* t *distribution (dashed line) compared to the normal curve (solid line).*

But even with sample sizes of 30 or more, the *t* distribution is nearly identical to the normal curve.

Shortly, you will learn how to find the cutoff using a *t* distribution, but let's first return briefly to the example of how much students in your dorm study each night. You finally have everything you need for Step 2 about the characteristics of the comparison distribution. We have already seen that the distribution of means in this example has a mean of 2.5 hours and a standard deviation of .2. You can now add that the shape of the comparison distribution will be a *t* distribution with 15 degrees of freedom.[2]

THE CUTOFF SAMPLE SCORE FOR REJECTING THE NULL HYPOTHESIS: USING THE *t* TABLE

Step 3 of hypothesis testing is determining the cutoff for rejecting the null hypothesis. There is a different *t* distribution for any particular degrees of freedom. However, to avoid taking up pages and pages with tables for each possible *t* distribution, you use a simplified table that gives only the crucial cutoff points. We have included such a **t table** in Appendix A (Table A–2).

t **table**

In the hours-studied example, you have a one-tailed test. (You want to know whether students in your dorm study *more* than students in general at your college study). You will probably want to use the 5% significance level, because the cost of a Type I error (mistakenly rejecting the null hypothesis) is not great. You have 16 participants, making 15 degrees of freedom for your estimate of the population variance.

Table 9–1 shows a portion of the *t* table from Appendix A. Find the column for the .05 significance level for one-tailed tests and move down to the row for 15 degrees of freedom. The crucial cutoff is 1.753. Thus, you will reject the null hypothesis if your sample's mean is 1.753 or more standard deviations above the mean on the comparison distribution. (If you were using a known variance, you would have found your cutoff from a normal curve table. The Z score to reject the null hypothesis based on the normal curve would have been 1.645.)

One other point about using the *t* table: In the full *t* table in Appendix A, there are rows for each degree of freedom from 1 through 30, then for 35, 40, 45, and so on, up to 100. Suppose your study has degrees of freedom between two of these higher values. To be safe, you should use the nearest degrees of freedom to yours given on the table that is *less* than yours. For example, in a study with 43 degrees of freedom, you would use the cutoff for *df* = 40.

THE SAMPLE MEAN'S SCORE ON THE COMPARISON DISTRIBUTION: THE *t* SCORE

Step 4 of hypothesis testing is figuring your sample's score on the comparison distribution. In Chapter 7, this meant finding the Z score on the comparison distribu-

---

[2]Statisticians make a subtle distinction in this situation between the comparison distribution and the distribution of means. (We avoid this distinction to simplify your learning of what is already fairly difficult.) The general procedure of hypothesis testing, as we introduced it in Chapter 7, can be described as comparing a Z score to your sample's mean, where $Z = (M - \mu)/\sigma_M$ and then comparing this Z score to a cutoff Z score from the normal curve table. We described this process as using the distribution of means as your comparison distribution. Statisticians would say that actually you are comparing your computed Z score to a distribution of Z scores (which is simply a standard normal curve). Similarly, for a *t* test, statisticians think of the procedure as figuring a *t* score (like a Z score, but figured using an estimated standard deviation) where $t = (M - \mu)/S_M$ and then comparing your computed *t* score to a cutoff *t* score from a *t* distribution table. Thus, according to the formal statistical logic, the comparison distribution is a distribution of *t* scores, not of means.

TABLE 9–1	Cutoff Scores for *t* Distributions with 1 Through 17 Degrees of Freedom (Highlighting Cutoff for Hours Studied Example)					
	One-Tailed Tests			Two-Tailed Tests		
df	.10	.05	.01	.10	.05	.01
1	3.078	6.314	31.821	6.314	12.706	63.657
2	1.886	2.920	6.965	2.920	4.303	9.925
3	1.638	2.353	4.541	2.353	3.182	5.841
4	1.533	2.132	3.747	2.132	2.776	4.604
5	1.476	2.015	3.365	2.015	2.571	4.032
6	1.440	1.943	3.143	1.943	2.447	3.708
7	1.415	1.895	2.998	1.895	2.365	3.500
8	1.397	1.860	2.897	1.860	2.306	3.356
9	1.383	1.833	2.822	1.833	2.262	3.250
10	1.372	1.813	2.764	1.813	2.228	3.170
11	1.364	1.796	2.718	1.796	2.201	3.106
12	1.356	1.783	2.681	1.783	2.179	3.055
13	1.350	1.771	2.651	1.771	2.161	3.013
14	1.345	1.762	2.625	1.762	2.145	2.977
15	1.341	1.753	2.603	1.753	2.132	2.947
16	1.337	1.746	2.584	1.746	2.120	2.921
17	1.334	1.740	2.567	1.740	2.110	2.898

tion—the number of standard deviations your sample's mean is from the mean on the distribution. You do exactly the same thing when your comparison distribution is a *t* distribution. The only difference is that, instead of calling this a *Z* score, because it is from a *t* distribution, you call it a **t score**. In terms of a formula,

t score

(9-7)

$$t = \frac{M - \mu}{S_M}$$

> The *t* score is your sample's mean minus the population mean, divided by the standard deviation of the distribution of means.

In the example, your sample's mean of 3.2 is .7 hours from the mean of the distribution of means, which amounts to 3.5 standard deviations from the mean (.7 hours divided by the standard deviation of .2 hours). That is, the *t* score in the example is 3.5. In terms of the formula,

$$t = \frac{M - \mu}{S_M} = \frac{3.2 - 2.5}{.2} = \frac{.7}{.2} = 3.5$$

DECIDING WHETHER TO REJECT THE NULL HYPOTHESIS

Step 5 of hypothesis testing is deciding whether to reject the null hypothesis. This step is exactly the same with a *t* test, as it was in those discussed in previous chapters. In the example, the cutoff *t* score was 1.753 and the actual *t* score for your sample was 3.5. Conclusion: Reject the null hypothesis. The research hypothesis is supported that students in your dorm study more than students in the college overall.

Figure 9–3 shows the various distributions for this example.

FIGURE 9–3 *Distributions for the hours studied example.*

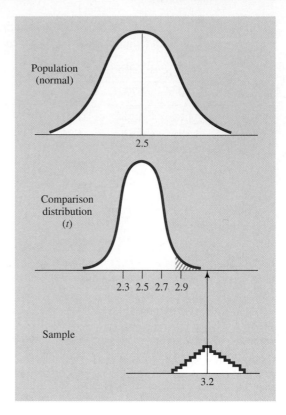

SUMMARY OF HYPOTHESIS TESTING WHEN THE POPULATION VARIANCE IS NOT KNOWN

Table 9–2 compares the hypothesis-testing procedure we just considered (for a *t* test for a single sample) with the hypothesis-testing procedure from Chapter 7 (for a *Z* test for a single sample). That is, we are comparing the current situation in which you know the population's mean but not its variance to the Chapter 7 situation where you knew the population's mean *and* variance.

ANOTHER EXAMPLE OF A *t* TEST FOR A SINGLE SAMPLE

Consider another fictional example. Suppose a researcher was studying the psychological effects of a devastating flood in a small rural community. Specifically, the researcher was interested in whether people felt more or less hopeful after the flood. The researcher randomly selected 10 people from this community to complete a short questionnaire. The key item on the questionnaire asked how hopeful they felt, using a 7-point scale from *extremely unhopeful* (1) to *neutral* (4) to *extremely hopeful* (7). The researcher wanted to know whether the responses would be consistently above or below the midpoint on the scale (4).

Table 9–3 shows the results and figuring for the *t* test for a single sample; Figure 9–4 shows the distributions involved. Here are the steps of hypothesis testing.

❶ **Restate the question as a research hypothesis and a null hypothesis about the populations.** There are two populations:

Population 1: People who experienced the flood
Population 2: People who are neither hopeful nor unhopeful

TABLE 9–2 Hypothesis Testing with a Single Sample Mean When Population Variance Is Unknown (*t* Test for a Single Sample) Compared to When Population Variance Is Known (*Z* Test for a Single Sample)

Steps in Hypothesis Testing	Difference From When Population Variance Is Known
❶ Restate the question as a research hypothesis and a null hypothesis about the populations.	No difference in method.
❷ Determine the characteristics of the comparison distribution:	
Population mean	No difference in method.
Population variance	Estimate from the sample.
Standard deviation of the distribution of sample means	No difference in method (but based on estimated population variance).
Shape of the comparison distribution	Use the *t* distribution with $df = N - 1$.
❸ Determine the significance cutoff.	Use the *t* table.
❹ Determine your sample's score on the comparison distribution.	No difference in method (but called a *t* score).
❺ Decide whether to reject the null hypothesis.	No difference in method.

The research hypothesis is that the two populations will score differently. The null hypothesis is that they will score the same.

   ❷ **Determine the characteristics of the comparison distribution.** If the null hypothesis is true, the mean of both populations is 4. The variance of these populations is not known, so you have to estimate it from the sample. As shown in Table 9–3, the sum of the squared deviations of the sample's scores from the sample's mean is 32.10. Thus, the estimated population variance is 32.10 divided by 9 degrees of freedom $(10 - 1)$, which comes out to 3.57.

   The distribution of means has a mean of 4 (the same as the population mean). Its variance is the estimated population variance divided by the sample size—3.57 divided by 10 equals .36. The square root of this, the standard deviation of the distribution of means, is .60. Its shape will be a *t* distribution for $df = 9$.

   ❸ **Determine the cutoff sample score on the comparison distribution at which the null hypothesis should be rejected.** The researcher wanted to be very cautious about mistakenly concluding that the flood made a difference. Thus, she decided to use the .01 significance level. The hypothesis was nondirectional (that is, no specific direction of difference from the mean of 4 was specified; either result would have been of interest), so the researcher used a two-tailed test. The researcher looked up the cutoff on Table 9–1 (or Table A–2 in Appendix A) for a two-tailed test and 9 degrees of freedom. The cutoff given on the table is 3.250. Thus, to reject the null hypothesis, the sample's score on the comparison distribution must be 3.250 or higher or −3.250 or lower.

   ❹ **Determine your sample's score on the comparison distribution.** The sample's mean of 4.7 is .7 scale points from the null hypothesis mean of 4.0. That

TABLE 9–3	Results and Figuring for a Single-Sample *t* Test for a Study of 10 People's Ratings of Hopefulness Following a Devastating Flood (Fictional Data)

Rating (X)	Difference From the Mean (X − M)	Squared Difference From the Mean (X − M)²
5	.3	.09
3	−1.7	2.89
6	1.3	1.69
2	−2.7	7.29
7	2.3	5.29
6	1.3	1.69
7	−2.3	5.29
4	− .7	.49
2	−2.7	7.29
5	.3	.09
Σ: 47		32.10

$M = \Sigma X/N = 47/10 = 4.7.$
$df = N - 1 = 10 - 1 = 9.$
$\mu = 4.0.$
$S^2 = SS/df = 32.10/(10 - 1) = 32.10/9 = 3.57.$
$S_M^2 = S^2/N = 3.57/10 = .36.$
$S_M = \sqrt{S_M^2} = \sqrt{.36} = .60.$
t with $df = 9$ needed for 1% significance level, two-tailed $= \pm 3.250.$
Actual sample $t = (M - \mu)/S_M = (4.7 - 4)/.6 = .7/.6 = 1.17.$

Decision: Do not reject the null hypothesis.

makes it 1.17 standard deviations on the comparison distribution from that distribution's mean ($.7/.6 = 1.17$); $t = 1.17$.

❺ **Decide whether to reject the null hypothesis.** The *t* of 1.17 is not as extreme as the needed *t* of ± 3.250. Therefore, the researcher cannot reject the null hypothesis. The study is inconclusive. (If the researcher had used a larger sample, giving more power, the result might have been quite different.)

SUMMARY OF STEPS FOR A *t* TEST FOR A SINGLE SAMPLE

Table 9–4 summarizes the steps of hypothesis testing when you have scores from a single sample and a population with a known mean but an unknown variance.

1. In what sense is a sample's variance a biased estimate of the variance of the population the sample is taken from? That is, in what way does the sample's variance typically differ from the population's?
2. What is the difference between the usual formula for figuring the variance and the formula for estimating a population's variance from the scores in a sample?

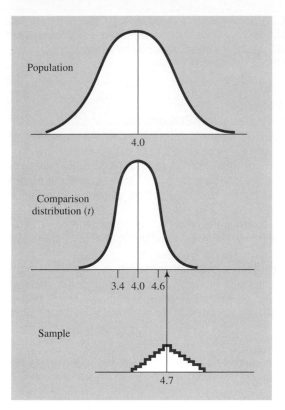

FIGURE 9–4 *Distributions for the example of how hopeful individuals felt following a devastating flood.*

3. (a) What are degrees of freedom? (b) How do you figure the degrees of freedom in a *t* test for a single sample? (c) What do they have to do with estimating the population variance? (d) What do they have to do with the *t* distribution?

4. (a) How does a *t* distribution differ from a normal curve? (b) How do degrees of freedom affect this? (c) What is the effect of the difference on hypothesis testing?

5. List three differences in how you do hypothesis testing for a *t* test for a single sample versus for a *Z* test for a single sample (what you learned in Chapter 7).

TABLE 9–4 Steps for a *t* Test for a Single Sample

---

❶ **Restate the question as a research hypothesis and a null hypothesis about the populations.**

❷ **Determine the characteristics of the comparison distribution.**

   a. The mean is the same as the known population mean.

   b. The standard deviation is figured as follows:

      i. Figure the estimated population variance: $S^2 = SS/df$.

      ii. Figure the variance of the distribution of means: $S_M^2 = S^2/N$.

      iii. Figure the standard deviation of the distribution of means: $S_M = \sqrt{S_M^2}$.

   c. The shape will be a *t* distribution with $N - 1$ degrees of freedom.

❸ **Determine the cutoff sample score on the comparison distribution at which the null hypothesis should be rejected.**

   a. Decide the significance level and whether to use a one-tailed or a two-tailed test.

   b. Look up the appropriate cutoff in a *t* table.

❹ **Determine your sample's score on the comparison distribution:** $t = (M - \mu)/S_M$.

❺ **Decide whether to reject the null hypothesis:** Compare the scores from Steps 3 and 4.

---

6. A population has a mean of 23. A sample of 4 is given an experimental procedure and has scores of 20, 22, 22, and 20. Test the hypothesis that the procedure produces a lower score. Use the .05 significance level. (a) Use the steps of hypothesis testing and (b) make a sketch of the distributions involved.

ANSWERS:

1. The sample's variance will in general be larger.
2. In the usual formula you divide by the number of participants (N); in the formula for estimating a population's variance from the scores in a sample, you divide by the number of participants in the sample minus 1.
3. (a) The number of scores free to vary. (b) The number of scores in the sample minus 1. (c) In estimating the population variance, the formula is the sum of squared deviations divided by the degrees of freedom. (d) t distributions differ slightly from each other according to the degrees of freedom.
4. (a) It has heavier tails; that is, more scores at the extremes. (b) The more degrees of freedom, the closer the shape (including the tails) to a normal curve. (c) The cutoffs for significance are more extreme for a t distribution than for a normal curve.
5. In the t test you (a) estimate the population variance from the sample (it is not known in advance); (b) you look up the cutoff on a t table in which you also have to take into account the degrees of freedom (you don't use a normal curve table); and (c) your sample's score on the comparison distribution, which is a t distribution (not a normal curve), is a t score (not a Z score).
6. (a) Steps of hypothesis testing:

   ❶ **Restate the question as a research hypothesis and a null hypothesis about the populations.** There are two populations:

   Population 1: People who are given the experimental procedure
   Population 2: The general population

   The research hypothesis is that Population 1 will score lower than Population 2. The null hypothesis is that Population 1 will not score lower than Population 2.

   ❷ **Determine the characteristics of the comparison distribution.** The mean of the distribution of means is 23. To figure the estimated population variance, you first need to figure the sample mean, which is $(20 + 22 + 22 + 20)/4 = 84/4 = 21$. The estimated population variance is $S^2 = SS/(N - 1) = [(20 - 21)^2 + (22 - 21)^2 + (22 - 21)^2 + (20 - 21)^2]/(4 - 1) = (-1^2 + 1^2 + 1^2 + -1^2)/3 = (1 + 1 + 1 + 1)/3 = 4/3 = 1.33$. The variance of the distribution of means is $S_M^2 = S^2/N = 1.33/4 = .33$. $S = \sqrt{S_M^2} = \sqrt{.33} = .57$. It's shape will be a t distribution for $df = 3$.

   ❸ **Determine the cutoff sample score on the comparison distribution at which the null hypothesis should be rejected.** From Table A–2, the cutoff for a one-tailed t test at the .05 level for $df = 3$ is -2.353.

   ❹ **Determine your sample's score on the comparison distribution.** $t = (M - \mu)/S_M = (21 - 23)/.57 = -2/.57 = -3.51$.

   ❺ **Decide whether to reject the null hypothesis.** The t of -3.57 is more extreme than the needed t of -2.353. Therefore, reject the null hypothesis; the research hypothesis is supported.

   (b) Sketches of distributions are shown in Figure 9–5.

THE *t* TEST FOR DEPENDENT MEANS

The situation you just learned about (the t test for a single sample) is for when you know the population mean but not its variance, and where you have a single sample of scores. It turns out that in most research you do not even know the population's *mean*; plus, in most research situations you usually have not one set, but *two* sets, of

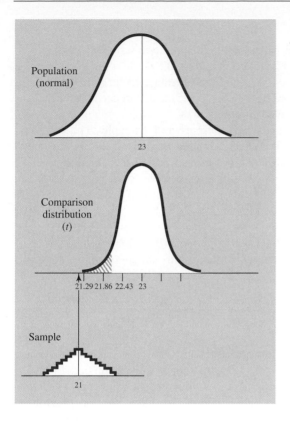

FIGURE 9-5 *Distributions for answer to "How Are You Doing?" question 6b.*

scores. These two things, not knowing the population mean and having two sets of scores, almost always go together. This situation is very common.

The rest of this chapter focuses specifically on this important research situation in which you have two scores from each person in your sample. This kind of research situation is called a **repeated-measures design** (also known as a *within-subjects design*). A common example is when you measure the same people before and after some psychological or social intervention. For example, an organizational psychologist might measure days missed from work for a sample of assembly workers before and after a new health promotion program was introduced.

The hypothesis-testing procedure for the situation in which each person is measured twice is a *t* **test for dependent means.** It has the name "dependent means" because the mean for each group of scores (for example, a group of before-scores and a group of after-scores) are dependent on each other in that they are both from the same people. (In Chapter 10, we consider the situation in which you compare scores from two different groups of people, a research design analyzed by a *t* test for *independent* means.)

The *t* test for dependent means is also called a *t test for paired samples, t test for correlated means,* and *t test for matched samples*. Each of these names comes from the same idea that in this kind of *t* test you are comparing two sets of scores that are related to each other in a direct way, such as each person being tested before and after some procedure.

You do a *t* test for dependent means exactly the same way as a *t* test for a single sample, except that (a) you use something called *difference scores,* and (b) you assume that the population mean is 0.

repeated-measures design

t test for dependent means

DIFFERENCE SCORES

difference scores

change scores

With a repeated-measures design, your sample includes two scores for each person instead of just one. The way you handle this is to make the two scores per person into one score per person! You do this magic by creating **difference scores**: For each person, you subtract one score from the other. If the difference is before versus after, difference scores are also called **change scores**.

Consider the health-promotion, absence-from-work example. The organizational psychologist takes the number of days missed from work during the month after the program minus the number of days missed during the month before the program. This gives an after-minus-before difference score for each worker. When the two scores are a before-score and an after-score, we usually take the after-score minus the before-score to indicate the *change*.

Once you have the difference score for each person in the study, you do the rest of the hypothesis testing with difference scores. That is, you treat the study as if there were a single sample of scores (scores that in this situation happen to be difference scores).[3]

POPULATION OF DIFFERENCE SCORES WITH A MEAN OF 0

Ordinarily, the null hypothesis in a repeated-measures design is that on the average there is *no difference* between the two groups of scores. For example, the null hypothesis in the health promotion study is that on the average there is no difference between absences from work before and after the health promotion program is started. What does *no difference* mean? Saying there is on the average no difference is the same as saying that the mean of the population of the difference scores is 0. Therefore, when working with difference scores, you are comparing the population of difference scores that your sample of difference scores comes from to a population of difference scores with a mean of 0. In other words, with a *t* test for dependent means, what we call Population 2 will ordinarily have a mean of 0.

EXAMPLE OF A *t* TEST FOR DEPENDENT MEANS

Olthoff (1989) tested the communication quality of engaged couples 3 months before and again 3 months after marriage. One group studied was 19 couples who had received ordinary premarital counseling from the ministers who were going to marry them. (To keep the example simple, we will focus on just this one group, and on only the husbands in the group. Scores for wives were similar, though somewhat more varied, making it a more complicated example for learning the *t* test procedure.)

The scores for the 19 husbands are listed in the "Before" and "After" columns in Table 9–5, followed by all the *t* test figuring. (The distributions involved are shown in Figure 9–6.) The crucial column for starting the analysis is the difference scores. For example, the first husband, whose communication quality was 126 before marriage and 115 after had a difference of −11. (You usually figure after minus before, so that an increase is positive and a decrease, as for this husband, is

---

[3]You can also use a *t* test for dependent means with scores from pairs of research participants, considering each pair as if it were one person, and figuring the difference score for each pair. For example, suppose you have 30 married couples and want to test whether husbands are consistently older than wives. You could figure for each couple a difference score of husband's age minus wife's age.

TABLE 9–5 *t* Test for Communication Quality Scores Before and After Marriage for 19 Husbands Who Received No Special Communication Training

Husband	Communication Quality		Difference (After – Before)	Deviation of Differences From the Mean of Differences	Squared Deviation
	Before	*After*			
A	126	115	− 11	1.05	1.1
B	133	125	− 8	4.05	16.4
C	126	96	− 30	−17.95	322.2
D	115	115	0	12.05	145.2
E	108	119	11	23.05	531.3
F	109	82	− 27	−14.95	233.5
G	124	93	− 31	−18.95	359.1
H	98	109	11	23.05	531.3
I	95	72	− 23	−10.95	119.9
J	120	104	− 16	− 3.95	15.6
K	118	107	− 11	1.05	1.1
L	126	118	− 8	4.05	16.4
M	121	102	− 19	− 6.95	48.3
N	116	115	− 1	11.05	122.1
O	94	83	− 11	1.05	1.1
P	105	87	− 18	− 5.95	35.4
Q	123	121	− 2	10.05	101.0
R	125	100	− 25	−12.95	167.7
S	128	118	− 10	2.05	4.2
Σ:	2,210	1,981	−229		2,772.9

For difference scores:

$M = -229/19 = -12.05.$

$\mu = 0$ (assumed as a no-change baseline of comparison).

$S^2 = SS/df = 2{,}772.9/(19-1) = 154.05.$

$S_M^2 = S^2/N = 154.05/19 = 8.11.$

$S_M = \sqrt{S_M^2} = \sqrt{8.11} = 2.85.$

t with $df = 18$ needed for 5% level, two-tailed $= \pm 2.101$.

$t = (M - \mu)/S_M = (-12.05 - 0)/2.85 = -4.23.$

Decision: Reject the null hypothesis.

Note: Data from Olthoff (1989).

negative.) The mean of the difference scores is −12.05. That is, on the average, these 19 husbands' communication quality decreased by about 12 points.

Is this decrease significant? In other words, how likely is it that this sample of difference scores is a random sample from a population of difference scores whose mean is 0?

❶ **Restate the question as a research hypothesis and a null hypothesis about the populations.** There are two populations:

FIGURE 9-6 *Distributions for the Olthoff (1989) example of a* t *test for dependent means.*

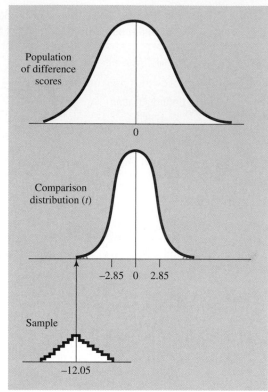

Population 1: Husbands who receive ordinary premarital counseling
Population 2: Husbands whose communication quality does not change from before to after marriage

The research hypothesis is that Population 1 is different from Population 2—that husbands who receive ordinary premarital counseling (such as the husbands Olthoff studied) *do* change in communication quality from before to after marriage. The null hypothesis is that the populations are the same—that the husbands who receive ordinary premarital counseling *do not* change in their communication quality from before to after marriage.

Notice that you have no actual information about Population 2 husbands. The husbands in the study are a sample of Population 1 husbands. If the research hypothesis is correct, Population 2 husbands do not even really exist. For the purposes of hypothesis testing, we set up Population 2 as a kind of straw man comparison group. That is, we set up a comparison group for purposes of the analysis of husbands who, if measured before and after marriage, would on the average show no difference.

❷ **Determine the characteristics of the comparison distribution.** If the null hypothesis is true, the mean of the population of difference scores is 0. The variance of the population of difference scores can be estimated from the sample of difference scores. As shown in Table 9–5, the sum of squared deviations of the difference scores from the mean of the difference scores is 2,772.9. With 19 husbands in the study, there are 18 degrees of freedom. Dividing the sum of squared deviation scores by the degrees of freedom gives an estimated population variance of 154.05.

The distribution of means (from this population of difference scores) has a mean of 0, the same as the population mean. Its variance is the estimated population variance (154.05) divided by the sample size (19), which gives 8.11. The standard deviation is 2.85, the square root of 8.11. Because Olthoff was using an estimated population variance, the comparison distribution is a *t* distribution. The estimate of the population variance is based on 18 degrees of freedom, so this comparison distribution is a *t* distribution for 18 degrees of freedom.

❸ **Determine the cutoff sample score on the comparison distribution at which the null hypothesis should be rejected.** Olthoff used a two-tailed test to allow for either an increase or decrease in communication quality. Using the .05 significance level and 18 degrees of freedom, Table A–2 shows a cutoff *t* score of ±2.101.

❹ **Determine your sample's score on the comparison distribution.** Olthoff's sample had a mean difference score of −12.05. That is, the mean was 12.05 points below the mean of 0 on the distribution of means. The standard deviation of the distribution of means is 2.85. Thus, the mean of the difference scores of −12.05 is 4.23 standard deviations below the mean of the distribution of means. So Olthoff's sample of difference scores has a *t* score of −4.23.

❺ **Decide whether to reject the null hypothesis.** The *t* of −4.23 for the sample of difference scores is more extreme than the needed *t* of ±2.101. Thus, you can reject the null hypothesis: Olthoff's husbands are from a population in which husbands' communication quality is different after marriage from what it was before (it is lower).

Olthoff's actual study was more complex. You may be interested to know that he found that the wives also showed this decrease in communication quality after marriage. But a group of similar engaged couples who were given special communication-skills training by their ministers (much more than the usual short session) had no significant decline in marital communication quality after marriage (see Figure 9–7). In fact, there is now a great deal of research showing that relationship quality of all kinds on the average declines from before to after marriage (e.g., Karney & Bradbury, 1997) and that intensive communication skills training can be very helpful in reducing or eliminating this decline (Markman et al., 1993).

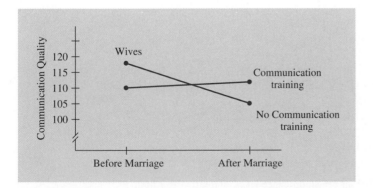

FIGURE 9–7 *Communication skills of wives given premarital communications training and wives not given such training. (Based on Olthoff, 1989.)*

A SECOND EXAMPLE OF A *t* TEST FOR DEPENDENT MEANS

Here is another example. A researcher is interested in the effect of noise on hand-eye coordination in surgeons. The researcher gives nine surgeons a standard test of hand-eye coordination under both quiet and noisy conditions—not while doing surgery, of course. The prediction is that surgeons' coordination is better under quiet conditions. (Ideally, any effects of practice or fatigue from taking the hand-eye coordination test twice would be equalized by testing half the surgeons under noisy conditions first, and half under quiet conditions first.

Table 9–6 shows the results for this fictional study. It also shows the figuring of difference scores and all the other figuring for the *t* test for dependent means. Figure 9–8 shows the distributions involved. Here are the steps of hypothesis testing:

❶ **Restate the question as a research hypothesis and a null hypothesis about the populations.** There are two populations:

Population 1: Surgeons like those tested in this study
Population 2: Surgeons whose coordination is the same under quiet and noisy conditions

The research hypothesis is that Population 1's mean difference scores (quiet minus noisy) is greater than Population 2's. That is, the research hypothesis is that sur-

---

TABLE 9–6 *t* **Test for a Study of Hand-Eye Coordination in Which Nine Surgeons Are Measured Under Noisy and Quiet Conditions (Fictional Data)**

Surgeon	Conditions		Difference	Deviation	Squared Deviation
	Quiet	*Noisy*			
1	18	12	6	$6 - 2 = 4$	16
2	21	21	0	-2	4
3	19	16	3	1	1
4	21	16	5	3	9
5	17	19	-2	-4	16
6	20	19	1	-1	1
7	18	16	2	0	0
8	16	17	-1	-3	9
9	20	16	4	2	4
Σ:	170	152	18		60

For difference scores:

$M = 18/9 = 2.0$.

$\mu = 0$ (assumed as a no-difference baseline of comparison).

$S^2 = SS/df = 60/(9 - 1) = 60/8 = 7.5$.

$S_M^2 = S^2/N = 7.50/9 = .83$.

$S_M = \sqrt{S_M^2} = \sqrt{.83} = .91$.

t for *df* = 8, needed for 5% significance level, one-tailed = 1.860.

$t = (M - \mu)/S_M = (2.00 - 0)/.91 = 2.20$.

Decision: Reject the null hypothesis.

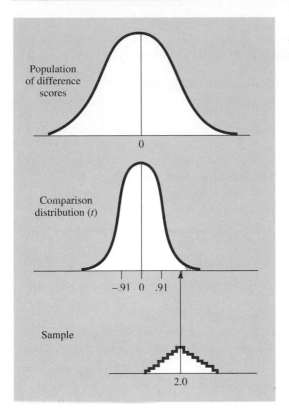

FIGURE 9-8 *Distributions for fictional study of hand-eye co-ordination under noisy and quiet conditions.*

geons perform better under quiet conditions. The null hypothesis is that Population 1's difference in performance is not higher than Population 2's. That is, the null hypothesis is that surgeons do no better under quiet conditions.

❷ **Determine the characteristics of the comparison distribution.** If the null hypothesis is true, the mean of the population of difference scores is 0. What is the variance of this population of difference scores? Estimating from the sample of difference scores, it is the sum of the squared deviations of the difference scores divided by the degrees of freedom. This is shown in Table 9–6 to be 7.5.

The mean of the comparison distribution is 0, the same as the null hypothesis population. The variance of the comparison distribution is .83 (the estimated population variance divided by the sample size). The standard deviation of the comparison distribution is the square root of this, .91. The comparison distribution is a *t* distribution for 8 degrees of freedom. It is a *t* distribution because we figured its variance based on an estimated population variance. It has 8 degrees of freedom because there were 8 degrees of freedom in the estimate of the population variance.

❸ **Determine the cutoff sample score on the comparison distribution at which the null hypothesis should be rejected.** This is a one-tailed test because there was a reasonable basis for predicting the direction of the difference. Using the .05 significance level with 8 degrees of freedom, Table A–2 shows a cutoff *t* of 1.860.

❹ **Determine your sample's score on the comparison distribution.** The sample's mean difference of 2 is 2.20 standard deviations (of .91 each) above the mean of 0 on the distribution of means.

❺ **Decide whether to reject the null hypothesis.** The sample's *t* score of 2.20 is more extreme than the cutoff *t* of 1.860. You can reject the null hypothesis. Sur-

TABLE 9–7	Steps for a *t* Test for Dependent Means

❶ **Restate the question as a research hypothesis and a null hypothesis about the populations.**

❷ **Determine the characteristics of the comparison distribution.**
    a. Make each person's two scores into a difference score. Do all the remaining steps using these difference scores.
    b. Figure the mean of the difference scores.
    c. Assume a population mean of 0: $\mu = 0$.
    d. Figure the estimated population variance of difference scores: $S^2 = SS/df$.
    e. Figure the variance of the distribution of means of difference scores: $S_M^2 = S^2/N$.
    f. Figure the standard deviation of the distribution of means of difference scores: $S_M = \sqrt{S_M^2}$.
    g. The shape is a *t* distribution with $df = N - 1$.

❸ **Determine the cutoff sample score on the comparison distribution at which the null hypothesis should be rejected.**
    a. Decide the desired significance level and whether to use a one-tailed or a two-tailed test.
    b. Look up the appropriate cutoff in a *t* table.

❹ **Determine your sample's score on the comparison distribution:** $t = (M - \mu)/S_M$.

❺ **Decide whether to reject the null hypothesis:** Compare the scores from Steps 3 and 4.

geons have better hand-eye coordination under quiet than under noisy conditions (in this fictional study).

SUMMARY OF STEPS FOR A *T* TEST FOR DEPENDENT MEANS

Table 9–7 summarizes the steps for a *t* test for dependent means.[4]

HOW ARE YOU DOING?

1. Describe the situation in which you would use a *t* test for dependent means.
2. When doing a *t* test for dependent means, what do you do with the two scores you have for each participant?
3. In a *t* test for dependent means, (a) what is usually considered to be the mean of the "known" population (Population 2), and (b) why?
4. Five individuals are tested before and after an experimental procedure; their scores are given below. Test the hypothesis that there is no change, using the .05 significance level. (a) Use the steps of hypothesis testing and (b) sketch the distributions involved.

[4]The steps of carrying out a *t* test for dependent means can be somewhat combined into computational formulas for *S* and *t* based on difference scores. For purposes of learning the ideas, we strongly recommend that you use the regular procedures as we have discussed them in this chapter for doing the practice problems. In a real research situation, the figuring is usually all done by computer. However, if you ever have to do a *t* test for dependent means for an actual research study by hand (without a computer), you may find these formulas useful.

D in the formulas below is for difference score:

$$S = \sqrt{\frac{\Sigma D^2 - (\Sigma D)^2 / N}{N - 1}} \qquad (9\text{-}8)$$

$$t = \frac{\Sigma D / N}{S / \sqrt{N}} \qquad (9\text{-}9)$$

Person	Before	After
1	20	30
2	30	50
3	20	10
4	40	30
5	30	40

ANSWERS:

1. It is used when you are doing hypothesis testing and you have two scores for each participant (such as a before-score and an after-score) and the population variance is unknown.
2. Subtract one from the other to create a difference or change score for each person. The *t* test is then done with these difference of change scores.
3. (a) 0. (b) Because you are comparing your sample to a situation in which there is no difference—a population of difference scores in which the average difference is 0.
4. (a) Steps of hypothesis testing (all figuring is shown in Table 9–8):

   ❶ **Restate the question as a research hypothesis and a null hypothesis about the populations.** There are two populations:

   Population 1: People like those tested before and after the experimental procedure.
   Population 2: People whose scores are the same before and after the experimental procedure.

   The research hypothesis is that Population 1's mean change scores (after minus before) is different than Population 2's. The null hypothesis is that Population 1's change is the same as Population 2's.

   ❷ **Determine the characteristics of the comparison distribution.** The mean of the comparison distribution is 0; its standard deviation is 6, It is a *t* distribution for 4 *df*.

   ❸ **Determine the cutoff sample score on the comparison distribution at which the null hypothesis should be rejected.** For a two-tailed test at the .05 level, the cutoff is ±2.776.

TABLE 9–8 **Figuring for Answer to "How Are You Doing?" Question 4**

Person	Score Before	Score After	Change (After − Before)	Deviation (Change − Mean)	Squared Deviation
1	20	30	10	6	36
2	30	50	20	16	256
3	20	10	−10	−14	196
4	40	30	−10	−14	196
5	30	40	10	6	36
Σ	140	160	20		720

For difference scores:

$M = 20/5 = 44.$

$\mu = 0.$

$S^2 = SS/df = 720/(5 - 1) = 720/4 = 180.$

$S_M^2 = S^2/N = 180/5 = 36.$

$S_M = \sqrt{S_M^2} = \sqrt{36} = 6.$

t for *df* = 4 needed for 5% significance level, two-tailed = ±2.776.

$t = (M - \mu)/S_M = (4 - 0)/6 = .67$

Decision: Do not reject the null hypothesis.

❹ **Determine your sample's score on the comparison distribution.** $t = (4 - 0)/6 = .67$.

❺ **Decide whether to reject the null hypothesis.** The sample's *t* score of .67 is not more extreme than the cutoff *t* of ± 2.776. Therefore, do *not* reject the null hypothesis.

(b) The distributions are shown in Figure 9–9.

ASSUMPTIONS

As we have seen, when using an estimated population variance, the comparison distribution is a *t* distribution. However, the comparison distribution will be exactly a *t* distribution only if the distribution of individuals follows a normal curve. Otherwise, the comparison distribution will follow some other (usually unknown) shape.

    Thus, strictly speaking, a normal population is a requirement within the logic and mathematics of the *t* test. A requirement like this for a hypothesis-testing procedure is called an **assumption.** That is, a normal population distribution is one assumption of the *t* test. The effect of this assumption is that if the population distribution is not normal, the comparison distribution will be some indeterminate shape other than a *t* distribution—and thus the cutoffs on the *t* table will be incorrect.

    Unfortunately, when you do a *t* test, you don't know whether the population is normal. This is because when doing a *t* test, usually all you have to go on are the scores in your sample. Fortunately, however, as we saw in Chapter 5, distributions in psychology research quite often do approximate a normal curve. (This also applies to distributions of difference scores.) Also, statisticians have found that, in practice, you get reasonably accurate results with *t* tests even when the population is rather far from normal. In other words, the *t* test is said to be *robust* over moderate violations of the

assumption

FIGURE 9–9 *Distributions for answer to "How Are You Doing?" question 4.*

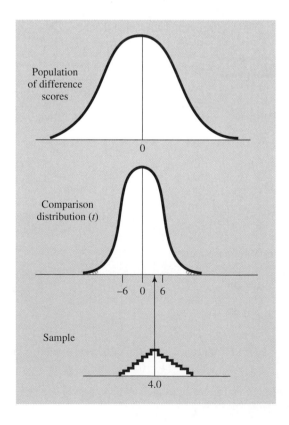

Population of difference scores

0

Comparison distribution (*t*)

−6   0   6

Sample

4.0

assumption of a normal population distribution. How statisticians figure out the **robustness** of a test is an interesting topic, which is described in Box 10–1 in Chapter 10.   **robustness**

The only very common situation in which using a *t* test for dependent means is likely to give a seriously distorted result is when you are using a one-tailed test and the population is highly skewed (is very asymmetrical, with a much longer tail on one side than the other). Thus, you need to be cautious about your conclusions when doing a one-tailed test if the sample of difference scores is highly skewed, suggesting the population it comes from is also highly skewed.

EFFECT SIZE AND POWER FOR THE *t* TEST FOR DEPENDENT MEANS

EFFECT SIZE

You can figure the effect size for a study using a *t* test for dependent means the same way as in Chapter 8. It is the difference between the population means divided by the population standard deviation: $d = (\mu_1 - \mu_2)/\sigma$. When using this formula for a *t* test for dependent means, μ_1 is for the predicted mean of the population of difference scores, μ_2 (the "known" population mean) is almost always 0, and σ is usually for the standard deviation of the populations of difference scores. The conventions for effect size for a *t* test for dependent means are also the same as you learned for the situation we considered in Chapter 8: A small effect size is .20, a medium effect size is .50, and a large effect size is .80.

Consider an example. A sports psychologist plans a study on attitudes toward teammates before versus after a game. She will administer an attitude questionnaire twice, once before and once after a game. Suppose that the smallest before–after difference that would be of any importance is 4 points on the questionnaire. Also suppose that based on related research, the researcher figures that the standard deviation of difference scores on this attitude questionnaire is about 8 points. Thus, $\mu_1 = 4$ and $\sigma = 8$. Applying the effect size formula, $d = (\mu_1 - \mu_2)/\sigma = (4 - 0)/8 = .50$. In terms of the effect size conventions, her planned study has a medium effect size.

To estimate the effect size after a study, you use the actual mean of your sample's difference scores as your estimate of μ_1 and you use S (for the population of difference scores) as your estimate of σ.

Consider our first example of a *t* test for dependent means, the study of husbands' change in communication quality. In that study, the mean of the difference scores was -12.05. The estimated population standard deviation of the difference scores would be 12.41. That is, we figured the estimated variance of the difference scores (S^2) to be 154.05; $\sqrt{S^2} = 12.41$. Therefore, the estimated effect size is $d = (\mu_1 - \mu_2)/\sigma = (M - 0)/S = (-12.05 - 0)/12.41 = -.97$. This is a very large effect size. (The negative sign for the effect size means that the large effect was a decrease.)

POWER

Table 9–9 gives the approximate power at the .05 significance level for small, medium, and large effect sizes and one-tailed and two-tailed tests. In the sports psychology example, the researcher expected a medium effect size ($d = .50$). If she planned to conduct the study using the .05 level, two-tailed, with 20 participants, the study would have a power of .59. This means that if the research hypothesis is true and has a medium effect size, there is a 59% chance that this study will come out significant.

TABLE 9–9 Approximate Power for Studies Using the *t* Test for Dependent Means for Testing Hypotheses at the .05 Significance Level

Difference Scores in Sample (*N*)	Effect Size		
	Small (*d* = .20)	Medium (*d* = .50)	Large (*d* = .80)
One-tailed test			
10	.15	.46	.78
20	.22	.71	.96
30	.29	.86	*
40	.35	.93	*
50	.40	.97	*
100	.63	*	*
Two-tailed test			
10	.09	.32	.66
20	.14	.59	.93
30	.19	.77	.99
40	.24	.88	*
50	.29	.94	*
100	.55	*	*

*Power is nearly 1.

The power table (Table 9–9) is also useful when you are reading about a nonsignificant result in a published study. Suppose that a study using a *t* test for dependent means has a nonsignificant result. The study tested significance at the .05 level, was two-tailed, and had 10 participants. Should you conclude that there is in fact no difference at all in the populations? Probably not. Even assuming a medium effect size, Table 9–9 shows that there is only a 32% chance of getting a significant result in this study.

Consider another study that was not significant. This study also used the .05 significance level, two-tailed. This study had 100 research participants. Table 9–9 tells you that there would be a 55% chance of the study's coming out significant if there were even a true small effect size in the population. If there were a medium effect size in the population, the table indicates that there is almost a 100% chance that this study would have come out significant. Thus, in this study with 100 participants, we could conclude from the results that in the population there is probably at most a small difference.

To keep Table 9–9 simple, we have given power figures for only a few different numbers of participants (10, 20, 30, 40, 50, and 100). This should be adequate for the kinds of rough evaluations you need to make when evaluating results of research articles.[5]

[5]Cohen (1988, pp. 28–39) provides more detailed tables in terms of numbers of participants, levels of effect size, and significance levels. If you use his tables, note that the *d* referred to is actually based on a *t* test for independent means (the situation we consider in Chapter 10). To use these tables for a *t* test for dependent means, first multiply your effect size by 1.4. For example, if your effect size is .30, for purposes of using Cohen's tables, you would consider it to be .42 (that is, .30 × 1.4 = .42). The only other difference from our table is that Cohen describes the significance level by the letter *a* (for "alpha level"), with a subscript of either 1 or 2, referring to a one-tailed or two-tailed test. For example, a table that refers to "$a_1 = .05$" at the top means that this is the table for *p* <.05, one-tailed.

| TABLE 9–10 | Approximate Number of Research Participants Needed for 80% Power for the *t* Test for Dependent Means in Testing Hypotheses at the .05 Significance Level |

	Effect Size		
	Small (*d* = .20)	Medium (*d* = .50)	Large (*d* = .80)
One-tailed	156	26	12
Two-tailed	196	33	14

PLANNING SAMPLE SIZE

Table 9–10 gives the approximate number of participants needed for 80% power for a planned study. (Eighty percent is a common figure used by researchers for the minimum power to make a study worth doing.) Suppose you plan a study in which you expect a large effect size and will use the .05 significance level, two-tailed. The table shows you would only need 14 participants to have 80% power. On the other hand, a study using the same significance level, also two-tailed, but in which you expect only a small effect size would need 196 participants in your study for 80% power.[6]

HOW ARE YOU DOING?

1. (a) What is an assumption in hypothesis testing? (b) Describe a specific assumption for a *t* test for dependent means. (c) What is the effect of violating this assumption? (d) What does it mean to say that the *t* test for dependent means is "robust"? (e) Describe a situation in which it is not robust.
2. How can you tell if you have violated the normal curve assumption?
3. (a) Write the formula for effect size; (b) describe each of its terms as they apply to a planned *t* test for dependent means; (c) describe what you use for each of its terms in figuring effect size for a completed study that used a *t* test for dependent means.
4. You are planning a study in which you predict the mean of the population of difference scores to be 40, and the population standard deviation is 80. You plan to test significance using a *t* test for dependent means, one-tailed, with an alpha of .05. (a) What is the predicted effect size? (b) What is the power of this study if you carry it out with 20 participants? (c) How many participants would you need to have 80% power?

ANSWERS

1. (a) It is a requirement that you must meet for the results of the hypothesis testing procedure to be accurate.
   (b) The population of individuals' difference scores is assumed to be a normal distribution.
   (c) The significance level cutoff from the *t* table is not accurate.
   (d) Unless you very strongly violate the assumption (that is, unless the population distribution is very far from normal), the cutoff is fairly accurate.
   (e) When doing a one-tailed test and the population distribution is highly skewed.
2. You look at the distribution of the sample of difference scores to see if it is dramatically different from a normal curve.
3. (a) $d = (\mu_1 - \mu_2)/\sigma$.

[6]More detailed tables, giving needed numbers of participants for levels of power other than 80% (and also for effect sizes other than .20, .50, and .80 and for other significance levels) are provided in Cohen (1988, pp. 54–55). However, see footnote 5 in this chapter about using Cohen's tables for a *t* test for dependent means.

(b) *d* is the effect size; μ_1 is for the predicted mean of the population of difference scores; μ_2 is the mean of the known population, which for a population of difference scores is almost always 0; σ is for the standard deviation of the populations of difference scores.

(c) To estimate μ_1, you use *M*, the actual mean of your sample's difference scores; μ_2 remains as 0; and for σ, you use *S*, the standard deviation of the population of difference scores.

4. (a) $d = (\mu_1 - \mu_2)/\sigma = (40 - 0)/80 = .5$. (b) .71. (c) 26.

CONTROVERSY: ADVANTAGES AND DISADVANTAGES OF REPEATED-MEASURES DESIGNS

The main controversies about *t* tests have to do with their relative advantages and disadvantages compared to various alternatives (alternatives we will discuss in Chapter 15). There is, however, one consideration that we want to comment on now. It is about all research designs in which the same participants are tested before and after some experimental intervention (the kind of situation the *t* test for dependent means is often used for).

Studies using difference scores (that is, studies using a repeated-measures design) often have much larger effect sizes for the same amount of expected difference between means than other kinds of research designs. That is, testing each of a group of participants twice (once under one condition and once under a different condition) usually produces a high-power type of study. In particular, this kind of study gives more power than dividing the participants up into two groups and testing each group once (one group tested under one condition and the other tested under another condition). In fact, studies using difference scores usually have even more power than those in which you have twice as many participants, but tested each only once.

Why do repeated-measures designs have so much power? The reason is that the standard deviation of difference scores is usually quite low. (The standard deviation of difference scores is what you divide by to get the effect size when using difference scores.) In a repeated-measures design, the only variation is in the difference scores. Variation among participants on each testing's scores are not part of the variation involved in the analysis. This is because difference scores are all comparing participants to themselves. William S. Gosset, who essentially invented the *t* test (see Box 9–1), made much of the higher power of repeated-measures studies in a historically interesting controversy over an experiment about milk, which is described in Box 9–2.

On the other hand, testing a group of people before and after an experimental procedure, without any kind of control group that does not go through the procedure, is a weak research design (Cook & Campbell, 1979). Even if such a study produces a significant difference, it leaves many alternative explanations for that difference. For example, the research participants might have matured or improved during that period anyway, or perhaps other events happened in between, or the participants not getting benefits may have dropped out. It is even possible that the initial test itself caused changes.

Note, however, that the difficulties of research that tests people before and after some intervention are shared only slightly with the kind of study in which participants are tested under two conditions, such as noisy versus quiet, with half tested first under one condition and half tested first under the other condition.

<u>BOX 9–2</u> The Power of Studies Using Difference Scores: How the Lanarkshire Milk Experiment Could Have Been Milked for More

In 1930, a major health experiment was conducted in Scotland involving 20,000 schoolchildren. Its main purpose was to compare the growth of a group of children who were assigned to drink milk regularly to those who were in a control group. The results were that those who drank milk showed more growth.

However, William Gosset, a contemporary statistician and inventor of the *t* test (see Box 9–1), was appalled at the way the experiment was conducted. It had cost about £7,500, which in 1930 was a huge amount of money, and was done wrong! Large studies such as this were very popular among statisticians in those days because they seemed to imitate the large numbers found in nature. Gosset, by contrast, being a brewer, was forced to use very small numbers in his studies—experimental batches of beer were too costly. And he was often chided by the "real statisticians" for his small sample sizes. But Gosset argued that no number of participants was large enough when strict random assignment was not followed. And in this study, teachers were permitted to switch children from group to group

if they took pity on a child whom they felt would benefit from receiving milk!

However, even more interesting in light of the present chapter, Gosset demonstrated that the researchers could have obtained the same result with 50 pairs of identical twins, flipping a coin to determine which of each pair was in the milk group (and sticking to it). Of course, the statistic you would use is the *t* test as taught in this chapter—the *t* test for dependent means.

More recently, the development of power analysis, which we introduced in Chapter 8, has thoroughly vindicated Gosset. It is now clear just how surprisingly few participants are needed when a researcher can find a way to set up a repeated-measures design in which difference scores are the basic unit of analysis. (In this case, each *pair* of twins would be one "participant.") As Gosset could have told them, studies that use the *t* test for dependent means can be extremely sensitive.

References: Peters (1987); Tankard (1984).

---

t TESTS IN RESEARCH ARTICLES

Research articles usually describe *t* tests in a fairly standard format that includes the degrees of freedom, the *t* score, and the significance level. For example, $t(24) = 2.80$, $p < .05$ tells you that the researcher used a *t* test with 24 degrees of freedom, found a *t* score of 2.80, and the result was significant at the .05 level. Whether a one-tailed or two-tailed test was used may also be noted. (If not, assume that it was two-tailed.) Usually the means, and sometimes the standard deviations, are given for each testing. Rarely is the standard deviation of the difference scores reported.

Had our student in the dormitory example reported the results in a research article, she would have written something like this: "The sample from my dormitory studied a mean of 3.2 hours ($SD = .80$). Based on a *t* test for a single sample, this was significantly different from the known mean of 2.5 for the college as a whole, $t(15) = 3.50$, $p < .01$, one-tailed." The researchers in our fictional flood victims example might have written up their results as follows: "The reported hopefulness of our sample of flood victims ($M = 4.7$, $SD = 1.89$) was not significantly different from the midpoint of the scale, $t(9) = 1.17$."

As we noted earlier, psychologists only occasionally use the *t* test for a single sample. We introduced it mainly as a stepping-stone to the more widely used *t* test for dependent means. Nevertheless, one does sometimes see the *t* test for a single sample in research articles. For example, Soproni et al. (2001), as part of a larger study, had pet dogs respond to a series of eight trials in which the owner would look at one of two bowls of dog food and the researchers measured whether the dog went to the correct bowl. (The researchers called these "at trials" because the owner looked directly *at* the target.) For each dog, this produced an average percentage correct that was compared to chance, which would be 50% correct. Here is part of their results: "During the eight test trials for gesture, dogs performed significantly above chance on at target trials: one sample *t* test, $t(13) = 5.3$, $p < .01 \ldots$" (p. 124).

As we have said, the *t* test for dependent means is much more commonly used. Olthoff (1989) might have reported his result in the example we used in this way: "There was a significant decline in communication quality, dropping from a mean of 116.32 before marriage to a mean of 104.26 after marriage, $t(18) = 2.76$, $p < .05$." The researcher in the fictional surgeons study could have written the following: "The mean performance for the quiet group was 18.89, while the performance for the noisy group was 16.89. This difference was not statistically significant at the .01 level, even with a one-tailed test, $t(8) = 2.20$."

As another example, Nakkula and Nikitopoulus (2001) examined scores on a measure of negotiation and social skills in a group of 205, 10 to 15 year-olds in Argentina before and after they participated in the Program for Youth Negotiators training program. Table 9–11 (reproduced from their Table 1) shows the results. Given the fairly large sample size, it is not surprising that a percent change of 4.8% was so very clearly significant. They do not give standard effect sizes, but it is possible to figure them out from the table. For example, for the first result, they give a standard error of .53—which, with an *N* of 205 works out to a standard deviation of the population of individuals of 4.02. The difference in means (3.12) divided by 4.02 comes out to an effect size of .78, a large effect size. However, the effect size for COLL (collaboration), even though significant, is quite small (.17).

TABLE 9–11 Means (and Standard Errors) for Negotiation and Psychosocial Competence ($N = 205$)

	Pretest	Posttest	Change	Percent Change	*t*
Negotiation	65.15 (.58)	68.27 (.59)	3.12 (.53)	4.8	5.84 ****
PI	12.58 (.19)	12.74 (.18)	.15 (.16)	1.2	.92
COMM	12.36 (.17)	12.75 (.17)	.39 (.17)	3.2	2.23 *
COLL	13.87 (.18)	14.27 (.18)	.41 (.17)	3.0	2.39 *
CBPT	13.01 (.19)	14.36 (.20)	1.34 (.22)	10.3	6.14 ****
CRES	13.33 (.18)	14.16 (.20)	.83 (.19)	6.2	4.49 ****
Psychosocial Competence	2.11 (.01)	2.16 (.01)	.05 (.01)	2.5	5.94 ****
IU	2.06 (.01)	2.10 (.01)	.04 (.01)	1.9	2.59 **
IS	2.28 (.01)	2.34 (.01)	.06 (.01)	2.6	4.63 ****
PM	1.95 (.01)	2.01 (.01)	.06 (.01)	3.2	4.51 ****

* $p < .05$, ** $p < .01$, *** $p < .001$, **** $p < .0001$
PI = Personal Initiative, COMM = Communication, COLL = Collaboration, CBPT = Conflict-Based Perspective Taking, CRES = Conflict Resolution Approach, IU = Interpersonal Understanding, IS = Interpersonal Skills, PM = Personal Meaning
(*Source:* Nakkula & Nikitopoulos, 2001)

SUMMARY

1. You use the standard steps of hypothesis testing even when you don't know the population variance. However, in this situation you have to estimate the population variance from the scores in the sample, using a formula that divides the sum of squared deviation scores by the degrees of freedom ($df = N - 1$).

2. When the population variance is estimated, the comparison distribution of means is a t distribution (with cutoffs given in a t table). A t distribution has slightly heavier tails than a normal curve (just how much heavier depends on how few degrees of freedom). Also, in this situation, a sample's number of standard deviations from the mean of the comparison distribution is called a t score.

3. You use a t test for dependent means in studies where each participant has two scores, such as a before-score and an after-score. In this t test, you first figure a difference or change score for each participant, then go through the usual steps of hypothesis testing with the modifications described in the paragraphs above and making Population 2 a population of difference scores with a mean of 0 (no difference).

4. An assumption of the t test is that the population distribution is a normal curve. However, even when it is not, the t test is usually fairly accurate.

5. The effect size of a study using a t test for dependent means is the mean of the difference scores divided by the standard deviation of the difference scores. You can look up power and needed sample size for any particular level of power in special tables.

6. The power of studies using difference scores is usually much higher than that of studies using other designs with the same number of participants. However, research using a single group tested before and after some intervening event, without a control group, allows for many alternative explanations of any observed changes.

7. t tests are reported in research articles using a standard format. For example, "$t(24) = 2.80, p < .05$."

KEY TERMS

assumption (p. 322)
biased estimate (p. 303)
change scores (p. 314)
degrees of freedom (df)
   (p. 303)
difference scores
   (p. 314)

repeated-measures design
   (p. 313)
robustness (p. 323)
t distribution (p. 305)
t score (p. 307)
t table (p. 306)
t tests (p. 300)

t test for a single sample
   (p. 300)
t test for dependent means
   (p. 313)
unbiased estimate of the
   population variance (S^2)
   (p. 303)

EXAMPLE WORKED-OUT COMPUTATIONAL PROBLEMS

t TEST FOR A SINGLE SAMPLE

Eight participants are tested after being given an experimental procedure. Their scores are 14, 8, 6, 5, 13, 10, 10, and 6. The population (of people not given this procedure) is normally distributed with a mean of 6. Using the .05 level, two-tailed, does the experimental procedure make a difference? (a) Use the steps of hypothesis testing and (b) sketch the distributions involved.

❶ **Restate the question as a research hypothesis and a null hypothesis about the populations.** There are two populations:

Population 1: People who are given the experimental procedure
Population 2: The general population

The research hypothesis is that the Population 1 will score differently than Population 2. The null hypothesis is that Population 1 will not score differently than Population 2.

❷ **Determine the characteristics of the comparison distribution.** The mean of the distribution of means is 6 (the known population mean). To figure the estimated population variance, you first need to figure the sample mean, which is $(14 + 8 + 6 + 5 + 13 + 10 + 10 + 6)/8 = 72/8 = 9$. The estimated population variance is $S^2 = SS/(N - 1) = 78/7 = 11.14$; the variance of the distribution of means is $S_M^2 = S^2/N = 11.14 / 8 = 1.39$. $S = \sqrt{S_M^2} = \sqrt{1.39} = 1.18$. It's shape will be a *t* distribution for $df = 7$.

❸ **Determine the cutoff sample score on the comparison distribution at which the null hypothesis should be rejected.** From Table A–2, the cutoff for a two-tailed *t* test at the .05 level for $df = 7$ is ± 2.365.

❹ **Determine your sample's score on the comparison distribution.** $t = (M - \mu) / S_M = (9-6)/1.18 = 3 / 1.18 = 2.54$.

❺ **Decide whether to reject the null hypothesis.** The *t* of 2.54 is more extreme than the needed *t* of ± 2.365. Therefore, reject the null hypothesis; the research hypothesis is supported.

Sketches of distributions are shown in Figure 9–10.

FIGURE 9–10 *Distributions for answer to "Examples of Worked-Out Computational Problems" for* t *test for a single sample.*

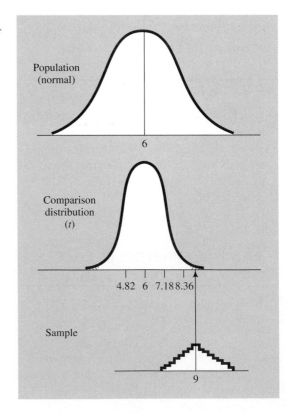

t TEST FOR DEPENDENT MEANS

A researcher tests 10 individuals before and after an experimental procedure. The results were as follows:

Participant	Before	After
1	10.4	10.8
2	12.6	12.1
3	11.2	12.1
4	10.9	11.4
5	14.3	13.9
6	13.2	13.5
7	9.7	10.9
8	11.5	11.5
9	10.8	10.4
10	13.1	12.5

Test the hypothesis that there is an increase in scores, using the .05 significance level. Use the steps of hypothesis testing and sketch the distributions involved.

Table 9–12 shows the results, including the figuring of difference scores and all the other figuring for the t test for dependent means. Figure 9–11 shows the distributions involved. Here are the steps of hypothesis testing:

❶ **Restate the question as a research hypothesis and a null hypothesis about the populations.** There are two populations:

Population 1. People like those who are given the experimental procedure
Population 2: People who show no change from before to after

The research hypothesis is that Population 1's mean change score is greater than Population 2's. The null hypothesis is that Population 1's mean change is not greater than Population 2's.

❷ **Determine the characteristics of the comparison distribution.** Its population mean is 0 change. The estimated population variance is shown in Table 9–12 to be .39. The comparison distribution will be a t distribution for 9 degrees of freedom with a mean of 0 and a standard deviation of .20. It will be a t distribution for $df = 9$.

❸ **Determine the cutoff sample score on the comparison distribution at which the null hypothesis should be rejected.** For a one-tailed test at the .05 level with $df = 9$, the cutoff is 1.833.

❹ **Determine your sample's score on the comparison distribution.** The sample's mean change of .14 is .70 standard deviations (of .20 each) on the distribution of means above that distribution's mean of 0.

❺ **Decide whether to reject the null hypothesis.** The sample's t of .70 is less extreme than the needed t of 1.833. Thus, you cannot reject the null hypothesis. The study is inconclusive.

PRACTICE PROBLEMS

These problems involve figuring. Most real-life statistics problems are done on a computer. However, even if you have a computer and statistics software, do these by hand (with the help of a calculator) to ingrain the method in your mind. Also, in all problems involving figuring, be sure to show your work.

TABLE 9–12	Figuring for Answer to "Examples of Worked-Out Computational Problems" for *t* Test for Dependent Means

Participant	Score		Change	Deviation	Squared Deviation
	Before	*After*			
1	10.4	10.8	.4	.26	.07
2	12.6	12.1	−.5	−.64	.41
3	11.2	12.1	.9	.76	.58
4	10.9	11.4	.5	.36	.13
5	14.3	13.9	−.4	−.54	.29
6	13.2	13.5	.3	.16	.03
7	9.7	10.9	1.2	1.06	1.12
8	11.5	11.5	0.0	−.14	.02
9	10.8	10.4	−.4	−.54	.29
10	13.1	12.5	−.6	−.74	.55
Σ:	117.7	119.1	1.4	0	3.49

For change scores:

$M = 1.4/10 = .14.$

$\mu = 0.$

$S^2 = SS/df = 3.49/(10 - 1) = 3.49/9 = .39.$

$S_M^2 = S^2/N = .39/10 = .039.$

$S_M = \sqrt{S_M^2} = \sqrt{.039} = .20.$

t for $df = 9$ needed for 5% significance level, one-tailed = 1.833.

$t = (M - \mu)/S_M = (.14 - 0)/.20 = .70.$

Decision: Do not reject the null hypothesis.

For practice in using a computer to solve statistics problems, refer to the computer section of each chapter of the *Student's Study Guide and Computer Workbook* that accompanies this text.

All data are fictional unless an actual citation is given.

Answers to Set I problems are given at the back of the book.

SET I

1. In each of the following studies, a single sample's mean is being compared to a population with a known mean but an unknown variance. For each study, decide whether the result is significant.

	Sample Size (*N*)	Population Mean (μ)	Estimated Population Variance (S^2)	Sample Mean (*M*)	Tails	Significance Level (α)
(a)	64	12.40	9.00	11.00	1 (low predicted)	.05
(b)	49	1,006.35	317.91	1,009.72	2	.01
(c)	400	52.00	7.02	52.41	1 (high predicted)	.01

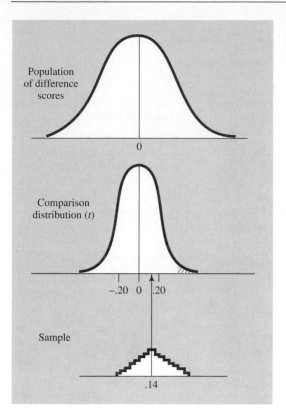

FIGURE 9-11 *Distributions for answer to "Examples of Worked-Out Computational Problems" for* t *test for dependent means.*

2. Suppose a candidate running for sheriff claims that she will reduce the average speed of emergency response to less than 30 minutes. (30 min. is thought to be the average response time with the current sheriff.) There are no past records, so the actual standard deviation of such response times cannot be determined. Thanks to this campaign, she is elected sheriff, and careful records are now kept. The response times for the first month are 26, 30, 28, 29, 25, 28, 32, 35, 24, and 23 min.

   Using the .05 level of significance, did she keep her promise? (a) Use the steps of hypothesis testing. (b) Sketch the distributions involved. (c) Explain your answer to someone who has never taken a course in statistics.

3. A researcher tests five individuals who have seen paid political ads about a particular issue. These individuals take a multiple choice test about the issue in which people in general (who know nothing about the issue) usually get 40 questions correct. The number correct for these five individuals was 48, 41, 40, 51, and 50.

   Using the .05 level of significance, two-tailed, do people who see the ads do better on this test? (a) Use the steps of hypothesis testing. (b) Sketch the distributions involved. (c) Explain your answer to someone who is familiar with the Z test for a single sample, but is unfamiliar with t tests.

4. For each of the following studies using difference scores, test the significance using a t test for dependent means.

Number of Difference Scores in Sample	Mean of Difference Scores in Sample	Estimated Population Variance of Difference Scores	Tails	Significance Level
(a) 20	1.7	8.29	1 (high predicted)	.05
(b) 164	2.3	414.53	2	.05
(c) 15	−2.2	4.00	1 (low predicted)	.01

5. A program to decrease littering was carried out in four cities in California's Central Valley starting in August 2001. The amount of litter in the streets (average pounds of litter collected per block per day) was measured during the July before the program started and then the next July, after the program had been in effect for a year. The results were as follows:

City	July 2001	July 2002
Fresno	9	2
Merced	10	4
Bakersfield	8	9
Stockton	9	1

Using the 1% level of significance, was there a significant decrease in the amount of litter? (a) Use the five steps of hypothesis testing. (b) Sketch the distributions involved. (c) Explain your answer to someone who understands mean, standard deviation, and variance, but knows nothing else about statistics.

6. A researcher assesses the level of a particular hormone in the blood in five patients before and after they begin taking a hormone treatment program. Results for the five are as follows:

Patient	A	B	C	D	E
Before	.20	.16	.24	.22	.17
After	.18	.16	.23	.19	.16

Using the 5% significance level, was there a significant change in the level of this hormone? (a) Use the steps of hypothesis testing. (b) Sketch the distributions involved. (c) Explain your answer to someone who understands the *t* test for a single sample but is unfamiliar with the *t* test for dependent means.

7. Figure the estimated effect size and indicate whether it is approximately small, medium, or large, for each of the following studies:

Study	a	b	c	d
Mean Change	20	5	.1	100
S	32	10	.4	500

8. What is the power of each of the following studies, using a *t* test for dependent means (based on the .05 significance level)?

Effect Size	N	Tails
(a) Small	20	One
(b) Medium	20	One
(c) Medium	30	One
(d) Medium	30	Two
(e) Large	30	Two

9. About how many participants are needed for 80% power in each of the following planned studies that will use a *t* test for dependent means with $p < .05$?:

Predicted Effect Size	Tails
(a) Medium	Two
(b) Large	One
(c) Small	One

10. Weller and Weller (1997) conducted a study of the tendency for the menstrual cycles of women who live together (such as sisters) to become synchronized. For their statistical analysis, they compared scores on a measure of synchronization of pairs of sisters living together they studied versus the degree of synchronization that would be expected by chance (lower scores mean more synchronization). Their key results (reported in a table not reproduced here) were synchrony scores of 6.32 for the 30 roommate sister pairs in their sample compared to an expected synchrony score of 7.76; they then reported a *t* score of 2.27 and a *p* level of .011 for this difference. Explain this result to a person who is familiar with hypothesis testing with a known population variance, but not with the *t* test for a single sample.

11. A psychologist conducts a study of perceptual illusions under two different lighting conditions. Twenty participants were each tested under both of the two different conditions. The experimenter reported: "The mean number of effective illusions was 6.72 under the bright conditions and 6.85 under the dimly lit conditions, a difference that was not significant, $t(19) = 1.62$." Explain this result to a person who has never had a course in statistics. Be sure to use sketches of the distributions in your answer.

12. A study was done of personality characteristics of 100 students who were tested at the beginning and end of their first year of college. The researchers reported the results in the following table:

Personality Scale	Fall		Spring		Difference	
	M	SD	M	SD	M	SD
Anxiety	16.82	4.21	15.32	3.84	1.50**	1.85
Depression	89.32	8.39	86.24	8.91	3.08**	4.23
Introversion	59.89	6.87	60.12	7.11	.23	2.22
Neuroticism	38.11	5.39	37.32	6.02	.89*	4.21

*$p < .05$. **$p < .01$.

(a) Focusing on the difference scores, figure the *t* values for each personality scale. (Assume that SD in the table is for what we have called *S*, the unbiased estimate of the population standard deviation.) (b) Explain to a person who has never had a course in statistics what this table means.

SET II

13. In each of the following studies, a single sample's mean is being compared to a population with a known mean but an unknown variance. For each study, decide whether the result is significant.

	Sample Size (N)	Population Mean (μ)	Estimated Standard Variance (S)	Sample Mean (M)	Tails	Significance Level (α)
(a)	16	100.31	2.00	100.98	1 (high predicted)	.05
(b)	16	.47	4.00	.00	2	.05
(c)	16	68.90	9.00	34.00	1 (low predicted)	.01

14. Evolutionary theories often emphasize that humans have adapted to their physical environment. One such theory hypothesizes that people should spontaneously follow a 24-hour cycle of sleeping and waking—even if they are not exposed to the usual pattern of sunlight. To test this notion, eight paid volunteers were placed (individually) in a room in which there was no light from the outside and no clocks or other indications of time. They could turn the lights on and off as they wished. After a month in the room, each individual tended to develop a steady cycle. Their cycles at the end of the study were as follows: 25, 27, 25, 23, 24, 25, 26, and 25.

Using the 5% level of significance, what should we conclude about the theory that 24 hours is the natural cycle? (That is, does the average cycle length under these conditions differ significantly from 24 hours?) (a) Use the steps of hypothesis testing. (b) Sketch the distributions involved. (c) Explain your answer to someone who has never taken a course in statistics.

15. In a particular country, it is known that college seniors report falling in love an average of 2.2 times during their college years. A sample of five seniors, originally from that country but who have spent their entire college career in the United States, were asked how many times they had fallen in love during their college years. Their numbers were 2, 3, 5, 5, and 2. Using the .05 significance level, do students like these who go to college in the United States fall in love more often than those from their country who go to college in their own country? (a) Use the steps of hypothesis testing. (b) Sketch the distributions involved. (c) Explain your answer to someone who is familiar with the *Z* test for a single sample but is unfamiliar with the *t* test.

16. For each of the following studies using difference scores, test the significance using a *t* test for dependent means.

Number of Difference Scores in Sample	Mean of Difference Scores	S^2 for Difference Scores	Tails	Significance Level
(a) 10	3.8	50	One (high)	.05
(b) 100	3.8	50	One (high)	.05
(c) 100	1.9	50	One (high)	.05
(d) 100	1.9	50	Two	.05
(e) 100	1.9	25	Two	.05

17. Four individuals with high levels of cholesterol went on a special crash diet, avoiding high-cholesterol foods and taking special supplements. Their total cholesterol levels before and after the diet were as follows:

Participant	Before	After
J. K.	287	255
L. M. M	305	269
A. K.	243	245
R. O. S.	309	247

Using the 5% level of significance, was there a significant change in cholesterol level? (a) Use the steps of hypothesis testing. (b) Sketch the distributions involved. (d) Explain your answer to someone who has never taken a course in statistics.

18. Five people who were convicted of speeding were ordered by the court to attend a workshop. A special device put into their cars kept records of their speeds for 2 weeks before and after the workshop. The maximum speeds for each person during the 2 weeks before and the 2 weeks after the workshop follow.

Participant	Before	After
L. B.	65	58
J. K.	62	65
R .C.	60	56
R. T.	70	66
J. M.	68	60

Using the 5% significance level, should we conclude that people are likely to drive more slowly after such a workshop? (a) Use the steps of hypothesis testing. (b) Sketch the distributions involved. (c) Explain your answer to someone who is familiar with hypothesis testing involving known populations, but has never learned anything about t tests.

19. The amount of oxygen consumption was measured in six individuals over two 10-minute periods while sitting with their eyes closed. During one period, they listened to an exciting adventure story; during the other, they heard restful music.

Participant	Story	Music
1	6.12	5.39
2	7.25	6.72
3	5.70	5.42
4	6.40	6.16
5	5.82	5.96
6	6.24	6.08

Based on the results shown, is oxygen consumption less when listening to the music? Use the 1% significance level. (a) Use the steps of hypothesis testing. (b) Sketch the distributions involved. (c) Explain your answer to someone who understands mean, standard deviation, and variance, but knows nothing else about statistics.

20. Five sophomores were given an English achievement test before and after receiving instruction in basic grammar. Their scores are shown below.

Student	Before	After
A	20	18
B	18	22
C	17	15
D	16	17
E	12	9

Is it reasonable to conclude that future students would show higher scores after instruction? Use the 5% significance level. (a) Use the steps of hypothesis testing. (b) Sketch the distributions involved (c) Explain your answer to someone who understands mean, standard deviation, and variance, but knows nothing else about statistics.

21. Figure the predicted effect size and indicate whether it is approximately small, medium, or large, for each of the following planned studies:

Study	a	b	c	d
Predicted Mean Change	8	8	16	16
σ	30	10	30	10

22. What is the power of each of the following studies, using a *t* test for dependent means (based on the .05 significance level)?

Effect Size	N	Tails
(a) Small	50	Two
(b) Medium	50	Two
(c) Large	50	Two
(d) Small	10	Two
(e) Small	40	Two
(f) Small	100	Two
(g) Small	100	One

23. About how many participants are needed for 80% power in each of the following planned studies that will use a *t* test for dependent means with $p < .05$?:

Predicted Effect Size	Tails
(a) small	Two
(b) medium	One
(c) large	Two

24. A study compared union activity of employees in 10 plants during two different decades. The researchers reported "a significant increase in union activity, $t(9) - 3.28, p <.01$." Explain this result to a person who has never had a course in statistics. Be sure to use sketches of the distributions in your answer.

25. Holden et al. (1997) compared mothers' reported attitudes towards corporal punishment of their children from before to 3 years after having their first child. "The average change in the women's prior-to-current attitudes was significant, $t(107) = 10.32, p <.001 \ldots$" (p. 485). (The change was that they felt more negatively about corporal punishment after having their child.) Explain this result to someone who is familiar with the *t* test for a single sample, but not with the *t* test for dependent means.

26. Table 9–13 (reproduced from Table 4 of Larson et al., 2001) shows ratings of various aspects of work and home life of 100 middle-class men in India who were fathers. Pick three rows of interest to you and explain the results to someone who is familiar with the mean, variance, and Z scores, but knows nothing else about statistics.

TABLE 9–13 Comparison of Fathers' Mean Psychological States in the Job and Home Spheres ($N = 100$)

Scale	Range	Sphere Work	Sphere Home	Work vs. home
Important	0–9	5.98	5.06	6.86***
Attention	0–9	6.15	5.13	7.96***
Challenge	0–9	4.11	2.41	11.49***
Choice	0–9	4.28	4.74	−3.38***
Wish doing else	0–9	1.50	1.44	0.61
Hurried	0–3	1.80	1.39	3.21**
Social anxiety	0–3	0.81	0.64	3.17**
Affect	1–7	4.84	4.98	−2.64**
Social climate	1–7	5.64	5.95	4.17***

Note: Values for column 3 are *t* scores; $df = 99$ for all *t* tests.
**$p < .01$. ***$p < .001$.
(*Source:* Larson et al., 2001.)

CHAPTER 10

THE *t* TEST FOR INDEPENDENT MEANS

***t* test for independent means**

Are You Ready?
What You Need to have Mastered Before Starting This Chapter:

- Chapters 1, 2, and 5 through 9.

This chapter examines hypothesis testing in the very common situation of comparing two samples, such as an experimental group and a control group. This is a *t* test situation because you don't know the population variances, so you have to estimate them. This time it is called a ***t* test for independent means** because it compares the means of two entirely separate groups of people whose scores are independent of each other. This is in contrast to the *t* test for dependent means, considered in the last chapter, in which there are two groups of scores, but both are for the same group of people (such as the same people measured before and after a health-promotion education program).

THE DISTRIBUTION OF DIFFERENCES BETWEEN MEANS

distribution of differences between means

The *t* test for independent means works like the hypothesis-testing procedures you already know, with one main exception: The key focus is on a difference between the means of two samples. Thus, the comparison distribution is a **distribution of differences between means.**

This special distribution is, in a sense, two steps removed from the populations of individuals: First, there is a distribution of means from each population of individuals. Second, there is a distribution of differences between pairs of means, one of each pair from each of these distributions of means.

Think of this distribution of differences between means as being built up as follows: (a) Randomly select one mean from the distribution of means for Population 1, (b) randomly select one mean from the distribution of means for Population 2, and (c) subtract. (That is, take the mean from the first distribution of means minus the mean from the second distribution of means.) This gives a difference score between the two selected means. Then repeat the process. This creates a second difference, a difference between the two newly selected means. Repeating this process a large number of times creates a distribution of differences between means.

THE LOGIC

Figure 10–1 diagrams the entire logical construction for a distribution of differences between means. At the top are the two population distributions. We do not know the characteristics of these population distributions, but we do know that if the null hypothesis is true, the two population means are the same. That is, the null hypothesis is that $\mu_1 = \mu_2$. We also can estimate the variance of these populations based on the sample information (these estimated variances will be S_1^2 and S_2^2).

Below each population distribution is the distribution of means for that population. Using the estimated population variance and knowing the size of each sample, you can figure the variance of each distribution of means in the usual way. (It is the variance of its parent population divided by the size of the sample.)

FIGURE 10–1 *A diagram of the logic of a distribution of differences between means.*

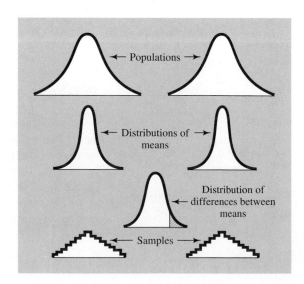

Below these two distributions of means, and built from them, is the crucial distribution of differences between means. This distribution's variance is ultimately based on estimated population variances. Thus, we can think of it as a *t* distribution. The goal of a *t* test for independent means is to decide whether the difference between the means of your two actual samples is a more extreme difference than the cutoff difference on this distribution of differences. The two actual samples are shown (as histograms) at the bottom.

Remember, this whole procedure is really a kind of complicated castle in the air. It exists only in our minds to help us make decisions based on the results of an actual experiment. The only concrete reality in all of this is the actual scores in the two samples. You estimate the population variances from these sample scores. The variances of the two distributions of means are based entirely on these estimated population variances (and the sample sizes). And, as you will see shortly, the characteristics of the distribution of differences between means is based on these two distributions of means.

Still, the procedure is a powerful one. It has the power of mathematics and logic behind it. It helps you develop general knowledge based on the specifics of a particular study.

With this overview of the basic logic, we now turn to five key details: (a) the mean of the distribution of differences between means, (b) the estimated population variance, (c) the variance and standard deviation of the distribution of differences between means, (d) the shape of the distribution of differences between means, and (e) the *t* score for the difference between the particular two means being compared.

MEAN OF THE DISTRIBUTION OF DIFFERENCES BETWEEN MEANS

In a *t* test for independent means, you are considering two populations—for example, one population from which an experimental group is taken and one population from which a control group is taken. In practice, you don't know the mean of either population. You do know that if the null hypothesis is true, these two populations have equal means. Also, if these two populations have equal means, the two distributions of means have equal means. (This is because each distribution of means has the same mean as its parent population of individuals.) Finally, if you take random samples from two distributions with equal means, the differences between the means of these random samples, in the long run, balance out to 0. The result of all this is the following: Whatever the specifics of the study, you know that if the null hypothesis is true, the distribution of differences between means has a mean of 0.

ESTIMATING THE POPULATION VARIANCE

In Chapter 9, you learned to estimate the population variance from the scores in your sample. It is the sum of squared deviation scores divided by the degrees of freedom (the number in the sample minus 1). To do a *t* test for independent means, it has to be reasonable to assume that the populations the two samples come from have the same variance. (If the null hypothesis is true, they also have the same mean. However, whether or not the null hypothesis is true, you must be able to assume the two populations have the same variance.) Therefore, when you estimate the variance from the scores in either sample, you are getting two separate estimates of what should be the same number. In practice, the two estimates will almost never be exactly identical. Since they are both supposed to be estimating the same thing,

**pooled estimate of the popula-
tion variance (S^2_{Pooled})**

weighted average

the best solution is to average the two estimates to get the best single overall estimate. This is called the **pooled estimate of the population variance (S^2_{Pooled})**.

In making this average, however, you also have to take into account that the two samples may not be the same size. If one sample is larger than the other, the estimate it provides is likely to be more accurate (because it is based on more information). If both samples are exactly the same size, you could just take an ordinary average of the two estimates. On the other hand, when they are not the same size, you need to make some adjustment in the averaging to give more weight to the larger sample. That is, you need a **weighted average,** an average weighted by the amount of information each sample provides. Also, to be precise, the amount of information each sample provides is not its number of scores, but its degrees of freedom (its number of scores minus 1).

Thus, your weighted average needs to be based on the degrees of freedom each sample provides. To find the weighted average, you figure out what proportion of the total degrees of freedom each sample contributes, multiply that proportion by the population variance estimate from that sample, and add up the two results. In terms of a formula,

The pooled estimate of the population variance is the proportion of the degrees of freedom in the first sample divided by the total degrees of freedom (from both samples) times the population estimate based on the first sample, plus the proportion of the degrees of freedom in the second sample divided by the total degrees of freedom times the population estimate based on the second sample.

$$S^2_{Pooled} = \frac{df_1}{df_{Total}}(S^2_1) + \frac{df_2}{df_{Total}}(S^2_2) \qquad (10\text{-}1)$$

In this formula, S^2_{Pooled} is the pooled estimate of the population variance. df_1 is the degrees of freedom in the sample from Population 1 and df_2 is the degrees of freedom in the sample from Population 2. (Remember, each sample's df is its number of scores minus 1.) df_{Total} is the total degrees of freedom ($df_{Total} = df_1 + df_2$). S^2_1 is the estimate of the population variance based on the scores in Population 1's sample; S^2_2 is the estimate based on the scores in Population 2's sample.

Consider a study in which the population variance estimate based on an experimental group of 11 participants is 60, and the population variance estimate based on a control group of 31 participants is 80. The estimate from the experimental group is based on 10 degrees of freedom (11 participants minus 1), and the estimate from the control group is based on 30 degrees of freedom (31 minus 1). The total information on which the estimate is based is the total degrees of freedom—in this example, 40 (that is, 10 + 30). Thus, the experimental group provides one quarter of the information (10/40 = 1/4), and the control group provides three quarters of the information (30/40 = 3/4).

You then multiply the estimate from the experimental group times 1/4, making 15 (that is, 60 × 1/4 = 15), and you multiply the estimate from the control group times 3/4, making 60 (that is, 80 × 3/4 = 60). Adding the two, this gives an overall estimate of 15 plus 60, or 75. Using the formula,

$$S^2_{Pooled} = \frac{df_1}{df_{Total}}(S^2_1) + \frac{df_2}{df_{Total}}(S^2_2) = \frac{10}{40}(60) + \frac{30}{40}(80)$$

$$= \frac{1}{4}(60) + \frac{3}{4}(80) = 15 + 60 = 75$$

Notice that this procedure does not give the same result as ordinary averaging (without weighting). Ordinary averaging would give an estimate of 70 (that is,

[60 + 80]/2 = 70). Our weighted estimate of 75 is closer to the estimate based on the control group alone than to the estimate based on the experimental group alone. This is as it should be, because the control group estimate in this example was based on more information.

Tip for Success
You know you have made a mistake in figuring S^2_{Pooled} if it does not come out between the two estimates. (You also know you have made a mistake if it does not come out closer to the estimate from the larger sample.)

FIGURING THE VARIANCE OF EACH OF THE TWO DISTRIBUTIONS OF MEANS

The pooled estimate of the population variance is the best estimate for both populations. (Remember, to do a *t* test for independent means, you have to be able to assume that the two populations have the same variance.) However, even though the two populations have the same variance, if the samples are not the same size, the distributions of means taken from them do not have the same variance. That is because the variance of a distribution of means is the population variance divided by the sample size. In terms of formulas,

(10-2)
$$S^2_{M_1} = \frac{S^2_{Pooled}}{N_1}$$

The variance of the distribution of means for the first population (based on an estimated population variance) is the pooled estimate of the population variance divided by the number of participants in the sample from the first population.

(10-3)
$$S^2_{M_2} = \frac{S^2_{Pooled}}{N_2}$$

The variance of the distribution of means for the second population (based on an estimated population variance) is the pooled estimate of the population variance divided by the number of participants in the sample from the second population.

Consider again the study with 11 in the experimental group and 31 in the control group, where we figured the pooled estimate of the population variance to be 75. For the experimental group, the variance of the distribution of means would be 75/11, which is 6.82. For the control group, the variance would be 75/31, which is 2.42. Using the formulas,

$$S^2_{M_1} = \frac{S^2_{Pooled}}{N_1} = \frac{75}{11} = 6.82$$

$$S^2_{M_2} = \frac{S^2_{Pooled}}{N_2} = \frac{75}{31} = 2.42$$

Tip for Success
Remember that when figuring estimated variances, you divide by the degrees of freedom. But when figuring the variance of a distribution of means, which does not involve any additional estimation, you divide by the actual number in the sample.

VARIANCE AND STANDARD DEVIATION OF THE DISTRIBUTION OF DIFFERENCES BETWEEN MEANS

The **variance of the distribution of differences between means** ($S^2_{Difference}$) is the variance of Population 1's distribution of means plus the variance of Population 2's distribution of means. (This is because in a difference between two numbers, the variation in each contributes to the overall variation in their difference. It is like subtracting a moving number from a moving target.) Stated as a formula,

variance of the distribution of differences between means ($S^2_{Difference}$)

The variance of the distribution of differences between means is the variance of the distribution of means for the first population (based on an estimated population variance) plus the variance of the distribution of means for the second population (based on an estimated population variance).

$$S^2_{\text{Difference}} = S^2_{M_1} + S^2_{M_2} \tag{10-4}$$

standard deviation of the distribution of differences between means ($S_{\text{Difference}}$)

The **standard deviation of the distribution of differences between means** ($S_{\text{Difference}}$) is the square root of the variance:

$$S_{\text{Difference}} = \sqrt{S^2_{\text{Difference}}} \tag{10-5}$$

The standard deviation of the distribution of differences between means is the square root of the variance of the distribution of differences between means.

In the example we have been considering, the variance of the distribution of means for the experimental group was 6.82, and the variance of the distribution of means for the control group was 2.42; the variance of the distribution of the difference between means is thus 6.82 plus 2.42, which is 9.24. This makes the standard deviation of this distribution the square root of 9.24, which is 3.04. In terms of the formulas,

$$S^2_{\text{Difference}} = S^2_{M_1} + S^2_{M_2} = 6.82 + 2.42 = 9.24$$

$$S_{\text{Difference}} = \sqrt{S^2_{\text{Difference}}} = \sqrt{9.24} = 3.04$$

STEPS TO FIND THE STANDARD DEVIATION OF DIFFERENCES BETWEEN MEANS

❶ **Figure the estimated population variances based on each sample**. That is, figure one estimate for each population using the formula $S^2 = SS/(N - 1)$.

❷ **Figure the pooled estimate of the population variance:**

$$S^2_{\text{Pooled}} = \frac{df_1}{df_{\text{Total}}} (S^2_1) + \frac{df_2}{df_{\text{Total}}} (S^2_2)$$

$$(df_1 = N_1 - 1 \text{ and } df_2 = N_2 - 1; df_{\text{Total}} = df_1 + df_2)$$

❸ **Figure the variance of each distribution of means:** $S^2_{M_1} = S^2_{\text{Pooled}}/N_1$ and $S^2_{M_2} = S^2_{\text{Pooled}}/N_2$

❹ **Figure the variance of the distribution of differences between means:** $S^2_{\text{Difference}} = S^2_{M_1} + S^2_{M_2}$

❺ **Figure the standard deviation of the distribution of differences between means:** $S_{\text{difference}} = \sqrt{S^2_{\text{Difference}}}$

SHAPE OF THE DISTRIBUTION OF DIFFERENCES BETWEEN MEANS

The distribution of differences between means is based on estimated population variances. Thus, the distribution of differences between means (the comparison distribution) is a *t* distribution. The variance of this distribution is figured based on population variance estimates from two samples. Therefore, the degrees of freedom for this *t* distribution are the sum of the degrees of freedom of the two samples. In terms of a formula,

The total degrees of freedom is the degrees of freedom in the first sample plus the degrees of freedom in the second sample.

$$df_{\text{Total}} = df_1 + df_2 \tag{10-6}$$

In the example we have been considering with an experimental group of 11 and a control group of 31, we saw earlier that the total degrees of freedom is 40 (that is, $11 - 1 = 10$; $31 - 1 = 30$; and $10 + 30 = 40$). To find the t score needed for significance, you look up the cutoff point in the t table in the row with 40 degrees of freedom. Suppose you are conducting a one-tailed test using the .05 significance level. The t table in Appendix A shows a cutoff of 1.684 for 40 degrees of freedom; that is, for a result to be significant, the difference between the means has to be at least 1.684 standard deviations above the mean difference of 0 on the distribution of differences between means.

THE t SCORE FOR THE DIFFERENCE BETWEEN THE TWO ACTUAL MEANS

Here is how you figure the t score for step 4 of the hypothesis testing: First, figure the difference between your two samples' means. (That is, subtract one from the other). Then, figure out where this difference is on the distribution of differences between means. You do this by dividing your difference by the standard deviation of this distribution. In terms of a formula,

(10-7)

$$t = \frac{M_1 - M_2}{S_{\text{Difference}}}$$

The t score is the difference between the two population means divided by the standard deviation of the distribution of differences between means.

For our example, suppose the mean of the first sample is 198 and the mean of the second sample is 190. The difference between these two means is 8 (that is, $198 - 190 - 8$). Earlier we figured the standard deviation of the distribution of differences between means in this example to be 3.04. That would make a t score of 2.63 (that is, $8/3.04 = 2.63$). In other words, in this example the difference between the two means is 2.63 standard deviations above the mean of the distribution of differences between means. In terms of the formula,

$$t = \frac{M_1 - M_2}{S_{\text{Difference}}} = \frac{198 - 190}{3.04} = \frac{8}{3.04} = 2.63$$

HOW ARE YOU DOING?

1. (a) When would you carry out a t test for independent means? (b) How is this different from the situation in which you would carry out a t test for dependent means?
2. (a) What is the comparison distribution in a t test for independent means? (b) Explain the logic of going from scores in two samples to an estimate of the variance of this comparison distribution. (c) Illustrate your answer with sketches of the distributions involved. (d) Why is the mean of this distribution 0?
3. Write the formula for each of the following: (a) pooled estimate of the population variance, (b) variance of the distribution of means for the first population, (c) variance of the distribution of differences between means, and (d) t score in a t test for independent means. (e) Define all the symbols used in these formulas.
4. Explain (a) why a t test for independent means uses a single pooled estimate of the population variance, and (b) why and (c) how this estimate is "weighted."
5. For a particular study comparing means of two samples, the first sample has 21 participants and an estimated population variance of 100; the second sample has 31 participants and an estimated population variance of 200. (a) What is the standard deviation of the distribution of differences between means? (b) What is its mean? (c) What will be its shape? (d) Illustrate your answer with sketches of the distributions involved.

ANSWERS:

1. (a) When you have done a study in which you have scores from two samples and you do not know the population variance. (b) In a t test for dependent means you have two scores from each of several individuals.

2. (a) A distribution of differences between means. (b) You estimate the population variance from each sample's scores; since you assume the populations have the same variance, you then pool these two estimates (giving proportionately more weight in this averaging to the sample that has more degrees of freedom in its estimate); using this pooled estimate, you figure the variance of the distribution of means for each sample's population by dividing this pooled estimate by the sample's number of participants; finally, since your interest is in a difference between means, you create a comparison distribution of differences between means that will have a variance equal to the sum of the variances of the two distributions of means (because the distribution of differences between means is made up of pairs of means, one taken from each distribution of means, and thus its variance is contributed to by both distributions of means). (c) Your sketch should look like Figure 10–1. (d) It will have a mean of zero because if the null hypothesis is true, the two populations have the same mean so that differences between means would on the average come out to zero.

3. (a) $S^2_{\text{Pooled}} = \dfrac{df_1}{df_{\text{Total}}}(S^2_1) + \dfrac{df_2}{df_{\text{Total}}}(S^2_2)$

   (b) $S^2_{M_1} = \dfrac{S^2_{\text{Pooled}}}{N_1}$

   (c) $S^2_{\text{Difference}} = S^2_{M_1} + S^2_{M_2}$

   (d) $t = \dfrac{M_1 - M_2}{S_{\text{Difference}}}$

   (e) S^2_{Pooled} is the pooled estimate of the population variance; df_1 and df_2 are the degrees of freedom in the samples from the first and second populations, respectively; df_{Total} is the total degrees of freedom (the sum of df_1 and df_2); S^2_1 and S^2_2 are the population variance estimates based on the samples from the first and second populations, respectively; $S^2_{M_1}$ is the variance of the distribution of means for the first population based on an estimated variance of the population of individuals; N_1 is the number of participants in the sample from the first population; $S^2_{\text{Difference}}$ is the variance of the distribution of differences between means based on estimated variances of the populations of individuals; t is the t score for a t test for independent means (the number of standard deviations from the mean on the distribution of differences between means); M_1 and M_2 are the means of the samples from the first and second populations, respectively; and $S_{\text{Difference}}$ is the standard deviation of the distribution of differences between means based on estimated variances of the populations of individuals.

4. (a) You assume that both populations have the same variance, thus the estimates from the two samples should be estimates of the same number. (b) We weight (give more influence to) an estimate from a larger sample because, being based on more information, it is likely to be more accurate. (c) The actual weighting is done by multiplying each sample's estimate by its proportion of the total information (the degrees of freedom); you then sum these two products.

5. (a) $S^2_{\text{Pooled}} = (20/50)(100) + (30/50)(200) = 40 + 120 = 160$

   $S^2_{M_1} = 160/21 = 7.62$; $S^2_{M_2} = 160/31 = 5.16$; $S^2_{\text{Difference}} = 7.62 + 5.16 = 12.78$; $S_{\text{Difference}} = \sqrt{12.78} = 3.57$

   (b) 0; (c) t distribution with $df = 50$; (d) Should look like Figure 10–1 with numbers written in.

HYPOTHESIS TESTING WITH A *t* TEST FOR INDEPENDENT MEANS

Considering the steps of hypothesis testing, there are three new wrinkles for a *t* test for independent means: (a) The comparison distribution is now a distribution of differences between means (this affects step 2); (b) the degrees of freedom for finding the cutoff on the *t* table is based on two samples (this affects step 3); and (c) your sample's score on the comparison distribution is based on the difference between your two means (this affects step 4).

EXAMPLE OF A *t* TEST FOR INDEPENDENT MEANS

Moorehouse and Sanders (1992) studied whether an adolescent boy's sense of how well he is doing in school is related to his mother's work situation. The boys were all in seventh to ninth grade and were all from families in which the mother worked full time. For purposes of this analysis, the boys were divided into two groups: those in which the mother's work gave her opportunities to solve problems (26 boys) and those in which the mother's work did not give her opportunities to solve problems (17 boys). All 43 boys were given a standard test of perceived academic competence (how successful they see themselves as being at school).

The scores and figuring for the *t* test are shown in Table 10–1. Figure 10–2 illustrates the distributions involved. Let's go through the steps of hypothesis testing.

❶ **Restate the question as a research hypothesis and a null hypothesis about the populations.** There are two populations:

Population 1: Boys whose mothers' work involves solving problems
Population 2: Boys whose mothers' work does not involve solving problems

Based on theory and previous research, Moorehouse and Sanders expected that boys whose mothers' work involved solving problems to have higher scores on the test of perceived academic competence. The research hypothesis was that Population 1 boys would score higher than Population 2 boys: $\mu_1 > \mu_2$. (That is, this was a directional hypothesis.) The null hypothesis was that the Population 1 boys would not score higher than the Population 2 boys.

❷ **Determine the characteristics of the comparison distribution.** The comparison distribution is a distribution of differences between means. Its mean is 0 (as it almost always is in a *t* test for independent means, because we are interested in whether there is more than 0 difference between the two populations). Regarding its standard deviation,

Ⓐ **Figure the estimated population variances based on each sample.** As shown in Table 10–1, S_1^2 comes out to 18.96 and $S_2^2 = 29.08$.

Ⓑ **Figure the pooled estimate of the population variance:** As shown in Table 10–1, the figuring for S_{Pooled}^2 gives a result of 22.91.

Ⓒ **Figure the variance of each distribution of means:** Dividing S_{Pooled}^2 by the N in each sample, as shown in Table 10–1, gives $S_{M_1}^2 = .88$ and $S_{M_2}^2 = 1.35$.

Ⓓ **Figure the variance of the distribution of differences between means:** Adding up the variances of the two distributions of means, as shown in Table 10–1, comes out to $S_{\text{Difference}}^2 = 2.23$.

TABLE 10–1 *t* Test for Independent Means for a Study of the Relation of the Work Situation of the Mothers of Adolescent Boys to the Boys' Perceived Academic Competence

Boys Whose Mothers' Work Involves Problem Solving			Boys Whose Mothers' Work Does Not Involve Problem Solving		
Score	Deviation from mean	Squared deviation from mean	Score	Deviation from mean	Squared deviation from mean
36.9	4.1	16.81	23.5	− 5.7	32.49
34.6	1.8	16.81	22.5	− 6.7	44.89
26.4	− 6.4	40.96	36.4	7.2	51.84
33.3	.5	.25	40.0	10.8	116.64
35.4	2.6	6.76	30.6	1.4	1.96
34.8	2.0	4.00	30.5	1.3	1.69
32.3	− 4.5	.25	34.5	5.3	28.09
34.5	1.7	2.89	31.3	2.1	4.41
36.0	3.2	10.24	19.4	− 9.8	96.04
24.5	− 8.3	68.89	29.6	.4	.16
31.6	− 1.2	1.44	24.8	− 4.4	19.36
36.1	3.3	10.89	25.0	− 4.2	17.64
36.8	4.0	16.00	28.8	− .4	.16
27.9	− 4.9	24.01	32.5	3.3	10.89
34.4	1.6	2.56	33.3	4.1	16.81
33.8	1.0	1.00	29.6	.4	.16
36.9	4.1	16.81	24.5	4.7	22.09
34.4	1.6	2.56			
31.7	− 1.1	1.21			
29.4	− 3.4	11.56			
34.1	1.3	1.69			
18.2	−14.6	213.16			
34.5	1.7	2.89			
35.3	2.5	6.25			
35.5	2.7	7.29			
33.4	.6	.36			
Σ: 852.7		473.97	496.8		465.32

$M_1 = 32.80$; $S_1^2 = 473.97/25 = 18.96$; $M_2 = 29.22$; $S_2^2 = 465.32/16 = 29.08$

$N_1 = 26$; $df_1 = N_1 - 1 = 25$; $N_2 = 17$; $df_2 = N_2 - 1 = 16$

$df_{Total} = df_1 + df_2 = 25 + 16 = 41$

$$S_{Pooled}^2 = \frac{df_1}{df_{Total}}(S_1^2) + \frac{df_2}{df_{Total}}(S_2^2) = \frac{25}{41}(18.96) + \frac{16}{41}(29.08)$$

$$= .61(18.96) + .39(29.08) = 11.57 + 11.34 = 22.9$$

$S_{M_1}^2 = S_{Pooled}^2/N_1 = 22.91/26 = .88$

$S_{M_2}^2 = S_{Pooled}^2/N_2 = 22.91/17 = 1.35$

$S_{Difference}^2 = S_{M_1}^2 + S_{M_2}^2 = .88 + 1.35 = 2.23$

$S_{Difference} = \sqrt{S_{Difference}^2} = \sqrt{2.23} = 1.49$

Needed *t* with $df = 41$ (using $df = 40$ in table), 5% level, one-tailed = 1.684

$t = (M_1 - M_2)/S_{Difference} = (32.80 - 29.22)/1.49 = 3.58/1.49 = 2.40$

Conclusion: Reject the null hypothesis; the research hypothesis is supported.

Note: Data from Moorehouse & Sanders (1992).

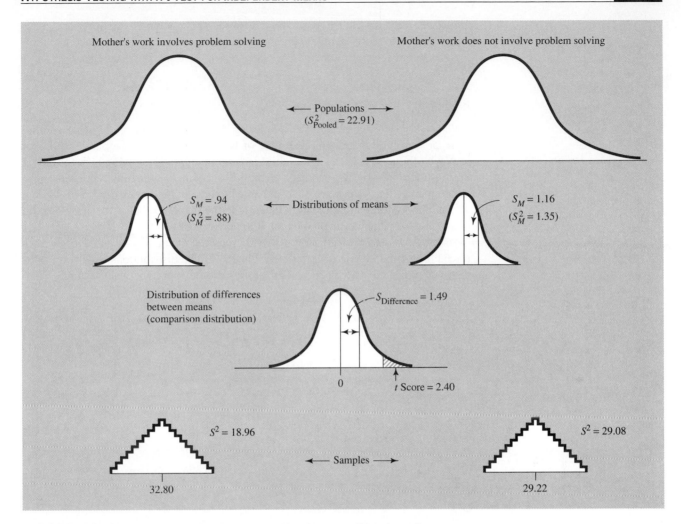

FIGURE 10-2 *The distributions in the example of a* t *test for independent means. (Data from Moorehouse & Sanders, 1992.)*

❶ **Figure the standard deviation of the distribution of differences between means:** $\sqrt{2.23} = 1.49$.

The shape of this comparison distribution will be a *t* distribution with a total of 41 degrees of freedom.

❸ **Determine the cutoff sample score on the comparison distribution at which the null hypothesis should be rejected.** This requires a one-tailed test because a particular direction of difference between the two populations was predicted. Since the *t* table in Appendix A (Table A–2) does not have exactly 41 degrees of freedom, you use the next lowest (40). At the .05 level, you need a *t* of at least 1.684.

❹ **Determine your sample's score on the comparison distribution.** The *t* score is the difference between the two sample means (32.80 − 29.22, which is 3.58), divided by the standard deviation of the distribution of differences between means (which is 1.49). This comes out to 2.40.

❺ **Decide whether to reject the null hypothesis.** The *t* score of 2.40 for the difference between the two actual means is larger than the needed *t* score of 1.684.

You can reject the null hypothesis. The research hypothesis is supported: Boys whose mothers' work involves solving problems see themselves as better at schoolwork than boys whose mothers' work does not involve solving problems.

A SECOND EXAMPLE OF A *t* TEST FOR INDEPENDENT MEANS

Valenzuela (1997) compared the mothering received by poor children who either were or were not undernourished. One of her measures was systematic ratings of how well the mother assisted her child in a standard puzzle-solving task (observed during home visits). The mothers of the 43 adequately nourished children had a mean quality of assistance of 33.1 and an estimated population variance of 201.64. The mothers of the 42 chronically undernourished children had a mean of 27.0 on this measure, with an estimated population variance of 134.56.

The scores and figuring for the *t* test comparing the quality of assistance scores for the two conditions are shown in Table 10–2. The distributions involved are illustrated in Figure 10–3. Next, we go through the steps of hypothesis testing.

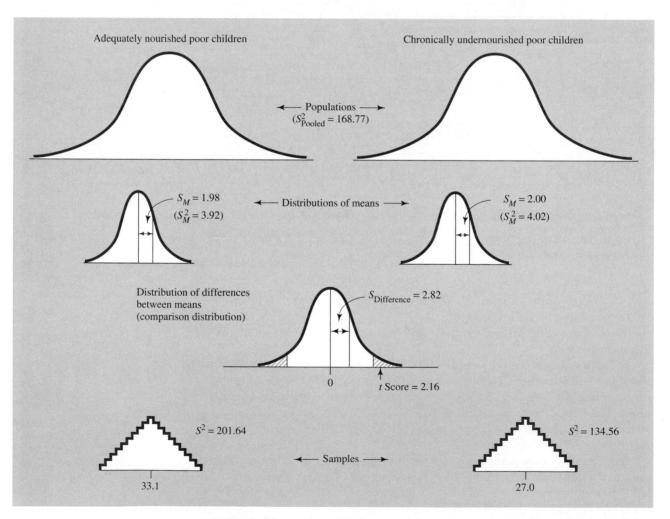

FIGURE 10–3   *The distributions in the example of mothers of adequately nourished versus chronically undernourished poor children. (Data from Valenzuela, 1997.)*

TABLE 10–2 *t* Test for Independent Means in Study of Quality of Assistance of Mothers of Adequately Nourished Versus Chronically Undernourished Poor Chilean Children

Adequately Nourished Children:
$$N_1 = 43; df_1 = N_1 - 1 = 42; M_1 = 33.1; S_1^2 = 201.64$$
Chronically Undernourished Children:
$$N_2 = 42; df_2 = N_2 - 1 = 41; M_2 = 27.0; S_2^2 = 134.56$$
$$df_{Total} = df_1 + df_2 = 42 + 41 = 83$$
$$S_{Pooled}^2 = \frac{df_1}{df_{Total}}(S_1^2) + \frac{df_2}{df_{Total}}(S_2^2) = \frac{42}{83}(201.64) + \frac{41}{83}(134.56)$$
$$= .51(201.64) + .49(134.56) = 102.84 + 65.93 = 168.77$$
$$S_{M_1}^2 = S_{Pooled}^2/N_1 = 168.77/43 = 3.92$$
$$S_{M_2}^2 = S_{Pooled}^2/N_2 = 168.77/42 = 4.02$$
$$S_{Difference}^2 = S_{M_1}^2 + S_{M_2}^2 = 3.92 + 4.02 = 7.94$$
$$S_{Difference} = \sqrt{S_{Difference}^2} = \sqrt{7.94} = 2.82$$
Needed *t* with $df = 83$ (using $df = 80$ in the table), 5% level, two-tailed $= 1.990$
$$t = (M_1 - M_2)/S_{Difference} = (33.1 - 27.0)/2.82 = 6.1/2.82 = 2.16$$
Conclusion: Reject the null hypothesis; the research hypothesis is supported.

Note: Data from Valenzuela (1997).

❶ **Restate the question as a research hypothesis and a null hypothesis about the populations.** There are two populations.

> **Population 1:** Mothers of adequately nourished poor children
> **Population 2:** Mothers of chronically undernourished poor children

The research hypothesis was that Population 1 mothers would score differently than Population 2 mothers on quality of assistance to their children. Valenzuela predicted that Population 1 would score higher than Population 2. However, following conventional practice in studies like this, she used a nondirectional significance test. (This had the advantage of allowing the possibility of finding significant results in the direction opposite to her prediction.) Thus, the research hypothesis actually tested was that Population 1 mothers would score differently from Population 2 mothers: $\mu_1 \neq \mu_2$. The null hypothesis was that the Population 1 mothers would score the same as Population 2 mothers: $\mu_1 = \mu_2$.

❷ **Determine the characteristics of the comparison distribution.** As usual, the mean of the distribution of differences between means will be 0. To find the standard deviation of this distribution,

 ❹ **Figure the estimated population variances based on each sample.** These are already figured for us: $S_1^2 = 201.64$ and $S_2^2 = 134.56$.

 ❺ **Figure the pooled estimate of the population variance:** As shown in Table 10–2, the figuring for S_{Pooled}^2 gives a result of 168.77.

 ❻ **Figure the variance of each distribution of means:** Dividing S_{Pooled}^2 by the *N* in each sample, as shown in Table 10–2, gives $S_{M_1}^2 = 3.92$ and $S_{M_2}^2 = 4.02$.

 ❼ **Figure the variance of the distribution of differences between means:** Adding up the variances of the two distributions of means, as shown in Table 10–2, comes out to $S_{Difference}^2 = 7.94$.

 ❽ **Figure the standard deviation of the distribution of differences between means:** $\sqrt{7.94} = 2.82$.

The shape of this comparison distribution will be a *t* distribution with a total of 83 degrees of freedom.

❸ **Determine the cutoff sample score on the comparison distribution at which the null hypothesis should be rejected.** The cutoff you need is for a two-tailed test at the usual .05 level, with 83 degrees of freedom. The *t* table in Appendix A (Table A–2) does not have a listing for 83 degrees of freedom. Thus, you use the next lowest *df* available, which is 80. This gives a cutoff of ± 1.990.

❹ **Determine your sample's score on the comparison distribution.** The *t* score is the difference between the two sample means divided by the standard deviation of the distribution of differences between means. This comes out to a *t* of 2.16. (That is, $t = 6.1/2.82 = 2.16$.)

❺ **Decide whether to reject the null hypothesis.** The *t* score of 2.16 for the difference between the means of the two conditions is more extreme than the needed *t* score of ± 1.99. Therefore, the researchers could reject the null hypothesis. The research hypothesis is supported: Mothers of adequately nourished children provide better quality of assistance to their children than do mothers of chronically undernourished children.

SUMMARY OF STEPS FOR A *t* TEST FOR INDEPENDENT MEANS

Table 10–3 summarizes the steps for a *t* test for independent means.[1]

HOW ARE YOU DOING?

1. List the ways in which hypothesis testing for a *t* test for dependent means is different from a *t* test for dependent means in terms of (a) step 2, (b) step 3, and (c) step 4.
2. Using the .05 significance level, two-tailed, figure a *t* test for independent means for an experiment comparing an experimental to a control condition. For the experimental condition, with 26 participants, $M = 5$, $S^2 = 10$; for the control condition, with 36 participants, $M = 8$, $S^2 = 12$. (a) Use the steps of hypothesis testing. (b) Sketch the distributions involved.

ANSWERS:

1. (a) The comparison distribution is now a distribution of differences between means.
   (b) The degrees of freedom is the sum of the degrees of freedom for the two samples.
   (c) The *t* score is based on a differences between means (divided by the standard deviation of the distribution of differences between means).
2. (a) Steps of hypothesis testing:
   ❶ **Restate the question as a research hypothesis and a null hypothesis about the populations.** There are two populations.

      Population 1: People given the experimental procedure
      Population 2: People given the control procedure

---

[1]The steps of figuring the standard deviation of the distribution of differences between means can be combined into a single overall computational formula:

$$S_{\text{Difference}} = \sqrt{\frac{(N_1 - 1)(S_1^2) + (N_2 - 1)(S_2^2)}{N_1 + N_2 - 2}\left(\frac{1}{N_1} + \frac{1}{N_2}\right)} \tag{10-8}$$

As usual, we urge you to use the full set of steps and the regular, definitional formulas, in your figuring when doing the practice problems in this book. Those steps help you learn the basic principles. However, this computational formula will be useful if statistics software is not available and you have to compute by hand a *t* test for independent means on scores from a real study with many participants in each group.

TABLE 10–3 Steps for a *t* Test for Independent Means

❶ **Restate the question as a research hypothesis and a null hypothesis about the populations.**

❷ **Determine the characteristics of the comparison distribution.**
  a. Its mean will be 0.
  b. Figure its standard deviation.

  ❹ **Figure the estimated population variances based on each sample**. For each population, $S^2 = SS/(N - 1)$.

  ❺ **Figure the pooled estimate of the population variance:**
  $$S^2_{\text{Pooled}} = \frac{df_1}{df_{\text{Total}}}(S^2_1) + \frac{df_2}{df_{\text{Total}}}(S^2_2)$$
  $(df_1 = N_1 - 1$ and $df_2 = N_2 - 1; df_{\text{Total}} = df_1 + df_2)$

  ❻ **Figure the variance of each distribution of means:**
  $S^2_{M_1} = S^2_{\text{Pooled}}/N_1$ and $S^2_{M_2} = S^2_{\text{Pooled}}/N_2$

  ❼ **Figure the variance of the distribution of differences between means:**
  $S^2_{\text{Difference}} = S^2_{M_1} + S^2_{M_2}$

  ❽ **Figure the standard deviation of the distribution of differences between means:** $S_{\text{Difference}} = \sqrt{S^2_{\text{Difference}}}$

  c. Determine its shape: It will be a *t* distribution with df_{Total} degrees of freedom.

❸ **Determine the cutoff sample score on the comparison distribution at which the null hypothesis should be rejected.**
  a. Determine the degrees of freedom (df_{Total}), desired significance level, and tails in the test (one or two).
  b. Look up the appropriate cutoff in a *t* table. If the exact *df* is not given, use the *df* below it.

❹ **Determine your sample's score on the comparison distribution:**
  $t = (M_1 - M_2)/S_{\text{Difference}}$

❺ **Decide whether to reject the null hypothesis:** Compare the scores from steps 3 and 4.

The research hypothesis was that Population 1 people score differently than Population 2 people: $\mu_1 \neq \mu_2$. The null hypothesis is that the Population 1 people score the same as Population 2 people: $\mu_1 = \mu_2$.

❷ **Determine the characteristics of the comparison distribution.** The mean of the distribution of differences between means is 0. For the standard deviation,

  ❹ **Figure the estimated population variances based on each sample.** $S^2_1 = 10$; $S^2_2 = 12$.

  ❺ **Figure the pooled estimate of the population variance:** $S^2_{\text{Pooled}} = (25/60)(10) + (35/60)(12) = 4.17 + 7.00 = 11.17$.

  ❻ **Figure the variance of each distribution of means:** $S^2_{M_1} = 11.17/26 = .43$ and $S^2_{M_2} = 11.17/36 = .31$.

  ❼ **Figure the variance of the distribution of differences between means:** $S^2_{\text{Difference}} = .43 + .31 = .74$.

  ❽ **Figure the standard deviation of the distribution of differences between means:** $\sqrt{.74} = .86$.

The shape is a *t* distribution with $df = 60$.

❸ **Determine the cutoff sample score on the comparison distribution at which the null hypothesis should be rejected.** The *t* cutoff for .05 level, two-tailed, $df = 60 = \pm2.001$.

❹ **Determine your sample's score on the comparison distribution.** $t = (5 - 8)/.86 = -3.49$.

❺ **Decide whether to reject the null hypothesis.** The *t* of -3.49 is more extreme than the needed *t* of ±2.001. Therefore, reject the null hypothesis.

(b) The distributions involved are shown in Figure 10–4.

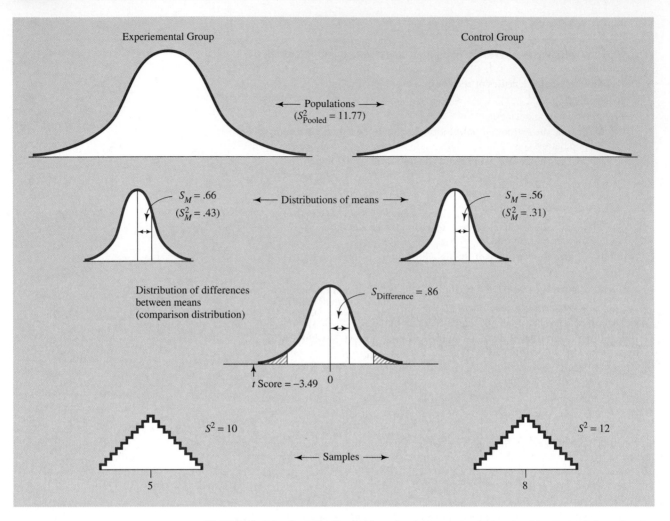

FIGURE 10-4   *The distributions for the answer to "How Are You Doing" Question 2.*

ASSUMPTIONS OF THE *t* TEST FOR INDEPENDENT MEANS

The first assumption for a *t* test for independent means is the same as that for any *t* test: Each of the population distributions is assumed to follow a normal curve. In practice, this is only a problem if you have reason to think that the two populations are dramatically skewed distributions, and in opposite directions. The *t* test holds up well even when the shape of the population distributions is fairly far from normal.

In a *t* test for independent means, you also have to be able to assume that the two populations have the same variance. (You take advantage of this assumption when you average the estimates from each of the two samples.) Once again, however, it turns out that in practice the *t* test gives pretty accurate results even when there are fairly large differences in the population variances, particularly when there are equal or near equal numbers of scores in the two samples. (How do we know that the *t* test holds up well to moderate violations of its assumptions? See Box 10–1 for a description of what are called "Monte Carlo Methods.")

BOX 10–1   Monte Carlo Methods: When Mathematics Becomes Just an Experiment, and Statistics Depend on a Game of Chance

The name for the methods, *Monte Carlo* (after the famous Monegasque casino resort city), has been adopted only in recent years. But the approach itself dates back at least a few centuries to when mathematicians would set down their pens or chalk and go out and try an actual experiment to test a particular understanding of a probability problem. For example, in 1777 Buffon described, in his *Essai d'Arithmétique morale,* a method of computing the ratio of the diameter of a circle to its circumference by tossing a needle onto a flat surface containing parallel lines. Assuming that the needle fell randomly into any position, one could compute the odds of its taking certain positions, such as touching the lines or not and lying at certain angles. The term *Monte Carlo* no doubt reflects the early understanding of mathematicians and statisticians that many of their problems were like those involving games of chance. (Recall Pascal and the problem of points from Chapter 5, Box 5–2.)

Wide use of Monte Carlo methods by statisticians became possible with the advent of computers. This is because the essence of Monte Carlo studies is the interaction of randomness and probabilities, which means testing out a great many possibilities. Indeed, the first application of Monte Carlo methods was in neutron physics, since the behavior of particles when scattered by a neutron beam is so complicated and so close to random that solving the problem mathematically from equations was practically impossible. But by artificially simulating the statistical conditions of what were essentially physical experiments, the physical world could be understood—or at least approximated in an adequate way.

Do you remember being shown Brownian motion in your chemistry or physics class in high school? Its study is a good example of a Monte Carlo problem. Here are atomic particles, more or less, this time in fluids, free to do an almost limitless number of almost random things. In fact, Brownian motion has been likened to a "random walk" of a drunkard. At any moment, the drunkard could move in any direction. But the problem is simplified by limiting the drunkard (or particle) to an imaginary grid.

Picture the grid of a city's streets. Further imagine that there is a wall around the city that the drunkard cannot escape (just as all particles must come to a limit—they cannot go on forever). At the limit, the wall, the drunkard must pay a fine, which also varies randomly. The point of this example is how much is random—all the movements and also all the ultimate consequences. So the number of possible paths is enormous.

The random walk example brings us to the main feature of Monte Carlo methods: They require the use of random numbers. And for an explanation of them, you can look forward to Chapter 15, Box 15–1.

Now, let's return to what interests us here—the use of Monte Carlo studies to check out what will be the result of the violations of certain assumptions of statistical tests. For example, the computer may set up two populations with identical means, but the other parameters are supplied by the statistical researcher so that these violate some important assumption. Perhaps the populations are skewed a certain way, or the two populations have different variances.

Then, samples are randomly selected from each of these two offbeat populations (remember, they were invented by the computer). The means of these samples are compared using the usual *t*-test procedure with the usual *t* tables with all their assumptions. A large number, often around 1,000, of such pairs of samples are selected, and a *t* test is computed for each. The question is, How many of these 1,000 *t* tests will come out significant at the 5% significance level? Ideally, the result would be about 5%, or 50 of the 1,000. But what if 10% (100) of these supposedly 5%-level tests come out significant? What if only 1% do? If these kinds of results arise, then this particular violation of the assumptions of the *t* test cannot be tolerated. But in fact, most violations (except for very extreme ones) checked with these methods do not create very large changes in the *p* values.

Monte Carlo methods are a boon to statistics, but like everything else, they have their drawbacks as well and consequently their critics. One problem is that the ways in which populations can violate as-

(continued)

sumptions are almost limitless in their variations. But even computers have their limits—Monte Carlo studies are tried on only a representative set of those variations. A more specific problem is that there is good reason to think that some of the variations that are not studied are far more like the real world than those that have been studied (see the discussion in Chapter 5 of the controversy about how common the normal curve really is). Finally, when we are deciding whether to use a particular statistic in any specific situation, we have no idea about the population our sample came from—is it like any on which there has been a Monte Carlo study performed, or not? Simply knowing that Monte Carlo studies have shown some statistic to be robust in the face of many kinds of assumption viola-

tions does not prove that it is so in a given situation. We can only hope that it increases the chances that using the statistic is safe and justifiable.

At any rate, Monte Carlo studies are a perfect example of how the computer has changed science. Shreider (1966) expressed it this way:

> Computers have led to a novel revolution in mathematics. Whereas previously an investigation of a random process was regarded as complete as soon as it was reduced to an analytic description, nowadays it is convenient in many cases to solve an analytic problem by reducing it to a corresponding random process and then simulating that process. (p. vii)

In other words, instead of math helping us analyze experiments, experiments are helping us analyze math.

However, the *t* test can give quite misleading results if (a) the scores in the samples suggest that the populations are very far from normal, (b) the variances are very different, or (c) there are both problems. In these situations, there are alternatives to the ordinary *t* test procedure, some of which we will consider in Chapter 15.

Many computer programs for figuring the *t* test for independent means actually provide two sets of results. For example, Table 10–4 shows part of the output using the SPSS for Windows computer program for the example comparing boys whose mothers' work involves versus does not involve solving problems. The first set of results, labeled "Equal variances assumed," figures the *t* test assuming the population variances are equal. This method is the standard one, the one you have learned in this chapter (the slight difference between the *t* of 2.393 in the computer output shown in Table 10–4 and the result we figured of 2.40 shown in Table 10–1 is just due to rounding error). The other method the computer uses, labeled "Equal variances not assumed," does not make this assumption. It uses an alternative procedure that takes into account that the population variances may be unequal. (But it still assumes the populations follow a normal distribution.) However, in most situations we can assume that the population variances are equal. In fact, in this example, where it was likely the populations did have about the same variance, you see that using the alternative procedure produced a very similar final result and that we

TABLE 10–4 Portion of Output from SPSS for Windows *t* Test for Independent Means for Adolescent Boys' Perceived Academic Competence Example

		t-test for Equality of Means			
		t	*df*	Sig. (2-tailed)	Mean Difference
ACADCOMP	Equal variances assumed	2.393	41	.021	3.5726
	Equal variances not assumed	2.287	29.157	.030	3.5726

(Data from Moorehouse & Sanders, 1992.)

would have made the same conclusion using either method (that is, in both analyses, $p < .05$). Thus, researchers usually use the standard procedure. Using the special approach has the advantage that you don't have to worry about whether you met the equal population variance assumption. But it has the disadvantage that if you have met that assumption, with this special method you have less power. That is, when you do meet the assumption, you are slightly less likely to get a significant result using the special method.

EFFECT SIZE AND POWER FOR THE *T* TEST FOR INDEPENDENT MEANS

EFFECT SIZE

Effect size for the *t* test for independent means is the figured in basically the same way as we have been using all along:

(10-9)
$$d - \frac{\mu_1 - \mu_2}{\sigma}$$

> The effect size is the difference between the population means divided by the population's standard deviation.

Cohen's (1988) conventions for the *t* test for independent means are the same as in all the situations we have considered so far: .20 for a small effect size, .50 for a medium effect size, and .80 for a large effect size.

Suppose that an environmental psychologist is working in a city with high levels of air pollution. This psychologist plans a study of number of problems completed on a creativity test over a 1-hour period. The study compares performance under two conditions. In the experimental condition, each participant takes the test in a room with a special air purifier. In the control condition, each participant takes the test in a room without the air purifier. The researcher expects that the control group will probably score like others who have taken this test in the past, which is a mean of 21. But the researcher expects that the experimental group will perform better, scoring about 29. This test is known from previous research to have a standard deviation of about 10. Thus, $\mu_1 = 29$, $\mu_2 = 21$, and $\sigma = 10$. Given these figures, $d = (\mu_1 - \mu_2)/\sigma = (29 - 21)/10 = .80$, a large effect size.

When you have results of a completed study, you estimate the effect size as the difference between the sample means divided by the pooled estimate of the population standard deviation (the square root of the pooled estimate of the population variance). You use the sample means because they are the best estimate of the population means, and you use S_{Pooled} because it is the best estimate of σ. Stated as a formula,

(10-10)
$$\text{Estimated } d = \frac{M_1 - M_2}{S_{\text{Pooled}}}$$

> The estimated effect size is the difference between the sample means divided by the pooled estimate of the population's standard deviation.

Consider Valenzuela's (1997) study of the quality of instructional assistance provided by mothers of poor children. The mean for the sample of mothers of the adequately nourished children was 33.1; the mean for the sample of mothers of chronically undernourished children was 27.0. We figured the pooled estimate of the population variance to be 168.77; the standard deviation is thus 12.99. The difference in means of 6.1, divided by 12.99, gives an effect size of .47—a medium effect size. In terms of the formula,

$$\text{Estimated } d = \frac{M_1 - M_2}{S_{\text{Pooled}}} = \frac{33.1 - 27.0}{12.99} = \frac{6.1}{12.99} = .47$$

POWER

Table 10–5 gives the approximate power for the .05 significance level for small, medium, and large effect sizes and one-tailed or two-tailed tests. Consider again the environmental psychology example of a planned study, where the researchers expected a large effect size ($d = .80$). Suppose this researcher plans to use the .05 level, one-tailed, with 10 participants. Based on Table 10–5, the study would have a power of .53. This means that even if the research hypothesis is in fact true and has a large effect size, there is only a 53% chance that the study will come out significant.

Now consider an example of a completed study. Suppose you have read a study using a *t* test for independent means that had a nonsignificant result using the .05 significance level, two-tailed. There were 40 participants in each group. Should you conclude that there is in fact no difference at all in the populations? This conclusion seems quite unjustified. Table 10–5 shows a power of only .14 for a small effect size. This suggests that even if such a small effect does indeed exist in the populations, this study would probably not come out significant. Still, we can also conclude that if there is a true difference in the populations, it is probably not large. Table 10–5 shows a power of .94 for a large effect size. This suggests that if a large effect exists, it almost surely would have produced a significant result.

TABLE 10–5 Approximate Power for Studies Using the *t* Test for Independent Means Testing Hypotheses at the .05 Significance Level

Number of Participants in Each Group	Effect Size		
	Small (.20)	Medium (.50)	Large (.80)
One-tailed test			
10	.11	.29	.53
20	.15	.46	.80
30	.19	.61	.92
40	.22	.72	.97
50	.26	.80	.99
100	.41	.97	*
Two-tailed test			
10	.07	.18	.39
20	.09	.33	.69
30	.12	.47	.86
40	.14	.60	.94
50	.17	.70	.98
100	.29	.94	*

*Nearly 1.
Note: Based on Cohen (1988), pp. 28–39.

POWER WHEN SAMPLE SIZES ARE NOT EQUAL

For a study with any given total number of participants, power is greatest when the participants are divided into two equal groups. Recall the example from the start of this chapter where the 42 participants were divided into 11 in the experimental group and 31 in the control group. This study has much less power than it would have if the researchers had been able to divide their 42 participants into 21 in each group.

There is a practical problem in figuring power from tables when sample sizes are not equal. Like most power tables, Table 10–5 assumes equal numbers in each of the two groups. What do you do when your two samples have different numbers of people in them? It turns out that in terms of power, the **harmonic mean** of the numbers of participants in two unequal sample sizes gives the equivalent sample size for what you would have with two equal samples. The harmonic mean sample size is given by this formula:

harmonic mean

$$(10\text{-}11) \qquad \text{Harmonic Mean} = \frac{(2)(N_1)(N_2)}{N_1 + N_2}$$

> The harmonic mean is 2 times the first sample size times the second sample size, all divided by the sum of the two sample sizes.

In our example with 11 in one group and 31 in the other, the harmonic mean is 16.24:

$$\text{Harmonic Mean} = \frac{(2)(N_1)(N_2)}{N_1 + N_2} = \frac{(2)(11)(31)}{11 + 31} = \frac{682}{42} = 16.24$$

Thus, even though you have a total of 42 participants, the study has the power of a study with equal sample sizes of only about 16 in each group. (This means that a study with a total of 32 participants divided equally would have had about the same power.)

PLANNING SAMPLE SIZE

Table 10–6 gives the approximate number of participants needed for 80% power for estimated small, medium, and large effect sizes using one-tailed and two-tailed tests, all using the .05 significance level.[2] Suppose you plan a study in which you

TABLE 10–6	Approximate Number of Participants Needed in Each Group (Assuming Equal Sample Sizes) for 80% Power for the *t* Test for Independent Means, Testing Hypotheses at the .05 Significance Level

	Effect Size		
	Small (.20)	Medium (.50)	Large (.80)
One-tailed	310	50	20
two-tailed	393	64	26

[2]Cohen (1988, pp. 54–55) provides fuller tables, indicating needed numbers of participants for levels of power other than 80%; for effect sizes other than .20, .50, and .80; and for other significance levels. If you just need a rough approximation, Dunlap and Myers (1997) have developed a shortcut for finding the approximate number of participants needed for studies using the *t* test for independent means. For 50% power, the number of participants needed per group is approximately $8/d^2 + 1$. For 80%–90% power, $16/d^2 + 2$.

expect a medium effect size and will use the .05 significance level, one-tailed. Based on Table 10–6, you need 50 people in each group (100 total) to have 80% power. However, if you did a study using the same significance level but expected a large effect size, you would need only 20 people in each group (40 total).

HOW ARE YOU DOING?

1. List two assumptions for the *t* test for independent means. For each, give the situations in which violations of these assumptions would be seriously problematic.
2. Why do you need to assume the populations have the same variance?
3. What is the effect size for a planned study in which Population 1 is predicted to have a mean of 17, Population 2 is predicted to have a mean of 25, and the population standard deviation is assumed to be about 20?
4. What is the power of a study using a *t* test for independent means, with a two-tailed test at the .05 significance level, in which the researchers predict a large effect size and there are 20 participants in each group?
5. What is the approximate power of a study using a *t* test for independent means, with a two-tailed test at the .05 significance level, in which the researchers predict a large effect size, and there are 6 participants in one group and 34 participants in the other group?
6. How many participants do you need in each group for 80% power in a planned study in which you predict a small effect size and will be using a *t* test for independent means, one-tailed, at the .05 significance level?

ANSWERS:

1. One assumption is that the two populations are normally distributed; this is mainly a problem if you have reason to think the two populations are strongly skewed in opposite directions. A second assumption is that the two populations have the same variance; this is mainly a problem if you believe the two distributions have quite different variances *and* the sample sizes are different, or you are also somewhat in violation of the normal distribution assumption.
2. Because you make a pooled estimate of the population variance. The pooling would not make sense if the estimates from the two samples were for populations with different variances.
3. $d = (17 - 25)/20 = -8/20 = -.4$.
4. .69
5. Harmonic mean $= (2)(6)(34)/(6 + 34) = 408/40 = 10.2$. Power for a study like this with 10 in each group $= .39$.
6. 310.

CONTROVERSY: THE PROBLEM OF TOO MANY *t* TESTS

A long-standing controversy is what is usually called the problem of "too many *t* tests." The basic issues here come up in all types of hypothesis testing, not just the *t* test. However, we introduce this problem now because it has traditionally been brought up in this context.

Suppose you do a large number of *t* tests for the same study. For example, you might compare two groups on each of 17 different measures—such as different indicators of memory on a recall task, various intelligence test subscales, or different aspects of observed interactions between infants. When you do several *t* tests in the same study, the chance of any one of them coming out significant at, say, the 5%

level is really greater than 5%. If you make 100 independent comparisons, on the average five of them will come out significant at the 5% level just by chance. That is, about five will come out significant even if there is no true difference at all between the populations the *t* tests are comparing.

The fundamental issue is not controversial. Everyone agrees that there is a problem in a study involving a large number of comparisons. And everyone agrees that in a study like this, if only a few results come out significant, these differences should be viewed very cautiously. The controversy is about how cautious to be and about how few is "only a few." One reason there is room for controversy is that in most cases, the many comparisons being made are not independent—the chance of one coming out significant is related to the chance of another coming out significant.

Here is an example. A study compares a sample of lawyers to a sample of doctors on 100 personality traits. Now suppose the researcher simply conducts 100 *t* tests. If these 100 *t* tests were truly independent, we would expect that on the average five would come out significant just by chance. In fact, tables exist that tell you quite precisely the chance of any particular number of *t* tests coming out significant. The problem, however, is that in practice these 100 *t* tests are *not* independent. Many of the various personality traits are probably related: If doctors and lawyers differ on assertiveness, they probably also differ on self-confidence. Thus, certain sets of comparisons may be more or less likely to come out significant by chance, so that 5 in 100 may not be what you should expect by chance. There is yet another complication: In most cases, differences on some of the variables are more important than on others. Some comparisons may directly test a theory or the effectiveness of some practical procedure; other comparisons may be more "exploratory."

Here is another kind of example. In studies using brain imaging procedures (such as functional magnetic resonance imagery or fMRI), the way the analysis works for a typical study is like this: A person's brain is scanned every few seconds over a 10 or 15 minute period. During this time, the person is sometimes looking at one kind of image, say a picture of a person smiling, and at other times is looking at a different kind of image, say a picture of the same person frowning. For each little area of the brain, the fMRI produces a number for how active that area was during each 2- to 3-second scan. Thus, for each little area of the brain, you might have 60 numbers for activation when looking at the smile and 60 numbers for when looking at the frown. Thus, for each little area, you can figure a *t* test for independent means. In fact, this is exactly what is done in this kind of research. The problem, however, is that you have a great many little areas of the brain. (Typically, in fMRI research, each little area may be about a ¼-inch cube or smaller.) Thus, you have several thousand *t* tests, and you would expect some of them to be significant just by chance. This whole situation is further complicated by the issue that some brain areas might be expected to be more likely to show different levels of activity for this kind of image. In addition, the situation is still further complicated by the fact that you might want to pay more attention when two or more little areas that are right next to each other show significant differences.

In these various examples, there are a variety of contending solutions. We introduce one kind of solution in Chapter 11 (the Bonferroni procedure), when we consider a related situation, one that comes up in studies comparing more than two groups. However, the issue remains at the forefront of work on the development of statistical methods.

THE *t* TEST FOR INDEPENDENT MEANS IN RESEARCH ARTICLES

A *t* test for independent means is usually described in a research article by giving the means (and sometimes the standard deviations) of the two samples, plus the usual way of reporting any kind of *t* test—for example, $t(38) = 4.72$, $p < .01$ (recall that the number in parentheses is the degrees of freedom). The result of the Moorehouse and Sanders (1992) example might be written up as follows: "The mean perceived academic competence for the boys whose mothers' work involved problem solving was 32.8 ($SD = 4.27$), and the mean for the boys whose mothers' work did not involve problem solving was 29.2 ($SD = 5.23$); $t(41) = 2.42$, $p < .05$, one-tailed."

Here is another example. Raymore and her colleagues (2001), as part of a large-scale study of U.S. young people, compared the socioeconomic idex (SEI) of students who went away from home to go to college versus those who stayed at home. Here is an excerpt from their results section: ". . . females who had left home were from higher SEI homes ($N = 115$, $M = 54.7$, $SD = 16.5$) than college females who had not left home ($N = 74$, $M = 44.8$, $SD = 14.8$) ($t = 4.19$, $df = 187$, $p < .05$)" (p. 211). (Notice that the degrees of freedom are given in a different from usual format in the scientific journal in which this paper appeared.)

The researchers in this example do not give the effect size. However, you could figure it out from what they do give. Usually in a research article, *SD* is the estimated population standard deviation (what in this book we label *S*). Thus, you can figure the pooled estimate of the population standard deviation using the numbers provided:

$$S^2_{\text{Pooled}} = (df_1/df_{\text{Total}})(S^2_1) + (df_2/df_{\text{Total}})(S^2_2)$$
$$= (114/187)(16.5^2) + (73/187)(14.8^2)$$
$$= (.61)(272.25) + (.39)(219.04) = 166.07 + 85.43$$
$$= 251.5$$

$$S_{\text{Pooled}} = \sqrt{S^2_{\text{Pooled}}} = \sqrt{251.5} = 15.86$$

You can then estimate the effect size:

$$\text{Estimated } d = (M_1 - M_2)/S_{\text{pooled}} = (54.7 - 44.8)/15.86 = 9.9/15.86 = .62.$$

This is a moderate effect size.

Table 10–7 is an example in which the results are given in a table. This table is taken from a study conducted by Frisch et al. (1995) in which 293 female medical students in Malaysia were surveyed on their views about smoking and on whether their family members and friends smoked. This table compares those students who have brothers who smoke to those who have brothers who don't smoke. The measures were Knowledge (of the health risks of being around smokers), Attitude (towards being around smokers), Efforts (to avoid being around smokers), and Physician's Responsibility (to inform patients of health risks of being around smokers). All scales were scored so that higher scores were pro-smoking. Lower scores meant more concern about the health risks.

The first line of the table shows that those with a brother who smokes scored higher on the Knowledge scale. This means that such students have less knowledge about the health risks of being around smokers. The second line shows those with a

| TABLE 10–7 | *t* Tests for Means on Passive Smoking Knowledge, Attitude, and Efforts According to Smoking Status, for Total Group and Men and Women |

	Brother Smoker	Brother Nonsmoker	*t*-Value	Sig.
Total Group	$N =$	$N =$		
Knowledge	2.03 (96)	1.88 (140)	2.61	.01
Attitude	1.95 (94)	1.70 (137)	3.29	.001
Efforts	2.36 (92)	2.23 (133)	1.88	.061
Phys. Resp.*	1.78 (95)	1.61 (142)	2.02	.04
Men				
Knowledge	2.15 (54)	1.92 (69)	2.97	.004
Attitude	2.08 (54)	1.83 (67)	2.12	.036
Efforts	2.50 (52)	2.31 (66)	1.87	.064
Phys. Resp.*	1.81 (54)	1.65 (69)	1.27	.207
Women				
Knowledge	1.87 (42)	1.85 (71)	.30	.767
Attitude	1.77 (40)	1.57 (70)	2.43	.018
Efforts	2.17 (40)	2.15 (67)	.26	.797
Phys. Resp.*	1.76 (41)	1.58 (73)	1.51	.136

*Physician's Responsibility.
Note: Data from Frisch, Shamsuddin, & Kurtz (1995).

brother who smokes have a more positive attitude toward being around smokers (that is, they do not see it as being as much of a health risk).

Note that some of these results were not significant. What should we conclude? Consider the students' beliefs about a physician's responsibility. In this comparison, there were 41 with smoker brothers and 73 with nonsmoker brothers. The formula for the harmonic mean indicates that for purposes of figuring power, there are 52.5 participants per group. That is,

$$\text{Harmonic Mean} = \frac{(2)(N_1)(N_2)}{N_1 + N_2} = \frac{(2)(41)(73)}{41 + 73} = \frac{5,986}{114} = 52.5$$

Once you know the sample size to use, you can look up power in Table 10–5, using 50 participants (the nearest number of participants in the table to 52.5) and a two-tailed test. From the table, the power of this study to find significance for a small effect size is only .17. On the other hand, the power of the study to find a medium effect size is .70 and a large effect size, .98. Thus, if in fact there is a small effect for having a brother who is a smoker, this would probably not have shown up in this study. On the other hand, suppose there was in fact a medium effect of this kind. In that case, the result of this study probably would have been significant. Almost certainly if there were a large effect, the study would have come out significant. Thus, we can fairly confidently take from this study that having a brother who is a smoker probably does not make a large difference for Malaysian female medical students' beliefs about a physician's responsibility to inform patients about the risks of being around smokers. However, we cannot conclude that there might not be a small effect of this kind.

SUMMARY

1. A *t* test for independent means is used for hypothesis testing with two samples of scores. The main difference from a *t* test for a single sample is that the comparison distribution is a distribution of differences between means of samples. This distribution can be thought of as being built up in two steps: Each population of individuals produces a distribution of means, and then a new distribution is created of differences between pairs of means selected from these two distributions of means.

2. The distribution of differences between means has a mean of 0 and is a *t* distribution with the total of the degrees of freedom from the two samples. Its standard deviation is figured in several steps:
   ❶ **Figure the estimated population variances based on each sample.**
   ❷ **Figure the pooled estimate of the population variance.**
   ❸ **Figure the variance of each distribution of means.**
   ❹ **Figure the variance of the distribution of differences between means.**
   ❺ **Figure the standard deviation of the distribution of differences between means.**

3. The assumptions of the *t* test for independent means are that the two populations are normally distributed and have the same variance. However, the *t* test gives fairly accurate results when the true situation is moderately different from the assumptions.

4. Effect size for a *t* test for independent means is the difference between the means divided by the population standard deviation. Power is greatest when the sample sizes of the two groups are equal. When they are not equal, you use the harmonic mean of the two sample sizes when looking up power on a table.

5. When you carry out many significance tests in the same study, such as a series of *t* tests comparing two groups on various measures, the possibility that any one of the comparisons may turn out significant at the .05 level by chance is greater than .05. There is controversy about how to adjust for this problem, though most agree that results should be interpreted cautiously in a situation of this kind.

6. *t* tests for independent means are usually reported in research articles with the means of the two groups plus the degrees of freedom, *t* score, and significance level. Results may also be reported in a table in which each significant difference is shown by stars.

KEY TERMS

distribution of differences between means (p. 342)
harmonic mean (p. 361)
pooled estimate of the population variance (S^2_{Pooled}) (p. 344)
standard deviation of the distribution of differences between means ($S_{Difference}$) (p. 346)
t test for independent means (p. 341)
variance of the distribution of differences between means ($S^2_{Difference}$) (p. 345)
weighted average (p. 344)

EXAMPLE WORKED-OUT COMPUTATIONAL PROBLEMS

FIGURE THE STANDARD DEVIATION OF THE DISTRIBUTION OF DIFFERENCE SCORES.

Figure $S_{Difference}$ for the following study: $N_1 = 40$, $S^2_1 = 15$; $N_2 = 60$; $S^2_2 = 12$.

❶ **Figure the estimated population variances based on each sample:** $S_1^2 = 15$; $S_2^2 = 12$.

❷ **Figure the pooled estimate of the population variance:**

$$df_1 = N_1 - 1 = 40 - 1 = 39; df_2 = N_2 - 1 = 60 - 1 = 59;$$
$$df_{Total} = df_1 + df_2 = 39 + 59 = 98.$$

$$S_{Pooled}^2 = \frac{df_1}{df_{Total}}(S_1^2) + \frac{df_2}{df_{Total}}(S_2^2) = (39/98)(15) + (59/98)(12)$$
$$= (.4)(15) + (.6)(12) = 6 + 7.2 = 13.2$$

❸ **Figure the variance of each distribution of means:**

$$S_{M_1}^2 = S_{Pooled}^2/N_1 = 13.2/40 = .33$$
$$S_{M_2}^2 = S_{Pooled}^2/N_2 - 13.2/60 =. 22$$

❹ **Figure the variance of the distribution of differences between means:**

$$S_{Difference}^2 = S_{M_1}^2 + S_{M_2}^2 = .33 + .22 = .55$$

❺ **Figure the standard deviation of the distribution of differences between means:**

$$S_{difference} = \sqrt{S_{Difference}^2} = \sqrt{.55} = .74$$

HYPOTHESIS TESTING USING THE t TEST INDEPENDENT MEANS

A researcher randomly assigns seven individuals to receive a new experimental pro cedure and seven to a control condition. At the end of the study, all 14 are measured. Scores for those in the experimental group were 6, 4, 9, 7, 7, 3, and 6. Scores for those in the control group were 6, 1, 5, 3, 1, 1, and 4. Carry out a t test for independent means using the .05 level of significance, two-tailed. Use the steps of hypothesis testing and sketch the distributions involved.

The figuring is shown in Table 10–8; the distributions are illustrated in Figure 10–5. Here are the steps of hypothesis testing.

❶ **Restate the question as a research hypothesis and a null hypothesis about the populations.** There are two populations:

Population 1: People like those who receive the experimental procedure
Population 2: People like those who receive the control procedure

The research hypothesis is that the means of the two populations are different: $\mu_1 \neq \mu_2$. The null hypothesis is that the means of the two populations are the same: $\mu_1 = \mu_2$.

❷ **Determine the characteristics of the comparison distribution.** The distribution of differences between means has a mean of 0.

    ❶ **Figure the estimated population variances based on each sample:** $S_1^2 = 4$; $S_2^2 = 4.33$.

    ❷ **Figure the pooled estimate of the population variance:** $S_{Pooled}^2 = 4.17$.

    ❸ **Figure the variance of each distribution of means:** $S_{M_1}^2 = .60$; $S_{M_2}^2 = .60$.

    ❹ **Figure the variance of the distribution of differences between means:** $S_{Difference}^2 = 1.20$

TABLE 10–8　**Figuring for Worked-Out Computational Problem for Hypothesis Testing Using the t Test Independent Means**

Experimental Group			Control Group		
Score	Deviation From Mean	Squared Deviation From Mean	Score	Deviation From Mean	Squared Deviation From Mean
6	0	0	6	3	9
4	−2	4	1	−2	4
9	3	9	5	2	4
7	1	1	3	0	0
7	1	1	1	−2	4
3	−3	9	1	−2	4
6	0	0	4	1	1
Σ: 42	0	24	21	0	26

$M_1 = 6$; $S_1^2 = 24/6 = 4$; $M_2 = 3$; $S_2^2 = 26/6 = 4.33$

$N_1 = 7$; $df_1 = N_1 - 1 = 6$; $N_2 = 7$; $df_2 = N_2 - 1 = 6$

$df_{\text{Total}} = df_1 + df_2 = 6 + 6 = 12$

$S_{\text{Pooled}}^2 = \dfrac{df_1}{df_{\text{Total}}}(S_1^2) + \dfrac{df_2}{df_{\text{Total}}}(S_2^2) = \dfrac{6}{12}(4) + \dfrac{6}{12}(4.33) = .5(4) + .5(4.33) = 2.00 + 2.17 = 4.17$

$S_{M_1}^2 = S_{\text{Pooled}}^2/N_1 = 4.17/7 = .60$

$S_{M_2}^2 = S_{\text{Pooled}}^2/N_2 = 4.17/7 = .60$

$S_{\text{Difference}}^2 = S_{M_1}^2 + S_{M_2}^2 = .60 + .60 = 1.20$

$S_{\text{Difference}} = \sqrt{S_{\text{Difference}}^2} = \sqrt{1.20} = 1.10$

Needed t with $df = 12$, 5% level, two-tailed $= \pm 2.179$

$t = (M_1 - M_2)/S_{\text{Difference}} = (6.00 - 3.00)/1.10 = 3.00/1.10 = 2.73$

Conclusion: Reject the null hypothesis; the research hypothesis is supported.

❷ **Figure the standard deviation of the distribution of differences between means:** $S_{\text{Difference}} = 1.10$.
The shape is a t distribution with $df = 12$.

❸ **Determine the cutoff sample score on the comparison distribution at which the null hypothesis should be rejected.** With $df = 12$, .05 significance level, two-tailed test, the cutoff is ± 2.179.

❹ **Determine the sample's score on the comparison distribution.** $t = 2.73$.

❺ **Decide whether to reject the null hypothesis.** The t of 2.73 is more extreme than ± 2.179. Thus, you can reject the null hypothesis. The research hypothesis is supported.

FINDING POWER WHEN SAMPLE SIZES ARE UNEQUAL

A planned study with a predicted small effect size has 22 in one group and 51 in the other. What is the approximate power for a one-tailed test at the .05 significance level?

$$\text{Harmonic Mean} = \frac{(2)(N_1)(N_2)}{N_1 + N_2} = \frac{(2)(22)(51)}{22 + 51} = \frac{2244}{73} = 30.7$$

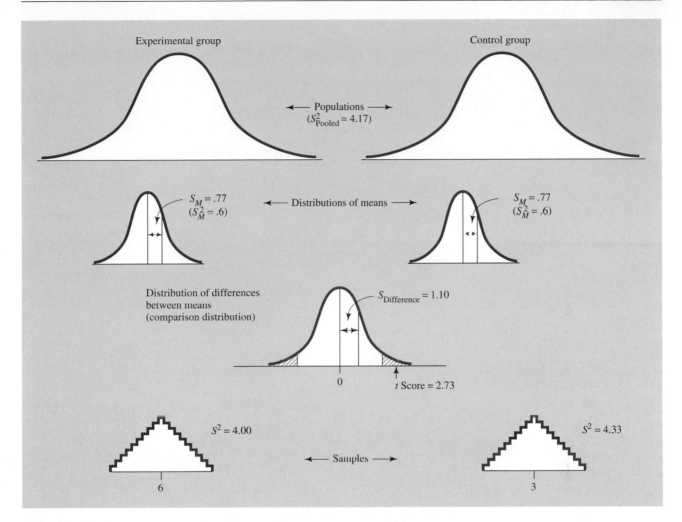

FIGURE 10-5   *The distributions in the worked-out computational problem for hypothesis testing using the* t *test independent means.*

From Table 10–5, for a one-tailed test with 30 participants in each group, power for a small effect size is .19.

PRACTICE PROBLEMS

These problems involve figuring. Most real-life statistics problems are done on a computer. However, even if you have a computer and statistics software, do these by hand (with the help of a calculator) to ingrain the method in your mind. Also, in all problems involving figuring, be sure to show your work.

For practice in using a computer to solve statistics problems, refer to the computer section of each chapter of the *Student's Study Guide and Computer Workbook* that accompanies this text.

All data are fictional unless an actual citation is given.

Answers to Set I problems are given at the back of the book.

SET I

1. For each of the following studies, say whether you would use a *t* test for dependent means or a *t* test for independent means.

   (a) A researcher randomly assigns a group of 25 unemployed workers to receive a new job-skills program and 24 other workers to receive the standard job-skills program, and then measures how well they all do on a job-skills test.

   (b) A researcher measures self-esteem in 21 students before and after taking a difficult exam.

   (c) A researcher tests reaction time of each of a group of 14 individuals twice, once while in a very hot room and once while in a normal-temperature room.

2. Figure $S_{Difference}$ for each of the following studies:

N_1	S_1^2	N_2	S_2^2
a. 20	1	20	2
b. 20	1	40	2
c. 40	1	20	2
d. 40	1	40	2
e. 40	1	40	4

3. For each of the following experiments, decide if the difference between conditions is statistically significant at the .05 level (two-tailed).

	Experimental Group			Control Group		
	N	M	S^2	N	M	S^2
(a)	30	12.0	2.4	30	11.1	2.8
(b)	20	12.0	2.4	40	11.1	2.8
(c)	30	12.0	2.2	30	11.1	3.0

4. A social psychologist studying mass communication randomly assigned 82 volunteers to one of two experimental groups. Sixty-one were instructed to get their news for a month only from television, and 21 were instructed to get their news for a month only from the radio. (Why the researcher didn't assign equal numbers to the two conditions is a mystery!) After the month was up, all participants were tested on their knowledge of several political issues. The researcher did not have a prediction as to which news source would make people more knowledgeable. That is, the researcher simply predicted that there is some kind of difference. These were the results of the study. TV group: $M = 24$, $S^2 = 4$; radio group: $M = 26$, $S^2 = 6$. Using the .01 level, what should the social psychologist conclude? (a) Use the steps of hypothesis testing; (b) sketch the distributions involved; and (c) explain your answers to someone who is familiar with the *t* test for a single sample, but not with the *t* test for independent means.

5. An educational psychologist was interested in whether using a student's own name in a story affected children's attention span while reading. Six children were randomly assigned to read a story under ordinary conditions (using names like Dick and Jane). Five other children read versions of the same story, but with each child's own name substituted for one of the children in the story. The researcher kept a careful measure of how long it took each child to read the story. The results are shown below. Using the .05 level, does including the

child's name make any difference? (a) Use the steps of hypothesis testing; (b) sketch the distributions involved; and (c) explain your answers to someone who has never had a course in statistics.

Ordinary Story		Own-Name Story	
Student	Reading Time	Student	Reading Time
A	2	G	4
B	5	H	16
C	7	I	11
D	9	J	9
E	6	K	8
F	7		

6. A developmental psychologist compares 4-year-olds and 8-year-olds on their ability to understand the analogies used in stories. The scores for the five 4-year-olds tested were 7, 6, 2, 3, and 8. The scores for the three 8-year-olds tested were 9, 2, and 5. Using the .05 level, do older children do better? (a) Use the steps of hypothesis testing; (b) sketch the distributions involved; and (c) explain your answers to someone who understands the t test for a single sample, but does not know anything about the t test for independent means.

7. Figure the estimated effect size for problems (a) 4, (b) 5, and (c) 6. (d) Explain what you have done in part (a) who understands the t test for independent means but knows nothing about effect size.

8. Figure the approximate power of each of the following planned studies, all using a t test for independent means at the .05 significance level, one-tailed, with a predicted small effect size:

	N_1	N_2
(a)	3	57
(b)	10	50
(c)	20	40
(d)	30	30

9. What are the approximate numbers of participants needed for each of the following planned studies to have 80% power, assuming equal numbers in the two groups and all using the .05 significance level? (Be sure to give the total number of participants needed, not just the number needed for each group.)

Study	μ_1	Expected μ_2	σ	Tails
a	107	149	84	1
b	22.5	16.2	31.5	2
c	14	12	2.5	1
d	480	520	50	2

10. Van Aken and Asendorpf (1997) studied 139 German 12-year-olds. All of the children completed a general self-worth questionnaire and were interviewed

about the supportiveness they experienced from their mothers, fathers, and class-mates. The researchers then compared the self-worth of those with high and low levels of support of each type. The researchers reported that "lower general self-worth was found for children with a low-supportive mother ($t(137) = 4.52$, $p < .001$, $d = 0.78$) and with a low-supportive father ($t(137) = 4.03$, $p < .001$, $d = 0.69$). . . . A lower general self-worth was also found for children with only low supportive classmates ($t(137) = 2.04$, $p < .05$, $d = 0.35$)." (a) Explain what these results mean to a person who has never had a course in statistics. (b) Include a discussion of effect size and power. (When figuring power, you can assume that the two groups in each comparison had about equal sample sizes.)

11. Gallagher-Thompson and her colleagues (2001) compared 27 wives who were caring for their husbands who had Alzheimer's disease to 27 wives in which neither partner had Alzheimers. The two groups of wives were otherwise simi-lar in terms of age, number of years married, and social economic status. Table 10–9 (reproduced from their Table 1) shows some of their results. (a) Focusing on the Geriatric Depression Scale (the first row of the table) and the Mutuality Scale for Shared Values (the last row in the table), explain these results to a person who knows about the *t* test for a single sample, but is unfamiliar with the *t* test for independent means.

Set II

12. For each of the following studies, say whether you would use a *t* test for depen-dent means or a *t* test for independent means.
    (a) A researcher measures the heights of 40 college students who are the first-born in their families and compares the 15 who come from large families to the 25 who come from smaller families.

TABLE 10–9   Comparison of Caregiving and Noncaregiving Wives on Select Psychosocial Variables

	Caregiving Wives ($n = 27$)			Noncaregiving Wives ($n = 27$)				
	M	*SD*	Range	*M*	*SD*	Range	*t*	*p*
Geriatric Depression Scale[a]	9.42	6.59	1–25	2.37	2.54	0–8	5.14	.0001
Perceived Stress Scale[b]	22.29	8.34	6–36	15.33	6.36	7–30	3.44	.001
Hope questionnaire[c]								
Agency	11.88	1.63	9–16	13.23	1.39	10–16	3.20	.002
Resilience	11.89	0.91	10–14	13.08	1.60	10–16	3.31	.002
Total	23.77	2.03	21–29	26.31	2.56	22–31	3.97	.0001
Mutuality Scale[d]								
Closeness	3.51	.81	.33–4	3.70	.41	2.67–4	−1.02	.315
Reciprocity	2.25	1.19	.17–4	3.25	.55	1.67–4	−3.68	.001
Shared pleasures	2.65	1.00	0–4	3.52	.61	1.75–4	−3.66	.001
Shared values	3.15	.89	0–4	3.46	.45	2.4–4	−1.51	.138

Note: For all measures, higher scores indicate more of the construct being measured.
[a]Maximum score is 30.
[b]Maximum score is 56.
[c]Four questions in each subscale, with a maximum total score of 32.
[d]Maximum mean for each subscale is 4.
Source: Gallagher-Thompson et al., 2001.

(b) A researcher tests performance on a math skills test of each of 250 individuals before and after they complete a one-day seminar on managing test anxiety.
(c) A researcher compares the resting heart rate of 15 individuals who have been taking a particular drug to the resting heart rate of 48 other individuals who have not been taking this drug.

13. Figure $S_{\text{Difference}}$ for each of the following studies:

	N_1	S_1^2	N_2	S_2^2
a.	30	5	20	4
b.	30	5	30	4
c.	30	5	50	4
d.	20	5	30	4
e.	30	5	20	2

14. For each of the following experiments, decide if the difference between conditions is statistically significant at the .05 level (two-tailed).

	Experimental Group			Control Group		
	N	M	S^2	N	M	S^2
(a)	10	604	60	10	607	50
(b)	40	604	60	40	607	50
(c)	10	604	20	40	607	16

15. A psychologist theorized that people can hear better when they have just eaten a large meal. Six individuals were randomly assigned to eat either a large meal or a small meal. After eating the meal, their hearing was tested. The hearing ability scores (high numbers indicate greater ability) are given below. Using the .05 level, do the results support the psychologist's theory? (a) Use the steps of hypothesis testing, (b) sketch the distributions involved, and (c) explain your answers to someone who has never had a course in statistics.

Big Meal Group		Small Meal Group	
Subject	Hearing	Subject	Hearing
A	22	D	19
B	25	E	23
C	25	F	21

16. Twenty students randomly assigned to an experimental group receive an instructional program; 30 in a control group do not. After 6 months, both groups are tested on their knowledge. The experimental group has a mean of 38 on the test (with an estimated population standard deviation of 3); the control group has a mean of 35 (with an estimated population standard deviation of 5). Using the .05 level, what should the experimenter conclude? (a) Use the steps of hypothesis testing, (b) sketch the distributions involved, and (c) explain your answer to someone who is familiar with the t test for a single sample, but not with the t test for independent means.

17. A study of the effects of color on easing anxiety compared anxiety test scores of participants who completed the test printed on either soft yellow paper or on harsh green paper. The scores for five participants who completed the test printed on the yellow paper were 17, 19, 28, 21, and 18. The scores for four participants who completed the test on the green paper were 20, 26, 17, and 24. Using the .05 level, one-tailed (predicting lower anxiety scores for the yellow paper), what should the researcher conclude? (a) Use the steps of hypothesis testing, (b) sketch the distributions involved, and (c) explain your answers to someone who is familiar with the *t* test for a single sample, but not with the *t* test for independent means.

18. Figure the estimated effect size for problems (a) 15, (b) 16, and (c) 17. (d) Explain your answer to part (a) to a person who understands the *t* test for independent means but is unfamiliar with effect size.

19. What is the approximate power of each of the following planned studies, all using a *t* test for independent means at the .05 significance level, two-tailed, with a predicted medium effect size?

	N_1	N_2
(a)	90	10
(b)	50	50
(c)	6	34
(d)	20	20

20. What are the approximate numbers of participants needed for each of the following planned studies to have 80% power, assuming equal numbers in the two groups and all using the .05 significance level? (Be sure to give the total number of participants needed, not just the number needed for each group.)

	Expected			
	μ_1	μ_2	σ	Tails
(a)	10	15	25	1
(b)	10	30	25	1
(c)	10	30	40	1
(d)	10	15	25	2

21. Escudero et al. (1997) videotaped 30 couples discussing a marital problem in their laboratory. The videotapes were later systematically rated for various aspects of the couple's communication, such as domineeringness and the positive or negative quality of affect (emotion) expressed between them. A major interest of their study was to compare couples who were having relationship problems with those who were not. The 18 couples in the group having problems were recruited from those who had gone to a marital clinic for help; they were called the Clinic group. The group not having problems were recruited through advertisements, and were called the Nonclinic group. (The two groups in fact had dramatically different scores on a standard test of marital satisfaction.) Table 10–10 presents some of their results. (You can ignore the arrows and plus and minus signs, which have to do with how they rated the interactions.

TABLE 10–10 Base-Rate Differences Between Clinic and Nonclinic Couples on Relational Control and Nonverbal Affect Codes Expressed in Proportions (SDs in Parentheses)

	Couple Status		Between-Group Differences
	Clinic Mean	Nonclinic Mean	t
Domineeringness ($\uparrow$)	.452 (107)	.307 (.152)	3.06*
Levelingness ($\rightarrow$)	.305 (.061)	.438 (.065)	5.77**
Submissiveness ($\downarrow$)	.183 (.097)	.226 (.111)	1.12
Double-codes	.050 (.028)	.024 (.017)	2.92*
Positive affect (+)	.127 (.090)	.280 (.173)	3.22*
Negative affect (−)	.509 (.192)	.127 (.133)	5.38**
Neutral affect (0)	.344 (.110*)	.582 (.089)	6.44**
Double-codes (+/−)	.019 (.028)	.008 (.017)	2.96*

Note. Proportions of each control and affect code were converted using arcsine transformation for use in between-group comparisons. *$p < .01$; **$p < .001$; (d.f. = 28).

Data from Escudero, V., Rogers, L. E., & Gutierrez, E. (1997), tab. 3. Patterns of relational control and nonverbal affect in clinic and nonclinic couples. *Journal of Social and Personal Relationships, 14*, 5–29. Copyright © 1997 by Sage Publications, Inc. Reprinted by permission of Sage Publications.

TABLE 10–11 Gender Differences in Internet Use and Potential Mediators

	Males[a]	Females[b]	t-value	df	p-value
E-mail use	4.16 (0.66)	4.30 (0.57)	2.81	626	.005
Web use	3.57 (0.67)	3.30 (0.67)	−4.84	627	.000
Overall internet use	3.86 (0.58)	3.80 (0.53)	−1.44	627	.130
Computer anxiety	1.67 (0.56)	1.80 (0.57)	4.03	612	.000
Computer self-efficacy	3.89 (0.52)	3.71 (0.62)	−3.49	608	.001
Loneliness	2.06 (0.64)	1.96 (0.64)	−1.88	607	.061
Depression	1.22 (0.32)	1.28 (0.34)	2.36	609	.019
E-mail privacy	4.04 (0.78)	4.10 (0.69)	−0.97	609	.516
E-mail trust	3.50 (0.77)	3.46 (0.75)	−0.65	610	.516
Web privacy	4.06 (0.74)	4.09 (0.71)	0.62	623	.534
Web trust	3.14 (0.73)	3.12 (0.73)	−0.28	624	.780
Web search success	4.05 (0.85)	4.13 (0.81)	1.12	568	.262
Importance of computer skills	2.54 (1.03)	2.31 (0.90)	−2.57	477	.011
Computers cause health problems	2.67 (1.00)	3.00 (1.08)	3.36	476	.001
Gender stereotypes about computer skills	3.45 (1.15)	4.33 (0.96)	−8.95	476	.000
Racial/ethnic stereotypes about computer skills	3.63 (1.17)	3.99 (1.07)	3.40	477	.001
Computers are taking over	3.08 (1.19)	2.87 (1.08)	−1.89	476	.059

Note: For the attitude items, 1 = strongly agree, 2 = strongly disagree. For gender, 1 = male. 2 = female. Numbers in parentheses are standard deviations.

[a]$n = 227$.

[b]$n = 403$.

Source: Jackson et al., 2001.

Also, ignore the note at the bottom about "arcsine transformation"—we will explain this in Chapter 15.) (a) Focusing on Domineeringness and Submissiveness, explain these results to a person who has never had a course in statistics. (b) Include a discussion of effect size and power. (When figuring power, you can assume that the two groups in each comparison had about equal sample sizes.)

22. Jackson et al. (2001) gave a questionnaire about internet usage to college students. Table 10–11 (their Table 1) shows their results comparing men and women. (a) Select one significant and one nonsignificant result and explain these two results to a person who understands the *t* test for a single sample but does not know anything about the *t* test for independent means. (b) Include a discussion of effect size and power.

23. Do men or women have longer first names? Take out a phone book and use the random numbers given here to select a page. On the first page (page 12), look for the first clearly female name, and write down how many letters it has. Do the same thing (find the page for the number, etc.) 16 times. Then continue, getting lengths for 16 male names. (You will have to exclude names for which you cannot tell the gender.) Carry out a *t* test for independent means using these two samples. (Be sure to note the city and year of the telephone book you used.)
12, 79, 10, 97, 53, 74, 15, 55, 41, 128, 57, 93, 94, 31, 68, 516, 60, 56, 7, 93, 43, 91, 57, 58, 38, 120, 14, 38, 57, 743, 98, 471, 38, 66, 20, 32, 60, 43, 78, 29, 39, 17, 31, 12, 61, 100, 80, 35, 31, 99, 22

CHAPTER 11

INTRODUCTION TO THE
ANALYSIS OF VARIANCE

Are You Ready?
What You Need to have Mastered Before Starting This Chapter:

- Chapters 1, 2, and 5 through 10.

Cindy Hazan and Philip Shaver (1987) arranged to have the *Rocky Mountain News,* a large Denver area newspaper, print a mail-in survey. The survey included the question shown in Table 11–1 to measure what is called attachment style. Those who selected the first choice are "secure"; those who selected the second, "avoidant"; and those who selected the third, "anxious-ambivalent." These attachment styles are thought to be different ways of behaving and thinking in close relationships that develop from a person's experience with early caretakers (e.g., Mickelson et al., 1997). Readers also answered questions about various aspects of love, including amount of jealousy. Hazan and Shaver then compared the amount of jealousy reported by people with the three different attachment styles.

    With a *t* test, Hazan and Shaver could have compared the mean jealousy scores of any two of the attachment styles. Instead, they were interested in differences among all three attachment styles. The statistical procedure for testing variation

TABLE 11–1	Question Used in Hazan and Shaver (1987) Newspaper Survey

Which of the following best describes your feelings. [Check One]

[ ] I find it relatively easy to get close to others and am comfortable depending on them and having them depend on me. I don't often worry about being abandoned or about someone getting too close to me.

[ ] I am somewhat uncomfortable being close to others; I find it difficult to trust them completely, difficult to allow myself to depend on them. I am nervous when anyone gets too close, and often, love partners want me to be more intimate than I feel comfortable being.

[ ] I find that others are reluctant to get as close as I would like. I often worry that my partner doesn't really love me or won't want to stay with me. I want to merge completely with another person, and this desire sometimes scares people away.

Note: From Hazan & Shaver (1987), p. 515.

analysis of variance
ANOVA

among the means of several groups is called the **analysis of variance,** sometimes abbreviated as **ANOVA.** (You could use the analysis of variance for a study with only two groups, but the *t* test, which gives the same result in that situation, is simpler.)

In this chapter, we introduce the analysis of variance, focusing on the situation in which the different groups being compared each have the same number of scores. We consider in Chapter 12 the more complicated situation, when the number of people in each group is not equal. We complete our introduction to analysis of variance in Chapter 13 by considering situations in which the different groups are arrayed across more than one dimension. For example, in the same analysis we might consider both gender and attachment style, making six groups in all (female secure, male secure, female avoidant, etc.), arrayed across the two dimensions of gender and attachment style. This situation is known as a "factorial analysis of variance." To emphasize the difference from factorial analysis of variance, what you learn in this chapter and the next is often called a *one-way analysis of variance.* (If this is confusing, don't worry. We will go through it slowly and systematically in Chapter 13. We only mention this now so that if you hear these terms, you will not be surprised.)

BASIC LOGIC OF THE ANALYSIS OF VARIANCE

The null hypothesis in an analysis of variance is that the several populations being compared all have the same mean. For example, in the attachment example, the null hypothesis is that the populations of secure, avoidant, and anxious-ambivalent people all have the same degree of jealousy. The research hypothesis would be that the degree of jealousy differs among these three populations.

Hypothesis testing in analysis of variance is about whether the means of the samples differ more than you would expect if the null hypothesis were true. This question about *means* is answered, surprisingly, by analyzing *variances* (hence, the name *analysis of variance*). Among other reasons, you focus on variances because when you want to know how several means differ, you are asking about the variation among those means.

Thus, to understand the logic of analysis of variance, we consider variances. In particular, we begin by discussing two different ways of estimating population variances. As you will see, the analysis of variance is about a comparison of the results of these two different ways of estimating population variances.

ESTIMATING POPULATION VARIANCE FROM VARIATION WITHIN EACH SAMPLE

With the analysis of variance, as with the *t* test, you do not know the true population variances. However, as with the *t* test, you can estimate the variance of each of the populations from the scores in the samples. Also, as with the *t* test, you assume in the analysis of variance that all populations have the *same* variance. Thus, you can average the estimates from each sample into a single pooled estimate, called the **within-groups estimate of the population variance.** It is an average of estimates figured entirely from the scores *within* each of the samples.

within-groups estimate of the population variance

One of the most important things to remember about this within-groups estimate is that it is not affected by whether or not the null hypothesis is true. This estimate comes out the same whether the means of the populations are all the same (the null hypothesis is true) or whether the means of the populations are very different (the null hypothesis is false). This estimate comes out the same because it focuses only on the variation inside of each population. Thus, it doesn't matter how far apart the means of the different populations are.

ESTIMATING THE POPULATION VARIANCE FROM VARIATION BETWEEN THE MEANS OF THE SAMPLES

There is also a second way to estimate the population variance. Each sample's mean is a number in its own right. If there are several samples, there are several such numbers, and these numbers will have some variation among them. The variation among these means gives another way to estimate the variance in the populations that the samples come from. Just how this works is a bit tricky, so follow the next two sections closely.

When the Null Hypothesis Is True. First, consider the situation in which the null hypothesis is true. In this situation, all samples come from populations that have the same mean. Remember, we are always assuming that all populations have the same variance (and also that they are all normal curves). Thus, if the null hypothesis is true, all populations are identical (they have the same mean, variance, and shape).

However, even when the populations are identical, samples from them will each be a little different. How different can the sample means be? That depends on how much variation there is within each population. If a population has very little variation in the scores within it, then the means of samples from that population (or any identical population) will tend to be very similar to each other.

What if several identical populations have a lot of variation in the scores within each? In that situation, if you take one sample from each population, the means of those samples could easily be very different from each other. Being very different, these means will have a great deal of variance among them.

The point is that the more variance within each of several identical populations, the more variance there will be between the means of samples when you take a random sample from each population.

Suppose you were studying samples of six children from each of three large playgrounds (the populations in this example). If each playground had children who were all either 7 or 8 years old, the means of your three samples would all be between 7 and 8. Thus, there would not be much variance among those means. However, if each playground had children ranging from 3 to 12 years old, the means of the three samples would probably vary quite a bit. What this illustrates is that the variation among the means of samples is related directly to the amount of variation within each of the populations from which the samples are taken. The more variation within each population, the more variation between the means of samples taken from those populations.

This principle is illustrated in Figure 11–1. The three identical populations on the left have small variances and the three identical populations on the right have

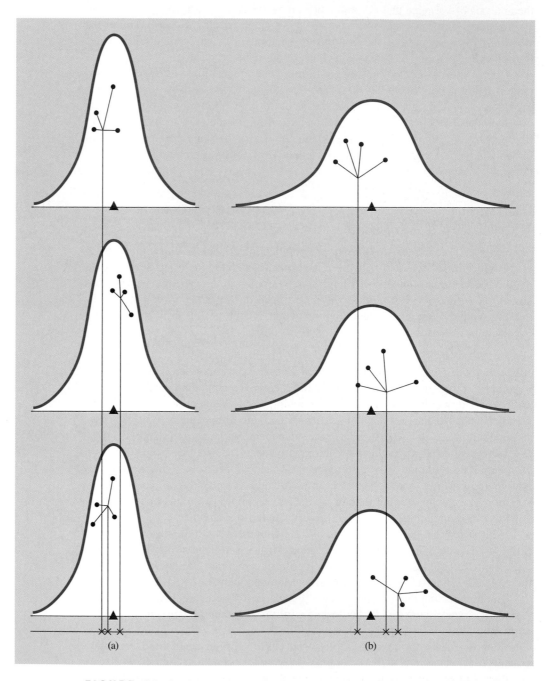

(a)   (b)

FIGURE 11–1 *Means of samples from identical populations will not be identical. (a) Sample means from populations with less variation will vary less. (b) Sample means from populations with more variation will vary more. (Population means are indicated by a triangle, sample means by an X.)*

large variances. In each set of three identical populations, even though the means of the populations are exactly the same, the means of the samples from those populations are not exactly the same. Most important, the means from the populations with less variance are closer together (have less variance among them). The means from the populations with more variance are more spread out (have more variance among them).

We have now seen that the variation among the means of samples taken from identical populations is related directly to the variation of the scores within each of those populations. This has a very important implication: It should be possible to estimate the variance within each population from the variation among the means of our samples.

Such an estimate is called a **between-groups estimate of the population variance.** (It has this name because it is based on the variation between the means of the samples, the "groups." Grammatically, it ought to be *among* groups, but *between* groups is traditional.) We take up how you actually figure this estimate later in the chapter.

between-groups estimate of the population variance

So far, all of this logic we have considered has assumed that the null hypothesis is true, so that there is no variation among the means of the *populations*. Let's now consider what happens when the null hypothesis is not true, and instead the research hypothesis is true.

When the Null Hypothesis Is Not True. If the null hypothesis is not true and the research hypothesis is true, the populations themselves have different means. In this situation, variation among means of samples taken from these populations is still caused by the variation within the populations. However, in this situation in which the research hypothesis is true, variation among the means of the samples *also* is caused by variation between the population means. That is, in this situation the means of the samples are spread out for two different reasons: (a) because of variation within each of the populations and (b) because of variation between the populations. The left side of Figure 11–2 shows populations with the same means and the means of samples taken from them. (This is the same situation as in both sides of Figure 11–1.) The right side of Figure 11–2 shows three populations with different means and the means of samples taken from them. (This is the situation we have just been discussing.) Notice that the means of the samples are more spread out in the situation on the right side of Figure 11–2. This is true even though the variations within the populations are the same for the situation on both sides of Figure 11–2. This additional spread (variance) for the means on the right side of Figure 11–2 is due to the populations having different means.

COMPARING THE WITHIN-GROUPS AND BETWEEN-GROUPS ESTIMATES OF POPULATION VARIANCE

Table 11–2 summarizes what we have seen so far about the within-groups and between-groups estimates of population variance, both when the null hypothesis is true and when the research hypothesis is true. When the null hypothesis is true, both estimates should be about the same. (Only *about* the same—these are estimates). Here is another way of describing this similarity of the between-groups estimate and the within-groups estimate when the null hypothesis is true: In this situation, the ratio of the between-groups estimate to the within-groups estimate should be approximately 1 to 1. For example, if the within-groups estimate is 107.5, the

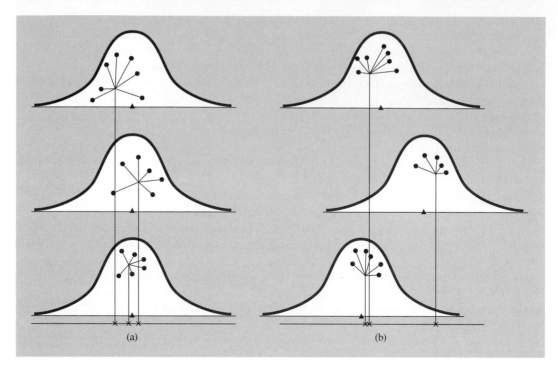

FIGURE 11–2 *Means of samples from populations whose means differ (b) will vary more than sample means taken from populations whose means are the same (a). (Population means are indicated by a triangle, sample means by an X.)*

between-groups estimate should be around 107.5, so that the ratio would be about 1. (A ratio is found by dividing one number by the other.)

The situation is quite different when the null hypothesis is not true. As shown in Table 11–2, when the research hypothesis is true, the between-groups estimate is influenced by two sources of variation: (a) the variation of the scores within each population and (b) the variation of the means of the populations from each other. Yet even when the research hypothesis is true, the within-groups estimate still is influenced only by the variation within the populations. Therefore, when the research hypothesis is true, the between-groups estimate should be larger than the within-group estimate. In this situation the ratio of the between-groups estimate to the within-groups estimate should be greater than 1. For example, the between-group

TABLE 11–2   **Sources of Variation in Within-Group and Between-Group Variance Estimates**

	Variation Within Populations	Variation Between Populations
Null hypothesis is true		
Within-groups estimate reflects	X	
Between-groups estimate reflects	X	
Research hypothesis is true		
Within-groups estimate reflects	X	
Between-groups estimate reflects	X	X

estimate might be 638.9 and the within-group estimate 107.5, making a ratio of 638.9 to 107.5, or 5.94.

This is the central principle of the analysis of variance: *When the null hypothesis is true, the ratio of the between-groups population variance estimate to the within-groups population variance estimate should be about 1. When the research hypothesis is true, this ratio should be greater than 1.* If you figure this ratio and it comes out much bigger than 1, you can reject the null hypothesis. That is, it is unlikely that the null hypothesis could be true and the between-groups estimate be a lot bigger than the within-groups estimate.

THE *F* RATIO

This crucial ratio of the between-groups to the within-groups population variance estimate is called an *F* **ratio.** (The *F* is for Sir Ronald Fisher, an eminent statistician who developed the analysis of variance; see Box 11–1.)

F ratio

THE *F* DISTRIBUTION AND THE *F* TABLE

We have said that if the crucial ratio of between-groups estimate to within-groups estimate (the *F* ratio) is a lot larger than 1, you can reject the null hypothesis. The next question is, just how much bigger than 1?

Statisticians have developed the mathematics of an *F* **distribution** and have prepared tables of *F* ratios. For any given situation, you merely look up in an *F* **table** how extreme an *F* ratio is needed to reject the null hypothesis at, say, the .05 level. (You learn to use the *F* table later in the chapter.)

F distribution
F table

For an example of an *F* ratio, let's return to the attachment style study. The results of that study, for jealousy, were as follows: The between-groups population variance estimate was 23.19, and the within-groups population variance estimate was .53. (You learn shortly how to figure these estimates on your own.) The ratio of the between-groups to the within-groups variance estimates (23.19/.53) came out to 43.91; that is, $F = 43.91$. This *F* ratio is considerably larger than 1. The *F* ratio needed to reject the null hypothesis at the .05 level in this study is only 3.01. Thus, the researchers confidently rejected the null hypothesis and concluded that amount of jealousy is different among the three attachment styles. (Mean jealous ratings were 2.17 for secures, 2.57 for avoidants, and 2.88 for anxious-ambivalents.)

AN ANALOGY

Some students find an analogy helpful in understanding the analysis of variance. The analogy is to what engineers call the signal-to-noise ratio. For example, your ability to make out the words in a staticky cell phone conversation depends on the strength of the signal versus the amount of random noise. With the *F* ratio in the analysis of variance, the difference among the means of the samples is like the signal; it is the information of interest. The variation within the samples is like the noise. When the variation among the samples is sufficiently great in comparison to the variation within the samples, you conclude that there is a significant effect.

HOW ARE YOU DOING?

---

1. When do you use an analysis of variance?
2. (a) What is the within-groups population variance estimate based on? (b) How and (c) why is it affected by the null hypothesis being true or not?

BOX 11-1   Sir Ronald Fisher, Caustic Genius of Statistics

Ronald A. Fisher, a contemporary of William Gosset (see Chapter 9, Box 9–1) and Karl Pearson (see Chapter 14, Box 14–1), was probably the brightest and certainly the most productive of this close-knit group of British statisticians. In the process of writing 300 papers and 7 books, he developed many of the modern field's key concepts: variance, analysis of variance, statistics (in the sense of describing a sample as opposed to parameters of a population), significance levels, the null hypothesis, and almost all of our basic ideas of research design, including the fundamental importance of randomization.

It is one of those family legends that little Ronald, born in 1890 in East Finchley, a northern suburb of London, was so fascinated by math that one day, at age 3, when put into his high chair for breakfast, he asked his nurse, "What is a half of a half?" Told it was a quarter, he asked, "What's half of a quarter?" To that answer he wanted to know what was half of an eighth. At the next answer he purportedly thought a moment and said, "Then I suppose that a half of a sixteenth must be a thirty-toof." Ah, baby stories.

Fisher was a sickly child with severe vision impairment, so he was forbidden to read by artificial light. He was fascinated by astronomy and mathematics by age 6 and soon was attending lectures on astronomy. At school, his math teacher taught him at night, using no paper, pencil, or other visual aids. As a result, Fisher developed a sense of geometrics which helped him solve difficult mathematic problems in novel ways—ways others often could not follow.

As a grown man, Fisher seems to have been difficult to get along with, in part because he sensed from the beginning that Karl Pearson, who had had the field almost to himself, was not going to be helpful. Fisher sent in to Pearson's journal (the most prestigious in statistics) a masterful work, and Pearson held it for a year, not believing the results and so having his students calculate tables using Fisher's equations. Finally Pearson published the resulting tables, with Fisher's important mathematical work as only a footnote!

Others suggest Fisher was always difficult, and ascribe this to a cold and unemotional mother, but whatever the reason, throughout his life the man was embroiled in bitter feuds, even with scholars who had previously been his closest allies and who certainly ought to have been comrades in research. When he was teased, apparently he responded with deadly seriousness; when others were anxious, he joked. William G. Cochran (a well-known statistician in his own right) reported a tale of their crossing a street together at a moment that was obviously unsafe. When Cochran hesitated, Fisher supposedly chided him: "Oh come on, a spot of natural selection won't hurt us." And Cochran sheepishly risked his neck.

Fisher's thin ration of compassion extended to his readers as well—not only was his writing hopelessly obscure, but it often simply failed to supply important assumptions and proofs. Gosset said that when Fisher began a sentence with "Evidently," it meant two hours of hard work before one could hope to see why the point was evident. Another statistician sought to excuse him, however, saying that "Fisher was talking on a plane barely understood by the rest of humanity." It is true that he was invariably admired and respected for his work, if not for his manners.

Indeed, his lack of empathy extended to all of humankind. Like Galton, Fisher was fond of eugenics, favoring anything that might increase the birthrate of the upper and professional classes and skilled artisans. Not only did he see contraception as a poor idea—fearing that the least desirable persons would use it least—but he defended infanticide as serving an evolutionary function. It may be just as well that his opportunities to experiment with breeding never extended beyond the raising of his own children and some crops of potatoes and wheat.

The greatest influence on Fisher was probably his 14 years working at an agricultural experimental station called Rothamsted, in Hertfordshire, 25 miles north of London. At Rothamsted there were shelves of leather-bound books with weekly records of fertilizers used, daily records of rainfall and temperature, and yearly records of harvests, all kept for 90 years. Fisher was hired for one year to do what he could with these (he stayed much longer, bringing in others to help him).

What Fisher did was amazing. He had only a hand-operated calculator called a Millionaire because it could handle numbers up to millions. This wonderful machine required a minute of hard labor to multiply something like 3562 by 57. (For example, you pulled on the handle 7 times to multiply by 7.) In his first important paper, "Studies in Crop Rotation I," it would have required eight months of 12-hour days of physical labor to prepare the tables for this article, not to mention the mental work. Yet in these papers he developed a large percentage of the theories and tools used today in statistics. They are filled with material that still teaches new ideas to those in the field. As David Salsburg puts it, "Seldom in the history of science has a set of titles [the six 'Studies of Crop Rotation'] been such a poor descriptor of the importance of the material they contain" (p. 43).

Fisher, like Gosset at his brewery in Dublin, faced all sorts of practical problems at Rothamsted, such as whether yearly applications of manure improved the yield of a field in the long run or was the cause of mysterious declines in production after many decades. Perhaps it was even this isolation from the personality disputes among London academics and this closeness to real issues that helped Fisher concentrate on developing statistics as a powerful research tool.

Although Fisher eventually became the Galton Professor of Eugenics at University College, his most influential appointment probably came when he was invited to Iowa State College in Ames for the summers of 1931 and 1936 (where he was said to be so put out with the terrible heat that he stored his sheets in the refrigerator all day). At Ames, Fisher greatly impressed George Snedecor, an American professor of mathematics also working on agricultural problems. Consequently, Snedecor wrote a textbook of statistics for agriculture that borrowed heavily from Fisher's work at Rothamsted. The book so popularized Fisher's ideas about statistics and research design that its second edition sold 100,000 copies.

While Fisher was at Ames, he also won over E. F. Lindquist, professor of education at the University of Iowa in Iowa City. Lindquist filled his next textbook with Fisher's ideas, introducing them to the fields of education and psychology, where they have played a major role to this day.

References: Peters (1987); Salsburg (2001); Stigler (1986); Tankard (1984).

3. (a) What is the between-groups population variance estimate based on? (b) How and (c) why is it affected by the null hypothesis being true or not?
4. What are two sources of variation that can contribute to the between-groups population variance estimate?
5. (a) What is the F ratio; (b) why is it usually about 1 when the null hypothesis is true; and (c) why is it usually larger than 1 when the null hypothesis is false?

ANSWERS:

1. Analysis of variance is used when you are comparing means of samples from more than two populations.
2. (a) The variation among the scores within each of the samples. (b) It is not affected. (c) Whether or not the null hypothesis is true has to do with whether or not the means of the populations differ. Thus, the within-groups estimate is not affected by whether or not the null hypothesis is true, because the variation within each population (which is the basis for the variation within each sample) is not affected by whether or not the population means differ.
3. (a) The variation among the means of the samples. (b) It is larger when the null hypothesis is false. (c) Whether or not the null hypothesis is true has to do with whether or not the means of the populations differ. When the null hypothesis is false, the means of the populations differ. Thus, the between-groups estimate is bigger when the null hypothesis is false, because the variation among the means of the populations (which is one basis for the variation among the means of the samples) is greater when the population means differ.
4. Variation among the scores within each of the populations and variation among the means of the populations.
5. (a) The ratio of the between-groups population variance estimate to the within-groups population variance estimate. (b) Because both estimates are based entirely on the same source of variation—the variation among the scores within each of the populations. (c) Because the between-groups estimate is also influenced by the variation among the means of the populations while the within-groups estimate is not. Thus, when the null hypothesis is

false (meaning that the means of the populations differ), the between-groups estimate will be bigger than the within-groups estimate.

CARRYING OUT AN ANALYSIS OF VARIANCE

Having considered the basic logic of the analysis of variance, we will go through an example to illustrate the details. (We use a fictional study to keep the numbers simple.)

Suppose a social psychologist is studying the influence of knowledge of previous criminal record on juries' perceptions of the guilt or innocence of defendants. The researcher recruits 15 volunteers who have been selected for jury duty (but have not yet served at a trial). The researcher shows them a videotape of a 4-hour trial in which a woman is accused of passing bad checks. Before viewing the tape, however, all of the research participants are given a "background sheet" with age, marital status, education, and other such information about the accused woman. The sheet is the same for all 15 participants, with one difference. For five of the participants, the last section of the sheet says that the woman has been convicted several times before of passing bad checks—we will call those participants the Criminal Record group. For five other participants, the last section of the sheet says the woman has a completely clean criminal record—the Clean Record group. For the remaining five participants, the sheet does not mention anything about criminal record one way or the other—the No Information group.

The participants are randomly assigned to the groups. After viewing the tape of the trial, all 15 participants make a rating on a 10-point scale, which runs from completely sure she is innocent (1) to completely sure she is guilty (10). The results of this fictional study are shown in Table 11–3. As you can see, the means of the three groups are different (8, 4, and 5). Yet there is also quite a bit of variation within each of the three groups. Population variance estimates from the score of these three groups are 4.5, 5.0, and 6.5.

You need to figure three numbers to test the hypothesis that the three populations are different: (a) a population variance estimate based on the variation of the

TABLE 11–3   Results of the Criminal Record Study (Fictional Data)

Criminal Record Group			Clean Record Group			No Information Group		
Rating	Deviation from Mean	Squared Deviation from Mean	Rating	Deviation from Mean	Squared Deviation from Mean	Rating	Deviation from Mean	Squared Deviation from Mean
10	2	4	5	1	1	4	−1	1
7	−1	1	1	−3	9	6	1	1
5	−3	9	3	−1	1	9	4	16
10	2	4	7	3	9	3	−2	4
8	0	0	4	0	0	3	−2	4
Σ: 40		18	20		20	25		26

$M = 40/5 = 8.$ $S^2 = 18/4 = 4.5.$ $M = 20/5 = 4.$ $S^2 = 20/4 = 5.0.$ $M = 25/5 = 5.$ $S^2 = 26/4 = 6.5.$

scores within each of the samples, (b) a population variance estimate based on the differences among the group means, and (c) the ratio of the two, the F ratio. (In addition, you need the significance cutoff from an F table.)

ESTIMATING POPULATION VARIANCE FROM THE VARIATION OF SCORES WITHIN EACH GROUP

You can estimate the population variance from any one group (that is, from any one sample) using the usual method of estimating a population variance from a sample. First, you figure the sum of the squared deviation scores. That is, you take the deviation of each score from its group's mean, square that deviation score, and sum all the squared deviation scores. Second, you divide that sum of squared deviation scores by that group's degrees of freedom. (The degrees of freedom for a group are the number of scores in the group minus 1.) For the example, as shown in Table 11–3, this gives an estimated population variance of 4.5 based on the Criminal Record group's scores, an estimate of 5.0 based on the Clean Record group's scores, and an estimate of 6.5 based on the No Information group's scores.

Once again, in the analysis of variance, as with the t test, we assume that the populations have the same variance, that the estimates based on each sample's scores are all estimating the same true population variance. The sample sizes are equal in this example, so the estimate for each group is based on an equal amount of information. Thus, you can pool these variance estimates by straight averaging. This gives an overall estimate of the population variance based on the variation within groups of 5.33 (that is, the sum of 4.5, 5.0, and 6.5, which is 16, divided by 3, the number of groups).

The estimated variance based on the variation of the scores within each of the groups is the within-groups variance estimate. This is symbolized as S^2_{Within} or MS_{Within}. MS_{Within} is short for *mean squares within*. The term *mean squares* is another name for the variance, because the variance is the mean of the squared deviations. (S^2_{Within} or MS_{Within} is also sometimes called the error variance and symbolized as S^2_{Error} or MS_{Error}.)

In terms of a formula,

(11-1)
$$S^2_{\text{Within}} \text{ or } MS_{\text{Within}} = \frac{S^2_1 + S^2_2 + \cdots + S^2_{\text{Last}}}{N_{\text{Groups}}}$$

The within-groups population variance estimate is the sum of the population variance estimates based on each sample, divided by the number of groups.

In this formula, S^2_1 is the estimated population variance based on the scores in the first group (the group from Population 1), S^2_2 is the estimated population variance based on the scores in the second group, and S^2_{Last} is the estimated population variance based on the scores in the last group. (The dots, or ellipses, in the formula show that you are to fill in the population variance estimate for as many other groups as there are in the analysis). N_{Groups} is the number of groups.

Using this formula for our figuring, we get

$$S^2_{\text{Within}} = \frac{S^2_1 + S^2_2 + \cdots + S^2_{\text{Last}}}{N_{\text{Groups}}} = \frac{4.5 + 5.0 + 6.5}{3} = \frac{16}{3} = 5.33$$

ESTIMATING POPULATION VARIANCE FROM THE DIFFERENCES BETWEEN GROUP MEANS

To figure the between-group estimate of the population variance, you first estimate from the means of your samples the variance of a distribution means; then, based on the variance of this distribution of means, you figure the variance of the population of individuals. That is, there are two steps:

❶ Estimate the variance of the distribution of means: Sum the sample means' squared deviations from the grand mean and divide it by the number of means minus 1.

You can think of the means of your samples as taken from a distribution of means. You follow the standard procedure of using the scores in a sample to estimate the variance of the population from which these scores are taken. In this situation, you think of the means of your samples as the scores and the distribution of means as the population from which these scores come. What this all boils down to are the following procedures. You begin by figuring the sum of squared deviations. (You find the mean of your sample means, figure the deviation of each sample mean from this mean of means, square each of these deviations, and then sum these squared deviations.) Then, divide this sum of squared deviations by the degrees of freedom, which is the number of means minus 1. In terms of a formula (when sample sizes are all equal),

> The estimated variance of the distribution of means is the sum of each sample mean's squared deviation from the overall mean, divided by the degrees of freedom for the between-group population variance estimate.

$$S_M^2 = \frac{\Sigma(M - GM)^2}{df_{\text{Between}}} \qquad (11\text{-}2)$$

In this formula, S_M^2 is the estimated variance of the distribution of means (estimated based on the means of the samples in your study). M is the mean of each of your samples. GM is the **grand mean,** the overall mean of all your scores, which is also the mean of your means. df_{Between} is the degrees of freedom in the between-group estimate, the number of groups minus 1. Stated as a formula,

grand mean

> The degrees of freedom for the between-groups population variance estimate is the number of groups minus 1.

$$df_{\text{Between}} = N_{\text{Groups}} - 1 \qquad (11\text{-}3)$$

In the criminal record example, the three means are 8, 4, and 5. The figuring of S_M^2 is shown in Table 11–4.

❷ Figure the estimated variance of the population of individual scores: Multiply the variance of the distribution of means times the number of scores in each group.

What we just figured in step A, from a sample of a few means, is the estimated variance of a distribution of means. From this we want to make an estimation of the variance of the population (the distribution of individuals) on which the distribution of means is based. We saw in Chapter 7 that the variance of a distribution of means is smaller than the variance of the population (the distribution of individuals) that it is based on. This is because means are less likely to be extreme than are individual scores (because several scores that are extreme in the same direction are unlikely to be included in any one sample). Specifically, you learned in Chapter 7 that the vari-

TABLE 11–4	Estimated Variance of the Distribution of Means Based on Means of the Three Experimental Groups in the Criminal Record Study (Fictional Data)

Sample Means	Deviation from Grand Mean	Squared Deviation from Grand Mean
(M)	$(M - GM)$	$(M - GM)^2$
4	-1.67	2.79
8	2.33	5.43
5	$- .67$	.45
Σ: 17	-0.01	8.67

$GM = \Sigma M/N_{\text{Groups}} = 17/3 = 5.67; S_M^2 - \Sigma(M - GM)^2/df_{\text{Between}} - 8.67/2 - 4.34.$

ance of a distribution of means is the variance of the distribution of individual scores divided by the number of scores in each sample.

Now, however, we are going to reverse what we did in Chapter 7. In Chapter 7 you figured the variance of the distribution of means by *dividing* the variance of the distribution of individuals by the sample size. Now you are going to figure the variance of the distribution of individuals by *multiplying* the variance of the distribution of means by the sample size. (See Table 11–5.) That is, to come up with the variance of the population of individuals, you multiply your estimate of the variance of the distribution of means by the sample size. The result of all this is the between-groups variance estimate. Stated as a formula (for when sample sizes are equal),

(11-4)
$$S_{\text{Between}}^2 \text{ or } MS_{\text{Between}} = (S_M^2)(n)$$

> The between-groups population variance estimate (or mean squares between) is the estimated variance of the distribution of means times the number of scores in each group.

In this formula, S_{Between}^2 or MS_{Between} is the estimate of the population variance based on the variation between the means (the between-groups population variance estimate). n is the number of participants in each sample.

Let's return to our example in which there were five participants in each sample and an estimated variance of the distribution of means of 4.34. In this example, multiplying 4.34 by 5 gives a between-groups population variance estimate of 21.7. In terms of the formula,

$$S_{\text{Between}}^2 \text{ or } MS_{\text{Between}} = (S_M^2)(n) = (4.34)(5) = 21.7$$

TABLE 11–5	Comparison of Figuring the Variance of a Distribution of Means from the Variance of a Distribution of Individuals, and the Reverse

* From distribution of individuals to distribution of means: $S_M^2 = S^2/N$

* From distribution of means to distribution of individuals: $S^2 = (S_M^2)(N)$

FIGURING THE F RATIO

The F ratio is the ratio of the between-groups to the within-groups estimate of the population variance. Stated as a formula,

> The F ratio is the between-groups population variance estimate (or mean squares between) divided by the within-groups population variance estimate (or mean squares within).

$$F = \frac{S^2_{\text{Between}}}{S^2_{\text{Within}}} \text{ or } \frac{MS_{\text{Between}}}{MS_{\text{Within}}} \qquad (11\text{-}5)$$

In the example, the ratio of between to within is 21.7 to 5.33. Carrying out the division gives an F ratio of 4.07. In terms of the formula,

$$F = \frac{S^2_{\text{Between}}}{S^2_{\text{Within}}} \text{ or } \frac{MS_{\text{Between}}}{MS_{\text{Within}}} = \frac{21.7}{5.33} = 4.07$$

THE F DISTRIBUTION

You are not quite done. You still need to find the cutoff for the F that is large enough to reject the null hypothesis. This requires a distribution of F ratios that you can use to figure out what is an extreme F ratio.

In practice, you simply look up the needed cutoff on a table. To understand where that number on the table comes from, you need to understand the F distribution. The easiest way to understand this distribution is to think about how you would go about making one.

Start with three identical populations. Next, randomly select five scores from each. Then, on the basis of these three samples (of five scores each), figure the F ratio. (That is, you use these scores to make a between-groups estimate and a within-groups estimate and divide the first by the second.) Let's say that you do this and the F ratio you come up with is 1.36. Now you select three new random samples of five scores each and figure the F ratio using these three samples. Perhaps you get an F of .93. If you do this whole process many, many times, you will eventually get a lot of F ratios. The distribution of all possible F ratios figured in this way (from random samples from identical populations) is called the F distribution. Figure 11–3 shows an example of an F distribution. (There are many different F distributions and each has a slightly different shape. The exact shape depends on how many samples you take each time and how many scores are in each sample. The general shape is like that shown in the figure.)

No one actually goes about making his or her own F distributions in this way. It is a mathematical distribution whose exact characteristics can be found from a formula. Statisticians can also prove that if you had the patience to follow this procedure of taking random samples and figuring the F ratio of each for a very long time, you would get the same result.

As you can see in Figure 11–3, the F distribution is not symmetrical but has a long tail on the right. The reason for the positive skew is that an F distribution is a distribution of ratios of variances. Variances are always positive numbers. (A variance is an average of squared deviations, and anything squared is a positive number.) A ratio of a positive number to a positive number can never be less than 0. Yet there is nothing to stop a ratio from being a very high number. Thus, the F ratio's

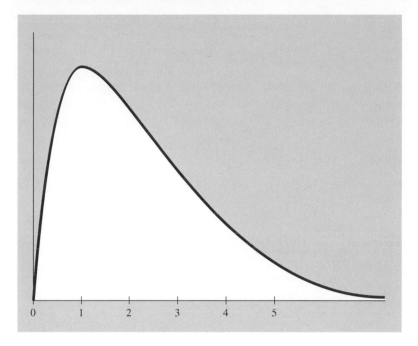

FIGURE 11–3   *An* F *distribution.*

distribution cannot be lower than 0 and can rise quite high.[1] (Most *F* ratios pile up near 1, but they spread out more on the positive side, where they have more room to spread out.)

THE *F* TABLE

The *F* table is a little more complicated than the *t* table. This is because there is a different *F* distribution according to both the degrees of freedom used in the between-groups variance estimate and the degrees of freedom used in the within-groups variance estimate. That is, you have to take into account two different degrees of freedom to look up the needed cutoff. One is the **between-groups degrees of freedom.** It is also called the **numerator degrees of freedom.** This is the degrees of freedom you use in the between-groups variance estimate, which is the numerator of the *F* ratio. The other is the **within-groups degrees of freedom,** also called the **denominator degrees of freedom.** This is the sum of the degrees of freedom from each sample you use when figuring out the within-groups variance estimate, the denominator of the *F* ratio.

The between-groups degrees of freedom is the degrees of freedom used in figuring the between-groups variance estimate. Stated as a formula,

between-groups degrees of
 freedom
numerator degrees of freedom
within-groups degrees
 of freedom
denominator degrees
 of freedom

---

[1]It is possible, by chance, for *F* to be larger or smaller than 1 in any particular situation. Both the between-groups and the within-groups estimates are only estimates and can each vary a fair amount even when the null hypothesis is true. If *F* is considerably larger than 1, you reject the null hypothesis that the populations all have the same mean. But what if *F* is substantially smaller than 1? This rarely happens. When it does, it could mean that there is *less* variation among the groups than would be expected by chance—something is restricting the variation between groups.

The degrees of freedom for the between-groups population variance estimate is the number of groups minus 1.

$$df_{\text{Between}} = N_{\text{Groups}} - 1 \qquad (11\text{-}6)$$

The within-groups degrees of freedom is the sum of the degrees of freedom used in figuring the within-groups population variance estimate. Since all groups are used, it is the sum of the degrees of freedom used in figuring each of the population variance estimates. Stated as a formula,

The degrees of freedom for the within-groups population variance estimate is the sum of the degrees of freedom used in making estimates of the population variance from each sample.

$$df_{\text{Within}} = df_1 + df_2 + \cdots + df_{\text{Last}} \qquad (11\text{-}7)$$

In the criminal record experiment example, the between-groups degrees of freedom is 2. (There are 3 means, minus 1.) In terms of the formula,

$$df_{\text{Between}} = N_{\text{Groups}} - 1 = 3 - 1 = 2.$$

The within-groups degrees of freedom is 12. This is because each of the groups has 4 degrees of freedom on which the estimate is based (5 scores minus 1) and there are 3 groups overall, making a total of 12 degrees of freedom. In terms of the formula,

$$df_{\text{Within}} = df_1 + df_2 + \cdots + df_{\text{Last}} = (5 - 1) + (5 - 1) + (5 - 1) = 4 + 4 + 4 = 12.$$

You would look up the cutoff for an F distribution "with 2 and 12" degrees of freedom. As shown in Table 11–6, for the .05 level, you need an F ratio of 3.89 to reject the null hypothesis. (The full F table is Table A–3 in Appendix A.)

TABLE 11–6   Cutoffs for the F Distribution (Portion)

Denominator Degrees of Freedom	Significance Level	Numerator Degrees of Freedom					
		1	2	3	4	5	6
10	.01	10.05	7.56	6.55	6.00	5.64	5.39
	.05	4.97	4.10	3.71	3.48	3.33	3.22
	.10	3.29	2.93	2.73	2.61	2.52	2.46
11	.01	9.65	7.21	6.22	5.67	5.32	5.07
	.05	4.85	3.98	3.59	3.36	3.20	3.10
	.10	3.23	2.86	2.66	2.54	2.45	2.39
12	.01	9.33	6.93	5.95	5.41	5.07	4.82
	.05	4.75	3.89	3.49	3.26	3.11	3.00
	.10	3.18	2.81	2.61	2.48	2.40	2.33
13	.01	9.07	6.70	5.74	5.21	4.86	4.62
	.05	4.67	3.81	3.41	3.18	3.03	2.92
	.10	3.14	2.76	2.56	2.43	2.35	2.28

Note: Full table is Table A–3 in Appendix A.

For part c of each question, use the following scores involving three samples: The scores in Sample A are 5 and 7 ($M = 6$), the scores in Sample B are 6 and 10 ($M = 8$), and the scores in Sample C are 8 and 9 ($M = 8.5$).

1. (a) Write the formula for the within-groups population variance estimate and (b) define each of the symbols. (c) Figure the within-groups population variance estimate for the above scores.
2. (a) Write the formula for the variance of the distribution of means when using it as part of an analysis of variance and (b) define each of the symbols. (c) Figure the variance of the distribution of means for the above scores.
3. (a) Write the formula for the between-groups population variance estimate based on the variance of the distribution of means and (b) define each of the symbols. (c) Figure the between-groups population variance estimate for the above scores. (d) Explain the logic behind this formula.
4. (a) Write the formula for the F ratio and (b) define each of the symbols. (c) Figure the F ratio for the above scores.
5. (a) Write the formulas for the between-groups and within-groups degrees of freedom and (b) define each of the symbols. (c) Figure the between-group and within-groups degrees of freedom for the above scores.
6. (a) What is the F distribution? (b) Why is it skewed to the right? (c) What is the cutoff F for the above scores for the .05 significance level?

ANSWERS

1. (a) $S^2_{Within} = (S^2_1 + S^2_2 + \cdots + S^2_{Last}) / N_{groups}$.
   (b) S^2_{Within} is the within-groups population variance estimate; S^2_1 is the estimated population variance based on the scores in the first group (the group from Population A); S^2_2 is the estimated population variance based on the scores in the second group, S^2_{Last} is the estimated population variance based on the scores in the last group; the dots show that you are to fill in the population variance estimate for as many other groups as there are in the analysis; N_{Groups} is the number of groups.
   (c) $S^2_1 = ([5 - 6]^2 + [7 - 6]^2)/(2 - 1) = (1 + 1)/1 = 2$;
   $S^2_2 = ([6-8]^2 + [10 - 8]^2)/(2-1) = (4 + 4)/1 = 8$;
   $S^2_3 = ([8 - 8.5]^2 + [9 - 8.5]^2)/(2 - 1) = (.25 + .25)/1 = .5$;
   $S^2_{Within} = (S^2_1 + S^2_2 + \cdots + S^2_{Last}) / N_{Groups} = (2 + 8 + .5) / 3 = 10.5 /3 = 3.5$.
2. (a) $S^2_M = \Sigma(M - GM)^2 / df_{Between}$.
   (b) S^2_M is the estimated variance of the distribution of means (estimated based on the means of the samples in your study). M is the mean of each of your samples. GM is the grand mean, the overall mean of all your scores, which is also the mean of your means. $df_{Between}$ is the degrees of freedom in the between-group estimate, the number of groups minus 1.
   (c) Grand mean is $(6 + 8 + 8.5)/3 = 7.5$.

$$S^2_M = \Sigma(M - GM)^2 / df_{Between} = ([6 - 7.5]^2 + [8 - 7.5]^2 + [8.5 - 7.5]^2) / (3-1)$$
$$= (2.25 + 2.25 + 1)/2 = 5.5/2 = 2.25.$$

3. (a) $S^2_{Between} = (S^2_M)(n)$.
   (b) $S^2_{Between}$ is the between-groups population variance estimate; S^2_M is the estimated variance of the distribution of means (estimated based on the means of the samples in your study); n is the number of participants in each sample.
   (c) $S^2_{Between} = (S^2_M)(n) = (2.25)(2) = 4.5$.
   (d) The goal is to have a variance of a distribution of individuals based on the variation among the means of the groups. S^2_M is the estimate of the variance of a distribution of means from the overall population based on the means of the samples. To go from the variance of a distribution of means to the variance of a distribution of individuals, you multiply by the size of each sample. This is because the variance of the distribution of means is always smaller than the distribution of individuals (because means of samples are less likely

to be extreme than are individual scores); the exact relation is that the variance of distribution of distribution of means is the variance of the distribution of individuals divided by the sample size; thus you reverse that process here.

4. (a) $F = S^2_{Between}/S^2_{Within}$
   (b) F is the F ratio; $S^2_{Between}$ is the between-groups population variance estimate; S^2_{Within} is the within-groups population variance estimate.
   (c) $F = S^2_{Between}/S^2_{Within} = 4.5/3.5 = 1.28$.

5. (a) $df_{Between} = N_{Groups} - 1$ and $df_{Within} = df_1 + df_2 + \cdots + df_{Last}$.
   (b) $df_{Between}$ is the between-groups degrees of freedom; N_{Groups} is the number of groups; df_{Within} is the within-groups degrees of freedom; df_1 is the degrees of freedom for the population variance estimate based on the scores in the first sample; df_2 is the degrees of freedom for the population variance estimate based on the scores in the second sample; df_{Last} is the degrees of freedom for the population variance estimate based on the scores in the last sample; the dots show that you are to fill in the population degrees of freedom for as many other samples as there are in the analysis.
   (c) $df_{Between} = N_{Groups} - 1 = 3 - 1 = 2$; $df_{Within} = df_1 + df_2 + \cdots + df_{Last} = 1 + 1 + 1 = 3$.

6. (a) The distribution of F ratios you would expect by chance. (b) F ratios, because they are a ratio of variances (which as averages of squared numbers have to be positive), are ratios of two positive numbers, which always have to be positive. Thus, they can't be less than 0. But there is no limit to how high an F ratio can be. Thus, the scores bunch up at the left (near 0) and spread out to the right. (c) 9.55.

HYPOTHESIS TESTING WITH THE ANALYSIS OF VARIANCE

Let's look at hypothesis testing in the criminal record experiment. The distributions involved are shown in Figure 11–4. Here are the steps of hypothesis testing.

❶ **Restate the question as a research hypothesis and a null hypothesis about the populations.** There are three populations:

Population 1: Jurors told that the defendant has a criminal record
Population 2: Jurors told that the defendant has a clean record
Population 3: Jurors given no information about the defendant's record

The null hypothesis is that these three populations have the same mean ($\mu_1 = \mu_2 = \mu_3$). The research hypothesis is that the populations' means differ.

❷ **Determine the characteristics of the comparison distribution.** The comparison distribution is an F distribution with 2 and 12 degrees of freedom.

❸ **Determine the cutoff sample score on the comparison distribution at which the null hypothesis should be rejected.** Using the F table for the .05 significance level, the needed F ratio is 3.89.

❹ **Determine your sample's score on the comparison distribution.** In the analysis of variance, the comparison distribution is an F distribution, and the sample's score on that distribution is thus its F ratio. In the example, the F ratio was 4.07.

❺ **Decide whether to reject the null hypothesis.** In the example, the F ratio of 4.07 is more extreme than the .05 significance level cutoff of 3.89. Thus, the researcher would reject the null hypothesis that the three groups come from populations with the same mean. This suggests that they come from populations with different means: that people exposed to different kinds of information (or no information) about the criminal record of a defendant in a situation of this kind will differ in their ratings of the defendant's guilt.

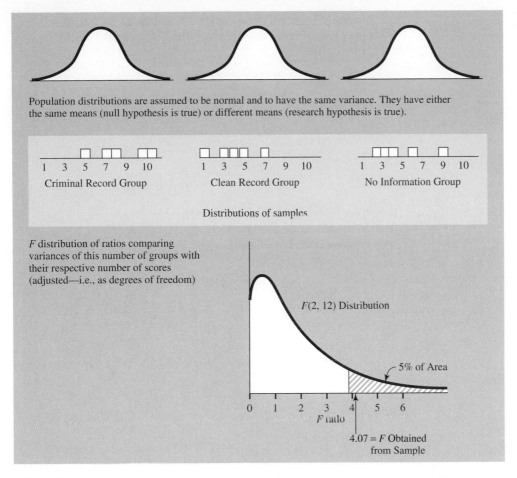

FIGURE 11-4 *The distributions involved in the criminal record study example (fictional data).*

You may be interested to know that several real studies have looked at whether knowing a defendant's prior criminal record affects the likelihood of conviction. The overall conclusion seems to be reasonably consistent with that of the fictional study described here. For a review of such studies, see Dane and Wrightsman (1982).

ANOTHER EXAMPLE

Mikulincer (1998) conducted a series of studies in Israel using the same attachment style classification measure we discussed earlier in the chapter (see Table 11–1). One of his studies included 30 college students (10 of each attachment style), all of whom were in serious romantic relationships. As part of the study, each evening the students wrote down whether during that day their partner had done something to violate their trust. Participants noted such events as the partner being very late for a promised meeting or "forgetting" to tell the participant about some important plan. The results, along with the analysis of variance figuring, are shown in Table 11–7. The distributions involved are shown in Figure 11–5. The steps of the hypothesis-testing procedure follow.

❶ **Restate the question as a research hypothesis and a null hypothesis about the populations.** There are three populations.

| TABLE 11-7 | Number of Trust Violation Events by Romantic Partners Over 3 Weeks Reported by Individuals of Three Attachment Styles |

	Attachment Style		
	Secure	Avoidant	Anxious-Ambivalent
n	10	10	10
M	2.10	3.70	4.20
S	1.66	1.89	1.93
S^2	2.76	3.57	3.72

F distribution:

$df_{\text{Between}} = N_{\text{Groups}} - 1 = 3 - 1 = 2$

$df_{\text{Within}} = df_1 + df_2 + \cdots + df_{\text{Last}} = (10-1) + (10-1) + (10-1) = 9 + 9 + 9 = 27$

F needed for significance at .05 level from F table, $df = 2, 27$: 3.36

Between-groups population variance estimate:

Table for finding S^2 for the three means

	M	Deviation	Squared Deviation
Secure	2.10	-1.23	1.51
Avoidant	3.70	.37	.14
Anxious-Ambivalent	4.20	.87	.76
	Σ: 10.00	$\Sigma (M - GM)^2$	2.41
	GM: 3.33		

$S_M^2 = \Sigma (M - GM)^2 / df_{\text{Between}} = 2.41/2 = 1.205$

S_{Between}^2 or $MS_{\text{Between}} = (S_M^2)(n) = (1.205)(10) = 12.05$

Within-groups population variance estimate:

$$S_{\text{Within}}^2 \text{ or } MS_{\text{Within}} = \frac{S_1^2 + S_2^2 + \ldots + S_{\text{Last}}^2}{N_{\text{groups}}} = \frac{2.76 + 3.57 + 3.72}{3} = \frac{10.05}{3} = 3.35$$

F ratio: $F = S_{\text{Between}}^2 / S_{\text{Within}}^2$ or $MS_{\text{Between}} / MS_{\text{Within}} = 12.05/3.35 = 3.60$

Note: Data from Mikulincer (1998).

Population 1: Students with a secure attachment style
Population 2: Students with an avoidant attachment style
Population 3: Students with an anxious-ambivalent attachment style

The null hypothesis is that these three populations have the same mean ($\mu_1 = \mu_2 = \mu_3$). The research hypothesis is that their means differ.

❷ **Determine the characteristics of the comparison distribution.** The comparison distribution will be an F distribution. Its degrees of freedom are figured as follows: The between-groups variance estimate is based on three groups, making 2 degrees of freedom. The within-groups estimate is based on 9 degrees of freedom (10 participants) in each of the three groups, making a total of 27 degrees of freedom.

❸ **Determine the cutoff sample score on the comparison distribution at which the null hypothesis should be rejected.** Using Table A–3 in Appendix A, look down the column for 2 degrees of freedom in the numerator and stop at the row for our denominator degrees of freedom of 27. We will use the .05 significance level. This gives a cutoff F of 3.36.

❹ **Determine your sample's score on the comparison distribution.** This step requires determining the sample's F ratio. You find the numerator, the between-groups variance estimate, in two steps.

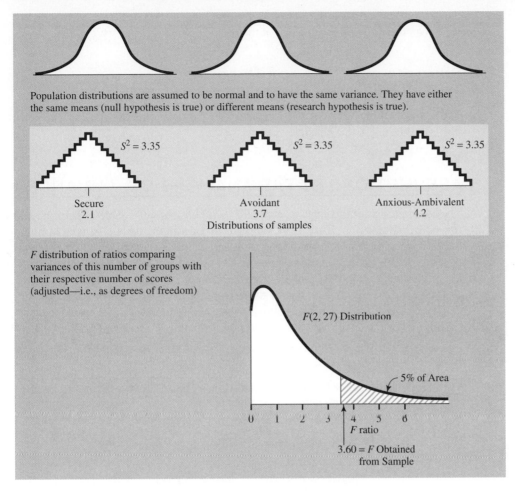

FIGURE 11–5 *The distributions involved in the trust violation example (data from Mikulincer, 1998).*

❹ **Estimate the variance of the distribution of means:** Sum the sample means' squared deviations from the grand mean and divided by the number of means minus 1. From Table 11–7, this comes out to 1.205.

❺ **Figure the estimated variance of the population of individual scores:** Multiply the variance of the distribution of means by the number of scores in each group. From Table 11–7, this comes out to 12.05.

The denominator of the F ratio, the within-groups variance estimate, is the average of the population variance estimates figured from each sample. (Be careful not to use estimates of the population standard deviation.) In this study, the average of 2.76, 3.57, and 3.72 comes out to 3.35. This is the denominator of the F ratio, the estimate of the population variance based on the variation within groups.

The F ratio is the between-groups estimate divided by the within-groups estimate, which comes out to 3.60 (that is, $12.05/3.35 = 3.60$).

❺ **Decide whether to reject the null hypothesis.** The F ratio of 3.60 is more extreme than the .05 significance level cutoff of 3.36. Therefore, Mikulincer rejected the null hypothesis. He was able to conclude that students having the three attachment styles differ in the number of trust violations by their romantic partners they reported over a 3-week period. This conclusion was consistent with Mikulincer's hypotheses based on attachment theory.

SUMMARY OF STEPS FOR HYPOTHESIS TESTING WITH THE ANALYSIS OF VARIANCE

Table 11–8 summarizes the steps of an analysis of variance of the kind we have been considering in this chapter.

ASSUMPTIONS IN THE ANALYSIS OF VARIANCE

The assumptions for the analysis of variance are basically the same as for the t test for independent means. That is, the cutoff F ratio from the table is strictly accurate only when the populations follow a normal curve and have equal variances. As with the t test, in practice the cutoffs are reasonably accurate even when your populations are moderately far from normal and have moderately different variances. As a general rule, if the variance estimate of the group with the largest estimate is no more than four or five times that of the smallest and the sample sizes are equal, the conclusions using the F distribution should be adequately accurate. In Chapter 15 we

---

TABLE 11–8 Steps for the Analysis of Variance (When Sample Sizes Are Equal)

❶ **Restate the question as a research hypothesis and a null hypothesis about the populations.**

❷ **Determine the characteristics of the comparison distribution.**
  a. The comparison distribution is an F distribution.
  b. The numerator degrees of freedom is the number of groups minus 1: $df_{Between} = N_{Groups} - 1$.
  c. The denominator degrees of freedom is the sum of the degrees of freedom in each group (the number in the group minus 1): $df_{Within} = df_1 + df_2 + \cdots + df_{Last}$

❸ **Determine the cutoff sample score on the comparison distribution at which the null hypothesis should be rejected.**
  a. Decide the significance level.
  b. Look up the appropriate cutoff in an F table, using the degrees of freedom from Step 2.

❹ **Determine your sample's score on the comparison distribution.** This will be an F ratio.
  a. Figure the between-groups population variance estimate ($S^2_{Between}$ or $MS_{Between}$).
    i. Figure the means of each group.
    ❶ **Estimate the variance of the distribution of means:** $S^2_M = \Sigma(M - GM)^2/df_{Between}$
    ❷ **Figure the estimated variance of the population of individual scores:** $S^2_{Between}$ or $MS_{Between} = (S^2_M)(n)$.
  b. Figure the within-groups population variance estimate (S^2_{Within} or MS_{Within}).
    i. Figure population variance estimates based on each group's scores: For each group, $S^2 = \Sigma(X - M)^2/(n - 1) = SS/df$.
    ii. Average these variance estimates: S^2_{Within} or $MS_{Within} = (S^2_1 + S^2_2 + \cdots + S^2_{Last})/N_{Groups}$
  c. Figure the F ratio: $F = S^2_{Between}/S^2_{Within}$ or $F = MS_{Between}/MS_{Within}$

❺ **Decide whether to reject the null hypothesis:** Compare the scores from Steps 3 and 4.

consider what to do when you have reason to think that your populations are a long way from meeting these assumptions.

1. A study compares the effects of three experimental treatments, A, B, and C, by giving each treatment to 16 participants and then assessing their performance on a standard measure. The results on the standard measure are, Treatment A group: $M = 20$, $S^2 = 8$; Treatment B group: $M = 22$, $S^2 = 9$; Treatment C group: $M = 18$, $S^2 = 7$. Using the .01 significance level, do the three experimental treatments create any difference among the populations these groups represent? (a) Use the steps of hypothesis testing and (b) sketch the distributions involved.
2. Give the two main assumptions for the analysis of variance.
3. Why do we need the equal variance assumption?
4. What is the general rule about when violations of the equal variance assumption is likely to lead to serious inaccuracies in results?

ANSWERS:

1. (a) Steps of hypothesis testing:

❶ **Restate the question as a research hypothesis and a null hypothesis about the populations.** There are three populations.

Population 1: People given experimental treatment A
Population 2: People given experimental treatment B
Population 3: People given experimental treatment C

The null hypothesis is that these three populations have the same mean ($\mu_1 = \mu_2 = \mu_3$). The research hypothesis is that their means differ.

❷ **Determine the characteristics of the comparison distribution.** The comparison distribution will be an F distribution. Its degrees of freedom are figured as follows: The between-groups variance estimate is based on three groups, making 2 degrees of freedom. The within-groups estimate is based on 15 degrees of freedom (16 participants) in each of the three groups, for a total of 45 degrees of freedom.

❸ **Determine the cutoff sample score on the comparison distribution at which the null hypothesis should be rejected.** Using Table A–3 in Appendix A, the cutoff for $df = 2, 45$ at the .01 level is 5.11.

❹ **Determine your sample's score on the comparison distribution.** For the between-groups variance estimate,

Ⓐ **Estimate the variance of the distribution of means**: Sum the sample means' squared deviations from the grand mean and divide by the number of means minus 1:

$$S^2_M = [(20 - 20)^2 + (22 - 20)^2 + (18 - 20)^2]/(3 - 1) = (0 + 4 + 4)/2 = 4.$$

Ⓑ **Figure the estimated variance of the population of individual scores:** Multiply the variance of the distribution of means by the number of scores in each group.

$$S^2_{Between} = (4)(16) = 64.$$

For the within-groups variance estimate, average the population variance estimates figured from each sample. $S^2_{Within} = (8 + 9 + 7)/3 = 9$.

The F ratio is the between-groups estimate divided by the within-groups estimate:
$F = 64/9 = 7.11$

❺ **Decide whether to reject the null hypothesis.** The F of 7.11 is more extreme than the .01 cutoff of 5.11. Therefore, reject the null hypothesis. The research hypothesis is supported; the different experimental treatments do produce different effects on the standard performance measure.

(b) The distributions involved are shown in Figure 11–6.
2. The populations are assumed to be normally distributed with equal variances.

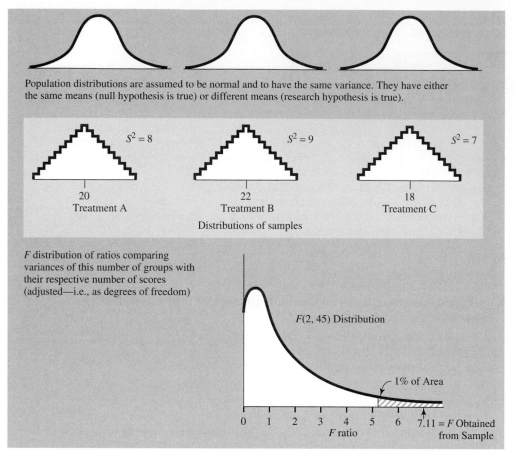

FIGURE 11–6   *The distributions involved in "How Are You Doing?" question 1.*

3. We need the equal variance assumption in order to be able to justify averaging the estimates from each sample into an overall within-groups population variance estimate.
4. The analysis can lead to inaccurate results when the variance estimate from the group with the largest estimate is more than four or five times the smallest variance estimate.

PLANNED COMPARISONS

When you reject the null hypothesis in an analysis of variance, this implies that the population means are not all the same. What is not clear, however, is which population means differ from which. For example, in the criminal record study, the Criminal Record group jurors had the highest ratings for the defendant's guilt ($M = 8$); the No Information group jurors, the second highest ($M = 5$); and the Clean Record group jurors, the lowest ($M = 4$). From the analysis of variance results, we concluded that the true means of the three populations these groups represent are not all the same. (That is, the overall analysis of variance was significant.) However, we do not know which particular populations' means are significantly different from each other.

In practice, in most research situations involving more than two groups, our real interest is not in an overall, or *omnibus*, difference among the several groups, but rather in more specific comparisons. For example, in the criminal record study, the researchers' prediction in advance would probably have been that the Criminal Record group would rate the defendant's guilt higher than the No Information group and that the Clean Record group would rate the defendant's guilt lowest. If, in fact, the researchers had made these predictions, these predictions would be examples of what are called **planned comparisons**.

planned comparisons

Researchers use planned comparisons to look at some particular, focused differences between groups that directly follow from some theory or are related directly to some practical application. Planned comparisons are also sometimes called *a priori comparisons,* because they have been planned in advance of the study. They may also be called *planned contrasts,* because they contrast (compare) specific groups. Finally, a general name you may see for most contrasts you would figure is *linear contrasts.*

FIGURING PLANNED COMPARISONS

The procedure to compare the means of a particular pair of groups is a direct extension of what you already know: You figure a between-groups population variance estimate, a within-groups population variance estimate, and an F.

The within-groups population variance estimate will be the same as for the overall analysis of variance. This is because regardless of the particular groups you are comparing, you are still assuming that all groups are from populations with the same variance—thus, your best estimate of that variance is the one that makes use of the information from all the groups, the average of the population variance estimates from each of the samples.

The between-groups population variance estimate, however, in a planned comparison is different from the between-groups estimate in the overall analysis. It is different because in a planned comparison you are interested in the variation only between a particular pair of means. Specifically, in a planned comparison between two group means, you figure the between-groups population variance estimate with the usual two-step procedure, but using just the two means of interest.[2]

Once you have the two variance estimates for the planned comparison, you figure the F in the usual way, and compare it to a cutoff from the F table based on the df that go into the two estimates, which are the same as the overall analysis for df_{Within} and are usually exactly 1 for $df_{Between}$ (because the between estimate is based on two means, and $2 - 1 = 1$).

AN EXAMPLE

Consider the planned comparison of the Criminal Record group ($M = 8$) to the No Information group ($M = 5$).

---

[2]Why not just use a t test to compare the two groups? If you used an ordinary t test, your pooled estimate of the population variance would be based on only these two groups. Thus, you would be ignoring the information about the population variance provided by the scores in the other groups. One way to deal with this would be to do the ordinary t test in the usual way at every step, except wherever you would ordinarily use the pooled estimate, you would instead use the within-groups population variance estimate from the overall analysis of variance. Also, you would determine your significance cutoff using the df for the overall within-groups estimate. Actually, this modified t test procedure for a planned comparison and the one we describe using the F test are mathematically equivalent and give exactly the same ultimate result in terms of whether or not your result is significant. (See Chapter 16 for a more general discussion of the relation of the t test to the analysis of variance.) We emphasize the F test approach here because it is more straightforward in terms of the rest of the material in this chapter.

The within-groups population variance estimate for a planned comparison is always the same as the within-groups estimate from the overall analysis: In the criminal record example S^2_{Within} was 5.33.

For the between-groups population variance estimate, you follow the usual two-step procedure, but using only the two means you plan to compare.

❶ **Estimate the variance of the distribution of means**: Sum the sample means' squared deviations from the grand mean and divide by the number of means minus 1. The grand mean for these two means would be 6.5 (that is, $[8 + 5]/2 = 6.5$) and df_{Between} when there are two means being compared is $2 - 1 = 1$. Thus,

$$S^2_M = \Sigma(M - GM)^2/df_{\text{Between}} = [(8 - 6.5)^2 + (5 - 6.5)^2]/1 = (1.5^2 + 1.5^2)/1$$
$$= 2.25 + 2.25 = 4.5.$$

❷ **Figure the estimated variance of the population of individual scores:** Multiply the variance of the distribution of means by the number of scores in each group. There are five in each group in this study. Thus,

$$S^2_{\text{Between}} = (S^2_M)(n) = (4.5)(5) = 22.5.$$

Thus, for this planned comparison, $F = S^2_{\text{Between}}/S^2_{\text{Within}} = 22.5/5.33 = 4.22$. The .05 cutoff for $df = 1, 12$ is 4.75. Thus, the planned comparison is not significant. You can conclude that the three means differ overall (from the original analysis of variance, which was significant), but you cannot conclude specifically that the Criminal Record condition makes a person rate guilt differently from being in the No Information condition.

A SECOND EXAMPLE

What about the other planned contrast of the Clean Record group to the No Information group? The difference in means here is even smaller (5 versus 4). Thus, if there was no difference in the first planned contrast, there can't be any here. Still, we can figure the comparison just to illustrate the process.

For the between-group population variance estimate,

❶ **Estimate the variance of the distribution of means**: Sum the sample means' squared deviations from the grand mean and divide by the number of means minus 1. The grand mean for these two means is $(5 + 4)/2 = 4.5$ and $df_{\text{Between}} = 2 - 1 = 1$. Thus,

$$S^2_M = [(5 - 4.5)^2 + (4 - 4.5)^2]/1 = .5^2 + .5^2 = .25 + .25 = .5.$$

❷ **Figure the estimated variance of the population of individual scores:** Multiply the variance of the distribution of means by the number of scores in each group:

$$S^2_{\text{Between}} = (S^2_M)(n) = (.5)(5) = 2.5.$$

The within-groups estimate, again, is the same as we figured for the overall analysis—5.33.

Thus, $F = S^2_{\text{Between}}/S^2_{\text{Within}} = 2.5/5.33 = .47$. An F less than 1 is never significant, and in any case, is clearly less than 4.75, the .05 cutoff for $df = 1, 12$.

SIMPLE AND COMPLEX COMPARISONS

simple comparisons
complex comparisons

Comparisons between two groups are called **simple comparisons**. Researchers sometimes also make **complex comparisons** in which they compare, for example, the average of two groups to a third. For example, in the attachment and trust study, you might want to compare the secure group to the average of the avoidant and anxious-ambivalent groups. Or, in a four-group analysis, you might compare the average of two of the groups to the average of the other two groups. Sometimes you even might set up a special kind of contrast in which you check to see whether the means follows a particular, more complex pattern, such as mean 1 being higher than mean 2, mean 3 higher than mean 2, and mean 4 higher than mean 3. Most statistical analysis software make any kind of complex contrast fairly easy to carry out. However, to keep manageable the amount you have to learn in this introductory book, we focus here only on the simple (and most common) comparisons of one mean versus another.[3]

THE BONFERRONI CORRECTION

There is a problem when you carry out several planned comparisons. Normally, when you set the .05 significance level, this means you have selected a cutoff so extreme that you have only a .05 chance of getting a significant result if the null hypothesis is true. However, with multiple comparisons, if you use the .05 cutoff, you can actually have much *more* than a .05 chance of getting a significant result if the null hypothesis is true!

The reason is this: If you are making several comparisons, each at the .05 level, the chance of any one of them coming out significant is more than .05. (It is like flipping coins. If you flip any one coin, it has only a 50% chance of coming up heads. But if you flip five coins, there is a lot better than 50% chance at least one of them will come up heads.) In fact, if you make two comparisons, each at the .05 significance level, there is about a .10 chance that at least one will come out significant just by chance (that is, if the null hypothesis is true). If you make three planned comparisons at the .05 level, there is about a .15 chance.

A widely used approach to dealing with this problem with planned comparisons is the **Bonferroni procedure** (also called *Dunn's test*). The idea of the Bonferroni procedure is that you use a more stringent significance level for each comparison. The result is that the overall chance of any one of the comparisons being mistakenly significant is still reasonably low. For example, if each of two planned comparisons used the .025 significance level, the overall chance of any one of them being mistakenly significant would still be less than .05. (That is, .05/2 = .025.) With three planned comparisons, you could use the .017 level (.05/3 = .017).

The general principle is that the Bonferroni corrected cutoff you use is the true significance level you want divided by the number of planned comparisons. Thus, if you want to test your hypothesis at the .01 level and you will make three planned comparisons, you would test each planned comparison using the .0033 significance level. That is, .01/3 = .0033.

If you are doing your analyses on a computer, it gives exact significance probabilities as part of the output—that is, it might give a *p* of .037 or .0054, not just whether you are beyond the .05 or .01 level. However, if you are using tables, nor-

Bonferroni correction

---

[3]You can do complex contrasts using the procedure of this chapter: When figuring the between-group estimate, instead of using the two group means, you would instead use the two averages you want to compare—such as the average of two groups and the mean of the other group. In this situation, however, you need to make a correction for the fact that it is harder to get by chance an extreme average of two means than a single mean. The corrections are these. When comparing the average of two groups to a third group, multiply the $S^2_{Between}$ you figure for this comparison by 1.33. When comparing the average of three groups to a fourth group, multiply your $S^2_{Between}$ for the comparison by 1.5. When comparing the average of two groups to the average of two other groups, multiply it by 2.

mally only the .01 or .05 cutoffs are available. Thus, for simplicity, when the Bonferroni corrected cutoff might be .017 or even .025, researchers, to be safe, may use the .01 significance level. Also, if there are only two planned comparisons (or even three), it is common for researchers not to correct at all.

HOW ARE YOU DOING?

1. (a) What is a planned comparison? (b) Why do researchers make them? (c) What is the difference between a simple and a complex comparison?
2. How is the procedure for figuring a planned comparison between two particular groups different from the overall analysis of variance?
3. A study has three groups of 25 participants each in the overall analysis of variance, and S^2_{Within} is 100. The researcher makes a single planned comparison between a group that has a mean of 10 and another group that has a mean of 16. Is it significant? (Use the .05 significance level.)
4. (a) Why do researchers making planned comparisons need to make the Bonferroni correction? (b) What is the principle of the Bonferroni correction?
5. If a researcher is making four planned comparisons using the .05 significance level, what would be the Bonferroni corrected significance level?

ANSWERS:

1. (a) A planned comparison is a focused comparison of two groups within an overall analysis of variance that the researcher planned in advance of the study based on theory or some practical issue.
   (b) Researchers make them because they are more likely to be of theoretical or practical interest than the overall difference among means.
   (c) A simple planned comparison compares the means of two groups; a complex comparison considers some combination of more than two groups, such as a comparison of the average of two groups compared to the third.
2. It is the same except that you make the between-groups estimate using only the means of the two groups being compared.
3. For the between-groups population variance estimate for the planned comparison,

   ❶ **Estimate the variance of the distribution of means:** $GM = (10 + 16)/2 = 13$; $df_{Between} = 2 - 1 = 1$.

   $$S^2_M = [(10 - 13)^2 + (16 - 13)^2]/1 = 18.$$

   ❷ **Figure the estimated variance of the population of individual scores:**

   $$S^2_{Between} = (18)(25) = 450.$$

   The within-groups estimate is the same as the overall within-group estimate, 100.
   $F = 450/100 = 4.5$.
   The cutoff for $df = 1,72$ (actually 1, 70, since 1, 72 is not in the table) is 3.98.
   You can reject the null hypothesis. The planned comparison is significant.
4. (a) Because with more than one comparison, the chance of any one coming out significant is greater than the direct significance level used.
   (b) You divide your overall desired true significance level by the number of comparisons. This way, the chance of any one of them coming out significant is taken into account.
5. Bonferroni corrected significance level is .05/4 = .0125.

CONTROVERSY: OMNIBUS TESTS VERSUS PLANNED COMPARISONS

The analysis of variance is commonly used in situations comparing three or more groups. (If you are comparing two groups, you can use a *t* test). However, following the logic we introduced earlier, Rosnow and Rosenthal (1989) argue that such diffuse or omnibus tests are not very useful. They say that in almost all cases, when we test the overall difference among three or more groups, "we have tested a question in which we almost surely are not interested" (p. 1281). In which questions *are* we interested? We are interested in specific comparisons, such as between two particular groups.

Rosnow and Rosenthal (see also Rosenthal et al., 1999) advocate that when figuring an analysis of variance, you should analyze *only* planned comparisons. These should replace entirely the overall F test (that is, the diffuse or omnibus F test) for whether you can reject the hypothesis of no difference among population means. Traditionally, planned comparisons, when used at all, are a supplement to the overall F test. So this is a rather revolutionary idea.

Consider an example. Orbach et al. (1997) compared a group of suicidal mental hospital patients (individuals who had made serious suicide attempts), nonsuicidal mental hospital patients with similar diagnoses, and a control group of volunteers from the community. The purpose of the study was to test the theory that suicidal individuals have higher tolerance for physical pain. The idea is that their higher pain threshold makes it easier for them to do the painful acts involved in suicide. The researchers carried out standard pain threshold and other sensory tests and administered a variety of questionnaires to all three groups. Here is how they describe their analysis:

> To examine the study hypothesis, we performed a set of two linear contrasts for each pain measure. . . . The first linear contrast, *suicidality contrast,* compared the suicidal group with the two nonsuicidal groups (psychiatric inpatients and control participants). The second contrast compared the two nonsuicidal groups. . . . We did not make a previous omnibus F because we conducted preplanned group comparisons testing the study hypothesis. Because of multiple comparisons needed, the critical alpha was set at .01, to avoid Type I error. . . .
>
> The suicidality contrast was significant for thermal sensation threshold, $F(1, 95) = 21.64, p < .01$; pain threshold, $F(1, 95) = 23.65, p < .01$; pain tolerance $F(1, 95) = 6.55, p < .01$; and maximum tolerance $F(1, 95) = 16.05$. No significant difference was found between the suicidal and nonsuicidal groups in the magnitude estimate measure. An examination of the means . . . supports our main hypothesis: Suicidal participants, as expected, had high sensation and pain thresholds, high pain tolerance, and were more likely to tolerate the maximum temperature administered than inpatients and control participants. Interestingly, the second set of contrasts revealed no significant differences between the psychiatric inpatients and control participants in any of the five pain measures. (p. 648)

The Orbach et al. study exemplifies Rosnow and Rosenthal's advice to use planned comparisons instead of an overall analysis of variance. But this approach has not yet been widely adopted and is still controversial, the main concern being much like the issue we considered in Chapter 7 regarding one-tailed and two-tailed tests. If we adopt the highly targeted, planned comparisons recommended by Rosnow and Rosenthal, critics argue, we lose out on finding unexpected differences not initially planned, and we put too much control of what is found in the hands of the researcher (versus nature).

ANALYSES OF VARIANCE
IN RESEARCH ARTICLES

Analyses of variance (of the kind we have considered in this chapter) are usually described in a research article by giving the F, the degrees of freedom, and the significance level. For example, $F(3, 67) = 5.81, p < .01$. The means for the groups usually are given in a table, although if there are only a few groups and only one or a few measures, the means may be given in the regular text of the article. Usually, there is also some report of follow-up analyses, such as planned comparisons.

Returning again to the criminal-record experiment example, we could describe the analysis of variance results this way: "The means for the Criminal Record, Clean Record, and No Information groups were 7.0, 4.0, and 5.0, respectively, $F(2, 12) = 4.07$, $p < .05$. We also carried out two planned comparisons, neither of which were significant at the .05 level: The Criminal Record versus the No Information condition, $F(1, 12) = 4.22$, $p < .10$; the Clean Record versus the No Information condition, $F(1, 12) = .47$, ns. The first comparison approached significance, but after a Bonferroni correction (for two planned contrasts), it would not even reach the .10 level."

Note that it is also common for researchers to report planned comparisons using t tests—these are not ordinary t tests for independent means, but are special t tests for the comparisons that are mathematically equivalent to the method we described—that is, the results in terms of significance are identical (see footnote 2).

SUMMARY

1. The analysis of variance (ANOVA) is used to test hypotheses based on differences among means of several samples. The procedure compares two estimates of population variance. One, the within-groups estimate, is the average of the variance estimates from each of the samples. The other, the between-groups estimate, is based on the variation among the means of the samples.

2. The F ratio is the between-groups estimate divided by the within-groups estimate. The null hypothesis is that all the samples come from populations with the same mean. If the null hypothesis is true, the F ratio should be about 1. This is because the two population variance estimates are based on the same thing, the variation within each of the populations. If the research hypothesis is true, so that the samples come from populations with different means, the F ratio should be larger than 1. This is because the between-groups estimate is now influenced by the variation both within the populations and between them. But the within-groups estimate is still affected only by the variation within each of the populations.

3. When the samples are of equal size, the within-groups population variance estimate is the ordinary average of the estimates of the population variance figured from each sample. The between-groups population variance estimate is done in two steps. First, you estimate the variance of the distribution of means based on the means of your samples. (This is figured with the usual formula for estimating population variance from sample scores.) Second, you multiply this estimate by the number of participants in each group. This step takes you from the variance of the distribution of means to the variance of the distribution of individual scores.

4. The distribution of F ratios when the null hypothesis is true is a mathematically defined distribution that is skewed to the right. Significance cutoffs are given on an F table according to the degrees of freedom for each population variance estimate, the between-groups (numerator) estimate being based on the number of groups minus 1, and the within-groups (denominator) estimate being based on the sum of the degrees of freedom within all samples.

5. The assumptions for the analysis of variance are the same as for the t test. The populations must be normally distributed, with equal variances. Like the t test, the analysis of variance is robust to moderate violations of these assumptions.

6. The overall results of an analysis of variance are often followed up by planned comparisons, based on theory or a specific practical need, that examine differences such as those between specific pairs of means. These comparisons are figured using the usual analysis of variance method, but with the between-groups estimate based on the variation among the two means being compared.

7. When making more than one planned comparisons, researchers often protect against the possibility of getting some comparisons significant just by chance by making a Bonferroni correction of the significance level (dividing the overall desired significance level by the number of comparisons).

8. Some experts recommend that instead of using an analysis of variance to make diffuse, overall comparisons among several means, researchers should plan in advance to conduct only specific planned comparisons, targeted directly to their theoretical or practical questions.

9. Analysis of variance results are reported in a standard fashion, such as $F(3, 67) = 5.81$, $p < .01$. Results of planned comparisons are also commonly reported (sometimes using special t tests instead of analysis of variance).

KEY TERMS

analysis of variance (ANOVA) (p. 378)
between-groups degrees of freedom ($df_{Between}$) (p. 391)
between-groups estimate of the population variance ($S^2_{Between}$ or $MS_{Between}$) (p. 381)
Bonferroni correction (p. 403)

complex comparison (p. 402)
denominator degrees of freedom (df_{Within}) (p. 391)
F distribution (p. 383)
F ratio (p. 383)
F table (p. 383)
grand mean (GM) (p. 388)
numerator degrees of freedom ($df_{Between}$) (p. 391)

planned comparison (p. 401)
simple comparison (p. 402)
within-groups degrees of freedom (df_{Within}) (p. 391)
within-groups estimate of the population variance (S^2_{Within} or MS_{Within}) (p. 379)

EXAMPLE WORKED-OUT COMPUTATIONAL PROBLEMS

OVERALL ANALYSIS OF VARIANCE

An experiment compares the effects of four treatments, giving each treatment to 20 participants and then assessing their performance on a standard measure. The results on the standard measure are Treatment 1: $M = 15$, $S^2 = 20$; Treatment 2: $M = 12$, $S^2 = 25$; Treatment 3: $M = 18$, $S^2 = 14$; Treatment 4: $M = 15$, $S^2 = 27$. Using the .05 significance level, does treatment matter? Use the five steps of hypothesis testing and sketch the distributions involved.

❶ **Restate the question as a research hypothesis and a null hypothesis about the populations.** There are four populations.

Population 1: People given experimental treatment 1
Population 2: People given experimental treatment 2
Population 3: People given experimental treatment 3
Population 4: People given experimental treatment 4

The null hypothesis is that these four populations have the same mean ($\mu_1 = \mu_2 = \mu_3 = \mu_4$). The research hypothesis is that their means differ.

❷ **Determine the characteristics of the comparison distribution.** The comparison distribution will be an F distribution. $df_{Between} = N_{Groups} - 1 = 4 - 1 = 3$; $df_{Within} = df_1 + df_2 + \cdots + df_{Last} = 19 + 19 + 19 + 19 = 76$.

❸ **Determine the cutoff sample score on the comparison distribution at which the null hypothesis should be rejected.** Using Table A–3 in Appendix A for $df = 3, 75$ (the closest below 3, 76) at the .05 level, the cutoff is 2.73.

❹ **Determine your sample's score on the comparison distribution.** For the between-groups variance estimate,

   ❹ **Estimate the variance of the distribution of means**: Sum the sample means' squared deviations from the grand mean and divide by the number of means minus 1.

$$GM = (15 + 12 + 18 + 15)/4 = 15.$$
$$S_M^2 = \Sigma(M - GM)^2/df_{Between} = ([15 - 15]^2 + [12 - 15]^2 + [18 - 15]^2 + [15 - 15]^2)/(4 - 1)$$
$$= (0 + 9 + 9 + 0)/3 = 18/3 = 6.$$

   ❸ **Figure the estimated variance of the population of individual scores:** Multiply the variance of the distribution of means by the number of scores in each group.

$$S_{Between}^2 = (S_M^2)(n) = (6)(20) = 120.$$

For the within-groups variance estimate,

$$S_{Within}^2 = (S_1^2 + S_2^2 + \cdots + S_{Last}^2)/N_{Groups} = (20 + 25 + 14 + 27)/4 = 86/4 = 21.5$$
$$F = S_{Between}^2/S_{Within}^2 = 120/21.5 = 5.58$$

❺ **Decide whether to reject the null hypothesis.** The F of 5.58 is more extreme than the .05 cutoff of 2.73. Therefore, reject the null hypothesis. The research hypothesis is supported; the different experimental treatments do produce different effects on the standard performance measure.

The distributions involved are shown in Figure 11–7.

PLANNED COMPARISONS

For the above study, figure a planned contrast comparing Treatment 2 to Treatment 3 using the .01 significance level.

For the between-group population variance estimate,

   ❹ **Estimate the variance of the distribution of means:** Sum the sample means' squared deviations from the grand mean and divide by the number of means minus 1. The grand mean for these two means is $(12 + 18)/2 = 15$ and $df_{Between} = N_{Groups} - 1 = 2 - 1 = 1$.

$$S_M^2 = \Sigma(M - GM)^2/df_{Between} = [(12 - 15)^2 + (18 - 15)^2]/1 = (3^2 + 3^2)/1$$
$$= (9 + 9)/1 = 18.$$

   ❸ **Figure the estimated variance of the population of individual scores:** Multiply the variance of the distribution of means by the number of scores in each group.

$$S_{Between}^2 = (S_M^2)(n) = (18)(20) = 360;$$

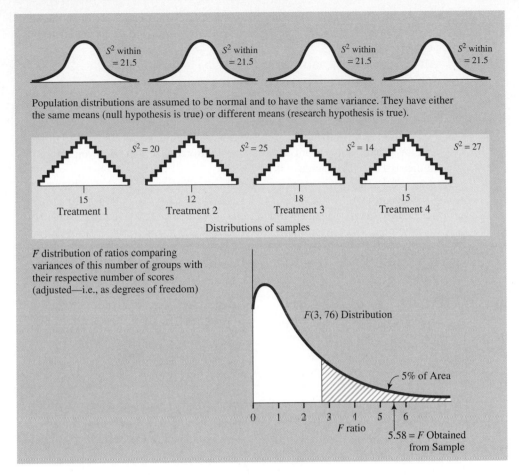

FIGURE 11–7 *The distributions involved in "Worked-Out Computational Problem" for overall analysis of variance.*

$$S^2_{\text{Within}} \text{ (from the overall analysis)} = 21.5;$$
$$F = S^2_{\text{Between}} / S^2_{\text{Within}} = 360/21.5 = 16.74.$$

The cutoff for .05, $df = 1$, 75 (the closest on the table below the true df of 1, 76) = 6.99.

Reject the null hypothesis; the comparison is significant.

BONFERRONI CORRECTION

What is the Bonferroni corrected significance level for each of six planned contrasts at the overall .05 significance level?

Bonferroni corrected significance = .05/6 = .0083.

PRACTICE PROBLEMS

These problems involve figuring. Most real-life statistics problems are done on a computer. However, even if you have a computer and statistics software, do these by hand (with the help of a calculator) to ingrain the method in your mind. Also, in all problems involving figuring, be sure to show your work.

For practice in using a computer to solve statistics problems, refer to the computer section of each chapter of the *Student's Study Guide and Computer Workbook* that accompanies this text.

All data are fictional unless an actual citation is given.

Answers to Set I problems are given at the back of the book.

SET I

1. For each of the following studies, decide if you can reject the null hypothesis that the groups come from identical populations. Use the .05 level. (Note that studies (b) and (c) provide S, not S^2.)

(a)	Group 1	Group 2	Group 3		
n	10	10	10		
M	7.4	6.8	6.8		
S^2	.82	.90	.80		
(b)	Group 1	Group 2	Group 3	Group 4	
n	25	25	25	25	
M	94	101	124	105	
S	24	28	31	25	
(c)	Group 1	Group 2	Group 3	Group 4	Group 5
n	25	25	25	25	25
M	94	101	124	105	106
S	24	28	31	25	27

2. For each of the following studies, decide whether you can reject the null hypothesis that the groups come from identical populations. Use the .01 level.

(a)	Group 1	Group 2	Group 3
	8	6	4
	8	6	4
	7	5	3
	9	7	5
(b)	Group 1	Group 2	Group 3
	12	10	8
	04	02	0
	12	10	8
	04	02	0

3. A psychologist at a private mental hospital was asked to determine whether there was any clear difference in the length of stay of patients with different categories of diagnosis. Looking at the last four patients in each of the three major categories, the results (in terms of weeks of stay) were as follows:

	Diagnosis Category	
Affective Disorders	Cognitive Disorders	Drug-related Conditions
7	12	8
6	8	10
5	9	12
6	11	10

Using the .05 level, is there a significant difference in length of stay among diagnosis categories? (a) Use the steps of hypothesis testing; (b) sketch the distributions involved; and (c) explain your answer to someone who understands everything involved in conducting a t test for independent means, but is unfamiliar with the analysis of variance.

4. A study compared the felt intensity of unrequited love among three groups: 50 individuals who were currently experiencing unrequited love, who had a mean experienced intensity $= 3.5$, $S^2 = 5.2$; 50 who had previously experienced unrequited love and described their experiences retrospectively, $M = 3.2$, $S^2 = 5.8$; and 50 who had never experienced unrequited love but described how they thought they would feel if they were to experience it, $M = 3.8$, $S^2 = 4.8$. Determine the significance of the difference among groups, using the 5% level. (a) Use the steps of hypothesis testing; (b) sketch the distributions involved; and (c) explain your answer to someone who has never had a course in statistics.

5. A researcher studying genetic influences on learning compares the maze performance of four genetically different strains of rats, using eight rats per strain. Performance for the three strains were as follows:

Strain	Mean	S
J	41	3.5
M	38	4.6
Q	14	3.8
W	37	4.9

Using the .01 significance level, is there an overall difference in maze performance among the four strains? (a) Use the steps of hypothesis testing; (b) sketch the distributions involved; and (c) explain your answer to someone who is familiar with hypothesis testing with known populations, but is unfamiliar with the t test or the analysis of variance.

6. Based on the study described in problem 3, figure planned comparisons for (a) affective disorders versus drug-related conditions and (b) cognitive disorders versus drug-related conditions. Test the significance of these comparisons using the .05 level (without a Bonferroni correction). (c) Explain your work to a person who understands analysis of variance but is unfamiliar with planned comparisons.

7. (a) Based on the study described in problem 4, figure a planned comparison for those who had previously experienced unrequited love and described their experiences retrospectively versus those who had never experienced unrequited love but described how they thought they would feel if they were to experience it. Test the significance of this comparison using the .05 level. (b) Explain your work to a person who understands analysis of variance but is unfamiliar with planned comparisons.

8. Based on the study described in problem 5, figure planned comparisons for (a) strain J versus strain M, (b) strain J versus strain Q, (c) strain J versus strain W, (d) strain Q versus strain M, and (e) strain Q versus strain W. Test the significance of each of these contrasts using an overall .05 level (that is, each contrast should be tested at a Bonferroni corrected level based on an overall level of .05). (f) Explain your work to a person who understands analysis of variance but is unfamiliar with planned comparisons and the Bonferroni correction.

9. What is the Bonferroni corrected significance level for each of the following situations?

Situation	(a)	(b)	(c)	(d)
Overall Significance Level	.05	.05	.01	.01
Number of Planned Comparisons	2	4	3	5

10. Grilo et al. (1997) are clinical psychologists interested in the relation of depression and substance use to personality disorders. Personality disorders are persistent, problematic traits and behaviors that exceed the usual range of individual differences. The researchers conducted interviews assessing personality disorders with adolescents who were psychiatric inpatients and had one of three diagnoses: those with major depression, those with substance abuse, and those with both major depression and substance abuse. The mean number of disorders was as follows: major depression $M = 1.0$, substance abuse $M = .7$, those with both conditions $M = 1.9$. The researchers reported, "The three study groups differed in the average number of diagnosed personality disorders, $F(2,112) = 10.18$, $p < .0001$." Explain this result to someone who is familiar with hypothesis testing with known populations, but is unfamiliar with the t test or the analysis of variance.

11. A researcher wants to know if the need for mental health care among prisoners varies according to the different types of prison facilities. The researcher randomly selects 40 prisoners from each of the three main types of prisons in a particular Canadian province and conducts exams to determine their need for mental health care. In the article describing the results, the researcher reported the means for each group and then added: "The need for mental health care among prisoners in the three types of prison systems appeared to be clearly different, $F(2, 117) = 5.62$, $p < .01$. A planned comparison of System 1 to System 2 was significant, $F(1, 117) = 4.03$, $p < .05$." Explain this result to a person who has never had a course in statistics.

12. Which type of English words are longer—nouns, verbs, or adjectives? Go to your dictionary, turn to random pages (using the random numbers listed below), and go down the column until you come to a noun. Note its length (in number of letters). Do this for 10 different nouns. Do the same for 10 verbs and then for 10 adjectives. Using the .05 significance level, (a) carry out an analysis of variance comparing the three types of words, and (b) figure a planned contrast of nouns versus verbs. (Be sure also to give the full bibliographic information on your dictionary—authors, title, year published, publisher, city.)

651, 73, 950, 320, 564, 666, 736, 768, 661, 484, 990, 379, 323, 219, 715, 472, 176, 811, 167, 612, 102, 452, 849, 615, 228, 352, 851, 981, 821, 834, 719, 525, 907, 448, 4, 335, 671, 118, 403.

SET II

13. For each of the following studies, decide if you can reject the null hypothesis that the groups come from identical populations. Use the .05 level.

(a)	Group 1	Group 2	Group 3
n	5	5	5
M	10	12	14
S^2	4	6	5
(b)	Group 1	Group 2	Group 3
n	10	10	10
M	10	12	14
S^2	4	6	5
(c)	Group 1	Group 2	Group 3
n	5	5	5
M	10	14	18
S^2	4	6	5
(d)	Group 1	Group 2	Group 3
n	5	5	5
M	10	12	14
S^2	2	3	2.5

14. For each of the following studies, decide whether you can reject the null hypothesis that the groups come from identical populations. Use the .01 level.

(a)	Group 1	Group 2	Group 3
	1	1	8
	2	2	7
	1	1	8
	2	2	7
(b)	Group 1	Group 2	Group 3
	1	4	8
	2	5	7
	1	4	8
	2	5	7

15. An organizational psychologist was interested in whether individuals working in different sectors of a company differed in their attitudes toward the company. The results for the three people surveyed in engineering were 10, 12, and 11; for the three in the marketing department, 6, 6, and 8; for the three in accounting, 7, 4, and 4; and for the three in production, 14, 16, and 13 (higher numbers mean more positive attitudes). Was there a significant difference in attitude toward the company among employees working in different sectors of the company at the .05 level? (a) Use the steps of hypothesis testing; (b) sketch the distributions involved; and (c) explain your answer to someone who understands everything involved in conducting a t test for independent means, but is unfamiliar with the analysis of variance.

16. Do students at various colleges differ in how sociable they are? Twenty-five students were randomly selected from each of three colleges in a particular region and were asked to report on the amount of time they spent socializing each day with other students. The results for College X was a mean of 5 and an estimated population variance of 2; for College Y, $M = 4$, $S^2 = 1.5$; and for College Z, $M = 6$, $S^2 = 2.5$. What should you conclude? Use the .05 level. (a) Use the steps of hypothesis testing, (b) sketch the distributions involved; and (c) explain your answer to someone who has never had a course in statistics.

17. A psychologist studying artistic preference randomly assigns a group of 45 participants to one of three conditions in which they view a series of unfamiliar abstract paintings. The 15 participants in the Famous condition are led to believe that these are each famous paintings; their mean rating for liking the paintings is 6.5 ($S = 3.5$). The 15 in the Critically Acclaimed condition are led to believe that these are paintings that are not famous but are very highly thought of by a group of professional art critics; their mean rating is 8.5 ($S = 4.2$). The 15 in the Control condition are given no special information about the paintings; their mean rating is 3.1 ($S = 2.9$). Does what people are told about paintings make a difference in how well they are liked? Use the .05 level. (a) Use the steps of hypothesis testing; (b) sketch the distributions involved; and (c) explain your answer to someone who is familiar with the t test for independent means, but is unfamiliar with analysis of variance.

18. Based on the study described in problem 15, figure planned comparisons for (a) engineering versus production, (b) marketing versus production, (c) accounting versus production, (d) engineering versus marketing, and (e) engineering versus accounting. Test the significance of each of these comparisons using the overall .05 level (with a Bonferroni correction for testing each comparison). (f) Explain your work to a person who understands analysis of variance, but is unfamiliar with planned comparisons or Bonferroni corrections.

19. Based on the study described in problem 16, (a) figure a planned comparison for College X versus College Y, using the .05 significance level and (b) explain your work to a person who understands analysis of variance, but is unfamiliar with planned comparisons.

20. Based on the study described in problem 17, figure planned comparisons for (a) Famous versus Control and (b) Critically Acclaimed versus Control. Use the .05 significance level (without any Bonferroni correction). (c) Explain your work to a person who understands analysis of variance, but is unfamiliar with planned comparisons.

21. What is the Bonferroni corrected significance level for each of the following situations?

Situation	(a)	(b)	(c)	(d)
Overall Significance Level	.01	.01	.05	.05
Number of Planned Comparisons	4	2	4	3

22. An experiment is conducted in which 60 participants each fill out a personality test, but not according to the way the participants see themselves. Instead, 15 are randomly assigned to fill it out according to the way they think their mothers see them (that is, the way they think their mothers would fill it out to describe the participants); 15 as their fathers would fill it out for them; 15 as their best friends would fill it out for them; and 15 as the professors they know best would fill it out for them. The main results appear in Table 11–9. Explain these results to a person who has never had a course in statistics.

23. Rosalie Friend (2001), an educational psychologist, compared three methods of teaching writing. Students were randomly assigned to three different experimental conditions involving different methods of writing a summary. At the

TABLE 11–9	Means for Main Personality Scales for Each Experimental Condition (Fictional Data)				
Scale	Mother	Father	Friend	Professor	$F(3, 56)$
Conformity	24	21	12	16	4.21**
Extroversion	14	13	15	13	2.05
Maturity	15	15	22	19	3.11*
Self-confidence	38	42	27	32	3.58*

*$p < .05$. **$p < .01$.

end of the two days of instructions, participants wrote a summary. One of the ways it was scored was the percentage of specific details of information it included from the original material. Here is a selection from her article describing one of the findings:

> The effect of summarization method on inclusion of important information was significant: $F(2, 144) = 4.1032$, $p < .019$. The mean scores (with standard deviations in parentheses) were as follows: Argument Repetition, 59.6% (17.9); Generalization, 59.8% (15.2); and Self-Reflection, 50.2% (18.0). (p. 14.)

Explain these results to a person who has never had a course in statistics. Also, using the information in the above description.

24. Cut up 100 little pieces of paper of about the same size and write a "1" on 16, "2" on 34, "3" on 34, and "4" on 16 of them. (You are making an approximately normal distribution). Put the slips into a bowl or hat, mix them up, draw out two, write down the numbers on them, and put them back. Then draw out another two, write down their numbers, and put them back; and finally draw another two, write down their numbers, and put them back. (Strictly speaking, you should sample "with replacement." That means putting each one, not two, back after writing its number down. But we want to save you a little time, and it should not make very much difference in this case.) Figure an analysis of variance for these three randomly selected groups of two each. Write down the F ratio, and repeat the entire drawing process and analysis of variance again. Do this entire process at least 20 times, and make a frequency polygon of your results. You are creating an F distribution for 2 (3 groups $-$ 1) and 3 (2 $-$ 1 in each of three groups) degrees of freedom. At what point do the top 5% of your F scores begin? Compare that to the 5% cutoff given on the F table in Appendix A for 2 and 3 degrees of freedom.

CHAPTER 12

THE STRUCTURAL
MODEL IN THE ANALYSIS
OF VARIANCE

structural model

Are You Ready?
What You Need to have Mastered Before Starting This Chapter:

- Chapters 1, 2, and 5 through 11.

Chapter 11 introduced the basic logic of the analysis of variance. Building on this understanding, in this chapter we explore an alternative but mathematically equivalent way of understanding the analysis of variance. This alternative is called the **structural model.** The core logic you learned in Chapter 11 still applies. However, the structural model provides a different and more flexible way of figuring the two population variance estimates. This new method makes it easier to handle the situation in which the number of individuals in each group is not equal, a major situation we consider in this chapter. Further, understanding the structural model provides deeper insights into the underlying logic of the analysis of variance, including helping you understand the way analysis of variance results are laid out in computer printouts. Finally, you need to understand the structural model approach to do factorial analysis of variance (the subject of the second half of Chapter 13).

PRINCIPLES OF THE STRUCTURAL MODEL

DIVIDING UP THE DEVIATIONS

The structural model is all about deviations. To start with, there is the deviation of a score from the grand mean. The grand mean is the mean of *all* the scores, regardless of the group they are in. In the criminal record example in Chapter 11 (see Tables 11–3 and 11–4) , the grand mean of the 15 scores was 85/15 = 5.67. In the attachment style and trust study examples from that chapter (see Table 11–7), the grand mean of the 30 trust violation scores was 3.33.

The deviation from the grand mean is just the beginning. You then think of this deviation from the grand mean as having two parts: (a) the deviation of the score from the mean of its group and (b) the deviation of the mean of its group from the grand mean. Consider a participant in the criminal-record study who rated the defendant's guilt as a 10. The grand mean of all participants' guilt ratings was 5.67. This person's score has a total deviation of 4.33 (that is, $10 - 5.67 = 4.33$). The mean of the Criminal Record group by itself was 8. Thus, the deviation of this person's score from his or her group's mean is 2 (that is, $10 - 8 = 2$), and the deviation of that group's mean from the grand mean is 2.33 (that is, $8 - 5.67 = 2.33$). Note that these two deviations (2 and 2.33) add up to the total deviation of 4.33. This is illustrated in Figure 12–1. We encourage you to study this figure until you grasp it well.

SUMMING THE SQUARED DEVIATIONS

The next step in the structural model is to square each of these deviation scores and add up the squared deviations of each type for all the participants. This gives a
sum of squared deviations

sum of squared deviations for each type of deviation score. It turns out that the sum of squared deviations of each score from the grand mean is equal to (a) the sum of the squared deviations of each score from its group's mean plus (b) the sum of the squared deviations of each score's group's mean from the grand mean. This principle can be stated as a formula:

The sum of squared deviations of each score from the grand mean is the sum of squared deviations of each score from its group's mean plus the sum of squared deviations of each score's group's mean from the grand mean.

$$\Sigma(X - GM)^2 = \Sigma(X - M)^2 + \Sigma(M - GM)^2$$
$$\text{or } SS_{\text{Total}} = SS_{\text{Within}} + SS_{\text{Between}}$$

(12-1)

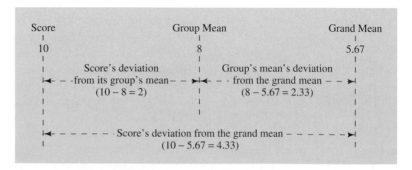

FIGURE 12–1   *Example from the fictional criminal-record study of the deviation of one individual's score from the grand mean being that individual's score's deviation from his or her group's mean plus that individual's group's mean's deviation from the grand mean.*

In this formula, $\Sigma(X - GM)^2$ or SS_{Total} is the sum of squared deviations of each SS_{Total}
score from the grand mean, completely ignoring the group a score is in. $\Sigma(X - M)^2$
or SS_{Within} is the sum of squared deviations of each score from its group's mean, SS_{Within}
added up for all participants. $\Sigma(M - GM)^2$ or $SS_{Between}$ is the sum of squared devia- $SS_{Between}$
tions of each score's group's mean from the grand mean—again, added up for all
participants.

This rule applies only to the *sums* of the squared deviations. For each individual score, the deviations themselves but not the squared deviations, always add up.

FROM THE SUMS OF SQUARED DEVIATIONS TO THE POPULATION VARIANCE ESTIMATES

Now we are ready to use these sums of squared deviations to figure the needed population variance estimates for an analysis of variance. To do this, you divide each sum of squared deviations by an appropriate degrees of freedom. The between-groups population variance estimate ($S^2_{Between}$ or $MS_{Between}$) is the sum of squared deviations of each score's group's mean from the grand mean ($SS_{Between}$) divided by the degrees of freedom on which it is based ($df_{Between}$, the number of groups minus 1). Stated as a formula,

(12-2)
$$S^2_{Between} = \frac{\Sigma(M - GM)^2}{df_{Between}} \text{ or } MS_{Between} = \frac{SS_{Between}}{df_{Between}}$$

> The between-groups population variance estimate is the sum of squared deviations of each scores's group's mean from the grand mean divided by the degrees of freedom for the between-groups population variance estimate.

The within-groups population variance estimate (S^2_{Within} or MS_{Within}) is the sum of squared deviations of each score from its group's mean (SS_{Within}) divided by the total degrees of freedom on which this is based (df_{Within}; the sum of the degrees of freedom over all the groups—the number of scores in the first group minus 1, plus the number in the second group minus 1, etc.). Stated as a formula,

(12-3)
$$S^2_{Within} = \frac{\Sigma(X - M)^2}{df_{Within}} \text{ or } MS_{Within} = \frac{SS_{Within}}{df_{Within}}$$

> The within-groups population variance estimate is the sum of squared deviations of each score from its group's mean divided by the degrees of freedom for the within-groups population variance estimate.

Notice that we have ignored the sum of squared deviations of each score from the grand mean (SS_{Total}). This sum of squares is useful mainly for checking our arithmetic. Recall that $SS_{Total} = SS_{Within} + SS_{Between}$.

Figure 12–2 again shows the division of the deviation score into two parts, but this time emphasizes which deviations are associated with which population variance estimates.

RELATION OF THE STRUCTURAL MODEL APPROACH TO THE CHAPTER 11 METHOD

The methods we have just described for figuring the within-groups and between-groups population variance estimates using the structural model approach give exactly the same result as the methods you learned in Chapter 11. (If you enjoy algebra, you might see if you can derive the earlier formulas from the ones you have just learned.) However, the procedures you follow to figure those estimates are

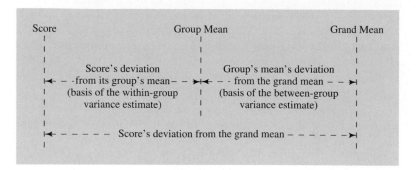

FIGURE 12-2   *The score's deviations from its group's mean is the basis for the within-group population variance estimate; the group's mean's deviation from the grand mean is the basis for the between-group population variance estimate.*

quite different. In this chapter's structural model approach, when figuring the within-groups variance estimate method, you never actually figure the variance estimate for each group and average them. Similarly, for the between-groups estimate, with the structural model approach, you never multiply anything by the number of scores in each sample. The point is that with either method, you get the same within-groups and between-groups variance estimates. Thus, either way, the ingredients for the F ratio are the same. And either way, the result comes out the same.[1]

The deeper logic of the analysis of variance with the structural model is also essentially the same as what you learned in Chapter 11, with a twist. What is the same is that if the null hypothesis is true, the two population variance estimates should be about equal; if the null hypothesis is false, the between-groups estimate should be greater (because differences among population means contribute to it) than the within-groups estimate. The twist is one of emphasis. The approach you learned in Chapter 11 emphasizes entire groups, comparing a variance based on differences among group means to a variance based on averaging variances of the groups. The structural model approach emphasizes individual scores. It compares a variance based on deviations of individual scores' groups' means from the grand mean to a variance based on deviations of individual scores from their group's mean. The Chapter 11 method focuses directly on what contributes to the overall population variance estimates; the structural model approach focuses directly on what contributes to the divisions of the deviations of scores from the grand mean.

These logical differences are fairly subtle, and in the end they boil down to the same thing. So if the computations and logic are both about the same, why have we

[1]Here is why they are the same: For the between-groups population variance estimate, the Chapter 11 method involves the squared deviation of each group's mean from the grand mean and then multiplying by the number in each group. In the structural model method, you figure for each score its group's mean's squared deviation from the grand mean. Since you are doing this as many times as there are scores within each group, it is the same thing as doing this using the group means just once and at the end multiplying by the number in each group. For the within-groups estimate, the Chapter 11 method involves the squared deviations of each score from its group's mean, dividing this by the degrees of freedom for the group, and then averaging over all groups. In the structural model, you take each score's squared deviation from its group's mean, add them all up, and divide at the end by the number of scores. Dividing the sum for each group by its *df* and averaging these comes out the same as dividing the overall sum by the total *df*.

BOX 12–1   Analysis of Variance as a Way of Thinking About the World

The analysis of variance is a wonderfully basic idea worth looking at a little more, not only because it is the way you will think more and more as you read or conduct research, but also because it is in fact the way you think already.

In conducting any research (or trying to decide on the quality of a study you are reading), you are interested in whether a certain variable really makes a difference. You organize two (or more) groups so that you can show that any difference in results is there purely because one group received the variable's influence and the other did not.

For example, to see the effect of entering into conversations on friendship formation, you have one group converse with a stranger every day for a week and one group do nothing special. Then, you look for a difference in number of new friendships. To be certain that a difference shows up, you equalize the impact on the two groups of anything else that might be able to cause that same difference—no one is to join any clubs or go to any parties that week. You also try to control any other "random" effects that could allow enough variation that it would be easy for one group to be different for extraneous reasons—you do not enlist people who differ greatly from normal in their physical attractiveness or who do not speak English fluently.

This sort of standard thinking about research design parallels the logic of analysis of variance, a purely statistical technique. As one of the classic textbooks on research design (Kerlinger, 1973) puts it, "The main technical function of research design is to control variance" (p. 306). That is, researchers want to maximize the variance of the variable of the research hypothesis (the numerator, or between-groups variance). And they want to control the extraneous variables not under study (which contribute to the denominator, or within-groups variance). So the analysis of variance is very similar to the way you think as you plan an experiment.

We also said, however, that the analysis of variance is similar to how you have always thought. Kelley (1971) suggested that we are all scientists at heart, forming hypotheses and testing them. And our method of making distinctions and deciding about causation uses analysis of variance reasoning. Suppose that you are new to a country, and as you travel, you observe a blond woman dropping letters into a bright blue domed box. If you see other blonde women dropping letters into green boxes, red bins, purple cylinders, and yellow canisters, you build up the data for the important variable being the hair color and gender of the person (you make the person the numerator, the between-groups variance). The container can vary and is unimportant (you make it the denominator, the within-groups variance). But if you see many other sorts of persons putting letters always into bright blue domed boxes, you know that the boxes are the between-group difference that matters, the persons just random stuff. (In Canada, they would be red boxes.)

Likewise, as naive psychologists, we may wonder about the concept called honesty. Is it a trait of certain people, or does everyone "have a price"? Doubtless you have observed people and situations throughout your life and have your own theory. Your theory reflects which you think is larger, the numerator, the trait of honesty, or the denominator, the effect of situations (such as the size of a bribe, whether others will know if one was honest, etc.).

If you are familiar with the developmental psychologist Jean Piaget, you will recognize that analysis of variance–type thinking is part of what he called "formal operations," the style of abstract thinking normally acquired around age 14. So you should have no trouble grasping the analysis of variance—you have been innocently using it for years!

asked you to learn two different ways of thinking about this? We taught you the Chapter 11 method mainly because it is more intuitive. It is especially useful for helping you grasp what the population variance estimates are about and why they should be the same when the null hypothesis is true and not the same when it isn't. In addition, with the Chapter 11 method, you can figure an analysis of variance in a straightforward way from means and variances of groups. You don't need to work directly with scores.

However, as we said at the start of this chapter, it is important to introduce you to the structural model because (a) it has been the most widely used (in part because it is closer to the computational formulas that so long dominated everyone's thinking), (b) it is more flexible and thus easier for you to use when working with unequal-sized groups and with factorial analysis of variance (introduced in Chapter 13), and (c) it is related to a fundamental mathematical approach to which we want to be sure to expose those of you who might be going on to more advanced statistics courses.

HOW ARE YOU DOING?

1. (a, b, and c) Describe three kinds of deviations in an analysis of variance and (d) their relation.
2. (a, b, and c) Describe three kinds of squared deviations in analysis of variance and (d) their relation.
3. Write the structural model formula for the within-groups population variance estimate and define each of the symbols.
4. Write the structural model formula for the between-groups population variance and define each of the symbols.
5. (a) When figuring an analysis of variance, are there any differences in results between the Chapter 11 method and the structural model approach? (b, c, and d) List three advantages of the structural model approach.

ANSWERS:

1. (a) Deviation of each score from the grand mean; (b) deviation of each score from its group's mean; and (c) deviation of each score's group's mean from the grand mean. (d) For each score, its deviation from its group's mean plus its group's mean's deviation from the grand mean add up to the score's deviation from the grand mean.
2. (a) Squared deviation of each score from the grand mean; (b) squared deviation of each score from its group's mean; and (c) squared deviation of each score's group's mean from the grand mean. (d) The sum, over all the scores, of the squared deviations of each score from its group's mean plus the sum of the squared deviations of each score's group's mean's from the grand mean, add up to the sum of squared deviations of each score from the grand mean.
3. $S^2_{\text{Within}} = SS_{\text{Within}} / df_{\text{Within}}$. S^2_{Within} is the within-groups population variance estimate; SS_{Within} is the sum of squared deviations of each score from its group's mean, added up for all participants; and df_{Within} is the degrees of freedom for the within-groups population variance estimate, the sum of the degrees of freedom for each group (for each group, the number of participants minus 1).
4. $S^2_{\text{Between}} = SS_{\text{Between}} / df_{\text{Between}}$. S^2_{Between} is the between-groups population variance estimate; SS_{Between} is the sum of squared deviations of each score's group's mean from the grand mean, added up for all participants; and df_{Between} is the degrees of freedom for the between-groups population variance estimate, the number of groups minus 1.
5. (a) No. (b) It has been the most widely used, (c) it is more flexible when working with unequal-sized groups and with factorial analysis of variance, and (d) it is related to a fundamental mathematical approach that is useful for understanding more advanced statistics.

USING THE STRUCTURAL MODEL TO FIGURE AN ANALYSIS OF VARIANCE

AN EXAMPLE

Table 12–1 shows all the figuring using the structural model for an analysis of variance for the criminal record study. This table shows all three types of deviations and squared deviations for each score. For example, for the first person, the deviation from the grand mean is 4.33 (the score of 10 minus the grand mean of 5.67). This deviation squared is 18.74. The deviation of the score from its group's mean is 2; this deviation squared is 4. Finally, the deviation of the score's group's mean from the grand mean is 2.33; this deviation squared is 5.43. Notice that the deviations of each score's group's mean from the grand mean (in this case, 2.33) is the same number for all the scores in a group. At the bottom of each column, we have also summed the squared deviations of each type.

The bottom part of Table 12–1 shows the analysis of variance figuring. First, you figure the three sums of squared deviations (SS_{Total}, SS_{Within}, and $SS_{Between}$). The next step is to check for accuracy. You do this following the principle that the sum of squared deviations of each score from the grand mean comes out to the total of the other two kinds of sums at squared deviations.

The degrees of freedom, the next step shown in the table, is figured the same way as in Chapter 11. Then, the table shows the figuring of the two crucial population variance estimates. You figure them by dividing each sum of squared deviations by the appropriate degrees of freedom. Finally, the table shows the figuring of the F ratio in the usual way—dividing the between-groups variance estimate by the within-groups variance estimate. All these results, degrees of freedom, variance estimates, and F, come out exactly the same (within rounding error) as we figured in Chapter 11 (for example, see Table 11–4).

ANALYSIS OF VARIANCE TABLES

An **analysis of variance table** lays out the results of an analysis of variance based on the structural model approach. These kinds of charts are automatically produced by most analysis of variance computer programs. A standard analysis of variance table has five columns. Table 12–2 shows an analysis of variance table for the criminal record study.

The first column in a standard analysis of variance table is labeled "Source"; it lists the type of variance estimate or deviation score involved ("between," "within," and "total"). The next column is usually labeled *"SS"*; it lists the different types of sums of squared deviations. The third column is *"df,"* the degrees of freedom of each type. The fourth column is *"MS"*; this refers to mean squares. That is, *MS* is *SS* divided by *df,* the variance estimate. *MS* is, as usual, the same thing as S^2. However, in an analysis of variance table the variance is almost always referred to as *MS*. The last column is *"F,"* the F ratio. Each row of the table refers to one of the variance estimates. The first row is for the between-groups variance estimate. It is usually listed under Source as "Between" or "Group," although you will sometimes see it called "Model" or "Treatment." The second row is for the within-groups variance estimate, though it is sometimes labeled as "Error." The final row is for the sum of squares based on the total deviation of each score from the grand mean. Note, however, that computer printouts will sometimes use a different order for the columns and will sometimes omit either *SS* or *MS,* but not both.

analysis of variance table

TABLE 12–1 Analysis of Variance for the Criminal Record Study (Fictional Data) Using the Structural Model Approach (Compare to Tables 11–3 and 11–4)

Criminal Record Group

X	X − GM		X − M		M − GM	
	Deviation	Squared Deviation	Deviation	Squared Deviation	Deviation	Squared Deviation
10	4.33	18.74	2	4	2.33	5.43
7	1.33	1.77	−1	1	2.33	5.43
5	− .67	.45	−3	9	2.33	5.43
10	4.33	18.74	2	4	2.33	5.43
8	2.33	5.43	0	0	2.33	5.43
40		45.13		18		27.14

$M = 40/5 = 8$

Clean record group

X	X − GM		X − M		M − GM	
	Deviation	Squared Deviation	Deviation	Squared Deviation	Deviation	Squared Deviation
5	− .67	.45	1	1	−1.67	2.79
1	−4.67	21.81	−3	9	−1.67	2.79
3	−2.67	7.13	−1	1	−1.67	2.79
7	1.33	1.77	3	9	−1.67	2.79
4	−1.67	2.79	0	0	−1.67	2.79
20		33.95		20		13.95

$M = 20/5 = 4$

No information group

X	X − GM		X − M		M − GM	
	Deviation	Squared Deviation	Deviation	Squared Deviation	Deviation	Squared Deviation
4	−1.67	2.79	−1	1	−.67	.45
6	.33	.11	1	1	−.67	.45
9	3.33	11.09	4	16	−.67	.45
3	−2.67	7.13	−2	4	−.67	.45
3	−2.67	7.13	−2	4	−.67	.45
25		28.25		26		2.25

$M = 25/5 = 5$

Sums of squared deviations:
$\Sigma(X - GM)^2$ or $SS_{Total} = 45.13 + 33.95 + 28.25 = 107.33$
$\Sigma(X - M)^2$ or $SS_{Within} = 18 + 20 + 26 = 64$
$\Sigma(M - GM)^2$ or $SS_{Between} = 27.14 + 13.95 + 2.25 = 43.34$
Check ($SS_{Total} = SS_{Within} + SS_{Between}$):
$SS_{Total} = 107.33$; $SS_{Within} + SS_{Between} = 64 + 43.34 = 107.34$
(slight difference due to rounding error)

Degrees of freedom:
$df_{Total} = N - 1 = 15 - 1 = 14$
$df_{Within} = df_1 + df_2 + \cdots + df_{Last} = (5 - 1) + (5 - 1) + (5 - 1) = 4 + 4 + 4 = 12$
$df_{Between} = N_{Groups} - 1 = 3 - 1 = 2$
Check ($df_{Total} = df_{Within} + df_{Between}$): $14 = 12 + 2$

Population variance estimates:
S^2_{Within} or $MS_{Within} = SS_{Within}/df_{Within} = 64/12 = 5.33$
$S^2_{Between}$ or $MS_{Between} = SS_{Between}/df_{Between} = 43.34/2 = 21.67$
F ratio: $F = S^2_{Between}/S^2_{Within}$ or $MS_{Between}/MS_{Within} = 21.67/5.33 = 4.07$

| TABLE 12–2 | Analysis of Variance Table for the Criminal Record Study (Fictional Data) | | | |

Source	SS	df	MS	F
Between	43.34	2	21.67	4.07
Within	64	12	5.33	
Total	107.33	14		

ANALYSIS OF VARIANCE WITH UNEQUAL-SIZED GROUPS

Whether each group has the same or different numbers of scores, the basic logic of the analysis of variance is the same: You compare estimates of the population variance based on between-groups versus within-groups variation. However, the procedures for figuring the within-groups and between-groups variance estimates you learned in Chapter 11 are quite difficult to use with unequal-sized groups. They require complex adjustments to give appropriate weighting to the information from the different-sized groups. On the other hand, the structural model approach works out so that it automatically makes the needed adjustments for unequal sized groups. (However, with unequal sized groups, you have to remember to figure GM as just the average of all the scores.)

AN EXAMPLE

Here is an example using some made-up scores based on results of a real study conducted by Clark et al. (1997). These researchers studied three groups of patients: those with panic disorder, those with generalized anxiety disorder, and those with social phobia. They also included a comparison group of nonpatients. As an initial part of their study, they compared the four groups on various standard measures. Table 12–3 is based loosely on Clark et al.'s actual findings on the anxiety tests. (The pattern of results is the same. However, to keep the example simple, we have used far fewer participants and have made the individual scores small whole numbers. The actual study results are shown in Table 12–11 later in the chapter.) Table 12–3 also shows the figuring and the analysis of variance table. The various distributions involved are illustrated in Figure 12–3. We will follow the usual hypothesis-testing procedure step by step.

❶ **Restate the question as a research hypothesis and a null hypothesis about the populations.** There are four populations:

Population 1: Nonpatients
Population 2: Panic disorder patients
Population 3: Generalized anxiety disorder patients
Population 4: Social phobia patients

The null hypothesis is that these four populations have the same mean level of anxiety. The research hypothesis is that they do not all have the same mean level of anxiety.

❷ **Determine the characteristics of the comparison distribution.** The comparison distribution in an analysis of variance is always an F distribution. You figure its degrees of freedom the same way we have all along. The between-groups degrees of freedom is the number of groups minus 1. There are four groups, so $df_{Between}$ is 3. The within-groups df is the number of scores minus 1 in each group.

TABLE 12–3   Analysis of Variance of Anxiety Scores Loosely Based on Clark et al. (1997) (Fictional Data)

Nonpatients Squared Deviations				Panic Disorder Patients Squared Deviations				Generalized Anxiety Disorder Patients Squared Deviations				Social Phobia Patients Squared Deviations			
X	$X-GM$	$X-M$	$M-GM$	X	$X-GM$	$X-M$	$M-GM$	X	$X-GM$	$X-M$	$M-GM$	X	$X-GM$	$X-M$	$M-GM$
7	9	1	4	11	1	0	1	10	0	1	1	11	1	0	1
8	4	0	4	10	0	1	1	12	4	1	1	11	1	0	1
10	0	4	4	12	4	1	1					11	1	0	1
7	9	1	4												
32	22	6	16	33	5	2	3	22	4	2	2	33	3	0	3

$M = 32/4 = 8$ $M = 33/3 = 11$ $M = 22/2 = 11$ $M = 33/3 = 11$

$GM = (32 + 33 + 22 + 33)/12 = 10$

$df_{Total} = N - 1 = 12 - 1 = 11$

$df_{Within} = df_1 + df_2 + \cdots + df_{Last} = (4 - 1) + (3 - 1) + (2 - 1) + (3 - 1) = 3 + 2 + 1 + 2 = 8$

$df_{Between} = N_{Groups} - 1 = 4 - 1 = 3$

F needed for $df = 3, 8$ at .05 level $= 4.07$

$SS_{Total} = 22 + 5 + 4 + 3 = 34$

$SS_{Within} = 6 + 2 + 2 + 0 = 10$

$SS_{Between} = 16 + 3 + 2 + 3 = 24$

ANALYSIS OF VARIANCE TABLE:

Source	SS	df	MS	F
Between	24	3	8	6.4
Within	10	8	1.25	
Total	34	11		

Conclusion: Reject the null hypothesis.

There are 3 degrees of freedom in the Nonpatients group (4 scores minus 1), 2 degrees of freedom in the Panic Disorder group, 1 in the Generalized Anxiety group, and 2 in the Social Phobia group; thus, df_{Within} is $3 + 2 + 1 + 2 = 8$. That is, this will be an F distribution for 3 and 8 degrees of freedom.

❸ **Determine the cutoff sample score on the comparison distribution at which the null hypothesis should be rejected.** Using the F table in Appendix A (Table A–3), for 3 degrees of freedom in the numerator and 8 degrees of freedom for the denominator, for the .05 significance level, the cutoff F is 4.07.

❹ **Determine your sample's score on the comparison distribution.** Because the comparison distribution is a distribution of F ratios, this step means figuring your sample's F ratio (using this chapter's method). The numerator is the between-groups variance estimate. It is based on the deviation of each score's group's mean from the grand mean. For example, the first score's group's mean is 8 and the grand mean is 10. This deviation is 2, making a squared deviation of 4. Summing all 12 squared deviations of this kind gives 24, which is shown in the analysis of variance table for SS in the Between row. Next, you divide this sum of squared deviations by the between-groups degrees of freedom ($df_{Between}$). The result, as shown in the analysis of variance table, under MS, comes out to 8. That is, 8 is the numerator, the between-groups population variance estimate.

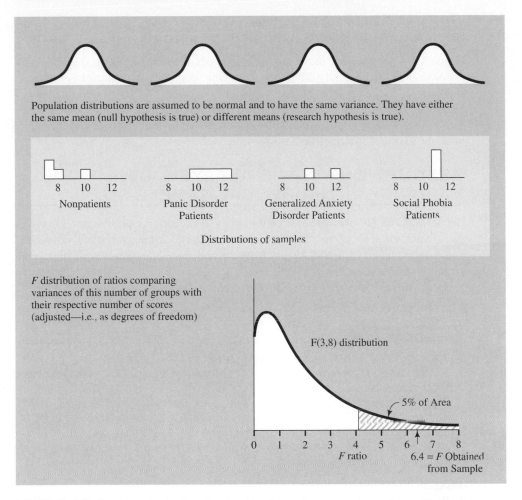

FIGURE 12–3 *The distributions involved in the analysis of variance for the fictional data loosely based on Clark et al. (1997).*

The denominator of the F ratio is the within-groups population variance estimate. It is based on the deviations of each score from its group's mean. For example, the first score is 7 and its group's mean is 8. This makes a deviation of -1 and a squared deviation of 1. Summing all 12 of the squared deviations of this kind gives 10. You divide 10 by the within-groups degrees of freedom, which is 8, giving 1.25.

The F ratio, as usual, is the between-groups estimate divided by the within-groups estimate. This comes out to 6.4.

When using this chapter's method and working by hand, it is wise at this point to figure the sum of squared deviations of each score from the grand mean, which is shown on the line in the table for Total. This way you can check your arithmetic, since this sum should equal the total of the other two sums of squared deviations. (In this case, 24 plus 10 does come out to 34.)

❺ **Decide whether to reject the null hypothesis.** The F ratio of 6.4 is more extreme than the .05 significance level cutoff F of 4.07. Thus, the researcher can reject the null hypothesis. The researcher can conclude that the four kinds of patients have different anxiety scores.

SUMMARY OF PROCEDURES FOR AN ANALYSIS OF VARIANCE USING THE STRUCTURAL MODEL

Table 12–4 summarizes the steps in an analysis of variance using this chapter's method. Note that the only difference from what you did in Chapter 11 is in step 4, substeps b through g (compare to Table 11–8). Table 12–5 shows an analysis of variance table with the symbols for all the parts put in each section where the numbers would usually go. It is followed by the same style of analysis of variance table with the various formulas filled in where the numbers would usually go.[2]

ASSUMPTIONS IN THE ANALYSIS OF VARIANCE WITH UNEQUAL SAMPLE SIZES

We considered the assumptions for the analysis of variance in Chapter 11. However, when the sizes of the groups are not close to equal, the analysis of variance is much more sensitive to violations of the equal-variance assumption. In fact, with unequal sample sizes, the analysis of variance becomes suspect when the most extremely different population variance estimates (among those from the different groups) are even as much as 1.5 times the other.

HOW ARE YOU DOING?

1. Name and describe the rows and columns of an analysis of variance table.
2. List the ways in which figuring an analysis of variance with the structural model approach is different from the Chapter 11 approach.
3. Figure an analysis of variance (at the .05 level) using the structural model approach for a study with the following scores: Group 1: 1 and 5; Group 2: 2 and 4; Group 3: 8, 11, and 11. (a) Use the steps of hypothesis testing and (b) sketch the distributions involved.
4. When considering whether an analysis of variance has met the assumptions, what is the effect of having unequal sample sizes?

ANSWERS:

1. Columns: Source (which kind of squared deviations); SS (sums of squared deviations); df (degrees of freedom); MS (mean squares, the population variance estimates); F (the F ratios). Rows: "Between" (the SS, df, and MS for the between-groups population variance estimate and the F for the overall analysis); "Within" (the SS, df, and MS for the within-groups population variance estimate); "Total" (the SS and df for the population variance estimate based on all the scores).
2. When figuring the between-groups population variance estimate, instead of finding the estimated variance of the distribution of means based on the variation among the means of the groups and then multiplying this by the number in each group, you add up for each score the squared deviation of its group's mean from the grand mean, then divide this by the de-

---

[2]There are also computational formulas for figuring an analysis of variance with the structural approach. For purposes of learning the ideas, we strongly recommend that you use the regular procedures as we have discussed them in this chapter for doing the practice problems. In a real research situation, the figuring is almost always done by computer. However, if you ever have to do an analysis of variance for an actual research study by hand (without a computer), you may find these formulas useful.

$$SS_{\text{Total}} = \Sigma X^2 - \frac{(\Sigma X)^2}{N} \tag{12-4}$$

$$SS_{\text{Between}} = \frac{(\Sigma X_1)^2}{n_1} + \frac{(\Sigma X_2)^2}{n_2} + \cdots + \frac{(\Sigma X_{\text{Last}})^2}{n_{\text{Last}}} - \frac{(\Sigma X)^2}{N} \tag{12-5}$$

$$SS_{\text{Within}} = SS_{\text{Total}} - SS_{\text{Between}} \tag{12-6}$$

$X_1, X_2, \ldots, X_{\text{Last}}$ are the scores in each group, and $n_1, n_2, \ldots, n_{\text{Last}}$ are the number of scores in each group.

TABLE 12–4 Hypothesis Testing Steps for an Analysis of Variance Using the Structural Model Approach (Equal- or Unequal-Sized Groups)

❶ **Restate the question as a research hypothesis and a null hypothesis about the populations.**

❷ **Determine the characteristics of the comparison distribution.**
   a. The comparison distribution will be an F distribution.
   b. The numerator degrees of freedom is the number of groups minus 1: $df_{Between} = N_{Groups} - 1$.
   c. The denominator degrees of freedom is the sum of the degrees of freedom in each group (the number of scores in the group minus 1): $df_{Within} = df_1 + df_2 + \cdots + df_{Last}$.
   d. Check the accuracy of your figuring by making sure that df_{Within} and $df_{Between}$ sum to df_{Total} (which is the total number of participants minus 1).

❸ **Determine the cutoff sample score on the comparison distribution at which the null hypothesis should be rejected.**
   a. Decide the significance level.
   b. Look up the appropriate cutoff in an F table.

❹ **Determine your sample's score on the comparison distribution.** This will be an F ratio.
   a. Figure the mean of each group and the grand mean of all scores.
   b. Figure the following deviations for each score:
      i. Its deviation from the grand mean $(X - GM)$.
      ii. Its deviation from its group's mean $(X - M)$.
      iii. Its group's mean's deviation from the grand mean $(M - GM)$.
   c. Square each of these deviation scores.
   d. Figure the sums of each of these three types of deviation scores (SS_{Total}, SS_{Within}, and $SS_{Between}$).
   e. Check the accuracy of your figuring by making sure that $SS_{Within} + SS_{Between} = SS_{Total}$.
   f. Figure the between-groups variance estimate: $SS_{Between}/df_{Between}$.
   g. Figure the within-groups variance estimate: SS_{Within}/df_{Within}.
   h. Figure the F ratio: $F = S^2_{Between}/S^2_{Within}$ or $F = MS_{Between}/MS_{Within}$.

❺ **Decide whether to reject the null hypothesis:** Compare scores from Steps 3 and 4.

TABLE 12–5 Analysis of Variance Table Showing Symbols and Formulas for Figuring the Analysis of Variance

Symbols Corresponding to Each Part of an Analysis of Variance Table

Source	SS	df	MS	F
Between	$SS_{Between}$	$df_{Between}$	$MS_{Between}$ (or $S^2_{Between}$)	F
Within	SS_{Within}	df_{Within}	MS_{Within} (or S^2_{Within})	
Total	SS_{Total}	df_{Total}		

Formulas for Each Part of an Analysis of Variance Table

Source	SS	df	MS	F
Between	$\Sigma(M - GM)^2$	$N_{Groups} - 1$	$SS_{Between}/df_{Between}$	$MS_{Between}/MS_{Within}$
Within	$\Sigma(X - M)^2$	$df_1 + df_2 + \cdots + df_{Last}$	SS_{Within}/df_{Within}	
Total	$\Sigma(X - GM)^2$	$N - 1$		

grees of freedom (number of groups minus 1). When figuring the within-groups population variance estimate, instead of estimating the population variance from each group's scores and averaging them, you add up for each score the squared deviation of its score from its group's mean, then divide this by the degrees of freedom (number in each group minus 1, added up for all groups).

3. (a) Table 12–6 shows the results, figuring, and the analysis of variance table.

❶ Restate the question as a research hypothesis and a null hypothesis about the populations. There are three populations:

Population 1: People like those in Group 1
Population 2: People like those in Group 2
Population 3: People like those in Group 3

The null hypothesis is that these three populations have the same mean. The research hypothesis is that they do not all have the same mean.

❷ Determine the characteristics of the comparison distribution. An F distribution with $df_{Between} = 2$, $df_{Within} = 4$.

❸ Determine the cutoff sample score on the comparison distribution at which the null hypothesis should be rejected. The cutoff for .05 with $df = 2, 4$ is 6.95.

❹ Determine your sample's score on the comparison distribution. The figuring on Table 12–6 shows an F of 10.5.

❹ Decide whether to reject the null hypothesis. The F ratio of 8 is more extreme than 6.95. Therefore, reject the null hypothesis.

(b) The various distributions involved are illustrated in Figure 12–4.

4. The analysis of variance is less robust to violations of the equal-variance assumption.

TABLE 12–6 Analysis of Variance Figuring for "How Are You Doing?" Question 3

	Group 1 Squared Deviations				Group 2 Squared Deviations				Group 3 Squared Deviations			
	X	$X-GM$	$X-M$	$M-GM$	X	$X-GM$	$X-M$	$M-GM$	X	$X-GM$	$X-M$	$M-GM$
	1	25	4	9	2	16	1	9	8	4	4	16
	5	1	4	9	4	4	1	9	11	25	1	16
									11	25	1	16
Σ	6	26	8	18	6	20	2	18	30	54	6	48
	$M = 6/3 = 3$				$M = 6/2 = 3$				$M = 30/3 = 10$			

$GM = (6 + 6 + 30)/7 = 6$
$df_{Total} = N - 1 = 7 - 1 = 6$
$df_{Within} = df_1 + df_2 + \cdots + df_{Last} = (2 - 1) + (2 - 1) + (3 - 1) = 1 + 1 + 2 = 4$
$df_{Between} = N_{Groups} - 1 = 3 - 1 = 2$
F needed for $df = 2, 4$ at .05 level $= 6.95$
$SS_{Total} = 26 + 20 + 54 = 100$
$SS_{Within} = 8 + 2 + 6 = 16$
$SS_{Between} = 18 + 18 + 48 = 84$

ANALYSIS OF VARIANCE TABLE:

Source	SS	df	MS	F
Between	84	2	42	10.5
Within	16	4	4	
Total	100	6		

Conclusion: Reject the null hypothesis.

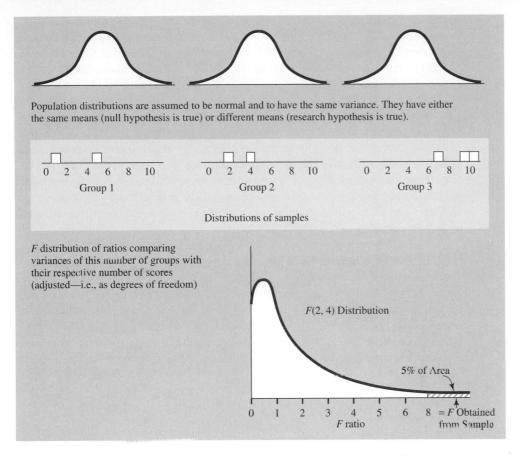

Population distributions are assumed to be normal and to have the same variance. They have either the same means (null hypothesis is true) or different means (research hypothesis is true).

Group 1   Group 2   Group 3

Distributions of samples

F distribution of ratios comparing variances of this number of groups with their respective number of scores (adjusted—i.e., as degrees of freedom)

$F(2, 4)$ Distribution

5% of Area

F ratio

$8 = F$ Obtained from Sample

FIGURE 12–4   *The distributions involved in the analysis of variance for "How Are You Doing?" question 3.*

POST HOC COMPARISONS

As we noted in Chapter 11, when you reject the null hypothesis in an analysis of variance, this implies that the population means are not all the same, but it does not tell you which population means differ from which. In Chapter 11, we also noted that researchers often plan specific comparisons based on theory or practical considerations. Sometimes, however, researchers take a more exploratory approach, for example, comparing all the different pairings of means to discover which ones do and do not differ significantly. That is, after the study is done, the researcher is fishing through the results to see which groups differ from each other. These are called **post hoc comparisons** (or *a posteriori comparisons*) because they are after the fact and not planned in advance.

    In post hoc comparisons, all possible comparisons have to be taken into account when figuring the overall chance of any one of them turning out significant. Using the Bonferroni procedure you learned in Chapter 11 for post hoc comparisons is safe, in the sense that you are confident you won't get too many results significant by chance. But in post hoc comparisons there are often so many comparisons to consider that the overall significance level is divided into such a small number by the Bonferroni procedure that getting any one comparison to come out significant would be a long shot. For example, with four groups, there are six possible pairs to compare, so using a Bon-

post hoc comparisons

ferroni correction and an overall significance level of .05, you would have to test each comparison at .05/6 or .0083. If there are five groups, there are 10 possible comparisons, so that .05 overall becomes .005 for each comparison. And so forth. Thus, the power for any one comparison becomes very low. In fact, the above only considers simple comparisons of one group to another. If you take into account possible complex comparisons, the number of possible post hoc comparisons is unlimited.

Of course, you might think, "I'll just test the pairs of means that have the biggest difference, so the number of comparisons won't be so great." Unfortunately, this strategy won't work. Since you did not decide in advance which pairs of means would be compared, when exploring after the fact, you have to take into account that any of the pairs might have been the biggest ones. So unless you made specific predictions in advance—and had a sound theoretical or practical basis for those predictions—all the possible pairings (and possibly complex comparisons as well) have to be counted.

For this reason, statisticians have developed a variety of procedures to use in these fishing expeditions. These procedures attempt to keep the overall risk of a Type I error at some level like .05, while at the same time not too drastically reducing power. You may see some of these referred to in articles you read, described by the names of their developers; the **Scheffé test** and **Tukey test** are the most widely used, with the *Neuman-Keuls* and *Duncan* procedures almost as common. Which procedure is best under various conditions remains a topic of dispute. You can learn the details about the possibilities and controversies in intermediate statistics.

Scheffé test
Tukey test

THE SCHEFFÉ TEST

As an example of a post hoc test, consider the Scheffé method. It has the advantage of being the most general in that it is the only one that can be used when you want to make both simple and complex comparisons. Its disadvantage, however, is that compared to the Tukey and other procedures, it is the most conservative. That is, for any given post hoc comparison, its chance of being significant using the Scheffé is usually still better than the Bonferroni, but worse than the Tukey or any of the other post hoc contrasts.

To use the Scheffé test, you first figure the F for your comparison in the usual way (as you learned in Chapter 11). But then you divide that F by the overall study's $df_{Between}$ (the number of groups minus 1) and then compare this to the overall study's F cutoff.[3]

Here is an example. Recall from Chapter 11 that for the comparison of the Criminal Record group versus the No Information group, we figured an F of 4.22. Since the overall $df_{Between}$ in that study was 2 (there were three groups), for a Scheffé test, you would actually consider the F for this contrast to be an F of only $4.22/2 = 2.11$. You would then compare this F of 2.11 to the cutoff F for the overall between effect (in this example, the F for $df = 2, 12$).

[3]Here is the idea behind the Scheffé method: For any comparison, the between-groups sum of squared deviations for the comparison can never be greater than the overall sum of squared deviations between groups. The numerator term you use for figuring a comparison in the method you learned in Chapter 11 is the same as the sum of squares for the comparison, because in these comparisons you only have one degree of freedom; thus MS equals SS. So, if you divide this number by the overall study's $df_{Between}$, it can never exceed the overall $MS_{Between}$. In this way, every possible contrast is being evaluated on at least as conservative a basis as the overall analysis.

1. What are post hoc comparisons, and (b) why do researchers make them?
2. (a) Why do researchers usually not use the Bonferroni procedure for post hoc comparisons?
   (b) What is the advantage over the Bonferroni of procedures such as the Tukey and Scheffé tests?
3. What are the (a) advantages and (b) disadvantages of the Scheffé procedure versus other post hoc tests (such as the Tukey)?
4. How do you do the Scheffé procedure?
5. Suppose in a study with four groups of 50 participants each, for a particular contrast, you figure an F of 12.60. Using a Scheffé test, is this significant at the .05 significance level?

ANSWERS:

1. (a) Comparisons figured after an analysis of variance, such as between two groups, that were not planned in advance.
   (b) As an exploratory procedure to see what patterns of relations among populations are suggested by the data over and above any comparisons that were planned in advance.
2. (a) In any follow-up analysis, there are so many possible post hoc comparisons (especially if you include complex comparisons) that if you used the Bonferroni procedure, your corrected significance level would be so extreme that it would be impossible for almost any result to be significant.
   (b)The effect of the Tukey and Scheffé tests, and others like them, when doing multiple post hoc comparisons and correctly adjusting for the many comparisons being made, is that a result does not have to be quite so extreme to be significant.
3. (a) You can use it for any number of comparisons, including complex comparisons.
   (b) It is more conservative: The chance of any comparison being significant is less.
4. Figure the comparison in the usual way (from Chapter 11), but divide the F by the overall study's $df_{Between}$ and use the overall study's F cutoff.
5. Overall study's $df_{Between} = 4 - 1 = 3$; $df_{Within} = 49 + 49 + 49 + 49 = 147$. Scheffé-corrected $F = 12.60/3 = 4.20$. Overall study's .05 cutoff $F (df = 3, 147$; closest on table $= 3$, 140) is 2.70. Thus, even with the Scheffé correction, this comparison is significant.

EFFECT SIZE AND POWER FOR THE ANALYSIS OF VARIANCE

EFFECT SIZE

Effect size for the analysis of variance is a little more complex than for a t test. With the t test, you took the difference between the two means and divided by the standard deviation. In the analysis of variance, you can still divide by the standard deviation. But what is the equivalent to the difference between the two means when you have three or more means?[4] Thus, in this section we consider a quite different approach to effect size, the **proportion of variance accounted for (R^2)**.[5]

proportion of variance accounted for (R^2)

---

[4]There actually *is* a kind of analysis of variance equivalent to the difference between means—the variation among the means. In fact, Cohen (1988) recommends using the standard deviation of the distribution of means. Thus, he defines what he calls f as an effect size for the analysis of variance, which is figured as the standard deviation of the distribution of means (estimated as S_M) divided by the standard deviation of the individuals (estimated as S_{Within}). However, this measure of effect size is rarely used in research articles and is less intuitively meaningful than the more common one we discuss here.

[5]If you have completed Chapter 4, you may recognize that we use the same symbol, R^2, for the proportion of variance accounted for in an analysis of variance as we do for the proportion of variance accounted for in multiple regression. In both cases, the proportion of variance accounted for describes how much of the variation in one variable can be accounted for (predicted or explained) by the other variable. In the prediction situation, we are thinking in terms of how much of the variation in the criterion variable is accounted for by the predictor variable. In analysis of variance, we are considering how much of the variance in the measured variable (such as ratings of guilt or satisfaction with treatment) is accounted for by the variable that divides up the groups (such as what experimental condition one is in or which treatment one receives). We have more to say in Chapter 16 about the many links between the analysis of variance and multiple regression.

To be precise, R^2 is the proportion of the total variation of scores from the grand mean that is accounted for by the variation between the means of the groups. You figure it using the sums of squares. It is the between-group sum of squares ($SS_{Between}$) divided by the total sum of squares (SS_{Total}). In terms of a formula,

| The proportion of variance accounted for is the sum of squared deviations of each score's group's mean from the grand mean, divided by the sum of squared deviations of each score from the grand mean. |

$$R^2 = \frac{SS_{Between}}{SS_{Total}}$$

(12-4)

Consider once again the criminal record study. In that example, the sum of squared deviations of the scores from the grand mean was 107.33. The sum of squared deviations of the scores' groups' means from the grand mean was 43.44. Thus, the proportion of the total variation accounted for by the variation between groups is 43.44/107.33, or 40%. In terms of the formula,

$$R^2 = \frac{SS_{Between}}{SS_{Total}} = \frac{43.44}{107.33} = .40$$

What if the sums of squares are not available, as is often true in published studies? It is also possible to figure R^2 directly from F and the degrees of freedom. The formula is

| The proportion of variance accounted for is the F ratio times the between-groups degrees of freedom (the degrees of freedom for the between-groups population variance estimate), divided by the sum of the F ratio times the between-groups degrees of freedom, plus the degrees of freedom for the within-groups population variance estimate. |

$$R^2 = \frac{(F)(df_{Between})}{(F)(df_{Between}) + df_{Within}}$$

(12-5)

(This formula is mathematically equivalent to Formula 12-4, but is reworked to allow you to directly use the information in a published study. If you are algebraically adventurous, you can try deriving formula 12-4 from 12-5, making use of the F ratio formula.)

For example, in the criminal record study,

$$R^2 = \frac{(F)(df_{Between})}{(F)(df_{Between}) + df_{Within}} = \frac{(4.07)(2)}{(4.07)(2) + 12}$$

$$= \frac{8.14}{8.14 + 12} = \frac{8.14}{20.14} = .40$$

eta **squared (η^2)**

You should also know that another common name for this measure of effect size (besides R^2) is $\boldsymbol{\eta^2}$, the Greek letter *eta* **squared**; η^2 is also known as the *correlation ratio*.

The proportion of variance accounted for is a useful measure of effect size because it has the direct meaning suggested by its name. (Further, researchers are familiar with R^2 from its use in regression, and its square root, R, is a kind of correlation coefficient that is very familiar to most researchers—see footnote 4 and Chapters 3 and 4.)

R^2 is a proportion of two positive numbers ($SS_{Between}/SS_{Total}$). Therefore, it has a minimum of 0. Also, $SS_{Between}$ can never be larger than SS_{Total}, so the proportion of variance accounted for has a maximum of 1. However, in practice it is rare for an

TABLE 12–7 Approximate Power for Studies Using the Analysis of Variance Testing Hypotheses at the .05 Significance Level

Participants per Group (n)	Effect Size		
	Small ($R^2 = .01$)	Medium ($R^2 = .06$)	Large ($R^2 = .14$)
Three groups ($df_{Between} = 2$)			
10	.07	.20	.45
20	.09	.38	.78
30	.12	.55	.93
40	.15	.68	.98
50	.18	.79	.99
100	.32	.98	*
Four groups ($df_{Between} = 3$)			
10	.07	.21	.51
20	.10	.43	.85
30	.13	.61	.96
40	.16	.76	.99
50	.19	.85	*
100	.36	.99	*
Five groups ($df_{Between} = 4$)			
10	.07	.23	.56
20	.10	.47	.90
30	.13	.67	.98
40	.17	.81	*
50	.21	.90	*
100	.40	*	*

*Nearly 1.

analysis of variance to have an R^2 even as high as .50. Cohen's (1988) conventions for R^2 are .01, a small effect size; .06, a medium effect size; and .14, a large effect size.

POWER

Table 12–7 shows the approximate power for the .05 significance level for small, medium, and large effect sizes; sample sizes of 10, 20, 30, 40, 50, and 100 per group; and three, four, and five groups.[6]

Consider a planned study with five groups of 10 participants each. This study has an expected large effect size (.14), and using the .05 significance level, this study would have a power of .56. Thus, even if the research hypothesis is in fact true and has a large effect size, there is only a little greater than even chance (56%) that the study will come out significant.

As we have noted in previous chapters, determining power is especially useful when interpreting the practical implication of a nonsignificant result. For example,

[6]More detailed tables are provided in Cohen (1988, pp. 289–354). When using these tables, note that the value of u at the top of each of his tables refers to $df_{Between}$, which for a one-way analysis of variance is the number of groups minus 1, not the number of groups as used in our Table 12–7.

TABLE 12–8	Approximate Number of Participants Needed in Each Group (Assuming Equal Sample Sizes) for 80% Power for the One-Way Analysis of Variance Testing Hypotheses at the .05 Significance Level

	Effect Size		
	Small ($R^2 = .01$)	Medium ($R^2 = .06$)	Large ($R^2 = .14$)
Three groups ($df_{Between} = 2$)	322	52	21
Four groups ($df_{Between} = 3$)	274	45	18
Five groups ($df_{Between} = 4$)	240	39	16

suppose that you have read a study using an analysis of variance with four groups of 30 participants each in which the researcher reports a nonsignificant result at the .05 level. Table 12–7 shows a power of only .13 for a small effect size. This suggests that even if such a small effect exists in the population, this study would be very unlikely to have come out significant. But the table shows a power of .96 for a large effect size. This suggests that if a large effect existed in the population, it almost surely would have shown up in that study.

PLANNING SAMPLE SIZE

Table 12–8 gives the approximate number of participants you need in each group for 80% power at the .05 significance level for estimated small, medium, and large effect sizes for studies with three, four, and five groups.[7]

For example, suppose you are planning a study involving four groups and you expect a small effect size (and will use the .05 significance level). For 80% power, you would need 274 participants in each group, a total of 1,096 in all. However, suppose you could adjust the research plan so that it was now reasonable to predict a large effect size (perhaps by using more accurate measures and a more powerful experimental manipulation). Now you would need only 18 in each of the four groups, for a total of 72.

HOW ARE YOU DOING?

1. (a) Why is the method of figuring effect size for analysis of variance quite different than that used for the t tests? (b) Explain the logic of why proportion of variance accounted for can serve as an effect size in analysis of variance.
2. (a) Write the formula for effect size in analysis of variance using sums of squares; (b) define each of the symbols; (c) give an alternative symbol for R^2; and (d) figure the effect size for a study in which $SS_{Between}$ is 20 and SS_{Total} is 200.
3. (a) Write the formula for effect size in analysis of variance from a study in which only the F ratio and degrees of freedom are available; (b) define each of the symbols; and (c) figure the effect size for a study with 18 participants in the first group, 20 in the second, and 14 in the third, and an F of 4.5
4. What is the power of a study with four groups of approximately 40 participants each to be tested at the .05 significance level, in which the researchers predict a large effect size?

[7]More detailed tables are provided in Cohen (1988, pp. 381–389). If you use these, see footnote 6 in this chapter.

5. About how many participants do you need in each group for 80% power in a planned study with five groups in which you predict a medium effect size and will be using the .05 significance level?

ANSWERS:

1. (a) With t tests, your focus is on the difference between two means; there is no direct equivalent in the analysis of variance. (b) You are figuring the percentage of the total variation among the scores that is accounted for by which group the participant is in.
2. (a) $R^2 = SS_{Between}/SS_{Total}$. (b) R^2 is the proportion of variance accounted for; $SS_{Between}$ is the sum of squared deviations of each score's group's mean from the grand mean; and SS_{Total} is the sum of squared deviations of each score from the grand mean. (c) η^2. (d) .10.
3. (a) $R^2 = [(F)(df_{Between})]/[(F)(df_{Between}) + df_{Within}]$. (b) R^2 is the proportion of variance accounted for; F is the F ratio from the study; $df_{Between}$ is the degrees of freedom for the between-groups population variance estimate (number of groups minus 1); and df_{Within} is the degrees of freedom for the within-groups population variance estimate (the sum of the degrees of freedom for each group's population variance estimate). (c) $df_{Between} = 3 - 1 = 2$; $df_{Within} = 17 + 19 + 13 = 49$. $R^2 = [(F)(df_{Between})]/[(F)(df_{Between}) + df_{Within}] = [(4.5)(2)]/[(4.5)(2) + 49] = 9/[9 + 49] = 9/58 = .16$.
4. .99.
5. 39.

CONTROVERSY: THE INDEPENDENCE ASSUMPTION AND THE UNIT OF ANALYSIS QUESTION

In addition to the assumptions we have emphasized of normal population distributions and equal population variances, the analysis of variance (and also the t test) assumes that each score is independent of the others. This is called the **independence assumption**. For example, we assume that any two scores within a particular group are no more linked to each other than are any other two scores. This is the usual situation in research.

independence assumption

There are, however, several somewhat common situations in which a study can easily violate this assumption. One such situation arises when the participants in a study include multiple individuals from within existing groups—such as families, businesses, teams, and so forth. Suppose, for example, that you want to compare the effectiveness of three drug-use prevention programs in the schools. One program is used in 10 schools, a second in 10 other schools, and a third in still 10 other schools. There are about 500 students in each school. After the programs have been in effect for 6 months, you give drug-use questionnaires to the students in all the schools. You then want to do an analysis of variance on the results to see is the three programs had different effects on the scores on the questionnaires. There were 5,000 students who received the first program—that is, 500 students in each of 10 schools. Thus, you might consider there to be 5,000 participants in each condition.

The problem, however, is that a student in one school is likely to fill out the questionnaire much more like another student at the same school than like a student at another school, even if the other school had the same program. This is because each school has its own culture and history around drugs and around programs from the outside, because people at the same school may be especially likely to talk to each other about the program, because people from the same school may be of more similar social-economic backgrounds, and so forth. Thus, this study seems to violate the independence assumption.

Another kind of research situation where this problem arises can be seen in a typical type of study on the effectiveness of treatment methods. Suppose 40 participants are given psychotherapy method A, a different 40 method B, and a third 40 method C. However, the researchers will probably not have 40 different therapists giving each method. Instead, considering method A for example, there may be four therapists, each of whom give method A to 10 participants. It does seem likely that the patients of the same therapist being given method A are likely to have more similar effects to each other than are patients of another therapist also giving method A.

There are actually a variety of approaches that have been proposed to deal with this problem, including setting up the study so the problem doesn't arise in the first place. But that is not always practical.

unit of analysis

Another solution to this problem is this: In the school example, instead of considering there to be 5,000 participants in each group, you could take the average for the 500 students in each school. That is, the **unit of analysis**, instead of the person, would be the school. If you took this approach, there would be 10 scores in each group (the average scores for the 500 students in each of the 10 schools in the group). Similarly, in the psychotherapy study, instead of an analysis of variance with 40 scores for each method, you could make patients of the same therapist the unit of analysis, making just four such units per method!

This approach of using the more inclusive unit of analysis is correct in the sense that there is now no problem with the independence assumption—the averages of any one school or of any set of patients of a particular therapist should be no more like any other in its group. The problem with this solution is that the power of the study may be very dramatically reduced. In the school study, instead of an overall sample size of 15,000, there is an overall sample size of only 30! In the therapy study, the sample is reduced from 120 to 16. This is partly made up for by the fact that averages should have less variance (following our usual principle from Chapter 7 that the mean of a group is less likely to be extreme than is an individual score). But the overall effect is still usually a great loss of power.

Yet another approach to the problem is to check for whether which group a person is in matters—whether in fact people in the same subgroup are more similar to each other than to people in other subgroups. Thus, the researcher in the schools example might do an analysis of variance just within one prevention program, using school as the group variable and person as the unit of analysis. If there was no significant difference and the effect size was very small, this would suggest that students at one school were not particularly more similar to each other than to students at other schools. If this was found for all three prevention programs, you might then feel confident in making person the unit of analysis.

Here is an example from an actual study where they followed that strategy: Sullivan and Feltz (2001) were interested in the relation of conflict between teams and cohesion (sense of togetherness) within teams. To test their predictions, they studied players in a number of hockey teams. However, they did not want to lose the power of studying individuals. Here is what they did: "Because the individual was the unit of analysis, it was necessary to determine if there were any team-level effects . . . A one-way ANOVA showed no significant differences among teams for any of the conflict scores. . . ." (pp. 347–348).

Statisticians have been aware of this issue for a long time, but it has only recently come front and center before the research community so that many new ideas are being tried, and there is much discussion of what is the best approach (see Kenny et al., 1998).

STRUCTURAL MODEL ANALYSIS OF VARIANCE AND POST HOC COMPARISONS IN RESEARCH ARTICLES

In Chapter 11 we described how analysis of variance results are typically reported in a research article in terms of the F and significance, as well as the results of any planned comparisons. Most computer programs provide an analysis of variance table of the type we considered in this chapter. For example, Table 12–9 is the output from SPSS for Windows for the criminal record study. Further, when researchers were less familiar with the details of how analysis of variance was done, it was common for research articles to include an abbreviated version of an analysis of variance table. Thus, you will sometimes see such tables in older articles. Today, analysis of variance is so widely used and understood that it is rare to see such a table in a research article.

There is one aspect of how analysis of variance is reported in research articles that we have not considered so far and which depends on the material in this chapter. Researchers often report results of post hoc comparisons among all pairs of means. The most common method of doing this is by putting small letters by the means in the tables. Usually, means with the same letter are not significantly different from each other; those with different letters are. For example, Table 12–10 presents the actual results on the love experience measures in the Hazan and Shaver (1987) study (our first example in Chapter 11). Consider the first row (the happiness results). The avoidant and anxious-ambivalent groups are not significantly different from each other, since they have the same letter (a). But both are significantly different on happiness compared to the secure group, which has a different letter (b). In the jealousy row, however, all three groups differ from one another.

As a second example, Table 12–11 is reproduced from the Clark et al. (1997) study we used as an example earlier in this chapter (with figures loosely based on its actual results as shown here).

When reading results of post hoc comparisons, you will see many different procedures named. For example, Table 12–10 (from the Hazan & Shaver study) explicitly mentions that the results are "according to Scheffé test."

SUMMARY

1. An alternative approach to the analysis of variance uses the structural model. In the structural model approach, the deviation of each score from the grand mean is divided into two parts: (a) the score's difference from its group's mean and (b) its group's mean's difference from the grand mean. These deviations, when squared, summed, and divided by the appropriate degrees of freedom, give the same within-groups and between-groups estimates as using the Chapter 11

TABLE 12–9 Portion of Output from SPSS for Windows Analysis of Variance for Criminal Record Example (Fictional Data)

ANOVA

GUILT

	Sum of Squares	df	Mean Square	F	Sig.
Between Groups	43.333	2	21.667	4.063	.045
Within Groups	64.000	12	5.333		
Total	107.333	14			

TABLE 12–10 Love Subscale Means for the Three Attachment Types (Newspaper Sample)

Scale Name	Avoidant	Anxious/ Ambivalent	Secure	$F(2, 571)$
Happiness	3.19_a	3.31_a	3.51_b	14.21***
Friendship	3.18_a	3.19_a	3.50_b	22.96***
Trust	3.11_a	3.13_a	3.43_b	16.21***
Fear of closeness	2.30_a	2.15_a	1.88_b	22.65***
Acceptance	2.86_a	3.03_b	3.01_b	4.66**
Emotional extremes	2.75_a	3.05_b	2.36_c	27.54***
Jealousy	2.57_a	2.88_b	2.17_c	43.91***
Obsessive preoccupation	3.01_a	3.29_b	3.01_a	9.47***
Sexual attraction	3.27_a	3.43_b	3.27_a	4.08*
Desire for union	2.81_a	3.25_b	2.69_a	22.67***
Desire for reciprocation	3.24_a	3.55_b	3.22_a	14.90***
Love at first sight	2.91_a	3.17_b	2.97_a	6.00**

Note: Within each row, means with different subscripts differ at the .05 level of significance according to a Scheffé test.
$*p < .05; **p < .01; ***p < .001$.
From Hazan, C., & Shaver, P. (1987), tab. 3. Romantic love conceptualized as an attachment process. *Journal of Personality and Social Psychology, 52,* 511–524. Copyright, 1987, by the American Psychological Association. Reprinted by permission.

method. However, the structural model is more flexible and can be applied to studies with unequal sample sizes.

2. Computations using the structural model are usually summarized in an analysis of variance table, with a column for source of variation (between, within, and total), sums of squared deviations (*SS*), degrees of freedom (*df*), population variance estimates (*MS,* which equals *SS/df*), and *F* (which equals $MS_{Between}/MS_{Within}$).

TABLE 12–11 Study 2: Means and Standard Deviations for Participant Characteristics

Variable	*M* (and *SD*) for Group			
	Panic Disorder ($n = 45$)	Generalized Anxiety Disorder ($n = 33$)	Social Phobia ($n = 73$)	Nonpatients ($n = 45$)
Age	33.0_a (7.1)	40.1_b (9.6)	34.9_a (8.9)	33.0_a (6.9)
STAI	48.8_b (12.1)	49.5_b (9.5)	46.4_b (10.0)	29.2_a (5.4)
Beck Depression Inventory	$15.3_{b,c}$ (8.6)	18.3_c (10.2)	12.8_b (7.8)	2.1_a (2.2)
VAS–Anxiety	23.0_b (18.6)	28.8_b (22.1)	25.0_b (18.2)	5.6_a (9.4)
VAS–Depression	21.8_b (21.1)	29.4_b (21.1)	24.7_b (18.5)	8.2_a (11.3)
VAS–Happiness	53.1_b (16.3)	55.7_b (17.0)	53.0_b (17.1)	74.5_a (15.1)

Note: Means with different subscripts differ significantly ($p < .01$). STAI = State–Trait Anxiety Inventory, State subscale; VAS = visual analogue scale.
Data from Clark, D. M., et al. (1997), tab. 3. Misinterpretation of body sensations in panic disorder. *Journal of Consulting and Clinical Psychology, 65,* 203–213. Copyright, 1997, by the American Psychological Association. Reprinted with permission.

3. Assumptions are the same as for any analysis of variance, though an analysis of variance with unequal-sized groups is more sensitive to violations of the equal population variance assumption.

4. An analysis of variance may be followed up by exploratory, post hoc comparisons. Such comparisons have to protect against the possibility of getting some significant results just by chance because of the great many comparisons that could be made. There are a number of methods for dealing with this problem that are not as severe as the Bonferroni correction (see Chapter 11). One such method, the Scheffé test, can be used even if the exploration includes comparisons of means and complex comparisons. In the Scheffé test you figure each comparison of interest in the usual way and then divide its F by the overall analysis' between-groups degrees of freedom.

5. The proportion of variance accounted for (R^2), also called eta squared (η^2), is a measure of analysis of variance effect size. It is $SS_{Between}$ divided by SS_{Total}. Power depends on effect size, number of people in the study, significance level, and number of groups.

6. An additional assumption of the analysis of variance is that scores be independent, such that no two scores are likely to be more similar to each other than any other two scores (other than as a result of which experimental group they are in). When this assumption is not met, for example, because scores come from subgroups within each experimental group, you can combine scores in subgroups to make a more inclusive unit of analysis, although this procedure drastically reduces power.

KEY TERMS

analysis of variance table (p. 423)

eta squared (η^2) (p. 434)

independence assumption (p. 437)

post hoc comparisons (p. 431)

proportion of variance accounted for (R^2) (p. 433)

Scheffé test (p. 432)

structural model (p. 417)

sum of squared deviations ($SS_{Between}$, SS_{Within}, SS_{Total}) (p. 418)

Tukey test (p. 432)

unit of analysis (p. 438)

EXAMPLE WORKED-OUT COMPUTATIONAL PROBLEMS

FIGURING AN ANALYSIS OF VARIANCE USING THE STRUCTURAL MODEL METHOD

A researcher at an alcohol treatment center conducts a study of client satisfaction with treatment methods A, B, and C. The researcher randomly assigns each of the available 10 clients to receive one of these treatments; 4 clients end up with Treatment A, 3 with Treatment B, and 3 with Treatment C. Two weeks later, the researcher measures client satisfaction with the three treatments on a scale from 1 (low satisfaction) to 20 (high satisfaction). Scores for Treatment A were 8, 13, 10, and 9. Scores for Treatment B were 7, 3, and 8. Scores for Treatment C were 6, 4, and 2. Figure an analysis of variance (at the .05 level) using the structural model approach. (a) Use the steps of hypothesis testing and (b) sketch the distributions involved.

Table 12–12 shows the figuring and the analysis of variance table.

❶ **Restate the question as a research hypothesis and a null hypothesis about the populations.** There are three populations:

TABLE 12–12 Analysis of Variance Figuring and Analysis of Variance Table for "Examples of Worked-Out Computational Problems" for a Alcohol Treatment Study (Fictional Data)

Treatment A							Treatment B							Treatment C						
X	X − GM		X − M		M − GM		X	X − GM		X − M		M − GM		X	X − GM		X − M		M − GM	
	Dev	Dev²	Dev	Dev²	Dev	Dev²		Dev	Dev²	Dev	Dev²	Dev	Dev²		Dev	Dev²	Dev	Dev²	Dev	Dev²
8	1	1	−2	4	3	9	7	0	0	1	1	−1	1	6	−1	1	2	4	−3	9
13	6	36	3	9	3	9	3	−4	16	−3	9	−1	1	4	−3	9	0	0	−3	9
10	3	9	0	0	3	9	8	1	1	2	4	−1	1	2	−5	25	−2	4	−3	9
9	2	4	−1	1	3	9														
40		50		14		36	18		17		14		3	12		35		8		27

$M = 40/4 = 10$ $M = 18/3 = 6$ $M = 12/3 = 4$

Note: Dev = Deviation; Dev² = Squared deviation

$GM = (40 + 18 + 12)/10 = 70/10 = 7$

$df_{Total} = N - 1 = 10 - 1 = 9$

$df_{Within} = df_1 + df_2 + \cdots + df_{Last} = (4 - 1) + (3 - 1) + (3 - 1) = 3 + 2 + 2 = 7$

$df_{Between} = N_{Groups} - 1 = 3 - 1 = 2$

F needed for $df = 2, 7$ at the .05 level $= 4.74$

$SS_{Total} = 50 + 17 + 35 = 102$

$SS_{Within} = 14 + 14 + 8 = 36$

$SS_{Between} = 36 + 3 + 27 = 66$

ANALYSIS OF VARIANCE TABLE:

Source	SS	df	MS	F
Between	66	2	33	6.42
Within	36	7	5.14	
Total	102	9		

Conclusion: Reject the null hypothesis.

Population 1: Alcoholics receiving Treatment A
Population 2: Alcoholics receiving Treatment B
Population 3: Alcoholics receiving Treatment C

The null hypothesis is that these three populations have the same mean. The research hypothesis is that they do not all have the same mean.

❷ **Determine the characteristics of the comparison distribution.** An F distribution; from Table 12–12, $df = 2, 7$.

❸ **Determine the cutoff sample score on the comparison distribution at which the null hypothesis should be rejected.** Using Table A–3, for $df = 2, 7$ and a .05 significance level, the cutoff F is 4.74.

❹ **Determine your sample's score on the comparison distribution.** From the figuring shown in Table 12–12, $F = 6.42$.

❺ **Decide whether to reject the null hypothesis.** The F ratio of 6.42 is more extreme than the .05 significance level cutoff F of 4.74. Thus, the researcher can reject the null hypothesis. If these were real data, the researcher could conclude that the three kinds of treatment have different effects on how satisfied clients like theirs are with their treatment.

(b) The various distributions involved are illustrated in Figure 12–5.

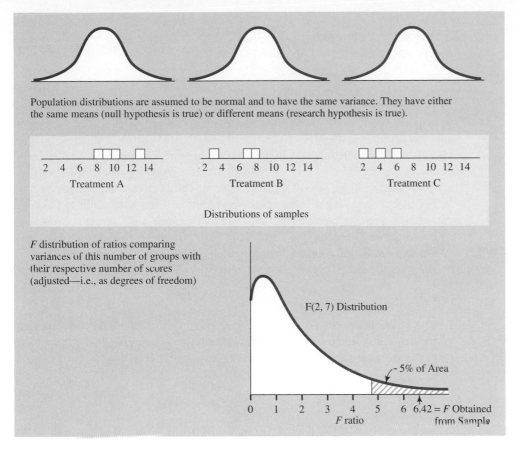

Population distributions are assumed to be normal and to have the same variance. They have either the same means (null hypothesis is true) or different means (research hypothesis is true).

2 4 6 8 10 12 14
Treatment A

2 4 6 8 10 12 14
Treatment B

2 4 6 8 10 12 14
Treatment C

Distributions of samples

F distribution of ratios comparing variances of this number of groups with their respective number of scores (adjusted—i.e., as degrees of freedom)

F(2, 7) Distribution

5% of Area

0   1   2   3   4   5   6 6.42 = F Obtained
F ratio   from Sample

FIGURE 12–5 *The distributions involved in the analysis of variance for the "Examples of Worked-Out Problems" for a alcohol treatment study (fictional data).*

FIGURING SIGNIFICANCE OF POST HOC COMPARISONS USING THE SCHEFFÉ METHOD

A study has five groups with 10 participants in each. Using a Scheffé test, is a comparison with a computed F of 11.21 significant at the .01 significance level?

> The overall study's $df_{Between} = 5 - 1 = 4$; $df_{Within} = 9 + 9 + 9 + 9 + 9 = 45$.
> The Scheffé-corrected F for this contrast is $11.21/4 = 2.80$.
> The overall study's .01 cutoff F ($df = 4, 45$) is 3.77.
> The contrast is not significant.

FIGURING EFFECT SIZE FROM SUMS OF SQUARES

What is the effect size in the alcoholism treatment study above?

$$R^2 = SS_{Between}/SS_{Total} = 66/102 = .65.$$

FIGURING EFFECT SIZE FROM F AND THE DESIGN OF THE STUDY

Figure the effect size for a study with four groups, 14 in the first group, 12 in the second, 15 in the third, and 15 in the fourth. F is 3.89.

$df_{Between} = 4 - 3 = 2; df_{Within} = 13 + 11 + 14 + 14 = 52$
$R^2 = [(F)(df_{Between})]/[(F)(df_{Between}) + df_{Within}] = [(3.89)(3)]/[(3.89)(3) + 52]$
$= 11.67/[11.67+52] = 11.67/63.67 = .18.$

PRACTICE PROBLEMS

These problems involve figuring. Most real-life statistics problems are done on a computer. However, even if you have a computer and statistics software, do these by hand (with the help of a calculator) to ingrain the method in your mind. Also, in all problems involving figuring, be sure to show your work (including, for analysis of variance problems, a full analysis of variance table as well as all the figuring behind it).

For practice in using a computer to solve statistics problems, refer to the computer section of each chapter of the *Student's Study Guide and Computer Workbook* that accompanies this text.

All data are fictional unless an actual citation is given.

Answers to Set I problems are given at the back of the book.

SET I

1. The scores below are the same as for problem 2a in Chapter 11. (a) Work out the same problem using the structural model approach and (b) compare your answer to what you found in Chapter 11 (use the .01 level).

Group 1	Group 2	Group 3
8	6	4
8	6	4
7	5	3
9	7	5

2. Figure an analysis of variance for the following data (using the 1% significance level). (a) Use the steps of hypothesis testing and (b) sketch the distributions involved.

Group 1	Group 2	Group 3	Group 4
71	82	68	78
67	82	70	76
	82		

3. Figure an analysis of variance for each of the data sets below using the structural model approach (at the 5% significance level). (a) Use the steps of hypothesis testing and (b) sketch the distributions involved.

	Group 1	Group 2	Group 3
(i)	3	0	1
	4	1	2
	5	2	3
(ii)	Group 1	Group 2	Group 3
	3	0	1
	5	0	3
		1	
		2	
		2	

4. A researcher is interested in the self-esteem levels of teachers of three different subjects. The levels of self-esteem for the four English teachers studied were 2, 2, 3, and 5. For the three math teachers studied, the self-esteem levels were 6, 4, and 5. For the five social studies teachers studied, the levels were 9, 6, 7, 10, and 13. Do the results support a difference in the mean self-esteem levels for the three types of teachers (at the .05 level)? (a) Use the steps of hypothesis testing, (b) sketch the distributions involved, and (c) explain your answer to someone who understands mean, variance, and estimated population variance (including the notions of sample, population, and degrees of freedom), but knows nothing else about statistics.

5. A study compared the effectiveness of smoking prevention programs. Around North America there are four programs using method A; their overall ratings are 13, 8, 10, and 9. Three programs use method B; their ratings are 5, 7, and 6. And three programs use method C; their ratings are 4, 6, and 2. On the basis of these samples, should we conclude that programs using different methods have different degrees of effectiveness? Use the .05 level. (a) Use the steps of hypothesis testing, (b) sketch the distributions involved, and (c) write a report to a government committee explaining your conclusions (the report should be written so that it will be understood by officials who may have never had a course in statistics).

6. For each of the following studies, test whether a comparison in which the researcher figures an F of 17.21 would be significant using the Scheffé method.

	Number of Groups	Participants in Each Group	Significance Level
(a)	5	10	.05
(b)	6	10	05
(c)	5	20	.05
(d)	5	10	.01

7. Figure the effect size using the sums of squares for problems (a) 1, (b) 2, (c) 3i, (d) 3ii, (e) 4, and (f) 5. (g) Explain your work for e to a person who is familiar with mean and variance but not with effect size.

8. Figure the effect size for the following completed studies:

	Study F	Participants Per Group
(a)	4.21	Group 1 = 10, Group 2 = 12, Group 3 = 10, Group 4 = 8
(b)	4.21	Group 1 = 12, Group 2 = 10, Group 3 = 10, Group 4 = 8
(c)	4.21	Group 1 = 10, Group 2 = 12, Group 3 = 10
(d)	4.21	Group 1 = 10, Group 2 = 12, Group 3 = 18
(e)	4.21	Group 1 = 10, Group 2 = 12, Group 3 = 19
(f)	8.42	Group 1 = 10, Group 2 = 12, Group 3 = 10, Group 4 = 8

9. What is the power of each of the following planned studies, using the analysis of variance with $p < .05$?

	Predicted Effect Size	Number of Groups	Participants in Each Group
(a)	Small	3	20
(b)	Small	3	30
(c)	Small	4	20
(d)	Medium	3	20

10. About how many participants do you need in each group for 80% power in each of the following planned studies, using the analysis of variance with $p < .05$?

	Predicted Effect Size	Number of Groups
(a)	Small	3
(b)	Large	3
(c)	Small	4
(d)	Medium	3

11. Based on Table 12–10 from the Hazan and Shaver (1987) study, indicate for which variables, if any, (a) the Avoidants are significantly different from the other two groups, (b) the Anxious-Ambivalents are different from the other two groups, (c) the Secures are different from the other two groups, and (d) all three groups are different. (e) Explain to a person who understands analysis of variance, but does not know anything about post hoc comparisons, what is meant in the table note that the results are "according to a Scheffé test."

12. Miller (1997) asked 147 women students to view slides of magazine ads that included, among other things, pictures of attractive men. The participants were measured for physiological arousal (skin conductance) while viewing the ads and also after viewing them; they were asked to rate the attractiveness and how much they would like to meet each person in the ads. As part of the analysis, Miller compared results for women dating no one, women in casual dating relationships, and women in exclusive dating relationships. Table 12–13 shows Miller's results. (a, b, and c) Describe the pattern of results on each variable. (d) Explain to a person who understands analysis of variance, but is unfamiliar with post hoc comparisons, what is meant in a general way by the table note that the results are based on "Duncan's multiple range test." (That is, you don't need to explain this specific test, but you do need to explain why a test like this was used and what it attempts to accomplish.)

SET II

13. Problem 15 in Chapter 11 was an analysis of variance problem about whether individuals working in different areas of a company differed in their attitudes

TABLE 12–13   Effects of Relationship Status

Dependent measure	Relationship Status		
	Dating No One	Casual Dating	Exclusive Dating
Skin conductance	19.5_b	19.1_b	15.8_a
Desire to meet target	14.6_b	15.3_b	11.2_a
Perceived physical attractiveness of target	15.6_b	17.1_b	13.8_a

Note: Higher numbers reflect greater arousal, desire to meet target, and perceived attractiveness; for the latter two items the possible range was 1–19. Within each row, means with different subscripts differ significantly ($p < .05$) by Duncan's multiple range test.
Data from Miller, R. S. (1997), tab. 4. Inattentive and contented: Relationship commitment and attention to alternatives. *Journal of Personality and Social Psychology, 73,* 758–766. Copyright, 1997, by the American Psychological Association. Reprinted with permission.

toward the company. The results, in terms of positiveness of attitudes, for the three people surveyed in engineering were 10, 12, and 11; for the three in the marketing department, 6, 6, and 8; for the three in accounting, 7, 4, and 4; and for the three in production, 14, 16, and 13. (a) Work out the same problem using the structural model approach, and (b) compare your answer to what you found in Chapter 11 (use the .05 level).

14. Figure an analysis of variance for the following data (at the 1% significance level). (a) Use the steps of hypothesis testing, and (b) sketch the distributions involved.

Group 1	Group 2	Group 3	Group 4	Group 5
1	3	2	2	4
7	11	12	8	10
		6		8

15. Figure an analysis of variance for each of the data sets below using the structural model approach (at the 5% significance level). (a) Use the steps of hypothesis testing, and (b) sketch the distributions involved.

	Group 1	Group 2	Group 3
(i)	0	0	4
	2	2	6
		0	
		2	

	Group 1	Group 2	Group 3
(ii)	0	0	4
	2	2	6
			5
			6

16. A sleep researcher compared the effect of three types of sleep disturbance (being woken at various intervals) on alertness the next morning. Originally, there were 12 research participants who were randomly assigned to one of the three conditions, making four per condition. However, one of the participants in the Disturbance Schedule I condition did not follow the instructions, and this participant's data could not be used in the analysis, making unequal sample sizes. The results on the alertness measure were as follows: Disturbance Schedule I: 120, 140, 140; Disturbance Schedule II: 130, 150, 120, 140; Disturbance Schedule III: 100, 90, 110, 120. Do the results support different effects on alertness for the three types of disturbance schedules (at the .05 level)? (a) Use the steps of hypothesis testing, (b) sketch the distributions involved, and (c) explain your answer to someone who understands mean, variance, and estimated population variance (including the notions of sample, population, and degrees of freedom), but knows nothing else about statistics.

17. Problem 16 in Chapter 10 was a t test for independent means for a study of the effects of color on easing anxiety. It compared anxiety test scores of individuals who completed the test printed on either soft yellow paper or harsh green paper. The scores for five participants who completed the test printed on yellow paper were 17, 19, 28, 21, and 18. The scores for four participants who

completed the test on the green paper were 20, 26, 17, and 24. Figure an analysis of variance for these same data. (You are using ANOVA for a situation with just two groups.) If you take the square root of the F ratio, it should come out the same (within rounding error) as the t score you figured using the t test for independent means. (We discuss this link between the t test and the analysis of variance in Chapter 16.)

18. For each of the following studies, test whether a comparison in which the researcher figures an F of 8.12 would be significant using the Scheffé method.

	Number of Groups	Participants in Each Group	Significance Level
(a)	4	30	.05
(b)	5	80	.05
(c)	4	5	.05
(d)	8	30	.01

19. Figure the effect size using the sums of squares for problems (a) 13, (b) 14, (c) 15i, (d) 15ii, (e) 16, and (f) 17. (g) Explain your work on (e) to a person familiar with the t test, but not with effect size.

20. Figure the effect size for the following completed studies:

	Study F	Participants Per Group
(a)	7.15	Group 1 = 8, Group 2 = 20, Group 3 = 20
(b)	3.10	Group 1 = 8, Group 2 = 20, Group 3 = 20
(c)	15.83	Group 1 = 8, Group 2 = 20, Group 3 = 20
(d)	7.15	Group 1 = 20, Group 2 = 20, Group 3 = 20, Group 4 = 20, Group 5 = 20

21. What is the power of each of the following planned studies, using the analysis of variance with $p < .05$?

	Predicted Effect Size	Number of Groups	Participants in Each Group
(a)	Small	4	50
(b)	Medium	4	50
(c)	Large	4	50
(d)	Medium	5	50

22. About how many participants do you need in each group for 80% power in each of the following planned studies, using the analysis of variance with $p < .05$?

	Predicted Effect Size	Number of Groups
(a)	Small	5
(b)	Medium	5
(c)	Large	5
(d)	Medium	3

TABLE 12–14 Means and Standard Deviations of the three Liking Measures According to Feedback and Picture prime (Study 6)

Feedback Condition	Picture prime			
	Secure Base	Positive	Neutral	No Picture
No feedback				
M	4.61_b	4.68_b	4.06_a	4.08_a
SD	1.17	1.18	1.13	1.05
Failure				
M	4.71_b	3.63_a	3.61_a	3.53_a
SD	1.35	1.03	1.09	1.22

Note: Means with different subscripts within rows are significantly different at $p < .05$.

23. Based on Table 12–11 from the Clark et al. (1997) study, indicate for which variables, if any, (a) the Panic Disorder patients were significantly different from the other three groups, (b) the Generalized Anxiety Disorder patients were different from the other three groups, (c) the Social Phobia patients were different from the other three groups, (d) the Nonpatients were different from the other three groups, and (e) any other patterns of differences among groups. (f) Explain to a person who understands analysis of variance but does not know anything about post hoc comparisons, what is the basis for these comparisons.

24. Mikulincer and his colleagues (2001) showed participants one of four kinds of pictures—a secure base picture (a Picasso painting of a mother and baby), a positive picture that had nothing to do with relationships (a photo of a smiling person), a neutral picture (a simple geometric figure), or no picture (a blank screen for the same amount of time as the other pictures). The pictures were flashed on very rapidly in the midst of another task they were doing, so that participants were unaware that they had even seen the pictures. (This is called "subliminal priming.") The other task they were doing was rating how much they like various Chinese ideographs. Also, before seeing the primes, participants completed a puzzle task; some were given no feedback about how they did; others were led to believe they had failed at the task. Table 12–14 shows the mean ratings for how much the participants liked the ideographs. Describe the pattern of results for (a) the No feedback participants and (b) the Failure participants. (c) Explain to a person who understands analysis of variance, but does not know anything about post hoc comparisons, why the researchers made comparisons among these conditions and what considerations they had to take into account in doing so.

CHAPTER 13

FACTORIAL ANALYSIS OF VARIANCE

Factorial analysis of variance

Are You Ready?
What You Need to have Mastered Before Starting This Chapter:

- For the first part of this chapter, you need to have read and understood Chapters 1, 2, and 5 through 11; for the second part of the chapter (on the computational procedures), you also need to have mastered the material in Chapter 12.

Factorial analysis of variance is an extension of the procedures you learned in Chapters 11 and 12. This method provides a highly flexible and efficient approach to analyzing results of certain types of experiments that are very widely used in psychology.

We begin by examining in depth the nature of the research approach used in these kinds of experiments, then go on to a briefer discussion of the reasoning and computational procedures for a factorial analysis of variance.

BASIC LOGIC OF FACTORIAL DESIGNS AND INTERACTION EFFECTS

AN EXAMPLE

Lambert and his colleagues (1997) were interested in how stereotypes affect the evaluations we make of others. For example, people often use age or gender stereotypes to evaluate whether someone will be successful in a particular job. Lambert et al. were especially interested in how the influence of stereotypes is affected (a) by awareness that a stereotype is inappropriate for a particular circumstance and (b) by mood. They believed that people are less affected by a stereotype when it is inappropriate and are particularly unaffected by stereotypes when in a sad mood.

Thus, Lambert et al. did the following experiment. Participants were asked to put themselves in the position of a job interviewer. Their task was to "form a preliminary evaluation of the suitability of an individual for a particular job" (p. 1010)—which for all participants was that of a flight attendant. The participants were then given a resume of an applicant that included a photo of a very attractive woman. Based on this information, the participants were asked how likely it was they would hire her, using a scale from 0 (not at all) to 10 (extremely). This experiment used the *attractiveness stereotype,* a stereotype that includes the tendency to think that good-looking people are especially competent.

The researchers put half the participants in a sad mood prior to reading the resume, supposedly as part of a separate experiment. These participants were asked to think about "an episode in your life that made you feel very sad and continues to make you sad whenever you think about it, even today" (p. 1004). This was the Sad Mood condition. The other half of the participants were not given any particular instructions. This was the Neutral Mood condition.

The other influence of interest to the researchers was appropriateness of the stereotype. Participants were given a description of a good flight attendant that differed according to how important attractiveness was for the job. For half the participants in each of the mood groups, the description emphasized the ability "to solve and analyze problems in a rational and analytic fashion" (p. 1010); this was the Stereotype Inappropriate condition. For the other participants, the description emphasized passenger satisfaction and how appearance contributed to it; this was the Stereotype Appropriate condition.

In sum, there were two experimental manipulations: sad versus neutral mood and the job description being stereotype appropriate versus stereotype inappropriate.

Lambert and his colleagues could have done two studies, one comparing sad versus neutral mood and one comparing stereotype appropriate versus inappropriate job descriptions. Instead, they studied the effects of both mood and stereotype appropriateness in a single study. They considered four groups of participants (see Table 13–1): (a) those in a sad mood with a stereotype appropriate description, (b) those in a sad mood with a stereotype inappropriate description, (c) those in a neutral mood with a stereotype appropriate description, and (d) those in a neutral mood with a stereotype inappropriate description.

TABLE 13–1 Factorial Design Employed by Lambert et al. (1997)

	Mood	
Stereotype	Sad	Neutral
Appropriate	a	c
Inappropriate	b	d

FACTORIAL RESEARCH DESIGN DEFINED

factorial research design

The Lambert et al. (1997) study is an example of a **factorial research design.** In a factorial research design the effect of two or more variables are examined at once by making groupings of every combination of the variables. In this example, there are two levels of mood (sad and neutral) and two levels of stereotype appropriateness (appropriate and inappropriate). This allows four possible combinations, and Lambert et al. used all of them in their study.

A factorial research design has a major advantage over conducting separate studies of each variable—efficiency. With a factorial design, you can study both variables at once, without needing twice as many participants. In the example, Lambert et al. were able to use a single group of participants to study the effects of mood and stereotype appropriateness. (The two "studies" don't get in each other's way because for each part of each comparison, there are equal numbers in each part of the other conditions.)

INTERACTION EFFECTS

There is an even more important advantage of a factorial research design. A factorial design lets you study the effects of combining two or more variables. In this example, mood and stereotype appropriateness might affect hiring in a simple additive way. By additive, we mean that their combined influence is the sum of their separate influences—if you are more of one and also more of the other, then the overall effect is the total of the two individual effects. For example, suppose being sad makes you more willing to hire someone; similarly, suppose the stereotype being appropriate makes you more willing to hire a person. If these two effects are additive, then participants in the sad, stereotype appropriate group will be most willing to hire the person; participants in the neutral, stereotype inappropriate group will be least likely to hire the person; and those in the other two conditions would have an intermediate likelihood of hiring the person.

It could also be that one variable but not the other has an effect. Or perhaps neither variable has any effect. In the additive situation, or the one in which only one variable or neither has an effect, looking at the two variables in combination does not give any interesting additional information.

However, it is also possible that the combination of the two changes the result. In fact, Lambert et al. predicted that the effect of stereotype inappropriateness would be especially strong in the sad mood condition. This prediction was based on the notion that when in a sad mood, we are more willing to revise our initial, unthinking, stereotype-based reactions.

A situation where the *combination* of variables has a special effect is called an **interaction effect.** An interaction effect is an effect in which the impact of one variable depends on the level of the other variable. In the Lambert et al. study, there was an interaction effect. Look at Table 13–2. The result was that the participants in the Appropriate-Sad group were most likely to hire the applicant, the Inappropriate-Neutral group was the next most likely, and the two other groups were least likely (to about an equal extent). Consider the bottom row of the results, the Inappropriate Stereotype group. This part of the result supported the researchers' theory that when in a sad mood, people are able to counteract their stereotypes. (What about the Appropriate-Sad being the most likely to hire? The researchers acknowledged that this result was "unexpected and difficult to explain" [p. 1011].)

Suppose the researchers had studied stereotype appropriateness and mood in two separate studies. They would have concluded that each factor had only a slight effect. The average likelihood of hiring for the appropriate is 6.77 (that is, the average of 5.8 and 7.73 comes out to 6.77) and for inappropriate is 6.29. The average likelihood of hiring for those in the sad mood condition was 6.78 versus 6.28 for those in the neutral mood condition. Thus, following the approach of two separate studies, they would have completely missed the most important result. The most important result had to do with the combination of the two factors.

interaction effect

TABLE 13–2 Mean Likelihood of Hiring in the Lambert et al. (1997) Study

Stereotype	Mood	
	Sad	Neutral
Appropriate	7.73	5.80
Inappropriate	5.83	6.75

SOME TERMINOLOGY

two-way analysis of variance
two-way factorial research design
one-way analysis of variance

The Lambert et al. study would be analyzed with what is called a **two-way analysis of variance** (it uses a **two-way factorial research design**). By contrast, the situations in Chapters 11 and 12 (such as the attachment-style study or the criminal-record experiment) used a **one-way analysis of variance.** Such analyses are called one-way because they consider the effect of only one variable that separates groups (such as a person's attachment style or information about a defendant's criminal record).

Some studies investigate the effect of three or more variables at a time. For example, Lambert et al. also wanted to be sure that their results were not affected by gender. Thus, in another analysis, they divided each of their four groups into two subgroups, women and men. This created eight combinations: sad-appropriate women, sad-appropriate men, sad-inappropriate women, and so forth. The complete set of groupings is diagrammed in Figure 13–1. In this analysis, they were studying the influence of three variables that separate groups at one time. It takes three dimensions to diagram such a study. Thus, this is an example of a *three-way factorial design.* (The result was that there were no significant effects for gender, either overall or in interaction with mood, stereotype appropriateness, or their combination.) You can do studies with four-way and higher factorial designs, though you can't diagram such studies in any simple way. However, most psychology research is limited to two-way and occasionally three-way factorial designs.

main effect

In a two-way analysis, each variable or "way" (each dimension in the diagram) is a possible **main effect.** If the result for a variable, averaging across the variable or variables crossed with it to divide up the groups another way, is significant, it is a main effect. This is entirely different from an interaction effect, which is based on the combination of variables. In the two-way Lambert et al. study, there was a possibility of two main effects and one interaction effect. The two possible main effects include one for stereotype appropriateness and one for mood. The possible interaction effect is for the combination of stereotype appropriateness and mood. In a two-way analysis of variance you are always testing two possible main effects and one possible interaction.

cell
cell mean

Each grouping combination in a factorial design is called a **cell.** The mean of the scores in each cell is a **cell mean.** In the Lambert et al. study, there are four cells and thus four cell means, one for each combination of the levels of stereotype appropriateness and mood. That is, one cell is Stereotype Appropriate and Sad Mood (as shown in Table 13–2, its mean is 7.73); one cell is Stereotype Inappropriate and Sad Mood (5.83); one cell is Stereotype Appropriate and Neutral Mood (5.80); and one cell is Stereotype Inappropriate and Neutral Mood (6.75).

FIGURE 13–1 *A three-way factorial design used in the Lambert et al. (1997) study.*

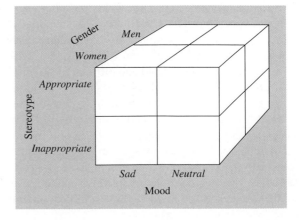

The means of one variable alone are called **marginal means.** For example, in the Lambert et al. study there are four marginal means, one mean for all the stereotype appropriate participants (as we saw earlier, 6.77), one for all the stereotype inappropriate participants (6.29), one for all the sad mood participants (6.78), and one for all the neutral mood participants (6.28). (Because we were mainly interested in the interaction, we did not show these marginal means in the tables.)

To look at a main effect, you focus on the marginal means. To look at the interaction effect, you focus on the pattern of individual cell means.

marginal means

HOW ARE YOU DOING?

1. (a) What is a factorial design? (b and c) Give two advantages of a factorial design over doing two separate experiments.
2. In a factorial design, (a) what is a main effect, and (b) what is an interaction effect?
3. Below are the means from a study in which participants rated the originality of paintings under various conditions. For each mean, indicate its grouping and whether it is a cell or marginal mean.

	Contemporary	Rennaissance	Overall
Landscape	6.5	5.5	6
Portrait	3.5	2.5	3
Overall	5	4	

4. In each of the following studies participant's performance on a coordination task was measured under various conditions or compared for different groups. For each study, make a diagram of the design and indicate whether it is a one-way, two-way, or three-way design: (a) a study in which people are assigned to either a high-stress condition or a low-stress condition, and within each of these conditions, half are assigned to work alone and half to work in a room with other people; (b) a study comparing students majoring in physics, chemistry, or engineering; (c) a study comparing people doing a task in a hot room versus a cold room, with half in each room doing the task with their right hand and half with their left hand, and within each of these various temperature/hand combinations, half are blindfolded and half are not.

ANSWERS:

1. (a) A research design in which the effect of two or more variables are examined at once by making groupings of every combination of the variables.
   (b) It is more efficient. For example, you can study the effects of two variables at once with only a single group of participants.
   (c) It makes it possible to see if there are interaction effects.
2. (a) The effect of one of the variables ignoring the pattern of results on the other variable.
   (b) The different effect of one variable according to the level of the other variable.
3. 6.5 = cell mean for Contemporary/Landscape group; 5.5 = cell mean for Rennaissance/Landscape group; 6 = marginal mean for Landscape groups; 3.5 = cell mean for Contemporary/Portrait groups; 2.5 = cell mean for Rennaissance/Portrait group; 3 = marginal mean for Portrait group; 5 = marginal mean for Contemporary groups; and 4 = marginal mean for Rennaissance groups.
4. (a) Two-way.

	Stress	
	High	Low
Alone		
With Others		

(b) One-way.

Physics	Chemistry	Engineering

(c) Three-way.

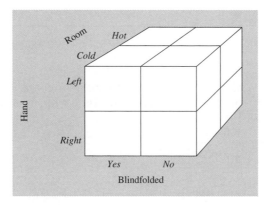

RECOGNIZING AND INTERPRETING INTERACTION EFFECTS

It is very important to understand interaction effects. In many experiments the interaction effect is the main point of the research. As we have seen, an interaction effect is an effect in which the impact of one variable depends on the level of another variable. The Lambert et al. results (Table 13–2) show an interaction effect. This is because the impact of stereotype appropriateness is different with a sad mood than with a neutral mood. You can think out and describe an interaction effect in three ways: in words, in numbers, or in a graph.

IDENTIFYING INTERACTION EFFECTS IN WORDS AND NUMBERS

You can think out an interaction effect in words by saying that an interaction effect occurs when the effect of one variable depends on the level of another variable—in the Lambert et al. example, the effect of stereotype appropriateness depends on the level of mood. (You can also say that the effect of mood depends on the level of stereotype appropriateness. Interaction effects are completely symmetrical in that you can describe them from the point of view of either variable.)

You can see an interaction effect numerically by looking at the pattern of cell means. If there is an interaction effect, the pattern of differences in cell means across one row will not be the same as the differences in cell means across another row. Consider the Lambert et al. example. In the Stereotype Appropriate row, the Sad Mood participants rated how likely they were to hire (7.33) much higher than the Neutral Mood participants (5.80). This was a positive difference of 1.93 (that is, 7.73 − 5.80 = 1.93). However, look at the Stereotype Inappropriate row. Those in a sad mood rated their likelihood of hiring (5.83) *lower* than those in the neutral mood (6.75). The difference for sad-versus-neutral mood for stereotype inappropriate participants was −.92.

Table 13–3 gives cell and marginal means for six possible results of a fictional two-way factorial study on the relation of age and education to income. Age has

TABLE 13–3 Possible Means for Results of a Study of the Relation of Age and Education to Income

	Result A			Result B			Result C		
	High School	College	Overall	High School	College	Overall	High School	College	Overall
Younger	40	40	40	60	40	50	20	60	40
Older	40	60	50	40	60	50	40	80	60
Overall	40	50		50	50		30	70	

	Result D			Result E			Result F		
	High School	College	Overall	High School	College	Overall	High School	College	Overall
Younger	20	20	20	40	60	50	40	60	50
Older	120	120	120	40	80	60	60	100	80
Overall	70	70		40	70		50	80	

two levels (younger, such as 25 to 29, versus older, such as 30 to 34) and education has two levels (high school versus college). These fictional results are exaggerated to make clear when there are interactions and main effects.

In Result A, there is an interaction. Note that in the Younger row, education makes no difference, but in the Older row, the college cell mean is much higher than the high-school cell mean. One way to say this is that for the younger group, education is unrelated to income; but for the older group, people with a college education earn much more than those with less education.

Result B is also an interaction. This is because in the Younger row the high-school mean income is higher than the college mean income, but in the Older row the high-school mean income is lower. Put in words, among younger people, those with only a high-school education make more money (perhaps because they entered the workplace earlier or the kinds of jobs they have start out at a higher level); but among older people, those with a college education make more money.

Result C is *not* an interaction effect. In the Younger row, the high-school mean is 40 lower than the college mean, and the same is true in the Older row. Whether young or old, people with college educations earn $40,000 more.

In Result D, there is also no interaction—in neither row is there any difference. Regardless of education, older people earn $100,000 more.

Result E is an interaction: In the Younger row, the college mean is 20 higher, but in the Older row, the college mean is 40 higher. So among young people, college-educated people earn a little more; but among older people, those with a college education earn much more.

Finally, Result *F* is also an interaction effect—there is a smaller difference in the Younger row than in the Older row. As with Result E, for people with a college education, income increases more with age than it does for those with only a high-school education.[1]

[1]Based on 1990 statistics from the U.S. Department of Education, the actual situation in the United States is closest to Result F, though not as extreme. People with a college education earn more than those with only a high school education in both age groups, but the difference is somewhat greater for the older group. However, it is important to keep in mind that whether or not people receive a college education is also related to the social class of their parents and other factors that may affect income as much or more than education does.

Table 13–4 shows possible results of another fictional study. In this factorial experiment, the two experimentally manipulated variables are difficulty of the task (easy versus hard) and level of physiological arousal (low, moderate, or high). Arousal in this study is how anxious the participant is made to feel about the importance of doing well. The variable being measured is how well the participant performs a set of arithmetic tasks. The interpretations of possible interactions are as follows:

Result A: No interaction. The cell means in the Easy row do not differ among themselves, and the cell means in the Hard row do not differ among themselves. There is one main effect: Task difficulty affects performance; arousal does not.

Result B: No interaction. The cell means in the Easy row increase by 10 from low to moderate and from moderate to high. The cell means in the Hard row do the same. Again, there is only a main effect: Arousal affects performance; task difficulty does not.

Result C: No interaction. The cell means in the Easy row increase by 10 from low to moderate and from moderate to high; the cell means in the Hard row do the same. In this example, there are two main effects: Arousal affects performance and task difficulty affects performance.

Result D: Interaction. The pattern of cell means in the Easy row is an increase of 10 from low to moderate and another increase of 10 from moderate to high. This pattern is not the same as the pattern of cell means in the Hard row, where there is again an increase of 10 from low to moderate, but there is an increase of 40 from moderate to high. Thus, in all cases, performance on easy and hard tasks tends to improve with greater arousal. However, the impact of high versus moderate arousal is much greater for hard than for easy tasks.

Result E: Interaction. The pattern of cell means in the Easy row is an increase of 10 and then a decrease of 10. This is quite different from the Hard row, where the pattern is a decrease of 10 and then an increase of 10. For easy tasks, performance is best under moderate arousal, but for hard tasks, performance is worst under moderate arousal.

Result F: Interaction. In the Easy row, the cell means increase as you go across; in the Hard row, they decrease as you go across. For easy tasks, the more arousal, the better; for hard tasks, arousal interferes with performance. (Result F is closest to a well-established finding in psychology known as the Yerkes-Dodson law.)

TABLE 13–4 **Some Possible Results of an Experiment on the Effect of Task Difficulty and Arousal Level on Performance (Fictional Data)**

	Result A				Result B				Result C			
	Arousal				*Arousal*				*Arousal*			
Task	*Low*	*Moderate*	*High*	*Overall*	*Low*	*Moderate*	*High*	*Overall*	*Low*	*Moderate*	*High*	*Overall*
Easy	10	10	10	10	10	20	30	20	10	20	30	20
Hard	20	20	20	20	10	20	30	20	20	30	40	30
Overall	15	15	15		10	20	30		15	25	35	

	Result D				Result E				Result F			
Easy	10	20	30	20	10	20	10	13.3	10	20	30	20
Hard	10	20	60	30	20	10	20	16.7	30	20	10	20
Overall	10	20	45		15	15	15		20	20	20	

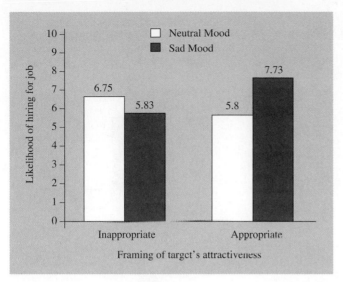

FIGURE 13–2 *Judgments of the physically attractive job candidate as a function of framing of attractiveness (inappropriate vs. appropriate) and manipulated mood (sad vs. neutral), Experiment 3. Higher numbers indicate a greater likelihood of hiring the target for the job. [From Lambert, A. J., Khan, S. R., Lickel, B. A., & Fricke, K. (1997), fig. 1. Mood and the correlation of positive versus negative stereotypes.* Journal of Personality and Social Psychology, 72, *1002–1016. Copyright, 1997, by the American Psychological Association. Reprinted with permission.]*

IDENTIFYING INTERACTION EFFECTS GRAPHICALLY

Another common way of making sense of interaction effects is by graphing the pattern of cell means. This is usually done with a bar graph.[2] Figure 13–2 is reproduced from Lambert et al.'s article. The graphs in Figures 13–3 and 13–4 show the graphs for the fictional results we just considered (shown in Tables 13–3 and 13–4, respectively).

One thing to notice about such graphs is this: Whenever there is an interaction, the pattern of bars on one section of the graph is different from the pattern on the other section of the graph. Thus, in Figure 13–2, the pattern for inappropriate is a step down, but the pattern for appropriate is a step up. The bars having a different pattern is just a graphic way of saying that the pattern of differences between the cell means from row to row is not the same.

Consider Figure 13–3. First look at Results C and D. In Result C the younger and older sets of bars have the same pattern—both step up by 40. In Result D, both are flat. Within both Results C and D, the younger bars and the older bars have the same pattern. These were the examples that did not have interactions. All the other results, which did have interactions, have patterns of bars that are not parallel. For example, in Result A, the two younger bars are flat, but the older bars show a step up. In Result B, the younger bars show a step down from high school to college, but the older bars show a step up from high school to college. In Results E and F, both younger and older bars show a step up, but the younger bars show a smaller step up than the older bars.

Consider Figure 13–4. Results A, B, and C show no interaction—within each result, the patterns of bars for low, moderate, and high arousal are the same. Result D is an interaction. You can see this in the figure as follows: The bars within low are flat and the bars within moderate are flat; but for the high arousal bars, there is a step up from easy to hard tasks. Result E's interaction shows steps up for low and high arousal, but a step down for moderate arousal. Result F's interaction is seen in there being a step up for low, flat for moderate, and a step down for hard.

---

[2]The use of bar graphs to show analysis of variance cell means where there is an interaction effect has become the standard in the last few years. Prior to this, it was more common to use line graphs. We discuss this and provide an example in the section on factorial analysis of variance in research articles.

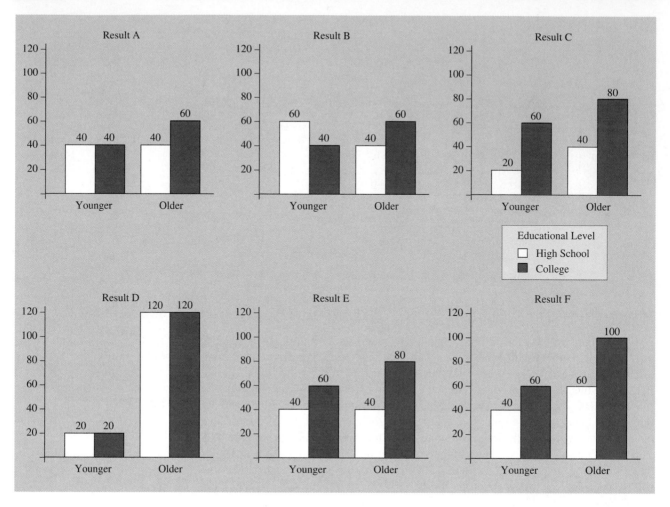

FIGURE 13-3   *Graphs of fictional results in Table 13-3.*

Figure 13–5 shows an alternate way of graphing the results from Table 13–4 than shown in Figure 13–4. Here we have grouped the bars according to hard versus easy. The easy-task bars for low, moderate, and high arousal are next to each other and the hard-task bars for low, moderate, and high arousal are next to each other. This alternate way of grouping is completely equivalent in meaning and leads to exactly the same conclusions. For example, in Result A the three hard-task bars are flat and the three easy-task bars are flat. In Result C, where there is also no interaction, the three easy-task bars rise up in the same step pattern as the three hard-task bars. However, consider Result D, where there is an interaction. The pattern of the easy-task bars is different from the pattern of the hard-task bars. There is a bigger step up from moderate to high arousal in the hard-task bars than there is in the easy-task bars.

You can also see main effects from these graphs. In Figure 13–3, a main effect for age would be shown by the bars for younger being overall higher or lower than the bars for older. For example, in Result C, the bars for older are clearly higher than the bars for younger. What about the main effect for the bars that are not grouped together—college versus high school in this example? With these bars, you have to see whether the overall step pattern goes up or down. For example, in Re-

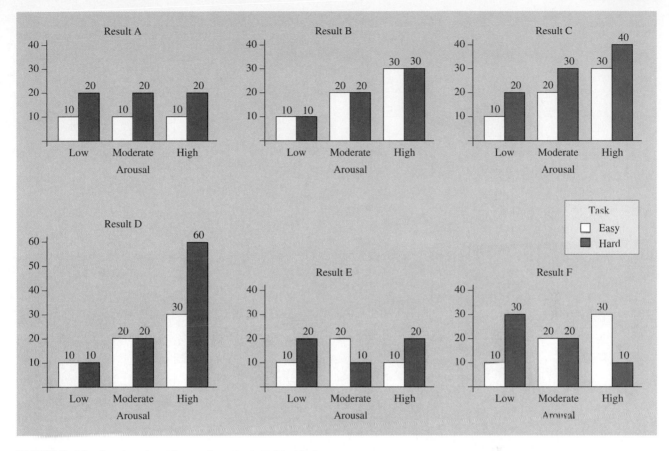

FIGURE 13–4 *Graphs of fictional results in Table 13–4.*

sult C, there is also a main effect for education, because the general pattern of the bars for high school to college goes up, and it does this for both the younger and older bars. Result D shows a main effect for age (the older bars are higher than the younger bars). But Result D does not show a main effect for education—the pattern is flat for both the older and younger bars. Result A in Figure 13–4 shows a main effect for task difficulty but no main effect for arousal. This is because the average heights of the bars are the same for low, moderate, and high arousal; while within each arousal level, the bars step up from easy to hard.

RELATION OF INTERACTION AND MAIN EFFECTS

Any combination of main and interaction effects can be significant. For example, they may all be significant, as in the pattern in Result F of Table 13–3. In this result, older students earn more (a main effect for age), college students earn more (a main effect for level of education), and how much more college students earn depends on age (the interaction effect). Similarly, in Result D of Table 13–4, on the average people perform better at hard tasks (a main effect for task difficulty) and at higher levels of arousal (a main effect for arousal level), but the effect of task difficulty only shows up at high levels of arousal (the interaction). (Notice, however, that the main effect for task difficulty—the higher average for hard tasks—is entirely due to the high arousal condition. We have more to say about this kind of situation shortly.)

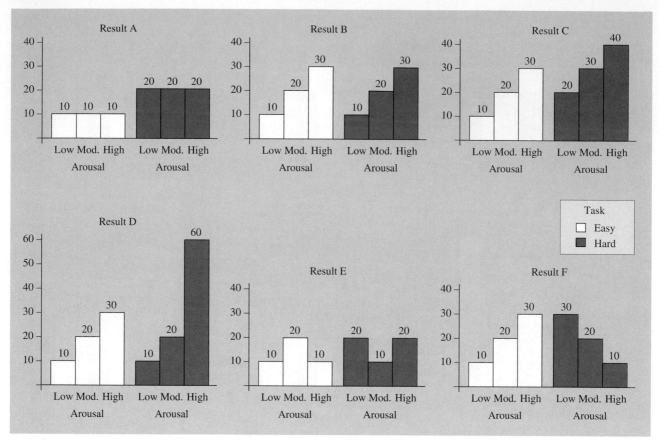

FIGURE 13-5   *Alternative graphs (compared to Figure 13–4) of fictional results in Table 13–4.*

There can also be an interaction effect with no main effects. Result B of Table 13–3 is an example. The average level of income is the same for younger and older (no main effect for age), and it is the same for college and high school (no main effect for level of education). Similarly, in Result F of Table 13–4, the average performance is the same for low, moderate, and high arousal (no main effect for arousal level) and is the same for easy and hard tasks (no main effect for task difficulty). However, in both examples there are clear interactions.

The Lambert et al. (1997) example we considered earlier is actually an example of an interaction with no main effects (see Table 13–2 or Figure 13–2). It is true that on the average the sad participants rated their likelihood to hire higher than the neutral mood participants. However, this difference was not large enough to be statistically significant. Similarly, the difference between stereotype appropriate and inappropriate conditions was not large enough to be significant. Only the interaction effect was significant.

It is also possible for there to be one main effect significant along with an interaction, one main effect significant by itself, or for there to be no significant main or interaction effects. How many of these possibilities can you identify in Tables 13–3 and 13–4?

When there is no interaction, a main effect has a straightforward meaning. However, when there is an interaction along with a main effect, you have to be cautious in drawing conclusions about the main effect. Consider Result D in the arousal and task difficulty example (Table 13–4). Presuming the differences are large enough to be significant, there are two main effects and an interaction. But as we noted earlier, the main effect for task difficulty is entirely due to the high arousal hard-task cell. It would be misleading to make any statement about hard versus easy tasks in general without noting that the effect really depends on the level of arousal.

Sometimes the main effect clearly holds up over and above any interaction. Consider again Result D in the arousal and task difficulty example. In this result, the main effect for arousal holds up over and above the interaction. It is true for both easy and hard tasks that low arousal produces the least performance, moderate the next most, and high arousal the most. (There is still an interaction because the degree that high arousal produces better performance than moderate arousal is more for hard than for easy tasks.)

HOW ARE YOU DOING?

Questions 1 to 3 are based on the results shown below of a fictional study of the effects of vividness and length of examples on number of examples recalled.

	Vividness		
	Low	High	Overall
Short	5	7	6
Long	3	1	2
Overall	4	4	

1. Describe the pattern of results in words.
2. Explain the pattern in terms of numbers.
3. Make two graphs of these results.
4. For a two-way factorial design, what are the possible combinations of main and interaction effects?
5. When there is both a main and an interaction effect, (a) under what conditions must you be cautious in interpreting the main effect, and (b) under what conditions can you still be confident in the overall main effect?

ANSWERS:

1. There is a main effect in which short examples are recalled better and an interaction effect such that there is a bigger advantage of short over long examples when they are highly vivid.
2. The main effect is that on the average people recall six short examples but only two long examples. The interaction effect is that for low vivid examples, people recall two more short than long; but for highly vivid examples, they recall six more short than long.
3. See Figure 13–6.
4. All possible combinations: no main or interaction effects, either main effect only, the interaction only, both main effects but no interaction effect, an interaction effect with either main effect, or an interaction effect with both main effects.
5. (a) When the main effect is found for only one level of the other variable or its direction is reversed at different levels of the other variable.
   (b) When the main effect holds and is in the same direction at each level of the other variable.

BASIC LOGIC OF THE TWO-WAY ANALYSIS OF VARIANCE

The statistical procedure for analyzing the results of a two-way factorial experiment is called a two-way analysis of variance. The basic logic is the same as you learned in Chapter 11. In any analysis of variance, you figure an F ratio, and this F ratio

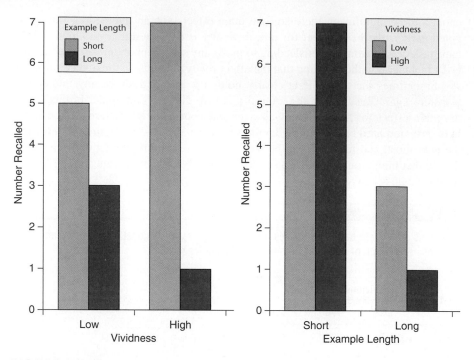

FIGURE 13–6   *Answer to "How Are You Doing?" question 3.*

compares a population variance estimate based on the variation *between* the means of the groupings of interest to a population variance estimate based on variation *within* groups.

THE THREE *F* RATIOS IN A TWO-WAY ANALYSIS OF VARIANCE

In a two-way analysis of variance, there are three *F* ratios: one for the column main effect, one for the row main effect, and one for the interaction effect. The numerator of each of these *F* ratios will be a between-group population variance estimate based on the groupings being compared for the particular main or interaction effect. The within-group variance estimate is the same for all three *F* ratios—it is always the average of the population variance estimates made from the scores within each of the cells.

LOGIC OF THE *F* RATIOS FOR THE ROW AND COLUMN MAIN EFFECTS

One way of understanding how the analysis is done for main effects is as follows. Consider the main effect for the columns. You figure the following *F* ratio: The numerator is a between-group variance estimate based on the variation between the column marginal means. The denominator is a within-group variance estimate based on averaging the variance estimates from each of the cells. Think of the Lambert et al. (1997) study example. The *F* ratio for mood (the columns variable, as we have drawn the chart) is figured as follows. The numerator, the between-group variance estimate, is based on the difference between the sad mood marginal mean and the neutral mood marginal mean. The denominator, the within-group variance esti-

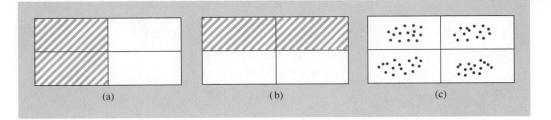

FIGURE 13-7 *A diagram to help you understand a 2 × 2 factorial analysis of variance: (a) the column between-group variance estimate as based on the difference between the mean of the participants in the first (shaded) and second (unshaded) columns, (b) the row between-group estimate as based on the difference between the mean of the participants in the top (shaded) and bottom (unshaded) row, and (c) the within-group variance estimate as based on the variation among scores in each cell.*

mate, is based on averaging the population variance estimates from within each of the four cells.

The procedure for the row main effect is the same idea. It is figured using a between-group variance estimate based on the difference between the two row marginal means. (The Lambert et al. study was designed so that the row marginal means are the mean for all the stereotype appropriate participants and the mean for all the stereotype inappropriate participants.)

Figure 13–7a shows the column between-group variance estimate as based on the difference between the mean of the scores in the first column (the shaded area) and the mean of the scores in the second column (the unshaded area). Figure 13–7b shows the row between-group estimate as based on the difference between the mean of the scores in its top row (the shaded area) and the mean of the scores in the bottom row (the unshaded area). And Figure 13–7c shows the within-group variance estimate (used for all the F ratios) as based on the variation among the scores in each of the cells.

LOGIC OF THE *F* RATIO FOR THE INTERACTION EFFECT

The logic of the F ratio for the interaction effect is a bit more complex. One approach is to think of the interaction effect as a description of the combinations left over after considering the row and column main effects. That is, in a 2 × 2 design, the main effects have grouped the four cells into rows and columns. But it is also possible to divide the cells into other kinds of groupings. Figure 13–8, based on the Lambert et al. study, shows a remaining possible organization of the four cells into two larger groupings: (a) one grouping of two cells consisting of the upper left cell

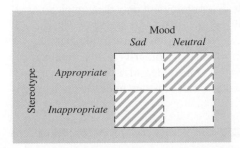

FIGURE 13-8 *Interaction as a comparison of the mean of scores in the shaded cells (neutral mood, stereotype appropriate and sad mood, stereotype inappropriate) to the mean of scores in the unshaded cells (sad mood, stereotype appropriate and neutral mood, stereotype inappropriate) in the study by Lambert et al. (1997).*

BOX 13–1   Personality and Situational Influences on Behavior: An Interaction Effect

In Chapter 12, Box 12–1, you saw that the analysis of variance mimics the way psychological researchers plan research and the way we all think. Knowing this parallel, whether researchers make the comparison consciously or not, they probably often use the crisp model of analysis of variance as a guide to their own logic. And they do this not only when analyzing data or even when designing research, but probably also use the analysis of variance as a metaphor when theorizing as well. In a certain sense, the study of statistics is training in a style of seeing the world.

A clear example of statistics influencing the way psychologists think about their subject matter, not just their data, is in the study of personality. In the 1960s, the field of personality was forever changed by the work of Walter Mischel (1968). Mischel appeared to have demonstrated that as a general rule, *situation* (a street signal turning red, for example, or a well-dressed person asking for help) is a far better predictor of how a person will act than any personality trait (for example, that a person is by nature cautious or altruistic). The embattled personality theorists, typically trained in psychodynamics, struggled to defend themselves within the rules of the game as Mischel had defined them—how much of the variance in behavior could really be predicted by their personality measures? That is, personality theorists were forced to think statistically.

One result of this challenge has been something called "interactionism" (e.g., Endler & Magnusson, 1976). This is the idea that behavior is best predicted by the interaction of person and situation. You can instantly guess what statistical method has had its influence (you are studying it in this chapter).

For example, according to this model, neither the personality trait of anxiety nor the situation of taking the SAT is nearly as good a predictor of anxiety as knowing that a person with a given tendency toward anxiety perceives the taking of the SAT as an anxiety-producing situation. The emphasis is that behavior is being altered constantly by the individual's internal disposition interacting with his or her perception of the changing situation. (In fact, even Walter Mischel now proposed a theory of this kind; Mischel & Shoda, 1995.)

Let's follow an anxious man through some situations. He may feel even more or even less anxiety while proceeding from the testing situation to a dark, empty parking lot, depending again on the interaction of his trait of anxiety and his perception of this new situation. The same is true as he proceeds to drive home on the highway, to open the garage door, to enter an empty house.

According to interactionism, the person is not a passive component but "an intentional active agent in this interaction process" (Endler & Magnusson, 1976, p. 968). The important part of the person aspect of the interaction is how a person thinks about a situation. The important part of the situation is, again, its meaning for the person.

Interactionists admit that this sort of statistical model is still too mechanical and linear. In the real world, there is constant feedback between situation and person, something more like a transaction than an interaction. But they say that to test these models requires more complicated statistical tools. They are coming—for example, Kenny (1995) predicted that within 10 years, event history analysis and multilevel modeling will be the standard tools for data analysis, a prediction that is already starting to come true. So, as the experts in statistics produce more complicated methodologies, personality theorists will adopt them—not only as tools for data analysis but also as models of the mutual influence of the inner person and that person's outer world.

This same influence of statistics on theory is happening in cognition, perception, and learning (Gigerenzer & Murray, 1987) among many other fields of psychology. In a sense, we could say that pioneers in statistics are now determining not only the complexity of psychological research that is possible but also the depth of theorizing itself. They are carving out the channels through which psychologists' actual thinking patterns flow and therefore, at least for the present, are shaping and directing much of our understanding of psychology.

(stereotype appropriate and sad mood) along with the lower right cell (stereotype inappropriate and neutral mood), and (b) another grouping of two cells consisting of the lower left cell (stereotype inappropriate and sad mood) and the upper right cell (stereotype appropriate and neutral mood). The between-group variance estimate for the interaction effect can then be figured from the variation between the means of these two groupings.

With a 2 × 2 design, there is only one organization of pairs of cells that is not already accounted for by the row and column organizations—the grouping pattern shown as in the example in Figure 13–8. But with a larger two-way design, such as a 2 × 3, there is more than one way to make the groupings, and all must be taken into account. Thus, it can be quite complicated to figure the between-group variance estimate for the interaction effect when dealing with situations other than a 2 × 2 design. Fortunately, it turns out that figuring the interaction between-group variance estimate is much more straightforward from the perspective of the structural model you learned in Chapter 12, to which we turn next.

HOW ARE YOU DOING?

1. In a two-way analysis of variance, what is the numerator of the F ratio for the row main effect?
2. In a 2 × 2 analysis of variance, what is the numerator of the F ratio for the interaction main effect?
3. In any two-way analysis of variance, what is the denominator of the F ratio for (a) each main effect and (b) the interaction?

ANSWERS:

1. The estimated population variance estimate based on the variation between the two row means.
2. The estimated population variance estimate based on the variation between the means of the two diagonals.
3. (a) The within-cell population variance estimate. (b) The within-cell population variance estimate.

FIGURING A TWO-WAY ANALYSIS OF VARIANCE

As just noted, to figure the interaction effect in a factorial analysis of variance beyond a 2 × 2 design, it is much easier to use the structural model approach of Chapter 12. Rather than mix approaches, researchers carry out the entire factorial analysis of variance using the structural model approach. Thus, in this section we first consider the structural model approach as it applies to factorial analysis of variance and then go into the details of how to do the figuring for a full factorial analysis of variance.

THE STRUCTURAL MODEL FOR THE TWO-WAY ANALYSIS OF VARIANCE

From the structural model perspective, each score's overall deviation from the grand mean can be divided into several components. In a two-way analysis, there are four parts of this overall deviation (see Figure 13–9):

1. The score's deviation from the mean of its cell (used for the within-group population variance estimate).

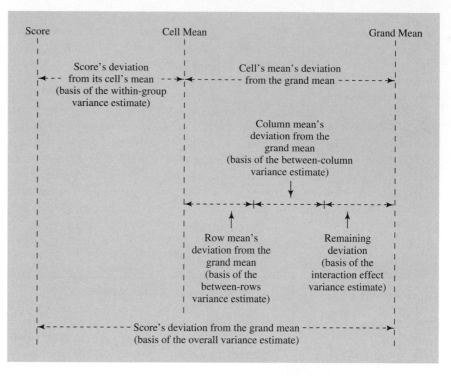

FIGURE 13–9   *Dividing up each score's deviation from the grand mean.*

2. The score's row's mean from the grand mean (used for the between-group population variance estimate for the main effect for the variable that divides the rows).

3. The score's column's mean from the grand mean (used for the between-group estimate for the main effect for the variable that divides the columns.)

4. What remains after subtracting out the other three deviations from the overall deviation from the grand mean (used for the between-group estimate for the interaction effect).

You might want to study Figure 13–9—it is the best way to understand and remember what's going on.

STEPS FOR THE TWO-WAY ANALYSIS OF VARIANCE

When figuring an analysis of variance using the structural model, you figure the F ratios as follows:

   ❶ **Figure the mean of each cell, row, and column, plus the grand mean of all scores.**

   ❷ **Figure all the deviation scores of each type.**

   ❸ **Square each deviation score.** This gives the squared deviations.

   ❹ **Add up the squared deviation scores of each type.** This gives the sums of squared deviations.

   ❺ **Divide each sum of squared deviations by its appropriate degrees of freedom.** This gives the variance estimates.

   ❻ **Divide the various between-group variance estimates by the within-group variance estimates.** This gives the F ratios.

In terms of formulas, the sums of squares are as follows:

(13-1)
$$SS_{Rows} = \Sigma(M_{Row} - GM)^2$$

The sum of squared deviations for rows is the sum of each score's row's mean's squared deviation from the grand mean.

(13-2)
$$SS_{Columns} = \Sigma(M_{Column} - GM)^2$$

The sum of squared deviations for columns is the sum of each score's column's mean's squared deviation from the grand mean.

(13-3)
$$SS_{Interaction} = \Sigma[(X - GM) - (X - M) - (M_{Row} - GM) - (M_{Column} - GM)]^2$$

The sum of squared deviations for the interaction is the sum of the squares of each score's deviation from the grand mean minus its deviation from its cell's mean, minus its row's mean's deviation from the grand mean, minus its column's mean's deviation from the grand mean.

(13-4)
$$SS_{Within} = \Sigma(X - M)^2$$

The sum of squared deviations within cells is the sum of each score's squared deviation from its cell's mean.

(13-5)
$$SS_{Total} = \Sigma(X - GM)^2$$

The sum of squared deviations total is the sum of each score's squared deviation from the grand mean.

In these formulas, SS_{Rows}, $SS_{Columns}$, $SS_{Interaction}$, and SS_{Within} are the sums of squared deviations for rows, columns, interaction, and within cells. The sum sign (Σ) tells you to add up over all scores (not just over all rows or columns or cells). GM is the grand mean; X is the score. M_{Row} and M_{Column} are the mean of a score's row or column, and M is the mean of a score's cell.

As usual, the different individual sums of squares add up to the total sums of squares. (You can use this as a check on your arithmetic.) Stated as a formula,

(13-6)
$$SS_{Total} = SS_{Rows} + SS_{Columns} + SS_{Interaction} + SS_{Within}$$

The sum of squared deviations total is the sum of squared deviations for rows, plus the sum of squared deviations for columns, plus the sum of squared deviations for the interaction, plus the sum of squared deviations within cells.

The formulas for the population variance estimates are, as usual, the sums of squares divided by the degrees of freedom:

(13-7)
$$S^2_{Rows} \text{ or } MS_{Rows} = \frac{SS_{Rows}}{df_{Rows}}$$

The population variance estimate based on the variation between rows is the sum of squared deviations for rows divided by the degrees of freedom for rows.

(13-8)
$$S^2_{Columns} \text{ or } MS_{Columns} = \frac{SS_{Columns}}{df_{Columns}}$$

The population variance estimate based on the variation between columns is the sum of squared deviations for columns divided by the degrees of freedom for columns.

The population variance estimate based on the variation associated with the interaction is the sum of squared deviations for the interaction divided by the degrees of freedom for the interaction.

$$S^2_{\text{Interaction}} \text{ or } MS_{\text{Interaction}} = \frac{SS_{\text{Interaction}}}{df_{\text{Interaction}}}$$

(13-9)

The population variance estimate based on the variation within cells is the sum of squared deviations within cells divided by the within-cells degrees of freedom.

$$S^2_{\text{Within}} \text{ or } MS_{\text{Within}} = \frac{SS_{\text{Within}}}{df_{\text{Within}}}$$

(13-10)

In these formulas, S^2_{Rows} or MS_{Rows} is the population variance estimate for rows; S^2_{Columns} or MS_{Columns} is the population variance estimate for columns; $S^2_{\text{Interaction}}$ or $MS_{\text{Interaction}}$ is the population variance estimate for the interaction; and S^2_{Within} or MS_{Within} is the within-group population variance estimate.

The F ratios are the population variance estimates for the different effects, each divided by the within-group population variance estimate:

The F ratio for the row main effect is the population variance estimate based on the variation between rows divided by the population variance estimate based on the variation within cells.

$$F_{\text{Rows}} = \frac{S^2_{\text{Rows}}}{S^2_{\text{Within}}} \text{ or } \frac{MS_{\text{Rows}}}{MS_{\text{Within}}}$$

(13-11)

The F ratio for the column main effect is the population variance estimate based on the variation between columns divided by the population variance estimate based on the variation within cells.

$$F_{\text{Columns}} = \frac{S^2_{\text{Columns}}}{S^2_{\text{Within}}} \text{ or } \frac{MS_{\text{Columns}}}{MS_{\text{Within}}}$$

(13-12)

The F ratio for the interaction effect is the population variance estimate based on the variation associated with the interaction divided by the population variance estimate based on the variation within cells.

$$F_{\text{Interaction}} = \frac{S^2_{\text{Interaction}}}{S^2_{\text{Within}}} \text{ or } \frac{MS_{\text{Interaction}}}{MS_{\text{Within}}}$$

(13-13)

In these formulas, F_{Rows} is the F ratio for the row main effect; F_{Columns} is the F ratio for the column main effect; and $F_{\text{Interaction}}$ is the F ratio for the interaction effect.

DEGREES OF FREEDOM IN A TWO-WAY ANALYSIS OF VARIANCE

Degrees of Freedom for Between-Group Variance Estimates for the Main Effects. The degrees of freedom for each main effect (each between-group variance estimate) is the number of levels of the variable minus 1. For example, if there are two levels, as in each main effect in the Lambert et al. study, there is 1 degree of freedom. In the arousal levels and task difficulty examples we considered earlier, the columns main effect (arousal level) had three levels. Thus, there were 2 degrees of freedom for this main effect.

Stated as formulas,

(13-14) $$df_{\text{Rows}} = N_{\text{Rows}} - 1$$

The degrees of freedom for the rows main effect is the number of rows minus 1.

(13-15) $$df_{\text{Columns}} = N_{\text{Columns}} - 1$$

The degrees of freedom for the columns main effect equals the number of columns minus 1.

In these formulas, N_{Rows} is the number of rows, and N_{Columns} is the number of columns.

Degrees of Freedom for the Interaction Effect Variance Estimate. The degrees of freedom for the variance estimate for the interaction effect is the total number of cells minus the number of degrees of freedom for both main effects, minus 1. In the Lambert et al. study, there were four cells and 1 degree of freedom for each main effect. This leaves 2 degrees of freedom, minus 1 more, leaving 1 for the interaction. In the arousal level and task difficulty examples, there were six cells. There were 2 degrees of freedom for the column effect and 1 for the row effect (easy versus hard task). This leaves 3 degrees of freedom. When 1 more is subtracted, there are 2 left for the interaction.

Stated as a formula,

(13-16) $$df_{\text{Interaction}} = N_{\text{Cells}} - df_{\text{Rows}} - df_{\text{Columns}} - 1$$

The degrees of freedom for the interaction effect is the number of cells minus the degrees of freedom for the row main effect minus the degrees of freedom for the column main effect minus 1.

In this formula N_{Cells} is the number of cells. Applying the formula to the Lambert et al. study,

$$df_{\text{Interaction}} = N_{\text{Cells}} - df_{\text{Rows}} - df_{\text{Columns}} - 1 = 4 - 1 - 1 - 1 = 1$$

Applying the formula to the arousal and task difficulty example,

$$df_{\text{Interaction}} = N_{\text{Cells}} - df_{\text{Rows}} - df_{\text{Columns}} - 1 = 6 - 1 - 2 - 1 = 2$$

Degrees of Freedom for the Within-Group Population Variance Estimate. As usual, the within-group degrees of freedom is the sum of the degrees of freedom for all the groups (in this case, all the cells). For each cell, you take its number of scores minus 1, then add up what you get for all the cells. In terms of a formula,

(13-17) $$df_{\text{Within}} = df_1 + df_2 + \ldots + df_{\text{Last}}$$

The degrees of freedom for the within-cells population variance estimate is the sum of the degrees of freedom for all the cells.

In this formula, df_1, df_2, ..., df_{Last} are the degrees of freedom for each cell (the number of scores in the cell minus 1), in succession, from the first cell to the last.

Total Degrees of Freedom. The total degrees of freedom, as usual, is the number of scores minus 1. In terms of a formula,

(13-18) $$df_{\text{Total}} = N - 1$$

The total degrees of freedom is the number of scores minus 1.

You can also figure the total degrees of freedom by adding up all the individual degrees of freedom (for columns, rows, interaction, and within). This provides a check of your arithmetic in figuring degrees of freedom. In terms of a formula,

> The total degrees of freedom is the degrees of freedom for the row main effect plus the degrees of freedom for the column main effect plus the degrees of freedom for the interaction effect plus the degrees of freedom for the within-cell population variance estimate.

$$df_{Total} = df_{Rows} + df_{Columns} + df_{Interaction} + df_{Within} \qquad (13\text{-}19)$$

TABLE FOR A TWO-WAY ANALYSIS OF VARIANCE

The analysis of variance table in a two-way analysis is similar to the ones in Chapter 12 (where you were doing one-way analyses of variance). However, with a two-way analysis of variance there is a line in the table for each between-group effect. Table 13–5 shows the layout.

EXAMPLE

Wong and Csikszentmihalyi (1991) had 170 high-school students carry beepers for a week. The students were beeped at random intervals (about every 2 waking hours). Whenever they were beeped, the students filled out a questionnaire about what they were doing at the moment. The study was a 2×2 factorial design for gender and whether students had a high or low desire to affiliate. One of the variables measured was number of times over the week that the student was engaged in social activities when beeped.

Results are shown in Table 13–6, exactly as reported by Wong and Csikszentmihalyi. However, to keep the example simple, we have made up scores that give the same cell and marginal means but with only 10 participants per cell. These scores and the figuring for all the deviations are shown in Table 13–7. Table 13–8 shows the cutoff F values and the analysis of variance table. Figure 13–10 graphs the results. We can explore the example following the usual step-by-step hypothesis-testing procedure.

❶ **Restate the question as a research hypothesis and a null hypothesis about the populations for each main effect and the interaction effect.** There are four populations:

Population 1, 1: Girls who are low on desire for affiliation
Population 1, 2: Girls who are high on desire for affiliation
Population 2, 1: Boys who are low on desire for affiliation
Population 2, 2: Boys who are high on desire for affiliation

The first null hypothesis is that the combined populations for girls (Populations 1, 1 and 1, 2) have the same mean number of times engaged in social activities as the combined populations for boys (Populations 2, 1 and 2, 2). This is the null hy-

TABLE 13–6 Cell and Marginal Means for Number of Times Engaged in Social Activities (Data from Wong & Csikszentmihalyi, 1991)

	Affiliation		
	Low	High	
Boys	10.30	9.22	9.76
Girls	15.75	18.51	17.13
	13.03	13.87	13.45

(Gender)

TABLE 13–5 Layout of an Analysis of Variance Table for a Two-Way Analysis of Variance

Source	SS	df	MS	F
Between:				
Columns	$SS_{Columns}$	$df_{Columns}$	$MS_{Columns}$	$F_{Columns}$
Rows	SS_{Rows}	df_{Rows}	MS_{Rows}	F_{Rows}
Interaction	$SS_{Interaction}$	$df_{Interaction}$	$MS_{Interaction}$	$F_{Interaction}$
Within	SS_{Within}	df_{Within}	MS_{Within}	
Total	SS_{Total}	df_{Total}		

TABLE 13–7 Scores, Squared Deviations, and Sums of Squared Deviations for Fictional Data Based on the Wong and Csikszentmihalyi (1991) Study

	Low Affiliation					High Affiliation				
X	$(X - GM)^2$	$(X - M)^2$	$(M_{Row} - GM)^2$	$(M_{Column} - GM)^2$	INT^2	X	$(X - GM)^2$	$(X - M)^2$	$(M_{Row} - GM)^2$	$(M_{Column} - GM)^2$	INT^2

Boys

X	$(X - GM)^2$	$(X - M)^2$	$(M_{Row} - GM)^2$	$(M_{Column} - GM)^2$	INT^2	X	$(X - GM)^2$	$(X - M)^2$	$(M_{Row} - GM)^2$	$(M_{Column} - GM)^2$	INT^2
12.1	1.82	3.24	13.62	.18	.92	11.1	5.52	3.53	13.62	.18	.92
11.4	4.20	1.21	13.62	.18	.92	10.4	9.30	1.39	13.62	.18	.92
11.2	5.06	.81	13.62	.18	.92	10.2	10.56	.96	13.62	.18	.92
10.9	6.50	.36	13.62	.18	.92	9.8	13.32	.34	13.62	.18	.92
10.3	9.92	.00	13.62	.18	.92	9.2	18.06	0.00	13.62	.18	.92
9.8	13.32	.25	13.62	.18	.92	9.1	18.92	.01	13.62	.18	.92
9.7	14.06	.36	13.62	.18	.92	8.9	20.70	.10	13.62	.18	.92
9.5	15.60	.64	13.62	.18	.92	8.7	22.56	.27	13.62	.18	.92
9.3	17.22	1.00	13.62	.18	.92	8.2	27.56	1.04	13.62	.18	.92
8.8	21.62	2.25	13.62	.18	.92	6.6	46.92	6.86	13.62	.18	.92
103.0	109.32	10.12	136.20	1.80	9.20	92.2	193.42	14.50	136.20	1.80	9.20

Girls

X	$(X - GM)^2$	$(X - M)^2$	$(M_{Row} - GM)^2$	$(M_{Column} - GM)^2$	INT^2	X	$(X - GM)^2$	$(X - M)^2$	$(M_{Row} - GM)^2$	$(M_{Column} - GM)^2$	INT^2
17.4	15.60	2.74	13.54	.18	.92	22.0	73.10	2.72	13.54	.18	.92
17.1	13.32	1.82	13.54	.18	.92	20.5	49.70	3.96	13.54	.18	.92
16.8	11.22	1.10	13.54	.18	.92	19.9	41.60	1.93	13.54	.18	.92
16.7	10.56	.90	13.54	.18	.92	19.1	31.92	.35	13.54	.18	.92
15.5	4.20	.06	13.54	.18	.92	18.5	25.50	0.00	13.54	.18	.92
15.3	3.42	.20	13.54	.18	.92	17.4	15.60	1.23	13.54	.18	.92
15.0	2.40	.56	13.54	.18	.92	17.0	12.60	2.28	13.54	.18	.92
15.4	3.80	.12	13.54	.18	.92	17.1	13.32	1.99	13.54	.18	.92
14.3	.72	2.10	13.54	.18	.92	17.1	13.32	1.99	13.54	.18	.92
14.0	.30	3.06	13.54	.18	.92	16.5	9.30	4.04	13.54	.18	.92
157.5	65.54	12.64	135.40	1.80	9.20	185.1	285.96	29.95	135.40	1.80	9.20

M	= mean of the score's cell
M_{Row}	= mean of the score's row
M_{Column}	= mean of the score's column
INT	= score's remaining deviation for the interaction

Examples of figuring of deviations, using the first score in the Low Boys cell:

        Ⓐ   **Ⓑ**   **Ⓒ**

$$(X - GM)^2 = (12.1 - 13.45)^2 = -1.35^2 = 1.82$$
$$(X - M)^2 = (12.1 - 10.30)^2 = 1.80^2 = 3.24$$
$$(M_{Row} - GM)^2 = (9.76 - 13.45)^2 = -3.69^2 = 13.62$$
$$(M_{Column} - GM)^2 = (13.03 - 13.45)^2 = -0.42^2 = .18$$
$$INT^2 = [(X - GM) - (X - M) - (M_{Row} - GM) - (M_{Column} - GM)]^2 = [(-1.35) - (1.80) - (-3.69) - (-.42)]^2$$
$$= (-1.35 - 1.80 + 3.69 + .42)^2 = .96^2 = .92$$

SS_{Total}	= 109.32 + 193.42 + 65.54 + 285.96 = 654.24	
SS_{Within}	= 10.12 + 14.50 + 12.64 + 29.95 = 67.21	
SS_{Row}	= 136.20 + 136.20 + 135.40 + 135.40 = 543.20	**Ⓓ**
SS_{Column}	= 1.80 + 1.80 + 1.80 + 1.80 = 7.20	
$SS_{Interaction}$	= 9.20 + 9.20 + 9.20 + 9.20 = 36.80	

Accuracy check: $SS_{Total} = 654.24$; $SS_{Within} + SS_{Rows} + SS_{Columns} + SS_{Interaction} = 67.21 + 543.20 + 7.20 + 36.80 = 654.41$ (results are within rounding error).

TABLE 13-8 Analysis of Variance Using Sums of Squares Based on the Wong and Csikszentmihalyi (1991) Study (Fictional Data)

F needed for Gender main effect ($df = 1, 36; p < .05$) = 4.12 ($df = 1, 35$ from table)
F needed for Affiliation main effect for ($df = 1, 36; p < .05$) = 4.12
F needed for interaction effect ($df = 1, 36; p < .05$) = 4.12

Source	SS	df	MS	F	
Gender	543.20	1	543.20	290.48	Reject the null hypothesis.
Affiliation	7.20	1	7.20	3.85	Do not reject the null hypothesis.
Gender × affiliation	36.80	1	36.80	19.68	Reject the null hypothesis.
Within cells	67.21	36	1.87		

pothesis for testing the main effect for gender (girls versus boys). The research hypothesis is that the populations of girls and boys have different means.

The second null hypothesis is that the combined populations for those low on desire for affiliation (Populations 1, 1 and 2, 1) have the same mean number of times engaged in social activities as the combined populations for those high on desire for affiliation (Populations 1, 2 and 2, 2). This is the null hypothesis for testing the main effect for desire for affiliation (low versus high). The research hypothesis is that populations high and low on desire to affiliate have different means.

The third null hypothesis is that the difference between the mean number of social activities of the two populations for girls (Population 1, 1 minus Population 1, 2) will be the same as the difference between the means of the two populations for boys (Population 2, 1 minus Population 2, 2). This is the null hypothesis for testing the interaction effect. (It could also be stated, with no change in meaning, as the difference between the two populations for lows equaling the difference between the two populations for highs.) The research hypothesis is that these differences will not be the same.

❷ **Determine the characteristics of the comparison distributions.** The three comparison distributions will be F distributions. The denominator degrees of freedom are the sum of the degrees of freedom in each of the cells (the number of scores in the cell minus 1). In this example, there are 10 participants in each of the four cells. This makes 9 degrees of freedom per cell, for a total of 36. The numerator for

FIGURE 13-10 *Graph of fictional (simplified) data based on the results of the Wong and Csikszentmihalyi (1991) study.*

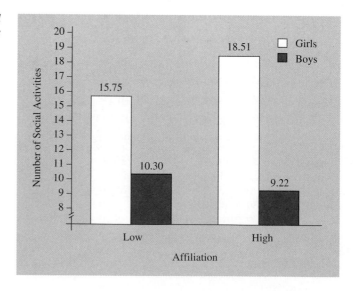

the comparison distribution for the gender main effect has 1 degree of freedom (2 rows minus 1); the numerator for the desire for affiliation main effect also has 1 degree of freedom; and the numerator degrees of freedom for the interaction effect is, again, 1 (it is the number of cells, four, minus the degrees of freedom for columns, minus the degrees of freedom for rows, minus 1). As a check of the accuracy of the degrees of freedom calculations, the three numerators plus the denominator degrees of freedom come out to $1 + 1 + 1 + 36 = 39$; this is the same as the total degrees of freedom figured as number of participants minus 1 (that is, $40 - 1 = 39$).

❸ **Determine the cutoff sample scores on the comparison distributions at which each null hypothesis should be rejected.** Using the .05 significance level, Table A–3 (Appendix A) gives a cutoff for 1 and 35 degrees of freedom of 4.12 (the closest available on the table below 1 and 36). The degrees of freedom and the significance level are the same in this example for both main effects and the interaction, so the cutoff is the same for all three.

❹ **Determine your samples' scores on each comparison distribution.** This requires figuring three F ratios.

    Ⓐ **Figure the mean of each cell, row, and column, plus the grand mean of all scores.** These are shown at the top of Table 13–7.

    Ⓑ **Figure all the deviation scores of each type.** To save space, Table 13–7 shows only the squared deviations. However, below the table of squared deviations, we show how we figured all the deviations for the first score. For example, the deviation of the first score from the grand mean is 12.1 minus 13.45.

    Ⓒ **Square each deviation score.** All of these squared deviations are shown in Table 13–7. For example, the first score's deviation of -1.35 from the grand mean, when squared, is 1.82.

    Ⓓ **Add up the squared deviation scores of each type.** For example, for the sum of squared deviations from the grand mean, the total in the first cell (Low Affiliation Boys) is 109.32; for the second cell, 193.42; for the third, 65.54; and for the fourth, 285.96. This adds up to a total of 654.24. That is, $SS_{Total} = 654.24$. Remember that the *sums* of the various squared deviations (SS_{Within}, SS_{Rows}, $SS_{Columns}$, $SS_{Interaction}$) add up. But within a single participant, the various squared deviations do not add up to the overall squared deviation of the score from the grand mean. Table 13–7 also shows the check for accuracy: The sum of the squared deviations from the grand mean equals the total of the sums of the other four kinds of squared deviations (within rounding error).

    (One other point about the figuring shown in Table 13–7: Ordinarily, in a 2×2 analysis, all of the squared deviations for rows are the same throughout (as are all the squared deviations for columns and all the squared deviations for interaction). The slight difference of 136.20 versus 135.40 between the squared row deviations for the bottom-row scores versus the top-row scores is due to rounding error in figuring the row means.)

    Ⓔ **Divide each sum of squared deviations by its appropriate degrees of freedom.** This is shown in Table 13–8. For example, the population variance estimate for Gender (the rows) comes out to 543.20, the sum of squares of 543.20 divided by the degrees of freedom of 1.

    Ⓕ **Divide the various between-group variance estimates by the within-group variance estimates.** This gives the F ratios and is shown in Table 13–8. For example, the F for Gender comes out to 290.48, the between-rows population variance estimate of 543.20 divided by the within-cells population variance estimate of 1.87.

❺ **Decide whether to reject the null hypotheses.** The F ratio for the gender main effect of 290.48 is much larger than the cutoff of 4.12. Thus, you can reject

Tip for Success

When figuring the deviation for the interaction effect, keep close track of the signs of the deviations you are subtracting and remember that this interaction deviation, prior to squaring, is figured from the original unsquared deviations, not the squared deviations.

the null hypothesis that the girls' and boys' populations have the same mean amount of social activity. That is, the gender main effect is significant. The F of 3.85 for the need for affiliation main effect did not quite reach the necessary 4.12 cutoff. This effect can be said to have approached statistical significance but not to have reached it. Finally, the interaction effect F of 19.68 exceeds 4.12, so the interaction effect is also significant. (In the actual study, the same basic pattern was found—the gender main effect and the interaction effect were significant, while the desire for affiliation main effect approached but did not quite reach significance.) Before reading further, you might try to put into words what this interaction means.

As can be seen in Figure 13–10 (and from the cell means in Table 13–6), the gender main effect is due to girls engaging in more social activities than boys. The interaction effect is due to desire for affiliation being associated with more social activities for girls but essentially unrelated to number of social activities for boys. That is, there was a difference in number of activities between girls who were high and those who were low on desire for affiliation. But among boys, the difference was almost nonexistent (and even slightly in the opposite direction). This is why, combining boys and girls overall, desire for affiliation appeared to have little or no influence on activities. You can see again how using an analysis of variance to look at interaction effects uncovered an interesting relationship among these variables.

SUMMARY OF PROCEDURES FOR A TWO-WAY ANALYSIS OF VARIANCE

Table 13–9 summarizes the steps of hypothesis testing and Table 13–10 shows the analysis of variance table and the formulas for a two-way analysis of variance.[3]

[3]There are also calculational formulas for the sums of squares that researchers used before the advent of the computer. These formulas make it easier to carry out the figuring by hand (or with a hand calculator) when working with the results of a real study with a large number of scores in each cell. However, we strongly urge you to use the definitional formulas and procedures shown in Tables 13–9 and 13–10 when working the practice problems in this book. These definitional formulas reinforce the underlying principles that are the main things you are trying to learn. However, should you have need of them, here are the computational formulas:

$$SS_{\text{Total}} = \Sigma X^2 - \frac{(\Sigma X)^2}{N} \tag{13-20}$$

$$SS_{\text{Between}} = \frac{(\Sigma X_1)^2}{n} + \frac{(\Sigma X_2)^2}{n} + \cdots + \frac{(\Sigma X_{\text{Last}})^2}{n} - \frac{(\Sigma X)^2}{N} \tag{13-21}$$

$$SS_{\text{Within}} = SS_{\text{Total}} - SS_{\text{Between}} \tag{13-22}$$

$$SS_{\text{Rows}} = \frac{(\Sigma X_{\text{Row}_1})^2}{n_{\text{Row}}} + \frac{(\Sigma X_{\text{Row}_2})^2}{n_{\text{Row}}} + \cdots$$
$$+ \frac{(\Sigma X_{\text{Row}_{\text{last}}})^2}{n_{\text{Row}}} - \frac{(\Sigma X)^2}{N} \tag{13-23}$$

$$SS_{\text{Columns}} = \frac{(\Sigma X_{\text{Column}_1})^2}{n_{\text{Column}}} + \frac{(\Sigma X_{\text{Column}_2})^2}{n_{\text{Column}}} + \cdots$$
$$+ \frac{(\Sigma X_{\text{Column}_{\text{last}}})^2}{n_{\text{Column}}} - \frac{(\Sigma X)^2}{N} \tag{13-24}$$

$$SS_{\text{Interaction}} = SS_{\text{Between}} - SS_{\text{Rows}} - SS_{\text{Columns}} \tag{13-25}$$

In these formulas, ΣX^2 is the sum of each squared score, $(\Sigma X)^2$ is the square of the sum of all the scores; N is the total number of scores; $(\Sigma X_1)^2$, $(\Sigma X_2)^2$, . . . , $(\Sigma X_{\text{Last}})^2$ are the squares of the sums of all scores within each cell; n is the number of participants in each cell; $(\Sigma X_{\text{Row}_1})^2$, $(\Sigma X_{\text{Row}_2})^2$, . . . , $(\Sigma X_{\text{Row}_{\text{last}}})^2$ are the squares of the sums of all scores within each row; n_{Row} is the number of participants in each row; $(\Sigma X_{\text{Column}_1})^2$, $(\Sigma X_{\text{Column}_2})^2$, . . . , $(\Sigma X_{\text{Column}_{\text{last}}})^2$ are the squares of the sums of all scores within each column; and N_{Column} is the number of participants in each column.

TABLE 13–9	Steps of Hypothesis Testing for a Two-Way Analysis of Variance

❶ **Restate the question as a research hypothesis and a null hypothesis about the populations for each main effect and the interaction effect.**

❷ **Determine the characteristics of the comparison distributions.**
   a. The numerator degrees of freedom for the F distribution for the columns main effect is the number of columns minus 1: $df_{Columns} = N_{Columns} - 1$.
   b. The numerator degrees of freedom for the F distribution for the rows main effect is the number of rows minus 1: $df_{Rows} = N_{Rows} - 1$.
   c. The numerator degrees of freedom for the F distribution for the interaction effect is the number of cells minus the degrees of freedom for columns minus the degrees of freedom for rows minus 1: $df_{Interaction} = N_{Cells} - df_{Columns} - df_{Rows} - 1$.
   d. The comparison distributions will be F distributions with denominator degrees of freedom equal to the sum of the degrees of freedom in each of the cells (the number of scores in the cell minus 1): $df_{Within} = df_1 + df_2 + \ldots + df_{Last}$.
   e. Check the accuracy of your figuring by making sure that all of the degrees of freedom add up to the total degrees of freedom: $df_{Total} = N - 1 = df_{Within} + df_{Columns} + df_{Rows} + df_{Interaction}$.

❸ **Determine the cutoff sample scores on the comparison distributions at which each null hypothesis should be rejected.**
   A. Determine the desired significance levels.
   B. Look up the appropriate cutoffs in an F table (Table A–3).

❹ **Determine your samples' scores on each comparison distribution.**
   ❶ **Figure the mean of each cell, row, and column, plus the grand mean of all scores.**
   ❷ **Figure all the deviation scores of each type.** For each score figure:
      i. Its deviation from the grand mean: $X - GM$.
      ii. Its deviation from its cell's mean: $X - M$.
      iii. Its row's mean's deviation from the grand mean: $M_{Row} - GM$.
      iv. Its column's mean's deviation from the grand mean: $M_{Column} - GM$.
      v. Its deviation from the grand mean minus all the other deviations: Interaction deviation = $(X - GM) - (X - M) - (M_{Row} - GM) - (M_{Column} - GM)$.
   ❸ **Square each deviation score.** This gives the squared deviations.
   ❹ **Add up the squared deviation scores of each type.** This gives the sums of squared deviations: SS_{Total}, SS_{Within}, $SS_{Columns}$, SS_{Rows}, and $SS_{Interaction}$.
   ❺ **Divide each sum of squared deviations by its appropriate degrees of freedom.** This gives the variance estimates. That is, $MS_{Columns}$ or $S^2_{Columns} = SS_{Columns}/df_{Columns}$; MS_{Rows} or $S^2_{Rows} = SS_{Rows}/df_{Rows}$; $MS_{Interaction}$ or $S^2_{Interaction} = SS_{Interaction}/df_{Interaction}$.
   ❻ **Divide the various between-group variance estimates by the within-group variance estimates.** This gives the F ratios: $F_{Columns} = S^2_{Columns} S^2_{Within}$ or $MS_{Columns}/MS_{Within}$; $F_{Rows} = S^2_{Rows}/S^2_{Within}$ or MS_{Rows}/MS_{Within}; $F_{Interaction} = S^2_{Interaction}/S^2_{Within}$ or $MS_{Interaction}/MS_{Within}$.

❺ **Decide whether to reject the null hypotheses.** Compare scores in steps 3 and 4.

ASSUMPTIONS IN THE TWO-WAY ANALYSIS OF VARIANCE

The assumptions for a factorial analysis of variance are the same as for the one-way analysis of variance except that the requirements of population normality and equal variances apply to the populations that go with each cell.

HOW ARE YOU DOING?

1. List the steps for figuring the F ratios in a two-way factorial analysis of variance.
2. Write the formula for the sum of squares for rows and define each of the symbols.
3. Write the formula for the sum of squares for the interaction and define each of the symbols.
4. Write the formula for the degrees of freedom for the interaction and define each of the symbols.
5. Here are the scores for participants A through H (a total of eight; two participants per cell) for the fictional study of the effects of vividness and length of examples on number of examples recalled used in an earlier "How Are You Doing?" question. Find the three F ratios (and test their significance at $p < .05$).

Participant	Number Recalled	Vividness Condition	Length Condition
A	6	Low	Short
B	4	Low	Short
C	9	High	Short
D	5	High	Short
E	2	Low	Long
F	4	Low	Long
G	1	High	Long
H	1	High	Long

6. What are the assumptions for a factorial analysis of variance?

ANSWERS

1. **Ⓐ Figure the mean of each cell, row, and column, plus the grand mean of all scores.**
   Ⓑ Figure all the deviation scores of each type.
   Ⓒ Square each deviation score.

TABLE 13–10   Analysis of Variance Table and Formulas for a Two-Way Analysis of Variance

Analysis of variance table:

Source	SS	df	MS	F
Between:				
Columns	$SS_{Columns}$	$df_{Columns}$	$MS_{Columns}$ (or $S^2_{Columns}$)	$F_{Columns}$
Rows	SS_{Rows}	df_{Rows}	MS_{Rows} (or S^2_{Rows})	F_{Rows}
Interaction	$SS_{Interaction}$	$df_{Interaction}$	$MS_{Interaction}$ (or $S^2_{Interaction}$)	$F_{Interaction}$
Within	SS_{Within}	df_{Within}	MS_{Within} (or S^2_{Within})	
Total	SS_{Total}	df_{Total}		

Formulas for each section of the analysis of variance table:

Source	SS	df	MS	F
Between:				
Columns	$\Sigma(M_{Column} - GM)^2$	$N_{Columns} - 1$	$SS_{Columns}/df_{Columns}$	$MS_{Columns}/MS_{Within}$
Rows	$\Sigma(M_{Row} - GM)^2$	$N_{Rows} - 1$	SS_{Rows}/df_{Rows}	MS_{Rows}/MS_{Within}
Interaction	$\Sigma[(X - GM)$ $- (X - M)$ $- (M_{Row} - GM)$ $- (M_{Column} - GM)]^2$	$N_{Cells} - df_{Columns} - df_{Rows} - 1$	$SS_{Interaction}/df_{Interaction}$	$MS_{Interaction}/MS_{Within}$
Within	$\Sigma(X - M)^2$	$df_1 + df_2 + \ldots + df_{Last}$	SS_{Within}/df_{Within}	
Total	$\Sigma(X - GM)^2$	$N - 1$		

Definitions of basic symbols:

Σ =   sum of the appropriate numbers for all *scores* (not all cells)
M =   mean of a score's cell
M_{Row} =   mean of a score's row
M_{Column} =   mean of a score's column
GM =   grand mean of all scores
N_{Cells} =   number of cells
N_{Rows} =   number of rows
$N_{Columns}$ =   number of columns
X =   each score
N =   total number of scores in the study

❶ Add up the squared deviation scores of each type.
❷ Divide each sum of squared deviations by its appropriate degrees of freedom.
❸ Divide the various between-group variance estimates by the within-group variance estimates.

2. $SS_{Rows} = \Sigma(M_{Row} - GM)^2$
SS_{Rows} is the sum of squared deviations for rows; Σ tells you to add up what follows over all scores; M_{Row} is the mean of a score's row; and GM is the grand mean (the mean of all the scores).

3. $SS_{Interaction} \Sigma[(X - GM) - (X - M) - (M_{Row} - GM) - (M_{Column} - GM)]^2$
$SS_{Interaction}$ is the sum of squared deviations for the interaction; Σ tells you to add up what follows over all scores; X is each score; GM is the grand mean (the mean of all the scores); M is the mean of a score's cell; and M_{Row} and M_{Column} are the means, respectively, of a score's row and column.

4. $df_{Interaction} = N_{Cells} - df_{Rows} - df_{Columns} - 1$
$df_{Interaction}$ is the degrees of freedom for the interaction effect; N_{Cells} is the number of cells; df_{Rows} is the degrees of freedom for rows (the number of rows $- 1$); and $df_{Columns}$ is the degrees of freedom for columns (the number of columns $- 1$).

5. The major figuring is shown in Table 13–11. For the Vividness effect, $F = 0$; not significant. For the Length effect, $F = 32$; significant. For the interaction effect, $F = 8$; significant.

6. The populations associated with each cell are normal and all have the same variance.

TABLE 13–11   Figuring for "How Are You Doing?" Question 5

F needed for main effect for Vividness ($df = 1, 4; p < .05$) = 7.71.
F needed for main effect for Length ($df = 1, 4; p < .05$) = 7.71.
F needed for interaction effect ($df - 1, 4, p < .05$) = 7.71.

			Low Vividness						High Vividness		
X	$(X - GM)^2$	$(X - M)^2$	$(M_{row} - GM)^2$	$(M_{column} - GM)^2$	INT^2	X	$(X - GM)^2$	$(X - M)^2$	$(M_{row} - GM)^2$	$(M_{column} - GM)^2$	INT^2
Short											
6	4	1	4	0	1	9	25	4	4	0	1
4	0	1	4	0	1	5	1	4	4	0	1
	4	2	8	0	2		26	8	8	0	2
Long											
2	4	1	4	0	1	1	9	0	4	0	1
4	0	1	4	0	1	1	9	0	4	0	1
	4	2	8	0	2		18	0	8	0	2

$SS_{Total} = \quad 4 + 26 + 4 + 18 = 52$
$SS_{Within} = \quad 2 + 8 + 2 + 0 = \quad 12$
$SS_{Rows} = \quad 8 + 8 + 8 + 8 = \quad 32$
$SS_{Column} = \quad 0 + 0 + 0 + 0 = \quad 0$
$SS_{Interaction} = 2 + 2 + 2 + 2 = \quad 8$
Accuracy check: $SS_{Total} = SS_{Within} + SS_{Rows} + SS_{Columns} + SS_{Interaction} = 12 + 32 + 0 + 8 = 52$

Source	SS	df	MS	F	
Length (rows)	32	1	32	32	Reject the null hypothesis.
Vividness (columns)	0	1	0	0	Do not reject the null hypothesis.
Interaction (Length × Vividness)	8	1	8	8	Reject the null hypothesis.
Within cells	52	4			

POWER AND EFFECT SIZE IN THE FACTORIAL ANALYSIS OF VARIANCE

You figure power and effect size in a factorial analysis of variance in about the same way as for a one-way analysis of variance (see Chapter 12), except that you figure power and effect size separately for each main effect and the interaction.

EFFECT SIZE

You can figure the effect size for each main and interaction effect as an R^2, the proportion of variance accounted for (also called eta^2) by the effect. In Chapter 12 we described the proportion of variance accounted for as the proportion of the squared deviations of the scores from the grand mean that was accounted for by the deviations of the groups' means from the grand mean. In a one-way analysis of variance, $R^2 = SS_{\text{Between}}/SS_{\text{Total}}$. Now, consider the situation of the row effect in a two-way analysis of variance. We can certainly substitute SS_{Rows} for SS_{Between}. It makes sense to think of the numerator of this proportion as the sum of squared deviations of the rows' means from the grand mean—the variance created by the effect of the variable that divides the groups across the rows and is otherwise not accounted for.

However, what about the denominator: the baseline, which is the variance that is to be accounted for in the proportion of variance accounted for? In a two-way analysis, the squared deviations of each score from the grand mean are now partly accounted for by the column and interaction effects as well as by the row effect. But the row effect should not be held responsible for variance already accounted for by the column and interaction effects—the squared deviations to be accounted for by rows should include only those squared deviations not already accounted for by columns or the interaction. To put this in terms of a formula,

| The proportion of variance accounted for by variation between columns is the sum of squared deviations for columns divided by the sum of squares total minus the sum of squared deviations for rows minus the sum of squared deviations for the interaction. |

$$R^2_{\text{Columns}} = \frac{SS_{\text{Columns}}}{SS_{\text{Total}} - SS_{\text{Rows}} - SS_{\text{Interaction}}} \qquad (13\text{-}26)$$

The same principle holds for the column and interaction effects. Stated as formulas,

| The proportion of variance accounted for by variation between rows is the sum of squared deviations for rows divided by the sum of squares total minus the sum of squared deviations for columns minus the sum of squared deviations for the interaction. |

$$R^2_{\text{Rows}} = \frac{SS_{\text{Rows}}}{SS_{\text{Total}} - SS_{\text{Columns}} - SS_{\text{Interaction}}} \qquad (13\text{-}27)$$

| The proportion of variance accounted for by the interaction is the sum of squared deviations for the interaction divided by the sum of squares total minus the sum of squared deviations for columns minus the sum of squared deviations for rows. |

$$R^2_{\text{Interaction}} = \frac{SS_{\text{Interaction}}}{SS_{\text{Total}} - SS_{\text{Columns}} - SS_{\text{Rows}}} \qquad (13\text{-}28)$$

Technically, each of these is a "partial" R^2 because it describes the proportion of variance accounted for by an effect after "partialing out" the other effects. (We say more about partial correlations in Chapter 17.)

In our example based on the Wong and Csikszentmihalyi (1991) beeper study, R^2 would be figured as follows:

$$R^2_{Columns} \text{ (Affiliation)} = \frac{SS_{Columns}}{SS_{Total} - SS_{Rows} - SS_{Interaction}}$$

$$= \frac{7.20}{654.24 - 543.20 - 36.80} = \frac{7.20}{74.24} = .10$$

$$R^2_{Rows} \text{ (Gender)} = \frac{SS_{Rows}}{SS_{Total} - SS_{Columns} - SS_{Interaction}}$$

$$= \frac{543.20}{654.24 - 7.20 - 36.80} = \frac{543.20}{610.24} = .89$$

$$R^2_{Interaction} \text{ (Interaction)} = \frac{SS_{Interaction}}{SS_{Total} - SS_{Columns} - SS_{Rows}}$$

$$= \frac{36.80}{654.24 - 7.20 - 543.20} = \frac{36.80}{103.84} = .35$$

Based on Cohen's conventions for R^2 in the analysis of variance (see Chapter 12), there is an enormous effect size—a high R^2—for gender and also a healthy effect size for the interaction. The nonsignificant effect for affiliation had a medium to large effect size. (In the actual study, the effect sizes were much smaller. The effect sizes are so large in the example because we made up data with much less variance than in the actual study. We did this to help you see the patterns very clearly.)

If a study provides only the Fs and degrees of freedom,

(13-29)

$$R^2_{Columns} = \frac{(F_{Columns})(df_{Columns})}{(F_{Columns})(df_{Columns}) + df_{Within}}$$

The proportion of variance accounted for by variation between columns is the product of the F ratio for columns times its degrees of freedom divided by the sum of the F ratio for columns times its degrees of freedom plus the degrees of freedom within cells.

(13-30)

$$R^2_{Rows} = \frac{(F_{Rows})(df_{Rows})}{(F_{Rows})(df_{Rows}) + df_{Within}}$$

The proportion of variance accounted for by variation between rows is the product of the F ratio for rows times its degrees of freedom divided by the sum of the F ratio for rows times its degrees of freedom plus the degrees of freedom within cells.

(13-31)

$$R^2_{Interaction} = \frac{(F_{Interaction})(df_{Interaction})}{(F_{Interaction})(df_{Interaction}) + df_{Within}}$$

The proportion of variance accounted for by the interaction is the product of the F ratio for the interaction times its degrees of freedom divided by the sum of the F ratio for the interaction times its degrees of freedom plus the degrees of freedom within cells.

For example, in the beeper study, affiliation was the column main effect. We figured $F_{Columns}$ to be 3.85, degrees of freedom for this effect ($df_{Columns}$) was 1, and the degrees of freedom within cells (df_{Within}) was 36. Thus,

$$R^2_{Columns} = \frac{(F_{Columns})(df_{Columns})}{(F_{Columns})(df_{Columns}) + df_{Within}}$$

$$= \frac{(3.85)(1)}{(3.85)(1) + 36} = \frac{3.85}{39.85} = .10$$

TABLE 13–12 Approximate Power for Studies Using 2 × 2 or 2 × 3 Analysis of Variance for Hypotheses Tested at the .05 Significance Level

N Per Cell	Effect Size		
	Small $(R^2 = .01)$	Medium $(R^2 = .06)$	Large $(R^2 = .14)$
All effects in a 2 × 2 analysis:			
10	.09	.33	.68
20	.13	.60	.94
30	.19	.78	.99
40	.24	.89	*
50	.29	.94	*
100	.52	*	*
Two-level main effect in a 2 × 3 analysis:			
10	.11	.46	.84
20	.18	.77	.99
30	.26	.92	*
40	.34	.97	*
50	.41	.99	*
100	.70	*	*
Three-level main effect and interaction effect in a 2 × 3 analysis:			
10	.09	.36	.76
20	.14	.67	.98
30	.21	.86	*
40	.27	.94	*
50	.32	.98	*
100	.59	*	*

*Nearly 1.

POWER

In a factorial analysis of variance, the power of each effect is influenced by the overall design. For example, a three-level column effect will have different power if it is crossed with a two-level row effect than if it is crossed with a three-level row effect. To keep things simple, we present power figures for only the three most common two-way analysis of situations: All effects in a 2 × 2 design, a two-level (two-row or two-column) main effect in a 2 × 3 design, and a three-level (three-row or three-column) main effect in a 2 × 3 design. (The power of the interaction in a 2 × 3 design is the same as for the three-level main effect.)

Table 13–12 presents approximate power at the .05 significance level for each of these situations for small, medium, and large effect sizes and for cell sizes of 10, 20, 30, 40, 50, and 100.[4]

Consider a planned 2 × 2 study with 30 participants in each cell and an expected medium effect size ($R^2 = .06$) for the row main effect (and using the .05 significance level). The row main effect for this planned study would have a power of .78, meaning that if the research hypothesis for this row main effect is in fact true

---

[4]More detailed tables are provided in Cohen (1988, p. 389–354). However, using these tables with a factorial design requires some preliminary figuring, as Cohen explains on pages 364–379.

TABLE 13–13 Approximate Number of Participants Needed in Each Cell (Assuming Equal Sample Sizes) for 80% Power for Studies Using a 2 × 2 or 2 × 3 Analysis of Variance, Testing Hypotheses at the .05 Significance Level

	Effect Size		
	Small ($R^2 = .01$)	Medium ($R^2 = .06$)	Large ($R^2 = .14$)
2 × 2: All effects	197	33	14
2 × 3: Two-level main effect	132	22	9
Three-level main effect and interaction	162	27	11

and has a medium effect size, the chance that the study will come out significant is about 78%.

Or, consider an example of a published study in which a nonsignificant result is found for an interaction effect in a 2 × 3 analysis of variance with 20 participants per cell. Based on the table, power is only .14 for a small effect size. This means that even if such a small effect exists in the population, this study would be very unlikely to have come out significant. By contrast, the table shows a power of .98 for a large effect size. This means that if a large interaction effect existed in the population, it would almost certainly have been significant in this study.

PLANNING SAMPLE SIZE

Table 13–13 gives the approximate number of participants per cell needed for 80% power at the .05 significance level for estimated small, medium, and large effect sizes for the same situations as were included in the power table.[5]

Suppose that you are planning a 2 × 3 analysis of variance in which you are predicting a large effect size for the main effect on the three-level variable and a medium effect size for the other main effect and interaction. For 80% power (at the .05 significance level), you need 11 participants per cell for the three-level main effect, 22 per cell for the two-level main effect, and 27 per cell for the interaction effect. Of course, you have to do the whole experiment at once. Thus, you need at least 27 per cell (unless you choose to risk lower power for the interaction effect). This would mean recruiting 162 participants (27 for each of the six cells of the 2 × 3 design).

EXTENSIONS AND SPECIAL CASES OF THE FACTORIAL ANALYSIS OF VARIANCE

The analysis of variance is an extremely versatile technique. We cannot, in this introductory book, go into the details of the statistical procedures for handling all the possibilities. (These are covered in most intermediate statistics texts in psychology as well as in what are often called "experimental design" textbooks.) However, it is

---

[5]More detailed tables are provided in Cohen (1988, pp. 381–389). If you use these, be sure to read Cohen's pages 396–403.

possible to describe some of the variations and considerations and to provide some insight into the basic modifications to what you have already learned.

THREE-WAY AND HIGHER ANALYSIS OF VARIANCE DESIGNS

The most straightforward extension of the two-way analysis of variance is to experiments involving three-way or higher designs. You do the analysis exactly as we have described in this chapter, except that there are additional main and interaction effects.

Sometimes an experiment involves variables that are of interest only if they interact with the major variables, such as order of presentation or which of two experimenters conducted the study for each participant. In these situations, the researcher may start with a multiway factorial analysis of variance. If these variables of secondary interest do not have significant interaction effects with the variables of primary interest, you run the analysis again, ignoring these secondary variables. The design then becomes a more manageable two-way or three-way analysis of variance. The resulting analysis is said to be *collapsed* over the variables that are being ignored. For example, in the mood and stereotype appropriateness study, Lambert et al. first did a three-way analysis that included gender (see Figure 13–1). When they found that there were no main or interaction effects for gender, they went ahead and did a two-way analysis, collapsed over gender (that is, gender was ignored in the two-way analysis).

REPEATED-MEASURES ANALYSIS OF VARIANCE

In all the situations in this chapter and Chapters 11 and 12, the different cells or groupings are based on scores from different individuals. Sometimes, however, a researcher measures the same individual in several different situations. (If there are only two such conditions, such as before and after some treatment, you can use a *t* test for dependent means, as described in Chapter 9.) Consider a study in which you measure speed of recognizing a syllable when embedded in three word types: familiar words, unfamiliar words, and nonword sounds. The result is that for each participant, you have an average number of errors for each word type. Or, suppose you do a study of psychotherapy effects testing patients on their depression before, immediately following, and again 3 months after therapy. In both examples, you have three groups of scores, but all three scores are from the same people. These studies are examples of repeated-measures designs.

repeated-measures analysis of variance

Repeated-measures designs are analyzed with a **repeated-measures analysis of variance.** It has this name because the same participants are being measured repeatedly. This kind of design and analysis is also called a *within-subject design* and *within-subject analysis of variance,* because the comparison is within, not between, the different participants or subjects. (The American Psychological Association recommends the use of the term "participants" rather than "subjects.")

Sometimes a repeated-measures variable is crossed in the same study with an ordinary between-participants variable. For example, in the therapy study, there might be a control group not getting the therapy but tested at the same three points in time. This would be a *mixed* 2 (therapy versus control group) $\times$ 3 (before, after, 3 months after) design in which the first variable is the usual between-participants type and the second is a repeated-measures type. It is even possible to have two repeated-measures factors or even more complicated combinations.

1. (a) How is the method of figuring effect size for a factorial analysis of variance similar to that for a one-way analysis of variance? (b) How and (c) why is it different?
2. (a) Write the formula for the effect size for rows in a two-way analysis of variance using sums of squares. (b) Define each of the symbols, and (c) figure the effect size for a study in which SS_{Rows} is 20, $SS_{Columns}$ is 10, $SS_{Interaction}$ is 5, and SS_{Total} is 100.
3. (a) Write the formula for effect size for rows in a two-way analysis of variance in which you know only the F ratio and degrees of freedom, (b) define each of the symbols, and (c) figure the effect size for a study with 10 participants per cell, four rows, two columns, and an F of 6.3.
4. (a) What is the power of the two-level main effect in a 2×3 analysis of variance with approximately 40 participants in each group to be tested at the .05 significance level, in which the researchers predict a medium effect size? (b) About how many participants do you need in each cell for 80% power in a planned 2×2 study in which you predict a medium effect size and will be using the .05 significance level?
5. (a) What does it mean when a research study reports that "results were collapsed over order of testing"? (b) How is a repeated-measures analysis of variance different from an ordinary between-participants analysis of variance? (c) What is a mixed design?

ANSWERS

1. (a) You divide the sum of squares for the effect of interest by the total sum of squares to be accounted for. (b) What you divide by, instead of the sum of squares total, is the sum of squares total minus the sums of squares for the other effects. (c) Because the sum of squares for the other effects are not part of the variation that needs to be accounted for by the effect of interest.
2. (a) $R^2_{Columns} = \dfrac{SS_{Columns}}{SS_{Total} - SS_{Rows} - SS_{Interaction}}$
   (b) R^2_{Rows} is the proportion of variance accounted for by variation between rows; SS_{Rows} is the sum of squared deviations for rows; SS_{Total} is the total sum of square deviations of each score from the grand mean; $SS_{Columns}$ is the sum of squared deviations for columns; and $SS_{Interaction}$ is the sum of squared deviations for the interaction.
   (c) $R^2_{Rows} = 20/(100 - 10 - 5) = .24$.
3. (a) $R^2_{Rows} = \dfrac{(F_{Rows})(df_{Rows})}{(F_{Rows})(df_{Rows}) + df_{Within}}$
   (b) R^2_{Rows} is the proportion of variance accounted for by variation between rows; F_{Rows} is F ratio for rows; df_{Rows} is the degrees of freedom for rows (number of rows minus 1); df_{Within} is the degrees of freedom within cells (the number of scores in each cell minus 1 added up over all cells).
   (c) $R^2_{Rows} = (6.3)(3)/[(6.3)(3) + 72] = 4.45/76.45 = .06$.
4. (a) .97. (b) 33.
5. (a) Which order of testing a participant was given is ignored in the analysis. (b) Each participant has a score in each of the groups or cells of the analysis; in an ordinary, between-participants analysis of variance, each participant has a score in only one group or cell. (c) One factor is a repeated-measures factor and one factor is between-participants.

CONTROVERSY: UNEQUAL CELL SIZES AND DICHOTOMIZING NUMERIC VARIABLES

In this section we discuss two longstanding controversies regarding factorial analysis of variance: one about when there is an unequal number of participants in the various cells and one about the situation in which one of the variables that divides the groups, instead of being categorical, is a quantitative, numeric variable.

UNEQUAL NUMBERS OF PARTICIPANTS IN THE CELLS

A *one-way* analysis of variance, using the structural model approach from Chapter 12, works just fine and noncontroversially for either equal or unequal numbers of participants in the different groups. The situation is more complicated, however, for a factorial analysis of variance. There has been much controversy about how to deal with the issue. Sometimes, frustrated researchers resort to randomly eliminating scores from cells with too many. But this approach wastes power. It is now widely thought that the best solution is the *least-squares analysis of variance*, and today most analysis of variance programs use this approach automatically unless you indicate otherwise. (This approach is based on multiple regression analysis, which you learned something about in Chapter 4.) When cell sizes are equal, this approach gives the same result as the ordinary approach.

The result of using the least-squares approach is that each cell's influence on the main and interaction effects is equalized. This is usually what you want. However, an influential paper (Milligan et al., 1987) suggested that this approach is especially sensitive to violations of the assumptions of normality or equal population variances. (Alas, other traditional approaches to the factorial analysis of variance with unequal cell sizes are just as oversensitive.) Thus, the best advice to researchers is to try to design studies that use equal cell sizes. It also turns out, just as was true for the *t* test, that for a given number of participants, power is greatest when the participants are divided equally among the cells.

DICHOTOMIZING NUMERIC VARIABLES

Suppose a developmental psychologist measured anxiety and social skills in a group of children. The psychologist then observed their behavior in a play group with other children, focusing on their aggressive responses. To examine the results of this study, the researcher divided the children in half on their anxiety scores, making a high anxiety and a low anxiety group; then divided them in half on social skills, making a high and low social skills group. The combinations resulted in four groups: high anxiety, high social skills; high anxiety, low social skills; and so forth. Having divided up the children in this way, the researcher then carried out a 2×2 analysis of variance of high versus low anxiety by high versus low social skills. With this analysis, the researcher could see whether there was a main effect of anxiety on aggression, a main effect of social skills on aggression, and/or an interaction effect of anxiety and social skills on aggression.

The thing to notice here is that the researcher divided up the children into two groups on anxiety and two groups on social skills. Consider anxiety first. In this study anxiety was a numeric, quantitative variable measured along a continuum. Nevertheless, the researcher ignored all the fine gradations and simply divided the group in half, making a high anxiety and a low anxiety grouping. This resulted in everyone in the high anxiety grouping being treated as having the same score and everyone in the low anxiety grouping being treated as having the same score.

dichotomizing

median split

This kind of division is called **dichotomizing**—making into a dichotomy, or two groupings. Since the dichotomizing is usually done by taking those above and below the median, it is also called making a **median split** of the scores. In this example, the researcher also dichotomized (made a median split) on social skills.

The advantage of dichotomizing numeric variables is that you can then do a factorial analysis of variance, with all of its advantages of efficiency and testing interaction effects. Also, most psychologists are familiar with factorial analysis of variance. Many psychologists are less familiar with alternative procedures (based on multiple regression) that accomplish much the same thing but do not require dichotomizing.

A major disadvantage of dichotomizing is that a great deal of information is lost when you reduce a whole range of scores to just two, high and low, making measurement less accurate. One result is that the effect size and power of a study that dichotomizes is lower than when using the original scores. Cohen (1983) calculated this reduction in power and effect size to be between 20% and 66%! It is equivalent, he suggested, to "discarding one-third to two-thirds of the sample" (p. 253).

On the other hand, many researchers dichotomize their variables, claiming that the effect is "conservative"—that while it may increase the chance of a Type II error (failing to reject the null hypothesis when in fact it is false), it does not increase the chance of a Type I error (rejecting the null hypothesis when it is true). Put another way, dichotomizing reduces accuracy so that it is harder, not easier, to get significant results.

However, even assuming that on the average, the effect of dichotomizing a single variable is conservative, there are still problems. One concern is that the analysis is now *overly* conservative in the sense that true results will go undiscovered (you will make Type II errors) and true effect sizes will be underestimated. There is also a general inaccuracy. Dichotomizing is conservative *on the average*. But in any particular case the inaccuracy in dichotomizing could happen to work in favor of the researcher's hypothesis, making a true nondifference come out significant in the study and a true large effect size come out smaller.

Further, Maxwell and Delaney (1993) have shown that when both variables in a two-way factorial design are dichotomized (as in our example of anxiety and social skills), the effect is *not* automatically conservative. Under a number of common conditions in psychology research, dichotomizing two variables can produce the opposite of conservative effects even on the average. According to Maxwell and Delaney, you should be especially skeptical of the results of studies using a two-way analysis of variance in which both variables have been dichotomized.

In spite of these various problems, dichotomizing (even of both variables in two-way analysis of variance) is still surprisingly common in psychology research. It is our impression, though, that it is rapidly dying out.

FACTORIAL ANALYSIS OF VARIANCE IN RESEARCH ARTICLES

In a factorial analysis of variance, researchers usually give a description plus a table. The description gives the F ratio and the information that goes with it for each main and interaction effect. The table gives the cell means and sometimes also the marginal means. If there is a significant interaction effect, there may also be a graph.

For example, here is how Lambert et al. described the result we used for our example:

> Analyses of participants' intentions to hire the target revealed only one significant effect, the predicted Mood X Job Type interaction, $F(1, 57) = 11.46$, $p < .001$. Data relevant to this interaction are displayed in Figure [13–2]. (p. 1011)

Here's another example. Brockner et al. (2001) studied the effect of cultural values about the appropriateness of power differentials on how employees feel about having input to managers about important decisions. Their participants were business students in China, a culture in which power differentials are considered appropriate and normal, a "high power distance" culture, and in the United States, a "low power distance" culture. The students were asked to imagine that they were working in a company and had just been put under the direction of a new manager; they were then assigned to one of three conditions—the new manager discouraged input from them (the low voice condition), the new manager encouraged input from them (high voice), or no information was given about the manager's style (the control condition). They then had the students answer some questions about how committed they would feel to the organization. Here is how they report the results:

> A two-factor ANOVA yielded a significant main effect of voice, $F(2, 245) = 26.30$, $p < .001$. As expected, participants responded less favorably in the low voice condition ($M = 2.93$) than in the high voice condition ($M = 3.58$). The mean rating in the control condition ($M = 3.34$) fell between these two extremes. Of greater importance, the interaction between culture and voice was also significant, $F(2, 245) = 4.11$, $p < .02$. . . . As can be seen in Table [13–14], the voice effect was more pronounced in the low power distance culture (the United States) than in the high power distance culture (the People's Republic of China). (p. 304)

Until recently, it was common for researchers to show interaction effects using a kind of line graph. Consider an example. Gump and Kulik (1997) tested a theory about the conditions that promote interpersonal affiliation. Specifically, they predicted that one is more likely to affiliate with another person when one is under threat and when the other person is facing the same threat. In their study, participants were randomly assigned to either expect or not expect a painful experimental procedure. This was the threat manipulation (high versus low). In all conditions there was another participant in the room. Half the participants were told this other participant was in the same experiment, and thus facing a similar situation of threat or nonthreat; for the other half, the other participant was supposedly taking part in a completely different experiment, and thus not expecting the same threatening or nonthreatening situation. This was the manipulation of similarity of situation (similar versus dissimilar). As the participant was being told about the threat over an earphone, the experimenters observed how much time each participant spent looking at his or her partner. The results were as predicted:

> In this analysis, a significant interaction between participant threat and situational similarity emerged, $F(1, 77) = 5.57$, $p = .02$. No other effects were significant. As can be seen in Figure [13–11], it is clear that high threat produced more looking at an affiliate who was believed to be facing the same, compared with a different, situation, whereas no such differentiation occurred for low-threat participants. (p. 309)

TABLE 13–14   **Mean Level of Organizational Commitment as a Function of Culture and Level of Voice (Study 1)**

Culture	Level of Voice		
	Low	High	Control
United States	2.63	3.57	3.17
(low power distance)	(0.72)	(0.56)	(0.66)
People's Republic of China	3.27	3.60	3.52
(high power distance)	(0.68)	(0.43)	(0.55)

Note: Scores could range from 1 to 5, with higher scores reflecting greater organizational commitment. Standard deviations are in parentheses.

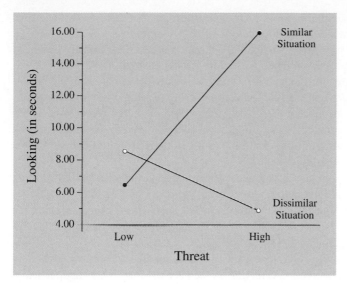

FIGURE 13–11 *Study 1: The effect of threat and situational similarity on time spent looking at an affiliate. [From Gump, B. B., & Kulik, J. A. (1997), fig. 1. Stress, affiliation, and emotional contagion.* Journal of Personality and Social Psychology, 72, *305–319. Copyright, 1997, by the American Psychological Association. Reprinted with permission.]*

The type of graph Gump and Kulik presented (Figure 13–11) has the advantage of making the pattern of interaction very vivid, even compared to the usual bar graph. The reason that line graphs like this have become less common in recent years is that they are slightly misleading in that the line implies that there is a continuum of effect. However, we only have information about the two extreme points. For example, in the Gump and Kulik study, there was a high threat and a low threat condition. The lines give the impression that the pattern for each similarity condition is continuous from low to high threat. Suppose the researchers had included an intermediate threat condition. It is possible that the result for this condition would be not at all where the line in the present graph says it should be. The bar graph approach, in contrast, does not imply anything about in-between levels—it simply shows the results at each level of the variable tested.

SUMMARY

1. In a factorial research design, participants are put into groupings according to the combinations of the variables whose effects are being studied. In such designs, you can study the effects of two variables without needing twice as many participants, and you can see the effects of combinations of the two variables.

2. An interaction effect is when the impact of one variable depends on the level of the other variable. A main effect is the impact of one variable, ignoring the effect of the other variable. Interaction effects and main effects can be described verbally, numerically, and graphically (usually on a graph with bars for each combination of the variables that divide the groups, with the height of the bar being the score on the measured variable).

3. In a two-way analysis of variance, there are three different between-groups variance estimates, one for differences on the variable dividing the rows, one for differences on the variable dividing the columns, and one for the interaction

of the row and column variables. The within-groups population variance estimate becomes a within-cells population variance estimate.

4. The figuring for a two-way analysis of variance uses an expanded version of the structural model approach. The within-groups estimate is based on deviations of each score from its cell's mean. The row effect is based on deviations between row means and the grand mean; the column main effect, on deviations between column means and the grand mean. The interaction effect is based on the deviation of scores from the grand mean remaining after subtracting out all the other deviations from the grand mean (deviations from the cell mean, the row means, and the column means).

5. To get the actual population variance estimates, the various deviations (within, rows, columns, and interaction) are squared, summed, and divided by their degrees of freedom. The F ratios for row, column, and interaction effects are the population variance estimates for each of these divided by the within-cells population variance estimate.

6. In a factorial analysis of variance, you figure effect size and power separately for each main and interaction effect. R^2 is the sum of squares for that particular effect divided by the part of the total sum of squares that remains after subtracting from it the sum of squares for the other two effects.

7. The factorial analysis of variance can be extended beyond two-way designs and can also be used for repeated-measures studies.

8. One longstanding controversy is about how to handle situations with unequal cell sizes. The least-squares approach is usually considered the best you can do, but the optimal solution is to have equal cell sizes. Another longstanding issue is about whether to dichotomize continuous variables in order to do an analysis of variance. This is a decreasingly common procedure; advanced procedures that use the full range of values of each variable are generally considered the better approach.

9. Results of factorial analyses of variance often include graphical descriptions of results, particularly when the interaction effect is significant. These are usually bar graphs, but sometimes include line graphs.

KEY TERMS

cell (p. 454)
cell mean (p. 454)
dichotomizing (p. 486)
factorial analysis of variance (p. 451)
factorial research design (p. 452)

interaction effect (p. 453)
main effect (p. 454)
marginal means (p. 455)
median split (p. 486)
one-way analysis of variance (p. 454)

repeated-measures analysis of variance (p. 484)
two-way analysis of variance (p. 454)
two-way factorial research design (p. 454)

EXAMPLE WORKED-OUT COMPUTATIONAL PROBLEM

In a 2 × 3 experiment, Variable A has three levels (1, 2 and 3) and Variable B has two levels (1 and 2). Four participants are randomly assigned to each combination of Variables A and B and are then observed on the measured variable. Scores of the 24 participants are given below:

	Variable B	
	Level 1	Level 2
Variable A Level 1	25	19
	20	24
	23	21
	24	20
Variable A Level 2	22	24
	19	18
	22	22
	21	20
Variable A Level 3	16	18
	19	21
	13	16
	16	17

Are there any significant main or interaction effects? Use the .05 significance level, follow the five steps of hypothesis testing, and make a graph of your results. Table 13 15 shows the figuring.

❶ **Restate the question as a research hypothesis and a null hypothesis about the populations for each main effect and the interaction effect.** There are six populations:

Population 1, 1: People given Level 1 of Variable A and Level 1 of Variable B.
Population 2, 1: People given Level 2 of Variable A and Level 1 of Variable B.
Population 3, 1: People given Level 3 of Variable A and Level 1 of Variable B.
Population 1, 2: People given Level 1 of Variable A and Level 2 of Variable B.
Population 2, 2: People given Level 2 of Variable A and Level 2 of Variable B.
Population 3, 2: People given Level 3 of Variable A and Level 2 of Variable B.

The first null hypothesis is that there is no difference among the means of the combined populations given Level 1 of Variable A (Populations 1, 1 and 1, 2), the combined populations given Level 2 of Variable A (Populations 2, 1 and 2, 2), and the combined populations given Level 3 of Variable A (Populations 3, 1 and 3, 2). This is the null hypothesis for testing the main effect for Variable A. The research hypothesis is that these three combined populations have different means.

The second null hypothesis is that the combined populations of those experiencing Level 1 of Variable B (Populations 1, 1; 2, 1; and 3, 1) have the same average scores as those experiencing Level 2 of Variable B (Populations 1, 2; 2, 2; and 3, 2). This is the null hypothesis for testing the main effect for Variable B. The research hypothesis is that the populations experiencing the two levels of Variable B are different.

The third null hypothesis is that the pattern of the means for the populations who all are given Level 1 of Variable B (Populations 1, 1; 2, 1; and 3, 1) will be the same as the pattern of the means of the three populations given Level 2 of Variable B (Populations 1, 2; 2, 2; and 3, 2). This is the null hypothesis for testing the interaction effect. The research hypothesis is that the pattern of the means of the three populations given Level 1 of Variable B differs from the pattern of the means of the three populations given Level 2 of Variable B.

❷ **Determine the characteristics of the comparison distributions.** The three comparison distributions will be F distributions: For the Variable A main effect, $df = 2$, 18; for the Variable B main effect, $df = 1$, 18; for the interaction effect, $df = 2$, 18.

TABLE 13–15 Figuring for Example Worked-Out Computational Problem

	Variable B		
	Public	Private	
Variable A Level 1	23	21	22
Level 2	21	21	21
Level 3	16	18	17
	20	20	20

F needed for main effect for Variable B ($df = 1, 18; p < .05$) = 4.41.
F needed for main effect for Variable A ($df = 2, 18; p < .05$) = 3.56.
F needed for interaction effect ($df = 2, 18; p < .05$) = 3.56.

	Variable B Level 1						Variable B Level 2				
X	$(X - GM)^2$	$(X - M)^2$	$(M_{Row} - GM)^2$	$(M_{Column} - GM)^2$	INT^2	X	$(X - GM)^2$	$(X - M)^2$	$(M_{Row} - GM)^2$	$(M_{Column} - GM)^2$	INT^2
Variable A Level 1											
25	25	4	4	0	1	19	1	4	4	0	1
20	0	9	4	0	1	24	16	9	4	0	1
23	9	0	4	0	1	21	1	0	4	0	1
24	16	1	4	0	1	20	0	1	4	0	1
	50	14	16	0	4		18	14	16	0	4
Variable A Level 2											
22	4	1	1	0	0	24	16	9	1	0	0
19	1	4	1	0	0	18	4	9	1	0	0
22	4	1	1	0	0	22	4	1	1	0	0
21	1	0	1	0	0	20	0	1	1	0	0
	10	6	4	0	0		24	20	4	0	0
Variable A Level 3											
16	16	0	9	0	1	18	4	0	9	0	1
19	1	9	9	0	1	21	1	9	9	0	1
13	49	9	9	0	1	16	16	4	9	0	1
16	16	0	9	0	1	17	9	1	9	0	1
	82	18	36	0	4		30	14	36	0	4

M = mean of the score's cell
M_{Row} = mean of the score's row
M_{Column} = mean of the score's column
INT = score's remaining deviation for the interaction

Sample figuring of deviations, using the first score in the Public Antiracist cell:

$$\overset{\text{Ⓐ}}{} \quad \overset{\text{Ⓑ}}{} \quad \overset{\text{Ⓒ}}{}$$

$$(X - GM)^2 = (25 - 20)^2 = 5^2 = 25.$$
$$(X - M)^2 = (25 - 23)^2 = 2^2 = 4.$$
$$(M_{Row} - GM)^2 = (22 - 20)^2 = 2^2 = 4.$$
$$(M_{Column} - GM)^2 = (20 - 20)^2 = 0^2 = 0.$$
$$INT^2 = [(X - GM) - (X - M) - (M_{Row} - GM) - (M_{Column} - GM)]^2 = (5 - 2 - 2 - 0)^2 = 1^2 = 1$$

TABLE 13–15 *Continued*

SS_{Total} = 50 + 18 + 10 + 24 + 82 + 30 = 214
SS_{Within} = 14 + 14 + 6 + 20 + 18 + 14 = 86
SS_{Column} = 0 + 0 + 0 + 0 + 0 + 0 =   0 ⓓ
SS_{Row} = 16 + 16 + 4 + 4 + 36 + 36 = 112
$SS_{Interaction}$ = 4 + 4 + 0 + 0 + 4 + 4 = 16

Accuracy check: SS_{Total} = 214; $SS_{Within} + SS_{Rows} + SS_{Columns} + SS_{Interaction}$ = 86 + 0 + 112 + 16 = 214

Source	SS	df	ⓔ MS	ⓕ F	
Variable B (columns)	0	1	0	0.1	Do not reject the null hypothesis.
Variable A (rows)	112	2	56	11.7	Reject the null hypothesis.
Interaction (columns × rows)	16	2	8	1.7	Do not reject the null hypothesis.
Within cells	86	18	4.8		

❸ **Determine the cutoff sample scores on the comparison distributions at which each null hypothesis should be rejected.** These are shown in Table 13–15.

❹ **Determine the samples' scores on each comparison distribution.** The figuring is shown on Table 13–15.

❺ **Decide whether to reject the null hypotheses.** Based on the results shown in Table 13–15, the main effect for Variable B is not significant; the main effect for Variable A is significant; and the interaction effect is not significant. Results are shown graphically in Figure 13–12.

PRACTICE PROBLEMS

These problems involve figuring. Most real-life statistics problems are done on a computer. However, even if you have a computer and statistics software, do these by hand (with the help of a calculator) to ingrain the method in your mind. Also, in all problems involving figuring, be sure to show your work.

For practice in using a computer to solve statistics problems, refer to the computer section of each chapter of the *Student's Study Guide and Computer Workbook* that accompanies this text.

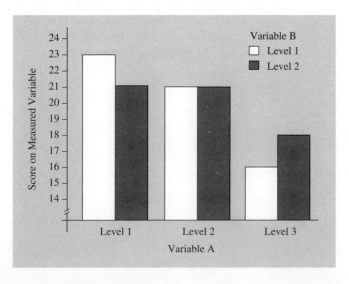

FIGURE 13–12 *Graph for Example Worked-Out Computational Problem.*

All data are fictional unless an actual citation is given.

Answers to Set I problems are given at the back of the book.

SET I

1. Each of the following is a table of means showing results of a study using a factorial design. Assuming that any differences are statistically significant, for each table, (a and b) make two bar graphs showing the results (in one graph grouping the bars according to one variable and in the other graph grouping the bars according to the other variable); (c) indicate which effects (main and interaction), if any, are found; and (d) describe the meaning of the pattern of means (that is, any main or interaction effects or the lack thereof) in words.

   (i) Measured variable: Income (thousands of dollars)

Class	Age	
	Young	Old
Lower	20	35
Upper	25	100

   (ii) Measured variable: Grade point average

College	Major	
	Science	Arts
Community	2.1	2.8
Liberal Arts	2.8	2.1

   (iii) Measured variable: Days sick per month

Group	Gender	
	Females	Males
Exercisers	2.0	2.5
Controls	3.1	3.6

2. Each of the following is a table of means showing results of a study using a factorial design. Assuming that any differences are statistically significant, for each table, (a and b) make two bar graphs showing the results (in one graph grouping the bars according to one variable and in the other graph grouping the bars according to the other variable); (c) indicate which effects (main and interaction), if any, are found; and (d) describe the meaning of the pattern of means (that is, any main or interaction effects or the lack thereof) in words.

   (i) Measured variable: Conversation length

Relationship	Topic	
	Nonpersonal	Personal
Friend	16	20
Parent	10	6

   (ii) Measured variable: Rated restaurant quality

Cost	City		
	New York	Chicago	Vancouver
Expensive	9	5	7
Moderate	6	4	6
Inexpensive	4	3	5

(iii) Measured variable: Ratings of flavor

	Coffee Brand		
	X	*Y*	*Z*
Regular	7	4	6
Decaf	5	2	6

(Type)

3. A sports psychologist studied the effect of a motivational program on injuries among players of three different sports. The chart below shows the design. For each of the following possible patterns of results, make up a set of cell means, figure the marginal means, and make a bar graph of the results: (a) a main effect for type of sport and no other main effect or interaction; (b) a main effect for program or not and no other main effect or interaction; (c) both main effects but no interaction; (d) a main effect for program or not and an interaction, but no main effect for type of sport; (e) both main effects and an interaction.

Measured Variable: Number of injuries per person over 10 weeks

	Sport		
	Baseball	*Football*	*Basketball*
With motivational program			
Without motivational program			

(Sport)

4. Carry out an analysis of variance for the following data set, including making a table of cell and marginal means and making a bar graph of the cell means. Use the .05 significance level.

Participant	Level of Variable I	Level of Variable II	Score
A	1	1	9
B	1	1	7
C	1	2	3
D	1	2	1
E	2	1	1
F	2	1	3
G	2	2	7
H	2	2	9
I	3	1	1
J	3	1	3
K	3	2	7
L	3	2	9
M	4	1	9
N	4	1	7
O	4	2	3
P	4	2	1

5. For each of the following data sets, carry out an analysis of variance, including making a table of cell and marginal means and making a bar graph of the cell means. Use the .05 significance level.

(i)

		Experimental Condition	
		A	B
Group 1		0	3
		1	2
		1	3
Group 2		3	0
		2	1
		3	1

(ii)

		Experimental Condition	
		A	B
Group 1		0	0
		1	1
		1	1
Group 2		3	3
		2	2
		3	3

(iii)

		Experimental Condition	
		A	B
Group 1		0	3
		1	2
		1	3
Group 2		0	3
		1	2
		1	3

6. Patients with two kinds of diagnoses were randomly assigned to one of three types of therapy. There were two patients per cell. Based on the results shown below, (a) carry out the analysis of variance; (b) make a table of cell and marginal means; (c) make a graph of the results; and (d) describe the results in words (indicate which effects are significant and, on the basis of the significant effects, how to understand the pattern of cell means). Use the .05 significance level.

	Therapy A	Therapy B	Therapy C
Diagnosis I	6	3	2
	2	1	4
Diagnosis II	11	7	8
	9	9	10

7. A psychologist who studies the legal system conducted a study of the effect of defendants' likability and nervousness on willingness to convict the defendant. Each participant read the same transcript, taken from an actual trial, in which the guilt or innocence of a male defendant was quite ambiguous. All participants also saw a brief videotape that supposedly showed the defendant on the witness stand. However, the way the actor played the part on the video-

tape differed for different participants, including the four possibilities of likable versus not and nervous versus not. After viewing the tape, participants rated the likelihood that the defendant is innocent (on a scale of 1, *very unlikely*, to 10, *very likely*). The results for the first 12 participants in the study were as follows:

	Likeable	Not Likeable
Nervous	7	3
	8	4
	6	2
Not nervous	3	7
	3	5
	3	9

(a) Carry out the analysis of variance. (b) Make a table of cell and marginal means. (c) Make a graph of the results. (d) Explain the results and the way you arrived at them to someone who is familiar with the one-way analysis of variance (including the structural model approach), but not with the factorial analysis of variance.

8. Figure the effect size for each main and interaction effect using the sums of squares for problems (a) 4, (b) 5a, (c) 5b, (d) 5c, (e) 6, and (f) 7.

9. Figure the effect size for the following completed studies:

	Effect F	df for the Effect	df_{Within}
(a)	6.12	1	40
(b)	6.12	1	20
(c)	6.12	2	40
(d)	6.12	3	40
(e)	3.06	1	40
(f)	12.24	1	40

10. What is the power of the effect in the following planned studies using the analysis of variance with $p < .05$?

	Predicted Effect Size	Overall Design	Number of Levels of the Effect	Participants Per Cell
(a)	small	2 × 2	2	30
(b)	small	2 × 2	2	50
(c)	small	2 × 3	2	30
(d)	small	2 × 3	3	30
(e)	medium	2 × 2	2	30

11. About how many participants do you need in each cell for 80% power in each of the following planned studies, using the analysis of variance with $p < .05$?

	Predicted Effect Size	Design	Effect
(a)	small	2×2	main effect
(b)	small	2×2	interaction effect
(c)	medium	2×2	main effect
(d)	small	2×3	2 level main effect
(e)	small	2×3	3 level main effect
(f)	small	2×3	interaction effect

12. Kunda and Oleson (1997) studied the effect on stereotypes of counterinforma-tion, learning about someone who is opposite to what you would expect from the stereotype. They predicted that extreme counterinformation may have a boomerang effect—making the stereotype even stronger. Participants were pre-selected to be in the study based on a questionnaire in which they rated public relations (PR) agents for their typical degree of extroversion: an "extreme-stereotype" group of participants who had rated PR agents as extremely extro-verted and a "moderate-stereotype" group of participants who had rated PR agents as only moderately introverted. During the actual study, some partici-pants were given a description of a particular PR agent who was highly intro-verted, the extreme deviant condition; the other participants were given no special description, the control condition. Finally, all participants were asked about their beliefs about PR agents.

Kunda and Oleson (1997) reported the results as follows:

> A 2 (prior stereotype) $\times$ 2 (condition) ANOVA yielded a significant inter-action, $F(1, 42) = 5.69$, $p < .05$, indicating that the impact of the target on participants' stereotypes depended on their prior stereotypes. As can be seen in Figure [13–13], extreme-stereotype participants exposed to the highly in-troverted target came to view PR agents as even more extroverted than did extreme controls. . . . [a] boomerang effect. . . . A different pattern was ob-served for the moderate-stereotype participants: Their stereotypes were un-affected by exposure to the same target. . . . The ANOVA also revealed a large effect for prior stereotypes, $F(1, 42) = 38.94$, $p < .0001$ indicating,

FIGURE 13–13 *Mean ratings of the extraversion of public relations (PR) agents made by participants with moderate or ex-treme prior stereotypes who were exposed to an extremely introverted PR agent or to no target (controls). Higher numbers indicate greater PR extraversion. [From Kunda, Z., & Oleson, K. C. (1997), fig. 4. When exceptions prove the rule: How extremity of deviance de-termines the impact of deviant examples in stereotypes.* Journal of Personality and Social Psychology, 72, *965–979. Copyright, 1997, by the American Psychological Association. Reprinted with permission.]*

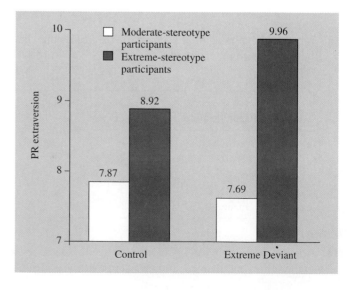

not surprisingly, that extreme-stereotype participants continued to view PR agents as more extroverted than did moderate-stereotype participants. There was also a marginal effect for condition, $F(1, 42) = 2.89$, $p < .10$, which was clearly due entirely to the extreme-stereotype participants. (p. 974)

Briefly describe the meaning of these results to a person who has never had a course in statistics. (Do not go into the computational details, just the basic logic of the pattern of means, the significant results, effect sizes, and issues of interpreting nonsignificant results.)

13. Yamagishi and Melara (2001) studied people's ability to separate visual images from the background. Participants were shown images differing from the background in either just chromacity (color) or just luminescence (brightness). Also, they made the figures more difficult to identify by degrading (distorting) either the contour (shape of the edges) or the surface of the figure. The key measure was "difference in sensitivity from baseline," which the researchers abbreviated as Δd_a. Here is an excerpt from their results (note that MS_e refers to mean squared error, which is the same as MS_{Within}, the population variance estimate based on the variation within cells).

> The only factor to yield a significant main effect was task [$F(1, 3) = 373.35$, $MS_e = 0.01$, $p < .001$]. Greater overall loss was observed in the chromacity tasks ($\Delta d_a = -0.86$) than in the luminance tasks ($\Delta d_a = -0.37$). . . . [T]he critical effect is found in the interaction between degradation and task. This interaction, depicted in Figure [13–14], was highly significant [$F(1, 3) = 178.77$, $MS_e = 0.02$, $p < .001$]. As one can see, figural identification in the luminance tasks was disrupted by contour degradation, but not by surface degradation. On the other hand, figural identification in the chromacity task was disrupted by both forms of degradation; however, surface degradation was twice as harmful to performance in these tasks as contour degradation. (p. 831)

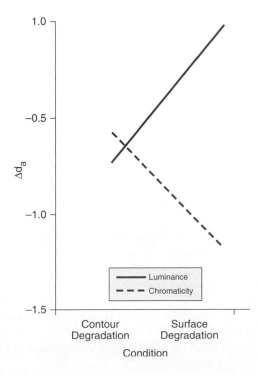

FIGURE 13–14 *Average difference in sensitivity from baseline (Δd_a) in luminance and chromaticity tasks under contour-degradation and surface-degradation conditions across Experiments 1A and 1B. Note the crossover interaction between degradation and task: Performance in the luminance tasks was most disrupted by contour degradation, whereas performance in the chromaticity tasks was most disrupted by surface degradation. [From Yamagishi, N., & Melara, R. D. (2001).* Perception & Psychologies, *63(5), 824–846.]*

Describe the meaning of these results to a person who understands one-way analysis of variance using the structural model approach, but is completely unfamiliar with factorial designs or the two-way analysis of variance.

SET II

14. Each of the following is a table of means showing results of a study using a factorial design. Assuming that any differences are statistically significant, for each table (a and b), make two bar graphs showing the results (in one graph grouping the bars according to one variable and in the other graph grouping the bars according to the other variable); (c) indicate which effects (main and interaction), if any, are found; and (d) describe the meaning of the pattern of means (that is, any main or interaction effects or the lack thereof) in words.

    (i) Measured variable: Degree of envy of another person's success

Degree of Success

Status of Other	Great	Small
Friend	8	5
Stranger	1	4

    (ii) Measured variable: Observed engagement in the activity

Play Activity

Situation	Blocks	Dress Up
Alone	4.5	2.5
With playmate	2.5	4.5

    (iii) Measured variable: Intensity of attention

Program

Type of Balletgoer	The Nutcracker	Modern
Regular	20	15
Sometime	15	15
Novice	10	5

15. Each of the following is a table of means showing results of a study using a factorial design. Assuming that any differences are statistically significant, for each table (a and b), make two bar graphs showing the results (in one graph grouping the bars according to one variable and in the other graph grouping the bars according to the other variable); (c) indicate which effects (main and interaction), if any, are found; and (d) describe the meaning of the pattern of means (that is, any main or interaction effects or the lack thereof) in words.

    (i) Measured variable: Right frontal neural activity in brain during memory task

Items Remembered

Times Presented	*Words*	*Pictures*
Once	45	68
Twice	30	30

(ii) Measured variable: Approval rating of the U.S. president

Region

Class	*West*	*East*	*Midwest*	*South*
Middle	70	45	55	50
Lower	50	25	35	30

(iii) Measured variable: Satisfaction with education

Gender

Time After Obtaining BA	*Females*	*Males*
1 month	3	3
1 year	4	4
5 years	9	9

16. In this study, English speaking participants were instructed to try to read a paragraph for a half hour in one of three languages they did not understand. They read the paragraph after either being told the main idea of the paragraph, told the main idea of the first sentence only, or not told anything about the meaning. They were given translations of some words. The researchers then measured how many of the other words they could correctly translate. The chart below shows the design. For each of the following possible patterns of results, make up a set of cell means, figure the marginal means, and make a bar graph of the results: (a) a main effect for language and no other main effect or interaction; (b) a main effect for knowledge of meaning and no other main effect or interaction; (c) both main effects but no interaction; (d) a main effect for language and an interaction, but no main effect for knowledge of meaning; (e) both main effects and an interaction.

Measured variable: Number of words not given that participant could correctly translate

Language

Knowledge of Meaning	*Dutch*	*Rumanian*	*Swedish*
Paragraph			
Sentence			
None			

17. Carry out an analysis of variance for the following data set, including making a table of cell and marginal means and making a bar graph of the cell means. Use the .05 significance level.

Participant	Level of Variable A	Level of Variable B	Score
1	1	1	8
2	1	1	6
3	1	2	6
4	1	2	8
5	2	1	5
6	2	1	1
7	2	2	1
8	2	2	5

18. For each of the following data sets, carry out an analysis of variance, including making a table of cell and marginal means and making a bar graph of the cell means. Use the .05 significance level.

(a)			Group	
			I	II
Experimental Condition	A		8	8
			6	6
	B		3	3
			1	1

(b)			Group	
			I	II
Experimental Condition	A		9	9
			5	5
	B		4	4
			0	0

19. A developmental psychologist studied the effects of loudness of a sudden noise on infants of different inherited temperaments. The infants were exposed either to a sudden loud noise or a sudden soft noise, and then the infants' startle reactions were observed. The startle reaction scores were as follows:

	Sudden Noise	
	Loud	Soft
Temperament K	14	7
	10	5
	9	9
Temperament R	3	8
	8	8
	7	2

(a) Make a table of cell and marginal means; (b) draw a bar graph of them; (c) carry out the five steps of hypothesis testing (use the .05 significance level); and (d) describe the results in words (indicate which effects are significant and, on the basis of the significant effects, how to understand the pattern of cell means).

20. In a particular high school, three types of videotaped teaching programs were each tried for English, history, and math. The researchers then measured amount learned. There were two students per cell. Based on the results shown below, (a) make a table of cell and marginal means; (b) draw a bar graph of them; (c) carry out the five steps of hypothesis testing (use the .05 significance level); and (d) explain the results and the way you arrived at them to someone who is familiar with the one-way analysis of variance (including the structural model approach), but not with the factorial analysis of variance.

	English	History	Math
Program Type A	3	15	2
	3	14	3
Program Type B	6	18	6
	8	10	5
Program Type C	1	13	2
	3	4	0

21. Figure the effect size for each main and interaction effect using the sums of squares for problems (a) 17, (b) 18a, (c) 18b, (d) 19, and (e) 20.

22. Figure the effect size for the following completed studies:

	Effect F	df for the Effect	df_{Within}
(a)	4.15	2	12
(b)	8.30	2	12
(c)	16.60	2	12
(d)	4.15	1	12
(e)	4.15	2	24
(f)	4.15	2	48

23. What is the power of the effect in the following planned studies using the analysis of variance with $p < .05$?

	Predicted Effect Size	Overall Design	Number of Levels of the Effect	Participants Per Cell
(a)	Small	2×2	2	10
(b)	Medium	2×2	2	10
(c)	Large	2×2	2	10
(d)	Medium	2×3	3	10
(e)	Medium	2×3	3	20
(f)	Medium	2×2	Interaction	20

24. About how many participants do you need in each cell for 80% power in each of the following planned studies, using the analysis of variance with $p < .05$?

	Predicted Effect Size	Design	Effect
(a)	medium	2×2	main effect
(b)	large	2×2	main effect
(c)	medium	2×2	interaction effect
(d)	medium	2×3	3 level main effect
(e)	large	2×3	3 level main effect
(f)	medium	2×3	interaction effect

25. Desmarais and Curtis (1997), two Canadian social psychologists, conducted a study related to how women and men evaluate their own worth as employees. Previous studies had shown that when given the chance to decide how much they should be paid for an experimental task, women usually paid themselves less. These researchers expected that this pattern would be affected by how much particular women and men had received in pay for actual work in the recent past. They conducted the usual experimental procedure in which women and men students were asked to allocate pay to themselves, but they also asked the participants how much they had earned the previous summer. Desmarais and Curtis reported their results as follows:

> Participants' self-payments were analyzed with a 2×3 (Gender of Participants X Recent Income Experience) analysis of variance (ANOVA). Contrary to the prediction that recent income would influence self-pay, the data revealed no pay allocation difference by income experience, $F(2, 66) = 1.99$, *ns* (see Table [13–16]). Also, there was no significant interaction of gender and income history, $F(2, 66) = 0.61$, *ns*. In keeping with previous research on perceived income entitlement, men paid themselves significantly more ($M = \$3.99$) than did women ($M = \$2.74$), $F(1, 66) = 5.86$, $p < .02$. (p. 143)

Briefly describe the meaning of these results to a person who has never had a course in statistics. (Do not go into the computational details, just the basic

TABLE 13–16 Mean Self-Payment for Experimental Task by Gender and Summer-Income Categories

	Summer Income					
	Low		Middle		High	
Gender	M	SD	M	SD	M	SD
Men	5.03	1.71	3.17	3.00	3.77	2.77
Women	3.13	1.68	2.65	1.89	2.44	1.65

Note: Students in the low-income category made less than \$6.00/hr; students in the middle-income cateogry made between \$7.50 and \$8.50/hr; students in the high-income category made over \$10.00/hr. For each cell, $n = 12$. Only the main effect for gender was significant, $p < .02$.

Data from Desmarais, S., & Curtis, J. (1997), tab. 1. Gender and perceived pay entitlement: Testing for effects of experience with income. *Journal of Personality and Social Psychology, 72*, 141–150. Copyright, 1997, by the American Psychological Association. Reprinted with permission.

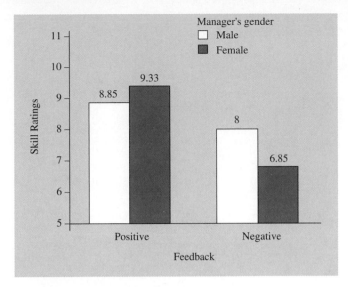

FIGURE 13–15 *Participants' ratings of the manager's skill at evaluating them as a function of feedback favorability and the manager's gender (Study 2). (From "Motivated Stereotyping of Women. She's Fine if She Praised Me but Incompetent If She Criticized Me" by Lisa Sinclair and Ziva Kunda.* Personality and Social Psychology Bulletin, *Vol. 26, No. 11, November 2000, p. 1336, copyright © 2000 by Society for Personality and Social Psychology, Inc. Reprinted by permission of Sage Publications Inc.)*

logic of the pattern of means, the significant results, effect sizes, and issues of interpreting nonsignificant results.)

26. Sinclair and Kunda (2000) tested the idea that if you want to think well of someone (for example, because they have said positive things about you), you are less influenced by the normal stereotypes when evaluating them. Participants filled out a questionnaire on their social skills and then either a male or female "manager in training" gave them feedback, rigged so that half the participants were given positive feedback and half, negative feedback. Finally, the participants rated the managers for their skill at evaluating them. The question was whether the usual tendency to stereotype women as less skillful managers would be undermined when people got positive ratings. Here are the results:

> Participants' ratings of the manager's skill at evaluating them were analyzed with a 2 (feedback) × 2 (manager gender) ANOVA. Managers who had provided positive feedback ($M = 9.08$) were rated more highly than were mangers who had provided negative feedback ($M = 7.46$), $F(1,46) = 19.44$, $p < .0001$. However, as may be seen in Figure [13–15], the effect was qualified by a significant interaction, $F(1, 46) = 4.71, p < .05 \ldots$ " (p. 1335–1336).

Describe the meaning of these results to a person who understands one-way analysis of variance using the structural model approach, but is completely unfamiliar with factorial designs or the two-way analysis of variance.

CHAPTER 14

CHI-SQUARE TESTS

Are You Ready?
What You Need to have Mastered Before Starting This Chapter:

- Chapters 1, 2, 5, 6, and 7. You will need Chapter 8 for understanding the section at the end of the chapter on power and effect size.

This chapter examines hypothesis-testing procedures for variables whose values are categories—such as religious preference or hair color. These procedures focus on the number of people in different categories rather than on mean scores on some dimension.

AN EXAMPLE

Harter et al. (1997) were interested in three styles of relating to romantic partners: a self-focused autonomy style, an other-focused connection style, and a mutuality style. Harter et al. conducted a newspaper survey that included items about the respondents' styles and also the respondents' perceptions of their partners' styles. One of the researchers' predictions was that men who described themselves as having the self-focused autonomy style would be most likely to describe their partners as having the other-focused style. And sure enough, of the 101 self-focused men in their study, 49.5% "reported the predicted pairing, compared to 25.5% who reported self-focused autonomous partners and 24.5% who reported partners displaying mutuality . . ." (p. 156). In terms of raw numbers, of the 101 self-focused men, 50 had other-focused partners, 26 had self-focused partners, and 25 had mutuality-style partners.

Suppose the partners of these men had been equally likely to be of each of the three relationship styles. If that were the situation, then about 33.66 (1/3 of the 101) of the partners of these men should have been of each style. This information is laid out in the Observed Frequency and Expected Frequency columns of Table 14–1. The Observed Frequency column shows the breakdown of relationship styles of partners actually *observed,* and the Expected Frequency column shows the breakdown you would *expect* if the different partner styles had been exactly equally likely.

Clearly, there is a discrepancy between what was actually observed and the breakdown you would expect if the partner styles were equally likely. The question is this: Should we assume that this discrepancy is no more than would easily occur just by chance for a sample of this size? Suppose that self-focused men in general (the population) are equally likely to have partners of all three styles. Still, in any particular sample from that population, you would not get a perfectly equal breakdown of partners' styles. But if the breakdown in the sample is a long way from equal, you would doubt that the partner styles in the population really are equal. In other words, you are in a hypothesis-testing situation, much like the ones we have been considering all along. But with a big difference too.

In the situations in previous chapters, the scores have all been numerical values on some dimension, such as a score on a standard achievement test, length of time in a relationship, an employer's rating of an employee's job effectiveness on a 9-point scale, and so forth. By contrast, relationship style of a man's partner is an example of what in Chapter 1 we called a *nominal variable* (or a *categorical variable*). A nominal variable is one in which the information is the number of people in each category. These are called nominal variables because the different categories or levels of the variable have names instead of numbers.

Hypothesis testing with nominal variables uses what are called chi-square tests. (Chi is the Greek letter χ; it is pronounced *ki,* rhyming with high and pie.) The chi-square test was originally developed by Karl Pearson (see Box 14–1) and is sometimes called the Pearson chi-square.

TABLE 14–1 Observed and Expected Frequencies for Relationship Styles of Partners of Self-Focused Autonomous Men

Partner Style	Observed Frequency[a] (O)	Expected Frequency (E)	Difference $(O - E)$	Difference Squared $(O - E)^2$	Difference Squared Weighted by Expected Frequency $(O - E)^2/E$
Other-Focused Connection	50	33.67	16.33	266.67	7.92
Self-Focused Autonomous	26	33.67	−7.67	58.83	1.75
Mutuality	25	33.67	−8.67	75.17	2.23

[a]Data from Harter et al. (1997).

THE CHI-SQUARE STATISTIC AND THE CHI-SQUARE TEST FOR GOODNESS OF FIT

The basic idea of any chi-square test is that you compare how well an observed breakdown of people over various categories fits some expected breakdown (such as an equal breakdown). In terms of the relationship style example, you are comparing the observed breakdown of 50, 26, and 25 to the expected breakdown of about 34 (33.67) for each style. A breakdown of numbers of people expected in each category is actually a frequency distribution, as you learned in Chapter 1. Thus, a chi-square test is more formally described as comparing an **observed frequency** distribution to an **expected frequency** distribution. Overall, what the hypothesis testing involves is first figuring a number for the amount of mismatch between the observed frequency and the expected frequency and then seeing whether that number is for a greater mismatch than you would expect by chance.

observed frequency
expected frequency

Let's start with how you would come up with that mismatch number for the observed versus expected frequencies. The mismatch between observed and expected for any one category is just the observed frequency minus the expected frequency. For example, in the Harter et al. study, for self-focused men with an other-focused partner, the observed frequency of 50 is 16.33 more than the expected frequency of 33.67 (recall the expected frequency is 1/3 of the 101 total). For the second category, the difference is −7.67. For the third, −8.67. These differences are shown in the Difference column of Table 14–1.

You do not use these differences directly. One reason is that some differences are positive and some are negative. Thus, they would cancel each other out. To get around this, you square each difference. (This is the same strategy we saw in Chapter 2 to deal with difference scores in figuring the variance.) In the relationship-style example, the squared difference for those with other-focused partners is 16.33 squared, or 266.67. For self-focused partners, it is 58.83. For those with mutuality style partners, 75.17. These squared differences are shown in the Difference Squared column of Table 14–1.

In the Harter et al. example, the expected frequencies are the same in each category. But in other research situations, expected frequencies for the different categories may not be the same. A particular amount of difference between observed and expected has a different importance according to the size of the expected frequency. For example, a difference of eight people between observed and expected is a much bigger mismatch if the expected frequency is 10 than if the expected frequency is 1,000. If the expected frequency is 10, a difference of 8 would mean that the observed frequency was 18 or 2, frequencies that are dramatically different from 10. But if the expected frequency is 1,000, a difference of 8 is only a slight mismatch. This would mean that the observed frequency was 1,008 or 992, frequencies that are only slightly different from 1,000.

How can you adjust the mismatch (the squared difference) between observed and expected for a particular category to take into account the expected frequency for that category? You can do this by dividing your squared difference for a category by the expected frequency for that category. Thus, if the expected frequency for a particular category is 10, you divide the squared difference by 10. If the expected frequency for the category is 1,000, you divide the squared difference by 1,000. In this way, you weight each squared difference by the expected frequency. This weighting puts the squared difference onto a more appropriate scale of comparison. In our example, for men with an other-focused partner, you would weight the mismatch by dividing the squared difference of 266.67 by 33.67, giving 7.92.

BOX 14–1 Karl Pearson, Inventor of Chi-Square and Center of Controversy

Karl Pearson, sometimes hailed as the founder of the science of statistics, was born in 1857, the son of a Yorkshire barrister. Most of both his virtues and his vices are revealed in what he reported to his colleague Julia Bell as his earliest memory: He was sitting in his high chair, sucking his thumb, when he was told to stop or his thumb would wither away. Pearson looked at his two thumbs and silently concluded, "I can't see that the thumb I suck is any smaller than the other. I wonder if she could be lying to me." Here we see Pearson's faith in himself and in observational evidence and his rejection of authority. We also see his tendency to doubt the character of people with whom he disagreed.

Pearson studied mathematics on a scholarship at Cambridge. Soon after he arrived, he requested to be excused from compulsory divinity lectures and chapel. As soon as his request was granted, however, he appeared in chapel. The dean summoned him for an explanation, and Pearson declared that he had asked to be excused not from chapel "but from *compulsory* chapel."

After graduation, Pearson traveled and studied in Germany, becoming a socialist and a self-described "free-thinker." Returning to England, he changed his name from Carl to Karl (in honor of Karl Marx) and wrote an attack on Christianity under a pen name. In 1885 he founded a "Men and Women's Club" to promote equality between the sexes. The club died out, but through it he met his wife, Maria Sharp.

Pearson eventually turned to statistics out of his interest in proving the theory of evolution, being especially influenced by Sir Francis Galton's work (see Box 3–1). Pearson, the better mathematician, saw in Galton's ideas of correlation a way to make fields such as psychology, anthropology, and sociology as scientific as physics and chemistry. He hoped to bypass the issue of causation through the use of this broader category of correlation, association, or contingency (ranging from 0, independence, to the "unity of causation," at 1). "No phenomena are causal," he said. "All phenomena are contingent, and the problem before us is to measure the degree of contingency."

Throughout his life, Pearson was controversial and strong-willed, especially when it came to "pseudoscience" and the masquerading of theology, metaphysics, or appeals to authority under the guise of science. He even thought physics should give up the use of words such as *atom, force,* and *matter* because they were not observable phenomena.

Most of Pearson's research from 1893 to 1901 focused on the laws of heredity and evolution. He sent young scientists out all over the world to measure the distributions of everything from skull sizes to the length of bird beaks. Then a legion of women "calculators" worked out the means and standard deviations. The results were published in the prestigious *Biometrika*, a journal funded by Galton. But Pearson knew he needed better statistical methods, leading him eventually to make his most famous contribution, the chi-square test. Pearson also invented the method of figuring correlation used today (see Chapter 3) and coined the terms *histogram, skew,* and *spurious correlation.* In his lifetime Pearson led statistics from its early position as a matter largely ignored to one central to the scientific method, especially in the natural sciences.

Unfortunately, Pearson was a great fan of eugenics, the "improvement" of the human race through selective breeding, and his work was later used by the Nazis as justification for their treatment of Jews and other ethnic minorities. Towards the end of his life he fought back, writing a paper using clear logic and data on Jews and Gentiles from all over the world to demonstrate that there was no Jewish or Aryan race and that the Nazis' ideas were sheer nonsense.

Indeed, throughout his life, Pearson's strong opinions led to a few devoted friendships and a long list of enemies, especially as other, younger statisticians passed him by, while he refused to publish their work in *Biometrika*. William S. Gosset (see Chapter 9, Box 9–1), inventor of the *t* test, was one of his friends. Sir Ronald Fisher, inventor of the analysis of variance and a man associated with even more extreme attitudes (as described in Chapter 11, Box 11–1), was one of Pearson's worst enemies. The kindly, peaceable Gosset, friends of both, was always trying to smooth matters between them. In 1933, Pearson finally retired, and Fisher, of all persons, took over his chair, the Galton Professorship of Eugenics at University College in London. In 1936, the two entered into their bitterest argument yet; Pearson died the same year.

References: Peters (1987); Salsburg, 2001; Stigler (1986); Tankard (1984).

For those with a self-focused partner, 58.83 divided by 33.67 gives 1.75. For those with a mutuality style partner, 75.17 divided by 33.67 gives 2.23. These adjusted mismatches (squared differences divided by expected frequencies) are shown in the rightmost column of Table 14–1.

What remains is to get an overall figure for the mismatch between observed and expected frequencies. This final step is done by adding up the results for all the categories. In the Harter et al. example, this would be 7.92 plus 1.75 plus 2.23, for a total of 11.90. This final number (the sum of the weighted squared differences) is an overall indication of the amount of mismatch between the expected and observed frequencies. It is called the **chi-square statistic.** In terms of a formula,

chi-square statistic

> Chi-square is the sum, over all the categories, of the squared difference between observed and expected frequencies divided by the expected frequency.

(14-1)
$$\chi^2 = \Sigma \frac{(O - E)^2}{E}$$

In this formula, χ^2 is the chi-square statistic. Σ is the summation sign, telling you to sum over all the different categories. O is the observed frequency for a category (the number of people actually found in that category in the study). E is the expected frequency for a category (in the Harter et al. example, it is based on what you would expect if there were equal numbers in each category).

Applying the formula to the example,

$$\chi^2 = \Sigma \frac{(O - E)^2}{E} = \frac{(50 - 33.67)^2}{33.67} + \frac{(26 - 33.67)^2}{33.67} + \frac{(25 - 33.67)^2}{33.67} = 11.90$$

STEPS FOR FIGURING THE CHI-SQUARE STATISTIC

Here is a summary of what we've said so far in terms of steps:

- ❶ **Determine the actual observed frequencies in each category.**
- ❷ **Determine the expected frequencies in each category.**
- ❸ **In each category, take observed minus expected frequencies.**
- ❹ **Square each of these differences.**
- ❺ **Divide each squared difference by the expected frequency for its category.**
- ❻ **Add up the results of Step E for all the categories.**

THE CHI-SQUARE DISTRIBUTION

Now we turn to the question of whether the chi-square statistic you have figured is a bigger mismatch than you would expect by chance. To answer that, you need to know how likely it is to get chi-square statistics of various sizes by chance. As long as you have a reasonable number of people in the study, the distribution of the chi-square statistic that would arise by chance follows quite closely a known mathematical distribution—the **chi-square distribution.**

chi-square distribution

The exact shape of the chi-square distribution depends on the degrees of freedom. For a chi-square test, the degrees of freedom are the number of categories that are free to vary, given the totals. In the partners' relationship-style example, there are three categories. If you know the total number of people and you know the number in any two categories, you could figure out the number in the third category—so only two are free to vary. That is, in a study like this one, if there are three categories, there are two degrees of freedom.

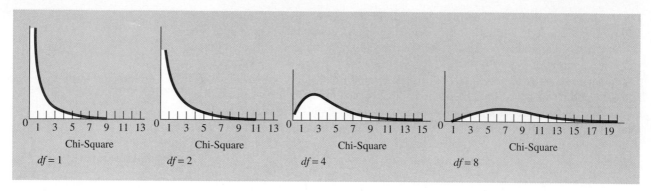

FIGURE 14-1 *Examples of chi-square distributions for different degrees of freedom.*

Chi-square distributions for several different degrees of freedom are shown in Figure 14–1. Notice that the distributions are all skewed to the right. This is because the chi-square statistic cannot be less than 0 but can have very high values. (Chi-square must be positive because it is figured by adding a group of fractions in each of which the numerator and denominator both have to be positive. The numerator has to be positive because it is squared. The denominator has to be positive because the number of people expected in a given category can't be a negative number—you can't expect less than no one!)

THE CHI-SQUARE TABLE

chi-square table

What matters most about the chi-square distribution for hypothesis testing is the cutoff for a chi-square to be extreme enough to reject the null hypothesis. A **chi-square table** gives the cutoff chi-squares for different significance levels and various degrees of freedom. Table 14–2 shows a portion of a chi-square table like the one in Appendix A (Table A–4). For our example, where there were two degrees of freedom, the table shows that the cutoff chi-square for the .05 level is 5.992.

THE CHI-SQUARE TEST FOR GOODNESS OF FIT

TABLE 14–2 Portion of a Chi-Square Table

df	Significance Level		
	.10	.05	.01
1	2.706	3.841	6.635
2	4.605	5.992	9.211
3	6.252	7.815	11.345
4	7.780	9.488	13.277
5	9.237	11.071	15.087

Note: Full table is in Appendix A.

chi-square test for goodness of fit

In the Harter et al. example, we figured a chi-square of 11.90. This is clearly larger than the chi-square cutoff (using the .05 significance level) of 5.992 (see Figure 14–2). Thus, the researchers rejected the null hypothesis. That is, they rejected as too unlikely that the mismatch they observed could have come about if in the population of self-focused men there were an equal number of partners of each relationship style. It seemed more reasonable to conclude that their truly were different proportions of relationship styles of the partners of such men.

We have just carried out a full hypothesis-testing procedure for the Harter et al. example. This example involved differing numbers of people at three levels of a particular nominal variable (the relationship style of partners of self-focused men). This kind of chi-square test involving levels of a single nominal variable is called a **chi-square test for goodness of fit.**

STEPS OF HYPOTHESIS TESTING

Let us review the chi-square test for goodness of fit using the same example, but this time systematically following the standard steps of hypothesis testing. In the process we also consider some fine points.

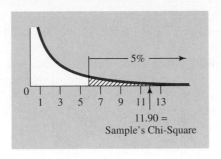

FIGURE 14–2 *For the Harter et al. (1997) example, the chi-square distribution (df = 2) showing the cutoff for rejecting the null hypothesis at the .05 level and the sample's chi-square.*

❶ **Restate the question as a research hypothesis and a null hypothesis about the populations.** There are two populations:

Population 1: Self-focused men like those in the study
Population 2: Self-focused men whose partners are equally of the three relationship styles

The research hypothesis is that the distribution of people over categories in the two populations is different; the null hypothesis is that they are the same.

❷ **Determine the characteristics of the comparison distribution.** The comparison distribution is a chi-square distribution with 2 degrees of freedom. (Once you know the total, there are only two category numbers still free to vary.)

(It is important not to be confused by the terminology here. The comparison distribution is the distribution to which we compare the number that summarizes the whole pattern of the result. With a *t* test, this number is the *t* score and we use a *t* distribution. With an analysis of variance, it is the *F* ratio and we use an *F* distribution. Accordingly, with a chi-square test, our comparison distribution is a distribution of the chi-square statistic. This can be confusing because when preparing to use the chi-square distribution, you compare a distribution of observed frequencies to a distribution of expected frequencies. Yet the distribution of expected frequencies is not a comparison distribution in the sense that we use this term in step 2 of hypothesis testing.)

❸ **Determine the cutoff on the comparison distribution at which the null hypothesis should be rejected.** You do this by looking up the cutoff on the chi-square table for your significance level and the study's degrees of freedom. In this example, we used the .05 significance level, and we determined in step 2 that there were 2 degrees of freedom. Based on the table, this gives a cutoff chi-square of 5.992 (see Figure 14–2).

❹ **Determine your sample's score on the comparison distribution.** Your sample's score is the chi-square figured from the sample. In other words, this is where you do all the figuring.

❿ **Determine the actual, observed frequencies in each category.** These are shown in the first column of Table 14–1.

❿ **Determine the expected frequencies in each category.** We figured these each to be 33.67 based on expecting an equal distribution of the 101 partners.

❿ **In each category, take observed minus expected frequencies.** These are shown in the third column of Table 14–1.

❿ **Square each of these differences.** These are shown in the fourth column of Table 14–1.

❿ **Divide each squared difference by the expected frequency for its category.** These are shown in the fifth column of Table 14–1.

❻ **Add up the results of step E for all the categories.** The result we figured earlier (11.90) is the chi-square statistic for the sample. It is shown in Figure 14–2.

❺ **Decide whether to reject the null hypothesis.** The chi-square cutoff to reject the null hypothesis (from step 3) is 5.992 and the chi-square of the sample (from step 4) is 11.90. Thus, you can reject the null hypothesis. The research hypothesis that the two populations are different is supported. That is, Harter et al. could conclude that the partners of self-focused men are not equally likely to be of the three relationship styles.

ANOTHER EXAMPLE

A fictional research team of clinical psychologists want to test a theory that mental health is affected by the level of a certain mineral in the diet, "mineral Q." The research team has located a region of the United States where mineral Q is found in very high concentrations in the soil. As a result, it is in the water people drink and in locally grown food. The researchers carry out a survey of older people who have lived in this area their whole life, focusing on mental health disorders. Of the 1,000 people surveyed, 134 had at some point in their life experienced an anxiety disorder, 160 had suffered from alcohol or drug abuse, 97 from mood disorders (such as major chronic depression), and 12 from schizophrenia; 597 had never experienced any of these problems. (In this example, we ignore the problem of what happens when a person had more than one of these problems.)

The psychologists then compared their results to what would be expected based on large surveys of the U.S. public in general. In these surveys, 14.6% of adults at some point in their lives suffer from an anxiety disorder, 16.4% from alcohol or drug abuse, 8.3% from mood disorders, and 1.5% from schizophrenia; 59.2% do not experience any of these conditions (Regier et al., 1984). If their sample of 1,000 is not different from the general U.S. population, 14.6% of them (146) should have had anxiety disorders, 16.4% of them (164) should have suffered from alcohol and drug abuse, and so forth. The question the clinical psychologists posed is this: On the basis of the sample we have studied, can we conclude that the rates of various mental health problems among people in this region are different from those of the general U.S. population?

Table 14–3 shows the observed and expected frequencies and the figuring for the chi-square test.

❶ **Restate the question as a research hypothesis and a null hypothesis about the populations.** There are two populations:

Population 1: People in the U.S. region with a high level of mineral Q
Population 2: The U.S. population

The research hypothesis is that the distribution of numbers of people over the five mental health categories is different in the two populations; the null hypothesis is that it is the same.

❷ **Determine the characteristics of the comparison distribution.** The comparison distribution is a chi-square distribution with 4 degrees of freedom (that is, 5 categories − 1 = 4). See Figure 14–3.

❸ **Determine the cutoff sample score on the comparison distribution at which the null hypothesis should be rejected.** We will use the standard 5% significance level and we have just seen that there are 4 degrees of freedom. Thus, Table 14–2 (or Table A–4 in Appendix A) shows that the clinical psychologists need a chi-square of at least 9.488 to reject the null hypothesis. This is shown in Figure 14–3.

TABLE 14–3 Observed and Expected Frequencies and the Chi-Square Goodness of Fit Test for Types of Mental Health Disorders in a U.S. Region High in Mineral Q Compared to the General U.S. Population (Fictional Data)

Condition	Observed (A)	Expected (B)
Anxiety disorder	134	146 (14.6% × 1,000)
Alcohol and drug abuse	160	164 (16.4% × 1,000)
Mood disorders	97	83 (08.3% × 1,000)
Schizophrenia	12	15 (01.5% × 1,000)
None of these conditions	597	592 (59.2% × 1,000)

Degrees of freedom = 5 categories − 1 = 4 ❷

Chi-square needed, $df = 4$, .05 level: 9.488 ❸

$$\chi^2 = \Sigma \frac{(O - E)^2}{E} = \frac{(134 - 146)^2}{146} + \frac{(160 - 164)^2}{164} + \frac{(97 - 83)^2}{83} + \frac{(12 - 15)^2}{15} + \frac{(597 - 592)^2}{592}$$

$$= \frac{-12^2}{146} + \frac{-4^2}{164} + \frac{14^2}{83} + \frac{-3^2}{15} + \frac{5^2}{592}$$

$$= \frac{144}{146} + \frac{16}{164} + \frac{196}{83} + \frac{9}{15} + \frac{25}{592}$$

$$= .99 + .10 + 2.36 + .60 + .04 = 4.09 \ ❻$$

Conclusion: Do not reject the null hypothesis. ❺

❹ **Determine your sample's score on the comparison distribution.** The chi-square figuring is shown in Table 14–3.

Ⓐ **Determine the actual observed frequencies in each category.** These are shown in the first column of Table 14–3.

Ⓑ **Determine the expected frequencies in each category.** These are figured by multiplying the expected percentage by the total number. For example, with 14.6% expected to have anxiety disorders, the actual expected number to have anxiety disorders is 146 (that is, 14.6% of 1000). All of the expected frequencies are shown in Table 14–3.

Ⓒ **In each category, take observed minus expected frequencies.** The result of these subtractions are shown in the numerators of the second formula line on Table 14–3.

Ⓓ **Square each of these differences.** The result of these squarings are shown in the numerators of the third formula line on Table 14–3.

Ⓔ **Divide each squared difference by the expected frequency for its category.** The result of these divisions are shown in the fourth formula line on Table 14–3.

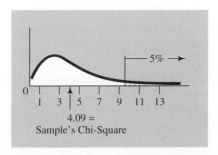

FIGURE 14–3 *For the mineral Q example, the chi-square distribution (df = 4) showing the cutoff for rejecting the null hypothesis at the .05 level and the sample's chi square.*

❻ Add up the results of step E for all the categories. The sum comes out to 4.09. The addition is shown on Table 14–3; the location on the chi-square distribution is shown in Figure 14–3.

❺ Decide whether to reject the null hypothesis. The sample's chi-square (from step 4) of 4.09 is less extreme than the cutoff (from step 3) of 9.488. The researchers cannot reject the null hypothesis; the study is inconclusive. (Having failed to reject the null hypothesis with such a large sample, it is reasonable to suppose that if there is any difference between the populations, it is quite small.)

HOW ARE YOU DOING?

1. In what situation do you use a chi-square test for goodness of fit?
2. List the steps for figuring the chi-square statistic and explain the logic behind each step.
3. Write the formula for the chi-square statistic and define each of the symbols.
4. (a) What is a chi-square distribution? (b) What is its shape? (c) Why does it have that shape?
5. Carry out a chi-square test for goodness of fit (using the .05 significance level) for a sample in which one category has 15 people, the other has 35 people, and the categories are expected to have equal frequencies. (a) Use the steps of hypothesis testing and (b) sketch the distributions involved.

Answers:

1. When you want to test whether a sample's distribution of people across categories represents a population that is significantly different from a population with an expected distribution of people across categories.
2. **❶ Determine the actual observed frequencies in each category.** This is the key information for the sample studied.

   ❷ Determine the expected frequencies in each category. Having these numbers makes it possible to make a direct comparison of what is expected to the observed frequencies.

   ❸ In each category, take observed minus expected frequencies. This is the direct comparison of the distribution for the sample versus the distribution representing the expected population.

   ❹ Square each of these differences. This gets rid of the direction of the difference (since the interest is only in how much difference there is).

   ❺ Divide each squared difference by the expected frequency for its category. This adjusts the degree of difference for the absolute size of the expected frequencies.

   ❻ Add up the results of step E for all the categories. This gives you a statistic for the overall degree of discrepancy.

3. $\chi^2 = \Sigma \dfrac{(O - E)^2}{E}$

   χ^2 is the chi-square statistic; Σ tells you to sum over all the different categories; O is the observed frequency for a category; E is the expected frequency for a category.
4. (a) For any particular number of categories, the distribution you would expect if you figured a very large number of chi-square statistics for samples from a population in which the distribution of people over categories is the expected distribution.

   (b) It is skewed to the right.

   (c) It has this shape because a chi-square statistic can't be less than 0 (since the numerator, a squared score, has to be positive, and its denominator, an expected number of individuals, also has to be positive), but there is no limit to how large it can be.
5. (a)

   ❶ Restate the question as a research hypothesis and a null hypothesis about the populations. There are two populations:

   Population 1: People like those in the sample.
   Population 2: People who have an equal distribution of the two categories.

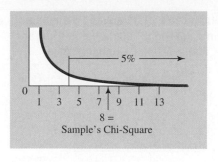

FIGURE 14–4 *For "How Are You Doing?" question 5, the chi-square distribution (df = 1) showing the cutoff for rejecting the null hypothesis at the .05 level and the sample's chi-square.*

The research hypothesis is that the distribution of numbers of people over categories is different in the two populations; the null hypothesis is that it is the same.

❷ **Determine the characteristics of the comparison distribution.** The comparison distribution is a chi-square distribution with 1 degree of freedom (that is, 2 categories − 1 = 1).

❸ **Determine the cutoff sample score on the comparison distribution at which the null hypothesis should be rejected.** At the .05 level with $df = 1$, cutoff is 3.841.

❹ **Determine your sample's score on the comparison distribution.**

Ⓐ **Determine the actual observed frequencies in each category.** As given in the problem, these are 15 and 35.

Ⓑ **Determine the expected frequencies in each category.** With 50 people total and expecting an even breakdown, the expected frequencies are 25 and 25.

Ⓒ **In each category, take observed minus expected frequencies.** These come out to −10 (that is, 15 − 25 = −10) and 10 (that is, 35 − 25 = 10).

Ⓓ **Square each of these differences.** Both come out to 100 (that is, $-10^2 = 100$ and $10^2 = 100$).

Ⓔ **Divide each squared difference by the expected frequency for its category.** These both come out to 4 (that is, 100/25 = 4).

Ⓕ **Add up the results of step E for all the categories.** 4 + 4 = 8.

❺ **Decide whether to reject the null hypothesis.** The sample's chi-square of 8 is more extreme than the cutoff of 3.841. Reject the null hypothesis; people like those in the sample are different from the expected even breakdown.

(b) See Figure 14–4.

THE CHI-SQUARE TEST FOR INDEPENDENCE

So far, we have looked at the distribution of one nominal variable with several categories, such as the relationship style of men's partners. In fact, this kind of situation is fairly rare in research. We began with an example of this kind mainly as a stepping-stone to a more common actual research situation, to which we now turn.

The most common use of chi-square is when there are two nominal variables, each with several categories. For example, Harter et al. might have studied whether the breakdown of partners of self-focused men was the same as the breakdown of partners of other-focused men. If that were their purpose, we would have had two nominal variables. Relationship styles of partners would be the first nominal variable. Men's own relationship styles would be the second nominal variable. Hypothesis testing in this kind of situation is called a **chi-square test for independence.** You learn shortly why it has this name.

Suppose researchers at a large university survey 200 staff members who commute to work about the kind of transportation they use as well as whether they are

chi-square test for independence

TABLE 14–4	Contingency Table of Observed Frequencies of Morning and Night People Using Different Types of Transportation (Fictional Data)			

		Transportation			Total
		Bus	*Carpool*	*Own Car*	
Sleep Tendency	Morning	60	30	30	120 (60%)
	Night	20	20	40	80 (40%)
	Total	80	50	70	200 (100%)

"morning people" (prefer to go to bed early and awaken early) or "night people" (go to bed late and awaken late). Table 14–4 shows the results. Notice the two nominal variables: types of transportation (with three levels) and sleep tendency (with two levels).

CONTINGENCY TABLES

contingency table

Table 14–4 is a **contingency table**—a table in which the distributions of two nominal variables are set up so that you have the frequencies of their combinations as well as the totals. Thus, in Table 14–4, the 60 in the bus-morning combination is how many morning people ride the bus. (A contingency table is similar to the tables in factorial analysis of variance that you learned about in Chapter 13; but in a contingency table, the number in each cell is a number of people, not a mean.)

Table 14–4 is a 3 × 2 contingency table because it has three levels of one variable crossed with two levels of the other. (Which dimension is named first does not matter.) It is also possible to have larger contingency tables, such as a 4 × 7 or a 6 × 18 table. Smaller tables, 2 × 2 contingency tables, are especially common.

INDEPENDENCE

The question in this example is whether there is any relation between the type of transportation people use and whether they are morning or night people. If there is no relation, the proportion of morning and night people is the same among bus riders, carpoolers, and those who drive their own cars. Or, to put it the other way, if there is no relation, the proportion of bus riders, carpoolers, and own car drivers is the same for morning and night people. However you describe it, the situation of no

independence

relation between the variables in a contingency table is called **independence**.[1]

SAMPLE AND POPULATION

In the observed survey results in the example, the proportions of night and morning people in the sample vary with different types of transportation. For example, the bus riders are split 60–20, so three-fourths of the bus riders are morning people. Among people who drive their own cars, the split is 30–40. Thus, a slight majority are night people. Still, the sample is only of 200. It is possible that in the larger population, the type of transportation a person uses is independent of the person's being

[1]Independence is usually used to talk about a lack of relation between two nominal variables. However, if you have studied Chapter 3, it may be helpful to think of independence as roughly the same as the situation of no correlation ($r = 0$).

a morning or a night person. The big question is whether the lack of independence in the sample is large enough to reject the null hypothesis of independence in the population. That is, you need to do a chi-square test.

DETERMINING EXPECTED FREQUENCIES

One thing that is new in a chi-square test of independence is that you now have to figure differences between observed and expected for each *combination* of categories—that is, for each **cell** of the contingency table. (When there was only one nominal variable, you figured these differences just for each category of that single nominal variable.) Table 14–5 is the contingency table for the example survey. This time, we have put in the expected frequency (in parentheses) next to each observed frequency.

    The key consideration in figuring expected frequencies in a contingency table is that "expected" is based on the two variables being independent. If they are independent, then the proportions up and down the cells of each column should be the same. In the example, overall, there are 60% morning people and 40% night people; thus, if transportation method is independent of being a morning or night person, this 60%–40% split should hold for each column (each transportation type). First, the 60%–40% overall split should hold for the bus group. This would make an expected frequency in the bus cell for morning people of 60% of 80, which comes out to 48 people. The expected frequency for the bus riders who are night people is 32 (that is, 40% of 80 is 32). The same principle holds for the other columns: The 50 carpool people should have a 60%–40% split, giving an expected frequency of 30 morning people who carpool (that is, 60% of 50 is 30) and 20 night people who carpool (that is, 40% of 50 is 20), and the 70 own-car people should have a 60%–40% split, giving expected frequencies of 42 and 28.

    Summarizing what we have said in terms of steps,

❶ **Find each row's percentage of the total.**

❷ **For each cell, multiply its row's percentage times its column's total.**
Applying these steps to the top left cell (morning persons who ride the bus),

❶ **Find each row's percentage of the total.** The 120 in the morning person row is 60% of the overall total of 200 (that is, $120/200 = 60\%$).

❷ **For each cell, multiply its row's percentage times its column's total.** The column total for the bus riders is 80; 60% of 80 comes out to 48 (that is, $.6 \times 80 = 48$).

    These steps can also be stated as a formula,

cell

(14-2)
$$E = \left(\frac{R}{N}\right)(C)$$

> A cell's expected frequency is the number in its row divided by the total, multiplied by the number in its column.

TABLE 14–5	Contingency Table of Observed (and Expected) Frequencies of Morning and Night People Using Different Types of Transportation (Fictional Data)

		Transportation			Total
		Bus	*Carpool*	*Own Car*	
Sleep Tendency	Morning	60 (48)[a]	30 (30)	30 (42)	120 (60%)
	Night	20 (32)	20 (20)	40 (28)	80 (40%)
	Total	80	50	70	200 (100%)

[a]Expected frequencies are in parentheses.

In this formula, E is the expected frequency for a particular cell, R is the number of people observed in this cell's row, N is the number of people total, and C is the number of people observed in this cell's column. (If you reverse cells and columns, the expected frequency still comes out the same.)

Applying the formula to the same top left cell,

$$E = \left(\frac{R}{N}\right)(C) = \left(\frac{120}{200}\right)(80) = (.60)(80) = 48$$

Looking at the entire Table 14–5, notice that the expected frequencies add up to the same totals as the observed frequencies. For example, in the first column (bus), the expected frequencies of 32 and 48 add up to 80, just as the observed frequencies in that column of 60 and 20 do. Similarly, in the top row (morning), the expected frequencies of 48, 30, and 42 add up to 120, the same total as for the observed frequencies of 60, 30, and 30.

FIGURING CHI-SQUARE AND SIGNIFICANCE

You figure chi-square the same way as in the chi-square test for goodness of fit, except that you now figure the weighted squared difference for each *cell* and add these up. Here is how it works for our survey example:

$$
\begin{aligned}
\chi^2 &= \Sigma \frac{(O - E)^2}{E} \\
&= \frac{(60 - 48)^2}{48} + \frac{(30 - 30)^2}{30} + \frac{(30 - 42)^2}{42} \\
&\quad + \frac{(20 - 32)^2}{32} + \frac{(20 - 20)^2}{20} + \frac{(40 - 28)^2}{28} \\
&= 3 + 0 + 3.43 + 4.5 + 0 + 5.14 = 16.07
\end{aligned}
$$

DEGREES OF FREEDOM

A contingency table with many cells may have relatively few degrees of freedom. In our example, there are six cells but only 2 degrees of freedom. Recall that the degrees of freedom are the number of categories free to vary once the totals are known. With a chi-square test of independence, the number of categories is the number of cells; the totals include the row and column totals—and if you know the row and column totals, you have a lot of information.

Consider the sleep tendency and transportation example. Suppose you know the first two cell frequencies across the top, for example, and all the row and column totals. You could then figure all the other cell frequencies just by subtraction. Table 14–6 shows the contingency table for this example with just the row and column totals and these two cell frequencies. Let's start with the Morning, Own Car cell. There is a total of 120 morning people and the other two morning-person cells have 90 in them (60 + 30). Thus, only 30 remain for the Morning, Own-Car cell. Now consider the three night person cells. You know the frequencies for all the morning people cells and the column totals for each type of transportation. Thus, each cell frequency for the night people is its column's total minus the morning people in that column. For example, there are 80 bus riders and 60 are morning people. Thus, the remaining 20 must be night people.

What you can see in all this is that with knowledge of only two of the cells, you could figure out the frequencies in each of the other cells. Thus, although there are

TABLE 14–6	Contingency Table Showing Marginal and Two Cells' Observed Frequencies to Illustrate Figuring of Degrees of Freedom

		Transportation			Total
		Bus	Carpool	Own Car	
Sleep Tendency	Morning	60	30	——	120 (60%)
	Night	——	——	——	80 (40%)
	Total	80	50	70	200 (100%)

six cells, there are only 2 degrees of freedom—only two cells whose frequencies are really free to vary once we have all the row and column totals.

As a general principle, in a chi-square test for independence, the degrees of freedom is the number of columns minus 1 times the number of rows minus 1. Put as a formula,

(14-3)
$$df = (N_{\text{Columns}} - 1)(N_{\text{Rows}} - 1)$$

> The degrees of freedom is the number of columns minus 1 times the number of rows minus 1.

N_{Columns} is the number of columns and N_{Rows} is the number of rows.

Using this formula for our survey example,

$$df = (N_{\text{Columns}} - 1)(N_{\text{Rows}} - 1) = (3 - 1)(2 - 1) = (2)(1) = 2.$$

HYPOTHESIS TESTING

With 2 degrees of freedom, Table 14–2 (or Table A–4) shows that the chi-square you need for significance at the .01 level is 9.211. The chi-square of 16.07 for our example is larger than this cutoff. Thus, you can reject the null hypothesis that the two variables are independent in the population.

STEPS OF HYPOTHESIS TESTING

Now let's go through the survey example again, this time following the steps of hypothesis testing.

❶ **Restate the question as a research hypothesis and a null hypothesis about the populations.** There are two populations:

Population 1: People like those surveyed
Population 2: People for whom being a night or a morning person is independent of the kind of transportation they use to commute to work

The null hypothesis is that the two populations are the same, that, in general, the proportions using different types of transportation are the same for morning and night people. The research hypothesis is that the two populations are different, that among people in general the proportions using different types of transportation are different for morning and night people.

Put another way, the null hypothesis is that the two variables are independent (they are unrelated to each other). The research hypothesis is that they are not independent (that they are related to each other).

❷ **Determine the characteristics of the comparison distribution.** The comparison distribution is a chi-square distribution with 2 degrees of freedom. As we have seen, in a 3×2 contingency table, if you know the numbers in two cells and the row and column totals, all the others can be determined. Or, using the rule for contingency tables, the number of cells free to vary is the number of columns minus 1 times number of rows minus 1.

❸ **Determine the cutoff sample score on the comparison distribution at which the null hypothesis should be rejected.** You use the same table as for any chi-square test. In the example, setting a .01 significance level with 2 degrees of freedom, your need a chi-square of 9.211.

❹ **Determine your sample's score on the comparison distribution.**

    ❶ **Determine the actual observed frequencies in each cell.** These are the results of the survey, as given in Table 14–4.

    ❷ **Determine the expected frequencies in each cell.** These are shown in Table 14–5. For example, for the bottom right cell (Night Person's Own Car cell),

        ❶ **Find each row's percentage of the total.** The 80 people in the night person's row are 40% of the overall total of 200 (that is, 80/200 = 40%).

        ❷ **For each cell, multiply its row's percentage times its column's total.** The column total for those with their own car is 70; 40% of 70 comes out to 28 (that is, $.4 \times 70 = 28$).

    ❸ **In each cell, take observed minus expected frequencies.** For example, for the Night Person's Own Car cell, this comes out to 12 (that is, $40 - 28 = 12$).

    ❹ **Square each of these differences.** For example, for the Night Person's Own Car cell, this comes out to 144 (that is, $12^2 = 144$).

    ❺ **Divide each squared difference by the expected frequency for its cell.** For example, for the Night Person's Own Car cell, this comes out to 5.14 (that is, $144/28 = 5.14$).

    ❻ **Add up the results of step E for all the cells.** As we saw, this came out to 16.07.

❺ **Decide whether to reject the null hypothesis.** The chi-square needed to reject the null hypothesis is 9.211 and the chi-square for our sample is 16.07 (see Figure 14–5). Thus, you can reject the null hypothesis. The research hypothesis that the two variables are not independent in the population is supported. That is, the proportions of type of transportation used to commute to work are different for morning and night people.

FIGURE 14–5 *For the sleep tendency and transportation example, chi-square distribution (df = 2) showing the cutoff for rejecting the null hypothesis at the .01 level and the sample's chi-square.*

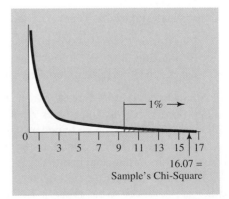

A SECOND EXAMPLE

Riehl (1994) studied the college experience of students who were the first generation in their family to attend college compared to other students who were not the
first generation in their family to go to college. (All students in the study were from
Indiana University.) One of the variables Riehl measured was whether or not students dropped out during their first semester.

Table 14–7 shows the results along with the expected frequencies (shown in
parentheses). Below the contingency table is the figuring for the chi-square test for
independence.

❶ **Restate the question as a null hypothesis and a research hypothesis
about the populations.** There are two populations:

Population 1: Students like those surveyed
Population 2: Students whose dropping out or staying in college their first semester is independent of whether or not they are the first generation in their
family to go to college

The null hypothesis is that the two populations are the same—that, in general,
whether or not students drop out of college is independent of whether or not they
are the first generation in their family to go to college. The research hypothesis is
that the populations are not the same. In other words, the research hypothesis is that
students like those surveyed are different from the hypothetical population in which
dropping out is unrelated to whether or not you are first generation.

TABLE 14–7 **Results and Figuring of the Chi-Square Test for Independence Comparing Whether
First-Generation College Students Differ from Others in First Semester Dropouts**

	Generation to Go to College		Total
	First	*Other*	
Dropped Out	Ⓐ 73 (57.7)	Ⓑ 89 (103.9)	162 (7.9%)
Did Not Drop Out	657 (672.3)	1,226 (1,211.1)	1,883 (92.1%)
	730	1,315	2,045

$df = (N_{\text{Columns}} - 1)(N_{\text{Rows}} - 1) = (2 - 1)(2 - 1) = (1)(1) = 1.$ ❷
Chi-square needed, $df = 1$, .01 level: 6.635. ❸

$$\chi^2 = \Sigma \frac{(O - E)^2}{E} = \frac{(73 - 57.7)^2}{57.7} + \frac{(89 - 103.9)^2}{103.9} + \frac{(657 - 672.3)^2}{672.3} + \frac{(1,226 - 1,211.1)^2}{1,211.1}$$

$$❹ = \frac{15.3^2}{57.7} + \frac{-14.9^2}{103.9} + \frac{-15.3^2}{672.3} + \frac{14.9^2}{1,211.1}$$

$$❺ = \frac{234.1}{57.7} + \frac{222}{103.9} + \frac{234.1}{672.3} + \frac{222}{1,211.1}$$

$$❻ = 4.06 + 2.14 + .35 + .18$$

$$= 6.73. ❼$$

Conclusion: Reject the null hypothesis. ❽

Notes. 1. With a 2×2 analysis, the differences and squared differences (numerators) are the same for all four cells. In this example, the
cells are a little difference due to rounding error. 2. Data from Riehl (1994). The exact chi-square (6.73) is slightly different from that reported in the article (7.2), due to rounding error.
Data from Riehl (1994).

❷ **Determine the characteristics of the comparison distribution.** This is a chi-square distribution with 1 degree of freedom.

❸ **Determine the cutoff sample score on the comparison distribution at which the null hypothesis should be rejected.** Using the .01 level and 1 degree of freedom. Table A–4 shows that you need a chi-square for significance is 6.635. This is illustrated in Figure 14–6.

❹ **Determine your sample's score on the comparison distribution.**

    Ⓐ **Determine the actual observed frequencies in each cell.** These are the results of the survey, as given in Table 14–7.

    Ⓑ **Determine the expected frequencies in each cell.** These are shown in parentheses in Table 14–7.

For example, for the top left cell (First Generation's Dropped Out cell),

    ❶ **Find each row's percentage of the total.** The Dropped Out row's 162 is 7.9% of the overall total of 2,045 (that is, 162/2,045 = 7.9%).

    ❷ **For each cell, multiply its row's percentage times its column's total.** The column total for the First Generation students is 730; 7.9% of 730 comes out to 57.7 (that is, .079 × 730 = 57.7).

    Ⓒ **In each cell, take observed minus expected frequencies.** These are shown in Table 14–7. For example, for the First Generation Dropped Out's cell, this comes out to 15.3 (that is, 73 − 57.7 = 15.3).

    Ⓓ **Square each of these differences.** These are also shown in Table 14–7. For example, for the First Generation Dropped Out's cell, this comes out to 234.1 (that is, $15.3^2 = 234.1$).

    Ⓔ **Divide each squared difference by the expected frequency for its cell.** Once again, these are shown in Table 14–7. For example, First Generation Dropped Out's cell, this comes out to 4.06 (that is, 234.1/57.7 = 4.06).

    Ⓕ **Add up the results of Step E for all the cells.** As shown in Table 14–7, this comes out to 6.73. Its location on the chi-square distribution is shown in Figure 14–6.

❺ **Decide whether to reject the null hypothesis.** Your chi-square of 6.73 is larger than the cutoff of 6.635. Thus, you can reject the null hypothesis. That is, judging from a sample of 2,045 Indiana University students, first generation students are somewhat more likely to drop out during their first semester than are other students. (Remember, of course, that there could be many reasons for this result.)

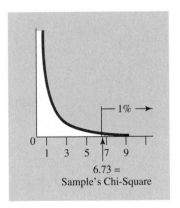

FIGURE 14–6 *For the example from Riehl (1994), chi-square distribution (df = 1) showing the cutoff for rejecting the null hypothesis at the .01 level and the sample's chi square.*

HOW ARE YOU DOING?

1. (a) In what situation do you use a chi-square test for independence? (b) How is this different from the situation in which you would use a chi-square test for goodness of fit?
2. (a) List the steps for figuring the expected frequencies in a contingency table. (b) Write the formula for expected frequencies in a contingency table and define each of its symbols..
3. (a) Write the formula for figuring degrees of freedom in a chi-square test of independence and define each of its symbols. (b) Explain the logic behind this formula.
4. Carry out a chi-square test for independence for the observed scores below (using the .10 significance level). (a) Use the steps of hypothesis testing, and (b) sketch the distributions involved.

		Nominal Variable A	
		Category 1	Category 2
Nominal Variable B	Category 1	10	10
	Category 2	50	10

ANSWERS:

1. (a) When you have the number of people in the various combinations of levels of two nominal variables and want to test whether the difference from independence in the sample is sufficiently great to reject the null hypothesis of independence in the population. (b) The focus is on the independence of two nominal variables, in a chi-square test for goodness of fit the focus is on the distribution of people over categories of a single nominal variable.

2. (a) ❶ Find each row's percentage of the total.

    ❷ For each cell, multiply its row's percentage times its column's total.

   (b) $E = \left(\dfrac{R}{N}\right)(C)$

   E is the expected frequency for a particular cell, R is the number of people observed in this cell's row, N is the number of people total, and C is the number of people observed in this cell's column.

3. (a) $df = (N_{Columns} - 1)(N_{Rows} - 1)$.

   df are the degrees of freedom, $N_{Columns}$ is the number of columns, and N_{Rows} is the number of rows.

   (b) df are the number of cell totals free to vary given you know the column and row totals. If you know the totals in all the columns but one, you can figure the total in the cells in the remaining column by subtraction. Similarly, if you know the total in all the rows but one, you can figure the total in the cells in the remaining row by subtraction.

4. (a)

   ❶ **Restate the question as a null hypothesis and a research hypothesis about the populations.** There are two populations:

   Population 1: People like those studied
   Population 2: People whose being in a particular category of Nominal Variable A is independent of their being in a particular category of Nominal Variable B.

The null hypothesis is that the two populations are the same; the research hypothesis is that the populations are not the same.

   ❷ **Determine the characteristics of the comparison distribution.** This is a chi-square distribution with 1 degree of freedom. That is, $df = (N_{Columns} - 1)(N_{Rows} - 1) = (2 - 1)(2 - 1) = 1$.

   ❸ **Determine the cutoff sample score on the comparison distribution at which the null hypothesis should be rejected.** From Table A–4, for the .10 level and 1 degree of freedom, the needed chi-square is 2.706.

   ❹ **Determine your sample's score on the comparison distribution.**

   ❹ **Determine the actual observed frequencies in each cell.** These are shown in the contingency table for the problem.

   ❽ **Determine the expected frequencies in each cell.**

   ❶ **Find each row's percentage of the total.** For the top row 20/80 = 25%; for the second row, 60/80 = 75%.

   ❷ **For each cell, multiply its row's percentage times its column's total.** For the top left cell, 25% × 60 = 15; for the top right cell, 25% × 20 = 5; for the bottom left cell, 75% × 60 = 45; for the bottom right cell, 75% × 20 = 15.

   ❸ **In each cell, take observed minus expected frequencies.** For the four cells, 10 − 15 = −5; 10 − 5 = 5; 50 − 45 = −5; 10 − 15 = −5.

   ❹ **Square each of these differences.** This is 25 for each cell (that is, $5^2 = 25$ and $-5^2 = 25$).

   ❺ **Divide each squared difference by the expected frequency for its cell.** These come out to 25/15 = 1.67, 25/5 = 5, 25/45 = .56, and 25/15 = 1.67.

   ❻ **Add up the results of step E for all the cells.** 1.67 + 5 + .56 + 1.67 = 8.9.

   ❺ **Decide whether to reject the null hypothesis.** The sample's chi square of 8.9 is larger than the cutoff of 2.706. Thus, you can reject the null hypothesis: Which category

TABLE 14–9	Approximate Power for the Chi-Square Test for Independence for Testing Hypotheses at the .05 Significance Level			
Total *df*	**Total *N***	**Effect Size**		
		Small	*Medium*	*Large*
1	25	.08	.32	.70
	50	.11	.56	.94
	100	.17	.85	*
	200	.29	.99	*
2	25	.07	.25	.60
	50	.09	.46	.90
	100	.13	.77	*
	200	.23	.97	*
3	25	.07	.21	.54
	50	.08	.40	.86
	100	.12	.71	.99
	200	.19	.96	*
4	25	.06	.19	.50
	50	.08	.36	.82
	100	.11	.66	.99
	200	.17	.94	*

*Nearly 1.

POWER

Table 14–9 shows the approximate power at the .05 significance level for small, medium, and large effect sizes and total sample sizes of 25, 50, 100, and 200. Power is given for tables with 1, 2, 3, and 4 degrees of freedom.[3]

Consider the power of a planned 2×4 study ($df = 3$) of 50 people with an expected medium effect size (Cramer's $\phi = .30$). The researchers will use the .05 level. From Table 14–9 you can find this study would have a power of .40. That is, if the research hypothesis is true, and there is a true medium effect size, there is about a 40% chance that the study will come out significant.

NEEDED SAMPLE SIZE

Table 14–10 gives the approximate total number of participants needed for 80% power with small, medium, and large effect sizes at the .05 significance level for chi-square tests of independence of 2, 3, 4, and 5 degrees of freedom.[4] Suppose you are planning a study with a 3×3 ($df = 4$) contingency table. You expect a large effect size and will use the .05 significance level. According to the table, you would only need 48 participants.

---

[3]Cohen (1988, pp. 228–248) gives more detailed tables. However, Cohen's tables are based on an effect size called *w*, which is equivalent to phi but not to Cramer's phi. He provides a helpful conversion table of Cramer's phi to *w* on page 222.

[4]More detailed tables are provided in Cohen (1988, pp. 253–267). When using these tables, see footnote 3. Also, Dunlap and Myers (1997) have shown that with a 2×2 table, the approximate number of participants needed for 80–90% power is $8/\phi^2$.

| TABLE 14–10 | Approximate Total Number of Participants Needed for 80% Power for the Chi-Square Test of Independence for Testing Hypotheses at the .05 Significance Level |

Total df	Effect Size		
	Small	Medium	Large
1	1,785	87	26
2	1,964	107	39
3	1,090	121	44
4	1,194	133	48

HOW ARE YOU DOING?

1. What are the assumptions for chi-square tests?
2. (a) What is the measure of effect size for a 2 × 2 chi-square test of independence? (b) Write the formula for this measure of effect size and define each of the symbols. (c) What are Cohen's conventions for small, medium, and large effect sizes? (d) Figure the effect size for a 2 × 2 chi-square test of independence in which there are a total of 100 participants and the chi-square is 12.
3. (a) What is the measure of effect size for a chi-square test of independence for a contingency table that is larger than 2 × 2? (b) Write the formula for this measure of effect size and define each of the symbols. (c) What is Cohen's convention for a small effect size for a 4 × 6 contingency table? (d) Figure the effect size for a 4 × 6 chi-square test of independence in which there are a total of 200 participants and the chi-square is 20.
4. What is the power of a planned 3 × 3 chi-square with 50 participants total and a predicted medium effect size?
5. About how many participants do you need for 80% power in a planned 2 × 2 study in which you predict a medium effect size and will be using the .05 significance level?

ANSWERS:

1. The only major assumption is that the numbers in each cell or category are from separate persons.
2. (a) The phi coefficient.

   (b) $\phi = \sqrt{\dfrac{\chi^2}{N}}$

   ϕ is the phi coefficient (effect size for a chi-square test of independence with a 2 × 2 contingency table); χ^2 is the sample's chi-square; and N is the number of participants in the study total.

   (c) .10 is a small effect size, .30 is a medium effect size, and .50 is a large effect size.

   (d) $\sqrt{(12/100)} = .35$.
3. (a) Cramer's phi.

   (b) Cramer's $\phi = \sqrt{\dfrac{\chi^2}{(N)(df_{Smaller})}}$ (14-5)

   Cramer's ϕ is Cramer's phi coefficient (effect size for a chi-square test of independence); χ^2 is the sample's chi-square; N is the number of participants in the study total; and $df_{Smaller}$ is the degrees of freedom for the smaller side of the contingency table.

   (c) .06.

(d) $\sqrt{20/[(200)(3)]} = .18$
4. .36.
5. 87.

CONTROVERSY: THE MINIMUM EXPECTED FREQUENCY

Over a half century ago, Lewis and Burke (1949) published a landmark paper on the misuse of chi-square. They listed nine common errors that had appeared in published papers, giving many examples of each. With one exception, their work has held up very well through the years. The errors are still being made, and they are still seen as errors. (If you follow the procedures of this chapter, *you* won't be making them!)

The one exception to this critical picture is the error that Lewis and Burke considered the most common weakness in the use of chi-square—expected frequencies that are too low. Now, it seems that low expected numbers in cells may not be such a big problem after all. Lewis and Burke, like most statistics textbook authors of their time, held that every cell of a contingency table (and every category of a goodness of fit test) should have a reasonable-sized expected frequency. They recommended a minimum of 10, with 5 as the bottom limit. Others recommended figures ranging from 1 to 20. Even Sir Ronald Fisher (1938) got into the act, recommending 10 as his minimum. Still others recommended that the minimum should be some proportion of the total or that it depended on whether the expected frequencies were equal or not. (Incidentally, notice that what was being debated were minimum *expected* frequencies, not observed frequencies.)

Since 1949, when Lewis and Burke published their article, there has been some systematic research on just what the effects of low expected frequencies are. (These studies use Monte Carlo methods—see Chapter 10, Box 10–1.) And what is the conclusion? As in most areas, the matter is still not completely settled. However, a major review of the research on the topic (Delucchi, 1983) draws two main conclusions:

1. "As a general rule, the chi-square statistic may be properly used in cases where the expected values are much lower than previously considered permissible" (p. 168). Even expected frequencies as low as 1 per cell may be acceptable in terms of Type I error, provided that there are a reasonable number of individuals overall. The most important principle seems to be that there should be at least five times as many individuals as there are cells. For example, a cell with a very low expected frequency would be acceptable in a 2×2 contingency table if there were at least 20 participants in the study overall.[5]

2. However, Delucchi cites one researcher as concluding that even though using chi-square with small expected frequencies may be acceptable (in the sense of not giving too many Type I errors in the long run), it may still not be a wise ap-

---

[5]Suppose you have a table larger than 2×2 with a category or cell that has an extremely small expected frequency (or even a moderately small expected frequency if the number of participants is also small). One solution is to combine related categories to increase the expected frequency and reduce the total number of cells. But this is a solution of last resort if you are making the adjustment based on the results of the experiment. The problem is that you are then taking advantage of knowing the outcome. The best solution is to add more people to the study. If this is not feasible, an alternative procedure, called Fisher's exact test, is sometimes possible. It is described in some intermediate statistics texts.

proach. This is because the chance of getting a significant result, even if your research hypothesis is true, may be quite slim. That is, with small expected frequencies, power is very low. Thus, you run the risk of Type II errors instead.

CHI-SQUARE TESTS IN RESEARCH ARTICLES

In research articles, chi-square tests usually include the frequencies in each category or cell as well as the degrees of freedom, number of participants, the sample's chi-square, and significance level. For example, Harter et al. reported their finding for the relationship style of the self-focused men as "$\chi^2(2, n = 101) = 11.89, p < .005$" (p. 156).

Here is another example of a chi-square test for goodness of fit. Sandra Moriarty and Shu-Ling Everett (1994) had graduate students go to 55 different homes and observe people watching television for 45-minute sessions. In one part of their results, they compared the number of people they observed who fell into one of four distinct categories:

> Flipping [very rapid channel changing], the category dominated by the most active type of behavior, occurred most frequently in 33% of the sessions ($n = 18$). The grazing category [periods of browsing through channels] dominated 24% of the sessions ($n = 13$), and 22% were found to be in each of the continuous and stretch viewing categories ($n = 12$). These differences were not statistically significant ($\chi^2 = 1.79, df = 3, p > .05$).

Published reports of chi-square tests for independence provide the same basic chi-square information. For example, Morgan et al. (2001) reported the following, based on a survey of 61 female and 55 male introductory psychology students:

> A 2 (Gender) $\times$ 3 (Work Plans) chi-square analysis was used to examine whether students' work plans involved traditional math and science fields, health-related applications of math and science, or non-math- or science-related work. The analysis was significant, $\chi^2(2, N = 116) = 6.68, p < .05$. Although both men and women were most likely to report work plans that were *not* math- or science-related plans, the difference was greater for women (65.6 and 3.3%, respectively, for non-math- or science- and math- or science-related) than for men (49.1 and 16.4%, respectively, for non-math- or science- and math- or science-related). (p. 302)

Morgan et al. do not give the actual number in each cell. Instead, as is fairly common in research articles, they give various totals and percentages. This information is usually of more direct interest to the reader than raw totals. However, this information is also everything you need to figure out the raw cell sizes if you need to do so. For example, consider the women non-math- or science-related cell. You know that there are 61 women (this was reported in the methods section of their article). You also are told that 65.6% of women are in the non-math- or science-area. Thus, this cell has 65.6% of 61, which is 40 women.

Morgan et al. also do not give the effect size for their significant result. However, you can figure this out from the chi-square, number of participants, and design of the study (2 $\times$ 3 in this example). Using the formula,

$$\text{Cramer's } \phi = \sqrt{\chi^2/[(N)(df_{\text{Smaller}})]} = \sqrt{6.68/[(116)(1)]}$$

$$= \sqrt{6.68/116} = \sqrt{.058} = .24$$

This suggests that there is something close to a moderate effect size.

SUMMARY

1. Chi-square tests are used for hypothesis tests with nominal variables. A sample's chi-square statistic shows the amount of mismatch between expected and observed frequencies over several categories. It is figured by finding, for each category or combination of categories, the difference between observed frequency and expected frequency, squaring this difference (eliminating positive and negative signs), and dividing by the expected frequency (making the squared differences more proportionate to the numbers involved). The results are then added up for all the categories or combinations of categories. The distribution of the chi-square statistic is known and the cutoffs can be looked up in standard tables.

2. The chi-square test for goodness of fit is used to test hypotheses about whether a distribution of frequencies over two or more categories of a nominal variable matches an expected distribution. (These expected frequencies are based, for example, on theory or on a distribution in another study or circumstance). In this test, the expected frequencies are given in advance or are based on some expected percentages (such as equal percentages in all groups). The degrees of freedom are the number of categories minus 1.

3. The chi-square test for independence is used to test hypotheses about the relation between two nominal variables—that is, about whether the breakdown over the categories of one variable has the same proportional pattern within each of the categories of the other variable. The frequencies are set up in a contingency table in which the two variables are crossed and the numbers in each combination are placed in each of the resulting cells. The frequency expected for a cell if the two variables are independent is the percentage of all the people in that cell's row times the total number of people in that cell's column. The degrees of freedom for the test of independence are the number of columns minus 1 times the number of rows minus 1.

4. Chi-square tests make no assumptions about normal distributions of their variables, but they do require that no individual be counted in more than one category or cell.

5. The estimated effect size for a chi-square test of independence (that is, the degree of association) for a 2×2 contingency table is the phi coefficient; for larger tables, Cramer's phi. Phi is the square root of the result of dividing your sample's chi-square by the number of persons. Cramer's phi is the square root of the result of dividing your sample's chi-square by the product of the number of persons times the degrees of freedom in the smaller side of the contingency table. These coefficients range from 0 to 1.

6. The minimum acceptable frequency for a category or cell has been a subject of controversy. Currently, the best advice is that even very small expected frequencies do not seriously increase the chance of a Type I error, provided that there are at least five times as many individuals as categories (or cells). However, low expected frequencies seriously reduce power and should be avoided if possible.

KEY TERMS

EXAMPLE WORKED-OUT COMPUTATIONAL PROBLEMS

CHI-SQUARE TEST FOR GOODNESS OF FIT

The expected distribution (from previous years) on an exam roughly follows a normal curve in which the highest scoring 2.5% of the students get A's; the next highest scoring 14%, B's; the next 67%, C's; the next 14%, D's; and the lowest 2.5%, F's. A class takes a test using a new grading system and 10 get A's, 34 get B's, 140 get C's, 10 get D's, and 6 get F's. Can you conclude that the new system produces a different distribution of grades (using the .01 level)? (a) Use the steps of hypothesis testing, and (b) make a sketch of the distributions involved.

Table 14–11 shows the observed and expected frequencies and the figuring for the chi-square test.

❶ **Restate the question as a research hypothesis and a null hypothesis about the populations.** There are two populations:

Population 1: Students graded with the new system
Population 2: Students graded with the old system

The research hypothesis is that the populations are different; the null hypothesis is that the populations are the same.

❷ **Determine the characteristics of the comparison distribution.** The comparison distribution is a chi-square distribution with 4 degrees of freedom (5 categories − 1 = 4).

❸ **Determine the cutoff sample score on the comparison distribution at which the null hypothesis should be rejected.** Using the .01 level and $df = 4$, Table 14–2 (or Table A–4) shows a needed chi square of 13.277.

❹ **Determine your sample's score on the comparison distribution.** As shown in Table 14–11, this comes out to 18.33.

TABLE 14–11 **Figuring for Chi-Square Goodness of Fit Test Example of Worked-Out Computational Problem**

Grade	Observed ❹	Expected ❻
A	10	5 (2.5% × 200)
B	34	28 (14.0% × 200)
C	140	134 (67.0% × 200)
D	10	28 (14.0% × 200)
F	6	5 (2.5% × 200)

Degrees of freedom = 5 categories − 1 = 4 ❷

Chi-square needed, $df = 4$, .01 level: 13.277 ❸

$$\chi^2 = \Sigma \frac{(O - E)^2}{E} = \frac{(10 - 5)^2}{5} + \frac{(34 - 28)^2}{28} + \frac{(140 - 134)^2}{134} + \frac{(10 - 28)^2}{28} + \frac{(6 - 5)^2}{5}$$

$$= \frac{5^2}{5} + \frac{6}{28} + \frac{6}{134} + \frac{-18^2 \,❸}{28} + \frac{1^2}{5}$$

$$= \frac{25}{5} + \frac{36}{28} + \frac{36 \,❶}{134} + \frac{324}{28} + \frac{1}{5}$$

$$= 5 + 1.29 + .27 + 11.57 + .20 = 18.33. \,❻$$

Conclusion: Reject the null hypothesis. ❺

FIGURE 14–8 *The Chi-Square Goodness of Fit Test Example of Worked-Out Computational Problem chi-square distribution (df = 4) showing the cutoff for rejecting the null hypothesis at the .01 level and the sample's chi-square.*

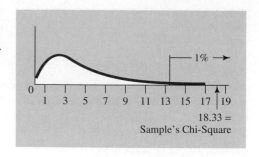

❺ **Decide whether to reject the null hypothesis.** The sample's chi square of 18.33 is more extreme than the needed chi-square of 13.277. Thus, you can reject the null hypothesis and conclude that the populations are different; the new grading system produces a different distribution of grades than the previous one. Figure 14–8 shows the distributions.

CHI-SQUARE TEST FOR INDEPENDENCE

Janice Steil and Jennifer Hay (1997) conducted a survey of professionals (lawyers, doctors, bankers, etc.) regarding the people they compare themselves to when they think about their job situation (salary, benefits, responsibility, status, etc.). One question of special interest was how much professionals compare themselves to people of their own sex, the opposite sex, or both. Here are the results:

	Participant Gender	
	Men	Women
Comparison:		
Same sex	29	17
Opposite sex	4	14
Both sexes	26	28

Can the researchers conclude that the gender of who people compare themselves to is different depending on their own gender (using the .05 level)? (a) Use the steps of hypothesis testing, and (b) make a sketch of the distributions involved.

Table 14–12 shows the figuring for the chi-square test.

❶ **Restate the question as a null hypothesis and a research hypothesis about the populations.** There are two populations:

Population 1: Professionals like those surveyed
Population 2: Professionals for whom own sex is independent of the sex of those to whom they compare their job situations

The null hypothesis is that the two populations are the same, that, in general, professional men and women do not differ in the sex of those to whom they compare their job situations. The research hypothesis is that the populations are not the same, that professionals like those surveyed are unlike the hypothetical population in which men and women do not differ in the sex of those to whom they compare their job situations.

❷ **Determine the characteristics of the comparison distribution.** This is a chi-square distribution with 2 degrees of freedom.

TABLE 14–12 Figuring for the Chi-Square Test of Independence Example of Worked-Out Computational Problem

Comparisons	Response: *Men*	Response: *Women*	Total
Same sex	Ⓐ 29 (23)	17 (23) Ⓑ	46 (39.0%)
Opposite sex	4 (9)	14 (9)	18 (15.3%)
Both sexes	26 (27)	28 (27)	54 (45.8%)
	59	59	118

$df = (N_{\text{Columns}} - 1)(N_{\text{Rows}} - 1) = (2 - 1)(3 - 1) = (1)(2) = 2.$ ❷

Chi-square needed, $df = 2$, .05 level: 5.992. ❸

$$\chi^2 = \Sigma\frac{(O-E)^2}{E} = \frac{(29-23)^2}{23} + \frac{(17-23)^2}{23} + \frac{(4-9)^2}{9} + \frac{(14-9)^2}{9} + \frac{(26-27)^2}{27} + \frac{(28-27)^2}{27}$$

$$= \frac{6^2}{23} + \frac{-6^2}{23} + \frac{-5^2}{9} + \frac{5^2}{9} + \frac{-1^2}{27} + \frac{1^2}{27} \quad \text{Ⓒ}$$

$$= \frac{36}{23} + \frac{36}{23} + \frac{25}{9} + \frac{25}{9} + \frac{1}{27} + \frac{1}{27} \quad \text{Ⓓ Ⓔ}$$

$$= 1.57 + 1.57 + 2.78 + 2.78 + .04 + .04 = 8.78. \quad \text{Ⓕ}$$

Conclusion: Reject the null hypothesis. ❺

Note. Data from Steil & Hay (1997). The chi-square computed here (8.78) is slightly different from that reported in their article (8.76) due to rounding error.

❸ **Determine the cutoff sample score on the comparison distribution at which the null hypothesis should be rejected.** Using the .05 level and 2 degrees of freedom, the needed chi-square for significance is 5.992.

❹ **Determine your sample's score on the comparison distribution.** As shown in Table 14–12, this comes out to 8.78.

❺ **Decide whether to reject the null hypothesis.** The chi square of 8.78 is larger than the cutoff of 5.992; thus you can reject the null hypothesis: The gender of the people with whom professionals compare their job situations is likely to be different for men and women. Figure 14–9 shows the distributions.

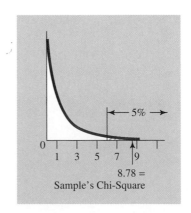

FIGURE 14–9 *The chi-square test for independence example of worked-out computational problem chi-square distribution (df = 2) showing the cutoff for rejecting the null hypothesis at the .05 level and the sample's chi-square. (Data from Steil & Hay, 1997.*

EFFECT SIZE FOR A 2 × 2 CHI-SQUARE TEST FOR INDEPENDENCE

Figure the effect size for a study with 85 participants and a chi-square of 14.41.

$$\phi = \sqrt{\chi^2/N} = \sqrt{14.41/85} = \sqrt{.170} = .41.$$

EFFECT SIZE FOR A CHI-SQUARE TEST FOR INDEPENDENCE WITH A CONTINGENCY TABLE GREATER THAN 2 × 2

Figure the effect size for a study with 3 × 7 study with 135 participants and the chi-square is 18.32.

$$\text{Cramer's } \phi = \sqrt{\chi^2/[(N)(df_{\text{Smaller}})]} = \sqrt{18.32/[(135)(2)]}$$
$$= \sqrt{18.32/270} = \sqrt{.068} = .26.$$

PRACTICE PROBLEMS

These problems involve figuring. Most real-life statistics problems are done on a computer. However, even if you have a computer and statistics software, do these by hand (with the help of a calculator) to ingrain the method in your mind. Also, in all problems involving figuring, be sure to show your work.

For practice in using a computer to solve statistics problems, refer to the computer section of each chapter of the *Student's Study Guide and Computer Workbook* that accompanies this text.

All data are fictional unless an actual citation is given.

Answers to Set I problems are given at the back of the book.

SET I

1. Carry out a chi-square test for goodness of fit for each of the following (use the .05 level for each):

(a) Category	Expected	Observed
A	20%	19
B	20%	11
C	40%	10
D	10%	5
E	10%	5

(b) Category	Expected	Observed
I	30%	100
II	50%	100
III	20%	100

(c) Category	Number in the Past	Observed
1	100	38
2	300	124
3	50	22
4	50	16

2. Carry out a chi-square test for goodness of fit for each of the following (use the .01 level for each). In each situation, the observed numbers are shown; the expected numbers are equal across categories.
   (a) Category A: 10; Category B; 10; Category C, 10; Category D, 10; Category E, 60.
   (b) Category A: 5; Category B; 5; Category C, 5; Category D, 5; Category E, 30.
   (c) Category A: 10; Category B; 10; Category C, 10; Category D, 10; Category E, 160.

3. A director of a small psychotherapy clinic is wondering if there is any difference in the use of the clinic during different seasons of the year. Last year, there were 28 new clients in the winter, 33 in the spring, 16 in the summer, and 51 in the fall. On the basis of last year's data, should the director conclude that season makes a difference? (Use the .05 level.) (a) Carry out the five steps of hypothesis testing. (b) Make a sketch of the distributions involved. (c) Explain

your answer to a person who has never taken a course in statistics. (Note: This problem is like the Harter et al. example in which you are doing a chi-square for a single nominal variable. This is not a chi-square test for independence and does not involve any contingency tables.)

4. Folwell et al. (1997) interviewed a group of adults, aged 54 and older, about their relationships with their siblings. One question they asked was whether there had been a change in emotional closeness over the years. They found that 43 of the respondents "perceived changes of emotional closeness in their sibling relationships . . . [and] 14 did not report a change in closeness in their sibling relationships" (p. 846). They also tested whether this difference was greater than you would expect by chance (which would be a 50–50 split). "A chi-square analysis revealed that respondents perceive changes in closeness in their sibling relationships ($\chi^2 = 14.75$, d.f. $= 1$, $\alpha = .05$)" (p. 846).
(a) Figure the chi-square yourself (your results should be the same, within rounding error). (b) Explain this result to a person who has never had a course in statistics.

5. Carry out a chi-square test for independence for each of the following contingency tables (use the .05 level).
   a.
20	40
40	0
   b.
20	0
40	40
   c.
20	40
0	40

6. Carry out a chi-square test for independence for each of the following contingency tables (use the .01 level).

(a)
10	16
16	10

(b)
100	106
106	100

(c)
100	160
160	100

(d)
10	16	10
16	10	10

(e)
10	16	16
16	10	16

(f)
10	16	10
16	10	16

7. A developmental psychologist is interested in whether children of three different ages (5, 8, and 11) differ in their liking for a certain kind of music. The psychologist studies 200 children at a local elementary school. The results are shown in the table below. Is there a significant relationship between these two variables? (Use the .05 level.) (a) Carry out the steps of hypothesis testing. (b) Make a sketch of the distributions. (c) Explain your answer to a person who has never taken a course in statistics.

		Age of Child		
		5	8	11
Liking for this kind of music	Yes	42	62	26
	No	18	38	14

8. A political psychologist is interested in whether the community a person lives in is related to that person's opinion on an upcoming water conservation ballot initiative. The psychologist surveys 90 people by phone with the results shown below. Is opinion related to community at the .05 level? (a) Carry out the steps of hypothesis testing. (b) Make a sketch of the distributions (c) Explain your answer to a person who has never taken a course in statistics.

	Community A	Community B	Community C
For	12	6	3
Against	18	3	15
No opinion	12	9	12

9. Figure the effect size for the results in problems (a) 5a, (b) 5b, (c) 5c, (d) 6a, (e) 6b, (f) 6c, (g) 6d, (h) 6e, (i) 6f, (j) 7, (k) 8.

10. Figure the effect size for the following studies:

	N	Chi-Square	Design
(a)	100	16	2×2
(b)	100	16	2×5
(c)	100	16	3×3
(d)	100	8	2×2
(e)	200	16	2×2

11. What is the power of the following planned studies using a chi-square test of independence with $p < .05$?

	Predicted Effect Size	Design	N
(a)	small	2×2	25
(b)	medium	2×2	25
(c)	small	2×2	50
(d)	small	2×3	25
(e)	small	3×3	25
(f)	small	2×5	25

12. About how many participants do you need for 80% power in each of the following planned studies using a chi-square test of independence with $p < .05$?

	Predicted Effect Size	Design
(a)	medium	2×2
(b)	large	2×2
(c)	medium	2×5
(d)	medium	3×3
(e)	large	2×3

13. Lydon and his associates (1997) conducted a study that compared long-distance to local dating relationships. The researchers first administered questionnaires to a group of students one month prior to their leaving home to begin their first semester at McGill University (Time 1). Some of these students had dating partners who lived in the McGill area; others had dating partners who lived a long way from McGill. The researchers contacted the participants again late in the fall semester, asking them about the current status of their original dating relationships (Time 2). Here is how they reported their results:

> Of the 69 participants . . . 55 were involved in long-distance relationships, and 14 were in local relationships (dating partner living within 200 km of them). Consistent with our predictions, 12 of the 14 local relationships were still intact at Time 2 (86%), whereas only 28 of the 55 long-distance relationships were still intact (51%), $\chi^2(1, N = 69) = 5.55, p < .02$. (p. 108).

(a) Figure the chi-square yourself (your results should be the same, within rounding error). (b) Figure effect size. (c) Explain this result to a person who has never had a course in statistics.

14. Wilfley et al. (2001), in a study of binge eating disorder, compared 37 women getting treatment in a clinic to a control group of 108 otherwise similar women from the general community. However, before beginning their analysis, they needed to check that the two groups were in fact not different in important ways. For example, they reported the following: "Equivalent proportions of women in the clinic ($N = 32$, 87%) and the community ($N = 89$, 82%) samples were obese . . . $\chi^2(1, N = 145) = 0.33, p = .56$" (p. 385).

(a) Figure the chi-square yourself (your results should be the same, within rounding error). (b) Figure effect size. (c) Explain this result to a person who has never had a course in statistics.

Set II

15. Carry out a chi-square test for goodness of fit for each of the following (use the .01 level for each):

(a)

Category	Expected	Observed
1	2%	5
2	14%	15
3	34%	90
4	34%	120
5	14%	50
6	2%	20

(b)

Category	Proportion Expected	Observed
A	1/3	10
B	1/6	10
C	1/2	10

16. Carry out a chi-square test for goodness of fit for each of the following (use the .05 level for each). In each situation, the observed numbers are shown; the expected numbers are equal across categories.

(a) Category I: 20; Category II; 20; Category III, 60.

(b) Category I: 20; Category II; 20; Category III, 20; Category IV, 60.

(b) Category I: 20; Category II; 20; Category III, 20; Category IV, 20; Category V, 60.

17. Carry out a chi-square test for goodness of fit for each of the following (use the .05 level for each). In each situation, the observed numbers are shown; the expected numbers are equal across categories.

(a) 5 10 5   (b) 10 15 10   (c) 10 20 10   (d) 5 15 5

18. A researcher wants to be sure that the sample in her study is not unrepresentative of the distribution of ethnic groups in her community. Her sample includes 300 whites, 80 African Americans, 100 Latinos, 40 Asians, and 80 others. In her community, according to census records, there are 48% whites, 12% African Americans, 18% Latinos, 9% Asians, and 13% others. Is her sample unrepresentative of the population in her community? (Use the .05 level.) (a) Carry out the steps of hypothesis testing. (b) Make a sketch of the distributions involved. (c) Explain your answer to a person who has never taken a course in statistics. (Note: This problem is like the Harter et al. example in which you are doing a chi-square for a single nominal variable. This is not a chi-square test for independence and does not involve any contingency tables.)

19. Stasser et al. (1989) conducted a study involving discussions of three different "candidates" which were described to participants in a way the researchers intended to make the candidates equally attractive. Thus, before analyzing their main results, they wanted to first test whether the three candidates were in fact seen as equally attractive. Of the 531 participants in their study, 197 initially preferred Candidate A; 120, Candidate B, and 214, Candidate C. Stasser et al. described the following analysis:

> The relative frequencies of prediscussion preferences . . . suggested that we were not entirely successful in constructing equally attractive candidates. . . . [T]he hypothesis of equal popularity can be confidently rejected, $\chi^2(2, N = 531) = 28.35, p < .001$. (p. 71)

(a) Figure the chi-square yourself (your results should be the same, within rounding error). (b) Explain this result to a person who has never had a course in statistics.

20. Carry out a chi-square test for independence for each of the following contingency tables (use the .05 level).

a.
0	18
18	0

b.
0	0	18
9	9	0

c.
0	0	9	9
9	9	0	0

d.
20	40
0	40

21. Carry out a chi-square test for independence for each of the following contingency tables (use the .05 level).

(a)
8	8
8	16

(b)
8	8
8	32

(c)
8	8
8	48

(d)
8	8	8
8	8	8
8	8	16

(e)
8	8	8
8	8	8
8	8	32

(f)
8	8	8
8	8	8
8	8	48

22. Below are results of a survey of a sample of people buying ballet tickets, laid out according to the type of seat they purchased and how regularly they attend. Is there a significant relation? (Use the .05 level.) (a) Carry out the steps of hypothesis testing. (b) Make a sketch of the distributions. (c) Explain your answer to a person who has never taken a course in statistics.

		Attendance	
		Regular	*Occasional*
Seating Category	*Orchestra*	20	80
	Dress circle	20	20
	Balcony	40	80

23. A comparative psychologist tests rats, monkeys, and humans on a particular learning task. The table below shows the numbers of each species that was and was not able to learn the task. Is there a relation between species and ability to learn this task (use the .01 level)? (a) Carry out the steps of hypothesis testing. (b) Make a sketch of the distributions. (c) Explain your answer to a person who has never taken a course in statistics.

		Species		
		Rat	Monkey	Human
Learned Task	Yes	2	4	14
	No	28	16	6

24. Figure the effect size for the results in problems (a) 20a, (b) 20b, (c) 20c, (d) 20d, (e) 21a, (f) 21b, (g) 21c, (h) 21d, (i) 21e, (j) 21f, (k) 22, (l) 23.

25. Figure the effect size for the following studies:

	N	Chi-Square	Design
(a)	40	10	2×2
(b)	400	10	2×2
(c)	40	10	4×4
(d)	400	10	4×4
(e)	40	20	2×2

26. What is the power of the following planned studies, using a chi-square test of independence with $p < .05$?

	Predicted Effect Size	Design	N
(a)	medium	2×2	100
(b)	medium	2×3	100
(c)	large	2×2	100
(d)	medium	2×2	200
(e)	medium	2×3	50
(f)	small	3×3	25

27. About how many participants do you need for 80% power in each of the following planned studies, using a chi-square test of independence with $p < .05$?

	Predicted Effect Size	Design
(a)	small	2×2
(b)	medium	2×2
(c)	large	2×2
(d)	small	3×3
(e)	medium	3×3
(f)	large	3×3

28. Everett et al. (1997) mailed a survey to a random sample of physicians. Half were offered $1 if they would return the questionnaire (this was the experimental group); the other half served as a control group. The point of the study was to see if even a small incentive would increase the return rate for physician surveys. Everett et al. report their results as follows:

> Of the 300 surveys mailed to the experimental group, 39 were undeliverable, 2 were returned uncompleted, and 164 were returned completed. Thus, the response rate for the experimental group was 63% ($164/300 - 39 = .63$). Of the 300 surveys mailed to the control group, 40 were undeliverable, and 118 were returned completed. Thus, the response rate for the control group was 45% ($118/300 - 40$) = .45). A chi-square test comparing the response rates for the experimental and control groups found the $1 incentive had a statistically significantly improved response rate over the control group [$\chi^2(1, N = 521) = 16.0, p < .001$].

(a) Figure the chi-square yourself (your results should be the same, within rounding error). (b) Figure effect size. (c) Explain this result to a person who has never had a course in statistics.

29. Irving and Berel (2001) compared the effects of four kinds of programs (three actual programs and a control group) designed to make women more skeptical of media portrayals of female body image. After completing each program, the 110 participants were given stamped, addressed postcards which they could mail to a media activism organization ("About Face") if they so chose. Here are some of their results:

> ... [P]ostcards were sent by approximately twice as many of the participants in the video-only condition (i.e., 36%) than in the internally oriented condition (19% of participants returned postcards) and the externally oriented condition (15% returned postcards). Only 5% of those in the no-intervention control group sent postcards to "About Face." Group differences in the rate of return were significant, $\chi^2(3, N = 110) = 8.79, p < .05$, suggesting that the intervention had a differential impact on intentions to engage in media activism. (p. 109)

(a) Figure the chi-square yourself (your results should be the same, within rounding error). (b) Figure effect size. (c) Explain this result to a person who has never had a course in statistics.

CHAPTER 15

STRATEGIES WHEN POPULATION DISTRIBUTIONS ARE NOT NORMAL:

DATA TRANSFORMATIONS AND RANK-ORDER TESTS

Are You Ready?
What You Need to have Mastered Before Starting This Chapter:

- Chapters 1, 2, and 5 through 11.

This chapter examines some strategies researchers use for hypothesis testing when the assumptions of normal population distributions and equal variances are clearly violated. (These assumptions underlie most ordinary hypothesis-testing procedures, such as the *t* test and the analysis of variance.) First, we briefly review the role of assumptions in the standard hypothesis-testing procedures. Then, we examine two approaches psychology researchers use when assumptions have not been met: data transformations and rank-order tests.

ASSUMPTIONS IN THE STANDARD HYPOTHESIS-TESTING PROCEDURES

As we saw in previous chapters, you have to meet certain conditions (the assumptions) to get accurate results with a *t* test or an analysis of variance. In these hypothesis-testing procedures, you treat the scores from a study as if they came from some larger, though unknown, populations. One assumption you have to make is that the populations involved follow a normal curve. The other main assumption you have to make is that the populations have equal variances.[1]

You also learned in previous chapters that you get fairly accurate results when a study suggests that the populations even very roughly meet the assumptions of following a normal curve and having equal variances. Our concern here, however, is with situations where it is clear that the populations are nowhere near normal, or nowhere near having equal variances. In such situations, if you use the ordinary *t* test or analysis of variance, you can get quite incorrect results. For example, you could do all the figuring correctly and decide to reject the null hypothesis based on your results. And yet, if your populations do not meet the standard assumptions, this result could be wrong—wrong in the sense that instead of there actually being only a 5% chance of getting your results if the null hypothesis is true, in fact there might be a 15% or 20% chance!

Remember: Assumptions are about populations and not about samples. It is quite possible for a sample not to follow a normal curve even though it comes from a population that does. Figure 15–1 shows histograms for several samples, each taken randomly from a population that follows a normal curve. (Notice that the smaller the sample, the harder it is to see that it came from a normal population.) Of course, it is quite possible for nonnormal populations to produce any of these samples as well. Unfortunately, the sample is usually all you have to go on when doing a study. One thing researchers do is make a histogram for the sample; if it is not drastically different from normal, the researchers assume that the population it came from is roughly normal. When considering normality, most psychology researchers consider a distribution innocent until proven guilty.

One common situation where you doubt the assumption that the population follows a normal distribution is when there is a ceiling or floor effect (see Chapter 1). Another common situation that raises such doubts is when the sample has outliers, extreme scores at one or both ends of the sample distribution. Figure 15–2 shows some examples of samples with outliers. Outliers are a big problem in the statistical methods we ordinarily use because these methods ultimately rely on squared deviations from the mean. Because it is so far from the mean, an outlier has a huge influence when you square its deviation from the mean. The result is that a single outlier, if it is extreme enough, can cause a statistical test to give a significant result even when all the other scores would not. An outlier can also make a result not significant that would be significant without the outlier.

---

[1] These two assumptions also apply when testing the significance of a correlation coefficient (Chapter 3). In that situation the assumptions include that the populations for each variable being correlated are normally distributed and that the variance of each variable is the same at each point along the other variable. This chapter uses as examples the *t* test and analysis of variance. However, you use data transformations and rank-order tests in the same ways to test hypotheses involving correlations.

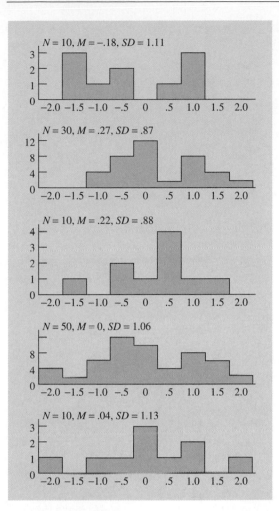

FIGURE 15-1 *Histograms for several random samples, each drawn from a normal population with* $\mu = 0$ *and* $\sigma = 1$.

1. What are the two main assumptions for *t* tests and the analysis of variance?
2. (a) How do you check to see if you have met the assumptions? (b) Why is this problematic?
3. (a) What is an outlier? (b) Why are outliers likely to have an especially big distorting effect in most statistical procedures?

ANSWERS:

1. The populations are normally distributed and have equal variances.
2. (a) You look at the distributions of the samples. (b) The samples, especially if they are small, can have quite different shapes and variances from the populations.
3. (a) An extreme score. (b) Because most procedures are based on squared deviations from the mean, so that the extremeness of an outlier is greatly multiplied when its deviation from the mean is squared.

DATA TRANSFORMATIONS

One widely used procedure when the scores in the sample do not appear to come from a normal population is to change the scores! Not by fudging—although at first it may sound that way, until we explain. The method is that the researcher applies

FIGURE 15–2 *Distributions with outliers at one or both ends.*

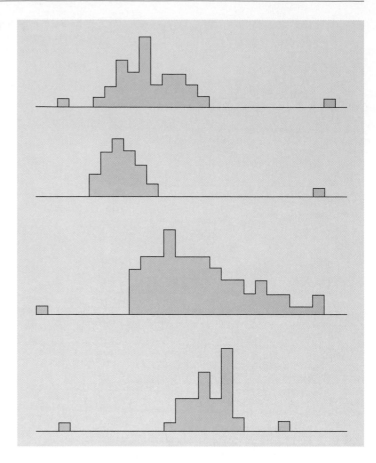

some mathematical procedure to each score, such as taking its square root, to make a nonnormal distribution closer to normal. (Sometimes this can also make the variances of the different groups more similar.) This is called a **data transformation.** Once you have made a data transformation, if the other assumptions are met, you can then go ahead with a usual *t* test or analysis of variance. Data transformation has an important advantage over other procedures of coping with nonnormal populations: Once you have made a data transformation, you can use familiar and sophisticated hypothesis-testing procedures.

    Consider an example. Measures of reaction time (such as how long it takes a research participant to press a particular key when a light flashes) are usually highly skewed to the right. There are many short (quick) responses and a few but sometimes quite long (slow) ones. It is unlikely that the reaction times shown in Figure 15–3 come from a population that follows a normal curve. The population of reaction-time scores itself is probably skewed.

    However, suppose you take the square root of each reaction time. Most reaction times are affected only a little. A reaction time of 1 second stays 1; a reaction time of 1.5 seconds reduces to 1.22. However, very long reaction times, the ones that create the long tail to the right, are much reduced. For example, a reaction time of 9 seconds is reduced to 3, and a reaction time of 16 seconds (the person was really distracted and forgot about the task) reduces to 4. Figure 15–4 shows the result of taking the square root of each score in the skewed distribution shown in Figure 15–3. After a **square-root transformation,** this distribution of scores seems much

data transformation

square-root transformation

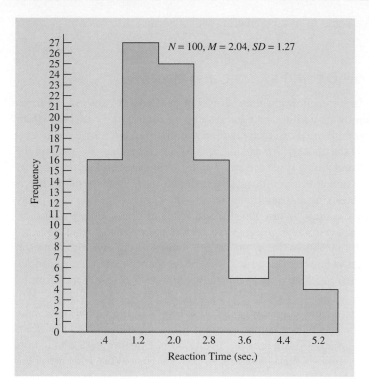

FIGURE 15-3 *Skewed distribution of reaction times (fictional data).*

$N = 100$, $M = 2.04$, $SD = 1.27$

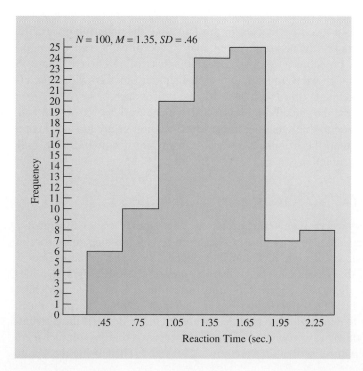

FIGURE 15-4 *Distribution of scores from Figure 15–3 after square-root transformation.*

$N = 100$, $M = 1.35$, $SD = .46$

more likely to have come from a population with a normal distribution (of transformed scores).

LEGITIMACY OF DATA TRANSFORMATIONS

Do you feel that this is somehow cheating? It would be if you did this only to some scores or in any other way did it to make the result come out more favorable to your predictions. However, in actual research practice, the first step after the data are collected and recorded (and checked for accuracy) is to see if the data suggest that the populations meet assumptions. If the scores in your sample suggest that the populations do not meet assumptions, you do data transformations. Hypothesis testing is done only after this checking and any transformations.

Remember that you must do any transformation for *all* the scores on that variable, not just those in a particular group. Most important, no matter what transformation procedure you use, the order of the scores always stays the same. A person with a raw score that is between the raw scores of two other participating people, will still have a transformed score between those same two people's transformed scores.

The procedure may seem somehow to distort reality to fit the statistics. In some cases, this is a legitimate concern. Suppose you are looking at the difference in income between two groups of Americans. You probably do not care about how much the two groups differ in the square root of their income. What you care about is the difference in actual dollars.

On the other hand, consider a self-esteem questionnaire. Scores on the questionnaire do not have any absolute meaning. Higher scores mean greater self-esteem; lower scores, less self-esteem. However, each scale-point increase on the test is not necessarily related to an equal amount of increase in an individual's self-esteem. It is just as likely that the square root of each scale point's increase is directly related to the person's self-esteem. Similarly, consider the example we used earlier of reaction time, measured in seconds. This would seem to have an absolute meaning—a second is a second. But even in this situation, the underlying variable, efficiency of processing of the nervous system, may not be directly related to number of seconds. It is probably a complex operation that follows some unknown mathematical rule (though we would still expect that shorter times go with more efficient processing and longer times with less efficient processing).

In these examples, the underlying "yardstick" of the variable is not known. Thus, there is no reason to think that the transformed version is any less accurate a reflection of reality than the original version. And the transformed version may meet the normality assumption.

KINDS OF DATA TRANSFORMATIONS

There are several types of data transformations. We already have illustrated a square-root transformation: Instead of using each score, you use the square root of each score. We gave an example in Figures 15–3 and 15–4. The general effect is shown in Figure 15–5. As you can see, a distribution skewed to the right becomes less skewed to the right after square-root transformation. To put it numerically, moderate numbers become only slightly lower and high numbers become much lower. The result is that the right side is pulled in toward the middle. (If the distribution is skewed the other way, you can *reflect* all the scores—that is, subtract them all from some high number so that they are now all reversed. Then, using the square

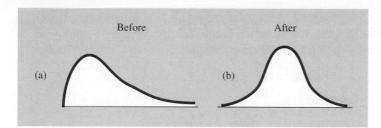

FIGURE 15–5 *Distributions skewed to the right before (a) and after (b) taking the square root of each score.*

root will have the correct effect. However, you then have to remember when look-ing at the final results that you have reversed the direction of scoring.)

There are many other kinds of transformations you will see in social and behav-ioral science research articles. One common type is called a *log transformation*. (In a log transformation, instead of the square root, the researcher takes the logarithm of each score.) Some other transformations you might see are *inverse transforma-tions* and *arcsine transformations*. We will not go into examples of all these kinds of transformations here. Just learning the square-root transformation will help you get the principle. The main thing to remember about other kinds of transformations is that they all use this same principle of taking each score and applying some arith-metic to it to make the set of scores come out more like a normal curve. Once again, whatever transformation you use, a score that is between two other scores always stays between those two other scores.

AN EXAMPLE OF A DATA TRANSFORMATION

Consider a fictional study in which four children who score high on a test of being "highly sensitive" are compared on the number of books read in the preceding year to four children who score low on the test. (The general idea of being a highly sensi-tive person is described in Aron, 1996, 2002; and Aron & Aron, 1997.) Based on theory, the researcher predicts that highly sensitive children will read more books. Table 15–1 shows the results.

Ordinarily, in a study comparing two independent groups, you would use a *t* test for independent means. Yet the *t* test for independent means is like all of the proce-dures you have learned for hypothesis testing (except chi-square): It requires that the parent populations of scores for each group be normally distributed. In this study, however, the distribution of the sample is strongly skewed to the right—the scores tend to bunch up at the left, leaving a long tail to the right. It thus seems likely that the population of scores of number of books read (for both sensitive and nonsensitive children) is also skewed to the right. This shape for the population distribution also seems reasonable in light of what is being measured. A child cannot read fewer than zero books; but once a child starts reading, it is easy to read a lot of books in a year.

Also note that the estimated population variances based on the two samples are dramatically different, 95.58 versus 584. This is another reason you would not want to go ahead with an ordinary *t* test.

However, suppose you do a square-root transformation on the scores (Table 15–2). Now both samples are much more like a normal curve—both samples have their middle scores bunch up in the middle (for example, for the Yes group, 6.00 and 6.71) and the more extreme (high and low) scores spread out a little from the mean (4.12 and 8.71). Also, the transformation seems reasonable in terms of the meaning of the numbers. Number of books read is meant as a measure of interest in

TABLE 15–1 Results of a Study Comparing Highly Sensitive and Not Highly Sensitive Children on the Number of Books Read in the Past Year (Fictional Data)

	Highly Sensitive	
	No	*Yes*
	0	17
	3	36
	10	45
	22	75
Σ:	35	173
M =	8.75	43.25
S² =	95.58	584.00

TABLE 15–2 Square-Root Transformation of the Scores in Table 15–1

Highly Sensitive			
No		*Yes*	
X	√X	X	√X
0	0.00	17	4.12
3	1.73	36	6.00
10	3.16	45	6.71
22	4.69	75	8.66

TABLE 15–3   Figuring for a *t* Test for Independent Means Using Square-Root Transformed Scores for the Study of Books Read by Highly Sensitive Versus Not Highly Sensitive Children (Fictional Data)

t needed for .05 significance level, $df = (4 - 1) + (4 - 1) = 6$, one-tailed $= -1.943$.

Highly Sensitive

	No	Yes
	0.00	4.12
	1.73	6.00
	3.16	6.71
	4.69	8.66
Σ:	9.58	25.49
$M =$	$9.58/4 = 2.40$	$25.49/4 = 6.37$
$S^2 =$	$12.03/3 = 4.01$	$10.56/3 = 3.52$

$$S^2_{Pooled} = 3.77$$

$S^2_M = $ $3.77/4 = .94$ $3.77/4 = .94$
$S^2_{Difference} = .94 + .94 = 1.88$
$S_{Difference} = \sqrt{1.88} = 1.37$
$t = (2.40 - 6.37)/1.37 = -2.90$

Conclusion: Reject the null hypothesis.

---

things literary. Thus, the difference between 0 and 1 book is a much greater difference than the difference between 20 and 21 books.

Table 15–3 shows the *t* test analysis using the transformed scores.

HOW ARE YOU DOING?

1. What is a data transformation?
2. Why is it done?
3. When is this legitimate?
4. Consider the following distribution of scores: 4, 16, 25, 25, 25, 36, 64. (a) Are they roughly normally distributed? (b) Why? (C) Carry out a square-root transformation for these scores (that is, list the square-root transformed scores) (d) Are the square-root transformed scores roughly normally distributed? (e) Why?

ANSWERS:

1. When each score is changed following some rule (such as take the square root of log).
2. In order to make the distribution more like a normal curve (or to make variances closer to equal across groups).
3. It is legitimate when it is done to all the scores, it is not done to make the results come out to fit the researcher's predictions, and the underlying meaning of the distance between scores is arbitrary.
4. (a) No. (b) They are skewed to the right. (c) 2, 4, 5, 5, 5, 6, 8. (d) Yes. (e) The middle scores are bunched in the middle and the extremes spread out evenly on both sides.

RANK-ORDER TESTS

Another way of coping with nonnormal distributions is to transform the scores to ranks. Suppose you have a sample with scores of 4, 8, 12, and 64. This would be a **rank-order transformation**   rather surprising sample if the population was really normal. A **rank-order trans-**

formation would change the scores to 1, 2, 3, and 4; the 1 referring to the lowest number in the group, the 2 to the second lowest and so forth. (A complication with a rank-order transformation occurs when you have two or more scores that are tied. The usual solution to ties is to give them each the average rank. For example, the scores 12, 81, 81, 107, and 154 would be ranked 1, 2.5, 2.5, 4, and 5.)

Changing ordinary scores to ranks is a kind of data transformation. But unlike the square-root transformations we just considered, with a rank-order transformation you aren't trying to get a normal distribution. The distribution you get from a rank-order transformation is rectangular, with equal numbers of scores (one) at each value. Ranks have the effect of spreading the scores out evenly.

There are special hypothesis-testing procedures, called **rank-order tests,** that make use of rank-ordered scores. They also have two other common names. You can transform scores from a population with any shaped distribution into ranks. Thus, these tests are sometimes called **distribution-free tests.** Also, the shape of distributions of rank-order scores are known exactly rather than estimated. Thus, rank-order tests do not require estimating any parameters (population values). For example, there is no need to estimate a population variance, because you can determine exactly what it will be if you know that ranks are involved. Hence, hypothesis-testing procedures based on ranks are also called **nonparametric tests.**

The *t* test and analysis of variance are examples of **parametric tests.** Chi-square, like the rank-order tests, is considered a nonparametric test, but it is distribution-free only in the sense that no assumptions are made about the shape of the population distributions. However, the terms *distribution-free* and *nonparametric* are typically used interchangeably; the subtleties of differences between them are a matter of ongoing debate among statisticians.

Rank-order tests also have the advantage that you can use them when the actual scores in the study are themselves ranks—for example, a study comparing the class standing of two types of graduates. Also, sometimes the exact numeric values of the numbers in a measure used in a study are questionable. For example, a researcher intends the measure to be numeric in the usual sense, with a 7 being as much above a 5 as a 12 is above a 10 (the researcher intends this to be equal-interval measurement—see Chapter 1). However, in reality the researcher is only sure that the numbers are correctly ordered, 7 is higher than 5, 10 is higher than 7, and so forth. In this case, the researcher might want to use rank-order measurement so as not to assume too much about the quality of the measurement.

The issue is actually somewhat controversial. Consider, for example, a scale marked "1 = Disagree, 2 = Mildly disagree, 3 = Mildly agree, and 4 = Agree." Are the underlying meanings of the numbers spread evenly across a numeric scale? It is clear that the results are meaningful as rank-order information—certainly, 2 shows more agreement than 1, 3 more than 2, and 4 more than 3. Hence, some psychologists argue that in most cases you should not assume that you have equal-interval measurements and should convert your data to ranks and use a rank-order significance test. Other researchers argue that even with true rank-order measurement, parametric statistical tests do a reasonably accurate job and that changing all the data to ranks can lose valuable information. The issue remains unresolved.

rank-order tests

distribution-free tests

nonparametric tests
parametric tests

OVERVIEW OF RANK-ORDER TESTS

Table 15–4 shows the name of the rank-order test that you would substitute for each of the parametric hypothesis-testing procedures you have learned. (Full procedures for using such tests are given in intermediate statistics texts.) For example, in a situ-

TABLE 15–4	Major Rank-Order Tests Corresponding to Major Parametric Tests
Ordinary Parametric Test	**Corresponding Rank-Order Test**
t test for dependent means	Wilcoxon signed-rank test
t test for independent means	Wilcoxon rank-sum test or Mann-Whitney U test
Analysis of variance	Kruskal-Wallis H test

ation with three groups, you would normally do a one-way analysis of variance. But if you want to use a rank-order method, you would use the Kruskal-Wallis *H* test.[2]

Next, we will describe how such tests are done in a general way, including an example. However, we do not actually provide all the needed information (such as the tables) for you to carry them out in practice. We introduce you to these techniques because you may see them used in articles you read and because their logic is the foundation of an alternative procedure that we do teach you to use (shortly). This alternative procedure does roughly the same thing as these rank-order tests and is closer to what you have already learned.

BASIC LOGIC OF RANK-ORDER TESTS

Consider a study with an experimental group and a control group. (The situation in which you would use a *t* test for independent means if all the assumptions were met.) If you wanted to use a rank-order test, you would first transform all the scores into ranks, ranking all the scores from lowest to highest, regardless of whether a score was in the experimental or the control group. If the two groups were scores randomly taken from a single population, there should be about equal amounts of high ranks and low ranks in each group. (That is, if the null hypothesis is true, the ranks in the two groups should not differ much.) Because the distribution of ranks can be worked out exactly, statisticians can figure the exact probability of getting any particular division of ranks into two groups if in fact the two groups were randomly taken from identical distributions.

The way this actually works is that the researcher changes all the scores to ranks, adds up the total of the ranks in the group with the lower scores, and then compares this total to a cutoff from a special table of significance cutoffs for totals of ranks in this kind of situation.

AN EXAMPLE OF A RANK-ORDER TEST

Table 15–5 shows the transformation to ranks and the figuring for the Wilcoxon rank-sum test for the kind of situation we have just described, using the books read by highly sensitive versus not highly sensitive children example. The logic is a little different from what you are used to, so be patient until we explain it.

---

[2]There are also rank-order tests you can use for correlation and testing the significance of the correlation—the most well known are Kendall's Tau and the Spearman Rho. There is also one widely used nonparametric test, besides chi-square tests, that is not based on rank-order scores at all. This is called the *sign test*. A sign test is used in place of a *t* test for dependent means. You create your set of difference scores, then you just add up the number of difference scores that are positive. If there is no average difference, about half the difference scores should be positive and half negative. Suppose your number of positives are substantially greater or substantially less than half. This result would argue against a null hypothesis that the true population of differences scores has an average difference of zero. Intermediate statistics texts usually have a table to look up the significance cutoffs for a sign test.

TABLE 15–5	Figuring for a Wilcoxon Rank-Sum Test for the Study of Books Read by Highly Sensitive Versus Not Highly Sensitive Children (Fictional Data)

Cutoff for significance: Maximum sum of ranks in the not highly sensitive group for significance at the .05 level, one-tailed (from a standard table) = 11.

Highly Sensitive

No		Yes	
X	Rank	X	Rank
0	1	17	4
3	2	36	6
10	3	45	7
22	5	75	8
Σ:	11		

Comparison to cutoff: Sum of ranks of group predicted to have lower scores, 11, equals but does not exceed cutoff for significance.

Conclusion: Reject the null hypothesis.

Notice that we first set the significance cutoff, as you would in any hypothesis-testing procedure. (This cutoff is based on a table you don't have but is available in most intermediate statistics texts.) The next step is to rank all the scores from lowest to highest, then add up the ranks in the group you expect to have the smaller total. You then compare the smaller total to the cutoff. In the example, the total of the ranks for the lower was not higher than the cutoff, so the null hypothesis was rejected.

We used the Wilcoxon rank-sum test, though we could have used the Mann-Whitney U test instead. It gives an exactly mathematically equivalent final result and is based on the same logic. It differs only in the computational details.

THE NULL HYPOTHESIS IN A RANK-ORDER TEST

The null hypothesis in a rank-order test is not quite the same as in an ordinary parametric test. A parametric test compares the means of the two groups; its null hypothesis is that the two populations have the same mean. The equivalent to the mean in a rank-order test is the middle rank (the median of the nonranked scores). For example, suppose five nonranked scores were 11, 12, 14, 19, and 20. Their corresponding ranks are 1, 2, 3, 4, and 5. The middle rank is 3; this corresponds to the median of the nonranked scores, which is the score of 14. Thus, we think of a rank-order test as comparing the medians of the two groups, that its null hypothesis is that the two populations have the same median.

NORMAL CURVE APPROXIMATIONS IN RANK-ORDER TESTS

Tables like those described for the maximum sum of ranks for rejecting the null hypothesis become quite cumbersome if moderate to large sample sizes with unequal groups have to be included. And the problem becomes truly unmanageable with more complicated designs. So, several approximations have been developed that use the rank sums in a formula to give a Z score. If the Z score is in the upper 5% (2.5% for a two-tailed test) of the normal curve, the result is considered significant. Often, when rank-order tests are reported in research articles, this Z score will be given.

TABLE 15–6	Figuring for a *t* Test for Independent Means Using Ranks Instead of Raw Scores for the Study of Books Read by Highly Sensitive Versus Not Highly Sensitive Children (Fictional Data)

t needed for .05 significance level, $df = (4 - 1) + (4 - 1) = 6$, one-tailed $= -1.943$

	Highly Sensitive	
	No	*Yes*
	1	4
	2	6
	3	7
	5	8
Σ	11	25
$M =$	$11/4 = 2.75$	$25/4 = 6.25$
$S^2 =$	$8.75/3 = 2.92$	$8.75/3 = 2.92$

$$S^2_{\text{Pooled}} = 2.92$$

$S^2_M =$	$2.92/4 = .73$	$2.92/4 = .73$

$S^2_{\text{Difference}} = .73 + .73 = 1.46$

$S_{\text{Difference}} = \sqrt{1.46} = 1.21$

$t = (2.75 - 6.25)/1.21 = -2.89$

Conclusion: Reject the null hypothesis.

USING PARAMETRIC TESTS WITH RANK-TRANSFORMED DATA

Two statisticians (Conover & Iman, 1981) have shown instead of using the special procedures for rank-order tests, you get approximately the same results if you transform the data into ranks and then apply the usual *t* test or analysis of variance procedures.

The result of using a parametric test with scores transformed into ranks will not be quite as accurate as either the ordinary parametric test or the rank-order test. It will not be quite as accurate as the ordinary parametric test because the assumption of normal distributions is violated. The distribution is, in fact, rectangular when ranks are involved. It will also not be quite as accurate as the rank-order test because the parametric test uses the *t* or *F* distribution instead of the special tables that rank-order tests use, which are based on exact probabilities of getting certain divisions of ranks. However, the approximation seems to be quite close for the *t* test and the one-way analysis of variance.[3]

Table 15–6 shows the figuring for an ordinary *t* test for independent means for the fictional sensitive children data, using each child's rank instead of the child's actual number of books read. Again we get a significant result. (In practice, carrying

---

[3]If you want to be very accurate, for a *t* test or one-way analysis of variance, you can convert your result to what is called an *L* statistic and look it up on a chi-square table (Puri & Sen, 1985). The *L* statistic for a *t* test is $([N - 1]t^2)/(t^2 + [N - 2])$, and you use a chi-square distribution with $df = 1$. The *L* statistic for a one way analysis of variance is $([N - 1][df_{\text{Between}}]F)/([df_{\text{Between}}]F + df_{\text{Within}})$, and you use a chi-square distribution with $df = df_{\text{Between}}$. The *L* for the significance of a correlation (see Chapter 3 appendix) is just $(N - 1)r^2$ and you use the chi-square table for $df = 1$. It is especially important to use the *L* statistic when using rank-transformed scores for more advanced parametric procedures, such as factorial analysis of variance (Chapter 13), multiple regression (Chapter 4), and those procedures discussed in Chapter 17. Thomas et al. (1999) give fully worked-out examples.

out an ordinary procedure like a *t* test with scores that have been transformed to ranks is least accurate with a very small sample like this. However, we used the small sample to keep the example simple.)

COMPARISON OF METHODS

We have considered two methods of carrying out hypothesis tests when samples appear to come from nonnormal populations: data transformation and rank-order tests. How do you decide which to use?

ADVANTAGES AND DISADVANTAGES

Data transformations have the advantage of allowing you to use the familiar parametric techniques on the transformed scores. But transformations will not always work. That is, there may not be any reasonable transformation that makes the scores normal in all groups. Also, transformations may distort the scores in ways that lose the original meaning.

Rank-order methods can be applied regardless of the distributions. They are especially appropriate when the original scores are ranks, and they are also useful when the scores do not clearly follow a simple numeric pattern (equal-interval), which some psychologists think is a common situation. Further, the logic of rank-order methods is simple and direct, requiring no elaborate construction of hypothetical distributions or estimated parameters.

However, rank-order methods are not as familiar to readers of research, and rank-order methods have not been developed for many complex situations. Another problem is that the simple logic of rank-order tests breaks down if there are many ties in ranks. Finally, like data transformation methods, rank-order methods distort the original data, losing information. For example, in the same sample, a difference between 6.1 and 6.2 could be one rank, but the difference between 3.4 and 5.8 might also be one rank.[4]

RELATIVE RISK OF TYPE I AND TYPE II ERRORS

How accurate are the various methods in terms of the 5% level really meaning that there is a 5% chance of incorrectly rejecting the null hypothesis? And how do the different methods affect power?

When the assumptions for parametric tests are met, the parametric tests are as good as or better than any of the alternatives. This is true for protection against both Type I and Type II errors. This would be expected, as these are the conditions for which the parametric tests were designed.

However, when the assumptions for a parametric test are not met, the relative advantages of the possible alternative procedures we have considered are not at all clear. In fact, the relative merits of the various procedures are topics of lively controversy, with many articles appearing in statistics-oriented journals every year.

---

[4]Another traditional advantage of rank-order tests has been that except for the labor of changing the scores to ranks, the actual figuring for most of these procedures is very simple compared to that of parametric tests. However, nowadays, with computers, it is as easy to figure either kind of procedure. With some standard statistical computer packages, there is actually less trouble involved in figuring the parametric test.

HOW ARE YOU DOING?

1. (a) What is a rank-order transformation? (b) Why is it done? (c) What is a rank-order test?
2. Transform the following scores to ranks: 5, 18, 3, 9, 2.
3. (a) If you wanted to use a standard rank-order test instead of a *t* test for independent means, what procedure would you use? (b) What are the steps of doing such a test? (c) What is the underlying logic?
4. Why do research articles sometimes report a *Z* value for a rank-order test?
5. (a) What happens if you change your scores to ranks and then figure an ordinary parametric test using the ranks? (b) Why will this not be quite accurate even assuming the transformation to ranks is appropriate? (c) Why will this result not be quite as accurate using the standard rank-order test? (d) What are the advantages of using this procedure over a standard rank-order test?
6. If conditions are not met for a parametric test (a) what are the advantages and (b) disadvantages of data-transformation over rank-order tests, and what are the (c) advantages and (d) disadvantages of rank-order tests over data transformation?

ANSWERS:

1. (a) Changing each score to its rank (order from lowest to highest) among all the scores.
(b) To make the distribution a standard shape, or because the true nature of the measurement may be rank-order.
(c) A special type of significance testing procedure designed for use with rank-ordered scores.
2. $5 = 3, 18 = 5, 3 = 2, 9 = 4$, and $2 = 1$.
3. (a) Wilcoxon rank-sum test or Mann-Whitney *U* test.
(b) Set the significance cutoff (based on a table) for the maximum sum of ranks for the group predicted to have the lower scores, change all scores to ranks (ignoring what group they are in), add up the ranks in the group predicted to have the lower scores, compare that total to the cutoff.
(c) The shape and details of a distribution of ranks is known, so statisticians can prepare tables based on figuring from exact probabilities of what is the maximum sum of ranks you would get any particular percent of the time (such as 5%) if the null hypothesis was true.
4. With large samples, rather than use the special tables, there are formulas for converting a sum of ranks to a *Z* score (based on an approximation to the normal curve).
5. (a) You get fairly similar results to doing the standard parametric test.
(b) Because the population distribution will be rectangular and not normal (an assumption for the *t* test).
(c) Because the rank-order test is based on knowing for sure the shape of the population distribution and using exact probabilities on that basis—with an ordinary *t* test of analysis of variance, usually at best the populations are only approximately normal and have only approximately equal variances.
(d) It is simpler when using a computer and you can do it with almost any statistical test (and there are not special rank-order tests for all the situations for which there are parametric tests).
6. (a) You can use the familiar parametric methods and the transformation may come closer to the true meaning of the underlying measurement.
(b) They will not always work and may distort underlying meaning of the measurement.
(c) They can be applied regardless of the distribution, rank order may better reflect the true meaning of the measurement, and rank-order tests are very accurate.
(d) They are often unfamiliar and have not been developed for may complex methods; also, ties in ranks (which are common) distort the accuracy of these tests.

CONTROVERSY: COMPUTER INTENSIVE METHODS

In recent years, thanks to the availability of computers, a whole new set of hypothesis-testing methods has become practical that some researchers argue should completely replace all the standard methods of hypothesis testing! The general name for these new procedures is **computer-intensive methods.** The main specific techniques are **randomization tests** and *bootstrap tests.* These procedures differ in important details, but their general logic is similar enough that we can give you the basic idea by focusing on one of them: randomization tests.

computer-intensive methods
randomization tests

Suppose that you have two groups of scores, one for an experimental group and one for a control group. Suppose also that the means of the two groups differ by some amount. Now consider what happens if all these scores were mixed up, ignoring which group they came from. If you figure the difference between the means of these two randomly set up groups, what is the chance that this whole process would result in a mean difference as big as the one found in the original, proper grouping of the scores?

If the mean difference between the original groupings is quite small, it is quite likely that you could get that big a mean difference through chance groupings. But if the mean difference for the original groupings is quite large, creating chance groupings would not often produce a difference as large. If chance groupings would produce a result as big as the original groupings less than 5% of the time, we would feel quite confident that the original groupings were quite different from what you would expect by chance. Thus, the approach of comparing an actual grouping to chance groupings of scores is a way of doing a significance test.

A randomization test for this kind of situation actually sets up rapidly, by computer, every single possible division of the scores into two groups of these sizes. Then it determines how many of these possible organizations have a difference as extreme as the actual observed differences between your two groups. If fewer than 5% of the possible organizations have differences this extreme, your result is significant. You can reject the null hypothesis that the two groups could have been this different by a chance division. (This logic is like that used for working out the probabilities for rank-order tests, but in this case, scores are not first converted to ranks.)

Table 15–7 shows what a computer would do for a randomization test for the example fictional two-group study of number of books read. Basically, what the table shows is the worked-out difference between means for every one of the 70 possible combination of eight scores into two groups of four scores each. Thus, for the actual two groups, the difference is 34.5; but for other ways of dividing up the eight scores, the difference in means can be as low as −37 and as high as +37. What is shown on the bottom, however, is that our particular result is one of the two highest of the 70—putting it in the top 5%. Thus, using this method, the researcher can conclude there is a significant difference—and do so without having made any assumptions whatsoever about population distributions!

Our example used a very small sample. Even so, there were 70 possible divisions of the scores. With larger (and more realistic) sample sizes, the number of different divisions quickly becomes unmanageable, even for most computers. For example, a comparison between two groups of seven participants each has 3,432 possible divisions; a comparison of 10 participants per group has 184,756. With 20 per group, there are 155,120,000! In practice, even most computers cannot handle true randomization tests with the size of samples common in psychology research.

To deal with this problem, statisticians have developed what are called *approximate randomization tests.* The computer randomly selects a large number of possible divisions of the sample—perhaps 1,000. The results using these randomly selected divisions are then considered representative of what you would find if you actually used every possible division. (This is similar to a Monte Carlo study, which we described in Chapter 10, Box 10–1. And how does something as orderly as a computer come up with so many random numbers? See Box 15–1.)

TABLE 15–7 Randomization Test Computations for the Study Comparing Highly Sensitive and Not Highly Sensitive Children on the Number of Books Read in the Past Year (Fictional Data)

Actual Results:

Highly Sensitive

	No	Yes
	0	17
	3	36
	10	45
	22	75
Σ	35	173
$M =$	8.75	43.25

Actual difference $= M_{Yes} - M_{No} = 34.5$

Needed to reject the null hypothesis: This mean difference must be in top 5% of mean differences. With 70 mean differences, it must be among the three highest differences.

All possible Divisions (70) of the Eight Scores Into Two Groups of Four Each:

Actual

	No	Yes		No	Yes		No	Yes		No	Yes		No	Yes		No	Yes		No	Yes
	0	17		0	22		0	22		0	22		0	22		0	10		0	10
	3	36		3	36		3	17		3	17		3	17		3	36		3	17
	10	45		10	45		10	45		10	36		10	36		22	45		22	45
	22	75		17	75		36	75		45	75		75	45		17	75		36	75
$M_{Yes} - M_{No}$	34.5			37			27.5			23			8			31			21.5	

	No	Yes		No	Yes		No	Yes		No	Yes		No	Yes		No	Yes		No	Yes
	0	10		0	10		0	10		0	10		0	10		0	10		0	10
	3	17		3	17		3	22		3	22		3	22		3	22		3	22
	22	36		22	36		17	45		17	36		17	36		36	17		36	17
	45	75		75	45		36	75		45	75		75	45		45	75		75	45
$M_{Yes} - M_{No}$	17			2			24			19.5			4.5			10			−5	

	No	Yes		No	Yes		No	Yes		No	Yes		No	Yes		No	Yes		No	Yes
	0	10		0	3		0	3		0	3		0	3		0	3		0	3
	3	22		10	36		10	17		10	17		10	17		10	22		10	22
	45	17		22	45		22	45		22	36		22	36		17	45		17	36
	75	36		17	75		36	75		45	75		75	45		36	75		45	75
$M_{Yes} - M_{No}$	−9.5			27.5			18			13.5			−1.5			20.5			16	

	No	Yes		No	Yes		No	Yes		No	Yes		No	Yes		No	Yes		No	Yes
	0	3		0	3		0	3		0	3		0	3		0	3		0	3
	10	22		10	22		10	22		10	22		22	10		22	10		22	10
	17	36		36	17		36	17		45	17		17	45		17	36		17	36
	75	45		45	75		75	45		75	36		36	75		45	75		75	45
$M_{Yes} - M_{No}$	1			6.5			−8.5			−13			14.5			10			−5	

	No	Yes		No	Yes		No	Yes		No	Yes		No	Yes		No	Yes		No	Yes
	0	3		0	3		0	3		0	3		0	3		0	3		0	3
	22	10		22	10		22	10		17	10		17	10		17	10		36	10
	36	17		36	17		45	17		36	22		36	22		45	22		45	22
	45	75		75	45		75	36		45	75		75	45		75	36		75	17
$M_{Yes} - M_{No}$	.5			−14.5			−19			3			−12			−16.5			−26	

	No	Yes		No	Yes		No	Yes		No	Yes		No	Yes		No	Yes		No	Yes
	17	0		22	0		22	0		22	0		22	0		10	0		10	0
	3	3		36	3		17	3		17	3		17	3		36	3		17	3
	10	10		45	10		45	10		36	10		36	10		45	22		45	22
	22	22		75	17		75	36		75	45		45	75		75	17		75	36
$M_{Yes} - M_{No}$	−34.5			−37			−27.5			−23			−8			−31			−21.5	

TABLE 15–7 (Continued)

No	Yes	No	Yes	No	Yes	No	Yes	No	Yes	No	Yes	No	Yes
10	0	10	0	10	0	10	0	10	0	10	0	10	0
17	3	17	3	22	3	22	3	22	3	22	3	22	3
36	22	36	22	45	17	36	17	36	17	17	36	17	36
75	45	45	75	75	36	75	45	45	75	75	45	45	75

$M_{Yes} - M_{No}$: −17   −2   −24   −19.5   −4.5   −10   5

No	Yes	No	Yes	No	Yes	No	Yes	No	Yes	No	Yes	No	Yes
10	0	3	0	3	0	3	0	3	0	3	0	3	0
22	3	36	10	17	10	17	10	17	10	22	10	22	10
17	45	45	22	45	22	36	22	36	22	45	17	36	17
36	75	75	17	75	36	75	45	45	75	75	36	75	45

$M_{Yes} - M_{No}$: 9.5   −27.5   −18   −13.5   1.5   −20.5   −16

No	Yes	No	Yes	No	Yes	No	Yes	No	Yes	No	Yes	No	Yes
3	0	3	0	3	0	3	0	3	0	3	0	3	0
22	10	22	10	22	10	22	10	10	22	10	22	10	22
36	17	17	36	17	36	17	45	45	17	36	17	36	17
45	75	75	45	45	75	36	75	75	36	75	45	45	75

$M_{Yes} - M_{No}$: −1   −6.5   8.5   13   −14.5   −10   5

No	Yes	No	Yes	No	Yes	No	Yes	No	Yes	No	Yes	No	Yes
3	0	3	0	3	0	3	0	3	0	3	0	3	0
10	22	10	22	10	22	10	17	10	17	10	17	10	36
17	36	17	36	17	45	22	36	22	36	22	45	22	45
75	45	45	75	36	75	75	45	45	75	36	75	17	75

$M_{Yes} - M_{No}$: −.5   14.5   19   −3   12   16.5   26

Seventy Differences Ordered From Lowest (Most Negative) to Highest:

−37, 34.5, 32, −27.5, −27.5, −26, −21.5, −24, −23, −20.5, −19.5, −16, −16.5, −17, −18, −19, −14.5, −14.5, −13.5, −13, −12, −10, −10, −9.5, −8.5, −8, −6.5, −5, −5, −4.5, −1.5, −3, −2, −1, −.5, .5, 1, 1.5, 2, 3, 4.5, 5, 5, 6.5, 8, 8.5, 9.5, 10, 10, 12, 13, 13.5, 14.5, 14.5, 16, 16.5, 17, 18, 19, 19.5, 20.5, 21.5, 23, 24, 26, 27.5, 27.5, 31, 34.5, 37

Conclusion: Actual mean difference is among the three highest. Reject the null hypothesis.

Computer-intensive methods, such as approximate randomization tests, do not require either of the two main assumptions of ordinary parametric tests. Further, like rank-order tests, they have a direct logic of their own that is very appealing, bypassing the whole process of estimated population distributions, distributions of means, and so forth. Computer-intensive methods are also extremely flexible. You can use them in almost any situation imaginable in which hypothesis testing could be applied. Thus, they can often be used when no existing test exists, parametric or otherwise.

The main disadvantage of the computer-intensive methods is that they are quite new, so the details and relative advantages of various approaches have not been well worked out. Further, because they are new, in most cases the standard computer statistical packages do not include them. Computer-intensive methods are only beginning to appear in published articles, but their use is likely to increase rapidly.

DATA TRANSFORMATIONS AND RANK-ORDER TESTS IN RESEARCH ARTICLES

The use of the procedures we have described in this chapter seems to wax and wane in popularity in different areas of psychology. In some fields, during certain years, you may see many studies using data transformations and never see a rank-order

BOX 15–1   Where Do Random Numbers Come From?

To be random, numbers must be selected with equal odds. That is, the odds of each number's appearance have to be totally independent of the odds of the numbers appearing before and after it. One of the many important uses of random numbers is in computer-intensive statistical methods, as discussed in this chapter. They are also essential to Monte Carlo studies (see Chapter 10, Box 10–1), which are used to test the effect of violating normality and other assumptions of parametric statistical tests—one way for psychologists to know whether they need to use the methods described in this chapter. But random numbers in themselves are an interesting topic.

The first random number table was created in 1927. Before that, mechanical methods such as shuffling devices were used. Remember William S. ("Student") Gosset (Chapter 9, Box 9–1)? To obtain his random numbers, he shuffled and drew from a deck of 3,000 cards. Then, in 1927, Karl Pearson encouraged L. H. C. Tippett to publish a table. Tippett found drawing numbered cards from a bag "unsatisfactory," so he selected digits from the 1925 census report. Later, in 1938, R. A. Fisher and Frank Yates published a list based on logarithms. At about the same time, a number of methods of checking for randomness were also introduced.

Later, more sophisticated physical solutions became common. Flashing a beam of light at irregular intervals onto a sectioned rotating disk was one. Another used the radiation of radioactive substances. It recorded the number of particles detected during a certain time span; if the number was odd, it set a counter to 1, and if even, to 0, and then generated lists of numbers from groupings of these binary digits. A third system employed an electronic valve that made noise that could be amplified; the fluctuating output values were random.

All of these physical methods were a nuisance: They required storing the numbers if they were to be reproduced or reused, and all this apparatus was hard to maintain. So, computers are now often used to create "pseudorandom numbers," using some special equation, such as squaring large numbers and taking a central group of the resulting digits. But these numbers are in some subtle sense not random, but predictable, because of the very fact that there was an intention in the equation's design—to create randomness (quite a paradox). There is also the problem of whether equations will "degenerate" and begin to repeat sequences. Finally, no matter how the list is generated, there is controversy about the consequences of repeated use of the same table.

The whole topic of how difficult it is to create something free of order or intelligence seems to say something. What that is, we will leave for you to decide.

---

test. In other areas, during the same years, you may see just the reverse. And the application of computer-intensive methods in psychology is such a new development that you are likely to encounter them in only a few of the most recent studies you read—often in circumstances where there is no obvious alternative procedure.

Data transformations are usually mentioned just prior to the description of the analysis, using the scores that were transformed. For example, Kawakami and Dovidio (2001), in a study of prejudice, begin a discussion of their reaction time (response latencies) results as follows: "Before analyzing the response latencies, . . . responses were subjected to a logarithmic transformation" (p. 220).

Here is an example of a rank-order test reported in a research study by Rotenstreich and Hsee (2001), focusing on the importance of subjective feeling in making risk-taking decisions. In one of their studies, one group of students was asked how much they would pay for having a 1% chance of winning a $500 coupon towards a European summer vacation and the other group was asked how much they would pay for having a 1% chance of winning a $500 coupon towards their tuition. Here are the results: "Although the two coupons had equivalent redemption value, the median price of the 1% chance of winning the European coupon was $20, whereas the median price of the 1% chance of winning the tuition coupon was only $5 ($p < 05$ by Mann-Whitney test . . .)" (p. 187).

SUMMARY

1. The t test, the analysis of variance, and other standard parametric tests all assume that populations follow a normal curve and have equal variances. When samples suggest that the populations are very far from normal or have different variances (for example, due to outliers), using the ordinary procedures gives incorrect results.

2. One approach when the populations appear to be violating these assumptions is to transform the scores, such as taking the square root of each score so that the distribution of the transformed scores appears to represent a normally distributed population. Other common transformations for skewed distributions are taking the log or inverse of each score. You can then use the ordinary hypothesis-testing procedures.

3. Another approach is to rank all of the scores in a study. Special rank-order tests (sometimes called nonparametric or distribution-free tests) use basic principles of probability to determine the chance of the ranks being unevenly distributed across groups. However, in many situations, using the rank-transformed scores in an ordinary parametric test gives a good approximation.

4. Data transformations allow you to use the familiar parametric techniques, but cannot always be applied and may distort the meaning of the scores. You can use rank-order methods in almost any situation, they are especially appropriate with rank or similar data, and they have a straightforward conceptual foundation. But rank-order methods are not widely familiar and they have not been developed for many complex data analysis situations. As with other data transformations, information may be lost or meaning distorted.

5. A randomization test is an example of a computer-intensive method that considers every possible rearrangement of the scores from a study to figure the probability that the actual arrangement (for example, the difference in means between the actual two groupings of scores) arose by chance. Computer-intensive methods have been proposed as an alternative to both parametric and nonparametric methods. They are widely applicable, sometimes to situations for which no other method exists. Also, they have an appealing direct logic. But they are unfamiliar to researchers; being new, their possible limitations are not well worked out, and they can be difficult to set up, as they are not provided on standard computer programs.

6. Research articles usually describe data transformations just prior to analyses using them. Rank-order methods are described much like any other kind of hypothesis test.

KEY TERMS

computer-intensive
   methods (p. 557)
data transformation
   (p. 546)
distribution-free tests
   (p. 551)

nonparametric tests
   (p. 551)
parametric tests (p. 551)
randomization tests
   (p. 557)
rank-order tests (p. 551)

rank-order transformation
   (p. 550)
square-root
   transformation (p. 546)

EXAMPLE WORKED-OUT COMPUTATIONAL PROBLEMS

The following problems are based on the scores below from a study with three groups:

Group A	Group B	Group C
15	21	18
4	16	19
12	49	11
14	17	

SQUARE-ROOT TRANSFORMATION

Carry out a square-root transformation.

Group A	Group B	Group C
3.88	4.58	4.24
2	4	4.36
3.46	7	3.31
3.74	4.12	

RANK-ORDER TRANSFORMATION

Carry out a rank-order transformation.

Group A	Group B	Group C
5	10	8
1	6	9
3	11	2
4	7	

PRACTICE PROBLEMS

These problems involve figuring. Most real-life statistics problems are done on a computer. However, even if you have a computer and statistics software, do these by hand (with the help of a calculator) to ingrain the method in your mind. Also, in all problems involving figuring, be sure to show your work.

For practice in using a computer to solve statistics problems, refer to the computer section of each chapter of the *Student's Study Guide and Computer Workbook* that accompanies this text.

All data are fictional unless an actual citation is given.

Answers to Set I problems are given at the back of the book.

SET I

1. For each of the following sample distributions, say whether it suggests that the population distribution is probably not normal, and why.

  (a) 41, 52, 74, 107, 617
  (b) 221, 228, 241, 503, 511, 521
  (c) .2, .3, .5, .6, .7, .9, .11
  (d) −6, −5, −3, 10
  (e) 11, 20, 32, 41, 49, 62

2. For each of the distributions below, make a square-root transformation:
  (a) 16, 4, 9, 25, 36
  (b) 35, 14.3, 13, 12.9, 18

3. For the distribution of 30 scores given below, (a) make a grouped frequencies histogram of the scores as they are (intervals 0–4.9, 5–9.9 10–14.9, etc.); (b) carry out a square-root transformation; and (c) make a grouped histogram of the transformed scores (0–.9, 1–1.9, etc.).
  9, 28, 4, 16, 0, 7, 25, 1, 4, 10, 4, 2, 1, 9, 16, 11, 12, 1, 18, 2, 5, 10, 3, 17, 6, 4, 2, 23, 21, 20

4. A researcher compares the typical family size in 10 cultures, 5 from Language Group A and 5 from Language Group B. The figures for the Group A cultures are 1.2, 2.5, 4.3, 3.8, and 7.2. The figures for the Group B cultures are 2.1, 9.2, 5.7, 6.7, and 4.8. Based on these 10 cultures, does typical family size differ in cultures with different language groups? Use the .05 level. (a) Carry out a t test for independent means using the actual scores. (b) Carry out a square-root transformation (to keep things simple, round off the transformed scores to one decimal place). (c) Carry out a t test for independent means using the transformed scores. (d) Explain what you have done and why to someone who is familiar with the t test for independent means but not with data transformation.

5. A researcher is studying the effect of sleep deprivation on recall. Six participants are each tested twice on a recall task, once on a day when well rested (they had plenty of sleep the night before) and once when sleep deprived (they have had no sleep for 48 hours. Here are the recall scores:

Participant	Well Rested	Sleep Deprived
A	16	5
B	18	2
C	10	10
D	7	3
E	20	16
F	10	9

Does sleep deprivation affect recall? (Use the .05 significance level.) (a) Carry out a t test for dependent means using the actual scores. (b) Carry out a square-root transformation of the difference scores (to keep things simple, round off the transformed scores to one decimal place). (c) Carry out a t test for dependent means using the transformed difference scores. (d) Explain what you have done and why to someone who is familiar with the t test for dependent means but not with data transformation.

6. A researcher randomly assigns participants to watch one of three kinds of films: one that tends to make peoples ad, one that tends to make people exuberant, and one that tends to make people angry. The participants are then asked to rate a series of photos of individuals on how honest they appear. The ratings for the sad-film group were 201, 523, and 614; the ratings for the angry-film group were 136, 340, and 301; and the ratings for the exuberant-film group were 838,

911, and 1,007. (a) Carry out an analysis of variance using the actual scores (use $p < .01$). (b) Carry out a square-root transformation of the scores (to keep things simple, round off the transformed scores to one decimal place). (c) Carry out an analysis of variance using the transformed scores. (d) Explain what you have done and why to someone who is familiar with analysis of variance but not with data transformation.

7. Miller (1997) conducted a study of commitment to a romantic relationship and how much attention a person pays to attractive alternatives. In this study, participants were shown a set of slides of attractive individuals. At the start of the results section, Miller notes, "The self-reports on the Attentiveness to Alternative Index and the time spent actually inspecting the attractive opposite-sex slides . . . were positively skewed, so logarithmic transformations of the data were performed" (p. 760). Explain what is being described here (and why it is being done) to a person who understands ordinary parametric statistics but has never heard of data transformations.

8. Prior to reporting the results for the latency ms scores (reaction time scores in milliseconds) on each trial, Teachman et al. (2001) reported the following: ". . . trial latency data were reciprocally transformed (1,000/latency in ms)" (p. 230). Explain what is being described here (and why it is being done) to a person who understands ordinary parametric statistics but has never heard of data transformations.

9. Make a rank-order transformation for the scores in problems (a) 2a and (b) 2b.

10. For the distribution of 30 scores given in problem 3, (a) carry out a rank-order transformation and (b) make a grouped frequency histogram of the ranked scores (0–4.9, 5–9.9, etc.).

11. For the data in problems (a) 4, (b) 5, and (c) 6, carry out the appropriate test using the original scores (if you have not done so already), carry out a rank-transformation of the scores, carry out the appropriate statistical test (t test or analysis of variance) using the rank-transformed scores, and explain what you have done and why to someone who is familiar with the ordinary parametric procedures but not with rank-order transformations or rank-order tests.

12. Ford et al. (1997) were interested in the relation of certain personality factors to treatment for post-traumatic stress disorder (a psychological condition resulting from a traumatic event such as might be experienced during war or as a result of a violent attack). The personality factor of interest to the researchers was based on a modern version of Freudian psychoanalytic theory called "object relations." This refers to the psychological impact of our earliest relationships, mainly with our parents (the "objects" of these early relationships). The researchers based their measure of object relations on a clinical interview focusing on such things as ability to invest in a close relationship and the ability to see others in a complex way (e.g., not seeing a person as all good or all bad). In reporting their results, they abbreviated the object relations clinical interview measure as "OR-C". The distribution of scores on the OR-C was not normal (it was bimodal).

One of their analyses focused on the relation of object relations to whether a person stays in treatment to completion or terminates prematurely. They reported their results as follows:

> Six of the 74 participants prematurely terminated. . . . The six premature terminators did not differ from the rest of the sample on any demographic or pretest variable. . . . They did differ statistically significantly from completers on OR-C ratings, scoring lower as tested by the nonparametric Mann-Whitney U Test ($Z = -3.43$, $p < .001$).(p. 554)

Explain the general idea of what these researchers are doing (and why they didn't use an ordinary *t* test) to a person who is familiar with the *t* test but not with rank-order tests.

SET II

13. For each of the following sample distributions, say (a) whether it suggests that the population distribution is probably not normal, and (b) why.
    (a) 281, 283, 287, 289, 291, 300, 302
    (b) 1, 4, 6, 6, 7, 7, 9, 13
    (c) 7, 104, 104, 104, 1,245, 1,247, 1,248, 1,251
    (d) 68, 74, 76, 1,938
    (e) 407.2, 407.5, 407.6, 407.9

14. For each of the distributions below, make a square-root transformation:
    (a) 100, 1, 64, 81, 121
    (b) 45, 30, 17.4, 16.8, 47

15. For the distribution of 20 scores given below, (a) make a histogram of the scores as they are; (b) carry out a square-root transformation; and (c) make a histogram of the transformed scores.
    2, 207, 894, 107, 11, 79, 112, 938, 791, 3, 13, 89, 1,004, 92, 1,016, 107, 87, 91, 870, 921

16. A study compared students' number of close friends during their first and second years in college. Here are the numbers of friends for five students tested.

Participant	First Year	Second Year
1	2	2
2	4	6
3	14	15
4	3	15
5	5	6

   Does the number of close friends increase from first to second year of college? (Use the .05 significance level.) (a) Carry out a *t* test for dependent means using the actual scores. (b) Carry out a square-root transformation of the difference scores (to keep things simple, round off the transformed scores to one decimal place). (c) Carry out a *t* test for dependent means using the transformed difference scores. (d) Explain what you have done and why to someone who is familiar with the *t* test for dependent means but not with data transformations.

17. A study compares performance on a novel task for people who do the task either alone, in the presence of a stranger, or in the presence of a friend. The scores for the participants in the alone condition are 1, 1, and 0; the scores of the participants in the stranger condition are 2, 6, and 1; and the scores for those in the friend condition are 3, 9, and 10. (a) Carry out an analysis of variance using the actual scores ($p < .05$). (b) Carry out a square-root transformation of the scores (to keep things simple, round off the transformed scores to one decimal place). (c) Carry out an analysis of variance using the transformed difference scores. (d) Explain what you have done and why to someone who is familiar with analysis of variance but not with data transformation.

18. A researcher conducted an experiment organized around a major televised address by the U.S. president. Immediately after the address, three participants

were randomly assigned to listen to the commentaries provided by the television network's political commentators. The other three were assigned to spend the same time with the television off, reflecting quietly about the speech. Participants in both groups then completed a questionnaire that assessed how much of the content of the speech they remembered accurately. The group that heard the commentators had scores of 4, 0, and 1. The group that reflected quietly had scores of 9, 3, and 8. Did hearing the commentary affect memory? Use the .05 level, one-tailed, predicting higher scores for the reflected-quietly group. (a) Carry out a *t* test for independent means using the actual scores. (b) Carry out a square-root transformation (to keep things simple, round off the transformed scores to one decimal place). (c) Carry out a *t* test for independent means using the transformed scores. (d) Explain what you have done and why to someone who is familiar with the *t* test for independent means but not with data transformation.

19. Carey et al. (1997) developed a program designed to enhance motivation for avoiding HIV infection risks. They then studied its effectiveness with a group of economically disadvantaged urban women who were randomly assigned to either receive the program or a control condition. All the women were measured before, 3 weeks after, and 12 weeks after the experimental group participated in the program. One of the measures in the study was sexual communication, such as the extent to which the women reported they had talked with their partners about safer sex and getting tested for HIV. Prior to describing their analyses on this variable, Carey et al. noted the following: "The communication scores were positively skewed at all three occasions; $\log_{10} (x + 1)$ transformations provided the best correction toward normality and were used in subsequent analyses" (p. 536). Explain what is being described here (and why it is being done) to a person who understands ordinary parametric statistics but has never heard of data transformations.

20. Connors et al. (1997) conducted a study focusing on the client-therapist alliance in alcoholism treatment. Prior to reporting the results of their study, they commented as follows:

> Variables such as percentage of days abstinent and drinks per day often depart from normality because of skewness and floor-ceiling effects. In response, the percentage of days abstinent variable was subjected to an arcsine transformation, and the drinks per drinking day variable was subjected to a square-root transformation, in each case to improve the distribution. (p. 592)

Explain what is being described here (and why it is being done) to a person who understands ordinary parametric statistics but has never heard of data transformations.

21. Martinez (2000) studied the link between homicide rates and immigrant status among Latinos in the United States. However, prior to presenting the results, Martinez noted, ". . . the dependent variables indicated skewed distributions. Thus, all Latino homicide types . . . were logarithmically transformed into natural logs." Explain what is being described here (and why it is being done) to a person who understands ordinary parametric statistics but has never heard of data transformations.

22. Make a rank-order transformation for the scores in problems (a) 14a and (b) 14b.

23. For the distribution of 20 scores given in problem 15, (a) carry out a rank-order transformation and (b) make a histogram of the ranked scores.

24. For the data in problems (a) 17 and (b) 18, carry out the appropriate test using original scores (if you have not done so already), carry out a rank-transforma-

tion of the scores, carry out the appropriate statistical test (*t* test or analysis of variance) using the rank-transformed scores, and explain what you have done and why to someone who is familiar with the normal parametric procedures but not with rank-order transformations or rank-order tests.

25. June et al. (1990) surveyed black students at a Midwestern university about problems in their use of college services. Surveys were conducted of about 250 students each time, at the end of the spring quarter over five different years. The researchers ranked the nine main problem areas for each of the years. One of their analyses then proceeded as follows: "A major question of interest was whether the ranking of most serious problems and use of services varied by years. Thus, a Kruskal-Wallis one-way analysis of variance (ANOVA) was performed on the rankings but was not significant. . . ." (p. 180). Explain why the researchers used the Kruskal-Wallis test instead of an ordinary analysis of variance and what conclusions can be drawn from this result.

26. As part of a larger study, Betsch et al. (2001) manipulated the attention to information presented in TV ads and then gave participants questions about the content of the ads as a check on the success of their manipulation. They report,

> Participants who were instructed to attend to the ads answered 51.5% . . . of the questions correctly. In the other condition, only 41.1% of questions were answered correctly. This difference is significant according to the Mann-Whitney U test, $U(84) = 2317.0$, $p < .01$. This shows that the attention manipulation was effective. (p. 248)

Explain the general idea of what these researchers are doing (and why they didn't use an ordinary *t* test) to a person who is familiar with the *t* test but not with rank-order tests.

CHAPTER 16

INTEGRATING WHAT YOU HAVE LEARNED:

THE GENERAL LINEAR MODEL

Are You Ready?
What You Need to Have Mastered Before Starting This Chapter:
- Chapter 1 through 13.

This chapter is intended to integrate and deepen your knowledge about the major statistical techniques you have learned—analysis of variance, t test, correlation, and regression. Equally important, it provides a thorough review of those techniques.

THE RELATIONSHIPS AMONG MAJOR STATISTICAL METHODS

More than 90% of the studies published in a typical year in the major social psychology journals use t tests, analysis of variance, correlation, or multiple regression (Reis & Stiller, 1992). This figure probably applies about equally well to all areas of psychology. By now you may have noticed many similarities among these four methods and the other statistical techniques that you have learned in this book. In fact, the techniques are more closely related than you might have realized: Many of them are simply mathematically equivalent variations of each other, and most of them can be derived from the same general formula. This is because there is a central logic behind all these methods based on a general formula that mathematical statisticians call the **general linear model.**

general linear model

So let's focus on the Big Four, which are all special cases of the general linear model and therefore systematically related. Perhaps in the process, many of your half-sensed intuitions about what you've learned will emerge into the light.

To put it all briefly (and then proceed in depth), the most general technique is multiple regression (Chapter 4), of which bivariate correlation (Chapter 3) is a special case. At the same time, the analysis of variance (chapters 11 to 13) is also a special case of multiple regression. Finally, the *t* test (chapters 9 and 10) can be derived directly from either bivariate correlation or the analysis of variance. Figure 16–1 shows these relationships.

When we say that one procedure is a special case of another, we mean that it can be derived from the formula for the other. Thus, when using the more specialized procedures, you get the same result as if you had used the more general procedure. To put this in more concrete terms, if you were going to a desert island to do psychology research and could take only one computer program with you to do statistical tests, you would want to choose multiple regression. With that one program, you could accomplish all of what is done by more specialized programs for bivariate correlation, *t* tests, and analyses of variance.

We explore these links in this chapter. First, we briefly review the idea of multiple regression from Chapter 4, and in this context consider a formal statement of the general linear model. Then, we look at each of the links in turn: multiple regression with bivariate correlation, analysis of variance with the *t* test, bivariate correlation with the *t* test, and multiple regression with the analysis of variance.

REVIEW OF THE PRINCIPLES OF MULTIPLE REGRESSION

Let us briefly review regression from Chapter 4. First, recall that the basic idea of bivariate prediction (also called bivariate regression) is that you come up with a systematic rule for predicting a person's score on a particular criterion variable by considering that person's score on a predictor variable. For example, we predicted happy mood from knowing how much sleep a person had the night before. Multiple regression is when you make your predictions using two or more predictor vari-

FIGURE 16–1 *The relationships among the four major statistical techniques.*

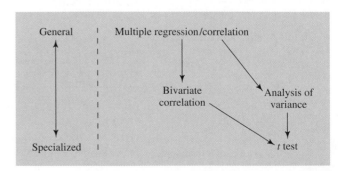

ables—when, for example, predicting happiness from amount of sleep, how well the person slept, and number of dreams the night before.

You can make prediction rules in either a Z-score form or a raw-score form. In this chapter, we focus on the raw-score form because that form makes it easier to see the relation to the general linear model. A multiple regression prediction rule with three predictor variables, when working with raw scores, goes like this:

(16-1)
$$\hat{Y} = a + (b_1)(X_1) + (b_2)(X_2) + (b_3)(X_3)$$

A person's predicted score on the criterion variable is the regression constant, plus the raw score regression coefficient for the first predictor variable times the person's score on the first predictor variable, plus the raw score regression coefficient for the second predictor variable times the person's score on the second predictor variable, plus the raw score regression coefficient for the third predictor variable times the person's score on the third predictor variable.

In this formula, $\hat{Y}$ is the predicted score on the criterion variable; a is the raw-score regression constant; b_1, b_2, and b_3 are the raw score regression coefficients for the first, second, and third predictor variables, respectively; and X_1, X_2, and X_3 are the person's scores on the first, second, and third predictor variables, respectively.

For example, in the sleep and mood study, a raw-score multiple regression model for predicting mood with three predictor variables might be as follows:

$$\hat{\text{Happiness}} = -5.89 + (1.24)(\text{hours slept}) + (.48)(\text{how well slept}) + (.25)(\text{number of dreams})$$

Suppose a particular person had slept 7 hours the night before, rated how well slept as a 3, and had 1 dream. Their predicted mood would be

$$\hat{\text{Happiness}} = -5.89 + (1.24)(7) + (.48)(3) + (.25)(1)$$
$$= -5.89 + 8.68 + 1.44 + .25 = 4.48.$$

It is also possible to describe the overall degree of association between the criterion variable and the combination of the predictor variables. This is called a multiple correlation coefficient and is symbolized by R. R must be at least as large as the smallest bivariate correlation of any of the predictor variables with the criterion variable. R^2 is the proportionate reduction in squared error gained by using the multiple regression prediction rule compared to simply predicting the criterion variable from its mean.

Finally, a multiple correlation (and the associated proportionate reduction in error) can be tested for significance using a procedure in which the null hypothesis is that in the population the multiple correlation is 0.

THE GENERAL LINEAR MODEL

One way of expressing the general linear model is as a mathematical relation between a criterion variable and one or more predictor variables. The principle is that any person's score on a particular criterion variable (such as happy mood) is the sum of several influences:

1. Some fixed influence that will be the same for all individuals—such as the nature of the testing procedure or the impacts of human biology and society.

2. Influences of other variables you have measured on which people have different scores—such as amount of sleep the night before, how well slept, and number of dreams.

3. Other influences not measured—this is what makes error.

Influence 1 corresponds to the regression constant (*a*) in the multiple regression equation. Influence 2 corresponds to all of the *b* and *X* pairs—$(b_1)(X_1)$, $(b_2)(X_2)$, and so forth—in a multiple regression equation. Influence 3 is about the errors in prediction. (If there were a 1.0 multiple correlation, there would be no Influence 3.) Thus, the general linear model can be stated in symbols as follows:

A person's actual score on the criterion variable is the regression constant, plus the raw score regression coefficient for the first predictor variable times the person's score on the first predictor variable, plus the raw score regression coefficient for the second predictor variable times the person's score on the second predictor variable, plus the raw score regression coefficient for the third predictor variable times the person's score on the third predictor variable, plus any additional regression coefficients times any additional scores on predictor variables, plus error.

$$Y = a + (b_1)(X_1) + (b_2)(X_2) + (b_3)(X_3) + \ldots + e \qquad (16\text{-}2)$$

In this formula, *Y* is a person's actual score on some criterion variable; *a* is the fixed influence that applies to all individuals (Influence 1); b_1 is the degree of influence of the first predictor variable (Influence 2); it is the raw score regression coefficient, which you then multiply by the person's raw score on the first predictor variable, X_1. b_2, b_3, and so forth are the influences of predictor variables 2, 3, and so forth. *e* is the error, the sum of all other influences (Influence 3) on the person's score on *Y*. That is, *e* is what is left over after everything else has been taken into account in making the prediction.

Notice that this formula is nearly identical to that for multiple regression, with two exceptions. First, instead of having the predicted *Y* value ($\hat{Y}$) on the left, you have the actual value of *Y*. Second, it includes an error term (*e*). This is because the formula is for the actual value of *Y* and because *a* and *b* values ordinarily don't predict perfectly. The error term (*e*) is added to account for the discrepancy from a perfect prediction of *Y*.

Thus, the general linear model is a statement of the influences that make up an individual's score on a particular variable. It is called a *linear model* because if you graphed the relationship between the criterion and predictor variables, the pattern would be a straight line. That is, the relationship would be constant in the sense of not being curvilinear. In mathematical terms, the equation is said to be linear because there are no squared (or higher power) terms in it.[1]

[1]There are clever ways of sneaking squared and higher power terms into linear model procedures. For example, you could create a new, transformed variable in which each score was squared. This transformed variable could then be used in a linear model equation as an ordinary variable. Thus, no squared term would actually appear in the equation. It turns out that this little trick can be extraordinarily valuable. For example, you can use this kind of procedure to handle curvilinear relationships with statistical methods designed for linear relationships (Cohen & Cohen, 1983; Darlington, 1990).

You may also have heard that various statistical procedures use a *least-squares criterion.* This means that the *a* and *b* values of the general linear model (or of a multiple regression prediction rule) for a particular criterion variable are figured in such a way as to create the smallest amount of squared error—an idea that we considered in Chapter 4.

THE GENERAL LINEAR MODEL AND MULTIPLE REGRESSION

The link between the general linear model and multiple regression is very intimate—they are nearly the same. Traditionally, they have not been equated because the general linear model is understood to be behind other techniques, such as bivariate correlation and the analysis of variance, in addition to multiple regression. However, in recent years psychologists have become increasingly aware that these other techniques can be derived from multiple regression as well as from the general linear model.

BIVARIATE REGRESSION AND CORRELATION AS SPECIAL CASES OF MULTIPLE REGRESSION

Bivariate regression, prediction from one predictor variable to one criterion variable, is a special case of multiple regression, which is prediction from any number of predictor variables to one criterion variable. Similarly, bivariate correlation, the association between one predictor variable and one criterion variable, is a special case of multiple correlation, the association of any number of predictor variables and one criterion variable.

HOW ARE YOU DOING?

1. (a) What does it mean for a procedure to be a "special case" of another procedure? (b) Describe which procedures are special cases of which.
2. Write the formula for raw-score multiple regression with two predictors and define each of the symbols.
3. Write the formula for the general linear model and define each of the symbols.
4. (a) How is the general linear model different from multiple regression? (b) Why?
5. How is bivariate regression a special case of multiple regression?

ANSWERS:

1. (a) The special case can be mathematically derived from the other procedure; it is mathematically identical except that it applies in a more limited set of situations.
   (b) *t* test is a special case of analysis of variance and of bivariate correlation; analyses of variance, bivariate correlation and multiple regression are both special cases of multiple regression.
2. $\hat{Y} = a + (b_1)(X_1) + (b_2)(X_2)$
   $\hat{Y}$ is the predicted score on the criterion variable; a is the raw-score regression constant; b_1 and b_2 are the raw score regression coefficients for the first and second predictor variables, respectively; and X_1 and X_2 are the person's scores on the first and second predictor variables, respectively.
3. $Y = a + (b_1)(X_1) + (b_2)(X_2) + (b_3)(X_3) + \ldots + e$
   Y is a person's actual score on some criterion variable; a is the fixed influence that applies to all individuals; b_1, b_2, and b_3 are the degrees of influence of the first, second and third predictor variables, respectively; X_1, X_2, and X_3 are the person's scores on the first, second, and third predictor variables, respectively; ". . ." is for additional influences and scores on predictor variables; and e is the error, the sum of all other influences on the person's score on Y.

4. (a) It is for the actual (not the estimated) score on the criterion variable and it includes a term for error. (b) To predict the actual score, you have to take into account that there will be error.
5. Multiple regression predicts the criterion variable from any number of predictor variables; bivariate regression is the special case in which you are predicting from only one predictor variable.

THE *t* TEST AS A SPECIAL CASE OF THE ANALYSIS OF VARIANCE

Both the *t* test and the analysis of variance test differences between means of groups. You use the *t* test when there are only two groups.[2] You usually use the analysis of variance, with its *F* ratio, only when there are more than two groups. However, you can use the analysis of variance with just two groups. When there are only two groups, the *t* test and the analysis of variance give identical conclusions.

The strict identity of *t* and *F* applies only in this two-group case. You cannot figure an ordinary *t* test among three groups. This is why we say that the *t* test is a *special case* of the analysis of variance. The test is mathematically identical to the analysis of variance in the particular case where there are only two groups.

INTUITIVE UNDERSTANDING OF THE RELATIONSHIP OF THE TWO PROCEDURES

One way to get a sense of the link of the two procedures is through the analogy of signal-to-noise ratio that we introduced in Chapter 11 to explain the analysis of variance. The idea is that the analysis of variance *F* ratio is a measure of how much the signal (analogous to the difference between group means) is greater than the noise (analogous to the variation within each of the groups). The same idea applies to a *t* test, which is also really about how much the signal (the difference between the two group means) is greater than the noise (the standard deviation of the distribution of differences between means, which is also based on the variation within the groups).

PARALLELS IN THE BASIC LOGIC OF THE TWO PROCEDURES

The analysis of variance *F* ratio is the population variance estimate based on the variation between the means of the groups divided by the population variance estimate based on the variation within each of the groups. That is, the *F* ratio is a fraction in which the numerator is based on the differences among the groups, comparing their means, and the denominator is based on the variation within each of the groups.

The *t* score is the difference between the means of the two groups divided by the standard deviation of the distribution of differences between means (and this

---

[2] In this chapter, we focus on the *t* test for independent means (and also the analysis of variance for between-subject designs). However, the conclusions are all the same for the *t* test for dependent means. It is a special case of the repeated-measures analysis of variance. Also, both the *t* test for dependent means and the repeated-measures analysis of variance are special cases of multiple regression/correlation. However, the link between these methods and multiple regression involves some extra steps of logic that we do not consider here to keep the chapter focused on the main ideas.

Box 16–1   The Golden Age of Statistics: Four Guys Around London

In the last chapter of his little book *The Statistical Pioneers,* James Tankard (1984) discusses the interesting fact that the four most common statistical techniques were created by four Englishmen born within 68 years of each other, three of whom worked in the vicinity of London (and the fourth, Gosset, stuck at his brewery in Dublin, nevertheless visited London to study and kept in good touch with all that was happening in that city). What were the reasons?

First, Tankard feels that their closeness and communication were important for creating the "critical mass" of minds sometimes associated with a golden age of discovery or creativity. Second, as is often the case with important discoveries, each man faced difficult practical problems or "anomalies" that pushed him to the solution at which he arrived. (None simply set out to invent a statistical method in itself.) Galton (Chapter 3, Box 3–1) was interested in the characteristics of parents and children, Pearson (Chapter 14, Box 14–1) in measuring the fit between a set of observations and a theoretical curve. Gosset's (Chapter 9, Box 9–1) problem was small samples caused by the economics of the brewery industry, and Fisher (Chapter 11, Box 11–1) was studying the effects of manure on potatoes. (Age was not a factor, Tankard notes. The age when these four made their major contributions ranged from 31 to 66.)

Tankard also discusses three important social factors specific to this "golden age of statistics." First, there was the role of biometrics, which was attempting to test the theory of evolution mathematically. Biometrics had its influence through Galton's reading of Darwin and Galton's subsequent influence on Pearson. Second, this period saw the beginning of mass hiring by industry and agriculture of university graduates with advanced mathematical training. Third, since the time of Newton, Cambridge University had been a special, centralized source of brilliant mathematicians for England. They could spread out through British industry and still, through their common alma mater, remain in contact with students and each other and conversant with the most recent breakthroughs.

Finally, about the entire history of this field, and its golden age in particular, Tankard has some warm, almost poetic words:

Indeed, it is difficult to see how statistics can be labeled as dull or inanimate. After peering beneath the surface of this practical and powerful discipline, we can see that it has succeeded more than once in eliciting strong passions and lively debate among people. And statistics, being a product of the human mind, it will doubtless continue to do so. (p. 141)

---

standard deviation is based mainly on a pooled variance estimate that is figured from the variation within each of the two groups). Thus, the *t* score is a fraction in which the numerator is the difference between the groups, comparing their means, and the denominator is based on the variation within each of the groups.

In other words, as shown in the top sections of Table 16–1, an *F* ratio and a *t* score are both fractions in which the numerator is based on the differences between the group means and the denominator is based on the variances within the groups.

NUMERIC RELATIONSHIP OF THE TWO PROCEDURES

The formula for a *t* score comes out to be exactly the square root of the formula for the *F* ratio in the situation where there are just two groups. Most students will not be interested in the precise derivation, but there is an important implication. If you figure a *t* score, it will come out to be exactly the square root of what you would get if you figured an *F* ratio for the same study. For example, if you figured a *t* of 3 and then you figured *F* for the same study, the *F* would come out to 9. Similarly, con-

TABLE 16–1	Some Links Between the *t* Test for Independent Means and the Analysis of Variance

t Test	Analysis of Variance
Numerator of *t* is the difference between the means of the two groups.	Numerator of *F* is partly based on variation between the means of the two or more groups.
Denominator of *t* is partly based on pooling the population variance estimates figured from each group.	Denominator of *F* is figured by pooling the population variance estimates figured from each group.
Denominator of *t* involves dividing by number of scores.	Numerator of *F* involves multiplying by number of scores. (Multiplying a numerator by a number has the same effect as dividing the denominator by that number.)
When using two groups, $t = \sqrt{F}$	When using two groups, $F = t^2$
$df = (N_1 - 1) + (N_2 - 1)$	$df_{\text{Within}} = (N_1 - 1) + (N_2 - 1) + \ldots + (N_{\text{Last}} - 1)$

sider the cutoffs in a *t* table. These are exactly the square roots of the cutoffs in the column of an *F* table for an analysis of variance for two groups (that is, the part of the *F* table with numerator $df = 1$).

An apparent difference between the two procedures is how they are affected by sample size. In the analysis of variance, the sample size is part of the numerator. As we saw in Chapter 11, the numerator of the *F* ratio is the population variance estimate using the difference among the means multiplied by the number of scores in each group. That is, $S^2_{\text{Between}} = (S^2_M)(n)$. In the *t* test, the sample size is part of the denominator. As we saw in Chapter 10, the denominator of the *t* test uses the pooled population variance estimate divided by the number of scores in each group. That is, $S_{\text{Difference}} = \sqrt{S^2_{\text{Difference}}}$ and $S^2_{\text{Difference}} = S^2_{M1} + S^2_{M2}$; $S^2_{M1} = S^2_{\text{Pooled}}/N_1$; $S^2_{M2} = S^2_{\text{Pooled}}/N_2$. This apparent contradiction is resolved, however, because multiplying the numerator of a fraction by a number has exactly the same effect as dividing the denominator by that number. For example, take the fraction 3/8. Multiplying the numerator by 2 gives 6/8, or 3/4; dividing the denominator of 3/8 by 2 also gives 3/4.[3]

WORKED-OUT EXAMPLE SHOWING THE IDENTITY OF THE TWO PROCEDURES

An example with all the figuring makes the equivalence more vivid. Table 16–2 shows the *t* and *F* figuring for the *t* test worked-out example computation problem from Chapter 10. Notice the following: (a) The pooled population variance estimate in the *t* test ($S^2_{\text{Pooled}} = 4.17$) is the same as the within-group population variance estimate for the analysis of variance ($S^2_{\text{Within}} = 4.17$), both figured as part of the denominator. (b) The degrees of freedom for the *t* distribution ($df = 12$) is exactly the same as the denominator degrees of freedom for the *F* distribution ($df_{\text{Within}} = 12$). (c) The cutoff *t* for rejecting the null hypothesis (2.179) is the square root of the cutoff *F* for rejecting the null hypothesis ($\sqrt{4.75} = 2.179$). (d) The *t* for these data (2.73) is the square root of the *F* ($\sqrt{7.55} = 2.75$, the slight difference being due to rounding error). And (e) the conclusion is the same. With both methods, you reject the null hypothesis.

---

[3]Other apparent differences (such as the seeming difference that the *F*-ratio numerator is based on a variance estimate and the *t* score numerator is a simple difference between means) are also actually the same when you go into them in detail.

TABLE 16–2 *t* Test and Analysis of Variance Computations for the Same Study (Fictional Data)

Experimental Group				Control Group		
X_1	$X_1 - M_1$	$(X_1 - M_1)^2$		X_2	$X_2 - M_2$	$(X_2 - M_2)^2$
6	0	0		6	3	9
4	−2	4		1	−2	4
9	3	9		5	2	4
7	1	1		3	0	0
7	1	1		1	−2	4
3	−3	9		1	−2	4
6	0	0		4	1	1
Σ 42	0	24		21	0	26

$M_1 = 6$ $S_1^2 = 24/6 = 4$ $M_2 = 3$ $S_2^2 = 26/6 = 4.33$

$N_1 - 7$ $df_1 = N_1 - 1 = 6$ $N_2 = 7$ $df_2 = N_2 - 1 = 6$

t test	ANOVA

Numerator

Mean difference = $6.00 - 3.00 = 3.00$

$$df_{Between} = N_{Groups} - 1 = 2 - 1 = 1$$
$$GM = (6 + 3)/2 = 9/2 = 4.5$$
$$\Sigma(M - GM)^2 = (6 - 4.5)^2 + (3 - 4.5)^2$$
$$= 1.52 + -1.52$$
$$= 2.25 + 2.25 = 4.5$$
$$S_{Between}^2 \text{ or } MS_{Between} = \left(\frac{\Sigma(M - GM)^2}{df_{Between}}\right)(n) = \left(\frac{4.5}{1}\right)(7) = 31.5$$

Denominator

$$S_{Pooled}^2 = \left(\frac{df_1}{df_{Total}}\right)(S_1^2) + \left(\frac{df_2}{df_{Total}}\right)(S_2^2) = \left(\frac{6}{12}\right)(4) + \left(\frac{6}{12}\right)(4.33)$$

$$= (.5)(4) + (.5)(4.33) = 2.00 + 2.17 = 4.17$$

$$S_{Difference}^2 = S_{M1}^2 + S_{M2}^2 = (S_{Pooled}^2/N_1) + (S_{Pooled}^2/N_2)$$

$$= (4.17/7) + (4.17/7)$$

$$= .60 + .60 = 1.20$$

$$S_{Difference} = \sqrt{S_{Difference}^2} = \sqrt{1.20} = 1.10$$

$$S_{Within}^2 \text{ or } MS_{Within} = \frac{S_1^2 + S_2^2 + \ldots + S_{Last}^2}{N_{Groups}} = \frac{4 + 4.33}{2}$$

$$= \frac{8.33}{2} = 4.17$$

Degrees of Freedom

$df_{Total} = df_1 + df_2 = 6 + 6 = 12$ $df_{Within} = df_1 + df_2 \ldots df_{Last} = 6 + 6 = 12$

Cutoff

Needed *t* with $df = 12$ at 5% level, two-tailed = ±2.179   Needed *F* with $df = 1, 12$ at 5% level = 4.75

Score on Comparison Distribution

$t - (M_1 - M_2)/S_{Difference} = (6.00 - 3.00)/1.10 = 3.00/1.10 = 2.73$ $F = S_{Between}^2/S_{Within}^2 \text{ or } MS_{Between}/MS_{Within} = 31.5/4.17 = 7.55$

Conclusions

Reject the null hypothesis; the research hypothesis is supported.   Reject the null hypothesis; the research hypothesis is supported.

HOW ARE YOU DOING?

1. When can you use a t test to do the same thing as an analysis of variance?
2. How is the numerator of a t test like the numerator of an F ratio in an analysis of variance?
3. How is the denominator of a t test like the denominator of an F ratio in an analysis of variance?
4. How is S^2_{Pooled} like S^2_{Within}?
5. When figured for the same scores, what is the relation of the t to the F?
6. What is the relation of the t cutoff to the F cutoff for the same study (involving two groups)?

ANSWER

1. When there are only two groups.
2. Both are about the difference or variation between the groups.
3. Both are about variation within groups.
4. The two are identical.
5. The t is the square root of the F.
6. The t cutoff is the square root of the F cutoff.

THE t TEST AS A SPECIAL CASE OF THE SIGNIFICANCE TEST FOR THE CORRELATION COEFFICIENT

The relationship of the correlation coefficient to the t test is far from obvious. Even many psychology researchers have only recently become aware of the link. The correlation coefficient is about the degree of association between two variables; the t test is about the significance of the difference between two population means. What is the possible connection?

One connection is that both use the t distribution to determine significance. In Chapter 3, we had not yet considered the logic of hypothesis testing, so we could discuss the significance of a correlation coefficient only in very general terms. With what you now understand, we can explain it more precisely. The procedure follows the standard steps of hypothesis testing. Its particular features are (a) the null hypothesis is that the population has a correlation of 0; (b) the comparison distribution is a t distribution with degrees of freedom equal to the number of participants minus 2; and (c) the score on the comparison distribution is a t score figured from the correlation coefficient using the formula $t = (r)(\sqrt{N-2})/\sqrt{1-r^2}$. (For more details, including an example and considerations of effect size and power, see the Chapter 3 Appendix.)

However, knowing about this procedure does not give much insight into *why* the correlation coefficient can be turned into a t score for purposes of hypothesis testing or of the connection between this t based on the correlation coefficient and the t test for the difference between means of two groups. It is to these issues that we now turn.

GROUP DIFFERENCES AS ASSOCIATIONS AMONG VARIABLES

We usually think of the correlation coefficient as the association between a predictor variable and a criterion variable. Testing the significance of a correlation coefficient asks whether you can reject the null hypothesis that in the population there is no association between the two variables (that in the population, $r = 0$).

TABLE 16–3	Relation between Correlation and *t* Test for Independent Means	
	Correlation	*t* Test
Variable 1	Predictor Variable	Variable that Divides the Groups
Variable 2	Criterion Variable	Measured Variable
Relation tested	High scores on predictor go with high scores on criterion	Those in one group on the variable that divides the groups have higher scores on the measured variable

The *t* test for independent means examines the difference between two population means, based on the means of two samples. The sample scores are on a measured variable that is like a criterion variable (you want to know the effect on it). The distinction between the two groups in a *t* test is like the predictor variable. In our example from the previous section, the variable that divides the two groups was whether participants were in the experimental or control group. Thus, you can think of the *t* test as about whether there is any association between the variable that divides the groups and the measured variable. (See Table 16–3.)

NUMERICAL PREDICTOR VARIABLES VERSUS TWO-CATEGORY NOMINAL VARIABLE THAT DIVIDES THE GROUPS

"But wait!" you may say. "The predictor variable in a correlation coefficient is a numerical variable, such as number of hours sleep or high school GPA. The variable that divides the groups in a *t* test for independent means is a variable with exactly two values, the two categories, such as experimental group versus control group." Yes, you are quite correct. This is precisely the difference between the situations in which you use a correlation coefficient and those in which you ordinarily use a *t* test for independent means.

How can this gap be bridged? Suppose that you arbitrarily give a number to each level of the two-category nominal variable that divides the groups. For example, you could make the experimental group a 1 and the control group a 2. (Using any other two numbers will, in the end, give exactly the same result when everything is changed to *Z* scores to figure the correlation coefficient. However, which group gets the higher number does determine the plus or minus sign of the final result.) Once you change the two-category nominal variable that divides the groups to a numerical variable, you can then figure the correlation between this two-valued numeric variable and the measured variable.

EXAMPLE OF THE NUMERIC EQUIVALENCE OF THE *T* TEST AND THE CORRELATION COEFFICIENT SIGNIFICANCE TEST

Table 16–4 shows the figuring for the correlation coefficient and its significance using the scores from the same *t* test example we used earlier. (To keep the table reasonably simple, we left out the figuring of the standard deviation of each variable that is used to change the raw scores to *Z* scores.) Notice that in this correlation setup, each individual has two scores: (a) a 1 or a 2, depending on whether the person is in the experimental group or the control group, and (b) a score on the measured variable.

TABLE 16–4   **Figuring of the Correlation Coefficient and a Hypothesis Test of the Correlation Coefficient Using the Data From Table 16–2 (and Table 10–8) and Changing the Variable that Divides the Groups Into a Numerical Variable Having Values of 1 (for the Experimental Group) or 2 (for the Control Group)**

Variable that Divides the Groups (Experimental Versus Control)		Measured Variable		Cross-Product
Raw	Z_X	Raw	Z_Y	$Z_X Z_Y$
1	−1	6	.62	− .62
1	−1	4	− .21	.21
1	−1	9	1.87	−1.87
1	−1	7	1.04	−1.04
1	−1	7	1.04	−1.04
1	−1	3	− .62	.62
1	−1	6	.62	− .62
2	1	6	.62	.62
2	1	1	−1.45	−1.45
2	1	5	.21	.21
2	1	3	− .62	− .62
2	1	1	−1.45	−1.45
2	1	1	−1.45	−1.45
2	1	4	− .21	− .21
Σ 21		63		−8.71
$M = 1.5$		4.5		$r = − .62$
$(SD = .5)$		$(SD = 2.41)$		

$df = N - 2 = 14 - 2 = 12$.

t needed with $df = 12$ at 5% level, two-tailed $= \pm 2.179$.

$t = r\sqrt{N-2}/\sqrt{1-r^2} = -.62\sqrt{14-2}/\sqrt{1-(-.62)^2} = -.62\sqrt{12}/\sqrt{1-.38} = -.62(3.46)/\sqrt{.62} = -2.15/.79 = -2.72$

Conclusion: Reject the null hypothesis; the research hypothesis is supported.

The resulting correlation is −.62. Using the formula for changing a correlation to a t score gives a t of −2.72. This t is the same, within rounding error, that we figured earlier (2.73) using the ordinary t-test procedures (see Chapter 10, Table 10–8 and Table 16–2 in this chapter). The difference in sign has to do with which group gets the 1 and which group gets the 2—a decision that is arbitrary. The degrees of freedom, and thus the needed t for significance and the conclusion, are also the same as for the t test for independent means.

In sum, the significance test of the correlation coefficient gives the same result as the ordinary t test. We say that the t test is a special case of the correlation coefficient, however, because you can use the t test only in the situation in which the predictor variable has exactly two values.

GRAPHIC INTERPRETATION OF THE RELATIONSHIP OF THE T TEST TO THE CORRELATION COEFFICIENT

Figure 16–2 shows the scatter diagram, including the regression line, for the scores in the example we have been following. The predictor variable (the variable that divides the groups) has just two values, so the dots all line up above these two values.

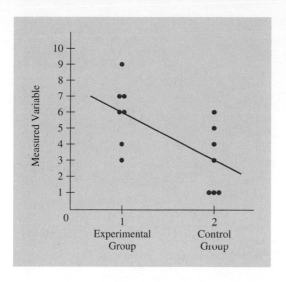

FIGURE 16-2 *Scatter diagram and regression line for the example, originally analyzed with a* t *test for independent means, with a value of 1 for the experimental group and 2 for the control group.*

Note that the regression line goes through the middle of each line of dots. In fact, when making a scatter diagram of the scores for a *t* test, the regression line always goes exactly through the mean of each set of dots. This is because the regression line shows the best predicted score at each level of the predictor variable, and for any group of scores, the best predicted score is always the mean.

Figure 16–3 shows some additional examples. In Figure 16–3a, the two means are nearly the same. Here, the slope of the regression line is about 0; the correlation is low and not significant. The correlation is .10; thus, with 20 participants, $t = r\sqrt{N-2}/\sqrt{1-r^2} = .1\sqrt{20-2}/\sqrt{1-.1^2} = .43$. Thinking in terms of a *t* test for independent means, because there is little difference between the means of the two groups, the *t* test will not be significant. The mean difference is $7.39 - 7.60 = .21$. The standard deviation of the distribution of differences between means is .48; thus, $t = (M_1 - M_2)/S_{\text{Difference}} = (7.39 - 7.60)/.48 - -.44$. This is the same result as you get using the correlation approach (within rounding error, and ignoring sign).

In Figure 16–3b the means of the two groups are somewhat different, but the dots in each group are even more widely spread out. Once again, the correlation coefficient is low and not significant. In the *t* test for independent means, the spread of the dots makes a large estimated population variance for each group, creating a large pooled variance estimate and a large standard deviation of the distribution of differences between means. In a *t* test you divide the mean difference by the standard deviation of the distribution of differences between means; thus, the larger this standard deviation, the smaller the *t* score. In the example the mean difference is .52 and the standard deviation of the distribution of differences between means is 1.21. This gives a *t* of .43, which is clearly not significant.

Finally, in Figure 16–3c there is a large difference between the means and less variation among the dots around each mean. Thus, the regression line is a very helpful predictor. Similarly, the large mean difference and small variance within each group make for a large *t* using a *t* test for independent means.

The principle that these figures illustrate is that the *t* test for independent means and the significance test for the correlation coefficient (which you know from Chapter 4 is the same as the square root of the proportionate reduction in error in regression) give the same results because both are largest when the difference between the two means is large and the variation among the scores in each group is small.

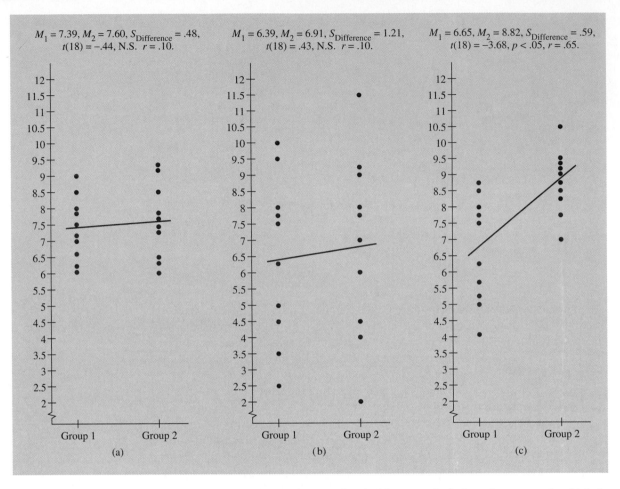

FIGURE 16-3   *Three possible scatter diagrams of scores analyzed with a* t *test for independent means, in which the means for the two groups are (a) nearly the same, (b) different but the scores are widely spread (large pooled variance and thus large standard deviation of the distribution of differences between means), and (c) very different, with the scores not widely spread.*

HOW ARE YOU DOING?

1. How can you understand a difference between groups on a measured variable in terms of an association between a predictor and a criterion variable?
2. How can you make a two-level nominal variable that divides the groups into a numeric variable that you can use in correlation or regression?
3. (a) What is the effect of the scores being spread out around their mean, and (b) why, for the *t* test for independent means?
4. (a) What is the effect of the scores being spread out around their mean, and (b) why, for the correlation coefficient?
5. When you make a scatter diagram for the scores in a *t* test for independent means, (a) what does it look like, and (b) where does the regression line go?

ANSWERS

1. A difference between groups on a measured variable is the same as an association between the variable that divides the groups (which is like the predictor variable in correlation or regression) and the measured variable (which is like the criterion variable in correlation or regression).

2. Make it in to a two-valued numeric variable by giving a score of, say, 1 on this variable to everyone in one group and a score of, say, 2 on this variable to everyone in the other group.
3. (a) It reduces the t.
   (b) The variance of each group will be greater, making the pooled estimate of the population variance greater, making the variance of the distribution of differences between means greater, making the standard deviation of the distribution of differences between means greater. You figure the t by dividing by the standard deviation of the differences between means. Thus, if it is bigger, the t is smaller.
4. (a) It reduces the r.
   (b) The scores are more spread out around the regression line, thus the amount of error is greater; if the error is greater, the squared error is greater, and the proportionate reduction in error is less. r is the square root of the proportionate reduction in error; so if it is less, r is less.
5. (a) The dots are all lined up above the points for the two levels of the variable that divides the groups.
   (b) It goes through the mean of each group.

THE ANALYSIS OF VARIANCE AS A SPECIAL CASE OF THE SIGNIFICANCE TEST OF MULTIPLE REGRESSION

The relationship between the analysis of variance and multiple regression parallels the relationship we just considered between the t test for independent means and the correlation coefficient. And in both, the solution is the same. The analysis of variance tests whether there is a difference on the measured variable between means of groups. The correlation or regression approach sees this as a relationship between a criterion variable (the measured variable) and a predictor variable (the different levels of the variable that divides the groups). For example, in the Hazan and Shaver (1987) study of attachment style and jealousy discussed in Chapter 11, the analysis of variance showed a significant difference in jealousy (the measured variable) among the three attachment styles (the variable that divides the groups). A correlation or regression approach, by contrast, would describe this result as a significant association between jealousy (the criterion variable) and attachment style (the predictor variable).

ANALYSIS OF VARIANCE FOR TWO GROUPS AS A SPECIAL CASE OF THE SIGNIFICANCE OF A BIVARIATE CORRELATION

The link between the analysis of variance and multiple regression/correlation is easiest to see if we begin with a two-group situation and (a) consider the correlation coefficient in terms of its being the square root of the proportionate reduction in error with raw scores (see Chapter 4), and (b) consider the analysis of variance using the structural model approach (Chapter 12). Table 16–5 shows the scores for our experimental versus control group example. However, this time we show the predicted raw scores and the errors and squared errors, as well as the figuring for the proportionate reduction in error. Table 16–6 shows the analysis of variance figuring, using the structural model approach, for the same scores.

There are several clear links. First, the sum of squared error figured in the correlation when using the bivariate prediction rule ($SS_{Error} = 50$) is the same as the within-group sum of squared deviations (SS_{Within}) for the analysis of variance. Why

TABLE 16–5 Figuring of the Proportionate Reduction in Error With Raw Scores Using the Data From Table 16–2 (and 10–8)

Predictor Variable (Experimental Versus Control)	Criterion Variable			
Raw	Score	Predicted	Difference	Squared Difference
1	6	6	0	0
1	4	6	−2	4
1	9	6	3	9
1	7	6	1	1
1	7	6	1	1
1	3	6	−3	9
1	6	6	0	0
2	6	3	3	9
2	1	3	−2	4
2	5	3	2	4
2	3	3	0	0
2	1	3	−2	4
2	1	3	−2	4
2	4	3	1	1

$$\Sigma = SS_{\text{Error}} = 50$$

Sum of squared error using the overall mean as a prediction rule (computation not shown): $SS_{\text{Total}} = 81.5$

$$\text{Proportionate reduction in squared error} = \frac{SS_{\text{Total}} - SS_{\text{Error}}}{SS_{\text{Total}}} = \frac{81.5 - 50}{81.5} = \frac{31.5}{81.5} = .39$$

$r^2 = .39; r = \sqrt{r^2} = \sqrt{.39} = \pm.62.$

are they the same? In regression, the error is a score's difference from the predicted value, and the predicted value in this situation of only two values for the predictor variable is the mean of the scores at each value (that is, the mean of each group's scores). In other words, in the regression, the sum of squared error comes from squaring and summing the difference of each score from its group's mean. In the analysis of variance, you figure the sum of squared error within groups as precisely the same thing—the sum of the squared deviations of each score from its group's mean.

Second, the sum of squared error total (SS_{Total}) is the same in regression and analysis of variance (in this example they are both 81.5). They are the same because in regression, SS_{Total} is the sum of the squared deviations of each criterion variable score from the overall mean of all the criterion variable scores and in the analysis of variance, SS_{Total} is the sum of the squared deviations of each measured variable score from the grand mean, which is the overall mean of all the measured variable scores.

Third, the reduction in squared error in regression—the sum of squared error using the mean to predict (81.5) minus the sum of squared error using the bivariate prediction rule (50)—comes out to 31.5. This is the same as the analysis of variance sum of squared error between groups (that is, $SS_{\text{Between}} = 31.5$). The reduction in error in regression is what the prediction rule adds over knowing just the mean. In this example, the prediction rule estimates the mean of each group, so the reduction in squared error for each score is the squared difference between the mean of that

TABLE 16–6   **Figuring of the Proportionate Reduction in Error with the One-Way Analysis of Variance Structural Model Approach Using the Data From Table 16–2 (and 10–8)**

One-way analysis of variance structural model calculation
$GM = 4.5$

	Experimental Group							Control Group						
X_1	$X - GM$		$X - M$		$M - GM$		X	$X - GM$		$X - M$		$M - GM$	
	Dev	Dev²	Dev	Dev²	Dev	Dev²		Dev	Dev²	Dev	Dev²	Dev	Dev²
6	1.5	2.25	0	0	1.5	2.25	6	1.5	2.25	3	9	−1.5	2.25
4	−.5	.25	−2	4	1.5	2.25	1	−3.5	12.25	−2	4	−1.5	2.25
9	4.5	20.25	3	9	1.5	2.25	5	.5	.25	2	4	−1.5	2.25
7	2.5	6.25	1	1	1.5	2.25	3	−1.5	2.25	0	0	−1.5	2.25
7	2.5	6.25	1	1	1.5	2.25	1	−3.5	12.25	−2	4	−1.5	2.25
3	−1.5	2.25	−3	9	1.5	2.25	1	−3.5	12.25	−2	4	−1.5	2.25
6	1.5	2.25	0	0	1.5	2.25	4	−.5	.25	1	1	−1.5	2.25
Σ:		39.75		24		15.75			41.75		26		15.75

Note: Dev = Deviation; *Dev²* = Squared deviation

Sums of squared deviations:
$\Sigma(X - GM)^2$ or $SS_{Total} = 39.75 + 41.75 = 81.5$
$\Sigma(X - M)^2$ or $SS_{Within} = 24 + 26 = 50$
$\Sigma(M - GM)^2$ or $SS_{Between} = 15.75 + 15.75 = 31.5$
Check ($SS_{Total} = SS_{Within} + SS_{Between}$): $81.5 = 50 + 31.5$

Degrees of freedom:
$df_{Total} = N - 1 = 14 - 1 = 13$
$df_{Within} = df_1 + df_2 + \ldots + df_{Last} = 6 + 6 = 12$
$df_{Between} = N_{Groups} - 1 = 2 - 1 = 1$
Check ($df_{Total} = df_{Within} + df_{Between}$): $13 = 12 + 1$

Population variance estimates:
S^2_{Total} or $MS_{Total} = SS_{Total}/df_{Total} = 81.5/13 = 6.27$
S^2_{Within} or $MS_{Within} = SS_{Within}/df_{Within} = 50/12 = 4.17$
$S^2_{Between}$ or $MS_{Between} = SS_{Between}/df_{Between} = 31.5/1 = 31.5$
F ratio: $F = S^2_{Between}/S^2_{Within}$ or $MS_{Between}/MS_{Within} = 31.5/4.17 = 7.55$
$R^2 = eta^2 = SS_{Between}/SS_{Total} = 31.5/81.5 = .39$

score's group and the overall mean. In analysis of variance, you figure $SS_{Between}$ by adding up, for each participant, the squared differences between the participant's group's mean and the grand mean.

Finally, the proportionate reduction in error in the regression ($r^2 = .39$) comes out to exactly the same as the proportionate reduction in error used as an effect size in analysis of variance (R^2 or $eta^2 = .39$). Both tell us the proportion of the total variation in the criterion (or measured) variable that is accounted for by its association with the predictor variable (the variable that divides the groups). That these numbers come out the same should be no surprise by now; we have already seen that the numerator and the proportionate reduction in error are the same for both.

Thus, the links between regression and the analysis of variance are quite deep. In fact, some researchers figure the significance of a correlation coefficient by laying it out as a regression analysis and plugging the various sums of squared error into an analysis of variance table and figuring F. The result is identical to any other way of figuring the significance of the correlation coefficient. If you figure the t for the correlation, it comes out to the square root of the F you would get using this procedure.

ANALYSIS OF VARIANCE FOR MORE THAN TWO GROUPS AS A SPECIAL CASE OF MULTIPLE CORRELATION

When considering the t test for independent means or the analysis of variance for two groups, we could carry out a correlation or regression analysis by changing the two categories of the nominal variable that divides the groups into any two different numbers (in the example, we used 1 for the experimental group and 2 for the control group). The problem is more difficult with an analysis of variance with more than two groups because the variable that divides the groups has more than two categories.

In the two-category situation, the particular two numbers you use do not matter (except for the sign). One way to understand this is to consider what happens when you figure a correlation in the way we described in Chapter 3, as the average of the cross-product of the Z scores. It turns out that in the two-group situation, you get the same two Z scores no matter what two numbers you pick. For example, with equal numbers in the two groups, the two Z scores always come out to $+1$ and -1. Thus, if you make the predictor variable scores for one group 1s and for the other group, 2s, you get Zs of -1 and $+1$. If you make one group 17s and the other group 698.88s, when you change these to Z scores, you still get -1s and $+1$s! (You can try this yourself with a few examples.)

However, when there are three or more groups, making up a predictor variable with arbitrary numbers for the different groups will not work. Whatever three numbers you pick imply some particular relation among the groups, and not all relations will be the same. For example, with three groups, making a predictor variable with 1s, 2s, and 3s gives a different result depending on which groups gets put in the middle. It also gives a different result than using 1s, 2s, and 4s.

Recall the example from Chapter 11 comparing ratings of a defendant's degree of guilt for participants who believed the defendant had either a criminal record or a clean record or in which nothing was said about the defendant's record. Suppose that we arbitrarily give a 1 to the first group, a 2 to the second, and a 3 to the third. This would imply that we consider these three levels to be equally spaced values on a numerical variable of knowledge about the criminal record. Changing these 1, 2, and 3 values to Z scores would not help, as they would still be evenly spread in this order. For this particular example, we might want to think of the three groups as ordered from criminal record to clean record, with the no information group in between. However, even then it would not be clear that the groups are evenly spaced on this dimension.

More generally, when you have several groups, you may have no basis in advance for putting the groups in a particular order, let alone for deciding how they should be spaced. For example, in a study comparing attitudes of four different Central American nationalities, nationality is the nominal variable that divides the groups. But you can't make these four nationalities into any meaningful four values of a single numerical variable.

There is a clever solution to this problem. When there are more than two groups, instead of trying to make the nominal variable that divides the groups into a single numerical variable, you can make it into several numerical predictor variables with two levels each.

Here is how this is done: Suppose that the variable that divides the groups has four categories—for example, four Central American nationalities: Costa Rican, Guatemalan, Nicaraguan, and Salvadoran. You can make one predictor variable for whether the participant is Costa Rican—1 if Costa Rican, 0 if not. You can then make a second predictor variable for whether the participant is Guatemalan, 1 or 0; and a third for whether the participant is Nicaraguan, 1 or 0. You could make a fourth for whether the participant is Salvadoran. However, if a participant has 0s on the first three variables, the participant has to be Salvadoran (because there are only the four possibilities).

In this example, you know any participant's nationality by the scores on the combination of the three two-value numerical variables. For example, a Costa Rican participant would have a 1 for Costa Rican and 0s for Guatemalan and Nicaraguan. Each Guatemalan participant would have a 1 for Guatemalan but 0s for Costa Rican and Nicaraguan. Each Nicaraguan participant would have 0s for Costa Rican and Guatemalan. Each Salvadoran participant would have 0s on all three variables. (Incidentally, you can use any two numbers for each two-valued nominal variable; we just used 1 and 0 for convenience.) Table 16–7 shows this coding for 10 participants.

This entire procedure is called **nominal coding.** The result in this example is that the variable that divides the groups, instead of being a nominal variable with four categories, is now three numerical variables but with only two values each. Creating several two-valued numerical variables in this way avoids the problem of creating an arbitrary ranking and distancing of the four levels.

nominal coding

Table 16–8 shows another example, this time for the criminal record study from Chapters 11 and 12. The variable that divides the groups, instead of being a nominal variable with three categories, is now two numerical variables (each with values of 1 or 0). More generally, you can code the nominal variable that divides the groups in an analysis of variance into several two-value numerical variables, exactly one less such two-valued numerical variables than there groups. (Not coincidentally, this comes out the same as the degrees of freedom for the between-group population variance estimate.)

TABLE 16–7 **Example of Nominal Coding for Participants of Four Central American Nationalities**

Participant	Nationality	Variable 1 Costa Rican or Not	Variable 2 Guatemalan or Not	Variable 3 Nicaraguan or Not
1	Guatemalan	0	1	0
2	Nicaraguan	0	0	1
3	Salvadoran	0	0	0
4	Nicaraguan	0	0	1
5	Costa Rican	1	0	0
6	Costa Rican	1	0	0
7	Salvadoran	0	0	0
8	Nicaraguan	0	0	1
9	Costa Rican	1	0	0
10	Guatemalan	0	1	0

TABLE 16–8   Example of Nominal Coding for the Criminal Record Example

		Predictor Variable		Criterion Variable
Participant	Experimental Condition	Variable 1: Criminal Record or Not	Variable 2: Clean Record or Not	Participant's Rating of Defendant's Guilt
1	Criminal record	1	0	10
2	Criminal record	1	0	7
3	Criminal record	1	0	5
4	Criminal record	1	0	10
5	Criminal record	1	0	8
6	Clean record	0	1	5
7	Clean record	0	1	1
8	Clean record	0	1	3
9	Clean record	0	1	7
10	Clean record	0	1	4
11	No information	0	0	4
12	No information	0	0	6
13	No information	0	0	9
14	No information	0	0	3
15	No information	0	0	3

Once you have done the nominal coding (changed the variable that divides the groups into two-value numerical variables), you then want to know the relation of this set of variables to the measured variable. You do this with multiple regression, using the set of two-value numerical variables as predictors and the measured variable as the criterion variable. Consider again the criminal record example. Having done the nominal coding, you can now figure the multiple regression of the two numerical predictor variables taken together with what you now think of as the criterion variable, rating of guilt. The result (in terms of significance level and R^2) comes out exactly the same as the analysis of variance.

The nominal coding procedure is extremely flexible and can be extended to the most complex factorial analysis of variance situations. In practice, researchers rarely actually do nominal coding—usually, a computer does it for you. We wanted you to see the principle so that you can understand how it is possible to make an analysis of variance problem into a multiple regression problem. There are, however, a number of analysis of variance research situations in which there are advantages to using the multiple regression approach (such as in a factorial analysis with unequal cell sizes). In fact, many analysis of variance computer programs do the actual computations not using the analysis of variance formulas, but by doing nominal coding and multiple regression.

CHOICE OF STATISTICAL TESTS

We have seen that the four major statistical procedures you have learned in this book can be considered special cases of multiple regression. You may now wonder why you don't learn just one technique, multiple regression, and do everything using it. You could. And you would get entirely correct results.

Box 16–2 Two Women Make a Point About Gender and Statistics

One of the most useful advanced statistics books written so far is *Using Multivariate Statistics* by Barbara Tabachnick and Linda Fidell (2001), two experimental psychologists at California State University at Northridge. These two met at a faculty luncheon soon after Tabachnick was hired. Fidell recalls that she had just finished a course on French and one on matrix algebra, for the pleasure of learning them ("I was very serious at the time"). She was wondering what to tackle next when Tabachnick suggested that Fidell join her in taking a belly dancing course. Fidell thought, "Something frivolous for a change." Little did she know.

Thus, their collaboration began. After the lessons, they had long discussions about statistics. In particular, the two found that they shared a fascination—and consternation—with the latest statistics made possible through all the new statistical packages for computers. The problem was making sense of the results.

Fidell described it this way: "I had this enormous data set to analyze, and out came lots of pretty numbers in nice neat little columns, but I was not sure what all of it meant, or even whether my data had violated any critical assumptions. I knew there were some, but I didn't know anything about them. That was in 1975. I had been trained at the University of Michigan; I knew statistics up through the analysis of variance. But none of us were taught the multivariate analysis of variance at that time. Then along came these statistical packages to do it. But how to comprehend them?" (You will be introduced to the multivariate analysis of variance in Chapter 17.)

Both Fidell and Tabachnick had gone out and learned on their own, taking the necessary courses, reading, asking others who knew the programs better, trying out what would happen if they did this with the data, what would happen if they did that. Now the two women asked each other, Why must this be so hard? And were others reinventing this same wheel at the very same time? They decided to put their wheel into a book.

"And so began years of conflict-free collaboration," reports Fidell. (That is something to compare to the feuds recounted in other boxes in this book.) The authors had no trouble finding a publisher, and the book, now in its fourth edition (Tabachnick & Fidell, 2001), has sold "nicely." (This despite the fact that their preferred titles—*Fatima and Scheherazade's Multivariate Statistics Book: A Thousand and One Variables; The Fuzzy Pink Statistics Book; Weight Loss Through Multivariate Statistics*—were overruled by the publisher. However, if you looked closely at the first edition's cover, you saw a belly dancer buried in the design.)

Fidell emphasizes that both she and Tabachnick consider themselves data analysts and teachers, not statistics developers or theorists—they have not invented methods, merely popularized them by making them more accessible. But they can name dozens of women who have risen to the fore as theoretical statisticians. In Fidell's opinion, statistics is a field in which women seem particularly to excel and feel comfortable. In teaching new students, the math-shy ones in particular, she finds that once she can "get them to relax," they often find that they thoroughly enjoy statistics. She tells them, "I intend to win you over. And if you will give me half a chance, I will do it."

Whatever the reason, statistics is a branch of mathematics that, according to Fidell, women often come to find "perfectly logical, perfectly reasonable—and then, with time, something they can truly enjoy." That should be good news to many of you.

Reference: Personal interview with Linda Fidell.

Why, then, should anyone use, say, a *t* test instead of an analysis of variance? The reason is that it is a procedure that is traditional and widely understood. Most researchers today expect to see a *t* test when two groups are compared. It seems strange, and somehow grandiose, to see an analysis of variance when a *t* test would do—though, in fact, the sense of grandiosity is simply a holdover from the days when all the figuring was done by hand and an analysis of variance was harder to do than a *t* test.

To use a correlation coefficient (and its associated significance test) in the two-group situation instead of an ordinary t test would confuse people who were not very statistically sophisticated (such as you before reading this chapter). Similarly, analyzing an experiment with several groups using multiple regression instead of analysis of variance would confuse those same unsophisticated readers.[4]

There is one advantage in using correlation and regression over the t test or an analysis of variance: The correlational approach automatically gives you direct information on the relationship between the variable that divides the groups and the measured variable as well as permitting a significance test. The t test and the analysis of variance give only statistical significance. (You can figure an effect size for either of these, but with a correlation coefficient or a multiple regression, you get the effect size automatically.)

HOW ARE YOU DOING?

1. Under what conditions can you use the analysis of variance to find the significance of a bivariate regression or correlation?
2. When there are only two groups, explain the similarity between analysis of variance structural model approach and regression in terms of (a) SS_{Total}, (b) SS_{Within} and SS_{Error}, (c) $SS_{Between}$ and $SS_{Total} - SS_{Error}$, and (d) proportionate reduction in error.
3. Based on what you have learned in previous sections, give an argument for why, when there are only two groups, the analysis of variance and correlation should give the same significance.
4. When changing a variable that divides groups in a two-group situation into a two-value numeric variable and then doing a correlation, why does it not matter which two numbers you use?
5. (a) What is nominal coding? (b) How is it done? (c) Why is it done? (d) Why can't you just use a single numeric variable with more than two values? (e) In a particular study, participants 1 and 2 are in Group A, participants 3 and 4 are in Group B, and participants 5 and 6 in Group C. Make a table showing nominal coding for these six participants.
6. (a) Why do researchers use t tests and analyses of variance when they could use correlation or regression instead? (b) What is an advantage of using regression and correlation over using analysis of variance and the t test.

ANSWERS

1. When the predictor variable has only two values.
2. (a) In analysis of variance, SS_{Total} is the sum of squared deviations of each measured variable score from the grand mean, which is the mean of all measured variable scores; in regression, SS_{Total} is the sum of squared deviations of each criterion variable score from the mean of all criterion variable scores. The measured variable in analysis of variance is the same as the criterion variable in regression. Thus, for the same study, SS_{Total} is the same in both.
   (b) SS_{Within} in analysis of variance is the sum of squared deviations of each measured variable score from the mean of the measured variable scores of its group. SS_{Error} in regression is the sum of squared deviations of each criterion variable score from the predicted criterion variable score. The mean of the measured variable scores of a particular group in analysis of variance is exactly what would be the predicted score for the criterion variable in

---

[4]Another reason for the use of different procedures is that the t test and analysis of variance have traditionally been used to analyze results of true experiments with random assignment to levels of the variables that divide the groups, while correlation and regression have been used mainly to analyze results of studies in which the predictor variable was measured in people as it exists, what is called a correlational research design. Thus, using a correlation or regression approach to analyze a true experiment, while correct, might imply to the not-very-careful reader that the study was not a true experiment.

regression if there are only two groups. Thus, for the same study, SS_{Within} and SS_{Error} is the same.

(c) In analysis of variance, $SS_{Total} = SS_{Between} + SS_{Within}$. Thus, $SS_{Between}$ has to equal $SS_{Total} - SS_{Within}$. We have already seen that SS_{Total} is the same in analysis of variance and regression, and that SS_{Within} in analysis of variance is the same as SS_{Error} in regression. Thus, for the same study, $SS_{Between}$ and $SS_{Total} - SS_{Error}$ are the same.

(d) Proportionate reduction in error in analysis of variance is $SS_{Between}/SS_{Total}$. The proportionate reduction in error in regression is $SS_{Total} - SS_{Error}/SS_{Total}$. We have already seen that the terms that make up these numerators and denominators are the same in analysis of variance and regression. Thus, in the same study, the proportionate reduction in error is the same.

3. In this situation, both the analysis of variance and the significance test of the correlation give the same results as the t test for independent means, thus they must give the same result as each other.

4. Because when figuring a correlation you first change the predictor variable scores to Z scores, and for any particular two-group situation, using any two numbers always gives the same two Z scores.

5. (a) Changing a nominal variable that divides groups into several two-value numeric variables.

(b) Participants in the first group are given a 1 on the first two-value numeric variable and a 0 on all others; participants in the second group are given a 1 on the second two-value numeric variable and a 0 on the rest; this continues up to participants in the last group, who are given a 0 on all the two-value numeric variables.

(c) It allows you to figure an analysis of variance using the two-value numeric variables as predictors in a multiple regression.

(d) The order of those values and the distance between them would influence the results.

(c) Participant	Score on Numeric Variable 1	Score on Numeric Variable 2
1	1	0
2	1	0
3	0	1
4	0	1
5	0	0
6	0	0

6. (a) Researchers are familiar with t tests and analysis of variance for testing differences between groups, they are traditional for this purpose, and some researchers are unfamiliar with and would be confused by the use of correlation and regression for this purpose.

(b) Correlation and regression automatically give you estimates of effect size and not just significance.

CONTROVERSY: WHAT IS CAUSALITY?

The general linear model itself is not very controversial; it is simply a mathematical statement of a relationship among variables. In fact, its role as the foundation of the major statistical techniques has not yet been widely realized among practicing researchers. There is, however, an area of controversy that is appropriate to mention here. It has to do with the role of statistics in science generally, but in practice it is most often raised in the context of the major general linear model-based procedures. This is the issue of causality. We have already addressed this issue at one level in

Chapter 3, where we considered the problem of inferring a direction of causality from a study that does not use random assignment to groups. But there is a still deeper level to the issue: What does causality mean?

Baumrind (1983) has outlined two main understandings of causality that are used in science. One, which she calls the *regularity theory of causality*, has its roots in philosophers like David Hume and John Stuart Mill (as well as early scientists, including Galileo). This view holds that we recognize X as a cause of Y if (a) X and Y are regularly associated, (b) X precedes Y, and (c) there are no other causes that precede X that might cause both X and Y. In psychology, we address the (a) part by finding a significant correlation between X and Y. We address the (b) part, if possible, by our knowledge of the situation (for example, in a correlation of whether one is the firstborn in one's family with anxiety later in life, you can rule out the possibility that anxiety later in life caused the person to be firstborn) or designing the study into an experiment (by manipulating X prior to measuring Y). The (c) part has to do with the issue of a correlation between X and Y being due to some third variable causing both. Ideally, we address this by random assignment to groups. But if that is not possible, various statistical methods of equating groups on proposed third factors are used as a makeshift strategy (we explore some of these in Chapter 17).

As psychologists, we are only sometimes in a position to do the kind of rigorous experimental research that provides a strong basis for drawing conclusions about cause and effect. Thus, much of the criticism and controversy involving research of practical importance, where it is usually least easy to apply rigorous methods, often hinges on such issues. For example, if marriage correlates with happiness, does marriage make people happier, or do happy people get and stay married?

There is another view of causality, a still more stringent view that sees the regularity theory conditions as a prerequisite to calling something a cause, but that these conditions are not sufficient alone. This other view, which Baumrind calls the *generative theory of causality*, has its roots in Aristotle, Thomas Aquinas, and Immanuel Kant. The focus of this view is on just *how X* affects *Y*. This is the way most nonscientists (and nonphilosophers) understand causality. The very idea of causality may have its roots as a metaphor of experiences such as willing your own arm to move (Event X) and it moves (Event Y). Scientists also take this view of causality very much to heart, even if it offers much more difficult challenges. It is addressed primarily by theory and by careful analysis of mediating processes. But even those who emphasize this view would recognize that demonstrating a reliable connection between X and Y (by finding statistical significance, for example) plays an important role at least in identifying linkages that require scrutiny for determining the real causal connection.

Finally, there are also those who hold—with some good arguments—that demonstrating causality should not be a goal of scientific psychology at all. But we have already had enough controversy for one chapter.

SUMMARY

1. The general linear model states that the value of a variable for any individual is the sum of a constant, plus the partial, weighted influence of each of several other variables, plus error. Bivariate and multiple correlation and regression (and associated significance tests), the *t* test, and the analysis of variance are all special cases of the general linear model.

2. Multiple regression is almost identical to the general linear model, and bivariate correlation and regression are the special cases of multiple regression/correlation in which there is only one predictor variable.

3. The t test for independent means can be mathematically derived from the analysis of variance. It is a special case of the analysis of variance in which there are only two groups. The t score for the same data is the square root of the F ratio. The numerators of both t and F are based on the differences between group means; the denominators of both are based on the variance within the groups; the denominator of t involves dividing by the number of participants, and the numerator of F involves multiplying by the number of participants; and the t degrees of freedom are the same as the F denominator degrees of freedom.

4. The t test for independent means is also a special case of the significance test for the correlation coefficient. A correlation is about the association of a predictor variable with a criterion variable. In the same way, by showing a difference between group means, the t test is about an association of the variable that divides the groups with the measured variable. If you give a score of 1 to each participant in one of the two groups and a 2 to each participant in the other group (or any two different numbers), then figure a correlation of these scores with the measured variable, the significance of that correlation will be the same as the t test. Drawing a scatter diagram of these data makes a column of scores for each group, with the regression line passing through the mean of each group. The more the means are different, the greater the proportionate reduction in error over using the grand mean and the greater the t score based on a comparison of the two groups' means.

5. The analysis of variance and correlation/regression also have many similarities. SS_{Total} in regression and in the analysis of variance are both about the deviations of each score from the mean of all the criterion or measured variable scores. The group means in an analysis of variance are the predicted scores for each individual in regression; thus, SS_{Error} and SS_{Within} are the same. The reduction in squared error ($SS_{Total} - SS_{Error}$) in regression is the same as the sum of squared deviations of scores' group's means from the grand mean ($SS_{Between}$) in the analysis of variance. Finally, regression's proportionate reduction in error (r^2 or R^2) is the same as the proportion of variance accounted for (R^2 or eta^2) effect size in analysis of variance.

6. An analysis of variance can be set up as a multiple regression by making the categories for the different groups into two-value numerical variables. The analysis of variance is a special case of multiple regression in which the predictor variables are set up in this way.

7. The t test, analysis of variance, and correlation can all be done as multiple regression. However, conventional practice leads to these procedures being used in different research contexts, as if they were actually different.

8. The regularity view identifies X as a cause of Y if X and Y are associated, X precedes Y, and no other third factors precede X that could cause them both. The generative view argues that in addition there must be a clear understanding of the mechanism by which X affects Y.

KEY TERMS

general linear model   nominal coding (p. 587)
  (p. 570)

PRACTICE PROBLEMS

These problems involve figuring. Most real-life statistics problems are done on a computer. However, even if you have a computer and statistics software, do these by hand (with the help of a calculator) to ingrain the method in your mind. Also, in all problems involving figuring, be sure to show your work.

For practice in using a computer to solve statistics problems, refer to the computer section of each chapter of the *Student's Study Guide and Computer Workbook* that accompanies this text.

All data are fictional.

Answers to Set I problems are given at the back of the book.

SET I

1. (a) Look up and write down the t cutoff at the .05 level (two-tailed) for 5, 10, 15, and 20 degrees of freedom. (b) Square each t cutoff and write it down next to the t. (c) Look up and write down, next to the squared ts, the cutoffs for F distributions with 1 degree of freedom in the numerator and 5, 10, 15, and 20 degrees of freedom as the denominators. (The results should be identical, within rounding error.)

2. Below are two data sets. For the first data set, in addition to the means and estimated population variances, we have shown the t test information. You should figure the second yourself. Also, for each, figure a one-way analysis of variance using the Chapter 11 method. Make a chart of the similarities of (a) t df to F denominator df, (b) t cutoff to square root of F cutoff, (c) S^2_{Pooled} to S^2_{Within}, and (d) the t score to the square root of the F ratio. (Use the .05 level throughout; t tests are two-tailed.)

	Experimental Group			Control Group			t test			
	N	M	S^2	N	M	S^2	df	t needed	S^2_{Pooled}	t
(i)	36	100	40	36	104	48	70	1.995	44	2.56
(ii)	16	73	8	16	75	6				

3. Below is data set a from Practice Problem 3 in Chapter 10. If you did not figure the t test for this with Chapter 10, do so now. Then, also figure a one-way analysis of variance using the Chapter 11 method. Make a chart of the similarities of (a) t df to F denominator df, (b) t cutoff to square root of F cutoff, (c) S^2_{Pooled} to MS_{Within}, and (d) the t score to the square root of the F ratio.

Experimental Group			Control Group		
N	M	S^2	N	M	S^2
30	12.0	2.4	30	11.1	2.8

4. Group A includes 10 people whose scores have a mean of 170 and a population variance estimate of 48. Group B also includes 10 people: $M = 150$, $S^2 = 32$.

Carry out a t test for independent means (two-tailed) and an analysis of variance (using the Chapter 11 method). Do your figuring on the two halves of the same page, with parallel computations next to each other. (That is, make a table similar in layout to the lower part of Table 16–2.) Use the .05 level for both.

5. For the scores listed below, figure a t test for independent means (two-tailed) and then figure an analysis of variance using the structural model approach from Chapter 12 (use the .05 level for both). Make a chart of the similarities of (a) t df to F denominator df, (b) t cutoff to square root of F cutoff, (c) S_{Pooled}^2 to MS_{Within}, and (d) the t score to the square root of the F ratio.

Group A	Group B
13	11
16	7
19	9
18	
19	

6. Below we list scores from practice problem 5 in Chapter 10. If you did not figure the t test for these with Chapter 10, do so now, using the .05 level, two-tailed. Then figure a one-way analysis of variance (also .05 level) using the structural model method from Chapter 12. Make a chart of the similarities of (a) t df to F denominator df, (b) t cutoff to square root of F cutoff, (c) S_{Pooled}^2 to MS_{Within}, and (d) the t score to the square root of the F ratio.

Ordinary Story		Own-Name Story	
Student	Reading Time	Student	Reading Time
A	2	G	4
B	5	H	16
C	7	I	11
D	9	J	9
E	6	K	8
F	7		

7. For the scores listed below, figure a t test for independent means and then figure an analysis of variance using the structural model approach from Chapter 12. Make a chart of the similarities of (a) t df to F denominator df, (b) t cutoff to square root of F cutoff, (c) S_{Pooled}^2 to MS_{Within}, and (d) the t score to the square root of the F ratio. (Use the .05 level throughout; the t test is two-tailed.)

Group A	Group B
.7	.6
.9	.4
.8	.2

8. Do the following for the scores in practice problems (a) 5, (b) 6, and (c) 7: (i) Figure a t test for independent means if you have not already done so, (ii) figure

the correlation coefficient (between the group that participants are in and their scores on the measured variable), (iii) figure the t for significance of the correlation coefficient (using the formula $t = r\sqrt{N-2}/\sqrt{1-r^2}$) and note explicitly the similarity of results, and (iv) make a scatter diagram. For (a), also (v) explain the relation of the spread of the means and the spread of the scores around the means to the t and correlation results.

9. Do the following for the scores in practice problems (a) 5, (b) 6, and (c) 7: (i) Figure the analysis of variance using the structural model approach from Chapter 12 if you have not done so already; (ii) figure the proportionate reduction in error based on the analysis of variance results; (iii) carry out a regression analysis (predicting the measured variable score from the group that participants are in); (iv) figure the proportionate reduction in error using the long method of figuring predicted scores, and finding the average squared error using them; and (v) make a chart showing the parallels in the results; for (a), also (vi) explain the major similarities. (Use the .05 level throughout.)

10. Participants 1, 2, and 3 are in Group I; participants 4 and 5 are in Group II; participants 6, 7, and 8 are in Group III; and participants 9 and 10 are in Group IV. Make a table showing nominal coding for these ten participants.

SET II

11. (a) Look up and write down the F cutoff at the .01 level for distributions with 1 degree of freedom in the numerator and 10, 20, 30, and 60 degrees of freedom in the denominator. (b) Take the square root of each and write it down next to it. (c) Look up the cutoffs on the t distribution at the .01 level (two-tailed) using 10, 20, 30, and 60 degrees of freedom, and write it down next to the corresponding F square root. (The results should be identical, within rounding error.)

12. Below are three data sets. For the first two data sets, in addition to the means and estimated population variances, we have shown the t test information. You should figure the third yourself. Also, for each, figure a one-way analysis of variance using the Chapter 11 method. Make a chart of the similarities of (a) t df to F denominator df, (b) t cutoff to square root of F cutoff, (c) S^2_{Pooled} to S^2_{Within}, and (d) the t score to the square root of the F ratio. (Use the .01 level throughout; t tests are two-tailed.)

	Experimental Group			Control Group			t test			
	N	M	S^2	N	M	S^2	df	t needed	S^2_{Pooled}	t
(i)	20	10	3	20	12	2	38	2.724	2.5	4
(ii)	25	7.5	4	25	4.5	2	48	2.690	3.0	6.12
(iii)	10	48	8	10	55	4				

13. Below we list scores from two data sets, both from practice problem 14 in Chapter 10. If you did not figure the t tests for these with Chapter 10, do so now, this time using the .01 level, two-tailed. Then, for each, also figure a one-way analysis of variance (also .01 level) using the Chapter 11 method. Make a chart of the similarities of (a) t df to F denominator df, (b) t cutoff to square root of F cutoff, (c) S^2_{Pooled} to S^2_{Within}, and (d) the t score to the square root of the F ratio.

	Experimental Group			Control Group		
	N	M	S^2	N	M	S^2
(i)	10	604	60	10	607	50
(ii)	40	604	60	40	607	50
(iii)	10	604	20	10	607	16

14. Group I consists of 12 people whose scores have a mean of 15.5 and a population variance estimate of 4.5. Group B also consists of 12 people: $M = 18.3$, $S^2 = 3.5$. Carry out a t test for independent means (two-tailed) and an analysis of variance (using the Chapter 11 method), figuring the two on two halves of the same page, with parallel computations next to each other. (That is, make a table similar in layout to the lower part of Table 16–2.) Use the .05 level.

15. For the scores listed below, carry out a t test for independent means (two-tailed) and an analysis of variance using the structural model method from Chapter 12. (Use the .05 level for both.) Make a chart of the similarities of (a) t df to F denominator df, (b) t cutoff to square root of F cutoff, (c) S^2_{Pooled} to MS_{Within}, and (d) the t score to the square root of the F ratio.

Group A	Group B
0	4
1	5
0	6
	5

16. For the scores below, figure a t test for independent means (.05 level, two-tailed) and an analysis of variance (.05 level) using the structural model method from Chapter 12. Make a chart of the similarities of (a) t df to F denominator df, (b) t cutoff to square root of F cutoff, (c) S^2_{Pooled} to MS_{Within}, and (d) the t score to the square root of the F ratio.

Group A	Group B
0	0
0	0
0	0
0	0
0	0
0	0
0	1
0	1
0	1
0	1
0	1
0	1
1	1
1	1
1	1
1	1

17. Below we list scores from practice problem 15 in Chapter 10. If you did not figure the t test for these with Chapter 10, do so now, using the .05 level, two-tailed. Then figure a one-way analysis of variance (also .05 level) using the structural model method from Chapter 12. Make a chart of the similarities of (a) t df to F denominator df, (b) t cutoff to square root of F cutoff, (c) S^2_{Pooled} to S^2_{Within}, and (d) the t score to the square root of the F ratio.

Big Meal Group		Small Meal Group	
Subject	Hearing	Subject	Hearing
A	22	D	19
B	25	E	23
C	25	F	21

18. Do the following for the scores in practice problems (a) 15, (b) 16, and (c) 17: (i) Figure a t test for independent means if you have not already done so, (ii) figure the correlation coefficient (between the group that participants are in and their scores on the measured variable), (iii) figure the t for significance of the correlation coefficient (using the formula $t = r\sqrt{N - 2}/\sqrt{1 - r^2}$) and note explicitly the similarity of results, (iv) make a scatter diagram, and (v) explain the relation of the spread of the means and the spread of the scores around the means to the t and correlation results.

19. Do the following for the scores in practice problems (a) 15, (b) 16, and (c) 17: (i) Figure the analysis of variance using the structural model approach from Chapter 12 if you have not already done so; (ii) figure the proportionate reduction in error based on the analysis of variance results; (iii) carry out a regression analysis (predicting the measured variable score from the group that participants are in); (iv) figure the proportionate reduction in error using the long method of figuring predicted scores, and finding the average squared error using them; and (v) make a chart showing the parallels in the results.

20. Participants 1 and 2 are in Group A; participants 3, 4, 5, and 6 are in Group B; and participants 7, 8, and 9 are in Group C. Make a table showing nominal coding for these nine participants.

CHAPTER 17

MAKING SENSE OF ADVANCED STATISTICAL PROCEDURES IN RESEARCH ARTICLES

Are You Ready?
What You Need to have Mastered Before Starting This Chapter:

- Chapters 1 through 11, and the first half of 13.

Most research you will read as a psychology student uses one or more of the statistical procedures you have learned in this book. However, often you will run into procedures that you will not learn to do yourself until you take more advanced statistics courses. Fortunately, most of these advanced procedures are direct extensions of what you have learned in this book. At the least, after reading this chapter, you should be able to make sense of the general idea of just about any statistical analysis in a research article.

The first part of this chapter considers some widely used advanced statistical techniques that focus on associations among variables. These are basically elaborations of what you learned in chapters 3 and 4 on correlation and regression. After a brief review of multiple regression as a foundation, we introduce hierarchical and stepwise multiple regression, partial correlation, reliability, factor analysis, and causal modeling. The second part of this chapter turns to advanced statistical techniques that focus on differences between groups. These are basically elaborations of what you learned in chapters 11, 12, and 13 on the analysis of variance. These procedures include the analysis of covariance, multivariate analysis of variance, and multivariate analysis of covariance. Finally, we consider what to do when you read a research article that uses a statistical technique you have never heard about.

BRIEF REVIEW OF MULTIPLE REGRESSION

You learned about multiple regression in Chapter 4 (and reviewed this material briefly in Chapter 16). Multiple regression is about predicting scores on a criterion variable from two or more predictor variables. For example, in the sleep and mood study example in that chapter, we discussed predicting a person's mood (the criterion variable) from three predictor variables, number of hours slept the night before, how well the person you slept, and number of dreams during the night.

A multiple regression prediction rule has a regression coefficient for each predictor variable. If you know a person's scores on the predictor variables, you multiply each predictor variable's score by that predictor variable's regression coefficient. The sum of these multiplications is the person's predicted score on the criterion variable. When working with Z scores, the regression coefficients are standardized and are called standardized regression coefficients or betas (βs). For example, with three independent variables, the form of the prediction rule is as follows:

$$\hat{Z}_Y = (\beta_1)(Z_{X_1}) + (\beta_2)(Z_{X_2}) + (\beta_3)(Z_{X_3})$$

The overall accuracy of a prediction rule, the amount of variation it accounts for in the criterion variable, is called the proportion of variance accounted for and is abbreviated as R^2. Multiple regression also gives you the statistical significance of both the overall proportion of variance accounted for, R^2, as well as for the regression coefficient for each predictor variable individually.

HIERARCHICAL AND STEPWISE MULTIPLE REGRESSION

HIERARCHICAL MULTIPLE REGRESSION

Sometimes researchers focus on the influence of several predictor variables in a sequential way. That is, they want to know how much of the variation in the criterion variable is accounted for by the first predictor variable, then how much is added to the overall variance accounted for in the criterion variable by including a second predictor variable. Then, perhaps, they want to know how much more is added by including a third predictor variable. And so on. Thus, when reporting results, a researcher usually describes the amount that each successive predictor variable adds to the overall prediction in terms of an increase in R^2. The procedure is known as **hierarchical multiple regression.**

hierarchical multiple regression

Consider an example. Armstrong-Stassen (2001) surveyed 187 employees of the Canadian federal government, once when major layoffs had just been announced (which she refers to as "T1" for time 1) and once again 20 months later (T2). (None of these employees had been laid off.) She then looked at how several variables measured at Time 1 predicted Time 2 "Threat of Job Loss," "Sense of Powerlessness," and "Organizational Commitment." Her results are shown in Table 17–1 (reproduced from her Table 4). Look at the results for T2 Threat of Job Loss. The first Time 1 variable considered, "Measure," refers to the same variable (Threat of Job Loss, in this case) from Time 1. This variable by itself had an R^2 of .29; the F (for the R^2) was clearly significant, as shown by the three stars, meaning $p < .001$ (as noted at the bottom of the table). The second step was to add two predictor variables at once having to do with background characteristics: Gender and job level. Adding these two predictor variables increased the R^2 from .29 to .33, an increase (ΔR^2) of .04. The table shows that the significance for the change (labeled ΔF) is significant at $p < .05$. At the next step, Armstrong-Stassen added Job Satisfaction and Sense of Powerlessness. (The table is a little confusing here. What it means is that for the analysis for T2 Threat of Job Loss, at this point she is adding in Sense of

TABLE 17–1   Hierarchical Regression Results for time 2 (T2) Job Security and T2 Organizational Commitment

Time 1	T2 Threat of Job Loss ß		T2 Sense of Powerlessness ß		T2 Organizational Commitment ß	
Measure	.36***		.21*		.40***	
R^2		.29		.31		.35
ΔF		67.12***		73.77***		87.43
Gender	−.14		−.11		.12	
Job Level	−.16*		−.29***		.10	
R^2		.33		.38		.39
ΔR^2		.04		.07		.04
ΔF		4.54*		9.75***		5.53**
Job Satisfaction	−.13		−.25**		.19*	
Job Loss Threat/						
Sense of Powerlessness	−.02		.02		.04	
R^2		.34		.44	.01	
ΔR^2		.01		.06		.43
ΔF		2.18		8.49**		.04
Organizational Commitment	.07		−.05			3.78*
Organizational Trust	−.00		−.16		.29***	
Organizational Morale	−.07		.03		−.10	
R^2		.35		.46		.48
ΔR^2		.01		.02		.05
ΔF		0.69		1.51		7.56***
Health Symptoms	.26**		.09		.07	
Burnout	−.15		−.14		−.06	
R^2		.38		.47		.48
ΔR^2		.03		.01		.00
ΔF		3.80*		1.27		0.33

Note: Beta coefficients are from the simultaneous regression with all variables entered.
*$p < .05$: **$p < .01$; ***$p < .001$.
From Armstrong-Stassen, 2001.

Powerlessness; but in the analysis for Sense of Powerlessness, at this point she is adding in Threat of Job Loss; and for the analysis for Organizational Commitment, at this point she is adding in both.) Adding these two variables increased the R^2 from .33 to .34, an increase (ΔR^2) of .01, which was not significant. At the next step, she added Organizational Commitment, Organizational Trust, and Organizational Morale. The addition of these three variables increased the R^2 from .34 to .35, another increase (ΔR^2) of just .01, which, again, was not significant. Finally, at the last step, Armstrong-Stassen added Health Symptoms and Burnout. Adding these two variables increased the R^2 from .35 to .38, an increase of .03, which was significant.

What this tells us is that a strong predictor of feeling the threat of job loss at T2 is threat of job loss at T1—that is, those who initially felt threatened continued to feel threatened. But over and above what is contributed by this initial feeling, gender and job level make an additional difference. You can look at the betas (which the table notes explain are for the overall prediction rule) and see that in both cases the predictions were negative. Elsewhere in the article, Armstrong-Stassen notes that "Gender was coded as 1 for men and 2 for women" and that "Job level was coded 1 for nonmanagement and 2 for management." Thus, threat of job loss was greater for men and for nonmanagement. The next couple of steps, in which all the other job related feelings were entered, did not add much to the ability to predict T2 feeling of threat, but it was predicted by having more health symptoms and less burnout.

STEPWISE MULTIPLE REGRESSION

stepwise multiple regression

Sometimes, especially in an exploratory study, you measure a great many variables that are possible predictors of the criterion variable, and you want to pick out which predictor variables make a useful contribution to the overall prediction. This is usually done with a controversial procedure called **stepwise multiple regression** (or *stepwise regression*, for short). The most common form of stepwise multiple regression works as diagrammed in Table 17–2: A computer program goes through a step-by-step procedure, first picking out the single variable that accounts for the most

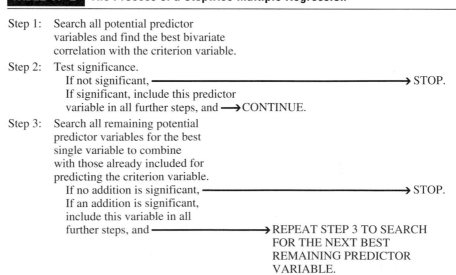

TABLE 17–2   **The Process of a Stepwise Multiple Regression**

Step 1:   Search all potential predictor variables and find the best bivariate correlation with the criterion variable.

Step 2:   Test significance.
             If not significant, ────────────────────────────→ STOP.
             If significant, include this predictor variable in all further steps, and ──→CONTINUE.

Step 3:   Search all remaining potential predictor variables for the best single variable to combine with those already included for predicting the criterion variable.
             If no addition is significant, ───────────────────→ STOP.
             If an addition is significant, include this variable in all further steps, and ─────────→ REPEAT STEP 3 TO SEARCH FOR THE NEXT BEST REMAINING PREDICTOR VARIABLE.

variance in the criterion variable. If this proportion of variance accounted for is not significant, the process stops, since even the best predictor is of no use. However, if this proportion of variance accounted for by this predictor is significant, the process goes on to the next step. The next step is to pick out the predictor variable that, in combination with this first one, has the highest R^2. The computer then checks to see whether this combination is a significant improvement over the best single predictor variable alone. If it is not, the process stops. If it is a significant improvement, the computer goes on. The next step is to pick out which of the remaining predictor variables, when combined with these first two, gives the highest R^2. Then, this combination is checked to see if it is a significant improvement in prediction over and above just the first two predictors. The process continues until either all the predictor variables are included or adding any of the remaining ones does not give a significant improvement. This procedure is called "stepwise" because it proceeds one step at a time.[1]

Schwartz and Cohen (2001) studied 223 schizophrenic patients of a Florida community agency, focusing on the variables that might predict suicidality (the tendency to think about suicide, intent to harm oneself, and the seriousness and feasibility of any current suicide plan). Because they had measured a great many variables that might predict suicidality, they used stepwise regression. Here are their results:

> . . . a stepwise regression procedure was used to obtain the most effective overall model for suicidality. Results suggest that depressive symptoms alone accounted for 28% of the variance in ratings of suicidality. When age was added to the prediction model as a second variable, the two-variable combination accounted for 33% of the variance in ratings of suicidality. After traumatic stress was entered into the prediction equation, the three- variable model accounted for 38% of the variance in ratings of suicidality. The addition of other [predictor] variables added only minimally (and insignificantly) to the prediction model. Therefore, although depressive symptoms were found to most strongly associate with ratings of suicidality, the most significant combination of risk factors was the three-variable model including depressive symptoms, age, and recent traumatic stress. (p. 317)

What the authors are telling us is that of the several potential predictors (there were 12), the proportion of variance accounted for by three of these variables was not significantly improved upon by also including any of the remaining variables.

One caution: We said earlier that stepwise regression is a controversial procedure. The reason it is controversial is that the prediction formula that results from this procedure is the best group of variables for predicting the criterion variable, *based on the sample studied.* However, it often happens that when the same variables are studied with a new sample, a somewhat different combination of variables turns out best. The reason this so often happens is that the variable selected at each step is one that adds the most to the overall prediction. The variable added has to make a significant improvement, but it doesn't have to make a significantly *larger*

---

[1]Technically, what we have described is "forward stepwise regression." Some researchers prefer to start with a prediction rule including all the predictor variables and then see how much predictability is lost when the least useful predictor is eliminated. If not much is lost, the next least useful is eliminated, and so forth. This process continues until eliminating the least useful remaining predictor significantly reduces the strength of the prediction. This alternative approach is called "backward stepwise regression." Usually, forward and backward stepwise regression give about the same results. There are other possibilities, some of which alternate backward and forward steps. Which of these procedures you use rarely makes much difference.

improvement than the next best variable—it only has to add the most, and the addition has to be significant. The next best variable might also make a significant addition, but just not quite as large an improvement. In a new sample from the same population, a slight difference in one predictor adding more than the other could well be reversed.

COMPARING HIERARCHICAL AND STEPWISE REGRESSION

Hierarchical and stepwise regression are similar in an important way. In both methods, you add variables a stage at a time and check whether the addition significantly improves the prediction. However, there is also an important difference. In hierarchical regression, the order of adding the predictor variables is based on some theory or plan, decided in advance by the researcher. In stepwise regression, there is no initial plan. The computer simply figures out the best variables to add until adding more makes no additional significant contribution.

Thus, hierarchical regression is used in research that is based on theory or some substantial previous knowledge. Stepwise regression is useful in exploratory research where you don't know what to expect. Stepwise regression is also useful in applied research where you are looking for the best prediction formula without caring about its theoretical meaning.

HOW ARE YOU DOING?

1. Write the formula for multiple regression with Z scores for three predictors and define each of the symbols.
2, (a) How does hierarchical regression work? (b) Why is it done?
3. Describe the results of the hierarchical regression in Table 17–1 for Organizational Commitment. (That is, describe it step by step and also summarize the overall conclusion.)
4. (a) How does stepwise regression work? (b) Why is it done? (c) What is a major limitation of this procedure?
5. How are hierarchical and stepwise regression (a) similar and (b) different?

ANSWERS:

1. $\hat{Z}_Y = (\beta_1)(Z_{X_1}) + (\beta_2)(Z_{X_2}) + (\beta_3)(Z_{X_3})$
   $\hat{Z}_Y$ is a person's predicted Z score on the criterion variable; β_1, β_2, and β_3 are the standardized regression coefficients (betas) for the first, second, and third predictor variables, respectively; and X_1, X_2, and X_3 are the person's Z scores for the first, second, and third predictor variables, respectively.
2. (a) You figure the R^2 for predicting the criterion variable from a predetermined particular predictor variable (or group of predictor variables); then you figure the R^2 for predicting that criterion variable from a prediction rule that includes the original predictor variable (or variables) *plus* a new, additional predictor variable (or variables), and then figure the *difference* (the increase) in R^2 and its significance. You can continue this process for many steps. The focus is on how much each additional predictor or group of predictors adds to those added at the previous step.
   (b) To test a theory about how particular variables predict a criterion variable over and above particular previous ones.
3. T1 Organizational Commitment accounts for 35% of the variance in T2 Organizational Commitment; adding gender and job level increases this to 39%, a 4% increase, which is significant (the betas suggest that women and management have more commitment); adding Job Satisfaction, Job Loss Threat, and Sense of Powerlessness raise it to 43%, another significant 4% increase; Organizational Trust and Organizational Morale raise it to 48%, a significant 5% increase; but Health Symptoms and Burnout add essentially nothing—the overall variance accounted for is still 48%. Overall, this tells you that a huge chunk of the variation is accounted for by the Time 1 measure, but even over and above what it con-

tributes, additional predictability is provided by background (gender and job level); that even accounting for T1 commitment and background, yet additional predictability is added by the job related items; that even over and above all this, still more predictability is added by organizational feelings; but once all these are taken into account, very little if any further predictability is added by health and burnout.

4. (a) You do a series of regressions for each variable predicting the criterion and select the one that gives the highest R^2. If this is not significant, you stop. But if it is, you do another series of regressions, each including the first variable and one of the remaining variables; from these you select the two-variable regression that gives the highest R^2. If this is not a significant *increase* in R^2, you stop the process with one predictor variable. If it is a significant increase, you continue the process, searching for the best three-variable prediction rule that includes the first two plus one of the remaining. This process goes on until adding the best remaining variable does not make a significant increase in R^2.
(b) To sort out, from a large number of possible predictors, the subset that are most useful in predicting the criterion.
(c) The best subset of predictors in this sample might not be the best subset in the population.

5. (a) Both involve systematically adding variables to a multiple regression prediction rule and testing whether the addition at each stage is significant.
(b) In hierarchical regression, you add variables in a planned sequence and continue to the end regardless if additions at earlier stages are significant; stepwise regression is an exploratory procedure that adds a variable at each stage according to which turns out to be the best additional predictor among all remaining variables, and you stop when the addition of the best remaining one is not significant.

PARTIAL CORRELATION

Partial correlation is widely used in personality, social, developmental, clinical, and various applied areas of psychology. Partial correlation is the amount of association between two variables, over and above the influence of one or more other variables. Suppose a researcher wants to know how the stress people experience in married life is related to how long they have been married. However, the researcher realizes that part of what might make marital stress and marriage length go together is whether the couples have children. Having children or not could make stress and length go together, because those married longer are more likely to have children and having children may create marital stress. Thus, simply figuring the correlation between marital stress and marriage length would be misleading. The researcher wants to know what the relation between stress and marriage length would be if everyone had the same number of children. Or, to put it another way, the researcher wants somehow to subtract out the influence of number of children from the relation between marital stress and length.

In this example, the researcher would figure a partial correlation between marital stress and length of marriage, **holding constant** number of children. Holding a variable constant is also called **partialing out**, **controlling for**, or **adjusting for**, the variable held constant (such as number of children). These terms (holding constant, partialing out, etc.) all mean the same thing and are used interchangeably. The actual statistic for partial correlation is called the **partial correlation coefficient.** Like an ordinary correlation coefficient, it goes from -1 to $+1$. Just remember that, unlike an ordinary correlation, some third variable is being controlled for.

Here is another way to understand partial correlations. In the marriage example, you could figure the ordinary correlation between stress and marriage length using only people who have no children, then figure an ordinary correlation between stress and marriage length for only those with one child, and so on. Each of

Partial correlation

**holding constant
partialing out
controlling for
adjusting for
partial correlation coefficient**

these correlations, by itself, is not affected by differences in number of children. (This is because the people included within any one of these correlations all have the same number of children.) You could then figure a kind of average of these various correlations, each of which is not affected by number of children. This average of these correlations is the partial correlation. It is literally a correlation that *holds constant* the number of children. (The figuring for a partial correlation is fairly straightforward, and you do not actually have to figure all these individual correlations and average them. However, the result amounts to doing this.)

Researchers often use partial correlation to help sort out alternative explanations for the relations among variables. For example, if a correlation between stress and length holds up, even after controlling for number of children, an alternative explanation about children is made unlikely.

Here is an example from an actual study. Shahinfar et al. (2001) studied violence and aggression in a sample of 110 adolescent boys in a juvenile detention facility who had been convicted of serious crimes. Here is part of their results section:

> Pearson correlations were computed among the measures of interest. Because age was significantly related to two of the social information-processing measures, partial correlations controlling for age are presented below the diagonal in Table [17–3]. As shown in Table [17–3], the significance of the results did not differ when age was controlled. (pp. 138–139)

For example, the ordinary ("Pearson") correlation between having been a victim of severe violence and Approval of Aggression was .24, which was significant at the .05 level (as shown by the one star). When controlling for age, this correlation was still .24 and was still significant at the .05 level. To take another example, being a witness of severe violence had an ordinary correlation of .28 with Perceived Consequences of Aggression with $p < .01$; after controlling for age, this was .27, with p still $< .01$.

RELIABILITY

The kinds of measures used in psychology research, such as questionnaires, systematic observation of behavior, physiological changes, and the like, are rarely perfectly consistent or stable over time. (We discussed this briefly in Chapter 3.) The

TABLE 17–3   **Correlations Among Measures**

Variable	1	2	3	4	5	6	7	8
1. Victim, severe violence	—	.22*	.28**	.32**	.19*	.18*	.24*	.08
2. Witness, severe violence	.13	—	.47**	.63**	.06	.04	.13	.28**
3. Victim, mild violence	.43**	.38**	—	.39**	−.04	−.08	.10	.13
4. Witness, mild violence	.21*	.57**	.25**	—	−.05	.01	.19*	.18*
5. Hostile bias	.19*	.06	−.03	−.05	—	.60**	−.02	−.16
6. Hostile social goals	.19*	.05	−.06	.01	.58**	—	−.18	−.19
7. Approval of aggression	.24*	.12	.08	.17	.01	−.15	—	.08
8. Perceived consequences of aggression	.07	.27**	.12	.17	−.13	−.24	.11	—

Note. Simple correlations are presented above the diagonal, and partial correlations controlling for age are presented below the diagonal.
* $p \le .05$. ** $p \le .01$.
From Shahinfar et al., 2001.

degree of consistency or stability of a measure is called its **reliability.** Roughly speaking, the reliability of a measure is how much you would get the same result if you were to give the same measure again to the same person under the same circumstances. You will often see reliability statistics in research articles.

One way to gauge a measure's reliability is to use the measure with the same group of people twice. The correlation between the two testings is called **test-retest reliability.** However, this approach often is not practical or appropriate. For example, you can't use this approach if taking a test once would influence the second taking (such as with an intelligence test).

For many measures, such as most questionnaires, you can also gauge their reliability by correlating the average of the answers to half the questions with the average of the answers to the other half. For example, you could correlate the average score on all the odd-numbered questions with the average score on all the even-numbered questions. If the person is answering consistently, this should be a high correlation. This is called **split-half reliability.**

A problem with the split-half method is deciding which way to split the halves. Using odd-versus-even items makes sense in most situations, but by chance it could give too low or too high a correlation. Fortunately, there is a more general solution. You can divide the test into halves in all possible ways and figure the correlation using each division, then average all these split-half correlations. A statistic called **Cronbach's alpha** (α), the most widely used measure of reliability, gives you what amounts to this average. Cronbach's alpha also can be thought of as telling you the overall consistency of the test, how much high responses go with highs and lows with lows over all the test questions In general, in psychology, a good measure should have a Cronbach's alpha of at least .6, and preferably closer to .9.

Finally, in some research, the main measures are observations of behavior or coding of material written or spoken by participants. In these situations, there are often two or more raters of each participant's behavior or material, so that reliability is the similarity of the ratings between raters. This is called **interrater reliability.** (It is also called *interjudge reliablity, interrater agreement,* or *interjudge agreement.*)

Reliabilities are nearly always discussed when a research article is mainly about the creation of a new measure. For example, Valk et al. (2001) developed a measure of disability in elderly nursing home residents. The test, which is filled out by staff about residents, initially included 26 items that assessed seven domains of functioning, such as Mobility (sample item, "Is the resident able to walk?") and Alertness (sample item, "Does the resident react if somebody speaks to him /her?"). They tested out their measure with 115 poorly functioning residents of Dutch nursing homes, with an average age of 81.5. For 111 of the residents, ratings were made by two different raters. All residents were assessed a second time a week later. Here is the reliability discussion from their results section:

> The associations of times with a domain, as measured by means of Cronbach's alpha, were obtained on each of the scales (lowest: Perception 0.54; highest: Mobility, 0.93). Table [17–4] presents the mean scores, *SD*, median, and Cronbach's alpha of the domains. The test-retest reliability was good to excellent; see Table [17–5]. Correlation coefficients ranged from 0.63 to 0.94. Interrater reliability for the scales Cognition, Incontinence, Mobility, and ADL was high (0.79 to 0.93), and moderate for Resistance to Nursing Assistance (0.51). Perception showed very low interrater reliability 0.33 (see Table [17–6]). (p. P188)

Looking at the tables, you can see, for example, that Alertness, with six items, has a Cronbach's alpha of .84, a test-retest reliability (labeled "Repro-

reliability

test-retest reliability

split-half reliability

Cronbach's alpha

interrater reliability

TABLE 17–4   Domains: Means, Standard Deviations, Cronbach's Alpha, and Range

Scale	n	Items	Mean	Median	SD	Cronbach's Alpha	Range
Incontinence	112	4	70.1	81.2	32.5	.88	0–8
Mobility	112	3	48.6	40	35.8	.93	0–10
Resistance	111	1	53.1	66.6	41.0	—	0–3
Alertness	111	6	30.8	27.7	22.0	.84	0–18
Cognition	112	7	69.3	72.7	28.9	.78	0–11
ADL	96	3	75.9	87.5	31.4	.90	0–8
Perception	88	2	.30	0	0.65	.54	0–4

From Valk et al., 2001.

TABLE 17–5   Reproducibility of the Questionnaire: After One Week

Scale	Correlation
Cognition	0.89
Mobility	0.94
ADL	0.90
Alertness	0.85
Incontinence	0.89
Resistance	0.63
Perception	0.76

Note: Spearman correlation coefficients, $p < .001$.
From Valk et al., 2001.

factor analysis

factor
factor loading

ducibility of the Questionnaire: After One Week") of .85, and an interrater reliablity of .71. This is thus a quite adequately reliable scale. On the other hand, consider Perception, which had two items. Here the reliabilities were .54, .76, and .33. Thus, Valk et al. dropped this domain (and its two items) from the scale, making the final scale 24 items assessing six domains. (Incidentally, you may have noticed from the notes at the bottom of the tables that the test-retest and interrater reliability were figured using the Spearman correlation. This is a rank-order correlation method of the kind discussed in Chapter 15. Valk et al. used this kind of correlation because the items used rank-order measurement. Ordinarily, however, these kinds of reliabilities are figured using ordinary correlation coefficients.)

FACTOR ANALYSIS

Suppose you have measured a group of people on a large number of variables (for example, you might have given a questionnaire that includes many different personality traits). You use **factor analysis** to tell you which variables tend to clump together—which ones tend to be correlated with each other and not with other variables. Each such clump (group of variables) is called a **factor.** The correlation of an individual variable with a factor is called that variable's **factor loading** on that factor. Variables have loadings on each factor but usually will have high loadings on only one. Factor loadings range from −1, a perfect negative correlation with the factor, through 0, no relation to the factor, to +1, a perfect positive correlation with the factor. Normally, a variable is considered to contribute meaningfully to a factor only if it has a loading at least above .3 (or below −.3).

The factor analysis is done using a fairly complex set of formulas that begin with the correlations among all the variables and end up with a set of factor loadings. (It also provides other information, including how much variance each factor accounts for of the total amount of variation among the variables.) There are, in fact, several somewhat different approaches to factor analysis. Thus, the researcher has some leeway and can select from a variety of methods, each of which may give slightly different results.

However, the most subjective part of the process is the name the researcher gives to a factor. When reading about a factor analysis in a research article, think closely about the name the researcher gives to each factor. Do the names really do a good job of describing the variables that make up the factor?

Here is an example of a factor analysis from organizational psychology. Koslowsky et al. (2001) gave 232 nurses in Israeli hospitals the following instructions:

> Think about a time when you were being supervised in doing some task. Suppose your supervisor asked you to do your job somewhat differently and, though you were initially reluctant, you did exactly what you were asked.
>
> On the following pages there are a number of reasons why you might have done so. . . . Decide how likely it would be that you complied for this reason. (p. 461)

The nurses responded on a 7-point scale from 1, "definitely not a reason," to 7, "definitely a reason," to items relating to 11 power sources, such as coercion or providing information. As part of their study, the researchers carried out a factor analysis of the 11 power sources. They reported the following results: "The analysis yielded a two-factor solution [see Table 17–7]. The first factor, which explained 41.9 per cent of the variance, included seven power sources [see Table 17–7]. . . . The second factor, which explained 15.5 percent of the variance, included four power bases [see Table 17–7]."

For example, Interpersonal coercion was included in the first factor because it had a high loading (.81) on this factor, but only a small loading (−.17) on the second factor. Expertise, on the other hand, was included in the second factor because it had a high loading on this factor (.78) but only a small loading (.16) on the first factor. Notice, however, that some items were not so clearly part of one factor or the other, such as Legitimate position, which had a loading of .53 on the first factor and .45 on the second. This makes sense, since having a legitimate right to use power is somewhere between the harshness of such things as coercion and the softness of persuading by providing information. Also notice that the names the researchers

TABLE 17–6 Interrater Reliability of the Questionnaire

Scale	Correlation
Cognition	0.79
Mobility	0.93
ADL	0.80
Alertness	0.71
Incontinence	0.88
Resistance	0.51
Perception	0.33

Note: Spearman correlation coefficients, $p < .001$.

From Valk et al., 2001.

TABLE 17–7 Factor Analysis Loadings for the Eleven Power Sources

	Loadings	
Power sources by factor	*Factor 1*	*Factor 2*
Harsh power bases		
Impersonal coercion	0.81	−0.17
Impersonal reward	0.80	0.05
Personal reward	0.78	0.31
Legitimate reciprocity	0.71	0.26
Personal coercion	0.66	0.32
Legitimate equity	0.61	0.17
Legitimate position	0.53	0.45
Soft power tactics		
Expertise	0.16	0.78
Information	−0.17	0.76
Reference	0.34	0.70
Legitimate dependence	0.36	0.56
Explained variance (%)	41.9	15.5
Internal consistency (alpha)	0.85	0.79

From Koslowsky et al., 2001.

chose to give to the factors seem reasonable in light of the variables included in them, though it is always possible that other researchers might see the commonalities within each factor as having a different meaning. Finally, notice that at the bottom of the table they also give the Internal consistency (alpha), by which they mean Cronbach's alpha for the items in each factor (that is, the ones with high loadings on a factor) if you were to think of them as a scale. (In fact, based on this factor analysis, the researchers went on to use the items in the two factors as two scales, which they then related to other variables such as the nurse's job satisfaction.)

HOW ARE YOU DOING?

1. (a) What is partial correlation? (b) What does it mean if a partial correlation is less than the original correlation? (c) What does it mean if a partial correlation is about the same as the original correlation? (d) How can partial correlation help sort out direction of causality in a correlational study?
2. In the Shahinfar et al. (2001) example of partial correlation (see Table 17–3), what is the (a) actual and (b) partial correlation (controlling for age) between being a victim of severe violence and Hostile bias? (c) What does this tell us?
3. (a) What is the reliability of a measure? (b, c, and d) List and define three kinds of reliability. (e) How does Cronbach's alpha relate to split-half reliability?
4. In the Valk et al. (2001) example of reliability (see tables 17–4, 17–5, and 17–6), (a) indicate which is the most reliable scale, and (b, c, and d) give its reliabilities.
5. (a) When do you use a factor analysis? (b) What information does it give you? (c) What is a factor? (d) What is a factor loading? (e) What is the most subjective part of factor analysis?
6. In the Koslowsky et al. (2001) example of factor analysis (see Table 17–7), what are personal reward's loadings on each factor?

ANSWERS:

1. (a) The correlation of two variables controlling for a third variable. (b) That the variable controlled for accounts for some of the association between the original two variables. (c) That the variable controlled for does not account for the correlation between the original two variables. (d) It helps test whether the correlation might be due to a third variable causing the association between the original two variables.
2. (a) .19. (b) .19. (c) This tells us that the association between being a victim of severe violence and hostile bias is not due to their association with age.
3. (a) Its consistency and stability. (b) Test-retest reliability, which is how much the measure gives the same results when taken twice by the same people. (c) Internal consistency reliability, which is how much the different parts of the measure give similar results. (d) Interrater reliability, which is how much different raters give the same results. (e) Cronbach's alpha is like the average of the correlations between all possible pairs of halves of the measure.
4. (a) Mobility; (b) internal consistency reliability (Cronbach's alpha) = .93; (c) test-retest reliability (Spearman's correlation coefficient) = .94; (d) interrater reliability (Spearman's correlation coefficient) = .93.
5. (a) When you have many measures of a group of people. (b) It tells you the groupings of variables that are highly correlated with each other but not very correlated with variables in other groupings. (c) One of these groupings. (d) The correlation of a variable with a factor. (e) Deciding what to name a factor based on the variables with high loadings on it.
6. The personal rewards loadings are .78 on the first factor and .31 on the second factor.

CAUSAL MODELING

As with factor analysis, you use causal modeling when you have measured people on a number of variables. Unlike factor analysis, the goal of causal modeling is to test whether the pattern of correlations among the variables fits with some specific theory of which variables are causing which.

Causal modeling methods are widely used in psychology. We first introduce the older (but still common) method of path analysis. It is often called *ordinary path analysis* to distinguish it from the new, more elaborate method of structural equation modeling (which is also a kind of path analysis) we describe in the next main section

PATH ANALYSIS

In **path analysis**, you make a diagram with arrows connecting the variables. Each arrow, or **path**, shows what the researcher predicts to be the cause-and-effect connections between variables. Then, based on the correlations of these variables in a sample and the path diagram predicted by the researcher, you can figure path coefficients for each path. The **path coefficient** is like a beta in multiple regression. In fact, if the path diagram is a correct description of the causal relationship among the variables, the path coefficient tells you how much of a standard deviation change on the variable at the end of the arrow is produced by a one standard deviation change in the predictor variable at the start of the arrow. (Also note that a path coefficient is like a partial correlation in that it is figured so that it partials out the influence of any other variables that have arrows to the variable at the end of the same arrow.)

Here is an example. Williamson and her colleagues (2001) studied 98 wives and 44 husbands who were caring for an elderly spouse living at home who was impaired in some way, such as with Alzheimer's disease. The research was testing a theory about what causes and what averts potentially harmful behavior by the caregiver towards the partner. Figure 17–1 shows their predicted pattern of cause and effect relationships (along with the path coefficients figured from their results) among these different variables. For example, the arrows in the path diagram tell you that Caregiver age is predicted to affect ADL (activities of daily living), which in turn is not predicted to affect any other variables in the model (that is, there are no arrows from ADL to other variables). However, Caregiver Age is also predicted to affect the degree of Care Recipient Dementia, which is one of the predicted

path analysis
path

path coefficient

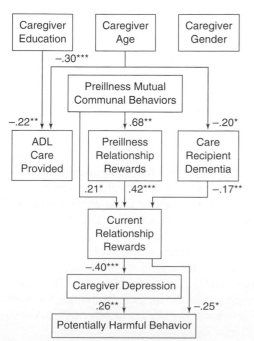

FIGURE 17–1 *Significant pathways emerging in path analyses predicting potentially harmful caregiver behavior. ADL = activities of daily living.* * p < .05. ** p < .01. *** p < .001. *Sources: Williamson et al., 2001.*

causes of Current Relationship Rewards, which in turn is predicted to affect Potentially Harmful Behavior in two ways: indirectly through Caregiver Depression—high levels of rewards leading to less depression, which then reduces the likelihood of Potentially Harmful Behavior—and directly, with high levels of rewards directly reducing the likelihood of Potentially Harmful Behavior. This path diagram lays out predictions based on a rich and complex theory.

Based on the correlations among these variables in their sample of caregivers, the path coefficients show the direction and degree of the predicted effects. The stars show the level of significance for a path. As is often done in ordinary path analyses, the researchers actually tested other possible paths, but only included in the diagram paths that were significant. (Thus, all paths in the model have at least one star.)

STRUCTURAL EQUATION MODELING

Structural equation modeling

Structural equation modeling is a special elaboration of ordinary path analysis. It also involves a path diagram with arrows between variables and path coefficients for each arrow. However, structural equation modeling has several important advantages over the older path analysis method. One major advantage is that structural equation modeling gives you an overall measure of the fit between the theory (as described by the path diagram) and the correlations among the scores in your sample, called a **fit index**. There are several different fit indexes, but for most, a fit of .9 or higher is considered a good fit. Recently, a fit index that works a little differently has become widely used. It is usually referred to by its abbreviation, **RMSEA** (root mean square error of approximation). The *smaller* the RMSEA, the better the fit. Fits below .05 are considered to be very good, below about .10, good.

fit index

RMSEA

In structural equation modeling, you can also do a kind of significance test of the fit. We say a "kind of significance test" because the null hypothesis is that the theory fits. Thus, a significant result tells you that the theory does *not* fit. In other words, a researcher trying to demonstrate a theory hopes for a nonsignificant result in this significance test!

latent variable

A second major advantage of structural equation modeling over ordinary path analysis is that it uses what are called latent variables. A **latent variable** is not actually measured, but stands for a true variable that you would like to measure but can only approximate with real-life measures. For example, a latent variable might be social class, which the researcher tries to approximate with several measured variables, such as level of income, years of education, prestige of occupation, and home square footage. No one of these measured variables by itself is a very good stand-in for social class.

In structural equation modeling, the mathematics is set up so that a latent variable is a combination of the measured variables, combined in such a way as to use only what they have in common with each other. What they have in common is the true score, the underlying variable they are all getting at parts of. (A latent variable is actually like a factor in factor analysis, in that the factor is not directly measured itself, but it represents a combination of several variables that make it up.)

In a structural equation modeling path diagram, the variables that are measured usually are shown in boxes and the latent variables, in circles or ovals. This is shown in Figure 17–2. Notice in the figure that the arrows from the latent variables (the ones in circles) go to the measured variables (the ones in boxes). The idea is that the latent variable is the underlying cause of the measured variables, the measured variables being the best we can do to get at the true latent variable.

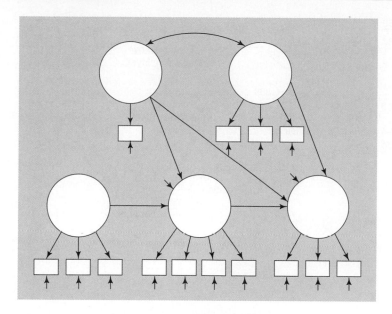

FIGURE 17-2 *A structural equation model path diagram.*

Also notice that all of the other arrows between variables are between latent variables. Structural equation modeling works in this way: The measured variables are used to make up latent variables, and the main focus of the analysis is on the causal relations (the paths) between the latent variables. (Notice, finally, the short arrows that seem to come from nowhere. These show that there is also error—other unmeasured causes—affecting the variable. These "error" or "disturbance" arrows are sometimes left out in published articles to keep the figure simple.)

AN EXAMPLE OF STRUCTURAL EQUATION MODELING

This example is from a study by Senecal and her colleagues (2001). They explain that

> The purpose of this study was to propose and test a model of work-family conflict . . . . The model posits that positive interpersonal factors both at work (i.e., one's employer) and at home (e.g., one's spouse) influence work and family motivation. Moreover, the model proposes that low levels of self-determined family and work motivation both contributed to family alienation, which in turn influences the experience of work-family conflict. Finally, work-family conflict leads to feelings of emotional exhaustion.

The researchers measured the various variables in this model in a sample of 786 French Canadians who were all working at least part time and were living with a relationship partner and at least one child.

Figure 17–3 shows the diagram of their model and the path coefficients. Notice that each latent variable (shown in ovals) has two to four measured variables associated with it. For example, Feeling Valued by One's Partner has three indicators (labeled V1, V2, and V3). The most important path coefficients are those between the latent variables. For example, Feeling Valued by One's Partner has a substantial path coefficient of .47 leading to Motivation Toward Family Activities. This means that if the path model correctly shows the patterns of causality, a 1 standard deviation increase in Feeling Valued causes .47 of a standard deviation increase in Motivation Toward Family Activities.

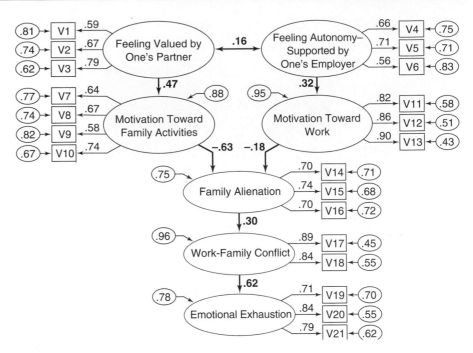

FIGURE 17–3   *Results of the hypothesized model. Source: Senecal, Vallerand, & Guay, 2001.*

Having laid out the model and figured the path coefficients, the authors then tested the fit of the correlations in their sample to the overall model: "The adequacy of the model was assessed by structural equation modeling. . ." (p. 181). In addition to looking at specific path coefficients, Senecal et al. considered the overall fit of their model, noting that all hypothesized paths had significant coefficients in the predicted direction and "the CFI = .94 and the NNFI = .93 [two fit indexes] were acceptable" (p. 182).

SOME LIMITATIONS OF CAUSAL MODELING

It is important to realize how little magic there is behind these wonderful methods. They still rely entirely on a researcher's deep thinking. All the predicted paths in a path analysis diagram can be significant and a structural equation model can have an excellent fit, and yet it is still quite possible that other patterns of causality could work equally well or better.

Alternatives could have arrows that go in the opposite direction or make different connections, or the pattern could include additional variables not in the original diagram. Any kind of causal modeling shows at best that the correlations in the sample are consistent with the theory. The same correlations could also be consistent with quite different theories. Ideally, a researcher tries out reasonable alternative theories and finds that the correlations in the sample do not fit them well. Nevertheless, there can always be alternative theories the researcher did not think of to try.

In addition, causal modeling and all of the other techniques we have considered so far rely basically on correlations. Thus, they are all subject to the cautions we emphasized in chapters 3 and 4. The most important caution is the one we just considered: Correlation does not demonstrate direction of causality. Further, these techniques take only linear relationships directly into account. Finally, results are distorted (usually toward smaller path coefficients) if there is a restriction in range.

So don't be bowled over by the mathematical sophistication of a technique such as latent variable modeling. It is useful—sometimes wonderfully useful—but if you haven't used random assignment to groups, the direction of cause and effect cannot be determined beyond a reasonable doubt. If the underlying relationships are curvilinear, or if other limitations apply, such as restriction in range, the more sophisticated procedures are generally even more likely to give misleading results than simple bivariate correlations.

HOW ARE YOU DOING?

1. What is the purpose of causal modeling?
2. (a) What is a path diagram? (b) What is a path? (c) What is a path coefficient? (d) In an ordinary path analysis, how do you evaluate whether there is a good fit of the model to the correlations in the sample?
3. (a) What is a fit index? (b) What is considered a good fit on most fit indexes? (c) What is considered a very good fit on the RMSEA?
4. (a) What is a latent variable? (b) What is its relation to measured variables? (c) What is the usual direction of causality between a latent variable and its associated measured variables? (d) Why?
5. (a) What is the meaning of a significance test of the overall fit in a structural equation model? (b) How is this different from an ordinary significance test?
6. What are two major limitations of structural equation modeling?

ANSWERS:

1. To test whether the correlations in a sample are consistent with a predicted pattern of cause and effect among those variables (and also to figure the size of the relations among the variables given the predicted pattern and the correlations).
2. (a) A drawing of the predicted causal relationships among variables, showing causality as arrows from cause to effect. (b) A predicted causal relation between two variables, shown as an arrow from the predicted cause to the predicted effect. (c) The size of the causal influence figured based on the correlations among the variables in the sample and assuming the predicted relations in the path diagram are correct. Assuming the pattern of the path diagram is correct, it tells you the fraction of a standard deviation change in the effect variable produced by a 1 standard deviation change in the causal variable. (d) You check whether the path coefficients are all in the predicted direction and significant.
3. (a) A number that tells you how well the predicted pattern of cause and effect in the path diagram is consistent with the correlations in the sample. (b) .90. (d) below .05.
4. (a) A variable that is not directly measured, but which stands for the true value of the concept the variable is about. (b) It is what they have in common. (c) From latent variable to measured variables. (d) Because the underlying latent variable is the cause of the observed, measured variables.
5. (a) The probability of getting the correlations in the sample if the predicted model shown in the path diagram is correct. (b) A significant result means there is a bad fit.
6. First, no matter how good the fit, you can never know if there might be some other model that would fit equally well. Second, it is based on correlations and thus has all their limitations (such as not giving conclusive support for a particular direction of causality, being based entirely on linear relationships and being distorted by restriction in range).

PROCEDURES THAT COMPARE GROUPS AND INDEPENDENT AND DEPENDENT VARIABLES

So far in this chapter, we have looked at statistical procedures about associations among variables, basically fancy elaborations of correlation and regression. Now we turn to procedures that focus on differences between group means, basically fancy elaborations of the analysis of variance (chapters 11, 12, and 13).

independent variable

In such procedures, there are two main kinds of variables. One is the kind that divides the groups from each other, such as experimental versus control group in a *t* test or the different groups in an analysis of variance (such as the chapter 11 and 12 criminal-record study example, which compared participants in the Criminal Record group, the Clean Record group, and the No Information group). A variable like this, especially when which group a person is in is based on the researcher having randomly assigned participants to conditions, is called an **independent variable**. In a two-way factorial analysis of variance, there are actually two independent variables—for example, mood (sad versus neutral) and stereotype (appropriate versus inappropriate) in the Lambert et al. (1997) study we considered in Chapter 13.

dependent variable

The other kind of variable in a study that compares groups is the variable that is measured—in the criminal record example, it was ratings of innocence; in the Lambert et al. study, it was ratings of how likely the participant would be to hire the person. A variable like this, which is measured and represents the effect of the experimental procedure, is called a **dependent variable**. It is dependent in the sense that any participant's score on this variable depends on what happens in the experiment.

Note that an independent variable in a *t* test or analysis of variance is like a predictor variable in regression, and a dependent variable in a *t* test or analysis of variance is like the criterion variable in regression. Often, in fact, when discussing regression results, even in formal research articles, researchers use the independent–dependent variable terminology instead of the predictor–criterion variable terminology. But it is rare for researchers doing a *t* test or analysis of variance to use the predictor–criterion variable terminology.

We did not need to introduce these terms (independent and dependent variables) before because the situations we considered were relatively straightforward. However, it would be difficult to understand the remaining procedures covered in this chapter without knowing about the difference between independent and dependent variables.

ANALYSIS OF COVARIANCE (ANCOVA)

analysis of covariance (ANCOVA)

One of the most widely used of the elaborations on the analysis of variance is the **analysis of covariance (ANCOVA).** In this procedure, you do an ordinary analysis of variance, but one which adjusts the dependent variable for the effect of unwanted additional variables. The analysis of covariance does for the analysis of variance what partial correlation does for ordinary correlation. Each of the variables controlled for (or "partialed out" or "held constant") is called a **covariate.** The rest of the results are interpreted like any other analysis of variance, with one main exception: When reporting results, instead of giving the means of each group, the researcher may give the **adjusted means**, the means of each group after adjusting (partialing out) the effect of the covariates.

covariate

adjusted means

Here is an example. Aron et al. (2000) had married couples come to their laboratory and participate in what they thought was an evaluation session in which they completed some questionnaires about the quality of their relationship, participated in a task together where they thought they were being observed for how they worked together during the task, and then completed some more questionnaires about their relationship. Actually, the first set of questionnaires was a pretest, the second set a posttest, and the task was experimentally manipulated so that some couples were randomly assigned to do a task together that was novel and physiologically arousing—they were tied together at the wrist and ankles and then had to push a foam cylinder back and forth across a 30 foot gym mat, including go over a 3 foot barrier in the middle, without using their hands or teeth, trying to beat a time limit. Other couples were randomly assigned to do a more mundane task—they simply went back and forth across the mat.

Based on a theoretical model, the researchers predicted that "shared participation in the novel-arousing activities, compared with shared participation in mundane activities, increases experienced relationship quality" (p. 279). They then went on to describe their statistical analysis and results:

> To test this hypothesis, we conducted an analysis of covariance (ANCOVA) comparing the two experimental groups on couple average posttest experienced relationship quality with couple average pretest relationship quality (and relationship length) as a covariate. . . . [The hypothesis] was clearly supported, $F(1, 24) = 6.07$, $p < .05$, partial r [a measure of effect size] = .45. The adjusted means on the posttest experienced relationship quality index . . were .30 for the novel-arousing-activity group and $-.35$ for the mundane-activity group. (pp. 279–280)

Notice that there were two covariates. First, the researchers wanted to look at change—so they compared posttest scores but adjusted them for pretest scores by making pretest scores a covariate. In addition, they wanted to be sure their results were not affected by differences in length of relationship, so they made length of relationship a second covariate. These are in fact the two main situations in which researchers use analysis of covariance. One is when they want to study change and they make the pretest measure a covariate. The other is when there are nuisance variables whose influence they want to hold constant.

MULTIVARIATE ANALYSIS OF VARIANCE (MANOVA) AND MULTIVARIATE ANALYSIS OF COVARIANCE (MANCOVA)

In all of the procedures discussed so far in this book, there is only one dependent variable. There may be two or more independent variables, as in the factorial analysis of variance. However, in all the situations we have considered, there has been only one dependent variable.

In this section we introduce **multivariate statistics**, which are procedures that can have more than one dependent variable. We will focus on the two most widely used multivariate procedures, multivariate versions of the analysis of variance and covariance.[2]

multivariate statistics

Multivariate analysis of variance (MANOVA) is an analysis of variance that can have more than one dependent variable. Usually, the dependent variables are different measures of approximately the same thing, such as three different political involvement scales or five different reading ability tests. Suppose you study three groups and measure each participant on four dependent variables. The MANOVA would give an overall F and significance level for the difference among the three groups, in terms of how much they differ on the combination of the four dependent variables. The overall F is figured differently from an ordinary analysis of variance. In fact, there are several slightly different ways of figuring it—but the most com-

Multivariate analysis of variance (MANOVA)

[2]There are also multivariate versions of correlation and regression in which there are more than one criterion variable, such as *canonical correlation*. But these are not widely used. Also, factor analysis and structural equation modeling, which are widely used, are technically considered multivariate procedures.

mon method is based on what is called *Wilk's lambda*, though you may also see other methods mentioned. However, it is still an *F* and it is interpreted in the same basic way—significance means you can reject the null hypothesis of no difference among groups in the population.

When you do find an overall significant difference among groups with MANOVA, this says that the groups differ on the combination of dependent variables. You then would want to know whether the groups differ on any or all of the dependent variables considered individually. Thus, you usually follow up a MANOVA with an ordinary analyses of variance for each of the dependent variables. These individual analyses of variance are called *univariate analyses of variance* (as opposed to the overall multivariate analyses), because each has only one dependent variable.

AN EXAMPLE

Phelps et al. (2001) compared Black university students from different cultures in terms of racial identity and related variables. They described their results as follows:

> . . . we conducted a one-way multivariate analysis of variance (MANOVA) with ethnic group (African, African American, West Indian/Caribbean) as the independent variable and the subscales of the CMI [Cultural Mistrust Inventory], MEIM [Multigroup Ethnic Identity Measure], and RIAS-B [Racial Identity Attitude Scale-B], Long Form, as the dependent variables. The Wilk's lambda indicated a statistically significant MANOVA, $F(20, 256) = 3.97$, $p < .001$. (p. 212)

Having identified an overall difference among groups, the researchers then wanted to sort out effects on specific variables. They explain: "Follow-up univariate analyses of variance (ANOVAs) were performed to determine which variables were statistically significant" (p. 212). For example, in one analysis, they report: "On the CMI subscales, African American students scored statistically higher . . . than did African and West Indian/Caribbean students, indicating more mistrust of Whites" (p. 212).

MULTIVARIATE ANALYSIS OF COVARIANCE

multivariate analysis of covariance (MANCOVA)

An analysis of covariance in which there is more than one dependent variable is called a **multivariate analysis of covariance (MANCOVA).** The difference between it and an ordinary analysis of covariance is just like the difference between a MANOVA and an ordinary analysis of variance. Also, you can think of a MANCOVA as a MANOVA with covariates (variables adjusted for).

OVERVIEW OF STATISTICAL TECHNIQUES

Table 17–8 lays out the various procedures considered in this chapter, along with the other parametric procedures covered throughout the book. Just to prove to yourself how much you have learned, you might cover the right-hand column and play "Name That Statistic."

HOW ARE YOU DOING?

1. In a *t* test or analysis of variance, (a) what is the independent variable, and (b) what is the dependent variable? (c) How do independent and dependent variables match up with criterion and predictor variables?
2. (a) What is an analysis of covariance? (b) How is it like partial correlation? (c) What is a covariate? (d) What are the two most common types of covariates?
3. How are multivariate statistics unlike all of the procedures covered previously in this book?

TABLE 17–8	Major Statistical Techniques			
Association or Difference	Number of Independent or Predictor Variables	Number of Dependent or Criterion Variables	Any Variables Controlled?	Name of Technique
Association	1	1	No	Bivariate correlation/regression
Association	Any number	1	No	Multiple regression (including hierarchical and stepwise regression)
Association	1	1	Yes	Partial correlation
Association	Many, not differentiated		No	Reliability coefficients, Factor analysis
Association	Many, with specified causal patterns			Path analysis, Structural equation modeling
Difference	1	1	No	One-way ANOVA, t test
Difference	Any number	1	No	factorial ANOVA
Difference	Any number	1	Yes	ANCOVA
Difference	Any number	Any number	No	MANOVA
Difference	Any number	Any number	Yes	MANCOVA

4. (a) What is multivariate analysis of variance, and how does it differ from an ordinary analysis of variance? (b) After finding a significant effect in a MANOVA, what is the usual next step? (c) What is multivariate analysis of covariance, and how does it differ from an ordinary analysis of covariance?
5. What method would you use if you had more than one independent variable, only one dependent variable, and one or more covariates?

ANSWERS:

1. (a) The variable that divides the groups. (b) The variable that is measured. (c) The independent variable is like the predictor variable; the dependent variable is like the criterion variable.
2. (a) An analysis of variance that controls (or adjusts for or partials out) one or more variables. (b) It finds results after controlling for another variable. (c) The variable that is partialed out (or controlled for or adjusted for). (d) Variables measured at pretest and nuisance variables that add unwanted variation to the analysis.
3. They can have more than one dependent variable.
4. (a) An analysis of variance with more than one dependent variable. (b) Carry out a series of univariate analyses of variance—that is, individual analyses of variance for each dependent variable. (c) An analysis of covariance with more than one dependent variable.
5. Analysis of covariance.

CONTROVERSY: SHOULD STATISTICS BE CONTROVERSIAL?

Most statistics books, this one included, teach you statistical methods in a fairly cut-and-dried way, almost as if imparting absolute truth. But we have also tried to mess up this tidy picture with our discussions of controversies. Usually, this is thought to confuse students. (Although, when you learned other fields of psychology, your understanding was built, we hope, from the presentation of controversy—this person's research demonstrated one thing, but this other person's study showed a flaw, while that one's student showed that this was an exception, and so forth.) So, in this last section on controversy, we are going to try to mess things up even more.

In Box 17–1, we describe the historical development of today's statistics out of a hybrid of two views, known as the Fisher and the Neyman-Pearson approaches.

BOX 17–1   The Forced Partnership of Fisher and Pearson

Let's take one final look at the history of the development of statistical methods in psychology, adding some tidbits of interest. We told you in Box 11–1 that Sir Ronald Fisher more or less invented the experimental method as it is now employed; that it arose from his work in agriculture (mostly on soil fertility, the weight of pigs, and the effect of manure on potato fields); that he was a difficult man to get along with; and that Fisher and another great British statistician, Karl Pearson, were particular enemies.

Well, Pearson had a son, Egon, who worked at his father's Galton Laboratory at University College, London. In 1925, the young Egon formed a lasting friendship with Jerzy Neyman, a youthful lecturer at the University of Warsaw who had just arrived at the Galton Laboratory. In the next years, the two worked very closely.

In 1933, Karl Pearson retired. Ironically, Fisher was given Pearson's old position as head of the department of eugenics, originally founded by Galton. And because of the feud between Fisher and the senior Pearson, a new department of statistics was created to smooth the retiring bird's feathers, to be headed by Pearson's son, Egon.

As hard as Pearson and his friend Neyman claim to have tried to avoid the continuation of the old feud between Sir Ronald and the senior Pearson, it was soon as bitter as ever. Pearson and Neyman actually were in many ways far more supportive of Fisher's ideas than of Karl Pearson's, but their extensions and elaborations of Fisher's approaches, intended to be friendly, infuriated the cranky Sir Ronald. (See, you don't want to change your major to history after all—keeping these names straight is at least as hard as learning statistics was!) Neyman immigrated to the United States when Hitler invaded Poland, starting the statistics program at the University of California, Berkeley, where he remained until his death in 1981.

He is especially remembered for his bringing David Blackwell, an African-American statistician, out of obscurity, because he had been unable to get a job due to his race. Neyman was also remembered for his afternoon department teas, ending with a toast to the "ladies," referring to the many women present, whose careers he also encouraged, leading to many prominent women statisticians.

Until Fisher died in 1962, Neyman was under constant attack from Fisher. What was at issue? To simplify a very complicated set of ideas, Fisher had rejected what is called Bayesian theory, a whole approach to statistics we touched on in Chapter 5, which holds the position that scientific research is conducted in order to adjust preexisting beliefs in the light of new evidence as it is collected. In disagreeing, Fisher held that inductive inference is carried out mainly by objectively disproving the null hypothesis, not by testing prior probabilities arrived at subjectively. Fisher was exceptionally dogmatic about his ideas, referring to his approach as "absolutely rigorous" and "perfectly rigorous." He called it the only case of "unequivocal inference." And he had a great mind. And he wrote a huge amount. He became very influential throughout the world.

Pearson and Neyman also rejected Bayesian theory, but they proposed the method of testing two opposing hypotheses rather than just the null hypothesis. As a result of this innovation, there would be two types of errors. Type I errors would be when the null hypothesis is rejected even though it is true (and they called its probability alpha, or the level of significance—does all this sound familiar?). Type II errors would be when the null hypothesis was not rejected even though it is false (and the probability of that error was beta—again familiar?). Which type of error you preferred to minimize depended on the impact of each on your purposes, as Neyman and Pearson were frequently thinking in terms of applied research. Fisher never talked about any hypothesis but the null and therefore never considered Type II errors.

Now you can see what happened: Statistics today is a hybrid of Fisher's ideas, with Pearson's and Neyman's added when they could no longer be ignored. The concept of testing the null hypothesis comes from Fisher, the only somewhat less influential concepts of Type II error, beta, power, and effect size, from his younger enemies.

It was a wedding none of them would have probably approved of, for both camps eventually came to see their approaches as fundamentally in opposition. Fisher compared Neyman and Pearson to the stereotype of the Soviets of his day in their determination to reduce science to technology "in the comprehensive organized effort of a five-year plan for the nation" and remarked sarcastically after Neyman gave a talk before the Royal Statistical Society in London that Neyman should have chosen a topic "on which he could speak with authority." Neyman, for his part, stated that Fisher's methods of testing were in a "mathematically specifiable sense worse than useless." Ah, how rational.

The current debate about the role of significance testing in psychology (see "Controversy" sections in Chapters 6, 7, and 8), while not quite so strident, does have some resonance of the old days. For example, two of the main disputants (Schmidt & Hunter, 1997) comment that "all of the objections" to arguments for their position "are logically deficient" (p. 38), that "each of these objections, although appearing plausible and even convincing to many researchers, is logically and intellectually bankrupt" (pp. 61–62). In an article published at about the same time, two of the main disputants from the opposite camp (Cortina & Dunlap, 1997) described the arguments of the other side as "built on faulty premises, misleading examples, and misunderstanding of certain critical concepts" (p. 170). Comments we have heard from both sides in less formal settings have been even less restrained.

As we have noted throughout these boxes, statistics is, for better and for worse, a product of human intellect and human passions operating together (ideally, for the sake of science, though the latter to a lesser extent). The results have not always been perfect, but they can be far more interesting than they might seem on the surface.

References for historical material: Peters (1987); Salsburg, 2001; Stigler (1986); Tankard (1984).

This wedding was supposed to end the feud as to which was the better method, but in fact, although most psychologists are content with this hybrid, others, such as Gigerenzer and his associates (Gigerenzer & Murray, 1987; Gigerenzer et al., 1989; Sedlmeier & Gigerenzer, 1989), are not at all content. Neither are Jacob Cohen (1990) and Robert Rosenthal (e.g., Rosnow & Rosenthal, 1989b), two psychologists who are very well known for their contributions to statistical techniques and whose work on topics such as power, effect size, the null hypothesis, meta-analysis, and other topics we have mentioned throughout the book.

Gigerenzer and Murray (1987) argue that the viewpoints of Fisher and of Pearson and Neyman—which to these early statisticians themselves were always fundamentally contradictory—have been misunderstood and misused as a result of being blended. The marriage was entirely one of convenience, with little thought given to long-term effects. Gigerenzer and Murray regard the hybrid as the result of so many of the first statistics textbooks having been written under the influence of the dogmatic and persuasive Sir Ronald Fisher (recall Box 11–1). But then, after World War II, the Pearson-Neyman view became known and had to be integrated without admitting that the original texts could have been wrong. (The desire was to present psychology as a science, having as its basis a unified, mechanical, flawless method of decision making.)

The result of all of this, Gigerenzer and Murray claim, is a neglect of controversy and of alternative approaches, and statistics textbooks "filled with conceptual confusion, ambiguity, and errors" (p. 23). Further, they argue that these dominant statistical methods, which were originally only tools, are now shaping the way psychologists view human cognition and perception itself (recall boxes 12–1 and 13–1).

More generally, the current hot debates about significance tests we considered in chapters 6, 7, and 8 are part of this larger trend of reopening the long-buried controversies.

As a last word on all this, we must say that the majority of psychologists and statisticians are fairly comfortable with the methods found in today's textbooks. Time and careful thinking will tell whether this majority ought to be so complacent. But no one is going to figure it out for us. We will have to do it together. Therefore, we truly hope that once you master the methods in this book, you will have the confidence to look further and not be content to continue applying these methods in a mindless, rote way 20 years from now. If you become a psychologist who either reads research or does it, then whatever else your interests, you must also be a good citizen within the larger discipline. Keep up at least a little with developments in methods of data analysis, accepting and even demanding change when it is warranted. After all, if our tools become dated, what hope is there for our findings?

HOW TO READ RESULTS USING UNFAMILIAR STATISTICAL TECHNIQUES

Based on this chapter and what you have learned throughout this book, you should be well prepared to read and understand, at least in a general way, the results in most psychology research articles. However, you will still now and then come up against new techniques (and sometimes unfamiliar names for old techniques). This happens even to well-seasoned researchers. So what do you do when you run into something you have never heard of before?

First, don't panic. Usually, you can figure out the basic idea. Almost always there will be a p level, and it should be clear just what pattern of results is being considered significant or not. In addition, there will usually be some indication of the degree of association or the size of the difference. If the statistic is about the association among some variables, it is probably stronger as the result gets closer to 1 and weaker as the result gets closer to 0. You should not expect to understand every word in a situation like this, but do try to grasp as much as you can about the meaning of the result.

Suppose you really can't figure out anything about a statistical technique used in a research article. In that situation, you can try to look up the procedure in a statistics book. Intermediate and advanced textbooks are sometimes a good bet, but we have to warn you that trying to make sense of an intermediate or advanced statistics text on your own can be difficult. Many such texts are heavily mathematically oriented. Even a quite accessible textbook will use its own set of symbols. Thus, it can be hard to make sense of a description of a particular method without having read the whole book. Perhaps a better solution in this situation is to ask for help from a professor or graduate student. If you know the basics as you have learned them in this book, you should be able to understand the essentials of their explanations.

If you are often coming upon statistics you don't understand, the best solution is to take more statistics courses. Usually, the next course after this one would be an intermediate course that focuses mainly on analysis of variance and may go into multiple regression to some extent. You will find such a course particularly useful if you are planning to go to graduate school in psychology, where statistics will be a crucial tool in all the research you do. It will help prepare you for graduate school.

Also, a strong performance in such a course is extremely impressive to those evaluating applications to the top graduate programs. (It is also our experience that you are especially likely to enjoy the other students you meet in such a course. Those who take the intermediate statistics course in psychology are not all whizzes at statistics, but they are almost always highly motivated, bright students who will share your goals.) In fact, some people find statistics so fascinating that they choose to make a career of it. You might too!

More generally, new statistical methods are being invented constantly. Psychologists all encounter unfamiliar numbers and symbols in the research articles they read. They puzzle them out, and so will you. We say that with confidence because you have arrived, safe and knowledgeable, at the back pages of this book. You have mastered a thorough introduction to a complex topic. That should give you complete confidence that, with a little time and attention, you can understand anything further in statistics. Congratulations on your accomplishment.

SUMMARY

1. In hierarchical multiple regression, predictor variables are included in the prediction rule in a planned, sequential fashion. This allows you to determine the contribution of each successive variable over and above those already included. Stepwise multiple regression is an exploratory procedure in which potential predictor variables are searched in order to find the best predictor; then the remaining variables are searched for the predictor that, in combination with the first, produces the best prediction. This process continues until adding the best remaining variable does not provide a significant improvement.

2. Partial correlation is the correlation between two variables while holding one or more other variables constant.

3. Reliability coefficients tell you how much scores on a test are internally consistent (usually with Cronbach's alpha), consistent over time (test-retest reliability), or give comparable scores from different raters (interrater reliability).

4. Factor analysis identifies groupings of variables, called factors, that correlate maximally with each other and minimally with other variables. A factor loading is the correlation of a variable with a factor.

5. Causal analysis examines whether the correlations in a sample are consistent with a systematic, hypothesized pattern of causal relationships among them. Path analysis describes these relationships with arrows, each pointing from cause to effect, and each with a path coefficient indicating the influence of the theorized causal variable on the theorized effect variable. Structural equation modeling is an advanced version of path analysis that includes latent, unmeasured variables (each of which represents the common elements of several measured variables). It also provides measures of the overall fit of the hypothesized causal pattern to the correlations in the sample.

6. In a t test, analysis of variance, and other procedures that compare groups, variables that divide the groups and are considered the cause are called independent variables; variables that are measured and considered the effect are called dependent variables.

7. The analysis of covariance (ANCOVA) is an analysis of variance that controls for one or more variables (called covariates). The multivariate analysis of variance (MANOVA) is an analysis of variance that can have more than one de-

pendent variable. The multivariate analysis of covariance (MANCOVA) is an analysis of covariance that can have more than one dependent variable.

8. In recent years psychologists have begun to reexamine the basics of the statistics they use, opening up the possibility of controversy about what had been in the past often taken as incontrovertible.

9. It is often possible to get the main idea of an unfamiliar statistical procedure by keeping in mind that it probably tells you about association among variables or differences among groups, that p values tell you about the significance of that association or difference, and that you will probably be given some numbers from which you can get a sense of the degree of association or amount of difference.

KEY TERMS

adjusted means (p. 616)
adjusting for (p. 605)
analysis of covariance (ANCOVA) (p. 616)
controlling for (p. 605)
covariate (p. 616)
Cronbach's alpha (α) (p. 607)
dependent variable (p. 616)
factor (p. 608)
factor analysis (p. 608)
factor loading (p. 608)
fit index (p. 612)
hierarchical multiple regression (p. 600)
holding constant (p. 605)

independent variable (p. 616)
interrater reliability (p. 607)
latent variable (p. 612)
multivariate analysis of covariance (MANCOVA) (p. 608)
multivariate analysis of variance (MANOVA) (p. 617)
multivariate statistics (p. 617)
partial correlation (p. 605)
partial correlation coefficient (p. 605)

partialing out (p. 605)
path (p. 611)
path analysis (p. 611)
path coefficient (p. 611)
reliability (p. 607)
RMSEA (p. 612)
split-half reliability (p. 607)
stepwise multiple regression (p. 602)
structural equation modeling (p. 612)
test-retest reliability (p. 607)

PRACTICE PROBLEMS

For the problems below that ask you to explain results, you need to explain only the general meaning of the results, using only the same level of detail as used when the procedures were described in the chapter. You do not need to describe the logic of the statistical procedures covered here in the way that you have been doing in previous chapters.

All studies for which we do not give an actual citation are fictional.

Answers to most Set I problems are given at the back of the book.

SET I

1. Part of a study conducted by Lindzey et al. (1997) examined how well mutuality (balance) in father–child interaction predicted social competence in preschool children. In this study, each child and the child's father were observed interacting in a standardized situation. The interactions were rated in ways that gave measures of who initiates play activities and the mutuality of complying with each other's initiation of play activities.

   The researchers also had the children's teachers rate each child's social competence. The researchers found a clear correlation between father–child mutuality and the teacher's social-competence rating for the child. However, the researchers were concerned that the measure of mutuality might be mixed up with the amount that children and fathers each initiated individually.

> We therefore conducted a series of hierarchical regression analyses to examine whether father–child mutual compliance . . . made unique contributions to the prediction of children's social competence after taking account of each individual's behavior. . . . Father initiation rate and child initiation rate were entered first and accounted for 3 percent ($p = .57$) of the variance. Father–child mutual compliance was entered second and accounted for an additional, significant 18 percent ($p = .01$) of the variance in teacher-rated social competence. (pp. 532–533)

Explain this method and result to a person who is familiar in a general way with ordinary multiple regression but has never heard of hierarchical multiple regression.

2. Mooney et al. (1991) were interested in what predicts women's adjustment to college. Thus, they studied 82 women who were in the fourth week of their first semester at college. The women in the study were all living away from home. The predictor variables were distance from home (in miles), perceived distance from home (a scale from *just right* to *too far*), a self-esteem scale, and an "academic locus of control" scale that measures how much a person feels in control over being successful at school. One purpose of the study was to find out whether all of these variables made their own unique contributions to predicting college adjustment. And if not all of them, which ones? The authors describe the procedure they used as follows:

> For this analysis, a stepwise procedure was employed. . . . Three predictors were retained: academic locus of control, perceived distance from home, and self-esteem. . . . With these variables in the equation, 59% of the variance in the dependent variable was accounted for ($R = .77$, $R^2 = .59$ . . .). The standardized beta coefficients [of the regression equation including these three predictor variables] indicated that academic locus of control was weighted the most, followed by self-esteem and perceived distance. . . . (p. 447)

Explain this method and result to a person who is familiar in a general way with ordinary multiple regression but is not familiar with stepwise multiple regression.

3. Zimmer-Gembeck et al. (2001) studied dating practices in a sample of 16 year olds in Minneapolis. As part of their study they examined the relation of dating involvement, experience, and quality with various aspects of self-concept and self-worth (that is, how positively the 16 year olds rated themselves on such things as scholastic competence, social acceptance, etc.). However, the researchers were concerned that the correlations among these variables would be inappropriately influenced by differences in appearance of physical maturity (how old the person looks). Thus, their results, shown in Table 17–9, provide correlations "controlling for appearance of physical maturity" (p. 327).

Explain this method and the pattern of a few example results to a person who is familiar with correlation and multiple regression, but is unfamiliar with partial correlation.

4. Boyd and Gullone (1997) studied anxiety and depression in a sample of 783 adolescents attending schools in and around Melbourne, Australia. To measure anxiety, they used the Revised Children's Manifest Anxiety Scale (RCMAS). In discussing the measure in their methods section, they note the following: "Alpha coefficient reliability estimates of internal consistency for the RCMAS range from .42 to .87" (p. 192). Explain these results to someone who is famil-

TABLE 17–9   Partial correlations (controlling for appearance of physical maturity) of dating and self-concept at age 16

Self-concept/self-worth	Overinvolvement with dating	Level of dating experience	Quality of romantic relationship
Scholastic competence	−0.10	0.08	−0.03
Social acceptance	0.04	0.24**	0.29**
Physical appearance	0.06	0.24**	0.11
Job competence	−0.12	0.12	0.07
Romantic appeal	0.10	0.35***	0.36***
Behavioral conduct	−0.33***	−0.17*	−0.04
Close friendahip	0.00	0.09	0.09
Global self-worth	−0.11	0.05	0.18*

N ranged from 125 (when examining quality of romantic relationships) to 166.
*$p < 0.05$, **$p < 0.01$, ***$p < 0.001$
From Zimmer-Gimbeck, Siebenbrumer, & Collins, 2001.

iar with correlation but is unfamiliar with reliability or the statistics associated with it.

5. Fawzi et al. (1997) studied whether the usual way of thinking about posttraumatic stress disorder (PTSD), as described in the fourth edition of the standard *Diagnostic and Statistical Manual of Mental Disorders* (DSM-IV), applies to Vietnamese refugees in the United States. As part of their study, 74 refugees were interviewed (in their native language) regarding various PTSD symptoms and the traumatic events they had experienced, such as torture. As expected, the number of PTSD symptoms correlated with the number of traumatic events. In a further analysis of the pattern of symptoms (which symptoms go together with which), they conducted a factor analysis that resulted in four factors.

> In correspondence with the DSM-IV, the first three factors represented dimensions of arousal, avoidance, and reexperiencing, respectively (see Table [17–10]). However, in contrast to the DSM-IV defined subcategories where avoidance represents one dimension of symptomatology, avoidance appeared to be separated into two factors in this sample. The second factor reflected avoidance associated with general withdrawal or numbing of responsiveness, with high factor loadings for "unable to feel emotions" and "less interest in daily activities." The fourth factor reflected avoidance of stimuli related to the traumatic event(s). (p. 104)

Explain these results to a person who is familiar with correlation but is unfamiliar with factor analysis.

6. MacKinnon-Lewis and her colleagues (1997) were interested in predictors of social acceptance by peers of 8–10-year-old boys. The main predictors they used were the child's rating of parental acceptance and rejection, peers' ratings of acceptance and aggression, and conflict with siblings as observed in a laboratory interaction. They tried several different possible causal models, and concluded that the best was what they called Model 1.

> The standardized path coefficients of Model 1 are presented in Figure [17–4], which shows that siblings whose mothers were perceived and observed to be more rejecting were observed and reported to be more aggressive with one another than were siblings whose mothers were less rejecting. Moreover, boys who experienced more aggressive sibling interactions were more likely to be nominated by their peers as being aggressive and were less accepted by their peers. Although fathering

TABLE 17–10 Factor Loadings for Principal Components Analysis of PTSD DSM-IV Symptoms for 74 Vietnamese Refugees

Symptom Dimension	Factor Loading
Arousal	
Recurrent nightmares	.79
Difficulty concentrating	.78
Feeling irritable/outburst of anger	.77
Inability to remember parts of the most traumatic events	.74
Trouble sleeping	.73
Avoiding activities that remind you of traumatic events	.70
Feeling jumpy, easily startled	.67
% Variance explained	44%
Avoidance/withdrawal	
Unable to feel emotions	.79
Less interest in daily activities	.70
Feeling detached or withdrawn	.65
Feeling jumpy, easily startled	.51
Feeling as if you don't have a future	.51
% Variance explained	24%
Reexperiencing	
Recurrent thoughts/memories of most terrifying events	.83
Feeling as though the event is happening again	.83
Sudden emotional or physical reaction when reminded of most traumatic events	.57
% Variance explained	22%
Avoidance of stimuli related to trauma event(s)	
Avoiding thoughts or feelings associated with traumatic events	.71
% Variance explained	11%

Note: Data from Fawzi, M. C. S., et al. (1997), tab. 1. The validity of posttraumatic stress disorder among Vietnamese refugees. *Journal of Traumatic Stress,* 10, 105. Copyright, 1997, by the International Society for Traumatic Stress Studies. Reprinted with permission.

> failed to evince a direct influence on sibling aggression, an indirect effect was evidence as a result of the fact that less accepting fathering was related to more rejecting mothering. (p. 1027)

Explain the method they used, illustrating it with some sample results, to a person who is familiar with multiple regression and partial correlation in a general way but not with path analysis.

7. Aron et al. (1998) studied experiences of unreciprocated love, loving someone who does not love you. One of their predictions focused on the intensity of the experience (how much you think about it, how much it disrupts your life). The researchers hypothesized that intensity would be predicted by desirability (how much the lover thought a relationship with the beloved would be wonderful), probability (how much the beloved had led the lover to believe a relationship might develop), and desirability of the state (how much the lover thought it was desirable to be in love, even though it was not reciprocated). Aron et al. carried out a structural equation model analysis testing this model. The results are shown in Figure 17–5 (reproduced from their Figure 1).

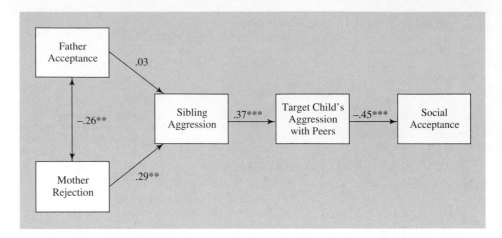

FIGURE 17–4   *Path model of associations among parenting variables, sibling aggression, peer aggression, and social acceptance. Standardized path coefficients are given. **p < .01. ***p < .001.*
[From MacKinnon-Lewis, C., Starnes, R., Volling, B., & Johnson, S. (1997), fig. 1. Perceptions of parenting as predictors of boys' sibling and peer relations. Developmental Psychology, *33, 1024–1031. Copyright, 1997, by the American Psychological Association. Reprinted with permission.]*

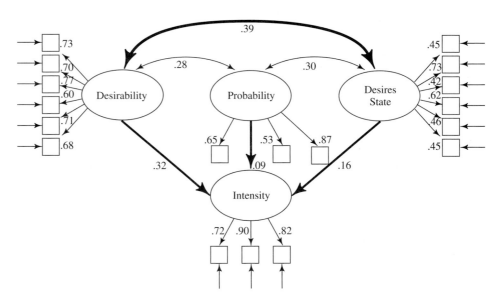

FIGURE 17–5   *Latent variable model based on a three-factor framework of motivation in unreciprocated love that was fitted to data for 743 participants who reported experiencing unreciprocated love.*
NOTE: Bentler-Bonnett normed fixed index (NFI) = .90; non-normed fit index (NNFI) = .92; average standardized residuals = .04; c2 (129) = 430.88; p < .01. All parameter estimates shown were significantly different from 0, at least at the .05 level. The key result is that each of the major causal paths to intensity, from desirability, probability, and desirability of the state, were positive and significant, confirming the hypothesis that each of these variables independently predicts intensity. (Figure 1 from "Motivations for Unreciprocated Love" by Aron and Aron, Personality and Social Psychology Bulletin, *Vol. 24 No. 8, August, 1998, p. 792.)*

(a) Explain the pattern of results. (b) Using this diagram as an example, explain the general principles of interpreting a path diagram (including the limitations) to a person who understands multiple regression in a general way but who is unfamiliar with path diagrams or structural equation modeling.

8. In each of the following studies, which variable is the independent variable and which is the dependent variable?

(a) A study comparing a group given two different kinds of medication on their level of anxiety.

(b) A study looking at heart rate change while watching one of three kinds of movies (horror movie, love story, or comedy).

(c) A study of number of touches between two infants playing in the same room, comparing when their mothers are present versus when their mothers are not present.

9. Roeser et al. (2001) conducted a cross-cultural study of self-esteem comparing adolescents from the United States and the Netherlands. In their article they had a section labeled "Covariates" in which they note that "A measure of social desirability was included in each analysis because prior research has shown that self-report measures of mental health often elicit socially desirable response patterns." (p. 120). (That is, social desirability was a kind of nuisance variable they were concerned would disturb their pattern of results.) They then reported a series of 2 (country) X 2 (gender) analyses of covariance. Here is one of their results: "ANCOVA results for the CBCL [a measure of emotional/behavioral problems] . . . revealed only one significant effect: After covarying out the effect of social desirability . . . , American adolescents reported significantly more externalizing problems than their Dutch peers, $F(1, 136) = 9.80$, $p \propto .01$, Eta squared = .07" (p. 123). Explain what is being done, using this result as an example, to someone who is familiar with ordinary analysis of variance and with partial correlation, but who is not familiar with the analysis of covariance.

10. Gire (1997) studied the preferred methods of resolving conflicts, comparing people in individualistic versus collectivistic cultures. Participants were 90 Nigerians (Nigeria was considered an example of a relatively collectivist society) and 95 Canadians (Canada was considered an example of a relatively individualistic society). All participants answered questions about how much they preferred each of five methods of resolving conflicts. Half the participants in each country answered the questions regarding an interpersonal conflict (a conflict between two neighbors) and half regarding an intergroup conflict (between two groups of neighbors). This created a 2 (culture) X 2 (interpersonal vs. intergroup conflict) factorial design, with five measures of conflict resolution preferences.

> These data were analyzed by using the multivariate analysis of variance (MANOVA) procedure. The 2-way MANOVA yielded a significant main effect of culture $F(5, 173) = 6.37$, $p < .001$. An examination of the univariate analyses and the means suggests that Nigerians preferred negotiation to a greater extent than Canadians, while the reverse was the case on arbitration, as predicted. There was also a significant culture by type of conflict interaction, $F(5, 173) = 3.84$, $p < .002$. The univariate analyses and the means, presented in Table [17–11], reveal that significant differences occurred on three procedures—threats, acceptance of the situation, and arbitration. (p. 41)

Explain these results to someone who understands factorial analysis of variance but is not familiar with multivariate analysis of variance.

TABLE 17–11	Method Preferences as a Function of Culture and Type of Conflict			
	Nigerians		Canadians	
Method	IP	IG	IP	IG
Threats*	2.09	1.50	1.35	1.61
Accept the situation*	2.72	3.16	3.43	2.71
Negotiation	6.07	6.11	5.56	5.64
Mediation	4.70	4.77	4.87	5.13
Arbitration*	3.05	4.90	5.20	5.42

Note: One asterisk (*) indicates that the means of the culture by type of conflict interaction on a given method was significant at $p < .05$ level. The larger the number, the higher the preference for the method. IP = Interpersonal Conflict; IG = Intergroup Conflict.

Data from Gire, J. T. (1997), tab. 1. The varying effect of individualism-collectivism on reference for methods of conflict resolution. *Canadian Journal of Behavioural Science, 29,* 38–43. Copyright, 1997, by the Canadian Psychological Association. Reprinted with permission.

11. For each of the following studies, what would be the most appropriate statistical technique?
   (a) A study in which the researcher has a complex theory of the pattern of cause and effect among several variables.
   (b) A study of the association between two variables.
   (c) A study of whether a questionnaire scale is consistent internally (that is, that the items correlate with each other) and consistent over time in giving the same result.
   (d) A 3 X 2 factorial design with three dependent measures.
   (e) A study in which seven variables have been measured that are thought to predict a particular criterion variable, and the researcher wants to determine which variables contribute significantly to the prediction (but has no theory about which ones might be the most likely).
   (f) A study in which a researcher measures 16 variables and wants to explore whether there are any simpler groupings of variables underlying these 16.
   (g) A study in which an experimental group and a control group are being compared on a single dependent variable.
   (h) A study comparing five groups of individuals on a single dependent variable.
   (i) A study of the effect of several predictor variables on a single criterion variable, in which the researcher has a specific theory about their relative importance and wants to check whether each successive additional predictor adds anything to what the preceding variables predict.

SET II

12. MacDonald and her colleagues (1997) studied the relation of various factors to war veterans' symptoms of posttraumatic stress disorder (PTSD). These psychologists recruited a community sample of 756 Vietnam War veterans in New Zealand, including 161 Maori individuals (the Maori are the indigenous Polynesian people of New Zealand). Table 17–12 shows the results of their hierarchical regression analysis. Explain the pattern of results and the method used to a person who is familiar in a general way with ordinary multiple regression but is unfamiliar with hierarchical multiple regression.

TABLE 17–12 Regression Coefficients, R_2 and R_2 Change Values for Combat Exposure, Vietnam Experience Variables, and Race Prediciting to PTSD

Predictor Variable	Standardized beta		
	Step 1	Step 2	Step 3
Combat exposure	.266**	.300**	.297**
Vietnam military experience			
Length Vietnam service		−.035	−.036
Rank		−.316**	−.314**
Combat role		.153*	.154*
Military specialization 1[a]		.015	.017
Military specialization 2[a]		.044	.044
Race[b]			−.024
R^2	.070***	.171**	.171**
R^2 change		.100*	.001

*p < .01; **p < .001.
[a]Dummy variables: military specialization 1 (infantry/non-infantry); military specialization 2 (artillery/nonartillery).
[b]Dichotomous variable (Maori/non-Maori).
Data from MacDonald, C., Chamberlain, K., & Long, N. (1997), tab. 2. Race, combat, and PTSD in a community sample of New Zealand Vietnam War veterans. *Journal of Traumatic Stress, 10,* 123. Copyright, 1997, by the International Society for Traumatic Stress Studies. Reprinted with permission.

13. Hermann and her colleagues (1997) conducted a study of children undergoing biofeedback treatment for migraine headaches. The purpose of the study was to identify variables that predict success of this kind of treatment, so the researchers measured headache activity (HA) at the end of the 8-week treatment program. Headache activity was a summary variable based on such factors as frequency and intensity of headaches. They also measured a number of predictor variables, including HA at "prebaseline" (before treatment began); behavior problems measured on the Child Behavior Checklist (CBCL), including internalizing and externalizing behavior; psychosomatic distress; age; and family variables as measured by the Family Environment Scale (FES), including the Family Relations Index, organization, and control. They reported their results as follows:

> Using hierarchical multiple regression, child characteristics (Model 1) and family environment (Model 2) were evaluated independently as predictors of treatment outcome. To control for baseline differences, HA activity during prebaseline was entered first. The variables reflecting child characteristics and aspects of family functioning, respectively, were entered as a set in Step 2. . . . As summarized in Table [17–13], Model 1 revealed externalizing behavior tendencies, psychosomatic distress, and age as significant predictors accounting for 39% of treatment success. By contrast, the quality of family relationships, control, and organization (Model 2) were not found to exert a significant influence on treatment outcome. There was no evidence for a significant relationship between prebaseline activity and treatment success. . . . (pp. 613–614)

Note that the researchers carried out *two* different hierarchical regressions, one which they called Model 1 and one which they called Model 2.

TABLE 17–13 Prediction of Treatment Outcome Using Hierarchical Multiple Regression

Model and Step	Total R^2	dfs	F	β	$R^2\Delta$	$F\Delta$
Model 1	.39	5, 26	3.3*			
Step 1. HA activity prebaseline				−0.04	.02	0.7*
Step 2. CBCL: internalizing behavior				−0.27	.37	3.9*
CBCL: externalizing behavior				0.57*		
Psychosomatic distress				0.37*		
Age				−0.43*		
Model 2	.03	4, 27	0.2			
Step 1. HA activity prebaseline				−0.18	.02	0.7*
Step 2. FES: Family Relationship Index				−0.04	.01	0.06
FES: organization				−0.06		
FES: control				−0.05		

Note: HA = headache; CBCL = Child Behavior Checklist; FES = Family Environment Scale.
*$p < .05$.
Data from Hermann, C., Blanchard, E. B., & Flor, H. (1997), tab. 5. Biofeedback treatment for pediatric migraine: Prediction of treatment outcome. *Journal of Consulting and Clinical Psychology, 65,* 611–616. Copyright, 1997, by the American Psychological Association. Reprinted with permission.

Explain the pattern of results and the method used to a person who is familiar in a general way with ordinary multiple regression but is unfamiliar with hierarchical multiple regression.

14. In another part of the same study about the predictors of the effectiveness of a biofeedback treatment program for children with migraine headaches, in addition to the hierarchical regressions, Hermann et al. also conducted a stepwise regression. They report it as follows:

> For exploratory purposes, a stepwise regression . . . was computed, allowing all predictor variables, with the exception of prebaseline HA activity, to compete directly with each other. Consistent with Model 1, age (β = 0.38), and psychosomatic distress (β = 0.39) emerged as significant outcome predictors, accounting for 35% of treatment outcome, $F(3, 28) = 4.9$, $p < .01$. (p. 614)

Explain the results and the method used to a person who is familiar in a general way with ordinary multiple regression but is not familiar with stepwise regression.

15. Frank and her colleagues (1997) studied adolescents' depressive concerns and their relation with their parents. These researchers focused on two aspects of depressive concerns, a self-critical preoccupation and an interpersonal preoccupation. They also focused on two aspects of what they called "separation-individuation conflict" with parents, how much the adolescents perceived their parents as constraining them (exerting strong control over their behaviors) and how insecure the adolescents felt about their parents. Frank et al. reported their analysis and results as follows:

> We then correlated the mother and father versions of the Perceived Constraint and Insecurity scales with scores for self-critical and interpersonal concerns. Bivariate and partial correlational analyses are summarized in Table [17–14]. Partial analyses controlled for one aspect of separation-individuation conflict . . . and each type of depressive concern.

Explain this method and illustrate your answer by focusing on some example results to a person who is familiar with correlation and, in a general way, with ordinary multiple regression but is unfamiliar with partial correlation.

TABLE 17–14	Bivariate and Partial Correlations Showing Relations Between the Constraint and Insecurity Scales and Self-Critical and Interpersonal Preoccupations

	Bivariate r		Partial r	
Scale	Interpersonal	Self-Critical	Interpersonal	Self-critical
Constraint				
Fathers	.12	.23***	.00	.18**
Mothers	.08	.23***	−.12*	.14**
Insecurity				
Fathers	.24***	.13	.20**	.02
Mothers	.33***	.12*	.29***	−.07

Note: Partial correlation analyses assessing relations between constraint (or insecurity) and depressive concerns control for insecurity (or constraint) as well as adolescent depression.
*$p < .05$. **$p < .01$. ***$p < .001$.
Data from Frank, S. J., Poorman, M. O., & Van Egeren, L. A. (1997), tab. 5. Perceived relationships with parents among adolescent inpatients with depressive preoccupations and depressed mood. *Journal of Clinical Child Psychology, 26*, 205–215. Copyright © 1997 by Lawrence Erlbaum Associates, Inc. Reprinted by permission.

16. Schmader et al. (2001), as part of a study of students' beliefs about ethnic injustice in a university setting, describe one of their key measures as follows: "Beliefs about systemic ethnic injustice were assessed with four items ($\alpha = .69$)" (p. 101). (Here is an example item: "Differences in status between ethnic groups are the result of injustice" p. 101.) Explain the meaning of "$\alpha = .69$" to someone familiar with correlation but not with reliability or Cronbach's alpha.

17. Crick et al. (1997) developed a teachers' rating measure of "relational aggression" in preschoolers. Ordinary, overt aggression harms others directly, but "relational aggression harms others through damage to their peer relationships (e.g., using social exclusion or rumor spreading as a form of retaliation)" (p. 579). As part of this study, they first administered a 23-item teacher rating scale of preschoolers' social behavior. They described the key analysis of this measure as follows:

> A principal components factor analysis . . . was first conducted to assess whether . . . relational aggression would emerge as a separate factor independent of overt aggression. The analysis yielded the four predicted factors, relational aggression, overt aggression, prosocial behavior, and depressed affect. (p. 582)

Table 17–15 shows the factor loadings. Explain their results to a person who is familiar with correlation but is unfamiliar with factor analysis.

18. Kwan and her colleagues (1997) predicted that the relation of self-esteem and social harmony to life satisfaction would be different in different cultures. In more communal cultures, such as many Asian cultures, social harmony would matter more. However, in more individualistic cultures, such as most North American and European cultures, self-esteem would matter more. As part of the focus on cultural differences, the researchers also measured independent self-construal (how much a person emphasizes personal development and achievement) and interdependent self-construal (how much a person emphasizes getting along and fitting in with others). The participants in the study were 389 college students from the United States and Hong Kong. Figure 17–6 shows their basic results. Note that Kwan et al. give two path coefficients for

TABLE 17–15 Factor Loadings for the Teacher Measure of Social Behavior (PSBS–T)

Item	Relational Aggression	Overt Aggression	Prosocial Behavior	Depressed Affect
Tells a peer that he or she won't play with that peer or be that peer's friend unless he or she does what this child asks	.84			
Tells others not to play with or be a peer's friend	.83			
When mad at a peer, this child keeps that peer from being in the play group	.81			
Tells a peer that they won't be invited to their birthday party unless he or she does what the child wants	.88			
Tries to get others to dislike a peer	.89			
Verbally threatens to keep a peer out of the play group if the peer doesn't do what the child asks	.85			
Kicks or hits others		.81		
Verbally threatens to hit or beat up other children		.75		
Ruins other peer's things when he or she is upset		.82		
Pushes or shoves other children		.72		
Hurts other children by pinching them		.83		
Verbally threatens to physically harm a peer in order to get what they want		.81		
Is good at sharing and taking turns			.76	
Is helpful to peers			.83	
Is kind to peers			.62	
Says or does nice things for other kids			.75	
Doesn't have much fun				.90
Looks sad				.87
Doesn't smile much				.82

Note: All cross-loadings were less than .40. PSBS–T = Preschool Social Behavior Scale—Teacher Form.
Data from Crick, N. R., Casas, J. F., & Mosher, M. (1997), tab. 1. Relational and overt aggression in preschool. *Developmental Psychology, 33,* 579–588. Copyright, 1997, by the American Psychological Association. Reprinted with permission.

each path–the ones not in parentheses are for the Hong Kong sample; those in parentheses are for the U.S. sample.

(a) Explain the pattern of results. (b) Using this diagram as an example, explain the general principles of interpreting a path diagram (including the limitations) to a person who understands multiple regression in a general way but is unfamiliar with path diagrams or structural equation modeling.

19. DeGarmo and Forgatch (1997) studied the social support divorced mothers received from their closest confidant. The researchers measured a number of variables and then examined the predicted relationships among the variables using structural equation modeling. Figure 17–7 shows the results.

(a) Explain the pattern of results. (b) Using this diagram as an example, explain the general principles of interpreting a path diagram (including the limitations) to a person who understands multiple regression in a general way but is unfamiliar with path diagrams or structural equation modeling.

20. In each of the following studies, indicate which variable is the independent variable and which is the dependent variable:

(a) A study of speed of performance on a complex task, in which one group does the task at night and the other in the morning.

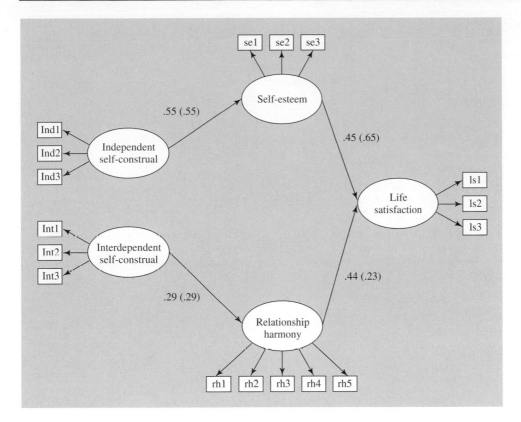

FIGURE 17–6 *The final Self-Construal Scale model.* N = *194 for the Hong Kong sample;* N = *184 for the U.S. sample. Ellipses represent latent constructs, boxes represent indicators, arrows pointing from latent constructs to indicators depict factor loadings, and arrows relating latent constructs represent path coefficients. Standardized path coefficients are shown; factor loadings and measurement errors are omitted for clarity. Numbers inside parentheses are coefficients for the U.S. sample; numbers outside parentheses are coefficients for the Hong Kong sample. All these coefficients were significant at* p < *.05 or less. [From Kwan, V. S., M. H. Bond, & T. M. Singelis, (1997), fig. 1. Pancultural explanations for life satisfaction: Adding relationship harmony to self-esteem.* Journal of Personality and Social Psychology, 73, *1038–1051. Copyright, 1997, by the American Psychological Association. Reprinted with permission.]*

   (b) A study comparing college women and men on their attitudes towards psychotherapy.

   (c) A study of voting preferences of people from three different regions of Canada.

21. Thompson et al. (2001) conducted a study of the "Mozart effect"—that listening to music written by Mozart improves performance on tasks involving spatial abilities. In their initial analysis, the researchers found that participants did better on a paper folding task after listening to a Mozart sonata than after an equivalent period of silence or after listening to a piece by another classical composer (an Albioni adagio). However, they then repeated their analyses, but this time

> . . . a series of analyses of covariance . . . tested whether the Mozart effect would remain in evidence when individual differences in enjoyment, arousal, and mood were statistically controlled. For each analysis . . . the covariate represented the scores on one of [these] measures. Although the Mozart effect remained significant

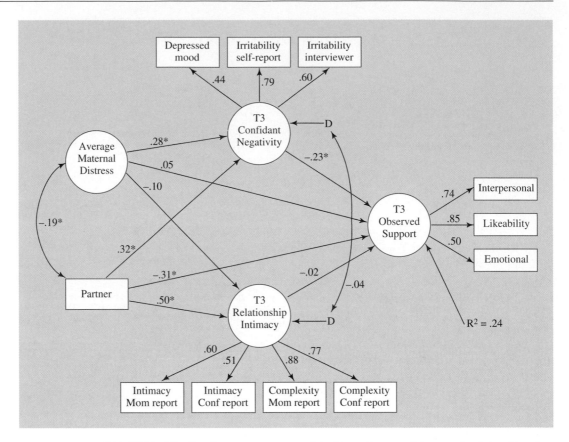

FIGURE 17–7 *Support process model with mother, confidant, and relationship characteristics, controlling for repartnering with a man and for change in maternal distress. T3 = Time 3; Conf = Confidant. $\chi^2(67, N = 138) = 84.82$, p = .07; comparative fit index = .963: *p < .05. [From DeGarmo, D. S., & M. S. Forgatch, (1997), fig. 1. Determinants of observed confidant support for divorced mothers.* Journal of Personality and Social Psychology, *72, 336–345. Copyright, 1997, by the American Psychological Association. Reprinted with permission.]*

when POMS mood scores were partialed out, $F(1, 10) = 12.93$, $p < .05$, it was no longer reliable when enjoyment ratings, POMS arousal scores, or subjective mood-arousal ratings were held constant. (p. 250)

Explain what is being done, using this result as an example, to someone who is familiar with ordinary analysis of variance, but who is not familiar with the analysis of covariance.

22. This question refers to another part of the study by DeGarmo and Forgatch (1997), described in problem 19. These researchers studied a group of divorced mothers, focusing on the support they received from their closest confidant. That confidant was sometimes a close friend, sometimes a family member, and sometimes a cohabiting partner. In the study, both the mothers and the confidants were interviewed on various measures; they were also videotaped interacting in a special laboratory task, and the interaction was systematically coded by the researchers. These various approaches created quite a few measures of the relationship between the mother and her closest confidant, including three measures of confidant support, four measures of confidant negativity, and four measures of the intimacy of their relationship.

One aspect of the study focused on how the relationship with the confidant differed for confidants who were friends, family members, or cohabiting partners. DeGarmo and Forgatch described the analysis as follows:

> Multivariate and univariate analyses of variance were conducted on the indicators of support, negativity, and intimacy for close friends, family members, and cohabiting partners. The mean values, tests of differences, and significant contrasts are displayed in Table [17–16].
>
> Significant differences were found among relationship types in the multivariate analysis of variance (MANOVA) on the indicators, $F(20, 254) = 4.10, p < .001$. (p. 340)

Degarmo and Forgatch then discussed the results of the univariate analyses of variance. For example, they noted that the "analysis of variance showed a pattern in which partners were observed to provide less support" (p. 340).

Explain these results to a person familiar with analysis of variance but not with MANOVA.

23. In a recent issue of a journal in an area of psychology that especially interests you, find an article that uses one of the statistical procedures described in this chapter. Write a brief summary of the study, referring specifically to the statistics. With your answer, include a photocopy or printout of the article, marking clearly the part that reports the statistics you describe.

24. In a recent issue of a journal in an area of psychology that especially interests you, find an article that uses a statistical procedure not covered anywhere in this book. Write a brief summary of the study you found, referring specifically to the statistics. With your answer, include a photocopy or printout of the article, marking clearly the part that reports the statistics you describe.

TABLE 17–16 Means and Standard Deviations for Construct Indicators by Confidant Relationship Types

Construct Indicator	Friend (1)		Family (2)		Partner (3)		$F(2, 135)$	Significant contrasts
	M	SD	M	SD	M	SD		
Observed confidant support								
Interpersonal	3.34	.67	3.35	.63	2.92	.65	5.93**	1, 2 > 3
Likeability	3.39	.86	3.24	.94	2.68	1.21	6.58**	1, 2 > 3
Emotional	1.04	.36	.96	.37	.69	.35	12.17***	1, 2 > 3
Confidant negativity								
Self-report, irritability	1.91	.84	1.70	.70	2.25	.65	5.27**	3 > 2
Intimacy-report irritability	1.36	.50	1.33	.35	1.48	.40	1.65	
Depressed mood	1.06	.32	.93	.36	.95	.34	2.02	
Relationship intimacy								
Mother-report intimacy	3.18	.73	3.19	.75	3.65	.58	5.94**	3 > 1, 2
Confidant-report intimacy	3.05	.78	3.29	.69	3.48	.64	4.62**	3 > 1
Mother-report complexity	1.91	.84	2.29	.74	2.87	.33	22.52***	3 > 1, 2
Confidant-report complexity	2.01	.74	2.19	.75	2.73	.55	13.36***	3 > 1, 2

Note: ns = 65, 33, and 40 for the friend, family, and partner relationship types, respectively.
** $p < .01$. ***$p < .001$.
Data from DeGarmo, D. S., & Forgatch, M. S. (1997), tab. 2. Determinants of observed confidant support for divorced mothers. *Journal of Personality and Social Psychology, 72,* 336–345. Copyright, 1997, by the American Psychological Association. Reprinted with permission

APPENDIX A

TABLES

TABLE A–1	Normal Curve Areas: Percentage of the Normal Curve Between the Mean and the Z Scores Shown				
Z	% Mean to Z	Z	% Mean to Z	Z	% Mean to Z
.00	.00	.24	9.48	.48	18.44
.01	.40	.25	9.87	.49	18.79
.02	.80	.26	10.26	.50	19.15
.03	1.20	.27	10.64	.51	19.50
.04	1.60	.28	11.03	.52	19.85
.05	1.99	.29	11.41	.53	20.19
.06	2.39	.30	11.79	.54	20.54
.07	2.79	.31	12.17	.55	20.88
.08	3.19	.32	12.55	.56	21.23
.09	3.59	.33	12.93	.57	21.57
.10	3.98	.34	13.31	.58	21.90
.11	4.38	.35	13.68	.59	22.24
.12	4.78	.36	14.06	.60	22.57
.13	5.17	.37	14.43	.61	22.91
.14	5.57	.38	14.80	.62	23.24
.15	5.96	.39	15.17	.63	23.57
.16	6.36	.40	15.54	.64	23.89
.17	6.75	.41	15.91	.65	24.22
.18	7.14	.42	16.28	.66	24.54
.19	7.53	.43	16.64	.67	24.86
.20	7.93	.44	17.00	.68	25.17
.21	8.32	.45	17.36	.69	25.49
.22	8.71	.46	17.72	.70	25.80
.23	9.10	.47	18.08	.71	26.11

TABLE A–1 (cont.)

Z	% Mean to Z	Z	% Mean to Z	Z	% Mean to Z
.72	26.42	1.19	38.30	1.66	45.15
.73	26.73	1.20	38.49	1.67	45.25
.74	27.04	1.21	38.69	1.68	45.35
.75	27.34	1.22	38.88	1.69	45.45
.76	27.64	1.23	39.07	1.70	45.54
.77	27.94	1.24	39.25	1.71	45.64
.78	28.23	1.25	39.44	1.72	45.73
.79	28.52	1.26	39.62	1.73	45.82
.80	28.81	1.27	39.80	1.74	45.91
.81	29.10	1.28	39.97	1.75	45.99
.82	29.39	1.29	40.15	1.76	46.08
.83	29.67	1.30	40.32	1.77	46.16
.84	29.95	1.31	40.49	1.78	46.25
.85	30.23	1.32	40.66	1.79	46.33
.86	30.51	1.33	40.82	1.80	46.41
.87	30.78	1.34	40.99	1.81	46.49
.88	31.06	1.35	41.15	1.82	46.56
.89	31.33	1.36	41.31	1.83	46.64
.90	31.59	1.37	41.47	1.84	46.71
.91	31.86	1.38	41.62	1.85	46.78
.92	32.12	1.39	41.77	1.86	46.86
.93	32.38	1.40	41.92	1.87	46.93
.94	32.64	1.41	42.07	1.88	46.99
.95	32.89	1.42	42.22	1.89	47.06
.96	33.15	1.43	42.36	1.90	47.13
.97	33.40	1.44	42.51	1.91	47.19
.98	33.65	1.45	42.65	1.92	47.26
.99	33.89	1.46	42.79	1.93	47.32
1.00	34.13	1.47	42.92	1.94	47.38
1.01	34.38	1.48	43.06	1.95	47.44
1.02	34.61	1.49	43.19	1.96	47.50
1.03	34.85	1.50	43.32	1.97	47.56
1.04	35.08	1.51	43.45	1.98	47.61
1.05	35.31	1.52	43.57	1.99	47.67
1.06	35.54	1.53	43.70	2.00	47.72
1.07	35.77	1.54	43.82	2.01	47.78
1.08	35.99	1.55	43.94	2.02	47.83
1.09	36.21	1.56	44.06	2.03	47.88
1.10	36.43	1.57	44.18	2.04	47.93
1.11	36.65	1.58	44.29	2.05	47.98
1.12	36.86	1.59	44.41	2.06	48.03
1.13	37.08	1.60	44.52	2.07	48.08
1.14	37.29	1.61	44.63	2.08	48.12
1.15	37.49	1.62	44.74	2.09	48.17
1.16	37.70	1.63	44.84	2.10	48.21
1.17	37.90	1.64	44.95	2.11	48.26
1.18	38.10	1.65	45.05	2.12	48.30

TABLE A–1 (cont.)

Z	% Mean to Z	Z	% Mean to Z	Z	% Mean to Z
2.13	48.34	2.44	49.27	2.75	49.70
2.14	48.38	2.45	49.29	2.76	49.71
2.15	48.42	2.46	49.31	2.77	49.72
2.16	48.46	2.47	49.32	2.78	49.73
2.17	48.50	2.48	49.34	2.79	49.74
2.18	48.54	2.49	49.36	2.80	49.74
2.19	48.57	2.50	49.38	2.81	49.75
2.20	48.61	2.51	49.40	2.82	49.76
2.21	48.64	2.52	49.41	2.83	49.77
2.22	48.68	2.53	49.43	2.84	49.77
2.23	48.71	2.54	49.45	2.85	49.78
2.24	48.75	2.55	49.46	2.86	49.79
2.25	48.78	2.56	49.48	2.87	49.79
2.26	48.81	2.57	49.49	2.88	49.80
2.27	48.84	2.58	49.51	2.89	49.81
2.28	48.87	2.59	49.52	2.90	49.81
2.29	48.90	2.60	49.53	2.91	49.82
2.30	48.93	2.61	49.55	2.92	49.82
2.31	48.96	2.62	49.56	2.93	49.83
2.32	48.98	2.63	49.57	2.94	49.84
2.33	49.01	2.64	49.59	2.95	49.84
2.34	49.04	2.65	49.60	2.96	49.85
2.35	49.06	2.66	49.61	2.97	49.85
2.36	49.09	2.67	49.62	2.98	49.86
2.37	49.11	2.68	49.63	2.99	49.86
2.38	49.13	2.69	49.64	3.00	49.87
2.39	49.16	2.70	49.65	3.50	49.98
2.40	49.18	2.71	49.66	4.00	50.00
2.41	49.20	2.72	49.67	4.50	50.00
2.42	49.22	2.73	49.68		
2.43	49.25	2.74	49.69		

TABLE A-2 Cutoff Scores for the *t* Distribution

df	One-Tailed Tests .10	.05	.01	Two-Tailed Tests .10	.05	.01
1	3.078	6.314	31.821	6.314	12.706	63.657
2	1.886	2.920	6.965	2.920	4.303	9.925
3	1.638	2.353	4.541	2.353	3.182	5.841
4	1.533	2.132	3.747	2.132	2.776	4.604
5	1.476	2.015	3.365	2.015	2.571	4.032
6	1.440	1.943	3.143	1.943	2.447	3.708
7	1.415	1.895	2.998	1.895	2.365	3.500
8	1.397	1.860	2.897	1.860	2.306	3.356
9	1.383	1.833	2.822	1.833	2.262	3.250
10	1.372	1.813	2.764	1.813	2.228	3.170
11	1.364	1.796	2.718	1.796	2.201	3.106
12	1.356	1.783	2.681	1.783	2.179	3.055
13	1.350	1.771	2.651	1.771	2.161	3.013
14	1.345	1.762	2.625	1.762	2.145	2.977
15	1.341	1.753	2.603	1.753	2.132	2.947
16	1.337	1.746	2.584	1.746	2.120	2.921
17	1.334	1.740	2.567	1.740	2.110	2.898
18	1.331	1.734	2.553	1.734	2.101	2.879
19	1.328	1.729	2.540	1.729	2.093	2.861
20	1.326	1.725	2.528	1.725	2.086	2.846
21	1.323	1.721	2.518	1.721	2.080	2.832
22	1.321	1.717	2.509	1.717	2.074	2.819
23	1.320	1.714	2.500	1.714	2.069	2.808
24	1.318	1.711	2.492	1.711	2.064	2.797
25	1.317	1.708	2.485	1.708	2.060	2.788
26	1.315	1.706	2.479	1.706	2.056	2.779
27	1.314	1.704	2.473	1.704	2.052	2.771
28	1.313	1.701	2.467	1.701	2.049	2.764
29	1.312	1.699	2.462	1.699	2.045	2.757
30	1.311	1.698	2.458	1.698	2.043	2.750
35	1.306	1.690	2.438	1.690	2.030	2.724
40	1.303	1.684	2.424	1.684	2.021	2.705
45	1.301	1.680	2.412	1.680	2.014	2.690
50	1.299	1.676	2.404	1.676	2.009	2.678
55	1.297	1.673	2.396	1.673	2.004	2.668
60	1.296	1.671	2.390	1.671	2.001	2.661
65	1.295	1.669	2.385	1.669	1.997	2.654
70	1.294	1.667	2.381	1.667	1.995	2.648
75	1.293	1.666	2.377	1.666	1.992	2.643
80	1.292	1.664	2.374	1.664	1.990	2.639
85	1.292	1.663	2.371	1.663	1.989	2.635
90	1.291	1.662	2.369	1.662	1.987	2.632
95	1.291	1.661	2.366	1.661	1.986	2.629
100	1.290	1.660	2.364	1.660	1.984	2.626
∞	1.282	1.645	2.327	1.645	1.960	2.576

TABLE A-3 Cutoff Scores for the *F* Distribution

Denominator df	Significance Level	Numerator Degrees of Freedom					
		1	2	3	4	5	6
1	.01	4,052	5,000	5,404	5,625	5,764	5,859
	.05	162	200	216	225	230	234
	.10	39.9	49.5	53.6	55.8	57.2	58.2
2	.01	98.50	99.00	99.17	99.25	99.30	99.33
	.05	18.51	19.00	19.17	19.25	19.30	19.33
	.10	8.53	9.00	9.16	9.24	9.29	9.33
3	.01	34.12	30.82	29.46	28.71	28.24	27.91
	.05	10.13	9.55	9.28	9.12	9.01	8.94
	.10	5.54	5.46	5.39	5.34	5.31	5.28
4	.01	21.20	18.00	16.70	15.98	15.52	15.21
	.05	7.71	6.95	6.59	6.39	6.26	6.16
	.10	4.55	4.33	4.19	4.11	4.05	4.01
5	.01	16.26	13.27	12.06	11.39	10.97	10.67
	.05	6.61	5.79	5.41	5.19	5.05	4.95
	.10	4.06	3.78	3.62	3.52	3.45	3.41
6	.01	13.75	10.93	9.78	9.15	8.75	8.47
	.05	5.99	5.14	4.76	4.53	4.39	4.28
	.10	3.78	3.46	3.29	3.18	3.11	3.06
7	.01	12.25	9.55	8.45	7.85	7.46	7.19
	.05	5.59	4.74	4.35	4.12	3.97	3.87
	.10	3.59	3.26	3.08	2.96	2.88	2.83
8	.01	11.26	8.65	7.59	7.01	6.63	6.37
	.05	5.32	4.46	4.07	3.84	3.69	3.58
	.10	3.46	3.11	2.92	2.81	2.73	2.67
9	.01	10.56	8.02	6.99	6.42	6.06	5.80
	.05	5.12	4.26	3.86	3.63	3.48	3.37
	.10	3.36	3.01	2.81	2.69	2.61	2.55
10	.01	10.05	7.56	6.55	6.00	5.64	5.39
	.05	4.97	4.10	3.71	3.48	3.33	3.22
	.10	3.29	2.93	2.73	2.61	2.52	2.46
11	.01	9.65	7.21	6.22	5.67	5.32	5.07
	.05	4.85	3.98	3.59	3.36	3.20	3.10
	.10	3.23	2.86	2.66	2.54	2.45	2.39
12	.01	9.33	6.93	5.95	5.41	5.07	4.82
	.05	4.75	3.89	3.49	3.26	3.11	3.00
	.10	3.18	2.81	2.61	2.48	2.40	2.33
13	.01	9.07	6.70	5.74	5.21	4.86	4.62
	.05	4.67	3.81	3.41	3.18	3.03	2.92
	.10	3.14	2.76	2.56	2.43	2.35	2.28
14	.01	8.86	6.52	5.56	5.04	4.70	4.46
	.05	4.60	3.74	3.34	3.11	2.96	2.85
	.10	3.10	2.73	2.52	2.40	2.31	2.24
15	.01	8.68	6.36	5.42	4.89	4.56	4.32
	.05	4.54	3.68	3.29	3.06	2.90	2.79
	.10	3.07	2.70	2.49	2.36	2.27	2.21

TABLE A-3 (cont.)

Denom- inator df	Signi- ficance Level	Numerator Degrees of Freedom					
		1	2	3	4	5	6
16	.01	8.53	6.23	5.29	4.77	4.44	4.20
	.05	4.49	3.63	3.24	3.01	2.85	2.74
	.10	3.05	2.67	2.46	2.33	2.24	2.18
17	.01	8.40	6.11	5.19	4.67	4.34	4.10
	.05	4.45	3.59	3.20	2.97	2.81	2.70
	.10	3.03	2.65	2.44	2.31	2.22	2.15
18	.01	8.29	6.01	5.09	4.58	4.25	4.02
	.05	4.41	3.56	3.16	2.93	2.77	2.66
	.10	3.01	2.62	2.42	2.29	2.20	2.13
19	.01	8.19	5.93	5.01	4.50	4.17	3.94
	.05	4.38	3.52	3.13	2.90	2.74	2.63
	.10	2.99	2.61	2.40	2.27	2.18	2.11
20	.01	8.10	5.85	4.94	4.43	4.10	3.87
	.05	4.35	3.49	3.10	2.87	2.71	2.60
	.10	2.98	2.59	2.38	2.25	2.16	2.09
21	.01	8.02	5.78	4.88	4.37	4.04	3.81
	.05	4.33	3.47	3.07	2.84	2.69	2.57
	.10	2.96	2.58	2.37	2.23	2.14	2.08
22	.01	7.95	5.72	4.82	4.31	3.99	3.76
	.05	4.30	3.44	3.05	2.82	2.66	2.55
	.10	2.95	2.56	2.35	2.22	2.13	2.06
23	.01	7.88	5.66	4.77	4.26	3.94	3.71
	.05	4.28	3.42	3.03	2.80	2.64	2.53
	.10	2.94	2.55	2.34	2.21	2.12	2.05
24	.01	7.82	5.61	4.72	4.22	3.90	3.67
	.05	4.26	3.40	3.01	2.78	2.62	2.51
	.10	2.93	2.54	2.33	2.20	2.10	2.04
25	.01	7.77	5.57	4.68	4.18	3.86	3.63
	.05	4.24	3.39	2.99	2.76	2.60	2.49
	.10	2.92	2.53	2.32	2.19	2.09	2.03
26	.01	7.72	5.53	4.64	4.14	3.82	3.59
	.05	4.23	3.37	2.98	2.74	2.59	2.48
	.10	2.91	2.52	2.31	2.18	2.08	2.01
27	.01	7.68	5.49	4.60	4.11	3.79	3.56
	.05	4.21	3.36	2.96	2.73	2.57	2.46
	.10	2.90	2.51	2.30	2.17	2.07	2.01
28	.01	7.64	5.45	4.57	4.08	3.75	3.53
	.05	4.20	3.34	2.95	2.72	2.56	2.45
	.10	2.89	2.50	2.29	2.16	2.07	2.00
29	.01	7.60	5.42	4.54	4.05	3.73	3.50
	.05	4.18	3.33	2.94	2.70	2.55	2.43
	.10	2.89	2.50	2.28	2.15	2.06	1.99
30	.01	7.56	5.39	4.51	4.02	3.70	3.47
	.05	4.17	3.32	2.92	2.69	2.53	2.42
	.10	2.88	2.49	2.28	2.14	2.05	1.98

TABLE A-3 (cont.)

Denom- inator df	Signi- ficance Level	Numerator Degrees of Freedom					
		1	2	3	4	5	6
35	.01	7.42	5.27	4.40	3.91	3.59	3.37
	.05	4.12	3.27	2.88	2.64	2.49	2.37
	.10	2.86	2.46	2.25	2.11	2.02	1.95
40	.01	7.32	5.18	4.31	3.83	3.51	3.29
	.05	4.09	3.23	2.84	2.61	2.45	2.34
	.10	2.84	2.44	2.23	2.09	2.00	1.93
45	.01	7.23	5.11	4.25	3.77	3.46	3.23
	.05	4.06	3.21	2.81	2.58	2.42	2.31
	.10	2.82	2.43	2.21	2.08	1.98	1.91
50	.01	7.17	5.06	4.20	3.72	3.41	3.19
	.05	4.04	3.18	2.79	2.56	2.40	2.29
	.10	2.81	2.41	2.20	2.06	1.97	1.90
55	.01	7.12	5.01	4.16	3.68	3.37	3.15
	.05	4.02	3.17	2.77	2.54	2.38	2.27
	.10	2.80	2.40	2.19	2.05	1.96	1.89
60	.01	7.08	4.98	4.13	3.65	3.34	3.12
	.05	4.00	3.15	2.76	2.53	2.37	2.26
	.10	2.79	2.39	2.18	2.04	1.95	1.88
65	.01	7.04	4.95	4.10	3.62	3.31	3.09
	.05	3.99	3.14	2.75	2.51	2.36	2.24
	.10	2.79	2.39	2.17	2.03	1.94	1.87
70	.01	7.01	4.92	4.08	3.60	3.29	3.07
	.05	3.98	3.13	2.74	2.50	2.35	2.23
	.10	2.78	2.38	2.16	2.03	1.93	1.86
75	.01	6.99	4.90	4.06	3.58	3.27	3.05
	.05	3.97	3.12	2.73	2.49	2.34	2.22
	.10	2.77	2.38	2.16	2.02	1.93	1.86
80	.01	6.96	4.88	4.04	3.56	3.26	3.04
	.05	3.96	3.11	2.72	2.49	2.33	2.22
	.10	2.77	2.37	2.15	2.02	1.92	1.85
85	.01	6.94	4.86	4.02	3.55	3.24	3.02
	.05	3.95	3.10	2.71	2.48	2.32	2.21
	.10	2.77	2.37	2.15	2.01	1.92	1.85
90	.01	6.93	4.85	4.01	3.54	3.23	3.01
	.05	3.95	3.10	2.71	2.47	2.32	2.20
	.10	2.76	2.36	2.15	2.01	1.91	1.84
95	.01	6.91	4.84	4.00	3.52	3.22	3.00
	.05	3.94	3.09	2.70	2.47	2.31	2.20
	.10	2.76	2.36	2.14	2.01	1.91	1.84
100	.01	6.90	4.82	3.98	3.51	3.21	2.99
	.05	3.94	3.09	2.70	2.46	2.31	2.19
	.10	2.76	2.36	2.14	2.00	1.91	1.83
∞	.01	6.64	4.61	3.78	3.32	3.02	2.80
	.05	3.84	3.00	2.61	2.37	2.22	2.10
	.10	2.71	2.30	2.08	1.95	1.85	1.78

TABLE A-4	Cutoff Scores for the Chi-Square Distribution

	Significance Level		
df	.10	.05	.01
1	2.706	3.841	6.635
2	4.605	5.992	9.211
3	6.252	7.815	11.345
4	7.780	9.488	13.277
5	9.237	11.071	15.087
6	10.645	12.592	16.812
7	12.017	14.067	18.475
8	13.362	15.507	20.090
9	14.684	16.919	21.666
10	15.987	18.307	23.209

TABLE A-5	Index to Power Tables and Tables Giving Number of Participants Needed for 80% Power

Hypothesis-Testing Procedure	Chapter	Power Table	Number of Participants Table
Correlation coefficient (r)	3	111	111
t test for dependent means	9	324	325
t test for independent means	10	360	361
One-way analysis of variance	12	435	436
Two-way analysis of variance	13	482	483
Chi-square test for independence	14	528	529

ANSWERS
TO SET I PRACTICE PROBLEMS

Chapter 1

1. (a) Satisfaction with the vocational counselor; (b) 1, 2, 3, or 4; (c) the particular rating the client makes.
2. (a) Nominal (or categorical); (b) numeric (or quantitative); more precisely, equal interval; (c) numeric (or quantitative); more precisely, rank order (or ordinal).
3. (a)

Number of Children	Frequency	Percent
6	1	5
5	0	0
4	1	5
3	2	10
2	7	35
1	5	25
0	4	20

(b) Histogram.

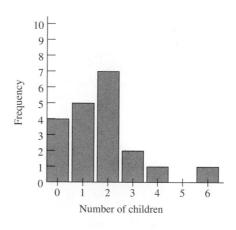

(c) Frequency polygon.

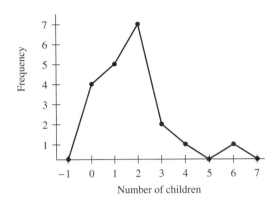

Number of children

(d) Unimodal, skewed to the right.

4. (a)

Hours	Frequency	Percent	Hours	Frequency	Percent
18	1	2	8	5	10
17	0	0	7	11	22
16	0	0	6	4	8
15	1	2	5	2	4
14	0	0	4	3	6
13	2	4	3	4	8
12	1	2	2	2	4
11	3	6	1	1	2
10	5	10	0	1	2
9	4	8			

(b) and (c) are based on frequency table above. See answer to question 3 for examples.

(d) Approximately unimodal; slightly skewed to the right.

5. (a)

Score	Frequency	Percent	Score	Frequency	Percent
96	1	4	83	2	8
95	0	0	82	0	0
94	0	0	81	1	4
93	0	0	80	1	4
92	1	4	79	0	0
91	1	4	78	0	0
90	0	0	77	0	0
89	0	0	76	2	8
88	0	0	75	2	8
87	1	4	74	1	4
86	0	0	73	1	4
85	1	4	72	0	0
84	0	0	71	1	4
70	1	4	59	1	4
69	1	4	58	0	0
68	2	8	57	0	0
67	1	4	56	0	0
66	0	0	55	0	0
65	0	0	54	0	0
64	2	8	53	0	0
63	0	0	52	0	0
62	0	0	51	0	0
61	0	0	50	1	4
60	0	0			

(b) based on frequency table above (see answer to Question 3b for an example).

(c)

Interval	Frequency	Percent
90–99	3	12
80–89	6	24
70–79	8	32
60–69	6	24
50–59	2	8

(d) is based on frequency table in c above. See answer to Question 3b for an example. (e) Unimodal, approximately symmetrical (slightly negatively skewed).

6. (a) Similar to 5a above. (b) is based on frequency table in a; see answer to Question 3c, for an example.

(c)

Interval	Frequency	Percent
80–89	10	29.4
70–79	0	0
60–69	5	14.7
50–59	0	0
40–49	5	14.7
30–39	7	20.6
20–29	7	20.6

(d) Histogram

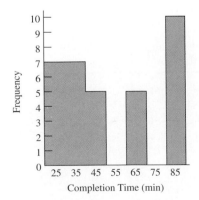

Completion Time (min)

(e) roughly rectangular
7. (a) Bimodal; (b) approximately normal (or unimodal or symmetrical); (c) multimodal.
8. Example answers:

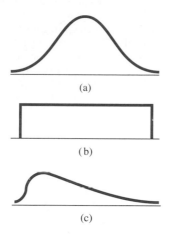

(a)

(b)

(c)

9. (a) A distribution is the way a group of numbers is spread out over the possible values the numbers can have. You can describe such a distribution with a graph, called a histogram—a kind of bar graph with one bar for each possible value with one unit of height for each time its particular value occurs. In a histogram, a symmetrical distribution has a symmetrical shape (the right and left halves are mirror images). A unimodal distribution is one in which this graph has a single high point, with the other values gradually decreasing around it.
   (b) A negatively skewed unimodal distribution is not symmetrical, and its tail—the long, low side—extends to the left (where the negative scores go on the graph).
10. (a) This is called a frequency table because it lays out how frequently (how many times) each category occurs for different categories. For example, of the 90 college students in the study, 19 gave bad news about Relationship with family (the first category). The table also gives the percentages. For example, 19 students is 19/90 of the total, or 21.1 percent.
   (b) The most bad news is given in four of the nine categories: Relationship with family, Relationship with actual/potential girlfriend/boyfriend, Relationship with friends, and Health of family member/friend. All of these categories had to do with family members or friends and most with relationships and there were few cases in the other categories (which had little directly to do with family or friends).

Chapter 2

1. (a) $M = \Sigma X/N = 261/9 = 29$; (b) 28; (c) $SS = \Sigma(X - M)^2 = (32 - 29)^2 + (28 - 29)^2 + (24 - 29)^2 + (28 - 29)^2 + (28 - 29)^2 + (31 - 29)^2 + (35 - 29)^2 + (29 - 29)^2 + (26 - 29)^2 = 86$; (d) $SD^2 = SS/N = 86/9 = 9.56$; (e) $SD = \sqrt{SD^2} = \sqrt{9.56} = 3.09$.
2. (a) 4; (b) 4; (c) 26; (d) 3.25; (e) 1.80.

3. The average temperature, in the sense of adding up the 10 readings and dividing by 10, was -7 degrees Celsius. This is the *mean*. However, if you line up the temperatures from lowest to highest, the middle two numbers are both -5 degrees. The middle number is the *median*. The specific temperature that came up most often is the *mode*—there are two modes, -1 and -5.
   As for the variation, one approach is the *variance*—the average of each temperature's squared difference from the mean temperature. You get a more direct sense of how much a group of numbers vary among themselves if you take the square root of the variance, the standard deviation—the square root of 46.8 is 6.84. This means, roughly, that on an average day the temperature differs by 6.84 degrees from the average of -7 degrees.
4. (a) .4; (b) .14; (c) like 3 above.
5. (a) $Z = (X - M)/SD = (91 - 79)/12 = 1$; (b) $-.92$; (c) 2.
6. (a) If IQ = 107, $Z = (X - M)/SD = (107 - 100)/16 = .44$; $X = (Z)(SD) + M = (.44)(41) + 231 = 249$.
   (We rounded off to a whole number because the actual score on the test is the number of items correct, which cannot be a fraction.). (b) $Z = -1.06$; $X = 188$; (c) $Z = 0$; $X = 231$.
7. Wife: $Z = (X - M)/SD = (63 - 60)/6 = .5$. Husband: $Z = (59 - 55)/4 = 1$. The husband has adjusted better in relation to other divorced men than the wife has adjusted in relation to other divorced women.
   For wives, a score of 63 is 3 points better than the average of 60 for divorced women in general. (The "mean" in the problem is the ordinary average—the sum of the scores divided by the number of scores.) There is, of course, some variation in scores among divorced women. The approximate average amount that women's scores differ from the average is 6 points—this is the *SD* (standard deviation) referred to in the problem. (*SD* is only approximately the average amount scores differ from the mean. To be precise, *SD* is the square root of the average of the square of the difference of each score from the mean.) Thus, the wife's score is only half as far above the mean of wives as wives' scores in general differ from the mean of wives' scores. This gives her what is called a *Z* score of $+.5$, which gives her location on a scale that compares her score to that of divorced women in general. Using the same logic, the husband's divorce adjustment is as much above the mean as the average amount that men differ from the mean; that is, he has a *Z* score of $+1$. What this all means is that both have adjusted better than average for their gender, but the husband has adjusted better in relation to other divorced men than the wife has adjusted in relation to other divorced women.
8. The "mean" is the ordinary arithmetic average—add up the total number of dreams and divide by the number of people. The average number of dreams reported over the 2 weeks was 6.84. The *SD* (standard deviation), roughly speaking, is the average amount that the numbers of dreams are spread out from their average—in this case, by 3.18 dreams. This is quite a lot of spread. To be more precise, you figure the standard deviation by taking each person's number of dreams and subtracting 6.84 from it and squaring this difference; the standard deviation is the square root of the average of these squared differences.

9. Like the answer to 8 above, focusing on means of 5.02, 5.11, 32.27, and 31.36 and on standard deviations of 2.16, 2.08, 20.36, and 21.08.

Chapter 3

1. (a) Curvilinear; (b) linear, positive, strong; (c) linear, negative, strong; (d) linear, positive, strong; (e) linear, positive, small to moderate; (f) no correlation.

2. (a)

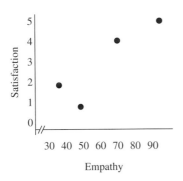

(b) Positive linear correlation—as therapist empathy goes up, so does patient satisfaction.

(c)

	Therapist Empathy		Patient Satisfaction		
	Raw	Z_X	*Raw*	Z_Y	$Z_X Z_Y$
1	70	.36	4	.63	.23
2	94	1.45	5	1.26	1.83
3	36	−1.17	2	− .63	.74
4	48	− .63	1	−1.26	.80
					$\Sigma = 3.60$

$$r = 3.60/4 = .90$$

(d) The first thing I did was make a graph, called a scatter diagram, putting one variable on each axis, then putting a dot where each person's pair of scores goes on that graph. This gives a picture of the pattern of relationship between the two variables. In this example, high scores generally go with highs and lows with lows. The scores going together in a systematic pattern make this a *correlation*; that highs go with highs and lows with lows makes this correlation *positive;* that the dots fall roughly near a straight line make this positive correlation *linear.*

Next, I figured the *correlation coefficient,* a number describing the degree of linear correlation (in a positive correlation, how consistently highs go with highs and lows with lows). To do this, I changed all the scores to Z scores because Z scores tell you how much a score is low or high relative to the other scores in its distribution. You figure the correlation coefficient by multiplying each person's two Z scores by each other, totaling up these products, and then averaging this total over the number of people. This will be a high number if highs go with highs and lows with lows, because with Z scores, highs are always positive and positive times positive is positive, and with Z scores, lows are always negative and negatives times negatives become positives too. Following this procedure, the highest number you can get, if the scores for the two variables are perfectly correlated, is $+1$. If there were no linear correlation between the variables, the result would be 0 (because highs would sometimes be multiplied by highs and sometimes by lows, giving a mixture of positive and negative products that would cancel out).

In this example, the products of the Z scores add up to 3.6, which when divided by the number of therapist–patient pairs is .90. This is called a *Pearson correlation coefficient* (r) of .9 and indicates a strong, positive linear correlation between satisfaction and empathy.

(e) (i) If a therapist has more empathy, this causes the patient to feel more satisfied (empathy causes satisfaction); (ii) if a patient feels more satisfied, this causes the therapist to feel more empathic toward the patient (satisfaction causes empathy); or (iii) some third factor, such as a good match of the patient's problem with the therapist's ability, causes clients to be more satisfied and therapists to be more empathic (third factor causes both satisfaction and empathy).

3. (a) See 2a above for example scatter diagram. (b) Positive linear correlation—as hours studied go up, so do test grades. (c) $r = 4.20/5 = .84$. (d) Like 2d above. (e) (i) Studying more hours causes improved test grades; (ii) getting a better test grade causes more hours studied—note that although this is theoretically possible, in reality it is not possible to have a future event (the score on the test) cause a previous event (hours studied); or (iii) a third factor, such as interest in the subject matter, could be causing the student to study more and also to do better on the test.

4. (a) See 2a above for example scatter diagram. (b) Curvilinear correlation (∩): As self-disclosure increases, liking increases—up to a point; but then as self-disclosure increases further, liking decreases. (c) $r = .93/10 = .09$.

5. Set A:

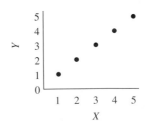

X		Y		Cross-Product of Z Scores
Raw	Z	Raw	Z	
1	−1.41	1	−1.41	2.0
2	− .71	2	− .71	.5
3	.00	3	.00	0
4	.71	4	.71	.5
5	1.41	5	1.41	2.0
$M = 3$; $SD = 1.41$				5.0
				$r = 5.0/5 = 1.00$.

Set B: $r = 4.5/5 = .90$; Set C: $r = −3.0/5 = −.60$; Set D: $r = 3.0/5 = .60$.

6. Possibility A:

Take Drug		Get Cold		Cross-Product of Z Scores
Raw	Z	Raw	Z	
0	−1	1	1	−1
0	−1	1	1	−1
0	−1	1	1	−1
0	−1	1	1	−1
1	1	0	−1	−1
1	1	0	−1	−1
1	1	0	−1	−1
1	1	0	−1	−1
				−8
				$r = −8/8 = −1.00$

Possibility B: $r = −4/8 = −.50$; Possibility C: $r = 0/8 = .00$; Possibility D: $r = −6.2/8 = −.775$.

7. (a) The measures may have low reliability, thus reducing (attenuating) the possible correlation between them. (b) There is restriction in range: Among millionaires, there may not be a very great range of comfort of living situation (they probably all have quite comfortable living situations), so the correlation with any variable (including happiness) is limited.

8. (a) This table shows the degree of association among scores on several measures given to pregnant women and their partners. (Here continue with an explanation of the correlation coefficient like that in 2d above; except in this problem you also need to explain the mean, standard deviation, and Z scores—which you do in the same way as in answering the problems in Chapter 2.) For example, the correlation of .17 between women's reports of stress and men's reports of women's stress indicates that the association between these two measures is quite weak. Thus, how much stress a woman is under is not highly related to how much stress her partner believes she is under. On the other hand, the correlation of .50 (near the middle of the first column of correlations) tells you that there is a much stronger association between a woman's report of stress and her depressed mood at the second interview. That is, women who report being under stress are also likely to report being depressed, those reporting being under not much stress are likely to report not being very depressed.

(b) In general the correlations shown in this table are strongest among the stress, support, and mood items; correlations of these variables with demographics (age, ethnicity, etc.) were fairly weak. Partner support seemed to be strongly correlated with stress and mood, and depressed mood at the second testing was particularly related to the other variables.

(c) Just because two variables are correlated, even strongly correlated, does not mean that you can know the particular direction of causality that creates that association. For example, there is a strong negative correlation between partner support at time 1 and depressed mood at time 2. There are three logically possible directions of causality here: Support can be causing lower depression, lower depression can be causing support, or some third factor can be causing both. You can rule out the second possibility, since something in the future (low depression) can't cause the past (initial support). However, the other two possibilities remain. It is certainly plausible that having her partner's support helps reduce depression. But it is also possible that a third factor is causing both. For example, consider level of income. Perhaps when a couple has more income, the partner has more time and energy to provide support and the greater comfort of living keeps depression down.

Chapter 4

1. (a) Score on knowledge of physiology; (b) number of injuries over subsequent year; (c) .4; (d) $\hat{Z}_{\text{Injuries}} = (.4)(Z_{\text{Score}})$. (e) (.4)(−2) = −.8; (f) −.4; (g) 0; (h) .4; (i) .8.
2. (a) $40 + (.5)(30) = 55$; (b) 60; (c) 65; (d) 70; (e) 75; (f) 80; (g) 85; (h) 90.
3. (a) Z_X (when $X = 0$) $= (0 − 10)/2 = −5$; $\hat{Z}_Y = (r)(Z_X) = (.4)(−5) = −2$; $\hat{Y} = (2)(−2) + 10 = 6$; $a = 6$
   Z_X (when $X = 1$) $= −4.5$; $\hat{Z}_Y = −1.8$; $\hat{Y} = 6.4$; $b = 6.4 − 6 = .4$; $\hat{Y} = 6 + (.4)(X)$
   (b) $\hat{Y} = 16 + (.4)(X)$; (c) $\hat{Y} = 2 + (.4)(X)$; (d) $\hat{Y} = 8 + (.2)(X)$.

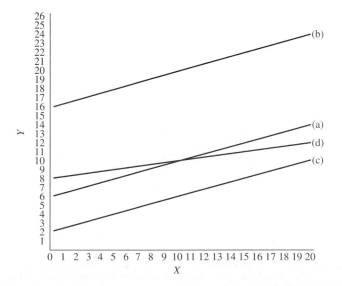

4. (a) Z_X (when $X = 0$) = $(0 - 6)/3.35 = -1.79$; $\hat{Z}_Y = (r)(Z_X) = (.84)(-1.79) = -1.5$; $\hat{Y} = (14.9)(-1.5)+73 = 50.65$; $a = 50.65$; Z_X (when $X = 1$) = -1.49; $\hat{Z}_Y = -1.25$; $\hat{Y} = 54.38$; $b = 54.38 - 50.65 = 3.73$; $\hat{Y} = 50.65 + (3.73)(X)$ or Predicted test grade = $50.65 + (3.73)$(hours studied).

(b) $50.65 + (3.73)(0) = 50.65$; 87.95; 73.03; 80.49; 73.03

(c)

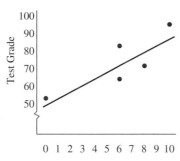

(d) Error = $52 - 50.65 = 1.35$, squared error = 1.82; 7.05, 49.70; 9.97, 99.40; -9.49, 90.06; -9.03, 81.54.

(e) $SS_{Error} = 322.52$; $r^2 = (SS_{Total} - SS_{Error})/SS_{Total} = (1,110 - 3.22.52)/1,110 = .71$.

(f) $\sqrt{.71} = .84$

(g) The most accurate method to predict a person's Z score on one variable (call it Y) based on that person's Z score on another variable (call it X) is to multiply the Z score on X by r. You can also use r and the means and standard deviations of your two variables to make a formula to predict the raw score on Y from a raw score on X. First you figure a number that gets added to the prediction no matter what value of X you are predicting from (the *regression constant*); this is the number that you predict for Y when $X = 0$. You figure this by finding the Z score for X when $X = 0$; then you multiply this Z score by r to get the Z score predicted for Y; then you convert this predicted Z score to a raw score on Y. In this example, this works out to 50.65. Next you figure how much to add to the predicted score on Y for each additional unit on X (called the *raw score regression coefficient*). (Since this is linear correlation, this number will be the same throughout.) You can come up with this number by first figuring what you would predict for Y when $X = 1$ using this same procedure of converting to a Z score, figuring the predicted Z score, and converting this back to a raw score (in this example, this comes out to 54.38). Then you subtract the predicted Y when $X = 0$ from the predicted Y when $X = 1$—this tells you how much predicted Y increases for each increase of 1 on X. In this example, this comes out to 3.73. Thus, the overall formula for predicting a person's test grade is to start with 50.65 and then add 3.73 times the number of hours studied. Applying this formula to the first student, you get 50.65 plus 3.73 times 0 hours studied, which comes out to a predicted test score of 50.65. For the second student, it is 50.65 plus 3.73 times 10 hours studied, which comes out

to a predicted test score of 87.95. I then followed the same procedure for the rest of the students.

After coming up with the formula, I made a scatter diagram in the usual way but then put in a line showing the predicted scores (called a *regression line*). Since the predicted values are for a linear correlation, they follow a straight line, so you can make this line by putting in a dot for any two predicted scores and drawing the line through them. This line is another way of showing the prediction formula.

I then took the following steps to evaluate the accuracy of the prediction formula. I first figured, for each student, how much error there is between what I predicted using the formula and the student's actual score, called the *error*. For example, for the first student, the error is $52 - 50.65$, which comes out to 1.35. Because the errors would all cancel each other out when adding them up (because some are negative and some positive), I squared the errors and added them all up to get the sum of squared errors when using the prediction formula. This came out to 322.52. I then compared the error I would make using the prediction formula to the error I would make predicting without it. The best I could do for prediction if I didn't have the prediction formula would be to predict that each student would have the mean test score. Thus, I would next figure the error, squared errors, and sum of squared errors if I had predicted the mean. However, in this problem, this number was given—1,110. The statistic that is used to compare these two kinds of errors (called the *proportionate reduction in error*) is the reduction in squared error from using the formula (the total squared error predicting from the mean minus the sum of squared error using the formula) divided by the total squared error when using the mean. This comes out to .71—meaning that I have reduced my squared error by 71% over just using the mean to predict. Since proportionate reduction in error is mathematically equivalent to the correlation coefficient squared, I checked my result by taking the square root of the proportionate reduction in error. The square root of .71 is .84, which is exactly the correlation coefficient.

5. (a) Z_X (when $X = 0$) = $(0 - 73)/14.9 = -4.9$; $\hat{Z}_Y = (r)(Z_X) = (.84)(-4.9) = -4.116$; $\hat{Y} = (3.35)(-4.116)+6 = -7.789$; $a = 7.789$; Z_X (when $X = 1$) = -4.832; $\hat{Z}_Y = -4.059$; $\hat{Y} = -7.598$; $b = -7.598 - -7.789 = .191$; $\hat{Y} = -7.789 + (.191)(X)$ or predicted hours studied = $-7.789 + (.191)$(test grade).

(b) $-7.789 + (.191)(52) = 2.14$; 10.36; 8.06; 5.77; 4.44.

(c) See 4c above for an example (this scatter diagram and regression line will not be exactly the same).

(d) Error = $0 - 2.14 = -2.14$, squared error = 4.58; $-.36$, $.13$; -2.06, 4.24; 2.23, 4.97; 1.56, 2.43.

(e) $SS_{Error} = 16.35$; $r^2 = (SS_{Total} - SS_{Error})/SS_{Total} = (56 - 16.35)/56 = .71$.

(f) $\sqrt{.71} = .84$

6. (a) Z_X (when $X = 0$) = $(0 - 62)/22.14 = -2.8$; $\hat{Z}_Y = (r)(Z_X) = (.9)(-2.8) = -2.52$; $\hat{Y} = (1.58)(-2.52) + 3 = -.982$; $a = -.982$; Z_X (when $X = 1$) = -2.755; $\hat{Z}_Y = -2.48$; $\hat{Y} = -.918$; $b = -.918 - -.982 = .064$; $\hat{Y} = -982 + (.064)(X)$ or Predicted satisfaction = $-982 + (.064)$(empathy).

(b) $-.982 + (.064)(70) = 3.50$; 5.03; 1.32; 2.09.

(c) See 4c above as an example.

(d) Error $= 4 - 3.50 = .50$, squared error $= .25$; $-.03$, .00; .68, .46; -1.09, 1.19.

(e) $SS_{Error} = 1.9$; $r^2 = (SS_{Total} - SS_{Error})/SS_{Total} = (10 - 1.9)/10 = .81$.

(f) $\sqrt{.81} = .90$

(g) Like 4g above.

7. (a) Z_X (when $X = 0$) $= (0 - 3)/1.58 = -1.899$; $\hat{Z}_Y = (r)(Z_X) = (.9)(-1.899) = -1.709$; $\hat{Y} = (22.14)(-1.709) + 62 = 24.163$; $a = 24.163$; Z_X (when $X = 1$) $= -1.266$; $\hat{Z}_Y = -1.139$; $\hat{Y} = 36.783$; $b = 36.783 - 24.163 = 12.62$; $\hat{Y} = 24.16 + (12.62)(X)$ or Predicted empathy $= 24.16 + (12.62)$(satisfaction).

(b) $24.16 + (12.62)(4) = 74.64$; 87.26; 49.40; 36.78.

(c) See 4c above as an example.

(d) Error $= 70 - 74.64 = -4.64$, squared error $= 21.53$; 6.74, 45.43; -13.40, 179.56; 11.22, 125.89.

(e) $SS_{Error} = 372.41$; $r^2 = (SS_{Total} - SS_{Error})/SS_{Total} = (2,068 - 372.41)/2,068 = .82$.

(f) $\sqrt{.82} = .91$. (The slight difference from the original r is due to rounding error.)

(g) Different: Prediction formula and predictions (since something different is being predicted), scatter diagram and regression line. Same (within rounding error): proportionate reduction in error, correlation coefficient.

8. First, explain regression, as in 4g above, plus the mean, standard deviation, Z scores, and the correlation coefficient as in answers to Chapter 2 and 3 problems. The two graphs show regression lines separately for each experimental group. The left graph shows that Expectation of Success provides little information to predict Number of Plans for either the Positive Fantasy or Negative Reality group, but for the Contrast group, there is a fairly strong positive relation between Expectation of Success and Number of Plans. The right graph, which shows the regression lines for predicting Taking Responsibility from Expectation of Success, indicates that there is a moderate negative relation for the Positive Fantasy group, a small negative relation for the Negative Reality group, and a strong positive relation for the Contrast group.

9. First, explain regression, as in 4g above. The researchers are using *multiple regression,* a method of predicting scores on a criterion variable from more than one predictor variable. Thus, for a multiple regression equation using Z scores with two predictor variables, you predict the Z score on the criterion variable as the first predictor variable's Z score times the standardized regression coefficient (beta) for the first predictor variable, plus the second predictor variable's Z score times the standardized regression coefficient for the second predictor variable. In Equation 1 for peer acceptance, the table shows standardized regression coefficients of .10 and .32. Thus, the predicted Z score on a child's peer acceptance is .10 times his or her mother's nonsocial teaching Z score plus .32 times his or her mother's social coaching Z score. This suggests that children's peer acceptance is most strongly related to their mothers' social coaching and much less strongly related to their mothers' nonsocial teaching.

It is important to note, however, that the regression coefficients reflect what each predictor contributes to the prediction, over and above what the other contributes. Thus, the ordinary correlations between each predictor variable and the criterion variable can show a quite different pattern. In the present example, the ordinary correlations show a similar pattern, though the difference between the two is not as great as when considering the standardized regression coefficients.

Another important piece of information in this table is the R^2. As with bivariate regression, this is the proportion of squared error in making predictions that is reduced by using this best prediction rule (in this case using two predictors) over just using the average peer acceptance rating to predict each score. The proportionate reduction in error is 14%. (The square root of this, .37, is the multiple correlation coefficient.)

10. (a) $\hat{Z}_{Peer\ Acceptance} = (.10)(Z_{Nonsocial\ Teaching}) + (.32)(Z_{Social\ Coaching})$. A: $(.10)(-2) + (.32)(0) = -.20$; B: 0; C: .20; D: $-.64$; E: .64; F: .84; G: $-.74$.

(b) $\hat{Z}_{Peer\ Acceptance} = (.27)(Z_{Responsive\ Style}) + (.29)(Z_{Social\ Coaching})$. A: $(.27)(-2) + (.29)(0) = -.54$; B: 0; C: .54; D: $-.58$; E: .58; F: 1.12; G: $-.85$.

Chapter 5

1. (a) 50%; (b) 16%; (c) 98%; (d) 84%; (e) 50%; (f) 84%; (g) 2%; (h) 16%.

2. (a) 50; (b) 45; (c) 40; (d) 35; (e) 30.

3. (a) From the normal curve table, 43% (.43) have Z scores between the mean and 1.5. By definition, 50% have Z scores below the mean. Thus, the total percentage below 1.5 is 50% + 43% = 93%. (b) 7%; (c) 7%; (d) 93%; (e) 2%; (f) 98%; (g) 33%; (h) 4%; (i) 5%.

4. (a) $Z = (16 - 15)/5 = .2$; from the normal curve table, percent between mean and $.2 = 7.93$; with 50% above the mean, the percent above .2 is 50% $- 7.93\% = 42.07\%$; (b) 34.46%; (c) 27.43%; (d) 72.57%; (e) 42.07%

5. (a) Top 40% means 10% between the mean and this score; the nearest Z score from the normal curve table for 10% is .25; a Z score of .25 equals a raw score of $(.25)(5) + 15 = 16.25$; (b) 17.6; (c) 19.2.

6. (a) 21.90%; (b) 22.24%; (c) 42.79%; (d) 44.06%; (e) 21.90%.

7. (a) The top 10% means 90% are below. Of this 90%, 50% are below the mean. Thus, the top 10% is the point where 40% of scores are between it and the mean. Looking this up in the normal curve table, 40.00 (the closest actual value is 39.97) is a Z score of $+1.28$. (b) 2.33.

8. (a) Needed $Z = 1.64$; this corresponds to raw score of 50 + $(10)(1.64) = 66.4$. (b) The scores for almost anything you measure, in nature and in psychology, tend approximately to follow the particular pattern shown below, called a normal curve. In a normal curve, most of the scores are near the middle with fewer but equal numbers of scores at each extreme. Because the normal curve is mathematically defined, the precise proportion of scores in any particular section of it can be calculated, and these have been listed in special tables. (Then explain mean, standard deviation, and Z scores as in answers to Chapter 2 problems.) The normal curve table tells the percentage of scores in the normal curve between the mean and any particular Z score.

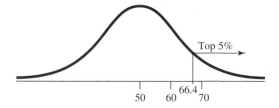

The coordination test scores are known to follow a normal curve. Thus, you can look up in the table the Z score for the point on the normal curve at which 45% of the scores are between it and the mean. The normal curve is completely symmetrical. Thus, 50% of the scores fall above the mean, leaving 5% above 45%. This is a Z score of 1.64 (actually, there is not an exact point on the table for 45%, so I could have used either 1.64 or 1.65). With a standard deviation of 10, a Z score of 1.64 is 16.4 points above the mean. Adding that to the mean of 50 makes the score needed to be in the top 5% turn out to 66.4.

9. (a) 10/50: $p = 10/50 = .2$; (b) .4; (c) (10 + 20)/50 = .6; (d) .6; (e) 1.

(f) The probability of a particular thing happening is usually defined as the number of possible ways the thing could happen (the number of *possible successful outcomes*) divided by the number of possible ways things like this could happen (the number of *all possible outcomes*). In this example, for part (a) there are 10 different drug/alcohol people you might pick out of a total of 50 people you are picking from. Thus, the probability is 10/50 = .2.

10. A *sample* is a group of people studied that represent the entire group to which the results are intended to apply, called the *population*. (In this example, the population is all Australian high school students.) You study a sample because it would be impractical or impossible to test the entire population. One way of ensuring that the sample is not systematically unrepresentative is to select the sample randomly. This does not mean haphazardly. For example, just taking the students who are easily available to test would be haphazard sampling. But this would not be a good method because whatever factors made them easily available—such as living in a nearby town—might make them unrepresentative of the population as a whole. An example of a truly random method would be to acquire a list of all the high school students in Australia, number each student, and then use a table of random numbers to pick as many as are to be surveyed.

11. Like 10 above.

Chapter 6

1. (a) The logical, statistical procedure for determining the likelihood of your study having gotten a particular pattern of results if the null hypothesis is true. (b) The situation in hypothesis testing in which you decide to reject the null hypothesis because the probability of getting your particular results if the null hypothesis were true is less than 5%. (c) A procedure used in hypothesis testing when the research hypothesis does not specify a particular direction of difference—it tests for extreme results that are either higher or lower than would be expected by chance.

2. It is possible that the research hypothesis is correct but the result in the particular sample was not extreme enough to be able to reject the null hypothesis.

3. (i) (a) Population 1: Canadian children of librarians; Population 2: All Canadian children. (b) Population 1 children have a higher average reading ability than Population 2 children. (c) Population 1's average reading ability is not higher than Population 2's. (d) One-tailed, because the question is whether they "score higher," so only one direction of difference is of interest.

(ii) (a) Population 1: People who live in a particular city; Population 2: All people who live in the region. (b) Populations 1 and 2 have different mean incomes. (c) Populations 1 and 2 have the same mean income. (d) Two-tailed, because the question is whether the income of the people in the city is "different" from those in the region as a whole, so a difference in either direction would be of interest.

(iii) (a) Population 1: People who have experienced an earthquake; Population 2: People in general. (b) Populations 1 and 2 have different mean levels of self-confidence. (c) Populations 1 and 2 have the same mean level of self-confidence. (d) Two-tailed, because they might have either more or less.

4.

Study	Cutoff	Z Score on Comparison Distribution	Decision
A	+1.64	2	Reject null hypothesis
B	±1.96	2	Reject null hypothesis
C	+2.33	2	Inconclusive
D	±2.57	2	Inconclusive
E	+1.64	1	Inconclusive

5.

Study	Cutoff	Z Score on the Comparison Distribution	Decision
A	+1.64	1	Inconclusive
B	±2.57	4	Reject null hypothesis
C	±2.57	3	Reject null hypothesis
D	±2.57	2.5	Inconclusive
E	−1.64	−2	Reject null hypothesis

6. ❶ **Restate the question as a research hypothesis and a null hypothesis about the populations. The two populations of interest are**

Population 1: Students who are prevented from using their sense of smell.
Population 2: Students in general.

The research hypothesis is that students prevented from using their sense of smell (Population 1) will do worse on the taste test than students in general (Population 2). The null hypothesis is that students prevented from using their sense of smell (Population 1) will not do worse on the taste test than students in general (Population 2). ❷ **Determine the characteristics of the comparison distribution.** The comparison distribution will be the same as Population 2. As stated in the problem, $\mu = 14$ and $\sigma = 4$. We assume it follows a normal curve. ❸ **Determine the cutoff sample score on the comparison distribution at which the null hypothesis should be rejected.** At the .05 level, one-tailed, the cutoff is -1.64. ❹ **Determine your sample's score on the comparison distribution.** The sample's score was 5. $Z = (5-14)/4 = -2.25$. ❺ **Decide whether to reject the null hypothesis.** A Z score of -2.25 is more extreme than the cutoff of -1.64. Thus, you can reject the null hypothesis. The research hypothesis is supported—not having a sense of smell makes for fewer correct identifications.

Explanation: In brief, you solve this problem by considering the likelihood that being without a sense of smell makes no difference. If the sense of smell made no difference, the probability of the student studied getting any particular number correct is simply the probability of students in general getting any particular number correct. We know the distribution of the number correct that students get in general. Thus, you can figure that probability. It turns out that it would be fairly unlikely to get only 5 correct—so the researcher concludes that not having the sense of smell does make a difference.

To go into the details a bit, the key issue is determining these probabilities. We assumed that the number correct for the students in general follows a normal curve—a specific bell-shaped mathematical pattern in which most of the scores are in the middle and there are fewer as the numbers get higher or lower. There are tables showing exactly what proportions are between the middle and any particular Z score on the normal curve.

When considering what to conclude from a study, researchers often use a convention that if a result could have happened by chance less than 5% of the time under a particular scenario, that scenario will be considered unlikely. The normal curve tables show that the top 5% of the normal curve begins with a Z score of 1.64. The normal curve is completely symmetrical; thus the bottom 5% includes all Z scores below -1.64. Therefore, the researcher would probably set the following rule: The scenario in which being without the sense of smell makes no difference will be rejected as unlikely if the number correct (converted to a Z score using the mean and standard deviation for students in general) is less than -1.64.

The actual number correct for the student who could not use the sense of smell was 5. The normal curve for students in general had a mean of 14 and a standard deviation of 4. Getting 5 correct is 9 below the mean of 14; in terms of standard deviations of 4 each, it is 9/4 below the mean. A Z of -2.25 is more extreme than -1.64. Thus, the researcher concludes that the scenario in which being without smell has no effect is unlikely. This is illustrated below.

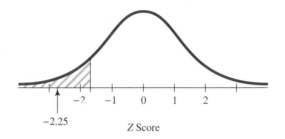

7. Cutoff (.01 level, one-tailed) $= -2.326$; Z score on comparison distribution for patient studied $= +1.2$; the experiment is inconclusive. Hypothesis testing steps, explanation, and sketch similar to 6 above.

8. Cutoff (.05 level, two-tailed) $= \pm 1.96$; Z score on comparison distribution for the police chief studied $= .81$; the experiment is inconclusive. Hypothesis testing steps, explanation, and sketch similar to 6 above.

9. The two Ms (5.7 and 4.8) and the $p < .05$ are crucial. M stands for *mean,* the average of the scores in a particular group. The average number of times per day the high narcissism participants looked in the mirrors was 5.7, while the average for the low narcissism participants was only 4.8. The $p < .05$ tells us that this difference is statistically significant at the .05 level. This means that if a person's level of narcissism made no difference in how often the person looked in the mirror, the chances of getting two groups of participants who were this different on looking in the mirror just by chance would be less than 5%. Hence, you can reject that possibility as unlikely and conclude that the level of narcissism does make a difference in how often people look in the mirror.

10. Similar to 9 above.

Chapter 7

1. There is less variation among means of samples of more than one score than there are among individual scores. This is because the likelihood of two extreme scores in the same direction randomly ending up in the same sample is less than the probability of each of those extreme scores being chosen individually.

2. (a) $\sigma^2 = 10^2 = 100$; $\sigma_M^2 = \sigma^2/N = 100/2 = 50$; $\sigma_M = \sqrt{\sigma_M^2} = \sqrt{50} = 7.07$; (b) 5.77; (c) 5; (d) 3.33.

3. (a) $\sigma^2 = 20^2 = 400$; $\sigma_M^2 = \sigma^2/N = 400/2 = 200$; $\sigma_M = \sqrt{\sigma_M^2} = \sqrt{200} = 14.14$; (b) 11.55; (c) 10; (d) 6.67.

4. (a) Lower limit $= M - (\sigma_M)(1.96) = 100 - (7.07)(1.96) = 86.14$; upper limit $= 100 + (7.07)(1.96) = 113.86$; (b) 88.69, 111.31; (c) 90.2, 109.8; (d) 93.47, 106.53.

5. (a) Lower limit $= M - (\sigma_M)(2.57) = 10 - (14.14)(2.57) = -26.34$; upper limit $= 10 + (14.14)(2.57) = 46.34$; (b) $-19.68, 39.68$; (c) $-15.7, 35.7$; (d) $-7.14, 27.14$.

6. (a) ❶ **Restate the question as a research hypothesis and a null hypothesis about the populations.** The two populations are:

Population 1: People given the experimental treatment
Population 2: People in general (who do not get the experimental treatment).

The research hypothesis is that the population given the experimental treatment (Population 1) has a different mean score than people in general (Population 2). The null hypothesis is that Population 1's mean is the same as Population 2's.
❷ **Determine the characteristics of the comparison distribution.** Comparison distribution is a distribution of means of samples of 10 taken from the distribution of Population 2. $\mu = 40$; $\sigma_M^2 = \sigma^2/N = 6^2/10 = 3.6$; $\sigma_M = \sqrt{3.6} = 1.90$. Because the population is normal, the distribution of means is normal.
❸ **Determine the cutoff sample score on the comparison distribution at which the null hypothesis should be rejected.** Using a two-tailed test at the .05 level, the cutoffs are ± 1.96.
❹ **Determine your sample's score on the comparison distribution.** $Z = (44 - 40)/1.90 = 2.11$.
❺ **Decide whether to reject the null hypothesis.** 2.11 is more extreme than 1.96. Thus, you can reject the null hypothesis. The research hypothesis is supported; those who receive the experimental treatment score differently from the general population.
Drawing of the distributions involved is shown below.

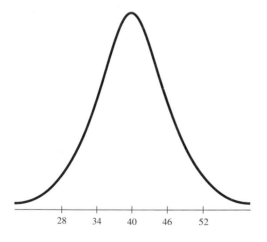

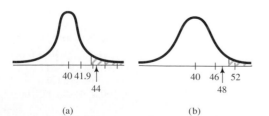

(a)   (b)

95% confidence interval: Lower limit $= M - (\sigma_M)(1.96) = 44 - (1.9)(1.96) = 40.28$; upper limit $= 47.72$.
(b) Hypothesis-testing steps similar to (a) above. $\sigma_M = 6$; $Z = (48 - 40)/6 = 1.33$; do not reject the null hypothesis; study is inconclusive as to whether those who those receive the experimental treatment are different from those in the general population. 95% confidence interval: 36.24 to 59.76.

7. Hypothesis-testing steps and drawing similar to 6 above. (a) $\sigma_M = .8$; $Z = (82 - 81)/.8 = 1.25$; do not reject the null hypothesis; 99% confidence interval: 79.94 to 84.06. (b) $\sigma_M = 2.53$; $Z = (84 - 81)/2.53 = 1.19$; do not reject the null hypothesis; 99% confidence interval: 77.5 to 90.5.

8. (a) and (b) Hypothesis-testing steps and drawing similar to 6 above. $\sigma_M = .1$; $Z = (1.5 - 1.8)/.1 = -3$; reject the null hypothesis. (c) 1.24 to 1.76.
   (d) This is a standard hypothesis-testing problem, with one exception. You can't compare directly the reaction times for the group of 25 women tested to a distribution of reaction times for individual women. The probability of a group of scores having an extreme mean just by chance is much less than the probability of any one individual having an extreme score just by chance. (When taking a group of scores at random, any extreme individual scores are likely to be balanced out by less extreme or oppositely extreme scores). Thus, you need to compare the mean of the group of 25 reaction times to a distribution of what would happen if you were to take many random groups of 25 reaction time scores and find the mean of each group of 25 scores.
   Such a distribution of many means of samples has the same mean as the original distribution of individual scores (there is no reason for it to be otherwise). However, it is a narrower curve. This is because the chances of extremes are less. In fact, its variance will be exactly the variance of the original distribution of individuals divided by the number of scores in each sample. In this example, this makes a distribution of means with a mean of 1.8 and a standard deviation of .1 (that is, the square root of $.5^2$ divided by 25). This will be a normal distribution because a distribution of many means from a normally distributed population is also normal.
   The cutoff for significance, using the .01 level and a one-tailed test, is -2.33. The mean rating of the group of 25 women who received the special program, 1.5, was 3 standard deviations below the mean of the distribution of means, making it clearly more extreme than the cutoff. Thus, you can reject the null hypothesis and conclude that the results support the hypothesis that elderly women who take part in the special program have lower reaction times.
   The confidence interval is an estimate (based on your sample's mean and the standard deviation of the distribution of means) of the range of values that is likely to include the true population mean for the group studied (Population 1; in this example, women who receive the special reaction-time program). A 99% confidence interval is the range of values you are 99% confident includes the true population mean. The lower limit of this interval is the mean of the lowest distribution of means that would have a 99% chance of including this sample mean; its upper limit is the mean of the highest distribu-

tion of means that would have a 99% chance of including this sample mean.

To figure the confidence interval, you first consider that the best single point estimate of the mean of Population 1 is the sample's mean (in this case, 1.5). You then assume that the standard deviation of the distribution of means for this population is the same as for the known population (which we figured earlier to be .1). Based on this information, if the true population mean was 1.5, 99% of the time, sample means would fall between a Z score of -2.57 (the point on the normal curve that includes 49.5% of the scores below the mean) and $+2.57$. In our example, these Z scores correspond to raw scores of 1.24 and 1.76.

It turns out that the values figured in this way are the limits of the confidence interval. Why? Suppose the true population mean was 1.24. In this case, there would be a .5% chance of getting a mean as large as or larger than 1.5. (That is, with a mean of 1.24 and a standard deviation of .1, 1.5 is exactly 2.57 standard deviations above the mean, which is the point that corresponds to the cutoff for the top .5% of this curve.) Similarly, if the true population mean was 1.76, there would be only a .5% chance of getting a mean lower than 1.5.

9. (a) and (b) Hypothesis-testing steps and drawing similar to 6 above. $\sigma_M = .2$; $Z = (5.9-5.5)/.2 = 2$; reject the null hypothesis. (c) 5.51 to 6.29. (d) Similar to 8d above, plus an explanation of material from previous chapters on hypothesis testing, normal curve, means, and standard deviations.

10. The lines that go above and into each bar show, for that particular group, the standard deviation of the distribution of means for people like those in this group. (Then explain a distribution of means as in 8d above.)

11. Similar to confidence interval part of 8d above.

(b) and (c) are similar to 4a above.

5. (a) A small positive effect size is .2; predicted $\mu_1 = \mu_2 + (d)(\sigma) = 15 + (.2)(2) = 15.4$; (b) 14; (c) 16.6; (d) 15.7; (e) 12.

6.

	Z Needed for Significance	σ_M	Score for Significance
(a)	1.64	.4	90.66
(b)	1.64	.4	90.66
(c)	1.64	.2	90.33
(d)	1.64	1.0	91.64
(e)	2.33	.4	90.93
(f)	1.96	.4	90.78

	Z for Significance on the Predicted Population	Beta	Power	Effect Size
(a)	$(90.66 - 91)/.4 = -.85$	.20	.80	1/4
(b)	$(90.66 - 92)/.4 = -3.35$	< .01	> .99	1/2
(c)	$(90.33 - 91)/.2 = -3.35$	< .01	> .99	1/2
(d)	$(91.64 - 91)/1 = .64$	.74	.26	1/4
(e)	$(90.93 - 91)/.4 = -.18$	.43	.57	1/4
(f)	$(90.78 - 91)/.4 = -.55$	.29	.71	1/4

Drawing of overlapping distributions for version (a) appears at the top of page 658.

Chapter 8

1. (a) The probability of falsely rejecting the null hypothesis. (b) The probability of failing to reject the null hypothesis when in fact the null hypothesis is false.

2. (a) $d = (\mu_1 - \mu_2)/\sigma = (19 - 25)/12 = -.5$, medium; (b) $-.25$, small; (c) 0, no effect; (d) .42, medium; (e) .83, large.

3. (a) $d = (\mu_1 - \mu_2)/\sigma = (50 - 50)/5 = 0$, no effect (b) .4, medium; (c) .8; large; (d) 1.2, large; (e) $-.6$, medium.

4. (a)

Conclusion from Hypothesis Testing	Real Situation	
	Null Hypothesis True	Research Hypothesis True
Research Hypothesis Supported (Reject null)	*Type I Error* Decide more recess time improves behavior but it really doesn't	*Correct Decision* Decide more recess time improves behavior and it really does
Study Inconclusive (Do no reject null)	*Correct Decision* Decide effect of recess time on behavior is not shown in this study; actually more recess time doesn't improve behavior	*Type II Error* Decide effect of recess time on behavior is not shown in this study; actually more recess time improves behavior

Sketch for (a):

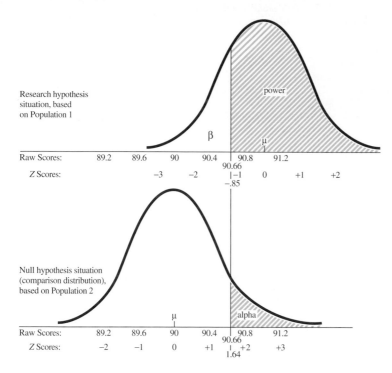

7. (a) ❶ $\sigma_M = 2$; ❷ significance cutoff: $Z = 1.64$; raw $= 50 + (1.64)(2) = 53.28$; ❸ corresponding Z on predicted distribution $= (53.28 - 55)/2 = -.86$; ❹ from Z table, power $= .81$, beta $= .19$.

(b)

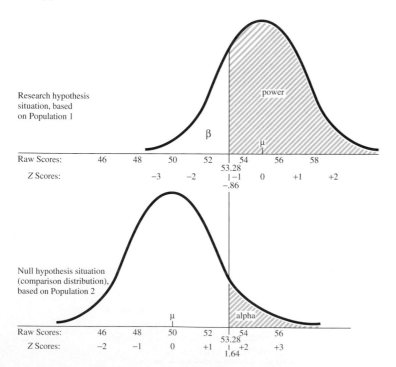

(c) Power is the chance of rejecting the null hypothesis if the research hypothesis is true. To find power, you first need the standard deviation of the comparison distribution (2 here) and the cutoff to reject the null hypothesis in raw score terms (this is a one-tailed test at the .05 level, so it is a Z of 1.64, which for this distribution's mean and standard deviation is 53.28). You also have to be able to assume that the distribution of both the known population (Population 2) and the distribution for the population based on the research hypothesis (Population 1) follow a normal curve and have the same variance. Then comes the power figuring. The researcher hypothesizes that the mean of the population of artists (Population 1) is 55. The distribution of means from this population would be normal with mean = 55 and σ_M = 2. We already figured that any mean above 53.28 will be significant in terms of the comparison distribution. But a score of 53.28 has a Z score of only −.86 on the distribution of means based on the researcher's hypothesis. Using the normal curve table, 81% is above −.86. Assuming that the researcher's predictions are correct, there is an 81% chance that a sample of 36 artists will produce a result high enough to reject the null hypothesis. That is, power is 81%.

8. (a) ❶ σ_M = .89; predicted mean on Population 1 = 11 + (.8)(.89) = 11.71. ❷ significance cutoff: Z = 2.57; raw = 11 + (2.57)(.89) = 12.52; ❸ corresponding Z on predicted distribution = (11.71 − 12.52)/.89 = −.91); ❹ from Z table, power = .82, beta = .18.
   8(b) and 8(c) are similar to 7b and 7c above.

9. (a) Not affected; (b) possibly of small importance; (c) Regarding situation (a), the significance level tells you the probability of getting your results if the null hypothesis is true; sample size is already taken into account in figuring the significance. Regarding situation (b), it is possible to get a significant result with a large sample even when the actual practical effect is slight—such as when the mean of your sample (and thus, your best estimate of the mean of the population that gets the experimental treatment) is only slightly higher than the mean of the known population. This is possible because significance is based on the difference between the mean of your sample and the known population mean divided by the standard deviation of the distribution of means. If the sample size is very large, then the distribution of means is very small (because it is figured by dividing the population variance by the sample size). Thus, even a small difference between the means when divided by a very small denominator can give a large overall result, making the study significant.

10. Similar to 7c above.

11. (a) Increases power; (b) decreases power; (c) increases power; (d) decreases power; (e) decreases power.

12. (a) When planning an experiment, to permit changes of various kinds (or even abandon the project) if power is too low. (Or possibly make the study less costly, for example, by reducing number of participants, if power is higher than reasonably needed.) (b) After a study is done that had nonsignificant results, to evaluate whether the result should be attributed to the null hypothesis's being false (in the high-power situation) or to inadequate power so that it is still reasonable to think that future research might have a chance of being significant. (Also, in the case of a significant result with a large sample, if power is very high, this suggests that a low effect size is possible, so that although the result is significant, it may not be very important.)

Chapter 9

1. (a) t needed (df = 63, $p < .05$, one-tailed) = −1.671; S_M = $\sqrt{S^2/N}$ = $\sqrt{9/64}$ = .38; t = $(M − \mu)/S_M$ = (11 − 12.40)/.38 = −3.68; reject null hypothesis. (b) t needed = 2.690; S_M = 2.55; t = 1.32; do not reject null hypothesis. (c) t needed = 2.364; S_M = .13; t = 3.15; reject null hypothesis.

2. (a) ❶ **Restate the question as a research hypothesis and a null hypothesis about populations.**

   Population 1: Response times under the new sheriff.
   Population 2: Response times under the old sheriff.

   The null hypothesis is that the two populations are the same. The research hypothesis is that the two populations are different.
   ❷ **Determine the characteristics of the comparison distribution.** Population 2: shape = assumed normal; μ = 30; σ^2 = unknown; S^2 = $\Sigma(X − M)^2/(N − 1)$ = 124/(10 − 1) = 13.78. Distribution of means: shape = t (df = 9); μ_M = 30; S_M = $\sqrt{S^2/N}$ = 1.17
   ❸ **Determine the cutoff sample score on the comparison distribution at which the null hypothesis should be rejected.** t needed (df = 9, $p < .05$, one-tailed) = −1.833.
   ❹ **Determine your sample's score on the comparison distribution.** M = $\Sigma X/N$ = 280/10 = 28; t = $(M − \mu)/S_M$ = (28 − 30)/1.17 = −1.71
   ❺ **Decide whether to reject the null hypothesis.** −1.71 is not more extreme than −1.833; do not reject the null hypothesis.
   (b)

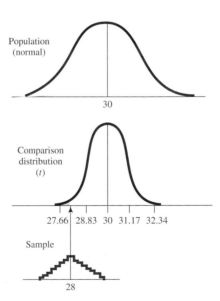

Population (normal)

30

Comparison distribution (t)

27.66   28.83   30   31.17   32.34

Sample

28

   (c) Similar to 5c below except instead of difference scores, actual scores are used here, and the expected population mean is the 30 minutes (1/2 hour) that the sheriff had promised to do better than when a candidate.

3. Hypothesis testing steps and sketch similar to 2a and b above. t needed = 2.776; t = $(M − \mu)/S_M$ = (46 − 40)/2.3 = 2.61; do not reject the null hypothesis.

4. (a) t needed ($df = 19$, $p < .05$, one-tailed) $= 1.729$.
   $S_M = \sqrt{S^2/N} = \sqrt{8.29/20} = \sqrt{.415} = .64$.
   $t = (M - \mu)/S_M = (1.7 - 0)/.64 = 2.66$.
   Reject null hypothesis.

   (b) t needed $= \pm 1.980$; $S_M = \sqrt{414.53/164} = 1.59$; $t = (2.3 - 0)/1.59 = 1.45$; do not reject null hypothesis.

   (c) t needed $= -2.624$; $S_M = .52$; $t = -4.23$; reject null hypothesis.

5. (a) ❶ **Restate the question as a research hypothesis and a null hypothesis about populations.**

   Population 1: Cities like those who participated in the anti-littering program.
   Population 2: Cities who do not change in the amount of litter over a one-year period.

   The research hypothesis is that Population 1 has a greater mean decrease in litter than Population 2. The null hypothesis is that Population 1 doesn't have a greater mean decrease in litter than Population .

   ❷ **Determine the characteristics of the comparison distribution.** Population 2: Shape = assumed normal; $\mu = 0$; σ^2 = unknown; $S^2 = 50/3 = 16.67$. Distribution of means: shape $= t$ ($df = 3$); $\mu_M = 0$; $S_M = \sqrt{S^2/N} = \sqrt{16.67/4} = 2.04$.

   ❸ **Determine the cutoff sample score on the comparison distribution at which the null hypothesis should be rejected.** t needed ($df = 3$, $p < .01$, one-tailed) $= 4.541$.

   ❹ **Determine your sample's score on the comparison distribution.** Change scores $= 7, 6, -1, 8$; $M = 20/4 = 5$; $t = (5 - 0)/2.04 = 2.45$.

   ❺ **Decide whether to reject the null hypothesis.** 2.45 is not more extreme than 4.541; do not reject the null hypothesis.

   (b)

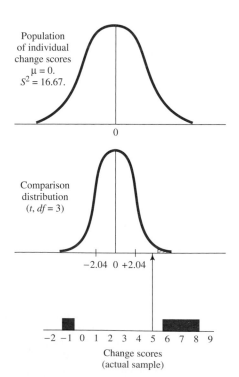

Population of individual change scores
$\mu = 0$.
$S^2 = 16.67$.

0

Comparison distribution
(t, $df = 3$)

−2.04 0 +2.04

−2 −1 0 1 2 3 4 5 6 7 8 9

Change scores
(actual sample)

(c) The first thing I did was to simplify things by converting the numbers to change scores—postprogram (2002) litter minus preprogram (2001) litter for each city—and found the mean of these change scores, which was 5. The next step was to see whether this result, found in these five cities, indicates some real difference more generally due to being in this program. The alternative is the possibility that this much change could have occurred in four randomly selected cities just by chance even if in general the program had no real effect (creates a mean change of 0).

I then considered just how much a group of four cities would have to change before I could conclude that they have changed too much to chalk up to chance. This required figuring out the characteristics of this imagined population of cities which, on the average, had no change. An average of no change is the same as saying it has a mean of 0 change. I didn't know the variance of this imaginary distribution, so I estimated it from the information in the sample of four cities. If the sample cities are just random examples from this distribution of no change, the variance of these cities should reflect the variance of this distribution (which would be the distribution they come from). However, the variance figured from a particular group (sample) from a larger population will in general be slightly smaller than the true population's variance. This is because the variance in the sample is based on squared deviations from the sample's mean. The sample mean is the perfect balance point for its scores, so that the sum of squared deviations from it will be smaller than the sum of squared deviations from any other number (such as the true population mean). Thus, instead of dividing the sum of the squared deviations by the number of scores, I divided it instead by the degrees of freedom, which is the number of scores minus 1—in this case, 3. (This adjustment exactly accounts for the tendency of the variance in the sample to underestimate the true population variance.) This gave an estimated population variance (S^2) of 16.67.

I was interested not in individual cities but in a group of four; I needed the characteristics of a distribution of means of samples of four drawn from this hypothetical population of individual city change scores. Such a distribution of means also has a mean of 0 (there is no reason to expect the means of such groups of four taken randomly to be systematically higher or lower than 0). But such a distribution will have a much smaller variance (because the average of a group of four scores is a lot less likely to be extreme than any individual score). Fortunately, it can be proved mathematically that the variance of a distribution of means is the variance of the distribution of individuals divided by the number of individuals in each sample. This works out here to be 4.17; the standard deviation, the square root of 4.17, is 2.04.

If you assume that the imaginary population of individual cities' change scores is normally distributed (and we have no reason to think otherwise), you can think of the distribution of means of samples from that distribution as having a precise known shape, called a t

distribution (which has slightly higher tails than a normal curve). Looking in a table for a t distribution for the situation in which there are 3 degrees of freedom used to estimate the population variance, the table shows that there is a less than a 1% chance of getting a score that is 4.541 standard deviations from the mean of this distribution.

The mean change score for the four cities was 5, which is 2.45 (that is, 5/2.04) standard deviations above the mean of 0 change on this distribution of means of change scores. This is not as extreme as 4.541, so there is more than a 1% chance that these results could have come from a hypothetical distribution with no change. Therefore, the researcher would not rule out that possibility, and the study would be considered inconclusive.

6. (a), (b), and (c). Hypothesis-testing steps, sketch, and explanation similar to 5 above. t needed $= \pm2.776$; $t = (M - \mu)/S_M = (.014 - 0)/.005 - 2.8$; reject the null hypothesis. (Note: This result is very close to the cutoff level; if you round off slightly differently, your result might not be significant. This is one of those rare situations in which different ways of rounding can produce different results.)

7. (a) Estimated $d = (M - 0)/S = (20 - 0)/32 = .625$, medium effect size; (b) .5, medium; (c) .25, small; (d) .2, small.

8. From Table 9–9: (a) .22; (b) .71; (c) .86; (d) .77; (e) .99.

9. From Table 9–10: (a) 33; (b) 12; (c) 156.

10. Similar to 5c above except focusing on this study and the simpler situation involving just a single sample and also does not need to explain the basic logic of hypothesis testing (only what is added when you have an unknown population variance).

11. Similar to 5b and 5c above except c should focus on this study and material on mean, standard deviation, and variance should be added, as in the answers to Chapter 2 problems.

12. (a) Anxiety: $S_M = \sqrt{S^2/N} = \sqrt{1.85^2/100} = .185$, $t = 1.50/.185 = 8.11$; Depression: $S_M = .423$; $t = 7.28$; Introversion: $S_M = .222$; $t = 1.04$; Neuroticism: $S_M = .421$; $t = 2.11$.

(b) Similar to 5c above except focusing on this study and material on mean, standard deviation, and variance should be added as in the answers to Chapter 2 problems.

$t = 2.00$; do not reject the null hypothesis. (c) $S^2_{\text{Pooled}} = 2.6$; $S_{\text{Difference}} = .417$; $t = 2.16$; reject the null hypothesis.

4. (a) ❶ **Restate the question as a research hypothesis and a null hypothesis about populations.**

Population 1: People who get their news from TV.
Population 2: People who get their news from radio.

The research hypothesis is that the two populations have different means. The null hypothesis is that the two populations have the same mean.
❷ **Determine the characteristics of the comparison distribution.** $S^2_{\text{Pooled}} = (60/80)(4) + (20/80)(6) = 4.5$; comparison distribution (distribution of differences between means): $M = 0$; $S_{\text{Difference}} = .54$; Shape = $t(80)$.
❸ **Determine the cutoff sample score on the comparison distribution at which the null hypothesis should be rejected.** t needed ($df - 80$, $p < .01$, two-tailed) $- \pm2.639$.
❹ **Determine your sample's score on the comparison distribution.** $t = (24 - 26)/.54 = -3.70$.
❺ **Decide whether to reject the null hypothesis.** -3.70 is more extreme than ±2.639; reject the null hypothesis; the prediction is supported by the experiment.
(b)

Chapter 10

1. (a) Independent; (b) dependent; (c) dependent.

2. (a) $S^2_{\text{Pooled}} = [df_1/(df_1 + df_2)](S^2_1) + [df_2/(df_1 + df_2)](S^2_2) = (19/38)(1) + (19/38)(2) = 1.5$; $S^2_{M1} = S^2_{\text{Pooled}}/N_1 = 1.5/20 = .075$; $S^2_{M2} = .075$; $S^2_{\text{Difference}} = S^2_{M1} + S^2_{M2} = .075 + .075 = .15$; $S_{\text{Difference}} = .39$.

(b) .35; (c) .1; (d) .27; (e) .35.

3. (a) t needed ($df = 58$, $p < .05$, two-tailed) $= \pm2.004$; $S^2_{\text{Pooled}} = [df_1/(df_1 + df_2)](S^2_1) + [df_2/(df_1 + df_2)](S^2_2) = (29/58)(2.4) + (29/58)(2.8) = 2.6$; $S^2_{M1} = S^2_{\text{Pooled}}/N_1 = 2.6/30 = .087$; $S^2_{M2} = .087$; $S^2_{\text{Difference}} = S^2_{M1} + S^2_{M2} = .174$; $S_{\text{Difference}} = .417$; $t = (M_1 - M_2)/S_{\text{Difference}} = (12 - 11.1)/.417 = 2.16$. Conclusion: Reject the null hypothesis. The difference is significant. (b) $S^2_{\text{Pooled}} = 2.7$; $S_{\text{Difference}} = .451$;

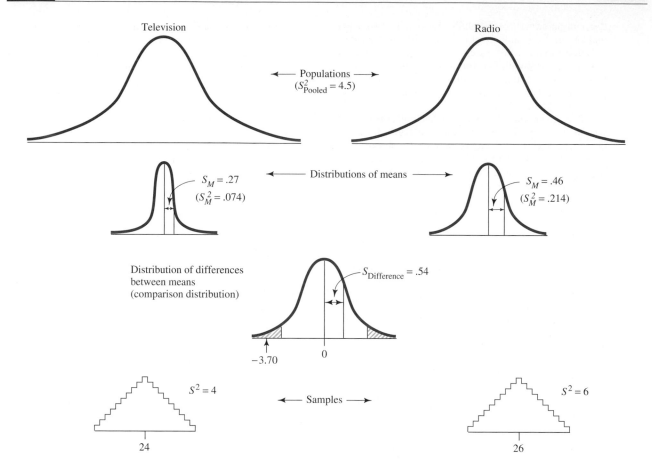

(c) In this situation I am testing whether the two samples come from identical populations. I have two estimates of those identical populations, one from each sample. Thus, to get the most accurate overall estimate, I can average the two. In order to give more weight to the estimate based on the larger degrees of freedom, I figure a weighted average, multiplying each estimate by its proportion of the total degrees of freedom and adding up the results. This pooled estimate of the population variance comes out to 4.5.

Because I was interested not in individual scores but in the difference between the mean of a group of 61 and the mean of another group of 21, I needed to figure out what would be the characteristics of a distribution of differences between means of groups of 61 and 21 that are randomly taken from the two identical populations whose variance I just estimated. This required two steps. First I figured the characteristics of the distribution of means in the usual way for the population associated with each sample, but using my pooled estimate for the variance of each population of individuals. This came out to .074 for the TV group and .214 for the radio group. The second step is directly about the distribution of differences between means. It is like a distribution you would get if you took a mean from the distribution of

means from the TV group and took one from the comparable distribution for the radio group and figured their difference. After doing this many times, the distribution of these differences would make up a new distribution, of differences between means. Because we are assuming (if radio versus TV made no difference) that the two original populations have the same means, the two distributions of means have the same mean. On average, the difference between a mean taken from the TV group and a mean taken from the radio group should come out to 0 (because sometimes one will be bigger and sometimes the other, but in the long run these random fluctuations should balance out). The variance of this distribution of differences between means is affected by the variation in both distributions of means—in fact, it is just the sum of the two. Thus, its variance is .074 plus .214, or .288. Its square root, the standard deviation of the distribution of differences, is .54.

Because this whole process is based on estimated variances, the distribution of means is a t distribution with degrees of freedom equal to the total number of degrees of freedom that went into the two estimates—thus $df = 80$. Looking this up on the t table for .01 two-tailed gives a cutoff needed of 2.639. The t for my sample is the difference between the two groups divided by the standard deviation of the distribution of differences between means: $24 - 26 / .54 = -3.70$. This is more extreme than the cutoff, so I can reject the null hypothesis.

5. (a), (b), and (c). Hypothesis-testing steps, sketch, and explanation similar to 4 above (except c also needs to include basic material as in answers to previous chapters' problems). t needed $= \pm 2.262$; $S^2_{\text{Pooled}} = (5/9)(5.6) + (4/9)(19.3) = 11.69$; $S^2_{\text{Difference}} = 1.95 + 2.34 = 4.29$; $t = (6 - 9.6)/2.07 = -1.73$. Do not reject the null hypothesis; the experiment is inconclusive as to whether including the child's name makes a difference. (Note: The scores in this problem seem to violate the assumption of equal population variances. However, because the result was not significant even using the ordinary procedure, it would probably not be significant using a modified procedure.)

6. (a), (b), and (c). Hypothesis-testing steps, sketch, and explanation similar to 4 above. t needed $= 1.943$; $S^2_{\text{Pooled}} = (2/6)(12.33) + (4/6)(6.7) = 8.58$; $S^2_{\text{Difference}} = 2.86 + 1.72 = 4.58$; $t = (5.33 - 5.2)/2.24 = .06$. Do not reject the null hypothesis; the experiment is inconclusive as to whether older children do better.

7. (a) $d = (24 - 26)/4.5 = -.94$; (b) 1.05; (c) .04.

8. (a) Harmonic mean $= (2)(N_1)(N_2)/(N_1 + N_2) = (2)(3)(57)/(3 + 57) = 5.7$, from Table 10–5 approximate power $= .11$; (b) harmonic mean $= 16.7$, power $= .15$; (c) harmonic mean $= 26.7$, power $= .19$; (d) power $= .19$.

9. (a) $d = (107 - 149)/84 = -.50$; medium effect size; needed N (from Table 10–6) $= 50$ per group, 100 total. (b) $d = .20$, needed $N = 393$ per group, 786 total. (c) $d = .80$, needed $N = 20$ per group, 40 total. (d) $d = -.80$; needed $N = 26$ per group, 52 total.

10. [Along with the following include a full explanation of all terms and concepts as in 4c and answers to previous chapters' explanation problems] This study shows that using a conventional .05 significance level, German children who receive low levels of support—whether from their mother, father, or classmates—showed lower levels of self-worth. Further, the effect sizes were fairly large ($d = .78$ and $d = .69$) with regard to support from mother or father; however, the effect size was only small to moderate ($d = .35$) with regard to support from classmates. This would seem to imply that support from parents is more important than support from classmates in terms of a child's feeling of self-worth. The power of the study for a large effect size is .98. (This assumes there were about equal numbers of children in the high and low support groups, that the test is two-tailed, and uses the figure for 50 in each group.) The power for a medium effect size is .70. Because we already know that the results are significant and we know the effect sizes, the power calculations are not very important.

11. Similar to 10 above.

Chapter 11

1. (a) F needed ($df = 2, 27$; $p < .05$) $= 3.36$; $S^2_{\text{Between}} = (SS/df)(n) = \{[(7.4 - 7)^2 + (6.8 - 7)^2 + (6.8 - 7)^2]/(3 - 1)\}(10) = 1.2$; $S^2_{\text{Within}} = (.82 + .90 + .80)/3 = .84$;

$F = 1.2/.84 = 1.43$; do not reject the null hypothesis. (b) F needed ($df = 3, 96$; $p < .05$) $= 2.70$ (actually using $df = 3, 95$); $S^2_{\text{Between}} = 4,116.75$; $S^2_{\text{Within}} = 736.5$; $F = 5.59$; reject the null hypothesis. (c) F needed ($df = 4, 120$; $p < .05$) $= 2.46$ (actually using $df = 4, 100$); $S^2_{\text{Between}} = 3,087.5$; $S^2_{\text{Within}} = 735$; $F = 420$; reject null hypothesis.

2. (a) F needed ($df = 2, 9$; $p < .01$) $= 8.02$; Group 1: $M = 8$, $S^2 = .67$; Group 2: $M = 6$, $S^2 = .67$; Group 3: $M = 4$, $S^2 = .67$; $S^2_{\text{Between}} = (4)(4) = 16$; $S^2_{\text{Within}} = .67$; $F = 16/.67 = 23.88$; reject the null hypothesis. (b) F needed ($df = 2, 9$; $p < .01$) $= 8.02$; Group 1: $M = 8$, $S^2 = 21.33$; Group 2: $M = 6$, $S^2 = 21.33$; Group 3: $M = 4$, $S^2 = 21.33$; $S^2_{\text{Between}} = 16$; $S^2_{\text{Within}} = 21.33$; $F = .75$; do not reject the null hypothesis.

3. (a) ❶ **Restate the question as a research hypothesis and a null hypothesis about populations.**

Population 1: Patients with affective disorders.
Population 2: Patients with cognitive disorders.
Population 3: Patients with drug-related conditions.

The research hypothesis is that the three population means differ. The null hypothesis is that the three populations have the same mean.
❷ **Determine the characteristics of the comparison distribution.** F distribution with 2 and 9 degrees of freedom.
❸ **Determine the cutoff sample score on the comparison distribution at which the null hypothesis should be rejected.** 5% level, $F(2,9)$ needed $= 4.26$
❹ **Determine your sample's score on the comparison distribution.** $S^2_{\text{Within}} = (.67 + 3.33 + 2.67) / 3 = 2.22$; $S^2_{\text{Between}} = (5.33)(4) = 21.32$; $F = 9.60$.
❺ **Decide whether to reject the null hypothesis.** 9.60 is more extreme than 4.26; reject the null hypothesis.
(b)

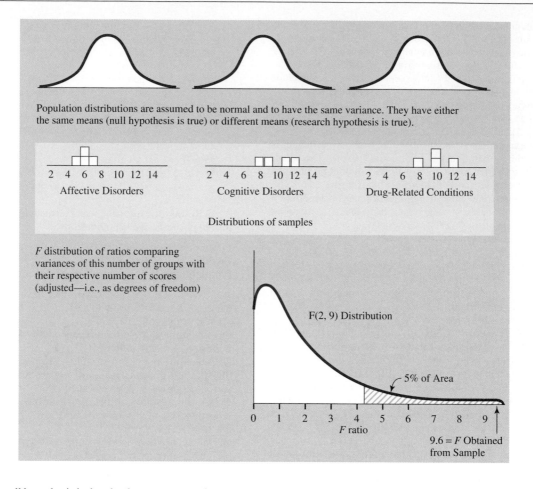

Population distributions are assumed to be normal and to have the same variance. They have either the same means (null hypothesis is true) or different means (research hypothesis is true).

2 4 6 8 10 12 14	2 4 6 8 10 12 14	2 4 6 8 10 12 14
Affective Disorders	Cognitive Disorders	Drug-Related Conditions

Distributions of samples

F distribution of ratios comparing variances of this number of groups with their respective number of scores (adjusted—i.e., as degrees of freedom)

F(2, 9) Distribution

5% of Area

0   1   2   3   4   5   6   7   8   9
F ratio

9.6 = F Obtained from Sample

(c) The null hypothesis is that the three groups are from populations of length-of-stay scores with equal means (and, as with a *t* test, you have to be able to assume that they have equal variances). If this null hypothesis is true, you can estimate the variance of these equal populations in two ways: (i) You can estimate from the variation within each of the three groups and then average them. (This is just what you would do in a *t* test for independent means, except now three are being averaged instead of just two; also in a *t* test we would weight these variances according to the degrees of freedom they contribute to the overall estimate. However, because all groups have equal *N*s, you simply average them—in effect weighting them equally.) This average, called the within-group population variance estimate, comes out to 2.22. (ii) You can also estimate the variance using the three means. If you assume the null hypothesis is true, the three samples are taken from identical populations, each of which will have an identical distribution of means. Thus, the amount of variation among my three means provides a basis for estimating the variation in this distribution of means. Using the usual formula for estimating a population variance, I get 5.33. However, the question is, what would be the distribution of individuals that would have a distribution of means with a variance of 5.33? To find the distribution of means from a distribution of individuals, you divide the variance of the distribution of individuals by the number in each sample. Now, you want to

do the reverse—multiply the variance of the distribution of means by the number in each sample to get the variance of the distribution of individuals. This comes out to 5.33 times 4, or 21.32. This is called the between-group estimate of the population variance.

If the null hypothesis is true, the two estimates should be about the same because they are estimates of the same population and the ratio of the between-group estimate divided by the within-group estimate, called the *F* ratio, should be about 1. However, suppose the null hypothesis is false (the three populations have different means). This will not affect the within-group estimate (because the variation within each group is not affected by whether the population means differ), but it will make the between-group estimate bigger (because the variation between group means will now be affected both by the variation within the distribution of means *and* the variation among the means of the populations). Thus, when the null hypothesis is false, the *F* ratio will be bigger than one. In this problem, the *F* ratio is 21.32/2.22 = 9.60.

Statisticians have made tables of what happens when you figure *F* ratios based on randomly taking a group of four scores from each of three identical populations—the null hypothesis situation for a study like this one. These tables show that there is less than a 5% chance of getting an *F* ratio larger than 4.26; my actual *F* ratio is bigger than this; thus I can reject the null hypothesis.

4. (a), (b), and (c). Hypothesis-testing steps, sketch, and explanation similar to 3 above (except c needs to include material similar to earlier chapters' explanations problems). F needed ($df = 2, 147; p < .05$) = 3.09 (actually using $df = 2, 100$); $S^2_{Between} = (.09)(50) = 4.5$; $S^2_{Within} = (5.2 + 5.8 + 4.8)/3 = 5.27$; $F = .85$; do not reject the null hypothesis.

5. (a), (b), and (c). Hypothesis-testing steps, sketch, and explanation similar to 3 above (except c needs to include material similar to earlier chapters' explanation problems.) F needed ($df = 3, 28; p < .01$) = 4.57; $S^2_{Between} = (155)(8) = 1240$; $S^2_{Within} = (3.5^2 + 4.6^2 + 3.8^2 + 4.9^2)/4 = 17.97$; $F = 69.0$; reject the null hypothesis.

6. (a) F needed ($df = 1, 9; p < .05$) = 5.12; $S^2_{Between}$ (for two means) = (8)(4) = 32; S^2_{Within} (from overall analysis) = 2.22; $F = 32/2.22 = 14.41$; reject the null hypothesis;
   (b) $S^2_{Between} = (0)(4) = 0$; $F = 0/2.22 = 0$; do not reject the null hypothesis.
   (c) In a study with more than two groups, researchers often make predictions for differences between specific pairs of groups; these are called planned comparisons. To test a planned comparison, you do a special analysis of variance in which the between-group estimate is based on just the two groups being compared, but the within-group estimate uses the information from all groups in the overall analysis of variance. (The variation in all populations is assumed to be the same, so this method lets you take advantage of the information in all the groups when figuring the within-group population variance estimate.) Thus, for the first planned comparison (Affective vs Drug-Related Conditions), I figured the between-group estimate using the estimated variance of the distribution of means based on means of these two groups (6 and 10, which came out to $S^2_M = 8$) and then multiplied this by the number in each group (4). The result was 32. Dividing this by the overall within-group estimate I'd figured earlier for Problem 3, which was 2.22, gave an F ratio of 14.41. This was bigger than the needed F for df of 1 (the number of df in figuring the between group estimate) and 9 (the df for the within-group estimate). Thus, I could reject the null hypothesis. Following the same procedure for the second contrast gave an F of 0, which of course was not significant.

7. (a) F needed ($df = 1, 147; p < .05$) = 3.94 (actually using $df = 1, 100$); $S^2_{Between}$ (for two means) = (.18)(50) = 9; S^2_{Within} (from overall analysis) = 5.27; $F = 9/5.27 = 1.71$; do not reject the null hypothesis.
   (b) Similar to 6c above.

8. (a) Bonferroni corrected significance level = .05/5 = .01; F needed ($df = 1, 28; p < .01$) = 7.64; $S^2_{Between}$ (for two means) = (4.5)(8) = 36, S^2_{Within} (from overall analysis) = 17.97, $F = 36/17.97 = 2.00$, do not reject the null hypothesis;
   (b) $S^2_{Between} = (364.5)(8) = 2916$, $F = 2916/17.97 = 162.27$, reject the null hypothesis;
   (c) $S^2_{Between} = (8)(8) = 64$, $F = 64/17.97 = 3.56$, do not reject the null hypothesis;
   (d) $S^2_{Between} = (288)(8) = 2304$, $F = 2304/17.97 = 128.21$, reject the null hypothesis;
   (e) $S^2_{Between} = (264.5)(8) = 2116$, $F = 2116/17.97 = 117.75$, reject the null hypothesis.
   (f) [Explanation of planned comparisons similar to 6c above.] Bonferroni correction is done to take into account that when testing many comparisons, the chance of any one of them coming out significant is greater than the supposed significance level. This is corrected for by using for each comparison a significance level based on dividing the overall significance level by the number of comparisons. In this problem with five comparisons and an overall significance level of .05, each of the five comparisons is tested at the .05/5 = .01 level of significance.

9. (a) .05/2 = .025; (b) .0125; (c) .0033; (d) .002.

10. Like 3c (and also including material from Chapter 10) but focusing on this study's results.

11. Similar to 3c and 6c (and also including material from previous chapters) but focusing on this study's results.

Chapter 12

1. (a) $df_{Total} = N - 1 = 12 - 1 = 11$; $df_{Within} = df_1 + df_2 + \ldots + df_{Last} = (4 - 1) + (4 - 1) + (4 - 1) = 9$; $df_{Between} = N_{Groups} - 1 = 3 - 1 = 2$; F needed ($df = 2, 9; p < .01$) = 8.02.

Group 1						
X	$X - GM$		$X - M$		$M - GM$	
	Dev	Dev^2	Dev	Dev^2	Dev	Dev^2
8	2	4	0	0	2	4
8	2	4	0	0	2	4
7	1	1	−1	1	2	4
9	3	9	1	1	2	4
Σ 32		18		2		16

$M = 32/4 = 8$

Group 2						
X	$X - GM$		$X - M$		$M - GM$	
	Dev	Dev^2	Dev	Dev^2	Dev	Dev^2
6	0	0	0	0	0	0
6	0	0	0	0	0	0
5	−1	1	−1	1	0	0
7	1	1	1	1	0	0
Σ 24		2		2		0

$M = 24/4 = 6$.

Group 3						
X	$X - GM$		$X - M$		$M - GM$	
	Dev	Dev^2	Dev	Dev^2	Dev	Dev^2
4	−2	4	0	0	−2	4
4	−2	4	0	0	−2	4
3	−3	9	−1	1	−2	4
5	−1	1	1	1	−2	4
Σ 16		18		2		16

$M = 16/4 = 4$.

$GM = (32 + 24 + 16)/12 = 72/12 = 6$.
$SS_{Total} = 18 + 2 + 18 = 38$.
$SS_{Within} = 2 + 2 + 2 = 6$.
$SS_{Between} = 16 + 0 + 16 = 32$.

(cont.)

Analysis of variance table:

Source	SS	df	MS	F
Between	32	2	16	23.88
Within	6	9	.67	
Total	38	11		

Conclusion: Reject the null hypothesis

(b) All df as in Chapter 11; $MS_{Between}$, MS_{Within}, and F are the same as $S^2_{Between}$, S^2_{Within}, and F of Chapter 11.

2. (a) and (b) Like 3a and b in Chapter 11. F needed ($df = 3, 5$; $p < .01$) = 12.06.

Source	SS	df	MS	F
Between	298.89	3	99.63	41.51
Within	12	5	2.4	

Conclusion: Reject the null hypothesis.

3. (a) and (b) for both parts Like 3a and b in Chapter 11.
   (i) $M_1 = 4$; $M_2 = 1$; $M_3 = 2$; $GM = 2.33$. F needed ($df = 2, 6$; $p < .05$) = 5.14.

Source	SS	df	MS	F
Between	14	2	7	7.00
Within	6	6	1	

Conclusion: Reject the null hypothesis.

(ii) $M_1 = 4$; $M_2 = 1$; $M_3 = 2$; $GM = 1.89$; F needed ($df = 2, 6$; $p < .05$) = 5.14.

Source	SS	df	MS	F
Between	12.89	2	6.45	4.85
Within	8.00	6	1.33	

Conclusion: Do not reject the null hypothesis.

4. (a and b) Like 3a and 3b in Chapter 11. F needed ($df = 2, 9$; $p < .05$) = 4.26.

Source	SS	df	MS	F
Between	84	2	42	9.95
Within	38	9	4.22	
Total	122	11		

Conclusion: Reject the null hypothesis.

(c) The overall logic is to examine whether the variation in self-esteem among the three samples could have occurred more than 5% of the time if in fact the three samples had been taken at random from three populations of teachers with the same mean self-esteem level. If they were just three random samples from populations with the same mean, the variation in self-esteem level for each group would be a reasonable basis for estimating the population's variation. Similarly, under these conditions, the variation of the means of the groups would also be a basis for estimating the overall population variance (this is because any variation among these means can only be due to variation in scores within the three populations). If both estimates are the same, their ratio should be 1:1, or 1.

But suppose the groups are really from populations with different means. In this situation, the estimate of the variation from the means of the groups should be larger than that based on the variation within each group of teachers. Thus, the ratio would be more than 1.

Because the number of scores in each group is unequal, when figuring an overall estimate the information provided by some groups should count more than others. The way this is handled uses the principle that for each score, its deviation from the overall mean of all scores is equal to its deviation from the mean of its own group plus the deviation of the mean of its group from the overall mean. It also turns out (and can be proved mathematically) that if you square each of these different deviations, the sum of all the squared deviations from the grand mean is equal to the sum of the squared deviations of each score from its mean plus the sum of the squared deviation of each score's group's mean from the grand mean. The latter two sums of squared deviations, when divided by the degrees of freedom involved in each computation, give you the two estimates of the population variance.

In the present problem, the sum of the squared deviations of each score's group's mean from the overall mean (of 6) was 84. The degrees of freedom are 2 because only three groups' means are involved; thus, the population variance estimate is 84/2, or 42. Similarly, the sum of each score's squared deviation from its group's mean was 38. The total degrees of freedom (each group's number of scores minus 1 for all groups) was 9; thus the population variance estimate using the within-group variations is 38/9, or 4.22. The ratio of the two estimates of the population variance is 42/4.22, or 9.95. The distribution of all possible ratios figured in this way for any particular degrees of freedom is known and can be looked up on a standard table. In this problem, a ratio of 4.26 or less would occur by chance 5% of the time—a figure much smaller than our 9.95. Thus, we can conclude that there is a less than 5% chance of getting this much variation among our groups if these self-esteem levels had been actually drawn by chance from three populations of teachers with the same mean.

5. (a) and (b). Similar to 3a and 3b in Chapter 11. F needed ($df = 2, 7$; $p < .05$) = 4.74.

Source	SS	df	MS	F
Between	66	2	33	9.62
Within	24	7	3.43	

Conclusion: Reject the null hypothesis.

(c) Similar to 4c and answers to previous chapters' problems.

6. (a) Effective F = computed $F/df_{Between}$ for overall analysis = $17.21/(5 - 1) = 4.30$; cutoff $F(df = 4, 45; p < .05) = 2.58$; significant. (b) Effective $F = 3.44$, cutoff $F = 2.29$; significant; (c) Effective $F = 4.30$, cutoff $F = 2.47$; significant; (d) Effective $F = 4.30$, cutoff $F = 3.77$; significant.

7. (a) $R^2 = SS_{Between}/SS_{Total} = 32/38 = .84$; (b) .99; (c) .70; (d) .62; (e) .69; (f) .73.

8. (a) $df_{Between} = 4 - 1 = 3$, $df_{Within} = 9 + 11 + 9 + 7 = 36$, $R^2 = [(F)(df_{Between})]/[(F)(df_{Between}) + df_{Within}] = [(4.21)(3)]/[(4.21)(3) + 36] = .26$; (b) .26; (c) .23; (d) .19; (e) .18; (f) .41.

9. From Table 12–7: (a) .09; (b) .12; (c) .10; (d) .38.

10. From Table 12–8: (a) 322; (b) 21; (c) 274; (d) 52.

11. (a) Acceptance, emotional extremes, jealousy; (b) emotional extremes, jealousy, obsessive preoccupation, sexual attraction, desire for union, desire for reciprocation, love at first sight; (c) happiness, friendship, trust, fear of closeness, emotional extremes, jealousy; (d) emotional extremes, jealousy.

(e) After conducting an overall analysis of variance among more than two groups, researchers often go on to conduct an exploratory analysis comparing each pair of groups; these are called a post-hoc (after the fact) comparisons. The problem is that with many comparisons it is possible that some will be significant just by chance more often than the supposed significance level of, say, 5%. When doing post-hoc tests, special procedures have been developed to protect against this problem so that the researcher can be confident that any difference found will be truly no more likely to have occurred by, say, 5% (if that is the significance level chosen) if the null hypothesis is true. The Scheffé test is an example of this kind of procedure.

12. (a), (b), and (c) For all three variables, exclusively dating women had significantly lower levels than each of the other two groups; (d) similar to 11d above.

Chapter 13

1. (i) (a) and (b)

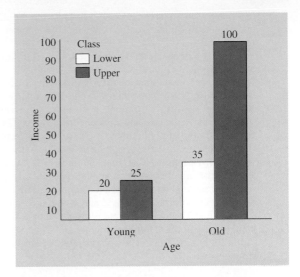

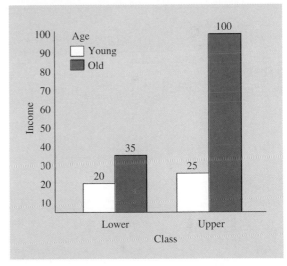

(c) Main effects for class and age, interaction effect; (d) income is greater in general for upper-class and for older individuals, but the combination of older and upper class has a higher income than would be expected just from the effects of either variable alone.

(ii) (a) and (b) Graphs of the same kind as in (i) (a) and (b) above; (c) no main effects, interaction effect; (d) neither type of college nor type of major, by itself, predicts grades, but there is a clear pattern if one considers the combinations: Grades are highest for community college arts majors and for liberal arts college science majors.

(iii) (a) and (b) Graphs of the same kind as in 1 (i) (a) and (b) above; (c) both main effects significant; no interaction. (d) Females miss fewer days per month than males; those who exercise miss fewer days per month than controls. Each combination misses the number of days you would expect knowing their level of each variable separately.

2. (i) (a) and (b) Graphs of the same kind as in 1 (i) (a) and (b) above; (c) main effect for relationship and an interaction.

(d) Conversations are longer with friends; but the difference is much greater for personal than for nonpersonal topics.

(ii) (a) and (b) Graphs of the same kind as in 1 (i) (a) and (b) above; (c) main effect for city and price range, plus an interaction. (d) Restaurant quality is different in different cities, with New York highest and Chicago lowest. Restaurant quality is different in different price ranges, with expensive the best and inexpensive the least. The two factors do not simply combine, however, as price makes more difference in New York than in the other cities.

(iii) (a) and (b) Graphs of the same kind as in 1 (i) (a) and (b) above; (c) main effects for brand and type and an interaction. (d) Flavor is rated on the average more positively for regular than decaf and brands Z and X are rated more favorably than Y. However, there is an interaction in which there is no difference between regular and decaf for brand Z, but for brands Z and Y, regular is rated 2 points higher.

3. Example answers.

Sport

(a)

Condition	Baseball	Football	Basketball	
With motivational program	10	5	6	7
Without motivational program	10	5	6	7
	10	5	6	

(b)

Condition	Baseball	Football	Basketball	
With motivational program	6	6	6	6
Without motivational program	10	10	10	10
	8	8	8	

(c)

Condition	Baseball	Football	Basketball	
With motivational program	6	7	8	7
Without motivational program	8	9	10	9
	7	8	9	

(d)

Condition	Baseball	Football	Basketball	
With motivational program	6	7	8	7
Without motivational program	10	9	8	9
	8	8	8	

(e)

Condition	Baseball	Football	Basketball	
With motivational program	6	7	8	7
Without motivational program	6	8	10	8
	6	7.5	9	

4. F needed for Variable I and interaction ($df = 3, 8$) = 4.07; for Variable II ($df = 1, 8$) = 5.32.

		Variable I				
		1	2	3	4	Overall
Variable II	1	8	2	2	8	5
	2	2	8	8	8	5
Overall		5	5	5	5	

Source	SS	df	MS	F	
Variable I	0	3	0	0	Do not reject null.
Variable II	0	1	0	0	Do not Reject null.
Interaction	144	3	48	24	Reject null.
Within cells	16	8	2		

(Graph of the same kind as in 1 (i) (a) or (b) above.)

5. F needed for each effect in a, b, and c ($df = 1, 8, p < .05$) = 4.26. Graphs of the same kind as in 1 (i) (a) or (b) above.

(i)

		Experimental Condition		
		A	B	Overall
Group	1	.67	2.67	1.67
	2	2.67	.67	1.67
Overall		1.67	1.67	

Source	SS	df	MS	F	
Group	0	1	0	0	Do not reject null.
Condition	0	1	0	0	Do not reject null.
Interaction	12	1	12	35.29	Reject null.
Within cells	2.68	8	.34		

(ii)

		Experimental Condition		
		A	B	Overall
Group	1	.67	.67	.67
	2	2.67	2.67	2.67
Overall		1.67	1.67	

Source	SS	df	MS	F	
Group	12	1	12	35.29	Reject null.
Condition	0	1	0	0	Do not reject null.
Interaction	0	1	0	0	Do not reject null.
Within cells	2.68	8	34		

Source	SS	df	MS	F	
Likability	0	1	0	0	Do not reject null.
Nervousness	0	1	0	0	Do not reject null.
Interaction	48	1	48	24	Reject null.
Within cells	12	8	2		

(iii)

		Experimental Condition		
		A	B	Overall
Group	1	.67	2.67	1.67
	2	.67	2.67	1.67
Overall		.67	2.67	

Source	SS	df	MS	F	
Group	0	1	0	0	Do not reject null.
Condition	12	1	0	35.29	Reject null.
Interaction	0	1	0	0	Do not reject null.
Within cells	2.68	8	.34		

6. (a) F needed for main effect for Diagnosis ($df = 1, 6$) = 5.99; for main effect for Therapy and interaction ($df = 2, 6$) = 5.14.

Source	SS	df	MS	F	
Therapy	8	2	4	1.33	Do not reject null.
Diagnosis	108	1	108	36	Reject null.
Interaction	0	2	0	0	Do not reject null.
Within cells	18	6	3		

(b)

Means:

	A	B	C	
I	4	2	3	3
II	10	8	9	9
	7	5	6	

(c) Similar to 1a above

(d) There is a significant difference in effectiveness between the two diagnostic categories—therapy is more effective for those with Diagnosis II. However, there is no significant difference among types of therapy, and the types of therapy are not significantly differentially effective for the different diagnostic types.

7. (a) F needed for each effect ($df = 1, 8$) = 5.14.

(b)

Means:

	Likable	Not Likable	
Nervous	7	3	5
Not Nervous	3	7	5
	5	5	

(c) Similar to 1a above

(d) These results indicate that there is a significant interaction between nervousness and likability: When the defendant is likable, he is more likely to be rated innocent if he is nervous; but if he is not likable, he is more likely to be rated innocent if he is not nervous. There was no overall significant effect for likable or not or for nervous or not—though with the very small sample sizes involved, failures to reject the null hypothesis should not be taken as evidence that such an effect does not exist.

The figuring of the significance is like a one-way analysis of variance using the structural model approach. The within-group sum of squares and degrees of freedom are figured in the usual way, considering each cell as its own group. However, the between-group deviations from the mean are divided into three parts: One is the variation between likability versus not (based on each participant's liking versus not-liking group's mean minus the grand mean); another is the variation between nervous versus not. The degrees of freedom for each is the number of levels (2 in each case) minus one.

However, following this procedure some of the between-group effect is left over—the variation between likability groups that is different according to which nervousness group they are in. This is an example of what is called an interaction effect. You figure its mean squares based on the deviation of the score from the overall grand mean minus the other three deviations (the score minus its group's mean and the two deviations of its group's mean from the grand mean). Its degrees of freedom are what are left over in the total between-group degrees of freedom (with four subgroups, between-group $df = 3$ minus 1 for likability and minus another 1 for nervousness).

8. (a) $R^2_{\text{Columns}} = SS_{\text{Columns}}/(SS_{\text{Total}} - SS_{\text{Rows}} - SS_{\text{Interaction}}) = 0/(160 - 0 - 144) = 0$, $R^2_{\text{Rows}} = 0$, $R^2_{\text{Interaction}} = .9$. (b) $R^2_{\text{Group}} = 0$, $R^2_{\text{Condition}} = 0$, $R^2_{\text{Interaction}} = .82$; (c) .82, 0, 0; (d) 0, .82., 0; (e) $R^2_{\text{Columns}} = .32$, $R^2_{\text{Rows}} = .86$, $R^2_{\text{Interaction}} = 0$; (f) $R^2_{\text{Columns}} = 0$, $R^2_{\text{Rows}} = 0$, $R^2_{\text{Interaction}} = .8$.

9. (a) $R^2 = $ (Effect F)(df for the effect)/[(Effect F)(df) + df_{Within}] = $(6.12)(1)/[(6.12)(1) + 40]$ = .13; (b) .23; (c) .23; (d) .31; (e) .07; (f) .23.

10. From Table 13–11: (a) .19; (b) .29; (c) .26; (d) .21; (e) .78.

11. From Table 13–12: (a) 197; (b) 197; (c) 33; (d) 132; (e) 162; (f) 162.

12. As expected, participants with extreme stereotypes about PR agents being extroverted, compared to participants with only moderate stereotypes of this kind, described PR agents as more extroverted. This result was statistically significant, meaning that you can be reasonably confident that the pattern of the result applies not just to the particular people studied, but to people like those studied in general. (More precisely, the researchers were able to conclude that if there was no average difference in the general population between extreme and moderate stereotype people, there is less than a .0001 chance that this experiment could have produced a result this strong.) Further, in relation to the effect size (proportion of variance accounted for) typically found in psychology studies, this difference was substantial. (Using the formula based on Fs, $R^2 = .48$.) In addition, and most important, this tendency was surprisingly much stronger for participants who were given a description of a particular PR agent who was highly introverted. This result was also statistically significant. (In this case, the chance was less than 5% of getting a result this strong if in the general population there was no average tendency of this kind.) The pattern of this result also had a fairly large effect size in relation to what is usually seen in psychology studies ($R^2 = .12$).

On average, those exposed to the extreme introvert tended to give higher ratings of extroversion. This result was of "marginal" statistical significance, meaning that it was on the borderline of being too unlikely to have come up if there were no true average difference in the population. More important, this result is not very interesting because, as you can see from the graph, it is entirely due to the extreme stereotype participants—if anything, the moderate stereotype participants showed an opposite pattern of effect.

13. Similar to 12 above.

Chapter 14

1. (a) χ^2 needed ($df = 5 - 1 = 4, 5\%$) = 9.488.

Category	O	Expected	$O - E$	$(O - E)^2$	$(O - E)^2/E$
A	19	(.2)(50) = 10	9	81	8.10
B	11	(.2)(50) = 10	1	1	.10
C	10	(.4)(50) = 20	-10	100	5.00
D	5	(.1)(50) = 5	0	0	0.00
E	5	(.1)(50) = 5	0	0	0.00
Total	50		50	0	$\chi^2 = 13.20$

Conclusion: Reject the null hypothesis

(b) χ^2 needed = 5.992, $\chi^2 = 44.45$, reject the null hypothesis; (c) χ^2 needed = 7.815, $\chi^2 = 1.23$, do not reject the null hypothesis

2. χ^2 needed for a, b, and c: ($df = 5 - 1 = 4, 1\%$) = 13.277;

(a)

Category	O	Expected	$O - E$	$(O - E)^2$	$(O - E)^2/E$
A	10	20	-10	100	5
B	10	20	-10	100	5
C	10	20	-10	100	5
D	10	20	-10	100	5
E	60	20	40	1600	80
Total	100	100	0		$\chi^2 = 100$

Conclusion: Reject the null hypothesis

(b) $\chi^2 = 50$, reject the null hypothesis; (c) $\chi^2 = 450$, reject the null hypothesis.

3. (a) ❶ **Restate the question as a research hypothesis and a null hypothesis about populations.**

Population 1: Clients like those of this psychotherapy clinic. **Population 2:** Clients for whom season makes no difference in when they start psychotherapy.

The research hypothesis is that the distribution over seasons of when clients start is different between the two populations. The null hypothesis is that the distribution over seasons of when clients start is not different between the two populations.
❷ **Determine the characteristics of the comparison distribution.** Chi-square distribution with 3 degrees of freedom ($df = 4 - 1 = 3$).
❸ **Determine the cutoff sample score on the comparison distribution at which the null hypothesis should be rejected.** .05 level, $df = 3$: χ^2 needed = 7.815.
❹ **Determine your sample's score on the comparison distribution.**

Season	O	Expected	$O - E$	$(O - E)^2$	$\dfrac{(O - E)^2}{E}$
Winter	28	(1/4)(128) = 32	-4	16	.50
Spring	33	(1/4)(128) = 32	1	1	.03
Summer	16	(1/4)(128) = 32	-16	256	8.00
Fall	51	(1/4)(128) = 32	19	361	11.28
Total	128		128	0	$\chi^2 = 19.81$

❺ **Decide whether to reject the null hypothesis.** 19.81 is larger than 7.815; reject the null hypothesis; the research hypothesis is supported.

(b)

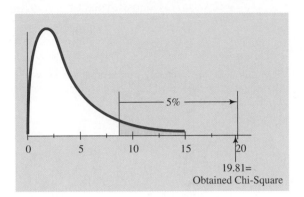

19.81=
Obtained Chi-Square

(c) If the seasons make no difference, you would expect about 25% of new clients each season (for last year, 25% of 128 is 32). Are last year's actual numbers in each season so discrepant from these expectations that you should conclude that in general the numbers of new clients are not equally distributed over the seasons? The chi-square statistic reflects the discrepancy between observed and expected results. For each category (such as the four seasons), you figure that discrepancy, square it, and divide by the expected number; then you add up the results. In the winter, 28 less 32 is −4, squared is 16, divided by 32 is 5. Doing the same for the other three seasons and adding up the four gives a total chi-square of 19.81. (Chi-square uses squared discrepancies so that the result is not affected by the directions of the differences. You divide by the expected number to reduce the impact of the raw number of cases on the result.)

Statisticians have determined mathematically what would happen if you took an infinite number of samples from a population with a fixed proportion of cases in each category and figured chi-square for each such sample. This distribution depends only on how many categories are free to take on different expected values. (The total number expected is the total number of cases; thus, if you know the expected for any three categories, you can just subtract to get the number expected for the fourth.) A table of the chi-square distribution when three categories are free to vary shows that there is only a 5% chance of getting a chi-square of 7.815 or greater. Because our chi-square is larger than this, the observed result differs from the expected more than you would reasonably expect by chance—the number of new clients, in the long run, is probably not equal over the four seasons.

4. (a) You should get same result within rounding error. (b) Similar to 3c above.

5. For (a), (b), and (c): $df = (N_{Columns} - 1)(N_{Rows} - 1) = (2 - 1)(2 - 1) = 1$; χ^2 needed $= 3.841$.
   (a)

20	(36)	40	(24)	60	(60%)
40	(24)	0	(16)	40	(40%)
60		40		100	

$\chi^2 = (20 - 36)^2/36 + (40 - 24)^2/24 + (40 - 24)^2/24 + (0 - 16)^2/16 = 44.45$
Reject the null hypothesis.
(b) $\chi^2 = 16.66$, reject the null hypothesis.
(c) $\chi^2 = 16.66$, reject the null hypothesis.

6. For (a), (b), and (c): $df = (N_{Columns} - 1)(N_{Rows} - 1)$
   $= (2 - 1)(2 - 1) = 1$; χ^2 needed $= 6.635$.
   (a)

10	(13)	16	(13)	26	(50%)
16	(13)	10	(13)	26	(50%)
26		26		52	

$\chi^2 = (10 - 13)^2/13 + (16 - 13)^2/13 + (16 - 13)^2 / 13 + (10 - 13)^2 / 13 = 2.76$. Do not reject the null hypothesis.
(b) $\chi^2 = .36$, do not reject the null hypothesis; (c) $\chi^2 = 27.68$, reject the null hypothesis.
   For 6. (d), (e), and (f): χ^2 needed $= 9.211$. (d) $\chi^2 = 2.76$, do not reject the null hypothesis; (e) $\chi^2 = 2.76$, do not reject the null hypothesis; (f) $\chi^2 = 3.71$, do not reject the null hypothesis.

7. (a) ❶ Restate the question as a research hypothesis and a null hypothesis about populations.
Population 1: Children like those surveyed.
Population 2: Children for whom age is independent of whether or not they like this kind of music.

The research hypothesis is that the two populations are different. The null hypothesis is that the two populations are the same.
❷ Determine the characteristics of the comparison distribution. Chi-square distribution with two degrees of freedom. $df = (N_{Columns} - 1)(N_{Rows} - 1) = (3 - 1)(2 - 1) = 2$
❸ Determine the cutoff sample score on the comparison distribution. .05 level, $df = 2$: $\chi^2 = 5.992$.
❹ Determine your sample's score on the comparison distribution.

		Age of Child			
		5	8	11	
Likes Type of Music	Yes	42 (39)	62 (65)	26 (26)	130 (65%)
	No	18 (21)	38 (35)	14 (14)	70 (35%)
		60	100	40	200

$\chi^2 = (42 - 39)^2/39 + (62 - 65)^2/65 + (26 - 26)^2/26 + (18 - 21)^2/21 + (38 - 35)^2/35 + (14 - 14)^2/14 = 1.06$.
❺ Decide whether to reject the null hypothesis. 1.06 is less extreme than 5.992; do not reject the null hypothesis; the study is inconclusive.

(b)

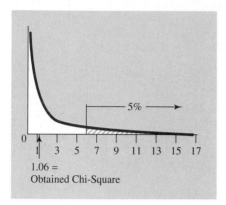

1.06 =
Obtained Chi-Square

(c) In this example, 65% of all children liked the particular kind of music. Thus, if age and liking of this kind of music are not related, 65% of the children in each age group should like this kind of music. For example, you'd expect 39 of the 60 8-year-olds to like this music. Are the survey results so discrepant from these expectations that you should conclude that age is related to what kind of music children like?

The chi-square statistic reflects the discrepancy between observed and expected results. For each combination of the 2×3 arrangement, you figure that discrepancy between observed and expected, square it, and divide by the expected number; then you add up the results. In the yes-8-year-old combination, 42 minus 39 is 3, squared is 9, divided by 39 is .23. Doing the same for the other five combinations and adding them all up gives 1.06. (Chi-square uses squared discrepancies so that the result is not affected by the directions of the differences. It is divided by the expected number to adjust for the impact of relatively different numbers expected in the combinations.)

The rest is similar to 5c above except for the following about degrees of freedom. For each age group, if you know the totals and the figure for children who like this kind of music, you can figure the number who do not by subtraction. And of the three age groups, if you know the total and any two of them, you can figure the third by subtraction. So only two combinations are "free to vary."

8. (a), (b), and (c) Similar to 7 (a), (b), and (c) above. χ^2 needed = 9.488; χ^2 = 8.55; do not reject the null hypothesis.

9. (a) $\phi = \sqrt{\chi^2/N} = \sqrt{44.45/100} = .67$; (b) .41; (c) .41; (d) .23; (e) .03; (f) .23; (g) Cramer's $\phi = \sqrt{\chi^2/(N)(df_{Smaller})}$ = $\sqrt{2.76/(72)(1)} = .20$; (h) .18; (i) .22; (j) .16; (k) .22.

10. (a) $\phi = \sqrt{\chi^2/N} = \sqrt{16/100} = .40$; (b) Cramer's $\phi = \sqrt{\chi^2/(N)(df_{Smaller})} = \sqrt{16/(100)(1)} = .40$; (c) Cramer's $\phi = .28$; (d) $\phi = .28$; (e) $\phi = .28$.

11. From Table 14–9: (a) .08; (b) .32; (c) .11; (d) .07; (e) .06; (f) .06.

12. From Table 14–10: (a) 87; (b) 26; (c) 133; (d) 133; (e) 39.

13. (a) You should get same result within rounding error. (b) $\phi = \sqrt{\chi^2/N} = \sqrt{5.55/69} = .28$; (c) Similar to 7c above.

14. (a) You should get same result within rounding error. (b) $\phi = \sqrt{\chi^2/N} = \sqrt{.33/145} = .05$; (c) Similar to 7c above.

Chapter 15

1. The following are probably not normal: (a) skewed right; (b) bimodal; (d) skewed right, (e) approximately rectangular.

2. (a) 4, 2, 3, 5, 6; (b) 5.92, 3.78, 3.61, 3.59, 4.24.

3. (a)

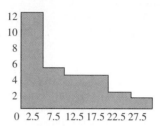

(b) 3, 5.3, 2, 4, 0, 2.6, 5, 1, 2, 3.2, 2, 1.4, 1, 3, 4, 3.3, 3.5, 1, 4.2, 1.4, 2.2, 3.2, 1.7, 4.1, 2.4, 2, 1.4, 4.8, 4.6, 4.5.

(c)

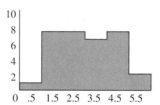

4. (a) t needed ($df = 8$, $p < .05$, two-tailed) = ± 2.306; Group A: $M = 3.8$, $S^2 = 5.06$; Group B: 5.7, 6.76; $S^2_{Pooled} = 5.91$; $S_{Difference} = 1.54$; $t = -1.23$; do not reject the null hypothesis. (b) Group A, 1.1, 1.6, 2.1, 1.9, 2.7; Group B, 1.4, 3.0, 2.4, 2.6, 2.2; (c) t needed = ± 2.306; Group A: $M = 1.88$, $S^2 = .35$; Group B: 2.32, .35; $S^2_{Pooled} = .35$; $S_{Difference} = .37$; $t = -1.19$; do not reject the null hypothesis.

(d) The first t test (using the actual scores) was not correct because the distributions of the samples were very skewed for both language groups, making it likely that the population distributions were also very skewed, violating the assumption for a t test that the underlying population distributions are normal. Thus, I took the square root of each score, which made the sample distributions closer to normal, thus suggesting that the population distributions of square roots of family sizes is nearly normally distributed. I realize that taking the square root of each family size distorts its straightforward meaning, but the impact for the individuals in the family of each additional child is probably not equal. That is, going from no children to 1 child has a huge impact. Going from 1 to 2 has less, and going from 7 to 8 probably makes much less difference for the family.

In any case, having taken the square root of each score, I then carried out a t test, again using the transformed scores. As with the original t test, the result was not significant—but at least I could be confident that I had done the analysis correctly.

5. (a) t needed ($df = 5$, $p < .05$, two-tailed) $= \pm 2.571$; $t = (M - 0)/S_M = (6 - 0)/2.54 = 2.36$; do not reject the null hypothesis. (b) 3.32, 4, 0, 2, 2, 1. (c) $t = (2.05 - 0)/.6 = 3.42$; reject the null hypothesis. (d) Similar to 4d above.

6. (a) F needed ($df = 2, 6$; $p < .01$) $= 10.93$; Sad: $M = 446$, $S^2 = 47,089$; Angry: 259, 11,272; Exuberant: 918.67, 7,184; $S^2_{\text{Between}} = 346,771$; $S^2_{\text{Within}} = 22,000$; $F = 15.76$; reject the null hypothesis. (b) 14.2, 22.9, 24.8; 11.7, 18.4, 17.3; 28.9, 30.2, 31.7. (c) 20.63, 31.94; 15.8, 12.91; 30.27, 1.96; $S^2_{\text{Between}} = 162.72$; $S^2_{\text{Within}} = 15.61$; $F = 10.42$; do not reject the null hypothesis. (d) Similar to 4d above, *except* note that the square root transformation does *not* solve the problem of skew and that it also creates distributions very likely to violate the assumption of equal population variances.

7. Miller wanted to examine the relationships among the variables he was studying, probably including various parametric hypothesis-testing techniques such as the t test or an analysis of variance (or testing the significance of bivariate or multiple correlation or regression results). All of these procedures are based on the assumption that the distributions of the variables in the population follow a normal curve. However, Miller first checked the distributions of the variables he was studying and found that scores on two key measures were skewed, suggesting that the population distributions for these variables probably violated the normal distribution assumption. (Rest of your answer similar to 4d above.)

8. Similar to 7 above.

9. (a) 2, 1, 3, 4; (b) 5, 3, 2, 1, 4.

10. (a) 16.5, 30, 10.5, 22.5, 1, 15, 29, 3, 10.5, 18.5, 10.5, 6, 3, 16.5, 22.5, 20, 21, 3, 25, 6, 13, 18.5, 8, 24, 14, 10.5, 6, 28, 27, 26.

(b)

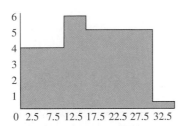

11. (a) Test using original scores in 4a above. Ranks: Group A, 1, 3, 5, 4, 9; Group B, 2, 10, 7, 8, 6; Group A: $M = 4.4$, $S^2 = 8.8$; Group B: 6.6, 8.8; $S^2_{\text{Pooled}} = 8.8$; $S_{\text{Difference}} = 1.88$; $t = -1.17$; do not reject the null hypothesis. Explanation: Similar to 4d above except instead of explaining square root transformation, explain rank-order transformation: I changed each of the scores to its rank among all the scores. This makes the distribution roughly rectangular. Some statisticians recommend that if the assumptions are questionable for an ordinary parametric test, you change the scores to ranks first and then proceed, and that gives more accurate results. There are special procedures you can use for a t test for independent means with ranks. But the figuring is mathematically equivalent to what you do with an ordinary t test using ranks. The difference is that the rank-order procedure goes with special tables that are more accurate in this situation than the t table. However, statisticians have found that the results using an ordinary t table in this situation are usually a good approximation.

(b) Ranks: 5, 6, 1, 3.5, 3.5, 2; $t = (M - 0)/S_M = (3.5 - 0)/.75 = 4.67$; reject the null hypothesis.

(c) Ranks: 2, 5, 6; 1, 4, 3; 7, 8, 9; $S^2_{\text{Between}} = 22.32$; $S^2_{\text{Within}} = 2.56$; $F = 8.72$; reject the null hypothesis.

12. Similar to answers to 4d and 11a, but note that researchers used one of the special rank-order tests.

Chapter 16

1.

df	5	10	15	20
(a) t	2.571	2.228	2.132	2.086
(b) t^2	6.61	4.96	4.55	4.35
(c) F	6.61	4.97	4.54	4.35

2. (i)

	(a) df	(b) Cutoff	(c) Within-Group Variance	(d) t or F
t	70	1.995	$S^2_{\text{Pooled}} = 44$	2.56
F	70	3.980	$S^2_{\text{Within}} = 44$	6.55
		($\sqrt{\ } = 1.995$)		($\sqrt{\ } = 2.56$)

(ii)

	(a) df	(b) Cutoff	(c) Within-Group Variance	(d) t or F
t	30	2.043	$S^2_{\text{Pooled}} = 7$	-2.13
F	30	4.170	$S^2_{\text{Within}} = 7$	-4.57
		($\sqrt{\ } = 2.042$)		($\sqrt{\ } = 2.14$)

3.

	(a) df	(b) Cutoff	(c) Within-Group Variance	(d) t or F
t	58	2.004	$S^2_{\text{Pooled}} = 2.6$	2.16
F	58	4.020	$S^2_{\text{Within}} = 2.6$	4.67
		($\sqrt{\ } = 2.005$)		($\sqrt{\ } = 2.16$)

4.

| | **t-Test** | **ANOVA** |

Numerator

$df_{Between} = N_{Groups} - 1 = 2 - 1 = 1$

Mean difference $= 170 - 150$ $GM = (170 + 150)/2$
                $= 20$ $= 160$

$\Sigma(M - GM)^2 = (170 - 160)^2$
                $+ (150 - 160)^2$
                $= 200$

$S^2_{Between}$ or $MS_{Between} =$
$$\frac{\Sigma(M - GM)^2}{df_{Between}}(n)$$
$$= (200/1)(10)$$
$$= 2,000$$

Denominator

$S^2_{Pooled} = (df_1/df_{Total})(S^2_1)$ S^2_{Within} or $MS_{Within} =$
$\qquad + (df_2/df_{Total})(S^2_2)$ $(S^2_1 + S^2_2 + \ldots$
$\qquad = (.5)(48) + (.5)(32)$ $\qquad + S^2_{Last})/(N_{Groups})$
$\qquad = 40$ $= (48 + 32)/2 = 40$

$S^2_{Difference}$
$= S^2_{M1} + S^2_{M2}$
$= (S^2_{Pooled}/N_1) + (S^2_{Pooled}/N_2)$
$= (40/10) + (40/10) = 8$

$S_{Difference}$
$= \sqrt{S^2_{Difference}}$
$= \sqrt{8} = 2.83.$

Degrees of Freedom

$df_{Total} = df_1 + df_2 = 9 + 9 = 18$ df_{Within}
$\qquad\qquad = df_1 + df_2 + \ldots + df_{Last}$
$\qquad\qquad = 9 + 9 = 18$

Cutoff

Needed t ($df = 18$, $p < .05$,   Needed F ($df = 1, 18$;
two-tailed): 2.101 $p < .05$): 4.41 ($\sqrt{} = 2.1$)

Score on Comparison Distribution

$t = (M_1 - M_2)/S_{Difference}$ $F = S^2_{Between}/S^2_{Within}$
$= 20/2.83$ or $MS_{Between}/MS_{Within}$
$= 7.07$ $= 2,000/40 = 50$ ($\sqrt{} = 7.07$)

Conclusions

Reject the null hypothesis.   Reject the null hypothesis.

5.

	(a) df	(b) Cutoff	(c) Within-Group Variance	(d) t or F
t	6	2.447	$S^2_{Pooled} = 5.67$	4.60
F	6	5.99	$MS^2_{Within} = 5.67$	21.16
		($\sqrt{} = 2.45$)		($\sqrt{} = 4.6$)

6.

	(a) df	(b) Cutoff	(c) Within-Group Variance	(d) t or F
t	9	2.262	$S^2_{Pooled} = 11.69$	-1.73
F	9	5.99	$MS_{Within} = 11.69$	3.02
		($\sqrt{} = 2.45$)		($\sqrt{} = 1.74$)

7.

	(a) df	(b) Cutoff	(c) Within-Group Variance	(d) t or F
t	4	2.776	$S^2_{Pooled} = .025$	3.1
F	4	7.71	$MS_{Within} = .025$	9.6
		($\sqrt{} = 2.78$)		($\sqrt{} = 3.1$)

8. (a) (i) $t = 4.6$ (see 5 above); (ii) $r = 7.06/9 = .88$; (iii) $t = (.88)(\sqrt{6})/\sqrt{1 - .88^2} = 4.49$. (result is same as 4.6 within rounding error).

(iv)

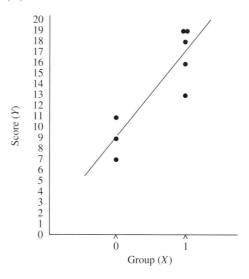

(v) A t test is the difference between the means divided by the standard deviation of the distribution of differences between means. The standard deviation of the distribution of differences is largely based on the variances in each sample, and the variance in each sample is an indication of how spread out the scores are around the mean. A correlation coefficient can be understood in terms of the scatter diagram as the degree of slope of the line and how closely the dots fall to that line. When the predictor variable has only two values, then the dots in the scatter diagram all go above the two values and the line that describes the dots goes through the mean of each set of dots. Thus, as in a t test, the correlation is bigger the more difference between the means and the closer the scores are to that mean.

(b) (i) $t = -1.73$ (see 6 above); (ii) $r = .50$; (iii) $t =$

$(-.5)(\sqrt{9})/\sqrt{1 - .5^2} = -1.72$; (iv) similar to 8 (a) (iv) above.

(c) (i) $t = 3.1$ (see 7 above); (ii) $r = .84$; (iii) $t = (.84)(\sqrt{4})/\sqrt{1 - .84^2} = 3.11$; (iv) similar to 8 (a) (iv) above.

9. (a) (v)

Regression	ANOVA
Mean of $Y = 14$	Grand mean $= 14$
$SS_{Total} = 154$	$SS_{Total} = 154$
Predicted Y for Group A $= 17$	Mean of Group A $= 17$
Predicted Y for Group B $= 9$	Mean of Group B $= 9$
$SS_{Error} = 34$	$SS_{Within} = 34$
Reduction in error $= 120$	$SS_{Between} = 120$
$r^2 = .77$	$R^2 = .78$

(vi) You can think of the analysis of variance as about the relationship between the variable on which the groups differ (Group A versus Group B in this problem) and the measured variable. If you think of the variable on which the groups differ as a predictor variable, regression is also about the same thing. In this problem you can consider those in Group A to have a score of 1 on this predictor and those in Group B to have a score of 2 on it. (Any two numbers would do; these are just examples). In fact, the underlying mathematics is the same. Here are some of the parallels. In both regression and the analysis of variance, you figure the total squared deviations from the overall mean (in both, this is SS_{Total}). A deeper link is that the best predictor for those in either group is the group's mean, so the regression equation predicts the mean for each group. The result is that the errors of predictions are deviations of the scores from the mean. If you square these and add them up, they are called SS_{Error} in regression and SS_{Within} in ANOVA. In regression, before figuring the proportionate reduction in error, you figure the reduction in error ($SS_{Total} - SS_{Error}$)—the amount of squared error that the regression formula saves over predicting from the overall mean of the criterion variable. This is the same as $SS_{Between}$ in ANOVA, because when there are only two group means, regression improves on prediction only to the extent that the means of the two groups are different. Finally, because SS_{Total} is the same in both regression and analysis of variance, and because reduction in error $= SS_{Between}$, r^2 in regression has to come out the same as R^2 figured as an effect size in ANOVA.

(b)

Regression	ANOVA
Mean reading time $= 7.64$	Grand mean $= 7.64$
$SS_{Total} = 140.55$	$SS_{Total} = 140.55$
Predicted reading time ordinary story $= 6$	Mean reading time ordinary story $= 6$
Predicted reading time own-name story $= 9.6$	Mean reading time own-name story $= 9.6$
$SS_{Error} = 105.2$	$SS_{Within} = 105.2$
Reduction in error $= 35.35$	$SS_{Between} = 35.35$
$r^2 = .34$	$R^2 = .34$

(c)

Regression	ANOVA
Mean of criterion variable $= .6$	Grand mean $= .6$
$SS_{Total} = .34$	$SS_{Total} = .34$
Predicted score for Group A $= .8$	Mean of Group A $= .8$
Predicted score for Group B $= .4$	Mean of Group B $= .4$
$SS_{Error} = .1$	$SS_{Within} = .1$
Reduction in error $= .24$	$SS_{Between} = .24$
$r^2 = .71$	$R^2 = .71$

10.

Participant	Group	Variable 1 (Group I or not)	Variable 2 (Group II or not)	Variable 3 (Group III or not)
1	I	1	0	0
2	I	1	0	0
3	I	1	0	0
4	II	0	1	0
5	II	0	1	0
6	III	0	0	1
7	III	0	0	1
8	III	0	0	1
9	IV	0	0	0
10	IV	0	0	0

Chapter 17

1. Hierarchical regression is a variation of ordinary multiple regression in which you add the predictor variables in predetermined stages and figure the additional contribution of each. In the Lindzey et al. study, the first two predictor variables considered were father and child initiation rates, which accounted for only 3% of the variance in children's social competence (the criterion variable). (This R^2 of .03 was far from significant with a p of 57!) Then, Lindzey et al. added an additional predictor variable—father–child mutual compliance—which increased the overall variance accounted for from .03 to .21, an increase of 18%, which was significant (with $p < .01$). In sum, when it comes to predicting children's competence, father and child initiation rates are not very important by themselves, but over and above these two predictors, mutual compliance is a substantial predictor.

2. Stepwise regression is a variation of ordinary multiple regression you use when you have a lot of predictor variables and you want to pick out the best ones. You first figure a regression of each predictor by itself and select the one that accounts for the most variance. If even this best one is not very good (for example, is not significant), you stop. If it is a good predictor, you figure a regression of each remaining predictor in combination with the first and select the additional predictor that adds the most variance accounted for to the prediction. If even this best addition does not make much of a contribution, you stop. If it is a good predictor, you continue in the same way—until you either run out of predictors or the next best addition is not very good. In the

Mooney et al. study, this procedure led to their keeping three of their four original predictors.

3. "Controlling for" refers to partial correlation, a procedure based on multiple regression in which you figure the correlation between two variables, subtracting out the influence of one or more other variables (the variables that are controlled for). It amounts to figuring the correlation between your variables at each level of the controlled-for variable and then averaging these correlations.

For example, in this study, the moderately strong correlation between romantic appeal and level of dating experience can't be explained as both being due somehow to appearance of physical maturity, because appearance at physical maturity is controlled for.

4. Boyd and Gullone are describing the reliability of the study's measures. Reliability is how much a test measures something consistently—if the test were taken again by the same person under identical circumstances, how close it would come to giving the same result. One method of assessing reliability is by looking at how one half of the test correlates with the other half of the test, the idea being that the same person is taking two tests (the two halves of the test) at the same time under the same circumstances. Alpha (or Cronbach's alpha), a common measure of reliability, is based on the average of correlations between every possible way of splitting the test in half. An alpha of .60 or .70 is usually considered a minimum adequate level of reliability—that some of Boyd and Gullone's measures had lower alphas means that some of the variables studied may not be giving very precise information.

5. You use a factor analysis to uncover the underlying pattern among a large number of variables—to find which variables group together in the sense of correlating with each other but not with variables in other grouping. Fawzi et al.'s results suggest that the best underlying pattern among the 16 PTSD symptom ratings has four groupings or factors (called "dimensions" in their table). The table shows the correlations, called "Factor Loadings," of each individual variable with the grouping. (In this table, the researchers listed only each symptom's factor loading on the factor on which it had the highest loading. Each variable has a loading on each factor, but ordinarily has a high loading on only one factor, and it is thought of as being part of that factor.) The researchers note that the first three factors correspond to the three key aspects of PTSD as it is usually understood. Their fourth factor (which has only one item), however, suggested that there is an additional and somewhat separate aspect of avoidance that had not been considered in previous work as being such a separate aspect.

6. The procedure described here is path analysis, an elaboration of ordinary multiple regression in which you make specific predictions about the pattern of causality among your variables (your causal model), usually including making a diagram showing the causality as arrows between boxes, as in MacKinnon-Lewis et al.'s figure. You then figure the regression coefficients (called "path coefficients"). These researchers tried several possible models, and the figure shows the one that they decided was best (in terms of the strongest coefficients overall). In this model, for example, father acceptance (after partialing out mother rejection) has little direct influence on sibling aggression, but mother rejection (after partialing out father acceptance) has a moderate effect on it. According to the rest of this model, sibling aggression has a moderate effect on aggression with peers, which in turn has a fairly large negative effect on social acceptance.

7. (a) In the context of the proposed model, the key result is that all three hypothesized paths to intensity were significant. However, you can also see that the path from desirability to intensity was strongest and the path from probability to intensity, though significant, was not very strong. This means that how intensely one feels unrequited love is very strongly predicted by how desirable one finds the beloved, moderately by how much one finds the state of being in love desirable, but only slightly by one's belief that the other will eventually reciprocate.

(b) In structural equation modeling you specify a pattern of causal relationships among variables, diagramed with arrows connecting each cause to its effects. You can also specify that some variables measured in the study are indicators of an underlying unmeasured "latent" variable. In this example, there are paths from the three motivational factors to intensity. Further, the three motivations (shown in ovals) are each latent variables indicated by several measured variables. Once the model is specified, path coefficients (like regression coefficients) are figured for each arrow ultimately based on the correlations among the variables. For example, the .32 path from desirability to intensity means that holding constant probability and desires state, for each standard deviation of change in desirability there would be .32 of a standard deviation of change in intensity.

8. (a) Independent, kind of medication; dependent, level of anxiety. (b) Independent, kind of movie; dependent, heart rate change. (c) Independent, whether or not mother is present; dependent, number of touches between the two infants.

9. ANCOVA, or analysis of covariance, is analysis of variance in which one or more variables have been controlled for—ANCOVA is to ordinary ANOVA as a partial correlation is to ordinary correlation. In this example, Roesser et al. are making the point that the country main effect in their factorial ANOVA holds up even after social desirability is controlled for.

10. MANOVA, or multivariate analysis of variance, is ordinary analysis of variance, except that it looks at the overall effect on more than one dependent variable. In this example, there were five measures of conflict resolution preference. The significant "main effect of culture" means that the two cultures differed significantly when considering the entire set of dependent variables at once. Similarly, the significant "culture by type of conflict interaction" means that the effect of culture on the set of dependent variables varies according to the type of conflict. To understand which of the several conflict resolution variables were accounting for these overall effects, the researchers carried out univariate analyses, ordinary analyses of variance on one dependent variable at a time. The pattern of results were quite different according to the specific dependent variable considered.

11. (a) Causal modeling (path analysis or structural equation modeling); (b) bivariate correlation and regression; (c) reliability statistics, such as Cronbach's alpha and test-retest reliability; (d) 3×2 multivariate analysis of variance, probably followed up by univariate 3×2 analyses of variance; (e) stepwise regression; (f) factor analysis; (g) t test for independent means; (h) one-way analysis of variance; (i) hierarchical multiple regression.

GLOSSARY

Numbers in parentheses refer to chapters in which the term is introduced or substantially discussed.

Adjusting for Same as *partialing out.* (17)

Alpha (α) probability of a Type I error; same as *significance level* (8). Also short for *Cronbach's alpha.* (17)

Analysis of covariance (ANCOVA) analysis of variance that controls for the effect of one or more unwanted additional variables. (17)

Analysis of variance (ANOVA) Hypothesis-testing procedure for studies with two or more groups. (11–13)

Analysis of variance table Chart showing the major elements in figuring an analysis of variance using the structural-model approach. (12, 13)

Assumption Condition, such as a population's having a normal distribution, required for carrying out a particular hypothesis-testing procedure; part of the mathematical foundation for the accuracy of the tables used in determining cutoff values. (9–15)

Beta (β) Standardized regression coefficient. (4) Also, probability of a Type II error in hypothesis testing. (8)

Between-groups degrees of freedom ($df_{Between}$) Same as *numerator degrees of freedom.* (11)

Between-groups estimate of the population variance ($S^2_{Between}$, $MS_{Between}$) In analysis of variance, estimate of the variance of the population distribution of individuals based on the variation among the means of the groups studied; same as *mean squares between.* (11)

Between-groups sum of squares ($SS_{Between}$) Same as *sum of squared deviations between groups.* (12)

Biased estimate Estimate of a population parameter that is likely systematically to overestimate or underestimate the true population value. For example, SD^2 would be a biased estimate of the population variance (it would systematically underestimate it). (9)

Bimodal distribution Frequency distribution with two approximately equal frequencies, each clearly larger than any of the others. (1)

Bivariate prediction Prediction of scores on one variable based on scores of one other variable. (4)

Bivariate regression Same as *bivariate prediction.* (4)

Bonferroni procedure Multiple-comparison procedure in which the total alpha percentage is divided among the set of comparisons so that each is tested at a more stringent significance level. (11)

Categorical variable Same as *nominal variable.* (1, 14)

Causal analysis Procedure, such as path analysis or structural equation modeling, that analyzes correlations among a group of variables in terms of a predicted pattern of causal relations among them. (17)

Ceiling effect Situation in which many scores pile up at the high end (creating skewness) because it is not possible to have a higher score. (1)

Cell In a factorial design, particular combination of levels of the independent variables. (13) In chi-square, particular combination of categories for two variables in a contingency table. (14)

Cell mean Mean of a particular combination of levels of the variables that divide the groups in a factorial design. (13)

Central limit theorem Mathematical principle that the distribution of the sums (or means) of scores taken at random from any distribution of individuals will tend to form a normal curve. (5, 7)

Central tendency Typical or most representative value of a group of scores. (2)

Change score After score minus before score; kind of *difference score*. (9)

Chi-square distribution Mathematically defined curve used as the comparison distribution in chi-square tests; distribution of the chi-square statistic. (14)

Chi-square statistic (χ^2) Statistic that reflects the overall lack of fit between the expected and observed frequencies; sum, over all the categories or cells, of the squared difference between observed and expected frequencies divided by the expected frequency. (14)

Chi-square table Table of cutoff scores on the chi-square distribution for various degrees of freedom and significance levels. (14)

Chi-square test for goodness of fit Hypothesis-testing procedure that examines how well an observed frequency distribution of a nominal variable fits some expected pattern of frequencies. (14)

Chi-square test for independence Hypothesis-testing procedure that examines whether the distribution of frequencies over the categories of one nominal variable are unrelated to the distribution of frequencies over the categories of another nominal variable. (14)

Comparison distribution Distribution used in hypothesis testing. It represent the population situation if the null hypothesis is true. It is the distribution to which you compare the score based on your sample's results and is made up of the same kinds of numbers as those of the sample's results (such as sample means, differences between sample means, *F* ratios, or chi squares). (6)

Complex comparison Comparison of particular means (following an analysis of variance) that involves more than two means (for example, the average of two means compared to a third). (11)

Computational formula Equation mathematically equivalent to the definitional formula; it is easier to use for hand computation but does not directly show the meaning of the procedure. (2)

Computer-intensive methods Statistical methods, including hypothesis-testing procedures, involving large numbers of repeated computations. (15)

Confidence interval Range of scores between particular upper and lower values likely to include the true population mean. (7)

Confidence limit Upper or lower value of a confidence interval. (7)

Contingency table Two-dimensional chart showing frequencies in each combination of categories of two nominal variables. (14)

Controlling for Same as *partialing out*. (17)

Conventional levels of significance ($p < .05, p < .01$) Levels of significance (alpha levels) widely used in psychology. (6)

Correlation Association between scores on two or more variables. (3)

Correlation coefficient (r) Measure of degree of linear correlation ranging from –1 (a perfect negative linear correlation) through 0 (no correlation) to +1 (a perfect positive correlation); average of the cross-products of Z scores of two variables; square root of the proportionate reduction in error. (3, 4)

Correlation matrix Common way of reporting the correlation coefficients among several variables in a research article; table in which the variables are named on the top and along the side and the correlations among them are all shown (only half of the resulting square, above or below the diagonal, is usually filled in, the other half being redundant). (3)

Covariate Variable controlled for in an analysis of covariance. (17)

Criterion variable (usually y) In regression, the variable that is predicted about. (4)

Cramer's phi Measure of association between two nominal variables; effect-size measure for a chi-square test of independence with a contingency table that is larger than 2 X 2; also known as Cramer's V and sometimes written as ϕ_C or V_C. (14)

Cronbach's alpha (α) Widely used measure of a test's reliability that reflects the average of the split-half correlations from all possible splits into halves of the items on the test. (17)

Curvilinear correlation Relation between two variables that shows up on a scatter diagram as dots following a systematic pattern that is not a straight line; any association between two variables other than a linear correlation. (3)

Cutoff sample score In hypothesis testing, point on the comparison distribution at which, if reached or exceeded by the sample score, you reject the null hypothesis. (6)

Data transformation Mathematical procedure (such as taking the square root) applied to each score in a sample, usually done to make the sample distribution closer to normal. (15)

Decision error Incorrect conclusion in hypothesis testing in relation to the real (but unknown) situation, such as deciding the null hypothesis is false when it is really true. (7)

Definitional formula Equation for a statistical procedure directly showing the meaning of the procedure. (2)

Degrees of freedom (df) Number of scores free to vary when estimating a population parameter; usually part of a formula for making that estimate—for example, in the formula for estimating the population variance from a single sample, the degrees of freedom is the number of scores minus 1. (9–14)

Denominator degrees of freedom (df_{Within}) Degrees of freedom used in the within-group estimate of the population variance in an analysis of variance, denominator of the F ratio; number of scores free to vary (number of scores in each group minus 1, summed over all the groups) in figuring the within-group population variance estimate; *within-groups degrees of freedom*. (11)

Dependent variable Variable considered to be an effect; usually a measured variable. (17)

Descriptive statistics Procedures for summarizing a group of scores or otherwise making them more comprehensible. (1)

Deviation score Score minus the mean. (2)

Difference score Difference between a person's score on one testing and the same person's score on another testing; often a change score (after score minus before score). (9)

Dimension In a factorial design, one of the variables that divides the groups that is crossed with another variable that divides the groups. (13)

Directional hypothesis Research hypothesis predicting a particular direction of difference between populations—for example, a prediction that one population has a higher mean than the other. (6)

Distribution-free test Approximately the same as a *nonparametric test*. (15)

Distribution of differences between means Distribution of differences between means of pairs of samples such that for each pair of means, one is from one population and the other is from a second population; the comparison distribution in a *t* test for independent means. (10)

Distribution of means Distribution of means of samples of a given size from a particular population (also called a *sampling distribution of the mean*); comparison distribution when testing hypotheses involving a single sample of more than one individual. (7)

Effect size Standardized measure of difference (lack of overlap) between population means. Effect size increases with greater differences between means and decreases with greater standard deviations in the populations, but is not affected by sample size. (8)

Equal-interval measurement Measurement in which the same difference between any two values represents an equal amount of difference in the underlying thing being measured. (15)

Error In prediction, the actual score minus the predicted score. (4)

Expected frequency In a chi-square test, number of people in a category or cell expected if the null hypothesis were true. (14)

Expected relative frequency Number of successful outcomes divided by the number of total outcomes you would expect to get if you repeated an experiment a large number of times. (5)

Factor In factor analysis, group of variables that correlate maximally with each other and minimally with variables not in the group. (17)

Factor analysis Statistical procedure that identifies groups of variables correlating maximally with each other and minimally with other variables. (17)

Factor loading In factor analysis, correlation of a variable with a factor. (17)

Factorial analysis of variance Analysis of variance for a factorial research design. (13)

Factorial research design Way of organizing a study in which the influence of two or more variables is studied at once by setting up the situation so that a group of people are tested for every combination of the levels of the variables; for example, in a 2 X 2 factorial research design there would be four groups, those

high on variable 1 and high on variable 2, those high on variable 1 but low on variable 2, those low on variable 1 but high on variable 2, and those low on variable 1 and low on variable 2. (13)

***F* distribution** Mathematically defined curve that is the comparison distribution used in an analysis of variance; distribution of *F* ratios when the null hypothesis is true. (11)

Fit index In structural equation modeling, measure of how well the pattern of correlations in a sample corresponds to the correlations that would be expected based on the hypothesized pattern of causes and effects among those variables; usually ranges from 0 to 1, with 1 being a perfect fit. (17)

Floor effect Situation in which many scores pile up at the low end of a distribution (creating skewness) because it is not possible to have any lower score. (1)

***F* ratio** In analysis of variance, ratio of the between-groups population variance estimate to the within-groups population variance estimate; a score on the comparison distribution (an *F* distribution) in an analysis of variance. (11–13)

Frequency distribution Pattern of frequencies over the various values; what a frequency table, histogram, or frequency polygon describes. (1)

Frequency polygon Line graph of a distribution in which the values are plotted along the horizontal axis and the height of each point is the frequency of that value; the line begins and ends at the horizontal axis, and the graph resembles a mountainous skyline. (1)

Frequency table Listing of number of individuals having each of the different values for a particular variable. (1)

***F* table** Table of cutoff scores on the *F* distribution for various degrees of freedom and significance levels. (11)

General linear model General formula that is the basis of most of the statistical methods covered in this text; describes a score as the sum of a constant, the weighted influence of several variables, and error. (16)

Grand mean (*GM*) In analysis of variance, overall mean of all the scores, regardless of what group they are in; when group sizes are equal, mean of the group means. (12)

Grouped frequency table Frequency table in which the number of individuals is given for each interval of values. (1)

Haphazard selection Procedure of selecting a sample of individuals to study by taking whoever is available or happens to be first on a list; should not be confused with true random selection. (5)

Harmonic mean Special average influenced more by smaller numbers; in a *t* test for independent means when the number of scores in the two groups differ, the harmonic mean is used as the equivalent of each group's sample size when determining power. (10)

Heavy-tailed distribution Distribution that differs from a normal curve by being too spread out so that a histogram of the distribution would have too many scores at each of the two extremes ("tails"). (1)

Hierarchical multiple regression Multiple regression procedure in which predictor variables are added one or a few at a time, in a planned sequential fashion, allowing you to figure the contribution to the prediction of each successive variable over and above those already included. (17)

Histogram Barlike graph of a frequency distribution in which the values are plotted along the horizontal axis and the height of each bar is the frequency of that value; the bars are usually placed next to each other without spaces, giving the appearance of a city skyline. (1)

Holding constant Same as *partialing out.* (17)

Hypothesis testing Procedure for deciding whether the outcome of a study (results for a sample) support a particular theory or practical innovation (which is thought to apply to a population). (6)

Independence Situation of no relationship between two variables; term usually used regarding two nominal variables in a chi-square test for independence. (14)

Independent variable Variable considered to be a cause. (17)

Inferential statistics Procedures for drawing conclusions based on the scores collected in a research study (sample scores) but going beyond them (to conclusions about a population). (1)

Interaction effect Situation in the factorial analysis of variance in which the combination of variables has an effect that could not be predicted from the effects of the two variables individually; situation in which effect of one variable that divides the groups on the measured variable depends on the level of the other variable that divides the groups. (13)

Intercept The point where the regression line crosses the vertical axis; the regression constant (a). (4)

Interval estimate Region of scores (that is, the scores between some specified lower and upper value) estimated to include a population parameter such as the population mean; a *confidence interval* is an example of an interval estimate. (7)

Kurtosis Extent to which a frequency distribution deviates from a normal curve, having tails that are too thick or too thin. (1)

Latent variable In structural equation modeling, unmeasured variable assumed to be the underlying cause of several variables actually measured in the study. (17)

Least-squares analysis of variance Recommended approach to the factorial analysis of variance when there are unequal numbers of participants in the different cells. (13)

Least-squares model Usual method of determining the optimal values of regression coefficients; these optimal values are those that produce the least squared error in the predicted values. (16)

Level of significance (α) Probability of getting statistical significance if the null hypothesis is actually true; probability of a Type I error. (6–8)

Levels of measurement Types of underlying numerical information provided by a measure, such as equal-interval, rank-order, and nominal (categorical). (1, 15)

Linear correlation Relation between two variables that shows up on a scatter diagram as the dots roughly following a straight line; a correlation of r unequal to 0. (3)

Log transformation Data transformation using the logarithm of each score. (15)

Long-run relative-frequency interpretation of probability Understanding of probability as the proportion of a particular outcome that you would get if the experiment were repeated many times. (5)

Main effect Difference between groups on one variable in a factorial design; result for a variable that divides the groups, averaging across the levels of the other variable that divides the groups. (13)

Marginal mean In a factorial design, mean score for all the participants at a particular level of one of the variables. (13)

Mean (M, μ) Arithmetic average of a group of scores; sum of the scores divided by the number of scores; also symbolized as $\overline{X}$. (2)

Mean squares between (MS_{Between}) Same as *between-group estimate of the population variance estimate* (S^2_{Between}). (11, 12)

Mean squares within (MS_{Within}) Same as *within-group population variance estimate* (S^2_{Within}). (11, 12)

Median Middle score when all the scores in a distribution are arranged from highest to lowest. (2)

Meta-analysis Statistical method for combining effect sizes from different studies. (8)

Mode Value with the greatest frequency in a distribution. (2)

Multicollinearity Situation in multiple regression in which the predictor variables are correlated with each other. (4)

Multimodal distribution Frequency distribution with two or more high frequencies separated by a lower frequency; a bimodal distribution is the special case of two high frequencies. (1)

Multiple comparisons Hypothesis-testing procedures for testing the differences among particular means in the context of an overall analysis of variance. (12)

Multiple correlation Correlation of a criterion variable with two or more predictor variables. (4)

Multiple correlation coefficient (R) Measure of degree of multiple correlation; positive square root of the proportionate reduction in error (R^2) in a multiple regression. (4)

Multiple regression Procedure for predicting scores on a criterion variable from scores on two or more predictor variables. (4)

Multivariate analysis of covariance (MANCOVA) Analysis of covariance with more than one dependent variable. (17)

Multivariate analysis of variance (MANOVA) Analysis of variance with more than one dependent variable. (17)

Multivariate statistics Statistical procedures involving more than one dependent variable. (17)

Negative correlation Relation between two variables in which high scores on one go with low scores on the other, mediums with mediums, and lows with highs; on a scatter diagram, the dots roughly follow a straight line sloping down and to the right; a correlation of r less than 0. (3)

95% confidence interval Confidence interval in which, roughly speaking, there is a 95% chance that the population mean is within this interval. (7)

99% confidence interval Confidence interval in which, roughly speaking, there is a 99% chance that the population mean is within this interval. (7)

No correlation No systematic relation between two variables. (3)

Nominal coding Converting a nominal (categorical) predictor variable in an analysis of variance into several two-level numerical variables that can be used in a multiple regression analysis. (16)

Nominal variable Variable with values that are categories (that is, they are names rather than numbers); same as *categorical variable*. (1, 14)

Nondirectional hypothesis Research hypothesis that does not predict a particular direction of difference between populations. (6)

Nonparametric test Hypothesis-testing procedure making no assumptions about population parameters; approximately the same as a *distribution-free test*. (15)

Normal curve Specific, mathematically defined, bell-shaped frequency distribution that is symmetrical and unimodal; distributions observed in nature and in research commonly approximate it. (1, 5)

Normal curve table Table showing percentages of scores in a normally distributed distribution between the mean and various numbers of standard deviations above the mean. (5)

Normal distribution Frequency distribution following a normal curve. (5)

Null hypothesis Statement about a relation between populations that is the opposite of the research hypothesis; statement that in the population there is no difference (or a difference opposite to that predicted) between populations; contrived statement set up to examine whether it can be rejected as part of hypothesis testing. (6)

Numerator degrees of freedom ($df_{Between}$) Degrees of freedom used in the between-group estimate of the population variance in an analysis of variance (the numerator of the F ratio); number of scores free to vary (number of means minus 1) in figuring the between-group estimate of the population variance; same as *between-group degrees of freedom*. (11)

Numeric variable Variable whose values are numbers (as opposed to a nominal variable). (1)

Observed frequency (O) In a chi-square test, number of individuals actually found in the study to be in a category or cell. (14)

One-tailed test Hypothesis-testing procedure for a directional hypothesis; situation in which the region of the comparison distribution in which the null hypothesis would be rejected is all on one side (tail) of the distribution. (6)

One-way analysis of variance Analysis of variance in which there is only one independent variable (as distinguished from a factorial analysis of variance). (11, 12)

Ordinal variable Same as *rank-order variable*. (1, 15)

Outcome Term used in discussing probability for the result of an experiment (or almost any event, such as a coin coming up heads or it raining tomorrow). (5)

Outlier Score with an extreme (very high or very low) value in relation to the other scores in the distribution. (2)

Parametric test Ordinary hypothesis-testing procedure, such as a t test or an analysis of variance, that requires assumptions about the shape or other parameters (such as the variance) of the populations. (15)

Partial correlation coefficient Measure of the degree of correlation between two variables, over and above the influence of one or more other variables. (17)

Partialing out In multiple regression, partial correlation, or analysis of covariance, removing the influence of a variable from the association among the other variables; same as *holding constant, controlling for,* and *adjusting for*. (17)

Path analysis Method of analyzing the correlations among a group of variables in terms of a predicted pattern of causal relations; usually the predicted pattern is diagramed as a pattern of arrows from causes to effects. (17)

Path coefficient Degree of relation associated with an arrow in a path analysis (including in structural equation modeling); same as a regression coefficient from a multiple regression prediction rule in which the variable at the end of the arrow is the criterion variable and the variable at the start of the arrow is the predictor, along with all the other variables that have arrows leading to that criterion variable. (17)

Phi coefficient (ϕ) Measure of association between two dichotomous nominal variables; square root of division of chi-square statistic by N; equivalent to correlation of the two variables if they were each given numerical values (for example, of 1 and 0 for the two categories); effect-size measure for a chi-square test of independence with a 2 X 2 contingency table. (14)

Planned comparisons Multiple comparisons in which the particular means to be compared were decided in advance; same as *planned contrasts*. (12)

Planned contrasts Same as *planned comparisons*. (11)

Pooled estimate of the population variance (S^2_{Pooled}) In a t test for independent means, weighted average of the estimates of the population variance from two samples (each estimate weighted by the proportion of the degrees of freedom for its sample divided by the total degrees of freedom for both samples). (10)

Population Entire group of people to which a researcher intends the results of a study to apply; larger group to which inferences are made on the basis of the particular set of people studied. (5)

Population mean (μ) Mean of the population (usually not known). (5)

Population parameter Actual value of the mean, standard deviation, and so on, for the population (usually population parameters are not known, though sometimes they are estimated); population parameters are usually symbolized by Greek letters. (5)

Population standard deviation (σ) Standard deviation of the population (usually not known). (5)

Population variance (σ^2) Variance of the population (usually not known). (5)

Positive correlation Relation between two variables in which high scores on one go with high scores on the other, mediums with mediums, and lows with lows; on a scatter diagram, the dots roughly follow a straight line sloping up and to the right; a correlation of r greater than 0. (3)

Post hoc comparisons Multiple comparisons, not designated in advance, among particular means; procedure conducted as part of an exploratory analysis after an analysis of variance. (12)

Power Same as *statistical power*. (8)

Power table Table for a hypothesis-testing procedure showing the statistical power of a study for various effect sizes and sample sizes. (8)

Prediction model Formula for making predictions; that is, formula for predicting a person's score on a criterion variable based on the person's score on one or more predictor variables. (4)

Predictor variable (usually X) In regression, variable that is used to predict scores of individuals on another variable. (4)

Probability (p) Expected relative frequency of a particular outcome; proportion of successful outcomes to all outcomes. (5)

Proportionate reduction in error (r^2, R^2) Measure of association between variables that is used when comparing associations found in different studies or with different variables; correlation coefficient squared; reduction in squared error, using a bivariate or multiple regression prediction rule, over the squared error using the mean to predict, expressed as a proportion of the squared error when using the mean to predict; correlation coefficient squared; variance of the predicted criterion variable scores (based on a regression formula) divided by the variance of the actual scores. Same as *proportion of variance accounted for*. (3, 4, 12, 13, 16, 17)

Proportion of variance accounted for (r^2, R^2) Same as proportional reduction in error. (4, 12, 13, 16, 17)

Quantitative variable Same as *numeric variable*. (1)

Random selection Method for selecting a sample that uses truly random procedures (usually meaning that each person in the population has an equal chance of being selected); one procedure is for the researcher to begin with a complete list of all the people in the population and select a group of them to study using a table of random numbers; should not be confused with haphazard selection. (5)

Randomization test Hypothesis-testing procedure (usually computer-intensive) that considers every possible reorganization of the data in the sample to determine if the organization of the actual sample data was unlikely to occur by chance. (15)

Rank-order test Hypothesis-testing procedure that makes use of rank-ordered data. (15)

Rank-order transformation Changing a set of scores to ranks, so that the highest score is rank 1, the next highest rank 2, and so forth. (15)

Rank-order variable Numeric variable in which the values are ranks, such as class standing or place finished in a race; also called *ordinal variable*. (1, 15)

Raw score Ordinary measurement (or any other number in a distribution before it has been made into a Z score or otherwise transformed). (2)

Raw-score prediction formula Prediction model in regression using raw scores. (4)

Raw-score regression coefficient (b) Regression coefficient in a prediction model using raw scores. (4)

Rectangular distribution Frequency distribution in which all values have approximately the same frequency. (1)

Regression coefficient (b, β) Number multiplied by a person's score on the predictor variable as part of a prediction model. (4)

Regression constant (a) In a prediction model using raw scores, particular fixed number added into the prediction. (4)

Regression line Line on a graph such as a scatter diagram showing the predicted value of the criterion variable for each value of the predictor variable. (4)

Reliability Consistency of a measure; extent to which, if you were to give the same measure again to the same person under the same circumstances, you would obtain the same result. (3, 17)

Repeated-measures analysis of variance Analysis of variance in which each individual is tested more than once. (13)

Repeated-measures design Research strategy in which each person is tested more than once; same as *within-subject design*. (9, 13)

Research hypothesis In hypothesis testing, statement about the predicted relation between populations (usually a prediction of difference between population means). (6)

Restriction in range Situation in which you figure a correlation but only a limited range of the possible values on one of the variables is included in the group studied. (3)

RMSEA (root mean square error of approximation) Widely used fit index in structural equation modeling; low values indicate a good fit. (17)

Robustness Extent to which a particular hypothesis-testing procedure is reasonably accurate even when its assumptions are violated. (9)

Sample Scores of the particular group of people studied; usually considered to be representative of the scores in some larger population. (5)

Scatter diagram Graph showing the relationship between two variables; the values of one variable (the predictor) are along the horizontal axis, the values of the other variable (the criterion) are along the vertical axis, with each score shown as a dot in this two-dimensional space; also called *scatter plot*. (3)

Scatter plot Same as *scatter diagram*. (3)

Scheffé test Method of figuring the significance of post-hoc comparisons that takes into account all possible comparisons that could be made. (12)

Score Particular person's value on a variable. (1)

Simple comparison Comparison of two groups' means following an analysis of variance. (11)

Skewness Extent to which a frequency distribution has more scores on one side of the middle as opposed to being perfectly symmetrical. (1)

Slope Steepness of the angle of a line on a two-variable graph, such as the regression line in a graph of the relation of a criterion and predictor variable; number of units the line goes up for every unit it goes across (in raw score regression, slope = b). (4)

Split-half reliability One index of a measure's reliability, based on a correlation of the scores of items from the two halves of the test. (17)

Squared deviation score Square of the difference between a score and the mean. (2)

Square-root transformation Data transformation using the square root of each score. (15)

Standard deviation (*SD, S, σ*) Square root of the average of the squared deviations from the mean; the most common descriptive statistic for variation; approximately the average amount that scores in a distribution vary from the mean. (2, 5, 9)

Standard deviation of the distribution of means (σ_M, S_M) Square root of the variance of the distribution of means; same as *standard error* (*SE*) (7, 9)

Standard error (*SE*) Same as *standard deviation of the distribution of means,* also called *standard error of the mean.* (7, 9)

Standardized regression coefficient (β) Regression coefficient in a prediction model using *Z* scores; also called a *beta weight.* (4)

Standard score *Z* score in a distribution that follows a normal curve; sometimes refers to any *Z* score. (2)

Statistical power Probability that the study will give a significant result if the research hypothesis is true. (8)

Statistically significant Conclusion that the results of a study would be unlikely if in fact there were no difference in the populations the samples represent; an outcome of hypothesis testing in which the null hypothesis is rejected. (3, 6)

Stepwise multiple regression Exploratory procedure in which all the potential predictor variables that have been measured are tried in order to find the predictor variable that produces the best prediction, then each of the remaining variables is tried to find the predictor variable which in combination with the first produces the best prediction; this process continues until adding the best remaining variable does not provide a significant improvement. (17)

Structural equation modeling Sophisticated version of path analysis that includes paths with latent, unmeasured, theoretical variables and that also permits a kind of significance test and provides measures of the overall fit of the data to the hypothesized causal pattern. (17)

Sum of squared deviations (*SS*) Total over all the scores of each score's squared difference from the mean. (2, 4, 12)

Structural model Way of understanding the analysis of variance as a division of the deviation of each score from the overall mean into parts corresponding to the variation within groups (its deviation from its group's mean) and between groups (its group's mean's deviation from the overall mean); an alternative

(but mathematically equivalent) way of understanding the analysis of variance. (12, 13)

Subjective interpretation of probability Way of understanding probability as the degree of one's certainty that a particular outcome will occur. (5)

Sum of squared deviations between groups (SS_{Between}) Sum of squared deviations of each score's group's mean from the grand mean; same as *between-groups sum of squares.* (12)

Sum of squared deviations total (SS_{Total}) In analysis of variance, sum of squared deviations of each score from the overall mean of all scores, completely ignoring the group a score is in. (12) In regression, sum of squared differences of each score from the predicted score when predicting from the mean. (4)

Sum of squared deviations within groups (SS_{Within}) Sum of squared deviations of each score from its group's mean; same as *within-group sum of squares.* (12)

Sum of squared errors (SS_{Error}) Sum of the squared differences between each score and its predicted score. (4)

Symmetrical distribution Distribution in which the pattern of frequencies on the left and right side are mirror images of each other. (1)

***t* distribution** Mathematically defined curve that is the comparison distribution used in a *t* test. (9)

Test-retest reliability One index of a measure's reliability, obtained by giving the test to a group of people twice; correlation between scores from the two testings. (17)

***t* score** On a *t* distribution, number of standard deviations from the mean (like a *Z* score, but on a *t* distribution). (9)

***t* table** Table of cutoff scores on the *t* distribution for various degrees of freedom, significance levels, and one- and two-tailed tests. (9)

***t* test** Hypothesis-testing procedure in which the population variance is unknown; it compares *t* scores from a sample to a comparison distribution called a *t* distribution. (9, 10)

***t* test for a single sample** Hypothesis-testing procedure in which a sample mean is being compared to a known population mean and the population variance is unknown. (9)

***t* test for dependent means** Hypothesis-testing procedure in which there are two scores for each person and the population variance is not known; it determines the significance of a hypothesis that is being tested using difference or change scores from a single group of people. (9)

***t* test for independent means** Hypothesis-testing procedure in which there are two separate groups of people tested and in which the population variance is not known. (10)

Two-tailed test Hypothesis-testing procedure for a nondirectional hypothesis; the situation in which the region of the comparison distribution in which the null hypothesis would be rejected is divided between the two sides (tails) of the distribution. (6)

Two-way analysis of variance Analysis of variance for a two-way factorial research design. (13)

Two-way factorial research design Factorial research design with two variables that each divide the groups. (13)

Type I error Rejecting the null hypothesis when in fact it is true; getting a statistically significant result when in fact the research hypothesis is not true. (8)

Type II error Failing to reject the null hypothesis when in fact it is false; failing to get a statistically significant result when in fact the research hypothesis is true. (8)

Unbiased estimate of the population variance (S^2) Estimate of the population variance, based on sample scores, which has been corrected (by dividing the sum of squared deviations by the sample size minus 1 instead of the usual procedure of dividing by the sample size directly) so that it is equally likely to overestimate or underestimate the true population variance. (2, 9)

Unimodal distribution Frequency distribution with one value clearly having a larger frequency than any other. (1)

Value Possible number or category that a score can have. (1)

Variable Characteristic that can have different values. (1)

Variance (SD^2, S^2, σ^2, MS) Measure of how spread out a set of scores are; average of the squared deviations from the mean; standard deviation squared. (2, 5, 9, 11)

Variance of a distribution of differences between means ($S^2_{\text{Difference}}$) Number figured as part of a t test for independent means; equals the sum of the variances of the distributions of means for each of two samples. (10)

Variance of a distribution of means (S^2_M, σ^2_M) Variance of the population divided by the number of scores in each sample. (7, 9)

Weighted average Average in which the scores being averaged do not have equal influence on the total, as in figuring the pooled variance estimate in a t test for independent means. (10)

Within-groups degrees of freedom (df_{Within}) Same as *denominator degrees of freedom.* (11)

Within-groups estimate of the population variance (S^2_{Within}, MS_{Within}) In analysis of variance, estimate of the variance of the distribution of the population of individuals based on the variation among the scores within each of the actual groups studied. (11)

Within-groups sum of squares (SS_{Within}) Same as *sum of squared deviations within groups.* (12)

Within-subject design Same as *repeated-measures design.* (9)

Z score Number of standard deviations a score is above (or below, if negative) the mean of its distribution; ordinary score transformed so that it better describes that score's location in a distribution. (2)

Z test Hypothesis-testing procedure in which there is a single sample and the population variance is known. (7)

GLOSSARY OF SYMBOLS

α Significance level; probability of a Type I error in hypothesis testing. (8)

β Standardized regression coefficient (4); also probability of a Type II error in hypothesis testing. (8)

μ Population mean. (5)

μ_M Mean of a distribution of means. (7)

σ Population standard deviation. (5)

σ_M Standard deviation of a distribution of means. (7)

σ^2 Population variance. (5)

σ_M^2 Variance of a distribution of means. (7)

Σ Sum of; add up all the scores following. (2)

ϕ Phi coefficient; effect size in chi-square analysis of a 2 X 2 contingency table. (14)

χ^2 Chi-square statistic. (14)

a Regression constant. (4)

b Raw score regression coefficient. (4)

d Effect size for studies involving one or two means. (8–10)

df Degrees of freedom. (9–14)

$df_1, df_2,$ **etc.** Degrees of freedom for the first group, second group, etc. (10–13)

df_{Between} Numerator degrees of freedom in the analysis of variance. (11)

$df_{\text{Columns}}, df_{\text{Rows}}, df_{\text{Interaction}}$ Degrees of freedom for columns, rows, and interaction (in the factorial analysis of variance). (13)

df_{Total} Total degrees of freedom over all groups. (10–13)

df_{Within} Denominator degrees of freedom in the analysis of variance. (11)

F **ratio** Ratio of between-groups population variance estimate to within-groups population variance estimate in the analysis of variance. (11)

GM Mean of all scores in the analysis of variance. (11–13)

M Mean. (2)

$M_1, M_2,$ **etc.** Mean of the first group, second group, etc. (10–13)

$M_{\text{Column}}, M_{\text{Row}}$ Mean of the scores in a particular column or a particular row (in the factorial analysis of variance). (13)

MS_{Between} Mean squares between. (11)

$MS_{\text{Columns}}, MS_{\text{Rows}}, MS_{\text{Interaction}}$ Mean squares between for columns, rows, interaction. (13)

MS_{Error} Mean squares error. (11)

MS_{Within} Mean squares within. (11)

n Number of scores in each group in the analysis of variance. (11)

N Number of scores overall. (2)

$N_1, N_2,$ **etc.** Number of scores in the first group, second group, etc. (10–13)

$N_{\text{Columns}}, N_{\text{Rows}}$ Number of columns, number of rows (in factorial analysis of variance). (13)

N_{Cells} Number of cells in a factorial design. (13)

N_{Groups} Number of groups in the analysis of variance.

p Probability. (5)

r Correlation coefficient. (3)

r^2 Proportionate reduction in error (proportion of variance accounted for) in bivariate regression. (3)

R Multiple correlation coefficient. (4, 12)

R^2 Proportionate reduction in error (proportion of variance accounted for) in multiple regression and analysis of variance. (4, 12, 13)

$R^2_{Columns}$, R^2_{Rows}, $R^2_{Interaction}$ Proportion of variance accounted for (measure of effect size in the factorial analysis of variance) for columns, rows, interaction. (13)

S Unbiased estimate of the population standard deviation. (9)

S^2 Unbiased estimate of the population variance. (9)

S^2_1, S^2_2, etc. Unbiased estimate of the population variance based on scores in the first sample, second sample, etc. (10–13)

$S^2_{Between}$ Between-group estimate of the population variance. (11)

$S^2_{Columns}$, S^2_{Rows}, $S^2_{Interaction}$ Estimated population variance between groups for columns, rows, interaction (in factorial analysis of variance). (13)

$S_{Difference}$ Standard deviation of the distribution of differences between means. (10)

$S^2_{Difference}$ Variance of the distribution of differences between means. (10)

S^2_{Error} Error variance. (4, 11)

S_M Standard deviation of the distribution of means based on an estimated population variance. (9)

S^2_M Variance of a distribution of means based on an estimated population variance in a t test or as estimated from the variation among means of groups in the analysis of variance. (9, 11)

S^2_{M1}, S^2_{M2}, etc. Variance of the distribution of means based on a pooled population variance estimate, corresponding to the first sample, second sample, etc. (10, 11)

S_{Pooled} Pooled estimate of the population standard deviation. (10)

S^2_{Pooled} Pooled estimate of the population variance. (10)

S^2_{Within} Within-groups population variance estimate. (11)

SD Standard deviation. (2)

SD^2 Variance. (2)

SS Sum of squared deviations. (2)

$SS_{Between}$ Sum of squared deviations between groups. (12)

$SS_{Columns}$, SS_{Rows}, $SS_{Interaction}$ Sum of squared deviations between columns or rows or due to interaction (in the factorial analysis of variance). (13)

SS_{Total} Total sum of squared deviations from the mean (or from the grand mean, in the analysis of variance). (4, 12, 13)

SS_{Within} Sum of squared deviations within groups (or within cells). (12, 13)

t score Number of standard deviations from the mean on a t distribution. (9)

X Score on a particular variable; in regression, X is usually for the predictor variable. (1–4)

X_1, X_2, etc. First predictor variable, second predictor variable, etc. (4)

$\overline{X}$ Mean of variable X. (2)

Y Usually, the criterion variable in regression. (3, 4)

$\hat{Y}$ Predicted value of variable Y. (4)

Z Number of standard deviations from the mean. (2)

Z_X Z score for variable X. (3, 4)

Z_{X1}, Z_{X2}, etc. Z score for the first predictor variable, Z score for the second predictor variable, etc. (4)

Z_Y Z score for variable Y. (3, 4)

$\hat{Z}_Y$ Predicted value of the Z score for variable Y. (4)

OTHER SYMBOLS

^ Predicted value of the variable. (4)

¯ Mean of the variable. (2)

REFERENCES

ABELSON, R. P. (1997). On the surprising longevity of flogged horses: Why there is a case for the significance test. *Psychological Science, 8,* 12–15.

ALTMAN, D. G., LEVINE, D. W., HOWARD, G., & HAMILTON, H. (1997). Tobacco farming and public health: Attitudes of the general public and farmers. *Journal of Social Issues, 53,* 113–128.

AMERICAN PSYCHOLOGICAL ASSOCIATION. (1994). *Graduate study in psychology.* Washington, DC: Author.

ANDERSON, J. E., CAREY, J. W., & TAVERAS, S. (2000). HIV testing among the general US population at increased risk: Information from national surveys, 1987–1996. *American Journal of Public Health, 90,* 1089–1095.

ARMSTRONG-STASSEN, M. (2001). Reactions of older employees to organizational downsizing: The role of gender, job level, and time. *Journal of Gerontology: Psychological Sciences, 56B,* 239.

ARON, A., & ARON, E. N. (1989). *The heart of social psychology.* Lexington, MA: Heath.

ARON, A., & ARON, E. N. (1997). Self-expansion motivation and including other in the self. In W. Ickes (Section Ed.) & S. Duck (Ed.), *Handbook of personal relationships* (2nd ed., Vol. 1, pp. 251–270). London: Wiley.

ARON, A., ARON, E. N., & NORMAN, C. C. (2001). The self expansion model of motivation and cognition in close relationships and beyond. In M Clark & G. Fletcher (Eds.), *Blackwell handbook in social psychology, Vol. 2: Interpersonal processes.* Oxford: Blackwell.

ARON, A., ARON, E. N., & ALLEN, J. (1998). Motivations for unreciprocated love. *Personality and Social Psychology Bulletin, 24,* 787–796.

ARON, A., NORMAN, C. C., ARON, E. N., MCKENNA, C., HEYMAN, R. E. (2000). Couples' shared participation in novel and arousing activities and experienced relationship quality. *Journal of Personality and Social Psychology, 78,* 273–284.

ARON, A., PARIS, M., & ARON, E. N. (1995). Falling in love: Prospective studies of self concept change. *Journal of Personality and Social Psychology, 69,* 1102–1112.

ARON, E. N. (1996). *The highly sensitive person.* New York: Birch/Lane.

ARON, E. N. (1999). High sensitivity as one source of fearfulness and shyness: Preliminary research and clinical implications. In L. A. Schmidt & J. Schulkin (Eds.), *Extreme fear, shyness, and social phobia: Origins, biological mechanisms, and clinical outcomes* (pp. 251–272). New York: Oxford.

ARON, E. N., & ARON, A. (1997). Sensory processing sensitivity and its relation to introversion and emotionality. *Journal of Personality and Social Psychology, 73,* 345–368.

BARRON, K. E., & HARACKIEWICZ, J. M. (2001). Achievement goals and optimal motivation: Testing multiple goal models. *Journal of Personality and Social Psychology, 80,* 715.

BAUMRIND, D. (1983). Specious causal attributions in the social sciences: The reformulated stepping-stone theory of heroin use as exemplar. *Journal of Personality and Social Psychology, 45,* 1289–1298.

BERNDSEN, M., MCGARTY, C., VAN DER PLIGT, J., & SPEARS, R. (2001). Meaning-seeking in the illusory correlation paradigm: The active role of participants in the categorization process. *British Journal of Social Psychology, 40,* 209–233.

BETSCH, T., PLESSNER, H., SCHWIEREN, C., & GUTIG, R. (2001). I like it but I don't know why: A value-account approach to implicit attitude formation. *Personality and Social Psychology Bulletin, 27,* 242–253.

BLOCK, N. (1995). How heritability misleads about race. *Cognition, 56,* 99–128.

BOURGEOIS, M. M. (1997). A powerful, effective statistics text. [Review of A. Aron & E. Aron, *Statistics for Psychology*]. *Contemporary Psychology, 42,* 993–994.

BOYD, C. P., & GULLONE, E. (1997). An investigation of negative affectivity in Australian adolescents. *Journal of Clinical Child Psychology, 26,* 190–197.

BREWER, J. K. (1972). On the power of statistical tests in the *American Education Research Journal. American Educational Research Journal, 9,* 391–401.

BRICKMAN, P., COATES, D., & JANOFF-BULMAN, R. (1978). Lottery winners and accident victims: Is happiness relative? *Journal of Personality and Social Psychology, 36,* 917–927.

BROCKNER, J., ACKERMAN, G., GREENBERG, J., GELFAND, M. J., FRANCESCO, A. M., CHEN, Z. X., LEUNG, K., BIERBRAUER, G., GOMEZ, C., KIRKMAN, B. L., & SHAPIRO, D. (2001). Culture and procedural justice: The influence of power distance on reactions to voice. *Journal of Experimental Social Psychology, 37,* 305.

BUSHMAN, B. J., & ANDERSON, C. A. (2001). Media violence and the American public: Scientific facts versus media misinformation. *American Psychologist, 56,* 477–489.

BUSS, D. M., & SCHMITT, D. P. (1993). Sexual strategies theory: An evolutionary perspective on human mating. *Psychological Review, 100,* 204–232.

CAREY, M. P., MAISTO, S. A., KALICHMAN, S. C., FORSYTH, A. D., WRIGHT, E. M., & JOHNSON, B. T. (1997). Enhancing motivation to reduce the risk of HIV infection for economically disadvantaged urban women. *Journal of Consulting and Clinical Psychology, 65,* 531–541.

CASPI, A., BEGG, D., DICKSON, N., HARRINGTON, H., LANGLEY, J., MOFFITT, T. E., & SILVA, P. A. (1997). Personality differences predict health-risk behaviors in young adulthood: Evidence from a longitudinal study. *Journal of Personality and Social Psychology, 73,* 1052–1063.

CASPI, A., & HERBENER, E. S. (1990). Continuity and change: Assortative marriage and the consistency of personality in adulthood. *Journal of Personality and Social Psychology, 58,* 250–258.

CATANZARO, D., & TAYLOR, J. C. (1996). The scaling of dispersion and correlation: A comparison of least-squares and absolute deviation statistics. *British Journal of Mathematical and Statistical Psychology, 49,* 171–188.

CHAPMAN, H. A., HOBFOLL, S. E., & RITTER, C. (1997). Partners' stress underestimations lead to women's distress: A study of pregnant inner-city women. *Journal of Personality and Social Psychology, 73,* 418–425.

CHASE, L. J., & CHASE, R. B. (1976). A statistical power analysis of applied psychological research. *Journal of Applied Psychology, 61,* 234–237.

CHIU, C., HONG, Y., & DWECK, C. S. (1997). Lay dispositionism and implicit theories of personality. *Journal of Personality and Social Psychology, 73,* 19–30.

CHOW, S. L. (1988). Significance test or effect size. *Psychological Bulletin, 103,* 105–110.

CHOW, S. L. (1996). *Statistical significance: Rationale, validity, and utility.* London: Sage.

CLARK, D. M., SALKOVSKIS, P. M., OST, L-G., BREITHOLTZ, E., KOEHLER, K. A., WESTLING, B. E., JEAVONS, A., & GELDER, M. (1997). Misinterpretation of body sensations in panic disorder. *Journal of Consulting and Clinical Psychology, 65,* 203–213.

COHEN, J. (1962). The statistical power of abnormal-social psychological research: A review. *Journal of Abnormal and Social Psychology, 65,* 145–153.

COHEN, J. (1988). *Statistical power analysis for the behavioral sciences.* Hillsdale, NJ: Erlbaum.

COHEN, J. (1990). Things I have learned (so far). *American Psychologist, 45,* 1304–1312.

COHEN, J. (1992). A power primer. *Psychological Bulletin, 112,* 155–159.

COHEN, J. (1994). The Earth is round ($p < .05$). *American Psychologist, 49,* 997–1003.

COHEN, J., & COHEN, P. (1983). *Applied multiple regression/correlation analysis for the behavioral sciences.* Hillsdale, NJ: Erlbaum.

COLEMAN, H. L. K., CASALI, S. B., & WAMPOLD, B. E. (2001). Adolescent strategies for coping with cultural diversity. *Journal of Counseling & Development, 79,* 356–362.

COMMISSION PAYMENTS TO TRAVEL AGENTS. (1978, August 8). *New York Times,* p. D–1.

CONNORS, G. J., CARROLL, K. M., DiCLEMENTE, C. C., LONGABAUGH, R., & DONOVAN, D. M. (1997). The therapeutic alliance and its relationship to alcoholism treatment participation and outcome. *Journal of Consulting and Clinical Psychology, 65,* 588–598.

CONOVER, W., & IMAN, R. L. (1981). Rank transformations as a bridge between parametric and nonparametric statistics. *American Statistician, 35,* 124–129.

COOK, T. D., & CAMPBELL, D. T. (1979). *Quasi-experimentation: Design and analysis issues for field settings.* Skokie, IL: Rand McNally.

COOPER, S. E., & ROBINSON, D. A. G. (1989). The influence of gender and anxiety on mathematics performance. *Journal of College Student Development, 30,* 459–461.

CORTINA, J. M., & DUNLOP, W. P. (1997). On the logic and purpose of significance testing. *Psychological Methods, 2,* 161–172.

CRICK, N. R., CASAS, J. F., & MOSHER, M. (1997). Relational and overt aggression in preschool. *Developmental Psychology, 33,* 579–588.

DAHLSTROM, W. G., LARBAR, D., & DAHLSTROM, L. E. (1986). *MMPI patterns of American minorities.* Minneapolis: University of Minnesota Press.

DANE, F. C., & WRIGHTSMAN, L. S. (1982). Effects of defendants' and victims' characteristics on jurors' verdicts. In N. L. Kerr & R. M. Bray (Eds.), *The psychology of the courtroom.* Orlando, FL: Academic Press.

DARLINGTON, R. B. (1990). *Regression and linear models.* New York: McGraw-Hill.

DAWES, R. M., FAUST, D., & MEEHL, P. E. (1993). Statistical prediction versus clinical prediction: Improving what works. In G. Keren & C. Lewis (Eds.), *A handbook for data analysis in the behavioral sciences: Methodological issues* (pp. 351–367). Hillsdale, NJ: Erlbaum.

DECARLO, L. T. (1997). On the meaning and use of kurtosis. *Psychological Methods, 2,* 292–307.

DEGARMO, D. S., & FORGATCH, M. S. (1997). Determinants of observed confidant support for divorced mothers. *Journal of Personality and Social Psychology, 72,* 336–345.

DELUCCHI, K. L. (1983). The use and misuse of chi-square: Lewis and Burke revisited. *Psychological Bulletin, 94,* 166–176.

DENNENBERG, V. H. (1999). A critique of Mody, Studdert-Kennedy, and Brady's "Speech perception deficits in poor readers Auditory processing or phonological coding?". *Journal of Learning Disabilities, 32,* 379–383.

DESMARIS, S., & CURTIS, J. (1997). Gender and perceived pay entitlement: Testing for effects of experience with income. *Journal of Personality and Social Psychology, 72,* 141–150.

DUNLAP, W. P., & MYERS, L. (1997). Approximating power for significance tests with one degree of freedom. *Psychological Methods, 2,* 186–191.

DWINELL, P. E., & HIGBEE, J. L. (1991). Affective variables related to mathematics achievement among high-risk college freshmen. *Psychological Reports, 69,* 399–403.

EBERHARDT MCKEE, T. L., & PTACEK, J. T. (2001). I'm afraid I have something bad to tell you: Breaking bad news from the perspective of the giver. *Journal of Applied Social Psychology, 31,* 246

ENDLER, N. S., & MAGNUSSON, D. (1976). Toward an interactional psychology of personality. *Psychological Bulletin, 83,* 956–974.

EPPLEY, K. R., ABRAMS, A. I., & SHEAR, J. (1989). Differential effects of relaxation techniques on trait anxiety: A meta-analysis. *Journal of Clinical Psychology, 45,* 957–974.

ESCUDERO, V., ROGERS, L. E., & GUTIERREZ, E. (1997). Patterns of relational control and nonverbal affect in clinic and nonclinic couples. *Journal of Social and Personal Relationships, 14,* 5–29.

EVANS, R. (1976). *The making of psychology.* New York: Knopf.

EVERETT, S. A., PRICE, J. H., BEDELL, A. W., & TELLJOHANN, S. K. (1997). The effect of a monetary incentive in increasing the return rate of a survey to family physicians. *Evaluation and the Health Professions, 20,* 207–214.

EYSENCK, H. J. (1981). *A model for personality.* Berlin: Springer-Verlag.

FAWZI, M. C. S., PHAM, T., LIN, L., NGUYEN, T. V., NGO, D., MURPHY, E., & MOLLICA, R. F. (1997). The validity of post-traumatic stress disorder among Vietnamese refugees. *Journal of Traumatic Stress, 10,* 101–108.

FISHER, B. (1978). *Fisher Divorce Adjustment Scale.* Boulder, CO: Family Relations Learning Center.

FISHER, R. A. (1938). *Statistical methods for research workers* (7th ed.). London: Oliver & Boyd.

FISHER, R. A., & YATES, F. (1938). Statistical Tables for Biological, Agricultural and Medical Research. London: Oliver and Boyd.

FISKE, S. T. (1998). Stereotyping, prejudice, and discrimination. In D. T. Gilbert, S. T. Fiske, & G. Lindzey, (Eds.) *The handbook of social psychology* (4th ed.). New York: McGraw-Hill.

FOERTSCH, J., & GERNSBACHER, M. A. (1997). In search of gender neutrality: Is singular *they* a cognitively efficient substitute for generic *he? Psychological Science, 8,* 106–112.

FOLWELL, A. L., CHUNG, L. C., NUSSBAUM, J. F., BETHEA, L. S., & GRANT, J. A. (1997). Differential accounts of closeness in older adult sibling relationships. *Journal of Social and Personal Relationships, 14,* 843–849.

FORD, J. D., FISHER, P., & LARSON, L. (1997). Object relations as a predictor of treatment outcome with chronic posttraumatic stress disorder. *Journal of Consulting and Clinical Psychology, 65,* 547–559.

FRANK, S. J., POORMAN, M. O., VAN EGEREN, L. A., & FIELD, D. T. (1997). Perceived relationships with parents among adolescent inpatients with depressive preoccupations and depressed mood. *Journal of Clinical Child Psychology, 26,* 205–215.

FRANZ, M. L. VON. (1979). *The problem of puer aeternus.* New York: Springer-Verlag.

FRICK, R. W. (1995). Accepting the null hypothesis. *Memory and Cognition, 23,* 132–138.

FRICK, R. W. (1996). The appropriate use of null hypothesis testing. *Psychological Methods, 1,* 379–390.

FRICK, R. W. (1998). Interpreting statistical testing: Process and propensity, not population and random sampling. *Behavior Research Methods, Instruments, and Computers, 30,* 527–535.

FRIEND, R. (2001). Effects of strategy instruction on summary writing of college students. *Contemporary Educational Psychology, 26,* 14.

FRISCH, A. S., SHAMSUDDIN, K., & KURTZ, M. (1995). Family factors and knowledge: Attitudes and efforts concerning exposure to environmental tobacco among Malaysian medical students. *Journal of Asian and African Studies, 30,* 68–79.

FRITZON, K. (2001). An examination of the relationship between distance traveled and motivational aspects of firesetting behaviour. *Journal of Environmental Psychology, 21,* 45–60.

GABLE, S., & LUTZ, S. (2000) Household, parent, and child contributions to childhood obesity. *Family Relations, 49,* 293–300.

GALLAGHER-THOMPSON, D., DAL CANTO, P. G., JACOB, T., & THOMPSON, L. W. (2001). A comparison of marital interaction patterns between couples in which the husband does or does not have Alzheimer's disease. *Journal of Gerontology: Social Sciences, 56B,* S144.

GALLUP, D. G. H. (1972). *The Gallup poll: Public opinion, 1935–1971.* New York: Random House.

GALTON, F. (1889). *Natural inheritance.* London: Macmillan.

GERBERT, B., BRONSTONE, A., MAURER, T., HOFMANN, R., & BERGER, T. (1999). Decision support software to help primary care physicians triage skin cancer: A pilot study. *Arch Dermatol, 135,* 187–192.

GIGERENZER, G., & MURRAY, D. J. (1987). *Cognition as intuitive statistics.* Hillsdale, NJ: Erlbaum.

GIGERENZER, G., SWIJTINK, Z., PORTER, Y., DASTON, L., BEATTY, J., & KRUGER, L. (1989). *The empire of chance.* Cambridge, England: Cambridge University Press.

GIRE, J. T. (1997). The varying effect of individualism-collectivism on preference for methods of conflict resolution. *Canadian Journal of Behavioural Science, 29,* 38–43.

GOIDEL, H. K., & LANGLEY, R. E. (1995). Media coverage of the economy and aggregate economic evaluations: Uncovering evidence of indirect media effects. *Political Research Quarterly, 48,* 313–328.

GONZAGA, G. C., KELTNER, D., LONDAHL, E. A., & SMITH, M. D. (2001). Love and the commitment problem in romantic relations and friendship. *Journal of Personality and Social Psychology, 81,* 251.

GOSSET, W. S. (1947). *"Student's" collected papers.* London: University College.

GOUGH, H., & HEILBRUN, A. (1983). *The Adjective Check List Manual.* Palo Alto, CA: Consulting Psychologist Press.

GRAHAM, S., WEINER, B., & ZUCKER, G. S. (1997). An attributional analysis of punishment goals and public reactions to O. J. Simpson. *Personality and Social Psychology Bulletin, 23,* 331–346.

GREENWALD, A. G. (1975). Consequences of prejudice against the null hypothesis. *Psychological Bulletin, 82,* 1–19.

GRILO, C. M., WALKER, M. L., BECKER, D. F., EDELL, W. S., & McGLASHAN, T. H. (1997). Personality disorders in adolescents with major depression, substance use disorders, and co-existing major depression and substance use disorders. *Journal of Consulting and Clinical Psychology, 65,* 328–332.

GUMP, B. B., & KULIK, J. A. (1997). Stress, affiliation, and emotional contagion. *Journal of Personality and Social Psychology, 72,* 305–319.

HAHLWEG, K., FIEGENBAUM, W., FRANK, M., SCHROEDER, B., & WITZLEBEN, I. V. (2001). Short- and long-term effectiveness of an empirically supported treatment for agoraphobia. *Journal of Counseling and Clinical Psychology, 69,* 375, 380.

HAMILTON, D. (1981). *Cognitive processes in stereotyping and intergroup behavior.* Hillsdale, NJ: Erlbaum.

HAMILTON, D., & GIFFORD, R. (1976). Illusory correlation in interpersonal perception: A cognitive basis of stereotypic judgments. *Journal of Experimental Social Psychology, 12,* 392–407.

HARRIS, R. J. (1997). Significance tests have their place. *Psychological Science, 8,* 8–11.

HARTER, S., WATERS, P. L., PETTITT, L. M., WHITESELL, N., KOFKIN, J., & JORDAN, J. (1997). Autonomy and connectedness as dimensions of relationship styles in men and women. *Journal of Social and Personal Relationships, 14,* 147–164.

HAZAN, C., & SHAVER, P. (1987). Romantic love conceptualized as an attachment process. *Journal of Personality and Social Psychology, 52,* 511–524.

HEIN, S. F., & AUSTIN, W. J. (2001). Empirical and hermeneutic approaches to phenomenological research in psychology: A comparison. *Psychological Methods, 6,* 3.

HERMANN, C., BLANCHARD, E. B., & FLOR, H. (1997). Biofeedback treatment for pediatric migraine: Prediction of treatment outcome. *Journal of Consulting and Clinical Psychology, 65,* 611–616.

HIGHLEN, P. S., & FINLEY, H. C. (1996). Doing qualitative analysis. In N. F. T. L. Leong & J. T. Austin (Eds.), *The psychology research handbook* (pp. 177–192). Thousand Oaks, CA: Sage.

HILGARD, E. R. (1987). *Psychology in America: A historical perspective.* Orlando, FL: Harcourt Brace Jovanovich.

HINDLEY, C., FILLIOZAT, A., KLACKENBERG, G., NICOLET-MEISTER, D., & SAND, E. (1966). Differences in age of walking in five European longitudinal samples. *Human Biology, 38,* 364–379.

HOLDEN, G. W., THOMPSON, E. E., ZAMBARANO, R. J., & MARSHALL, L. A. (1997). Child effects as a source of change in maternal attitudes. *Journal of Social and Personal Relationships, 14,* 481–490.

HOLZWORTH, R. J. (1996). Policy capturing with ridge regression. *Organizational Behavior and Human Decision Processes, 68,* 171–179.

HOPKINS, K. D., & GLASS, G. V. (1978). *Basic statistics for the behavioral sciences.* Englewood Cliffs, NJ: Prentice Hall.

HUNTER, J. E. (1997). Needed: A ban on the significance test. *Psychological Science, 8,* 3–7.

HUSSERL, E. (1970). *The crisis of European sciences and transcendental phenomenology: An introduction to phenomenological philosophy* (D. C. Carr, Trans.). Evanston, IL: Northwestern University Press.

HYDE, J. S. (1993). Gender differences in mathematics ability, anxiety, and attitudes: What do meta-analyses tell us? In L. A. Penner, G. M. Batsche, H. M. Knoff, & D. L. Nelson, *The challenge in mathematics and science education: Psychology's response* (pp. 237–249). Washington, DC: American Psychological Association.

HYDE, J. S., FENNEMA, E., & LAMON, S. J. (1990). Gender differences in mathematics performance: A meta-analysis. *Psychological Bulletin, 107,* 139–155.

IRVING, L. M., & BEREL, S. R. (2001). Comparison of media-literacy programs to strengthen college women's resistance to media images. *Psychology of Women Quarterly, 25,* 103–111.

JACKSON, L. A., ERVIN, K. S., GARDNER, P. D., & SCHMITT, N. (2001). Gender and the Internet: Women communicating and men searching. *Sex Roles, 44,* 372–373.

JESSOR, R. (1996). Ethnographic methods in contemporary perspective. In R. Jessor, A. Colby, & R. A. Shweder (Eds.), *Ethnography and human development: Context and meaning in social inquiry* (pp. 3–14). Chicago: University of Chicago Press.

JOHNSON, C., & MULLEN, B. (1994). Evidence for the accessibility of paired distinctiveness in distinctiveness-based illusory correlation in stereotyping. *Personality and Social Psychology Bulletin, 20,* 65–70.

JUDD, C. M., MCCLELLAND, G. H., & CULHANE, S. E. (1995). Data analysis: Continuing issues in the everyday analysis of psychological data. *Annual Review of Psychology, 46,* 433–465.

JUNE, L. N., CURRY, B. P., & GEAR, C. L. (1990). An 11-year analysis of black students' experience of problems and use of services: Implications for counseling professionals. *Journal of Counseling Psychology, 37,* 178–184.

KAGAN, J. (1994). *Galen's prophecy: Temperament in human nature.* New York: Basic Books.

KARNEY, B. R., & BRADBURY, T. N. (1997). Neuroticism, marital interaction, and the trajectory of marital satisfaction. *Journal of Personality and Social Psychology, 72,* 1075–1092.

KELLEY, H. H. (1971). *Attribution in social interaction.* Morristown, NJ: General Learning Press.

KENNY, D. A. (1995). Relationship science in the 21st century. *Journal of Social and Personal Relationships, 12,* 597–600.

KENNY, D. A., KASHY, D. A., & BOLGER, N. (1998). Data analysis in social psychology. In D. Gilbert, S. Fiske, & G. Lindzey (Eds.), *Handbook of social psychology* (4th ed., Vol. 1, pp. 233–265). Boston, MA: McGraw-Hill.

KERLINGER, F. N. (1973). *Foundations of behavioral research.* New York: Holt, Rinehart and Winston.

KLEINMUNTZ, B. (1990). Why we still use our heads instead of formulas: Toward an integrative approach. *Psychological Bulletin, 107,* 296–310.

KOSLOWSKY, M., SCHWARZWALD, J., & ASHURI, S. (2001). On the relationship between subordinates' compliance to power sources and organisational attitudes. *Applied Psychology: An International Review, 50,* 455–476.

KRAEMER, H. C., & THIEMANN, S. (1987). *How many subjects? Statistical power analysis in research.* Newbury Park, CA: Sage.

KUNDA, Z., & OLESON, K. C. (1997). When exceptions prove the rule: How extremity of deviance determines the impact of deviant examples on stereotypes. *Journal of Personality and Social Psychology, 72,* 965–979.

KWAN, V. S. Y., BOND, M. H., & SINGELIS, T. M. (1997). Pancultural explanations for life satisfaction: Adding relationship harmony to self-esteem. *Journal of Personality and Social Psychology, 73,* 1038–1051.

LAMBERT, A. J., KHAN, S. R., LICKEL, B. A., & FRICKE, K. (1997). Mood and the correction of positive versus negative stereotypes. *Journal of Personality and Social Psychology, 72,* 1002–1016.

LARSON, R., DWORKIN, J., & VERMA, S. (2001). Men's work and family lives in India: The daily organization of time and emotions. *Journal of Family Psychology, 15,* 206–224.

LEE, K., BYATT, G., & RHODES, G. (2000). Caricature effects, distinctiveness, and identification: Testing the face-space framework. *Psychological Science, 11,* 379–385.

LEVENTHAL, L., & HUYN, C-L. (1996). Directional decisions for two-tailed tests: Power, error rates, and sample size. *Psychological Methods, 1,* 278–292.

LEWIS, D., & BURKE, C. J. (1949). The use and misuse of the chi-square test. *Psychological Bulletin, 46,* 433–489.

LI, K. Z. H., LINDERBERGER, U., FREUND, A. M., & BALTES, P. B. (2001). Walking while memorizing: Age-related differences in compensatory behavior. *Psychological Science, 12,* 230–237.

LINDZEY, E. W., MIZE, J., & PETTIT, G. S. (1997). Mutuality in parent-child play: Consequences for children's peer competence. *Journal of Social and Personal Relationships, 14,* 523–538.

LYDON, J., PIERCE, T., & O'REGAN, S. (1997). Coping with moral commitment to long-distance dating relationships. *Journal of Personality and Social Psychology, 73,* 104–113.

MacDONALD, C., CHAMBERLAIN, K., & LONG, N. (1997). Race, combat, and PTSD in a community sample of New Zealand Vietnam War veterans. *Journal of Traumatic Stress, 10,* 117–124.

MacKINNON-LEWIS, C., STARNES, R., VOLLING, B., & JOHNSON, S. (1997). Perceptions of parenting as predictors of boys' sibling and peer relations. *Developmental Psychology, 33,* 1024–1031.

MARKMAN, H. J., RENICK, M. J., FLOYD, F. J., STANLEY, S. M., & CLEMENTS, M. (1993). Preventing marital distress through communication and conflict management training: A 4- and 5-year follow-up. *Journal of Consulting and Clinical Psychology, 61,* 70–77.

MARTINEZ, R. (2000). Immigration and urban violence: The link between immigrant Latinos and types of homicide. *Social Science Quarterly, 81,* 363–374.

MAXWELL, S. E., & DELANEY, H. D. (1990). *Designing experiments and analyzing data.* Belmont, CA: Wadsworth.

MAXWELL, S. E., & DELANEY, H. D. (1993). Bivariate median splits and spurious statistical significance. *Psychological Bulletin, 113,* 181–190.

McCONNELL, A. R. (2001). Implicit theories: Consequences for social judgment of individuals. *Journal of Experimental Social Psychology, 37,* 215–227.

McConnell, A. R., Sherman, S. J., & Hamilton, D. L. (1994). Illusory correlation in the perception of groups: An extension of the distinctiveness-based account. *Journal of Personality and Social Psychology, 67,* 414–429.

McCracken, G. (1988). *The long interview.* London: Sage.

McLaughlin-Volpe, T., Aron, A, & Reis, H. T. (2001, February). *Closeness during interethnic social interactions and prejudice: A diary study.* Paper presented at the Annual Meeting of the Society for Personality and Social Psychology, San Antonio, TX.

McLaughlin-Volpe, T., Aron, A, & Reis, H. T. (1998, August). Closeness during interethnic social interactions and prejudice: A diary study. In A. Aron (Chair), *Intergroup contact and personal relationships.* Symposium conducted at the Annual Convention of the American Psychological Association, San Francisco, CA.

McLeod, J. (1996). Qualitative research methods in counseling psychology. In R. Woolfe & W. Dryden (Eds.), *Handbook of counseling psychology* (pp. 65–86). London: Sage.

Meehl, P. E. (1954). *Clinical versus statistical prediction: A theoretical analysis and a review of the evidence.* Minneapolis: University of Minnesota Press.

Meyers, A. W., Coleman, J. K., Whelan, J. P., & Mehlenbeck, R, S. (2001). Examining careers in sport Psychology: Who is working and who is making money? *Professional Psychology: Research and Practice, 32,* 5–11.

Micceri, T. (1989). The unicorn, the normal curve, and other improbable creatures. *Psychological Bulletin, 105,* 156–166.

Mickelson, K. D., Kessler, R. C., & Shaver, P. R. (1997). Adult attachment in a nationally representative sample. *Journal of Personality and Social Psychology, 73,* 1092–1106.

Mikulincer, M. (1998). Attachment working models and the sense of trust: An exploration of interaction goals and affect regulation. *Journal of Personality and Social Psychology, 74.*

Mikulincer, M., Hirschberger, G., Nachmias, O., & Gillath, O. (2001). The affective component of the secure base schema: Affective priming with representations of attachment security. *Journal of Personality and Social Psychology, 81,* 305.

Miller, L. C., & Fishkin, S. A. (1997). On the dynamics of human bonding and reproductive success: Seeking windows on the adapted-for human-environmental interface. In J. Simpson & D. T. Kenrick (Eds.), *Evolutionary social psychology* (pp. 197–235). Hillsdale, NJ: Erlbaum.

Miller, R. S. (1997). Inattentive and contented: Relationship commitment and attention to alternatives. *Journal of Personality and Social Psychology, 73,* 758–766.

Milligan, G. W., Wong, D. S., & Thompson, P. A. (1987). Robustness properties of nonorthogonal analysis of variance. *Psychological Bulletin, 101,* 464–470.

Mirvis, P., & Lawler, E. (1977). Measuring the financial impact of employee attitudes. *Journal of Applied Psychology, 62,* 1–8.

Mischel, W. (1968). *Personality and assessment.* New York: Wiley.

Mischel, W., & Shoda, Y. (1995). A cognitive-affective system theory of personality: Reconceptualizing situations, dispositions, dynamics, and invariance in personality structure. *Psychological Review, 102,* 246–268.

Mize, J., & Pettit, G. S. (1997). Mothers' social coaching, mother-child relationship style, and children's peer competence: Is the medium the message? *Child Development, 68,* 312–332.

Mody, M., Studdert-Kennedy, M and Brady, S. (1997). Speech perception deficits in poor readers: Auditory processing or phonological coding? *Journal of Experimental. Child Psychology, 64,* 1–33.

Mooney, S. P., Sherman, M. F., & Lo Presto, C. T. (1991). Academic locus of control, self-esteem, and perceived distance from home as predictors of college adjustment. *Journal of Counseling and Development, 69,* 445–448.

Moorehouse, M. J., & Sanders, P. E. (1992). Children's feelings of school competence and perceptions of parents' work in four sociocultural contexts. *Social Development, 1,* 185–200.

Moorehouse, E., & Tobler, N. S. (2000). Preventing and reducing substance use among institutionalized adolescents. *Adolescence, 35,* 1–28.

Moriarty, S. E., & Everett, S-L. (1994). Commercial breaks: A viewing behavior study. *Journalism Quarterly, 71,* 346–355.

Mouradian, V. E. (2001). Applying schema theory to intimate aggression: Individual and gender differences in representation of contexts and goals. *Journal of Applied Social Psychology, 31,* 376

Mueller, J. H., Elser, M. J., & Rollack, D. N. (1993). Test anxiety and implicit memory. *Bulletin of the Psychonomic Society, 31,* 531–533.

Myers, D. G. (1991). Union is strength: A consumer's view of meta-analysis. *Personality and Social Psychology Bulletin, 17,* 265–266.

Nakkula, M. J., & Nikitopoulos, C. E. (2001). Negotiation training and interpersonal development: An exploratory study of early adolescents in Argentina. *Adolescence, 36,* 12–20.

Nezlek, J. B., Kowalski, R. M., Leary, M. R., Blevins, T., & Holgate, S. (1997). Personality moderators of reactions to interpersonal rejection: Depression and trait self-esteem. *Personality and Social Psychology Bulletin, 23,* 1235–1244.

Nickerson, R. S. (2000). Null hypothesis significance testing: A review of an old and continuing controversy. *Psychological Methods, 5,* 241–301

Norcross, J. C., Hanych, J. M., & Terranova, R. D. (1996). Graduate study in psychology: 1992–1993. *American Psychologist, 51,* 631–643.

NOWNES, A. J. (2000). Policy conflict and the structure of interest communities: A comparative state analysis. *American Politics Quarterly, 28,* 309–327.

OAKES, M. (1982). Intuiting strength of association from a correlation coefficient. *British Journal of Psychology, 73,* 51–56.

OETTINGEN, G., SCHNETTER, K., & PAK, H. (2001). Self-regulation of goal setting: Turning free fantasies about the future into binding goals. *Journal of Personality and Social Psychology, 80,* 736–753.

OLTHOFF, R. K. (1989). *The effectiveness of premarital communication training.* Unpublished doctoral dissertation, California Graduate School of Family Psychology, San Francisco.

ONWUEGBUZIE, A. J. (1994). Examination-taking strategies used by college students in a statistics course. *College Student Journal,* 28(2), 163–174.

ONWUEGBUZIE, A. J. (2001). I'll begin my statistics assignment tomorrow: The relationship between statistics anxiety and academic procrastination. *Stress and Coping in Education,* 1, 6.

ORBACH, I., MIKULINCER, M., KING, R., COHEN, D., & STEIN, D. (1997). Thresholds and tolerance of physical pain in suicidal and nonsuicidal adolescents. *Journal of Consulting and Clinical Psychology, 65,* 646–652.

PAYNE, B. K. (2001). Prejudice and perception: The role of automatic and controlled processes in misperceiving a weapon. *Journal of Personality and Social Psychology, 81,* 185.

PEARSON, K. (1978). *The history of statistics in the 17th and 18th centuries.* London: Griffin.

PECUKONIS, E. V. (1990). A cognitive/affective empathy training program as a function of ego development in aggressive adolescent females. *Adolescence, 25,* 59–76.

PELLEGRINI, A. D., & BARTINI, M. (2000). An empirical comparison of methods of sampling aggression and victimization in school settings. *Journal of Educational Psychology, 92,* 360–366.

PETERS, W. S. (1987). *Counting for something: Statistical principles and personalities.* New York: Springer-Verlag.

PETTIGREW, T., & MEERTEN, R. W. (1995). *European Journal of Social Psychology, 25,* 57–75.

PHELPS, R. E., TAYLOR, J. D., & GERARD, P. A. (2001). Cultural mistrust, ethnic identity, racial identity, and self-esteem among ethnically diverse black university students. *Journal of Counseling and Development, 79,* 112.

PIASECKI, R., WYRICK, M., & HUFF, T. (2001). The relationship among test anxiety, personality, and perceived test characteristics.

PHILLIPS, L. D. (1973). *Bayesian statistics for social scientists.* London: Nelson.

PRENDA, K. M., & LACHMAN, M. E. (2001). Planning for the future: A life management strategy for increasing control and life satisfaction in adulthood. *Psychology and Aging, 16,* 207.

PRENTICE, D. A., & MILLER, D. T. (1992). When small effects are impressive. *Psychological Bulletin, 112,* 160–164.

PURI, M. L., & SENN, P. K. (1985). *Nonparametric methods in general linear models.* New York: Wiley.

RAYMORE, L. A., BARBER, B. L., & ECCLES, J. S. (2001). Leaving home, attending college, partnership and parenthood: The role of life transition events in leisure pattern stability from adolescence to young adulthood. *Journal of Youth and Adolescence, 30,* 197–223.

REBER, P. J., & KOTOVSKY, K. (1997). Implicit learning in problem solving: The role of working memory capacity. *Journal of Experimental Psychology: General, 126,* 178–203.

REGIER, D., MYERS, J., KRAMER, M., ROBINS, L., BLAZER, D., HOUGH, R., EATON, W., & LOCKE, B. (1984). The NIMH Epidemiologic Catchment Area Program. *Archives of General Psychiatry, 41,* 934–941.

REICHARDT, C. S., & GOLLOB, H. F. (1999). Justifying the use and increasing the power of a t test for a randomized experiment with a convenience sample. *Psychological Methods, 4,* 117–128.

REIS, H. T., & STILLER, J. (1992). Publication trends in *JPSP:* A three-decade review. *Personality and Social Psychology Bulletin, 18,* 465–472.

REISSMAN, C., ARON, A., & BERGEN, M. R. (1993). Shared activities and marital satisfaction: Causal direction and self-expansion versus boredom. *Journal of Social and Personal Relationships, 10,* 253–254.

RIEHL, R. J. (1994). Academic preparation, aspirations, and first-year performance of first-generation students. *College and University, 70,* 14–19.

ROBINS, R. W., & JOHN, O. P. (1997). Effects of visual perspective and narcissism on self-perception: Is seeing believing? *Psychological Science, 8,* 37–42.

ROSENTHAL, R, ROSNOW, R. L., & RUBIN, D. B. (1999) *Contrasts and Effect Sizes in Behavioral Research: A Correlational Approach.* Cambridge University Press, Cambridge, U.K.

ROSNOW, R. L., & ROSENTHAL, R. (1989) Statistical procedures and the justification of knowledge in psychological science. *American Psychologist, 44,* 1276–1284.

ROTTENSTREICH, Y., & HSEE, C. K. (2001). Money, kisses, and electric shocks: On the affective psychology of risk. *Psychological Science, 12,* 185–190.

RUSCIO, J. (2000). The role of complex thought in clinical prediction: Social accountability and the need for cognition. *Journal of Consulting and Clinical Psychology, 68,* 145–154.

SALSBURG, D. (2001). *The lady tasting tea: How statistics revolutionized science in the twentieth century.* New York: Freeman.

SAWILOWSKY, S. S., & BLAIR, R. C. (1992). A more realistic look at the robustness and Type II error properties of the *t* test to departures from population normality. *Psychological Bulletin, 111,* 352–360.

SCARR, S. (1997). Rules of evidence: A larger context for the statistical debate. *Psychological Science, 8,* 16–17.

SCHMADER, T., MAJOR, B., GRAMZOW, R. H. (2001). Coping with ethnic stereotypes in the academic domain: Perceived injustice and psychological disengagement. *Journal of Social Issues, 57,* 101.

SCHMIDT, F. L. (1996). Statistical significance testing and cumulative knowledge in psychology: Implications for training of researchers. *Psychological Methods, 1,* 115–129.

SCHMIDT, F. L., & HUNTER, J. E. (1997). Eight common but false objections to the discontinuation of significance testing in the analysis of research data. In L. L. Harlow, S. A. Mulaik, & J. H. Steiger (Eds.), *What if there were no significance tests?* (pp. 37–64). Mahwah, NJ: Erlbaum.

SCHWARTZ, R. C., & COHEN, B. N. (2001). Risk factors for suicidality among clients with schizophrenia. *Journal of Counseling & Development, 79,* 314–319.

SCHNEIDER, W. J., & NEVID, J. S. (1993). Overcoming math anxiety: A comparison of stress inoculation training and systematic desensitization. *Journal of College Student Development, 34,* 283–287.

SCHRAM, C. M. (1996). A meta-analysis of gender differences in applied statistics achievement. *Journal of Educational and Behavioral Statistics, 21,* 55–70.

SEDLMEIER, P., & GIGERENZER, G. (1989). Do studies of statistical power have an effect on the power of studies? *Psychological Bulletin, 105,* 309–316.

SENECAL, C., VALLERAND, R. J., & GUAY, F. (2001). Antecedents and outcomes of work-family conflict: Toward a motivational model. *Personality and Social Psychology Bulletin, 27,* 176–186.

SHAHINFAR, A., KUPERSMIDT, J. B., & MATZA, L. S. (2001). The relation between exposure to violence and social information processing among incarcerated adolescents. *Journal of Abnormal Psychology, 110,* 136–141.

SHAPIRO, D. A., & SHAPIRO, D. (1983). Comparative therapy outcome research: Methodological implications of meta-analysis. *Journal of Consulting and Clinical Psychology, 51,* 42–53.

SHELINE, Y. I., SANGHAVI, M., MINTUN, M. A., & GADO, M. H. (1999). Depression duration but not age predicts hippocampal volume loss in medically healthy women with recurrent major depression. *Journal of Neuroscience, 19,* 5034–5043.

SHREIDER, YU. A. (1966). Preface to the English edition. In N. P. Bushlenko, D. I. Golenko, Yu. A. Shreider, L. M. Sobol, & V. G. Sragovich (Yu. A. Shreider, Ed.), *The Monte Carlo method: The method of statistical trials* (G. J. Tee, Trans.), (p. vii). Elmsford, NY: Pergamon Press.

SIEGEL, M., & BIENER, L. (1997). Evaluating the impact of statewide anti-tobacco campaigns: The Massachusetts and California Tobacco Control Programs. *Journal of Social Issues, 53,* 147–168.

SIGALL, H., & OSTROVE, N. (1975). Beautiful but dangerous: Effects of offender attractiveness and nature of the crime on juridic judgments. *Journal of Personality and Social Psychology, 31,* 410–414.

SINCLAIR, L., & KUNDA, Z. (2000). Motivated stereotyping of women: She's fine if she praised me but incompetent if she criticized me. *Personality and Social Psychology Bulletin, 26,* 1329–1342.

SKINNER, B. F. (1956). A case history in scientific method. *American Psychologist, 11,* 221–233.

SOPRONI, K., MIKLOSI, A., CSANYI, V., & TOPAL, J. (2001). Comprehension of human communicative signs in signs in pet dogs *(canis familiaris). Journal of Comparative Psychology, 115,* 124.

SPEED, A., & GANGSTEAD, S. W. (1997). Romantic popularity and mate preferences: A peer-nomination study. *Personality and Social Psychology Bulletin, 23,* 928–937.

SPENCER, S. J., STEELE, C. M., & QUINN, D. M. (1999). Stereotype threat and women's math performance. *Journal of Experimental Social Psychology, 35,* 4–28.

STASSER, G., TAYLOR, L. A., & HANNA, C. (1989). Information sampling in structured and unstructured discussions of three- and six- person groups. *Journal of Personality and Social Psychology, 57,* 67–78

STEELE, C. M. (1997). A threat in the air: How stereotypes shape intellectual identity and performance. *American Psychologist, 52,* 613–629.

STEEN, L. A. (1987). Forward. In S. Tobias, *Succeed with math: Every student's guide to conquering math anxiety* (pp. xvii–xviii). New York: College Entrance Examination Board.

STEERING COMMITTEE OF THE PHYSICIANS HEALTH STUDY RESEARCH GROUP. (1988). Preliminary report: Findings from the aspirin component of the ongoing Physicians Health Study. *New England Journal of Medicine, 318,* 262–264.

STEIL, J. M., & HAY, J. L. (1997). Social comparison in the work place: A study of 60 dual-career couples. *Personality and Social Psychology Bulletin, 23,* 427–438.

STIGLER, S. M. (1986). *The history of statistics.* Cambridge, MA: Belknap Press.

STIPEK, D. J., & RYAN, R. H. (1997). Economically disadvantaged preschoolers: Ready to learn but further to go. *Developmental Psychology, 33,* 711–723.

SUH, E., DIENER, E., & FUJITA, F. (1996). Events and subjective well-being: Only recent events matter. *Journal of Personality and Social Psychology, 70,* 1091–1102.

SULLIVAN, P. J., & FELTZ, D. L. (2001). The relationship between intrateam conflict and cohesion within hockey teams. *Small Group Research, 32,* 347–348.

TABACHNICK, B. G., & FIDELL, L. S. (2001). *Using multivariate statistics* (4th ed.). New York: HarperCollins.

TANKARD, J., JR. (1984). *The statistical pioneers.* Cambridge, MA: Schenkman.

TARIS, R., & FEIJ, J. A. (2001). Longitudinal examination of the relationship between supplies-values fit and work outcomes. *Applied Psychology: An international Review, 50,* 59.

TEACHMAN, B. A., GREGG, A. P., & WOODY, S. R. (2001). Implicit associations for fear-relevant stimuli among individuals with snake and spider fears. *Journal of Abnormal Psychology, 110,* 330.

THOMAS, J. R., NELSON, J. K., & THOMAS, K. T. (1999). A generalized rank-order method for nonparametric analysis of data from exercise science: A tutorial. *Research Quarterly for Exercise and Sport, 70,* 11–27.

THOMPSON, W. F., SCHELLENBERG, E. G., & HUSAIN, G. (2001). Arousal, mood, and the Mozart effect. *Psychological Science, 12,* 248–251.

TOBIAS, S. (1982, January). Sexist equations. *Psychology Today,* pp. 14–17.

TOBIAS, S. (1995). *Overcoming math anxiety (revised).* New York: W. W. Norton.

TUFTE, E. R. (1983). *The visual display of quantitative information.* Cheshire, CT: Graphic Press.

U.S. BUREAU OF THE CENSUS. (1990). *Statistical abstracts of the United States.* Washington, DC: U.S. Government Printing Office.

U.S. DEPARTMENT OF EDUCATION. (1990). *The condition of education.* Washington, DC: U.S. Government Printing Office.

VALENZUELA, M. (1997). Maternal sensitivity in a developing society: The context of urban poverty and infant chronic undernutrition. *Developmental Psychology, 33,* 845–855.

VALK, M., POST, M. W. M., COOLS, H. J. M., & SHRIJVERS, G. A. J. P. (2001). Measuring disability in nursing home residents: Validity and reliability of a newly developed instrument. *Journal of Gerontology: Psychological Sciences, 56B,* P187–P191.

VAN AKEN, M. A. G., & ASENDORPF, J. B. (1997). Support by parents, classmates, friends, and siblings in preadolescence: Covariation and compensation across relationships. *Journal of Social and Personal Relationships, 14,* 79–93.

WALBERG, H. J., STRYKOWSKI, B. F., ROVAI, E., & HUNG, S. S. (1984). Exceptional performance. *Review of Educational Research, 54,* 87–112.

WELLER, A., & WELLER, L. (1997). Menstrual synchrony under optimal conditions: Bedouin families. *Journal of Comparative Psychology, 111,* 143–151.

WHITECOTTON, S. M. (1996). The effects of experience and a decision aid on the slope, scatter, and bias of earnings forecasts. *Organizational Behavior and Human Decision Processes, 66,* 111–121.

WILCONSON, L., & TASK FORCE ON STATISTICAL INFERENCE. (1999). *American Psychologist, 54,* 594–604.

WILFLEY, D. E., DOHM, F., FAIRBURN, C. G., STRIEGEL-MOORE, R. H., & PIKE, K. M. (2001). Bias in binge eating disorder: How representative are recruited clinic samples?. *Journal of Counseling and Clinical Psychology, 69,* 385.

WILLIAMSON, G. M., SHAFFER, D. R., & THE FAMILY RELATIONSHIPS IN LATE LIFE PROJECT. (2001). Relationship quality and potentially harmful behaviors by spousal caregivers: How we were then, how we are now. *Psychology and Aging, 16,* 217–226.

WISEMAN, H. (1997). Interpersonal relatedness and self-definition in the experience of loneliness during the transition to university. *Personal Relationships, 4,* 285–299.

WONG, M. M., & CSIKSZENTMIHALYI, M. (1991). Affiliation motivation and daily experience: Some issues on gender differences. *Journal of Personality and Social Psychology, 60,* 154–164

YAMAGISHI, N., & MELARA, R. D. (2001). Informational primacy of visual dimensions: Specialized roles for luminance and chromacity in figure-ground perception. *Perception and Psychophysics, 63,* 824–846.

ZEIDNER, M. (1991). Statistics and mathematics anxiety in social science students: Some interesting parallels. *British Journal of Education, 61,* 319–329.

ZIMMER-GIMBECK, M. J., SIEBENBRUNER, J., & COLLINS, A. W. (2001). Diverse aspects of dating: Associations with psychosocial functioning from early to middle adolescence. *Journal of Adolescence, 24,* 313–336.

INDEX